T5-ARG-500

FIFTH EDITION

CONSUMER HEALTH

A Guide to Intelligent Decisions

HAROLD J. CORNACCHIA, ED.D.
Professor of Health Education, Emeritus
San Francisco State University
San Francisco, California

STEPHEN BARRETT, M.D.
Psychiatrist and Consumer Advocate
Allentown, Pennsylvania

FIFTH EDITION

with 98 illustrations

St. Louis Baltimore Boston Chicago London Philadelphia Sydney Toronto

Dedicated to Publishing Excellence

Editor-in-Chief: James M. Smith
Acquisitions Editor: Vicki Malinee
Developmental Editors: Cathy Waller, Cheryl Gelfand-Grant
Editorial Project Manager: Jolynn Gower
Production Assistant: Colleen E. Foley
Designer: David Zielinski

FIFTH EDITION

Copyright © 1993 Mosby–Year Book, Inc.

Previous editions copyrighted 1976, 1980, 1985, 1989

All rights reserved. No part of this publication may be reproduced, stored in a retrieval system, or transmitted, in any form or by any means, electronic, mechanical, photocopying, recording, or otherwise, without prior written permission from the publisher.

Permission to photocopy or reproduce solely for internal or personal use is permitted for libraries or other users registered with the Copyright Clearance Center, provided that the base fee of $4.00 per chapter plus $.10 per page is paid directly to the Copyright Clearance Center, 27 Congress Street, Salem, MA 01970. This consent does not extend to other kinds of copying, such as copying for general distribution, for advertising or promotional purposes, for creating new collected works, or for resale.

Printed in the United States of America

Mosby–Year Book, Inc.
11830 Westline Industrial Drive
St. Louis, Missouri 63146

Library of Congress Cataloging in Publication Data

Cornacchia, Harold J.
Consumer health : a guide to intelligent decisions / Harold J. Cornacchia, Stephen Barrett.—5th ed.
p. cm.
Includes bibliographical references and index.
ISBN 0-8016-6747-X
1. Medical care. 2. Health products. 3. Quacks and quackery. 4. Consumer education. 5. Medical care—United States. I. Barrett, Stephen. II. Title.
RA410.5.C67 1992
362.1—dc20 92-26457
CIP

362.1
C812

94 95 96 GW/VH 9 8 7 6 5 4 3 2

About the Authors

Harold J. Cornacchia, Ed.D., who lives in San Francisco, is a prominent educator, consultant, administrator, author, and consumer advocate. He is Emeritus Professor of Health Education at San Francisco State University and has been a lecturer with faculty appointments at four other universities. During his 35-year career, he has developed, promoted, and administered health education programs in elementary and secondary schools throughout the United States. He introduced and taught consumer health at San Francisco State University and has conducted workshops on this subject for teachers, in consultation with the FDA and the California Medical Society. He has appeared on radio and television programs, spoken at conferences on health frauds and quackery, contributed numerous articles to lay and professional publications, and served as a board member of the National Council Against Health Fraud. He was the director of a National Training Center in Drug Education, sponsored by the U.S. Office of Education. The National Fire Prevention Association program on fire safety that he developed for elementary schools has saved hundreds of lives. His 16 coauthored books include *Health in Elementary Schools, Drugs in the Classroom,* and *Shopping for Health Care.*

Stephen Barrett, M.D., who practices psychiatry in Allentown, Pennsylvania, is a nationally renowned author, editor, and consumer advocate. He edits and publishes *Nutrition Forum Newsletter* and has been a frequent contributor to *Priorities Magazine, Healthline Newsletter,* and *Consumer Reports on Health.* He is a board member of the National Council Against Health Fraud and chairs its Task Force on Victim Redress. He is medical editor of Prometheus Books and a scientific and editorial advisor to the American Council on Science and Health. He is a scientific consultant to the Committee for the Scientific Investigation of Claims of the Paranormal (CSICOP) and co-chairman of its paranormal health claims subcommittee. He operates a clearinghouse for information on health frauds and quackery. He has edited or coauthored 33 books, including *The Health Robbers; Health Schemes, Scams, and Frauds; Your Guide to Good Nutrition;* and *Vitamins and "Health" Foods: The Great American Hustle.* In 1984 he won the FDA Commissioner's Special Citation Award for Public Service in fighting nutrition quackery. In 1986 he was awarded honorary membership in the American Dietetic Association. In 1987 he began teaching health education at Pennsylvania State University.

FOREWORD

You can gain a great deal from this book if you're interested in:

- Nutrition
- Physical fitness
- Bodybuilding
- High-level wellness
- Choosing trustworthy health-care professionals
- Avoiding health rip-offs
- Getting more for your health dollar

More is known about achieving and maintaining good health today than ever before. Life expectancy is at an all-time high; and, although there is still room for improvement, health-related accomplishments have exceeded the fondest dreams of past visionaries. In 1890, when life expectancy was 37 years of age, the imaginative Jules Verne predicted that in 1000 years the life expectancy would reach 58 years! In fact, it has doubled to more than 74 years in less than a century. This progress has been due, in part, to a biologically safer environment: cleaner water, food, and living space. But we hear plenty of bad news about these, and it worries us. Medical care, both preventive and therapeutic, has made important contributions, yet we worry about the risks associated with immunization, cancer therapies, prescription drugs, surgery, and many other treatment modalities. How can we resolve our concerns and reap the benefits of what modern science is discovering about health? The key is to be informed about what is happening in the health marketplace.

Unfortunately, the explosion in knowledge about health has been matched by enormous increases in health misinformation. Worse yet, health misinformation is much more readily available than the sound information people really want. In 1984 a congressional subcommittee reported that Americans wasted billions of dollars on worthless and unproven health remedies. Medical quackery was found to be the number one consumer fraud problem among the nation's elderly population. The congressional report estimated that more is spent on cancer and arthritis quackery than is spent on research into cures for those diseases. The promotion of dubious health practices is not limited to the elderly or sick. Young, healthy people are the targets of supplements, devices, weight-control plans, and products aimed at fulfilling dreams of the body beautiful, superior athletic performance, exceptional mental ability, and more. Quackery has something for everyone because we all have wishes that exceed reality.

The entrepreneurs who market dubious health practices are clever and persistent. They exploit the public's enthusiasm for healthful living and self-help. Their promotions far outstrip school and public health education efforts aimed at consumer protection and encouragement of positive health behavior. In fact, the spread of health misinformation has itself become an industry and is the foundation upon which the purveyors of dubious health products and services rely. Individuals who spread the misinformation are protected by the First Amendment, which guarantees freedom of speech. A myriad of writers produce books, magazine articles, newsletters, and pamphlets that promote quackery. Misinformation that would be illegal on a product label or in an advertisement is spread by modern mass media techniques. Health theories and claims are repeatedly extolled on radio and television talk shows whose celebrity hosts make such claims appear legitimate.

Another aspect of modern quackery's modus operandi is multilevel marketing. Its pyramid-type schemes capitalize on people's financial ambitions. Its participants encourage their friends and relatives to become "satisfied users" so that they too can "believe in" their products—an essential factor for successful selling. Their judgment becomes clouded by self-interest and a general inability to separate the real effects from the imagined effects of health practices. Cable television may be used to amplify testimonials into the siren call of quackery on a national scale. Average consumers are no match for such promotionalism.

Health hucksters are aided by those who claim that consumer protection laws constitute over-regulation. "Freedom of choice" is their battle cry, but a careful examination reveals this argument to be a red herring. It is quacks who seek the freedom to sell worthless and unproven health products and services to unwary consumers. True freedom of choice cannot be exercised by people who have been deceived or driven by desperation.

Consumers exist in a crisis of confidence, and wonder who can be trusted for reliable health information. Many self-appointed "consumer advocates" do not act in the public's interest. Although some are sincere and make a contribution, others use their role to simply engage in irrational business-bashing, to advance political causes, or to act from motives of personal aggrandizement. Occasionally, business trade associations and lobbies can pose as "consumer groups" and seek self-serving legislation. This is where academic consumer health education comes in. Consumer protection laws are based on fundamental principles—inseparable from those of science—including the Consumer Bill of Rights. These provide standards that can unmask the pretenders to consumerism.

As peer-reviewed scholars, the authors of *Consumer Health* are trustworthy because they are accountable to the academic and scientific communities. Dr. Cornacchia is a respected scholar and teacher with a thorough knowledge of his field. Dr. Barrett brings to this book a medical background plus his experience as one of the nation's leading consumer activists. As a psychiatrist, he adds an important dimension of understanding what motivates both patient and practitioner involvement in dubious health care. Dr. Cornacchia believes that most health behavior can be analyzed as a type of consumer behavior, and that people's lifestyles are reflected by the products and services they use. Dr. Barrett stresses that people generally believe what they hear most and that health-related advertising significantly impacts health behavior. I agree with both of these ideas.

Consumer Health offers a kaleidoscopic view of today's complex and exciting health marketplace. Its message is twofold: "You can do much for yourself through good decision-making," but "buyer beware!" It reveals the tremendous innovation of the purveyors of quackery at a time when more caution than ever is needed in making choices in the health marketplace. This book provides the information needed to protect both your money and your health.

William T. Jarvis, Ph.D.

Professor of Public Health and
Preventive Medicine
Loma Linda University School of Medicine
President, National Council Against
Health Fraud, Inc.

PREFACE

Consumers must regularly confront the complicated and confusing health marketplace where caveat emptor (let the buyer beware) is the dominant philosophy. The rapid expansion of medical science has created innumerable opportunities for new health products and services. Many of these receive considerable publicity before they have been adequately or completely exposed to scientific study.

Consumers often have difficulty in making intelligent decisions about the purchase and use of products and services that are useless, worthless, or hazardous. Quacks, pseudoscientists, many advertisers, and a multitude of well-intentioned promoters spread vast amounts of misinformation. Frauds and deception are rampant. Consumers are bilked out of billions of dollars each year, and many suffer loss of health as well. Unfortunately, government and community agencies provide far less protection than most people realize. Navigating the legitimate avenues of the health marketplace can also be difficult and complex.

Consumers who wish to protect their health and their pocketbooks therefore must shop with great care. They must become accurately informed. They must learn how to identify and use reliable sources of information. They must accept responsibility and speak out when they are victims of fraud and deception. They must raise objections to dubious products and services and report them to the appropriate regulatory agencies.

Goal for this Revision

This fifth edition of *Consumer Health* continues to emphasize the economic aspects of health and the social and psychological factors that influence consumer choices. As with previous editions, *the book's fundamental purpose is to provide factual information and guidelines to enable consumers to select health products and services intelligently.*

This edition is the most comprehensive and thoroughly researched text on consumer health ever published. The data have been selected from thousands of reliable reports in books, scientific journals, and other periodicals, as well as original investigations done by the authors. Consumers will find the information useful in applying the caveat vendor (let the seller beware) concept to the health marketplace.

The underlying principles of consumer health were clearly identified in the Consumer Bill of Rights promulgated by President John F. Kennedy and have guided the development of this textbook. President Kennedy declared that consumers have the right to purchase safe products and services, to be correctly informed, to freely choose products and services, and to be heard by the government and others when injustices occur. We strongly support consumer awareness and advocacy of these rights.

Intended Audience

Consumer Health will be helpful to teachers, health educators, health professionals, and to the general public. It can be used as a basic text or for supplementary reading in courses such as consumer health, health education, consumer education, sociology, psychology, home economics, social welfare, and business. School districts will find *Consumer Health* useful as a reference for teachers and students, as well as an aid in curriculum development. Professional health-care providers can use this text to prepare for public presentations and can make it available in their offices for perusal by clients.

New to This Edition

The modifications in this edition were guided by suggestions from college and university instructors and the authors' analysis of new information and trends in the health marketplace.

- Two entirely new chapters have been added (Chapter 16: Cardiovascular Disease and Chapter 24: Coping with Dying), and Arthritis, Cancer, and AIDS are now covered in separate chapters (17, 18, 19) instead of being combined into one.
- Many chapters now contain vignettes ("Personal Glimpses") to stimulate reader interest and boxes

that emphasize key points. New photographs and cartoons have been added to several chapters. Many checklists and "It's Your Decision" boxes related to "real-life" decisions have been added throughout the text.

- Chapter 10, Self-Care, has been reorganized to improve the sequence and clarity of the information.
- Chapter 12, Basic Nutrition Concepts, has been revised to integrate the 1989 U.S. Dietary Guidelines, the more recent guidelines from the U.S. Department of Agriculture, and other advice from prominent government and scientific groups.
- Chapter 15, Exercise Concepts, Devices, and Services, has been expanded and contains a new chart to facilitate the analysis of exercise equipment.
- Chapter 16, Cardiovascular Disease, has been added in light of the enormous attention this topic has received from the scientific community. It stresses preventive measures and the latest diagnostic and treatment procedures for coronary heart disease. The discussion of diet and cholesterol, covered under basic nutrition in the previous edition, has been expanded and moved into this chapter.
- Chapter 19, AIDS, provides a thorough discussion of this very serious public health threat.
- Chapter 20, Drug Products, has been thoroughly revised to make it simpler yet more practical.
- Chapter 24, Coping with Dying, covers new material on the emotional aspects of terminal illness and death, advanced directives, living wills, euthanasia, organ donations, and quackery related to aging. It also includes hospice care, which was included in a different chapter in previous editions.
- Chapter 25, Health Insurance, has been reorganized and expanded to cover new information on managed care, long-term care, Medicare fraud, and proposals for national health insurance.
- Chapter 26, Health Care Economics, contains updated tables and several new ones.
- More than 150 toll-free hotlines have been added to the list of reliable information sources in the Appendix.

Additional Changes

Glossary. The glossary has been lengthened to include many useful items that are not discussed elsewhere in the book.

Tables. Most charts and tables have been updated, and several new ones have been added as teaching aids.

References. The reference lists have been expanded. References that may be especially useful for students seeking additional information are identified with asterisks. These publications are "classic" resources that are available in many libraries. Some references are listed merely to help readers judge the credibility of cited material.

Latest Information. An extensive search of the scientific literature and personal investigation by the authors have provided information to update and greatly expand the content of this edition. New and enriched areas include: advertising regulation, AIDS quackery, birth control methods, ayurvedic medicine, cardiac rehabilitation, chiropractic, cholesterol guidelines, coronary bypass surgery and angioplasty, dental x-ray guidelines, Edgar Cayce, heart attack treatment, hospital morbidity statistics, immuno-augmentative therapy (IAT) for cancer, infertility, macrobiotic diets, meditation, the mercury-amalgam scam, multilevel marketing, natural hygiene, naturopathy, nutrition labeling, periodic medical examinations. Sargenti root canal treatment, sources of reliable information, subliminal tapes, and stress testing.

Organization

The book has been reorganized to provide a more meaningful and useful understanding of the consumer health concept and its practical application. The text is broadly divided into six parts: dynamics of the health marketplace; approaches to health care; nutrition and fitness; major health problems; other products and services; and protection of the consumer.

Part I: Dynamics of the Health Marketplace focuses on past and present problems. After providing an historical perspective, it discusses frauds and quackery, how to separate fact from fiction, and the influence of advertising.

Part II: Approaches to Health Care covers basic medical care, the services of many types of scientific and nonscientific practitioners, self-care, and health care facilities.

Part III: Nutrition and Fitness integrates what consumers need to know about the extremely important topics of nutrition, weight control, and exercise. Its chapters provide the necessary tools for distinguishing between scientifically based methods and fads, fallacies, and scams.

Part IV: Major Health Problems covers four of the leading causes of death and/or disability in our society: cardiovascular disease, arthritis, cancer, and AIDS.

Part V: Other Products and Services covers a myriad of other subjects that affect most, if not all, consumers. Among them are drug products, skin and beauty aids, birth control methods, vision aids, hearing aids, and other health devices.

Part VI: Protection of the Consumer focuses on legal and economic issues involved in protecting consumers. These include death-related issues, health insurance, other economic issues, consumer protection laws and agencies, and a summary of strategies for the intelligent consumer.

The Appendix provides comprehensive lists of agencies, organizations, publications, and toll-free hotlines that offer reliable information.

Acknowledgments

No book like this could have been written without help from many experts. The authors offer special thanks to: Janet B. McDonald, Ph.D., R.D., public affairs specialist, U.S. Food and Drug Administration; John E. Dodes, D.D.S., president, New York Council Against Health Fraud; Stephen Moss, D.D.S., M.S., Professor of Dentistry, New York University College of Dentistry; William T. Jarvis, Ph.D., Professor of Public Health and Preventive Medicine, Loma Linda University; Daniel Goldfarb, M.D., psychiatrist, Allentown, Pa., Judith N. Barrett, M.D., family practitioner, Allentown, Pa.; Alice C. Cornacchia, housewife, San Francisco; and attorney Geoffrey Drucker of the U.S. Postal Service's Consumer Protection Division.

In addition, the authors would like to thank the following professionals for their insightful reviews of the last edition and their excellent suggestions for this one:

Nancy Baldwin
Edinboro University

Steve Furney
Southwest Texas State University

Mary Hawk
Western Washington University

Daniel Kniffin
Texas A&M University

William London
Kent State University

Ray Petersen
Brigham Young University

Harold J. Cornacchia, Ed.D.
Stephen Barrett, M.D.

Consumer Health Decisions

People frequently face decisions about purchasing and using a variety of health products and services.

- How should one select a physician, a dentist, or other health specialist?
- What aspirin or aspirin-like products should be purchased? Is aspirin better than acetaminophen or ibuprofen? When should they be used?
- Should contact lenses be purchased? Are hard lenses better than soft lenses? Are extended-wear contacts safe?
- Which health or dental insurance coverage provides the best protection?
- When should one visit a physician? A dentist?
- What should be done about excessive or unreasonable physicians' or dentists' fees? How can health costs be controlled or reduced?
- How can reliable sources of health information be identified and located?
- Are television, radio, newspapers, magazines, and books reliable sources of health information?
- When is it appropriate to use supplementary vitamins and minerals? Is vitamin E helpful?
- What is the safe way to lose and control weight? Are diet pills helpful or harmful?
- Which cosmetics are safe to use? Which are effective?
- Should organic or health foods be purchased? Are they more expensive than other foods?
- Can vitamin C prevent colds? Cure colds? Cure cancer? Is it hazardous to use?
- How can the best protection against sun exposure be provided?
- What agencies and organizations help protect the consumer?
- How should one select a nursing or convalescent home? A hospital?
- Should dental repair kits be used to fix dentures?
- What kinds of toothbrushes and dentifrices are most effective?
- Are the ingredients in over-the-counter drug products safe and effective for menstrual cramps?
- Is the vaginal sponge a safe and effective contraceptive?
- Are over-the-counter pregnancy test kits reliable?
- If a physician recommends surgery, when is it appropriate to obtain a second opinion?
- Who can help determine the need for hearing aids? Eyeglasses?
- Does the patenting of a health device ensure its safety and effectiveness?
- Can electric vibrators and massage equipment help one to lose weight?
- Can special foods and medicines prevent or control arthritis?
- Are any AIDS remedies safe and effective?
- Can laetrile prevent or control cancer?
- When can self-diagnosis and self-medication be appropriately used?
- How does one register a complaint about a health product? A health service?
- Are periodic health examinations necessary? How often? How much should they cost?
- Should laxatives be used?
- Can wearing a copper bracelet help arthritis?
- Can any products help to grow, restore, or remove hair?
- Can wrinkles be removed? Can plastic surgery help?
- Should generic or brand name drugs be purchased? Which are less expensive?
- How can quacks and quackery be recognized?
- Which exercise equipment provides the greatest benefits? The fewest benefits?
- How should people budget for health care?
- What should a consumer do when fraud and quackery have been discovered in the health marketplace?
- How should consumers analyze advertisements for health products and services?
- Should consumers use unorthodox health care services and products?
- Should consumers use ambulatory health care centers?
- Can mouthwashes and dentifrices control the development of plaque on teeth?

- Should a person who wishes to become fit join a health club or exercise center?
- How trustworthy are chiropractors, naturopaths, and acupuncturists?
- How can a consumer judge whether the findings of a research study reported in the media are reliable and valid?
- Can laundry bleach be used to clean dentures?
- What actions can consumers take to limit "heroic" medical care if they are terminally ill?
- Under what circumstances are dental implants appropriate?
- What products are appropriate for a home medicine cabinet?
- How can a consumer judge whether exercise equipment may be beneficial?
- Is radial keratotomy a safe and effective procedure?
- Do silver-amalgam fillings pose any health hazard?
- What forms of birth control are safest and most effective?
- What can women do about premenstrual syndrome (PMS)?
- Can any food or diet influence the course of arthritis or cancer?
- How much money should be budgeted for health care?

To make intelligent decisions, a consumer must be well informed.

Contents

DYNAMICS OF THE HEALTH MARKETPLACE

CHAPTER ONE

Introduction to the Health Marketplace

"It's only a damned house call!"

Today you can cheat an honest man, not only easily but often.

GENTRY: VULNERABLE AMERICANS

In 1989 the FDA concluded that 38 million have tried at least one fraudulent health product and 1 in 10 were adversely affected.

MODERN MATURITY, FEB/MAR 1990

Quackery—the promotion and sale of useless remedies promising relief from chronic and critical health conditions—exceeds $10 billion a year. The cost of quackery in human terms, measured in disillusion, pain, relief forsaken or postponed because of reliance on unproven methods, is more difficult to measure, but nonetheless real. All too often the purchaser has paid with his life.

CONGRESSMAN CLAUDE PEPPER[1]
QUACKERY—A $10 BILLION SCANDAL

POOR CONSUMER DECISIONS

In 1990, in Duluth, Georgia, before getting ready for his high school prom, a teenager drank water mixed with two teaspoons of *Somatomax PM,* a powdery substance a friend had bought at a health food store. He had heard it would give him a "high." It did not. Within 20 minutes, he became comatose. Fortunately, his parents found him in time, but without prompt emergency treatment he might not have survived.

The substance was gamma hydroxybutyrate (GHB), a product touted to build muscle, reduce fat, and induce sleep. It was sold under various names in health food stores, bodybuilding and fitness centers, and through the mail. GHB is dangerous and was never approved for general distribution by the Food and Drug Administration (FDA). After the agency collected 57 cases of GHB-related illness, it initiated criminal charges against the local manufacturer. Poisonings were reported in at least nine states.[2] No deaths occurred, but most patients required emergency room care.

CONSUMER DECISIONS

What actions should consumers take to act intelligently in the health marketplace?

INTELLIGENT CONSUMERS

The beginning of wisdom is doubt.
Statements about health products and services that appear to be true should not be accepted at face value
Nothing should be believed because someone wishes you to believe it.
Skepticism serves to puncture platitudes and eliminate lies.
Intelligent consumers must be skeptical about what they read and hear.

Despite the many economic gains that have occurred in the United States, people must still work hard to survive. People generally seek ways to ease their burdens, acquire more free time, and above all, attain good health. They wish to alleviate discomfort quickly and easily. They also wish to remain youthful and attractive, to live longer, and to fully enjoy the pleasures of living a productive and rewarding life. Many people seek a fountain of youth or a panacea (cure-all) for their ailments.

In light of the economic, social, scientific, and technologic advances that have occurred, it is not surprising that many people have come to believe that health—like any material item—is purchasable. This attitude was expressed clearly by René Dubos[3] who, many years ago, reported this proclamation by one of the leaders of American medicine:

> The modern American is encouraged to believe that money can create drugs for the cure of heart disease, cancer, and mental disease, but he makes no worthwhile effort to recognize, let alone correct, the mismanagements of his everyday life that contribute to the high incidence of these conditions.

Dubos also stated, "To ward off disease or recover health, men as a rule find it easier to depend on healers than to attempt the more difficult task of living wisely."

Many quacks, manufacturers, and other entrepreneurs are aware of consumers' desires to purchase health easily and quickly. They flood the marketplace with products and services of every description to accommodate people who want a pleasurable and pain-free life. Promoters use advertisements, supermarket tabloids, direct-mail circulars, television talk shows, radio commercials, and word-of-mouth to sell their wares. Some of these materials have little or no use, some are costly and may cause direct harm. These hucksters often use pseudoscientific approaches to mislead and misrepresent products and services. They know that scientific information is important but often is confusing. The media encourage self-diagnosis and self-treatment but often provide inaccurate information. Self-diagnosis and self-treatment are valuable when the products are safe and effective and consumers know when a physician should be consulted. For the most part, however, consumers are at the mercy of sellers (*caveat emptor*—let the buyer beware).

This book is designed to help consumers understand the variety of influences they will encounter in the health marketplace. It should enable individuals to make intelligent decisions about health products and services. It attempts to help consumers make informed choices to protect their health and their pocketbook and to implement the principle of *caveat vendor* (let the seller beware).

This chapter provides an introduction to consumer health by identifying the problems found in the health marketplace. It briefly describes the development of the consumer movement and its basic principles, provides a conceptual definition of "consumer health," lists the characteristics of intelligent consumers, and offers guidelines for making decisions about health matters.

Problems in the Health Marketplace

Many problems in the health marketplace make it difficult for consumers to make prudent choices. These problems have influenced large segments of the population, the elderly in particular, to resort to nonscientific health-care methods, and to self-care. People often fail to receive accurate scientific information with which to make intelligent decisions about health products and services.

Health care costs have risen about 11% a year since 1960 and reached 12.2% of the gross national product (GNP), up from 11.6% in 1989. This upward spiral of expenditures does not appear to be diminishing. In 1990, health expenditures were $666.2 billion or 11.6% of the GNP. Personal health expenditures included $125.7 billion for physician services, $34 billion for dental services, $54.6 billion for drugs and sundries, and $12.1 billion for vision products.[4]

In 1990, per capita health expenditures averaged $2566. Private insurance paid almost one-third of all personal health care costs. In 1988, the average daily hospital rate was $586 per day, while the average daily cost per hospital was $4207.[5] In 1989, the cost of an office visit to a general practitioner was $24 to $36 and for other specialists was $30 to $55 for an established patient.[6]

AIDS has killed over 130,000 people since it was recognized 10 years ago, including 31,000 people during 1990 (see Chapter 19). The Centers for Disease Control identified it as the second leading cause of death in men between 25 and 44 years of age and probably fifth among killers of women of the same age group.[7] John Renner, M.D.,[8] stated that quacks have run rampant, marketing such dubious remedies as blue-green algae (pond-scum) at $20 per bottle, injections of hydrogen peroxide, herbal capsules found to contain poisonous metals, chlorine bleach solution to bathe the body, and exposing the genitals and rectum to the sun's rays at 4:00 P.M.

A substantial segment of the population has become disenchanted with the quality of medical care and with physicians in general. A survey conducted by the American Medical Association in 1984 revealed that two-thirds of Americans were losing faith in doctors.[9] Many of the respondents thought that physicians had excessive interest in money matters and provided insufficient information and advice to patients.

In 1986, *The Washington Post* reported on a survey in which 48% of the respondents thought doctors made too much money.[10] The abundance of medical advertising on television and radio, in newspapers, telephone directories, and direct mail, and in other media has added to consumer concern about the financial status of physicians.

More recently Slatella[11] reported a nationwide movement in which patients and families are abandoning their blind faith in the establishment and are asking more questions about the quality of medical care.

Consumers have also been displeased with medical practitioners who:

1. Fail to consider the psychologic aspects of illness.
2. Fail to provide sufficient time to discuss and clarify illnesses and conditions.
3. Fail to adequately inform patients of effective alternative treatments.
4. Use too many drugs in treatment. The New York State Health Department has been investigating practitioners who they believe prescribe too many drugs.[13]
5. Subject patients to unnecessary tests. The U.S. Department of Health and Human Services[14] claimed in 1987 that patients were subjected to $28 million of medical tests they did not need.
6. Perform unnecessary surgery. Many hysterectomies and cesarean sections continue to be unnecessary[19] (see Chapter 22). The U.S. Center for Health Statistics stated the rate of cesareans in 1989 was 23.8%.[15]

The American College of Obstetricians & Gynecologists[16] has claimed that 20% to 40% of Pap smear tests done today fail to detect cancer or precancerous cell abnormalities.

The Public Citizen Health Research Group[17] believes that the system of disciplinary action against

Personal Glimpse

Dare to Ask

A family doctor saw a patient in the emergency room and diagnosed appendicitis. He called in a popular young surgeon who agreed with him. The patient was operated on within the hour and was cured. The family doctor whistled when he heard the bill for the operation was $865, but he choked when he saw that the surgeon had also charged $125 just to see the patient in the emergency room . . . Then, demonstrating monumental chutzpah, that surgeon had charged $95 more "to admit the patient."

My fee for the whole business would have been around $650, not $1085. And that is the way we all used to charge, but nowadays the idea is to make it a la carte and get away with murder. . . .

Don't be afraid to ask what something will cost, even if you are well insured; if we don't spare the insurer, the premiums will just go up for all of us . . . Then when it is all over and you have the doctor and hospital bills, do go over them carefully. Mistakes are often made and include some treatments you didn't get, some tests not done, or some of these a la carte things that should be part of, not an addition to, the larger fee. You have the right to ask for an explanation from the hospital or doctor. You might get a reduction. . . . Even if you just feel abused and have no proof of wrongdoing, you can still tell the doctor who referred you to the offender. You may not get justice but you will diminish that greedy person and he or she may be more careful in the future.

George B. Markle, IV, M.D.[12]

physicians to protect the public from poor health care is uncoordinated and often ineffective. It has identified 9479 questionable doctors (1.7% of physicians) who were disciplined for a variety of offenses that include overprescribing/misrepresenting, incompetency/negligent care, and drug and alcohol abuse.

A *Newsday* survey of 1100 doctors in the New York metropolitan area found that 29.7% said that malpractice suits were the result of error half the time and 13.8% claimed they knew of impaired physicians who were in practice.[18]

In 1988, 87% of the people who live in the United States were covered by some form of health insurance.[5] Only 75% had major medical protection and 50% were covered by dental insurance. It is estimated that 35 to 40 million people have no health insurance. An additional 20 million are underinsured and cannot afford crucial medical care. Health insurance premiums, deductibles, and copayments are skyrocketing. Approximately 120 million people have no dental insurance. Many of the insured individuals do not know what their policies cover because they have not read them or are unable to understand them. Frequently these policies have important limitations, exclusions, and other gaps in coverage, and offer benefits so low that a family could face financial disaster if a serious illness or injury were to strike. The elderly are often exposed to eager salespersons who offer medigap policies (supplementary to Medicare) and who provide pressure to purchase multiple policies. This action results in overlapping coverage and unnecessary expense. The federal government is planning to limit the number of policies available to the elderly.

Health information can be confusing and complex. It can be confusing because of the variety of sources and the difficulty in determining their reliability. It is complex because evidence from research is often unclear or incomplete. Conclusions often are not black and white. Scientific data often are insufficient to prove or disprove a supposed fact. Finding reliable sources of information can be challenging to the consumer (see Chapter 3 and the Appendix).

Despite the greater general awareness about health matters, people continue to undermine good health with their lifestyle choices. The resulting illnesses make them more susceptible to quackery and increases the cost of health care in our society. In a recent Louis Harris and Associates poll[20] of 1254 adults 18 years of age or older, 22% said they maintained a proper weight, 34% said they performed strenuous exercise, 56% said they limited fat intake, 74% said they did not smoke, and 91% said they drank alcohol moderately. The *Mayo Clinic Health Letter*[21] stated that 40% of Americans do not exercise and 90% do not exercise adequately.

Entrepreneurs often interpret preliminary research findings to suit their convenience when selling useless and sometimes harmful products and services. For example, a single study done on a few rats or even humans may provide important evidence. However, until a larger and more representative population is used and the conclusions are reviewed and replicated by other scientists, the results should not be accepted as significant (see Chapter 3).

The media exert tremendous influence on people. The number of informational sources is huge. Thousands of radio and television stations broadcast, and many employ one or more physicians to disseminate health information. Approximately 11,500 magazines, 10,000 newspapers (1700 daily), 50,000 new books (9000 in medicine, science, and technology), and hundreds of thousands of books and pamphlets are published each year. People often do not receive accurate scientific information with which to make intelligent decisions about health products and services. Partial information and misinformation are spread through newspapers, radio and television talk shows and through advertising (see Chapters 4 and 5) using "show biz" personalities. *Star, Globe, National Enquirer,* and other tabloids sell millions of copies weekly and have great influence on people's health behavior. Over 2000 books in print recommend unproven and nonscientific nutrition practices.

Large numbers of consumers seek help from nonscientific health care providers such as chiropractors, acupuncturists, naturopaths, faith healers, and so-called holistic practitioners (see Chapter 9).

The desire to self-diagnose and self-treat has positive and negative aspects (see Chapter 10). The health marketplace provides many useful and helpful products (see Table 1-1). However, some of these products are abused or used unnecessarily as a result of deceptive advertising.

Quacks are numerous, and quackery is extensive in the United States. The Food and Drug Administration[22] has listed the following as the top 10 health frauds: (1) fraudulent arthritis products, (2) bogus AIDS cures, (3) instant weight-loss schemes, (4) fraudulent sexual aids, (5) spurious cancer clinics, (6) quack baldness remedies and other appearance modifiers, (7) false nutritional schemes, (8) unproven use of muscle stimulators, (9) chelation therapy (claimed to clean out clogged arteries), (10) treatment for nonexistent yeast infections. The *Mayo Clinic Health Letter*[23] reported that one in four persons in the United States will use a quack product each year.

In its 1984 report, *Quackery—a $10 Billion Scandal,* the U.S. House of Representatives Select Committee on Aging stated that senior citizens represent 11% of the population and 60% of these citizens are victims of health fraud.[1] The elderly are a prime target since 80% have at least one chronic health condition. Many con artists have sold false hope for the restoration of youth, relief from pain, and delay of death. Many clinics in Mexico, the United States, and elsewhere use unproven and questionable remedies.

CONSUMER TIP

Health frauds are difficult to curtail and control; like crabgrass, they sprout up here, there, and everywhere.

THE CONSUMER MOVEMENT

The consumer movement began about 35 years ago when people noticed how much the business world was influencing their life. Consumerism emerged because many people concluded that making money should not be the only object of our economic system. The so-called consumer revolution resulted from a growing public demand for justice and fair play in the marketplace. This represented a significant change in the national value system.

The consumer movement has had considerable impact on society. It has stimulated passage of many laws and the formation of many voluntary consumer organizations. It has resulted in the publication of magazines, pamphlets, and books to help educate people. The media have focused considerable attention on consumer health issues. Despite this increased awareness of fraudulent practices, quackery continues to flourish.

Deception in the marketing of food, drugs, and cosmetics has frequently been deliberate. In the early days of the movement the lack of the application of ethical principles in dealing with consumers was attested to by Ralph Lee Smith and Senator Edward M. Kennedy. Smith[25] wrote:

> The language of modern advertising is suited to hiding, partially or completely, the truths of science . . . The great new advances in medical knowledge lend themselves easily to such trickery. Language is debased and science exploited to bring profits by misrepresenting the facts about personal health.

TABLE 1–1

OVER-THE-COUNTER DRUGS AND HEALTH AND BEAUTY AIDS SOLD IN THE UNITED STATES IN 1990[24]

Product		Sales
Toiletries and personal care products		$15,900,000,000
Over-the-counter drugs		10,300,000,000
Analgesics, digestive and others (laxatives, stomach and diarrhea remedies, internal analgesics, arthritis remedies, hemorrhoidal preparations, sleeping tablets, diet aids, vitamins)	5,800,000,000	
Cough, cold, and flu remedies (nasal sprays, cough syrups, cough drops, cold and sinus remedies, throat lozenges)	2,700,000,000	
External/other remedies (foot and acne remedies, eye drops and lotions, external analgesics, early pregnancy tests, topical hydrocortisones, contact lens care, diaper cream)	1,700,000,000	
Paper goods (sanitary protections, disposable diapers, premoistened towelettes)		5,200,000,000
Selected remaining toiletries (deodorants, talc/dusting powder, feminine douches, cotton swabs, women's fragrances, women's contraceptives, baby powder, baby bath)		3,000,000,000
Oral hygiene (toothbrushes, mouthwash, dental floss, dental cleaners, dental adhesions, dentifrices)		2,900,000,000
Skin care (suntan lotions and oils, baby lotions and oils, depilatories, facial creams, hand and body lotions)		2,100,000,000
Color cosmetics (eye and lip makeup, nail color, face makeup)		1,900,000,000
Men's products (after shave colognes, blades and razors, shaving cream)		1,700,000,000
Hair care (conditioners, shampoos, hair color, hair fixtures, hair preparations, home permanents)		1,600,000,000
Selected sundries (batteries, pet flea collars, insect repellants)		1,500,000,000
Total		$46,100,000,000

From The OTC/HBA battleground, Drug Topics 135:52-53, April 22, 1991.

The need for consumer protection led to emphasis of the *let the seller beware* (caveat vendor) concept rather than the *let the buyer beware* (caveat emptor) concept and led to the promulgation of the Consumer Bill of Rights by President John F. Kennedy.

Let the Buyer Beware (Caveat Emptor)

The concept of caveat emptor in the business world prevailed with little challenge until the advent of the consumer movement. Products could be advertised and sold with little consideration of their efficacy or safety. Services could be rendered without much regulation. Many sellers did not act responsibly toward consumers. Although the Food and Drug Administration (FDA) and the Federal Trade Commission (FTC) had existed for many years, these federal agencies were not able to exert much influence on the products and services that were available (see Chapter 2). There was need for greater consumer involvement. The advent of the Consumer Bill of Rights in 1962 gave impetus to the concept of caveat vendor.

Let the Seller Beware (Caveat Vendor)

Virginia H. Knauer,[26] a former special assistant to the President for consumer affairs, stated that our greatest challenge is to heighten consumers' awareness of their rights and to educate them about the marketplace and their role in it:

> We need a concerned public that shops for value, demands more information about products, is discriminating about advertisements, suspects offers of something-for-nothing and is vocal about the abuses of the marketplace. The individual learns to play his role as a citizen, organizes for citizen action, and makes his voice heard.

Citizen-advocate Ralph Nader[27] supported and amplified Knauer's comment:

> There can be no daily democracy without daily citizenship. If we do not exercise our civil rights, who will? If we do not perform our civic duties, who can? The fiber of a just society in the pursuit of happiness is a thinking, active citizenry. That means you.

In 1968 the Consumer Protection and Environmental Health Service was established in the U.S. Department of Health, Education, and Welfare. Several years later its environmental programs were transformed into a new agency, the Environmental Protection Agency, and the Office of Consumer Affairs was established in the Office of the Secretary of Health, Education, and Welfare. Similar offices were established in a number of other federal agencies. Senators Jacob Javits, Gary Hart, Warren Magnuson, George McGovern, Charles Percy, and others were active in promoting the cause of the consumer. Since 1973, legislation has been introduced with the goal of creating a high-level government agency with considerable power to intervene for the consumer, but it was never granted congressional approval. For several years federal funds to support consumer education were available from the Office of Education.

Today many state and local agencies protect consumers. Many voluntary organizations actively promote the caveat vendor concept. These groups serve notice on the business world that they have a responsibility to consumers and that their efforts in this regard will be under scrutiny. These groups introduce, help modify, and stay informed of legislation that affects the public. They also educate the community, monitor the media, and act to prevent fraud and quackery.

Consumerism has achieved much social visibility through the efforts of Ralph Nader and, in the health field, of Sidney Wolfe, M.D., of the Public Citizen Health Research Group. Numerous publications have made people aware of the consumer movement. *Consumer Reports* (circulation over 4 million), The *FDA Consumer, Kiplinger's Personal Financial Magazine* (formerly called *Changing Times*), and a variety of other magazines and newsletters have stimulated concern and provided much useful information. Radio and television stations have become active in this movement. Many national, state, and local consumer organizations have emerged. The national groups have included Action for Children's Television, Council on Children, American Council on Consumer Interests, Consumer Federation of America, National Consumers League, National Council Against Health Fraud, and American Council on Science and Health.

The consumer movement has led to changes in such areas as advertising, packaging, labeling information, product content, and warranty provisions. Some industries have established consumer representatives who meet with consumer groups, recall products, and are active in the marketplace. The FTC has taken aggressive actions against misleading advertising, and the FDA has taken major steps in controlling the safety and efficacy of drug, cosmetic, and food products. Court decisions now permit doctors, dentists, and other health practitioners to advertise. The public has been awakened to the need for expanded social consciousness and social action to ensure equity, fair play, and justice in the business world.

Consumer Bill of Rights

President John F. Kennedy recognized the need for consumer protection and gave considerable recognition and status to the movement when he outlined a Consumer Bill of Rights in a message to Congress on March 15, 1962. The basic principles in this Bill of Rights continue to serve as guidelines for the entire consumer movement.[28]

The right to safety: To be protected against the marketing of goods that are hazardous to health or to life.

The right to be informed: To be protected against fraudulent, deceitful, or grossly misleading information, advertising, labeling, or other practices, and to be given the facts needed to make informed choices.

The right to choose: To be assured, whenever possible, access to a variety of products and services at competitive prices, and in those industries in which competition is not workable and government regulation is substituted, an assurance of satisfactory quality and service at fair prices.

The right to be heard: To be assured that consumer interests will receive full and sympathetic consideration in the formulation of government policy, and fair and expeditious treatment in its administrative tribunal.

The Consumer Bill of Rights calls for social action by individuals and groups in both the public and private sectors of society. For maximum consumer protection, individuals, government, and voluntary agencies and organizations must all be involved in a joint effort to assure the safety and efficacy of products, to increase the communication of accurate information, and to guard against the promotion of misleading information.

Some years ago Betty Furness,[29] a prominent consumer advocate, said that "informed and alert consumers are the greatest defenders of the free enterprise system." Resources for providing information to consumers and for hearing complaints from consumers must be available. Individuals must use these resources to become informed if they expect to make intelligent choices about the purchase and use of health products and services. They must also be willing to object and to take needed action when deceptive practices occur. People must be afforded the opportunity to express grievances to government agencies, business enterprises, and consumer advocate groups when they have been victimized.

What Is Consumer Health?

Consumer health could be defined to include any or all aspects of the health care delivery system as well as all phases of health education. However, this book uses a narrower definition of consumer health: *the decisions individuals make about the purchase and use of health products and services that may have a direct effect on their health.* This definition provides a unique health orientation because of its specific relationship to the consumer's pocketbook.

Products are those substances, materials, or equipment prepared or manufactured for consumer purchase and used in the treatment, care, and maintenance of health. Services refers to health actions, information, or work furnished or supplied to help satisfy the needs or wants of consumers: things people do to and for people.

Consumer health involves the economic, or monetary, aspects of health over which individuals have control. It includes self-motivated or self-initiated action, which may include the purchase of a bottle of aspirin tablets or a dentifrice or the selection of a physician, dentist, or nursing home. It is not what health departments or others do to control disease or the environment through clinics, information, or in other ways. However, a consumer's decision to seek and use such products, services, or information is consumer health.

Positively, consumer health involves the information and understanding that enable individuals to make wise decisions about health services and products. Negatively, it refers to the avoidance of unwise decisions based on frauds, fads, fallacies, and superstitions. Some years ago Dr. Herbert Ratner[30] of the Stritch School of Medicine, Loyola University, referred to consumer health in another way that is still applicable:

> Modern man ends up a vitamin-taking, antacid-consuming, barbiturate-sedated, aspirin-alleviated, benzedrine-stimulated psychosomatically diseased, surgically despoiled animal; nature's highest product turns out to be a fatigued, peptic-ulcerated, tense, headachy, overstimulated, neurotic, tonsilless creature.

FIGURE 1-1. Where do you get most of your health information?
(From: The Image Bank—Janeart Ltd.)

The Intelligent Health Consumer

Consumers who wish to protect themselves against frauds, misleading and inaccurate information, purveyors of quackery, and con artists must learn to act intelligently. Such action will involve perseverance and at times a great deal of effort.

1. *The intelligent consumer is well informed and knows how to make sound decisions.* Becoming well informed takes considerable effort, but only well informed individuals can cope with the complexity of the health marketplace.
2. *The intelligent consumer seeks reliable sources of information.* Most physicians, dentists, allied health professionals, and specialists in the health field, as well as scientists and health educators, are reliable. Federal, state, and local government agencies and professional and many voluntary organizations involved in health such as the FDA, the FTC, the American Medical Association, the American Cancer Society, the American Dental Association, the Arthritis Foundation, the U.S. Public Health Service, are generally dependable sources (for more information see Chapter 3 and the Appendix).
3. *The intelligent consumer is appropriately skeptical about health information and does not accept statements appearing in the news media or advertising at face value.* Do not hesitate to ask questions in regard to accuracy, scientific evidence, sources of information, and proponent credentials, among others (see Chapters 3 and 5).
4. *The intelligent consumer is wary of inept practitioners, pseudopractitioners, and pitchmen in the business and medical worlds and can identify quacks and quackery.* They often sell science or pseudoscience in a brand of gobbledygook that sounds technical and scientific because they use valid terms.

TABLE 1–2

INTELLIGENT HEALTH CONSUMER PROFILE

This exercise can help determine the extent to which consumers act intelligently when exposed to misleading and inaccurate information, to health fraud, and to health quackery. Place an X in the column to the right that best represents your answer:

	VM	M	S	L	N
Are you sufficiently informed to be able to make sound decisions?					
Where do you go for information when needed?					
Professional health organizations/individuals					
Health books, magazines, newsletters					
Government health agencies					
Advertisements					
Newpapers/magazines					
Radio/television					
People you know					
To what extent do you accept statements appearing in news reports or advertisements at face value?					
To what extent can you identify quacks, quackery, fraudulent schemes, and hucksters?					
When selecting health practitioners to what extent do you:					
Talk with or visit before first appointment					
Check/inquire regarding qualifications/credentials					
Ask friend/neighbor about reputation					
Inquire about fees and payment procedures					
When you have been exposed to a fraudulent practice, quack, quackery, or a poor product or service, to what extent do you report your experience?					

Key: VM = very much; M = much; S = some; L = little; N = none;

5. *The intelligent consumer selects practitioners with great care and questions fees, diagnoses, treatments, and alternative treatments.* These inquiries should be done in a discreet manner. The purpose is not to be antagonistic but to ensure the clarity and validity of information received.
6. *The intelligent consumer willingly "speaks out" by reporting frauds, quackery, and wrongdoing to appropriate agencies and law enforcement officials.*

Table 1-2 can help consumers review their knowledge and behavior regarding the products and services they purchase and use. It offers a rough appraisal to help identify areas of consumer health that need attention.

IT'S YOUR DECISION

What would you do if you had a back pain that was severe at times and has been with you for some weeks, months or longer? Would you:

		Reason
1. ______	Obtain a painkiller from a drug store?	______
2. ______	Apply a heating pad for at least 30 minutes every night for 1 week?	______
3. ______	Visit a chiropractor?	______
4. ______	Obtain an acupuncture treatment?	______
5. ______	See a medical doctor?	______
6. ______	Other	______

You have heard a so-called health expert proclaim that a special substance or product available in the health marketplace will help relieve back pain. What action would you take to help you decide whether to purchase and use this product?

SUMMARY

Changes in life-style resulting from scientific and technologic advances in the United States have created consumer problems in the health marketplace. The spiraling costs of medical care, the questioning of the quality of medical care, consumer displeasure with medical services, the confusion and complexity of health information, the inadequate health insurance coverage of a large segment of the population, the marketing of worthless, fraudulent, and harmful health products and services, and the promotion of nonscientific practices have led to increased consumer protection activities. Consumer focus in the marketplace has changed from emphasis on caveat emptor to caveat vendor. The Consumer Bill of Rights—safety, freedom of choice, informed choice, and freedom to speak out—emerged.

This background led to the authors' definition of consumer health: *decisions people make to purchase and use health products and services that have a direct effect on their health.* Consumers must make intelligent choices, but they need accurate information to freely select health products and services.

DISCUSSION QUESTIONS

1. What effect have the scientific and technologic changes in the United States had on health values in the United States?
2. Name five problems in the health marketplace that deserve consumer attention. What can be done about them? How has AIDS contributed to these problems?
3. What factors were involved in the development of the consumer protection movement in the United States?
4. What is the caveat emptor/caveat vendor concept? What is its relationship to the consumer movement? What are its implications for health products and services purchased and used by consumers?
5. What are the basic principles of consumer protection found in the Consumer Bill of Rights? How can they be applied to the health marketplace?
6. What is *consumer health?* What are its positive and negative aspects?
7. What actions will enable people to become intelligent consumers?

REFERENCES

*1. Pepper C: Quackery—a $10 billion scandal. A report by the chairman of the Subcommittee on Health and Human Services of the Select Committee on Aging, House of Representatives, Washington, DC, 1984, U.S. Government Printing Office.

*Recommended reading

2. Farley F: Prom night leads to GHB prosecutions, FDA Consumer 25(5):34-35, 1991.
3. Dubos R: Mirage of health, Garden City, NY, 1959, Doubleday & Co.
4. Levit KR et al: National health expenditures, Health Care Financing Review 13(1):29-54, 1991.
*5. Health Insurance Association of America: Sourcebook of Health Insurance Data, Washington, DC, 1990, The Association.
6. Gonzales ML: Socioeconomic characteristics of medical practice, Chicago, 1991, American Medical Association.
7. AIDS epidemic, The Nation's Health, Feb 1991.
8. Segal M: Defrauding the desperate, FDA Consumer 21(8):16-19, 1987.
9. American Medical Association: Physicians' opinion on health care issues (Survey and opinion research), Chicago, 1984, The Association.
10. Polling the patient, The Washington Post, Health Section, p 97, April 16, 1986.
11. Slatella M: No more blind faith: more consumers asking questions, Newsday, Nov 13, 1990.
12. Markle GB: Dare to ask the cost, Public Citizen Health Research Group Health Letter 5(5):10-11, 1989.
13. Three hundred scrutinized in overprescriptions, The New York Times, p 8, Mar 8, 1990.
14. McLeod D: Unneeded medical tests are focus of HHS probe, AARP Bulletin, March 1990.
15. Rate of caesarean births has leveled off. The Nation's Health, Aug 1991.
16. The pap test misses much cervical cancer through lab errors, The Wall Street Journal, pp 1, 22, Nov 2, 1987.
*17. 9479 questionable doctors, Public Citizen Health Research Group 7(7):1-5, 1991. Health Letter. July 1991.
18. Richards CF: What bothers doctors. Newsday Magazine, Jan 13, 1991.
19. Women's health alert, Public Citizen Health Research Group Health Letter 7(4):3, 1991.
20. The Prevention Index '91: A report card on the nation's health, Emmaus Pa, 1991, Rodale Press Inc.
21. State of your health, Mayo Clinic Health Letter, 8(10):6, 1990.
*22. Top 10 health frauds, FDA Consumer, 23(8):29-31, Oct 1989.
23. Quackery, Mayo Clinic Health Letter, Medical Essay, June 1988.
24. The OTC/HBA battleground, Drug Topics 135:52-53, 1991.
25. Smith RL: The health hucksters, New York, 1960, Thomas Y Crowell Co, Inc.
26. Coniff J: You can make a big business care, Today's Health 49:16-19, 1971.
27. McGarrah RG, Jr: A consumer's directory of Prince George's County (Maryland) doctors, Washington DC, 1974, Health Research Group.
28. Consumer Advisory Council, Executive Office of the President: First report, Washington DC, 1963, US Government Printing Office.
29. Bishop J, Jr and Hubbard HW: Let the buyer beware, Washington DC, 1969, National Press Inc.
30. US Senate Special Committee on Aging: Consumer frauds and elderly persons: a growing problem, Washington DC, April, 1983, US Government Printing Office.
31. Ray RD and Rogers PG: There's too much uncertainty in medical care, The Wall Street Journal, p 36, Oct 13, 1987.
32. Sullivan R: New York starts effort to slow cesarean rate, The New York Times, p B4, Nov 24, 1987.

CHAPTER TWO

A Historical Perspective

I know it's common to speak of the "good old days" of snake oil and soothing syrup as though they were gone forever. The amazing fact is that to a very great extent those good old days, so called, are still with us.

George P. Larrick, Former Commissioner,
Food and Drug Administration

Consumer health had its beginnings many years ago. Numerous treatments once thought effective have been abandoned by scientific practitioners, but many fads, fallacies, and myths continue to influence the decisions people make about their health. This chapter provides an historical perspective on consumer health, with emphasis on medical practice, patent medicines, quackery, drug laws, and food faddism.

CONSUMER DECISIONS

What fads, fallacies, and myths advocated long ago still influence consumer decisions about health products and services?

MEDICAL PRACTICE

The Greeks introduced a quasiscientific approach to medicine in the fifth century BC. The Oath of Hippocrates that emerged as the code of ethics for modern physicians came from this era.[1] In AD 100 the Greek physician and writer Galen set forth the theory that disease was caused by cold (although heat was also needed) and "plethora" (excess blood and fluid). As a result bleeding and purging (with enemas) were used for centuries. They were still among the most common healing methods used in the United States during the first half of the nineteenth century.

Most doctors in the Middle Ages were monks. Divine intervention was sought as the main treatment for illness, as diseases were thought to be caused by demonic or evil influence. Priests, believed to have divine healing power, employed incantation and prayer. Prayer and the laying on of hands were considered necessary treatment procedures.

The early American Indians used plants with healing properties; most of these were emetics or cathartics (for example, jalap, cascara). The Incas discovered cinchona bark, which contains quinine (used for treating malaria).

In colonial times there were few trained physicians and no medical school in the United States. Furthermore, the United States had no provisions for certification or supervision; incompetence in medical practice was prevalent. Virtually anyone could practice medicine, but it was common for a young man to apprentice himself to a practitioner for 7 years at $100 per year.

The first American medical school did not open until 1765. However, in prerevolutionary America, there were 3500 practitioners, 400 of whom had obtained medical degrees from foreign universities. Many were immigrants. Benjamin Rush, a signer of the Declaration of Independence, is considered the father of American medicine. He began his training in America as an apprentice and obtained his medical degree from the University of Edinburgh in 1768.

Death rates were high during the eighteenth century. The major killers were infectious diseases, but the causes of infection were not known. Cathartics and various herbal concoctions were used for treatment. When purging was combined with bleeding, many patients became so weak that they died. Two measures that actually helped to control infectious diseases were the use of cinchona bark against malaria and vaccination against smallpox.

American medicine went from bad to worse in the nineteenth century. Many medical schools opened, but most had few if any standards of competence.[2] Programs were generally 2 years long, with little scientific training and no laboratory or clinical instruction. In 1870 the head of the Harvard Medical School said that written examinations could not be given because most of the students could not write well enough.[3] Dozens of schools sold diplomas, some for as little as $5. Many of the so-called healers were illiterates who peddled narcotic "cure-alls."

In 1900 a study revealed that physicians had trouble making enough money to succeed during the first 5 years after taking the Hippocratic Oath. Three-quarters of American medical school graduates turned to other ways of earning a living.[4]

In the 1800s self-diagnosis and self-medication were practiced extensively. Most families had a supply of medical books, herbs, and other nostrums. People who could nurse the sick were generally available, but doctors were seldom called when illness occurred. Few doctors were competent, patients lived considerable distances from physicians, and treatment was often too severe.

Medicines used before 1900 were generally not curative. About all that could be done for patients was to provide some measure of relief and nursing care. A wide variety of patient medicines and nostrums were marketed. Charlatans flourished without interference from the law.

Until the work of Louis Pasteur, Joseph Lister, and Robert Koch established the bacterial theory of disease in the 1870s, no one had a clear idea of the cause of infections. Pasteur was a chemist who studied contagious disease in animals and discovered the anthrax bacillus. He developed diphtheria antitoxin, rabies vaccine, and a process for killing disease-causing bacteria in milk (pasteurization). Lister used carbolic acid for antiseptic surgery. Koch discovered the bacillus that causes tuberculosis. By the 1880s, antiseptic and aseptic methods were incorporated into medical practice.

In 1904 the American Medical Association and the Carnegie Foundation commissioned Dr. Abraham Flexner to investigate medical schools in the United States. His report, published in 1910, recommended standards for curriculum, admission, and clinical teaching and led to the closing of half of these schools. By the 1930s, substandard medical schools were eliminated, and licensing and accreditation procedures had been established. By 1944 only 69 medical schools remained. Today 141 medical and osteopathic schools offer accredited training in the United States.

FIGURE 2-1.
From *The Great Patent Medicine Era* by Adelaide Hechtlinger, © 1970 by Grosset & Dunlap, Inc. Reprinted by permission.

HERBAL REMEDIES

Herbal remedies have been used throughout history. The Persians, Romans, Greeks, Hebrews, and Babylonians were familiar with the practice of herbal medicine. By trial and error, accident or design, it was concluded that certain roots, plants, barks, and seeds possessed medicinal properties. In the second century BC, the Egyptians used myrrh, cumin, peppermint, caraway, fennel, and oil of cloves for various ailments. Licorice was especially esteemed. Sarsaparilla, the dried root of the similax, a climbing vine native to tropical regions of the Americas, was introduced in Europe in the sixteenth century as a tonic for venereal disease and later for chronic rheumatism, scrofula, and skin disease. In the latter part of the nineteenth century its use as a medicine was abandoned, but it became popular as a syrup for soft drinks.

Although a few plant substances have been used in modern medical practice, most have been replaced by products that are safer or more effective or have fewer unpleasant side effects. For example, reserpine, found naturally in snakeroot (rauwolfia), was one of the earliest effective remedies against high blood pressure and was used extensively during the 1950s and 1960s until better synthetic drugs were developed. Curare, used to paralyze muscles during surgical procedures, has been replaced by synthetic derivatives. Foxglove leaves contain digitalis, a drug used to treat heart failure and abnormal heart rhythms. But the use of dried leaves has given way to extracts and synthetic drugs whose dosages are precisely controlled.

PATENT MEDICINES

Dr. Oliver Wendell Holmes knew well enough that it was difficult to tell a mushroom from a toadstool, that many promoters of nostrums were sincere and kindly men and not unscrupulous rogues, though their handiwork might be hazardous to their customers.[5]

John Harvey Young, Ph.D.
The Toadstool Millionaires

Patent medicines were also known as nostrums and proprietary medicines. Nostrums are remedies recommended by their preparers, usually without scientific proof of effectiveness. Strictly speaking, patent medicines are those for which patents have been obtained from the U.S. Patent Office to deter other manufacturers from copying them. (A patent permits a 17-year monopoly.) However, many products referred to as "patent remedies" were actually never patented. A proprietary medicine is one whose name, composition, or manufacturing process is protected from use by competitors.

Nostrums have been used for many centuries. For example, great curative powers were attributed to snake skin. Herbs, roots, and decoctions have been used in thousands of medicinal preparations. Patent medicines are part of the American heritage. They were imported from England and Continental Europe. During the 1750s many appeared in America and were sold by postmasters, grocers, booksellers, tailors, and painters. The worse a substance tasted, the greater its curative powers were assumed to be. Some compounds included soil fertilizers and urine.

The nineteenth century has been referred to as the "patent medicine era" because of the extensive variety of materials sold to the public. The patent medicine business was a lucrative one. Many of the products were actually neither helpful nor toxic. However, some were poisonous.

The reasons patent medicines were used during the nineteenth century included:

1. Skepticism of physicians.
2. The continued use of bloodletting and purging. People were easily persuaded to try cheap, quick, and painless ways to health.
3. The need for symptomatic relief from widespread biliousness (dyspepsia) due to overeating, particularly of starchy foods, salt-cured meats, and fat-fried foods.
4. A desire to reduce the high mortality rate. The average American life expectancy was 40 years in 1850 and 50 years in 1900.
5. Public ignorance.
6. The high alcohol and narcotic content of many substances.
7. The scarcity of doctors, particularly competent ones.

Some patent medicines were designed for specific ailments while others were supposedly cure-alls. They were claimed to affect such afflictions as "female weakness," "worn-out kidneys," yellow fever, goiter, cancer, paralysis, and "piles" (hemorrhoids). Tonics, bitters, and other substances were widely used, but their ingredients were kept secret. Toxic substances and addictive narcotics could be legally marketed. Some patent medicines were as hazardous as the ministrations of the doctors practicing "heroic" medicine of the period.

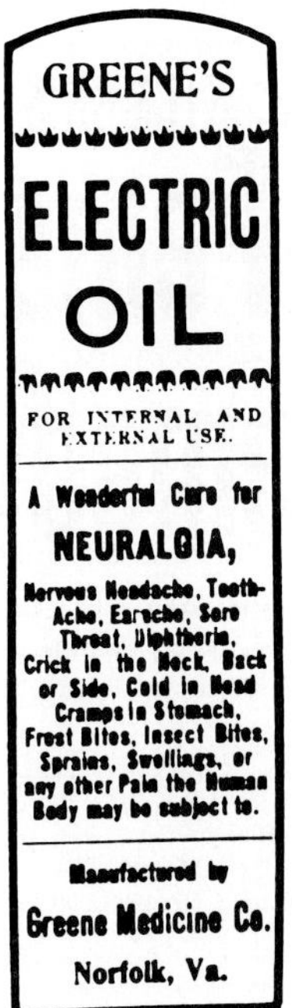

FIGURE 2-2.
From *The Great Patent Medicine Era* by Adelaide Hechtlinger, © 1970 by Grosset & Dunlap, Inc. Reprinted by permission.

Whiskey was considered the all-purpose remedy on the frontier. It was used as an antiseptic, painkiller, and courage builder. Tonics and cough medicines were popular because of their alcoholic content, as illustrated by these products: *Hood's Sarsaparilla* (18%), *Hotstetter's Bitters* (44%), *Parker's Tonics* (42%), and *Lydia E. Pinkham's Vegetable Compound* (18%). Most hard liquors today are about 40% to 45% alcohol.

Most patent remedies were basically of vegetable origin, including the leaves, flowers, seeds, bark, and roots of bittersweet, buckthorn, chicory, castor oil, hemlock, holly, juniper bush, violets, alder, alfalfa, allspice, and almond. The Indians used onion, mustard, elder, garlic, dandelion, ginger root, hops, horsemint, horse chestnuts, horseradish, mullein, hemlock, licorice, and sassafras. The *Indian Vegetable Family Instructor* included these uses:

For cough: Take dried leaves of rosemary, shred small and smoke them in a tobacco pipe.

To stop vomiting: Take green wheat and green grass, pound it and pour on boiling water, and sweeten with loaf sugar; press out the juice and drink a tablespoonful every 10 minutes.

DR. KILMER'S Female Remedy.

Symptoms and Conditions for which Female Remedy is Recommended.

If you have chronic weakness, bearing down, or perversions incident to life-change.

If you have uterine catarrh, suppressed or painful periods, or ovarian dropsy.

If you have suspicious growths, disposed to tumor or cancer, or hemorrhage.

If you have painful or irregular menstruation, leucorrhœa, or are unwell most of the time.

If you are suffering from retroversion or falling of the womb, induration or enlargement, hypertrophy, ulceration or drainage, and the many attending evils that are present in CHRONIC female complaints.

So Pure and natural are the herbal ingredients in **Female Remedy** THAT NO HARM CAN FOLLOW ITS USE, even when taken by the most delicate invalid.

At Druggists; Price, $1.00.

DR. KILMER'S

LADIES' HOME TREATMENT.

With these excellent remedies at hand, every lady can be her own physician.

She can treat herself without revealing her condition to any one, or subjecting her womanly modesty to an unnecessary examination by a physician.

Ladies need not submit to the use of pessaries, local manipulations and tamperings so much resorted to in practice. Such means are often fruitful cause of malignant maladies inviting more serious troubles (uterine tumor and cancer).

Ladies: If your case would seem to require the Female Remedy, Herbal Extract and the U & O Anointment, and you have decided to get them, **remember** to see that Dr. Kilmer's **likeness and address**, Binghamton, N. Y., are on outside and inside wrappers.

U & O Anointment, 25 or 50-cent sizes.
Herbal Extract, - - - 50 cts.

Sold by Druggists, or sent by mail on receipt of price.

ADDRESS,

Dr. Kilmer & Co., Binghamton, N. Y.

FIGURE 2-3.

From *The Great Patent Medicine Era* by Adelaide Hechtlinger, © 1970 by Grosset & Dunlap, Inc. Reprinted by permission.

FIGURE 2-4.

For rheumatism: Take a tablespoon of pitch from a white pine log, the same quantity of sulphur, and a spoonful of honey; add 2 quarts of the best fourth-proof brandy and shake till dissolved; cork it tightly for use; take a tablespoon three times daily.

Cure for corns: Spread a plaster of white turpentine, put it on corn, let it stay till the corn comes off of its own accord.[6]

Advertising

Advertising played an important role in the patent medicine business. Newspapers contributed to the growth of this industry. By 1860 there were 4000 newspapers, including 400 dailies. By 1900 there were 100 magazines in production. In 1804 about 100 patent medicines were being marketed. By 1858 over 1500 substances were advertised, not only in newspapers and magazines but also on handbills, the surfaces of rocks, templed hills, buildings, and steamboat decks.

There was no legislation to control advertising in the nineteenth century, and product claims by manufacturers were never modest. These were the main techniques used by advertisers:

1. Make the product's name memorable: Burdock's Blood Bitters, Swift's Sure Specific.
2. Distribute books and pamphlets giving medical advice.
3. Use cures from afar (e.g., China, Turkey).
4. Promote the American Indian and his healing care.
5. Invoke mythology (Hygeia, the minerva pill for syphilis).
6. Indicate that diseases may lead to pain and death.
7. Use biblical quotations and testimonials from ministers.
8. Use testimonials from supposedly satisfied customers. Some of these people later died from the disease the medicine was supposed to have cured.
9. Use a doctor's name or picture on the label.
10. Give away free items such as an almanac or booklet; offer a money-back "guarantee."

In 1905 Samuel Hopkins Adams, a freelance journalist, began a campaign against patent medicines in 10 articles he wrote for *Collier's* magazine. He called the products "the great American fraud," and said that gullible Americans were spending more than $75 million annually to purchase patent medicines that included large quantities of alcohol and opiates and a wide assortment of drugs. He investigated "Dr. King's New Discovery for Consumption," which had been proclaimed as the only sure cure for tuberculosis in the world, and found that the product contained morphine, chloroform, and 28% alcohol. The chloroform was to allay the cough, and the morphine and alcohol drugged the patient into deceptive cheerfulness. The label did not reveal the nature of the ingredients or their possible hazardous effects. Adams claimed that patent medicine testimonials were gathered from "gullible ignoramuses or secured through various pressures from people in public life."[5]

KICKAPOO INDIAN OIL FOR ALL PAIN. 

MAN AND CHIEF. MEDICINE MAN.

One Bottle Cured Him.

I had chills and fever for years. Visited doctors in Boston and elsewhere, but got no relief, and was very much discouraged. I paid hundreds of dollars to the doctors without benefit, and then bought a bottle of Kickapoo Indian Sagwa for one dollar, and the second dose stopped the chills, one bottle effected a permanent cure.

MARTIN CONNELLY.

Worcester, Mass.

Chills Take Flight.

I have suffered three years from chills, was all worn out and discouraged. Doctors failed to relieve me. Took Kickapoo Indian Sagwa, and my chills have taken flight. I am cured. NEWTON MAYS.

Spring Hill, Kans.

Impure Blood.

The vital fluid which circulates through the body, giving it nourishment and strength, is of the highest importance. There cannot be a healthy condition of the body if the blood is impure. The germs of scrofula, salt rheum, and many other diseases, which sooner or later undermine the health, all arise from impure blood. To insure good health, this state of things must be changed; the blood must be cleansed from all impurities, and allowed free and unobstructed circulation through both veins and arteries. Kickapoo Indian Sagwa is the acknowledged Blood Renovator. Its equal cannot be found in all the science of medicine and chemistry. In all cases of blood disease, Sagwa works like magic.

A Great Sufferer.

I have been a great sufferer from eczema for the past five years, and have been treated by three different doctors, without receiving any benefit from them. Have now tried the Kickapoo Indian Sagwa in connection with the Kickapoo Indian Salve, and find they will do just what is claimed of them, that is, purify the blood and cure skin diseases. I have used the remedies for ten days and the eczema has nearly disappeared, and I earnestly recommend all those afflicted with any kind of skin disease to procure these great Indian Remedies at once. They will surely give relief in a short time.

MRS. C. W. LEIGHTON.

Gossville, N. H.

My Mother-in-law.

My mother-in-law, Mrs. Turbit, of Indiana, was paying us a visit last spring, and as she had a peculiar running sore just under the ear—that was called by doctors whom she consulted scrofula, erysipelas, and cancer—I requested her to try the Kickapoo Indian Remedies. She had not much faith, as so many doctors had failed to help her; nevertheless I got her a bottle of Indian Sagwa and a box of Indian Salve. She consented to give them a trial, and in just three days there was a marked improvement in her condition; in two weeks she was entirely well The old sore healed, and save for a small scar it would be hard to tell it ever was there.

GEORGE RUSSELL,
Chief of Fire Department.

W. Bay City, Mich.

Scrofula.

In olden times of superstition this disease was believed to be cured by the patient being touched by the royal hand of the king. It was from this that the disease took the name of "king's evil." A terrible evil it is; and yet more terrible is the fact that in the veins of the majority of

Kickapoo Indian Sagwa cures Scrofula.

FIGURE 2-5.
From *The Great Patent Medicine Era* by Adelaide Hechtlinger, © 1970 by Grosset & Dunlap, Inc. Reprinted by permission.

Prominent Promoters and Remedies

Thousands of patent medicines were produced and distributed in the United States with sales reaching their peak during the nineteenth century and the first part of the twentieth century.

In 1796 Samuel H.P. Lee, a doctor from Windham, Connecticut, became the first American to prepare a patent medicine, which he called "Bilious Pills." The ingredients were gamboge, aloe, soap, and nitrate of potassium. The pills supposedly would cure biliousness, yellow fever, jaundice, dysentery, dropsy, worms, and female complaints.

In the 1800s a man named Thomas W. Dyott became king of the nostrum makers in America. His products contained large quantities of alcohol. He assumed the title of M.D. and fabricated experience as a doctor. By 1830 his income was $25,000 per year, and when he died, his estate was valued at $250,000.

Samuel Thomson, a New Hampshire farmer in the 1800s, devised a system of medical treatment intended to make every man his own physician. He believed that the diminished "power of heat" and water caused an imbalance of body elements. The cure was to restore heat with a 30-minute steam bath, which was followed by washing the body with cold water, taking a powerful vomitive containing herbs mixed in brandy, drinking warm water until vomiting occurs, taking another bath, resting in bed, and taking two herbal enemas.[7] This treatment was repeated for several days. Thomson was labeled "the sweating and steaming doctor."

The home-remedy books of the early 1800s promoted patent medicines as well as home remedies. Among these volumes were *Indian Doctor's Dispensatory, Dr. John Williams' Last Legacy, A Useful Family Herbal, Dr. Chase's Recipes, Gunn's Domestic Medicine,* and *Poor Man's Friend in Pain and Sickness.* Granny cures found in these books included:

> *Hard breasts:* Apply turnips roasted till soft, then mashed and mixed with a little oil of roses; change this mixture twice a day, keeping the breast very warm with flannel.
>
> *Baldness:* Rub head morning and night with onion till red, and rub afterwards with honey.
>
> *Cold:* Drink a pint of cold water while lying in bed.
>
> *Nosebleed:* Chew a newspaper; put a small piece of paper between the upper teeth and lower lip; chew gum.

Lydia E. Pinkham's Vegetable Compound was advertised in 1873 for female weaknesses, irregular menstruation, inflammation, and ulceration of the womb. The Bureau of Investigation of the American Medical Association could find no medical evidence to support these claims. The compound originally contained 18% alcohol. Eventually vitamins and minerals were added and the alcohol content was reduced. The company appealed to women disenchanted with their doctors by suggesting that the grandmotherly Mrs. Pinkham was compassionate and understood their needs. *The Pinkham Guide for Women,* a publication important to the product's success, had over 1 million copies distributed.

In 1890 Dr. Samuel Brubaker Hartman produced *Peruna,* which he claimed could cure catarrh of the lungs, disorders of the stomach, head, kidneys, bladder, and pelvis, and other conditions. Peruna contained 25% alcohol. For 25 years no other patent medicine in the United States devoted as much newspaper space to testimonials.

Medicine Shows

During the nineteenth century patent medicine promoters often met their customers face-to-face. They went to towns and villages, especially during fairs, setting up platforms, putting on shows, delivering spiels, selling their remedies, and then moving on. The performances evolved into full evenings of drama, vaudeville, musical comedy, bands, parades, and other spectacles. This was all considered respectable, as were the sidewalk exhibits in store windows that lured young men to "free exhibits" inside, where they were terrified into believing they suffered from some strange disease. The men were then spirited into examining rooms, where "doctors" asked a few hasty questions and pressured them into buying secret remedies. Often the cost was the exact amount of money found in their wallets.

Perhaps the greatest spectacle of the day was produced by John A. Healy and Charles Bigelow and their Kickapoo Indian Medicine Company.[8] The entertainment consisted of Indians and Wild West performers who were professional actors. Healy's "liver pads" supposedly contained a mixture of roots, bark, gum, leaves, oils, and berries prepared by the Kickapoo Indians. Actually they contained sawdust, red pepper, and glue!

Dudley J. LeBlanc, a Louisiana state senator, introduced *Hadacol* to the public in 1943. It was an elixir containing 12% alcohol, B-vitamins, iron, calcium and phosphorus, diluted hydrochloric acid, and honey. An 8-ounce bottle sold for $1.25, and a 24-ounce bottle cost $3.50. A pamphlet entitled "Good Health—Life's Greatest Blessing," produced by LeBlanc in 1948, contained testimonials by people supposedly cured of such conditions as anemia, arthritis, asthma, diabetes, epilepsy, heart trouble, and high and low blood pressure. It was claimed that a 13-year-old boy who lacked the energy to ride his bicycle took *Hadacol* and became a center on his football team.

LeBlanc revived the old-time medicine show. In 1950 a caravan of 130 vehicles, including steam calliopes, toured 3800 miles through the South. LeBlanc's medicine troupe played one-night stands in 18 cities with an average of 10,000 people attending. *Hadacol* boxtops were accepted as admission to hear a Dixieland band play "Hadacol Boogie" and "Who Put the Pep in Grandma?" In August 1951, shortly after LeBlanc claimed sales of $75 million, he sold his business for $8 million.

Quackery

> The story of quackery is a never-ending tale. Theorist after theorist propounds new gospels of healing . . . False prophet after false prophet arises, surrounds himself with

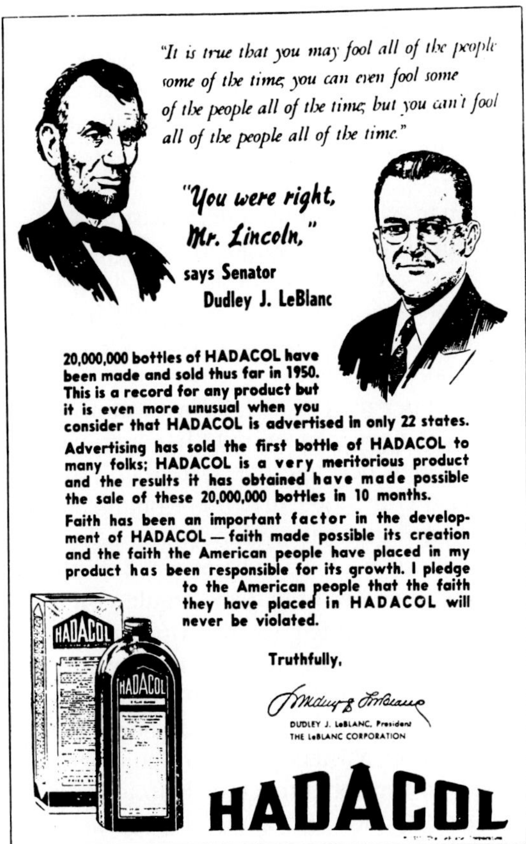

FIGURE 2-6.
James Harvey Young, From *The Medical Messiahs.* Copyright © 1967 by Princeton University Press. Used by permission.

fanatical followers, builds himself a sort of distinction while lolling in the lap of luxury, and then departs this mundane realm, leaving it a sadder if not wiser world.[9]

Morris Fishbein

A quack is a fraudulent health practitioner who disregards and/or misinterprets scientific evidence for personal gain. Quackery refers to methods that are questionable, useless, and possibly harmful. Its claims often parallel scientific discoveries by drawing upon current concepts but carrying them too far. Historian James Harvey Young has summarized the history of quackery by saying: "Quacks never sleep."

Animal Magnetism

The concept of a dreamlike or hypnotic state during which cures of symptoms are attempted has existed for centuries. Hypnosis was employed in ancient Greece and the Orient.

Franz Anton Mesmer, born in Austria in 1733, acquired three doctoral degrees, including one in medicine. He derived his concept of "animal magnetism" from astrology and believed that a magnetic force from the planets influenced body ailments. He assumed that this force was composed of invisible waves in gas form. He developed a doctrine of mental healing, in contrast to a physical healing approach. Although the theory of "animal magnetism" was unfounded, Mesmer's strong personality and suggestive approach succeeded with some patients who had hysterical or psychosomatic symptoms. Today hypnosis plays a modest role in the treatment of emotional problems.

Hydrotherapy

People of primitive societies found that hot and cold water could ease many ailments. Early in history, ways were discovered to sweat away fevers and other problems. People were placed in boxes built over steaming springs or volcanic caverns. The Romans and Greeks used cold baths at gymnasia to stimulate and refresh their bodies. Public baths appeared in Rome during the second century BC.

Hydrotherapy as a supposed curative agent enjoyed great popularity in the United States during the late 1800s and early 1900s; it has legitimate uses today in relieving muscular aches and helping people to relax. Spas are still popular in some parts of Europe, and in the United States today there are hundreds of such places.

Father Sebastian Kneipp, a parish priest in Germany, revived the use of water as a dominant pseudomedical force from 1840 to 1890. He claimed to have been ill constantly and to have recovered by doing such things as walking barefoot in the rain and in cold streams, and dousing his body with water. In *My Water Cure* he claimed that water dissolved poisonous elements in the blood, withdrew unhealthy water and purified the system, and strengthened and braced one's constitution. In 1892, he dispatched Benedict Lust to the United States as a missionary for his treatment. Lust went on to become the major promoter of naturopathy (see Chapter 9).

Device Quackery

Elisha Perkins, a practicing physician from Norwich, Connecticut, invented the Perkins Metallic Tractors in 1796. These were two rods of brass and iron about 3 inches long, rounded at one end and pointed at the other. They were produced at a time when electricity was considered a powerful force despite lack of knowledge of its properties. Dr. Perkins had observed during surgery that muscles may contract when touched by a metallic instrument, and concluded that metallic substances influenced nerves and muscles. He believed that his tractors could draw diseases from the body and could help against inflammation, rheumatism, and pains in the head, face, and breast. Although the state medical society was skeptical of Perkins's claims, it has been said that President George Washington, Supreme Court Justice Oliver Ellsworth, and Chief Justice John Marshall all purchased tractors.

Dr. Albert Abrams was born in San Francisco. He became professor of pathology at Cooper Medical College in San Francisco and in 1889 was appointed vice president of the California State Medical Society. In 1910 he published *Spondylotherapy*, in which he theorized that the reflex center in the spinal cord could be stimulated by rapid percussion (tapping). He believed that every disease had a vibratory rate and that diagnoses could be made by tapping the spine and abdomen to discover the patient's disease frequency. He claimed that he could determine the exact part of the body where an ailment was localized as well as its severity. He traveled throughout the country giving courses that cost $50 to $200.

Dr. Abrams also claimed he could determine a person's age, sex, and even religion from a drop of blood and could diagnose ailments from a handwriting sample. Later he introduced the reflexophone and said he could diagnose a person's condition by telephone.

Dr. Abrams treated illnesses with his oscilloclast, a sealed box with a rheostat, condenser, ohmmeter, and various wires. He claimed that the device would cure by sending into the body electrical waves that duplicated the rate of disease vibrations. He trained others to use his devices; several thousand individuals, including mechanotherapists, electrotherapists, sanipractors, naturopaths, and chiropractors became "electronic practitioners."[10] Some nonscientific practitioners use similar devices today (see Chapter 9).

A blue-ribbon committee created by *Scientific American* magazine investigated Dr. Abrams and concluded that his methods were "at best an illusion, at worst a colossal fraud." When he died in 1924, Abrams left several million dollars to his Electronic Medical Foundation to perpetuate the devices. Some may still be in use in the United States.

Dr. Ruth B. Drown, a chiropractor, developed and sold a variety of supposed diagnostic and therapeutic instruments. She conducted business with her daughter in the Los Angeles area for about 40 years.[11]

A woman with a lump in her breast was advised by her doctor in 1948 to go to a hospital for the treatment of cancer. Instead she visited Dr. Drown who "diagnosed" her condition by placing a drop of her blood on a blotter, which was then inserted into a small black box as Dr. Drown ran a finger across a rubber plate. The lady was informed that she did not have cancer but that a fungus had spread through her digestive system and liver. Dr. Drown also concluded that the woman had gallstones, a nonfunctioning kidney, and a deficiency of hydrochloric acid. The victim was told that her conditions could be cured if she would visit a practitioner, recommended by Dr. Drown, near her home in Chicago. Despite treatment by this practitioner (at $50 per visit) and further reassurance from Dr. Drown, the woman died of breast cancer.

Dr. Drown was persuaded to demonstrate the supposed power of her machine before scientists at the University of Chicago in 1949. Blood was drawn from ten patients whose health status had previously been determined by medical examination. Dr. Drown provided diagnoses for three of these individuals. She said the first patient had cancer of the left breast that had spread to the ovaries and pancreas; actually the patient had tuberculosis of the right lung. The diagnosis for the second patient was an improperly functioning uterus, but the actual condition was high blood pressure. The third patient, diagnosed as having cancer of the prostate, was a healthy young physician on the hospital staff.

Dr. Drown was brought to trial in 1950. The mechanical device she promoted was examined and found to be a very simple electrical circuit with a variety of wires. The galvanic instrument generated small voltages that would register on a dial. The dials were apparently irrelevant to treatment and the dried blood on the blotter was in no way linked to the galvanic circuit. Yet Dr. Drown was able to present testimony from 19 patients who spoke of marvelous benefits from her therapy. Dr. Drown was found guilty in 1951, fined $1000, and given a 1-year suspended sentence with 5 years probation. It cost the government $50,000 to prosecute the case.

Thereafter Dr. Drown stopped distributing her

devices in interstate commerce but continued to practice in California, eventually treating a total of 35,000 individuals. In 1963, following extensive investigation by the California State Bureau of Food and Drug Inspection, she was indicted for grand theft. An undercover agent from the district attorney's office had submitted samples of blood that were supposedly from her three children but actually came from a healthy turkey. At $50 per diagnosis, a report was returned claiming the children suffered from chickenpox and mumps. The agent was told how to use a Drown-supplied device to treat these conditions. Dr. Drown died at the age of 74 while awaiting trial.

Deluded Physician

William Horatio Bates received his M.D. degree from Cornell University in 1885. He was an attending physician at the New York Eye Infirmary and taught ophthalmology at the New York Postgraduate School from 1886 to 1891. In 1920 Dr. Bates wrote *Cure of Imperfect Eyesight by Treatment Without Glasses.* He stated (incorrectly) that the lens of the eye was not a factor in accommodation, and that refractive errors were simply "strain due to an abnormal condition of the mind" that could be helped through various prescribed eye exercises. He also advocated looking directly at the sun for short moments to "strengthen" the eyes. Although his methods have no validity, they are still advocated by a few practitioners today.

Narcotic Drugs

Brecher[13] described nineteenth-century America as a "dope fiend's paradise." Opium was sold legally at low prices. Morphine was commonly used, and heroin was marketed toward the end of the century. Opiates could be purchased as easily as aspirin is today. Physicians dispensed them in prescriptions, drugstores sold them over the counter, grocery and general stores made them available, and they could be ordered by mail.

More than 600 patent medicines and other products contained opium. They were widely advertised in newspapers and on billboards as effective against pain, cough, and other problems. Physicians prescribed them for pain, cough, diarrhea, dysentery, and other illnesses. Opiates were used as a substitute for alcohol. They apparently helped to calm rather than excite the baser passions and hence were considered less conducive to violent or criminal behavior. Many physicians converted alcoholics into narcotic addicts because morphine addiction was thought to be far less damaging than chronic alcoholism.

During the Civil War men who had been injured in battle were given large doses of opium to ease their pain. Soldiers often left hospitals cured of their wounds but addicted to narcotics. This affliction acquired the name "soldier's sickness." However, addiction was more widespread among civilians.

Personal Glimpse

A Demonstration of Great Strength

In 1912, Bernarr Macfadden toured midwestern cities to spark interest in his courses in "physical culture." One of the muscular youths who accompanied him was 18-year-old Forrest C. Shaklee, who went on to become a chiropractor and later founded the Shaklee Corporation, a large company that markets "natural" products through person-to-person sales (see Chapter 13). Shaklee literature describes how young Forrest helped Macfadden's promotion:

> Parades were held on the main street of each town, and consisted of a pride of muscular youths, some musicians, and a flatbed wagon . . .When enough of a crowd had been gathered around the flatbed, each of the youths was to exercise with a given piece of equipment. This was preceded by a discourse from Macfadden, extolling health through nature, diet and especially non-diet (he tended to look upon fasting as a blanket cure-all) and, of course, strenuous exercise . . . .
>
> The *pièce de résistance* of these outdoor displays was the lifting of an iron ball which appeared to weigh easily 500 pounds. Secured to the ball was a massive link chain, which one of the youths would grasp and which, with much concentration and apparent straining, he would raise gradually over his head. The crowds watching in awed silence at the beginning of the feat, would break into cheers and applause when the ball was finally raised. When it was his turn at the ball, Forrest discovered that lifting it was easily accomplished; the ball was hollow![12]

Federal Laws

The widespread use of narcotics in patent medicines and their accessibility through physicians, together with the extensiveness of quackery, gave impetus to passage of the Pure Food and Drug Act of 1906 and the Harrison Narcotic Act of 1914. Two leaders in the struggle for passage of the former were Dr. Harvey W. Wiley, chief chemist for the Department of Agriculture, and his crusading journalist follower, Samuel Hopkins Adams. Wiley's main concern had been the prevalence of fraudulent food products, but he also fought hard for the regulation of patent medicines. He wanted legislation to cover every kind of medicine for external and internal use, especially the proprietary medicines. Wiley believed that no remedy should be sold without its formula on the label and that no remedy containing alcohol or cocaine should be sold except by a doctor's prescription.

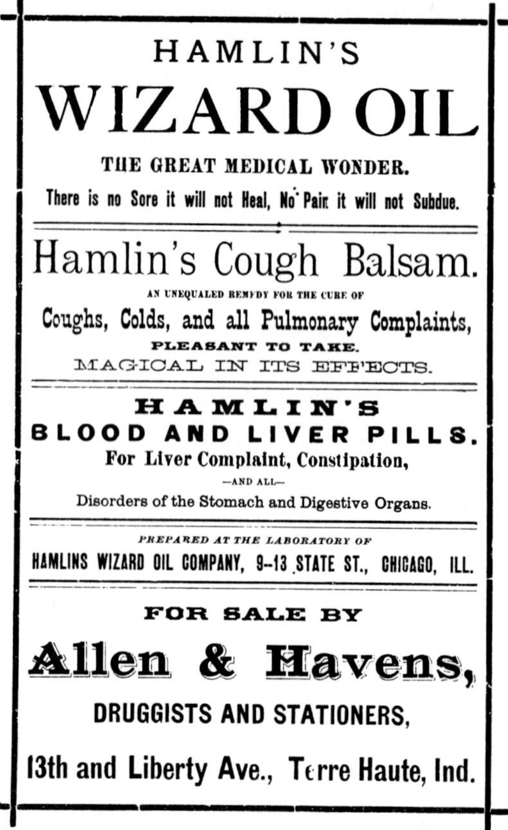

Figure 2-7.
From *The Great Patent Medicine Era* by Adelaide Hechtlinger, © 1970 by Grosset & Dunlap, Inc. Reprinted by permission.

Truth in Labeling

The Pure Food and Drug Act of 1906 required that medicine labels tell the truth—not the whole truth, but certain significant aspects. Labels had to state the presence and amount of certain dangerous drugs such as alcohol, opiates, and acetanilid. It was not necessary to identify other ingredients unless the proprietor wished to do so. The label could not provide false or misleading statements about the medicine or its ingredients.

The new law did not prevent self-medication but attempted to make it safer. It was assumed that the average person was intelligent enough to avoid risks when ingredients were known.

Many product labels changed drastically after 1906. Occasionally when the law was violated the government went to court, where it won a majority of such cases. However, fines were usually $50 or less, sometimes as low as one cent.

The first court trial under the Pure Food and Drug Act of 1906 was brought against Cuforhedake Brane-Fude (cure-for-headache brain food), a product that contained acetanilid (an analgesic and antipyretic), antipyrine, caffeine, sodium and potassium bromide, and alcohol. The label stated that the product contained 30% alcohol and 16 grams of acetanilid, but analysis of the product revealed only 24% alcohol. The government claimed that the label and an accompanying pamphlet that read: "a most wonderful certain and harmless relief . . . no . . . poisonous ingredients of any kind" were misleading. Samuel Hopkins Adams discovered that 22 people had died from acetanilid poisoning. Dr. Wiley concluded that the trade name was misleading and appeared to be an evasive spelling for a headache cure and that none of the ingredients was food for the brain. The manufacturer was found guilty of misbranding, was fined $700, and was forced to relabel the product. Some two million bottles of this substance had been sold for $1 each before the 1908 verdict. This illustrates how the selling of quack remedies can be very profitable despite government enforcement action—a situation that holds true today.

Truth in Advertising

The Pure Food and Drug Act had little effect upon misleading advertising. The Supreme Court ruled in 1911 that the Act's prohibition against false labeling did not apply to therapeutic claims, because the misbranding section of the law did not explicitly refer to curative promises. Congressman Swager Sherley of Kentucky sought to correct this dilemma by obtaining passage in 1912 of an amendment stating that an article would be misbranded "if its package of label shall bear or contain any statement, design, or device regarding the curative or therapeutic effect of such article or any of the ingredients or substances contained therein which is false and fraudulent."[6]

By 1915 the food and drug laws still had not controlled the problem of false and misleading advertising of patent medicines. Some observers claimed that conditions had worsened. Several of the reasons advanced were:

1. The job was too big for a small regulating staff.
2. Penalties were too light; fines were small and often unpaid.
3. Second offenders could be sent to jail for one year, but none had ever been sent.
4. Many dangerous drugs were not covered by the law.
5. Advertisements in newspapers needed to be attacked.

The Harrison Narcotic Act of 1914 was intended to authorize physicians to prescribe drugs solely to cure diseases and to alleviate suffering. The law was intended to ensure the orderly marketing of narcotics but was also used to prohibit the supplying of narcotic addicts, even by a physician's prescription.

The Proprietary Association opposed governmental control of advertising but was aware of the need to curb excesses. In 1915 it developed a code of ethics that included these provisions: (1) elimination of narcotics for children; (2) narcotics in adult medicines should comply with the Harrison Narcotic Act; (3) ingredients in medicines should not endanger life and health if used according to the instructions on the package; (4) alcohol should be used minimally; (5) package statements regarding therapeutic effects must be neither unreasonable nor demonstrably false; and (6) preparations must not be advertised or recommended as cures for diseases or conditions that are generally recognized as incurable. Unfortunately, the association's efforts to protect the public against patent medicines had little impact.

Increased Safety Requirements

The 1938 Food, Drug, and Cosmetic Act increased public protection but did not clearly distinguish between drugs requiring medical supervision and those suitable for self-medication. The hazard of permissive refills of prescribed drugs also remained. In the Midwest, a mother of three children was discovered upon admission to a hospital to be a barbiturate addict. She had received a prescription for 30 capsules that had been refilled 16 times

It cures from head to foot.

Puritana

Trade Mark Registered

Nature's Cure

For diseases of the STOMACH,
LIVER,
BLOOD,
KIDNEYS,

And for WEAK LUNGS,
STARVED NERVES,
FAGGED BRAIN.

It cures after everything else has failed. It cures cases that have been given up as hopeless. It cures pleasantly. It cures positively. It cures permanently.

It cures from head to foot.

Puritana is the prize formula of Prof. Dixi Crosby, M. D., LL. D., for over 30 years at the head of Dartmouth Medical College.

If you are a sufferer, get of your druggist this great disease-conquering discovery (the price is $1 for the complete treatment, consisting of one bottle of Puritana Compound, one bottle of Puritana Pills, and one bottle of Puritana Tablets), or write to the undersigned, and you will bless the day when you heard of Puritana. The Puritana Compound Co., Concord, N. H.

FIGURE 2-8.
From *The Great Patent Medicine Era* by Adelaide Hechtlinger, © 1970 by Grosset & Dunlap, Inc. Reprinted by permission.

within 3 months. Another woman mildly afflicted with high blood pressure was found dead in her bed. During the preceding 6 months she had received 23 refills of a prescription for 20 barbiturate capsules. Such evidence led to passage in 1951 of the Durham-Humphrey Amendment, which prohibited the refilling of prescriptions without specific authorization of the physician. It also gave the FDA the power to classify drugs as prescription drugs.

Young[6] calls the 25-year period following passage of the 1938 Act "the chemotherapeutic revolution." Its impact on self-medication was enormous. Americans spent less than $200 million per year for nonprescription medications in the 1930s, but by 1957 the sum had reached $2 billion. (Today it is over $30 billion.) This increase was partially due to extensive advertising. Unscrupulous promoters of pseudomedicine were prevalent during this period and their appeals became more sophisticated. Promotions included pamphlets, newspapers, roadside signs, lecturers (some speakers collected $25,000 weekly from fees and sales), and door-to-door salespeople.

Increased Efficacy Requirements

Critics charged in 1961 that the chemotherapeutic revolution had produced a therapeutic nightmare, especially with respect to prescription medications. Although many new drugs could save lives and reduce pain and suffering, many were improperly used, and drug-induced ailments occurred with increasing frequency. Some of the blame was attributed to physicians because (1) drugs were sometimes prescribed when none was needed; (2) new therapeutic agents were sometimes used without considering their potential dangers; and (3) physicians at times relied too much on the claims of drug manufacturers and salespeople.

Thalidomide, a generic drug, had been marketed in 1957 in West Germany as a sleeping tablet, sedative, and antiemetic for use by pregnant women. In 1960 the manufacturer submitted a new drug application to the FDA, indicating that thalidomide would be marketed under the trade name Kevadon. But Dr. Frances O. Kelsey, an FDA physician, suspected that the drug was hazardous to the unborn child. As a result of her action the drug application was withdrawn in March 1962. It soon became clear that babies born to mothers who took thalidomide during pregnancy had a high incidence of congenital malformations. The drug was never marketed in the United States; unfortunately, some Americans obtained it in Europe.

The thalidomide tragedy led to passage in October 1962 of the Kefauver-Harris Amendment to the Food, Drug, and Cosmetic Act. It provided that no new drug could be released to the public unless the manufacturer provided evidence acceptable to the FDA that the drug was effective as well as safe. Drug companies also had to notify the FDA immediately whenever they became aware that an approved drug might have adverse effects. Prior to this new legislation, the burden of proof efficacy was on the FDA.

Mail-order Frauds

Postal authorities were able to counter fraud by 1872 and, by 1895, could stamp letters "fraudulent" and return them to senders. But it was not until 1901 that the postmaster general, in collaboration with Dr. Wiley in the Department of Agriculture's Bureau of Chemistry, began acting against the misuse of the mails for the sale of patent medicines. Postal authorities assailed the most outrageous quacks who promised sure cures for such problems as cancer, consumption, epilepsy, blindness, deafness, a drug habit, a tobacco habit, "lost manhood," and "failing womanhood." Proving fraud was easiest against devices said to restore lost manhood or cure all human ills. During the late 1920s, frauds involving nostrums for tuberculosis and venereal disease were common. Most mail frauds today involve "miracle" diets and products claimed to enhance beauty, sexual function, or athletic prowess.

Nutrition Fads, Fallacies, and Myths

Nutrition-related fads, myths, and frauds have existed throughout the ages. It has been alleged that foods can sustain or interfere with general health and that some foods can cause or cure various illnesses. Some properties have been attributed to foods according to whether they are "natural" or not.

Food prejudices and taboos were rampant in early times. The Greeks ate grasshoppers for liver disorders and believed that fevers were helped by eating seven bugs from the skin of a bear. The Romans thought lettuce cleansed the senses, garlic gave physical strength, and truffles increased sexual potency. They also believed that good health came only with sacrifice, discomfort, self-discipline, and dour attitudes—a concept still common among health faddists.

Before the sixteenth century, physicians applied worms for lung diseases, deer fat for nerves, goose fat for piles, and, for undiagnosable conditions, moss grown on the skull of a hanged man. There was no understanding of human physiology or the origin of disease. Unusual or repulsive foods often were selected to prevent or treat ailments. For example, the Egyptians believed that a sick child should be fed skinned mice. The Romans believed that artichoke juice stopped falling hair. Pregnant Chinese women ate pigs' feet, and the Sultan of Turkey ate special clay from the Island of Lemnos to keep out demons. In the 1700s certain foods were regarded as potency-restorers and aphrodisiacs. Lettuce, for a time, was considered a sexual stimulant.

FIGURE 2-9.
From *The Great Patent Medicine Era* by Adelaide Hechtlinger, © 1970 by Grosset & Dunlap, Inc. Reprinted by permission.

Food faddism was extensive during the nineteenth century. During this period indigestion and dyspepsia were common because the American diet was rich in pork fat and pie. Some prominent promoters of food fads are presented next.

Sylvester Graham was considered the "prophet of whole wheat." He had been ordained as a Presbyterian minister in 1826 but was influenced by Philadelphia's Bible Christian Church. He practiced homeopathy and lectured on temperance, cholera, fresh air, taking baths, and sexual advice for young men.

Graham claimed that the true cause of disease was the removal of bran from flour during processing. Thus dark bread or brown bread reappeared in the marketplace and was called Graham bread. He also introduced the Graham cracker. At the time, nothing was known about the vitamin and mineral content of bran.

Graham believed that meat excited vile tempers and drove men to sexual excesses. He claimed that cholera was the result of too much lewdness and the eating of chicken pie. He also claimed that people did not bathe enough and needed external applications of cold water at least weekly. Partly as a result of his advocacy, Saturday night baths and setting-up exercises before open windows became common practices.

James Caleb Jackson introduced Granula and a variety of other food items. He had been a farmer in upstate New York and became a medical doctor by serving as an apprentice. His health had failed due to heart and kidney trouble together with dyspepsia. He believed that he had become well by consuming 30 to 40 glasses of water daily. In 1858 he opened a sanitarium at which women could get out of corsets and into bloomers; Jackson relieved them of their false hair, fed them fruits, Graham crackers and bread, and had them take naps and walks. He advocated vegetarianism and water in his program. To supplement the Graham crackers, Jackson prepared broken bits of rock-hard baked wheat with water, which he called Granula. He packaged this mixture and sold the product through the Our Home Granula Company. He developed a cereal coffee called So Mo, as well as other items. These were probably the first "health foods" sold in the United States.

Ellen Harmon White, who established the Seventh-Day Adventist Church in 1863, also advocated vegetarianism. She developed her own theories about food, and after a stay at Dr. Jackson's sanitarium, opened the Western Health Reform Institute in Battle Creek, Michigan in 1866. She was opposed to eating meat because she believed it stirred animal passions. She recommended eating Graham bread, fruits, and vegetables, drinking water, and refraining from salt and condiments, lard, cola, or alcohol.

John Harvey Kellogg, the physician employed by Sister White in 1876, introduced and promoted a variety of nutrition fads and health practices at her Battle Creek sanitarium. This facility, which was a leading health resort or spa of its day, had all the newest and most impressive mechanical devices for watering, rubbing, and feeding people. It was a place where tired businessmen and overweight women could go for relaxation and rejuvenation.

According to Deutsch,[5] Battle Creek became a fountainhead of faddism, the nation's chief clearinghouse for an array of nostrums, misinformation about foods, messianic food promoters, and millionaire cranks. In the process, John Harvey Kellogg became the first man to make a million dollars from food faddism. He produced over 80 books on health and disease, many of which were required reading for individuals at the sanitarium.

Kellogg claimed that 90% of ills were centered in the stomach and bowels. He advocated ridding the digestive tract of "poisons" derived from meat-eating, drinking, smoking, condiments, or anything pleasurable. He believed that bowel eliminations should occur frequently. The enema machine was used for bowel cleaning, with as many as 15 gallons run through an individual at one time. Tablespoons of sterilized bran were given to patients at every meal for laxative purposes. Roughage in the form of lettuce and bran for breakfast were commonly given. Kellogg said, "Bran does not irritate, it titillates." He wanted people to eat raw foods such as carrots at every meal. No salt or other condiments or fried foods were provided at the sanitarium. Other practices introduced by Kellogg included the use of unpasteurized milk, the chopping of peanuts to make peanut butter, and electrical stimulation of the skin.

Kellogg produced toasted or dextrinized cereals that while dry and crisp could easily be eaten without milk or cream. Thus the cereal flake was created in 1895. The first products were wheat flakes called Granose, later renamed Toasted Wheat Flakes. W.K. Kellogg, the brother of John Harvey, capitalized on these products and established what today is the Kellogg Company.

Charles W. Post had been a patient at Kellogg's sanitarium in 1891, suffering from a vaguely defined illness. He believed he was cured through his study of the power of the mind, including Christian Science, and dogged repetition to himself of the phrase, "I am well." In 1892 he established an inn where diet and mental healing were combined. Meat was allowed but not other "poisons." His cures were alleged to be quick, some occurring within minutes. He supposedly could cure dyspepsia and bladder complaints by having individuals shut their eyes and repeat, "I am well." He wrote books and published a magazine, *Good Health*.

Post marketed Postum Cereal Food Coffee and sold it in paper bags in Battle Creek. He claimed that Postum (which contained no caffeine) would cure such conditions as "coffee neuralgia" and "coffee heart." He developed a hard-baked wheat cracker, which he broke into small pieces and called Grape Nuts. It was sold as a health food in 1898 and advocated as a food for the brain and a cure for appendicitis, loose teeth, consumption, and malaria. Post netted $1 million from his products in 1901 alone.

Alfred W. McCann, born in Pennsylvania in 1879, was a "pure food" crusader who opened a new era of health faddism in 1911. He used scientific facts about vitamins and other aspects of nutrition and distorted them in his writings. His books, *Starving America* (1914) and *The Science of Eating* (1917), claimed that refined foods were deficient in nutrients and poisoned the eater.

Horace Fletcher was the "high priest of mastication" (chewing). His book, *Fletcherism: What It Is, How I Became Young at Sixty* (1913), contained the motto, "Nature will castigate those who don't masticate." He believed one should eat only when hungry, selecting foods that are most appealing, and chewing each mouthful 30 to 70 times. He said it was bad for the digestive process to swallow food before it had been reduced to a liquid state in which it "swallowed itself." Even soup and milk had to be "Fletcherized" by rolling them about the mouth until thoroughly mixed with saliva.

Adolphus Hohensee marketed Vita Health Foods in 1942. He acquired an honorary M.D. degree from the Kansas City University of Physicians and Surgeons, an unaccredited school that was closed the following year by the Missouri State Board of Medical Examiners. He added doctorates in Naturopathy to his credentials from schools in Oklahoma and Indiana without having attended classes in either of these states. In 1946 he passed an examination in Nevada and became licensed to practice chiropractic.

In his early lecturing days Hohensee sold Adolphus Brand products, including peppermint, soybean, lecithin, B-complex vitamins, wheat germ oil, mineral capsules, calcium tablets, an herbal laxative, and a tar shampoo. He produced such pamphlets as "High Blood Pressure," "Arthritis and

Rheumatism," "Better Eyes Without Glasses," and "Your Personality Glands." The FDA estimated that sales of his products during one lecture series in a single city would gross $40,000 to $50,000.

Hohensee's lectures attracted many people. He was humorous, quoted the Bible, told suggestive stories, frightened listeners with the horrors of disease, and described how the normal diet stagnated the blood and corroded the blood vessels. He paraded himself as a noble man abused by powerful enemies including the AMA and the FDA. He claimed that most disease was due to improper diet and could be helped by using his products.

Hohensee's commercial success came despite considerable legal difficulty. He was charged with selling drugs without a license in 1943 in Seattle; he pleaded guilty and was fined $50. The next spring in San Francisco he paid a $300 fine for posing as a doctor and a $200 fine for selling drugs without a license. The FDA brought him to trial in 1948 for false and deceptive labeling practices. He was found guilty of misbranding and fined $1000. In 1955, alert reporters caught him eating a meal of "forbidden foods." Beginning in 1962, he served 18 months in prison for using false claims to sell honey.

Dr. DeForest C. Jarvis wrote *Folk Medicine: A Vermont Doctor's Guide to Good Health* in which he advocated honey and apple cider vinegar for treating and preventing diseases from the common cold to arthritis. Dr. Fredrick Stare, chairman of Harvard's nutrition department, called the book "claptrap" and said that it "belongs on the fiction list."[4] In 1960 the FTC ordered the publisher to stop advertising that the methods advocated by the book were effective and had been scientifically tested. Despite these criticisms, however, the book sold over 500,000 copies and still is popular today.

Gayelord Hauser, who became a popular author, lecturer and syndicated newspaper columnist, was born in Germany in 1895. He claimed that he came to the United States, contracted incurable tuberculosis of the hip, and returned to Europe to die. There he found a man who told him he could stay alive only by eating living foods such as fruits, vegetables, and herbs. While recovering, he developed a strong interest in naturopathy and naprapathy (a type of chiropractic manipulation).

Hauser returned to the United States in his 20s and began practicing naprapathy. He turned to writing and lecturing and went to Hollywood in 1927. His followers included Greta Garbo, Paulette Goddard, the Duchess of Windsor, and Baron Phillipe de Rothschild. In 1984, after he had died at age 89 from complications of pneumonia, the *Los Angeles Times* reported that his fourteen books had sold nearly 50 million copies.

Hauser's *Look Younger, Live Longer* (1950) identified five supposed wonder foods: skim milk, brewer's yeast, wheat germ, yogurt, and blackstrap molasses. He stated that blackstrap molasses would cure insomnia, nervousness, menopausal problems, baldness, and low blood pressure. He also claimed that the diet recommended in this book could add 5 years to a person's life. However, Gardner[14] noted that the five wonder foods contain nothing one could not obtain less expensively from ordinary foods. In 1951, the FDA seized a quantity of Hauser's book because it was being illegally used to help market blackstrap molasses.

Another best-seller, *Mirror, Mirror on the Wall* (1960), suggested that women could achieve beauty by following a "cosmetic diet" through the intake of large amounts of vitamins, minerals, and proteins. Nutritionist Fredrick J. Stare, M.D., Ph.D., remarked that the book was "filled with misstatements, with falsehoods, with all kinds of errors and implications." After William Bates' book *Cure of Imperfect Eyesight by Treatment Without Glasses* became a best seller, Hauser claimed that eyes could be improved by combining use of his diets and Bates' exercises.

During the mid-1930s, the FDA took action against an "antidiabetic" tea and four other misbranded products marketed by Modern Products of Milwaukee, a company in which Hauser was a partner. The company still sells "natural" food products and spices using booklets that contain his recipes, excerpts of his philosophy, and a glowing description of his career.[15]

Lelord Kordel, who wrote 20 books, recommends high-protein foods, lecithin ("the miracle nutrient"), and vitamin and mineral supplements for everyone. According to court records, he began producing and marketing supplements in 1941, operating under various trade names. In 1946, he was convicted of misbranding and fined $4000. One product in the case was "Gotu Kola," an herbal tablet said to restore youth and "produce erect posture, sharp eyes, velvety skin, limbs of splendid proportions, deep chests, firm bodies, gracefully curved hips, flat abdomens" and even "pleasing laughter."

Thirteen other products were falsely claimed to be effective against various conditions including heart disease, liver troubles, tuberculosis, bone infections, and impotence.

Kordel had a brush with the FTC in 1957 and two more with the FDA in 1961. In 1963, when he was president of Detroit Vital Foods, Inc., products shipped by the company were found to be misbranded because they were accompanied by Kordel publications that falsely claimed these nutritional products could treat practically all diseases. After the appeals process ended in 1971, Kordel was fined $10,000 and served 1 year in prison. Current catalogues from Vital Foods, Inc., describe him as "America's leading vitamin and diet expert" and claim that he has never been ill.

Although the development of nutrition science during the twentieth century has provided a basis for sorting out nutrition facts from fictions, it has not stopped the promotion of nutrition fads and quackery. The discovery of vitamins, for example, has enabled charlatans to add enormous numbers of "dietary supplements" to their product lines. This subject is discussed in detail in Chapter 13.

Enemas and Laxatives

Many faddists have claimed that the intestines ("bowels") are a major source of health problems. One unfounded theory ("autointoxication") suggests that intestinal sluggishness leads to the absorption of poisons; another suggests that fecal material collects on the lining of the intestine and causes trouble unless removed by laxatives or enemas.

The concept of enemas may have originated from observations of the Ibis bird, which supposedly uses its curved beak to give itself a rectal infusion of Nile water. The Egyptians gave enemas with beer, oil, or other fluids, adding such ingredients as honey, herbs, hemp, or ox brain. Enemas were used to "resist poison," to nourish weak and consumptive patients (wine), to prevail against dropsy (urine), and to exorcise devils from possessed nuns (holy water). In eighteenth century England, tobacco enemas were used to attempt to resuscitate drowned persons. In the United States in the 1930s, children were often subjected to colonic irrigation for all sorts of complaints. Today, various fringe practitioners still use colonics to "detoxify" the body.

Elie Metchnikoff, a Russian chemist who won the 1908 Nobel Prize for his contributions to immunology, was a strong proponent of yogurt. His book *The Prolongation of Life* (1907) described his search for the elixir of life and his discovery of Bulgarians who supposedly lived to the age of 100.[4] He concluded that the sour milk (yogurt) they consumed was the cause of this extended life. Metchnikoff claimed that putrefaction of proteins in the intestines released poisons that caused disease. He called this "auto-intoxic action" and said that yogurt drove out the poisons by supplying microorganisms that were gentle, friendly, and happy.

Dr. Kellogg, who had advocated an immaculate bowel, capitalized on Metchnikoff's theory and changed his treatment at Battle Creek. He did not permit putrescible foods and "disinfected" all fruit with chemicals. Patients would have the "poisons" flushed out of the alimentary canal by taking half a pint of whey culture by mouth and injecting another half pint into the colon by enema.

Kellogg probably was more responsible than any other person for the common belief that a daily bowel movement is necessary. He built a giant laxative industry in the United States by proposing the use of bran for human intestines.

Cancer Quackery

As cancer began to receive considerable attention in the twentieth century, many cancer patients became the victims of pseudoscientists and charlatans. A few such individuals are mentioned here; more are discussed in Chapter 18.

Members of the Hoque family had no medical training, yet they exploited a cancer-cure salve that contained a corrosive substance. In 1902 and 1908 F.M. Hoque of San Jose, California, was found guilty of practicing medicine without a license. In 1929, W.F. Hoque, a stepson, was found guilty and fined $500 for violation of the Medical Practice Act.

O.A. Johnson of Kansas City, Missouri, sold an alleged treatment called "Mild Combination Treatment for Cancer." In 1910 he was charged with misbranding the product. Later the postal authorities forced him to sign a pledge that he would stop using the mails to sell his product. When two cases concerning women he claimed to have cured were investigated, it was found that both had died of their cancers.

The Hoxsey method of cancer therapy, developed by Harry M. Hoxsey, a naturopath, has been promoted since the early 1920s. It involved three elements: a liquid for internal use, a corrosive external compound, and supportive treatment. The internal substance contained potassium iodide (an expectorant), licorice, red clover, burdock root, stillingia root, herberis root, poke root, cascara (an herbal laxative), prickly ash bark, and buckthorn bark. The external substance was a yellow powder, a red paste, or a clear solution containing one or more chemicals capable of destroying cancerous tissues on contact. Unfortunately, they destroy healthy tissue as well. The supportive treatment included preparations containing iron, urinary antiseptics, vitamins, laxatives, and antacids.

Three times during the late 1920s, Hoxsey was convicted of practicing medicine without a license. In 1930, he was permanently enjoined for violating the Iowa Medical Practice Act. In 1936, after unsuccessful attempts to practice in other states, he moved to Dallas, Texas, where he maintained a thriving practice until vigorous action by the FDA drove him to Mexico.

In various trials against Hoxsey, the government presented scientific evidence that his "cured" patients fell into three categories: (1) those who never had cancer; (2) those who had been cured before going to his office; and (3) those who still had their disease or died under the Hoxsey treatment. One case involved a 16-year-old boy who developed cancer of the bone following a football injury.[6] The boy's parents did not wish the boy's leg to be amputated as recommended by his physician and took the boy to a Hoxsey clinic, where the medical director guaranteed a cure. Four months of tonics were not helpful, and death occurred several months later. The physician who had recommended amputation felt that the boy might have survived had it been performed. Hoxsey, who based his defense on testimonials from 22 patients, won the case. However, the FDA, which suspected that the judge had once been a Hoxsey patient, appealed the case and had the decision reversed. In 1963, after Hoxsey's appeal to the Supreme Court failed, he moved his clinic to Tijuana. He died in 1973, but the clinic is still operated by a nurse who worked with him for many years.

In every decade since 1940, at least one questionable cancer remedy has attracted a large following and become a national issue. Today's approaches, discussed in Chapter 18, tend to emphasize diet and lifestyle changes.

Exercise and Fitness

Exercise and fitness, of great importance in ancient Greece and Rome, have been repopularized during the twentieth century. The need for exercise became a social concern after World War I, as thousands of young men had been rejected as physically unfit for military duty. This led to the introduction of physical training activities for the general public and in the schools. In the 1920s, as the science of exercise developed, school programs came to be known as physical education.

During the early 1950s, tests of muscular fitness showed that American children were not as fit as European children. This finding and others led President Dwight D. Eisenhower to convene a conference of national authorities on fitness to propose ways to improve the fitness level of Americans. President John F. Kennedy was also interested in this effort and the Office of Sports and Fitness (now the President's Council on Physical Fitness and Sports) was established in Washington, D.C. Awareness of the importance of physical fitness continued to increase, and physical education became more closely related to all-around fitness and health.

In the late 1960s, cardiologist Kenneth Cooper wrote a popular book *Aerobics,* which provided fitness programs for adults and stressed heart-lung efficiency. The jogging boom, which began during the 1970s, has been followed by a surge of interest in strength training with weights and body-building machines. Today close to half of American adults exercise regularly.

Physical Culture and the "Bare-Torso King"

Bernarr Macfadden, who was born in 1868 and was one of the early proponents of exercise, advocated a variety of strange practices as well. During his youth he supposedly was sickly and unable to walk. His mother died of tuberculosis when he was six. He claimed that during his teens his uncle had told him he too was consumptive and would not live for more than a year. As a result, Macfadden relocated so he could enjoy outdoor life and obtain a decent diet. His strength eventually returned on this regimen, and he believed it had cured him of tuberculosis. At the age of 15 Macfadden discovered the gymnasium and began developing his body. To build his strength, he carried a 10-pound lump of lead wherever he went. He gained his chief education as a physical education instructor in a school in Bunker Hill, Illinois.

Macfadden's *Physical Culture* magazine appeared in 1890. In two years it had 100,000 subscribers, and its readership eventually grew to 1 million. Concern for physical culture was timely since there was a growing distrust of patent medicines and the health reform movement advocated a simpler, more natural form of hygiene.

Macfadden believed he had learned the true secrets of health without using scientific investigation. He concluded that health problems could be resolved by eating less and by fasting, which would give the body more time for repairs. For cancer he recommended fasting for a few days and a diet consisting of large quantities of grapes.

Macfadden's ideas for health may have contributed to the use of enriched flour, bed boards, scanty swimsuits, and sunbathing. His other beliefs included:

1. Fasting could cure 30 diseases, including heart disease and diabetes.
2. Food should be chewed until it becomes liquid.
3. Upon rising in the morning, a person should drink a cup of hot water and perform "exercises."
4. Walking to work, preferably barefoot, was advisable.
5. The perfect diet was one of nuts and fruits.
6. A person should eat when hungry and drink plenty of water; one-half gallon in the morning would strengthen the heart and conquer constipation.
7. The teeth should be exercised by eating hard crackers or zwieback.
8. People should sleep on the floor.
9. Cancer should be treated by fasting followed by exercises and a "vitality-building regimen."

Macfadden was claimed to be worth $31 million in 1931. He died in 1955 at the age of 87.

SUMMARY

This chapter illustrates some of the many ways in which questionable health products, services, and theories were promoted while medical science was in its infancy. Medical science has made great strides in understanding and treating disease, and consumer protection laws have had considerable impact. But it is important to recognize that the promoters described in this chapter have their modern counterparts, that many of their irrational ideas still are popular, and that quackery still is a serious problem.

DISCUSSION QUESTIONS

1. What were some characteristics of medical practice in the United States before the twentieth century?
2. Why has the nineteenth century been called "the patent medicine era"?
3. What are some of the reasons patent medicines were used during the nineteenth century?
4. What techniques were used by advertisers to promote patent medicines?
5. What techniques were used during medicine shows to promote patent medicines? Name some of the promoters and their products.
6. What were some quack medical procedures used during the eighteenth and nineteenth centuries? Identify their methods, the discoverer or promoter, and the period in which they were popular.
7. What narcotic drugs were found in patent medicines? Why were they used? How widely were they used?
8. What factors led to passage of federal laws to control patent medicines? What were these laws?
9. Who were some of the leading food fad promoters before the twentieth century, and what did they promote?
10. Discuss the "autointoxication" theory, its originator, and what followed as a result of this concept.
11. What is the Hoxsey method of cancer treatment? What legal problems did Hoxsey have?
12. What events led to the development of exercise and fitness programs in the United States in the twentieth century?
13. Who was the "Bare-Torso King," and what were his beliefs about exercise and diet?

REFERENCES

1. Atkinson DT: Magic, myths and medicine, New York, 1956, Fawcett Publications.
2. Starr P: The social transformation of American medicine, New York, 1982, Basic Books Inc, Publishers.
3. Lasagna L: The doctor's dilemma, New York, 1962, Harper & Brothers.

4. Deutsch RM: The new nuts among the berries, Palo Alto, Calif, 1977, Bull Publishing Co.
5. Young JH: The toadstool millionaires, Princeton, NJ, 1961, Princeton University Press.
6. Young JH: The medical messiahs, Princeton, NJ, 1992, Princeton University Press.
7. Whorton JC: Traditions of folk medicine in America, JAMA 257:1632-1635, 1987.
8. McNamara B: Step right up, Garden City, NJ, 1976, Doubleday & Co.
9. Fishbein M: The medical follies, New York, 1925, Boni & Liveright.
10. Smith RL: The strange world of mechanical quackery, Today's Health 42:42-47, 1984.
11. Smith RL: The incredible Drown case, Today's Health 46:46, 1968.
12. Spunt G: When nature speaks—the life of Forrest C Shaklee, Sr., New York, 1977, Frederick Fell Publishers. (Marketed by the Shaklee Corporation to its distributors)
13. Brecher EM and the editors of Consumer Reports: Licit and illicit drugs, Boston, 1972, Little, Brown & Co Inc.
14. Gardner M: Fads and fallacies in the name of science, New York, 1957, Dover Publications.
15. Gayelord Hauser's gourmet health recipes & beauty secrets. Undated 32-page brochure distributed in the late 1980s by Modern Products, Inc., Milwaukee.
16. Hechtlinger A: Great patent medicine era, New York, 1970, Grosset & Dunlop, Inc.
17. Cook J: Remedies and rackets: the truth about patent medicine today, New York, 1958, Norton Publishers.
18. Karolevitz RF: Doctors of the old west, Seattle, 1967, Superior Publishing Co.
19. Shyrock RH: Medicine in America, Baltimore, 1966, The Johns Hopkins University Press.
20. Kallet A and Schlink FJ: 100,000 guinea pigs: dangers in everyday foods, drugs, and cosmetics, New York, 1933, Vangard Press.

CHAPTER THREE

SEPARATING FACT FROM FICTION

One of the factors that makes America great is our freedom of speech. To maintain this freedom, we must also run a risk. False prophets can get up on pedestals and tell you almost anything they please.[1]

GABE MIRKIN, M.D.

Finding the occasional straw of truth awash in a great ocean of confusion and bamboozle requires intelligence, vigilance, dedication and courage. But if we don't practice these tough habits of thought . . . we risk becoming a nation of suckers, up for grabs by the next charlatan who comes along.[2]

CARL SAGAN

Be careful about reading health books. You might die of a misprint.

MARK TWAIN

The interest that Americans have developed in maintaining and improving their health has been accompanied by a tremendous increase in the volume of information available through the media. Thousands of books about health are published each year. Radio and television stations conduct special programs on health issues, employ physicians as commentators, and provide talk shows on which health matters are discussed. Newspapers cover health issues in news articles and feature stories. Health products are advertised frequently. Information is also spread by laypersons who share their ideas and experiences. Unfortunately, much of the health information circulating within our society is inaccurate.

Consumers who wish to make intelligent decisions about health matters must address several questions: What are scientific facts? How can they be identified? To what extent should people believe what they read and hear about health? Where can individuals find valid information? This chapter explains how the scientific method is used to determine facts, how health information is disseminated, and how reliable information can be obtained.

Consumer Decisions

How can consumers determine what is fact and what is fiction regarding health products and services?

How are statistics and statistical procedures misused in the health marketplace?

How can consumers determine the reliability of sources of information in order to make intelligent health decisions?

How Facts Are Determined

Reliable health information comes primarily through using the scientific method, a procedure for exposing hypotheses (assumptions) to critical examination and experimental testing. Harper[3] states that the more we eliminate false information, the closer we get to what is true. The scientific method offers an objective way to evaluate information to determine what is false.

The Scientific Method

Medical scientists use the scientific method to seek truths and find solutions to problems. This method does not rely on testimonials as evidence of fact. Rather, it provides an objective way to collect and evaluate data. Astronomer Carl Sagan has said that "science is a way of thinking much more than it is a body of knowledge."

Scientific research requires proper sampling techniques, the highest possible accuracy of measurement or observation, and appropriate statistical analysis of the findings, to reach valid conclusions. These conclusions then form the basis for developing new theories or modifying old ones. As noted by Sagan:[2]

> At the heart of science is an essential tension between two seemingly contradictory attitudes—an openness to new ideas, no matter how bizarre and counterintuitive they may be, and the most ruthless skeptical scrutiny of all ideas, old and new. This is how deep truths are winnowed from deep nonsense. Of course, scientists make mistakes in trying to understand the world, but there is a built-in error-correcting mechanism: The collective enterprise of creative thinking and skeptical thinking together keeps the field on track.

The scientific method has three special characteristics. First, it is self-correcting. Scientists do not assume that this method discovers absolute truth but rather that it produces conclusions that may be modified by subsequent studies. In this sense, science is cumulative. Second, the scientific method requires objectivity. Findings must not be contaminated by the personal beliefs, perceptions, biases, values, or emotions of the researcher. Only when the results can speak for themselves can the conclusions be considered valid. Often the results of research lead to new questions that need further exploration. Third, experiments must be replicable. One study, taken alone, seldom proves anything. To be valid, one researcher's findings must be repeatable by others.

The scientific method is designed to minimize error by following procedures accepted by the scientific community. The steps in scientific research include:

1. A question or problem is identified. (Example: What is the effect of vitamin C on the common cold?)
2. A hypothesis is formulated. (Supplementation with vitamin C can reduce the incidence of colds.)

3. A limited aspect of the hypothesis is selected for testing. (Will daily administration of 1000 mg of vitamin C prevent colds?)
4. A study is designed. (Sixty adults will be given 1000 mg tablets of vitamin C daily for four months, and sixty of comparable age, race, sex, and health status will be given an inactive substance [placebo].)
5. The study is conducted. (Volunteers are obtained and instructed on how to proceed.)
6. Data are collected, recorded, and tabulated. (There were six colds in the vitamin-C group and seven in the placebo group.)
7. Statistical techniques are used to analyze the data to determine whether the results appear significant or were likely to occur by chance alone. (The small difference between the two groups could easily have occurred by chance alone and therefore is not "statistically significant.")
8. A determination is made on whether hypotheses have been proved or disproved. (The hypothesis was not supported. The experiment found no evidence that vitamin C supplements reduce the incidence of colds.)
9. The study may be repeated by the researchers or by others to verify their results or conclusions. (Many double-blind experiments have found that vitamin C does not prevent colds. See Chapter 13.)

Science writer Rodger Doyle[4] identifies three types of studies used by medical scientists to investigate health and disease:

1. Case studies: systematic observation of the sick.
2. Laboratory experiments: study of animals, living tissue, cells, and disease-causing agents.
3. Epidemiology: statistical analysis of data from groups of healthy and sick individuals.

It is important that research findings not be overgeneralized. Conclusions based on data from one population may not apply to another population, and the results obtained from animal or test-tube studies cannot be applied with certainty to humans.

Doyle[4] states that controlled clinical trials offer the most credible evidence. He notes that competent medical researchers may use anecdotal reports for suggesting new hypotheses, but never as supporting evidence. The fact that an individual recovers after doing something is rarely sufficient to demonstrate that the recovery was caused by the action taken and is not simply coincidental. Moreover, reports of personal experiences can be biased, inaccurate, or even fraudulent. Well-designed experiments involving many people are needed to establish that a treatment method is effective.

Manufacturers are quick to take advantage of preliminary research that may appear to support increased use of their products. In 1988 the Physicians' Health Study Group[6] reported that aspirin use every other day had reduced the incidence of heart attacks among 11,000 generally healthy physicians. The researchers concluded that although aspirin might have some role in preventing heart attacks, the study's results should not be applied to the general population and that doctors should weigh potential risks as well as benefits when advising their patients. Within days after publication of the report, aspirin ads began referring to it and suggesting that consumers ask their doctors whether aspirin might help them. The FDA Commissioner, who believed that the ads were likely to encourage inappropriate self-medication, told manufacturers that aspirin did not have FDA approval for preventing heart attacks in healthy people and that continuing the ads would trigger regulatory action. Fish oils, calcium supplements, and high-fiber food products have also been marketed in ways that oversimplify or exaggerate the significance of research findings.

The Scientific Method in Action

In 1978 researchers at Mt. Sinai Hospital in Miami Beach compared the effects of chicken soup, cold water, and hot water on the clearance rate of nasal mucus. Each liquid was consumed through a straw from a covered cup or open vessel. A videotaping system was used to record the advance of tiny radioactive discs as mucus carried them out the nose. Cold water slowed mucus flow, but chicken soup and hot water sipped from an open cup speeded it up. Since chicken soup outperformed hot water; the researchers concluded that it appeared to have a special ability to clear a stuffy nose.[5] Momma was right.

Statistics

Statistics is a discipline that uses mathematical principles to analyze data derived from observations of specific phenomena. It includes collecting data (such as the frequency of an event), testing hypotheses, determining probabilities, and drawing conclusions. The brief discussion below explains some of the basic concepts used to interpret data. More detailed information can be obtained from a textbook on statistics or from an expert at a university or medical center.

There are two major types of statistical approach:

1. *Descriptive statistics* is used to reduce quantities of data or information into manageable form and to describe them precisely in terms of averages, differences, relationships, and in other ways (for example, numbers of people who use alcoholic beverages; relations between smoking and lung cancer).
2. *Inferential statistics* is used to determine the probability that the result of a study or experiment performed on a single sample reflects the status in the population or whether it happened purely by chance. The conclusions or generalizations drawn or inferred from the data are qualitative assessments (for example, that 60% of the people who smoke one package of cigarettes daily will get lung cancer; or that Laetrile is not effective in the treatment of lung cancer).

Certain fundamental concepts are important in understanding statistical procedures and may help consumers interpret scientific writings and studies reported in the media.

Measurements and observations: These are numerical observations or scores (for example, number of smokers, number of people who acquire lung cancer).

Population or universe: The total number of observations of the same type: a complete set of individuals, objects, or measurements with some observable characteristic (for example, the number of 36-year-old bald men with one leg).

Sample: A portion of a population or universe; a subgroup of a population.

Random selection or sample: A sample in which every member of a population has an equal chance of being selected.

Variable: A characteristic that can differ from subject to subject or vary over time and influence a study's conclusions (for example, weight, age, cholesterol level).

Experimental design: There are many ways to design experimental studies. One design used extensively in medical research is the controlled clinical trial. This compares an experimental group of people who receive the treatment being tested and a control group of people who receive a different treatment or no treatment. For example, members of the experimental group may receive a pill with active ingredients, whereas those in the control group receive an equivalent treatment or placebo. Studies may be conducted "blind" or "double-blind" to prevent any bias from interfering with collection or interpretation of the data. In blind studies, the participants do not know which treatment they receive. In a double-blind study, neither the people administering the treatment nor the experimental subjects know who gets what. In crossover studies, participants in two or more groups are switched from one intervention to another after a specified period of time. Some studies do not use control groups.

Large, randomized, placebo-controlled, double-blind studies in which several medical centers participate are considered the gold standard of research trials.[7] Since such studies are very expensive to conduct, they are reserved for questions of great importance.

Misuse of Statistics

There are three kinds of lies: lies, damned lies, and statistics.

Mark Twain

Many people tend to accept statistical data without question. To them, any information presented in quantitative form is correct.

Advertisers, quacks, pseudoscientists, and others often cite invalid data or misrepresent valid data to promote their theories, products, or services. The following statistical errors can cause confusion:

Bias: Attitudes of participants in a study may cause them to make erroneous observations. For example, in a study of vitamin C and the common cold, participants who knew they were taking vitamin C reported fewer colds than those who were taking vitamin C but did not know it.[8]

Omission of an important factor: Many individuals who feel helped by an unorthodox remedy have taken it together with effective treatment but credited the unorthodox remedy.

Non sequitur: Data may be interpreted illogically.

Noncomparable data: Valid comparisons can be made only if data are logically comparable.

Confusion of association and causation: Things that occur together may not be causally related. Care must be taken to be sure that those who recover after taking a remedy were helped by it rather than simply recovering spontaneously.

Insufficient data: Small amounts of data result in a high degree of uncertainty. Thus tests done on small numbers of individuals must usually be confirmed by larger studies.

Unrepresentative data: Improper sampling techniques (lack of random sampling) may yield data that do not accurately represent the population or universe. For example, to determine what car the average American likes best, it would not be appropriate to poll only owners of one make of car.

In *How To Lie With Statistics,* Darrell Huff[9] calls attention to procedures used to misrepresent data from drug research. These include biased samples, meaningless averages, purposeful omissions, apples-and-peaches comparisons, illogical conclusions, and deceptively drawn charts. He notes that a basic technique used by charlatans when they present testimonial evidence is the *post hoc, ergo propter hoc* fallacy: this happened after that, therefore this was caused by that. The fact that someone who smokes 50 cigarettes and drinks heavily each day lives to age 95 does not mean that these habits are healthful. Huff says that to analyze a statement, one should ask, "Who says so? How does he know? How did he find out? Is anything missing? Does it all make sense?"

Peer Review

Peer review is a process in which the work of a scientist or group is reviewed by others who have equal or superior knowledge. It may be used during the development or execution of a study as well as afterward. When studies are completed, researchers strive to publish their results in journals so that others can use or criticize the findings, and science can advance. The best scientific journals are peer-reviewed; papers submitted for publication are reviewed and approved, modified or rejected by the editor and several expert reviewers.

The two most prestigious American medical journals are the *Journal of the American Medical Association (JAMA)* and *The New England Journal of Medicine. JAMA* has more than 3000 names in its reviewer-referee file. Reports from over 2600 peer-reviewed scientific journals are listed in the *Index Medicus,* which is available at hospital and medical school libraries. Peer review is also done by scientific organizations. Several that have established formal review processes given great weight by the medical community are described here.

The American Medical Association's Council on Scientific Affairs studies many mechanical issues and makes reports to the AMA's House of Delegates. Once accepted, these reports help shape AMA public policies and may be published in *JAMA*.

The AMA Diagnostic and Therapeutic Technology Assessment (DATTA) project was established in 1982 by the AMA to evaluate drugs, devices, procedures, and techniques, covering about ten items per year. More than 1000 clinician-scientists from all areas of medicine have been selected by the AMA Council on Scientific Affairs to participate in the project. Evaluations typically take 3 to 4 months and represent a consensus of panelists considered expert in the technology under consideration; they judge whether it shall be considered safe and effective, investigational, indeterminate, or unacceptable. The topics selected are considered substantially important or controversial.

The National Institutes of Health Consensus Development Program, begun in 1977, has held about 90 consensus conferences in which experts meet for several days to discuss a topic and issue a report.

The National Academy of Sciences produces the Recommended Dietary Allowances (see Chapter 12) and many other reports by expert committees.

The Office of Technology Assessment (OTA) is a nonpartisan support agency that provides congressional committees with analyses of emerging, difficult, and highly technical issues. In 1990 it prepared an excellent report on unconventional cancer treatments (see Chapter 18).

The American College of Physicians' Clinical Efficacy Assessment Project focuses primarily on relatively new procedures.

In 1989, the U.S. Preventive Services Task Force published its recommendations for preventive services that prudent health professionals should provide their patients in the course of routine clinical care. These recommendations, which represent the pooled judgment of many experts, are discussed in Chapter 6.

In 1990 the RAND Corporation, a private research organization in Santa Monica, California teamed with the AMA and a 12-member medical school consortium to launch its Clinical Appropiateness Initiative. The project, which began publishing monographs in 1992, will prepare guidelines for a large number of medical and surgical procedures.

Scientific Fraud

Occasionally, individual scientists publish or attempt to publish faked research. The extent of this type of fraud is not known, but its existence presents one more argument for replicating studies. During the past 20 years, several instances of faked research have come to light at prominent medical centers.

In 1974 William T. Summerlin, a researcher at Sloan-Kettering Institute for Cancer Research, reported that he had found a way to prepare mouse skin so that it could be grafted onto an unrelated recipient without being rejected. Other researchers could not replicate his results. It was discovered that he had blackened the fur of white mice to make it appear as though skin grafts had succeeded.[10]

In 1980 and 1981 the world of science was jolted by cheating scandals at Yale University School of Medicine, Boston's Massachusetts General Hospital (an affiliate of Harvard University), Boston University Medical Center, Cornell University, and the University of California.[11] At Yale, Associate Professor Vijay R. Soman, a respected endocrinologist, was accused by a researcher from the National Institute of Health of plagiarism and the falsification of data in a published research paper about a study of conditions under which human blood cells "find" molecules of insulin. Dr. John Long of Massachusetts General Hospital, who was studying the characteristics of Hodgkin's disease in cell cultures from human patients, modified data to achieve specific results. At the Boston University Medical Center a $1 million cancer research project was found to contain falsified data. Harvard University researcher John Roland Darsee, who had published nearly 100 papers and abstracts, confessed to falsifying data for a study assessing whether certain drugs limit damage to heart attack victims.[12] Emory University's School of Medicine reported that a majority of the research done by Dr. Darsee while he was a resident and clinical fellow in cardiology at Emory probably should be considered invalid.[13] *The New England Journal of Medicine,* in a move unprecedented in its 171-year history, retracted two heart research papers by Dr. Darsee, who admitted they were based on fraudulent data.[14]

In 1985, after being questioned about duplicate data in two of his papers, Dr. Robert A. Slutsky resigned his positions as radiology resident and associate clinical professor at the University of California, San Diego. Subsequent investigation by a faculty committee concluded that out of 137 articles he had published, 77 were valid, 48 were questionable, and 12 were fraudulent.[15]

In 1988, Stephen H. Bruening, Ph.D., pleaded guilty in federal court to two counts of lying on federal grant applications he had made to the National Institute of Mental Health. He was sentenced to a half-way house for 60 days and 5 years of probation during which he would do no more research. He was also ordered to perform 250 hours of community service and to repay $11,352 of his former salary. The charge resulted from an investigation of faked research on the use of drugs for retarded children and adults. According to press reports, he had published numerous reports, based on fabricated data, purporting to show that mentally retarded people should be treated with fewer tranquilizers and more stimulants.[16,17]

Experts have expressed differing opinions about the frequency of fraud among research scientists. Gardner[18] states that scientists overeager for recognition and greedy for research grants sometimes rush amazing claims into print, and that "the history of science swarms with cases of outright fakery and instances of scientists who unconsciously distorted their work." However, Philip Handler,[19,20] former president of the National Academy of Sciences, testified in 1981 that the problem of fraud among scientists had been exaggerated in the press. He said that the scientific community has self-correcting mechanisms (peer review, high-quality journals, and demand for replication) that make detection inevitable when fraud occurs. The investigators in the Slutsky case concluded that (1) although research fraud is probably rare compared to the size of the research establishment, it may evade detection; (2) emphasis on competition and pressure to produce, while intended to advance the discovery of truth, can foster a conflict between personal career goals and the intellectual motivation of scientists to seek the truth; and (3) some scientists are prepared to take an appreciable risk by submitting inaccurate statements for publication.[15]

Sources of Health Information

Consumers obtain health information from individuals, educational institutions, and the media.

The first category may be subdivided into nonprofessionals, pseudoscientists, and professionals. Nonprofessionals include friends, neighbors, relatives, and others who relate their experiences and ideas through informal talks and meetings. The pseudoscientists include charlatans who may be considered quacks (see Chapter 4) who mislead and deceive consumers. The professionals include practicing physicians and dentists, research scientists, and others with specialized training and education who provide services and information. Educational institutions are schools at all levels that offer not only formal education through courses and programs provided by teachers and professors, but also informal education through personal student contacts. The largest and perhaps most influential source of health information is the media. Thousands of radio and television stations broadcast health programs. Thousands of magazines, journals, and newspapers publish health articles. Thousands of health books and health-related pamphlets are distributed each year in the United States.

TALK TO AN EXPERIENCED DOCTOR ANYTIME YOU WANT.

Doctors'TeleCare is not a recording. You'll talk to an experienced physician who wants to answer your questions, 24 hours a day, 7 days a week. You'll get the facts you need in plain English, not in confusing medical terms.

Call Doctors'TeleCare:

☎ For Questions About Medications.
☎ When You Can't Reach Your Own Doctor.
☎ When You Want A Second Opinion.
☎ For explanations of Lab Results.
☎ For help Choosing A Specialist.
☎ For Full Information About Diseases And Their Symptoms.

Doctors'TeleCare™
1-900-933-3737
$4.00 Per Minute. First Minute Is Free.
Call (714) 253-6920 For More Information.

Figure 3-1. Ad for a telephone service that offers medical information from a physician.

Reliability of Sources

It can be extremely difficult for consumers and sometimes even for health professionals to determine the reliability of health information. Separating fact from fiction can be a complex and time-consuming process. Some of the reasons for this difficulty are as follows:

1. Testimony from friends, neighbors, and others may be hearsay rather than scientific data. Factual information, especially when several individuals are involved, is often distorted in transmission.
2. Preliminary and limited scientific studies may be overly stressed by the media, misinforming the public and causing them to arrive at incorrect conclusions.
3. Research data published by experts may conflict sufficiently to cause public confusion.
4. Inaccurate health information may be disseminated by individuals, companies, and media outlets purely for reasons of self-interest or profit (Figure 3-1).

Nonprofessionals. Many consumers have misconceptions about the factors that influence health (see Chapter 1). People who share their personal experiences and knowledge may believe in unproven and unscientific procedures and treatments. Such people often are highly motivated to spread their beliefs. Testimonials from movie stars, professional athletes, and other celebrities are commonly used to promote questionable health methods. National organizations exist to promote "alternative" cancer remedies (Chapter 18), the Feingold diet (Chapter 7), and other dubious methods. More than a million individuals have been involved in the sale of food supplements through multilevel organizations such as Shaklee Corporation and Amway Corporation (Chapter 13).[21]

Pseudoscientists. Some individuals who pretend to have special expertise can be considered pseudoscientists. Common in this category are "nutrition consultants" with "degrees" from nonaccredited schools and diploma mills. Pseudoscientists misuse and distort scientific evidence to lend support to whatever products or services they promote or sell. They may use scientific terminology and data to develop theories that seem plausible to laypersons. They are often sophisticated in manipulating situations to gain notoriety and acceptance. They can be intelligent and effective in presenting information. They may write magazine articles and books and may also reach consumers through television and radio programs. Such pseudoscientists typically are deluded quacks (see Chapter 4).

Several observers have described characteristics that can help consumers distinguish pseudoscientists from true scientists. Hatfield,[22] for example, has noted:

> Generally speaking, an establishment scientist has attended and graduated from an accredited university, belongs to one or more well-respected professional organizations, conducts carefully-controlled and documented research, and reports these findings in professional journals that maintain high standards for accepting research papers.
>
> By contrast, those claiming to be an alternative to establishment science have no common set of standards or practices from which measurements and comparisons can be made or quality of performance judged. Personal testimonies and causal observations quite often serve as the basis of their research rather than act as the impetus to begin research.

Peterson[23] has likened improperly designed research to a man rowing a boat from only one side:

> No matter how long or how hard he works, he never succeeds in doing anything except going in a circle, never realizing that it isn't his dedication of his strength but his method that is flawed. Until fringe research puts both oars in the water, it is doomed to remain where it has always been: spinning aimlessly on the shores of science.

True medical scientists have no philosophical commitment to particular treatment approaches, only a commitment to develop and use methods that are safe and effective for an intended purpose. Arseneau and Thigpen[24] have noted that pseudoscientists use hypotheses and data differently from scientists. While scientists test hypotheses, abandon disproved ones, and welcome review of their findings and conclusions, pseudoscientists reject findings that contradict their beliefs and accuse critics of prejudice and conspiracy.

In this regard, Criss[25] warns that people with strange ideas should not be assumed to be modern Galileos:

> To be a true analogy, these people would have to do experiments, make observations, and bring these results for all to see and question in an open forum. Further, they would have to be denied freedom of speech and press, or any expression all over the land—for that was the injunction against Galileo in 1616! It was as a result of this experience that the scientific method was adopted among scientists. . . . It has allowed the replacement of old ideas with new ones, and has provided a means of judging, and discarding, unfounded ideas.

Professionals. Most health professionals give reliable advice, but scientific training does not guarantee reliability. For example, Adelle Davis promoted inaccurate and dangerous nutrition advice despite adequate training in nutrition. As noted in Chapter 13, scientific studies she cited to back up her theories often had no relevance to them. Dr. Andrew Ivy, a highly respected scientist, withdrew from the scientific community at the height of his career to promote the quack cancer remedy krebiozen (see Chapter 18). Chapters 4, 7, 8, 9, 13, and 18 of this book provide considerable information on how to identify professionals who engage in unscientific practices.

During the past few years, several lines of questionable nutrition products have been marketed with endorsements by scientists with prominent credentials. The most notable case occurred with United Science of America, Inc., a multilevel company that sold food supplements claimed to be effective in preventing cancer, heart disease, and many other ailments (see Chapter 13). Literature from the company said that its products had been designed and endorsed by a 15-person scientific advisory board. However, four members of the board told investigators that they had neither designed nor endorsed them. A few other multilevel companies claim to be guided by scientific boards, and a few supplement manufacturers have used endorsements by individual practitioners in advertisements. Barrett,[26] who believes that all such practitioners hold minority viewpoints, has warned that "vitamin product endorsements by doctors—no matter how prestigious they are—should be viewed with extreme caution. All I have seen so far have included claims that were unproved and also illegal."

Educational institutions. Educational standards are maintained through a system of accred-

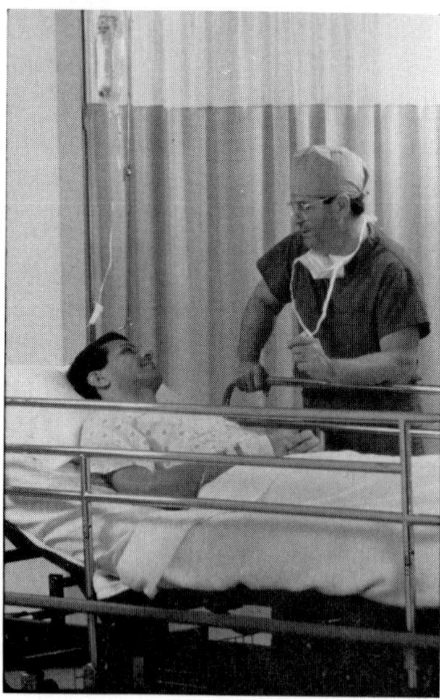

FIGURE 3-2. A good bedside manner is very important to most patients.
(From: The Image Bank—Jay Freis)

itation by agencies approved by the U.S. Secretary of Education or the Council on Postsecondary Accreditation. Almost all licensed practitioners of the healing arts must be graduates of accredited schools. Accredited institutions tend to have well-trained faculty members and to provide reliable guidance for their students. Schools of chiropractic, naturopathy, and acupuncture are exceptions because much of their subject matter is based on false beliefs (see Chapter 9). Nonaccredited schools that teach health subjects tend to be unreliable, and many are diploma mills that issue "degrees" and certificates whose only requirement is the payment of a fee. Chapter 13 discusses the problem of bogus nutrition credentials.

Many elementary and high school teachers of health subjects have had minimal formal training in what they teach and thus acquire misconceptions in the same manner as the general public. As a result, many misconceptions are passed from teacher to student. Dr. Roger Lederer, professor of biology, and Dr. Barry Singer, associate professor of psychology, California State University,[27] note that a problem exists even at universities:

> In recent years the teaching of pseudoscience and quackery in universities has become common and apparently accepted under the aegis of academic freedom. Typically the material is not formally presented as "Pseudoscience 101," but is offered as a component of a regular course.

Lederer and Singer, stating that pseudoscience is more evident in extension courses offered by institutions of higher learning, cite these examples:

1. The manipulation of cranial bones can straighten teeth.
2. If infants were born by the Leboyer method, world peace would be achieved.
3. A course approved for continuing education for nurses and pharmacists taught that high-frequency electronics can detect "the human aura, in all its various colors," that variations in auras may indicate the onset or presence of disease, and that "healing energy" can be transmitted by the laying on of hands.
4. A course entitled "Spiritual Hypnosis" was claimed to help individuals probe multiple consciousness in numerous physical dimensions to make contact with spiritual guides for help with mental disorders.
5. A conference sponsored by San Diego University offering relicensure credits for nurses and social workers advocated the use of mental imaging to cure cancer. It claimed that psyche and emotion are critical in the development of cancer and therefore hold the key to its treatment.

The Media

Max Gunther[28] succinctly describes the role of the media in disseminating health information:

> The media have four main functions: to entertain, to inform, to carry advertisements, and to make money for their stockholders. Because of the ways in which these functions are carried out, and the peculiar and intricate ways in which they are connected, an appalling amount of misinformation—ranging from the faintly biased to the downright wrong—is fed every day to an unfortunately gullible public. Hardly anywhere is this more evident than in the fields of medicine and its unwanted cousin, medical quackery.

Publicity is obviously a major factor in the success of quackery. Controversy often works to the advantage of quacks. During the mid-1970s, Laetrile promoters skillfully orchestrated publicity to increase their public following. Court cases of children whose parents wished to withhold therapy became a rallying point. Laetrile supporters who sincerely believed that their lives had been saved by Laetrile gained access to national television, where they appeared to be quite credible.[29] During the past few years, chiropractic, homeopathy, and other "alternative" methods have received considerable publicity in mainstream publications with little or no attempt to examine their shortcomings.

When the media attempt to present health information, these problems are often evident: (1) coverage of a subject is inadequate because of the limited time allotment; (2) selection or screening of speakers or subject areas is poor; (3) pseudoscientific claims often are presented without rebuttal from qualified experts; (4) attempts are made to sensationalize and overdramatize preliminary or new findings, especially about cancer, heart disease, and arthritis; and (5) a desire is evident to appeal to specific audiences or to attract large audiences with claims that nonscientific (alternative) methods are effective. Koren and Klein[30] have noted that the media have a natural tendency to report more on positive studies than negative ones. This tendency contributes to the difficulty laypersons have in placing medical news in perspective.

Herbert and Barrett[31] note additional factors in the spread of misinformation by the media:

1. Magical claims about health methods tend to be regarded as more newsworthy than established facts. Nationally televised talk shows provide enormous publicity for promoters of quackery.
2. Time works to quackery's advantage. It is much easier to report a lie as a straight news event than it is to investigate it.
3. Some journalists who have been misled by false ideas cannot write accurate papers.
4. Most promoters of health misinformation are regarded as underdogs in a struggle against the establishment. As such, they tend to be treated with undeserved sympathy. Most editors insist that articles which attack false ideas be balanced so that the apparent underdog gets a fair hearing. Even science editors rarely feel a duty to issue effective public warnings against misinformation.
5. Many more people are actively promoting misinformation than are actively opposing it. The sheer force of numbers works against the truth.
6. Publications that accept ads for food supplements may be unwilling to risk offending their advertisers. For example, when *Self* magazine published an article by a freelance writer listing money-saving tips from the 1980 edition of this book, a tip about spending less money on vitamins was deleted from the writer's manuscript by the magazine's editors.
7. Many editors fear that attacks on nutrition quackery will stir up controversy from readers who regard nutrition as their religion.
8. Editors may be afraid that attacking the credibility of a promoter of quackery will provide a libel suit.

Although libel suits related to health issues are extremely rare, other forms of economic reprisal are not. Cigarette manufacturers, for example, routinely cancel ads when magazines run articles about the dangers of smoking, and "alternative" practitioners often initiate letter-writing campaigns or cancel their subscriptions when publications criticize their methods. Following publication of the last two editions of this book, chiropractors attempted to execute a boycott[32] and bring other pressure on Mosby–Year Book to make the book's discussion of chiropractic more favorable.

Lack of peer review. Scientists are generally eager to point out the deficiencies in each other's theories and experimental techniques in establishing scientific truths. The comparable goal of most journalists is to report what happens. Journalists almost never publicly criticize each other's coverage of the news. This is particularly true when health topics are involved.

The National News Council was founded in 1973 "to serve the public interest by . . . advancing accurate and fair reporting of news." It investigated complaints alleging unfairness, inaccuracy, or breaches of ethical standards by wire services, newspapers, news syndicates, news magazines, and television and radio networks and stations. The Council exerted some pressure on media outlets, but its findings were not widely publicized. It ceased operation in 1984, citing lack of media support as the primary reason.

Advertisements. What people encounter through the media influences their decisions to purchase and use health products and services. Most media outlets depend on advertising revenue. Many health-related magazines contain many pages of health product ads. Consumers are encouraged to buy vitamins and minerals, wrinkle removers, weight reducers, headache-relief drugs, pep pills, and many other products. Advertising, however, is frequently misleading—often deliberately so. The intent is to capitalize on the ignorance of the reader by describing a product in terms of a mystical ingredient rather than in terms of specific contents or values. Advertising claims often have multiple meanings, one or more of which may be false.

Max Gunther[28] claims, "Fear of losing good advertisers is one of the common reasons why worthless medicines and gadgets and treatment methods get free plugs and why you do not see honest medical rebuttals printed as often as could be wished." (See Chapter 5 for more details.)

Newspapers. Many newspapers use overdramatization of incidents, inaccurate or exaggerated reports, quotations from unreliable sources, and misleading headlines to attract reader interest and attention. The weekly tabloids are notorious for this. Headlines like the following from tabloid newspapers should be given no credibility:

Breast-Feeding Can Prevent Pregnancies
Doctors Reveal Amazing Healing Powers of Water
Men Who Eat Slowly Make Better Lovers
Miracle of the Roses . . . Blooms From Shrine Are Curing Cancer, Arthritis and Even AIDS!
Pizza Cuts Heart Attack Risk
Researchers Claim Vasectomies May Lead to Heart Disease
Stars Use Crystals to Cure All Their Ills
Thousands Claim Cures From Radioactive Caves
Tomorrow's Drugs Will Make You Happier, Smarter, and More Creative
Vitamins—Guaranteed to Boost Energy and Slow Aging
World's Greatest Diet Pill—Eat What You Want and Still Lose 20 Pounds a Month

In 1987, Dr. Stephen Barrett[33] analyzed 322 articles on health, nutrition, and psychology appearing in five tabloid newspapers during a 3-month period and concluded that only 135 (42%) were reliable (see Table 3-1). One article in the *National Examiner*, for example, claimed that "a miraculous diet pill will flatten your tummy . . . and you can do it fast without a complicated diet program." The article discusses the Optifast system of weight control, a reputable medically supervised program. However, the program is not simple, the results are not instant, and the pills involved do not cause weight loss but simply add nutrients to the low-calorie program. Another article, "Bug Spray Makes Your Bosom Bigger," was accompanied by a photo captioned, "Flat-chested girls could look like Dolly Parton." The article stated that 30 men, who are suing a federal detention center, claim that exposure to a chemical intended to kill lice caused their breasts to undergo painful enlargement. Nothing in the article indicated that the chemical is useful for women.

Dr. Barrett also examined 247 articles involving supernatural beliefs, faith healers, psychics, alleged kidnappings by space aliens, and similar topics. All but eight presented such occult events as factual.

Consumers should be wary of reports indicating that studies were completed on small numbers of subjects, done in foreign countries (evidence of accuracy is more difficult to ascertain), or based on animal studies alone. Preliminary findings can be important, but they do not become established as facts unless additional studies support them.

Even well-written articles about preliminary developments sometimes carry misleading headlines or begin with words that exaggerate their significance. For example, an article in the San Francisco *Sunday Examiner and Chronicle* contained this headline: "New Hay Fever Drug May Replace Antihistamines." The article said the substance needed to be inhaled, would require two-thirds fewer antihistamine tablets to control symptoms, and would not cause drowsiness. Later in the article, however, an allergy authority said it would work only for a small number of patients and would not replace antihistamines.[34]

Magazines and newsletters. Magazines and newsletters differ widely in the accuracy of the information they publish. Table 3-2 summarizes an evaluation by the American Council on Science and Health[35] of the nutrition information in 25 popular magazines. At least twenty articles from each magazine were examined using these criteria:

1. Is the information in the articles scientifically sound and factual?
2. Do the articles make inaccurate claims that certain foods or nutrients have special health benefits?
3. What are the credentials of the supposed experts who write or act as sources for the articles?
4. Are featured weight-loss diets safe, sensible, and effective?

TABLE 3–1

RELIABILITY OF TABLOID ARTICLES

Reliable: Provides accurate information and appropriate advice.
Questionable: Mostly factual, but exaggerates, lacks perspective, or has headline that overstates contents of the article.
Unreliable: Contains serious factual errors or gives advice that is illogical or unscientific.

	Health	Nutrition	Psychologic	Total
National Enquirer				
Reliable	31	4	15	50 (57%)
Questionable	15	2	2	19 (21.5%)
Unreliable	5	10	4	19 (21.5%)
Globe				
Reliable	28	7	1	36 (44%)
Questionable	9	2	0	11 (13%)
Unreliable	13	13	9	35 (43%)
Sun				
Reliable	19	6	4	29 (44%)
Questionable	2	3	2	7 (11%)
Unreliable	15	7	8	30 (45%)
Weekly World News				
Reliable	6	1	0	7 (27%)
Questionable	5	0	2	7 (27%)
Unreliable	8	2	2	12 (46%)
National Examiner				
Reliable	11	2	0	13 (22%)
Questionable	9	0	2	11 (19%)
Unreliable	22	9	5	36 (59%)

© 1987 Stephen Barrett, M.D.

The major news magazines, *Time, Newsweek,* and *U.S. News & World Report,* are good sources of news on general health topics. Articles in these publications are usually timely, well-written, and based on interviews with recognized experts. During the past few years, however, all three of these magazines have publicized news about "alternative" health methods without appropriate critical analysis.

Three monthly magazines specializing in health topics deserve special comments: *Health* (formerly *In Health*), *American Health,* and *Prevention.* All three carry articles on a wide variety of topics. The articles on noncontroversial topics are generally well written, but articles on controversial topics occasionally give undeserved credibility to proponents of dubious methods. *Prevention* contains brief reports of preliminary research findings that can be difficult for readers to put into perspective. It also tends to exaggerate the ability of "positive thinking" to benefit health. Although the majority of their advertisers are reputable, none of these magazines has maintained rigorous advertising standards for health products or services.

In 1987 an expert panel assembled by *U.S. News & World Report* compared 13 health and nutrition periodicals, awarding up to 4 points each for accuracy, readability, and timeliness.[36] Only four (indicated with asterisks below) received perfect ratings for accuracy. The five highest overall scores (out of 12 possible points) were:

Tufts University Diet and Nutrition Letter 11.75*

Table 3–2

Nutrition Coverage in 25 Major Magazines

Magazine	Rating	Comments
Excellent		
Consumer Reports	90	Aggressively fights misrepresentation and myths with thoughtful scientific analysis
Saturday Evening Post	80	Thoughtful analysis, sometimes too technical
Good		
Vogue	79	Well-balanced, accurate articles
Redbook	76	Serious and factual articles
Reader's Digest	74	Could better utilize other sources
Parents	74	Good mix of professionally written articles
Good Housekeeping	73	Covers a wide spectrum of topics with good sources
Changing Times	72	Consistently reliable stories and good sources
Women's Day	71	Presents reliable, practical advice
Modern Maturity	71	Relatively accurate and well-presented
Seventeen	71	Reporting could be more complete
McCall's	70	Generally good, noncontroversial coverage
Fair		
Better Homes & Gardens	69	Fair, noncontroversial reporting
Glamour	69	Limited in-depth coverage of topics
Self	68	Some reliance on sensational reporting
Prevention	68	Large improvement seen, but still overemphasizes supplements
American Health	67	Objective reporting that is intelligent and practical
Health	67	Educational and informative, but overemphasizes supplements
Consumers Digest	66	Tendency toward advocacy—promoting one food or nutritional theory
Essence	64	Needs more scientific sources
Mademoiselle	62	Needs to expand nutrition sources
Family Circle	61	Effective at discussing issues in lay terms
Cosmopolitan	61	Makes some exaggerated claims. Heavy emphasis on slimming
Poor		
Gentlemen's Quarterly	58	Inconsistent treatment of topics, focusing on fads. Needs more sound information
Ladies Home Journal	52	Over-reliance on anecdotes and generalities

Source: Kroger M et al. 1989.[35]

University of California, Berkeley Wellness Letter 11.75*
Harvard Medical School Health Letter 11.25*
Mayo Clinic Health Letter 11.25
Nutrition Forum Newsletter 11.00*

Several other newsletters have begun publication during the past few years. Table 3-3 provides Dr. Barrett's analysis of their contents.

Books and pamphlets. The First Amendment of the Constitution protects free speech and thus, unfortunately, permits authors to embellish or distort facts and data and publish inaccurate and misleading health information. Writers and publishers, however, are subject to laws of libel if they unfairly

Table 3–3

Health and Nutrition Periodicals Aligned with the Scientific Community

Each of the newletters and magazines in the chart below presents valuable information. Some deal with controversial topics much more than others, while some deal with them less accurately than others. Some cover many topics superficially, while others cover fewer topics deeply. Some balance this mix according to the importance of the topic. Generally the broader the scope, the less thorough, and vice-versa.

A = How accurate?
D = How thorough?
P = How practical?
S = How broad a scope?
T = How timely?

4 = Excellent
3 = Good
2 = Fair
1 = Inconsistent

Publication	Cost	General Topics					Quackery			Comments
		A	D	P	S	T	A	S	T	
General health newsletters										
Consumer Reports on Health	24.00	4	4	4	4	4	4	3	4	Outstanding; packed with useful information
Edell Health Letter	24.00	4	2	3	3	3	4	2	3	Mostly summarizes journal articles without placing them in perspective
Executive Health's Good Health Report	34.00	3	3	2	2	2	1	2	2	Articles on controversial topics are inconclusive
George Washington University Personal Health Letter	48.00	4	3	4	3	3	—	—	—	Seldom covers controversial topics
Harvard Health Letter	24.00	4	4	4	4	4	4	4	4	Outstanding; especially good interpretation of research findings
Health Over 50	24.00	4	4	4	3	4	4	3	4	Excellent and timely
Healthline	21.00	3	3	4	4	3	3	3	3	Book reviews are not consistently reliable
Lahey Clinic Health Letter	18.00	4	4	4	4	4	—	—	—	Seldom covers controversial topics
Mayo Clinic Health Letter	24.00	4	3	4	4	4	4	4	4	Excellent and timely
Mirkin Report	32.00	4	2	4	4	4	4	4	4	Summarizes journal articles and provides practical tips
Public Citizen HRG Health Letter	18.00	2	3	1	1	4	2	2	2	Unduly negative about health marketplace. Some reports based on poor data sampling
The Health Letter	22.50	4	4	4	4	4	—	—	—	Seldom covers controversial topics
Univ. of Berkeley, California Wellness Letter	24.00	3	4	4	4	4	3	4	4	Some articles on "alternative methods" have been inaccurate
University of Texas Health Letter	24.00	4	4	4	4	4	—	—	—	Seldom covers controversial topics
Women's Health & Fitness News	18.00	3	4	3	2	3	1	2	2	Many articles on controversial topics have been inaccurate

Continued.

TABLE 3–3

HEALTH AND NUTRITION PERIODICALS ALIGNED WITH THE SCIENTIFIC COMMUNITY—cont'd

Publication	Cost	General Topics A	D	P	S	T	Quackery A	S	T	Comments
Nutrition newsletters										
Environmental Nutrition	36.00	3	3	4	3	4	2	3	4	Best features are news and book reviews. Some articles about vitamins have been inaccurate.
Nutrition Action	19.95	3	3	3	1	3	1	1	3	Alarmist attitude toward nutrition and food safety
Nutrition Forum	35.00	4	4	3	3	4	4	4	4	Emphasizes quackery and investigative reports. Much unique and original material.
Obesity and Health	59.00	4	4	4	—	4	4	4	4	Deals only with topics related to weight control.
Tufts Diet and Nutrition Letter	20.00	4	4	4	3	4	4	2	3	Deals primarily with food
Magazines										
American Health	14.97	4	3	4	4	4	1	3	4	Some articles on alternative methods have been atrocious.
FDA Consumer	12.00	4	4	4	3	4	4	3	4	Focuses mainly on foods and drug topics
Health (formerly *In Health*)	18.00	4	4	4	4	4	3	2	3	Too sympathetic toward "alternative" methods
Living Well	5.99	4	4	4	4	4	—	—	—	Outstanding new AMA/Good Housekeeping joint venture. Extent of quackery coverage not yet clear
Prevention	16.97	3	3	1	2	4	2	1	2	Emphasizes lifestyle improvements. Generally accurate but overemphasizes news about vitamin supplements and "positive thinking." Many articles encourage inappropriate self-treatment
Priorities	25.00	4	4	4	3	4	4	4	4	Emphasizes public health and environmental issues
Shape	17.97	3	4	4	3	4	3	2	3	Focused on nutrition and fitness
Your Health & Fitness	16.50	4	4	4	4	4	4	2	4	Much practical information

The following are not recommended because they promote unscientific and/or unproven methods:
Newsletters: *Alternatives, Cancer Chronicles, The Choice, The Doctor's People, Health & Healing, Health Facts, Men's Health Newsletter, Natural Living Newsletter, Nutrition News* (published by Siri Khalsa), *Second Opinion, People's Medical Society Newsletter*
Magazines: *Better Nutrition for Today's Living, Body, Mind & Spirit, Delicious!, East West Natural Health, Health Counselor, Health World, Let's Live, Longevity, Muscle & Fitness, New Age Journal, Senior Health, Total Health, Vegetarian Times, Your Health*
© 1992, Stephen Barrett, M.D.

demean the character of any individual. In 1992, *Vegetarian Times* published a rebuttal[37] and paid $21,000 in an out-of-court settlement to the National Council Against Health Fraud and four of its board members who charged that they had been unfairly criticized in a 1991 article about "quackbusters."[38]

FTC laws protect consumers against false and misleading advertising. Federal laws and some state food and drug laws provide protection against improper labeling of products and advertising with false or unproved health claims. However, many books and pamphlets extol the virtues of unproved products. Consumers should be alert to this maneuver and be aware that such action is frequently taken by food supplement manufacturers and publicists who support unproven methods.

Best-seller lists often contain one or more books on diet and fitness. These popular books are rarely accurate. *The Beverly Hills Diet* by Judy Mazel sold over a million copies and was on the bestseller list for many weeks. It is a bizarre diet primarily based on eating fruit and avoiding combinations of foods that supposedly cannot be digested at the same time. *Life Extension* by Dirk Pearson and Sandy Shaw is based on the dubious premise that animal experiments suggest that taking various nutrients can prolong human life to 150 years. The book stimulated sales of various substances said by the book to have "anti-aging" properties. Factually written books on health topics seldom become best sellers.

Many publishers are willing to publish books on unproven theories if they think that the books will be profitable. Only a few are unwilling to do so. The most noteworthy publishers of medical books for the general public are: Consumer Reports Books, which originates and reprints many books on health topics; Random House, which, in cooperation with the American Medical Association, is publishing the AMA Health Library; Prometheus Books, which specializes in books debunking quackery and paranormal claims; and Bull Publishing, which specializes in nutrition books written by experts.

Television and radio. Television and radio provide a great deal of health information. Cable television has one channel (The Lifetime Network) primarily devoted to health matters. Many stations use physicians as commentators or consultants. Although news reports tend to be presented accurately, radio and television talk shows give frequent exposure to promoters of quackery. *Donahue* and *The Merv Griffin Show* have been most significant in this regard.[41]

Stations sometimes take corrective action when they receive complaints about their health programming. In 1982, the California Council Against Health Fraud and the Greater Los Angeles Nutrition Council were instrumental in getting a Los Angeles radio station to drop a weekly program on nutrition because its information had been inaccurate. In 1983, radio station KNST-AM (Tucson, Arizona) offered extensive rebuttal time to critics following a talk show appearance in which Kurt Donsbach (see Chapter 13) promoted a product not approved for sale by federal authorities.

Telephone advice. In recent years there has been a proliferation of sources of telephone advice available to consumers. Many reliable agencies and groups operate toll-free hotlines (listed in the Appendix) through which callers can obtain printed information or ask questions to knowledgeable parties. Some hospitals, organizations, and individual practitioners sponsor phone lines through which consumers can select tape recordings on various topics.

Several commercial services, accessed through 900 numbers, provide direct contact with physicians or pharmacists who answer questions (see Figure 3-1). The charges for these calls (typically $2 to $3 per minute) are then billed through the telephone company. Critics of these services have warned that their advice has limited value because the person giving advice is unable to physically examine the caller. Proponents argue that the services can still provide valuable information. Scientific studies concerning the quality and cost-effectiveness of commercial telephone advice have not been published.

Suggestions for Consumers

Individuals must act intelligently to protect themselves from misleading and fraudulent practices that abound in the health marketplace.

Johnson and Goldfinger[39] provide these tips for evaluating medical or health information:

1. Proof that a new treatment is effective requires controlled studies that compare treatment under discussion to other treatments or to no treatment. Controls help to remove bias, and with large enough numbers the study can be statistically valid.

CONSUMER TIP

The following questions may be helpful in determining reliable sources of information:

1. What is the purpose of the book, presentation, or statement? Is it to sell products or ideas and the make money? Or is it to present data or to make a professional contribution?
2. What is the procedure and style of presentation? Is it presented in an educational or scientific manner? Are propaganda devices used, such as testimonials, broad generalities, name-calling, and misleading statements? Does the information contain exaggerated claims or use gross superlatives?
3. What are the qualifications of the author, speaker, organization, or agency? What is the educational background, professional experience, and training of the individual? If he has scientific credentials, are they in the field in which he is making claims? What is the standing of the individual in the professional community? Is the person listed in any recognized biographical sources such as *American Men and Women of Science* or in directories of health specialists?
4. Are the data based on appropriate research by experts in the health field or on the testimony or opinions of one or a few individuals? Is the information based on scientific facts or on emotional appeal?
5. Has the information been published in peer-reviewed professional journals and generally accepted as valid by the scientific community?
6. Where there appear to be conflicting claims about a health matter, what is the extent of the evidence supporting or refuting the claims? Has the claimant generalized from a particular incident or from broad research?

2. Reports should be based upon studies published in peer-reviewed medical journals.
3. Safety is not an absolute phenomenon but a relative one. All life activities, including medical treatment, involve some risk. The question is whether the risk is justified in comparison to other treatments and to the potential gain.
4. Be wary of claims of unusual remedies for chronic or incurable diseases. The burden of proof rests with those who make the claims.

Fleiger[40] advises consumers to be skeptical of news of major drug "breakthroughs" because many such reports are exaggerated or inaccurate interpretations of scientific findings. He states that truly significant advances in drugs and drug therapy are rare and gives these tips:

1. News stories about drugs producing complete cures, especially in patients with cancer, severe arthritis, AIDS, or other grave illnesses, are likely to be wrong. Except for antibiotics, drugs that make a disease disappear totally and permanently are few.
2. The results of one study of a small number of patients are seldom, if ever, conclusive. News stories may place undue importance on these reports and jump to conclusions that the researchers themselves know are unjustified.
3. Consider whether the report was made by a reporter or news service that regularly covers health and medical affairs and assigns reporters specializing in the subject. Be skeptical if the source emphasizes sensational stories on a regular basis.
4. Ask your doctor. While physicians cannot know everything, they are likely to be aware of truly important medical advances.

To stay informed, consumers should do the following:

1. Read reliable magazines and newsletters such as those recommended in Table 3-3. The two most practical are *Consumer Reports on Health* and the *Harvard Health Letter*.
2. Read the health and medical news in *Time, Newsweek,* and *U.S. News & World Report,* but be wary of their coverage of "alternative" health methods.
3. Take courses at accredited schools, colleges, and universities.
4. Select health professionals and health educators carefully.
5. Obtain information from federal, state, and local government agencies and reputable professional and voluntary organizations, such as the FDA, the AMA, the American Cancer Society, the American Dental Association, the Arthritis Foundation, the U.S. Public Health Service, and others listed in Chapter 27 and the Appendix.

It's Your Decision

According to a local newspaper report, a researcher at a medical center claims to have discovered a new substance that shows great promise for curing severe acne. How can consumers determine whether the report is factual, misleading, or fictional? What questions should be raised about the characteristics of the scientific method used, the use or misuse of statistics, scientific fraud, and whether the study has been peer-reviewed? How can you check the reliability of this information?

Summary

Consumers obtain health information from nonprofessional, professional, and pseudoprofessional individuals as well as from educational institutions and from the media. Unfortunately, much of this information is misleading, inaccurate, or false. Even scientists at times can find it difficult to sort fact from fiction. The intelligent health consumer should follow these practices:

1. Maintain a healthy degree of skepticism toward health information received through the media.
2. Select practitioners with great care.
3. Become well-informed before making decisions to purchase and use health products and services; pay little or no attention to health advertising.
4. Seek reliable sources of information.
5. Be familiar with the fundamental concepts used in the scientific method, including statistical concepts.

Discussion Questions

1. Describe the scientific method. What steps are used in the scientific method to carry out experiments?
2. Identify several characteristics of well-designed experiments.
3. What cautions are prudent in interpreting research findings?
4. What is statistics? Identify the two major types of statistical approaches. Describe three statistical concepts that can help consumers analyze studies reported in the media.
5. Describe five statistical errors used by advertisers to mislead consumers.
6. What is peer review? How does the scientific community use it? Name several scientific review bodies that are highly respected by the medical profession.
7. List several reasons why scientists may engage in fraudulent research.
8. From what sources do consumers obtain health information? Which ones have the greatest impact?
9. Why is it often difficult to determine the reliability of health information?
10. Identify some characteristics that can help consumers distinguish between true scientists and pseudoscientists.
11. What are the main functions of the media? How are they related to the ways in which misinformation is disseminated?
12. What factors help misinformation and quackery to spread through the media?
13. How does the First Amendment of the Constitution contribute to the spread of misinformation about health?
14. Name five magazines or newsletters that supply reliable information about health.
15. Discuss the possible advantages and limitations of telephone advice offered by commercial services.
16. Name at least five things consumers can do to obtain reliable information and protect themselves against misinformation.

References

1. Mirkin G: In Herbert V and Barrett S: Vitamins and "health" foods: the great American hustle, Philadelphia, 1981, George F Stickley Co.
*2. Sagan C: The fine art of baloney detection, Parade Magazine, p 12-13, Feb 1, 1987.
3. Harper AE: Mythical thinking vs scientific thinking, ACSH News & Views 4(2):4-5, 1983.
*4. Doyle RP: The medical wars, New York, 1983, William Morrow & Co Inc.
5. Sakethoo K et al: Effects of drinking hot water, cold water, and chicken soup on nasal mucous velocity and airflow resistance, Chest 74:408-410, 1978.
6. Physicians' Health Study Group: Preliminary report: findings from the aspirin component of the ongoing Physicians' Health Study, N Engl J Med 318:262-264, 1988.

*Recommended reading

*7. The gold standard of research trials, Harvard Heart Letter 2(2):6-7, 1991.
*8. Karlowski TR et al: Ascorbic acid for the common cold: a prophylactic and therapeutic trial, JAMA 246:2235-2237, 1975.
9. Huff D: How to lie with statistics, New York, 1954, WW Norton & Co Inc.
10. Begley S: Why scientists cheat, Newsweek, p 89-90, Feb 8, 1982.
11. Hunt M: A fraud that shook the world of science, New York Times Magazine, Nov 1, 1981.
12. Broad W: Harvard delays in reporting fraud, Science 215:478-482, 1982.
13. Probe of faked medical research widening, San Francisco Chronicle, April 25, 1983.
14. Doctor admits research fraud in journal, San Francisco Examiner, June 10, 1983.
15. Engler RL et al: Misrepresentation and responsibility in medical research, N Engl J Med 317:1383-1389, 1987.
16. Brand D and Nash J: "It was too good to be true," Time, p 59, June 1, 1987.
17. Researchers' help sought in fraud fight, American Medical News, p 40, Nov. 25, 1988.
18. Gardner M: Science, good, bad and bogus, Buffalo, NY, 1981, Prometheus Books.
19. House Committee on Science and Technology, Subcommittee on Investigation of Scientific Fraud, Washington, DC, March 30–April 1, 1980, US Government Printing Office.
20. Walton S: Data falsification: Congress asks how much and why, Bioscience 31:355-358, 1981.
*21. Barrett S: The multilevel mirage, Priorities, p 38-40, Summer 1991.
22. Hatfield D: In defense of the establishment, ACSH News & Views 6(2):6-7, 1985.
23. Peterson S: Spinning on science's shores, The Skeptical Inquirer 13(4):6, 1989.
24. Arseneau JC and Thigpen JT: The new quack: pseudoscience, public relations and politics, J Miss State Med Assoc, p 202-207, Aug 1981.
25. Criss M: Science and nonscience, The Rocky Mountain Skeptic 5(2):5-8, 1987.
26. Barrett S: Be wary of medical endorsements, ACSH News & Views 8(3):3-4, 1987.
27. Lederer RJ and Singer B: Pseudoscience in the name of the university, The Skeptical Inquirer 7(3):57-62, 1983.
28. Gunther M: Quackery and the media. In Barrett S, ed: The health robbers, ed 2, Philadelphia, 1980, George F Stickley Co.
29. Wilson B: The rise and fall of Laetrile, Nutrition Forum 5:33-40, 1988.
30. Koren G and Klein N: Bias against negative studies in newspaper reports of medical research, JAMA 266:1824-1826, 1991.
31. Herbert V and Barrett S: Vitamins and "health" foods: the great American hustle, Philadelphia, 1981, George F Stickley Co.
32. Kansas D.C. fights anti-chiropractic testbook—nationwide effort urged, ACA Journal of Chiropractic 25(12):19-20, 1988.
*33. Barrett S: Truth or trash? Health-related information in the tabloids, Priorities, p 27-30, Summer 1989.
34. Saltus R: New hay fever drug may replace antihistamines, San Francisco Sunday Examiner and Chronicle, May 15, 1983.
*35. Kroger M et al: The 1986-1988 ACSH survey on nutritional accuracy in American magazines, New York, 1989, American Council on Science and Health.
36. Carey J: Rating the health advisors, US News & World Report, p 54-55, Sept 7, 1987.
37. Barrett S et al: "Quackbusters" respond, Vegetarian Times, p 10-14, March 1992.
38. Bloyd-Peshkin S: The health-fraud cops—are the quackbusters consumer advocates or medical McCarthyites? Vegetarian Times, p 49-59, Aug 1991.
39. Johnson GT and Goldfinger SE, eds: The Harvard Medical School health letter book, Cambridge, Mass, 1981, Harvard University Press.
40. Fleiger K: A skeptic's guide to medical "breakthroughs," FDA Consumer 21(9):13, 1987.
41. Butler K: Tabloid journalism. In: A consumers guide to "alternative medicine," Buffalo, Prometheus Books, 1992.

CHAPTER FOUR

FRAUDS AND QUACKERY

"He couldn't find a thing wrong with me—the quack."
(Reprinted from The Saturday Evening Post ©1963 The Curtis Publishing Company.)

There is nothing men will not do, there is nothing they have not done to recover their health and save their lives. They have submitted to being half-drowned in water, and half-choked with gases, to being buried up to their chins in earth, to being scarred with hot irons like galley slaves, to being crimped with knives like codfish, to having needles thrust into their flesh, and bonfires kindled in their skins, to swallowing all sorts of abominations, and to pay for all this, as if to be singed and scalded were a costly privilege, as if blistering were a blessing and leeches a luxury.

OLIVER WENDELL HOLMES

There's a sucker born every minute.

P.T. BARNUM

There's also a crook born every hour who can take care of 60 suckers.

ANONYMOUS

Consumer Decisions

How can people identify fraudulent and quack products, services, practices, and practitioners?

What action can consumers take to avoid being victims of health frauds and quackery?

What action should consumers take when they encounter fraud and quackery in the health marketplace?

Despite the tremendous advances in medical science and health education, health frauds and quackery are still common. Newspapers, magazines, radio, and television provide entrepreneurs with enormous opportunities to promote their wares to the public. Laws intended to control fraud and quackery have not been particularly successful in reducing the extent of this problem. This chapter provides practical definitions of health fraud and quackery, explains why people are vulnerable, and tells how to identify and avoid them. The remaining chapters in the text offer more detailed information about the practices listed as well as many others that deserve attention.

Definitions

Quackery is derived from the word *quacksalver* (someone who boasts about his salves). Dictionaries define quack as "a pretender to medical skill; a charlatan" and "one who talks pretentiously without sound knowledge of the subject discussed." These definitions suggest that the promotion of quackery involves deliberate deception, despite the fact that many promoters sincerely believe in what they are doing. The FDA defines health fraud as "the promotion, for profit, of a medical remedy known to be false or unproven." This also can cause confusion because in ordinary usage—and in the courts—the word "fraud" connotes deliberate deception. Dr. William T. Jarvis,[1] president of the National Council Against Health Fraud, stresses that the essential characteristic of quackery is *promotion* ("Quacks quack!") rather than fraud, greed, or misinformation.

Quack methods are sometimes referred to as "alternatives." However, since ineffective methods are not true alternatives to effective ones, the terms *unscientific, nonscientific,* or *dubious* are more appropriate. This book generally uses these terms or places the word "alternative" in quotation marks when using it to describe unscientific methods.

Most people think of quackery as being promoted by quacks and charlatans who deliberately exploit their victims. Actually, most people promoting quackery are its victims who share misinformation and personal experiences with others. Customers of multilevel companies that sell overpriced vitamin supplements typically have been persuaded by friends, relatives, and neighbors who use them because they believe they are effective. Quackery is involved, but no "quacks." Pharmacists also profit from the sale of nutrition supplements that few customers need. In most cases, pharmacists do not promote the products but simply profit from the misleading promotions of others. Much quackery is involved in telling people something is bad for them (such as food additives) and selling a substitute (such as "organic" or "natural" food). Quackery is also involved in misleading advertising of nutrition supplements and other nonprescription drugs. Again, no "quack" is involved—just deception by advertising agencies.

Quackery is not all-or-nothing. A practitioner may be scientific in many respects and only minimally involved in unscientific practices. Also, products can be useful for some purposes but worthless for others.

To avoid semantic problems, some experts suggest that quackery be defined as "anything involving overpromotion in the field of health." This broader definition would include questionable ideas as well as questionable products and services, regardless of the sincerity of their promoters. In line with this definition, the word *fraud* would be reserved only for situations in which deliberate deception is involved.

Unproven methods are not necessarily quackery. Those that are consistent with established scientific concepts may be considered experimental. Legitimate researchers do not promote unproven procedures in the marketplace but engage in responsible studies with proper protocols (see Chapter 3). Methods that are inconsistent with established scientific concepts are more properly classified as nonsensical or disproven rather than experimental.

Frauds and Quackery Today

At least $10 billion is spent yearly on products and services that are falsely claimed to prevent or treat health problems. Some experts believe this figure is too conservative, but no precise data are available. Millions of dollars yearly are wasted on health devices (see Chapter 23), exercise equipment (see Chapter 15), unnecessary and ineffective drug and beauty products (Chapters 1, 20, and 21), and worthless and possibly harmful cancer remedies (Chapter 18). The Arthritis Foundation states that $1 billion yearly goes for quack remedies (Chapter 17). They add that 60% of patients continue to try questionable diets and nostrums such as alfalfa seed, sea brine, liniments, and iodine baths, even when under professional care. Billions are spent annually for spurious food remedies, fraudulent weight reduction schemes and products, fad diets, "organic" and "natural" foods, and unnecessary vitamins and minerals (see Chapters 13 and 14).

The California Medical Association[2] has listed the following practices as questionable: acupuncture, acupressure, applied kinesiology, bogus arthritis treatments, "cellular therapy," cellulite removal, chelation therapy, clinical ecology, colonic irrigation, cytotoxic testing, DMSO (dimethyl sulfoxide), enzymes and "glandular extracts," faith and psychic healing, figure enhancers, hair analysis, homeopathy, immune system protectors, iridology, Laetrile (amygdalin) treatment for cancer, live cell analysis, nutrition remedies for cancer, polarity therapy, reflexology, touch for health, vitamin megadoses, and youth prolongers.

A U.S. House of Representatives subcommittee report[3] lists numerous fraudulent and quack procedures that include: (1) clinics inside and outside the United States that provide bogus treatments for chronic and terminally ill patients using nonsurgical therapy—diet, drugs, enemas for arthritis, cancer, heart disease, and other ailments; (2) foundations that encourage the use of unproven remedies; and (3) phony healers who use a religious healing image or claim powers generated by Satan or witchcraft.

Why People Are Vulnerable

Despite the advanced state of medical science, many people with health problems turn to unscientific and unproven methods. Faced with the prospect of chronic suffering, deformity, or death, many individuals are tempted to try anything that offers relief or hope. The terminally ill, the elderly, and various cultural minorities are especially vulnerable to health frauds and quackery. Former Arthritis Foundation official Jerry Walsh, who was stricken at age 18 with rheumatoid arthritis, admitted that during the early years of his illness he spent thousands of dollars on quack remedies—everything from radium gadgets to magic buckeyes.

Even intelligent and well-educated individuals may resort to unorthodox medical procedures in the belief that anything is better than nothing. At age 16, the son of the famous writer, John Gunther, developed a brain tumor. The intelligent and generally well-informed family obtained the services of the best neurologists and brain surgeons at a well-known medical center. The parents were told there was no hope of saving the youth's life, but they felt compelled to try anything and everything. They turned to whatever hearsay remedies were available, including health foods, vegetable juices, and freshly squeezed juice of calf's liver. There were brief intervals of improvement from time to time. The physicians did not raise objections to the family's activities, and it appeared as though they acknowledged there was some benefit to be derived from them.[4]

Specific reasons why people turn to questionable and unproven methods include the following:

1. Individuals may underestimate the degree of illness or may delay obtaining assistance because they believe they cannot afford such services.
2. Religious and cultural beliefs can foster acceptance of faith healers, prayer, magic, sorcery, and the like. For example, a Chinese person may consider acupuncture and herbal remedies to be the orthodox form of treatment and the type of medicine practiced in the United States totally foreign.
3. Physicians may be unable to communicate in language their patients understand. Patients may be unable to ask questions of physicians; they may lack knowledge or may fear inquiries.
4. Patients may distrust physicians or question the quality of medical care. Doctors sometimes appear more concerned with treating illnesses than with treating the total patient.
5. Some people harbor extreme distrust of the medical profession, the food industry, drug

companies, and government agencies. Some feel deeply antagonistic toward scientific medicine but are attracted to methods that are "natural" or otherwise unorthodox.

6. Pride and modesty cause some individuals to avoid physicians. Some individuals with cancer or venereal disease prefer to receive treatment secretly. Others may not wish to undress before physicians or to subject themselves to what they believe to be indignities or interference with their privacy during health examinations.
7. People fear social unacceptability, pain, death, and growing old (wrinkles, loss of hair, decrease of sexual potency). Elderly individuals are particularly vulnerable in this regard.
8. Many people faced with a serious health problem that doctors cannot solve become desperate enough to try almost anything that arouses hope. Many victims of cancer, arthritis, multiple sclerosis, and AIDS fall prey to unscrupulous entrepreneurs. Some waste their life's savings searching for a "cure."
9. Many people suffer from chronic aches, pains, or other discomforts that are not well defined and for which medicine cannot offer clear-cut diagnosis or treatment. The more chronic the condition, the more susceptible the sufferer will be to promises of a "cure." Many people in this category fall into the hands of doctors who make fad diagnoses such as hypoglycemia or candidiasis hypersensitivity (see Chapter 9).
10. Patients may not receive help from physicians for psychological problems. Evidence indicates that 50% to 70% of individuals who go to general practitioners have emotional difficulties.
11. Many individuals are gullible because of their ignorance of health matters. People also tend to believe what others tell them about personal experience. Many people believe that any health-related claim in print or in a broadcast must be true, and are attracted by promises of quick, painless, or drugless solutions to problems.
12. The mass media provide a great deal of false and misleading information in advertisements, news reports, feature articles, and books, and on radio and television talk shows. News tends to focus on sensational developments, stimulating false hopes and arousing widespread fears. Radio and television talk shows abound with promoters of quackery.
13. People fail to realize that some serious illnesses (even cancer and arthritis) have ups and downs. The remission or down period may be mistakenly attributed to whatever product or service was used before it occurred.
14. People do not understand the nature of the placebo effect (discussed below).
15. Self-confidence, which quacks tend to exude, is a powerful persuader.

The box below contains the condensed testimony of a defense witness in the 1990 trial of a Canadian couple whose infant daughter had died of malnutrition under the care of an unlicensed naturopath. The couple was charged with criminal negligence, but eventually was acquitted.

Hazards of Frauds and Quackery

Consumers should be aware of quackery's dangers. Financial harm can range from minor expense to

Self-Confidence Sells

The herbalist was a very impressive man. He just glowed with health and was very charismatic, very jovial, charming, friendly, very nice, very knowledgeable. There was not a question that you could ask that he would not have an answer for. And he told a lot of stories about people who had come to see him and been cured by following his course of treatment. It's a very difficult thing to communicate just how mesmerizing this man was. He was so good, so positive. He just exuded this powerful aura about him. He told my father that his cancer was completely curable. He had to change his diet because this was the cause of the cancer. He would have to eat strictly fruits and vegetables, raw, or juices of those fruits and vegetables, and by doing this, the tumor would be dissolved. When my father lost weight, the herbalist said this was just the body ridding itself of toxins and poisons. During his final two weeks, my father developed a hole near his rectum and a lesion that grew bigger each day. The herbalist said it was just the radiation coming out, which was a good thing. I now know it was a gangrenous tumor. I look back now and can't believe that I fell under this man's spell.[5]

loss of one's life savings. Improper diagnosis can lead to greater illness and injury. Unsafe procedures can cause irreparable harm. Delay in getting proper treatment can have serious or fatal consequences. The following examples, which have received considerable publicity, illustrate quackery's serious potential for harm:

In 1961, the parents of 8-year-old Linda Epping charged that a chiropractor had bilked them out of $739 by falsely promising to cure her of cancer of the eye. Linda had been scheduled for surgery to remove her left eye and surrounding tissue. Her doctors thought cure was possible because it did not look like the tumor had spread. But shortly before the operation was to be performed, Linda's parents met a couple who said that a chiropractor had cured their son's brain tumor without using surgery. After the chiropractor agreed to help by "balancing" Linda's body, her parents removed her from the hospital and took her for treatment with "spinal adjustments," vitamins, food supplements and laxatives (up to 124 pills plus 150 drops of iodine solution daily). Despite the new "treatment," the tumor grew quickly. Within 3 weeks, it was the size of a tennis-ball and had pushed Linda's eye out of its socket. She died within a few months. The chiropractor was subsequently convicted of second degree murder and sentenced to prison.

Ruth Conrad, an Idaho woman, consulted one of the state's many unlicensed naturopaths. While seeking treatment for a sore shoulder, she also complained of a bump on her nose. The naturopath stated that it was cancer and gave her a black herbal salve to apply directly. Within a few days, her face became very painful and she developed red streaks that ran down her cheeks. Her worried phone call to the naturopath brought the explanation that the presence of the lines was a good sign because they "resemble a crab, and cancer is a crab." He also advised her to apply more of the black salve. Within a week, a large part of her face, including her nose, sloughed off. It took 3 years and 17 plastic surgery operations to reconstruct her face.

During the 1980s the amino acid L-tryptophan was marketed with unproven claims that it could help insomnia, weight reduction, premenstrual syndrome, and several other problems. In 1989 L-tryptophan was implicated in an outbreak of eosinophil-myalgia syndrome, a rare disorder characterized by muscle and joint pain, weakness, swelling of the arms and legs, fever and skin rash. More than 1500 cases were reported, including at least 28 deaths and many cases of paralysis and other severe disability. Although the outbreak probably was by a contaminant rather than L-tryptophan itself, there was no scientific justification for marketing L-tryptophan products in the first place. Hundreds of victims have filed lawsuits.

Common Misconceptions About Quackery

There are many misconceptions about quackery. Among those identified by Jarvis and Barrett are the following.[6]

Quacks are frauds and crooks. Most promoters of quackery sincerely believe in what they do. They may not willingly or deliberately deceive people.

Most quackery is dangerous. Most victims of quackery are harmed economically rather than physically. Sometimes an unproven approach will relieve emotionally related symptoms by lowering a person's tension level. Although such an experience is likely to be perceived as beneficial, it can prove harmful in the long run if the individual decides to rely upon unproven approaches for future health problems.

The media are reliable. Most media are willing to publicize sensational viewpoints they believe are newsworthy and will increase their audience. Radio and television and talk shows abound with promoters of nutrition quackery. General magazines that carry vitamin ads almost never publish articles advising readers not to waste their money on vitamins.

Personal experience is the best way to tell whether a treatment works. When someone feels better after having used a product or procedure, it is natural to give credit to whatever was done. However, this is unwise. Most ailments are self-limiting, and even incurable conditions can have sufficient day-to-day variation to enable quack methods to gain large followings. In addition, taking action often produces temporary relief of symptoms (a placebo effect). Scientific experimentation is almost always necessary to establish whether health methods are really effective. Thus, it is extremely important for consumers to understand the concepts of spontaneous remission and the placebo effect.

Spontaneous Remission

Where ailments are self-limiting, the quack makes nature his secret ally.[7]

James Harvey Young, Ph.D.
Professor of History, Emory University

Recovery from illness, whether it follows self-medication, treatment by a scientific practitioner, or treatment by an unscientific practitioner, may lead individuals to conclude that the treatment received was the cause of the return to good health. As Dr. Young points out:[7]

John Doe does not usually realize that most ailments are self-limiting and improve with time regardless of treatment. When a symptom goes after he doses himself with a remedy, he is likely to credit the remedy with curing him. He does not realize that he would have gotten better just as quickly if he had done nothing! Thousands of well-meaning John and Jane Does have boosted the fame of folk remedies and have signed sincere testimonials for patent medicines, crediting them instead of the body's recuperative power for a return to well-being.

It is commonly said that if you treat a cold it will disappear in a week, but if you leave it alone it will last 7 days. Even many serious diseases have ups and downs. Rheumatoid arthritis and multiple sclerosis are prime examples. On rare occasions even cancer can inexplicably disappear (although most testimonials for quack cancer remedies are based on faulty original diagnosis or simultaneous administration of effective treatment).

Placebo Effect

You must know that the will is a
powerful adjuvant of medicine.
Paracelsus

The power of suggestion has been demonstrated by many investigators in a variety of circumstances. In a classroom, for example, a professor sprayed plain water about the room and asked the students to raise their hands as soon as they detected an odor. Seventy-three percent managed to smell a nonexistent odor.

Persons with a dominant or persuasive personality often have considerable impact on others through their ability to create confidence, which enhances suggestibility. Many individuals who are taken in by charlatans later tell their doctors, ". . . but he talked to me; he explained things; he was so nice."

Individuals who are psychologically susceptible to suggestion often feel better under the influence of counseling or reassurance. One woman remarked, "I take a multivitamin pill that *Consumer Reports* says is useless. But I don't care. It makes me happy." Gullibility and wishful thinking are common human characteristics. People are willing to believe in untrue things in varying ways and to varying degrees. Even scientifically sophisticated people may respond to the power of suggestion.

In medicine the effect of suggestion is referred to as the "placebo effect." The Latin word *placebo* means "I shall please." A placebo effect is a response to a substance, device, or procedure that cannot be accounted for on the basis of pharmacological or other direct physical action. Feeling better when the physician walks into the room is a common example of the placebo effect.

A placebo may be used in medicine to satisfy a patient that something is being done. By lessening anxiety, placebo action may alleviate symptoms that are the result of the body's reaction to tension (so-called psychogenic, psychosomatic, or psychophysiologic symptoms). In certain circumstances a lactose tablet (sugar pill) may relieve not only anxiety but also pain, nausea, vomiting, palpitations, shortness of breath, and other symptoms. The patient expects the "medication" to make him or her feel better; often it does.

Many studies have shown that placebos may relieve a broad range of symptoms. In many disorders, one third or more of patients will get relief from a placebo. Temporary relief has been demonstrated, for example, in arthritis, hay fever, headache, cough, high blood pressure, premenstrual tension, peptic ulcer, and even cancer. The phychologic aspects of many disorders also work to the healer's advantage. A large percentage of symptoms either have a psychologic component or do not arise from organic disease. Hence, treatment offering some lessening of tension can often help. A sympathetic ear or reassurance that no serious disease is involved may prove therapeutic by itself.

Confidence in the treatment—on the part of the patient and the practitioner—makes it more likely that a placebo effect will occur. But power of suggestion may cause even a nonbeliever to respond favorably. The only requirement for a placebo effect is the awareness that something has been done. Perry and Heidrich[8] claim that 75% of patients sometimes respond to placebos. Lasagna[9] states that it is not possible to predict accurately or easily a particular patient's reaction to a placebo at a particular moment. However, the psychologic predisposition to respond positively to placebos is present to some extent in most people. Some are very likely to obtain relief from placebos in a wide variety of situations, whereas others are very unlikely to do so. Most people's response lies somewhere between the two extremes. Another factor that can mislead people is selective affirmation—a tendency to look for positive responses when improvement is expected.

 PERSONAL GLIMPSE

Placebo Response

Myths

1. Placebos work on the imagination—not the body.
2. Placebos make patients feel better—not get better.
3. Placebos may help—but they cannot hurt.
4. Placebos work primarily on suggestible patients.
5. Placebo response is not so important if the active drug really works.
6. Placebo response depends on the patient—not on the nurse, physician, or practitioner.

Facts

1. Placebos affect people physiologically as well as psychologically. Emotions can affect the hypothalamus, which triggers the pituitary gland to release hormones that can affect the thyroid and adrenal glands.
2. Placebos may enhance the curative mechanism of the body.
3. Adverse reactions can occur. Patients may complain of dry mouth, nausea, headache, drowsiness, sleep disturbance, or rash.
4. All kinds of people in a variety of settings with many kinds of illnesses respond. There does not appear to be a recognized personality profile.
5. Patients often respond to placebos as well as to active drugs; a placebo can make an active drug more effective.
6. How the placebo is given and by whom influences the outcome more than any characteristic of the patient.

The extent of placebo action depends on such factors as the patient's feelings toward the practitioner, the patient's attitudes toward the ailments, and the nature of the disease itself. The physician's manner of dealing with the individual, the patience and consideration given, and the confidence imparted are all important factors. The more a physician can induce trust, the more effective the medication is likely to be.

Placebo effects can also be negative. In one experiment, for example, some subjects who were warned of possible side effects of a drug were given injections of a placebo instead. Many of them reported dizziness, nausea, vomiting, and even mental depression.

The placebo effect in treatment is not restricted to drugs but may also result from procedures. Devices and physical techniques often have a tremendous psychologic impact. Various nonmedical practitioners, such as chiropractors, naturopaths, and physical culturists, use heat, light, diathermy, hydrotherapy, manipulation, massage, and a variety of gadgets. In addition to any physiologic effects, these devices and procedures exert a potent psychologic force that may be reinforced by the relationship between the patient and the practitioner. Of course, devices and procedures used by orthodox practitioners can also have placebo effects.

Barrett has expressed serious misgivings about overreliance on the placebo effect in clinical practice:

> Doctors are confronted by many people who complain of tiredness or a variety of vague symptoms that are reactions to nervous tension. Far too often, instead of finding out what is bothering them, doctors tell them to take a tonic, a vitamin, or some other type of placebo.
>
> I am against people being misled. The quack who relies on a placebo effect is also pretending he knows what he is doing—that he can tell what is wrong with you and that he has effective treatment for just about everything. His customers are playing Russian roulette. The medical doctor who uses vitamins as placebos may not be as dangerous, but he is encouraging people to form lifelong habits of using things they don't need.
>
> Most people who use placebos do not get relief from them. So we're talking about practices that are not only misleading. They are also a financial rip-off.[10]

RECOGNIZING QUACKERY

Fraud and quackery are so extensive and pervasive that laws and enforcement agencies are unable to adequately police or resolve the problem by themselves. Consumers must be alert for the purveyors of quackery and be able to recognize how they operate in the health marketplace.

Quacks can be classified into three groups:

Dumb quacks. These people know not, and do not know that they know not. They may be uneducated, ignorant people who believe they have the secret formula or cure-all that no one else possesses. Generally they are small-time operators.

Deluded quacks. These people know but have been misled into knowing not. They often have some educational background and may even have a medical degree. Their beliefs are based on faulty observations and equally faulty reasoning. They may command large audiences and thereby be dangerous.

Dishonest quacks. These people know not, and know that they know not. Their primary goal is money. They have no scruples.

Jarvis and Barrett warn that modern health quacks are supersalespeople.[6]

> Seldom do their victims realize how often or how skillfully they are cheated. Does the mother who feels good as she hands her child a vitamin think to ask herself whether he really needs it? Do buyers of "extra-strength pain relievers" wonder what's in them or whether an unadvertised brand might cost less? Do subscribers to "health food" publications realize that articles are slanted to stimulate business for their advertisers? Not usually.
>
> Most people think that quackery and health frauds are easy to spot. Some are, but most are not. Their promoters wear the cloak of science. They use scientific terms and quote (or misquote) scientific references. On talk shows, they may be introduced as "scientists ahead of their time." The very word "quack" helps their camouflage by making us think of an outlandish character selling snake oil from the back of a covered wagon—and of course no intelligent people would buy snake oil nowadays, would they?
>
> Well, maybe snake oil isn't selling so well, lately. But acupuncture? "Organic" foods? Mouthwash? Hair analysis? The latest diet book? Megavitamins? "Stress formulas"? Chelation therapy? Cholesterol-lowering teas? Homeopathic remedies? "Cures" for AIDS? Or shots to pep you up? Business is booming for health quacks. Their annual take is in the *billions.* Spot reducers, "immune boosters," water purifiers, "ergogenic aids," bust creams, spinal adjustments, devices to increase manhood, systems to "balance body chemistry," cults to give life new meaning, special diets for arthritis. The list is endless.
>
> What sells is not the quality of their goods and services, but their ability to influence their audience. To those in pain, they promise relief. To the incurable, they offer hope. To the nutrition-conscious, they say, "Make sure you have enough." To a public worried about pollution, they say, "Buy natural." To one and all, they promise better health and a longer life. Modern quacks can reach people emotionally, on the level that counts the most.

To make matters even more complicated, a method or product may be scientific when used in one context and quackery when used in another. What counts is the presence of false or exaggerated claims. Vitamin B_{12} shots are lifesaving when given for the treatment of pernicious anemia, but given them three times a week to "pep you up" is a form of medical fraud.

The following behavior patterns are characteristic of practitioners and promoters of quackery.

1. They promise quick, dramatic, simple, painless, or drugless treatment or cures.
2. They use anecdotes, case histories, or testimonials to support claims. Prominent people such as actors, writers, baseball players, and even physicians may be used in testimonials. Because people tend to believe what they hear about the personal experience of others, testimonials can be powerful persuaders. Years ago, Smith made this observation, which is still noteworthy:[11]

> Personal testimonials are not used in scientific medicine to prove or disprove the validity of therapies, and for good reason. There has never been a worthless or fraudulent treatment that could not produce a legion of persons who would swear that it helped or cured them.

3. They use disclaimers couched in pseudomedical or pseudoscientific jargon. Instead of promising to treat or cure a specific illness or condition, they offer to "detoxify" the body, "strengthen the immune system," "balance body chemistry," or bring the body into "harmony with nature."
4. They may display credentials or use titles that might be confused with those of the scientific or medical community. Use of the terms professor, doctor, or nutritionist may be spurious. Their credentials may be from an unaccredited school or an organization that promotes nonscientific methods.
5. The results they claim have not been verified by others or published in a reputable scientific journal.
6. They claim that a single product or service can cure a wide range of unrelated illnesses.
7. They claim to have a secret cure or one that is recognized in other parts of the world but not yet known or accepted in the United States.
8. They claim to be persecuted by organized medicine and that their treatment is being suppressed because it is controversial or because the medical establishment does not want competition.
9. They state that medical doctors should not be trusted because surgery, x-rays, and drugs cause more harm than good. They say most doctors are "butchers" and "poisoners."

10. They claim that most disease is due to a faulty diet and can be treated by nutritional methods.
11. They use scare tactics to encourage use of the product or service advocated. They say lack of adequate intake of vitamins and minerals results in poor nutrition that may cause troublesome conditions. They state that food additives and preservatives may poison people.
12. They claim that most Americans are poorly nourished and need "nutrition insurance."
13. They advise vitamins and "health foods" for everyone.
14. They use hair analysis to determine nutritional needs.
15. They claim that natural vitamins are better than synthetic ones.

The Freedom-of-Choice Issue

Promoters of quackery tend to disparage accepted scientific methods as well as consumer protection laws. They argue that personal experience determines what works and that patients should be free to select any therapy they wish (Figure 4-1). They also argue that everyone should be free to market methods without the responsibility of ensuring that they are effective. The American Council on Science and Health[12] views this version of "health freedom" as "nothing more than a hunting license for quacks." Jarvis[1] describes it as a ploy:

> The "health freedom" argument is a classic example of deception by misdirection. . . . The reality is that patients may freely choose to do a variety of things. Patients may refuse treatments, swallow vitamins, eat apricot pits or the whole tree if they wish. However, they may not sell their pet remedies in the marketplace if those remedies have not been proven safe and effective. The reason that patients clamor for dubious treatments is that they have been deceived into believing that these therapies offer hope. By focusing attention on the patients, the deceivers direct attention away from themselves.

Several groups espousing unscientific methods are crusading to weaken consumer protection laws. They include the National Health Federation (NHF), the National Council for Improved Health (NCIH), the Foundation for the Advancement of Innovative Medicine (FAIM), the Health Issues Cooperative Association, People for Cancer, and the Committee for Freedom of Choice in Medicine (CFCM). To promote their legal strategies, these groups lobby, stage news events, and/or generate letter-writing campaigns to legislators and government agencies. During the mid-1970s, for example, NHF and CCFM (then called the Committee for Freedom of Choice in Cancer Therapy) spearheaded passage of laws to permit the marketing of Laetrile (a bogus cancer remedy) within the borders of nearly half the states (Chapter 18 provides details). During the past two years, FAIM has pressed for passage of a law that would place physicians sympathetic to its views on New York State's medical board and protect physicians who use "alternative" methods.

There is no question that consumers should have considerable right to choose the health products and services they wish to use. However, freedom of choice will benefit consumers only to the extent that the marketplace is trustworthy and consumers are well informed.

WE THE PEOPLE of the United States, propose AMENDMENT XXVII to be known as the HEALTH CARE RIGHTS AMENDMENT, which should read as follows:

HEALTH CARE RIGHTS AMENDMENT
SECTION 1.
Congress shall make no law that restricts any individual's right to choose and to practice the type of health care they shall elect for themselves or their children for the prevention or treatment of any disease, injury, illness, or ailment of the body or the mind.

Figure 4-1. A now-defunct "consumer group" gathered close to 100,000 signatures supporting its proposed constitutional amendment supporting "health freedom." If it were enacted, government agencies could no longer stop the marketing of unproven or dangerous remedies so long as a single consumer objects. Anyone, licensed or not, could engage in any practice labeled "health care" so long as a single consumer wishes it to continue. Compulsory immunization would end, and courts could no longer protect children from parents who deny them access to effective treatment, even if such neglect will result in their death.

Consumer Action

People often are timid or reluctant to act when they have been harmed by excess charges, misleading information, poor products and services, or inadequate treatment. However, the Consumer Bill of Rights encourages consumers to take action to protect society at large as well as themselves. This is necessary to make the caveat vendor (let the seller beware) principle operational. Table 27-2 (Where to Complain) will be useful when frauds and quackery are detected.

SUMMARY

Despite the tremendous advances in medical science and health education, health frauds and quackery are still common. Americans waste huge amounts of money on unproven and unscientific approaches to health care. Faced with the prospect of chronic suffering, deformity, or death, many individuals are tempted to try anything that offers relief or hope. Health frauds and quackery can cause both financial and physical harm.

It is extremely important for consumers to understand the concepts of spontaneous remission and the placebo effect. The mere fact that someone feels better after trying a remedy does not prove that the remedy was effective. Most diseases are self-limiting, and placebos can relieve a broad range of symptoms.

Modern health quacks can be difficult to recognize. However, certain behavior patterns should help consumers identify them. It also is important for consumers to complain to appropriate authorities when they encounter deception in the marketplace.

CONSUMER TIP

Protecting Yourself Against Fraud and Quackery

These consumer actions will help protect against fraud and quackery in the health marketplace:

1. Be an intelligent health consumer by using the procedures identified in Chapter 1.
2. Speak out whenever fraud or quackery surfaces by registering complaints; be assertive but discreet, as well as explicit and factual.

WANT TO DO SOMETHING ABOUT QUACKERY?

FIGURE 4-2.
Used by permission of the National Council Against Health Fraud, Inc., a private voluntary health agency dedicated to combating health misinformation, fraud and quackery.

DISCUSSION QUESTIONS

1. Define the terms "health fraud," "quack" and "quackery."
2. What is the scope of health fraud and quackery in the United States? Identify several dubious products and procedures.
3. Why do people become victims of fraud and quackery? How do spontaneous remission and the placebo effect mislead people?
4. Identify the hazards of frauds and quackery.
5. What types of quacks are encountered by consumers? How may they be recognized?
6. Discuss how entrepreneurs use the "freedom-of-choice" concept to support frauds and quackery.
7. How can consumers protect themselves against frauds and quackery?

IT'S YOUR DECISION

One of your parents is seriously ill with cancer, with little hope of recovery. Treatment at a large medical center has not succeeded in curing or alleviating the condition. You have been told that your parent has only six months to live. A friend of your parents told them he was helped by a clinic in Mexico that uses a substance, unavailable in the United States, that cures a high percentage of cancer patients who receive it. Despite its high cost, your parents are considering a trip to Mexico. What should you do to help your parents reach an intelligent decision? How sensible would it be for them to spend their life savings for the treatment?

How Can You Suspect Fraud or Quackery in a Health-Care Proposal?

Does the practitioner or promoter exhibit these characteristics?	**Yes**	**No**
Promises quick, painless, drugless treatment or cure	☐	☐
Uses anecdotes or testimonials to support claim	☐	☐
Displays questionable credentials/titles	☐	☐
Uses pseudoscientific terminology	☐	☐
Claims that a single treatment can cure a wide range of illness	☐	☐
Claims persecution by organized medicine	☐	☐
States that many illnesses can be treated by nutrition	☐	☐
Advises use of vitamins/"health foods" for everyone	☐	☐
States surgery/x-rays/drugs do more harm than good	☐	☐
Espouses "freedom of choice" to use unproven approaches	☐	☐
Claims to have cure that is secret or known only in a remote part of the world	☐	☐

Any positive response should be regarded as suspicious.

REFERENCES

*1. Jarvis WT: How quackery is promoted. In Barrett S and Cassileth BR, eds: Dubious cancer treatment—a report on "alternative" methods and the practitioners and patients who use them, Tampa, Fla, 1991, Florida Division of the American Cancer Society.

2. The California Medical Association: The professional's guide to health and nutrition fraud, San Francisco, 1987, The Association.

*3. United States House of Representatives, Select Committee on Aging, Subcommittee on Health and Long-term Care: Quackery—a $10 billion scandal, May 31, 1984, Washington, DC, US Government Printing Office.

4. Gordon WH: The keys to quackery, Proceedings of the National Congress on Medical Quackery, Chicago, 1961, American Medical Association.

5. Bianchini M: Testimony in Her Majesty the Queen v. Sonia Atikian and Khachadour Atikian, Toronto, June 28, 1991.

*6. Jarvis W and Barrett S: How quackery sells, New York, (in press), American Council on Science and Health.

*7. Young JH: Why quackery persists. In Barrett S, ed: The health robbers, ed 2, Philadelphia, 1980, George F Stickley Co.

8. Perry SW and Heidrich G: Placebo response: myth and matter, Am J Nurs 81:720–725, 1981.

9. Lasagna L: The doctor's dilemma, New York, 1962, Harper & Row Publishers Inc.

10. Barrett S: Health frauds and quackery, FDA Consumer 11(9):12–17, 1977.

*11. Smith RL: At your own risk: the case against chiropractors, New York, 1969, Pocket Books.

*12. Barrett S: The unhealthy alliance: crusaders for "health freedom," New York, 1988, American Council on Science and Health.

*Recommended reading

CHAPTER FIVE

ADVERTISING

"By God! You *can* fool all of the people all of the time!"
(©1982 Medical Economics Company.)

The public is constantly being bombarded by those who wish to promote their own views, sell a bill of goods, convert others to a cause or convince us that they have discovered a special truth or have found a unique road to salvation [to health].

PAUL KURTZ, PH.D.[1]

All things should be laid bare so that the buyer may not be in any way ignorant of anything the seller knows.

CICERO

Freedom of speech doesn't give a person the right to shout "fire" in a crowded theater (Oliver Wendell Holmes, Jr.). Nor should it give con artists the right to promote health frauds through ads in print or on the air. Yet, health fraud lives and thrives . . . because of successful advertising.

ROGER MILLER[2]
CRITIQUING QUACK ADS
FDA CONSUMER, 1985

CONSUMER DECISIONS

How should consumers analyze advertisements for such health products and services as face lifts, collagen implants, liquid diets, herbal heat wraps, wrinkle creams, cellulite reduction, breast lifts or reductions, exercise equipment?

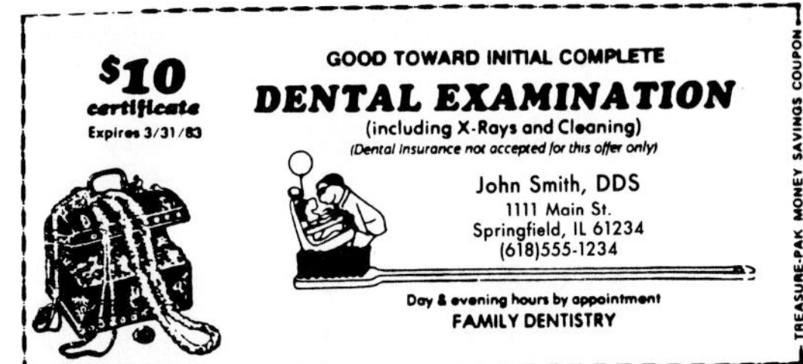

FIGURE 5-1. Straightforward ad with discount for first visit.

The prevailing philosophy of the free enterprise system is based on the profit motive. It permits sellers to supply what consumers want, and buyers to select the products they believe will be advantageous. In the health marketplace, consumers should be wary of advertising and should follow the principle of caveat emptor (let the buyer beware).

The purpose of advertising is to persuade people to make purchases. Business leaders view advertising in different ways. One has said, for example, that "the solution to marketing problems is not one of giving consumers what they want, but rather to make consumers want what we, the marketers, want them to want." Another has stated that advertisers are "concerned not with finding an audience to hear their message, but rather with finding a message to hold their audience." Another has stated that advertising has the obligation to communicate messages clearly, accurately, honestly, and with interest and impact.[3] Health professionals tend to be far more cautious and conservative than the business community concerning advertising, but abuses exist among health professionals also.

This chapter describes the nature of advertising and how it can mislead consumers. It also examines problems with the advertising of mail-order health products, professional services, drug products, foods and food supplements, exercise and fitness products, and weight-control products and services.

HIDDEN MOTIVATORS

The business world uses insights from psychology and the social sciences to manipulate consumer behavior. Many advertisers are able to persuade people to make purchases in a predictable manner. Advertising campaigns use strategies based on motivation analysis. Motivation research can determine what stimulates people's choices. Ads are often designed to reach the subconscious mind where preferences can be determined by factors that individuals may not be aware of. Much of what people want is psychological rather than material.

Cosmetics manufacturers, for example, are not selling merely lanolin, but fantasies involving attractiveness. Women who normally would pay only 50¢ for a bar of soap might be willing to pay $5 or more for a skin cream that they hope will make them beautiful. What they are buying is a promise. Purchasers of a cosmetic alleged to remove wrinkles are seeking everlasting attractiveness and social acceptance. Television ads for headache remedies often use soothing background music to promote their particular brand of pain-reliever.

Advertising messages attempt to convey simple answers to people's needs, ambitions, yearnings, fears, hopes, and feelings of guilt and inadequacy. Ads suggest products to enhance sexual performance or provide relief from a boring or lonely life. They offer quick, simple, painless methods of treatment. They encourage pill-taking as a panacea for insomnia, tension, and lack of energy. Ads for baldness remedies, weight control methods, deodorants, cures for impotence, bust developers, and penis enlargers exploit feelings of inferiority and suggest that using these products will lead to social success. Table 5-1 illustrates common techniques.

Visual imagery is often used to emphasize or exaggerate the truth. For example, Crest toothpaste has shown a "fluoride eraser" rubbing out a substantial black carious area on a tooth. Fluoridated toothpaste can help prevent cavities in their early stages by helping teeth remineralize. The picture suggests that Crest can cure large cavities, which it cannot do.[4]

Many ads encourage self-diagnosis and self-treatment. Increased consumer interest in self-care

TABLE 5–1

TECHNIQUES USED IN ADVERTISING

Technique	Questions to raise
Power words to gain attention	
"Strengthens immune system"	Is this possible? Will it help treat AIDS?
"Helps . . ."	Does it? What way? How much?
"Fights . . ."	How? Is it effective?
"Provides relief three times longer"	Longer than what? Why not four times?
"Free . . . money back"	What is free? Is this a come-on? What do you pay for?
"It's natural"	Is anything natural? Meaning? Is it better? More expensive?
"Amazing breakthrough"	Who says? What evidence? How effective?
"Less salt, fat, calories"	Than what? Than previous product? Is it still high?
"Cholesterol-free"	Is it undesirably high in fat?
Misleading comparisons to encourage consumers to jump to conclusions	
"Contains twice as much . . ."	As what? Is it better? More economical?
"Wrinkle eraser"	Does it really erase? Or cover temporarily?
"Isn't it time you tried . . ."	Why? Because everybody does?
"Contains X"	What is X? What does it do? Is it better than the ingredient(s) of competing products?
"Up to 8-hour relief"	What is "up to"?
"Fast-acting" "Inexpensive"	How does it compare to other products?
"Guaranteed purity, potency, and quality"	Does the product work?
"Clinically proven safe and effective"	What's the evidence?
Imagery to appeal to emotion	
"Quiet world is like taking a vacation from tension"	Will it help you escape from problems? The real world?
"Beautiful people, places, things"	Will the product help you achieve this?
"The Marlboro man"	Is smoking macho or stupid?
"Look younger instantly"	How quickly? Possible? Temporary?
"Created by research scientist (or specialist)"	Aren't most products? Qualifications?
"Miracle beauty secret, no surgery"	What is? Why secret? Does it work?
"Used extensively in Europe?"	Why not in United States. Not FDA approved?

(Chapter 10) has made more people vulnerable to advertising.

Consumer Reports has noted that some companies have found ways to plug health-related products by issuing press releases or canned video news reports.[5] The resultant press coverage may have greater impact and cost the manufacturer less than regular ads. Prescription drug manufacturers often use this way to call public attention to new products or preliminary scientific reports.

PUFFERY, WEASEL WORDS, AND HALF-TRUTHS

Puffery lies to you and it deceives you, but the law says it doesn't.

Ivan I. Preston[6]

In many ads the primary technique is puffery, which Preston defines as advertising that praises an item with opinions, superlatives, or exaggerations, vaguely or generally, but states no specific facts. In

The Great American Blow-Up, Preston provides this illustration:

> The book you are about to read is a superior piece of work. It demonstrates the sheerest true excellence in its treatment of one of the outstanding important topics of our time. You will find every moment informative and entertaining to a degree you have never before encountered in the world of fine literature. This much-applauded volume has earned for its author a rightful place as one of the top writers on the contemporary scene.

He then states:

> The paragraph you have just read is the purest baloney. . . . It is puffery. It is the pretentious opinion of salesmen and advertisers exaggerating their wares, magnifying value, quality and attractiveness to the limits of plausibility and beyond. It is false, and I know it is false. I do not believe it. If you had believed it, and had bought this book because you relied upon the belief, you would have gotten less than you had bargained for in the marketplace. You would have been cheated.

In the health marketplace, puffery is often used to promote nonprescription drugs. For example, Bayer aspirin has been said to "work *wonders,*" and Pepto-Bismol has been touted to have "the *famous* coating action." Pain-relievers, vitamins, and other products are identified as "advanced formulas." The most egregious puffs, however, appear on the jacket of books said to offer a *"revolutionary"* diet, *"amazing* health secrets," or the like.

Another selling trick is the use of "weasel words." These create the illusion of a promise but permit the advertiser to "weasel" out of the deal later. Here is an example from the catalog of a laboratory that supplies "glandular" products to chiropractors. These products are composed of dehydrated animal organs but contain no hormone or other pharmacologically active ingredient. They are mainly ordinary proteins made into pills or capsules. But according to the catalog:

> These glandular concentrates *reportedly* go directly to the aid of the gland of the same name . . . liver to liver, eye to eye, prostate to prostate, and so forth. *Theoretically,* the nutrients found in glands *may* contain essential factors and when taken as a supplement, will *help* the body's glands reach and maintain proper functioning levels.

The weasel words are italicized. Despite the illusion that the products are useful, the ad actually promises nothing. Another example would be a promised weight loss of "*up* to 20 pounds in 30 days."

Thomas Rosch,[7] former director of the FTC Bureau of Consumer Protection, has observed many instances in which words or statements used in advertising, although literally true, could be misunderstood by consumers to mean things that are not true. For example, a claim that one food product has more "food energy" than its competition may be literally true, because "food energy" is simply a synonym for calories and nothing more. Yet the consuming public may relate "food energy" to feeling energetic and interpret the claim to mean something that is untrue. Rosch also said that he had seen ad claims that have multiple meanings, one of which may be false or unsubstantiated. To some consumers a better product may mean better than competing products. To others it may mean better or superior as compared with past versions of the advertised product itself. If a product is claimed to be better, consumers should ask, "Better than what?"

About 10 years ago, a *Harvard Business Review* poll of 2700 executives found that two out of three executives believed that advertising failed to present a true picture of the product advertised. They were uneasy about the truthfulness and the social impact of ads.[8] A similar poll of business school deans rated honesty in advertising to be 13%.[9]

PERSONAL GLIMPSE

Would You Buy This Book?

Scientists confirm age-old wisdom: "Miracle Foods" are your best medicine; onions as a heart drug, broccoli to prevent cancer, chili peppers to fight colds. Let food be your medicine [Hippocrates]. Overwhelming evidence from over 300 scientists, 5000 research reports, scores of leading doctors, and dozens of respected universities. Exclusive offer of this book, *The Food Pharmacy,* from Prevention for $1.95. Obtainable by joining the Prevention Book Club.

CONSUMER TIP

Many advertisers believe they have license to lie in their commercials as long as nothing is said.

Advertising Outlets

The number of advertising outlets is enormous. There are tens of thousands of daily and weekly newspapers, magazines, and radio and television stations. Products also are marketed through direct mail and by word of mouth. Some sellers use less obvious marketing strategies in which free publicity is obtained through the use of public relations agencies and various types of public appearances that generate news reports. It has been estimated that the average American is exposed to 1500 advertising messages a day.

The cost of advertising depends mainly on the size of the audience it can reach. Ads can cost anywhere from a few dollars for a 30-second radio spot on a small station up to as much as $850,000 for a 30-second nationwide television ad aired during the Super Bowl. In 1990 between $20 and $50 millions each were spent on Anacin, Advil, Alka-Seltzer, Bayer aspirin, Benadryl, Crest toothpaste, Dexatrim, and Tylenol.

The extent of health-related advertising raises serious questions about its effect on people's health. What kind of society is being produced by the information transmitted? Is the selling of more health products and services a good thing for consumers? Does a belief in caveat emptor absolve the seller from encouraging behavior detrimental to health? Is it proper to profit by playing on people's hopes, fears, and anxieties? Concerned citizens believe there is need for more truth and honesty in advertising. Nevertheless, consumers should still protect themselves by invoking the caveat vendor (let the seller beware) principle and intelligently analyzing the ads they encounter.

Professional Advertising

Medical and dental societies traditionally have frowned on the use of advertising to solicit patients. Years ago, members who advertised might be expelled, and many state laws banned or severely restricted advertising by health professionals. In recent years, however, court decisions and pressure by the FTC have forced professional societies to abolish their ethical restraints on advertising.

The FTC is legally responsible for helping to foster competition in the marketplace and prevent price-fixing. In 1978 an FTC judge ruled that the American Medical Association (AMA) could no longer forbid member physicians from engaging in advertising or other competitive practices. In 1982 the U.S. Supreme Court upheld the FTC order permitting physicians and dentists to advertise without interference from their professional organizations. The Supreme Court decision forced the AMA and the American Dental Association to change their guidelines. The AMA Council on Ethical and Judicial Affairs now places no restrictions on advertising "except those that can be specifically justified to protect the public from deceptive practices. . . . The key issue is whether advertising or publicity, regardless of format or content, is true and not materially misleading." However, the Council has cautioned that statements relating to the quality of medical services may be a problem because they may be difficult or impossible to measure by objective standards.[10]

The FTC believed that advertising would lower prices due to greater competition in the marketplace and would provide consumers with additional information that would help them make appropriate decisions. Critics of this policy warned that (1) deceptive advertising would be more difficult to stop; (2) advertising would enable the least qualified practitioners to try to lure patients through salesmanship rather than demonstrations of competence; and (3) advertising would not lower fees because it would increase both the demand for services and the cost of delivering them. Figure 5-1 shows an ad that attempts to attract patients by offering a discount coupon for a dental examination.

In 1987, Folland[11] concluded that fewer than 10% of doctors planned to advertise, but the percentage would increase if competition increased. So far, those advertising the most have been plastic surgeons, ophthalmologists (radial keratotomy, lens implants), dermatologists (wrinkle relief, hair transplants), urologists (sexual dysfunction), obstetrics and gynecology specialists (free pregnancy tests) and orthopedists (sport injuries).

Margo[12] noted that advertisements for ophthalmology services are almost exclusively designed to promote surgery. He stated that ads may mislead the public about the risks and indications for surgery. In cataract surgery the risk of complications is small, but it is unfair and cruel to claim that it is quick, simple, and without risks, or that there may be no alternative to surgery. *Flamboyant* advertising is probably a sign of low-quality, mass-production service.

Yarborough[13] has expressed doubts about whether ads by individual physicians will better inform patients, reduce health-care costs, improve the quality of care, or reduce the incidence of malpractice litigation. He said that the primary reasons for advertising by most physicians are to persuade rather than inform, to increase their practice, and to make money. Their focus of health care therefore is placed on convenience, friendliness, and personal attention rather than quality of care. He urges physicians to resist advertising unless their objective is to benefit patients rather than boost their personal income and prestige. O'Brien[14] believes the most appropriate approach in advertising is one that informs the public of facilities and services offered.

Gray[15] has documented how advertising can draw very large responses. For example, a Southern California ophthalmologist advertised radial keratotomy and had 900 phone calls in 3 days. A Virginia plastic surgeon who spent $20,000 monthly attracted enough patients to perform 40 cosmetic operations per week. On the other hand, ads placed by a West Coast radiologist antagonized colleagues on whom he depended for referrals, and consequently his business suffered. And a large clinic that spent $280,000 advertising its services attracted many new patients, but it lost most of them because the patients did not want to wait 1½ hours for service.

The amount of professional advertising in telephone directories has increased sharply during the past few years. The 1990-1991 volume of the San Francisco *Yellow Pages* contained 56 pages for physicians, 32 for dentists, 12 for chiropractors, 8 for podiatrists, 5 for psychologists, 2½ for physical therapists, and 2 for acupuncturists. Some of the ads occupy a full page.

In 1983, a review of the Hartford, Connecticut telephone directory found that 12% of 946 physicians were not board-certified in the specialty under which they were listed.[16] However, it should be noted that some physicians who are qualified to practice as specialists may not have completed the requirements for board-certification.

Telephone companies have shown little or no interest in preventing unqualified individuals from misrepresenting their credentials. In Allentown, Pennsylvania, for example, an anesthesiologist with an interest in hypnosis for pain relief was permitted to advertise himself as a psychiatrist despite protests made to both the telephone company and the state medical board. To counter this type of problem, the American Board of Medical Specialties[17] has been placing lists of board-certified physicians in many of the *Yellow Pages*. However, most board-certified physicians are not participating in the program because they do not wish to pay the required fee (over $200 per year).

Ads by professional societies tend to be useful and informative (Figure 5-2). Figure 5-3 shows an informative ad by an individual dentist.

Figure 5-4 shows portions of an ad for a medical discount plan. Analysis by consumers should include the following:

1. Despite the emphasis on individualized services

FIGURE 5-2. Dental Association ad promoting dental care.

The 10,000 Bite Check Up

Preventive maintenance for your Teeth and Gums is essential to a total health program. So every 10,000 bites or every 6 months, which ever comes sooner, be sure to have a dental check up.

Robert Smith, DDS
1000 Duncan Rd.
Mapleville, NJ 07000
555-1234

Traditional Dentistry In A Relaxed Country Setting

FIGURE 5-3. Attracts attention because of allusions to auto maintenance.

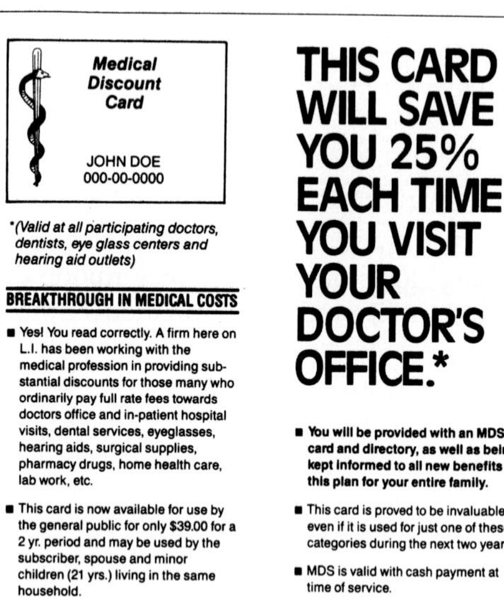

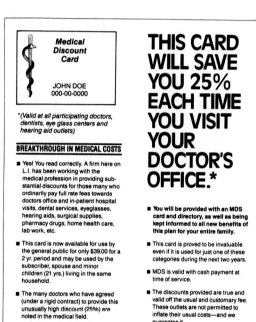

FIGURE 5-4. Ad for medical discount plan.

to be provided, how many types of doctors were involved? Of the 39 identified in the representative sampling, (names not printed here) not all were physicians: 22 were D.D.S.s or D.M.D.s (dentists), 11 were M.D.s (medical doctors), 3 were D.C.s (chiropractors), and 3 were D.P.M.s (podiatrists).

2. How is the guaranteed claim of discount provided? What recourse is there when a discount is not provided? What are the procedures to be followed?
3. Will hundreds of dollars per year be saved with an enrollment cost of $39? (Is this puffery? Is it truthful?) How many visits per year does an individual make to these various doctors?
4. Is cost savings more important than the quality of service provided?
5. Is it ethical and appropriate for doctors to offer discounts?
6. Is it realistic to believe that large numbers of competent health professionals would be willing to offer large discounts in this manner?

Marketing by Hospitals

Rising overhead costs and decreased occupancy rates have placed many hospitals in a precarious financial position. In many communities, hospitals are engaged in extensive marketing plans intended to ensure that they fill their beds. These may include ads for emergency services, outpatient clinics, programs for alcoholism, drug addiction, and chronic pain, fitness and smoking cessation programs, medical referral services, community lecture programs, and other items designed to boost community awareness of the hospital and its facilities. Hospitals have also offered new services such as Saturday surgery (for convenience), gourmet food, newsletters to former patients, and free transportation. A few have used such gimmicks as a "$10-off" coupon for emergency room services. Many hospitals spend hundreds of thousands of dollars to market themselves. Figure 5-5 shows a straightforward ad for people with anxiety-related symptoms.

Prescription Drug Advertising

Prescription drug advertising traditionally has been directed toward physicians, dentists, and other health care personnel in professional and technical magazines. The FDA regulates this advertising and requires that the ads carry considerable information about effectiveness, side effects, adverse reactions, precautions, and contraindications. Pharmaceutical companies now spend $2 billion a year promoting prescription drugs to physicians. This includes not

ANXIETY . . . in the ELDERLY

Doctors at the Medical College of Pennsylvania are offering free screening evaluations for people 60 or older, who experience the following symptoms:

- **Anxiety**
- **Worries**
- **Irritability**
- **Insomnia**
- **Shakiness**
- **Upset Stomach**
- **Difficulty Concentrating**
- **Fatigue**
- **Lump in the Throat**
- **Sweating**

These evaluations will be offered as part of a new program designed to find out more about how anxiety affects your daily lives, and to offer opportunities for relief.

Call Natalie Carter, RN, at 555-5683 for more information.

Hospital

The Medical College of Pennsylvania

3300 Henry Avenue, Philadelphia, Pennsylvania 19129

FIGURE 5-5. Straightforward ad for a hospital program that includes a free evaluation for anxiety-related symptoms.

only advertising but free samples, company-sponsored educational activities, and other perks.

For many years the FDA was reluctant to permit the advertising of prescription drugs because the information needed to make an intelligent decision about them generally is too complex to place in a brief advertisement. In 1983, a few manufacturers began advertising prescription drugs to consumers on television and in magazines. Shortly afterward, the FDA proposed a moratorium on direct-to-consumer ads in order to gather information before preparing regulations. This proposal was honored by the pharmaceutical industry. The FDA withdrew its voluntary moratorium in 1985 after it concluded that its regulations provided sufficient safeguards to protect the consumers.

Since that time manufacturers have spent millions of dollars advertising prescription products in magazines and newspapers, and on television. Some ads mention a product by name, while others encourage people with certain health problems to seek further medical advice. Most drugs in the latter category are either the only drug, or are the market leader in a category of drugs, that can be of help. The products have included: Seldane, an antihistamine that does not cause drowsiness, Rogaine (minoxidil), an antibaldness drug that is somewhat effective for some people, and Nicorette, a gum that can help people stop smoking. Figures 5-6 and 5-7 provide helpful, informative messages.

The FDA requires ads for drugs to include "adequate directions for use." For prescription drugs, this includes full product information of the type found in package inserts and the *Physicians Desk Reference*. Advertising messages to the public are unable to include this much information and some of it is too technical for laypersons to understand. The FDA is permitting manufacturers to provide limited information provided the ads make no claims of effectiveness for specific products.[18]

Although prescription drug ads call attention to useful products, their primary purpose is to sell products. Some observers believe that direct advertising educates patients, alerts consumers to new treatments, encourages people to seek medical advice for conditions that would otherwise go untreated, and generally results in a more informed public.[19] Others argue that advertising of prescription drugs interferes with the physician-patient relationship, confuses patients, increases the cost of drugs, puts undue emphasis on drug treatment alternatives, pressures doctors to prescribe products, and results in unnecessary use.[20]

Consumer Reports Health Letter[21] has noted that consumer drug ads can call attention to symptoms that require medical attention, can publicize a vaccine, and can alert consumers to products that are safer, cheaper or more convenient than those a person is using. But it warns:

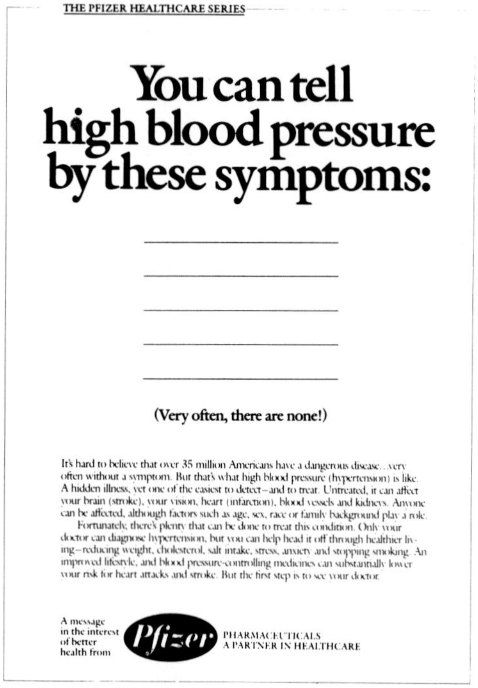

THE PFIZER HEALTHCARE SERIES

You can tell high blood pressure by these symptoms:

(Very often, there are none!)

It's hard to believe that over 35 million Americans have a dangerous disease...very often without a symptom. But that's what high blood pressure (hypertension) is like. A hidden illness, yet one of the easiest to detect—and to treat. Untreated, it can affect your brain (stroke), your vision, heart (infarction), blood vessels and kidneys. Anyone can be affected, although factors such as age, sex, race or family background play a role.

Fortunately, there's plenty that can be done to treat this condition. Only your doctor can diagnose hypertension, but you can help head it off through healthier living—reducing weight, cholesterol, salt intake, stress, anxiety and stopping smoking. An improved lifestyle, and blood pressure-controlling medicines can substantially lower your risk for heart attacks and stroke. But the first step is to see your doctor.

A message in the interest of better health from Pfizer PHARMACEUTICALS A PARTNER IN HEALTHCARE

FIGURE 5-6. Informative ad advising people that it is possible to have high blood pressure without knowing about it. The ad mentions no product, but the manufacturer knows that some people who are discovered to have "silent" hypertension will be appropriately treated with one of its products.

> Drug pitches are not public service messages—they're commercial advertisements . . . designed with the drug manufacturer's health in mind. Even when the ad seems to be merely alerting you to symptoms that may require drug treatment, the message is usually overstated. . . . You should regard consumer drug ads with the same type of skepticism as you would any other type of salesmanship.

It notes, for example, that Rogaine has tried to hook worried men by asking whether "an emerging bald spot" can "damage your ability to get along with others" or "influence your chances of obtaining a job or a date." And a similar pitch for Estraderm, a female hormone, called attention to what it called "myth number one: No man in his right mind would be interested in a menopausal woman." The Rogaine ad fails to mention that only a small percentage of men can benefit from the product and that it is extremely expensive. The Estraderm ad fails to consider risks and side effects or whether a drug actually is needed to counteract menopausal symptoms.

Nonprescription Drug Advertising

In 1972, the FDA began a lengthy review process that has led to the removal of many ineffective ingredients from nonprescription drugs (see Chapter 20). At the same time, regulatory actions by the FTC have persuaded many major manufacturers to stop making blatantly misleading claims. As a result, most nonprescription drugs sold today contain at least one effective ingredient, and ads for such products tend to be more truthful than they used to be. However, at least three problems remain:

1. Ads often fail to disclose the ingredients of the product. This makes it more difficult for consumers to choose the most suitable product or compare one product to another. Products promoted for the relief of colds, for example, may contain combinations of ingredients that may not be better than products that contain fewer ingredients or a single ingredient.
2. Many ads use imagery, puffery, or testimonials to suggest that a product is more effective than it actually is. Pain-relievers, for example, may be described as "advanced," "new," and "extra-strength" even though they are identical or substantially similar to competing products.
3. Commercial television viewers, bombarded with ads, may incorrectly conclude that many of life's problems can be solved by drugs. Ads for "Excedrin headaches" are a classic example in which the viewer is encouraged to use medication to relieve tension headaches with no mention that it would be prudent to try to resolve the underlying problem.

Consumer Tip

Prescription Drug Ads

- Remember that the primary purpose of the ad is to sell the product.
- Do not assume that the ad gives you the full story.
- Seek additional information from the company (a toll-free number may be given), a reliable drug reference book (see Chapter 20), and your physician.

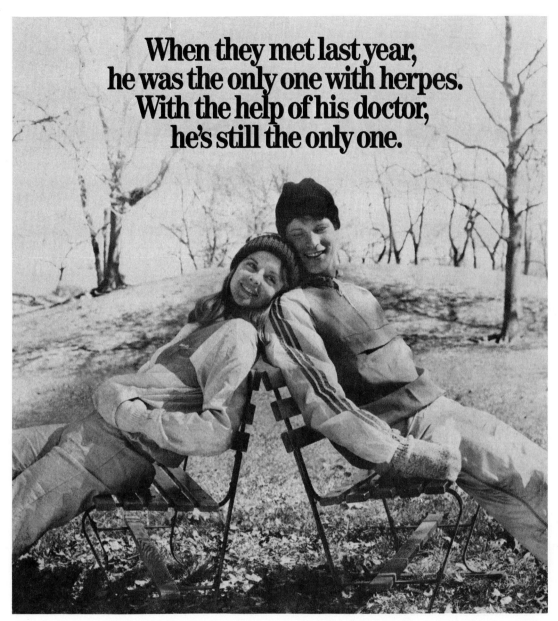

When they met last year, he was the only one with herpes. With the help of his doctor, he's still the only one.

Whether you have a mild, intermediate or severe case of genital herpes, you should see your doctor to help gain new control over your outbreaks—especially if you haven't seen your doctor within the past year.

The medical profession now has more information than ever before about the treatment of herpes, as well as effective counselling and treatment programs that can help you reduce the frequency, duration and severity of your outbreaks.

If in the past you were told that nothing could be done for herpes, it's no longer true. Herpes *is* controllable.

Ask your doctor about these treatment programs, and whether one of them would be suitable for you.

See your doctor...there is help for herpes

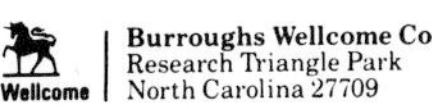

Burroughs Wellcome Co.
Research Triangle Park
North Carolina 27709

© 1986 BURROUGHS WELLCOME RH-86-BW-6

FIGURE 5-7. A useful message from the manufacturer of the prescription drug that can help control the symptoms of genital herpes and reduce its transmission.

Consumer Tip

Rational Choice of Over-the-Counter (OTC) Drugs

- Ignore advertising hype. Be wary of ads that claim "special," "secret," or "foreign" formula, use testimonials from satisfied customers, or promote a "miracle" or "wonder" cure that medicine has not yet discovered.
- Become informed with the help of a reference book plus guidance as needed from a physician.
- Select products according to their ingredients rather than advertising claims.
- Buy mostly single-ingredient products rather than combination products.

Many regulatory actions have targeted misleading ads for pain-relievers. In 1983, the FTC made it clear that manufacturers would be penalized if they continued to make unsubstantiated claims that their products were safer or more effective than similar products. The Commission ruling settled parallel actions against the manufacturers or advertisers of Bayer Aspirin, Vanquish, Cope, Midol, Bufferin, and Excedrin. The FTC ruled that it was deceptive to claim that any of these products contained special or unusual ingredients when they actually contained ingredients commonly used in other drugs. The Commission also found no basis for claims that Bayer aspirin had greater purity, stability, freshness, and disintegration speed than similar products.[22]

Food Advertising

Critics of food advertising have noted three main types of problems: (1) advertising tends to promote dietary imbalance; (2) many foods have been advertised with deceptive health claims; and (3) many labeling terms have not been standardized.

A study of messages related to food and eating behavior found that between 8:00 pm and 11:00 pm, food references occurred 4.8 times per 30 minutes of programming time.[23] About 60% were for low-nutrient beverages and sweets. Foods were also typically consumed as snacks. The most frequently expressed messages were claims of good taste and of food being "fresh and natural." Ads for fast-food restaurants, which were more frequent than those of any other category, did not mention salad bars. Of 261 commercials aired, only 3 mentioned fruit and none mentioned vegetables, although fruits and vegetables were pictured in 36% of the ads. The authors concluded that the "prime-time diet" is inconsistent with the U.S. dietary guidelines (see Chapter 12).

The American Academy of Pediatrics wants to stop television food advertising aimed at children. In an updated policy statement, the Academy charged that the primary goal of children's television is to sell products to children. According to the Academy, young children cannot distinguish between programs and commercials and do not understand that commercials are designed to sell products. The policy statement also noted: "Television shows promote toys. The same toys are used to promote cereals and other foods. Commercials for the cereals, named after the toys, indirectly promote the toy and the toy-based program as well as the cereal and other related products."

The recent public focus on the relationships between diet and various diseases, particularly heart disease and cancer, has spawned an enormous number of related advertising claims. In the mid-1980s, many food manufacturers began suggesting that their products might protect, or help protect, against certain diseases. Many of these claims were misleading because they stressed individual foods rather than overall diet. In addition, ads for certain foods stressed a potentially helpful quality (such as being low in cholesterol), when another quality (such as high fat content) would negate any benefit.

In 1990, the FDA[24] sent letters to six companies warning them to remove unsubstantiated health claims from foods that contained oats, oat bran, and fiber. One of the products, Oat Chex, a cereal made by the Ralston Purina Company, had been advertised that it "may help reduce cholesterol levels." The FDA stated the label suggesting that a serving provides "a nutritionally significant amount of fiber" is misleading because the product does not contain enough fiber to justify such a claim. In 1991, the agency proposed lengthy regulations intended to stop misleading health claims for foods (see Chapter 12). The proposals include definitions of "light," "low-fat," "high-fiber," and other previously unregulated terms.

Dietary Supplements

There is a great deal of false advertising for vitamins, minerals, and other types of food supplements.

Many companies falsely suggest that supplements be taken because it is difficult or impossible to meet nutrient needs with ordinary foods or in times of stress. Many products are marketed with false and illegal claims that they can prevent or treat various diseases.

Supplements also are promoted through books, radio and television broadcasts, oral claims from person to person, and many other channels. Claims through these channels are protected by the doctrines of free speech and freedom of the press as long as they are not directly tied to the sale of specific products. These problems are described in Chapter 13.

Weight-Related Claims

The $30-billion weight-control marketplace is rife with misleading ads for mail-order "diet" products, weight-loss clinics, spot-reducers, cellulite-removers, and other similar products. The FDA has stated that there is no scientific or clinical evidence to support the use of body wraps or sauna suits for controlling weight. Nor are there any data to back up promoters' claims that these products eliminate cellulite and bulging fat, make spot-reductions possible, improve calorie burn rate, or control appetite.[2]

A Pebble Beach, California company that sold items to increase the size of breasts (Mark Eden) and decrease midriffs (Astro-Trimmer and Slim-Skins) was indicted by a federal grand jury in San Jose, California, in May 1982 on charges of mail fraud in advertising their products. The ads included such statements as "Fifteen and a half inches slimmer in just 25 minutes with Slim-Skins," and "I watched it happen right in my own mirror—3 inches the first day, over 4 inches in 5 days." The ad for bust developing featured a smiling, well-endowed girl making the latter statement. The company settled out of court by paying a fine in excess of $1 million to the government and agreeing not to produce or market such items.[25]

Weight-loss clinics have come under heavy fire during the past few years. This topic is covered in Chapter 14.

Personal Glimpse

Would You Buy this Newsletter?

You have just received in the mail a 20-page booklet promoting a new newsletter.[26] The booklet's cover pictures the editor, a medical doctor, who is making the following claims:

"Give Me 90 Days And I'll Help You . . .

- Avoid headaches, sleep problems, depression and other everyday maladies . . .
- Unclog heart arteries that cause high blood pressure, stroke and heart attack . . .
- Tap your body's natural reserves to beat fatigue and have the energy to do the things you love . . .
- Avoid—and even reverse—the symptoms of arthritis and most forms of diabetes . . .
- Disease-proof your body and add many good years to your life! *Life-enriching program boosts your body's amazing power to heal itself!"*

The booklet describes the doctor as "America's leading advocate of a safer, gentler approach to better health." It also identifies him as "a leading member of the American College of Advancement in Medicine" and states that his clinic in California "helps thousands to find a healthier, non-toxic approach to life, and to reverse heart disease, arthritis, diabetes, and many other illnesses."

Do these claims seem credible? How can you investigate them?

Mail-Order Advertising

Many people believe that advertising claims for health products must be true or somehow they would not be "allowed." Many assume that media outlets screen such ads carefully, and some even think that the Postal Service licenses mail-order advertisers. Each of these beliefs is erroneous. Several large studies have shown that the vast majority of advertisements for mail-order health products are misleading.

In 1977, the Pennsylvania Medical Society Committee on Quackery conducted a study of magazine advertisements for health products sold by mail. One fourth of 500 nationally circulated magazines screened one summer were found to contain health advertisements. Not one product sold by mail appeared to be capable of living up to its advertised claims. The Committee advised extreme skepticism about buying health products by mail from such magazine ads.

In 1985 the FDA conducted a 1-month survey of advertisements for health products in American newspapers and magazines. The survey found 435 questionable ads, 249 of them for weight-loss products (mostly diet pills). Gross deceptions appeared in ads for waist wraps, vibrating belts, and sauna suits advertised to help lose weight. There were 89 ads for hair restoration schemes, 42 for products and 47 for "clinics." Wrinkle removers were also common. Other ads found in the survey included products for hemorrhoids, varicose veins, and indigestion; "rear end" kits for shaping; pills for the "ultimate orgasm;" and cheap, quick ways to treat arthritis, heart disease, alcoholism, depression, and high blood pressure.[2]

In 1991 the American Council on Science and Health (ACSH)[27] published the results of a study of magazines, tabloid newspapers, direct-mail catalogs, television infomercials, multilevel companies, and other channels through which health-related mail-order products are marketed. Table 5-2 identifies products typically sold through these channels. Figure 5-8 illustrates ads from the FDA and ACSH surveys.

The study included a survey of one issue each of 463 magazines in national circulation during the summer of 1990. Dubious ads appeared in 56 out of 423 (13%) general audience magazines and 23 out of 40 (58%) health and fitness magazines. In the general magazines, about 50 companies advertised about 70 dubious products. In health-food publications, 15 companies advertised 24 dubious products. In fitness and bodybuilding magazines, 26 companies advertised more than 60 products. All but one product (a sweat-reducing device) were misrepresented. Tabloid newspapers (*Globe, National Examiner, Sun, National Enquirer,* and *Weekly World News*), which were surveyed for several months, contained several misleading ads per issue.

ACSH's report advises that no mail-order product can (1) cause effortless weight loss; (2) erase scars, wrinkles, or "cellulite;" (3) selectively reduce one part of the body; (4) increase bust or penis size; (5) prevent or cure hair loss; increase stamina, endurance, strength, or muscle mass; "prevent aging;" (6) prolong life, prevent senility; (7) increase memory; or (8) increase sexual stimulation or pleasure.

Table 5–2

The Mail-Order Health Marketplace

Communication channel	Typical products
Magazines, astrology	Psychic help with health problems
Magazines, fitness/bodybuilding	"Ergogenic aids"
Magazines, general audience	Youth and beauty aids
Magazines, health	Nonprescription drugs sold through drugstores and supermarkets
Magazines, health food	Supplement products sold through health food stores. Misleading claims tend to be made through articles rather than ads
Magazines, pornographic	Sex aids
Newspapers, general	Weight-reduction schemes
Newspapers, tabloid	Weight-reduction schemes, psychic healing
Classified ads	Mostly information and product catalogs rather than specific products
Direct mail	Weight reduction schemes, anti-aging products, sex aids
Post-It ads	Weight reduction schemes, anti-aging products, pinhole eyeglasses
Prizes (mail or phone)	Vitamins, water purifiers
Catalogs from mail-order supplement distributors	A multitude of "dietary supplement" products with misleading therapeutic claims
Multilevel companies	A multitude of supplement products with illegal claims made through brochures, videotapes, and word-of-mouth
Infomercials	Weight-loss schemes, beauty aids, hair-loss remedies

Source: Barrett S: 1991.[27]

Advertisement

Diet Pill Sweeping U.S.

New Grapefruit 'Super Pill' Gives Fast Weight Loss

No Dieting - Eat All You Want Pill Does All the Work

BEVERLY HILLS, CA. (Special) An amazing new "super" grapefruit pill has recently been developed and perfected that reportedly "guarantees" that you will easily lose at least 10 pounds in 10 days. Best of all, it allows you to "eat as much as you want of your favorite foods and still lose a pound a day or more starting from the very first day until you achieve the ideal weight and figure you desire."

This "super" grapefruit pill is a dramatically improved version of the world famous grapefruit diet. It is far more effective than the original and eliminates "the mess, fuss, and high cost of eating half a fresh grapefruit at every meal."

"Pill Does All the Work"

According to the manufacturer, "the pill itself does all the work while you quickly lose weight with NO starvation "diet menus" to follow, NO calorie counting, NO exercise, and NO hunger pangs." It is 100% safe. You simply take the pill with a glass of water before each meal and the amazing combination of powerful ingredients are so effective they take over and you start losing weight immediately.

Pill Has ALL Daily Vitamins

The powerful and unique combination of ingredients are what make this a "super-pill". It contains highly potent grapefruit concentrate and a diuretic to help eliminate bloat and puffiness. No need to take any vitamins to maintain your good health and energy. The pill is fortified with ALL (100%) of the U.S. Government daily vitamin requirements.

Contains Japanese 'Glucomannan'

Each pill also contains an amazingly effective amount of "glucomannan", the remarkable natural dietary fiber discovery from Japan (used successfully for over 1500 years) that expands in your stomach and gives you a full and satisfied feel-

For Bosom Beauty

Try the one tested, trusted body creme that contains a full 40,000* units of ESTROGENIC HORMONES

If you believe that your body is the true key to feminine allure—then the one name you should remember from now on is LA VIVE . . . because LA VIVE Body Creme has helped thousands for more than 20 years! This superior formula features 20,000 units of natural estrons and estrogenic hormones per jar plus additional beneficial oils, especially designed to moisturize and lubricate . . . yet will not alter structure. No wonder so many grateful women have expressed their thanks in letters of praise! Stop envying others! Instead, try the 60-day supply of LA VIVE Hormone Creme. It's guaranteed — you must be absolutely thrilled with results or return for money back! 60-Day Supply (mailed in plain wrapper) only $6.98. *SPECIAL: Double ... postpaid. No COD.

Dandruff? Thinning? Balding?

Hair Growth is Possible according to reports on scientific experiments.

Professional, health and medical publications have reported on successful results with **several** substances that have not only **stopped hair loss** and dandruff but have actually **regrown hair.**

A recently reported test of 600 men, one hundred of whom were practicing doctors, revealed the following fantastic results: 85 to 90% of the patients diagnosed as suffering from hereditary baldness **stopped further balding within 6 to 8 weeks** after using an applied solution.

Further reports state that up to about 75% of certain test subjects **grew new hair.**

New hair was described as hair naturally colored, of **substantial density**, and at least **three quarters of an inch long.**

Healthy Hair Growth Requires More Than One Solution

Other researchers of hair loss and balding have reported on several substances that are vital for the growth of healthy hair. Among these substances are

BEFORE

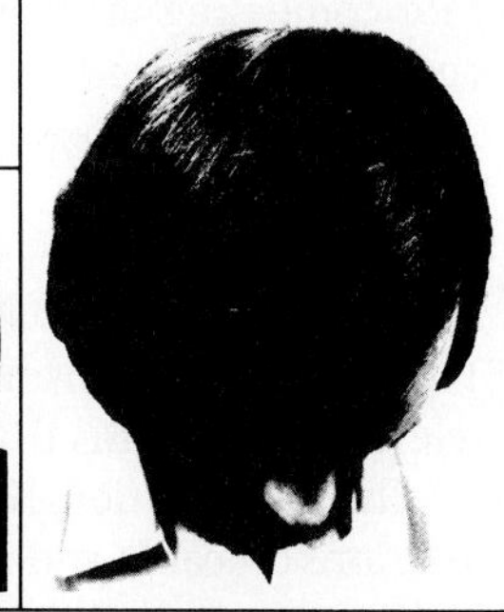

AFTER

PROGRAM YOUR MIND FOR SUCCESS

AS LOW AS $2.95 EACH

with the Finest Subliminal Tapes at the Lowest Prices Ever!

NEW BREAKTHROUGH IN MIND POWER! REMARKABLE RESULTS!

The exciting breakthrough of subliminal programming has been featured in such respected publications as the *Wall Street Journal Psychology Today*, and the *New York Times*. In fact, subliminal techniques are currently being used by leading hospitals and professional therapists worldwide.

But now the subliminal process has been propelled to unparalleled heights with amazing new **Subliminal Success™** cassettes. Known within the industry as the *"Rolls Royce" of mind reconditioning*, these **ultra-powerful, high-quality subliminal tapes** combine years of scientific research with state-of-the-art technology to stimulate fast, permanent, and

Studies have shown that this synchronization can speed up the learning process two to five times while dramatically increasing the receptivity of your subconscious mind.

Subliminal Success™ cassettes utilize this special music as the soothing background for the potent subliminal message directed to specific areas of yo your conscious mind relaxes designed sounds, your subcon ed like a powerful laser beam manifest all the positive change deserve in your life.

3. The 100,000 Repetition Fa

At the beginning of each exc Success™ cassette your subco instructed to accept each liste same impact as if you had lister *times.* Once your subconscio statement to be true, it in fact be *unique programming makes th working & most effective sublim*

SUPER LOW PRI WHY PAY MOR

As a special introductory off any 20 Subliminal Success™ That's a savings

NOTE: Due To High Demand, We Must Limit All Orders To Twenty Tapes Per Customer.

YES! I want to program my mind for success. Please rush me the titles I've checked below: (Indicate Quantity)

☐ ASC01. **PERMANENT WEIGHT LOSS**

☐ ASC02. **STOP SMOKING FOREVER**

Lose 4-6 inches of bulging fat BEFORE we cash your check!

Let Us Take The Risk!

Use the Shrink Wrap System to reduce a combination of your waist and hips, *FAST!* Just fill out the coupon below and postdate your check for 30 days from today! You'll pay nothing now (not for 30 days), but we *will* send your Shrink Wrap System NOW! Try it. Use it. Watch inches disappear. If for any reason you are not delighted, send it back. We will return your check or money order, UNCASHED! Even if you send it back later, we'll still refund your purchase price. Over 186,000 satisfied customers make us bold enough to make this super guarantee!

That's right! 4–6 inches starting the very first day! Science has known about this principle for years. In fact, right now, professional and amateur athletes the world over are using it in their training programs. And many famous entertainers who have to trim down fast rely on this method. Now, *you* can melt away inches from your waist, your hips—anywhere!

Don't Hold Fat In . . . Lose It!

Plastics and elastics are merely flimsy imitations. Girdles just squeeze it in. But the Shrink Wrap System takes it off . . . *fast!* The belt is adjustable, so you can put isometrics to work toning loose muscle tissue whenever you want. And, our easy exercise program helps you shed unsightly inches even more rapidly.

If you want to go even further, your waistline, hips, and other problem areas will continue to shrink when you use the Shrink Wrap System lo-cal eating plans that won't leave you hungry. You can use it as often as you need it to keep those inches off. It's working right now for thousands of satisfied buyers and it can be working for *you*, if you order now!

Here are the impressive stories (all sworn and notarized) of a few outstanding users. Everyone may not do as well, but if they can do this well, just think how many pounds and inches you will lose quickly with the Shrink Wrap System!

before after

"I lost 6 inches in 16 days!"
Doug Fink of Asheville, North Carolina

"I've lost 5" from my waist and 6" from my hips over a 12 day period. My weight loss was 18 lbs."
Dr. J. Lee Briers of New Castle, Delaware

"I lost 5 inches off my waist & 5 inches off my hips! I am amazed at the way the Shrink Wrap System works. I'll recommend it to everyone!" Helena Smith of Vandalia, Michigan

"I lost 9 pounds & 4 inches off my waist in 2 weeks! It's just unbelievable that it took so little time and effort to produce such amazing results!"
Robert N. Nilsen of Mechanicsburg, Pennsylvania

© 1982 The New Body Boutique, Inc.

FREE HOLONOMIC STEREO HEADPHONES

THE EASY WAY TO LOSE WEIGHT AND KEEP IT OFF

OR YOUR MONEY BACK!

Lose all the weight you want through this easy and incredible system.

Weight Loss Experts create powerful program that combines Oriental secrets and recent scientific breakthroughs!

SEXUAL VIGOR

Vigor-X is a new all natural supplement made from the SWISS OAT *(avena sativa)*, which has been scientifically proven to STIMULATE MALE AND FEMALE SEX hormones for MAXIMUM performance.

VIGOR-X

★ INCREASES VIRILITY & VIGOR ★ INCREASES SEXUAL FUNCTIONS
★ INCREASES STAMINA & ENERGY ★ SEEN ON POPULAR TALK SHOWS
★ INCREASES SEXUAL AROUSAL & SENSITIVITY

FREE GIFT WITH ORDER

GUARANTEED TO WORK

30-DAY MONEY BACK GUARANTEE

To order a 1-month supply (60 capsules) send $19.95 + $3.00 shipping and handling to: FUTURE SCIENCE LABS, INC., 3230 E. Flamingo Rd., Ste. 322, Las Vegas, NV 89121, Dept. S09-10. **SAVE!!** And buy a 60-day supply for $32.00 + $4.00 shipping and handling.

Name______ Address______

City______ State______ Zip______

34 — SUN — January 15, 1991

TRIM-AWAY 4000

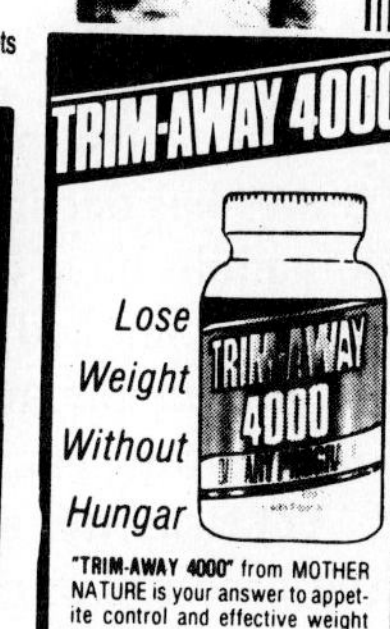

Lose Weight Without Hungar

"TRIM-AWAY 4000" from MOTHER NATURE is your answer to appetite control and effective weight loss. How? Glucamannan and our exclusive Fiber Blend are the most effective appetite suppressants available without side effects or prescription. These natural fibers expand in the stomach to make you feel full. This automatically makes you eat less. Also, they burn fat and eliminate excess water weight.

$17.95

plus $2.90 shipping & handling

Send check or money order to:

MOTHER NATURES
781 University Ave.
St. Paul, MN 55104

Or for faster service call:

1-800-458-1613

C.O.D. or VISA

FIGURE 5-8. Ads for mail-order health products.

The U.S. Postal Service has the primary responsibility for combating mail-order fraud. Chapter 27 describes how the agency works and some of its recent enforcement actions.

Infomercials

The FTC has warned consumers to be aware that some television programs that look like talk shows are actually program-length commercials. Many such programs on cable and independent television stations have promoted bogus weight-loss plans, hair-growth products, skin-rejuvenation products, body contouring programs, cosmetics, exercise aids, and other health-related products that supposedly provide great results with little effort or risk. Some of these programs used a movie star, athlete, or other celebrity as a host or guest, plus one or more "experts" who are referred to as "doctor." Testimonials from satisfied users also are a common feature.

One way to recognize an infomercial, says the FTC, is that the product promoted during "commercial breaks" is related to the program's content. Since 1988 the agency has filed complaints against at least seven companies marketing health-related products through infomercials.[28] The consent agreements ban false claims for the products and also require that future program-length ads be clearly identified as ads throughout the program.

Tobacco Products

Although the consumption of cigarettes in the United States has declined in the last 20 years and 38 million adults have quit smoking (nearly half of those who ever smoked), over 430,000 deaths each year are attributable to smoking and additional deaths occur from causes related to secondhand smoke.[29] Yet cigarettes are the second most heavily advertised products in newspapers and magazines, following automobiles.

Advertising has been banned on television and radio, and warnings are required on the labels of cigarettes and smokeless tobacco products. These products are extensively promoted through sporting and cultural events, and sales have greatly increased in foreign countries. In 1988 promotional expenditures in the United States reached an all-time high at $3.27 billion.[30]

Tobacco advertisements associate smoking with affluence, glamour, visceral satisfaction, escape from worry, romance, popularity, winning friends, gaining independence, relaxation, fitness, and getting ahead. Former U.S. Surgeon General C. Everett Koop,[31] has identified several tobacco ads that send contrary and dangerous signals about the use of tobacco to readers. He said one that uses the slogan, "Alive With Pleasure" perhaps should be changed to "Dying in Agony" in view of the deaths and other problems created by smoking cigarettes. A recent study of 20 leading magazines by the American Council on Science and Health found that those carrying the most cigarette ads tended to publish the least about smoking's dangers.[32]

In 1985, R.J. Reynolds used the denial-of-death theme in an editorial-type ad suggesting that a major federal study had cast doubt that cigarette smoking was a factor in causing heart disease. The FTC charged that the ad was deceptive because it misrepresented the study and omitted important findings. The company signed a consent agreement barring it from misrepresenting scientific studies in the future.[33]

Although tobacco companies claim that present cigarette promotions are not aimed at groups of people who are most at risk, ads do appear to be focused on youth, minorities, women, and the poor.[34] Camel cigarettes are being promoted to young people by a cartoon figure of a cigarette-smoking camel smoking who is described as a "smooth character." One of its ads includes offering a cigarette to break the ice on its list of "smooth moves" when dating a woman. The Public Citizen Health Research Group has charged that the ad also promotes male violence against women.[35] A recent study of logo recognition found that 30% of 3-year-old children and 91% of 6-year-old children were able to match Camel's cartoon figure with a picture of a cigarette and that the 6-year-olds were as familiar with "Old Joe" as they were with Mickey Mouse.[36]

Joe B. Tye, president of STAT (Stop Teenage Addiction to Tobacco), has identified 43 movies involved in covert advertising that encourages cigarette smoking. For example, in *Beverly Hills Cop II*, Eddie Murphy holds up a pack of Luckies and says, "These are very popular cigarettes with the children." *Superman II* has scenes that call attention to Marlboro cigarettes more than two dozen times.[37]

Cigarette companies are encouraging their customers to speak out for "smokers' rights."[38] R.J. Reynolds has published a *Smokers' Rights Action Guide*, which advises how to overcome what the company portrays as "discrimination" against smokers. Philip Morris has launched an "accommodation" program to "revive public smoking," mainly in restaurants.

The American Medical Association has called for a total ban on cigarette advertising. In 1991 the *Journal of the American Medical Association* listed more than 150 magazines that carry no ads for tobacco products.[39] They include: *American Health, Consumer Reports, Golf Illustrated, Good Housekeeping, Harvard Business Review, Health, Modern Maturity, Reader's Digest, Saturday Evening Post,* and *Seventeen.*

Youth and Beauty Aids

Many products and services are falsely advertised with claims that they can make people appear more youthful and attractive. In 1989 the FTC[40] charged Revlon and Charles Revson, Inc. with making unsubstantiated claims about the effectiveness of its Ultima II ProCollagen Anti-cellulite body complex. Revlon claimed the product significantly reduced cellulite and reduced the skin's bumpy texture, ripples, or slackness. The complaint said the claims were false and misleading because the company did not have reliable scientific evidence to support its claims. Additional information about bogus youth and beauty aids is provided in Chapter 21.

Adult Diapers

Two of the nation's biggest manufacturers of adult diapers, Procter & Gamble and Kimberly-Clark Corporation, agreed to alter their advertising in New York State that implied use of their products were the only way to cope with incontinence. There is evidence that pelvic exercise, biofeedback technique, surgery, and medication will help or cure 90% of people with such a problem.[41]

Exercise and Fitness

Regulatory agencies have paid much less attention to exercise and fitness products than they have to foods and drugs. The agencies appear to believe that misleading claims for these products generally have less potential to cause harm.

"Ergogenic aids" that are concoctions of vitamins, minerals, and amino acids have been promoted through fitness and bodybuilding magazines. In 1985, the market leader, Weider Health and Fitness, agreed not to falsely claim that two of its products could help build muscles or were effective substitutes for anabolic steroids (see Chapter 27). Weider still markets these and similar products with testimonial ads featuring bodybuilding champions and other athletes. Many other companies use similar ads, and some advertise with blatantly false claims.

The FTC also has acted against misleading representations by health and fitness facilities. In 1989 the agency stopped two individuals from falsely claiming that their electric muscle stimulation treatments produced the same effect as exercise.[40] Additional problems with health and fitness facilities are discussed in Chapter 15.

The FTC charged Fitness Quest, Inc., with making false and unsubstantiated claims about the effectiveness of its "Gut Buster" exercise device and with failing to disclose that the device could break and cause injury to the user. The complaint charged the product was falsely represented to be able to significantly flatten the user's stomach, improve the user's waistline by strengthening or toning the stomach muscles and reduce stomach fat. Also the user could not achieve these results by use of the Gut Buster for 5 minutes daily.[42]

Government Regulation

The FDA has jurisdiction over the labeling of foods and prescription drugs, but can intervene when illegal therapeutic claims are made for nonprescription products. The FTC has jurisdiction over the advertising of products and services except for prescription drugs. The U.S. Postal Service has jurisdiction over products marketed through the mail. Various state and local agencies have jurisdiction over advertising within their own state. In many cases, more than one agency may have authority to act against a particular ad. Chapter 27 discusses the role of each of these agencies in detail.

In recent years, the FDA has been severely criticized for failure to stop many misleading promotions for foods and nutrition-related products.[43] In 1991, however, it proposed tighter regulations for these products (see Chapter 12) and stepped up its enforcement program considerably. The FTC has been criticized for moving too slowly and for ignoring the vast majority of promotions it learns about. During the mid-1980s, it averaged only five or six health-related cases per year. Recently, however, this number has increased sharply. The Postal Service has a vigorous regulatory program that has stopped many promoters of mail fraud. State agencies vary considerably in their attitude toward health frauds. Some states handle many cases, while others handle few or none. Even when a promotion is stopped within one state, however, it may be able to continue in the rest. Consumers should keep in mind that the problem of health fraud is so vast that government agencies cannot stop the majority of violations they detect.[44]

Industry Self-Regulation

In 1971, when the FTC was initiating a new advertising substantiation program, the National Advertising Review Board (NARB) was formed "to promote higher standards of truth and accuracy in national and regional advertising." Its sponsors were the American Advertising Federation, American Association of Advertising Agencies, Association of National Advertisers, and Council of Better Business Bureaus. The review process is done primarily by the Council's National Advertising Division (NAD), which investigates questionable ads, draws conclusions, and sometimes negotiates settlements. Parties that disagree with NAD's findings can appeal to the NARB. Few cases go to the NARB.

NAD may initiate action as a result of its own monitoring of the advertising media. Complaints are also initiated by competing companies, local Better Business Bureaus, individual consumers, consumer groups, professional and trade associations, and government agencies. When NAD decides to investigate a complaint, it asks the advertiser for substantiation, which may then be shown to the complaintant for rebuttal. Closed cases are classified in the monthly *NAD Case Reports* as "substantiated" or "modified or discontinued." NAD closes about 100 cases a year. Anyone can initiate a complaint by sending a letter to NAD with a description of the ad (including a copy if it has been printed) and the reasons why it appears to be invalid.

NAD's impact on the health marketplace is very small. Dr. Stephen Barrett, who has complained about more than 20 health-related ads, has noticed that NAD refuses to open cases involving: (1) products or companies it does not consider basically legitimate; (2) dietary supplements whose manufacturers are making illegal therapeutic claims; (3) services by licensed health professionals; and (4) ads that are not distributed nationally. NAD's investigations tend to be slow, and even ads that are discontinued as a result of an NAD inquiry usually have run long enough to achieve their intended purposes. NAD's after-the-fact findings are rarely reported in the news media.

Consumer Analysis of Advertising

Consumers need to be critical of advertisements and must protect themselves by analyzing information that is provided or included. The following excerpts from ads in health magazines illustrate this need.

Advertisement 1

MAXIMUM STRENGTH PANADOL

Discover world-proven PANADOL . . . acetaminophen . . . fast pain relief . . . contains no aspirin . . . provides as strong a pain reliever as any you can buy and it won't upset your stomach . . . 1000 mg strong . . . from Europe to Australia, millions around the world.

World-proven by whom? Is a drug safe and effective to use because people in other countries use it? Acetaminophen has no effect on inflammation, and individuals who need this effect therefore should not use this chemical.

Is Panadol better because it contains more acetaminophen, because it is as strong a pain reliever as you can buy? A 1000-mg dose is equivalent to about three 5-grain tablets. The usual dose taken by adults is two 5-grain tablets at one time. If a person takes Panadol every 6 hours, the daily total ingested would be 4000 mg, which is 1000 mg more per day than is considered safe.

Advertisement 2

BEMINAL STRESS PLUS

"Stress burnout." Find out if you have it, why you have it, and how to combat it. "Stress burnout" occurs when, as the result of physical stress or lack of proper nutrition, your body does not get the vitamins it needs. Beminal Stress Plus vitamins are a protective step.

The term stress burnout is one invented by the advertiser to provide novelty or to attract attention. There is no such physiologic or medical term. Extra vitamins are not needed to protect against life's ordinary stresses (see Chapter 13).

Analysis of Claims

Table 5-3 provides guidelines for critically analyzing health advertisements. Ads should first be checked by identifying the claims used, noting these techniques in the *Claims used* column. The next step

Table 5–3

Consumer Analysis of Advertising

Appeal techniques	Some claims	Questions to be asked	Comments: Claims used	Comments: Questions/ replies
Bandwagon	All people use Used in hospitals and labs People rely on	Who says? Is it true?		
Costs	Less expensive	Than what? Are they really?		
Effectiveness	Relief of pain, aches, itches, burns; soothes Comforts, protects, prevents, easy to use	How long? Does it really? Who says? Evidence?		
Endorsements/ testimonials	By physicians, dentists, actors/actresses, athletes, others	Qualifications? Are they opinions? Do they use items themselves? Evidence?		
Generalizations	Winning with Anacin World-proven Every body needs milk Body may not get vitamins it needs	Win what? By whom? Do they? How often does this happen?		
Imagery/visuals	Subliminal, through music, animation, color, beauty of people, environment, photos, other	Is this for attention? Were photos modified? Are visuals realistic?		
Novelty/mystical aspects	New, different, mystical ingredient, contains X, from Europe, China, etc., nature's beauty secrets, special substance	What is new? Different? What is the substance? Mystical ingredient? Does it work as claimed?		
Slogans, symbols, humor	Lyrics, phrases, jokes, trademarks, other	Are these for attention, interest?		
Power words	Say-nothing words: strength, helps, fights, relief, natural, improves, pure, works harder, gentle, long-lasting, enriched	What? How? Possible? How long?		
Misleading comparisons	Virtually germ-free Up to 8-hour relief Relieve pain fast Contains twice as much	Is this significant? Will it prevent disease? How much? Could there be none? How fast? Is more better?		
Mood changes/ emotions/attitudes	Feel better, relieve tensions, improve ego, remove loneliness, fatigue, tastes good, easy to apply, promotes self-awareness	Evidence for this? Do they really?		

Continued.

TABLE 5–3

CONSUMER ANALYSIS OF ADVERTISING—cont'd

Appeal techniques	Some claims	Questions to be asked	Comments: Claims used	Comments: Questions/ replies
Rebates/rewards	Money back, reduced price, special book/ pamphlet, free, bonus, coupons, other	Does this increase price? Why? Is product better?		
Scientific studies/ evidence	Most doctors, dentists; study completed; shows promise; clinical tests show, research shows, created by research scientists, other	How many? Who? What tests? Research? On animals? Humans? Limited/ preliminary study? Controlled study?		
Superiority	Stronger, more of, better, best, leading, no others, greater, increased	How much? Are these differences significant?		
Social	Socially acceptable Smell nice Look better, attractive	Does product work?		

Consumer analysis summary*—comments

Appeals claims used

Conclusion regarding accuracy, truthfulness, misleading or deceptive statements

*Consumers should check reliable sources for information (see Chapter 23 and the Appendix).

should be to supply responses to *Questions to be asked* in the space provided. Finally, the specific *Claims used* should be analyzed to determine whether they are truthful or misleading. Some research will be necessary. Chapters 4, 6, 12, 20 and 27 identify reliable sources of information.

Figure 5-9 is a checklist for evaluating whether an advertisement may be fraudulent. It is not a sophisticated assessment but can help in making intelligent decisions.

SUMMARY

Puffery is the primary communication technique used in ads to sell health products and services. It attempts to appeal to people's psychologic as well as physiologic needs. Advertising frequently uses terminology to sell a promise, to stimulate fantasy

IT'S YOUR DECISION

Prepare a copy of the advertisement in Figure 5-10, "Specializing in weight reduction . . ." and a copy of Table 5-3, "Consumer Analysis of Advertising." Use a colored pen to underline the appeal techniques found in the ad by referring to Table 5-3. Complete Table 5-3 with the information identified in the advertisement. What conclusions can you draw? Do you need further information? Would you recommend this program to others? Why? Why not?

Product Name ______________________________

Place a check to the right in the box that applies:

	Yes	No
Is the product:		
"Fast/safe/easy"		
"Guaranteed"		
"Painless"		
"Exciting"		
"FDA-approved"		
"Fantastic"		
"Amazing"		
"Miraculous"		
"A breakthrough"		
"An exciting foreign discovery"		
Promoted with testimonials from users		
Does the product:		
"Cure serious diseases"		
"Work while you sleep"		
"Reverse aging"		
"Cure baldness"		
"Improve your romantic life"		
Show before-and-after pictures?		
"Prevent calorie absorption"		
"Improve your popularity"		
Does the advertiser claim		
"You can eat all you want and not gain weight"		
"The medical community is jealous"		

Key: 1 yes = Be suspicious
2 yesses = High probability of fraud
3 yesses = Save your money

FIGURE 5-9. Health fraud checklist.

yearnings and hopes, and often to convey simple answers to individual desires. Consumers should also be alert to the hidden motivational procedures used by manufacturers and sellers. They must be able to identify the unsubstantiated, misleading and possibly incorrect claims for health products and services to which they are constantly exposed in the media. Government agencies can stop many false and misleading promotions. But regulatory action provides only limited protection and cannot substitute for intelligent consumer behavior. Figure 5-10 provides tips on how to see through misleading claims.

Discussion Questions

1. What are the hidden motivators used in advertising campaigns? Is it ethical to use such motivators?
2. What techniques are used in advertising to sell products?
3. What is the meaning of puffery as used in ad-

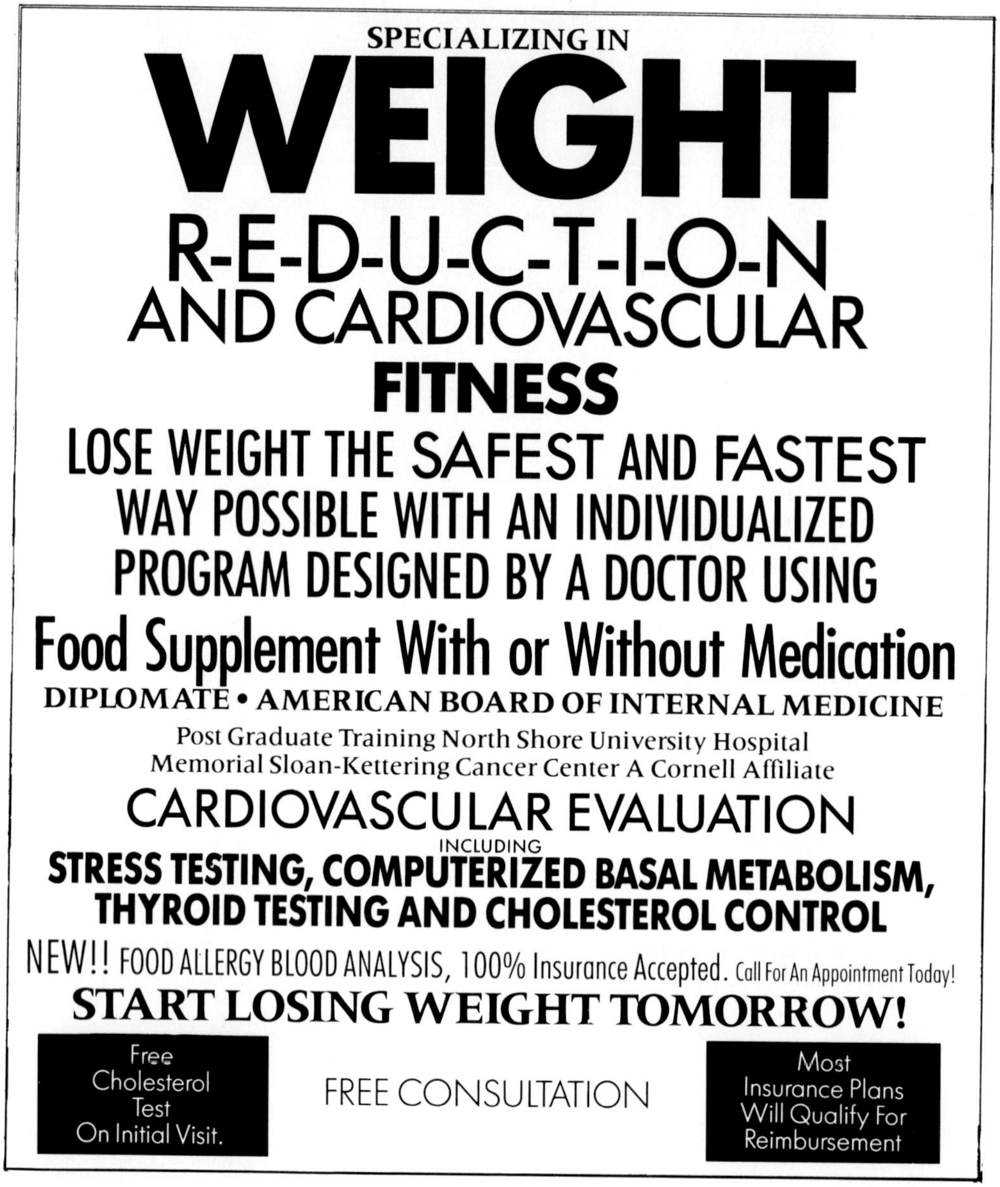

SPECIALIZING IN
WEIGHT
R-E-D-U-C-T-I-O-N
AND CARDIOVASCULAR
FITNESS
LOSE WEIGHT THE SAFEST AND FASTEST
WAY POSSIBLE WITH AN INDIVIDUALIZED
PROGRAM DESIGNED BY A DOCTOR USING
Food Supplement With or Without Medication
DIPLOMATE • AMERICAN BOARD OF INTERNAL MEDICINE
Post Graduate Training North Shore University Hospital
Memorial Sloan-Kettering Cancer Center A Cornell Affiliate
CARDIOVASCULAR EVALUATION
INCLUDING
STRESS TESTING, COMPUTERIZED BASAL METABOLISM,
THYROID TESTING AND CHOLESTEROL CONTROL
NEW!! FOOD ALLERGY BLOOD ANALYSIS, 100% Insurance Accepted. Call For An Appointment Today!
START LOSING WEIGHT TOMORROW!
Free Cholesterol Test On Initial Visit.
FREE CONSULTATION
Most Insurance Plans Will Qualify For Reimbursement

FIGURE 5-10. Advertisement for analysis.

vertising? Give examples. How does this action relate to the FTC Act against false advertisements? Are there true puffs?

4. Discuss the points for and against professional health advertising. What effect has the loosening of government restraints had on advertising by health professionals?
5. What questions might be raised about advertising by hospitals?
6. What are the pros and cons of prescription drug advertising?
7. Why has the U.S. Postal Service had problems combating mail-order fraud?
8. What are some of the abuses of advertising found in the health marketplace?
9. What action should consumers take when faced with health marketplace abuses?
10. What has industry done to self-regulate advertising? Is the process effective?
11. How effective is government regulation of advertising?
12. How can a consumer analyze advertising to

make intelligent decisions about the purchase of products?

13. What direction are tobacco companies taking with advertisements? Why is this taking place?
14. What are infomercials? How can consumers identify them?
15. What are 10 key words or phrases that will enable a consumer to identify a fraudulent health advertisement?

REFERENCES

1. Kurtz P: The responsibilities of the media and paranormal claims, Skeptical Inquirer 9(4):362, 1985.
2. Miller R: Critiquing quack ads, FDA Consumer 19(2):10-13, 1985.
3. Howard JA and Hulbert J: A staff report to the Federal Trade Commission: advertising and public interest, From FTC hearings on modern advertising practices, New York, 1973, The Commission.
4. Oler C: "Low blows" in television advertising, Can Dent Assoc J 7:482, 1985.
5. Advertising in disguise, Consumer Reports 51:179-181, 1986.
6. Preston IL: The great American blow-up: puffery in advertising and selling, Madison, Wis, 1975, University of Wisconsin Press.
7. FTC News Notes, May 6, 1983.
8. DeBaggio T: Advertising image: puffery or effrontery, The Nation 214:79-83, 1982.
9. Advertising Age, Dec. 7, 1981.
10. AMA Council on Ethical and Judicial Affairs: Current opinions, Chicago, 1989, American Medical Association.
11. Folland SF: Advertising by physicians: behavior and attitudes, Med Care 25:148-156, 1987.
12. Margo CE: Sounding board: selling imagery, N Engl J Med 314:1575-1576, 1986.
13. Yarborough M: Physician advertising: some reasons for caution, Southern Med J 82:1538-1544, 1989.
14. O'Brien JP: Legal issues need not hinder proper hospital advertising, Hospitals 56:57-61, 1982.
15. Gray J: The selling of medicine, Medical Economics p 180-194, Jan. 20, 1986.
16. Reade JM and Ratzan RM: Yellow professionalism: physicians in the Yellow Pages, N Engl J Med 21:1315-1319, 1987.
17. Edwards KS: The new ABMS listings, Ohio Medicine 86:653, 1990.
18. Kessler DA and Pines WL: The federal regulation of prescription drug advertising and promotion, JAMA 264:2409-2415, 1990.
19. Masson A and Rubin PH: Matching prescription drugs and consumers, N Engl J Med 313:513-515, 1985.
20. Cohen EP: Direct-to-the-public advertisement of prescription drugs, N Engl J Med 318:373-375, 1988.
21. Lipman MM: Office visit: pitching prescription drugs to consumers, Consumer Reports Health Letter 3:22, 1991.
22. FTC News Notes, Aug. 5, 1983. The prime time diet: a content analysis of eating behavior and food messages in television program content and commercials, AM J Pub Health 80:738–740, 1990.
23. Story M, Faulkner P: The prime time diet: a content analysis of eating behavior and food messages in television program content and commercials, Am J Pub Health 80:738–740, 1990.
24. Six food companies told to remove health claims, FDA Consumer 24(9):2, 1990.
25. Breast-building ads called falsies, San Francisco Chronicle, May 5, 1982.
26. Wellness today, a special supplement to Health & Healing, Potomac, Md, 1991, Phillips Publishing, Inc.
27. Barrett S: Quackery by mail, New York, 1991, American Council on Science and Health.
28. FTC News Notes, July 1991.
29. Tobacco advertising and the First Amendment, JAMA 264:1593-1594, 1990.
30. Cigarette advertising—United States 1988, JAMA 263:2872-2875, 1990.
31. Koop CE: A parting shot at tobacco, JAMA 262:2894-2895, 1989.
32. Beck B: 1990 ACSH survey: An evaluation of reporting on the health hazards of smoking in American magazines, New York 1991, American Council on Science and Health.
33. R.J. Reynolds abuses MR FIT, Consumer Reports Health Letter 2:44, 1990.
34. Tobacco foes attack ads that target women, minorities, teens and the poor, JAMA 264:1505-1506, 1990.
35. Camel ad: Is male violence a "smooth move?" The Public Citizen Health Research Group Health Letter 5(9):11-12, 1989.
36. Fischer M et al: Brand logo recognition by children aged 3 to 6 years, JAMA 266:3145-3148, 1991.
37. Tye JB: The silver screen covert cigarette ads in movies, Priorities, Summer 1991.
38. Tobacco companies "guide" smokers to action against nonsmokers, The Public Citizen Health Research Group Health Letter 5(9):4, 1989.
39. Magazines without tobacco advertising, JAMA 266:3099-3102, 1991.
40. FTC News Notes, Sept. 18, 1989.
41. Makers of adult diapers agree to alter ads, New York Times, Dec. 8, 1990.
42. FTC News Notes, Jan. 8, 1990.
43. Barrett S: Quackery and the FDA: a complicated story, Nutrition Forum 8:42-45, 1991.
44. Barrett S: Federal regulation of quackery: improvement is needed, Priorities, p 35-36, Fall 1990.

APPROACHES TO HEALTH CARE

CHAPTER SIX

SCIENTIFIC HEALTH CARE

"None of my friends could diagnose the symptoms, Doctor. You're my last hope!"

110 MEDICAL ECONOMICS/MAY 30, 1983

The good physician treats the disease; the great physician treats the patient who has the disease.

SIR WILLIAM OSLER

Knowing about your problem will help you assert yourself in the doctor's office. And the more you know, the more intelligently you're apt to follow—or question—your doctor's advice.

MARVIN LIPMAN, M.D.[1]

CONSUMER DECISIONS

How can one find a good physician or other health professional?

What should be included in a complete health examination, and how frequently should one be performed?

What guidelines can help determine whether to undergo recommended surgery?

How can a consumer determine the quality of health care received from a practitioner?

Scientific health care is the prevention, diagnosis, and treatment of disease based on the principles of modern science. Most people in the United States accept physicians as the primary health authorities and healers of the sick. Aligned with physicians are other scientifically trained practitioners and auxiliary (allied) providers. These people espouse scientifically based concepts of disease such as the germ theory. They advocate research based on scientific principles, and prevention and treatment based on proven methods. They also espouse a strict code of professional ethics and rigorous procedures for education, licensure, and accountability.

This chapter discusses the training and work of medical and osteopathic physicians, podiatrists, optometrists, nurses, pharmacists, and various allied personnel. Mental health, dental, and nutrition professionals are discussed in Chapters 7, 8, and 12, respectively.

HEALTH CARE PERSONNEL

Scientific health care practitioners are regulated by state licensing laws. To obtain a license, one must first complete a specified amount of training at an accredited institution and then complete a licensing examination. Based on laws that define their scope of practice, practitioners may be divided into three groups:

1. Independent practitioners, whose scope of practice is theoretically unlimited: medical and osteopathic physicians.
2. Independent practitioners, whose scope of practice is restricted to particular parts of the body: dentists, podiatrists, optometrists, and psychologists (in some states).
3. Ancillary providers, who usually must practice under some degree of medical supervision: nurses, physicians' assistants, physical and occupational therapists, pharmacists, and many types of technicians.

In many states, practitioners must participate in continuing education to maintain their license or membership in their professional association.

Medical Doctors

The doctor of medicine (M.D.) degree requires four years of training at a medical school accredited by the Liaison Committee on Medical Education, a joint committee of the AMA Council on Medical Education and the Association of American Medical Colleges. The first two years of medical training cover basic and preclinical science courses, including anatomy, physiology, biochemistry, histology, pathology, epidemiology, and pharmacology. The last two years stress clinical work in a variety of hospital and clinic settings. A minimum of three years of premedical college work is required for admission to medical school, but 96% of matriculants have at least a baccalaureate degree.[2]

Currently there are 125 accredited 4-year medical schools in the United States.[2] Graduates of these schools must take state or national board examinations to become licensed. Some states require an additional year or two of postgraduate training at a hospital. Graduates of foreign medical schools must take postgraduate education in the United States before they are eligible to take licensing examinations in most states.

Because of the vast scope of modern medical knowledge, most medical school graduates take additional training before entering clinical practice. Those choosing to become specialists take three or more years of specialty training. The recognized standard-setting organization is the American Board of Medical Specialties, which is composed of 23 primary medical specialty boards and six associate members: the AMA, American Hospital Association, Association of American Medical Colleges, Council of Medical Specialty Societies, Federation of State Medical Boards of the United States, and National Board of Medical Examiners. The recognized specialties and subspecialties are:

Administrative medicine: Operation and management of organizations and institutions such as health departments, hospitals, clinics, and health care plans

Aerospace medicine: Subspecialty of preventive medicine dealing with problems of aviation and space flight

Allergy and immunology: Subspecialty of internal medicine

Anesthesiology: Administration of drugs to prevent pain or to induce unconsciousness during surgical operations or diagnostic procedures

Cardiovascular disease (cardiology): Subspecialty of internal medicine that deals with the heart and blood vessels

Child psychiatry: Subspecialty of psychiatry that deals with nervous and emotional problems of children

Colon and rectal surgery (proctology): Diagnosis and treatment of disorders of the lower digestive tract

Dermatology: Diagnosis and treatment of skin diseases

Emergency medicine: Diagnosis and treatment of emergencies

Endocrinology and metabolism: Subspecialty of internal medicine that deals with glandular and metabolic disorders

Family practice: General medical services for patients and their families

Forensic pathology: Subspecialty of pathology that deals with medicine and the law

Gastroenterology: Subspecialty of internal medicine that deals with disorders of the digestive tract

General surgery: Surgery of parts of the body that are not in the domain of specific surgical specialties (some areas overlap)

Geriatrics: Care of problems of the elderly. Family practitioners and internists can become certified with added qualifications in geriatric medicine. Psychiatrists can become certified with added qualifications in geriatric psychiatry.

Head and neck (otolaryngology): Care of diseases of the head and neck except for those of the eyes or brain

Infectious disease: Subspecialty of internal medicine

Internal medicine: Diagnosis and nonsurgical treatment of internal organs of the body of adults

Neonatal-perinatal medicine: Subspecialty of pediatrics that deals with disorders of newborn infants, including premature infants

Neurological surgery (neurosurgery): Diagnosis and surgical treatment of diseases of the brain, spinal cord, and nerves

Neurology: Diagnosis and nonsurgical treatment of diseases of the brain, spinal cord, and nerves

Nuclear medicine: Use of radioactive substances for diagnosis and treatment

Obstetrics and gynecology (ob/gyn): Care of pregnant women and treatment of disorders of the female reproductive system

Occupational medicine: Subspecialty of preventive medicine that deals with the special physical and psychologic risks in industry

Ophthalmology: Medical and surgical care of the eye, including the prescription of glasses

Orthopedic surgery (orthopedics): Care of injuries and disorders of the muscles, bones, and joints

Pathology: Examination and diagnosis of organs, tissues, body fluids, and excrement

Pediatrics: Care of children from birth through adolescence

Pediatric allergy: Subspecialty of pediatrics

Pediatric hematology-oncology: Subspecialty of pediatrics concerned with the treatment of blood disorders and cancers

Pediatric nephrology: Subspecialty of pediatrics that deals with kidney disorders

Pediatric surgery: Subspecialty of pediatrics

Physical medicine and rehabilitation (physiatry): Treatment of convalescent and physically handicapped patients

Plastic surgery: Surgery to correct or repair deformed or mutilated parts of the body, or to improve facial or body features

Preventive medicine: Prevention of disease through immunization, good health practice, and concern with environmental factors

Psychiatry: Treatment of mental and emotional problems

Public health: Subspecialty of preventive medicine that deals with promoting the general health of the community

Pulmonary disease: Subspecialty of internal medicine that deals with diseases of the lungs

Radiology: Use of radiation for the diagnosis and treatment of disease

Rheumatology: Subspecialty of internal medicine that deals with arthritis and related disorders

Thoracic surgery: Surgical treatment of the lungs, heart, and large blood vessels within the chest cavity

Urology: Treatment of male sex organs and urinary tract and treatment of female urinary tract

Medical specialty boards require high standards of training and performance and ensure them by rigid examinations. Successful applicants receive diplomas and are considered "board-certified." They are also referred to as "diplomates" in their particular specialties. Physicians who complete all requirements for certification except the examination may be identified as "board-eligible." A few boards require periodic recertification. Currently there are about 570,000 medical doctors in the United States, about half of whom belong to the AMA.

Osteopathic Physicians

The principles of osteopathy originally were expressed by Andrew Taylor Still, M.D., in 1874, when medical science was in its infancy. Still, a medical doctor, believed that diseases were caused by mechanical interference with nerve and blood supply and were cured by manipulation of "deranged, displaced bones, nerves, muscles—removing all obstructions—thereby setting the machinery of life moving." His autobiography states that he could "shake a child and stop scarlet fever, croup, diphtheria, and cure whooping cough in three days by a wring of its neck."

Still was antagonistic toward the drug practices of his day and regarded surgery as a last resort. Rejected as a cultist by organized medicine, he founded the first osteopathic medical school in Kirksville, Missouri in 1894.

As medical science developed, osteopathy gradually incorporated all its theories and practices.[3] Today, except for slight additional emphasis on musculoskeletal diagnosis and treatment, the scope of osteopathy is identical to that of medicine.

Currently there are about 32,000 practitioners of osteopathy and 15 accredited colleges of osteopathic medicine in the United States. Admission to osteopathic school requires three years of preprofessional college work, but almost all those enrolled have a baccalaureate or higher degree. The doctor of osteopathy (D.O.) degree requires more than 5000 hours of training over 4 academic years. The faculties of osteopathic colleges are about evenly divided between doctors of osteopathy and holders of Ph.D. degrees, with a few medical doctors at some colleges. Graduation is followed by a 1-year rotating internship at an approved teaching hospital. About half of osteopaths enter general practice. Those who specialize follow internship with 1 to 6 years of residency training, depending on the specialty. Specialties include anesthesiology, dermatology, emergency medicine, general practice, internal medicine, neurology, obstetrics, ophthalmology, orthopedics, pathology, pediatrics, proctology, psychiatry, radiology, rehabilitation medicine, surgery, and a number of subspecialties.

Osteopathic physicians are fully licensed to practice in all states and are legally equivalent to medical doctors. Most states have a single licensing board for doctors of medicine and doctors of osteopathy, with the board made up of both medical and osteopathic physicians, but some states have a separate board for each profession. A few states have boards made up of only medical doctors that license members of both professions.

Many observers believe that osteopathy and medicine should merge.[4] But osteopathic organizations prefer to retain a separate identity and have exaggerated the minor differences between osteopathy and medicine in their advertising. According to a recent brochure from the American Osteopathic Association: (1) osteopathy is "the only branch of mainstream medicine that follows the Hippocratic approach," (2) the body's musculoskeletal system is central to the patient's well-being, (3) osteopathic manipulation is a proven technique for many hands-on diagnoses and often can provide an alternative to drugs and surgery, and (4) osteopathic medicine cooperates with other branches of medical services but maintains its professional independence to sustain and develop as a unique and comprehensive system of health care.

Podiatrists

Doctors of podiatric medicine (D.P.M.) are independent practitioners whose responsibilities include diagnosis, prevention, and treatment of problems of the human foot. Podiatrists are licensed in all states to prescribe corrective devices, drugs, and physical therapy. They may perform minor foot surgery in their offices, and, if deemed qualified by a hospital, may also perform major foot surgery at that hospital.

Podiatry has its roots in the practice of chiropodists, practitioners who treated corns, warts, bunions, and other ailments of the foot. The terms "chiropodist" and "chiropody" became obsolete during the mid-1960s.

Podiatric licensure requires a minimum of 3 years of undergraduate course work plus 4 additional years of study at one of the seven accredited colleges of podiatric medicine in the United States. Residency programs for 1 to 3 years of additional training are available to graduates. Podiatrists may become commissioned officers in the armed forces and the U.S. Public Health Service. There are about 11,500 podiatrists in the United States, most of whom belong to the American Podiatric Medical Association. About 90% of podiatrists are general practitioners, and the rest are specialists in such areas as podogeriatrics, podopediatrics, podiatric dermatology, foot surgery, foot orthopedics, and sports medicine.

Optometrists

Doctors of optometry (O.D.) are graduates of one of the 16 accredited colleges of optometry in the United States. They are trained to examine the eyes and related structures to detect vision problems, eye disease, and other abnormalities. They principally perform vision examinations for the purpose of prescribing glasses and contact lenses. During the course of an eye examination, an optometrist may use a tonometer or other instrument to detect glaucoma and an ophthalmoscope and other instruments to examine the exterior and interior of the eyes. Optometrists do not perform surgery but can use diagnostic drugs to help them examine the eyes. In 30 states they are also permitted to use drugs to treat certain eye diseases.

The educational program leading to the doctor of optometry degree includes a minimum of 2 or 3 years of undergraduate work, although, as in medicine, few matriculants have less than a baccalaureate degree. This is followed by 4 years of optometry school. In some states an internship is required. A license is obtained by passing a state board examination. Currently there are about 27,000 practicing optometrists in the United States, three fourths of whom belong to the American Optometric Association.

Nurses

Registered nurses (R.N.) are graduates of accredited nursing schools and have passed a state board examination for licensure. Their education may be acquired in three different ways. Two-year programs leading to an associate degree are offered at community colleges or vocational technical schools. Three-year programs leading to a diploma are offered at hospital-based schools of nursing. Four-year programs leading to a baccalaureate degree (B.S.N.) are offered by colleges and universities. About two million registered nurses are licensed to practice in the United States.

Registered nurses can become certified in any of 22 areas of practice by the American Nurses Credentialling Center (ANCC), a subsidiary of the American Nurses Association (ANA), if they meet educational and practice requirements and pass an examination. Those who are certified at the generalist level can use the designation Registered Nurse, Certified (R.N.,C.). Beginning in 1998, all applicants for these positions must hold a baccalaureate or higher degree in nursing. Certified clinical nurse specialists (R.N.,C.S.) are registered nurses who function either as clinical specialists or as nurse practitioners. They must have a master's or higher degree in nursing, meet practice requirements, and pass an examination. Certification is also available in nursing administration at both the generalist and advanced level. As of January 1992, over 90,000 nurses held current ANCC certification. ANCC certification examinations are based on standards of practice developed by ANA Councils. Several are offered by ANCC in collaboration with other specialty nursing organizations. Certification is available in additional areas of nursing practice through other specialty nursing organizations.

Registered nurses may work in hospitals, clinics, physicians' offices, public and voluntary health agencies, schools, industries, or independent practice. Some states require additional training for those who wish to work as school nurses.

Work as a public health nurse usually requires at least a bachelor's degree. Specialization in public health may be acquired through nursing schools offering a master of nursing (M.S.N.) degree. Schools of public health offer programs leading to a master of public health (M.P.H.) degree.

Nurse anesthetists are RNs who complete a 2-year program in anesthesia, usually at the master's level. Certified registered nurse anesthetists (C.R.N.A.) must pass an examination administered by the American Association of Nurse Anesthetists.

Nurse practitioners are registered nurses who undergo additional nursing education, usually at the master's level, to enable them to function (in some states) as primary care providers. ANCC certification for nurse practitioners (designated as

R.N.,C.S.) is available in pediatric, adult, family, gerontological, and school nurse practice.

Nurse-midwives are registered nurses who have completed an additional 1 to 2 years of training from an approved school of midwifery. By passing an examination given by the American College of Nurse-Midwives, they can earn a certified nurse-midwife (C.N.M.) certificate that allows them to practice midwifery in most states. Nurse-midwives care for mothers during pregnancy, manage labor and delivery, and watch for signs that a physician's attention is needed. They also help the mother care for herself and the baby and may serve as members of obstetrical teams in medical centers and other community institutions.

Practical and vocational nurses (L.P.N. and L.V.N.) are graduates of state-approved schools of nursing who must pass a state board examination for licensing. Their training involves 12 to 18 months of work following a minimum of 2 years of high school. They usually work under the direction of a registered nurse.

Pharmacists

Pharmacy is concerned with safety and efficacy in the procuring, storing, dispensing, and use of medications, related substances, and appliances. Pharmacists are also trained in methods of compounding and manufacturing drugs and testing them for purity and potency, although in actual practice most items they dispense are compounded by drug manufacturers.

There are 74 colleges of pharmacy in the United States that are accredited by the American Council on Pharmaceutical Education. A minimum of 5 years of study is required for a bachelor of science (B.S.) in pharmacy or a bachelor of pharmacy (B.Pharm.) degree. A doctoral degree (Pharm.D.) is offered at 74 colleges; some of those require a 6-year undergraduate program and others require a longer program. A curriculum of most schools of pharmacy includes clinical practice under the supervision of a faculty member.

Pharmacists practice in a number of work environments: community pharmacies, hospitals, clinics, extended care facilities, and nursing homes. A license to practice is required in all states. To obtain a license, one must graduate from an accredited college of pharmacy, spend a prescribed period of internship (in most states), and pass an examination given by the state board of pharmacy. Pharmacists with doctoral degrees, referred to as "clinical pharmacists," may teach in schools of pharmacy or medicine, provide patient care services in teaching hospitals, and engage in clinical research.[5] Currently there are about 160,000 pharmacists in the United States. In 1986 Florida passed a law that permits pharmacists to prescribe fluorides and a limited number of drugs. However, the majority have chosen not to do so.

Allied Health Care Personnel

More than 70 types of allied health care personnel offer clinical services to the public.[6] The AMA Committee on Allied Health Education and Accreditation accredits training programs for 26 occupations. Some types of allied health personnel are licensed, while others are not. They include:

Audiologists test patients and recommend hearing aids. Work in this field requires a master's degree in audiology.

Emergency medical technicians (EMTs) respond to medical emergencies and provide immediate care to the critically ill or injured. Rating as an EMT requires completion of an 81-hour course approved by the U.S. Department of Transportation. Rating as an EMT-dispatcher requires an additional 2-day communication course. An EMT-paramedic rating requires a minimum 500-hour approved course with 6 to 12 months of prior EMT experience. EMT-paramedics can work in mobile intensive care vehicles under a physician's direction through voice contact relayed from a medical center. They may administer drugs intravenously or use a defibrillator to shock a stopped heart into action. The basic courses are given by hospitals, community colleges, and health, police, and fire departments. Advanced training is given by hospitals. Some 2-year associate degree programs exist.

Medical assistants help physicians to examine patients. They may also obtain laboratory specimens, function as receptionists, complete insurance forms, and order supplies. Their training may be a 2-year community college program, after which certification may be obtained from the American Association of Medical Assistants, or on-the-job training by physician-employers.

Medical technologists are college graduates whose education includes at least 1 year of clinical training in the performance of various laboratory tests and procedures. They may be assisted in their work by laboratory technicians.

Nurse's aides and orderlies provide basic patient care under direct nursing supervision. They may bathe and feed patients, change linens, and make beds. No formal training is required: most hospitals or nursing homes first hire persons and then provide 6 to 8 weeks of on-the-job training.

Occupational therapists help physically and emotionally handicapped persons with vocational or recreational activities. They are college graduates whose education includes at least 2 years of specialized training.

Opticians give auxiliary support to optometrists and ophthalmologists. They are responsible for fitting, supplying, and adjusting glasses to prescriptions. They do not examine eyes and are not legally authorized to prescribe lenses.

Physical therapists help to rehabilitate individuals who have temporary or permanent physical handicaps or other ailments. Their treatment methods include exercises to improve muscle strength, flexibility, and coordination, and the application of heat, cold, or electricity to relieve pain or to change the patient's condition. Physical therapists are college graduates whose education includes 1 or more years of special training. Traditionally they work under physician supervision, but some states permit direct access to patients.

Patient representatives work mainly in hospitals, where they help patients interpret policies and procedures, respond to patient complaints, and help staff members understand how patients perceive the hospital experience. Academic training is not required, though most are college graduates and a few have master's degrees in health advocacy.

Physician assistants (PAs) under physician supervision perform many tasks traditionally done by physicians. PAs perform physical examinations, treat certain ailments, prescribe certain drugs, and counsel patients on health problems. Training at community colleges, universities, medical schools, or the military usually takes 1½ to 2 years. Some training programs require prior college and/or patient care experience. Most PAs work in physicians' offices, but some work in hospitals, health maintenance organizations (HMOs), prisons, and community clinics.

Respiratory therapists, on physician's orders, treat patients with heart or lung problems, administering oxygen and various types of gases or aerosol drugs. They may also test respiratory function. Therapists complete a minimum of 2 years' training in a college or hospital.

Social workers help people with their jobs, families, financial problems, and daily living tasks, particularly when their needs are related to illness or disability. They are usually college graduates.

Speech pathologists test patients and provide corrective therapy. Work in this field requires a master's degree in speech pathology.

Auxiliary dental, mental health, and nutrition personnel are discussed in other chapters.

Choosing a Physician

In the past, basic medical care of individuals and families was provided by family physicians. Typically they were general practitioners who did not limit themselves to one area of medicine. Many delivered babies, and some even performed major surgery. When a specialist was needed, the family physician remained as the primary contact and medical advisor, with the specialist serving as a consultant.

Over the past few decades this situation has changed. As medicine became more complex, the number of physicians becoming specialists increased and the number of general practitioners gradually dwindled. As our society has become more mobile, group practices and walk-in facilities have increased in number and many people consult specialists without coordination and referral by a family physician. These factors tend to foster fragmentation of medical care. Managed-care programs, in which primary physicians act as gatekeepers, attempt to decrease fragmentation and cut costs without compromising the quality of care.

The Good Physician

Because of the complexity of medical practice, it is difficult to construct yardsticks by which consumers can judge the quality of their medical care. In addition, what is good for one patient may not be what another needs or prefers. The following box lists qualities of a good physician.

Alper[7,8] suggests that marginal physicians can sometimes be identified by lack of an appropriate rationale for handling common infections (e.g., overuse of antibiotics, insufficient use of cultures), overdiagnosis of rare metabolic diseases (e.g., hypothyroidism, adrenal insufficiency, hypoglycemia), and overuse of tranquilizers and injections (e.g., B_{12} shots).

CONSUMER TIP

A good physician:

1. Is intelligent and knowledgeable
2. Is sympathetic and interested in the patient
3. Is sufficiently organized to maintain a reasonably smooth appointment schedule
4. Takes a detailed history and gives the patient enough time to discuss problems
5. After examination, gives the patient a clear explanation of the diagnosis and treatment
6. May indicate that knowledge or diagnosis is lacking
7. Knows his or her limitations and suggests referral to specialists when needed
8. Is conservative about recommending surgery
9. Will not abandon a patient once treatment has begun.
10. Is available for appropriate telephone consultations
11. Is available for emergencies or provides a competent backup physician
12. Charges reasonable fees and is willing to discuss them
13. Is on the staff of an accredited hospital
14. Keeps up-to-date by reading journals and attending educational meetings.

Locating Prospective Physicians

Medical authorities are unanimous in recommending affiliation with a primary care provider—a personal physician who becomes familiar with a patient's medical needs and can coordinate care with other physicians should consultations become necessary. A board-certified family practitioner (for adults and children), internist (for adults only), or pediatrician (for children only), is likely to be a good choice, since all of them have taken advanced training in the diagnosis and treatment of general medical problems.

Staff affiliation with a hospital connected with a medical school indicates that a physician is working with up-to-date colleagues and is therefore likely to keep abreast of current medical developments and techniques. A teaching appointment at a medical school and affiliation with a hospital that trains residents are favorable signs. Lack of hospital affiliation is suspect because it may mean that the physician is isolated from the scientific mainstream of the community. Worse yet, it could mean that the physician's standard of practice is not high enough to merit membership on a hospital staff.

Because a personal physician may significantly affect a person's health (and even life), considerable care should be exercised in looking for one. The best time to look is before becoming ill. Prospective names can be obtained from many sources:

1. The department of family practice and/or department of medicine at a nearby medical school
2. A local accredited hospital
3. Another local health care professional such as a dentist, nurse, or pharmacist
4. The county medical society (names are usually given out on a rotating basis from a list of available members)
5. Friends, neighbors, co-workers
6. The person's physician from a previous community

Several years ago, the Medical Association of Alabama asked people what counted most in choosing a family doctor. Following are some of the categories queried and the percentages of respondents who thought they were "important" or "very important":

Willingness to talk about your illness	100%
Access to a hospital you want	89%
Length of time to get an appointment	88%
Personality or appearance	84%
Fees	75%
Years of experience	73%
Office location	66%
Weekend and evening office hours	66%
Doctor's involvement in civic organizations	37%
Listing in Yellow Pages and other directories	30%

The *Washington Consumers' CHECKBOOK* has suggested asking friends the following questions:

1. Does your physician seem to understand your symptoms when you describe them?
2. Does your physician take time to explain your medical problems and their treatment?
3. Is it easy to talk with your physician about concerns, however silly they may seem?
4. How long do you usually have to wait for an appointment for a nonemergency medical problem?
5. How long must you usually wait for an appointment for a full physical examination?

6. How long do you usually wait in the physician's office?
7. Is it usually easy to reach the physician by phone?
8. Will the physician advise you on the phone?
9. Do the physician's fees seem reasonable?

Credentials may be ascertained by contacting the physician's office and may be verified by consulting the medical societies and hospitals with which the physician is affiliated. They are also located in the *Directory of Medical Specialists*, the *ABMS Compendium of Certified Medical Specialists*, and the *American Medical Directory*, which are commonly available at hospitals and public libraries. Most physicians identified as specialists in the Yellow Pages listings have completed accredited specialty training. However, telephone directory publishers rarely attempt to verify credentials, so self-proclaimed specialists may be listed also. The American Board of Medical Specialties has a toll-free number for finding out whether a physician is board-certified. The Board also has been placing lists of board-certified physicians in many telephone directories, but most board-certified physicians are not included because they do not wish to pay the required fee (over $200 per year).

Meeting the Physician

An excellent way to begin a relationship with a new physician is to have an evaluation that includes a thorough physical examination. Such an examination will provide the physician a baseline against which any future changes can be compared. Those who do not wish to have a complete physical examination might still wish to schedule a brief "get-acquainted" visit with the prospective physician.

Fundamental Elements of the Patient-Physician Relationship

The following report of the AMA Council on Ethical and Judicial Affairs was adopted by the AMA House of Delegates on June 26, 1990.

From ancient times, physicians have recognized that the health and well-being of patients depends on a collaborative effort between physician and patient. Patients share with physicians the responsiblity for their own health care. The patient-physician relationship is of greatest benefit to patients when they bring medical problems to the attention of their physicians in a timely fashion, provide information about their medical condition to the best of their ability, and work with their physicians in a mutually respectful alliance. Physicians can best contribute to this alliance by serving as their patient's advocate and by fostering the following rights:

1. The patient has the right to receive information from physicians, and to discuss the benefits, risks, and costs of appropriate treatment alternatives. Patients should receive guidance from their physicians as to the optimal course of action. Patients are also entitled to obtain copies or summaries of their medical records, to have their questions answered, to be advised of potential conflicts of interest that their physicians might have, and to receive independent professional opinions.

2. The patient has the right to make decisions regarding the health care that is recommended by his or her physician. Accordingly, patients may accept or refuse any recommended medical treatment.

3. The patient has the right to courtesy, respect, dignity, responsiveness, and timely attention to his or her needs.

4. The patient has the right to confidentiality. The physician should not reveal confidential communications or information without the consent of the patient, unless provided for by law or by the need to protect the welfare of the individual or the public interest.

5. The patient has the right to continuity of health care. The physician has an obligation to cooperate in the coordination of medically indicated care with other health care providers treating the patient. The physician may not discontinue treatment of a patient as long as further treatment is medically indicated without giving the patient sufficient opportunity to make alternative arrangements for care.

6. The patient has a basic right to have available adequate health care. Physicians, along with the rest of society, should continue to work toward this goal. Fulfillment of this right is dependent on society providing resources so that no patient is deprived of necessary care because of an inability to pay for the care. Physicians should continue their traditional assumption of a part of the responsibility for the medical care of those who cannot afford essential health care.

This will provide an opportunity to observe the physical characteristics of the office, to bring up health questions that may be troubling the person, and to judge the physician's personality. If satisfied, one can also sign a release form that the new physician can use to obtain past medical records.

Advance registration has an additional advantage. Some physicians will not accept new patients under emergency conditions, particularly outside of regular office hours. Once a patient is accepted, however, the doctor has a legal obligation either to treat the patient or to provide a substitute.

Having chosen a primary physician, it is a good idea to try to learn the doctor's routine. Most well-organized doctors have printed information sheets for this purpose. If these are not available, ask questions. What are the office hours? Which are the days off? Who will cover in the doctor's absence? Does the doctor make house calls? Which hospital does the doctor use? Knowing the hospital affiliation is particularly important. In an emergency, unless instructed differently, ambulance drivers usually take patients to the nearest hospital. The doctor may not be able to take care of a person who goes to the wrong hospital.

Emergency Care

In an emergency, one should try to telephone the doctor immediately rather than just show up at the hospital emergency room. Advance notice may enable one's doctor to provide the necessary service. It also will enable the doctor to alert the emergency room personnel so that they may begin treatment or arrange for necessary tests.

Should an emergency arise before a doctor has been selected, one's best bet is to go to the emergency room of the nearest accredited hospital. If a private practitioner is preferred, some medical societies maintain an emergency roster of doctors who are on call 24 hours a day.

If an ambulance is needed, one can be obtained by contacting a company listed in the Yellow Pages of the telephone directly, contacting the police, or dialing 911 or another community emergency number. Those who are subject to epilepsy, severe allergies, diabetes, or other ailments that may require emergency attention should wear a bracelet identifying the condition or carry an emergency medical identification card that lists the person's name, next of kin, medical problems, medications taken, and doctor's name.

Many cities now have freestanding emergency centers that offer health care services and fees in between those of office practitioners and emergency rooms. The advantages and disadvantages of using such facilities are discussed in Chapter 11. Elderly or ailing individuals who live alone can wear or install special devices for emergencies; by pressing a button they can signal that help is urgently needed.

Finding a Doctor Abroad

Americans traveling in foreign countries can locate suitable treatment facilities through the International Association for Medical Assistance to Travelers (IAMAT). Established in 1960, IAMAT is a voluntary organization of hospitals, health care centers, and physicians who pledge to provide travelers with physicians who speak their language, meet IAMAT standards, and adhere to a fixed fee schedule similar to that in the United States. When medical assistance is needed, the traveler can telephone the nearest center listed in the IAMAT directory to obtain a list of local physicians. *Health Information for International Travel,*[9] updated annually by the U.S. Centers for Disease Control, provides information on required vaccinations, prevention of foodborne diseases, and other valuable tips for travelers.

Basic Medical Care

The belief that people should have regular health examinations has been popularized by the medical profession, and a large segment of the public in the United States regards an annual examination as a necessity for health maintenance. The traditional assumption has been that routine examinations can detect diseases in their early stages so that treatment can prevent suffering and save lives. Glaucoma, high blood pressure, and certain types of cancer are among the diseases that may be influenced significantly if detected early. Annual screening examinations also help physicians to get better acquainted with their patients and provide good opportunities for patient education and reassurance.

On the other hand, most authorities doubt that *complete* annual physical examinations of symptom-free individuals are cost-effective in terms of either money or physician time. The fact that such examinations may be financed by third parties (insurance companies, employers, or government agencies) and that the examining physician may not be the patient's personal physician (which may cause wasteful duplication of services) add further dimensions to the problem.

Consumers Union's medical consultants[10] believe that any test given regularly should satisfy three basic requirements:

1. It should be able to detect a serious or potentially serious disease before symptoms make the individual aware that something is wrong.
2. There should be good reason to expect treatment begun at that early stage to produce a better outcome than treatment begun after symptoms have appeared.
3. The procedure should be targeted at those most likely to benefit from it.

The AMA Council on Scientific Affairs[11] has noted that while scientific organizations may differ somewhat on the recommended content and frequency of periodic examinations, most groups agree that they are valuable, especially when combined with fitness evaluation and counseling about nutrition, exercise, accident prevention, and other aspects of a healthy lifestyle.

History and Physical Examination

A thorough health evaluation consists of four phases: (1) the medical history, (2) the physical examination, (3) the clinical or laboratory tests, and (4) the report to the patient. It is likely to take 30 to 90 minutes and to cost from $60 to $125 for the doctor's time plus the cost of any clinical or laboratory tests. Internal medicine specialists tend to charge more than family practitioners.

The history should involve more than 100 detailed questions about past medical problems, current symptoms, social and family history, and health habits. It is obtained most efficiently with a questionnaire that is filled out by the patient (or parent) or administered by a member of the physician's staff. Before the physician sees the patient, an assistant also measures height, weight, temperature, pulse rate, respiratory rate, blood pressure, and, sometimes, visual acuity. The physician then reviews the questionnaire and asks further questions.

The physical examination usually includes the following:

General appearance: Abnormal nutritional states, skin disorders, and physical deformities are noted.

Eyes: Appearance, movement, pupillary reflexes, and visual fields are checked. Ophthalmoscope is used to examine insides of eyes. Tonometer may be used to measure internal eye pressure.

Ears: Otoscope is used to inspect eardrums and external canals. Hearing is tested with audiometer or wristwatch.

Nose: Inside is inspected for polyps or deviated septum.

Oral cavity and pharynx: Dental caries, tumors, and other indications of disease are noted.

Neck: Palpation is used to detect enlargement of lymph nodes or thyroid gland. Veins are inspected for distention. Stethoscope may be used to listen for arterial murmurs.

Lungs: Chest is percussed. Stethoscope is used to hear breath sounds.

Heart: Rate and rhythm are noted. Heart is palpated for abnormal rhythms and percussed to determine size. Stethoscope is used to check heart sounds.

Breasts: Inspection and palpation are done to detect tumors.

Lymph nodes: Armpits and groin are palpated.

Back: Percussion with fist may be used to detect kidney tenderness.

Abdomen: Deep palpation is used to detect tumors or enlarged liver or spleen. Stethoscope is used to hear bowel sounds and arterial murmurs.

Sex organs, male: Inspection, palpation, and a check for hernias are performed.

Sex organs, female: External genitalia are inspected. Cervix is visualized with vaginal speculum. Uterus and ovaries are palpated by means of bimanual examination.

Rectum and anus: Rectum and prostate are palpated with gloved finger. Anal area is inspected for hemorrhoids. Sigmoidoscopic examination may be performed.

Legs: Varicose veins are noted.

Feet: Pedal pulses are palpated.

Bones and joints: Swelling or deformities are noted.

Reflexes: Knee jerk, ankle jerk, and other reflexes are noted.

Laboratory Tests and Procedures

A urinalysis and complete blood count are normally ordered as part of a routine physical evaluation. Whether other tests are ordered varies according to the age of the patient, the style of the physician, the patient's history, and the physical findings. A list of commonly performed laboratory tests and procedures follows. Any but the thyroid and stress tests might be included as part of a general evaluation.

Urinalysis: The urine is tested for the presence of sugar, protein, cells, crystals, and other sediment. The presence of sugar might indicate diabetes. White blood cells might indicate infection. Red blood cells might indicate tumor or inflammation within the urinary system. Protein or other sediment may indicate kidney disease.

Complete blood count: Hemoglobin is measured and red blood cells are examined to determine the presence of anemia. White blood cells are counted and examined to help diagnose various infections or leukemia.

Blood sugar (glucose): A variety of tests may be used to diagnose diabetes or hypoglycemia.

Blood lipids (including cholesterol and triglycerides): Elevation may indicate a tendency toward heart disease.

Rapid plasma reagin (RPR): A serological test for syphilis.

Blood chemistry: Various tests are available to measure kidney function, liver function, certain enzyme activities, and many abnormal metabolic states. T_3, T_4, and T_7 are blood tests of thyroid function. Computerized equipment can perform many tests at one time, often at less cost to the patient than a few tests done singly. One common test panel, a chemistry profile, typically has 24 components.

Tine test: A skin test for tuberculosis.

Feces: Feces may be examined for occult blood or indications of parasites. Because their presence can be intermittent, specimens are usually collected for 3 consecutive days.

Papanicolaou (PAP) test: This is primarily a screening test for cervical cancer, but it may also indicate the presence of infection and the status of certain hormones.

Electrocardiogram (ECG): By analyzing electrical patterns of the heart, abnormal rhythms and other forms of heart disease can be diagnosed. Stress tests (ECGs performed during exercise) are discussed in Chapter 16.

Prostate-specific antigen (PSA): A screening test for prostate cancer.

Although screening tests provide considerable information at relatively low cost, they are not hazard-free. Minimal departures from "normal" can occur in health individuals, and "false positive" reports can result from errors in the testing or reporting procedures. The *Harvard Medical School Health Letter* has observed:

> The needless worry generated by an abnormal result, as well as the more expensive and sometimes risky diagnostic tests that are apt to follow, raises legitimate doubt about ordering too many tests on healthy people. Nobody has yet devised a solution to the problem of having too much information.[12]

Frequency of Examinations

Individual consumers must decide whether to invest in complete evaluations and how often to do so. For young adults who are symptom-free, once every 5 years is a reasonable frequency. Complete examinations might be practical every 3 to 5 years after age 40, every 2 to 3 years after age 50, and annually after age 60. However, individuals who feel more comfortable having annual checkups are certainly free to obtain them.

Those who consult their physician several times a year for acute or chronic problems can achieve the equivalent of periodic complete examinations if their physician examines a few extra parts of the body during each visit. This system can be both effective and economical.

At specific ages, certain medical procedures have special significance because they may prevent problems or detect potentially serious problems that are treatable in their early stages. In 1989, the U.S. Preventive Services Task Force[13] published its assessment in 169 interventions for 60 potentially preventable diseases and conditions. Its 20-member panel was helped by more than 300 experts from the United States, Canada, and Great Britain. Funded by the U.S. Public Health Service and the Kellogg Foundation, the panel was created in 1984 to determine what types of periodic physical examinations, laboratory tests, immunizations, counseling and other measures are scientifically-based and cost-effective.

The panel recommended that annual physicals that are similar for all patients be replaced by interventions based on age, gender and other risk factors pertinent to the individual patient. It also thought that doctors should spend more time counseling patients about healthy living and less time doing routine screening tests. The counseling recommendations are related to the leading causes of death and disability in each age group. The recommendations for cancer screening are somewhat less vigorous than those of the American Cancer Society.

Table 6-1 presents a simplified version of the panel's advice. Consumers who wish additional detail should examine the task force report.

Cancer Screening Tests

Since breast cancer occurs in one out of nine women, it is extremely important for women to examine their own breasts. Literature illustrating the procedure can be obtained from a physician or an office of the American Cancer Society, but it is best to review the technique under direct supervision of a physician. Monthly frequency is important to ensure familiarity with one's breasts so that changes can be noticed—and also for early detection of tumors. Women who menstruate should examine their breasts two or three days following a period when the breasts are least likely to be swollen or tender. Those who no longer menstruate should pick a regular day, such as the first day of the month, for the examination.

Mammography uses x-rays to examine the female breast for cancer. Demonstration projects indicate that one third of breast cancers occur in women between ages 35 and 49 and have found that most of these cancers can be detected by mam-

Table 6–1

Periodic Health Examinations

Birth through 18 months: Five visits required for immunizations

Screening	Parent counseling	Preventive procedures
Height and weight Hemoglobin & hematocrit once during infancy Hearing test for high-risk groups	Breastfeeding Nutrient intake, especially iron-rich foods Injury prevention* Baby bottle tooth decay Effects of passive smoking	First week: ophthalmic antibiotics, T_4/TSH, phenylalanine Vaccination against diphtheria, tetanus, pertussis, polio, hemophilus influenza type b Fluoride supplements for children in nonfluoridated areas (see Chapter 8)

Ages 2 through 6: one visit required for immunizations; others at doctor's discretion

Screening	Parent counseling	Preventive procedures
Height and weight Blood pressure Eye exam at age 3-4 Urinalysis for bacteria Hearing and tuberculin test for high-risk groups	Dietary counseling Selection of exercise program Toothbrushing and dental visits Injury prevention* Effects of passive smoking Skin protection from sunlight	Vaccination against diphtheria, tetanus, pertussis, polio Fluoride supplements for children in nonfluoridated areas (see Chapter 8)

Ages 7 through 12: one visit required for immunizations: others at doctor's discretion

Screening	Patient and parent counseling	Preventive procedures
Height and weight Blood pressure Tuberculin test for high-risk groups	Dietary counseling Selection of exercise program Regular toothbrushing and dental visits Injury prevention* Skin protection from sunlight	Vaccination against diphtheria, tetanus, pertussis, polio Fluoride supplements for children in nonfluoridated areas (see Chapter 8)

Continued.

TABLE 6–1

PERIODIC HEALTH EXAMINATIONS—*cont'd*

Ages 13 through 18: one visit required for immunizations; others at doctor's discretion

Screening	Counseling	Preventive procedures
Dietary intake Physical activity Tobacco/alcohol/drug use Sexual practices Height and weight Blood pressure For high-risk groups: Pap smear and test for rubella antibodies, sexually transmitted diseases, tuberculosis, and hearing impairment	Dietary counseling Selection of exercise program Tobacco/alcohol/drug use Sexual behavior: partner selection, disease prevention, and birth control Regular toothbrushing, flossing, and dental visits Injury prevention* Skin protection from sunlight	Tetanus-diphtheria booster Fluoride supplements for children in nonfluoridated areas (see Chapter 8)

Ages 19 through 39: visit every 1 to 3 years

Screening	Counseling	Preventive procedures
Dietary intake Physical activity Tobacco/alcohol/drug use Sexual practices Height and weight Blood pressure Pap smear every 1-3 years Blood cholesterol screening For high-risk groups: ECG, mammography, colonoscopy, fasting blood sugar, and tests for bacteria in urine, sexually transmitted diseases, tuberculosis, and hearing impairment	Dietary counseling Selection of exercise program Tobacco/alcohol/drug use Sexual behavior: partner selection, disease prevention, and birth control Regual toothbrushing, flossing, and dental visits Injury prevention* Skin protection from sunlight	Tetanus-diphtheria booster every 10 years For high-risk groups: Hepatitis B vaccine

mogram. Recent improvements in mammography have resulted in much lower radiation doses and better detection ability. The American Cancer Society recommends (1) a baseline mammogram between the ages of 35 and 40, (2) mammograms every year or 2 from ages 40 through 49, and (3) annual mammograms from age 50 on. The AMA Council on Scientific Affairs has published similar advice.[14] The Preventive Services Task Force stated that it may be prudent to begin screening at age 35 for women whose mother or sister developed breast cancer prior to menopause. For others, however, it advises mammography every 1 to 2 years beginning at age 50 and concluding at about age 75 unless an abnormality has been detected.

Testicular cancer, while much less common than breast cancer, is still the most common cancer in males between the ages of 15 and 34. Although it is easy to detect and one of the most curable cancers when discovered early, 50% of testicular cancers are diagnosed after the cancer has spread beyond the testicles. Testicular self-examination is a 3-minute, monthly self-examination best done after a bath or shower when the scrotal skin is most relaxed. Each testicle should be rolled gently between the thumb and fingers of both hands to look for hard lumps.

The American Cancer Society recommends an

Table 6–1

Periodic Health Examinations

Ages 40 through 64: visit every 1 to 3 years

Screening	Counseling	Preventive procedures
Dietary intake Physical activity Tobacco/alcohol/drug use Sexual practices Height and weight Blood pressure Blood cholesterol screening Pap smear every 1-3 years Mammagram every 1-2 years beginning at age 50 For high-risk groups: ECG, fasting blood sugar, and tests for bacteria in urine, sexually transmitted diseases, tuberculosis, hearing impairment, bone mineral density, and fecal occult blood/sigmoidoscopy	Dietary counseling Selection of exercise program Tobacco/alcohol/drug use Sexual behavior: partner selection, disease prevention, and birth control Regular toothbrushing, flossing, and dental visits Injury prevention* Skin protection from sunlight For high-risk groups: discussion of estrogen replacement therapy, aspirin therapy	Tetanus-diphtheria booster every 10 years For high-risk groups: Hepatitis B vaccine

Ages 65 and over: visit evey year

Screening	Counseling	Preventive procedures
Symptoms of coronary artery disease Dietary intake Physical activity Tobacco/alcohol/drug use Functional status at home Height and weight Blood pressure Visual acuity Dipstick urinalysis Mammogram every 1-2 years Breast examination annually Blood cholesterol screening Thyroid tests for women For high-risk groups: ECG, fasting blood sugar, Pap smear, and tests for tuberculosis, and fecal occult blood/sigmoidoscopy/colonoscopy	Dietary counseling Selection of exercise program Tobacco/alcohol/drug use Sexual behavior: partner selection, disease prevention, and birth control Regual toothbrushing, flossing, and dental visits Injury prevention* Skin protection from sunlight Glaucoma testing For high-risk groups: discussion of estrogen replacement therapy, aspirin therapy	Tetanus-diphtheria booster every 10 years Influenza vaccine every year Pneumococcal vaccine For high-risk groups: Hepatitis B vaccine

Adapted from the report of the U.S. Preventive Services Task force, 1989[13]
*Injury prevention measures include age-appropriate advice about preventing falls, fires, and burns, childhood poisoning, bicycling and motor vehicle injuries, drowing, gunshot injuries, and violent behavior.

Table 6–2

Summary of American Cancer Society Recommendations for the Early Detection of Cancer in Asymptomatic People

	Population		
Test or procedure	**Sex**	**Age**	**Frequency**
Sigmoidoscopy	M & F	50 and over	Every 3 to 5 years based on advice of physician
Stool Guaiac Slide Test	M & F	Over 50	Every year
Digital Rectal Examination	M & F	Over 40	Every year
Pap Test	F	18* (or when sexual activity begins)	Every 1 to 3 years based on advice of physician
Pelvic Examination	F	18-40	Every 1-3 years with Pap test
		Over 40	Every year
Endometrial Tissue Sample	F	At menopause, Women at high risk†	At menopause
Breast Self-examination	F	20 and older	Every month
Breast Clinical Examination	F	20-40	Every 3 years
		Over 40	Every year
Mammography‡	F	40-49	Every 1-2 years
		50 & over	Every year
Health Counseling and Cancer Checkup§	M & F	Over 20	Every 3 years
	M & F	Over 40	Every year

*All women who are or who have been sexually active, or have reached age 18, should have an annual Pap test and pelvic examination. After a woman has had three or more consecutive satisfactory normal annual examinations, the Pap test may be performed less frequently at the discretion of her physician.
†History of infertility, obesity, failure to ovulate, abnormal uterine bleeding, or estrogen therapy.
‡Screening mammography should begin by age 40.
§To include examination for cancers of the thyroid, testicles, prostate, ovaries, lymph nodes, oral region, and skin.
American Cancer Society, 1992[15]

annual pelvic examination and Pap test for all women who are sexually active or have reached age 18. Once three or more consecutive tests are normal, the frequency may be decreased at the discretion of the physician. Table 6-2 summarizes the society's[15] overall recommendations for cancer screening.

A recent study has found that, for detecting prostate cancer in its early stages, a prostate-specific antigen (PSA) test plus a digital rectal examination is more effective than a rectal examination alone.[16] If either test is suspicious, an ultrasound examination of the prostate will be advised. It has not been proven that early detection of prostate cancer actually saves lives. However, the study's authors are optimistic that the PSA test will eventually be proven cost-effective for screening men after age 50. The National Cancer Institute has planned a long-term study to resolve this matter.

Immunizations

Immunizations should be part of routine health care obtained through one's personal physician (or in some instances, through one's local health department). Long-lasting protection is available against measles, mumps, German measles (rubella), poliomyelitis, tetanus (lockjaw), whooping cough (pertussis), and diphtheria. Immunization against all of these is recommended by the American Academy of Pediatrics and the Immunization Practices Advisory Committee of the U.S. Public Health Service. The academy estimates that an average of $10 is saved in later health care costs for every dollar spent on immunization.

All states now require proof of immunization or other evidence of immunity against some of the above diseases for admission to school. However, the requirements vary from state to state, and exemptions may be granted for medical, moral, or religious reasons. In 1985 the FDA approved a vaccine that protects against *Haemophilus influenza* type b, a bacterium that can cause meningitis with death or neurologic damage to young children. Administration of this vaccine is recommended in a single dose at age 2.

In recent years, various individuals and groups that promote scientific practices have claimed that pertussis vaccine is prone to cause seizures and other neurologic complications. However, three studies totaling about 230,000 children and 713,000 immunizations have found no causal relationship between pertussis vaccine and any type of permanent neurologic illness.[17]

Immunization is also important for adults. Those unprotected against any of the above diseases (except whooping cough) should consult their physicians. Tetanus boosters should be administered every 10 years. Flu shots (which give only seasonal protection) and immunization against pneumococcal pneumonia are recommended for high-risk patients, elderly individuals, and certain institutional populations. Protection against hepatitis B is appropriate for health care workers in contact with blood products, travelers going to endemic areas, and individuals whose sexual behavior places them at high risk for acquiring the infection. Smallpox is now considered eradicated worldwide, so that vaccination is no longer recommended.

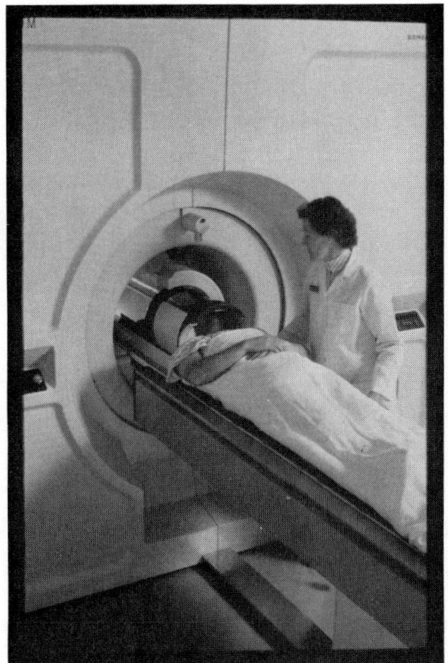

FIGURE 6-1. CAT Scan.
(From: The Image Bank-Jay Freis)

Medical Imaging

X-ray films can yield valuable diagnostic information. Because ionizing radiation is potentially dangerous, however, the possible benefits should be weighed against the risk involved in its use. In most cases, the physician is in a better position to do this than is the patient, but the following points may help one avoid unnecessary radiation:

1. If the physician suggests x-ray films, the patient should understand why they are needed. One should not be afraid to ask questions.
2. One should ask whether a lead-lined shield is available to protect the reproductive organs.
3. When changing physicians, the patient should request that recent x-ray reports be sent to the new physician.
4. Annual chest x-ray films are not considered appropriate for routine screening purposes. (They still may be appropriate for certain high-risk groups such as heavy smokers.)
5. The developing fetus is especially sensitive to radiation. X-ray films of the abdominal and pelvic regions of pregnant women should be postponed if possible, especially during the first 3 months of pregnancy. Some physicians prefer to avoid pelvic films during the last half of the menstrual cycle lest the woman be pregnant.

Advances in diagnostic scanning have enabled physicians to obtain a great deal of precise, detailed information about internal body structures. The procedures described below do not invade the body and pose no risk, or little risk compared to procedures (such as arteriography) that invade the body. The procedures require expensive equipment and can be costly.

Computerized axial tomography uses an x-ray source focused on specific planes of the body and rotated to obtain pictures from multiple angles. The data are fed into a computer and processed to create a cross-sectional depiction of density that resembles a photograph. The procedure is commonly referred to as a *CT scan* or *CAT scan*. Used selectively, it is invaluable and has replaced many invasive diagnostic procedures that were dangerous and often less reliable.

Conventional x-ray procedures and CT scans use a machine to generate and project x-rays through the body to produce a visual image. In *radionuclide imaging,* this set-up is reversed: radioactive chemicals are introduced into the body and taken up by various body structures. These structures then emit gamma rays that produce an image on a special camera outside the body. Radionuclide imaging can detect tumors, infections, circulatory blockage, and other types of problems. The parts of the body commonly scanned are the bones, brain, heart, thyroid gland, gallbladder, liver, kidneys, and lungs. The radioactive substances usually lose most of their radioactivity or are excreted from the body within hours or days.

Single photon emission computerized tomography (SPECT) is a specialized form of nuclear scanning that produced images similar to those of a CT scanner.

Positron emission tomography (PET) combines the use of radioactive substances and computers to produce vivid color-coded pictures. PET scans are useful for studying diseases of the heart and brain. However, they are very expensive and are used primarily in research settings.

Magnetic resonance imaging (MRI)—sometimes called *nuclear magnetic resonance (NMR)*—uses radio waves, a strong magnetic field, and a computer to produce cross-sectional images of the body. In some cases the picture can differentiate between adjacent soft tissues that might look the same on an x-ray film. To produce the NMR picture, the patient is placed inside a large magnetic coil. When the magnetic field is turned on, it causes hydrogen nuclei within the body to line up in one direction. Then the radio waves flip these particles in another direction. When the radio waves are turned off, the particles flip back again, releasing an electromagnetic signal that the computer translates into an image. The technique involves no radiation but it cannot be used with patients who have a pacemaker, metallic artificial joint, or other metallic implant.

Ultrasonography is done with a device that transmits sound waves through body tissues, records the echoes as the sounds encounter structures within the body, and transforms the recordings into a photographic image. No radiation is involved. Recent developments have greatly increased the variety and usefulness of diagnostic ultrasound procedures.[18] Ultrasound therapy is discussed in Chapter 23.

Magnetic source imaging (also called *biomagnetic imaging*) uses a device that coverts magnetic fields into electrical signals that are amplified and displayed on a computer screen for interpretation. It is used mainly for pinpointing the location of abnormal brain function in epileptics and for diagnosing other disorders of the brain.

Surgical Care

Contemporary surgery in the United States is very good, probably the best in the world. Improvements in preoperative preparation, anesthesia, surgical techniques, and postoperative supervision have greatly reduced the discomfort and dangers that were a part of most operations in the past. But surgery should never be taken lightly. Any operation carries some risk, both from the surgical procedure and from the anesthetic. To be justified, surgery must be appropriate and the benefits must exceed the hazards.

Unnecessary Surgery

Few issues called to the attention of consumers in the United States have aroused the heat that surrounds the question of unnecessary surgery. During the early 1970s it was noticed that the number of operations performed was rising faster than the growth in population. Critics have charged that 10% to 20% of the operations performed annually in the United States are unnecessary. Criticism has been directed primarily against elective (nonemergency) surgery, with hysterectomy, tonsillectomy, dilation and curettage (D & C), cesarean section, and back, knee, and prostate operations among the leading suspects. Dr. Sidney Wolfe called unnecessary operations "the greatest single curse in medicine."

Studies by John E. Wennberg, M.D.,[19] professor of epidemiology at Dartmouth Medical School, have shown that surgical rates are closely related to the density of surgeons and the number of beds in many communities. Dr. Wennberg has also noted that hospital admission rates for nonsurgical conditions can vary just as widely. He believes that considerable research is needed to determine what practice patterns may be optimal and that questionable local trends tend to decrease when studies are done.

One strategy to reduce the amount of unnecessary surgery has been to encourage or require that patients covered by insurance programs consult a second surgeon when elective surgery is recommended. Under these plans, the second surgeon is not permitted to do the operation and thus has no possible financial incentive for agreeing that surgery is needed. Dr. Eugene McCarthy, professor of public health at Cornell University Medical Center, has studied the effects of second opinion programs on the rates of surgery and concluded that many operations were done unnecessarily. Defenders of surgery in the United States have countered by saying that the mere fact that a consultant disagrees does not guarantee that an operation is unnecessary. Many other studies have been done to determine the effects of second-opinion programs on the quality of care and on overall health care costs.[20]

Other strategies to reduce surplus surgery involve the development and publication of criteria that can be used to measure the appropriateness of surgery. The criteria can then be used for preoperative screening (a preventive measure) or for postoperative review, either of which can be performed by hospital committees or outside agencies. As managed care and precertification programs have increased, the use of second opinion programs has dropped sharply.[21]

Physician responsibility. Each hospital accredited by the Joint Commission on Accreditation of Healthcare Organizations is required to maintain several active committees of physicians to assess the quality of care at the hospital. A utilization review committee determines the appropriateness of hospital admissions and lengths of hospital stay, a tissue committee reviews operative work, and audit committees examine for defective as well as unnecessary care. A physician whose work is judged by his or her colleagues to be substandard can have privileges curtailed or terminated. Some nonaccredited hospitals also have such committees; others do not.

Many insurance plans offer second opinions to their subscribers. The Blue Cross and Blue Shield Association, for example, has established a National Second Opinion Consultation Panel with more than 26,000 board-certified surgeons available to provide second or consulting opinions to many planholders. Association officials believe that direct savings will be increased by a "sentinel effect," in which the likelihood of nonconforming second opinions may make the original physicians' recommendations more conservative.

Patient responsibility. Although the ultimate responsibility for preventing unnecessary surgery lies with medical experts, consumers can take a number of steps to protect themselves.

If one needs to consult a surgeon, preference should be given to one who is board certified and on the staff of an accredited hospital. If surgery is recommended, a reasonable explanation of what it entails and why it is recommended should be sought. One should ask if a medical alternative is available and should consider getting a second opinion from another surgeon. Alper[7] suggests that if one's primary physician has been selected with care, the physician's opinion may be as valuable as that of a second surgeon, or even more valuable:

> A capable personal physician who is familiar with the surgeon's work will not let his patients be stampeded into an unnecessary operation. He will ask the surgeon to justify the procedure to him as well as to you.

The Department of Health and Human Services maintains a toll-free number (800-638-6833) to provide Medicare patients with the names of local doctors who can be consulted for second opinions. The Health Benefits Research Center, which Dr. McCarthy directs, maintains a toll-free number (800-522-0036) for patients of all ages. Medicare and some insurance companies provide 80% reimbursement for second opinions.

Ambulatory Surgery

Hundreds of different operations can be done in an outpatient setting. These include sterilization procedures, some hernia repairs, D & C, oral surgery, breast biopsy, tonsillectomy, cataract removal, and various forms of plastic and orthopedic surgery. Experts estimate that at least 20% of the nation's surgery could be done safely—at reduced cost—outside of a hospital. As noted by *New York Times* personal health reporter Jane Brody: "When appropriate, 1-day surgery in a hospital outpatient facility, freestanding clinic, or doctor's office, can save time and money, prevent family disruptions, and greatly reduce the psychological and physical trauma of having an operation."

To be suitable for outpatient surgery, one must be in good general health and have people available to provide any necessary postoperative care at home.

Surgery in the News

The following discussion describes recent developments relating to various operations. Laser surgery is a rapidly developing technology that has great potential. Laparoscopic cholecystectomy is a new procedure that appears better than cutting open the abdomen for gallbladder removal. Circumcision is discussed because its benefits have not been firmly established. Coronary bypass surgery (Chapter 16), cosmetic surgery (Chapter 21), therapeutic abortions (Chapter 22), and refractive keratotomy (Chapter 23) are discussed elsewhere.

Laser is an acronym for "*l*ight *a*mplification by *s*timulated *e*mission of *r*adiation." The laser beam is an intense and narrow beam of light that has one wavelength. Laser beams can be focused to cut, coagulate, or vaporize small areas of tissue with minimal bleeding or disturbance to neighboring tissues. In some cases, "laser scalpel" can slice as thin as the width of a cell without damaging surrounding tissues. Medical laser devices include a source of electricity, mirrors to direct the beam, a crystal or gas that is stimulated to emit the light, and tubing to deliver the energy. Lasers are classified according to their light source. The carbon dioxide laser is effective for cutting tissue. The argon laser is especially useful for sealing off blood vessels and destroying cancerous tumors; it heats tissues and acts somewhat like a welder. The YAG laser can be directed through fiberoptic instruments to reach less accessible places in the body. The excimer laser delivers energy in the form of rapid pulses, which allows greater control over the depth of tissue being cut and does not heat healthy tissue near the target area.

Lasers are commonly used to treat problems of the retina of the eye (bleeding, glaucoma, and retinal tears),[22] blockages in coronary arteries, skin disorders (moles, freckles, and various birthmarks),[23] gynecological disorders (genital warts, blocked fallopian tubes, endometriosis), tumors and bleeding within the digestive tract, and many other diseases and conditions. Many laser procedures can be conducted on an outpatient basis. Because of the danger of burns and destruction of normal tissues near the target, it is important that laser surgery be done by a competent specialist. These guidelines should be helpful to consumers who are considering laser surgery:

1. Select a surgeon with care; ask your family physician for a recommendation.
2. Ask about surgeon's qualifications, experience, and success rate with the condition to be treated.
3. If applicable, ask your family physician and the laser surgeon about the risks and benefits of conventional versus laser surgery.
4. If uncertain about proposed laser treatment, seek a second opinion.
5. Additional information about treatment procedures, risks, and benefits, and recommendations for laser surgeons can be obtained from the American Society for Laser Medicine and Surgery, 2404 Stewart Sq., Wausau, WI 54401.

Abdominal (open) cholecystectomy typically costs $6000 to $10,000 and requires a 5 to 7 day hospital stay and about a month to recover. Laparoscopic laser cholecystectomy (popularly called "keyhole laser surgery"), is faster and less invasive. A typical hospital stay is 36 hours or less, with return to full activities within a week. During the procedure, the instruments are inserted through four small cuts in the umbilicus and abdominal wall and manipulated while the operators observe their progress through a video monitor. An AMA Diagnostic and Therapeutic Technology Assessment has concluded that laparoscopic laser cholecystectomy is an appropriate treatment for uncomplicated gallstones.[24] Although its use was first reported in 1989, the laparoscopic procedure has become more common than the open procedure.

Circumcision has been practiced for religious reasons since ancient times and for health reasons for more than a century. In the United States, most newborn males are still circumcised, although in recent years the rate appears to be falling. Circumcision may decrease the incidence of cancer of the penis, a rare condition that occurs almost exclusively in uncircumcised men. Poor hygiene and certain sexually transmitted diseases also correlate with the incidence of cancer of the penis. The exact incidence of postoperative complications of circumcision (local infection and bleeding) is unknown but appears to be in the range of 0.2% to 0.6%. During the 1970s an American Academy of Pediatrics task force concluded that "there are no valid medical indications for circumcision in the neonatal period."[25] In 1989, after new studies suggested that uncircumcised males might be more prone to urinary tract infections, the American Academy of Pediatrics concluded that more research is needed, that there is no clear-cut medical answer on circumcision, and that the decision is best made by parents in consultation with their physician. In 1992, another study was published showing a higher incidence of urinary tract infection among uncircumcised young male adults attending a sexually transmitted disease clinic.[26]

Quality of Medical Care

The medical care system in the United States unquestionably provides the best care in the world. The physicians are well trained, and most of them practice in an ethical manner. Despite these credentials, however, there is concern about the quality, distribution, and cost of health services. Among the problem areas are incompetence, negligence, financial abuses, overutilization, impersonal care, and iatrogenic illness.

Incompetence

Incompetence can be the result of drug addiction, alcoholism, mental illness, senility, or failure to keep abreast of new medical developments. The AMA has developed a model "impaired physician" law, which has been adopted in some form by most states. The physician is first asked to seek help voluntarily. Next, hospital staffs are encouraged to find ways to care for their errant colleague. Failing that, county medical societies must step in. If a physician is not attached to a hospital or medical society, the state licensing board must act. State medical societies in every state operate programs to rehabilitate impaired physicians. For example, in Georgia a committee of recovered alcoholic or drug-addicted physicians reaches out to problem physicians to offer a treatment plan.

To keep abreast of medical developments, physicians talk with colleagues, read medical journals, attend meetings, and participate in other types of educational programs. Some authorities believe that continuing education should be formal and mandatory. Many states require a minimum number of hours per year for license renewal.

According to Alper,[8] promiscuous use of injections may be a sign of incompetence. Some injections should not be given, and others should be used sparingly. For example, antibiotics can usually be given by mouth, male hormones are unlikely to cure impotence, vitamin shots are inappropriate therapy for fatigue, and cortisone injections into joints can cause long-term harm if given too often.

The number of unfit and unethical physicians is unknown. A small number of physicians are involved with the use of diagnostic and therapeutic methods not recognized by the scientific community. This subject is covered in Chapter 9.

The Essence of a Doctor

Reared in poverty, Freddie Brant stopped school after the fifth grade. During World War II he was in the Army for four years. In 1949, along with a fellow paratrooper, he was sentenced to seven years in the penitentiary for bank robbery. Working in the prison hospital, he began his "medical education." Finally released, he worked for four years as a laboratory and x-ray technician for Dr. Reid L. Brown of Chattanooga, Tennessee. There he picked up not only more medical lore but also the diplomas of his employer.

Posing as Dr. Reid L. Brown, he obtained a license by endorsement and served for three years at a State Hospital in Texas. One day, while stopping at the village of Groveton, Texas, he treated the injured leg of a child. Groveton had long been without a doctor and its people were clamoring for medical care. "Dr. Brown" soon became established as the town physician and as a community leader. He might still be carrying on his thriving practice in Groveton, Texas, had he not run afoul of a computer. By coincidence he ordered drugs from a pharmaceutical firm used by the real Dr. Reid Brown. Its computer gagged when it discovered orders on the same day from two physicians with identical names. Following an investigation, Freddie Brant was charged with forgery and with false testimony.

Brant's exposure caused great consternation in Groveton, but its citizens rallied around him. He was not convicted. A Chicago newspaper said that justice was thwarted because of a "lava flow of testimonials to the effect that Freddie Brant was a prince of a medical man, license or no license." The paper said that the people of Groveton should have known that Reid Brown was not a doctor because he did too many things wrong. He made house calls for five dollars and charged only three dollars for an office visit. He approved of Medicare and would drive for miles to visit a patient, often without fee if the patient was poor. Besides, his handwriting was legible.

What were the reasons for Freddie Brant's success as an impersonator? The main ones were his readiness to refer any potentially complicated case to doctors in nearby towns, a personality that inspired confidence, and a willingness to take time to listen to his patients.

Robert C. Derbyshire, M.D.[27]

Malpractice

Every physician makes mistakes. Those that are serious enough to cause damage may lead to malpractice suits. Diagnostic error is the leading cause of suits. Foreign objects (such as a sponge) left in patients during surgery are another common cause. Malpractice allegations also arise from burns resulting from the application of heat, chemicals, or x-rays. Among the suits that are settled, those for misdiagnosis of fractures and dislocations are the most common.

Contrary to popular belief, the physicians who are sued the most are not necessarily those who are incompetent. Top-notch specialists, who attract a high percentage of complicated cases, inevitably have many patients with unfavorable treatment outcomes. Such patients are more likely to file suit.

Fear of malpractice suits has caused most physicians to practice "defensive medicine." This term refers to the ordering of tests that are not really necessary for medical purposes but that will protect the doctor from later being accused of negligently overlooking something. Following minor accidents, for example, x-ray films often are ordered for "legal reasons."

Financial Abuse

Many insurance companies base their coverage on the physician's "usual and customary fee." Some physicians charge insured patients more than uninsured ones but represent to the insurance companies that the higher fee is the usual one, when in fact it is not. While the motivation of this may or may not be admirable, the practice is illegal.

Another illegal procedure is the "unbundling" of claims, in which a practitioner bills separately for procedures that normally are covered by a single fee. An example would be a podiatrist who operates on three toes and submits claims for three separate operations.

Impersonal Care

Individuals have a right to receive much more from physicians than mere attention to scientific therapy. Intelligent consumers want compassion and concern. They also want the right to participate in the treatment by knowing what is wrong and how it should be handled.

It appears, however, that some physicians are more concerned with the number of patients they see than the quality of their interaction with patients. Such physicians may consider medical practice to be an episodic, impersonal affair. They spend brief amounts of time with patients, attending to their immediate complaints in rapid, mechanical fashion without allowing time for questions or for complaints about other ailments. Rarely do they take the time to form a relationship and inquire about the patient's life-style in order to suggest improvements of a preventive nature. Many people contribute to this situation by seeking medical care only when they are ill.

Some physicians are habitually late in keeping scheduled appointments. These doctors may attempt to justify their lateness by stating that urgent cases and emergencies make their schedule unpredictable and that some patients take longer than expected. However, doctors who wish to be punctual can leave room in their daily schedules for patients who need extra time or must be seen on short notice.

If a doctor falls significantly behind schedule, patients in the waiting room should be apprised of this fact so they can decide whether to wait, leave and return later, or reschedule for another day.

A few years ago the Shawnee Mission (Kansas) Medical Center found a novel way to approach this problem. After surveys showed that their patients' main complaint was wasting time in the waiting room, the doctors began lending beepers to those who wished to use nearby shopping facilities and be paged when the office was ready for them.[28]

Iatrogenic Illness

The word *iatrogenic* is derived from the Greek words *iatros* (physician) and *genesis* (production). It is broadly applied to mean any adverse condition produced in a patient as the result of diagnostic procedures or treatment. Dr. Ralph Greene,[29] clinical professor of pathology at Northwestern University Medical School, notes that the incidence of iatrogenic illness is growing despite and because of the growth of medical knowledge, technological advances, and the use of new drugs to treat previously incurable illnesses. His book *Medical Overkill* includes the following points:

1. If people have enough tests, abnormal results that occur by chance may led to extensive, expensive, and occasionally dangerous follow-up testing.
2. Doctors sometimes order tests because they fear legal liability if they do not.

3. All effective forms of treatment have the potential for troublesome side effects.
4. New treatments may have unforeseeable adverse long-term consequences.
5. Close to half of our hospital beds are occupied by patients who could be treated just as well or better at home. Of the rest, half have "self-inflicted," therefore preventable, illness.
6. Hospital-acquired infections are a serious enough problem that hospitalization should be avoided whenever possible.
7. Hospitalized patients should do as much as possible to avoid becoming the victim of a careless error. They should, for example, know the names and purposes of prescribed medications and know their blood type so they can check the labeling of blood being transfused.

Some degree of iatrogenesis is obviously inevitable. One's best protection, Dr. Greene concludes, is to become well informed, to choose the most competent physician available, and to speak up when doubts arise.

Discipline of Physicians

Four types of agencies are involved in the surveillance and discipline of physicians: medical societies, hospitals, state licensing boards, and agencies that administer or oversee government funded insurance programs.

Medical societies only have the ability to reprimand or expel members. Such action may be embarrassing or lower a physician in the eyes of colleagues, but it does not curtail the right to practice medicine.

Hospital officials have the ability to reduce, suspend, or revoke a physician's treatment privileges at their particular hospital. This could be devastating to a surgeon in a one-hospital community. But practitioners who work primarily in private offices or who have privileges at another hospital are affected less. Physicians who belong to neither a medical society nor a hospital staff are unaffected by the disciplinary efforts of these organizations.

Agencies that administer Medicare and Medicaid have the ability to terminate a practitioner's participation in these programs in cases of fraud or overutilization. Such an action will have considerable impact on physicians accustomed to seeing many patients under these programs.

State licensing boards have the authority to revoke or suspend a practitioner's license. This is a powerful action, but several factors can hamper the effectiveness of state boards. A state board cannot take action unless it receives a complaint, and patients and professional colleagues often are afraid that making a complaint might involve them in an unpleasant confrontation or even a lawsuit. Equally important, many state boards have insufficient staff and funds to do their job properly.

Until recently, medical licensing laws have been rather weak. During the 1960s most revocations resulted from narcotics offenses and other felonies. Incompetence was not even a ground for action in most states. Today it is grounds for revocation in most states, but not all. Revocation by one state does not necessarily stop a physician from practicing in another. In many states disciplinary action in another state is not a reason for revocation. Moreover, because the physician's livelihood is at stake, the courts are inclined to offer considerable protection. The situation noted years ago by Derbyshire[30] is still true today:

> The best efforts (of the boards) are often hampered by the capriciousness of the courts which do not hestitate to substitute their judgment for that of the boards. They often issue stay orders in cases in which the boards have revoked the licenses of physicians. Furthermore, these stay orders permit the defendant to continue his depredations during the long delays before his appeal is finally heard.

In response to public and medical society pressure, licensing laws have been tightened in many states during the past several years. Although court interference and underfunding still are problems, actions against physicians by state licensing boards have increased. The Federation of State Medical Boards states that the number of disciplinary actions against medical and osteopathic physicians totalled 1871 in 1984, 2183 in 1985, 2501 in 1986, 2873 in 1987, 2815 in 1988, 2957 in 1989, 3232 in 1990, and 3140 in 1991. The 1991 figure includes 959 license losses or suspensions, 1110 license restrictions, and 735 other prejudicial actions. *Medical Economics* magazine has calculated that the percentage of doctors formally disciplined rose steadily from 0.38% in 1984 to 0.57% in 1990.[31] In addition, state boards engage in many informal actions that significantly affect the behavior of the doctors involved.

The Public Citizen Health Research Group

(HRG)[32] has published the names of 9479 practitioners who were formally disciplined by state or federal agencies. The roster includes 8523 physicians, 896 dentists, chiropractors, and podiatrists, and 60 other practitioners whose degree was not specified. The data, most of which covered the period from 1985 through 1990, were obtained from 40 state medical boards and several federal agencies. Some actions involved late payment of fees and other matters unrelated to the quality patient care, but most were for more serious infractions. In 41% of the cases, the reporting agency did not specify any reason why the actions were taken. HRG believes that many state boards still are underfunded, understaffed, slow-moving, and overly lenient.[33]

The National Practitioner Data Bank, which began operating in September 1990, was mandated by the Health Care Quality Improvement Act of 1989. It is administered by the Bureau of Health Professions within the U.S. Public Health Service's Health Resources and Services Administration. Its purpose is to hinder the movement of "problem practitioners" from state to state. Among other things, this law requires hospital administrators to query the Data Bank when appointing or reappointing medical staff and to report disciplinary actions that negatively affect a doctor's clinical privileges for more than 30 days. Malpractice insurance carriers are required to report all settlements against physicians, dentists, and other health care providers. During its first year of operation, the Data Bank received 18,561 reports, 15% pertaining to adverse actions and 85% pertaining to malpractice actions.[34] It will be several years before the program's public impact can be assessed.

Bioethics

Explosive progress in medical technology has raised troublesome new ethical questions and intensified old ones. Some examples follow.

What is the value of life? Who is to decide when it shall start and when it shall stop? Should life be terminated when pain is great? Or when the cost of prolonging it places a heavy financial burden on the family or on society? To what extent should individuals determine whether their existence should be continued?

The AMA Judicial Council says that it is ethical to stop or withhold life-support treatment to let a terminally ill patient die, but that a physician should not intentionally cause death. The Council also has ruled that when the duty to prolong life conflicts with the duty to relieve suffering, the physician, patient and/or family have discretion to resolve the conflict.[35] Most states have *living will* laws that enable people to specify or limit the treatment they would receive should they become helpless and terminally ill. These subjects are discussed in Chapter 24.

Suppose physicians have provided all possible medical assistance to a patient. Should the patient be kept alive by means of special equipment when it is obvious that recovery is impossible? For how long? Suppose the expense has grown to $100,000 and the family cannot afford it. What happens then? If a hospital has equipment to keep alive only ten comatose patients, what happens when the eleventh and twelfth arrive? Who should be permitted to live? The ten who got there first? The youngest? The healthiest? The richest? Who should make these decisions, and how should they be made?

Should individuals have the right to sell their own body parts? Should a pregnancy be terminated because it is an inconvenience to the woman? Or because some government decides to limit population size? Should test-tube fertilization and surrogate motherhood be permitted? How should the use of scarce resources be allocated? Should surgical procedures costing tens or hundreds of thousands of dollars be financed by tax or insurance dollars?

Should individuals who appear to be mentally ill but have not harmed anyone be hospitalized against their will? Can physicians determine who is "dangerous" and who is not? Should psychotic individuals be forced to take tranquilizers to improve their mental state if they do not want to? Is psychosurgery ever justified? Are there adequate safeguards in our society so that nonconforming individuals and political dissidents cannot be classified as "mentally ill" to interfere with their freedom?

How confidential are medical records? Should the results of health examinations be centralized into a computer? Who should have access to such information? Insurance companies? Employers? Should patients have a right to inspect their own records, even when physicians believe that this would be detrimental to their welfare? How should extremely sensitive data such as the results of tests for AIDS be handled?

Medical progress depends on experimentation.

Who should be selected for experiments? Should people be allowed to volunteer as control subjects even if it means they may be deprived of an effective treatment? (This does not apply to new cancer treatments, which are tested by comparing them to older ones rather than placebos.) Should institutionalized mental patients or prison inmates be allowed to volunteer? Can such people actually exercise free choice? To what extent should animal experimentation be used? Do experiments in which genes are manipulated pose special risks to society?

Which should take precedence, producing and operating expensive equipment (such as kidney dialysis machines) for the benefit of a small number of persons, or upgrading basic medical care for a large number of underprivileged citizens?

The Intelligent Patient

Good medical care should be a partnership between patient and physician. The intelligent patient learns to consult a physician at appropriate times (see Chapter 10), makes careful observations when symptoms occur, communicates efficiently and openly, strives to understand the nature of any ailment and its treatment, and takes appropriate action if a grievance arises.

Effective Communication

When consulting a doctor, try to present a detailed and well-rorganized account of present symptoms and relevant past history. Before contacting the doctor, it may help to draw up a list to guide one's presentation. If there is more than one problem, start with the most important one. If medications are being taken, either write down their names and dosages or bring the medications to the appointment.

Physicians know much more about medicine than lay people do, but they may not always be good communicators. They may sometimes be authoritarian and even patronizing; it is an occupational hazard, the result of years of counseling and treating others. Patients should not accept this behavior. Consumers have the right to be partners in their care and to receive a clear explanation of the physician's findings and proposed treatment. There is no good reason why a physician cannot provide this. A friendly comment that you want to be able to follow the physician's advice properly usually establishes the desired relationship.

It is important that feelings of fear, embarrassment, or even resentment not be permitted to create a barrier between patient and physician. Put these feelings to good use by sharing them with the physician. Physicians are not mind-readers. A person who fears an examination or is shy about body parts should say so. Discomfort during an examination is something else the physician wants to know about. If the physician makes a sound or comment that causes concern, ask what it means.

If in doubt about a diagnosis or treatment plan, discuss these doubts. If a particular treatment is objectionable, the physician may be able to suggest an acceptable alternative. If necessary a consultation with another physician should be requested. Similarly, if the physician suggests consultative action, the patient should appreciate this concern and be receptive to the proposal.

Some consumer advocates recommend questioning doctors closely about the need for diagnostic tests and about alternatives to whatever treatment is proposed. However, challenging everything is likely to antagonize the doctor and could result in dismissal as a patient. The best approach is to select a doctor who makes sensible and cost-effective recommendations without prodding. Questions can then be used to enhance one's understanding rather than trying to outthink the doctor.

Be sure to have a clear understanding of fees involved. This matter is usually handled by the receptionist.

Personal Glimpse

Consultations

Diagnostic proficiency is directly related to the range and depth of the doctor's experience with any particular illness. If you're informed you have a problem and that it is rare or unusual, one that that appears serious or that involves a considerable amount of treatment or medication, you might want to ask your doctor the following questions:

- What is your experience with this problem?
- Would a consultation be warranted with a doctor who has had more experience with this problem?

David R. Stutz, M.D.
Bernard Feder, Ph.D.
The Savvy Patient[36]

Telephone Tips

Proper use of the telephone can do a great deal to make the physician's life easier while helping the patient to receive better service. Before calling the office take a moment to organize your thoughts. What is the problem? When did it begin? If there is a pain, does it come and go or is it steady? Does anything bring it on or relieve it? If there is an infection or any other reason to suspect a fever, the temperature should be taken. Try to decide whether the problem is urgent.

It is not unusual for a busy physician to receive 50 to 100 telephone calls a day—many more than could possibly be handled alone—so when you call, don't start by asking to speak with the physician. The receptionist or nurse is trained to assemble the information needed for a preliminary evaluation of the situation. This person usually knows which matters to handle alone and which ones the physician must handle personally. After talking to the receptionist or nurse, if you still believe it is necessary to speak with the physician, that is the time to ask.

When you telephone, have a pad and pencil handy to write down any instructions. Human memory is notoriously faulty. Call as early in the working day as possible. That way the physician can handle the problem most efficiently: the physician's assistants are on duty to help, and hospitals and laboratories are able to give their best services.

When calling for a prescription refill, know the phone number of the drugstore. The request should be made during the physician's office hours and before you are down to the last pill. That way the physician can review the office record to see whether the medication is still needed, whether the dosage should be changed, and so on. Such a review makes medical care safer. If you telephone outside of office hours, many physicians (especially those covering another's practice) order only enough medication for a few days. That is the safest way in the absence of medical records, but it does increase the cost of medication.

Handling a Grievance

If you choose a physician carefully and communicate effectively, it is unlikely that a serious grievance will develop. However, should you believe that a physician has overcharged for services or treated you in an incompetent, unethical, or unprofessional manner, there are measures that can be taken.

It's Your Decision

You are moving to a new community and want to find a competent physician, dentist, or other health professional. What would you do?

How would you know whether you have found the right person?

When you visit a physician for a physical examination, what should you expect it to include? What kinds of laboratory tests should take place? Why? Should such an examination occur yearly?

What should the cost be? What questions should you ask the physician about the findings of the examination?

A doctor has advised you to have surgery (hernia repair, gall bladder removal, hysterectomy, or tonsillectomy) within the next few weeks. What action should you take to decide about the surgery?

The grievance should first be discussed directly with the physician. It may turn out to be based on a simple misunderstanding. Or it may be possible to negotiate a satisfactory resolution. If discussion with the physician is not effective, the next step should be a complaint to the local medical society. Some people hesitate to do this, thinking that "doctors will always stick up for each other." Although physicians do have sympathy for each other, this feeling is balanced by an antipathy toward seriously unethical conduct, which reflects on the medical profession as a whole. Moreover, if other complaints against the same individual have been received, the society may already be suspicious of that physician.

If the physician is on the staff of a hospital, a complaint can also be made to the hospital administrator. Contacting the Better Business Bureau is unlikely to be effective because that organization ordinarily refers medical complainants to the local medical society.

If the medical society fails to resolve the concern, the next step should be a complaint to the state licensing board. Although the board will give priority to matters of incompetence, fraud, and illegal behavior, it may also take action in less serious situations.

If one believes a significant injury has resulted from negligence or carelessness, an attorney may be consulted to determine whether a malpractice suit is appropriate.

Summary

Intelligent consumers should locate and use a primary physician (or medical group) who provides care that is scientific, considerate, and compassionate. They should take an active role in dealing with health professionals. They should endeavor to understand the nature of any health problem they experience and the mechanisms and potential hazards of treatment. They should not hesitate to ask questions about fees or request consultations for complicated problems. Good medical care should be a partnership between patient and physician. It should include preventive approaches and periodic examinations as well as effective two-way communication.

Discussion Questions

1. What is scientific health care? How does it differ from nonscientific care?
2. What are the essential requirements for a physician to practice medicine in the United States?
3. Identify and briefly describe the medical specialties and subspecialties. What additional requirements are needed to practice as a specialist?
4. What are the similarities and differences between medical and osteopathic doctors?
5. What are the essential requirements for licensing of podiatrists, optometrists, nurses, and pharmacists in the United States?
6. What types of auxiliary health care personnel are consumers likely to deal with?
7. What guidelines and procedures should be used to select physicians?
8. Discuss the nature, purpose, and recommended frequency of physical examinations, laboratory tests and procedures, immunizations, and x-ray examinations.
9. Discuss the nature and purposes of recently developed types of medical imaging.
10. What are the patient and physician responsibilities regarding surgery? How can consumers help to prevent unnecessary surgery?
11. Discuss the newsworthy features of laser surgery, laparoscopic cholecystectomy, and circumcision.
12. What problems and practices affect the quality of medical care in the United States?
13. What are iatrogenic diseases? What are some ways to protect against them?
14. Who can discipline incompetent physicians? What action can be taken?
15. Discuss bioethics and its implications for health care.
16. How can a consumer be an intelligent patient?

REFERENCES

1. Lipman, M: Speak up to your doctor, Consumer Reports Health Letter 3:46, 1991.
2. Jonas HS, Etzel SI, and Barzansky B: Educational programs in U.S. Medical Schools, JAMA 286:913-920, 1991.
3. Gevitz N: The D.O.'s—Osteopathic medicine in America, Baltimore, 1982, The Johns Hopkins University Press.
4. Gevitz N: Sectarian medicine, JAMA 257:1636-1640, 1987.
5. Blies JA: The doctor of pharmacy, JAMA 249:1157-1160, 1983.
6. National Health Council: 200 ways to put your talent to work in the health field. New York, 1983, The Council.
7. Alper PR: Avoiding the marginal medic. In: Barrett S, editor: The health robbers, ed 2, Philadelphia, 1980, George F Stickley Co.
8. Alper PR: Who's a shot doctor? Medical Economics, p: 121-126, Aug 5, 1974.
9. Centers for Disease Control: Health information for international travel, Washington, DC, 1990, US Government Printing Office.
10. Those costly annual physicals. Consumer Reports 45:601-606, 1980.
11. AMA Council on Scientific Affairs: medical evaluations of healthy persons, JAMA 249:1626-1633, 1983.
12. Bennett W: A primer on routine lab tests, Harvard Medical School Health Letter 10(12):4-6, 1985.
*13. Lawrence RS et al: Guide to clinical preventive services, report of the US preventive services task force, Baltimore, 1989, Williams & Wilkins.
14. AMA Council on Scientific Affairs: Mammographic screening in asymptomatic women aged 40 years and older, JAMA 261:2535-2542, 1989.
15. Update January 1992: The American Cancer Society's recommendations for the cancer-related checkup. Ca-A Journal for Clinicians 42(1):44-45, 1992.
16. Catalona WJ et al: Measurement of prostate-specific antigen in serum as a screening test for prostate cancer, N Engl J Med 324:1156-1161, 1991.
17. Cherry JD: 'Pertussis vaccine encephalomyelopathy': it is time to recognize it as the myth that it is, JAMA 263:1679-1680, 1990.
18. AMA Council on Scientific Affairs: Medical diagnostic ultrasound instrumentation and clinical interpretation. Report of the Ultrasonography Task Force, JAMA 265:1155-1159, 1991.
19. Wennberg JE: Variations in medical practice and hospital costs, Conn Med, 49:444-453, 1985.
20. Crane M: Second opinions: where are the savings? Medical Economics, p: 174-194, Feb 2, 1987.

*Recommended reading

21. Crane M: Are third parties denying patients the surgery they need? Medical Economics, p: 79-82, April 8, 1991.
22. Patlak M: Light for sight: lasers beginning to solve vision problems, FDA Consumer 24(6):15-18, 1990.
23. Lewis R: Erasing skin marks with lasers, FDA Consumer 26(2):23-26, 1992.
24. AMA Diagnostic and Therapeutic Technology Assessment: laparoscopic cholecystectomy, JAMA 265:1585-1586, 1991.
25. Wallerstein E: Circumcision: the uniquely American medical enigma, In Symposium on Advances in Pediatric Urology, Urological Clinics of North America 12(1):123-132, 1985.
26. Spach D et al: Lack of circumcision increases the risk of urinary tract infections in young men, JAMA 267:679-681, 1992.
27. Condensed from Derbyshire RC: The medical imposters. In Barrett S: The health robbers. Philadelphia, 1980, George F. Stickley Co.
28. Beeper-tagged patients roam till summoned. Medical World News, Feb 14, 1983.
29. Greene R: Medical overkill, Philadelphia, 1983, George F. Stickley Co.
30. Derbyshire RC: Medical licensure and discipline in the United States, Baltimore, 1969, The Johns Hopkins University Press.
31. Gray J: Why bad doctors aren't kicked out of medicine, Medical Economics 69(2):126-149, 1992.
32. Van Tuinin I, McCarthy P, and Wolfe S: 9479 questionable doctors, Washington DC, 1990, Public Citizen Health Research Group.
33. Wolfe S: 9479 questionable doctors, Public Citizen Health Research Group Health Letter 7(7):1-5, 1991.
34. Mullan F et al: National Practitioner Data Bank: report for the first year, JAMA 268:73-79, 1992.
35. AMA Council on Judicial Affairs: Current opinions, Chicago, 1989, American Medical Association.
*36. Stutz DR and Feder F: The savvy patient—how to be an active participant in your medical care. New York, 1991, Consumer Reports Books.

CHAPTER SEVEN

MENTAL HEALTH CARE

"Leave us alone! I am a behavior therapist! I am helping my patient overcome a fear of heights!"

(From Hospital Tribune, Feb. 3, 1975.)

Present-day theories about how people become emotionally ill are exceeded in number only by the available remedies for making them well again.

LEWIS R. WOLBERG M.D.[1]
CLINICAL PROFESSOR OF PSYCHIATRY
NEW YORK UNIVERSITY MEDICAL SCHOOL

CONSUMER DECISIONS

When should a mental health professional be consulted?

How can a competent practitioner be selected?

How can consumers evaluate the effectiveness of mental healthcare?

Although excellent help is available for emotional problems, selecting a suitable therapist can be difficult. There is a wide array of practitioners, many of whom are incompetent. This chapter outlines the various types of practitioners, their treatment methods, and guidelines for distinguishing between proper and improper treatment. It also describes questionable self-help methods marketed to the public. Organizations that offer additional information are listed in the Appendix.

PSYCHIATRIC TREATMENT

For discussion purposes, psychiatric treatment may be divided into two types: "organic" and "psychodynamic." The organic model is basically an authoritarian one in which the patient is a passive recipient of the treatment. The assumption is often made, or at least implied, that the patient has a physical or biochemical abnormality that needs to be controlled or corrected. The organic therapist diagnoses a mental illness and prescribes treatment for the patient: a drug, electroconvulsive therapy, or very rarely psychosurgery.

The psychodynamic model assumes that the patient's mental state is not the result of biochemical factors but has been caused by past and present experiences and feelings. Using a primarily conversational approach, therapist and patient explore the patient's feelings and behavior and seek ways to alter them by persuasion, enviromental manipulation, or the development of new ways to react.

In actual practice there is no sharp dividing line between the two philosophies, and most psychiatrists use both in their approach to patients.

Drug Therapy

Drugs are commonly prescribed for the treatment of anxiety states, depression, psychomatic disorders, and psychoses.

Antipsychotic agents (sometimes referred to as major tranquilizers) are used primarily to treat psychotic reactions (thought disorders manifested by hallucinations, delusions, or loss of contact with reality). Since the early 1950s these drugs have rev-

TABLE 7–1

COMMON PSYCHOPHARMACOLOGICAL AGENTS

Drug	Reasons for use	Adverse reactions
Antipsychotic medications		
Chlorpromazine (Thorazine)* Chlorprothixene (Taractan) Fluphenazine (Permitil, Prolixin)* Haloperidol (Haldol)* Loxapine (Loxitane)* Mesoridazine (Serentil)* Molindone (Moban)* Perphenazine (Trilafon)* Thioridazine (Mellaril)* Thiothixene (Navane)* Trifluoperazine (Stelazine)*	Psychotic reactions	Stiffness, dry mouth, drowsiness, tremors, and other involuntary movements (tardive dyskinesia), constipation, impotence (these vary from drug to drug)
Clozapine (Clozaril)	Intractable psychosis	Drowsiness, aplastic anemia, seizures

TABLE 7–1

COMMON PSYCHOPHARMACOLOGICAL AGENTS—cont'd

Drug	Reasons for use	Adverse reactions
Antianxiety agents		
Alprazolam (Xanax)* Chlorazepate (Tranxene)* Chlordiazepoxide (Librium, Libritabs)* Diazepam (Valium)* Lorazepam (Ativan)* Oxazepam (Serax)* Prazepam (Centrax)	Anxiety reactions, Panic attacks, Psychophysiological disorders, Temporary relief of insomnia	Drowsiness, possible addiction
Flurazepam (Dalmane)* Temazepam (Restoril)* Triazolam (Halcion)	Insomnia	Possible addiction, amnesia, next day sedation
Buspirone (BuSpar)	Chronic anxiety	Agitation, dizziness, gastrointestinal distress
Anti-obsessive-compulsive agents		
Clomipramine (Anafranil)	Uncontrollable repetitive thoughts or actions	Seizures, dry mouth, constipation, increased appetite, impotence
Antidepressive agents		
Amitryptyline (Elavil, Endep)* Amoxapine (Asendin) Desipramine (Norpramin, Pertofrane)* Doxepin (Adapin, Sinequan)*	Severe or moderate depression, Panic attacks	Drowsiness, dry mouth, blurred vision, profuse sweating, constipation, difficulty urinating, weight gain
Fluoxetine (Prozac) Imipramine (Tofranil)* Maprotiline (Ludiomil)* Nortriptyline (Pamelor) Protriptyline (Vivactil)	Fluoxitine also used for obsessive-compulsive disorders	Fluoxetine can cause anxiety, gastrointestinal distress
Trazodone (Desyrel)* Trimipramine (Surmontil)		Trazodone can cause priapism (prolonged erection), dizziness
Isocarboxazid (Marplan) Phenelzine (Nardil) Tranylcypromine (Pamate)	Treatment-resistant depression, Atypical depression, Panic attacks	Agitation, dry mouth, restlessness, blurred vision, hypotension, adverse interactions with certain foods and drugs
Antimanic agents		
Lithium carbonate (Lithane, Eskalith)*	Mania, manic-depressive psychosis	Nausea and vomiting, tremor, excessive thirst, excessive urination, diarrhea, depressed thyroid function

*These drugs are available in generic forms that are considerably less expensive than name brands. However, generic antidepressants may be unsuitable for some patients because the blood levels they achieve may not be as high as those of name brands.

©1992, Stephen Barrett, M.D. Prepared with help from Daniel D. Goldfarb, M.D., Allentown, PA.

olutionized the field of psychiatry. Many patients who otherwise would have required lengthy (even lifelong) hospital stays are now able to improve or recover quickly. In addition, large numbers of previously institutionalized patients have been able to return to their communities.

Antianxiety agents (sometimes referred to as minor tranquilizers) are used for the treatment of anxiety states and psychosomatic disorders. Americans have been accused (with some justification) of being a "drugged society" because of their high use of alcohol and antianxiety agents such as diazepam (Valium). Although most people who receive antipsychotic medications probably need them, it is clear that physicians often prescribe antianxiety agents or antidepressants when it would be more appropriate to help patients identify and correct what is troubling them. Physicians are not entirely to blame for this, however; patients often press for instant and total relief.

The danger of addiction to Valium has been grossly exaggerated by the media, particularly in the motion picture, *I'm Running as Fast as I Can.* The central character in this film is an anxiety-ridden woman who takes huge amounts of Valium, suddenly stops taking the drug, and becomes severely ill and develops convulsions. Although addiction develops occasionally with a normally prescribed dosage of Valium, the ordinary precaution of tapering off a dosage, rather than stopping suddenly, will prevent a withdrawal reaction from occurring.

Antidepressants are available to counteract severe depressions (those manifested by loss of appetite, weight loss, severe insomnia, feelings of hopelessness, or psychomotor retardation or agitation). These drugs usually require from 3 days to several weeks to take effect. They are not intended for use in countering the minor upsets that are part of ordinary living.

Antidepressants and antipsychotic drugs often can be prescribed as a single bedtime dose. This method reduces the cost of the medication, usually aids sleep, and reduces the likelihood of annoying side effects.

All psychoactive drugs have the potential for adverse reactions, some serious and some not. In each case the value to the patient must be weighed against the nuisance or danger involved. Table 7-1 lists some of the common psychopharmacologic drugs, their uses, and their adverse reactions.

One complication of particular concern is tardive dyskinesia, an involuntary movement disorder characterized by twitching and tongue-thrusting, which can occur with a prolonged high dosage of antipsychotic medications. Although uncommon, it is often irreversible. Since the dangers of psychosis far outweigh the risk of tardive dyskinesia, there is no reason to withhold antipsychotic medication from individuals who are psychotic. However, it is poor medical practice to prescribe these drugs for nonpsychotic anxiety.

Drugs in the News

During the past 2 years, three psychiatric drugs have received considerable attention from the news media: clozapine (Clozaril), triazolam (Halcion), and fluoxetine (Prozac).

Clozaril is very valuable for treating psychotic patients who have not responded to other drugs. It has a 1% to 2% incidence of aplastic anemia, a life-threatening condition in which the body stops producing blood cells. However, when weekly blood tests are used to detect early signs of lowered blood cell production, the drug can almost always be stopped in time to avoid severe trouble. When marketing of Clozaril began, it could not be purchased separately from a company-endorsed management system that prevented patients from obtaining the drug without taking the weekly tests. Many psychiatrists, government agencies, and patient advocacy groups protested that the total cost was so high (about $25 a day) many patients who could benefit from Clozaril were unable to get it. In 1991 Sandoz Pharmaceuticals Corporation signed an FTC consent agreement, permitting patients to obtain Clozaril from any facility that appropriately monitors the drug. This permits dispensing by local pharmacists who follow a company-approved protocol that is inexpensive to administer. However, the drug itself still costs about $15 per day.

Halcion, the most widely prescribed sleeping pill, occasionally causes overexcitement, amnesia, or mental confusion. The manufacturer now advises that Halcion should not be given to patients with depression (treating the depression should alleviate the insomnia), and that elderly patients should be given half the normal dosage. In 1989 the FDA also required that the drug carry a warning statement about its potential to cause amnesia. In 1991 critics claimed that the manufacturer's own data show that Halcion also can cause paranoia and hallucinations, charges that the manufacturer disputes.[2] In response to the charges, Britain banned the drug.

The FDA did not, but announced it was reviewing the data closely. It also required the manufacturer to revive Halcion's labeling to emphasize that the drug is indicated for a short-term (7 to 10 days) treatment of insomnia and should be prescribed in the lowest effective dose.

Prozac, the most widely prescribed antidepressant drug, was attacked by the Citizen's Commission on Human Rights (CCHR). CCHR was established in 1969 by the Church of Scientology, which describes the Commission as "dedicated to the eradication of psychiatric violations of human rights."[3] In addition to Prozac, CCHR's targets have included electroconvulsive therapy, psychosurgery, the use of Ritalin for hyperactivity in children, and "psychotherapist sex crimes." CCHR has more than 100 offices in 18 countries.[4] In 1990 CCHR petitioned the FDA to withdraw Prozac from the market, claiming that it is addictive and causes suicide, violent behavior, and abnormal body movements. The FDA concluded that the charges were unfounded and rejected the petition.[5] Joseph English, M.D., president-elect of the American Psychiatric Association (APA), applauded the FDA's refusal:

> The Food and Drug Administration has chosen science over sensationalism . . . This medicine, carefully prescribed . . . will continue to be lifesaving for many thousands of persons suffering from depression . . . The CCHR and the Church of Scientology have a right to their opinions and ideologies. But . . . the real objective of this campaign, and similar efforts in the past, is the elimination of treatment for mental illnesses.[6]

Electroconvulsive Therapy

Electroconvulsive therapy (ECT) (also referred to as EST [electroshock therapy] and shock treatment) is a method of inducing a convulsion by giving a brief stimulus to the brain. To receive the treatment, the patient lies down and is rendered unconscious either by an electrical stimulus or by a short-acting barbiturate given intravenously. To protect against injury, a curare-like drug is also given so that the patient's muscles do not actually contract during the convulsion. Electrodes are applied to one or both temples and a small amount of current is transmitted to induce the convulsion. After the treatment the patient usually remains unconscious for about 15 to 30 minutes. A series of treatments may cause memory difficulty that clears up in a few weeks except for specific memories of some events during the months before, during, or after the period of treatment. However, the ability to acquire new information or remember information from the past is rarely impaired.[7]

Although its mechanism of action is unknown, ECT can be dramatically successful in certain types of severe depression and is sometimes helpful in severe psychotic reactions. However, it is seldom appropriate unless medication alone fails to produce results.

Psychosurgery

Psychosurgery is a method of diminishing a patient's reactions to unpleasant sensations by severing various nerve pathways within the brain. Before the era of pharmacotherapy, psychosurgery was widely used to reduce disturbed behavior in severely disturbed patients. Today, although it is still regarded as an effective mode of treatment, it is appropriate for consideration only when all other treatments have failed.

Psychotherapy

Psychotherapy may be defined as any type of persuasive or conversational approach that helps the patient. Although there are numerous schools of thought, most have in common a wish to understand the patient and help the patient alter emotional and/or behavioral patterns.

In *analytically oriented psychotherapy* the patients say what comes to mind (free association) and are helped by the therapist to understand their feelings, mental mechanisms, and relationships with people. Insights are used to help patients develop healthier ways of dealing with feelings and life situations. This type of therapy usually involves one or two 50-minute sessions per week. It is especially appropriate for people who communicate well and are motivated to change. Psychoanalysis is a more sensitive form of psychotherapy in which free association is done while lying on a couch. It requires three to five sessions per week. Few people can afford its high costs.

Behavioral therapy (also called behavioral modification) is the systematic application of learning theory to the treatment of disorders of behavior. The therapist first analyzes the patient's maladaptive responses—the behaviors that cause stress, limit satisfaction, and affect important areas of the patient's life. Treatment techniques can include systematic desensitization (gradually facing stressful situations to master them), relaxation training, positive reinforcement (being rewarded for behaving more maturely), and aversive therapy (associating an unpleasant stimulus with undesirable behavior).

According to the AMA Council on Scientific Affairs,[8] aversive techniques include: verbal rebukes, imagined noxious scenes, unpleasant tastes, physical restraint, hitting, pinching, electric shocks, and drug-induced nausea and vomiting. After reviewing the use of these techniques for obesity, tobacco smoking, alcoholism, drug abuse, homosexuality, sexual offenses, thumbsucking, and dangerous behavior in mentally retarded individuals, the Council concluded that: (1) few well-designed studies have been performed, (2) the most positive results have been reported with rapid smoking for smoking cessation, emetic therapy for alcoholism, electric shock for self-injurious behavior in mentally retarded individuals, and covert sensitization for sexual offenders; (3) some studies have found nonaversive techniques equally effective; and (4) much more research should be done before definitive conclusions can be drawn.

Biofeedback is a relaxation technique that can help people learn to control certain body functions. The patient is connected to a machine that continuously signals the heartbeat, degree of muscle contraction, or other body mechanisms. The patient is instructed to relax so that the signals decrease to a desirable level. Biofeedback can help people achieve deep relaxation, but the same mental state can be accomplished without electronic monitoring. It has also been tried for a variety of psychophysiologic ailments that include headaches, high blood pressure, and cardiac arrhythmias.

In 1980 a task force of the APA concluded the following:[9]

1. Biofeedback has not been found useful in severe psychiatric disorders but has been effective as an adjunct to psychiatric treatment to control anxiety and relieve specific psychosomatic complaints.
2. The few available studies indicate that hypnotic therapy, meditation, or relaxation training are equally effective.
3. There is no psychiatric condition for which biofeedback as such is the treatment of choice.
4. Biofeedback therapists should not be credentialed as independent professionals because medical and/or psychologic training is needed for the overall management of patients who might be suitable for biofeedback.

Battery-operated skin temperature monitors ($20 to $80) and devices that measure muscle or brain-wave activity ($200 to $400) have been marketed through the mail for home use. The *Harvard Medical School Health Letter* has cautioned that these devices have not been systematically evaluated and are likely to "have a short working life before they wind up in a closet or attic, gathering dust."[10]

Hypnosis is a temporary condition of altered attention during which suggestibility is greatly enhanced. The trance state may be used to uncover repressed material or to increase the patient's control over a symptom or behavior. Hypnosis is not a treatment in itself but may accelerate the treatment process in properly selected cases. It has also been used for anesthesia during childbirth and dental procedures and for relief of headaches and other painful conditions. Because everyone is not amenable to hypnosis, the therapist must have adequate training in both the administration of the procedure and the selection of patients.

Group therapy is a method whereby several persons, usually eight to ten, meet with a therapist for discussion. Groups may be homogeneous (composed of people with similar problems or backgrounds) or heterogeneous. The discussion may focus on specific topics or may deal with whatever comes up. Group discussions often help people feel less alone in their feelings and provide a "laboratory" for analysis of an individual's behavior in a group situation. Reticent individuals may find group sessions, in which they can sit and listen, preferable to individual sessions, which may be relatively silent.

Marriage counseling is a process whereby husband and wife meet individually and/or together with a therapist to help them identify current marital conflict. Acting as a referee, the therapist helps the couple communicate more effectively to negotiate solutions to their dispute. In *family therapy* the therapist meets with the family as a group to help resolve current family conflicts. *Sexual therapy* is most appropriate for couples who basically get along well but have a problem with sex. Couples with a sexual problem whose general relationship is poor will probably be better off with marital counseling or individual psychotherapy.[11]

Psychosomatic Problems

From time to time all individuals experience symptoms that are physical reactions to tension. Common examples are headaches, diarrhea, constipation, nausea, dizziness, muscle cramps, dry mouth, cold hands, indigestion, excessive sweating, and palpitations of the heart. Whether treatment is needed depends on the severity or frequency of the symptom. They may require no treatment, self-medication with an over-the-counter product, medical care, or psychiatric treatment.

These so-called psychosomatic or psychophysiologic reactions are mediated through the autonomic nervous system and are related to the action of adrenaline and related hormones on various parts of the body. Diarrhea before an examination, for example, is caused by increased intestinal motility. Tension headaches are caused by muscular tension in the back of the neck. Indigestion may be caused by excessive production of acid in the stomach. The symptoms of acute anxiety attacks—sweating, rapid heartbeat, palpitation, and a feeling of dread—are caused by release of adrenaline. Anxiety can also trigger *hyperventilation syndrome*, in which a feeling of shortness of breath is accompanied by lightheadedness and numbnesss of the hands and feet. On the more serious side, asthma, peptic ulcer, high blood pressure, backache, and ulcerative colitis can have significant emotional components.

Psychophysiologic reactions may be treated with: (1) drugs that prevent the hormones from affecting the target organs, (2) antianxiety drugs to reduce tension, (3) psychotherapy to attack the underlying causes of the tension, or (4) a combination of these. A large percentage of the ailments for which people seek medical attention are significantly related to tension.

PERSONAL GLIMPSE

An Attack from Within

An acute anxiety attack is of sudden onset and may even begin without any apparent precipitating event. The patient is suddenly extremely apprehensive. He is aware of palpitations. Perspiration becomes profuse and breathing is difficult . . . The patient often fears that a medical calamity is taking place within his body. Particularly during the first such attack, the patient is apt to feel that he will faint, or die, or lose control of himself or of his mind. In the severe anxiety attack, the patient literally reaches a panic state where he feels overwhelmed and completely helpless. He is aware of a tremendously strong impulse to run away from wherever he is. He knows not from what he runs, nor even clearly where safety lies. Even following the attack, the patient remains chronically fearful lest he suffer another such unpleasant attack. This, of course, creates . . . additional anxiety which only tends to aid in the precipitation of further attacks.

O. SPURGEON ENGLISH, M.D.
STUART M. FINCH, M.D.[12]

MENTAL HEALTH PRACTITIONERS

Many types of practitioners profess to help people with mental, emotional, and personal problems. The training, professional standards, and legal status of the different types of practitioners vary considerably.

Psychiatrists are physicians (M.D. or D.O.) who have completed at least 3 years of specialized training in psychiatry after graduation from medical or osteopathic school. *Child psychiatrists* have a minimum of 4 years of psychiatric training that includes 2 years in adult psychiatry and 2 years in child psychiatry. *Geriatric psychiatrists* are psychiatrists who have acquired additional certification by passing an examination in geriatric psychiatry. About half of the 35,000 psychiatrists and 60% of the 4000 child psychiatrists in the United States are certified by the American Board of Psychiatry and Neurology.

Psychoanalysts are practitioners who have undergone personal psychoanalysis and completed an additional 7 to 10 years of part-time training in the theories and specialized techniques of psychoanalysis. Most are psychiatrists, but a few have backgrounds in psychology or other nonmedical disciplines.

Psychologists are persons whose academic training has been the study of human behavior. Students of psychology study the mental, emotional, biologic, and social basis for human behavior, as well as theories that account for individual differences and abnormal behavior. They are also instructed in research methodology, statistics, psychologic testing, and a variety of skills applicable to their specialty if they intend to practice. The major recognized specialties are counseling, clinical psychology, school psychology, and industrial-organizational psychology.

Currently there are about 50,000 licensed or certified psychologists, about 35,000 of whom are health service providers. Common service settings for psychologists include: community mental health centers, mental hospitals, general hospitals, schools, rehabilitation centers, private individual and group practices, and residential facilities for emotionally disturbed children. Payment for treatment by a psychologist is deductible as a medical expense for federal income tax purposes and is covered by many insurance plans.

In most states, licensing or certification for independent practice as a psychologist requires as a minimum: (1) a doctoral degree from one of the 238 accredited training programs, (2) additional years of supervised clinical experience, and (3) passing of an examination. The *National Register for Health Services Providers in Psychology*, published by the Council for the National Register, lists licensed psychologists whose doctoral degrees and supervised experience meets the Register's standards. A few states allow persons with master's level training to work as psychologic associates or assistants under the supervision of licensed or certified professionals.

Social workers practice in private offices as well as under the auspices of public, voluntary, and proprietary agencies and institutions. They are licensed or regulated in all states except Wisconsin. More than 65,000 have been certified as *clinical social workers* or other specialties by the Academy of Certified Social Workers (ACSW). This requires: (1) a master's or doctoral degree from a school of social work that is recognized by the Council on Social Work Education, (2) 2 years or 3000 hours of postgraduate experience under supervision of a master's level social worker, and (3) passing a written examination given by the ACSW. The *NASW Register of Clinical Social Workers* lists clinical social workers who have had 2 years of supervised clinical work and either are licensed or certified by the state in which they practice or have met ACSW standards. The National Association of Social Workers states that clinical social workers provide over 65% of counseling and psychotherapy services in the United States. Private practitioners typically charge about $70 per hour.

Certified *clinical mental health counselors* work in agencies, schools, colleges, and independent practice. They must have an appropriate master's degree (or equivalent training) plus 2 years of counseling experience. They must pass a written examination conducted by the National Academy of Certified Clinical Mental Health Counselors. They are licensed or certified in 35 states. About 12,000 clinical mental health counselors belong to the American Mental Health Counselors Association.

Specialists in psychiatric nursing are registered nurses (RNs) who usually hold a master's degree from a program that lasts 1½ to 2 years, but the term psychiatric nurse may also be applied to any nurse who has worked in a psychiatric setting. The American Nurses' Association certifies psychiatric nurses on two levels. Certification as a psychiatric and mental health nurse requires 2 years of experience in a mental health setting, current clinical practice, and passage of an examination. Certification as a clinical specialist requires, in addition, a master's degree in psychiatric nursing (or equivalent training) and 2 years of postgraduate clinical experience. The *Directory of Specialists in Psychiatric Mental Health Nursing* provides names of clinical specialists in psychiatric nursing. Some psychiatric nurses conduct their own groups or serve as cotherapists in mental hospitals and clinics. Master's level psychiatric nurses may function as primary psychotherapists in community mental health centers. Some have set up private practices, providing both individual and family therapy.

Marital and family therapists are licensed or certified in 26 states. The American Association for Marriage and Family Therapy (AAMFT) is a professional organization with more than 18,000 members in the United States and Canada. Its members must have appropriate master's- or doctoral-level training plus 2 years of clinical graduate experience with couples and families under the supervision of an AAMFT-approved supervisor. The AAMFT also accredits training programs.

Sexual therapists specialize in the treatment of sexual problems that can be helped by simple techniques and increased communication between sexual partners. They may or may not be able to deal with underlying emotional problems that require additional psychotherapy. Certification is available from the American Association of Sex Educators, Counselors and Therapists (AASECT), an interdisciplinary interest group. Certification as a sex therapist requires: (1) a master's or doctoral degree, (2) licensure or certification in an appropriate professional discipline, (3) 90 hours of specialized education, (4) 90 hours of sex-therapist training, (5) 500 hours of supervised therapy, (6) 100 to 200 hours of individual or group supervision, and (7)

12 hours of structured group experience focused on attitudes about sexuality. Certification as a *sex counselor* has similar requirements but can be obtained with a bachelor's degree. AASECT publishes a register of those it has certified.

Since sexual therapy is neither defined nor regulated by law, anyone can adopt the title of "sexual therapist" or "sexual counselor." For this reason, it is important to check the reputation of a prospective therapist. Those practicing at university-affiliated clinics can be presumed competent. Information about other therapists may be obtained from your family physician, the local medical society, a clergyman, or the local family service agency.

Consumer Tip

When Does Someone Need Professional Help?

If you, or someone you know is experiencing the following symptoms, professional help is advisable.

Depression

Persistent feelings of sadness
Low self-esteem
Insomnia
Loss of interest in activities
Loss of appetite
Weight loss
Suicidal feelings

Anxiety

Intense anxiety that interferes with ability to function
Phobias
Panic attacks
Psychosomatic disorders

Rigidity

Obsessive thoughts
Self-defeating behavior

Impulsivity

Intense flightiness
Alcohol abuse

Impaired sociability

Excessive shyness
Socially inappropriate behavior
Strong feelings of discomfort in social situations

Unreality

Depersonalization (feelings that one's body is changing in size)
Delusions (rigidly held false beliefs)
Hallucinations (hearing voices)

Repeated failure

An overall "batting average" in life that remains well below a person's ability

There are many other types of mental health practitioners whose activities are not defined by law or regulated by licensure. Included in this category are caseworkers, social-work aides, clergymen, school counselors, and a wide variety of self-proclaimed therapists. Some have sound training, but others do not.

There are several reasons why finding a suitable therapist for a mental or emotional problem may be more difficult than finding one for a physical problem or for general medical care:

1. There is a wide range of types of practitioners.
2. Some types of practitioners lack standardization of training and credentials.
3. There may be many different approaches used by practitioners within each professional group.
4. The person seeking help may have no idea which type of treatment approach is most appropriate.
5. A personality fit between patient and therapist is more important in psychologic treatment than it is in the treatment of physical problems.
6. A sizable number of practitioners use questionable practices, some of which may be very difficult to recognize.

Who Should Seek Help?

Professional help is appropriate when mental or emotional problems significantly interfere with a person's ability to function, or the problems produce symptoms beyond an individual's tolerance. Psychiatrist Ronald Pies[13] identifies the most common symptoms as depression, anxiety, rigidity, impulsivity, impaired sociability, unreality, and repeated failure.

Selecting a Therapist

Several basic questions should be considered during the process of seeking mental-health treatment: (1) What type of help is wanted? (2) Which practitioners can provide such help? (3) Are they available in the community? and (4) How much can the patient afford to pay?

If medication is desired, one must see a physician. Most nonpsychiatric physicians are competent to prescribe appropriate antianxiety agents and antidepressants for patients who are not severely disturbed. For antipsychotic drugs, a high dosage of antidepressants, or any type of long-range treatment, it is best to consult a psychiatrist.

If a conversational form of treatment is preferred, a recommendation may be obtained from a personal physician, clergyman, school counselor, or friend. Psychoanalytic institutes located in some major cities and the departments of psychiatry at most medical schools can provide names of psychiatrists who specialize in psychotherapy. Additional names of psychiatrists can be obtained from the local medical society and the Yellow Pages. Information about the training and credentials of a prospective psychiatrist can be obtained from the biographical directory of the APA, the local medical society, or the psychiatrist directly. Those who have trained at university hospitals are more likely to be primarily interested in psychotherapy than those who have trained at state hospitals. "Do you do psychotherapy primarily?" is a good screening question.

Certification by the American Board of Psychiatry and Neurology is a good indication that a psychiatrist is qualified to administer organic forms of treatment, but this certification is not as useful a guideline in selecting a psychotherapist. Some analytically oriented psychiatrists are not motivated to become certified because they believe the board is primarily oriented toward organic psychiatry.

If one decides to consult a therapist who is not a psychiatrist, names may be obtained from a personal physician, clergyman, school counselor, friend, local professional society, or the Yellow Pages. Most national professional organizations publish biographical membership directors, and most certifying organizations publish directories of the professionals that they have certified. Some of these publications are available at public, hospital, and medical-school libraries. Credentials can also be checked by contacting the national professional organizations listed in the Appendix.

The current cost of psychotherapy with a private practitioner is usually $60 to $150 for a 50-minute session. Psychiatrists tend to charge more than nonpsychiatrists. In many communities, people who cannot afford private care can receive treatment at a mental health clinic where fees are based on the ability to pay. Most psychotherapy at community clinics is done by psychologists and social workers. A limited amount of counseling is available without charge to students at most colleges and universities.

Pies[13] advised consultation with a physician whenever mental problems are associated with any of the following symptoms: blackouts; memory lapses (such as trouble recalling recent events); persistent headaches; significant unintentional weight loss; numbness; tingling or other strange sensations; generalized weakness; dizzy spells; significant pain of any sort; difficulty walking; shortness of breath; seizures of any type; inability to control urination; unduly rapid and/or forceful heartbeats; frequent, heavy sweating; tremor; or slurred speech.

Self-Help Groups

Self-help groups, the goal of which is to encourage the emotional growth of their members, are growing throughout the nation. People in them believe that sharing their problems with others and receiving the support of an interested group allow members to gain more control over their emotional problem.

Recovery, Inc., is a self-help group that tries to prevent recurrences of mental illness of former mental patients and to prevent chronicity in nervous patients. Individuals are taught how to recognize symptoms of approaching difficulties and to head them off. Alcoholics Anonymous (AA) sponsors group meetings for people with drinking problems. Secular Organizations for Sobriety (SOS) also helps problem drinkers but has a nonreligious orientation. Neurotics Anonymous has a program similar to that of AA but is suitable for people with many different types of problems. The addresses of these groups are listed in the Appendix.

Hospital Care

There are four basic situations in which psychiatric hospital care is indicated: (1) the patient is considered dangerous to himself because he is suicidal or is not eating enough to sustain life, (2) the patient is considered dangerous to others, (3) the patient has regressed to the point where he cannot care for

FIGURE 7-1. Self-help groups are growing in numbers throughout the United States.
(From Ray and Ksir. Drugs, society, and human behavior, 5th ed., St Louis, 1989, Mosby–Year Book)

himself in the community, or (4) specialized treatment that is available only on an inpatient basis is needed.

Many communities have day-care or "partial-hospitalization" programs where patients spend 6 to 8 hours per day in a therapeutic atmosphere. Some hospitals have night-care programs. In some communities, halfway houses are available to ease the transition from hospital to community living.

Patients who are judged sufficiently dangerous to themselves or others can be committed involuntarily to either inpatient or outpatient treatment. Contrary to popular opinion, court decisions and state laws tend to define "dangerousness" rather narrowly. As a result, commitment against a person's will can be difficult to initiate or sustain.

During the past few years, a new type of "living will" has been used to provide seriously mentally ill people who are in remission with a way to consent to treatment if they decompensate. These documents describe when and how treatment should be implemented if the patient becomes incompetent to make a rational voluntary decision.

Questionable Practices

A wide variety of questionable practices exists among practitioners who profess to treat mental, emotional, and personal problems. Since terms such as therapist, psychotherapist, and counselor are not defined by law, anyone may use these titles to represent himself. The fields of sensitivity training, sexual counseling, marriage counseling, hypnosis, and encounter groups contain many self-proclaimed therapists who have little or no training. Other types of unqualified practitioners masquerade under such titles as metaphysician, astrolotherapist, autohypnotist, palmist, past-life therapist, reader-adviser, graphologist (handwriting analyst), and character analyst. Some have certificates from diploma mills, while others do not.

In addition, there are practitioners with orthodox training and credentials who engage in methods that are not based on the scientific evidence of their efficacy, who have personal problems that interfere with proper care of their patients, or who exploit their patients.

The trouble with questionable mental-health

treatment is not merely lack of efficacy. A disillusioning experience can cause the patient to abandon further effort to obtain help or can trigger a personal disaster such as suicide. Some of the common types of questionable mental-health practices are included in the following discussion.

Sensitivity Training

Sensitivity training began in the 1950s with training groups (T-groups) whose purpose was to help community leaders ease social tensions in their communities. This was accomplished by an intense small-group experience that encouraged self-disclosure and expression of strong feeling while focusing on the attitudes and interactions of group members. The process was never intended for the treatment of emotionally disturbed individuals.

Over the years there has been a proliferation of such groups under a variety of names such as: marathon groups, growth centers, encounter groups, and human-relations laboratories. Unfortunately, many leaders of these groups are incompetent.

The following factors should be considered before participating in a sensitivity group: (1) the psychologic condition and motivation of the individual, (2) the reputation and accountability of the sponsoring organization, (3) the qualifications of the group leaders and consultants, (4) the methods used to prescreen participants, and (5) the stated agenda and goals of the program.

Sensitivity training can be very upsetting to individuals who are not self-confident enough to handle the confrontation and emotional expression that can take place at such meetings. Depression, psychosis, major personality disorganization, anxiety reactions, homosexual panic, and physical injuries have resulted from improperly conducted meetings.

The stated purpose of encounter groups is to help people experience personal growth by learning to express their feelings more openly. The groups may take a variety of forms. Participants may talk under the guidance of a group leader. They may emphasize physical comfort or contact such as touching. They may have supportive and/or aggressive confrontations.

Dianetics and "Purification"

Dianetics, an approach promoted by the Church of Scientology, is described by its proponents as "an exact pastoral counseling technology for the location and elimination of unwanted emotional conditions and physical problems that are of spiritually induced origin."[14] Dianetics was developed by L. Ron Hubbard (1911-1986), who also founded the Church of Scientology and was a prolific science fiction writer.[14] Hubbard's book, *Dianetics: The Modern Science of Mental Healing,*[15] was originally published in 1950 and has undergone several revisions. It is widely advertised as "the owner's manual for the human mind" and said to have sold over 14 million copies.[3] Individuals who return an inquiry card from the book may receive thousands of follow-up solicitations for Scientology publications and seminars.

According to Hubbard, the "analytical" (conscious) mind is a perfect recorder, computer, and solver of problems. It is incapable of error except when interfered with by "engrams," recordings made by the "reactive" (unconscious) mind when the analytic mind is turned off by traumatic events. Hubbard's book states that engrams stored in the reactive memory bank cause neuroses, psychoses, and psychosomatic disorders. The goal of Dianetic therapy is to "clear" (erase) all engrams from the reactive bank. This is accomplished through a procedure called "auditing," in which the auditor may use an "E-meter" to help the patient recall traumatic events.

Time Magazine has described the E-Meter as "a simplified lie-detector . . . designed to measure electrical changes in the skin while subjects discussed intimate details of their past."[16] In 1963 the FDA seized more than 100 E-meters at the headquarters of the Founding Church of Scientology in Washington, DC. During the lengthy litigation that followed, Judge Gerhardt A. Gesell[17] concluded:

> Hubbard and his fellow Scientologists developed the notion of using an E-Meter to aid auditing. Substantial fees were charged for the meter and for auditing sessions using the meter. They repeatedly and explicitly represented that such auditing effectuated cures of many physical and mental illnesses. An individual processed with the aid of the E-meter was said to reach the intended goal of "clear" and was led to believe that there was reliable scientific proof that once cleared, many, indeed, most illnesses would automatically be cured. Auditing was guaranteed to be successful. All this was and is false.

Upholding the FDA's charges that the E-Meter was misbranded, Judge Gesell ordered that future use of the E-Meter be confined to "bona fide religious counseling" and that the device be prominently labeled with this warning notice:

> The E-Meter is not medically or scientifically useful for the diagnosis, treatment, or prevention of any disease. It is not medically or scientifically capable of improving the health or bodily functions of anyone.[18]

The copyright page of *Dianetics* states that the E-Meter "is not intended or effective for the diagnosis, treatment or prevention of any disease, or for the improvement of health or any bodily function."[15]

HealthMed, a chain of clinics run by Scientologists, offers a "purification program" of saunas, exercise, high doses of niacin, and other vitamins and minerals. The program, designed by Hubbard, is said to rid the body of "chemicals and poisons" that can dull awareness, mental acuteness, emotions, and "make a person feel dead, dull and lifeless."[19]

Megavitamin Therapy

During the early 1950s a few psychiatrists began adding massive doses of nutrients to the treatment of severe mental problems. The original substance used was vitamin B_3, (nicotinic acid or nicotinamide), and the therapy was termed megavitamin therapy. Since that time the treatment regimen has been expanded to include other vitamins, minerals, hormones, and diets, any of which may be combined with conventional drug therapy and/or ECT.

Today the treatment is called orthomolecular psychiatry, which is a term meaning "the treatment of mental disease by the provision of optimum molecular environment for the mind, especially substances normally present in the human body." Proponents suggest that abnormal behavior is caused by molecular imbalances that are correctable by administration of the "right" nutrient molecules at the right time. (*Ortho* is Greek for right.) The orthomolecular approach is now used to treat many other diseases (see Chapter 13).

A special task force of the APA has investigated the claims of the megavitamin and orthomolecular therapists. Its 1973 report noted that orthomolecular psychiatrists use unconventional methods not only in treatment but in diagnosis. The conclusion of the report follows. It is perhaps the most strongly worded statement ever published by a scientific review body:

> This review and critique has carefully examined the literature produced by megavitamin proponents and by those who have attempted to replicate their basic and clinical work. It concludes in this regard that the credibility of the megavitamin proponents is low. Their credibility is further diminished by a consistent refusal over the past decade to perform controlled experiments and to report their new results in a scientifically acceptable fashion.
>
> Under these circumstances this Task Force considers the massive publicity which they promulgate via radio, the lay press and popular books, using catch phrases which are really misnomers like "megavitamin therapy" and "orthomolecular treatment," to be deplorable.[20]

The Research Advisory Committee of the National Institute of Mental Health reviewed pertinent scientific data through 1979 and agreed that megavitamin therapy is ineffective and may be harmful. After the U.S. Defense Subcommittee looked into this therapy, it was removed as a treatment covered by CHAMPUS, the insurance program for military dependents.

Feingold Diet

A large number of school-age children have been labeled "hyperactive" or "hyperkinetic." In 1973 Dr. Benjamin Feingold, a pediatric allergist from California, proposed that salicylates, artificial colors, and artificial flavors were causes of hyperactivity. To treat or prevent this condition, he suggested a diet that was free of these additives.

Adherence to the Feingold diet requires drastic changes in family life-style and eating patterns. Virtually all manufactured baked goods, luncheon meats, ice cream, powdered puddings, candies, sodas, and punches must be eliminated. Coffee, tea, margarine, colored butter, and most commercially produced condiments are excluded. In addition, many nonfood items such as mouthwash, toothpaste, cough drops, perfume, and some over-the-counter and prescription drugs are prohibited. Eating in restaurants is practically impossible on the Feingold diet. "Convenience" foods are generally restricted because they contain artificial colors and flavors. Homemade foods prepared "from scratch" are therefore necessary for all family meals. Feingold strongly recommends that the hyperactive child be included in the preparation of the special foods, and he encourages the entire family to participate in the dietary program.

Many parents who have followed Feingold's recommendations have reported an improvement in their children's behavior. In fact, many families have banded together to promote the dietary program. The Feingold Association of the United States (FAUS), which has local chapters throughout the country, claims that fidgetiness, poor sleeping habits, short attention span, self-mutilation, antisocial traits, muscle incoordination, memory deficits, asthma, bedwetting, headaches, hives, seizures, and many other problems may respond to the Feingold program.[21] However, in 1980 an expert task force concluded that carefully designed experiments had failed to support the Feingold hypothesis, and the changes described in some reports had no practical significance.[22]

Because the Feingold diet does no physical harm, it might appear to be helpful in some instances due to its impact on the family. The potential benefits, however, must be weighed against the potentially harmful impact of teaching children to "blame" food ingredients for their difficulties when other factors are more likely to be responsible.

Subliminal Self-Help

Thousands of videotapes and audiotapes containing repeated messages are being marketed with claims that they can help people: lose weight, stop smoking, enhance athletic performance, quit drinking, think creatively, raise IQ, make friends, reduce pain, improve vision, restore hearing, cure acne, conquer fears, read faster, speak effectively, handle criticism, relieve depression, enlarge breasts, and do many other things. At least one company sells subliminal tapes for children, including a toilet-training tape for toddlers. Many tapes contain music said to promote relaxation. Most of the tapes are claimed to contain messages that are inaudible or barely audible, but some are barely or fully audible. Videotapes may feature images, said to be relaxing, combined with repeated messages shown so briefly that they cannot be seen.

One researcher who tested subliminal audiotapes from several companies concluded that they contained no embedded messages that could conceivably influence behavior.[23] Another research team tested volunteers for a study of tapes said to improve memory and self-esteem, but switched the tapes for half of the participants (to create a control group). Regardless of the tape used, about half of the volunteers claimed to achieve the results they were told to expect—but objective tests of memory and self-esteem showed no change.[24] A National Research Council committee has concluded that although many people claim that subliminal self-help tapes contribute to self-improvement there is no scientific evidence to support such claims.[25] Thus, there is no reason to believe that musical tapes with subliminal messages can do anything more for physical or mental well-being than listening to ordinary music. Moore[26] states that there is no scientific evidence that inaudible messages are unconsciously or subconciously perceived or can influence behavior.

Meditation

Meditation is generally defined as a class of techniques intended to influence an individual's consciousness through the regulation of attention. It may involve lying quietly or sitting in a particular position, attending to one's breathing (yoga), adopting a passive attitude, attempting to be at ease, or repeating a word aloud or to oneself (transcendental meditation). A National Research Council committee has concluded that people who meditate regularly may have a more restful life-style and that a variety of relaxation techniques might be appropriate for stress-reduction. However, the committee found no scientific evidence that meditation reduces stress more than does simply resting quietly or that meditation alone provides lasting benefits such as reducing high blood pressure or other unhealthy responses to stress.[25]

Overuse of Electroconvulsive Therapy

Psychiatrists who give ECT to a large proportion of their patients, particularly young adults, should be viewed with suspicion. Although ECT can be useful in some patients, most patients will respond to medication or psychotherapy.

Simplistic Advice

A deep understanding of the dynamics of a patient may enable a therapist to give good advice that appears to be simple in content. But sometimes therapists give advice without taking into consideration the complexity of the patient's situation. Such ill-conceived action may be the result of inadequate training, an emotional problem of the therapists, or both. The following composite cases illustrate this point:

A 60-year-old business man complained of insomnia and depression. Worry about his business was keeping him awake. The physician advised him to take a vacation to "get away from it all so you can stop worrying." The man went to a seaside resort but found he could not relax. He thought that his business would suffer from his absence, and idleness merely served to intensify his worrying.

A 35-year-old junior executive sought treatment for headaches and abdominal fullness. The physician correctly diagnosed that these were bodily reactions to tension, which was generated primarily at work. The patient believed he was being asked to do more than his share, but was afraid to speak up about it. The physician encouraged the man to express his resentment, but failed to discuss how to do this in a constructive manner. The patient "told off" his boss and quit in a huff, a decision he later regretted.

A middle-aged couple who consulted a counselor spent the entire first two sessions berating each other for one thing after another. Seeing only the hostility in the relationship, the counselor advised them to get a divorce. A more qualified therapist would have realized that they could not have remained together for many years without a positive side to their relationship. The therapist should have terminated the verbal slugfest, explored the positive aspects of the relationship, identified the issues in conflict, and tried to help the couple resolve them.

A 30-year-old housewife sought help to understand why she became angry with important people in her life, particularly her husband. The therapist encouraged discussion of her childhood and analyzed similarities between her father and her husband. The connection was made that "you get angry with your husband when he reminds you of your father." Feeling that this information justified her resentment, the patient acted more nastily toward her husband, and their relationship deteriorated. Actually, the marital situation had been far more complex than the therapist realized. He should have explored the patient's contribution to the marital friction and helped her learn better ways to handle her feelings.

Mismanagement of Psychotherapy

Psychotherapy should not only help patients resolve their problems, but it should also (with rare exception) help them become independent of the therapist. Just as children must learn to handle situations without always running to their mother, patients must learn to handle upset feelings between sessions without the direct help of the therapist. A therapist who permits or encourages frequent telephone calls is also encouraging overdependence. Therapists who receive many such calls from many patients are likely to have an unconscious problem, such as a neurotic need to have people depend on them, which interferes with treatment of the patients.

A more subtle example of this problem is the therapist who cannot adhere to a schedule. Patients are scheduled for particular times, but sessions are allowed to run considerably overtime when patients are upset or appear to be talking about particularly meaningful material. Although an occasional brief extension may be justified, a general policy of this type encourages patients to manipulate the therapist to gain more attention.

IT'S YOUR DECISION

Should you or a family member need help with an emotional or mental problem, which of the following actions would you take, and why?

		Reason
_____	Check Yellow Pages	_____
_____	Ask a local physician for help	_____
_____	Check with a religious counselor	_____
_____	Call the local health department	_____
_____	Discuss the matter with spouse or friend	_____
_____	Try sensitivity therapy	_____
_____	Take large amounts of vitamins	_____
_____	Other	_____

Should a family member have an alcohol problem, what action or actions might you take to assist this person, and why?

		Reason
_____	Check with religious counselor	_____
_____	Call one of the self-help groups in the community	_____
_____	Talk with a family relative or friend	_____
_____	Talk with family member about obtaining help	_____
_____	Call your local physician	_____
_____	Other	_____

A more malignant type of therapist's behavior is that of exploiting patients. Although it is not unusual for therapist and patient to feel a personal or physical attraction toward each other, acting on such feelings is not therapeutic. A composite case history illustrates what can happen:

> An unmarried 27-year-old woman entered therapy to overcome shyness, feelings of inadequacy, and fear of involvement with men. Few men had seemed interested in her, and she had rarely dated. As therapy proceeded, she developed an intense fondness for the therapist, based largely on the fact that he was the first man who ever spent time with her on a regular basis. At this point, instead of helping her learn how to attract suitable dates, the therapist suggested that sex with him would help her become more comfortable with men. She consented, hoping that marriage to the therapist would result. Her eventual disillusionment was a shattering experience that led to suicide.

Almost all psychiatrists believe that sexual contact with a patient is inappropriate and is usually harmful. Several state have laws forbidding such contact. In some states, it is a criminal offense, while in others it is considered malpractice and can lead to a loss of license. In 1990 a California jury awarded $1.5 million to a woman who claimed that she had been exploited by a psychiatrist who had treated her. Testimony during the trial indicated that they began dating after almost 2 years of treatment. The patient said that although she was extremely happy during the beginning of their affair, she became severely depressed when it ended.[27]

Summary

Although excellent help is available for the treatment of mental problems, selecting a suitable therapist can be difficult. Some people respond best to a conversational approach, some to medication, and some to both. Before seeking treatment, it is advisable to understand the types of help available and the training that various types of practitioners undergo. Although most practitioners with accredited training are competent, some engage in practices that are unscientific or reflect underlying problems of their own. For this reason, consumers should also be able to recognize the common signs of inappropriate therapy.

Discussion Questions

1. Define and briefly discuss the two general types of psychiatric treatment.
2. Identify and briefly discuss the treatment procedures used by psychiatrists.
3. What are the general types, the reasons for use, and the adverse reactions of the drugs used in psychiatric treatment?
4. Define psychotherapy, and discuss the nature and types of therapy used in the treatment of patients with psychologic problems.
5. What the term "psychosomatic" mean? How can psychosomatic problems be treated?
6. What are the types, qualifications and training, and services rendered by mental health practitioners?
7. When should people seek professional help for a mental or emotional problem?
8. How should a mental health practitioner be selected?
9. Identify several self-help groups and briefly discuss the services rendered.
10. Identify and briefly discuss questionable practices related to mental health.

References

1. Wolberg LR: The technique of psychotherapy, New York, 1977, Grune & Stratton.
2. Kolata G: Critics say Upjohn hid data on drug, The New York Times, Jan 21, 1992.
3. Church of Scientology International: The story that *Time* couldn't tell, Los Angeles, 1991, The Church.
4. Block S: Cleaning up, Psychiatry Update, Vol 1, 1991.
5. FDA denies Scientology petition against Prozac, FDA Talk Paper, Aug 1, 1991.
6. American Psychiatric Association: Press release, No 91-11, Washington, DC, Aug 1, 1991, The Association.
7. Task Force on Electroconvulsive Therapy: The practice of electroconvulsive therapy: recommendations for treatment, training, and privileging, Washington DC, 1990, American Psychiatric Association.
8. AMA Council on Scientific Affairs: Aversion therapy, JAMA 258:2562-2566, 1987.
9. Orne MT et al: APA Task Force Report 19: biofeedback. Washington DC, 1980, American Psychiatric Association.
10. Biofeedback: Harvard Medical School Health Letter 15(10):1-4, 1990.

*11. Callan J: Your guide to mental health, Philadelphia, 1982, George F Strickley Co.

*12. English OS and Finch SM: Introduction to psychiatry, New York, 1954, WW Norton & Co Inc.

*13. Pies RW: Inside psychotherapy: the patient's handbook, Philadelphia, 1983, George F Strickley Co.

---

*Recommended reading

14. US Churches of Scientology: New viewpoints, Los Angeles, 1976, The Church.
15. Hubbard LR: Dianetics: the modern science of mental health, Los Angeles, 1985, Bridge Publications Inc.
16. Behar R: The thriving cult of greed and power, Time Magazine, pp. 50-57, May 6, 1991.
17. *United States v Hubbard E-Meter*, 333 F(supp)357, 1971.
18. Food Drug Cosmetic Reports: *United States v Hubbard E-Meter*, p 842, Mar 12, 1973.
19. Hubbard LR: Clear body, clear mind, Los Angeles, 1990, Bridge Publications.
*20. Lipton M et al: Task force report on megavitamin and orthomolecular therapy in psychiatry, Washington DC, 1973, American Psychiatric Association.
21. The Feingold Association of the United States, The Feingold handbook, Alexandria, VA, 1986.
22. Wender EH and Lipton MA: The national advisory committee report on hyperkinesis and food additives—final report to The Nutrition Foundation, Washington DC, 1980, The Nutrition Foundation.
23. Merikle PM: Subliminal auditory messages: an evaluation, Psychology and Marketing 5:355-372, 1989.
24. Greenwald AG, Spangenberg ER, and Pratkanis AR: Double-blind tests of subliminal self-help audiotapes, Psychological Science 2:119-122, 1991.
25. Bjork RA et al: In the mind's eye: enhancing human performance, Washington DC, 1991, National Academy Press.
26. Moore TE: Subliminal perception: facts and fallacies, Skeptical Inquirer 16:273-281, 1992.
27. Rubsamen D: Psychiatrist's seduction of patient results in $1.5 million jury verdict, Psychiatric News, p 15, Mar 15, 1990.

CHAPTER EIGHT

DENTAL CARE

"I don't care if it does run up the light bill . . . brush them!"

(Copyright 1969 by Consumers Union of United States, Inc., Mount Vernon, N.Y. 10550. Reprinted by permission from Consumer Reports, March, 1969.)

Few pleasures match the enjoyment of eating. Ask anyone who has lost the ability to chew and you will realize that good teeth contribute not only to appearance but to the quality of life as well.

WILLIAM T. JARVIS, PH.D

The majority of dentists work in the privacy of their own office where they usually are not subject to review by knowledgeable colleagues. This situation, plus the fact that the harm done by poor dental care may not become apparent for many years, makes it difficult for consumers to evaluate the quality of the treatment they receive.

JOHN E. DODES, D.D.S.[1]

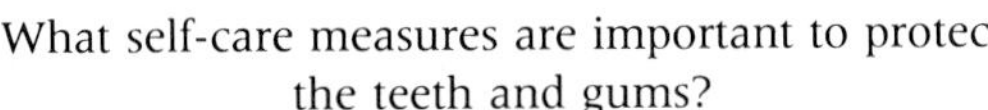

How important is fluoride for protecting against tooth decay?

What self-care measures are important to protect the teeth and gums?

How can a good dentist be located?

How do the potential benefits of dental x-ray films compare to the risks of radiation involved in obtaining them?

When is orthodontic care appropriate?

Do mercury-amalgam fillings pose any hazard?

Dental diseases are among the most prevalent ailments in the United States. Tooth decay (caries) affects almost everyone, and periodontal disease results in greater tooth loss than any other cause. The 1990 toll in dental bills was about $34 billion. Misconceptions about dental disease are common. Misinformation is spread by advertisers, food faddists, news media, and poorly informed health care professionals. This chapter covers the causes, prevention, and treatment of dental problems. It also contains a brief discussion of smokeless tobacco products.

DENTISTS

Dentists are licensed practitioners who hold either a doctor of dental surgery (D.D.S.) or the equivalent doctor of medical dentistry (D.M.D.) degree. Becoming a dentist requires a minimum of 2 years of predental college work followed by 4 years of dental school. However, almost all students entering dental school have a baccalaureate degree. There are 56 accredited dental schools in the United States. The first 2 years of dental school consist largely of basic and preclinical sciences and dental treatment under faculty supervision. State licensure is then accomplished by passing national and state board examinations. Dentists who wish to practice one of the dental specialties spend 2 or more years in advanced training. To become board certified, they must then pass a rigid examination under the auspices of a specialty examining board recognized by the American Dental Association (ADA). The eight recognized specialties are:

Endodontics: Prevention and treatment of diseases of the root pulp and related structures (root canal)

Oral and maxillofacial surgery: Tooth extractions; surgical treatment of diseases, injuries, and defects of the mouth, jaw, and face

Oral pathology: Diagnosis of tumors, other diseases, and injuries of the head and neck

Orthodontics: Diagnosis and correction of tooth irregularities and facial deformities

Pediatric dentistry: Dental care of infants and children

Periodontics: Treatment of diseases of the gums and related structures

Prosthodontics: Treatment of oral dysfunction through the use of prosthetic devices such as crowns, bridges, and dentures

Public health dentistry: Prevention and control of dental disease and promotion of community dental health

The ADA estimates that 141,000 dentists are professionally active in the United States, with about 129,700 in private practice. About 73.5% of dentists belong to the ADA.

AUXILIARY DENTAL PERSONNEL

Dentists are assisted by three categories of personnel: dental assistants, dental hygienists, and dental laboratory technicians.

Dental assistants have been part of the dental health care team since 1885. Most are women, but men also enter this vocation. The duties they may legally perform vary from state to state and can depend on the extent of their training. They may include preparing patients, sterilizing instruments, preparing materials, keeping records, and taking x-ray films. Many assistants are trained by their employer-dentist. Others have taken a short commercial course or received special training for expanded functions. Assistants must pass a special examination to be allowed to take x-ray films. Additional training is required to become a Registered Dental Assistant (RDA) who is permitted to polish teeth. Registered Dental Assistants in Extended Functions (RDAEFs) are legally permitted to apply sealants.

Dental hygienists provide clinical and educational services in private dental offices, schools, industrial plants, and public health and other government agencies. Their activities include performing oral prophylaxis (cleaning and polishing teeth), taking and processing x-ray films, conducting caries screening, and teaching oral health care. The training of dental hygienists takes 2 years for an A.A. degree or 4 years for a B.S. degree. They then can become registered by passing a state licensing examination. The scope of what dental hygienists may do varies from state to state and is gradually expanding.

Dental laboratory technicians are trained to construct and repair oral appliances such as crowns, bridges, and dentures. Some train by apprenticeship, and others attend educational programs of 1 to 2 years in length. Some of these programs are accredited, but others are not. Many junior or community colleges include a dental technology program as part of their vocational training. Dental laboratory technicians usually work under the direction of a dentist, either in the dentist's office or in a commercial laboratory. Those who work independently, selling directly to the public, are referred to as denturists. Denturism is illegal in most states.

Tooth Decay

Tooth decay (caries) is caused by bacteria in the mouth that produce acids that attack the tooth enamel. It is a highly complex phenomenon that also involves the interaction of hereditary factors, bacteria, nutritional factors, dietary habits, oral hygiene, and time. Animal studies suggest that caries can be controlled by reducing the number of decay-producing bacteria in the mouth. Caries occurs at its greatest intensity during adolescence.

Although most people know that sugar consumption has an effect on dental caries, few people know how it actually works in the decay process. The amount of sugar in the diet is not as important as the frequency of eating, the acid-buffering capacity of the saliva, the availability of fluoride, or the individual's oral hygiene practices.

Faddists teach that honey, raw sugar, and other "natural" sweets are nutritionally superior, and that white sugar is bad because it is "empty calories." They also suggest that natural sugars are less apt to produce tooth decay. Both of these ideas are incorrect. The vitamin content of natural sugars is minuscule. Honey is at least as cariogenic as refined sugar (sucrose) in the same concentration. The faddists' suggestion to substitute granola for conventional presweetened cereals is also foolish. (Granolas are made with oats, honey, dried fruit, and brown sugar.)

Decay-causing germs make no distinction between sugars from different sources. They digest them all and produce acids that attack (demineralize) the tooth enamel. The more frequently a person eats between meals, and the longer fermentable carbohydrates remain in contact with the teeth (which is more apt to happen with sticky sweets), the more the teeth are subjected to demineralization. However, remineralization (healing) occurs between periods of exposure to acids. The amount of decay depends upon the balance between demineralization and remineralization.[2] Remineralization is aided by the presence of fluoride ions.

Cases have been reported of tooth damage in users of vitamin C (ascorbic acid) tablets who chew the tablets rather than swallow them. Ascorbic acid is strong enough to erode tooth enamel over a period of time.[3]

Dental Sealants

Sealants are thin plastic coatings that can protect the chewing surfaces (but not the sides) of the back teeth (molars) from decay. Sealants fill the pits and fissures and harden soon after application. They usually last for years and can be reapplied if necessary. They are most effective for children between the ages of 5 and 14 when applied soon after the permanent teeth erupt. Friedman[4] cautions that sealants should be used only for pits and fissures that are defective:

> Not all pits and fissures need to be sealed but only those in which the sharp dental probe sticks firmly. Because molars are most likely to develop cavities, many dentists recommend sealing the . . . chewing surface whether or not defective; however, this creates an additional expense that may not be necessary.

Fluoridation

Fluoride is a mineral found naturally in most water supplies. When sufficient quantities of fluoride are available, especially during the process of tooth development, the resultant teeth are stronger and more resistant to decay.[5] Fluorides also work topically to prevent decay.

In the early 1900s a Colorado dentist named

Frederick McKay suspected that something in water was responsible for the brown stains on the teeth of members of his community. The mottled teeth also were remarkably free of decay. By 1931 a new technique for water analysis enabled Dr. McKay to identify excessive fluoride as the cause. Subsequent testing determined that the ideal concentration for prevention of caries without mottling is approximately one part of fluoride per million parts of water.[6] The first controlled fluoridation program began in 1945 in Grand Rapids, MI.

Today more than 135 million people in the United States drink water that is fluoridated, either artificially or naturally. Strident claims have been made that fluoridation causes cancer, birth defects, Down's syndrome, allergies, and a wide variety of other maladies. But none of these claims has held up to scrutiny by qualified scientists.[7-9] According to William T. Jarvis, Ph.D., president of the National Council Against Health Fraud:

> These charges seem to grow out of a mentality of distrust. Antifluoridation groups are led by many of the same people who oppose immunization, pasteurization, sex education, mental health programs, and other public health advances. Most are closely connected with sellers of alternatives to medically accepted products and services. The so-called "health food" industry justifies its existence by declaring that our conventional sources of food, water, and health care are misguided.

Too much fluoride can cause dental fluorosis, which, in its mildest form, causes small, white, virtually invisible opaque areas on teeth. In severe form, fluorosis causes brownish mottling. However, dental fluorosis does not result from artificial fluoridation alone, because the levels are kept low enough to avoid this effect.

Lifesavers Guide to Fluoridation, by John Yiamouyiannis, Ph.D., an antifluoridation pamphlet, distributed in virtually every community where fluoridation is considered, cites 250 references to back up claims that fluoridation is ineffective and unsafe. However, experts from the Ohio Department of Health traced the references and found that almost half had no relevance to community water fluoridation and that many others actually support fluoridation but were selectively quoted and misrepresented.[10]

Consumers Union has concluded:

> The simple truth is that there's no "scientific controversy" over the safety of fluoridation. The practice is safe, economical, and beneficial. The survival of this fake controversy represents one of the major triumphs of quackery over science in our generation.[8]

In 1990 an article in *Newsweek* magazine suggested that fluoridation was ineffective and dangerous.[11] The article was triggered by unauthorized release of preliminary data from an experiment at the National Institute of Environmental Health Sciences in which rats and mice were exposed to a high dosage of fluoride. A few of the animals had developed bone cancer. However, thorough review by a U.S. Public Health Service expert panel concluded that the data were insignificant and that fluoridation posed no risk of cancer or any other disease.[12] Dr. Stephen Barrett[13] called the *Newsweek* article "the most irresponsible analysis of a public health topic ever published by a major national news outlet."

Fluoridation Alternatives

At present, fluoridation reduces the incidence of cavities 20% to 40% in children and 15% to 35% in adults.[14] The reduction is less than it was 20 to 40 years ago, probably due to improved dental hygiene and widespread use of fluoride toothpaste. Children in areas with negligible amounts of fluoride in the drinking water should be given dietary supplementation with drops or tablets prescribed by a physician or dentist. Table 8-1 gives the recommended dosage. Children who drink adequately fluoridated water should not be given supplements.

When the recommended supplement schedule is followed conscientiously from birth through early adolescence, the level of caries protection approaches that of water fluoridation. However, since few parents have sufficient motivation to carry out such a program, water fluoridation is considered vastly superior from a public health standpoint. Topical methods apply fluoride directly to the surfaces of the teeth. They have merit but are not as effective as ingested fluorides. Fluoride toothpastes and mouth rinses are available for individual use; and gels, pastes, and solutions are available for administration by dentists. Topical fluoride methods can be used in nonfluoridated communities and also offer additional caries protection in fluoridated communities.

Water fluoridation, which costs about 50 cents per person per year, is considerably more economical than other methods of fluoride administration. Every dollar invested saves an estimated $80 in

Table 8–1

Supplemental Fluoride Dosage Milligrams of Fluoride per Day*

Age (years)	Concentration of fluoride in water (parts per million) 0.0 to 0.3	0.3 to 0.7	Over 0.7
Birth to 2	0.25	0	0
2 to 3	0.50	0.25	0
3 to 13	1.00	0.50	0

*2.2 mg of sodium fluoride contains 1 mg of fluoride.
Recommended by the American Dental Association, the American Academy of Pediatrics, and the American Society for Pediatric Dentistry. Includes nursing infants who usually consume little exogenous water. Commercial formulas contain no fluoride.

Table 8–2

Cavities Prevented by Various Methods per $100,000 Spent

Method	Number of cavities prevented
Community water fluoridation	440,000
School water fluoridation	106,000
Fluoride rinses	45,500
Fluoride toothpast	21,600
Topical fluoride, applied by dentist	18,900
Fluoride tablets (school)	13,500
Fluoride tablets (home)	8,000
Restoring decayed teeth	8,000

From U.S. Public Health Service. Based on 1980 data.

dental treatment costs.[15] Table 8-2 compares the cost-effectiveness of various methods of cavity prevention.

Periodontal Disease

Periodontal disease (also called pyorrhea) is the general term for inflammatory and degenerative diseases of the gums and other structures that surround the base of the teeth. It is the most common reason for tooth loss between the ages of 50 and 70. It is usually triggered by accumulation of plaque below the gum line.

There are several types of periodontal disease, all resulting from a bacterial infection that attacks the gums, bone, and ligaments that support and hold the teeth in the jaw. Without adequate bone and connecting fibers to hold the teeth, they become loose and are lost. Since this damage is irreversible, it is imperative that early signs of periodontal disease be recognized and proper action be taken. The earliest stage is gingivitis, which develops as toxins in the plaque irritate the gums, making them red, tender, swollen, and likely to bleed. The next stage, periodontitis, occurs when toxins destroy the tissues anchoring the teeth to the bone. Gums become detached from the teeth, forming pockets that fill with more plaque. Advanced periodontitis is present when the teeth lose more attachments because the supporting bone is destroyed. Without treatment, the tooth becomes loose and may fall out or require removal by a dentist.

Brushing, flossing, and periodic dental care are the first lines of defense against periodontal disease—as they are against caries. Adequate daily oral hygiene can prevent or minimize periodontal disease. Gingivitis, a sign that something is wrong, is evidenced by redness or bleeding of the gums but no discomfort. Pink coloring on the toothbrush bristles may present the first clue that gingivitis is present. The ADA states that more than half the people over the age of 18 have at least the early stage of some type of periodontal disease.[16]

Cleaning prophylaxis by a dentist or dental hygienist is advisable at least once a year to remove calculus (also called tartar or scale), prevent gingivitis, and reduce the risk of periodontal disease. Professional cleaning is a meticulous procedure in which all the tartar, above and below the gumline, is carefully removed with metal instruments called scalers. An ultrasonic device can be used to remove calculus, but its use should be followed with hand-scaling to ensure that the teeth are clean and smooth. The teeth are polished after the scaling.

In the late 1970s an oral hygiene program called the Keyes technique was widely promoted as a non-surgical alternative for treating advanced periodontal disease. The technique includes microscopic examination of the plaque and cleaning the teeth and gums with a mixture of salt, baking soda, and peroxide. At least three well-designed studies have shown that surgical treatment is more effective. A recent study found that while the baking soda mixture helped maintain oral health, it was no more effective than ordinary toothpaste. The researchers also found that people using the baking soda regimen were three times as likely to stop their program because it was inconvenient. It seems unlikely that the Keyes technique can contribute more toward healthy gums than can brushing with ordinary toothpaste and using dental floss.[1]

Self-Care

Although individuals can greatly influence their oral health, many people do not take dental problems seriously until it is too late. Losing one's teeth may not be as serious as losing an eye, a hand, or a foot, but people who lose their teeth are handicapped. Dentures are not as comfortable or as functional as normal, healthy teeth and can result in difficulty in eating as well as adverse effects on personality.

Brushing and Flossing

Teeth should be cleaned to remove plaque, which is the soft, sticky, colorless film of bacteria that is constantly forming on their surface. Acids produced by these bacteria are a major factor in both tooth decay and periodontal disease. Plaque changes in both quantity and destructive character with the passage of time. It takes about 24 hours for plaque to become sufficiently concentrated to begin causing damage. Pits, fissures, and areas between the teeth where toothbrushes cannot reach provide hideaways for plaque and thus furnish the sites for most dental problems.

One thorough daily cleaning, involving both brushing and flossing, is usually sufficient to break up the colonies of plaque that oral microorganisms are building. A fluoridated dentifrice should be used. Brushing after meals is primarily for the purpose of dislodging food particles and should be accompanied by a thorough rinsing of the mouth. Surface plaque can be identified with disclosing solutions or tablets. These dye the plaque bright red and enable a person to see areas that are missed when cleaning the teeth. If plaque is allowed to remain on the teeth, it can harden to form calculus. Calculus is a gum irritant and can host bacteria that cause periodontal disease. Once calculus builds up, a visit to the dentist will be required to remove it.

Myth of "Detergent Foods"

One of the myths concerning oral health is that eating so-called detergent foods (crunchy foods such as apples and popcorn) help to clean the teeth by removing plaque. Even official government publications have made this claim. Although coarse foods may provide exercise for the teeth and gums, they are not a substitute for oral hygiene. Studies on a variety of foods have shown that, at best, chewing can affect plaque on the upper third of the teeth. Areas under the gums where periodontal disease occurs are completely unaffected.

Dental Products

The ADA maintains a continual independent review of commonly used dental products that are commercially manufactured. Those judged to be safe and effective are permitted to carry statements of ADA acceptance on their packages and in their advertising.

Dentifrices

Dentifrices commonly contain abrasives, binding agents, sudsers, moisturizers, flavoring agents, and water. Many contain a fluoride compound. A dentrifice should be abrasive enough to prevent plaque and stain accumulation but not so harsh that it injures teeth or gums. The more abrasive toothpastes have little effect on the hard enamel in teeth, but cementum, the soft layer of the tooth just under the gum, is more vulnerable.[17] As a person gets older, the gums may recede and expose the cementum to possible damage by abrasion. Some products may also irritate the gums themselves.

Fluoride dentifrices inhibit dental caries even in adults. They are not a substitute for the fluoridation of community drinking water but are a useful adjunct. Many have been accepted by the ADA Council on Dental Therapeutics as: "an effective decay preventive dentifrice that can be of significant value when used in a conscientiously applied program of oral hygiene and regular professional care." Dentists can recommend fluoride-containing products that are within the proper range of abrasiveness based on their patients' individual needs.

Some dentrifice advertisements make claims regarding the *whitening* and *brightening* of teeth. The basic color of the teeth, as determined early in life, cannot be made whiter. Claims that toothpaste can remove calculus or retard new calculus formation also are questionable. Abrasive toothpastes may remove minor tooth discoloration caused by substances taken into the mouth, but abrasive toothpastes can easily damage the softer parts of the teeth. Toothpastes containing urea peroxide or hydrogen peroxide can exert bleaching action. However, the wisest course of action for consumers who are concerned about tooth discoloration is to discuss the matter with their dentist.

If gums recede so that cementum is exposed, the teeth can become sensitive. Use of a dentifrice that contains potassium nitrate (Promise, Denquel) lessens this sensitivity for some people.[18]

Fluoride Mouth Rinses

The ADA Council on Dental Therapeutics has accepted several nonprescription fluoride mouth rinses as "effective decay preventive rinses that can be of significant value when used regularly in conjunction with a decay-preventive fluoride dentrifice in a conscientiously applied program of oral hygiene and regular professional care." These can be helpful to people who live in nonfluoridated communities or whose teeth are very susceptible to decay.

Toothbrushes

Most dentists suggest a flat brushing surface with tufts of approximately equal length throughout the brush and a head small enough for comfort, regardless of the number of rows. The head of the brush must be small enough to reach all important surface areas of the mouth. Soft nylon bristles are flexible, clean teeth efficiently, and usually do not damage the gums. These bristles enable the user to get below the gum margin to help remove plaque. Toothbrushes with hard bristles should not be used because they can cause abrasive damage to the teeth and gums, especially when combined with a highly abrasive toothpaste. The type of toothbrush is much less important than the way it is used. To be effective, a brush must be manipulated properly.

Electric toothbrushes are useful but are not panaceas. Careful manual brushing can be just as effective as mechanical brushing, although recent studies report that certain electric toothbrushes, such as Interplak and Rotadent, remove plaque more efficiently than manual brushing. An electric toothbrush is particularly helpful for people with poor coordination due to mental or physical disabilities, patients with orthopedic bands on their teeth, and/or those who are unwilling to spend sufficient time for proper brushing by hand.

Consumers Union's consultants advise replacing one's toothbrush every 4 to 6 weeks because worn bristles make it less efficient at removing plaque. They also warn that commercially-marketed ultraviolet "toothbrush sterilizers" have no practical value because there is no danger from using a toothbrush that carries germs from one's own mouth.[19]

Dental Floss and Toothpicks

Dental floss comes waxed or unwaxed. Although may dentists recommend the unwaxed type as doing the better job of removing plaque, people with tightly spaced teeth may find it easier to use the waxed type. The important point is to use floss daily in the manner prescribed by the dentist or dental hygienist. Floss holders are available for individuals who have difficulty manipulating the floss by hand. Some dentists recommend a toothpick (sometimes a specially shaped one such as Stim-u-dent) or a rubber interdental tip as a supplement to dental floss.

Dental Irrigators

Oral irrigating devices use a direct spray of water to remove loose food particles and other large materials from about the teeth. Oral irrigators cannot substitute for either brushing or flossing, but patients with orthodontic bands, fixed bridges, or excessive spacing between the teeth may find them helpful. Incorrect use of an irrigating device can injure oral tissues. For this reason, persons using such devices should get instructions from their dentist about proper use.

Mouthwashes

Advertising has suggested that mouthwash is effective against bad breath, can help clean the teeth, prevent or treat colds and sore throats, and help control dental plaque. Each of these claims is questionable.[20]

A mouthwash can freshen the breath for a few minutes, but it cannot prevent infectious diseases. Some mouthwashes have a high alcohol content that can cause excessive drying of the mouth. People who are troubled with bad breath should understand that this is a symptom whose cause, whether oral or systemic, should be ascertained. Common causes of bad breath are poor oral hygiene, postnasal drip, gum disease, and the consumption of aromatic substances such as alcohol, garlic, and onions. Halitosis may also be a symptom of infections, tumors, diabetes, and a variety of other diseases.

For many years—until stopped by federal enforcement actions—manufacturers suggested in their ads that mouthwashes can help prevent or cure infections. It is true that antiseptic mouthwashes can kill some germs on contact, but this does not have medical significance. Germs in the tiny crevices in the mouth and within infected tissues cannot be reached or washed out. Germs that are washed off the surface of infected areas are quickly replaced.

The plaque-control situation is less clear-cut. In 1986 the FDA approved Peridex mouthrinse, a prescription drug that contains 0.12% chlorhexidine, as safe and effective in helping to control plaque. Chlorhexidine can reduce plaque below the gumline. In 1987 the ADA Council on Dental Therapeutics concluded that: "Listerine Antiseptic has been shown to help prevent and reduce supragingival (above the gumline) plaque accumulation and gingivitis when used in a conscientiously applied program of oral hygiene and regular professional care. It has not been shown to have a therapeutic effect on periodontitis." Listerine does not affect plaque below the gumline and is not nearly as effective as Peridex. Mouthwashes are not substitutes for brushing and flossing and are appropriate mainly for individuals under dental care in which other measures are unable to control gingivitis.

In 1990 the FDA asked Listerine's manufacturer and two other companies to stop making claims that their mouthwash can fight plaque and prevent gingivitis. After further review, the agency may issue guidelines on what claims, if any, are permissible, or whether the products must go through the approval process for nonprescription drugs.

Plax, another mouthwash claimed to reduce plaque, uses sodium benzoate as its principle ingredient. Consumers Union's dental consultants believe that Plax has has not been shown to produce a clinically meaningful reduction in plaque.[21]

A recent National Cancer Institute[22] survey found that the use of mouthwash containing high amounts of alcohol (25% or more) was associated with an increased incidence of cancer of the mouth and pharynx. The study was done because it is known that these cancers are more common among people who drink large amounts of alcoholic beverages. Although the findings do not establish a cause-and-effect relationship, they do indicate that further research should be done.

Sugar-Free Gum

Chewing gum that contains sugar can contribute to tooth decay. Thus, sugar-free gum would be a better choice for people who chew gum frequently. Certain gums that contain xylitol are marketed with claims that it actually decreases the incidence of decay. John E. Dodes, D.D.S., an expert on dental quackery, states that this claim is not supported by solid scientific evidence.

Do-It-Yourself Bleaching

Dentists have been bleaching teeth in their offices for decades. This is a legitimate procedure that requires care to ensure that the patient is not injured by the caustic bleaching agent. Recently, there has been a flurry of advertising for tooth-bleaching agents for home use. None of these "do-it-yourself" products has been proven safe and effective by well-designed studies.[23] Experts have warned that self-bleaching may not be effective and might be dangerous. The FDA has ruled that bleaching products containing carbamide or hydrogen peroxide are "drugs" because they alter the structure of the tooth. In 1991 the FDA ordered 20 manufacturers to stop selling them until they are demonstrated to be safe and effective. A case has been reported of an Illinois boy who had permanently damaged his teeth with seven applications of bleach over a 2-month period. The bleach gradually stripped off the enamel, causing teeth to turn darker instead of whiter.[24] Products that use abrasives or white polish to brighten teeth are considered cosmetics and can still be marketed.

Pain Relievers

People with toothaches sometimes seek temporary relief through the purchase of nonprescription pain relievers that are applied to the teeth. Usually these products contain clove oil, anesthetics, and aspirin. Clove oil is a powerful germicide (8 times as strong as phenol). It is uncertain whether its action is due to a local anesthetic effect or to its irritant activity. Anesthetics such as benzocaine and butane sulfate can give minor relief from pain, if the decayed area of the tooth is exposed and accessible. Aspirin has no demonstrated topical anesthetic action. It should never be packed into a carious tooth or placed onto the adjacent gum, since its acidic nature can traumatize a nerve ending and produce ulceration of the mucous membrane of the mouth. Ibuprofen (Advil, Nuprin), taken internally, can be effective against dental pain.

Dental Restorations

The most common material used to restore decayed teeth is silver amalgam, a mixture of an alloy of silver, tin, copper, and zinc, with an equal amount of mercury. Tooth-colored plastic fillings can be used in front teeth or for small visible back fillings. If much tooth structure has been lost as the result of decay or an accident, then a cast restoration is used, preferably gold.

A cemented restoration that covers only part of the tooth is called an inlay or onlay. Cast metal, porcelain, and composite plastic materials can be used for this purpose. When not enough tooth is present to hold an inlay, a crown is needed. This restores the entire tooth that is visible above the gumline. Crowns are usually made of a combination of metal (preferably gold or palladium alloy) and porcelain. A front crown, sometimes called a cap, is usually made of solid porcelain.

When teeth are missing, the teeth on either side of the space can be crowned and artificial teeth (a bridge) can be permanently joined to the crowns. A bridge that is cemented to adjacent teeth is called a fixed bridge. Fixed bridgework is generally superior to removable bridgework, but there are situations where fixed bridges cannot be used.

The "Maryland Bridge," a type of fixed bridge developed by researchers at the University of Maryland, utilizes recently invented materials that bond metal to tooth structures. This method enables the dentist to replace missing teeth with a cemented restoration, without placing crowns on the adjacent teeth. It costs half or less than a conventional fixed bridge, but it is not as durable.

"Drill-less Fillings"

The Caridex is a trademarked device that uses a warm solution of sodium hydroxide, sodium chloride, sodium hypochlorite, and aminobutyric acid as its active ingredient to soften decay so that it is easily scraped from the tooth with a metal instrument. This procedure is safe and allows some patients to be treated without an injection of anesthetic. However, most cavities are not sufficiently exposed, so drilling is still needed for the great majority of patients.

Laser Drilling

Some dentists use a laser device to drill cavities and advertise that this method is quicker, more precise, and less apt to require anesthesia than normal dril-

Toxic Television

In 1990, CBS-TV's *60 Minutes* aired a half-hour program called "Poison in Your Mouth," which suggested that mercury-amalgam fillings were dangerous. The most powerful segment featured a woman who said that her symptoms of multiple sclerosis had disappeared overnight after her fillings were taken out. The fact that multiple sclerosis normally has ups and downs was not mentioned during the program. Nor did the program mention that the removal process temporarily *raises* the body's mercury load and could not possibly cause an overnight cure.[26] The broadcast induced many viewers to seek replacement of their fillings with other materials.

Consumer Reports responded with an article that concluded: "Given their solid track record and a risk that's still conjecture, amalgam fillings are still your best bet."[27] A few months later, a reader responded:

> My mother, who was diagnosed with Lou Gehrig's disease more than two years ago, had her mercury fillings removed immediately after the show aired. After she had spent $10,000 and endured more than 18 hours of dental work so painful she once fainted in the waiting room, her condition did not improve. The pain was outweighed only by the monumental disappointment she and the whole family experienced as we lived through one more false hope.

ling. The device is not FDA-approved for this purpose. *Consumer Reports*[25] has cautioned that the device has not been proven safe and effective for removing tooth decay and that in many patients a regular drill is still required to get through the enamel on molars.

Bonding

Bonding is a popular method of correcting cosmetic problems in patients with healthy gums and adequate tooth structure to which bonding material can be applied. Most dentists employ this procedure. Bonding is not an alternative to crowning. Crowns are needed if teeth are badly broken down or must anchor permanent or removable bridges.

To prepare a tooth for bonding, an acid solution is applied to increase adhesion. A liquid plastic is then painted on, and a paste made of plastic and finely ground quartz, glass, or silica gel is layered onto the tooth. Each layer is hardened in minutes either chemically or by shining a very bright light on the plastic. Finally, the bonded surface is polished. Cosmetic results can also be achieved by bonding very thin plastic or porcelain veneers to the acid-etched tooth enamel.

Bonding is usually painless, faster, and cheaper than crowning. However, it is not permanent and may need to be repeated after several years, since the bonding material wears away. Some dentists claim to specialize in "cosmetic dentistry," but this is not a recognized specialty.

Endodontics (Root Canal Therapy)

Teeth are hollow and contain living, sensitive tissue commonly called the "nerve" but referred to by dentists as the pulp. In infections of the pulp caused by decay or accidents, the pulp can be removed and replaced with an inert material (gutta-percha). Endodontics is expensive (typically several hundred dollars per tooth) but should be painless. Teeth often need an artificial crown and post (to increase retention of the crown) following root canal therapy, but millions of teeth have been saved through this therapy alone.

Sargenti root canal therapy is a treatment that sometimes may save a tooth, but is much less predictable than standard endodontic treatment. It is performed with a paste that is easier and faster to place than gutta-percha. However, the paste contains paraformaldehyde, and when in contact with water it forms formaldehyde, a toxic substance used in embalming fluid. The pressure needed to reach the tip of the root can force the paste into surrounding tissues where it can cause serious injury. The FDA has banned interstate marketing of Sargenti-type pastes, but pharmacists can prepare them for dentists in their community.

Proponents of the Sargenti method have formed the American Endodontic Society, which has little or no standing within the scientific dental community. The recognized endodontic specialty group is the American Association of Endodontists. In September 1991 the ADA Council on Dental Therapeutics abandoned its long-held neutral position on the Sargenti method and resolved:

> In view of the fact that sufficient data have not been submitted to the Council on Dental Therapeutics to establish the safety of paraformaldehyde-containing root canal filling materials and that the FDA has not approved any products with this formulation, the council cannot recommend use of these products at this time.[28]

A few months later the council asked interested parties to submit the evidence needed to make a final determination.

Orthodontics

The goal of the orthodontist is to improve the health and function of the mouth as well as one's physical appearance. Twenty million adults and children receive orthodontic treatment annually, though many others with correctable malocclusions do not. The ADA recommends consultation with an orthodontist for children 4 to 7 years old if the family dentist suspects that the teeth are badly aligned. There is no age limit for orthodontic treatment, provided oral tissues are basically healthy. At least 15% of orthodontic patients are now between the ages of 20 and 60.

Before beginning treatment, the orthodontist obtains facial measurements, x-ray films, and plaster casts to aid in diagnosis and treatment planning. Some orthodontists also use computer analysis. Teeth responsible for overcrowding may need to be extracted. Braces are prepared, cemented or bonded to the teeth, and wired together. Slight pressure is then maintained on the bands and wires so that the teeth are gradually brought into correct alignment. Some discomfort may be present during the first few days after braces are applied, but severe pain normally does not occur during orthodontic treatment. When proper occlusion has been achieved, the braces are removed and a retaining appliance is substituted. The average length of treatment is 18 to 24 months for children and adolescents. Adult treatment, which is more likely to involve removable appliances, generally takes longer. A full course of orthodontic treatment can cost $2000 to $3000 or more.

Dentures

The preparation of dentures is a complex procedure that is done best by a dentist with the help of a dental laboratory technician. Poorly fitted dentures can cause serious problems, including difficulty in eating and speaking, disturbances of the temporomandibular joint (TMJ), and irreversible destruction of bone needed for denture support. Constant irritation from an ill-fitting denture, if continued over a long period, may cause open sores or inflammation. Full lower or upper dentures typically cost about $500 each. Poorly fitted dentures can cost the patient more in the long run, when the damage they cause has to be corrected.

Denturists

Denturists are a relatively small number of technicians who provide dentures directly to the public and are seeking to be licensed independently from dentists. Denturism is illegal in most states. Denturists in Maine, Arizona, and Colorado can practice under the supervision of a licensed dentist. Denturists are allowed to practice independently only in Oregon, Idaho, and Montana. However, in a recent study, investigators hired by the Arizona Dental Association found that only 3 out of the state's 13 denturists advised callers to see a dentist before visiting them.[29]

Denturists assert that they can fit dentures as competently as dentists and more cheaply. However, Canadian data indicate that fees charged by denturists in that country are similar to those charged by dentists. The major objection to denturism is that complete examination of the mouth and proper fitting of the teeth often require skills that denturists do not possess. Denturists are not competent to diagnose cancers or other diseases within the mouth, to screen for underlying disease, or to recognize when structural problems of the mouth (such as unseen roots of teeth) can lead to injury if not corrected prior to the installation of dentures. In 1991 an Arizona dental board noted that complaints concerning the state's denturists were many times more common than complaints about the state's dentists.[29]

The ADA is strongly opposed to denturism and has encouraged dental societies to sponsor community programs in which professionally acceptable dentures can be offered to financially disadvantaged individuals at a reduced cost. Programs of this type exist in most states. In addition, low-cost may be available from dentists whose fees are comparable to denturists.

Denture Cleaning and Repair

If plaque accumulates on dentures, it can cause mouth odors and lead to the formation of calculus that can irritate the soft tissue of the mouth. Therefore, dentures should be brushed daily with a commercially available denture cleaner.

Some people have used laundry bleach (liquid sodium hypochlorite) or baking soda as denture cleaners. Although laundry bleach partially removes beverage and tobacco stains, it has the potential to burn tissues inside the mouth. It can also tarnish metal denture parts and fade the color of the plastic material. Baking soda has been found to be less effective than the better commercial cleaners. White vinegar can soften calculus on a denture.

In time dentures may loosen and need rebuilding or repair. Adhesives, repair kits, and reliner kits are available to the public, but the do-it-yourself approach to denture repair is hazardous. The FTC has warned major manufacturers of denture adhesives that it is unlawful to advertise that: (1) a denture adhesive will remedy biting and chewing problems of denture wearers unless retention represents their entire dental problem, or that (2) a denture adhesive will enable all denture wearers to eat foods that are hard to bite, such as apples and corn-on-the-cob.[30]

Dental Implants

Implants are artificial root substitutes that are placed within the jaw bone to anchor artificial teeth. They are usually made of titanium. The cost typically ranges from $800 to $1800 per implant for the surgical phase, plus an additional amount for the replacement teeth. For many years implants that were not sufficiently tested in the laboratory were used in patients, often with disastrous results. Today there are implant systems that provide a good chance of success with little danger of serious complications. The best researched of these is the osteointegrated Brånemark implant that was developed in Sweden. Several other systems also look promising.

An important factor in the success of implants is to minimize chewing pressure on them for 3 to 6 months. This can be accomplished by hiding the base of the implant under the gum until the bone has healed sufficiently. Then surgery is performed to expose the implant for attachment of the artificial teeth. Consumers should carefully investigate the experience of any dentist they consult and request complete information about the type of implant and possible complications. An oral surgeon or periodontist is likely to have the best surgical skills for placing implants, but some general dentists have sufficient training to do the surgery properly.

Dental X-Ray Procedures

X-ray films are a necessary part of modern dental practice. Usually they involve little radiation and are inexpensive, but so many are obtained that dental films are second only to chest examinations in frequency and overall cost. America's annual bill for dental radiographs is more than a billion dollars. Since any amount of radiation exposure involves some risk, the dental profession has worked hard to minimize radiation exposure. This has been accomplished by: (1) reducing exposure time by combining high-voltage equipment with high-speed film, (2) using collimators to reduce the area of the exposure, (3) filtering out unnecessary radiation, (4) eliminating unnecessary repetition of x-ray films, and (5) using lead aprons to shield the rest of the body.

Dentists typically obtain full-mouth radiographs of all the teeth at the beginning of the patient's care and every 3 to 5 years thereafter. However, a history and clinical examination should be completed before deciding what type of dental radiography, if any, should be obtained. A full set normally consists of two to four bite-wing x-ray films, which show the areas between the teeth and the parts of the teeth that are outside of or just below the gums; and 14 periapical films, which reveal the deeper dental structures that include the tips of the roots of two or three teeth per film.

For bite-wing and periapical views, the film is placed inside the patient's mouth and the x-ray source is a stationary machine. Panoramic views are obtained with a machine that swings the x-ray camera around the head, enabling all the teeth to be included in a single picture. This procedure is quicker and more comfortable for the patient because the film is positioned outside the patient's mouth. Unfortunately, the resultant picture is not as detailed. Therefore bite-wing and periapical films are used to diagnose decay and periodontal disease, while panoramic films are appropriate for detecting diseases and infections in the jaw bones, orthodontic problems, and impactions (unerupted teeth).

Children and adults generally do not need an x-ray examination each time they see a dentist if they are not at high risk for decay and show no other signs of dental disease. (Young children rarely need x-rays because baby teeth usually are spaced so that all surfaces are visible to the naked eye.) Bite-wing x-ray films are appropriate annually for most patients and may be obtained more frequently if rampant caries exist. On such a schedule the diagnostic benefit clearly outweighs the minimal risk of radiation that is involved. What little risk exists is greatly reduced by the use of a lead apron. An expert panel has concluded that the above guidelines need not be altered during pregnancy because the amount of radiation reaching the pelvis is insignificant.[31]

If recent films are available, it may not be necessary to obtain new ones. Dental radiographs often yield more information when compared with previous films. Thus, if consulting a new dentist, bring previous films or have them forwarded to the new dentist.

Dubious Dentistry

Dodes[1] and Jarvis[32] have noted that a significant number of dentists have gone overboard in espousing pseudoscientific theories, particularly in the area of nutrition. Such practitioners use hair analysis and computer analysis of diet as a basis for recommending vitamins and minerals to "balance the body chemistry" of their patients. Hair analysis is not a reliable tool for measuring the body's nutritional state (see Chapter 13). Computer analysis is useful in determining the composition of a person's diet and can be a useful part of dietary counseling. However, few dentists are qualified to perform dietary counseling, and computerized "nutrient deficiency tests" are not legitimate (see Chapter 13).

Disorders of the TMJ (jaw joint) and facial muscles can cause facial pain and restriction in opening of the mouth. Clicking alone is not considered a problem. Allegations that TMJ problems can affect disease processes in other parts of the body (such as scoliosis, premenstrual syndrome, and sexual problems) are unsupported by scientific evidence. Scientific studies show that 80% to 90% of patients with TMJ pain will get better within 3 months if treated with nonprescription analgesics, moist heat, and exercises. Dodes[1] warns that correction of a "bad bite" can involve irreversible treatments such as grinding down the teeth or building them up with dental restorations:

> The most widespread unscientific treatment involves placing a plastic appliance between the teeth. These devices, called mandibular orthopedic repositioning appliances (MORAs), typically cover only some of the teeth and are worn continuously for many months or even years. When worn too much, MORAs can cause the patient's teeth to move so far out of proper position that orthodontics or facial reconstructive surgery is needed to correct the deformity.

Believers in "cranial osteopathy" claim that cranial bones can be manipulated to relieved pain, especially TMJ pain. This is impossible because the bones of the skull are fused to each other.

Auriculotherapy is a variant of acupuncture based on the notion that the body and organs are represented on the surface of the ear. Proponents claimed it is effective against facial pain and ailments throughout the body. Its practitioners twirl needles or administer small electrical currents at points on the ear that supposedly represent diseased organs. Courses on auriculotherapy are popular among holistic dentists. Although complications from unsterilized and broken needles have been reported, this bizarre practice is touted as "quick, easy, inexpensive, effective and completely reversible."

A few hundred dentists claim that the mercury in silver-amalgam fillings is toxic and causes a wide range of health problems including multiple sclerosis, arthritis, headaches, Parkinson's disease, and emotional stress. They recommend that mercury fillings be replaced with either gold or plastic ones and that vitamin supplements be taken to prevent trouble during the process.

These dentists typically use an industrial mercury detector to indicate that "toxic" amounts of mercury are being released. To use the device, the dentist asks the patient to chew vigorously for 10 minutes, which may cause tiny amounts of mercury to be released from the fillings. Although this exposure lasts for just a few seconds and most of the mercury will be exhaled rather than absorbed by the body, the machine gives a high readout, which the dentist interprets as dangerous.[33] The most commonly used device multiplies the amount of mercury it detects in a small sample of air by a factor of 8000. This gives a reading for a cubic meter, a volume far greater than the human mouth. The proper way to determine mercury exposure is to measure blood and urine levels, which indicate how much has been absorbed by the body. Scientific testing has shown that the amount of mercury absorbed from fillings is only a small fraction of the average daily intake from food and is insignificant.[34] The ADA Council on Ethics, Bylaws, and Judicial Affairs considers the unnecessary removal of silver-amalgram fillings "improper and unethical."[35]

Smokeless Products

Chewing tobacco and snuff contain tobacco leaf and various sweeteners, flavorings, and scents. Nicotine from the tobacco is absorbed into the blood stream and produces mental effects described by users as relaxing or stimulating. The popularity of these products—especially among teenagers—is related to advertising that associates use of the products with "macho" images and athletic prowess.

Smokeless tobacco can cause bad breath, decreased ability to taste, tooth discoloration and decay, and recession of the gums (especially where the tobacco is habitually placed). Smokeless products contain three types of chemicals known to produce cancer: polycyclic aromatic amines, nitrosamines, and polonium 210, which is radioactive. A 1988 study found that 46% of 423 professional baseball players who had used smokeless products within the previous week had precancerous changes (leukoplakia) in their mucous membranes.[36] Dr.Gregory Connolly, director of the dental division of the Massachusetts Department of Public Health, calls smokeless tobacco use "a chemical time bomb ticking in the mouths of hundreds of thousands of boys in this country."

The nicotine content of smokeless tobacco makes it highly addictive. Some users even keep it in their mouth while sleeping. A study conducted at East Carolina University found that only 1 of 41 participants at quit-smokeless-tobacco clinics was able to stop for more than 4 hours. Other chemicals are believed to pose risks to developing babies when smokeless products are used during pregnancy.

The Comprehensive Smokeless Tobacco Health Education Act of 1986 requires manufacturers of chewing tobacco and snuff to include the following warnings on package labels:

Rep. Henry Waxman (D-CA), who played a major role in passage of the law, hopes the warning labels will make it obvious to children that "smokeless tobacco products are not bubblegum."

Choosing a Dentist

Good dentists take a personal interest in patients and their health. They are prevention oriented, but not faddists. They use x-ray films and probably suggest a full-mouth study unless suitable films are available from the patient's previous dentists. According to Dodes:

> Dental work can last a lifetime but, unfortunately, this is not always the case. In a good dentist's office the vast majority of work lasts a very long time, while in the office of Dr. Poorwork the majority of dental work falls out or decays out in a few years. The price of dental work is not the best way to judge quality, rather, pay attention to the time the dentist takes to do the work. Good quality dentistry cannot be done assembly-line style, it takes time and meticulous attention to detail.

A good oral examination includes inspection of the teeth, gums, tongue, inside of the cheek, and palate. In adults a periodontal probe should be inserted between the gums and teeth to detect abnormally large crevices. The frequency of maintenance care (including scaling, and x-ray examinations) should be based on an assessment of the frequency of cavity formation, the rate of calculus formation, the condition of the gums, and any other special problem. Once current treatment has been completed, the patient should be placed on a recall schedule and notified when the next check-up is due.

Friedman[6] warns that flamboyant advertising is likely to signify an emphasis on mass production rather than quality care. When the fees charged per service are low, the number of services performed may be greater than needed, resulting in higher overall cost. He also states that dentists who advertise "twilight sleep", cosmetic dentistry, and one-visit comprehensive treatment are seldom in-

Consumer Tip

Suggestions for Locating a Qualified Dentist

- √ Friends, neighbors, or co-workers may be asked to recommend dentists with whom they are pleased.
- √ If there is a dental school in the area, faculty members may be able to suggest practitioners in the community.
- √ A nearby hospital with an accredited dental service should be able to offer suggestions.
- √ The local dental society or an *ADA Directory*, copies of which can be found in dental school libraries and many public libraries, may be helpful.
- √ One's family physician may be able to recommend a dentist.
- √ Visiting a prospective dentist's office prior to making an appointment may reveal whether it is clean and run efficiently.

It's Your Decision

1. You have discovered that your gums bleed when you brush your teeth. Which of the following actions should you take?

		Reason
_____	Stop brushing your teeth for while.	_____
_____	Purchase a new toothbrush	_____
_____	Try a different toothpaste or toothbrush	_____
_____	Try using a mouthwash	_____
_____	Try flossing the teeth and use dental stimulants	_____

2. A dentist has suggested that all your silver-amalgam fillings should be replaced with other fillings because of health dangers from the mercury found in your fillings. The dentist also states that you need to take vitamin supplements while this change is taking place. Should you follow this advice or look for another dentists? Why?

terested in long-term maintenance care that does not generate high income. He recommends avoiding dentists who use intravenous sedation; recommend automatic amalgam replacement; or "specialize" in cosmetic dentistry or in treating headaches, backaches, myofacial pain, or TMJ treatment.

It makes sense to become acquainted with a family dentist before an emergency arises. One should not be embarrassed to ask about fees and payment plans. Most dentists prefer patients to initiate discussion of fees because patients are aware of their own financial situations and the current dentist is not.

Summary

A combination of nutrition, oral hygiene, and professional care will enable most people to maintain their teeth in good condition throughout their lifetime. Adequate amounts of fluoride during childhood will help make teeth resistant to decay. The most efficient way to accomplish this is through water fluoridation and daily use of fluoridated toothpaste. Daily brushing and flossing of the teeth can prevent tooth decay and periodontal disease. Professional care may include administration of sealants, removal of calculus (tartar), restoration of decayed or missing teeth, and cosmetic measures. Most dentists furnish competent care, but consumers should be careful to avoid dental quackery.

Discussion Questions

1. What qualifications are required for a dentist to practice in the United States?
2. Identify and describe the types and required training of dental specialists in the United States.
3. What are the types and duties of auxiliary personnel?
4. Define tooth decay and periodontal disease. Identify the procedures used to prevent these conditions.
5. What are the benefits of fluoridation and its alternatives?
6. For whom is orthodontics suitable? What procedures does it utilize?
7. What dental products are commonly used in self-care? Discuss the purposes and effectiveness of each one.
8. What methods are used to restore teeth?
9. Who should prepare, clean, and repair dentures? What should be the role of denturists?
10. What dangers are involved in using snuff and chewing tobacco?
11. Why are cranial osteopathy, the Sargenti method, the Keyes technique, and mercury-amalgam removal considered dubious procedures?
12. How should a dentist be selected?
13. What principles should determine the appropriate frequency of routine dental care?

References

1. Dodes J: Dubious dental care, New York, 1991, American Council on Science and Health.
2. Rovin S: Tooth decay: a delicate balance, Nutrition Forum 1:22-23, 1984.
3. Dannenberg JL: Vitamin C enamel loss, J Am Dent Assoc 105:172, 1982.
*4. Friedman JW et al: Complete guide to dental health—how to avoid being overcharged and overtreated, New York, 1991, Consumer Reports Books.
5. Newbrun E: Effectiveness of water fluoridation, J Public Health Dent (special issue):49(5)279-289, 1989.
6. McClure FJ: Water fluoridation: the search and the victory, Washington DC, 1970, US Department of Health, Education, and Welfare.
7. Barrett S and Rovin S, eds: The tooth robbers: a pro-fluoridation handbook, Philadelphia, 1980, George F Stickley Co.
*8. Fluoridation, Consumer Reports, 43:392-396, 480-482, 1978.
9. Newbrun E: Fluorides and dental caries, ed 3, Springfield, Ill, 1986, Charles C Thomas, publisher.
10. Wulf C et al: Abuse of the scientific literature in an anti-fluoridation pamphlet, ed 2, Columbus, Ohio, 1988, American Oral Health Institute.
11. Begley S: Don't drink the water? Brush your teeth, but the fluoride from your tap may not do much good—and may cause cancer, Newsweek, pp 60-61, Feb 5, 1990.
12. Review of fluoride benefits and risks, Report of the Ad Hoc Subcommittee on Fluoride of the Commmittee to Coordinate Environmental Health and Related Progıams, Washington DC, 1991, US Public Health Service.
13. Barrett S: Fluoridation attacked unfairly, Nutrition Forum, 7:15, 1990.
14. American Dental Association: Facts about fluoride, 1991, The Association.
15. Fluoridation of community water systems, JAMA 267:3264-3265, 1992.
*16. American Dental Association: Periodontal diseases, Chicago, 1988, The Association.
17. Toothpastes, Consumer Reports, pp 138-140, March 1984.
18. American Dental Association Council on Dental Therapeutics: Accepted dental therapeutics, Chicago, 1984, The Association.

*Recommended reading

19. A toothbrush tanning booth? Consumer Reports Health Letter, 2:40, 1990.
20. Mouthwashes, Consumer Reports, 49:143-146, 1984.
21. Plax retracts, Plax 'pre-brushing dental rinse' promises less than it used to. What does it deliver? Consumer Reports Health Letter, 3:21, 1991.
22. Winn DM et al: Mouthwash use and oral conditions in the risk of oral and pharyngeal cancer, Cancer Res 51:3044-3047, 1991.
23. Berry JM: What about whiteners? Safety concerns explored, J Am Dent Assoc 121:223-225, 1990.
24. Sears C: FDA orders tooth bleaches off market, American Health, 11(1):22, 1992.
25. A tale of two lasers, Consumer Reports, 56:538, 1991.
*26. Barrett S: Toxic television: the mercury amalgam scam, Priorities, pp 35-37, Fall 1991.
*27. The mercury in your mouth, Consumer Reports, pp 316-319, 1991.
28. McCann D: CDT won't recommend Sargenti paste, ADA News, October 21, 1991.
29. McCann D: Cameras capture unlicensed dentist, ADA News, July 15, 1991.
30. FTC warns pharmaceutical companies on unfair ads for denture products, File No 792 3155, June 18, 1979.
31. Matteson SR et al: The selection of patients for x-ray examinations: dental radiographic examinations, HHS publications FDA 88-8273 and 8274, Washington DC, 1988, US Government Printing Office.
32. Jarvis WT: Dubious dentistry, In Barrett S, ed: The health robbers, ed 2, Philadelphia, 1980, George F Stickley Co.
*33. The mercury-amalgam scare, In Barrett S et al eds: Health schemes, scams, and frauds, New York, 1990, Consumer Reports Books.
34. Mackert JR: Dental amalgam and mercury, J Am Dent Assoc 122:54-61, 1991.
35. Berry JH: Questionable care: what can be done about dental quackery? J Am Dent Assoc 115:679-685, 1987.
36. Ernster VL et al: Smokeless tobacco use and health effects among baseball players, JAMA 264:218-224, 1990.
*37. Schultz D: Fluoride—cavity fighter on tap, FDA Consumer 26(1):34-38, 1992.

CHAPTER NINE

NONSCIENTIFIC HEALTH CARE

"When normal treatment fails, Mrs. Blaine, we sometimes resort to traditional folk remedies. Pass me the afflicted finger. I am going to kiss it and make it better."
(©Punch—Rothco.)

Some patients won't accept the diagnoses we doctors lay on them. . . . If the medical profession can't help them, then somewhere, somehow, they'll find someone who will.[1]

WILLIAM A. NOLAN, M.D.

Every system—be it based on the position of the stars, the pattern of lines in the hand, the shape of the face or skull, the fall of the cards or the dice, the accidents of nature, or the intuitions of a "psychic"—claims its quota of satisfied customers.[2]

RAY HYMAN, PH.D.

When you are well, what you think may not matter. But when you are sick, your beliefs can kill you.

WILLIAM T. JARVIS, PH.D.

CONSUMER DECISIONS

What factors influence the beliefs that people develop about the methods described in this chapter?

Under what circumstances would you rely on any of these methods?

Nonscientific health care practitioners differ from scientific ones because their concepts and methods are not based on acceptable scientific evidence. Nonscientific practitioners are sometimes referred to as cultists, marginal practitioners, unorthodox practitioners, or alternative practitioners. Those who claim to possess or provide a focus for psychic or supernatural healing powers are commonly referred to as faith healers. Many nonscientific practitioners attempt to enhance their status by identifying themselves as part of a "holistic" or "New Age" movement.

A complete listing of nonscientific approaches to health would be a monumental task, if not an impossible one. This chapter therefore identifies some approaches that have achieved notoriety. Chapters 7, 8, 13, 14, 16, 17, 18, and 19 cover additional practices related to mental health, dental care, nutrition, weight control, cardiovascular disease, arthritis, cancer, and AIDS. Chapter 4 discusses the general characteristics of quackery and health frauds.

ACUPUNCTURE

Beware of physicians bearing needles who think they're acupuncturists. You may get stuck.

CHINESE PROVERB

Acupuncture has been used in ancient Chinese and Eastern medicine for thousands of years. Traditional acupuncture, as now practiced, involves the insertion of stainless steel needles into various body areas. A low-frequency current may be applied to the needles to produce greater stimulation. Other procedures used separately or together include: moxibustion (burning of floss or herbs applied to the skin); injection of sterile water, procaine, morphine, vitamins, or homeopathic solutions through the inserted needles; applications of laser beams; placement of needles in the external ear (auriculotherapy); and acupressure (use of manual pressure).

"Chinese medicine" (also called Oriental medicine) is based on a philosophical and mystical viewpoint of life.[3] It states that the body's vital energy ("Ch'i" or "Qi") circulates through 14 hypothetical channels called meridians, which have branches connected to bodily organs and functions. Illness and disease are attributed to imbalance or interruption of Ch'i (see Figure 9-1). Acupuncture is claimed to restore balance by removing the interruptions. The treatment is applied to "acupuncture points," which are said to be located throughout the body. Skrabanek[4] states that originally there were 365 such points, corresponding to the days of the year, but the number identified by proponents during the past 2000 years has increased gradually to over 2000. Some practitioners place needles at or near the site of disease, while others select points on the basis of symptoms. In traditional or classical acupuncture a combination of points is usually used. However, the existence of "acupuncture points" has never been scientifically validated.

The diagnostic process used by acupuncturists may include questioning (medical history, lifestyle), observations (skin, tongue, color), listening (breathing sounds), and pulse-taking. Six pulses said to correlate with body organs or functions are checked to determine which meridians are "deficient" in Ch'i. (Medical science recognizes only one pulse, corresponding to the heartbeat, which can be felt in the wrist, neck, feet, and several other places throughout the body.) Some acupuncturists state that the electrical properties of the body may become imbalanced weeks or even months before health problems are apparent on a physical level.[5] These practitioners claim that acupuncture can be used to treat conditions when the patient just "doesn't feel right," even though no disease condition is apparent.

The conditions claimed to respond to acupuncture include: chronic pain (neck and back pain, migraine headaches), acute injury-related pain (strains, muscle and ligament tears), gastrointestinal problems (indigestion, ulcers, constipation, diarrhea), cardiovascular conditions (high and low blood pressure), genitourinary problems (menstrual irregularity, frigidity, impotence), muscle and nerve conditions (paralysis, deafness), and behavior-related problems (overeating, drug dependence,

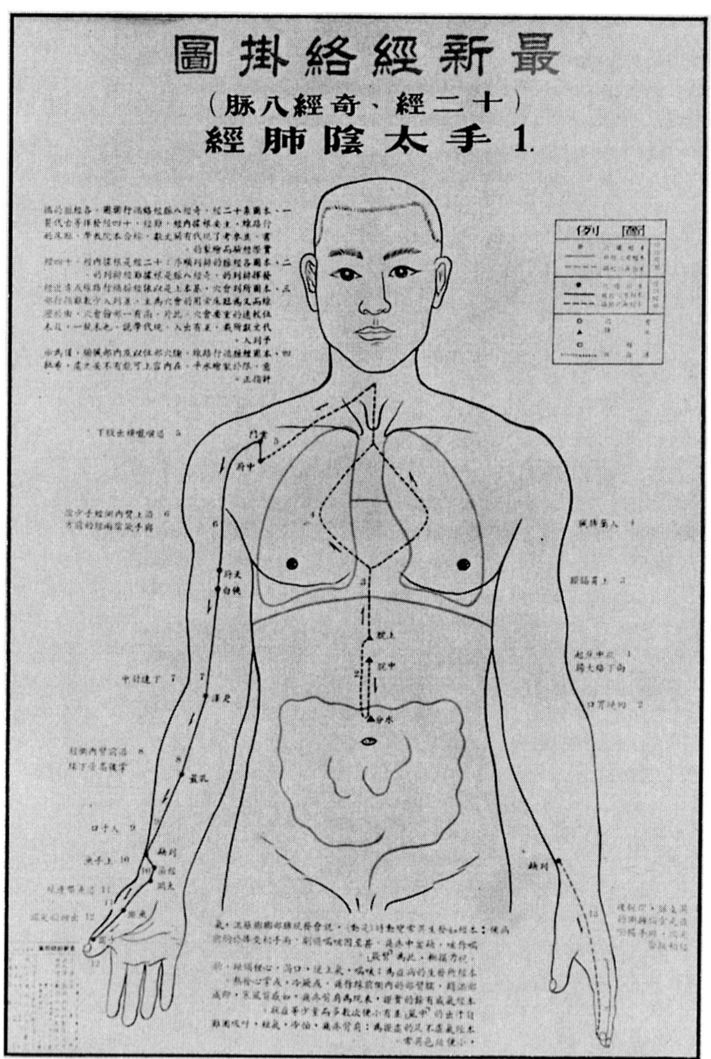

FIGURE 9-1. This chart identifies the locations for treatment of the lungs. The lung "meridian" runs along the inner arm and into the shoulder.

smoking). However, the evidence supporting these claims consists mostly of practitioners' observations and poorly designed studies.[6] A controlled study found that auriculotherapy (electro-acupuncture of the ear) was no more effective than placebo stimulation (light touching) against chronic pain.[7] In 1990 three Dutch epidemiologists analyzed 51 controlled studies of acupuncture for chronic pain and concluded that "the quality of even the better studies proved to be mediocre. . . . The efficacy of acupuncture in the treatment of chronic pain remains doubtful."[8]

Acupuncture anesthesia is not used for surgery in the Orient to the extent that its proponents suggest. In China physicians screen out patients who appear to be unsuitable. Acupuncture is not used for emergency surgery, and often is accompanied by inducing local anesthesia and/or giving the patient an analgesic such as a narcotic medication.

The reason acupuncture may relieve pain is unclear. One theory suggests that pain impulses are blocked from reaching the spinal cord or brain at various "gates" to these areas. Another theory suggests that acupuncture stimulates the body to produce narcotic-like substances called endorphins, which reduce pain. Other theories suggest that the placebo effect, external suggestion (hypnosis), and cultural conditioning are important factors. Melzack and Wall[9] note that plan relief produced by acupuncture can also be produced by many other types of sensory hyperstimulation, such as electricity and heat at acupuncture points and elsewhere in the body. They conclude that "the effectiveness of all of these forms of stimulation indicates that acupuncture is not a magical procedure but only one of many ways to produce analgesia [pain relief] by an intense sensory input."

Ulett[10] believes that "devoid of metaphysical thinking, acupuncture becomes a rather simple technique that can be useful as a nondrug method of pain control." However, in 1981 the American Medical Association Council on Scientific Affairs[11] concluded:

1. At this time, it cannot be said that acupuncture has any more certain effect on pain than a placebo or a sham acupuncture (needles inserted at random points rather than at the meridians).
2. It can produce substantial analgesia in selected patients but the mechanism does not operate consistently or reproducibly in the majority of people and does not operate at all in some people.
3. It can alleviate pain, but provides only temporary relief for patients with chronic pain.

Acupuncture can have serious complications that include: fainting, local hematoma (bleeding from punctured blood vessel), pneumothorax (punctured lung), convulsions, local infections, hepatitis B (from unsterile needles), bacterial endocarditis, contact dermatitis, and nerve damage. The herbs used by acupuncture practitioners are not regulated for safety, potency, or effectiveness. There is also the risk that an acupuncturist whose approach to diagnosis is not based on scientific concepts will fail to diagnose a dangerous condition.

In 1971 an acupuncture boom occurred in the United States because of stories about visits to China by various American dignitaries. Entrepreneurs, both medical and nonmedical, began using flamboyant advertising techniques to promote clinics, seminars, demonstrations, books, correspondence courses, and do-it-yourself kits. Today most states restrict the use of acupuncture to physicians or persons operating under the direct supervision of physicians. In some states acupuncture is permitted without medical supervision.

An attempt is being made to set standards through voluntary certification by the National Commission for the Certification of Acupuncturists (NCCA). Several thousand practitioners have become certified and some states have states adopted the NCCA exam as all or part of their criteria for licensing. The credentials used by acupuncturists include C.A. (certified acupuncturist), M.A. (master acupuncturist), D.A. (diplomate of acupuncture), and O.M.D. (Oriental medical doctor). These credentials are not recognized by the scientific community. In 1990 the U.S. Secretary of Education recognized the National Accreditation Commission for Schools and Colleges of Acupuncture and Oriental Medicine as an accrediting agency. However, such recognition is not based upon the scientific validity of what is taught but upon other criteria.

The National Council Against Health Fraud has concluded: (1) acupuncture is an unproven modality of treatment, (2) its theory and practice are based on primitive and fanciful concepts of health and disease that bear no relationship to present scientific knowledge, (3) research during the past 20 years has not demonstrated that acupuncture is effective against any disease, (4) perceived effects of acupuncture are probably due to a combination of expectation, suggestion, counter-irritation, operant conditioning, and other psychologic mechanisms, (5) the use of acupuncture should be restricted to appropriate research settings, (6) insurance companies should not be required by law to cover acupuncture treatment, (7) licensure of lay acupuncturists should be phased out, and (8) consumers who wish to try acupuncture should discuss their situation with a knowledgeable physician who has no commercial interest.[6]

CONSUMER TIP

Be Wary of Acupuncture

- Acupuncture is an invasive procedure (penetrates the skin). Although its complication rate is not high, acupuncture can cause serious complications.
- Many practitioners of acupuncture do not have adequate training and use unscientific approaches to the diagnosis and treatment of health problems.
- There is no evidence that acupuncture can influence the course of any organic disease.
- Pain relief from acupuncture, if it occurs, is likely to be short-lived.
- Consumers who wish to try acupuncture should choose a practitioner who is medically trained and does not espouse "Chinese medicine" or any other nonscientific approach described in this chapter.

REFLEXOLOGY

Reflexology, also known as zone therapy, is based on the notion that pressing on the hands or feet can help relieve pain and remove the underlying cause of disease in other parts of the body. Proponents claim that: (1) the body is divided into ten zones which begin or end in the hands and feet, (2) each organ or part of the body is represented on the hands and feet, (3) the practitioner can diagnose abnormalities by feeling the feet, and (4) massaging or pressing each area can stimulate the flow of energy, blood, nutrients, and nerve impulses to the corresponding body zone. Their fees typically range from $35 to $100 per session.

One prominent proponent claims that foot reflexology can cleanse the body of toxins, increase circulation, assist in weight loss and improve the health of organs throughout the body. Other proponents have reported success in treating: earaches, anemia, bedwetting, bronchitis, convulsions in an infant, hemorrhoids, hiccups, deafness, loss of hair, emphysema, prostate trouble, heart disease, overactive thyroid gland, kidney stones, liver trouble, rectal prolapse, undescended testicles, intestinal paralysis, cataracts, and hydrocephalus (a condition in which an excess of fluids surrounding the brain can cause pressure that damages the brain). One practitioner even claims to have lengthened a leg that was an inch shorter than the other. Figure 9-2 shows a simple reflexology chart.

CHIROPRACTIC

Louis Sportelli, D.C., who has been chairman of the board of governors of the American Chiropractic Association, describes chiropractic's basic theory as follows:

> A science based on the premise that good health depends, in part, upon a normally functioning nervous system. Body structure such as cells and organs function by the impulses carried through nerves. When these nerve impulses travel unhampered, the organs and cells of the body are able to function normally. When there is an interference (too much or not enough nerve supply), the tissues or organs cannot function properly and a state of malfunction may begin, predisposing the body to a disease state.[12]

Chiropractic is unique among nonscientific approaches because its practitioners are licensed in all 50 states. Chiropractors help some people with musculoskeletal ailments, but the problems described in this section are widespread and, in some cases, integral to the philosophy and practice of chiropractic.

Origin of Chiropractic

Various forms of spinal manipulation have been noted throughout recorded history.[13] The "discovery" of chiropractic was announced in 1895 by Daniel David Palmer, a grocer and "magnetic healer" who practiced in Davenport, Iowa. Palmer believed that he had restored the hearing of a deaf janitor by "adjusting" a bump on his spine. After further study, he theorized that the basic cause of disease was nerve interference caused by misaligned spinal bones.[14] The basic treatment advocated by Palmer was adjustment of the spine by hand. He rejected the germ theory and had an aversion to drugs, surgery, and medical diagnosis. The word "chiropractic" was derived from the Greek words *cheir* (hand) and *praktikos* (practice).

Soon after his discovery, Palmer opened a school to teach his methods to others. The basic entrance requirement, as it was in many medical schools around the turn of the century, was the ability to pay tuition.[15] One of the first students was Palmer's son, Bartlett Joshua, who is commonly referred to as "B.J." The son, who was an astute businessman, is credited with being the developer of chiropractic.

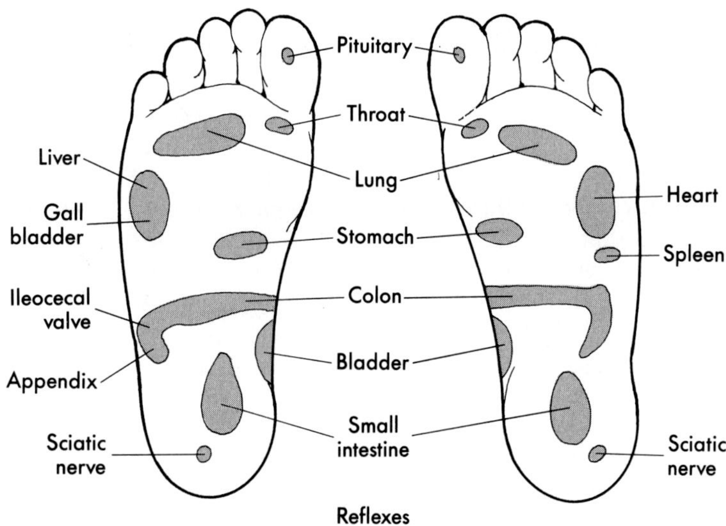

FIGURE 9-2. Simple reflexology chart. According to proponents, pressing on the shaded areas influences the parts of the body that are listed.

In 1906 D.D. Palmer was briefly jailed for practicing medicine without a license. After his release he sold his interest in the Palmer School of Chiropractic to B.J. At that time about 100 chiropractors were practicing. Today there are over 45,000.

The first area to license chiropractors was the District of Columbia in 1806. Between 1913 and 1933, 40 states passed licensing laws; other states gradually followed suit, with Louisiana being the last to do so in 1974. According to chiropractic sources, total expenditures for chiropractic care were approximately $2.7 billion in 1990.[16]

Rejection of Chiropractic

The concept that nerve interference is a major cause of disease has been consistently rejected by the scientific community because it does not conform to established anatomical facts. Dr. Edmund Crelin, a prominent anatomist from Yale University, has subjected Palmer's theory to an actual test.[17] During the early 1970s Dr. Crelin collected the spines of six persons within 3 to 6 hours after their death. Using instruments to twist their spines, he observed the spinal nerves and the opening through which they passed. No nerve compression took place regardless of the force applied. In a later memorandum he commented further:

> Only 24 of the 43 pairs of nerves that pass from the brain and spinal cord to various parts of the body could ever be impinged upon in the vertebral foramina (openings) by the excessive displacement of vertebrae. Why these 24 pairs should be causing disease, exclusive of all the others, defies a rational explanation. . . .
>
> Complete severance of spinal nerves to the heart, glands (salivary, thyroid, liver, pancreas, etc.) and smooth muscles of the lungs, stomach, intestines, etc., has only transient effects. The gland cells and smooth and cardiac muscles not only survive, but function normally. They surely do not become diseased.[18]

A team of Japanese physicians who observed chiropractors at work reported great discrepancies between what they claimed and what is anatomically possible. In 1990 they reported that "the methods of spinal palpation varied largely from one practitioner to another . . . and are not based on knowledge of human anatomy." The researchers also concluded that chiropractors claim to be able to palpate (feel) spinal structures that are too deep within the body to be felt from the outside.[19] American chiropractic organizations denounced the report as biased.

Despite their shortcomings, chiropractors have lobbied successfully in most states for laws that force insurance companies to pay for certain chiropractic services. In 1972 Congress provided coverage under Medicare for "treatment by means of manual manipulation of the spine to correct a subluxation demonstrated by x-rays to exist." The International Chiropractors Association states that passage of this bill was spurred by upwards of ten million letters received by members of Congress.[20]

Types of Chiropractors

National Council Against Health Fraud president William T. Jarvis, Ph.D., whose doctoral thesis was a study of chiropractic, notes that, "chiropractic's uniqueness is not in its use of manipulation but in its theoretical basis for doing so." He describes chiropractic as "a conglomeration of factions in conflict, bound together only by opposition to outside critics."[21]

Although philosophy and treatment vary greatly from one practitioner to another, chiropractors may be divided into two main types: "straights" and "mixers." Straights cling strictly to Palmer's basic doctrine that almost all disease is caused by misaligned vertebrae ("subluxations") that can be corrected by spinal adjustment. Mixers tend to acknowledge that factors such as germs and hormones play a role in disease, but they tend to regard mechanical disturbances of the nervous system as the underlying cause of lowered resistance to disease. In addition to spinal manipulation, mixers may use nutritional methods and various types of physiotherapy, such as heat, cold, traction, exercise, massage, and ultrasound. Straights tend to disparage medical diagnosis, claiming that examination of the spine is the proper way for chiropractors to analyze their patients. Mixers are more likely to diagnose medical conditions in addition to spinal abnormalities, and to refer patients to medical practitioners for treatment.

The two largest chiropractic organizations are the American Chiropractic Association (ACA, mixers), with about 23,000 members, including 6000 students, and the International Chiropractors Association (ICA, straights), with about 8000 members, including 3000 students. The two groups have considered merging, but they are unable to agree upon the definition and scope of chiropractic.

About 300 chiropractors belong to the National Association for Chiropractic Medicine, a reformist group that has openly renounced D.D. Palmer's basic theories. Its members limit their practice to musculoskeletal problems and have denounced the unscientific methods used by many of their colleagues. The group's application form includes a pledge to "openly renounce the historical chiropractic philosophical concept that subluxation is the cause of disease."

Many chiropractors still support D.D. Palmer's idea that spinal misalignments are the primary cause of disease. A 1980 survey of 1000 chiropractors on the ACA mailing list found that only 37 of 268 respondents (14%) "do not believe that the chiropractic subluxation is a significant cause of disease."[22] Asked whether "the chiropractic monocausal theory is scientifically supported," 12 of 260 (5%) said "completely," 195 (75%) said "partially," and 53 (20%) said "not at all."

Sid Williams, D.C., president of Life Chiropractic College and a former president of the ICA, states:

> . . . Interference with nervous system function can disrupt homeostasis, resulting in malfunction and disease. Subluxations of the vertebra are capable of interfering with normal nervous system function. Vertebral subluxations can be located or reduced or corrected by chiropractic adjustments. A nervous system restored to normal function is capable of restoring normal homeostasis."[23]

Dr. Sportelli's statement on page 154 also is consistent with D.D. Palmer's theory, but adds "in part" to the first sentence, which makes it sound less all-inclusive.

Professional Preparation of Chiropractors

In 1974 the U.S. Office of Education (USOE) approved the Council on Chiropractic Education (CCE) to accredit chiropractic schools. Currently, 14 of the 18 schools in the United States have CCE accreditation. Admission to a CCE-accredited school requires 2 years of prechiropractic college education with at least a C average. To receive the doctor of chiropractic (D.C.) degree, students must complete a minimum of 4200 hours of study over a 4-year period. Courses include anatomy, biochemistry, microbiology, pathology, public health, diagnosis and x-ray examination, related health sciences, and chiropractic principles and practice.[24] A second accrediting agency for chiropractic schools, the Straight Chiropractic Academic Standards Association (SCASA), received USOE approval in 1988.

In 1968 a comprehensive study by the U.S. Department of Health, Education, and Welfare concluded that chiropractic education does not prepare its practitioners to make an adequate diagnosis and provide appropriate treatment.[25] Although chiropractic schools have improved considerably since that time, they do not provide the depth of diagnostic and therapeutic training that physicians receive. Among other things, the range of ailments seen in patients attending clinics at chiropractic schools is far narrower than that of patients seen at medical school clinics, and chiropractic students receive little or no hospital training. Critics also point out that since much of chiropractic is based on a false premise, neither length of study nor accreditation of its schools can ensure the competence of its practitioners.

After graduation, many chiropractors take courses to help build their practices. These courses teach efficient office management, but some teach unethical methods of recruiting and retaining patients. Practice-building courses operated by Dr. Williams, for example, have distributed a textbook outlining a systematic plan to persuade all comers to have monthly spinal examinations.[26]

A 1986 report by the Office of the Inspector General (OIG) concluded that "practice-building courses, popular with many chiropractors, advocate advertising techniques which suggest the universal efficacy of chiropractic treatment for every ailment known to humans." It also concluded that despite evidence of an increased emphasis on science and professionalism in the training and practice of chiropractors, "there also exist patterns of activity and practice which at best appear as overly aggressive marketing—and, in some cases, seem deliberately aimed at misleading patients and the public regarding chiropractic care."[27] A subsequent OIG report noted that the two most common reasons for disciplinary actions by state chiropractic boards are billing abuses (relating to utilization or fees) and advertising abuses.[28] In 1990 Medicare paid about $181 million for chiropractic services.

Scope of Practice

Musculoskeletal disorders are the problems most often treated by chiropractors. However, charts and other materials relating the spine to the full range of illnesses can still be found in many chiropractic offices (see Figure 9-3).

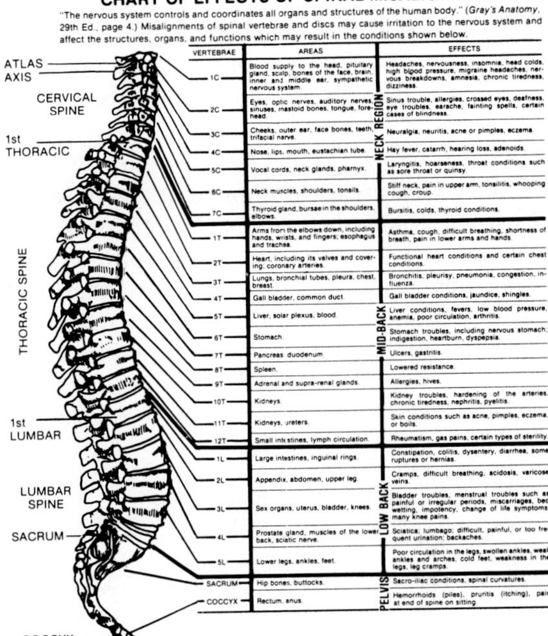

CHART OF EFFECTS OF SPINAL MISALIGNMENTS

"The nervous system controls and coordinates all organs and structures of the human body." (*Gray's Anatomy*, 29th Ed., page 4.) Misalignments of spinal vertebrae and discs may cause irritation to the nervous system and affect the structures, organs, and functions which may result in the conditions shown below.

VERTEBRAE	AREAS		EFFECTS
1C	Blood supply to the head, pituitary gland, scalp, bones of the face, brain, inner and middle ear, sympathetic nervous system.	NECK REGION	Headaches, nervousness, insomnia, head colds, high blood pressure, migraine headaches, nervous breakdowns, amnesia, chronic tiredness, dizziness.
2C	Eyes, optic nerves, auditory nerves, sinuses, mastoid bones, tongue, forehead.	NECK REGION	Sinus trouble, allergies, crossed eyes, deafness, eye troubles, earache, fainting spells, certain cases of blindness.
3C	Cheeks, outer ear, face bones, teeth, trifacial nerve.	NECK REGION	Neuralgia, neuritis, acne or pimples, eczema.
4C	Nose, lips, mouth, eustachian tube.	NECK REGION	Hay fever, catarrh, hearing loss, adenoids.
5C	Vocal cords, neck glands, pharnyx.		Laryngitis, hoarseness, throat conditions such as sore throat or quinsy.
6C	Neck muscles, shoulders, tonsils.		Stiff neck, pain in upper arm, tonsilitis, whooping cough, croup.
7C	Thyroid gland, bursae in the shoulders, elbows.		Bursitis, colds, thyroid conditions.
1T	Arms from the elbows down, including hands, wrists, and fingers; esophagus and trachea.		Asthma, cough, difficult breathing, shortness of breath, pain in lower arms and hands.
2T	Heart, including its valves and covering; coronary arteries.		Functional heart conditions and certain chest conditions.
3T	Lungs, bronchial tubes, pleura, chest, breast.		Bronchitis, pleurisy, pneumonia, congestion, influenza.
4T	Gall bladder, common duct.		Gall bladder conditions, jaundice, shingles.
5T	Liver, solar plexus, blood.	MID-BACK	Liver conditions, fevers, low blood pressure, anemia, poor circulation, arthritis.
6T	Stomach.	MID-BACK	Stomach troubles, including nervous stomach; indigestion, heartburn, dyspepsia.
7T	Pancreas duodenum.	MID-BACK	Ulcers, gastritis.
8T	Spleen.		Lowered resistance.
9T	Adrenal and supra-renal glands.		Allergies, hives.
10T	Kidneys.		Kidney troubles, hardening of the arteries, chronic tiredness, nephritis, pyelitis.
11T	Kidneys, ureters.		Skin conditions such as acne, pimples, eczema, or boils.
12T	Small intestines, lymph circulation.		Rheumatism, gas pains, certain types of sterility.
1L	Large intestines, inguinal rings.		Constipation, colitis, dysentery, diarrhea, some ruptures or hernias.
2L	Appendix, abdomen, upper leg.		Cramps, difficult breathing, acidosis, varicose veins.
3L	Sex organs, uterus, bladder, knees.	LOW BACK	Bladder troubles, menstrual troubles such as painful or irregular periods, miscarriages, bed wetting, impotency, change of life symptoms, many knee pains.
4L	Prostate gland, muscles of the lower back, sciatic nerve.	LOW BACK	Sciatica; lumbago; difficult, painful, or too frequent urination; backaches.
5L	Lower legs, ankles, feet.		Poor circulation in the legs, swollen ankles, weak ankles and arches, cold feet, weakness in the legs, leg cramps.
SACRUM	Hip bones, buttocks.	PELVIS	Sacro-iliac conditions, spinal curvatures.
COCCYX	Rectum, anus.	PELVIS	Hemorrhoids (piles), pruritis (itching), pain at end of spine on sitting.

FIGURE 9-3. Chart from a chiropractic brochure. Various charts like this help chiropractors explain how "spinal misalignments" (also called "subluxations") can cause more than 100 diseases and conditions. Many chiropractors claim that health can be restored by "adjusting" the spine to correct the misalignments. Do you think this claim is valid?

Osteopaths, physical therapists, athletic trainers, and some medical doctors also use manipulative techniques for certain musculoskeletal problems. According to orthopedist Stephen M. Levin, M.D., former president of the North American Academy of Manipulative Medicine (now called the North American Academy of Musculoskeletal Medicine), about 8000 physicians worldwide use manipulative techniques. He states:

> The prevailing scientific viewpoint is that manipulation relieves pain and secondary muscle spasm by restoring the mobility of joints that have a mechanical malfunction. When I meet with scientifically oriented chiropractors, including educators at some of their better schools, we talk the same language. In fact, some of them say that patients who aren't better within two weeks should be referred elsewhere.[29]

Studies of Effectiveness

In 1990 a British research team concluded that: "For patients with low back pain in whom manipulation is not contraindicated, chiropractic almost certainly confers worthwhile, long term benefit in comparison with hospital outpatient management . . . mainly in those with chronic or severe pain."[30] The study involved 741 patients between the ages of 18 and 65 who lacked signs of spinal nerve root compression, infectious disease, or other conditions that require medical intervention. The chiropractic treatment spanned up to 30 weeks (versus 12 weeks for hospital-based treatment) and cost about 50% more. The outcome was measured by a self-administered questionnaire about pain intensity, not a clinical evaluation. Patients with no prior history of back pain showed no difference in outcomes. Among patients with a prior history of back pain, those in the chiropractic treatment group scored significantly better than those in the hospital-based group at 6-, 12-, and 24-month follow-up intervals. The researchers cautioned that their findings may not apply to all patients with back pain. Jarvis agrees, but adds further reasons:

> The real value of any study is its applicability to the real world. . . . This study lost much of its applicability by screening patients carefully . . . accepting only those with no contraindications to manipulation. . . . There is no reason for anyone familiar with chiropractic practices to believe that similar screening is regularly done by most chiropractors. On the contrary, chiros are notorious for their overuse of manipulation, applying it for conditions for which there is no justification.[31]

The RAND Corporation, the UCLA School of Medicine, and two chiropractic research organizations have cosponsored a 3-part study of the appropriateness of spinal manipulation for low-back pain. In the first phase, a 7-member interdisciplinary panel identified 67 relevant articles and 9 books published between 1955 and 1989. From this review, the panelists concluded:

1. Data from 22 controlled studies support the use of manipulation for acute low-back pain in patients showing no signs of lower-limb nerve root involvement.
2. Scientific reports provide no help in deciding when spinal manipulative treatment should be stopped, with respect to either improvement or worsening of symptoms. It is not clear how many, if any, manipulations are necessary after a patient has become pain-free.[32]
3. There has been no systematic study of the frequency of complications from spinal manipulation for low-back pain. Although the risk appears small when compared to the large number of manipulations performed, no firm conclusions may be drawn because there are few data in the scientific literature.

Although chiropractors have promoted the RAND study as an endorsement of chiropractic, it is not. It merely supports the use of manipulation in carefully selected patients. Only a few of the reports identified by the RAND panel involved manipulation by chiropractors; most were done by medical doctors.[32a]

Some chiropractors have advertised that "chiropractic prolongs life." However, inspection of the *ACA Journal of Chiropractic* suggests otherwise. The percentage of chiropractors receiving chiropractic care is higher than that of the general population. If chiropractic could prolong life, it would be logical to conclude that chiropractors themselves would live longer. From 1976 through 1981, the ACA journal contained more than 200 obituary notices that specified the age at which the chiropractor had died. The average age was only 66, which was several years less than the American average.

Problems for Consumers

Critics of chiropractic list the following additional concerns:

1. Patients who are lulled into a false sense of security by exaggerated chiropractic claims may delay obtaining more appropriate care.[33]
2. Manipulation, particularly of the neck, can be dangerous. Strokes and broken bones have been reported.[34]
3. Although they are not qualified by training to understand the use of prescription drugs, many chiropractors discourage their use.[35]
4. Many chiropractors prescribe unnecessary vitamins and irrational "food supplement" formulations. Many sell these products in their offices at 2 to 3 times their cost.[36,37]
5. Many chiropractors obtain x-ray films of some or all of their patients to look for "subluxations." A few chiropractors still use a 14 × 36-inch x-ray film of the full spine, which yields little or no diagnostic information but subjects sexual organs to high levels of radiation.
6. Many chiropractors use dubious diagnostic approaches such as inappropriate muscle-testing (see "applied kinesiology" on page 160, hair analysis (see Chapter 13), thermography (see glossary), and gadgets that detect subluxations.
7. Many chiropractors suggest unnecessary "spinal adjustments," sometimes using scare tactics to do so.[14,36] During the 1970s the Lehigh Valley [PA] Committee Against Health Fraud[39] sent three healthy volunteers to a total of 16 local chiropractors for "checkups." Although no two chiropractors agreed on what was wrong with any of the volunteers, 15 recommended treat-

FIGURE 9-4. Bumper sticker distributed to chiropractors by the American Chiropractic Association during 1991.

ment for nonexistent conditions. Committee volunteers also asked 35 local practitioners, "How often should individuals who feel well have their spines checked?" The majority of answers ranged from 4 to 12 times per year.

During 1989 William M. London, Ed.D., assistant professor of health education at Kent State University, visited 23 chiropractors in Ohio and Florida who had advertised free consultations or examinations. Each one espoused subluxation theory either during the consultation or in waiting room literature, and all but two recommended periodic preventive maintenance. Seventeen performed examinations. Of these, three identified subluxations (at differing locations), three said his left leg was shorter than his right leg, and two said his right leg was shorter than his left one. Seven recommended treatment.[35]

The Vertebral Subluxation Research Institute teaches chiropractors how to convert "research volunteers" into "lifetime chiropractic patients." Its chiropractic clients are taught how to use telemarketing and other techniques to ask people to volunteer for "a nationwide study on spinal conditions." During the first office visit they are examined and given a brochure ("The Silent Killer") explaining the supposed dangers of subluxations. During the second visit—during a "report of findings"—they are advised to have their subluxations treated.[40]

Recent Developments

In 1976 chiropractors began a series of lawsuits against the AMA, other professional organizations, and several individual critics, charging that they had conspired to destroy chiropractic and to illegally deprive chiropractors of access to laboratory, x-ray, and hospital facilities. At various times, most of the defendant groups agreed in out-of-court settlements that their physician members were free to decide for themselves how to deal with chiropractors.

In 1987 a federal court judge concluded that during the 1960s "there was a lot of material available to the AMA Committee on Quackery that supported its belief that all chiropractic was unscientific and deleterious." The judge also noted that chiropractors still took too many x-rays. However, she ruled that the AMA had engaged in an illegal boycott. She concluded that the dominant reason for the AMA's antichiropractic campaign was the belief that chiropractic was not in the best interests of patients. But she ruled that this did not justify attempting to contain and eliminate an entire licensed profession without first demonstrating that a less restrictive campaign could not succeed in protecting the public.[41] The AMA appealed, but the U.S. Supreme Court declined to consider the case further. Although chiropractors trumpet the antitrust ruling as an endorsement of their effectiveness, it is important to understand that the case was decided on narrow legal grounds (restraint of trade) and was not an evaluation of chiropractic methods.

A 1979 report of a three-member government commission in New Zealand concluded that chiropractors had special expertise in treating back problems, but noted that they "do not provide an alternative comprehensive system of health care, and should not hold themselves out as doing so."[42] However, a report by the U.S. Congress Office of Technology Assessment (OTA)[43] noted that the commission did not include anyone familiar with the judgment of medical and scientific evidence. OTA also stated that the clinical studies considered by the commission did not justify any conclusion that spinal adjustment as done by chiropractors was either safe or effective. Dr. Jarvis,[44] who testified at commission hearings, has noted that in drawing their conclusions the commissioners ignored a broad range of valid critical testimony.

When plaintiffs in the antitrust suit against the AMA tried to have the New Zealand report admitted as evidence that chiropractic was a valid health care profession, the judge refused. She stated that the OTA review was well reasoned and that the New Zealand report was not trustworthy.[41]

Advice to Consumers

The terms "chiropractic," and "chiropractic treatment," are ambiguous and are not synonymous with "spinal manipulation." Chiropractic is both a philosophy and a treatment approach. Chiropractic treatment may include a wide variety of dubious measures in addition to appropriate or inappropriate manipulation. Thus, the potential usefulness of spinal manipulation may not counterbalance the unscientific philosophy or methods commonly embraced by chiropractors. The National Council Against Health Fraud believes that "a health care delivery system as confused and poorly regulated as is chiropractic constitutes a major consumer health problem."[45]

Barrett[46] advises consumers to avoid any chiropractor who: (1) claims that weekly or monthly spinal adjustments are needed to ensure health, (2) advertises that common vague symptoms are warning signs of serious disease in need of chiropractic care, or (3) recommends many spinal adjustments with a discount for advance payment—all of which indicate a tendency to promote unnecessary treatment. Consumers Union has advised consumers to avoid chiropractors entirely.[35]

Applied Kinesiology

Applied kinesiology is a system of diagnosis and treatment based on the notion that every organ dysfunction is accompanied by a specific muscle weakness, which enables diseases to be diagnosed through muscle-testing procedures. Its practitioners—most of whom are chiropractors—also claim that nutritional deficiencies, allergies, and other adverse reactions to food substances can be detected by placing substances in the mouth so that the patient salivates. "Good" substances will make specific muscles stronger, whereas "bad" substances will cause specific weaknesses. "Treatment" may include special diets, food supplements, acupressure, and spinal manipulation.

Applied kinesiology should be distinguished from kinesiology (biomechanics), which is the scientific study of movement. Applied kinesiology is considered a pseudoscience because its concepts do not conform to scientific facts about the causes of disease. Controlled studies have found no difference between the results with test substances and with placebos.[47]

Naturopathy

Naturopathy, sometimes referred to as "natural medicine," is a system of healing said to rely solely on "nature." Naturopaths claim to remove the underlying cause(s) of disease and to stimulate the body's natural healing processes.[48] They state that diseases are the body's effort to purify itself, and that cures result from increasing the patient's "vital force" by ridding the body of waste products and "toxins." They tend to oppose immunization procedures. The American Association of Naturopathic Physicians[49] claims that: "Naturopathic medicine has its own unique body of knowledge, evolved and refined for centuries."

Like many chiropractors, most naturopaths believe that virtually all diseases are within the scope of their practice. They offer treatment at their offices and at spas where patients may reside for several weeks. Their current methods include fasting, "natural food" diets, vitamins, herbs, tissue minerals, cell salts, manipulation, massage, exercise, colonic enemas, acupuncture, Chinese medicine, natural childbirth, minor surgery, and applications of water, heat, cold, air, sunlight, and electricity. Radiation may be used for diagnosis, but not for treatment. Prescription drugs are limited to compounds that are components of body tissues. The most comprehensive naturopathic publications, *A Textbook of Natural Medicine* (for students and professionals)[50] and *Encyclopedia of Natural Medicine* (for laypersons),[51] recommend special diets, vitamins, minerals, and/or herbs for more than 70 health problems ranging from acne to AIDS.

The term naturopathy was coined in 1895 by John Scheel, a practitioner in New York City, to describe his methods of health care. In 1902 he sold rights to the term to Benedict Lust, who had come to the United States in 1892 to promote hydrotherapy (see Chapter 2). Lust was largely responsible for naturopathy's growth in this country.[52] After acquiring chiropractic, osteopathic, naturopathic, and homeopathic medical degrees, he went on to found the American Naturopathic Association in 1919. Another prominent developer of naturopathy was Bernarr Macfadden, who promoted "physical culture" (see Chapter 2).

Before 1961, the doctor of naturopathy (N.D.) degree could be obtained at a number of chiropractic schools; now it is available only from two full-time schools of naturopathy and a few correspondence schools. Training at the full-time schools follows a pattern similar to that of chiropractic schools: 2 years of basic science courses and 2 years of clinical naturopathy. Two years of preprofessional college work are required for admission. In 1987 the U.S. Secretary of Education approved the Council on Naturopathic Medical Education as an accrediting agency for the full-time schools. As with acupuncture and chiropractic schools, this recognition is not based upon the scientific validity of what is taught but upon other criteria. Bastyr College, the leading naturopathy school, is providing retailers and their employees with home-study programs that espouse "natural" approaches for the gamut of disease.

Naturopaths are licensed as independent practitioners in seven states and Washington, D.C., and may legally practice in a few others as well. The American Association of Naturopathic Physicians has about 400 members. The total number of practitioners is unknown but includes chiropractors and acupuncturists who practice naturopathy. Naturopathic services are not covered by Medicare or most insurance policies.

Natural Hygiene

Natural Hygiene is a philosophy of health and "natural living" that denounces most medical treatment and advocates eating a "raw food" diet of vegetables, fruits, and nuts. It also advocates periodic fasting and "food combining" (avoiding food combinations it considers detrimental).[53] Its best-known advocates are Harvey and Marilyn Diamond, authors of *Fit For Life* (discussed in Chapter 14).

According to *Health Science*, the magazine of the American Natural Hygiene Society (ANHS), the Natural Hygiene movement was founded during the 1830s by Sylvester Graham, but declined until "resuscitated" from "almost dead" by Herbert M. Shelton (1895-1985). ANHS was founded in 1948 by Shelton and several associates and now has about 6500 members. Its headquarters is in Tampa, Florida. The society has been active in promoting certification of "organic foods" and opposing compulsory immunization, fluoridation, and food irradiation. *Health Science* lists 20 practitioners on its "professional referral list." Most of them are chiropractors, but a few hold medical, osteopathic, or naturopathic degrees.

Iridology

"Iridiagnosis" is based on the belief that each area of the body is represented by a corresponding area in the iris of the eye (the colored area surrounding the pupil), as shown in Figure 9-5. According to this viewpoint, a person's state of health and disease can be diagnosed from the color, texture, and location of various pigment flecks in the eye. Iridology practitioners claim to diagnose "imbalances" that can be treated with vitamins, minerals, herbs, and similar products. They may also claim that the eye markings can reveal a complete history of past

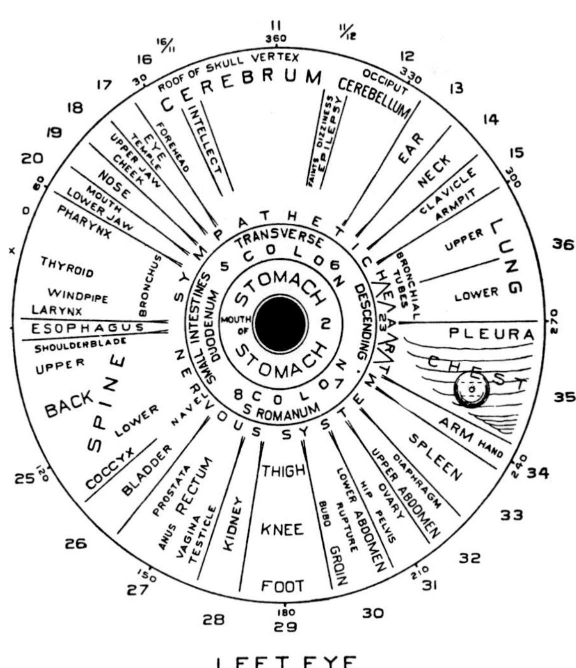

Figure 9-5. Iridology chart developed by a prominent naturopath more than 70 years ago.

illnesses as well as previous treatment. One textbook, for example, states that a white triangle in the appropriate area indicates appendicitis, but a black speck indicates that the appendix had been removed by surgery.

Bernard Jensen, D.C.,[54] the leading American iridologist, states that, "Nature has provided us with a miniature television screen showing the most remote portions of the body by way of nerve reflex responses." He also claims that iridology analyses are more reliable and "offer much more information about the state of the body than do the examinations of Western medicine." However, in 1979 he and two other proponents failed a scientific test in which they examined photographs of the eyes of 143 persons in an attempt to determine which ones had kidney impairments. (Forty-eight had been so diagnosed on the basis of creatinine clearance tests, and the rest had normal kidney function.) The three iridologists showed no statistically significant ability to detect which patients had kidney disease and which did not. One iridologist, for example, diagnosed 88% of the normal patients as having kidney disease, while another judged that 74% of the patients sick enough to need artificial kidney treatment were normal.[55]

According to Worrell[56]:

> Many of the conditions detected by practitioners of iridology are "diseases" whose existence has been disrupted or discredited by scientific investigation. . . . It would be difficult to agree on a standard diagnosis where the existence of the disease itself is in dispute.

Worrell notes that at least 20 iridology charts exist, but that all have differences in the location and interpretation of many of their iris signs. He also points out how incorrect "diagnoses" by iridologists can have serious consequences, as illustrated by the case of an accountant who consulted a chiropractor:

> During the course of treatment an iridology workup was recommended. The results indicated, among many other health problems, the presence of cancer. Overwhelmed, the patient spent the day in torment. Unable to consult his family physician . . . he finally sought my advice. After a lengthy discussion, I was able to allay his fears. . . . He wondered how an intelligent person such as himself could be caught up in such a deep emotional web over such a diagnosis. The story fortunately had a pleasant ending. However, the outcome could have been much more serious since the patient is also suffering from a heart condition, which was not noted on the iridology evaluation!

In 1981 the AMA Council on Scientific Affairs noted that iridology charts are similar in concept to those used years ago in "phrenology," the pseudoscience that related protuberances of the skull to the mental faculties and character of the individual. Regarding iridology's appeal, the council suggested:

> Iridology may stimulate interest among those turning to alternative methods of managing disease processes, and it does offer the dual attraction of simplicity and mystery without the inconvenience, and sometimes positive discomfort, that often accompanies diagnostic medical procedures; nevertheless, iridology has not yet been established as having any merit as a diagnostic technique.[11]

Stalker and Glymour[57] have noted:

> Chiropractors, iridologists, reflexologists, tongue diagnosers, zone therapists, and many others all claim to treat or diagnose the whole from some anatomical part. Of course, they differ about which part, but that does not seem to bother either them or the editors of holistic books.

HOMEOPATHY

Homeopathy dates back to the late 1700s when Samuel Hahnemann (1755-1843), a German physician, began formulating its basic principles. Hahnemann was justifiably distressed about bloodletting, leeching, purging, and other "heroic" medical procedures of his day that did far more harm than good. He was also critical of medications like calomel (mercurous chloride), which was given in doses that caused mercury poisoning. Instead, he developed his "law of similars": the symptoms of disease can be cured by substances that produce similar symptoms in healthy people. The word homeopathy is derived from the Greek words *homeo* (similar) and *pathos* (suffering or disease).

Hahnemann and his early followers conducted "provings" in which they administered herbs, minerals, and other substances to healthy people, including themselves, and kept detailed records of what they observed. Later these records were compiled into lengthy reference books called *materia medica*, which are used to match a patient's symptoms with a "corresponding" drug.

Hahnemann believed that diseases represent a disturbance in the body's ability to heal itself and that only a small stimulus is needed to begin the healing process. In line with this—and to avoid toxic side effects—he experimented to see how little medication could be given and still cause a healing response. At first he used small doses of accepted medications. But later he used enormous dilutions and concluded that the smaller the dose, the more powerful the effect—a principle he called the law of infinitesimals. This is opposite to what pharmacologists believe today.

Homeopathic drugs are prepared as follows: If the medicinal substance is soluble, 1 part is diluted in either 9 or 99 parts of a water and/or alcohol solution and shaken vigorously; if insoluble, it is finely ground and pulverized in similar proportions with powdered lactose (milk sugar). One part of the diluted medicine is diluted, and the process is repeated until the desired concentration is reached. Dilutions of 1 to 10 are designated by the Roman numeral X ($1X = 1/10$, $2X = 1/100$, $3X = 1/1,000$, $6X = 1/1,000,000$, and so on). Similarly, dilutions of 1 to 100 are designated by the Roman numeral C ($1C = 1/100$, $2C = 1/10,000$, $3C = 1/1,000,000$, and so on). Most remedies today range from 6X to 30C.

According to the laws of chemistry, there is a limit to the dilution that can be made without losing the original substance altogether. This limit, called Avogadro's number (6.022×10^{-23}), corresponds to homeopathic potencies of 12C or 24X (1 part in 10^{24}). Hahnemann himself realized there is virtually no chance that even one molecule of original substance would remain after extreme dilutions. But he believed that the vigorous shaking ("succussion") or pulverizing with each step of dilution leaves behind a spirit-like essence that is curative by reviving the body's "vital force."

Hahnemann's theories have never been accepted by scientifically oriented physicians who charge that homeopathic remedies are placebos (inert substances). However, because homeopathic remedies were actually less dangerous than those of nineteenth century medical orthodoxy, many medical practitioners began using them. At the turn of the century, homeopathy had some 14,000 practitioners and 22 schools in the United States alone. As medical science and medical education advanced, homeopathy declined sharply, particularly in America, where its schools either closed or converted to using modern methods. The last pure homeopathic school in the United States closed during the 1920s.[58]

Homeopathic remedies were given legal status by the 1938 Federal Food, Drug, and Cosmetic Act, which was shepherded through Congress by Senator Royal Copeland (D-NY), who was also a prominent homeopathic physician. One provision of this law recognized drugs as all substances included in the *Homeopathic Pharmacopeia of the United States.* Now in its ninth edition, this book lists more than 1000 substances and the historical basis for their inclusion: not by modern scientific testing, but by homeopathic "provings" conducted as long as 150 years ago.

The 1990 directory of the National Center for Homeopathy, now located in Alexandria, Virginia lists about 350 licensed practitioners, approximately half of them are physicians and the rest are mostly dentists, veterinarians, nurses, chiropractors, and naturopaths. Consumers interested in homeopathic self-treatment can obtain guidance through lay study groups, books, and courses sponsored by the Center. Most homeopathic practitioners still rely on *materia medica* in choosing among the thousands of remedies available. But a few use computerized electrical devices that they claim can help match the remedies to the patient's diseased organs.[59]

Homeopathic remedies are available from practitioners, health food stores, drugstores, and manufacturers who sell directly to the public. A few products are sold person-to-person through multilevel marketing coompanies. Homeopathic remedies appeal to some people who are afraid of more potent drugs. Manufacturers cater to this fear by claiming that their remedies are "the safer alternative" and "work without side effects." Many proponents claim that homeopathy not only cures but removes the predisposition to disease.

Some homeopathic manufacturers market "cell salts." The theory behind their use is that the basic cause of disease is mineral deficiency, correction of which will enable the body to heal itself. This system of healing claims that one or more of twelve salts are effective against a wide variety of diseases, including appendicitis (ruptured or not), baldness, deafness, insomnia, and worms. Development of this method is attributed to nineteenth-century physician W.H. Schuessler.

Promoters of homeopathic remedies sometimes recommend products called "glandulars" or "glandular extracts". The theory behind their use—like the magical thinking of primitive tribes—is that enzymes or other protein substances found in animal organs will strengthen or rejuvenate human body processes that involve similar substances. Thus, an extract of animal pancreas might be recommended to strengthen a person's pancreas, an animal heart extract might be suggested for the heart, and so on. When these substances are present in homeopathic dilution, they have no effect on the body. Even in higher concentration when taken by mouth, they are digested by the stomach and intestines. Since they are proteins, they are broken down into their component amino acids so that no "glandular substances" actually reach the cells they are supposed to help.

During the past decade, many homeopathic products have been marketed with illegal claims of efficacy against serious diseases. In 1983, for example, Biological Homeopathic Industries of Albuquerque, New Mexico, marketed BHI Anticancer Stimulating, BHI Antivirus, BHI Stroke, and 50 other types of tablets that the company claimed were effective against serious diseases. In 1984 the FDA forced the company to stop distributing several of the products and to tone down its claims for the rest.[60]

During 1988, the FDA took action against companies marketing "diet patches" with false claims that they could suppress one's appetite. The largest such company, Meditrend International, of San Diego, had instructed users to place one or two drops of a "homeopathic appetite control solution" on a patch and wear it all day affixed to an "acupuncture point" on the wrist to "bioelectrically" suppress the appetite control center of the brain.[61]

In most states, homeopathy can be practiced by any physician or other practitioner whose license includes the ability to prescribe drugs. Three states—Arizona, Nevada and Connecticut—have separate homeopathic licensing boards. The Nevada situation is notable because some of its practitioners acquired licenses as homeopaths after other states revoked their medical licenses for cancer quackery.

In 1986 the North Carolina Board of Medical Examiners revoked the license of George A. Guess, M.D., the state's only licensed homeopathic physician, after concluding that he was "failing to conform to the standards of acceptable and prevailing medical practice." The Board's decision was upheld by the North Carolina Supreme Court, but is being appealed to a federal court with help from the American Civil Liberties Union.

Public protection regarding drugs is based on a framework of federal laws and regulations that require drugs to be safe, effective, and properly labeled. However, the FDA has not applied these rules to homeopathic remedies. Because most homeopathic remedies are supposed to contain no detectable amount of any active ingredient, it is impossible to test whether their ingredients are those stated on their labels. They have been presumed safe, but unlike most other drugs, they have not been proven effective against disease by scientific means (such as double-blind testing). If the FDA were to require such proof for homeopathic drugs to remain on the market, the industry would not survive unless the United States Congress granted the industry new privileges.

In 1987 *Consumer Reports* concluded:

> Unless the laws of chemistry have gone awry, most homeopathic remedies are too diluted to have any physiological effect. . . . Consumers Union's medical consultants believe that any system of medicine embracing such remedies involved a potential danger to patients whether the prescribers are M.D.s, other licensed practitioners, or outright quacks. Ineffective drugs are dangerous drugs when used to treat serious or life-threatening disease. Moreover, even though homeopathic drugs are essentially nontoxic, self-medication can still be hazardous. Using them for a serious illness or undiagnosed pain instead of obtaining proper medical attention could prove harmful or even fatal.[62]

Faith Healing

Faith healing refers to practices based on a belief that religious faith can bring about recovery, or that prayer and faith in a healer can result in a cure through divine intervention. The terms spiritual healing, psychic healing, and paranormal healing are often used interchangeably. According to Ireland,[63] "the central element in such healing is to inspire such a high degree of confidence in the patient that he sincerely believes in the efficacy of the healer." However, Jarvis[64] notes that nonreligious individuals have sometimes been healed or acted as healers, and that healing has taken place in secular settings. Secular healers usually claim to have an intrinsic power of their own—such as a healing touch—which they attempt to demonstrate by such means as Kirlian photography (see p. 167).

Attempts at healing by faith and magic have existed throughout history. Ancient medicine functioned with the belief that diseases were caused by demons. Early Assyrian tablets describe methods of curing illnesses by driving out demons with magic, charms, incantations, and rituals. In the famous Greek temples of Aesculapius, religious methods of healing were employed. Christian history is replete with examples of widespread belief in the efficacy of faith healing. Jesus Christ, the best-known healer, was also remarkable for the variety of methods he used. Shrines such as Lourdes in France still attract large numbers of people who hope to be cured by an intense religious experience.

Christian Science

In about 1850 Phineas Parkhurst Quimby of Maine used Mesmer's ideas of animal magnetism to develop his own healing approach. Quimby would place his hands on a sick patient's head and abdomen to encourage the magnetic healing forces to flow through. He held that diagnosis and cure of illness resulted from the faith that individuals had in him. He was convinced that conventional medicine was useless, that disease itself was "error," and that only health was "truth."

In 1862 Quimby treated Mary Baker Glover for a spinal problem that had failed to respond to orthodox medical care. The water massage and hypnotism that he used apparently had a positive effect. On awakening from her trance, Glover found herself cured. She concluded, however, that her cure was not due to Quimby but to "truth in Christ." In 1875 she published *Science and Health,* which described her theories about religion based on the Bible and some of Quimby's ideas. She said that God was the author and that she was only the writer. In 1877 she married for the third time, becoming Mary Baker Eddy, and named her new philosophy Christian Science. The Church of Christ, Scientist was founded in 1879.

Mary Baker Eddy regarded herself as the supreme healer and believed she was as infallible as Christ. She claimed to be able to perform miracles and thought she had healed many people with crippling disabilities. She demanded absolute obedience to her system as well as to her person. She could not bear to be contradicted or found wrong. In her determination to justify herself on all counts, she frequently twisted evidence and facts to her purposes. Her writings contain numerous contradictions.

Christian Science contends that illness is an illusion caused by faulty beliefs, and that prayer heals by replacing bad thoughts with good ones. Christian Science practitioners work by trying to argue the sick thoughts out of the patient's mind. Consultations can take place in person, by telephone, or even by mail. Individuals may also be able to attain correct beliefs by themselves through prayer or mental concentration.

A pamphlet of the Christian Science Publishing Society states that "every student of Christian Science has the God-given ability to heal the sick." To become a practitioner, an individual takes 2 weeks of "primary class instruction" from a qualified teacher. The course is based on questions and answers from *Science and Health.* When training is completed, "C.S." may be placed after the person's name. After 3 years of full time practice, a practitioner may apply for the 6-day "normal class." Completion merits the degree of Bachelor of Christian Science (C.S.B.) and certifies the person as a teacher who may give primary instruction to 30 pupils a year. The February 1991 *Christian Science Journal* listed 1450 churches and about 2200 practitioners and teachers in the United States.

Devout Christian Scientists do not use medications and usually do not rely on medical aid. They are opposed to vaccination, immunization, and quarantine for contagious diseases, although official church policy is to advise members to comply with state laws. A physician or midwife may be used during childbirth. A physician may also be used to set a broken bone if no medication is involved.

The weekly magazine, *Christian Science Sentinel,* publishes several "testimonies" in each issue. To be considered for publication, an account must merely be "verified" by three individuals who "can vouch for the integrity of the testifier or know of the healing." In recent issues, believers have claimed that prayer has brought about recovery from anemia, arthritis, blood poisoning, corns, deafness, defective speech, multiple sclerosis, skin rashes, total body paralysis, visual difficulties, and various injuries. Most of these accounts contain little detail, and many of the diagnoses were made without medical consultation.

Christian Scientists may legally practice in all states. Medicare and some insurance companies cover care given by Christian Science practitioners, and their services are also tax deductible as a medical expense for federal income tax purposes. It is not known how many members continue to fully accept Mary Baker Eddy's premise that disease is an illusion, or how many members continue to visit practitioners instead of physicians. Eyeglasses, hearing aids, and dental treatment are being used by some members who still believe that illness is the consequence of mental error, but who find it easier to remove their discomfort than to remove their error.

Rita Swan, Ph.D., whose 16-month-old son Matthew died of meningitis under the care of two Christian Science practitioners in 1977, quickly collected allegations of 75 deaths and 95 serious injuries to children of Christian Scientists.[65] Angered by her experience, she formed CHILD, Inc., to work for legal reforms that can protect children from inappropriate treatment by faith healers.[66] She also sued the church but did not win the case. During the proceedings, church officials testified that the church had no training, workshops, or meetings for practitioners that include any discussion on how to evaluate the seriousness of a child's condition.[67]

A recent study compared alumni records from Principia College, a Christian Science school in Elsah, Illinois, with records from the University of Kansas in Lawrence, Kansas. Even though Christian Science tenets forbid the use of alcohol and tobacco, the death rates among those who had graduated from Principia between 1934 and 1948 were higher than those of their University of Kansas counterparts (26.2% vs. 20.9% in men, and 11.3% vs. 9.9% in women).[68] A subsequent study comparing the mortality of Christian Scientists and Seventh-day Adventists (who also are admonished to abstain from cigarettes and alcohol) found even greater differences.[69]

Prominent Individuals

In recent years there have been many evangelical faith healers in the United States. Some of the more prominent ones have been Billy Graham, Kathryn Kuhlman, Oral Roberts, Olga Worrell, Reverend Ralph DiOrio, Peter Popoff, and W.V. Grant. All have claimed to possess a gift of "miracle healing," but some have professed faith in the medical profession as well.

Kathryn Kuhlman, for many years the queen of faith healers in the United States, was an energetic woman who attracted large crowds to her healing services. A typical service would last several hours, during which Kuhlman would preach, pray, announce that individuals with various afflictions had been healed, and urge them to come forward to acknowledge their healing. She claimed that she herself did not heal, but was merely an instrument of the Holy Spirit. She had a number of medical doctors who would "certify" her healings.

A close evaluation of her work, however, was unfavorable. William Nolen, M.D.,[1] a Minnesota surgeon, was given permission to attend one of her services as an usher. Afterward, he examined or interviewed many people who had claimed to have been healed during the service. Not one person with organic disease had been helped. Ms. Kuhlman died in 1976, not long after undergoing open heart surgery.

In 1981 Oral Roberts opened the City of Faith, a $250 million medical center where "prayer and scientific medicine can be merged." Roberts, who claims to receive messages from God, has a large following of "prayer partners" who receive computer-generated letters about once a month from the Oral Roberts Evangelistic Association in Tulsa, Oklahoma. He promotes the idea that money donated to him (which he calls seed-faith) can bring to its donors rich rewards from God. He invites the prayer partners to indicate their spiritual and health needs so that he can pray for them in a special prayer tower at Oral Roberts University of Tulsa. The mailings, which ask for donations, often offer objects (for example, prayer cloth, prayer rope, prayer plaque, or prayer coin) "to touch and hold when you need a miracle."

In 1983 Roberts announced, "God has called this ministry to declare war on cancer and dread diseases." In 1987 he told his followers that God had ordered him to raise $8 million for scholarships at Oral Roberts Medical School and would "call him home" unless he did so. He obtained the money, but the appeal set off a storm of protest from television executives and religious leaders. In 1989 he announced that unfilled beds—a problem from the beginning—had forced him to close the school and shut down his hospital. At its peak, the 777-bed facility had only 148 inpatients.

Several years ago, magician James Randi and associates intercepted radio transmissions that proved that Peter Popoff was not getting information about the ailments of his audiences from God, as he claimed, but from his wife who was backstage. The investigators also saw that people capable of walking were placed in wheelchairs before W.V. Grant's performances, so that later he could help "cripples" walk. After extensive investigation, Randi concluded:

> I honestly see a strong parallel between the rock concert, the pro wrestling scene and the faith healing phe-

nomenon . . . *no one ever stops to ask out loud the one most important question:* IS IT FOR REAL?

Claims made by faith healers are nothing more than hollow boasts, and do not stand up to examination. Prepared culturally to expect miracles, convinced they are helpless without supernatural intervention, and bullied into supporting their gurus far beyond their means, the pathetic victims of the healers become a disillusioned subculture playing a dangerous game. . . . They are the dupes of clever, glib, highly-organized swindlers who are immune from justice and are confidently aware of that fact.[70]

Kirlian Photography

Kirlian photography is alleged by some faith healers to register their healing force or "aura" in photographs taken with a special apparatus. However, Randi[71] has demonstrated that the nature of the picture produced can be controlled by the degree of finger pressure applied to the apparatus as well as the amount of electrical grounding produced by contact between the apparatus and the subject's body. Other researchers have demonstrated that the photographic images are also affected by perspiration.

Psychic Surgery

Most "psychic surgeons" practice in the Philippines, but a few have made lucrative tours within the United States. They purport to heal without leaving a skin wound. However, skilled observers have noted that they use sleight-of-hand to create the illusion that surgery is being performed.[1,71] A false thumb may be used to store "blood" (a red dye) that appears as the skin is "cut." Animal parts or cotton wads soaked in the dye are palmed and then exhibited as "diseased organs" supposedly removed from the patient's body. In 1975 the FTC issued a cease-and-desist order against three Pacific Coast travel agencies that were promoting tours to the Philippines for psychic surgery as treatment for cancer and other ailments. The FTC called the practice "pure fakery." The American Cancer Society has concluded that "all demonstrations to date of psychic surgery have been done by various forms of trickery," and several practitioners have been prosecuted for theft and/or practicing medicine without a license.[72]

Problems of Faith Healing

Stanley Dean, M.D., professor of psychiatry at the University of Miami, has listed a number of problems that can occur with faith healers:

1. Faith healers are unskilled in making accurate diagnoses.
2. Patients may be accepted without adequate screening or referral.
3. Healers tend to assume a "panacea" (cure-all) complex and tend to downgrade other treatment techniques.
4. There is danger of delaying appropriate treatment in serious cases.
5. Although testimonials abound, no records are kept and there is not adequate follow-up.
6. Faith healers are not subject to professional, legal, or other restraints as are licensed health professionals.

The parents of Wesley Parker, an 11-year-old diabetic boy in San Bernardino, California, threw away their son's insulin after he was treated by a faith healer. The pastor of the First Assembly of God Church, together with his congregation, ministered through prayer. The preacher said the church believed in divine healing and also believed in physicians. He had led the parents to believe that the boy had been healed. Wesley Parker died. He was not buried immediately because his mother and father were told he would be resurrected. Lawrence and Alice Parker, Wesley's parents, were charged with involuntary manslaughter and endangering the health of the child. Found guilty, they were sentenced in September 1974 to five years' probation. The story was dramatized in the motion picture *Promised a Miracle,* which indicates how they became disillusioned.

The *Fort Wayne News-Sentinel* has documented that at least 103 persons—most of them children—have died since 1973 because they or their parents followed the teachings of the Faith Assembly Church, a Indiana-based religious sect that relies on faith healing rather than doctors.

Evaluation of Faith Healing

Many cures attributed to faith healing are actually cases of spontaneous remission (including some in which the original diagnosis was in error), but physicians recognize that the power of faith can affect the condition of many sick people. This is especially true in the case of psychosomatic and hysterical disorders. Such ailments can sometimes be relieved by the ministrations of a faith healer—or, for that matter, by the reassurances of a medical doctor.

It has been suggested that some people with

deep-seated psychosomatic ailments that do not respond to medical care need "an inner sense of forgiveness or cleansing" that only a ritual can produce.[64] Many people with chronic or incurable diseases will desperately reach for help from any source. Faith healers appeal to such people's need for hope. However, Reverend Lester Kinsolving[65] points out that although faith healers give some people a mental lift, there is a psychologic danger:

> Believers who are not helped may blame themselves. They may become sicker or severely depressed by such contemplations as: "Faith always heals; I'm not healed; I'm being punished! What have I done wrong? What's wrong with me?"

Dr. Louis Rose, a British psychiatrist, investigated hundreds of alleged faith healing cures. As his interest became well known, he received communications from healers and patients throughout the world. He sent each correspondent a questionnaire and sought corroborating information from physicians. After nearly 20 years, he concluded, "I have been unsuccessful. . . . I have yet to find one 'miracle cure'; and without that (or, alternatively, massive statistics which others must provide) I cannot be convinced of the efficacy of what is commonly termed faith healing."[73] His published analysis of 95 purported faith cures indicates:

1. In 58 cases it was not possible to obtain medical or other records; therefore the claims remained unconfirmed.
2. In 22 cases records were so much at variance with the claims that it was considered useless to continue the investigation further.
3. In two cases the evidence in the medical records suggested that the healer may have contributed to amelioration of an organic condition.
4. In one case demonstrable organic disability was relieved or cured after intervention of the healer.
5. In three cases the individual improved but relapsed.
6. In four cases a satisfactory degree of improvement in function was shown, although reexamination and comparison of medical records revealed no change in the organic state.
7. In four cases there was improvement when healing was received concurrently with orthodox medical treatment.
8. In one case, examined before and after treatment by the healer, the patient gained no benefit and continued to deteriorate.

C. Eugene Emery, Jr., a science writer for the *Providence Journal,* has looked closely at the work of Reverend Ralph DiOrio, a Roman Catholic priest whose healing services attract people by the thousands. In 1987 Emery attended one of DiOrio's services and recorded the names of nine people who had been blessed during the service and nine others who had been proclaimed to be cured. DiOrio's organization provided ten more cases that supposedly provided irrefutable proof of the priest's ability to cure. During a 6-month investigation, Emery found no evidence that any of these individuals had been helped.[74]

In 1988 Witmer and Zimmerman[75] reported that their exhaustive study of the scientific literature had located only three controlled examinations of the effects of prayer by third parties on people who were unaware of the prayers. Of these, one claimed benefit but was poorly designed, while the others found no benefit and were well designed. Surprised by the small number of published studies, Witmer and Zimmerman asked 38 journal editors whether they had ever received but rejected a manuscript on the subject of intercessary prayer. They also asked the editors to ask their readers whether they knew of any such study, published or unpublished. No editor or reader responded affirmatively.

Occult Practices

The occult refers to that which is mysterious, hidden, or obscure. It involves divination, incantation, and magic. Occult practices include: auric healing, color healing, phrenology, palmistry, numerology, I Ching, tarot, dowsing, extrasensory perception (ESP), pseudoreligious ceremonies, Krishna consciousness, humanistic mysticism, exorcism, monastic contemplation, Indian runic, and various types of witchcraft. Many persons with severe psychiatric disorders deeply identify with occult or mystical beliefs.

For some people, occultism can be a source of support and may help reduce anxiety. People who are lonely or timid, for example, may find that the sharing of occult beliefs provides them with companionship or an intriguing hobby. However, cult members may be vulnerable to exploitation by unscrupulous leaders. The occult can also be a breeding ground for psychosis.

Spiritualism and the "New Age"

The spiritualist movement was launched in 1848 when Margaret and Kate Fox claimed they were able to communicate with the dead. Through a series of rapping noises, the "spirits from beyond" gave advice, made predictions, and consoled loved ones. The Fox sisters performed in large arenas and charged clients for the opportunity to communicate with spirits. Soon after the Fox sisters began performing, thousands of mediums around the world claimed similar abilities. Years later, Margaret Fox admitted that she and her sister had been perpetrating a hoax.

Although many mediums have been exposed as fakes by magicians Harry Houdini, James Randi, and others, their activities persist. "Trance-channeling" is a current fad. Channeling can be defined as the communication of information to, or through, a live person (the medium or channel) from a source purported to be from another dimension or reality. One well-known practitioner is J.Z. Knight, who claims that a 35,000-year-old man named Ramtha uses her body to speak words of wisdom. Another is actress Shirley MacLaine, who claims that channeling provides useful information about "past lives." The Committee for the Scientific Investigation of Claims of the Paranormal (CSICOP), which has offered to test trance-channelers under laboratory conditions, has warned:

> [We] find it surprising that trance-channelers have been allowed to make uncorroborated and unverified claims, charge people hundreds or thousands of dollars for public and private audiences, and offer advice on business and personal matters without providing evidence that they indeed have contact with discarnate beings. Many people have been harmed by such practices. . . . We suggest that the public be extremely cautious about these claims.[76]

Aligned with spiritualism is the "New Age" movement, whose loosely defined philosophy includes such things as: "human potential, holistic health, recycling, organic foods, grassroots activism, practical spirituality, meditation, ecology, appropriate technology, feminism and progressive politics . . . a form of utopianism, the desire to create a better society, a 'new age' in which humanity lives in harmony with the cosmos."[77] *Time Magazine* described New Age as, "a whole cornucopia of beliefs, fads [and] rituals" to which some followers subscribe and others do not.[78] The beliefs include crystal healing (said to help the body balance and realign its "energy fields"), therapeutic touch, healing through mental imagery, pendulum power, and dozens of others.

"Cold reading" is a factor in most contacts between "psychic" practitioners and their individual clients. This process can lead a client to conclude that a practitioner ("reader"), met for the first time, knows all about the individual's personality and problems. According to Hyman, the most powerful technique involves encouraging the client to reinterpret the reader's *general* statements in terms of the client's own vocabulary and life.[2] Other techniques include: (1) using the client's reactions to general statements to formulate more specific ones, (2) posing questions that will be perceived as "hits" when they apply, but are not counted when they do not apply, and (3) rephrasing what the client says, relying on the fact that people often reveal things without remembering that they did so.

Lamar Keene,[79] a former professional psychic, has warned that some American psychics exchange information with each other about some of their clients, but pretend to derive this information by psychic means.

Astrology

Astrology as applied to health and illness involves the use of a horoscope to determine the diseases and infirmities to which one is allegedly predisposed. Stellar patterns at the time of birth are said to indicate potential illness, which may be triggered by subsequent transit of the planets over sensitive areas of the natal chart. "Medical astrologers" may claim (based on "astrological influences") that a part of the body is prone to weakness at certain times, or that particular times (based on the phases of the moon) may be ideal for surgery or fertility planning. Some also give dietary advice.

People are convinced of astrology's value because it "works." By this they mean that it supplies them with feedback that "feels right"—that convinces them that the horoscope provides a basis for understanding themselves and ordering their lives. It has personal meaning for them.[2]

Many experiments have demonstrated that people are likely to believe that a personality sketch fits them well, even when it was not compiled with them in mind. More than 40 years ago, psychologist Bertram Forer[80] administered a personality test to the students in one of his courses. A week later he gave each a typed personality sketch with the student's name on it—the "results" of the tests. Unknown to the students, however, each one actually received an identical list of 13 statements that Forer had copied from an astrology book:

1. You have a great need for other people to like and admire you.
2. You have a tendency to be critical of yourself.
3. You have a great deal of unused capacity which you have not turned to your advantage.
4. While you have some personality weaknesses, you are generally able to compensate for them.
5. Your sexual adjustment has presented problems for you.
6. Disciplined and self-controlled outside, you tend to be worrisome and insecure inside.
7. At times you have serious doubts as to whether you have made the right decision or done the right thing.
8. You prefer a certain amount of change and variety and become dissatisfied when hemmed in by restrictions and limitations.
9. You pride yourself as an independent thinker and do not accept other's statements without satisfactory proof.
10. You have found it unwise to be too frank in revealing yourself to others.
11. At times you are extroverted, affable, sociable, while at other times you are introverted, wary, reserved.
12. Some of your aspirations tend to be pretty unrealistic.
13. Security is one of your major goals in life.

After reading the sketch, students were asked to rate how well it revealed their basic personality characteristics. On a scale of 0 (poor) to 5 (perfect), 34 out of 39 rated it 4 or better, and 16 of these rated it as perfect. Many other investigators have confirmed and added to these findings.

People's tendency to accept vague, ambiguous, and general statements as descriptive of their unique personality is known as "the Barnum effect." Named after P.T. Barnum, it applies to any form of personality assessment, including personal interviews, standard psychologic tests, palmistry, tarot cards, and handwriting analysis. French et al[81] have noted:

> The typical horoscope is a mix of general statements and rather more specific ones. People tend to be impressed by the specific details that appear to fit (and pay less attention to those that do not), while the general Barnum-type statements provide readily acceptable "padding."

In 1984 CSICOP asked all 1200 American newspapers that published astrology columns to carry a disclaimer saying: "Astrological forecasts should be read for entertainment value only. Such predictions have no reliable basis in scientific fact." More than 40 papers are doing this, and a few others have reported CSICOP's request as a news item.

Biorhythms

Biorhythm theory suggests that behavior is characterized by three innate cycles: a 23-day physical cycle, a 28-day emotional cycle, and a 33-day intellectual cycle. The physical cycle influences tasks of a physical nature: physical strength, endurance, energy, resistance, and confidence. The emotional curve takes on increased importance in areas of high emotional content: sensibility, nerves, feelings, intuition, cheerfulness, moodiness, and creative ability. The intellectual cycle is of particular importance in pursuits requiring cognitive activity: intelligence, memory, mental alertness, logic, reasoning power, reaction, and ambition.

Each cycle begins at the exact moment of birth and oscillates up and down with absolute precision for the entire life. When the cycles are high, people are likely to be at their best; when they are low, the opposite is true. On critical days, when the cycles are changing, people are easily distracted and most prone to accidents. The three-cycle pattern repeats itself only once every $23 \times 28 \times 33$ days (58.1 years).

A Biolator calculator is available for quick measurement of cycles. Using this instrument, Bainbridge[82] performed nine statistical studies and concluded that biorhythm theory is "without value." In another study, he asked 108 students whether their biorhythms, which he calculated for them on a particular day, were valid. The majority said yes. Unknown to them, however, he had determined their values by flipping a coin.

Transcendental Meditation

Transcendental meditation (TM) is one of a variety of meditation techniques developed during the past 30 years. To use the method, a person sits in a comfortable position with eyes closed, twice a day for 15 to 20 minutes, initially directing attention to a secret Sanskrit mantra. This word, chosen for each individual by the teacher, is then repeated many times. The process can be learned for an initiation fee that covers two introductory lectures, an initiation, and four small-group meetings.

In 1992 the fee was $600 for families, $400 for individual adults, $155 for college students.

TM is alleged to help people think more clearly, improve their memory, recover immediately from stressful situations, stay younger, and enjoy life more fully. Proponents also claim that "stress is the basis of all illness" and that TM is "the single most effective thing you can do to improve all aspects of health and to increase inner happiness and learning ability."[83]

Eric Woodrum,[84] a sociologist who spent a year as a participant-observer of TM activities, has divided the TM movement into three phases. From 1959 to 1965 TM was interpreted as the most important component of a holistic program of spiritual evolution, nonattachment of the material realm, and attainment of nirvana. The program also included yoga exercises, silent prayer, dietary practices, and attendance at meditation courses. At the end of 1965, only one teacher of TM and about 220 practitioners lived in the United States.

During the next 4 years, the movement expanded rapidly as it won major publicity by identifying with aspects of the counterculture. The goal of "cosmic consciousness" was redefined in terms of bliss, energy, and peace, without reference to material nonattachment. By 1969 there were about 200 TM teachers and 12,000 meditators in the United States, but the movement had to redefine itself again as a result of two circumstances. One was the termination (for lack of attendance) of a rock concert-TM lecture tour by the movement's founder, Maharishi Mahesh Yogi, and the other was bitter criticism of him as materialistic by counterculture spokespeople.

Since 1970 the movement has emphasized the practical, physiologic, material, and social benefits of TM for conventional persons, with almost no other-worldly references. The movement produces a steady stream of evidence of "scientific validation" through an organizational arm, Maharishi International University. TM is also promoted through the American Foundation for the Science of Creative Intelligence, the World Plan Executive Council, and the World Medical Association for Perfect Health. In 1986 proponents claimed that Maharishi had trained 20,000 TM teachers and that 3,000,000 people worldwide had learned the TM technique.[83]

Woodrum divided TM participants into two subgroups. He said that average meditators have practical motivations for practicing TM, which they regard simply as a useful mental exercise. They consider the technique of TM separable from its quasireligious belief system, in which they have little interest. Members of the small inner movement, however, have philosophical motivations for practicing TM and participating in the movement. These individuals regard TM primarily as a path to "cosmic consciousness." They evaluate the technique in metaphysical terms according to the Science of Creative Intelligence (SCI), which has profound significance for their personal lives. They state that the TM movement can transform the world in keeping with the seven goals of their world plan:

1. To develop the full potential of the individual
2. To improve governmental achievements
3. To realize the highest ideal of education
4. To solve the problems of crime and all behavior that brings unhappiness to the family of man
5. To maximize intelligent use of the environment
6. To bring fulfillment to the economic aspirations of the individual and society
7. To achieve the spiritual goals of mankind in this generation

According to Woodrum, average meditators lend credibility to the secularized, practical image of TM, which is basic to its current broad appeal, whereas the members of the inner movement supply the man-hours and dedication that actualize the TM movement's potential for growth.

In 1987 a federal court jury awarded $137,890 to a man who contended that TM organizations had falsely promised that he could learn to levitate, reduce stress, improve his memory, and reverse the aging process. In 1988 an appeals court ordered a new trial.

Chapter 7 contains additional information about meditation.

Ayurvedic Medicine

TM organizations are now promoting ayurvedic medicine, which proponents say is a traditional Indian approach (ayurveda means "life knowledge") that combines "herbs, purifying therapies, and rejuvenation techniques to alleviate disease and promote longevity in the most natural way possible." The American Association for Ayurvedic Medicine, which claims to have 600 members, was founded in 1985 by Deepak Chopra, M.D., who states that "remaining healthy is actually a conscious choice."[85]

Ayurvedic theory states that individuals are endowed at birth with irreducible physiologic principles called "doshas," and that imbalance in these doshas is responsible for various disorders. Proponents claim that the pulse at the wrist can be used to detect diabetes, cancer, musculoskeletal disease, asthma, and "imbalances at early stages when there may be no other clinical signs and when mild forms of intervention may suffice."[86] The treatment modalities include: "pacifying diets," massage, exercise, transcendental meditation, and herbal compounds.

Ads from Maharishi Ayur–veda Products, Inc., state that in 1986 three ayurvedic physicians revived an ancient herbal formula called Maharishi Amrit Kalash, which is said to "have brought perfect health to the Vedic civilization thousands of years ago" and to "restore balance and order to the entire physiology by enlivening the connection between mind and body." A 1-month supply costs $45 in the form of Ambrosia herbal tablets or $50 as Nectar herbal fruit concentrate. Stephen Barrett, M.D., visited a Maharishi Ayur–veda exhibit at a recent health exposition and reported:

> After completing a brief questionnaire to determine my "body type," I was informed . . . that my "doshas" were imbalanced and offered . . .a tea to correct this. When I indicated that my health was good, [the exhibitor] replied that achieving balance through Ayurvedic measures would prevent future trouble.[87]

An investigative report published in the *Journal of the American Medical Association* stated that the ayurvedic movement's marketing practices reveals what appears to be "a widespread pattern of misinformation, deception, and manipulation of lay and scientific news media."[88]

Yoga Therapy

Yoga is said to be a practice whereby the body is brought to a state of unexcelled health and well-being that brings peace and serenity to the mind. Yoga therapy is based on ancient Indian beliefs about human existence. Its philosophy postulates five "sheaths" of existence: the physical body, the vital body, the mind, the higher intellect, and the abode of bliss (universal consciousness). The vital body is said to be composed of *prana,* life energy that flows through invisible channels. Disease is said to arise through imbalance of the three lower sheaths. In the healthy state, the positive energy of the highest sheath percolates through the lower ones and brings total harmony and balance to all of the individual's faculties.

Modern proponents state that infections, injuries, and other problems with a strong physical basis should be handled by conventional medicine, but psychosomatic ailments and degenerative disorders require more.[89] The recommended exercises include: yogic breathing, meditation, other relaxation techniques, bending, stretching, holding various postures, dietary measures, and "emotion culturing" (evoking positive emotions and diffusing negative ones). Yoga's effects can include: physical and mental relaxation, slow breathing, lowered blood pressure, reduction in metabolic activity, decreased heartbeat, and control of involuntary muscles.

Visual Training

"Vision therapists" claim to strengthen eyesight through a series of exercises and the use of eyeglasses. They emphasize exercising hand-eye coordination, watching a series of blinking lights, focusing on a string of objects, and sleeping in a certain position. Promoters say this regimen can improve school and athletic performance, increase the I.Q., and help overcome learning disabilities. Training sessions may take place once or twice a week and can cost $1000. However, according to the *Mayo Clinic Health Letter,* there is no scientific evidence that the approach works.[90]

Some optometrists claim that vision therapy is valuable for children with learning disabilities. The American Academy of Pediatrics and several other professional groups have stated that muscle exercises have no proven value for learning disabilities.[91] A committee of the National Research Council concluded that although certain visual abilities may improve with practice, visual training has not been proven to enhance athletic ability.[92]

Other Unorthodox Practices

Inglis and West[93] and Olson[94] have identified more than 70 "alternative therapies," including:

Alexander technique: A manipulative "bodywork" system that aims to reduce stress and to prevent and treat various disorders by correcting poor postural habits.

Aromatherapy: Based on the theory that plant oils

rubbed into the skin emit odors that can help heal hundreds of diseases and conditions.

Autogenic training: A system of mental exercises claiming to be effective against stress and psychosomatic conditions.

Bach remedies: Scents of various flowers are said to restore health by correcting negative emotional states that underlie all disease.

Feldenkrais technique: An exercise system claiming to reprogram the brain so the whole body-mind system works more efficiently.

Magnet therapy: Various systems of using magnets to "balance energy" within the body. Some proponents claim to be influencing the flow of energy along acupuncture meridians. Others claim to be balancing positive and negative magnetic energy that is detected with a device.

Polarity therapy: A system of manipulation, stretching exercises, clear thinking, and diet, which claims to restore health by removing blocks and balancing the flow of "life energy" between the positive (head) and negative poles (feet) of the body.

Radionics and radiesthesia: Practices based on claims that vibrations emanating from nature can be detected with pendulums, dowsing rods, black boxes, and other apparatus.

Reiki: A system whose practitioners are said to harness and transmit "universal life energy" by placing their hands in specific positions on or near the body, or through absentee healing. Also called the Radiance Technique, it is claimed to be useful for mental, emotional, physical, and spiritual balancing.

Rolfing: A system of massage and manipulation that seeks to liberate the body so it is able to align itself "properly with respect to gravity."

In 1987 the magazine *New Age Journal* reported that almost 100% of its readers who responded to a questionnaire had used "alternative" health methods and that 97% would be willing to choose such methods for treatment of a potentially life-threatening illness. The respondents reported using the following methods with mostly satisfactory results: acupressure (used by 42%), acupuncture (33%), aromatherapy (26%), chiropractic (56%), colonic (21%), crystal healing (25%), energy therapy (25%), Feldenkrais bodywork (13%), herbal medicines (47%), homeopathy (47%), iridology (19%), macrobiotic diet (26%), meditation (85%), mental imagery (70%), polarity therapy (24%), reflexology (38%), rolfing (19%), and yoga (53%). Despite the popularity of these methods, 73% of the respondents said that an alternative practice had been harmful and 57% felt that closer regulation was needed—preferably by "experts in various holistic therapies." The methods most often judged harmful were chiropractic, acupuncture, colonics, fasting, and various "natural" diets. Almost all of the respondents felt that "maintaining an emotional, physical, and spiritual balance" and "maintaining a positive attitude" were vital to good health, but only 57% thought it was important to have regular checkups by a medical doctor.[95]

Unscientific Medical Practices

A small percentage of physicians are making diagnoses and prescribing treatment considered invalid by the vast majority of physicians. Some of these practices have just a few proponents, while others have several hundred. Many of these practitioners feel alienated from orthodox medical practices and promote their beliefs to the public through publications, lectures, and talk show appearances.

Fad Diagnoses

Years ago many nervous or tired people were said to have adrenal insufficiency, a serious glandular disorder that is actually quite rare. The vast majority of these people were not only misdiagnosed but were also treated with adrenal gland extract, a substance they did not need and that is potentially harmful. Today a diagnosis of hypoglycemia (low blood sugar) is sometimes used to explain certain symptoms of nervousness or fatigue. Doctors who are "true believers" in hypoglycemia are apt to diagnose it in a large number of their patients. However, it is actually quite rare and should be diagnosed only after careful interpretation of blood glucose tests.

Herbert[36] states that a diagnosis of functional hypoglycemia should not be considered unless a person on a balanced diet gets symptoms 2 to 4 hours after eating, develops blood glucose levels below 45 mg per 100 ml whenever symptoms occur, and is immediately relieved of symptoms when the blood glucose level is raised. Bennion[96] cautions that the commonly performed glucose tolerance test is not reliable for evaluating most cases of suspected hypoglycemia. Low blood glucose levels without symptoms occur commonly in normal individuals fed large amounts of sugar. These incidents are of no diagnostic significance.

Clinical ecology is based on the belief that multiple symptoms are triggered by hypersensitivity to common foods and chemicals. Advocates of this belief describe themselves as "ecologically oriented" and consider their patients to be suffering from "environmental illness," "cerebral allergy," "allergy to everything," or "twentieth-century disease," which can mimic almost any other illness. Clinical ecologists speculate that: (1) although one substance may not have an effect, low doses of different substances can add or multiply their effects, (2) hypersensitivity develops when the total load of physical and psychologic stresses exceeds what a person can tolerate, and (3) hypersensitivities may be related to "immune system dysregulation" that can be difficult to diagnose and treat.[97]

According to proponents, potential stressors include practically everything that modern humans encounter, such as: urban air, diesel exhaust, tobacco smoke, fresh paint or tar, organic solvents and pesticides, certain plastics, newsprint, perfumes and colognes, medications, gas used for cooking and heating, building materials, permanent press and synthetic fabrics, household cleaners, rubbing alcohol, felt-tip pens, cedar closets, tap water, and electromagnetic forces. The signs and symptoms are said to include: depression, irritability, mood swings, inability to concentrate or think clearly, poor memory, fatigue, drowsiness, diarrhea, constipation, sneezing, running or stuffy nose, wheezing, itching eyes and nose, skin rashes, headaches, muscle and joint pains, frequent urination, pounding heart, swelling of various parts of the body, and even schizophrenia.

To diagnose "ecologically related" disease, practitioners take a history that emphasizes dietary habits and exposure to environmental chemicals they consider harmful. Various nonstandard tests and elimination and rotation diets are used with the hope of identifying foods that cause problems. In severe cases, patients may spend several weeks in an environmental control unit designed to remove them from exposure to airborne pollutants and synthetic substances that might cause adverse reactions.

Generally, patients are instructed to modify their diet and to avoid such substances as: scented shampoos, aftershave products, deodorants, cigarette smoke, automobile exhaust fumes, and synthetic fibers contained in clothing, furniture and carpets. Extreme restrictions can include staying at home for months and avoiding physical contact with family members. "Ecologically ill" patients may think of themselves as immunologically disabled in a hostile world of dangerous foods, chemicals, and an uncaring medical community. In many cases their life becomes centered around their illness.

The American Academy of Allergy and Immunology (AAAI), the nation's largest professional organization of allergists, has warned:

> Although the idea that the environment is responsible for a multitude of health problems is very appealing, to present such ideas as facts, conclusions, or even likely mechanisms without adequate support is poor medical practice.[98]

Clinical ecologists base their diagnoses primarily on the results of "provocation" and "neutralization" tests, which are performed by having the patient report symptoms that occur within 10 minutes after suspected harmful substances are administered under the tongue or injected into the skin. If any symptoms occur, the test is considered positive and lower concentrations are given until a dose is found that "neutralizes" the symptoms. Researchers at the University of California have demonstrated that these procedures are not valid.[99] In a double-blind study, 18 patients each received three injections of suspected food extracts and nine of normal saline over a 3-hour period. The tests were conducted in the offices of proponents who had been treating them. In unblinded tests, these patients had consistently reported symptoms when exposed to food extracts and no symptoms when given saline injections. But during the experiment, they reported as many symptoms following saline injections as they did after food extract injections, indicating that their symptoms were nothing more than placebo reactions. "Neutralizing" doses were equally effective whether they were food extracts or saline. The symptoms included nasal stuffiness, dry mouth, nausea, fatigue, headaches, and feelings of disorientation or depression.

In 1991 a jury in New York State awarded $489,000 in actual damages and $411,000 in punitive damages to the estate of a man who committed suicide after several years of treatment by a prominent clinical ecologist. Testimony at the trial indicated that although the man was a paranoid schizophrenic who thought "foods were out to get him," the doctor had diagnosed him as a "universal reactor" and advised that, to remain alive, he must live in a "pure" environment, follow a restrictive diet, and take supplements. During the trial the doctor admitted that since 1974, when he began practicing clinical ecology, he had diagnosed every patient who consulted him as environmentally ill.[100]

"Candidiasis hypersensitivity" is a supposed condition with multiple symptoms that may include: fatigue, depression, inability to concentrate, hyperactivity, headaches, skin problems (including hives), abdominal pains and bloating, constipation, diarrhea, respiratory symptoms, and problems of the urinary and reproductive organs. According to proponents, if a careful checkup does not reveal a cause for such symptoms, and a medical history includes antibiotic usage, "it's possible or even probable that your health problems are yeast-connected."

The proposed treatment program includes food supplements, special diets, and treatment with antifungal drugs. Proponents claim that the diagnosis is confirmed if the patient improves after taking antifungal drugs. However, the AAAI regards the concept of candidiasis hypersensitivity as "speculative and unproven," and notes that everyone has some of its supposed symptoms from time to time. In a strongly worded position paper, AAAI has warned that some patients who take the inappropriately prescribed antifungal drugs will suffer side effects, and that overuse of these drugs could lead to the development of resistant germs that endanger everyone.[98] In 1990 a double-blind trial found the antifungal drug nystatin was no better than a placebo for relieving systemic or psychologic symptoms of "candidiasis hypersensitivity syndrome."[101]

Many physicians accustomed to making the above "fad diagnoses" have added "chronic fatigue syndrome" (CFS) to their list. This is a controversial diagnosis that may be appropriate only for a small percentage of people who experience chronic fatigue. Because no cause has been discovered, some doctors doubt that CFS actually is a disease.

According to criteria developed by the U.S. Centers for Disease Control, the diagnosis should never be made unless the fatigue persists or recurs for at least 6 months and is severe enough to reduce the patient's activity level by more than half. In addition, the fatigue should be accompanied by several other symptoms, such as severe headaches, low-grade fever, joint or muscle pain, general muscle weakness, sleep disturbance, and various psychologic symptoms.[102] Other likely causes of fatigue must be carefully ruled out. Testing for antibodies to the Epstein-Barr virus, which is the usual cause of mononucleosis, is not useful for evaluating severe fatigue because 80% of healthy adults have positive antibody tests, presumably from mild or unapparent infection at an earlier age. No treatment has been proven effective for chronic disease syndrome, although antidepressant drugs may help relieve certain symptoms.

Consumer Reports[103] advises conservative measures: a balanced diet, adequate sleep, avoidance of excess stress, gradually increasing exercise without overdoing it, and—above all—patience. Calling CFS "a magnet for quacks," the magazine warns that "some practitioners create CFS patients by finding the syndrome in people who clearly don't have it." In 1990 its medical writer visited three "CFS specialists" and said he had been tired for 8 months. The first said the reporter's system was "sluggish" and needed to be "detoxified." He charged $185 and recommended blood tests costing $922.50. The others ordered Epstein-Barr tests, among others, and said the results were abnormal. One prescribed a drug used to treat heroin addiction and the other recommended vitamin injections to "bolster the immune system." Experts said that neither the tests, the diagnosis, or the recommended treatments were appropriate.

Chelation Therapy

Chelation therapy involves injection of an artificial amino acid called disodium edetate or EDTA into the bloodstream. The therapy is claimed to be effective against: kidney and heart disease, arthritis, Parkinson's disease, emphysema, multiple sclerosis, gangrene, psoriasis, and many other serious conditions. However, no controlled trial has shown that chelation therapy can help any of them, and manufacturers of EDTA do not list them as appropriate for EDTA treatment. A course of treatment, consisting of 20 to 50 intravenous infusions, can cost thousands of dollars.

Chelation therapy is heavily promoted as an alternative to coronary bypass surgery. It is sometimes claimed to be a "chemical Roto-Rooter" that can clean out atherosclerotic plaque from the body's arteries. It is not. After reviewing the pertinent literature, the American Heart Association's

PERSONAL GLIMPSE

Court Sides With Science

In 1991 a federal court judge in Georgia dismissed a claim asserted by a woman who suffered a stroke following surgery in 1989 for partial blockage of her left carotid artery. The woman had charged that her neurosurgeon had committed malpractice by failing to inform her that a chelation therapy was a possible alternative to the surgery. Georgia's informed consent law requires physicians, before performing surgery, to inform their patients of the risks and of "practical alternatives . . . which are generally recognized and accepted by reasonably prudent physicians." The judge ruled that the plaintiff had failed to prove that this standard had been violated.[2] Chelation therapy is a series of intravenous infusions containing an artificial amino acid (EDTA) and various other substances. Proponents claim chelation is an alternative to surgery because it can remove atherosclerotic plaque from the body's arteries.

In explaining his reasoning, the judge noted that chelation therapy is not taught in medical schools, is not FDA-approved for treating blocked arteries, and has been criticized as unproven by the American Medical Association, the American Heart Association, the American College of Cardiology, and the American College of Physicians. Even the doctors who testified as expert witnesses on the woman's behalf had admitted that chelation therapy is unpopular and not recognized as effective against cardiovascular disease by the great majority of physicians.

Task Force on New and Unestablished Therapies has concluded that there is no scientific evidence to demonstrate any benefit.[104]

A controlled trial whose protocol was approved by the FDA is now under way to test whether chelation therapy is effective against intermittent claudication, a condition in which impaired circulation to the legs causes pain when the person walks. Critics of chelation therapy believe this experiment will find no benefit. Even if it does, that would not prove it is safe or effective for treating heart disease.

Inspired by the claims for chelation therapy, many entrepreneurs have marketed a multitude of vitamin concoctions claimed to do the same thing as chelation therapy when taken by mouth. The FDA has ordered manufacturers to stop marketing these products, but a few are still doing so.

HOLISTIC MEDICINE

The term holistic (also spelled wholistic) is frequently used in both scientific and nonscientific circles. However, considerable confusion surrounds its use. Scientific practitioners regard holistic medicine as treatment of the "whole patient," with due attention to emotional and spiritual factors as well as the patient's life-style. But most others who label their approach holistic use nonscientific methods of diagnosis and treatment. Stalker and Glymour,[57] who have studied the holistic movement closely, consider it "a pablum of common sense and nonsense offered by cranks and quacks and failed pedants who share an attachment to magic and an animosity to reason." Some people espouse the holistic approach as an important modern development in the health care field. Critics reply that good physicians have always considered their patients as whole beings and that the term holistic is a dangerous banner under which practitioners of nonscientific methods have been rallying.

Chiropractors have been particularly active in organizing "holistic" or "wellness" centers that offer "natural" treatments and "preventive" services, but the methods recommended usually include unnecessary vitamin supplements, unnecessary spinal adjustments, and exercise programs of unproven value. In contrast, wellness programs run by scientific practitioners stress attention to risk factors. These programs offer help in stopping smoking, dietary counseling to promote weight control and nutrient balance, and exercise methods that increase heart strength and endurance. Since the holistic label is a potential source of public confusion, informed observers have recommended that scientific practitioners abandon its use.[105]

Unorthodox Groups

Physicians engaged in nonscientific practices tend to be politically supportive of one another, and many have banded together in professional groups. Some of these groups admit health care providers who are not physicians. Some publish a journal, and some have set up a "specialty board" that can certify applicants, but these undertakings lack standing within the scientific community.

The International Academy of Preventive Medicine (IAPM) was founded in 1971 "to create an atmosphere conducive to open discussion of preventive medical practices among physicians, dentists, Ph.D.'s and health-related professions." Subsequently, it merged with a similar group, the International College of Applied Nutrition, to form the International Academy of Nutrition and Preventive Medicine.

The American Holistic Medical Association (AHMA) was founded in 1978 by physicians who supposedly wished to use nontraditional methods as adjuncts to traditional ones. It has about 500 members, all of whom are medical or osteopathic physicians. Its conferences have included such topics as: acupuncture theory, anthroposophic medicine, ayurvedic medicine, balancing body chemistry, "exploring the new cosmology," imagery and healing, "a peek at the treasure of homeopathy," spiritual well-being, nontraditional methods of diagnosis, rolfing, psychosynthesis, rejuvenation exercises, metaphysics, alignment through music, psychoelectronics, renewal and personal awakening, and holistic treatment of inoperable cancer (by a Mexican physician who is a leading dispenser of Laetrile). Chalmers,[106] who evaluated the issues of AHMA's *Journal of Holistic Medicine* from 1980 through 1982, found only two well-designed studies among their 47 articles. The journal has not been published since 1986.

The American College of Advancement in Medicine (formerly called the American Academy of Medical Preventics) is composed mainly of medical and osteopathic physicians who have a special interest in chelation therapy. Most members of these groups prescribe or recommend megavitamins and questionable dietary practices for a wide variety of ailments. These approaches are discussed further in Chapters 7 and 13. Megavitamin proponents have formed the Orthomolecular Medical Society. "Clinical ecologists" have banded together to form the American Academy of Environmental Medicine (originally callled the Society for Clinical Ecology) and the American Academy of Otolaryngic Allergy. The International Association of Dentists and Physicians, formed in 1991, is open to all types of licensed or "certified" health care providers. Described as a "minority trade association," it hopes to set standards for unorthodox methods that will be recognized by insurance companies, regulatory agencies, and the courts.

Consumers Union believes that state licensing boards should systematically evaluate the work of medical and osteopathic physicians who engage in megavitamin therapy, clinical ecology, chelation therapy, homeopathy, or other dubious practices, to determine whether they are qualified to remain in practice.[107]

IT'S YOUR DECISION

Your back hurts after playing volleyball. Upon the advice of a friend, you see a chiropractor who examines you, obtains an x-ray film, manipulates your spine, and advises you to return the next day for a full report. The next day you feel better but keep the appointment anyway. The chiropractor is pleased about your apparent recovery but says you have a curvature of your spine that may make you prone to further difficulty. He recommends weekly visits for a few weeks followed by monthly checkups and adjustments for "preventative maintenance." What should you do?

SUMMARY

Nonscientific practitioners, as defined in this book, espouse a wide variety of theories and methods not based on scientific evidence. Some of these practitioners are sincere in their beliefs, while others are clear-cut frauds. In some cases, they mix effective methods with ineffective ones. In some cases their approach may relieve symptoms that are related to tension. In many cases, they claim credit for spontaneous improvements. Some unorthodox practitioners know their limitations, while others will attempt to treat any ailment. Consumers should be wary of the practitioners described in this chapter and use them cautiously, if at all. Licensure does not guarantee that a practitioner will render appropriate care.

DISCUSSION QUESTIONS

1. What are the general differences between scientific and nonscientific methods of health care?
2. Identify the various forms of nonscientific care.
3. What is acupuncture? What is its current status?

4. What is chiropractic? What is its origin? Why has its basic theory been rejected by the scientific community?
5. What are the types of chiropractors? How are chiropractors trained, and what services do they render?
6. What problems may be encountered by consumers who go to chiropractors?
7. What is naturopathy? How are its practitioners trained?
8. Briefly discuss reflexology, iridology, and applied kinesiology.
9. Discuss the history, philosophy, and current status of homeopathy.
10. Discuss faith healing and some of its prominent practitioners. What have evaluative studies of faith healing shown?
11. What are psychic surgery and Kirlian photography?
12. What is Christian Science? How has it affected the health of its followers?
13. Briefly discuss occult methods, including astrology, spiritualism, and other New Age practices.
14. What is "cold reading"? Why is it significant?
15. What are transcendental meditation and yoga? What effects do they have on people? How do they differ?
16. Briefly discuss chelation therapy.
17. Why are hypoglycemia, adrenal insufficiency, candidiasis hypersensitivity, environmental illness, and chronic fatigue syndrome classified as fad diagnoses?
18. Briefly discuss some professional organizations that promote nonscientific methods.
19. What is holistic medicine? What does it encompass?

REFERENCES

*1. Nolen W: Healing—a doctor in search of a miracle, New York, 1974, Random House Inc.
2. *Moore J v Baker RP*, US District Court for the Southern District of Georgia, Brunswick Division, Sept 5, 1991.
3. Porkert M and Ullmann C: Chinese medicine, New York, 1988, William Morrow & Co Inc.
*4. Skrabanek P: Acupuncture: past, present, and future, In Stalker D and Glymour C eds: Examining holistic medicine, Buffalo, 1985, Prometheus Books.
5. Introduction to oriental medicine, Seattle, 1991, John Bastyr College Publications.
*6. Sampson W et al: Acupuncture—the position paper of the National Council Against Health Fraud, Clin J Pain, 7:162-166, 1991.
7. Melzack R and Katz J: Auriculotherapy fails to relieve chronic pain—a controlled crossover study, JAMA 251:1041-1043, 1984.
8. Ter Reit G, Kleijnen J and Knipschild P: Acupuncture and chronic pain: a criteria-based meta-analysis, Clin Epidemiol 43:1191-1199, 1990.
9. Melzack R, Wall PD: The challenge of pain, New York, 1983, Basic Books Inc, Publishers.
10. Ulett GA: Acupuncture update 1984, South Med J 78:233-234, 1985.
11. American Medical Association Council on Scientific Affairs: Reports of the Council on Scientific Affairs of the American Medical Association, 1981, Chicago, 1982, The Association.
12. Sportelli L: Introduction to chiropractic, ed 7, Palmerton PA, 1983.
13. Lomax E: Manipulative therapy: a historical perspective from ancient times to the modern era, In Goldstein M, ed: The research status of spinal manipulative therapy, Monograph 15, 1975, National Institute of Neurological and Communicative Disorders and Stroke.
14. Maynard J: Healing hands: the story of the Palmer family, discoverers and developers of chiropractic, Mobile AL, 1977, Jonorm Publishers.
*15. Smith RL: At your own risk: the case against chiropractic, New York, 1969, Pocket Books.
16. Foundation for the Advancement of Chiropractic Tenents and Science: A study of chiropractic worldwide, Arlington, VA, Facts Bulletin, 4:5, 1992.
*17. Crelin E: A scientific test of the chiropractic theory, American Scientist, 61:574-580, 1973.
18. Crelin E: Discussion of the newspaper advertising of Richard T LaBarre, DC, in the Bethlehem Globe-Times 1974-1975, prepared for the district attorney of Northampton County, PA, in 1976.
19. Miura Y: Medical research on manipulative therapy for diseases of spinal origin, Ministry of Health and Welfare, Tokyo, Japan, 1990. English translation distributed by International Chiropractors Association.
20. Williams SE: Chiropractic science & practice in the United States, Arlington, VA, 1991, International Chiropractors Association.
*21. Jarvis WT: Chiropractic: a skeptical view, Skeptical Inquirer 12(4):47-55, 1987.
22. Quigley WH: Chiropractic's monocausal theory of disease, ACA Journal of Chiropractic, pp 52-60, June 1981.
23. Williams SE: Good philosophy produces good science, Chiropractic Research Journal 2(1):1-3, 1991.
24. Schafer RL and Sportelli L: Opportunities in chiropractic health careers, Lincolnwood IL, 1987, VGM Career Horizons.
25. US Department of Health, Education and Welfare: Independent practitioners under Medicare: a report to Congress, Washington DC, 1968.
26. Williams SE: Dynamic essentials of the chiropractic principle, practice and procedure ("blue senior textbook"), Marietta GA, (undated), Si-Nel Publishing Co.
27. Moran MC et al: Inspection of chiropractic services under

*Recommended reading

Medicare, Chicago, 1986, US Department of Health and Human Services.
28. Kusserow RP: State licensure and discipline of chiropractors, Office of Inspector General, Jan 1989.
29. Levin S: Interview by Dr. Stephen Barrett, 1989, In Barrett S et al, eds: Health schemes, scams, and frauds, New York, 1990, Consumer Reports Books.
30. Meade TW et al: Low back pain of mechanical origin: randomised comparison of chiropractic and hospital outpatient treatment, Br Med J 300:1421-1437, 1990.
31. Jarvis WT: Personal communication Nov 1990.
32. Shekelle PG et al: The appropriateness of spinal manipulation for low-back pain. Part I: project overview and literature review, Santa Monica CA, 1991, RAND.
*32a. Barrett S: Don't let chiropractors fool you, Priorities, pp 36-38, Spring 1992.
33. Modde PJ: Malpractice is an inevitable result of chiropractic philosophy and training, Legal Aspects of Medical Practice, pp 20-23, Feb 1979.
34. Kleynhans AM: Complications and contraindications to spinal manipulative therapy, In Haldeman S, ed: Modern developments in the principles and practice of chiropractic, New York, 1980, Appleton-Century-Crofts.
*35. Chiropractic: still not recommended, In Barrett S et al, eds: Health schemes, scams, and frauds, New York, 1990, Consumer Reports Books.
36. Herbert V and Barrett S: Vitamins and "health" foods: the great American hustle, Philadelphia, 1981, George F Stickley Co.
*37. "Nutrition" against disease: a close look at a chiropractic seminar, Nutrition Forum 5:25-28, 1988.
38. Barrett S: Chiropractic: inching ahead? Private Practice, pp 31-35, May 1982.
39. Barrett S: The spine salesmen, In Barrett S, ed: The health robbers, ed 2, Philadelphia, 1980, George F Stickley Co.
40. How to win patients and influence people, Consumer Reports Health Letter 3:11, 1991.
41. Getzendanner S: Memorandum opinion and order in *Wilk et al v AMA et al*, No. 76 C 3777, US District Court for the Northern District of Illinois, Eastern Division, August 27, 1987.
42. Inglis BD: Chiropractic in New Zealand, Wellington NZ, 1979, PD Hasselberg, Government Printer.
43. Banta D: Review of the report "Chiropractic in New Zealand," Washington DC, April 1980, US Congress Office of Technology Assessment.
44. Jarvis WT: The New Zealand chiropractic report: an evaluation, New Zealand Journal of Physiotherapy, pp 6-10, April 1980.
*45. National Council Against Health Fraud: Position paper on chiropractic, 1985, Loma Linda CA, The Council.
46. Barrett S: Letter, Prevention Magazine, p 78, Oct 1986.
*47. Kenny JJ, Clemens R and Forsythe KD: Applied kinesiology unreliable for assessing nutrient status, J Am Diet Assoc 88:698-704, 1988.
48. Pizzorno JE: What is a naturopathic physician? Let's Live, p 64, Feb 1988.
49. American Association of Naturopathic Physicians: Twenty questions about naturopathic medicine, Seattle, 1989, The Association.
50. Pizzorno JE and Murray MT, eds: A textbook of natural medicine, Seattle, 1985-1990, John Bastyr College Publications.
51. Pizzorno JE and Murray MT: Encyclopedia of natural medicine, Rocklin CA, 1990, Prima Publishing & Communications.
52. Cody, G: History of naturopathic medicine, In Pizzorno JJ and Murray MT eds: A textbook of natural medicine, Seattle, 1985-1990, John Bastyr College Publications.
*53. Raso J: Natural hygiene: still alive and dangerous, Nutrition Forum 7:33-36, 1990.
54. Jensen B: Iridology simplified, Escondido CA, 1980, Iridologists International.
55. Simon A et al: An evaluation of iridology, JAMA 242:1385-1387, 1979.
56. Worrell RS: Iridology: diagnosis or delusion? Skeptical Inquirer 7(3):23-35, 1983.
57. Stalker D and Glymour C: Engineers, cranks, physicians, magicians, N Engl J Med 308:960-964, 1983.
*58. Kaufman M: Homeopathy in America, Baltimore, 1971, The Johns Hopkins University Press.
*59. Barrett S: My visit to the Nevada Clinic, Nutrition Forum 4:6-8, 1987.
*60. Barrett S: Homeopathy: is it medicine? Nutrition Forum 4:1-6, 1987.
*61. Fringe medicine, In Barrett S et al, eds: Health schemes, scams, and frauds, New York, 1990, Consumer Reports Books.
*62. Homeopathic remedies: these 19th century medicines offer safety, even charm, but efficacy is another matter, Consumer Reports 52:60-62, 1987.
63. Ireland RR: Powwow: faith healing Pennsylvania style, Pennsylvania Medicine, pp 32-35, Aug 1973.
64. Jarvis W: Faith healing: taming the therapeutic miracle, Unpublished manuscript, 1977.
65. Kinsolving L: The miracle merchants, In Barrett S ed: The health robbers, Philadelphia, 1980, George F Stickley Co.
66. Swan R: Faith healing, Christian Science, and the medical care of children, New Engl J Med 309:1639-1641, 1983.
67. Swan R and Swan D: Civil suits against Christian Science providers; no standards established, CHILD Newsletter, No 1, 1991.
68. Simpson WF: Comparative longevity in a college cohort of Christian Scientists, JAMA 262:1657-1658, 1989.
69. Comparative mortality of two college groups, CDC Mortality and Morbidity Weekly Report 40:579-582, 1991.
*70. Randi J: The faith healers, Buffalo, 1987, Prometheus Books.
71. Randi J: Flim-flam! psychics, ESP, unicorns and other delusions, Buffalo, 1982, Prometheus Books.
*72. American Cancer Society: Unproven methods of cancer management—"psychic surgery", CA 40:184-188, 1990.
73. Rose L: Faith healing, Baltimore, 1971, Penguin Books.
74. Emery CE: Are they really cured? Providence Sunday Journal Magazine, January 15, 1989.
75. Witmer J and Zimmerman M: Intercessory prayer as medical treatment? an inquiry. Skeptical Inquirer, pp 177-180, 1991.
76. Kurtz P et al: CSICOP on trans-channelers, The Pseudoscientific Monitor, p 4, Nov 1987.

77. Adolph J: What is new age? In: The 1988 guide to new age living, Brighton MA, 1988, Rising Star Associates.
78. New age harmonies, Time Magazine, pp 62-72, Dec 7, 1987.
79. Keene ML: The psychic mafia, New York, 1976, St Martin's Press Inc.
80. Forer BR: The fallacy of personal validation: a classroom demonstration of gullibility, Journal of Abnormal and Social Psychology 44:118-123, 1949.
81. French C et al: Belief in astrology—a test of the Barnum effect, Skeptical Inquirer 15(2):166-172, 1991.
*82. Bainbridge WS: Biorhythms: evaluating a pseudoscience, Skeptical Inquirer 3(2):40-56, 1978.
83. World Plan Executive Council: The transcendental meditation television special: home video version, 1986, The Council.
*84. Woodrum E: The development of the transcendental meditation movement, The Zetetic, pp 38-48, Spring/Summer 1977.
85. Chopra D: Creating health: beyond prevention, toward perfection, Boston, 1987, Houghton Mifflin Co.
86. Sharma HM, Brihaspati DT and Chopra D: Maharishi ayur-veda: modern insights into ancient medicine, JAMA 265:2633-2636, 1991.
87. Barrett S: My quick tour of Whole Life Expo, Nutrition Forum 8:7, 1991.
88. Skolnik A: Maharishi Ayur-Veda: guru's marketing scheme promises the world eternal 'perfect health,' JAMA 266:1741-1750, 1991.
89. Monro R, Nagarantha R and Nagendra NR: Yoga for common ailments, New York, 1990, Simon & Schuster Inc.
90. "Visual therapy": a waste of your time and money, Mayo Clinic Health Letter, p 2, Feb. 1987.
91. Silver LB: The "magic cure": a review of the current controversial approaches for treating learning disabilities, Journal of Learning Disabilities 20:498-504, 512, 1987.
92. Swets JA et al: Enhancing human performance: issues, theories, and techniques, Washington DC, 1988, National Academy Press.
93. Inglis B and West R: The alternative health guide, New York, 1983, Alfred A Knopf Inc.
94. Olsen KG: The encyclopedia of alternative health care, New York, 1989, Simon & Schuster Inc.
95. Health survey: the results, New Age Journal, pp 57-58, Sept/Oct 1987.
*96. Bennion LJ: Hypoglycemia: fact or fad? New York, 1983, Crown Publishers Inc.
*97. Barrett S: Unproven "allergies": an epidemic of nonsense, Nutrition Today 24(2):6-11, 1989.
*98. American Academy of Allergy and Immunology: Position statements on clinical ecology and candidiasis hypersensitivity syndrome, J Allergy Clin Immunol 78:269-273, 1986.
*99. Jewett DL, Fein G and Greenberg MH: A double-blind study to determine food sensitivity, N Engl J Med 323:429-433, 1990.
*100. Medical malpractice—treatment of paranoid schizophrenia by "clinical ecology"—wrongful death—punitive damages, The New York Jury Verdict Reporter 10(23):1-2, 1991.
101. Dismukes W: A randomized, double-blind trial of nystatin therapy for the candidiasis hypersensitivity syndrome, N Engl J Med 323:1717-1723, 1990.
*102. National Institute of Allergy and Infectious Diseases: Chronic fatigue syndrome—a pamphlet for physicians, Bethesda, National Institutes of Health Publication 90-484, Oct 1990.
*103. Chronic fatigue: all in the mind? Consumer Reports 55:671-675, 1990.
*104. American Heart Association: questions and answers about chelation therapy, Dallas, 1985, The Association.
*105. Sampson WI: Wolves in sheep's clothing? In Barrett S, ed: The health robbers, ed 2, Philadelphia, 1980, George F Stickley Co.
106. Chalmers TC: Scientific quality and the Journal of Holistic Medicine, In Stalker D, Glymour C eds: Examining holistic medicine, Buffalo, 1985, Prometheus Books.
107. What can be done? In Barrett S et al, eds: Health schemes, scams, and frauds, New York, 1990, Consumer Reports Books.
*108. Butler K: A consumer's guide to "alternative medicine," Buffalo, 1992, Prometheus Books.

CHAPTER TEN

SELF-CARE

(© 1983 Medical Economics Company.)

You can do more for your health than your doctor can . . . you can save money and time. . . . You can learn to treat many medical problems at home. . . . Most . . . visits (to the doctor) are made for relatively minor medical problems . . . as many as 70 percent of visits to the doctor have been termed "unnecessary."

DONALD M. VICKERY, M.D.[1]
JAMES F. FRIES, M.D.

CONSUMER DECISIONS

When should ill people consult a physician?

To what extent should individuals self-diagnose and self-medicate when ill?

What guidelines are available to help consumers make intelligent decisions about self-care and self-help groups?

The American "self-care movement" obtained great impetus in the 1970s because of increasing healthcare costs and increased public interest in achieving a healthier life-style. These factors encouraged people to seek greater control over their own health, and to educate themselves for greater participation in their own care.[2]

The definition of self-care that emerged from this movement is:

> Functioning on one's own behalf in the promotion of health, the detection of disease, and the prevention and treatment of illness and injuries in activities taken separately or in participation with other laypersons or professionals.[3]

The extent to which consumers participate in self-care activities is not known. The best guess is that many millions are involved, since it is estimated that over $3 billion is spent each year on self-care products, devices, and services. Goldsmith[4] has estimated that 10 to 15 million people participate in 500,000 self-help groups. Further indications of the popularity of self-help are: (1) many books about self-care are published each year, (2) more than 1 million telephone calls are placed daily to *Tel-Med*, which plays audiotapes on health topics, and (3) there has been a proliferation of services that use computers that tap into large databases and issue comprehensive reports. Some services limit themselves to a few topics, while others address virtually any topic.

This chapter does not cover all aspects of self-care and is limited to products and services related to minor, self-limiting illnesses and injuries. Self-help groups that assist with special health problems are also discussed.

TYPES OF SELF-CARE

The spectrum of self-care activities can be categorized as follows:

Diagnostic and therapeutic: for example, common injuries, relaxation techniques, breast and cervical self-examination, sore throats, colds, insect bites

Rehabilitative: for example, Mastectomy, Inc., Mended Hearts, Fraternity of the Wooden Leg

Chronic disease support groups: for example, Arthritis Foundation, American Diabetes Association, Emphysema Anonymous

Prevention, maintenance, and behavior modification: for example, exercise, alcoholism, drug addiction, weight problems, stress reduction, smoking

Support groups for people whose spouses, parents, or children have problems: for example, Al-Anon and Alateen (spouses and children of alcoholics), physically handicapped, mentally retarded

REASONS FOR SELF-CARE

The reasons for self-care include:

1. People want control over their own body and life.
2. Consumers realize that they are exposed to many health risks related to life-style, environmental conditions, and failure to follow preventive practices.
3. Medical costs continue to escalate.
4. Consumers may lower their medical expenses by making fewer visits to doctors.
5. Advertising of over-the-counter drugs, devices, and equipment encourages self-diagnosis and self-medication.
6. Increased awareness of women's health resulting from the women's movement.
7. Ineffectiveness and inability of community health agencies to meet the special needs of patients with chronic illnesses.
8. Many consumers are dissatisfied with the quality of medical care: impersonal services, lack of communication, unnecessary surgery, and other problems.

INDIVIDUAL SELF-CARE

Individual self-care activities include the following:

1. *Self-diagnosis.* Many common symptoms and conditions do not require a visit to a physician. These include upper respiratory infections, injuries, muscle aches and pains, childhood dis-

eases, digestive disorders, and headaches. Fletcher[5] reported that 70% to 80% of all physician visits are unnecessary because they involve problems that are self-limiting and amenable to self-care.

2. *Self-testing.* This includes the use of home-care products for checking blood pressure, conducting urinalyses, and testing for pregnancy. There are also products and/or procedures for checking body parts including breasts (for cancer), cervix (for uterine cancer), ears (for wax or infection), mouth and teeth (for cavities or infection), and feet (for warts or bunions).
3. *Self-treatment.* This refers to the use of over-the-counter products, prescribed medicines and equipment, home remedies, vitamins, and contraceptives, first aid and emergency care (e.g., CPR, care of wounds and fractures), weight control, exercise, nutritional aids, physical therapy, support groups, and educational activities regarding injections, activities, diets, and tests.

Fletcher[5] stated that only 20% of the patients with minor symptoms consult a physician; however, 30% of the patients with various conditions should have consulted a physician earlier (see *When to consult a physician*, p. 184). Woods[6] conducted a survey of married women between the ages of 20 and 40 and found these self-care modalities used regularly: vitamins (used by 52% of the respondents), contraceptives (22%), prescription medications (16.6%), diets (4.9%), and over-the-counter medications (0.9%). She also found these self-care modalities used at a time of illness: over-the-counter drugs (42%), change of activity (28%), use of prescription drugs (16%), home remedies (5.4%), consultation with a professional (3.2%), and altered diet (2.2%). A study of parents conducted by the Harry Heller Research Corporation[7] revealed that half of the more than 9000 instances of identified health problems were self-treated.

Self-Diagnosis

He who has himself for a physician has a fool for a doctor and an ass for a patient.

Anonymous

Self-diagnosis is practiced by everyone to some extent. It would be impractical and a waste of medical expertise to have physicians deal with every cough, twinge, ache, and sore. However, individuals must be able to distinguish between minor and major health problems to determine when professional help is needed. Most conditions appropriate for self-treatment have symptoms that are easily recognized, occasional, and temporary. Examples include: the common cold, simple headaches, occasional indigestion, muscle aches and pains, slight burns, cuts and bruises, occasional sleeplessness, some skin infections, diarrhea, itching, and mild allergic reactions.

Self-diagnosis of a serious or chronic condition is another matter. Both overdiagnosis and underdiagnosis can lead to trouble. For example, a person who misdiagnoses a minor ache as arthritis may become needlessly upset; or someone who assumes that shortness of breath is the result of a bad chest cold when it is actually caused by heart failure may fail to seek timely corrective treatment. Even when self-diagnosis of a serious or chronic condition is correct, one's health may be threatened if a physician is not consulted. A physician's therapeutic resources far surpass any that are available to a layperson.

The classic survey of health practices and opinions done by the FDA[8] asked nearly 3000 randomly selected adults whether they had ever had various serious ailments and who had diagnosed them. Almost everyone who reported heart trouble, high blood pressure, and diabetes had the diagnoses made by a physician. But a sizable percentage of those reporting arthritis (20%), asthma (22%), allergies (28%), and hemorrhoids (32%) had made the diagnosis themselves without consulting a health-care professional.

People are less likely to recognize or seek help for illnesses that develop slowly, whereas illnesses with acute symptoms, such as severe abdominal pain, high fever, or excessive bleeding, are more easily recognized and brought to the physician's attention. It has been estimated that three of every four people with acute illnesses go to a physician, whereas only one of five people with chronic disease seeks medical attention. The following are possible reasons for not seeing a physician:

1. Lack of money
2. High cost of care
3. Inability to recognize symptoms of illnesses
4. Individual differences of opinion about the significance and importance of illness
5. Fear of the physician, diagnosis, or surgery
6. Apathy about one's health

7. Belief that illness is punishment for improper behavior
8. Belief that it is shameful to be ill
9. Lack of transportation
10. Too busy; unable to get away from work

When to Consult a Physician

A physician should be consulted when: (1) a symptom or condition is too severe to be endured (e.g., severe abdominal or chest pain); (2) an apparently minor symptom persists for a few days with no easily identifiable cause; (3) symptoms return repeatedly for no apparent reason (e.g., digestive distress); or (4) there is doubt about the nature of the condition.

A system of self-treatment for the common cold might include aspirin or acetaminophen for fever or muscular aches, adequate intake of liquids, limiting use of a nasal decongestant to once a day at bedtime if absolutely necessary, and a cough suppressant for dry, hacking cough. The physician should be visited in all cases of earache or in cases of sore throat accompanied by severe malaise. In addition, the physician should be consulted if a fever or dry cough persists for more than 48 hours.

When unsure about whether to visit a physician, a telephone call to the physician's office may help. If the symptoms are outlined, the nurse or receptionist (consulting with the physician if necessary) will advise whether a visit to the office should be scheduled.

Self-Treatment

Self-treatment involves a variety of procedures that are identified in this chapter and throughout the book.

Chronic Diseases

Home treatment may be practical and economical for individuals with chronic conditions such as allergies, asthma, diabetes, arthritis, and high blood pressure, and for some patients who need kidney dialysis. Physicians should be consulted about such possibilities.

Allergic individuals who are being desensitized by allergy shots may find it practical to administer the shots themselves, or have a friend or family member administer the shots. Home administration should not be done until it is clear that the shots are well tolerated; occasionally they produce a severe reaction.

Asthmatics (and their families) can learn how to use medications to minimize the frequency and severity of acute attacks. Some patients with arthritis can receive physical therapy at home.

Two conditions in which self-testing is of great value are diabetes and high blood pressure. Patients with diabetes, particularly those taking insulin, should regularly check their urine for the presence of sugar. The frequency of testing should be determined by the severity of the individual's condition; four urine tests a day, two days a week, may be appropriate for a patient with diabetes whose condition seems to be under control. Blood-glucose testing may also be practical to do at home. Monthly testing may be sufficient for an individual whose diabetes is under control. Daily testing may be needed for a patient with diabetes who has been diagnosed recently or whose disease needs very close monitoring. Accurate home-use devices are available to monitor blood-glucose levels (see Table 10-3).

Individuals whose high blood pressure is being medically treated can save time and money by checking their pressure at home as part of a medical program. Checks by a physician every 3 months may be sufficient if pressure is satisfactory and stable.

Home care for patients needing hemodialysis (kidney) is gaining popularity. However, the patient must realize and accept the responsibility for medications, diet, and care between treatments.

Self-Help Books

The number of self-care books published has greatly increased in recent years. Before relying on a self-help book, consumers should take careful steps to check its credibility. The mere fact that a book is published—even if written by a physician—does not guarantee that it is reliable. Table 10-1 shows how a three-member expert panel assembled by *U.S. News and World Report* magazine rated 10 popular drug guidebooks written for laypersons. Table 10-2 shows how a second three-member panel rated 10 popular medical books. Two members of this panel were medical experts; the third was the president of the People's Medical Society (discussed later in this chapter). Chapter 3 identifies many additional sources of reliable health information.

Two examples of self-help books follow. The first is a very practical volume that has been validated by scientific testing. The second contains reliable information but lacks practical guidelines for its use.

TABLE 10–1

RATINGS OF POPULAR DRUG REFERENCE BOOKS

Book	Price	Comments	Rating*
The Complete Drug Reference (Consumer Reports Books, 1991)	$39.95	Authoritative, comprehensive, best overall, but costly and more detailed than some people want; includes nonprescription drugs	9.4
The Essential Guide to Prescription Drugs (Harper/Collins, 1991)	$14.95	Strong section on drug treatment for specific conditions and diseases; too much technical lingo in some spots	8.7
The Pill Book (Bantam Books, 1990)	$5.95	A good buy; explanations are brief and, in parts, shallow; has no section on diseases or their drug treatment	8.2
Worst Pills, Best Pills (The Public Citizen Health Research Group, 1988)	$12.00	Strong focus on dangers of overusing certain drugs	7.8
Prescription Drugs (Beekman Publishers Inc, 1990)	$6.95	Thorough but poorly organized by generic drug names; outdated in parts, despite being promoted as "most current book" of its kind	7.6
Complete Guide to Prescription and Non-Prescription Drugs (The Body Press, 1991)	$15.95	Concise, but lacks depth; no section on diseases and their treatment	7.6
The ABCs of Prescription Drugs (Ivy Books, 1987)	$4.95	Organized by medical condition, with brief descriptions of typical drugs	6.5
Prescription Drugs and Their Side Effects (Perigee Books, 1991)	$9.95	Limited to the 396 most prescribed drugs; superficial throughout	6.4
Physicians' Desk Reference (Medical Economics Books, 1991)	$49.95	Very detailed but written for physicians, not the general public	5.8
Graedon's Best Medicine (Bantam Books, 1991)	$14.95	Has big gaps but also solid information; includes discussions of herbal remedies	5.7

*Based on a 10-point scale with 10 being the highest rating.
Modified from: Findley S and Burke S: Best books, US News and World Report pp 80-82, May 20, 1991.

Table 10–2

Ratings of Popular Medical Reference Books

Book	Price	Comments	Rating*
Mayo Clinic Family Health Book (William Morrow & Co Inc, 1990)	$34.95	Thorough and comprehensive; good prevention approach; no section on self-diagnosis	8.8
The American Medical Association Family Medical Guide (Random House Inc, 1987)	$29.95	Detailed self-diagnosis symptom, "flow charts," and helpful illustrations	8.7
The American Medical Association Encyclopedia of Medicine (Random House Inc, 1989)	$44.95	Best of medical encyclopedias with excellent illustrations but limited disease discussions	8.5
The Merck Manual (Merck & Co. 1987)	$21.50	Authoritative and detailed but designed for health professionals	7.3
The Columbia University College of Physicians and Surgeons Complete Home Medical Guide (Crown Publishers Inc, 1989)	$39.95	Clear general discussions, helpful first aid section, but lacks depth in parts	7.2
Better Homes and Gardens New Family Medical Guide (Meredith Corp, 1989)	$19.95	Good buy with a solid emergency section but not comprehensive	7.2
Take Care of Yourself (Addison-Wesley Publishing Co Inc, 1989)	$16.95	Not meant as a comprehensive guide; strong prevention and self-care format; good supplement to the other books	7.2
The New Good Housekeeping Family Health and Medical Guide (Hearst Books, 1989)	$24.95	Easy to use but bland, a bit dated, elementary in parts, with gaps in discussions	6.7
Family Health and Medical Guide (Signet, 1989)	$5.95	Pocket-size guide that is easy to read, accurate, a good value, but mostly superficial	6.5
The New Illustrated Medical Encyclopedia (Galahad Books, 1986)	$19.98	Question-and-answer format limits scope and depth; some weak questions and more than a few weak answers	6.3

*Based on a 10-point scale with 10 being the highest rating.

Modified from: Findley S, Burke S: Best books, US News and World Report, pp. 80-82, May 20, 1991.

Take Care of Yourself: A Consumers' Guide to Medical Care, by Donald M. Vickery, M.D., and James F. Fries, M.D.,[1] is a practical, comprehensive, and attractive text that focuses primarily on medical problems that consumers can act upon. The book includes information about avoiding illness, prevention, finding the right doctor, avoiding medical fraud, reducing medical costs, and the home pharmacy. A special feature is the section containing 100 Decision Charts for managing common health problems. The charts—set up as flow sheets—indicate when to apply home care and when to consult a physician. Consumers will find this a very useful reference.

Do-It-Yourself Medical Testing, by Cathey Pinckney and Dr. Edward R. Pinckney,[9] received a great deal of publicity at the time it was published. The book claims to provide "everything you need to know about performing 160 medical tests on yourself and your family." However, the book appears to be of little practical use for several of the following reasons:

1. It gives insufficient guidance about when the tests are appropriate to use.
2. Some of the tests are rarely used by doctors because other tests give more important information.
3. Some tests give positive results only when a person is so ill that the need to see a physician is obvious; in some cases, if a doctor is consulted after a home-test is positive, the doctor will repeat the test—which means that home testing may have provided nothing more than extra expense.
4. Some of the tests (such as determination of reflexes) have great value when used appropriately by physicians, but are of no use in the hands of patients. For example, it makes no sense to purchase a reflex hammer to check one's reflexes, because anyone having symptoms for which such tests are needed should see a doctor; no doctor confronted with symptoms suggesting neurologic disease would fail to perform the simple tests suggested by this book.
5. Most of the tests involving expenditure of money are not worth the expense involved. The Pinckneys suggest that home-testing can save money, but they fail to indicate which tests fall into this category and which do not. For example, buying a bottle of 100 urine dipsticks will not save money if the product loses its effectiveness in a few months and the test is performed only once.

Another book by the Pinckneys, *The Patient's Guide to Medical Tests,*[10] provides comprehensive information about the risks and benefits of more than 1000 medical tests and how doctors interpret them.

Thousands of self-help books, audiotapes, and videotapes have been marketed to the public with claims that they can help people function better mentally, improve relationships with others, relieve anxiety or depression, or achieve other desired emotional changes. Dr. Gerald Rosen,[11] former chairman of the American Psychological Association's Task Force on Self-Help Therapies, has noted the following:

1. Although some of these materials may be helpful, most have not been tested to see if they are valid.
2. Many self-help materials are promoted with extravagant and ethically questionable claims.
3. The fact that a technique is useful when included as part of a therapy program does not mean the technique will work as a self-help measure. Self-help books are more likely to be helpful during periods of therapy than when used alone.
4. Few do-it-yourself books have provisions to protect readers against failing to comply with instructions. Should treatment failure occur, the readers may inappropriately blame themselves, become skeptical as to whether they can be helped, and fail to seek professional assistance.

Gambrill notes that many self-help books exaggerate people's ability to alter themselves or their environment and that failure to achieve unrealistic goals offered by these books can make people more depressed.[11a]

Self-Care Devices

Numerous self-care health devices and products are available. Although some have merit, others have little or no practical value and are not as effective as their advertising suggests.

Home Pharmacy

Another way to help with self-care is to have a "home pharmacy" that is stocked with useful items for the self-management of minor illnesses, injuries, and certain emergency situations. Chapter 20 contains a list of suggested items.

Self-Testing

It is estimated that consumers spend $2 billion a year on home-use health tests and equipment. More tests are being developed for breast cancer, allergies, illegal drugs, and thyroid disorders. Tests that have failed to gain FDA approval for home-use include Pap smear and rapid strep throat tests used by physicians, and tests for AIDS and other sexually transmitted diseases.

There are two basic types of home tests: (1) continuous monitoring (e.g., blood pressure for hypertension, blood-glucose in diabetes), and (2) diagnostic screening (e.g., pregnancy, gonorrhea, occult blood in stools).

The *Johns Hopkins Medical Letter*[13] estimated that one in seven tests, including those administered professionally, result in false findings. The report adds that the risk of error in tests administered by laypersons is potentially higher. No test should ever be considered as the only criterion for diagnosis. A physician is needed to evaluate test results in light of symptoms and medical history.

Self-testing can lead some people to make an appointment with a doctor if they suspect a health problem. However, several physician surveys reveal these concerns: (1) patients may substitute the tests for physicians' opinions, (2) users may not be proficient in the administration of the test, and (3) tests may not be reliable. Table 10-3 identifies some of the self-diagnostic test kits.[14] Table 10-4 identifies some questionable home-care tests.

When home tests are appropriate, their best use is in cooperation with a physician. For example, when taking blood pressure the doctor shows the patient how it should be done and how to check the proper working condition of the equipment.

Blood-Pressure Devices

Blood-pressure kits for home resemble the devices used by physicians. They usually include a sphygmomanometer to measure blood pressure in the arteries and a stethoscope to listen to the arterial pulsations in the arm. Blood pressure is measured in millimeters of mercury (mm Hg); two numbers are recorded. Systolic pressure, the higher reading, is the pressure when the heart contracts to pump blood through the arteries. Diastolic pressure, the lower reading, reflects the pressure recorded between heart beats. Normal systolic pressure for adults is about 120 mm Hg. Diastolic readings above 90 are considered abnormal (see Chapter 16 for more detailed information).

There are three types of blood-pressure devices:

Mercury: A column of mercury rises in a tube as cuff pressure is increased and falls as pressure is decreased.

Mechanical aneroid (without liquid): A needle moves clockwise on a dial as pressure is increased and counterclockwise as pressure is decreased.

Electronic aneroid: A microphone under the cuff is used to register arterial sounds on a dial rather than project them aurally with a stethoscope.

The mercury type is highly accurate and does not need calibration, but is most difficult to use. *Consumer Reports* does not recommend this type for home use. The mechanical-aneroid type requires dexterity, good hearing to use the stethoscope, good eyesight to read the dial, some practice to use correctly. This type should be calibrated annually to maintain accuracy. There are two types of electronic devices: one with a cuff that must be manually inflated, and the other with a cuff that automatically inflates. The electronic instruments are easier to use because they provide digital readings and do not require listening to the sounds with a stethoscope. However, they require more frequent calibration to maintain accuracy.

Consumer Reports[15] studied 24 devices and concluded that the mechanical aneroid monitors offered the best value because they are less expensive and, when used correctly, are generally more accurate than electronic arm models. The top-rated models were:

MECHANICAL

- Marshall 104 ($29)
- Omron HEM-18 ($30)
- Walgreens 2001 ($20)
- Lumiscope 100-021 ($30)
- Sunmark 100 ($22)

ELECTRONIC WITH MANUAL INFLATION

- Sunbeam 7621 ($62)
- AND UA-701 ($45)
- Sunmark 144 ($48)

ELECTRONIC WITH AUTOMATIC INFLATION

- Omron HEM-704C ($130)
- Sunbeam 7650 ($115)
- Lumiscope 1081 ($100)
- Marshall 91 ($118)

Four electronic finger models included in the test were judged unacceptable because they performed inaccurately.

The consumer should be aware that: (1) adequate instruction in the use of a blood-pressure device is necessary to ensure accurate readings, (2)

Table 10–3

Self-Diagnostic Test Kits

Brand name	Manufacturer	How it works	Time for results	Manufacturer's suggested retail price	Stated accuracy
Pregnancy					
e.p.t. Plus	Warner-Lambert Company	Urine is dropped into test tube containing chemicals and monoclonal antibodies — pink color indicates presence of urinary HCG	10 minutes	$11	98%
Advance	ORTHO Pharmaceutical Corporation	A dipstick test using monoclonal antibodies — blue color indicates presence of urinary HCG	30 minutes	$10-12	98%
Acu-test	Beecham Products	Ring forms on bottom of test tube containing a few drop of urine to indicate presence of HCG	2 hours	$11 for single test, $16 for double test	98%
Diabetes — urinary glucose self-monitoring					
Tes-Tape	Eli Lilly and Company	A strip of tape is dipped into urine and color compared to chart to indicate urine glucose level	A few seconds	$6.50 for 100 strips	96%
Clinitest	Ames Division of Miles Laboratories	A pill is dropped into urine and color compared to chart to indicate urine glucose level	15 seconds	$6 for 100	99%

Continued.

TABLE 10–3

SELF-DIAGNOSTIC TEST KITS — cont'd

Brand name	Manufacturer	How it works	Time for results	Manufacturer's suggested retail price	Stated accuracy
Diabetes — blood glucose self-monitoring					
Reagent strips	Various manufacturers	A drop of blood is placed on reagent strip and color change compared to chart to indicate blood glucose level	2 minutes	$30-50 for bottle of 100	96%
Glucometer II	Ames Division of Miles Laboratories	A drop of blood on reagent strip is inserted into electronic digital meter to measure blood glucose level	1-2 minutes	$150	99%
Early colon cancer					
ColoScreen Self-Test	Helena Laboratories, Inc.	Pad dropped in toilet turns reddish if blood in stool	30 seconds	$7	As effective as lab test
Early Detector	Warner-Lambert Company	Chemically treated tissue paper turns blue if blood in stool	1 minute	$5-7	As effective as lab test
Hemoccult Home Test	Menley & James Laboratories	A paper slide turns blue if blood in stool sample	15 minutes	$7.50	As effective as lab test

TABLE 10–3

SELF-DIAGNOSTIC TEST KITS — cont'd

Brand name	Manufacturer	How it works	Time for results	Manufacturer's suggested retail price	Stated accuracy
Ovulation					
Ovutime	ORTHO Pharmaceutical Corporation	A test dipstick turns blue when mixed with urine and chemicals containing monoclonal antibodies for urinary LH	60 minutes	$35 for 6	96%
First Response	Tambrands, Inc.	Urine dropped into solution in test tube turns blue to indicate LH	20 minutes	$25 for 6	85% to 99%
Urinary tract infections					
Microstix-Nitrite	Ames Division of Miles Laboratories	Test strip dipped into urine changes color to indicated nitrite	30-40 seconds	$39 for 25	94% (with 3 consecutive morning specimens)
Venereal disease: gonorrhea					
V. D. Alert	Medical Frontiers, Inc.	Urethral sample collected on slide and mailed to lab	Within 2 days	$14-19	96%

From Fuerst ML: Home diagnostic tests: self-help health? Generics, pp 42-44, July 1986.

Table 10–4

Questionable Home-Care Tests

Type of test	Function as advertised	Cost	Remarks
Diabetes detector	Once diagnosed, diabetes can be controlled, but more than 5 million Americans have undiagnosed diabetes and may be risking their life. This test provides basic diabetes information, warning signs, and a simple, reliable urine test which enables you to monitor your risk	$15	It is not cost-effective to monitor everyone's urine several times a year to protect against a tiny chance that the onset of diabetes will present as a life-threatening problem. An occasional urinalysis as part of a periodic examination makes more sense.
Urine screening test	Simple urine test detects dozens of health problems from infections to diabetes. Tests for leukocytes, protein, glucose, ketones, hemoglobin, and blood. Simply dip the strip into specimen and one minute later compare color changes with the chart on box.	$39	The kit costs 2-3 times as much as a urinalysis at a laboratory or medical office. Few if any individuals would have reason to test themselves often enough to warrant the expense.
Bladder infection test	Simple dip-and-read strips allow early detection of the torment of variously known conditions such as cystitis, bladder infection, urinary tract infection. Also tests for leukocytes, nitrites. Early detection allows early treatment—often without a physician visit.	$32	The conditions named are unlikely to be diagnosed before symptoms strike. Once symptoms appear, a doctor should be consulted because all require treatment by a physician.
One-step pregnancy test	Hold the absorbent tip in urine stream and wait three minutes for result. Laboratory tests show test more than 99% accurate even as early as 1st day of a missed period.	$18	The test still may need medical interpretation. Some doctors will insist on retesting by a commercial laboratory.

a noisy environment can cause high readings during measurement, (3) elevated readings are not adequate for a diagnosis—it can only be made by a physician, and (4) a monitor may be a good investment for a hypertensive person who is under the care of a physician.

The coin-operated blood-pressure machines in shopping malls, supermarkets, drugstores, airports, and other places should be used with caution because their reliability is limited. The accuracy of these machines depends on how recently they have been calibrated.

Pregnancy Test Kits

A *pregnancy-test kit* involves a procedure whereby a few drops of urine are added to a test tube containing special chemicals. If human chorionic gonadotropin (HCG: a hormone found in pregnant women's urine) is present, this is a positive result that indicates pregnancy. The e.p.t. and First Response kits contain monoclonal antibodies that detect minute traces of HCG in urine. Most manufacturers recommend repeating the test a few days later to confirm results. Iannucci[16] stated that although manufacturers claim 99% accuracy of their tests, in actual use there are many more inaccurate results. Results can be affected by using a test past its expiration date, exposing the specimen to the sun, or having protein or blood in urine. The presence of cancer could also give inaccurate results.

Tests results will not be accurate unless the instructions are explicitly followed. Some of these instructions include: (1) the test must be conducted at room temperature, (2) the urine container must be free from dirt, (3) the result must not be read too early or too late, and (4) the urine must not be placed in the sun. The new e.p.t. Plus kit used to be the fastest test commercially available. It can be used 1 day after a woman misses her period and it provides results in 10 minutes. Whitehall Laboratories has marketed a new one-step product, Clearblue Easy, that gives results in 3 minutes and informs the user when the test is done improperly.

A study by Valanis and Perlman[17] reported that the incidence of false-negative results, the test incorrectly indicates no pregnancy, was over 24% for pregnancy-test kits. Louise Tyrer, M.D., vice-president for medical affairs of the Planned Parenthood Federation of America, said "You can't diagnose pregnancy without a pelvic exam and some physical assessment."[18] A positive result indicates pregnancy; therefore a visit to a physician is necessary. The physician will probably insist on confirming the diagnosis, and the woman will ultimately pay for two pregnancy tests.

PERSONAL GLIMPSE

Do-It-Yourself Abortions?

A self-help abortion effort that has received some notoriety in the United States in the past few years, apparently is an effort to ensure that women can still obtain abortions if the Supreme Court and state legislatures make them illegal. The movement's leaders advocate the use of menstrual extraction and are investigating abortion methods that include: the use of herbs, over-the-counter medications, and other simple but riskier methods that do not require devices or drugs. The Executive Director of the National Abortion Federation said her organization's position was against women performing such procedures. A vice-president of the Planned Parent Federation of American said women who participate expose themselves to the risk of infection and a perforated uterus.[18]

What is your reaction to this effort? Would you be willing to try any of these methods?

Other Test Kits

The *colon-rectal test* for home use is intended to screen people for cancer. The test is conducted by placing a stool specimen in contact with peroxide and guaiac (a chemical that reacts to blood). If the chemical turns to a specified color, hidden (occult) blood is present. Positive results do not always indicate cancer; they may be caused by bleeding gums, nonmalignant polyps, heavy use of aspirin, diverticulitis, hemorrhoids, or other conditions. Negative results may lull patients into a false sense of security. The American Cancer Society (ACS) recommends that three consecutive tests be completed to be certain the findings are accurate. The findings may be difficult to interpret and the patient will need the help of a physician.[2] The ACS states that the guaiac test for occult blood should be taken once a year after age 50 and should be used to supplement an examination with a proctoscope.

A *diabetes test* involves the self-monitoring of glucose in blood and urine to help control insulin levels. Self-monitoring should be done with a physician's guidance.

The *venereal-disease test* is performed by collecting a specimen of pus from the sexual organ, the sample is then sent to a laboratory for analysis to determine the presence of gonorrheal bacteria. If the results are negative, the analysis may reveal the presence of other sexually transmitted diseases.

The *urinary-tract infection test* determines the presence of nitrite in urine. The drawback of this test is that 1 in 10 bacterial infections does not react to the test's reagent, resulting in a false-negative result. If other symptoms are present, such as frequent, painful urination or a puslike discharge, a physician should be consulted.

The *ovulation-prediction test* is designed to predict the peak periods of a woman's fertility during a given menstrual cycle. This test attempts to discover luteinizing hormone (LH) in urine, because ovulation is triggered by a sudden increase in LH. The test may help couples with fertility problems, as it may be more accurate than recording basal body temperatures (another method used to predict ovulation). Fertility experts recommend taking basal body temperatures along with the test to see if the two measures of ovulation coincide. Some tests are available over-the-counter, but one's choice of product depends on individual needs. Physician guidance may be necessary.[19] Ovulation tests must be performed for several days in a row (see Table 10-1). If menstrual periods are irregular, testing may need to be conducted for a longer period of time. Inaccurate results can occur if the woman is entering menopause or using other hormones to treat infertility.

Cholesterol testing at fairs and supermarkets has been performed by inadequately trained people. Some tests are conducted under unsatisfactory conditions such as danger of infection and some machines to test blood samples are not calibrated properly. Questions have also been raised about the accuracy and practicality of such tests. Richard P. Kusserow, Inspector General of the Department of Health and Human Services, stated that these tests should be regulated more tightly.[20]

Vision may be tested using the Amsler Grid, which can detect the early signs of one form of senile macular degeneration. The test also includes procedures for detecting visual acuity and glaucoma. It is obtainable from the Minnesota Society for the Prevention of Blindness and Preservation of Hearing, 1208 Pioneer Bldg., St. Paul, MN 55101.

AIDS tests for self-use have been marketed without FDA approval. One kit that cost $30 required the consumer to prick a finger, draw some blood, and mail it to a laboratory for analysis. The lab would then notify the individual of the results by telephone. The accuracy of this test can be impaired if too much time elapses before the sample is mailed, or if the sample is exposed to severe temperature changes.

No home-use tests for AIDS have been approved by the FDA. On July 5, 1991, two companies stopped selling OraSure (saliva collection kit) and Epitope, products that claimed to detect AIDS virus antibodies. The FDA[21] had threatened severe regulatory action because the kits had not been proven safe and effective for use at home. An FDA advisory panel stated that such tests could be used improperly if available.[22] The Association of State and Territorial Public Health Laboratory Directors oppose the use of AIDS tests without adequate counseling. They state that positive findings may cause individuals to become suicidal and negative findings may falsely lead people to think they are not infected.

Home-immunization kits, consisting of alcohol, water solutions, and sugar pills, were allegedly sold by an Idaho naturopath as protection from numerous childhood diseases. Apparently these kits were manufactured by a company in Twin Falls, Idaho and sold to naturopaths, parents, and regional distributors in many states. The FDA did not approve these kits and stated that they did not afford protection from the diseases.[23]

CONSUMER TIP

Suggestions for Consumers

These suggestions will help consumers who are considering the use of home health care tests:

- Consult with a doctor or other healthcare professional before buying a test and ask which brand to purchase.
- Check the expiration date because chemicals lose their potency with time and the results could be affected.
- Store products as directed; they may be affected by hot and cold temperatures.
- Read labels and package instructions carefully and follow directions exactly. If questions remain, check the package for a toll-free number, consult your doctor, or consult the pharmacist at the place of purchase.
- Understand the limitations and purposes of the test.
- Test results should be obtained carefully and accurately; use a stopwatch if precise timing is necessary.
- Note special precautions such as avoiding certain foods or limitation of physical activity prior to testing. Failure to follow these instructions may invalidate results.
- If one must collect a stool, do exactly as advised.
- If a urine sample is necessary and a container is not included, wash a bottle with soap and hot water, and rinse away all traces of soap with distilled water.
- Know what action to take if results are positive, negative, or unclear. It may be advisable to repeat the test or consult a physician.

EFFECTIVENESS OF INDIVIDUAL SELF-CARE

Segal and Goldstein[24] reported that little is known about self-care behavior. Although it is clear that laypersons frequently evaluate and self-treat many health problems of daily living, the nature and extent of these self-care practices are not well understood. Nor has there been much research to demonstrate the effectiveness of self-care procedures.

The first and probably the most extensive study of self-care educational programs was sponsored by the Centers for Disease Control of the Public Health Service, which received responses from 723 programs out of 2284 that were contacted.[2] The survey results revealed the following benefits from self-care programs:

Increased wellness status	94%
Reduced established risk factors	86%
Prevented onset of illness or injury	79%
Prevented further deterioration or spread of present illness	63%

Several additional studies have provided promising but inconclusive results. Three University of Washington physicians attempted to discover whether people could take care of their minor ailments by reading an early edition of the book *Take Care of Yourself: A Consumers' Guide to Medical Care.* The results showed that 84% of the 1700 persons had read part of the book. Changes in attitude occured through improved confidence in being able to deal with health problems, but the reduction in visits to a physician was not statistically significant.[25]

Zapka and Averill[26] reported that a program conducted at a self-care facility at the University of Massachusetts resulted in a significantly large decrease in visits to a physician for the common cold. It was estimated that over a 2-year period some $46,000 would be saved as a result. The study incorporated health education; each participant studied a checklist of symptoms and received other informational handouts.

Roberts et al[27] conducted a double-blind study of a health education program at a University of Missouri family medical clinic to determine whether self-care instructions could reduce unnecessary visits to physicians for minor respiratory illnesses. A list of "cold severity criteria" was distributed to patients to help determine the need for a clinic visit. Physician-visit rates for colds dropped in the "informed" patient group compared with a control population that did not receive the criteria list. The informed patients recovered uneventfully and had no increase in complications.

Kemper[28] reported a study of 900 HMO members using the reference book *The Health Use Handbook* and a workshop technique did not reveal a lessening of clinic visits or a reduction in costs. However, 81% said they had read at least half of the book and 83% said the workshop had improved the health care of their families.

Berg studied 49 families in the Health Cooperative of Puget Sound in terms of health maintenance, common acute illnesses, and chronic disorders.[29] He concluded that self-care education programs did not reduce costs, except in those cases dealing with the chronic diseases (diabetes, home hemodialysis for kidney failure, hemophilia). He said his first choices for self-care education were the conditions of fever, ear problems, and cough.

The Arthritis Self-Care Project[30] for the treatment of chronic disease, which was conducted at the Stanford University Arthritis Center, involved 100 patients whose average age was 78. The project demonstrated that pain could be reduced by 20% with regular exercise and the performance of other self-care activities.

Consumers should be aware that there are limitations and hazards in the use of nonprescription drugs (see Chapter 20). Despite the safety and efficacy of over-the-counter medications, they are not without hazards, and therefore should be used cautiously according to their instructions. In fact, self-medication for more than a few days is often unwise. The risks include overlooking an advancing disease, postponing proper medical treatment, masking of symptoms, and an increase in expense and suffering. For example, a person who relies on ordinary cough syrup to ease a chronic cough may be postponing the diagnosis of lung cancer, which could be cured if found in its early stages. An individual who has indigestion and continues to take bicarbonate of soda or an antacid preparation day after day could have a stomach ulcer that eventually hemorrhages or perforates the stomach wall.

SELF-HELP GROUPS

It is better to light a candle than to curse the darkness.

Self-help or mutual-aid groups are diverse and loosely defined. Generally their members have a common condition, situation, heritage, or experience, and are largely self-governing. They emphasize self-reliance and usually offer a face-to-face or phone-fellowship network, often available without charge.[31] It is estimated that 9- to 12-million adults in the United States participate in these groups. They range from well-known organizations with local chapters, such as Alcoholics Anonymous (AA), to small one- or two-chapter organizations, such as All But Dissertations (ABD).

These groups may be categorized according to the factors that have influenced their formation:

1. Failure by professionals to treat a condition, (AA and Recovery, Inc)
2. Need for help to cope with physical, social, or psychologic problems following medical treatment (Mended Hearts and Make Today Count [for cancer victims and their families.])
3. Tragic life experiences such as death (AMEND [Aiding a Mother Experiencing Neonatal Death], and Coping with Grief)

Self-help groups provide opportunities to: (1) share feelings of fear, anger, uncertainty, helplessness, guilt, and depression, (2) meet others who have had similar experiences, (3) locate services that can help with material needs, and (4) obtain information. Services are rendered through group meetings, telephone conversations, home and hospital visits, practical help (such as transportation, shopping), and residential care. Organizations such as Mended Hearts and the Stroke Club, sponsored by the American Heart Association, help patients adjust their life-style after a serious cardiovascular illness. Reach to Recovery, sponsored by the American Cancer Society, helps patients with the psychologic problems resulting from a mastectomy (removal of a breast).

Hundreds of self-help groups in the United States can assist people with many health-related problems. The list that follows is a sample of currently functioning groups, some of which can be located in the Appendix of this book. All can be located through the *Encyclopedia of Medical Organizations and Agencies* (available at many libraries) or the National Health Information Clearinghouse.

CANCER

- Candlelighters (childhood cancer)
- Make Today Count

MENTAL AND EMOTIONAL PROBLEMS

- Divorce Anonymous
- Emotions Anonymous
- Neurotics Anonymous International Liaison
- Parents Anonymous (child abuse)
- Recovery, Inc.

OBESITY

- Buxom Belles, International
- TOPS Club
- Weight Watchers International

SUBSTANCE ABUSE

- Al-Anon
- Alateen
- Alcoholics Anonymous
- Calix Society (Catholic alcoholics)
- Families Anonymous (drugs, behavior problems)
- Gam-Anon International
- Gamblers Anonymous
- Narcotics Anonymous
- Secular Organizations for Sobriety
- Women for Sobriety

SURGERY-RELATED

- International Association of Laryngectomees
- Mended Hearts
- Reach to Recovery (breast cancer)
- United Ostomy Association

MISCELLANEOUS

- Mothers of AIDS Patients
- Mothers of Asthmatics
- National Rare Blood Club
- Meniere's Network
- Phoenix Society (burns)
- Emphysema Anonymous

The National Self-Help Clearinghouse, the Self-Help Center, and the National Mental Health Consumer Self-Help Clearinghouse can provide information about existing self-help groups and help people start new ones. Some national self-help organizations have local chapters listed in the Yellow or Blue Pages of the telephone directory.

People's Medical Society

In 1982 Rodale Press launched the People's Medical Society (PMS) and asked *Prevention* readers for financial support through donations and memberships. Present yearly dues are $15. Members of PMS receive a bimonthly newsletter that contains valuable consumer suggestions, but most of its articles are slanted to undermine trust in orthodox practitioners. The first newsletter stated the organization's goals as follows:

> Every part of the medical system is organized very effectively—except the customers. You and me. What we need is to create an umbrella of "civilian" control over the management of the medical system. Not a palace revolt, but a demand to get back to what is and ought to be rightfully ours.
>
> That's what the People's Medical Society is all about. That's why we exist: to plan a major drive against medical

costs, to demand that the medical establishment be more accessible and more accountable. We are not anti-doctor, we are anti-abuse. And we are pro-knowledge.

From time to time, PMS encourages its 80,000 members to write letters to legislators or government officials. Some letters have involved anti-quackery legislation (PMS opposes this), funds for organic farming (favors), licensing of nutritionists (opposes), and food irradiation (opposes).

PMS has published many books, booklets, and special reports. Some contain valuable information, but others promote unscientific methods of health care and make them appear to be equivalent to scientific ones. The PMS booklet *Options in Health Care,* for example, uncritically promotes the theories and practices of acupuncture, acupressure, Chinese medicine, chiropractic, homeopathy, hydrotherapy, metabolic therapy, naturopathy, orthomolecular therapy, psychic healing, and reflexology. These practices are discussed in Chapter 9. PMS bibliographies on various health topics include unscientific publications as well as reputable ones. For example, a bibliography on arthritis includes a book that claims that a food allergy is a major cause of arthritis; a bibliography on cancer includes one boosting macrobiotic diets; and a bibliography on nutrition includes several unscientific books. The 1983 PMS report, *Deregulating Doctoring,* suggests that unorthodox practitioners be allowed to practice with minimal regulation by state governments.

Publicity materials for one of its books describe PMS as "the largest consumer health organization in America" and state that it is run "by the people" and "for the people."[32] However, its president and board of directors are not elected and newsletters give no clear indication that its activities and policies are determined by anyone other than the group's president, Charles Inlander. Rodale Press terminated its affiliation with PMS about 4 years ago.

Although some of its stated goals are laudable, consumers should be skeptical of the People's Medical Society because much of its advice is unreliable.

Effectiveness of Self-Help Groups

Evaluations of some self-help groups have revealed positive results. People who attend express feelings of usefulness, importance, and increased satisfaction with life. However, there is evidence that some groups may not be helpful and that research is needed.

Burnell and Burnell, who studied bereaved parents, reported that most of them obtained comfort by knowing that others have similar problems and pain.[32a] Brown and Griffiths[33] expressed the belief that cancer self-help groups were effective in helping people face difficulties. Lieberman and Videka-Sherman[34] studied the impact of self-help groups on widows and widowers and indicated that participation in these groups had a positive effect on their mental health.

DiPasquale[37] reported on a National Institute of Health (NIH) study of a weekly support group of alcohol abusers who had AIDS. During a 3-month period, group discussions included the transmission of AIDS and its social stigma, the need for comfort and reassurance, caretaking performed by the NIH and its physicians, homosexuality, and trust. Findings indicated that the experience was helpful and should continue. The group experience provided support and strength for those with AIDS. DiPasquale studied 24 men and 8 women with the AIDS virus and found that there were psychologic benefits from this support group.

Spiegel,[38] a Stanford University psychiatrist, found that patients with advanced breast cancer who received psychotherapy lived longer than those not receiving therapy. He believes it may have been the result of less depression, improved appetite, better nutrition, or control of pain.

Taylor et at[35] stated that unqualified endorsement of self-support groups based on preliminary evidence may be premature. Whether the services intended to help solve personal emotional problems are more helpful than other services remains to be determined.

Peele[36] reported that alcohol treatment programs in the United States have not been proven effective by scientific studies. These programs include AA and treatment centers that include group therapy, individual counseling, and alcohol-related education.

Trojan[39] said that self-help group research is still unsatisfactory. However, he added that his review of 232 members from 65 disease-related groups indicated most members reported considerable positive changes. These changes resulted from support of other group members, more independent coping with disease, reduction of stress, feeling safe and sheltered, and reduction of fear of disease crisis.

Table 10–5

Smoking-Cessation Programs

Program	Method	Success rate*	Cost	Comment
Self-Help				
FreshStart (American Cancer Society)	Educational materials without counseling or direct intervention	15-20%	Nominal fee	Call local organization
Freedom from Smoking (American Lung Association)			Nominal fee	Call local organization
Clearing the Air (National Cancer Institute)			Free	Call 1-800-4-CANCER for information
Quit clinics/group therapy				
American Cancer Society American Lung Assn. Seventh-day Adventist	Trained facilitator, often a layperson who is an ex-smoker	28%	5-$75	Call local organization
SmokeEnders (for-profit program)	Clinics with group meetings		$495	Claims to have served 650,000 smokers, but no hard data available
Behavioral therapy				
Aversive smoking	Therapists apply shocks with each puff	Highly variable	n/a	Not recommended
Rapid smoking	Patient puts up money and is paid back with each week of abstinence	21%	n/a	Abstinence alone may be better
Self-reward or contingency management		27%	n/a	May be helpful with counseling
Medical approaches				
Medical advice	Simple warning by physician	5%+	n/a	People who have had heart attack or other serious smoking-related illness respond best
Nicotine gum	Chew gum for 20-30 minutes; provides sufficient nicotine to relieve craving	40-50% with counseling 20% without counseling	$23 for 90 pieces; $500 for 3 month supply	Best for heavy smokers; Problems with large doses; palpitations, dizziness, mouth sores, ulcers

*Success rates refer to continued abstinence for at least 1 year. Success probably depends more on individual motivation than any other factor.

Modified from: Public Citizen Health Research Group Health Letter.[40]

Smoking Cessation

Since 1964 over 41 million people have quit smoking, 90% of them without formal medical intervention. Most strongly motivated people can quit regardless of the method used. Many profit-oriented smoking-cessation companies claim high success rates because they do not follow up all patients for a year; do not verify abstience by checking nicotine products in the saliva, urine, or blood; and report on small numbers of highly selected and motivated individuals.

Table 10-5 lists the success rates, methods, and costs of a variety of smoking-cessation programs.

Ineffective Approaches to Smoking

Public Citizen Health Research Group[40] has identified the following as ineffective:

Products

"One Step at a Time" is a filter system by *Water Pik* that progressively blocks the smoke inhaled from cigarettes. People who used this method decrease the amount of tar and nicotine per cigarette, but tend to increase the number of cigarettes smoked.

Bantron tablets contain lobeline, which mimics the effects of nicotine and other chemicals. Lobeline products are useless for stopping cigarette smoking.

Health-break and Ban Smoke contain a variety of herbs, silver acetate, and benzocaine (a local anesthetic) that do nothing to help stop smoking.

Methods

Sensory deprivation was claimed by one researcher to have a 24% success rate and apparently is no longer available.

Hypnosis claims of up to 88% success are exaggerated and may be in the 15% to 20% range

Acupuncture also has not been scientifically demonstrated to help people stop smoking.

Table 10-6 summarizes the success rates of smoking-cessation methods.

Table 10–6

Effectiveness of Smoking-Cessation Methods

Method	1-Year success rate
No intervention	3-5%
Doctor's advice	5%
Self-help brochures	15-20%
Hypnosis	15-20%
Nicotine gum alone	8-20%
Aversive therapy	21%
Self-reward	27%
Group therapy/clinics	28%
Nicotine gum & counseling	47%

Note: No over-the-counter product has been proven effective. Modified from Public Citizen Health Research Group Health Letter, 4(10):1-6, 1988.[40]

Consumer Guidelines

Consumers who wish to participate in self-care should understand that illnesses and conditions need various kinds of attention. The guidelines that follow will help consumers make wise decisions.

Self-Care Tips

1. Determine whether the product or equipment is the most economical way to take care of the illness or injury.
2. Determine whether the items are safe and effective; ask a pharmacist or physician if in doubt.
3. Realize that products are only for temporary relief or emergency care.
4. Follow the directions exactly.
5. When using test kits with chemicals, note the expiration date and check whether protection is needed from extreme temperatures.
6. The signs and symptoms of an illness or injury may require a physician's interpretation and analysis.
7. Read books, such as the one by Vickery and Fries,[1] to increase your understanding of self-care practices.
8. Acquire adequate skills for the use of self-care equipment by conferring with your own physician.

Choosing a Self-Help Group

1. Check one of the resources listed in the Appendix to locate desired organizations.
2. Determine whether the organization or group will be able to satisfactorily serve your needs and goals.

IT'S YOUR DECISION

You think you may be pregnant and you want to obtain confirmation of your condition. Which of the following actions would you take, and why?

		Reason
1. _____	Ask a friend or parent what to do.	_____
2. _____	Purchase a self-diagnostic pregnancy test kit.	_____
3. _____	Ask a pharmacist for a product that will enable you to determine your condition.	_____
4. _____	Purchase a self-help book or acquire one from the library.	_____
5. _____	Immediately consult a physician.	_____
6. _____	Other.	_____

3. Obtain literature from the group about its purposes, program, costs, professional care, and other matters.
4. Visit the main office of the group to meet and talk with administrators, counselors, and other professionals to obtain more information on the qualifications of its staff, the methods used, and how the organization is run.
5. Make several visits to observe activities and programs.
6. Ask for the names and telephone numbers of individuals who have been members of the self-help group.
7. Check with a local health agency or organization about the quality of services and the reputation of the self-help group.

SUMMARY

Self-care refers to action taken by lay persons on their own behalf for the promotion of health; detection, prevention, and treatment of disease; activities taken separately or in participation with professionals.

Self-care may be categorized as diagnostic, therapeutic, or rehabilitative; prevention, maintenance, and behavior modification; and support groups. It has increased tremendously in recent years because of the high cost of medical care, increased advertising, dissatisfaction with medical care, and people's wish to be more in control of their life.

Most forms of health care involve at least some degree of self-care. Consumers need to learn how to distinguish between major and minor illnesses, and when to consult a doctor. Individuals with certain chronic conditions can monitor and help treat themselves. Consumers also can gain health knowledge by reading scientific books and magazines that provide accurate information.

Home health care tests should be carefully checked by consumers for safety, reliability, and accuracy. Consumers should become acquainted with guidelines for purchasing and using these tests.

There are numerous self-care health devices in the marketplace; some may not be useful and others may even be hazardous to use.

Many self-help groups aid individuals with specific health problems. Research has not been sufficiently extensive to determine the effectiveness of these groups, but there is a great deal of empirical data to support their value.

There are helpful guidelines that will enable consumers to make wise decisions regarding self-care and self-help groups.

DISCUSSION QUESTIONS

1. How would you define individual and group self-help care?
2. What are the types of self-care? Identify one example for each type.
3. What are some of the hazards and benefits of self-diagnosis and self-treatment of illness or injury?
4. When should a person consult a physician?
5. What are the reasons that people participate in individual and group self-care?
6. What are the general and specific types of home health care tests? What are their related problems in need of consideration?
7. What suggestions will help consumers when they plan to purchase and use home health care tests?
8. What are three of the leading medical and drug

books that have been highly rated by *U.S. News and World Report.* Why were they rated highly?

9. Discuss several self-care health devices, including claims made by their manufacturers and problems resulting from their use.
10. How can self-help groups be defined? What factors have influenced their formation?
11. What has been the effectiveness of individual and group self-care?
12. Name three smoking-cessation programs. Identify the methods used and the success rate for quitting. Identify two programs that do not work.
13. What are the guidelines that consumers should follow on the selection of individual and group activities?

REFERENCES

*1. Vickery DM and Fries JF: Take care of yourself: a consumers' guide to medical care, ed 4, Reading, Mass, 1990, Addison-Wesley Publishing Co Inc.
2. DeFreise GH: From activated patient to pacified activists: a study of self-care movement in the United States, Soc Sci Med 29:195-204, 1989.
3. Haug MR et al: Self-care among older adults, Soc Sci Med 29:189, 1989.
4. Goldsmith MF: Proliferating "self-help" groups offer wide range of support, seek physician rapport, JAMA 261:2474-2475, 1989.
*5. Fletcher D: Self-care: how to help patients share responsibility for their health, Postgrad Med 78:213-220, Aug 1985.
6. Woods NF: Self-care practices among young adult married women, Res Nurs Health 8:227-233, 1985.
7. Harry Heller Research Corporation: Health care practices and perceptions: a consumer survey of self-medication, Washington DC, 1984, The Proprietary Association.
8. Food and Drug Administration: A study of health practices and opinions, Springfield VA, 1972, National Technical Information Service.
9. Pinckney C and Pinckney ER: Do-it-yourself medical testing, New York, 1983, Facts on File Inc.
10. Pinckney C and Pinckney ER: The patient's guide to medical tests, ed 3, New York, 1986, Facts on File Inc.
11. Rosen GM: Self-help treatment books and the commercialization of psychotherapy, Am Psychol 42(1):40-56, 1987.
11a. Gambrill E: Self-help books. Pseudoscience in the guise of science. Skeptical Inquirer 16(4):389-399, 1992.
12. How much salt? For $45 you can take a wild guess. Consumer Reports 55:73, 1990.
13. Which home tests are worth it? Johns Hopkins Medical Letter, Health After 50 2(2):6-7, 1990.
14. Fuerst ML: Home diagnostic tests: self-help health? Generics 2:42-44, July 1986.
15. Blood pressure monitors, Consumer Reports 57:295-299, 1992.
16. Iannucci L: The perplexity of pregnancy. FDA Consumer 24(9):17, 1990.
17. Valanis BG and Perlman CS: Home pregnancy testing kits: prevalence of use, false-negative rates, and compliance with instructions. Am J Pub Health 72:1034-1036, 1982.
18. Kolata G: A new tactic, do-it-yourself abortions, The New York Times, Oct 23, 1985.
19. Fisher AC and Worth W: Ovulation prediction kits: who really needs them, ACSH News & Views 7(5):3-5, 1986.
20. Leary WE: Federal official faults public cholesterol tests, The New York Times, Nov 28, 1989.
21. Sale of unapproved test kits stopped, FDA Consumer, (25)8:7, 1991.
22. FDA urged to reject home tests for AIDS, San Francisco Chronicle, July 7, 1990.
23. Home immunization kits unapproved and ineffective, FDA Consumer 24(1):4, 1990.
24. Segal A and Goldstein J: Exploring the correlates of self-provided health care behavior, Social Science and Medicine 29:153-161, 1989.
25. Vickery DM et al: Effect of self-care education program on medical visits, JAMA 250:2952-2956, 1983.
26. Zapka J and Averill BW: Self-care for colds: a cost-effective alternative to upper respiratory infection management, Am J Public Health 19:814-816, 1979.
27. Roberts CR et al: Reducing physician visits for colds through consumer education, JAMA 250:1986-1989, 1983.
28. Kemper DW: Self-care education: impact on HMO costs, Med Care 10:710-718, 1982.
*29. Berg AO: Targeting symptoms for self-care health education, Medical Care 8:551-555, 1980.
30. Lorig KR: Effective education for the old elderly, Paper presented at the 110th annual meeting of the American Public Health Association, Montreal, Nov 1982.
31. Lieberman MA: A group therapist perspective on self-help groups, Int J Group Psychother 40:251-278, 1990.
32. The goals and philosophy of the People's Medical Society, News from Pantheon Books, undated, released in 1988.
32a. Burnell GRT and Burnell AL: The compassionate friends: a support group for bereaved parents, J Fam Pract 72:295-296, 1986.
33. Brown T and Griffiths P: Cancer self-help groups: an inside view, British Medical Journal 292:1503-1504, 1986.
34. Lieberman MA and Videka-Sherman L: The impact of self-help groups on the mental health of widows and widowers, Am J Orthopsychiatry 56:435-39, 1986.
35. Taylor SE et al: Social support groups and cancer the patient, J Consult Clin Psychol 54:608-615, 1986.
36. Peele S: Research issues in assessing addiction treatment efficacy: how cost-effective are Alcoholics Anonymous groups and private treatment centers? Drug Alcohol Depend 25:179-182, 1990.
37. DiPasquale JA: The psychological effects of support groups on individuals infected with AIDS virus, Cancer Nurs 13:278-285, 1990.
38. Support groups lengthen your life, Johns Hopkins Medical Letter, Health After 50 2(9):1-2, 1990.
39. Trojan A: Benefits of self-help groups: a survey of 232 members of 65 disease-related groups, Soc Sci Med 29:225-232, 1989.
40. Smoking cessation: The best ways to kick the deadliest most expensive addiction. Public Citizen Health Research Group Health Letter 4(10):1-6, 1988.

*Recommended reading

CHAPTER ELEVEN

Health Care Facilities

"I don't see any parade."

(Reprinted from The Saturday Evening Post © 1963, The Curtis Publishing Company.)

Improvement in quality [of hospital services] can occur at no additional cost, or even at cost savings, if physicians adopt more effective and more efficient strategies of care.

S.T. Fleming[1]

It is estimated that one half of the women and one third of the men reaching 65 years of age in 1990 will be expected to use a nursing home sometime before they die.

C.M. Murtaugh et al[2]

CONSUMER DECISIONS

How should a person select a good hospital, nursing home, or ambulatory care center? How can consumers select the best ambulatory care center for services when needed?

Where can help be obtained to locate long-term health-care services?

What are the available alternatives to nursing home care?

At some time in their life consumers will need to use health care facilities found in their communities. Thus it is important to be prepared to make intelligent decisions about the use of these facilities when the need arises. On a short-term basis, the use of a hospital may be necessary. In an emergency, a hospital emergency room or ambulatory care center may be helpful. An older person, a parent or a friend, may need the services of a nursing home that provides convalescent care as well as custodial care. When these occasions arise, consumers should be knowledgeable about community facilities and the services they offer.

The purpose of this chapter is to provide useful information that will enable consumers to locate and select hospitals, ambulatory health care centers, and nursing homes that will best serve their needs.

HOSPITALS

Hospitals in the United States are classified by types, organizational control for operation, services rendered, or length of patient stay as follows:

1. Types
   a. Community: All nonfederal, short-term general, and other special hospitals whose facilities and services are available to the public
   b. Noncommunity: Federal hospitals, psychiatric hospitals, hospitals treating tuberculosis and other respiratory diseases, chronic disease hospitals, institutions for the mentally retarded, and alcoholism and chemical dependency treatment facilities
2. Organizational control for operations
   a. Government, federal
   b. Government, nonfederal
   c. Nongovernment
      (1) Not-for-profit
      (2) Investor-owned for profit
3. Length of stay
   a. Short-term: under 30 days
   b. Long-term: more than 30 days
4. Types of services
   a. General medical and surgical
   b. Psychiatric, including care for the mentally retarded and the treatment of alcoholism and other chemical dependencies
   c. Treatment for tuberculosis and other respiratory diseases
   d. All other speciality services such as obstetrics and gynecology, rehabilitation, orthopedics, chronic disease, and eye, ear, nose, and throat treatment

In 1988 there were 6780 hospitals in the United States, with a total of 1,248,000 beds and an average daily patient load of 863,000. Of these, 81.5% (5533) were community hospitals, and 10% (670) were for-profit hospitals. The number of investor-owned, for-profit hospitals has increased in recent years.[3] Many are chains owned by corporations listed on the stock market.

The total number of hospitals in the United States has been declining since 1982. There are fewer rural and small hospitals. Five percent of all hospitals have fewer than 50 beds, 15% have fewer than 100 beds, and 21.5% have over 500 beds. Generally, the larger hospitals are better equipped and staffed to provide comprehensive healthcare. Table 11-1 shows the percentage of selected services rendered by community hospitals in 1988 in the United States.

Accreditation

Two procedures used to foster quality medical care in hospitals are licensing and accreditation. Licensing by government agencies is the method established by state law to grant permission for hospital operation. Health departments, through their professional health personnel, generally are responsible for the granting of licenses, with standards varying from state to state. The most prominent accrediting body for health care facilities is the Joint Commission on Accreditation of Healthcare Organizations. The Joint Commission also

Table 11–1

Percentage of Community Hospitals Offering Selected Services in 1988

Service	Percent
Ambulatory	95.1
Birthing Rooms	63.3
Emergency department	94.1
Outpatient alcoholism/chemical dependency	18.9
Physical therapy	85.5
Trauma care	13.4
Volunteer services	66.3
Open heart surgery	15.6
Organ transplantation	7.5
CT scanner	63.8
Magnetic resonance imagery	12.5
Megavoltage radiation therapy	18.4
AIDS-related treatment	59.4
Skilled nursing unit	17.9
Home care	34.5
Hospice care	14.6

From American Hospital Association: 1989-1990 AHA hospital statistics, Chicago, 1990, The Association.

conducts accreditation programs for hospitals, psychiatric facilities, substance abuse and rehabilitation programs, community mental health centers, long-term care facilities, home care, and ambulatory health care organizations. About 5400 hospitals and 3600 other health care facilities participate in the accreditation process.

The Joint Commission's board of commissioners, which oversees standard-setting and accrediting policies, has seven representatives from the American Hospital Association, seven from the American Medical Association, three from the American College of Physicians, three from the American College of Surgeons, one from the American Dental Association, and three public members appointed by the board itself.

Participation in the accreditation process is voluntary. A hospital, however, must be accredited to receive direct payments for services from Medicare and Medicaid, and to be able to maintain a recognized residency program for physicians. The Joint Commission's hospital standards, some of which are minimal and others of which are quite rigorous, include the following:[4]

1. A safe, clean, uncrowded hospital with enough beds to handle the patient load.
2. A well-organized administration with a chief executive and a governing body.
3. Provision of such services as a pharmacy, a diagnostic x-ray department, a clinical laboratory, surgical facilities, nursing, and food service, each staffed and supervised by qualified professionals. (For example, the nursing services must be supervised by registered nurses, and the pharmacy must be maintained by a registered pharmacist.)
4. Procedures by which physicians apply for staff membership and are evaluated in terms of experience, judgment, ability, and competence.
5. Establishment of rules and regulations for the medical staff to follow, including the maintenance of committees to review the quality of medical care of its members. (For example, a tissue committee must review the appropriateness of surgical procedures and a utilization review process must evaluate the appropriateness of patient admissions and lengths of stays.)
6. Maintenance and safeguarding of complete and continuous medical records on each patient.
7. Maintenance of infection control procedures; minimum danger of infection of mothers and infants, with obstetric department separated from other service areas.
8. Regularly scheduled case conferences and other educational activities for the staff.

The Joint Commission grants accreditation for three years. An organization can be accredited with commendation, accredited, conditionally accredited, or not accredited.

About 80% of the hospitals in the United States are accredited. Also accredited are 1188 psychiatric facilities, 1306 long-term care facilities, 2200 home care organizations, and 445 ambulatory healthcare organizations. Hospitals with fewer than 50 beds are less likely than larger hospitals to be accredited.

The Joint Commission has been developing new procedures for collecting, analyzing, and using quality-of-care data under its Agenda for Change initiative. Present standards, using the structural process (number of physicians, lab tests, etc.), do not adequately measure the quality of care in these organizations.

Problems

Accreditation of a hospital using structured criteria is no guarantee that a high level of medical care

Table 11-2

Average Occupancy Percentage in Selected Hospitals in U.S. 1988

Type of hospital	Beds filled (%)
Total community	65.5
Not-for-profit community	68.2
Investor-owned for-profit	50.9
Nonfederal long-term	87.3
State or local government short-term	63.8

Modified from American Hospital Association: 1989-1990 AHA hospital statistics, Chicago, 1990, The Association.

will be provided in that facility. It merely indicates that certain *quantitative* standards have been met. The number of square feet of floor space, the appropriate laboratory equipment, and the provision of adequate medical staff bylaws, although necessary, are of less significance to patients than the effectiveness of the service they received.

The Public Citizen Health Research Group[5] reported that a 1986-88 survey of 17 hospitals revealed the following problems in meeting these standards:

40% Had safety standard deficiencies
51% Lacked adequate monitoring of unnecessary surgery
50% Failed to adequately monitor patients in intensive and coronary care
56% Failed to monitor and evaluate the quality of care given by medical staff

These findings led New York State to refuse acceptance of accreditation by the Joint Commission and to conduct its own inspection of the hospitals in New York.

The Joint Commission hopes to establish norms by which reviewers can judge diagnostic accuracy, treatment effectiveness, surgical necessity, and the extent of infant and maternal mortality.

Hospitals today are faced with a variety of problems that are compounding their ability to provide quality services and cost-effectiveness:

1. *Some hospitals are operating as profit-making corporations rather than as facilities that function primarily to provide services to patients.* The expansion of hospital companies has been referred to as the "medical-industrial complex." Some corporations own or manage as many as 100 hospitals. There are 670 (10%) investor-owned hospitals in the United States.[6] The unanswered question is whether "cost-effective" hospital procedures affect the quality of care. The National Council of Senior Citizens[7] reported that higher patient costs in profit-making hospitals lead to price increases in not-for-profit hospitals. The investor-owned hospital chains have offered a variety of special treatment services to generate increased profits and attract more patients. These services include psychiatric care to treat depression, schizophrenia, phobias, and substance abuse. The action has resulted in the creation of thousands of hospital beds that experts believe may be unnecessary.
2. *Increased cost of services.* This has been the result of:
   a. Surplus hospital beds. Despite greater use in recent years, estimates indicate that over 30% of the nation's hospital beds are empty. Smaller hospitals tend to have more vacancies. In 1988 the average occupancy rate in U.S. hospitals was 69.2%. Table 11-2 shows the occupancy percentage for different types of hospitals. Investor-owned for-profit hospitals had the lowest occupancy percentages.

      National guidelines advise that a hospital's annual bed occupancy should be at least 80% in order to cover costs. In 1987 in New York City and Long Island, occupancy rates sharply increased to over 86% of capacity. Municipal hospitals were over 90% full, and some were completely full. The factors contributing to the increase were: (1) large numbers of AIDS patients, (2) patients who stayed longer because of lack of long-term health care facilities, and (3) conversion of beds to special uses.

   b. Insufficient use of services such as obstetrics, pediatrics, radiation therapy, open-heart surgery, and renal dialysis to support their continuance on a full-time basis in all hospitals. It has been recommended that these facilities and services should be available on a regional basis to be cost-effective.
   c. Need for new and sophisticated equipment, such as CT and MRI scanners. Progress in research and development occurs so rapidly that expensive equipment becomes obsolete quickly.

d. Increased cost of salaries, supplies, and equipment because of inflation.
e. Increased malpractice suit awards. These lawsuits result in very high insurance rates for both physicians and hospitals.
f. Medicare rules create pressure for shorter hospital stays or refusal of treatment for many patients. To standardize costs, payments are made according to the patient's diagnosis rather than the length of hospital stay or the extent of treatment provided. About 500 diagnosis-related groups (DRGs) have been established for this purpose. If a patient stays in the hospital longer than anticipated by the DRG system, the hospital may lose money. Because early releases tend to generate profits, hospitals sometimes discharge patients before it is medically proper to do so. Financial pressures have also led many hospitals to refuse to admit indigent patients or others who might prove unprofitable to treat. In 1986 the U.S. Congress passed the Emergency Medical Treatment Act, which outlawed the discharge or transfer of severely ill patients without adequate safeguards, a practice called "dumping." However, since its enactment, 140 hospitals have been charged with violations. The penalties include suspension or termination from Medicare problems and a fine of up to $50,000 per violation.[8] The DRG system also has led some hospitals to charge higher rates to privately insured patients who are not involved in the Medicare program.
g. The increased number and costs of AIDS patients, especially in public hospitals. The nationwide trend is toward the concentration of AIDS cases in a few large hospitals in large metropolitan areas. In 1987, 5% of the nation's hospitals were treating 50% of the AIDS patients. Public hospitals have provided more than half of inpatient and nearly 78% of outpatient care for people with AIDS. In 1987 the losses on inpatient AIDS treatment averaged $5818 per patient in public hospitals and $2381 in private hospitals. The average cost for treating an AIDS patient is now about $32,000 per year.[9]

3. *Complexity of communication between patients and staff.* To address this problem over 3000 hospitals (almost 50%) now have a patient representative, advocate, or ombudsman.
4. *Unnecessary operations and hospital-acquired illnesses and injuries.* Although hysterectomy and cesarian section rates have been stabilizing in recent years, they continue to be high. Two studies in several Boston hospitals identified a variety of hazards to patients: infection, mistakes in the operating room, falls, and reactions to medicines. In one study 36% of the patients (290 out of 815) suffered illness from drugs and therapy of diagnostic procedures. In 1987 Popescu[10] reported that 6% of hospital patients acquired nosocomial (hospital-acquired) infections. About 40% of these were urinary tract infections, 25% were surgical wound infections, and 19% were pneumonias. These infections added an average of four days and $1800 in expenses to the patient's hospital costs. A small percentage of these infections caused death.

   The Harvard Medical Practice Study[3] found that 99,000 (3.7%) of 2.7 million patients entering 51 New York hospitals in 1984 were harmed as a result of the care provided. One tenth of these patients or their families filed malpractice suits. Of those injured, 27,000 (1%) were victims of negligence—half during operations. The majority of those injured received minimal or temporary disability.
5. *Use of advertising.* Hospitals have found it necessary to be more competitive in the marketplace. The diminishing profits and the low bed-occupancy rates are some of the reasons hospitals are offering new services and other inducements to attract patients (see Chapter 5). Pettit[11] reported that in regions served by many competing hospitals, medical costs are higher.
6. *Inadequate assessment of the quality of care.* In 1972 the U.S. Congress established Professional Standard Review Organizations (PSROs) to monitor and improve the quality and appropriateness of services provided to hospitalized Medicare and Medicaid patients. These organizations set standards and review the quality of medicine practiced. Some PSROs were successful in reducing unnecessary surgery and improving other services. However, there has been no consistency in review procedures, proven overall impact, or uniform method of rating the quality of performance.

In 1987 Medicare officials released data on the death rates (percent of patients who died within 30 days of admission) for hospitalized patients in over 6000 participating hospitals. Of these, 146 (2.4%) had death rates exceeding the upper end of a predicted range, and 180 (3%) had mortality rates lower than predicted.[12] This action has been considered one way to evaluate the quality of patient care. Consumers might find this information helpful in the selection of hospitals. Critics fear, however, that the information will not be useful to judge hospital performance because the data do not take into account the severity of the patient's illness upon entering the hospital.[13]

Fink et al[14] stated the adequacy of the mortality data, when used as a complete measure of the quality of hospital care, has not yet been determined. He indicated that hospitals are undertaking plans to develop measures that reflect morbidity and disability outcomes. Jencks et al[15] studied outcome data for 5888 patients who were treated for stroke, pneumonia, heart attack, or congestive heart failure; they concluded that risk-adjusted death rates should be supplemented by a review of the actual care rendered before conclusions are drawn regarding the effectiveness of hospital care.

The DRG system has pressured hospitals to become more efficient. Fleming[1] claimed that improvements in the quality of services can be achieved at no additional cost and possibly less cost. Improvement of the health status of patients is necessary; two factors must become operative: (1) physicians must use the available resources more effectively, and (2) physicians must select the most appropriate strategies when treating patients.

Hospitals frequently have other quality-control problems. Medical records may be inadequate and incomplete and tissue committee reports to determine whether surgery was necessary may be insufficient. Although the number of autopsies performed should be at least 20% of the number of people who die in a hospital, the autopsy rate may fall below that figure. Staff privileges may not be clearly delineated, so physicians may not know their responsibilities and limitations. Physician privileges, once established, may be periodically reviewed, but the process frequently does not consider the quality of services rendered. Infant and maternal mortality may be too high. Hospitals may omit documented clinical reviews assessing the quality of care. Hospitals may lack required consultations for any patient whom the attending physician regards as a high medical or surgical risk, for whom the diagnosis is obscure, or for whom there is doubt concerning the best therapeutic measures. These problems are more likely to be found in unaccredited hospitals.

Consumers should be aware of these hospital problems, be familiar with the characteristics of a good hospital, and use the hospital-selection procedures that are presented in this chapter.

Characteristics of a Good Hospital

The characteristics that identify a quality hospital have not been precisely defined; however, there are essential components agreed on by experts.

1. A good hospital is accredited by the Joint Commission on Accreditation of Healthcare Organizations. It is a teaching hospital affiliated with a medical school and approved for the training of resident physicians, medical students, and nurses. A high-quality hospital also has a variety of research programs underway. The care is likely to be best when practitioners have up-to-date medical knowledge available. It is a voluntary hospital operating on a not-for-profit basis. This is not meant to disparage all proprietary or for-profit hospitals, but to indicate that not-for-profit facilities are more likely to be concerned with community service than with income.
2. A good hospital has a wide range of diagnostic and treatment facilities and services that are fully departmentalized; for example, it includes a pathology laboratory, a fully equipped emergency room, an outpatient department, and an intensive care unit.
3. A good hospital has a wide range of specialists, most of whom are board-certified, and employs registered nurses and nursing aides licensed by the state.
4. A good hospital uses peer review to maintain medical standards and makes an effort to keep physicians and staff up-to-date through a variety of educational programs, including visiting speakers, telephone clinics, films, video cassettes, and closed-circuit television.
5. A good hospital has an established tissue review committee. This committee should be composed of at least three physicians from the medical staff, one of whom is a pathologist. The committee reviews pathology reports on tissue specimens obtained during surgery to determine whether the surgery was justified. If a physician

PERSONAL GLIMPSE

Do You Know?

Upon admission to a hospital you are entitled to a copy of the *Patient's Bill of Rights.* It can be obtained by contacting the patient ombudsman or the admission's office. Here are several important rights to which you are entitled:

1. Considerate and respectful care
2. Complete current information from the physician about diagnosis, treatment, and prognosis in terms that the patient (or an appropriate person in the patient's behalf) can understand, and the name of the physician handling the case
3. Information from the physician that enables the patient to give informed consent before any procedure or treatment starts, and the name of the person who will administer it. This information should include a clear explanation of the risks, benefits, and possible alternatives to the treatment; this should not be merely a prepared statement for the patient to sign
4. To refuse treatment to the extent that the law allows, and to know the medical consequences of the choice
5. Privacy in the medical care program including: discreet conduct of examination and treatment, confidentiality in discussion of the case, and permission from the patient to allow anyone not directly involved to be present at a case discussion, consultation, examination, and treatment
6. Confidentiality of communications and records kept
7. Reasonable response to requests for services as indicated by the urgency of the case; complete information as to the reasons for transfer to another institution if necessary (including the alternatives to such transfer), and the knowledge that the other institution has accepted the patient for transfer.

   One hospital in Pennsylvania has instituted a program called "Satisfaction Guaranteed." Patients are invited to speak up and can obtain rapid correction or refunds when services other than medical treatment have been unsatisfactory. These services include room cleanliness, confidentiality, food quality, employees' courtesy and performance, timely treatment, and clear and concise explanations of tests and procedures
8. Information about any relationship between the hospital and other health care or educational institutions, as far as it concerns the patient's case, and about any professional relationships among individuals (by name) who are treating the patient
9. Knowledge of any hospital proposal to conduct human experimentation affecting the patient's treatment, and refusal to participate in such research
10. Expectation of reasonable continuity of care (including knowledge of appointment times, physicians, and their locations and to have the physician or a delegate inform the patient of the continuing health care requirements after discharge
11. Examination and explanation of the hospital bill, regardless of who pays for it
12. Knowledge of what hospital rules and regulations apply to the patient's conduct

appears in error, the committee requires an explanation. A physician who performs several questionable operations might be requested to appear before the executive committee of the medical staff of the hospital. When violations are sufficiently flagrant, the physician could be barred from practice at the hospital.

6. Consultations with other physicians are required in a good hospital when diagnoses are questionable, when great risk is involved, or when treatment procedures are in doubt.
7. A good hospital holds weekly meetings of an ambulatory care advisory committee to determine ways to run the hospital more efficiently and humanely. It provides the services of some type of ombudsman, or patient services representative, who communicates with patients and is concerned with their general welfare. The hospital also supports and abides by the *Patient's Bill of Rights* (see box above).

PERSONAL GLIMPSE

Doctor Charged with "Patient Dumping"[29]

In December 1986 an uninsured woman gave birth in an ambulance at the side of a road after being transferred from a hospital emergency room by an on-call obstetrician. The doctor noted that the woman's blood pressure was the highest he had ever seen in a pregnant woman—a condition that can lead to life-threatening complications. He ordered the woman transferred to a public hospital 170 miles away where a sophisticated neonatal unit was available. Within an hour after the ambulance began its trip, the woman gave birth. She then returned to the original hospital and was admitted. Fortunately, both she and the baby did well.

This incident led to the first case of a financial penalty against a doctor for violating a 1986 federal law intended to stop the practice known as patient dumping. The doctor appealed the proposed penalty, claiming that the transfer was done to provide superior medical care and that doctors should have the right to determine who they treat. He also said he was afraid that he might be sued for malpractice if complications arose. Others involved in the case, however, insisted that the original hospital had adequate facilities and that it was improper to transfer a patient who was about to give birth.

CONSUMER TIP

How to Survive in a Hospital[16]

Be alert. Alertness may be needed to avoid receiving the wrong medication or undergoing a procedure intended for someone else. Ask questions; if you are too ill to do so, ask a family member or a friend to assist you.

Check medications. Before taking any new drug, have the nurse check your name and any drug allergies listed on your wristband. Also ask the name of the drug and check its appearance. If it does not look like what you have previously received or what your doctor indicated, have the nurse check the order book or contact your physician.

Check tests and procedures. You should be informed of the purpose of a test or procedure and the risk or discomfort that may result. Make sure you know about any special preparations such as the use of laxatives, enemas, and fasting. Be sure the test or procedure is for you and is relevant for your condition.

Ask questions of doctors. Several doctors treating you may provide conflicting information. Raise questions and ask the doctors to communicate with each other before they talk with you.

Speak up. If there are problems with your food, delayed responses by nurses, curt replies to your requests, or other significant difficulties, talk to the nurse, dietitian, physician, or the hospital's patient advocate or ombudsman.

8. A good hospital encourages community participation in the conduct of the hospital. It has a consumer board or a consumer representative who participates in hospital planning sessions and makes recommendations for improvement of services. The hospital should be involved in community activities, such as programs for cancer screening, smoking cessation, the treatment of alcoholism and drug abuse, consumer education, and development of a neighborhood health center.

Selecting a Hospital

There is no simple way for the average consumer to determine whether a hospital is providing high-quality care; selection of a facility can be difficult.

In an emergency, minutes count and you must get to the nearest hospital. For effective surgery and long-time hospital care, however, *The New England Journal of Medicine*[17] identified these characteristics of a good hospital:

1. It has the best-trained physicians; highest percentage of board-certified specialists
2. It has the best-trained nurses; highest percentage of registered nurses (RNs) as opposed to licensed practical nurses (LPNs)
3. It has the highest level of technologic sophistication; cardiac-catheterization and facilities for magnetic resonance imagery (MRI), open-heart surgery, and organ transplantation

In the final analysis, this matter can be accomplished only by the professionals themselves, who periodically should conduct peer reviews and other evaluations to determine the current conditions.

The professionals should then bring about any necessary changes to ensure effective health care. Nevertheless, there are clues consumers should know.

In addition, they should ask questions and seek information to help them select a hospital. Physicians should be asked which hospital or hospitals they use for patients, and whether the patient has a choice. Doctors should be asked which hospital will best serve the patient's needs. If relevant, find out the nature of the physician's surgical privileges at the hospital. If the nature of surgical privileges is "major" or "full," the physician is likely to be board-certified and have extensive experience. With regard to staff privileges, ask whether the practitioner is a consulting, active, or courtesy staff member. A consulting staff member position is usually a specialized appointment filled by a physician with considerable skill and experience who is board-certified. An active staff member is one well known to hospital personnel, serves on committees, and has voting privileges. A courtesy staff member is one who can admit patients but is not active in hospital affairs.

Check whether the hospital is accredited by the Joint Commission and has many of the characteristics of a good hospital. One should also inquire whether it is a teaching hospital and has a strong research program. Check to see if it is aware of the *Patient's Bill of Rights* (p. 208), adheres to these principles, and is listed in the *American Hospital Association Guide to the Health Care Field.* This reference, available in larger libraries, contains basic information on health care institutions.

Before entering the hospital, find out about fees and charges, including the method of resolving these financial aspects. Ask the physician to help you understand the costs. Information should be obtained on whether the services are paid completely or partially by Medicare, Medicaid, prepaid health insurance, or in some other way. One should attempt to obtain estimates of the costs for which the patient will be charged and also identify which routine laboratory tests may be completed prior to admittance. Sometimes prepaid health insurance will pay for such procedures prior to admittance. Consideration should be given to the type of room service desired. A semiprivate room may be less expensive than a private room. Try not to enter on a weekend if the services you need are unavailable.

Home-Care Services

Home care can be defined as the provision of equipment and services to the patient at home for the purpose of restoring and maintaining the patient's maximum level of comfort, function, and health.[18] Home care is not just one service; it is a wide range of services with one common goal: to preserve the home and to improve the quality of life by providing help in the home.

Most hospitals in the United States offer home-care services. Many patients are discharged earlier because home care can be achieved at a much lower cost.

Many home-care services are designed to meet the patient's needs at home during recuperation after a hospital or nursing home stay. These services generally include medical and skilled nursing care; speech, respiratory, physical, or occupational therapy; intravenous drug therapy; nutrition or dietary services; hospice services for terminal illness (see Chapter 24); and personal care (bathing, dressing, and eating). Long-term home-care services for elderly and homebound individuals are covered later in the chapter.

Home-care services cost more in rural communities than in large metropolitan areas. They also are higher for intensive treatment than for occasional or limited service. Charges are usually made on a per-visit basis, although they may be made on an hourly basis. Some home-care services are covered by Medicare, Medicaid, and private insurance plans. These are some of the costs for services:[19]

Registered/practical nurse	$60 to $85 per visit (1-2 hours) $45 to $70 per hour
Therapists/social worker	same as nurses
Home health aide	$35 to $65 per visit (2-4 hours) $9 to $12 per hour

Sources of information about home health care include: (1) physician or hospital-based social and home-care offices, (2) the Visiting Nurse Association (check local telephone directory), (3) organizations such as the National Association for Home Care, National Homecaring Council, and American Federation of Home Health Agencies (see Appendix for addresses). Private agencies may be listed in the Yellow Pages of the telephone directory under the headings "home health services" or "nurses."

When searching for home health care, these questions will be helpful to ask:[20]

1. What services are available?
2. Is the agency or organization licensed or certified by the state health department? By Medicare and Medicaid?
3. Does the agency confer with your doctor before providing services?
4. Is care provided on weekends or after regular hours?
5. How does the agency handle emergencies?
6. Does the agency provide a written list of services and costs? What does Medicare, Medicaid, or private insurance cover?
7. Are employees screened and trained by the agency? How are they supervised? Are RNs or LPNs on staff?
8. If uncertain about an agency or service whom should be asked for information? One of the agencies listed? Local health department? Local hospital? Better Business Bureau?

Ambulatory Medical Care

Ambulatory medical care refers to facilities other than doctors' offices or hospitals where care is available on a walk-in/walk-out basis.[21] There are two types: *urgent* or *emergency care* facilities and *surgicenters.*

Urgent care facilities—also called freestanding emergency centers—provide treatment by a physician for minor medical emergencies, such as cut fingers, nosebleeds, sprained ankles, and simple fractures. These facilities also provide treatment for a wide variety of other health problems that require only one visit or a small number of visits. Some urgent care centers have expanded their services to function as family medical centers, offering long-term care as well as episodic care. Some typical names are Emcare, Medstop, Health Stop, Medfirst, Medic, Emergicenter, and Doctor Care.

Surgicenters are surgical units located outside of a hospital. They perform minor surgery that does not require an overnight stay in a hospital, such as: tonsil and adenoid removal, hernia repair, dilation and curettage, sterilization, biopsies, and removal of cysts, hemorrhoids, and warts.

Using an urgent or emergency care center is a consumer's choice; neither facility requires an appointment. However, one cannot simply walk into a surgicenter for an operation. A physician's recommendation is required.

It is estimated that there are 3000 to 4000 urgent care centers and over 500 surgicenters; almost all hospitals have surgicenters. Hospitals are increasing their ambulatory care services. It is estimated that by the year 2000, outpatient revenues will account for 50% of net hospital revenues.[22]

Most urgent care centers are located in the suburbs in small shopping centers, malls, and other busy thoroughfares. Surgicenters are located in large urban areas because there are enough physicians and surgeons who will refer cases to the center rather than to the local hospitals. These centers usually are owned by one or more physicians. The American College of Emergency Physicians recommends that centers be owned and operated by specialists who are board-certified in emergency medicine.

The staff in urgent care centers usually consists of medical doctors (full-time and part-time), nurses, and clerical help. Large centers may have a radiologist and laboratory technicians. Often part-time physicians are used. Surgicenters are staffed with medical directors, anesthesiologists, pathologists, surgeons, nurses, and clerical personnel.

Walk-in centers have proliferated because of: (1) the high cost of hospital services, (2) the realization that people can become ill or injured at any time of the day, (3) competition for patients as a result of a surplus of physicians in some communities, (4) insurance companies' desire to reduce hospital costs by lowering reimbursements to hospitals for emergency room services, (5) the reluctance of physicians to make house calls, (6) lack of physicians in some areas, (7) the tendency of physicians to refer patients to hospital emergency rooms after office hours, and (8) consumer dissatisfaction with the emergency room environment.

In 1985 the National Association for Ambulatory Care compared the costs of treating specific conditions in urgent care centers and in hospital emergency rooms and documented these approximate costs: simple fracture—$71 in an urgent care center versus $159 in a hospital; influenza—$30 versus $159; laceration and suturing of arm—$75 versus $133. In an urgent care center these were some average costs per patient visit: general physical examination—$75; musculoskeletal pain—$57; urinary tract infection—$43; and gastrointestinal abdominal pain—$40. The average hospital emergency room service charge in seven cities ranged from $73 to $170.[23] Surgicenters, in addition to surgery charges, have a patient fee for the use of facilities related to the cost of the attending surgeon, anesthesiologist, and pathologist. These fees could result in significant additional cost to the patient.

Patients are expected to pay cash or use a credit card following service in a walk-in center. However, if an urgent care center is accredited and licensed, Medicare pays the cost at rates similar to those for regular doctors' office visits. Blue Shield/Blue Cross and numerous commercial insurers, HMOs, and PPOs are also reimbursing these centers. Surgicenters that are certified generally have no problem with reimbursement from third-party payers.

AIDS patients have received innovative treatments at many of these outpatient centers. They have received help not only to improve their quality of life but also to live longer.[24] Institutions rendering these services, however, are being squeezed by rising costs, growing demand, and inadequate reimbursement from Medicaid and other third-party payers. In 1988 the average cost of an outpatient visit by an AIDS patient to these centers was $342, but income averaged $99.

Positive and Negative Features

These are some of the positive features of urgent or emergency care centers:

1. Open 7 days a week for 12 or more hours; some are open 24 hours daily
2. Convenient and easily accessible
3. No appointment necessary; walk in and pay; waiting time for service may be 14 to 20 minutes
4. Cheaper than hospital emergency rooms; may cost more than a standard physician's office visit
5. Facilities generally more comfortable than emergency clinics
6. Many well equipped with fully trained personnel (some not so well equipped and staffed)

These are some of the negative features of urgent or emergency care centers:

1. May fail to take a comprehensive medical history because of limited visitation time and provision for temporary care
2. Patient may lose continuity of care; may see different physicians if more than one visit is required, or treatment may not be coordinated with that of other physicians
3. By using the word "emergency" in their names, centers may mislead the public to believe that the staff can take care of major medical emergencies at any time
4. Part-time physicians may feel less responsibility to follow up on patients; some part-time physicians are hospital residents who are moonlighting

Surgicenters have these positive features: (1) costs are generally lower, (2) patients can go home a few hours after surgery, and (3) surgeons are usually staff members of local hospitals. Some critics have said, however, that hospitals are safer places for surgical procedures.

Table 11-3 summarizes the advantages and disadvantages of a variety of outpatient healthcare facilities.

Chesteen et al[25] completed a study of patient satisfaction with services at four freestanding clinics. These are some of the findings: 75% were satisfied with the waiting time (average 15.6 minutes), 74% with time spent with the physician (average 13.7 minutes), 78% with courtesy shown by physicians, 69% with out-of-pocket expenses (average $19.54), and 75% with the overall quality of the care received.

Urgent care centers are not licensed in most states because they generally are considered an extension of the doctors' offices. Few centers are accredited. Surgicenters are licensed in every state, but not many are accredited. The Accreditation Association for Ambulatory Health Care (AAAHC) and the Joint Commission on Accreditation of Healthcare Organizations are accrediting urgent care centers.

Quality of Care

The quality of care in ambulatory centers has not been evaluated to any great extent, and questions have been raised about their effectiveness. Brook et al[4] reported on a RAND survey of centers in six Eastern cities to determine the quality of ambulatory care received by 5986 adults and children with a variety of 17 chronic conditions such as acne, allergy, asthma, and hypertension. The RAND survey discovered that the centers achieved 81% of their outcome criteria (vision corrected properly, anemia controlled) and 62% of their process outcomes (examinations, tests).

Cashman et al[26] asked physicians to rate their levels of satisfaction while working in a major chain of investor-owned walk-in centers (83 centers in 5 cities and 31 Health Stop offices). With 10 being

TABLE 11–3

ADVANTAGES AND DISADVANTAGES OF OUTPATIENT HEALTH CARE FACILITIES

Facility	Advantages	Disadvantages
Medical office	Maximum personal attention Low cost per visit	Limited hours
Multispecialty group practice	Low cost per visit Consultations may be more readily available	Same physician may not always be seen (varies with set-up of group) May have less choice of consultants
Emergicenter (urgent care center)	Costs less than hospital emergency room Open long hours Convenient appointment times	Costs more than private office May not be ideal set-up for follow-up care When care is episodic, doctor does not get to know patient as an individual
Hospital emergency room	Open 24 hours a day Able to handle serious emergencies Sophisticated equipment available	Highest cost Nonemergency cases may not receive much attention Follow-up care may be minimal Care is episodic and less personal
Hospital outpatient clinic	Fees may be reduced for individuals who cannot afford private care	Patients may have to wait a long time to be seen Tend to have high staff turnover so different doctors may be seen
Ambulatory surgical facilities (surgicenter)	Surgery costs less than it would in a hospital	Unsuitable for major surgery

© 1988 Stephen Barrett, MD.

the highest level of satisfaction, they found the following: (1) physicians employed at the facilities (most for less than 10 months) averaged 6.5, and (2) physicians who had been fired or quit averaged 3.9.

Most physicians claimed management placed too much emphasis on revenue generation rather than patient services. The *New England Journal of Medicine*[27] printed several letters from physicians formerly employed by walk-in centers who claimed that the owners were more interested in profits than in quality care. Some centers were heavily involved in dispensing drugs for profit and some used laboratory tests and x-rays rather heavily. Physicians were often ranked monthly by corporations according to the total medications sold and their total revenue from patients. Those physicians who exceeded a certain base rate were given a percentage of those funds.

Selecting an Urgent-Care Facility

Urgent care centers can provide care for accidents or illnesses that occur when one's personal physician is not available. These centers do not require an appointment and generally provide quick service. They provide an alternative for people who do not have a regular physician and dislike the idea of going to a hospital emergency room. It is important to understand, however, that walk-in centers offer fragmentary care, their costs may be higher, their quality of care may be questionable, and they generally do not provide preventive health care. In addition, a doctor who knows a patient well is usually in a better position to meet the patient's needs. Therefore, it is prudent for consumers to have a primary care physician who can provide complete care. The following guidelines on selecting a walk-in center are intended mainly for consumers who choose to ignore this advice.

1. Check the Yellow Pages.
2. Inquire at the local Chamber of Commerce or the Better Business Bureau for names of businesses.
3. If you belong to an HMO or PPO, ask whether it has a center as part of their services.
4. Check your local public health or social service agency for assistance.

5. Write to the National Association for Ambulatory Care or the Free-Standing Ambulatory Association. Addresses are in the Appendix.
6. Check for accreditation with the AAAHC or the Joint Commission.
7. Ask friends or neighbors who have used the center about its reputation. Visit several centers before help is needed to check the extent and quality of the facilities; request literature about the services, staff specialization and other information; and ask to talk with staff members to check the physicians' credentials and qualifications.
8. Ask staff members these questions:
   a. How long has the center been in operation?
   b. Will a doctor see you in an emergency or will it be someone else? Is a doctor always available when the center is open?
   c. What are the charges and how can they be paid? Are reimbursements available from Medicare and other insurance carriers?
   d. How will follow-up care be handled, such as the removal of a cast or additional laboratory tests? Will another charge be made on the next visit?
   e. How does the center work with local hospitals and with emergency ambulance services?
   f. How are records maintained? Will the clinic communicate directly with my own or other physicians? How?
   g. Is it possible to talk with a doctor to discuss the purpose of my visit and to ask some questions?

Selecting a Surgicenter

Consumers usually have little choice in the selection of a surgicenter because the facility must be one that is used by their surgeon. In addition, people who believe that their doctor is competent and thorough will accept their recommendations with few or no questions. However, individuals who are uncertain about their physician or are new patients may wish to obtain answers to these questions:

1. How long has the center been in operation?
2. Is it licensed and accredited?
3. Have any complaints about the center been filed with the local medical society or the health departments?
4. What kinds of operations have been conducted in the center in the last year or two? Has this specific type of surgery been performed here and with what frequency?
5. Is the referring physician employed by the center? In what capacity?
6. What are the qualifications of the surgeon performing the operation in terms of education, training, and experience?
7. With what hospitals is the surgeon affiliated?
8. Who is the anesthesiologist and what is this person's training and experience?
9. How do charges for surgery compare with hospital charges?
10. Will my insurance cover the surgical fees?
11. Is there a separate facility fee in addition to the surgeon's fee?

Long-Term Care

Americans are living longer as the result of medical technology, improved health care, and many social and economic changes in society. Today the average 65-year-old person can expect to live another 17 years. In the past a nursing home may have been the only option for families that were unable to provide for ill or disabled elderly people. However, many social agencies and organizations now provide services that enable elderly individuals to live independently in their community. Home health care is one option that is more convenient and may be more affordable than the services available in a hospital or nursing home.

Long-term care refers to a wide range of nursing, medical, and social services provided to an individual over a prolonged period of time. These services may not be needed solely by the elderly and may not be exclusively provided by health professionals. Family members, lay volunteers, and others may provide various aspects of long-term care.

Long-Term Care Options

Long-term healthcare services may take place within the home as well as outside the home. Consumers need to be aware of the options available and know how to obtain help when it is needed.[28] Costs for these services vary from one part of the country to another. The Nursing Home section later in this chapter has additional suggestions under Alternatives to Nursing Home Care.

Services within the home

1. *Companion Services.* Companion services help to

ease loneliness; may be provided by volunteers or paid helpers.

2. *Respite Care.* Family members may receive a break from their responsibilities by using respite care; available through adult-care centers, hospitals, and nursing homes.
3. *Transportation and Escort Services.* These services are for people who need transportation for health care, shopping, banking, and other activities.
4. *Home Observation Programs.* Patients may need periodic checks for illness and injury; generally performed by letter carriers, utility workers, and others who regularly visit areas; they report findings to social agencies and local authorities; family members and neighbors may also be involved.

Services outside the home

A variety of living arrangements includes:

1. *Congregate Housing.* Rental apartments are provided for older people; may provide meals, housekeeping, healthcare, and other services; also known as "sheltered" or "enriched" housing.
2. *Life-Care Communities.* Life-care communities combine lifetime housing with a range of services that include medical and nursing care when needed; may also include meals, housekeeping, personal grooming, and transportation. Entrance fees may be $35,000 to $150,000 or higher, with monthly fees from $600 to $1500. Although 29 states have enacted legislation regulating life-care agencies, there are no federal or widespread state standards to regulate these communities. There has been a history of intentional fraud and unintentional mismanagement, according to the National Consumers League.[30] Some life-care communities have encountered difficulty in their meeting expenses while fulfilling the obligations of their contracts. One study reported on 50 communities between 1980 and 1985 in which 10% defaulted on their debts and another 14% failed to meet occupancy rates deemed crucial to success. Thus if a community goes bankrupt, residents lose their entry fees and have no equity in their housing units. Some of the communities have been guilty of misrepresentation of financial risks of the organization, profit status, religious affiliation, mortgage-lender's interest, and false advertising. Consumers interested in these communities should obtain a copy of *A Consumer Guide to Life-Care Communities*[30] from the National Consumers League (see Appendix for address).
3. *Shared Housing.* Small groups of unrelated people are brought together in a house or apartment; each person has their own bedroom; operated by a public or private agency; provides cleaning, shopping, cooking, and other services.
4. *Board and Care Homes or Adult Care, Sheltered Care, Residential Care.* Rooms and baths are provided and sometimes shared; meals, housekeeping, and personal care are also available.

Locating Facilities and Services

Information on long-term care facilities and services may be obtained from any of the following:

1. Local hospitals when patients are discharged
2. Social service agency professionals
3. Local and county health departments
4. Check all sections of the telephone directory
5. Write to the National Association of Area Agencies on Aging (address in the Appendix)

Nursing Homes

From both humanitarian and cost-containment perspectives, long-term care for elderly persons with chronic health problems has become a significant societal problem. There are 70% to 80% of elderly Americans who cannot afford nursing home care even for one year, since the cost now averages more than $22,000. As a result, many chronically ill elderly have their assets depleted to the point where they qualify for Medicaid coverage.[31] Individuals who contemplate placing an elderly person in a nursing home need to be aware of available facilities, the quality of care, how to handle complaints, alternatives to nursing care, and how to select a home.

Nursing homes accept patients for reasons of infirmity, advanced age, illness, injury, convalescence, chronic physical disability, and mental incompetence. They do not admit patients suffering from a communicable disease, alcoholism, drug addiction, or acute mental illness. There is apparently no uniform definition of a nursing home. The phrase may refer to out-of-home facilities that offer a range of services from those found in a hospital to homes providing no more than room and board. Other titles for nursing homes include rest homes,

homes for the aged, convalescent homes or hospitals, and sanitariums.

There were few nursing homes in the United States before 1935. In that year the Social Security Act made federal funds available to the impoverished aged. This gave impetus to the development of nursing homes. In 1965 amendments to the Social Security Act created Medicare, Medicaid, and provided for extended services for people over 65 years of age.[2]

Approximately 2 million people are housed in over 15,600 nursing homes throughout the United States. Many of these homes are privately owned and operated for profit. The average resident is 78 years old and poorer than most other elderly people. About 33% of the residents stay 1 to 3 years, 15% stay 3 to 5 years, and 16% stay 5 years or longer. The cost per resident typically is $65 to $75 per day or about $24,000 yearly. Typical monthly costs range from $1000 to $3000. Two thirds of the patients who pay for their care are impoverished within 1 year.

Types of Facilities

The various types of nursing homes provide different levels of service. Individual needs will dictate the type of facility that is most appropriate.

Skilled nursing or extended care facilities provide continuous nursing service on a 24-hour basis for convalescent patients. The RNs, LPNs, and nurses' aides provide services prescribed by the patient's physician, with emphasis on medical nursing care. Restorative therapy, physical therapy, occupational therapy, and other types are also provided.

Intermediate care facilities provide regular medical, nursing, and social services in addition to room and board for persons not capable of complete independent living. The level of nursing care is less than that provided by skilled nursing facilities.

Residential care facilities provide safe, hygienic, sheltered living to individuals capable of "functional independence." Social needs rather than medical needs are met.

Adult day-care facilities provide nursing and nutritional services and medical monitoring in a nonresidential environment.

Mental health care facilities provide long-term care with comprehensive psychosocial services, therapeutic intervention, and remedial education in a home-like setting.

Types of Care

The three general types of services available in nursing homes are nursing, personal, and residential care. *Nursing care services* require the professional skills of an RN or LPN. They include administering oral medications and injections and carrying out procedures ordered by attending physicians. Posthospital stroke, heart, or orthopedic care is available with related services, such as physical and occupational therapy, dental services, dietary consultation, laboratory and x-ray services, and a pharmaceutical dispensary. *Personal care services* include help with walking, getting in and out of bed, bathing, dressing, and eating, as well as preparation of special diets as prescribed by a physician. *Residential care* involves general supervision and a protective environment, including room and board. The facility may also provide for the social and spiritual needs of the resident.

Quality of Care Problems

All states require the licensing of nursing homes and home-care facilities. The minimal standards for qualification usually pertain to facilities, staffing, and services. Many qualified homes participate in peer review in consultation with state affiliate members of the American Health Care Association and the Long-Term Care Council of the Joint Commission.

Despite periodic inspections, nursing homes vary considerably within the established criteria. In addition, conformity with the law does not guarantee the skill of the staff, the provision of a friendly atmosphere, or the quality of the care rendered. Flagrant abuse in facilities that provide care for the elderly continues to be evident in numerous homes.

The Institute of Medicine (IOM), a component of the National Academy of Sciences, conducted a 2½-year study of nursing homes.[32] Many good facilities were found; however, poor-quality facilities outnumbered very good ones. The IOM stated that in many government-certified facilities residents received very inadequate—sometimes shockingly deficient—care likely to hasten a patient's deterioration. They found that discrimination existed against low-income patients. In addition there were patterns of lax enforcement and repeated noncompliance with quality standards. The IOM made these recommendations:

1. *Skilled nursing and intermediate care facilities:* Sep-

arate sets of certification standards should be abolished because both facilities provide similar services.

2. *Quality care:* The government should assess the quality of care in nursing homes. Currently inspections to certify compliance with federal standards are completed mainly by reviewing records.
3. *Patient needs:* All patients should receive the highest quality care that meets their individual physical, mental, and psychologic needs. A patient's needs should be assessed upon entrance to a home, and treatment plans should be updated every 3 months.
4. *Patient rights:* These should be clearly and concisely stated and practiced. They should include access to the ombudsman's office, the right to participate in resident councils, to meet visitors, to participate in social, religious, and political activities, and the right to dignity and privacy.
5. *Nursing care:* All nurse's aides should be required to have approved training from an approved state institution. Over 19% of the homes employ people with no experience or education. There are high levels of dissatisfaction and personnel turnover. More professional nurses should be provided.
6. *Inspections:* These should be based on key indicators of the quality of life and care. Information should be obtained from residents, their advocates and from other sources. Some inspections should not be announced in advance.

A 1987 federal law relating to nursing homes became operative in October 1990. It was anticipated that the quality of care would improve because the new law required the following: training of licensed nurses, round-the-clock nursing care, and the presence of a RN for at least 8 hours daily. The law also forbade restraining patients with drugs, belts, or vests unless medical necessity has been established. However, some experts believe that residents are no better off than they were before the law was passed.[33]

A study of 1500 nursing homes reported by the Health Care Financing Administration (HCFA)[34] found these problems: 37% failed federal standards for storage, preparation, and service of food under sanitary conditions; 23.6% were cited for not administering drugs according to physician's orders; 23% of the patients did not receive daily hygiene and good skin and dental care; 17.4% failed to provide needed care and rehabilitation training for residents with bowel and bladder problems; and 17.4% did not encourage residents to get maximum exercise to prevent paralysis or loss of ability to walk or move.

A study of 60 nursing homes in eight western states found that 20% of the residents received tranquilizers for which no medical need had been documented. A study of 12 nursing homes in Connecticut showed that 59% of the residents had been physically restrained in various ways to prevent them from falling, despite lack of evidence that this action had made them safe.[35] The Inspector General of the U.S. Department of Health and Human Services[36] identified the following common forms of nursing home abuse:

Physical abuse: Infliction of pain or injury
Misues of restraints: Chemical or physical control of a resident beyond their physician's orders or outside of accepted medical advice
Verbal-emotional abuse: Infliction of mental or emotional suffering
Physical neglect: Disregard for the necessities of daily living
Medical neglect: Lack of care for existing medical problems
Verbal-emotional neglect: Creating situations harmful to the resident's self-esteem
Personal property abuse: Illegal or improper use of a resident's property for personal gain

Selecting a Nursing Home

It is important to understand that attempting to locate and select a nursing home that meets an individual's needs takes time, effort, and patience. There is no easy solution to finding an extended care facility that provides quality services.[37] However, the following steps should help consumers arrive at intelligent decisions:

1. Prepare a list of nursing homes that appear suitable. Several of the following sources may provide the desired information: the local health department, local medical society, social security district office, welfare and family assistance office, and local council of social agencies or social service referral center, physicians, clergy members, relatives, friends, and possibly the Yellow Pages. If the community has prepared a directory of nursing homes and helping agencies, its use

will save the consumer time in making this list.
2. Telephone a number of homes to determine the types of services they provide and whether they have the level of care needed. Friends, neighbors, physicians, and the local health department may be asked for recommendations and reactions to the facilities under consideration.
3. Visit the facility to tour, evaluate (see guidelines on next page), review the home's inspection reports, inquire about and peruse the *Patient's Bill of Rights,* and obtain information about fees and methods of payment for care.
4. Visit additional facilities that appear to have the necessary services. An appointment should be made to see an administrator for at least an hour in midmorning or midafternoon to obtain information, discuss a variety of matters mentioned in #3, and tour the home.

Home inspections. The administrator should be asked for permission to read the most recent licensing, certification, and other reports. If the person is unwilling to accede to this request, it is possible to obtain the information elsewhere.

The Social Security Act was changed in 1972 to mandate routine disclosure of information obtained from inspections of nursing homes and other facilities for Medicare and Medicaid programs. These inspections occur at least annually, and the law requires the information to be available through the 1200 offices of the Social Security Administration.

Some state health departments inspect nursing homes and make this information available to the public. The California State Department of Health is responsible for licensing and certifying homes and conducts inspections four times a year. These investigations include checking the number and qualifications of the staff, the quality of the food, and the accuracy of the administration of medicine. Reports describe any noncompliance with state and federal standards noted by the inspectors. These public documents are open for review by interested persons at the regional offices of the Facilities Licensing Section of the State Department of Health.

The California State Department of Health has a medical-social review team that conducts unannounced inspections of homes once a year. The team checks the quality of patient care and the appropriateness of the placement of MediCal (low-income) patients. These reports have been made available through county social service and welfare offices.

Cautions about fees and payments. Complete information about costs, payment policies, and other details should be obtained. One should inquire about daily and monthly room rates and about extra charges for services and supplies (for physician, physical therapist, and private nursing services, medications, laundry, and special diets). One should also find out whether the fees are to be paid weekly, monthly, or in advance. If they are to be paid in advance, the policy concerning refunds for unused portions should be discussed. It should be noted that higher costs for services may mean that facilities have more nurses and other staff members. Greater costs, however, do not necessarily guarantee better care.

It has been said that good nursing homes are expensive, but poor ones are not cheap. The Better Business Bureau advises consumers to be wary of homes that want individuals to sign a life-care contract. It cannot be canceled, and the necessary intensive care, if needed, may not be provided. The Bureau suggests to be cautious if a large initial deposit is requested. When someone's resources are depleted, it may be impossible to leave if the facility proves unsatisfactory. If a deposit must be made, explore the possibility of arranging monthly payments rather than liquidating assets. It might be helpful to retain a lawyer to supervise the arrangements.

The Better Business Bureau states that some nursing homes accept a patient only if all assets, such as real estate, jewelry, stocks, and bonds, are signed over to become the property of the home when the patient dies. This is more likely to occur when the individual is unable to pay the full cost of the care. The Bureau recommends that before agreeing to such an arrangement, the individual should have a full understanding of all stipulations. Here, too, it is strongly advisable to have help from a knowledgeable lawyer or social agency.

Institutional care may be paid for by Medicare, Medicaid, health insurance, or private funds. Medicare covers up to 100 days (20 days fully, 80 days partially) in a Medicare-certified nursing home, provided that such care follows a stay of at least 3 continuous days in an acute care hospital and the individual's condition meets certain criteria. Medicare does not pay for care in residential or intermediate care facilities. Medicaid, a federal-state program, covers eligible low-income persons for long-term care in a residential care home, intermediate care facility, or nursing home. Local welfare offices should be contacted for help.

Health insurance and prepaid health care plans sometimes include nursing home care as a benefit. The care usually is referred to as extended care. The cost may be high. Inquiry should be made about the criteria for coverage.

Private payments usually are necessary for those who are not covered by Medicare, Medicaid, or a health insurance plan. However, publicly supported care may be available in instances where none of the above sources are available. The local or state department of public welfare or some charitable organization might be contacted for more information.

Contract provisions. Before signing a contract for admission to a nursing home it is advisable to have an attorney review it. These provisions are undesirable:

1. Absolving the home from financial liability for injury or theft
2. Waiving the right to be informed in advance of changes in patient care or charges for services
3. Guaranteeing to pay all costs of litigation, including a nursing home attorney, if the home is sued
4. Preventing cancellation of a life-care contract unless a reasonable trial period (minimum of 60 days) has been allowed

The contract should include these provisions:

1. Permission for the patient or family to purchase supplies, medications, and equipment on the open market if so desired
2. A clear statement of the behavior or financial condition that will precipitate eviction
3. A refund for unused time when a patient is discharged, dies, or is evicted for behavior problems

Final selection. After narrowing the choices of nursing homes to one or two, an unannounced visit should be made during a mealtime to determine the quality of the food and how it is served. A night visit might be advisable as well. This will also provide an opportunity to raise questions and concerns that may have arisen since the first visit. Observe the activities and talk with the patients: do they seem interested in life? Does the staff show concern for the patients?

Patients' Bill of Rights

One should inquire whether the facility adheres to the nursing home *Patients' Bill of Rights.* Homes wishing to be certified by Medicare and Medicaid must meet federal standards that include these rights. The 1987 federal law strengthened the protection of residents through these basic provisions:

1. The right to choose your own doctors and to help plan your course of treatment
2. Freedom from physical and mental abuse and from any restraints not medically required
3. Use of pharmacologic drugs by prescription and only for the symptoms for which they are prescribed
4. Right to privacy
5. Confidentiality of records
6. Right to services tailored to the resident's individual needs and advanced notice before room or roommate is changed
7. Right to voice grievances
8. Right to organize and participate in resident groups
9. Right to participate in social, religious, and community activities
10. Right to examine the most recent report of the facility and to review plans to correct deficiencies
11. Any other right established by the Secretary of Health and Human Services

Handling Complaints

Laws alone cannot ensure that all nursing homes provide quality care. Family members or other concerned parties must not only be discriminating in selecting places for elderly and chronically ill persons, but must also speak out, ask questions, investigate, and register complaints when they believe that services are inadequate. The appropriate action varies according to the nature of the problem, but there are many resources to telephone, visit, or contact by mail. The nursing home administrator should be visited for clarification and modification of the problem. The local Social Security district office functions as a clearinghouse for complaints about institutions receiving government funds. If the patient is covered by Medicaid, the patient's caseworker or the county welfare office can be contacted. The state Medicaid agency also can be contacted if the home is certified by Medicaid. A nursing home ombudsman may be a good resource. Contact may be made to the following: the state board responsible for licensing homes and administrators; local, state, or federal legislators; the local Better Business Bureau; a reputable lawyer or legal aid society; the local hospital association; and the local medical society. One can also contact the state association for nursing homes or homes for the aging, government agencies that deal with consumer affairs, and departments of public health and mental hygiene.

The 1987 federal law concerning nursing home standards requires nursing-home staff to draw up an annual plan for each patient's care after consulting with the patient. Plans must be updated every 3 months. Failure to fulfill a plan's terms can be grounds for daily fines of $10,000 or more. Family members are urged to request a copy of the plan of care and monitor its implementation. Complaints should go to the nursing-home staff and, if necessary, to the state's long-term care ombudsman.

The *Johns Hopkins Medical Letter, Health After 50,*[38] reported that at some time during 1989, 40% (500,000) of nursing home residents were restrained. It suggests the following actions to ensure that residents are not unnecessarily restrained:

1. If legally responsible for the resident, tell the administrators that you want no restraint to be used until you or your physician provide informed consent
2. Request an explanation from the administrator that details the specific reasons when a restraint is the only recourse, should they intend to use one
3. Ask for an estimate of when the restraint will be removed, reinforcing the notion that restraints should be used as little as possible
4. Spend as much time as you can participating in the resident's care. Restraints may be applied if a patient being tube-fed through the nose pulls out the tube; offering to feed the patient might circumvent this problem.
5. When shopping for a nursing home, inquire about the policy regarding the use of restraints.

Alternatives to Nursing Home Care

Before reaching a decision about nursing home care, it is advisable to determine the level of care needed by the person and whether an alternative is available. A physician, public health nurse, social service worker, and family members can help with these determinations. The needed care may include 24-hour care, daily medical supervision, minimal assistance with daily activities (help with shopping, cleaning, and cooking meals), or other services. The following alternatives may help elderly persons enjoy more independence:

1. *Home healthcare:* Visiting nurses, therapists, medical social workers, home health aides; estimate that rates begin at $50 to $60 per month or more
2. *Homemaker services:* Light housekeeping, shopping, and other services; rates $8 to $12 per hour
3. *Day-care centers for ambulatory patients:* Day activities, meals, recreational and social activities, and other services; rates may be $30 to $45 per day
4. *Food service* (such as Meals on Wheels) *and/or transportation services* (many communities offer transportation to doctors' appointments and other necessary activities)
5. *Telephone reassurance:* Provided by senior citizen groups, other volunteer organizations, or family members
6. *Emergency response systems:* An elderly person can press a button carried on his or her body to activate the telephone; this alerts a central monitoring system that can reach the fire department, hospital, health facility, social service agency, or family member; costs include installation (about $100) plus a monthly service fee of $30 to $40
7. *Special housing:* Small apartment buildings designed for the elderly with payment on a rental basis
8. *Personal care facility:* Residents have their own room and receive all the necessary services from the facility in return for a monthly fee in the range of $1500 to $2500
9. *Congregate-life housing:* Supervised apartments for "well elderly" in a life-care community; these include close medical monitoring, dietary and housekeeping services, social, recreational, and spiritual services; cost is a one-time fee of approximately $40,000 to $100,000 and monthly fees of $500 to $1500; less expensive for a board and lodging facility only
10. *Geriatric clinics or day hospitals:* Many services are planned for those with physical and mental impairments requiring daytime support and supervision. They may also provide: (a) counseling, (b) supervision by a nurse or social worker, (c) doctors and nurses to make home visits, (d) medication and monitoring, and (e) various types of therapy. The yearly cost approximates $12,000 to $15,000

It's Your Decision

On a 1 to 5 point scale, with 5 being the highest rating, how would you rate the hospital or nursing home that you, a friend, or a member of your family entered recently?

Criteria	Rating of hospital or nursing home
Extent of needs served	______
Accredited/licensed	______
Adequacy of physical condition of facility	______
Services rendered	
Quality of care	______
Courtesy of personnel	______
Food quality	______
Ombudsman available	______
Fees/charges	______
Total score =	______

Rating:
- Under 16 points = poor to very poor
- 17 to 23 points = fair
- 24 to 32 points = good
- 33 to 40 points = excellent

11. *Institutes for geriatric care:* Help elderly with major illnesses and injuries; cost is approximately $10,000 for a 3-month period
12. *Respite care:* Homes and centers that admit elderly individuals on a temporary basis; may help in recovery from illness or enable a family to take a vaction
13. *Domiciliary Care Program* (Pennsylvania): For Medicaid-eligible elderly, physically impaired, mentally ill, and mentally retarded people; foster homes with personal care; 24-hour supervision if necessary with meals, laundry, and household services; cost is approximately $8000 to $10,000 annually

Summary

The more than 6700 hospitals in the United States can be classified by type (community or noncommunity), organizational control (government or nongovernment), financial structure (for-profit or not-for-profit), length of stay (short or long), and by types of services (general, medical, surgical, psychiatric, and others). The procedures used to foster a high quality of care in hospitals are licensing and accreditation. Licensing is a state function. The Joint Commission on Accreditation of Healthcare Organizations establishes standards and is primarily responsible for accreditation. Hospitals are faced with numerous problems, such as: increasing costs, competition from other hospitals, unnecessary surgeries, malpractice suits, Medicare reimbursement limits (DRGs), and quality-of-care assessment.

Most hospitals now offer a variety of alternative healthcare services including home healthcare, wellness centers, and rehabilitation services. They may also provide health insurance as an HMO or PPO. Selecting a hospital is not easy for the average consumer, but there are guidelines that can help.

Over 4000 ambulatory healthcare centers exist in the United States. Most are for-profit centers staffed by full- and part-time physicians and nurses. They provide urgent or emergency care and perform minor surgery. Their positive features include: long hours of operation, convenient locations, better atmospheres than hospital emergency rooms, and lack of the need for an appointment. However, urgent care facilities usually cost more than medical office visits and may lead to fragmentation of medical care (loss of continuity with one's personal physician). They should not be regarded as a substitute for a personal physician. Surgicenters can provide services at a lower cost than hospitals, but may not be as safe as hospitals for some procedures.

Long-term care refers to a variety of services available to the elderly and others whereby people can be assisted while living at home or in a nursing home facility.

Nursing homes can offer three levels of services: skilled nursing care, personal care, and residential care. All states require that nursing homes be licensed, but this action does not ensure the quality of care provided. Abuses continue despite a 1987 law intended to improve matters; these include the use of unprescribed tranquilizers, physical restraints, unhygienic conditions, and poor quality of food. Consumers should use the guidelines for selection found in this text when planning long-term care services. When choosing a nursing home, careful consideration should be given to administration and staffing, physical aspects, psychological and social climate, quality of services, and costs.

Discussion Questions

1. What are the various types of hospitals in the United States?
2. What are the two procedures used to ensure quality of care in hospitals? Who is responsible for implementing these procedures?
3. What are some of the standards and requirements that must be met by hospitals seeking accreditation?
4. Name five problems facing hospitals in their efforts to provide quality healthcare.
5. What five characteristics can help identify a good hospital?
6. What procedures should be followed by consumers in the selection of hospitals?
7. Name four home healthcare services performed by hospitals. What guidelines are useful in the selection of these services?
8. What is the meaning of the term ambulatory care and how is this service classified?
9. Name three advantages and three disadvantages of using urgent or emergency healthcare centers.
10. How can consumers locate and select urgent healthcare centers?
11. What is long-term care? Identify four types of services available both inside and outside the patient's home.
12. What are nursing homes? Why are they needed?
13. What are the types of nursing homes? What services do each type provide?
14. What can be said about the quality of care in nursing homes? Name three common forms of abuse that continue to be found in these facilities.
15. What guidelines should consumers follow for locating and selecting a nursing home?
16. What cautions about fees and payments to nursing homes are important for consumers to consider?

REFERENCES

1. Fleming ST: The relationship between the cost and quality of medical care: a review of the literature, Med Care Rev 47:476-501, Winter, 1990.
2. Murtaugh CM et al: The risk of nursing homes later in life, Med Care 28:952-954, 1990.
3. American Hospital Association: 1989-1990 AHA hospital statistics, Chicago, 1990, The Association.
4. Brook RH et al: Quality of ambulatory care, Med Care 28:392-407, 1990.
5. JCAHO–Has its time come? Public Citizen Health Research Group Health Letter 6(1):10-11, 1990.
6. Freudenheim M: Specialty health care bonus: high profits, The New York Times, Feb 11, 1985.
7. National Council for Senior Citizens: For-profit hospital care—who profits/who cares? Washington DC, 1986, The Council.
8. JCAHO–140 hospitals named for patient dumping violations, Public Citizen Health Research Group Health Letter 7(5):1-7, 1991.
9. Hallinger FJ: Forecasting the medical care costs of the HIV epidemic: 1991–1994, Inquiry 28(3):213–225, 1991.
10. Popescu CB: When hospitals make patients sick, ACSH News and Views 8(2):1-2,14, 1987.
11. Pettit C: Hospital competition no boon to consumers, study suggests, San Francisco Chronicle, June 19, 1987.
12. Pear R: Mortality data released for 6000 hospitals, The New York Times, Dec 18, 1987.
13. McIlrath S: Despite objections, HCFA to publish hospital-by-hospital mortality data, American Medical News, Aug 28, 1987.
14. Fink A et al: The condition of the literature on differences in hospital mortality, Med Care 27:315-335, 1989.
15. Jencks SF et al: Interpreting hospital mortality data—the role of clinical risk adjustment, JAMA 260:3611-3616, 1988.
16. Lipman MM: Surviving a stay in the hospital, Consumer Reports Health Letter 3:30, 1991.
17. Choosing the Right Hospital, The Johns Hopkins Medical Letter, Health After 50 2(2):1-2, 1990.
18. Scott WC et al: Home care in the 1990s, JAMA 263:1241-1244, 1991.
19. National Consumers League: A consumer guide to health care, Washington DC, 1991, The League.
20. Friedman JA: Hospital care comes home, American Health 4:64-65, June 1987.
21. Dunn S: Fast medicine: doc-in-the-box, American Health 4:34-37, June 1985.
22. Ambulatory care growth charges CEO priorities, Hospitals 65:44, Feb 5, 1991.
23. Coleman B: A consumer's guide to ambulatory care, Washington DC, Feb 1986, National Consumers League.
24. Outpatient AIDS care squeezed by high costs, low payments, Hospitals 65:40, May 5, 1991.
25. Chesteen SB et al: A comparison of family practice clinics and free-standing emergency centers: organizational characteristics, process of care and patient satisfaction, J Med Prac 23:377-382, 1986.
26. Cashman SB et al: Physician satisfaction in a major chain of investor-owned walk-in centers, Health Care Manage Rev 15:47-57, Summer, 1990.
27. Pressure to keep prices high at a walk-in clinic, N Engl J Med 320:183-185, 1989 (editorial).
28. Sherwood S et al: Alternative paths to long-term nursing home care: nursing home geriatric day hospital, senior center and domiciliary care options, Amer J Pub Health 76:38-44, 1986.
29. JCAHO–Patient dumping case goes to court, Public Citizen Health Research Group Health Letter 7(5):3, 1991.
30. National Consumers League: A consumer guide to life-care communities, Washington DC, 1990, The League.
31. Tail EJ et al: Life care at home: a new model for financing and delivering long-term care, Inquiry 24:245-252, 1987.

32. IOM Panel: Many nursing homes are deficient: new rules needed, The Nation's Health, Apr 1986.
33. McLeod D: Assessing nursing home reform, AARP Bulletin 33:4-5, 1991.
34. Most nursing homes pass test but failures abound, AARP Bulletin 31:16, 1990.
35. McLeod D: Nursing homes said to restrain patients, AARP Bulletin 32:13, 1991.
36. McLeod D: Abuse abounds: nursing home residents still vulnerable, AARP Bulletin 31:10, 1990.
37. Montgomery J: Making the decision everybody hates: choosing a nursing home for ill patient, The Wall Street Journal, Feb 11, 1985.
38. Restraints on nursing home restraints, The Johns Hopkins Medical Letter, Health After 50 2(9):6, 1990.

NUTRITION AND FITNESS

CHAPTER TWELVE

BASIC NUTRITION CONCEPTS

"According to his lawyer, making him eat spinach is a violation of his civil rights. He's suing us for a million dollars."

It is not necessary to understand a car's inner workings to be a good driver. *Similarly, it is not necessary to know a great deal about the science of nutrition in order to eat properly.*

FREDRICK J. STARE, M.D., PH.D.[1]
VIRGINIA ARONSON, R.D., M.S.
STEPHEN BARRETT, M.D.

CONSUMER DECISIONS

How can foods be selected to ensure adequate nutrition?

How are nutrition labels useful?

Where can reliable nutrition information be obtained?

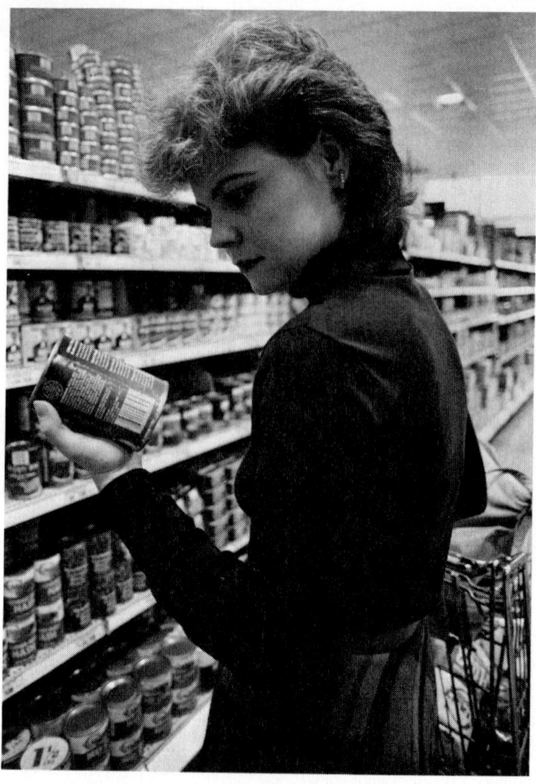

Shopper reading a food label.

Nutrition is the science of food and how the body uses it in health and in disease. A working knowledge of basic nutrition will help consumers make intelligent food selections and protect themselves against the vast array of nutrition myths and fads circulating in our society.

This chapter introduces basic nutrition concepts with emphasis on the major food components, the essential nutrients and their food sources, dietary guidelines, food labeling, and sources of reliable nutrition information. Food faddism and weight control will be discussed in the following two chapters. The relationships between diet and heart disease are covered in Chapter 16.

MAJOR FOOD COMPONENTS

The major nutrient components of food are proteins, carbohydrates, fats, vitamins, minerals, and water. Proteins, carbohydrates, and fats supply energy (calories) and are needed in large amounts. They are called *macronutrients.* (*Makros* is a Greek word that means large.) Practically all foods contain mixtures of proteins, fats, and carbohydrates, although they are commonly classified according to the predominant one. Vitamins and minerals are needed in relatively small amounts to help regulate body functions. They are called *micronutrients.* Water is the major component in both foods and the human body, which is about 60% water.

The body's digestive system breaks food down into molecules small enough to be absorbed through the stomach and intestinal walls into the blood stream. The absorbed substances are metabolized further and used for energy, growth and repair, and a myriad of other body functions.

Proteins

Proteins, the body's main structural component, are used to make bone, connective tissue, muscle, skin, hair, and cell membranes. Proteins also function as enzymes, hormones, antibodies, and as part of the compounds that transport oxygen to the tissues (hemoglobin and myoglobin).

The proteins in food are too large to be absorbed through the intestines, so they are broken down during digestion into their component amino acids. These smaller components are then absorbed from the intestines and reassembled as needed into the 50,000 or more proteins needed by the body. Amino acids not used for this purpose are used for energy. There are 20 amino acids, 8 or 9 of which are considered essential because they cannot be manufactured by the body and must be included in the diet. The essential amino acids are isoleucine, leucine, lysine, methionine, phenylalanine, threonine, tryptophan and valine; for infants, histidine also is essential. Protein sources are considered *complete* or high quality if they supply all of the essential amino acids in adequate amounts and *incomplete* or poor quality if they do not.

Carbohydrates

Carbohydrates are excellent sources of energy and supply about half of the calories consumed in the average American's diet. The most abundant sources are starches, sugars (mainly glucose, fructose, and lactose), and cellulose.

Starches (found in breads and cereals, potatoes, other vegetables, pasta, rice, and other grains) and most types of dietary fiber are *complex carbohydrates* composed of long chains of glucose molecules. Sugars, such as table sugar (sucrose), honey, and corn syrup, contain one or two sugar molecules and are called *simple carbohydrates.*

Glucose has been called the universal sugar because it is the basic form of food energy for life. All carbohydrates must be metabolized into glucose for the energy within them to be used by the body. Glucose circulates in the blood and is stored in the form of glycogen, mainly in the liver and the muscles. However, most extra calories are stored as fat, a more concentrated energy storage form than glycogen. If carbohydrate is not supplied in the diet, the body must use a less efficient process (described in Chapter 14) to break down fats and proteins for energy.

Many food faddists claim that sucrose is a "deadly poison," while complex carbohydrates are safer and more desirable. Foods that contain complex carbohydrates are an important part of a balanced diet. However, according to Stare, Aronson, and Barrett:[1]

> It is ridiculous to claim that one type of digestible carbohydrate is dangerously inferior to the others when all become glucose in the body anyway. All edible carbohydrates are safe when eaten in moderate amounts.

Dietary fiber. Dietary fiber (also called bulk or roughage) refers to plant components that are resistant to digestion by human gastrointestinal secretions. It includes a heterogenous group of carbohydrate compounds (cellulose, hemicellulose, mucilages, pectin, and gums) and the noncarbohydrate, lignin. All foods of vegetable origin contain fiber in various quantities. Whole-grain foods are a major source of dietary fiber. Bran has 9% to 12% crude fiber; dry beans, lentils, and soybeans have over 4%; roasted nuts have 2.3% to 2.6%. Most fruits and vegetables contain 0.5% to 1.0% of fiber, although some can be lost during processing.

Fiber in the intestinal tract holds water, making the feces bulkier and softer and enabling them to pass more quickly and easily through the intestines. Low-fiber diets result in constipation. Epidemiologic data provides evidence that prolonged lack of dietary fiber is associated with a broad spectrum of gastrointestinal, circulatory, and metabolic problems such as: diverticulitis (inflamed outpouches in the large intestine), varicose veins, deep vein thrombosis, hemorrhoids, colon cancer, increased serum lipid levels, obesity, and diabetes.

Naturally occurring fibers in food are usually a mixture of *soluble fibers* (pectins, gums, and mucilages), *insoluble fibers* (cellulose and lignin), and combinations of insoluble and soluble fibers (hemicelluloses). Oat bran and oatmeal contain relatively large amounts of soluble fiber, and whole wheat contains relatively large amounts of insoluble fiber.

Populations consuming diets rich in fiber-containing foods have significantly lower rates of cancer of the colon, rectum, and several other organs. Populations consuming diets low in fiber and high in fat, especially saturated fat, tend to have higher rates of heart disease, obesity, and certain cancers. It is known that increasing the amount of soluble fiber may help lower high blood-cholesterol levels and that increasing total dietary fiber is useful in treating constipation and hemorrhoids. Since foods high in fiber have a variety of fiber components and tend to be low in fat, it is difficult to design studies that can test for specific effects of fiber. Much research needs to be done to determine which components, if any, might be most useful and the amounts of these components that would be optimal.

All major scientific groups that have issued dietary guidelines agree that it is desirable for people to consume adequate amounts of dietary fiber. The Food and Drug Administration (FDA), however, does not believe sufficient evidence exists for manufacturers to claim that the amount of fiber in *individual food products* can help prevent cancer or lower the risk of cardiovascular disease.[2] The importance of soluble fiber in the treatment of high blood-cholesterol levels is covered in Chapter 16.

A study prepared for the FDA by the Life Sciences Research Office of the Federation of American Societies for Experimental Biology (FASEB) recommends an intake range of 20 to 35 g of fiber per day for healthy American adults, which corresponds to approximately 10 to 13 g per 1000 calories of food. The report concluded that achieving this level of intake is feasible by selecting ordinary foods that are currently available and that many Americans already did so.[3] Individuals who wish to increase their fiber intake can do so be eating more whole-grain breads and cereals, fruits, vegetables, legumes, and nuts. But even fiber that occurs naturally should be eaten in moderation. A high-fiber diet can cause one to feel stuffed or bloated, can cause diarrhea, and can interfere with the absorption of iron, copper, zinc, and calcium. Purified fibers or fiber supplements are generally not recommended for individuals who are able to obtain fiber from food.[4]

Fats (Lipids)

Lipid is the general term for fatty substances, including triglycerides (fats and oils), phospholipids (such as lecithin), and sterols (including cholesterol). In common usage, fats are lipids that are solid at room temperature, and oils are lipids that are liquid at room temperature.

Triglycerides are the fats commonly found in foods and in the body. Triglyceride molecules are composed of glycerol (an alcohol) plus three chain-like fatty acids. Fatty acids differ in the length of their molecular chains and the degree of saturation with hydrogen. Those filled to capacity with hydrogen are called *saturated* fatty acids. Those chains that have room for two hydrogen atoms are called *monounsaturated* fatty acids. Those with room for four or more hydrogen atoms are called *polyunsaturated.* Linoleic acid, which is polyunsaturated, is the only lipid nutrient recognized as essential for humans. Lipids in the diet contain many other fatty acids, but these can be synthesized from other substances and are not essential.

Triglycerides can contain combinations of fatty acids of all types. The dominant type of fatty acid determines the characteristics of the triglyceride. Oils tend to be richer in polyunsaturates, but palm oil and coconut oil are saturated. Other saturated fats are of animal origin, or are vegetable oils that have had hydrogen added by hydrogenation.

Cholesterol, an important component of cell membranes, is transported through the blood stream in three main cholesterol-protein combinations: high-density lipoproteins (HDL—"good cholesterol"), low-density lipoproteins (LDL—"bad cholesterol"), and very-low-density lipoproteins (VLDL). Actually, HDL and LDL are not types of cholesterol but are fat-protein compounds that transport cholesterol through the blood. HDL tends to carry cholesterol away from the arterial walls and LDL tends to deposit it there. When cholesterol is attached to a lipoprotein, the entire complex is properly referred to as HDL- or LDL-cholesterol. However, the terms HDL and LDL are more commonly used. The relationships between diet, lipoproteins, and heart disease are discussed thoroughly in Chapter 16.

Vitamins

Vitamins are organic (carbon-containing) substances required in tiny amounts to promote one or more specific biochemical reactions. Only tiny amounts are needed because vitamins are catalysts (substances that initiate or speed up chemical reactions but remain unchanged while performing their tasks repeatedly). Vitamins do not provide energy directly but are part of the enzyme systems required for the release of energy from carbohydrates, fats, and proteins. There are 13 known vitamins for humans: four are fat soluble (A, D, E, and K) and nine are water soluble (C and the eight B-complex vitamins: thiamine, riboflavin, niacin, B_6, B_{12}, folic acid, biotin, and pantothenic acid). Since patients can survive for many years without becoming ill on intravenous feedings fortified with these substances, it appears that no vitamins remain to be discovered.

Most vitamins must be obtained from food because the human body cannot manufacture them, but a few are also made within the body. Vitamin D is made in the skin when it is exposed to sunlight, and biotin and vitamin K are made by intestinal bacteria.

Vitamin deficiency diseases are rare in the United States because vitamins are plentiful in the food supply. Population groups at risk for deficiency are identified in Chapter 13.

Minerals

Minerals are inorganic compounds needed in relatively small amounts to help regulate body functions, aid in growth and maintenance of body tissues, and act as catalysts for the release of energy. The 17 essential minerals may be categorized as *major minerals* (macrominerals) or *trace minerals* (microminerals). The macrominerals are those present in the body in amounts exceeding 5 g: calcium, phosphorus, magnesium, sodium, potassium, chloride, and sulfur. Sodium, potassium, and chloride are called *electrolytes;* in water they completely dissociate into component ions that conduct electrical currents. The essential trace minerals are chromium, cobalt, copper, fluoride, iodide, iron, manganese, molybdenum, selenium, and zinc.

Human Nutrient Needs

Many sets of guidelines are available to help people make intelligent dietary choices. The Recommended Dietary Allowances (RDA), the U.S. Recommended Daily Allowances (U.S. RDA), and the Recommended Dietary Intakes (RDI) are related to the prevention of deficiency. Food group systems are simple methods of food classification for planning or evaluating the nutrient adequacy of one's diet. The Dietary Guidelines for Americans, the Nine Dietary Guidelines, and the Infant Dietary Guidelines are intended to help prevent certain diet-related diseases. The recently released USDA Food Guide Pyramid addresses both nutrient adequacy and disease prevention.

Recommended Dietary Allowances

The RDA are the levels of intake of essential nutrients "adequate to meet the known needs of practically all healthy persons," established by the Committee on Dietary Allowances of the Food and Nutrition Board of the National Research Council.[5] These standards usually are revised every 5 to 6 years. Table 12-1 contains the current values for protein, 11 vitamins, and 7 minerals. There also are "estimated safe and adequate daily dietary intakes" (ESADDI) for 7 additional vitamins and minerals as shown in Table 12-2. ESADDI are essential nutrients for which there are enough data to estimate a range of requirements, but not enough data to develop RDA.

A balanced diet of foods as described in Table 12-3 can provide adequate amounts of all essential nutrients. Most individuals do not need supplementary vitamins, minerals, or proteins. Table 12-4 identifies the functions and best food sources of the major nutrients.

In 1985 the RDA committee recommended lowering the RDAs for vitamins A, C, and B_6, and the minerals magnesium, iron, and zinc, and raising the RDA for calcium. The committee also wanted to redefine the RDAs as the amounts needed to "protect practically all healthy persons from nutritional deficiencies." However, no 1985 RDA report was published because certain members of the Food and Nutrition Board objected to some of these changes and thought that the RDA committee should try to determine "optimal" nutrient values. The RDA committee, whose viewpoints are favored by most nutrition scientists, replied that this is impossible because no data exist to make such determinations.[6] The report finally was published, in slightly edited form, in 1989.

Biochemical Individuality

RDAs are recommended daily averages. They are neither requirements nor minimums, and they do take into account the differing needs of individuals. Stare, Aronson, and Barrett have noted:

> Intakes equivalent to half of the RDAs are usually adequate. . . . Anyone who advises healthy persons to take doses of vitamins and minerals higher than the RDAs "to be sure they get enough" is bypassing the collective wisdom of the scientific nutrition community.[1]

Dr. Victor Herbert, a member of the 1980-1985 RDA committee, has noted:

> Health hustlers misrepresent the concept of "biochemical individuality" to imply that individuals should consume more than the RDAs in case they have greater-than-average needs. . . . RDAs are deliberately set higher than most people require in order to encompass the range of individual variations.[7]

Many supplements are supposedly formulated to meet the "special" needs of athletes, executives, housewives, teenagers, elderly individuals, and so on. The intended target group is suggested by the product's name (for example, Coach's Formula, Exec-30, Teenplex, Ger-E-Time). However, the idea that these groups have special needs that make supplementation advisable is without scientific foundation.

U.S. RDA/RDI

Labels on various food and drug products refer to U.S. RDA (United States Recommended Daily Allowances). These were determined by the FDA using the highest values for various age groups from the 1968 RDA table. Food labels state the percentage of U.S. RDA per portion of food for each nutrient present in significant amounts. Labels for vitamin and mineral products state the percentage of the U.S. RDA per dose. In 1991 the FDA[8] proposed

Text continued on p. 236.

Table 12–1

Recommended Dietary Allowances (1989)[5]

	Age (years)	Wt. (lbs)	Height (inches)	Fat-soluble vitamins				Water-soluble vitamins						
				A[a] (μg RE)	D[b] (μg)	E (mg α-TE)[c]	K (μg)[d]	C (mg)	Thiamin (mg)	Riboflavin (mg)	Niacin (mg)	B_6 (μg)	Folate (μg)	B_{12} (μg)
Infants	0.0-0.5	13	24	375	7.5	3	5	30	0.3	0.4	5	0.3	25	0.3
	0.5-1.0	20	28	375	10	4	10	35	0.4	0.5	6	0.6	35	0.5
Children	1-3	29	35	400	10	6	15	40	0.7	0.8	9	1.0	50	0.7
	4-6	44	44	500	10	7	20	45	0.9	1.1	12	1.1	75	1.0
	7-10	62	52	700	10	7	30	45	1.0	1.2	13	1.4	100	1.4
Males	11-14	99	62	1,000	10	10	45	50	1.3	1.5	17	1.7	150	2.0
	15-18	145	69	1,000	10	10	65	60	1.5	1.8	20	2.0	200	2.0
	19-24	160	70	1,000	10	10	70	60	1.5	1.7	19	2.0	200	2.0
	25-50	174	70	1,000	5	10	80	60	1.5	1.7	19	2.0	200	2.0
	51+	170	68	1,000	5	10	80	60	1.2	1.4	15	2.0	200	2.0
Females	11-14	101	62	800	10	8	45	50	1.1	1.3	15	1.4	150	2.0
	15-18	120	64	800	10	8	55	60	1.1	1.3	15	1.5	180	2.0
	19-24	128	65	800	10	8	60	60	1.1	1.3	15	1.6	180	2.0
	25-50	138	64	800	5	8	65	60	1.1	1.3	15	1.6	180	2.0
	51+	143	63	800	5	8	65	60	1.0	1.2	13	1.6	180	2.0
Pregnant				800	10	10	65	70	1.5	1.6	17	2.2	400	2.2
Lactating, 1st 6 months				1,300	10	12	65	95	1.6	1.8	20	2.1	280	2.6
Lactating, 2nd 6 months				1,200	10	11	65	90	1.6	1.7	20	2.1	260	2.6

TABLE 12–1

RECOMMENDED DIETARY ALLOWANCES (1989)[5] — cont'd

	Age (years)	Weight (lbs)	Height (inches)	Protein (grams)	Minerals						
					Calcium (mg)	Phosphorus (mg)	Magnesium (mg)	Iron (mg)	Zinc (mg)	Iodine (μg)	Selenium (μg)
Infants	0.0-0.5	13	24	13	400	300	40	6	5	40	10
	0.5-1.0	20	28	14	600	500	60	10	5	50	15
Children	1-3	29	35	16	800	800	80	10	10	70	20
	4-6	44	44	24	800	800	120	10	10	90	20
	7-10	62	52	28	800	800	170	10	10	120	30
Males	11-14	99	62	45	1,200	1,200	270	12	15	150	40
	15-18	145	69	59	1,200	1,200	400	12	15	150	50
	19-24	160	70	58	1,200	1,200	350	10	15	150	70
	25-50	174	70	63	800	800	350	10	15	150	70
	51+	170	68	63	800	800	350	10	15	150	70
Females	11-14	101	62	46	1,200	1,200	280	15	12	150	45
	15-18	120	64	44	1,200	1,200	300	15	12	150	50
	19-24	128	65	46	1,200	1,200	280	15	12	150	55
	25-50	138	64	50	800	800	280	15	12	150	55
	51+	143	63	50	800	800	280	10	12	150	55
Pregnant				60	1,200	1,200	320	30	15	175	65
Lactating, 1st 6 months				65	1,200	1,200	355	15	19	200	75
Lactating, 2nd 6 months				62	1,200	1,200	340	15	16	200	75

[a]1 RE (retinol equivalent) = 1 μg retinol or 6 μg beta-carotene
[b]As cholecalciferol; 10 mg cholecalciferol = 400 International Units (IU) of vitamin D
[c]1 mg α-TE = approximately 1 IU
[d]1 μg = one millionth of a g
These values, expressed as daily averages, are intended to provide for individual variations among normal persons as they live in the United States under usual environmental stresses. The heights and weights are medians for Americans in the listed ranges. The National Research Council recommends that diets should be based on a variety of common foods to provide other nutrients for which human requirements are less well defined.

TABLE 12–2

ESTIMATED SAFE AND ADEQUATE DAILY DIETARY INTAKES (ESADDI)

		Vitamins		Trace elements				
	Age (years)	Biotin (μg)	Pantothenic acid (mg)	Copper (mg)	Manganese (mg)	Fluoride (mg)	Chromium (μg)	Molybdenum (μg)
Infants	0.0-0.5	10	2	0.4-0.6	0.3-0.6	0.1-0.5	10-40	15-30
	0.5-1.0	15	3	0.6-0.7	0.6-1.0	0.2-1.0	20-60	20-40
Children	1-3	20	3	0.7-1.0	1.0-1.5	0.5-1.5	20-80	25-50
and	4-6	25	3-4	1.0-1.5	1.5-2.0	1.0-2.5	30-120	30-75
adoles-	7-10	30	4-5	1.0-2.0	2.0-3.0	1.5-2.5	50-200	50-150
cents	11+	30-100	4-7	1.5-2.5	2.0-5.0	1.5-2.5	50-200	75-250
Adults		30-100	4-7	1.5-3.0	2.0-5.0	1.5-4.0	50-200	75-250

Because there is less information on which to base allowances, these figures are not given in the main table of RDA but are provided in the form of ranges of recommended intakes. Since the toxic levels for many trace elements may be only several times higher than usual intakes, the upper levels given in this table should not be exceeded habitually.
From Food and Nutrition Board: Recommended daily allowances, ed 10, Washington, DC, 1989, National Academy Press.

TABLE 12–3

A PATTERN FOR DAILY FOOD CHOICES

Food group	Suggested daily servings	What counts as a serving?
Breads, cereals, and other grain products Whole-grain Enriched	6-11 servings from entire group (Include several servings of whole-grain products daily.)	1 slice of bread ½ hamburger bun or english muffin a small roll, biscuit, or muffin 3 to 4 small or 2 large crackers ½ cup cooked cereal, rice, or pasta 1 ounce of ready-to-eat breakfast cereal
Fruits Citrus, melon, berries Other fruits	2-4 servings from entire group	a whole fruit such as a medium apple, banana, or orange a grapefruit half a melon wedge ¾ cup of juice ½ cup of berries ½ cup cooked or canned fruit ¼ cup dried fruit
Vegetables Dark-green leafy Deep-yellow Dry beans and peas (legumes) Starchy Other vegetables	3-5 servings from entire group (Include all types regularly; use dark-green leafy vegetables and dry beans and peas several times a week.)	½ cup of cooked vegetables ½ cup of chopped raw vegetables 1 cup of leafy raw vegetables, such as lettuce or spinach
Meat, poultry, fish, and alternates (eggs, dry beans and peas, nuts, and seeds)	2-3 servings from entire group	Amounts should total 5 to 7 ounces of cooked lean meat, poultry, or fish a day. Count 1 egg, ½ cup cooked beans, or 2 tablespoons peanut butter as 1 ounce of meat.

TABLE 12–3

A PATTERN FOR DAILY FOOD CHOICES—cont'd

Food group	Suggested daily servings	What counts as a serving?
Milk, cheese, and yogurt	2 servings from entire group (3 servings for women who are pregnant or breastfeeding and for teens; 4 servings for teens who are pregnant or breastfeeding)	1 cup of milk 8 ounces of yogurt 1½ ounces of natural cheese 2 ounces of process cheese
Fats, sweets, and alcoholic beverages	Avoid too many fats and sweets. If you drink alcoholic beverages, do so in moderation.	

From U.S. Department of Agriculture, 1989.

TABLE 12–4

SOURCES AND FUNCTIONS OF MAJOR NUTRIENTS

Nutrient	Major functions in body	Best food sources
Protein 4 calories per g	Forms cell structure; supports growth, maintenance, and repair of tissue; needed for enzymes and hormones	Meat and alternates group Milk and cheese group
Carbohydrate 4 calories per g	Serves as primary energy source; can provide fiber for proper digestive function	Grain and cereal group Fruit and vegetable groups
Fat 9 calories per g	Serves as concentrated energy source; supplies essential fatty acid; carries fat-soluble vitamins	Milk and cheese group: whole milk products Meat and alternates group: meats, nuts, peanut butter Other sources: butter, margarine, oils, salad dressing, fried foods, and many processed foods
Vitamins and minerals	Perform various functions to help regulate body processes; necessary to obtain energy from foods	Fruit and vegetable groups: vitamins A, C Grain and cereal group: B vitamins Milk and cheese group: calcium, phosphorus, riboflavin Meat and alternates group: B vitamins, iron
Water	Transports nutrients; helps regulate body temperature; aids in digesttion	Water Other fluids Fruit and vegetables groups Milk and cheese group: milk

Reproduced with permission. Modified from Stare F, Aronson V, and Barrett S, Your guide to good nutrition, Buffalo, 1991, Prometheus Books.

replacing them with a new system of Reference Daily Intakes (RDI) for protein, 13 vitamins, and 13 minerals, based mainly on the 1989 RDA and ESADDI. The values are still more than most people need.

Food-Group Systems

The fundamental principles of healthy eating are *moderation, variety,* and *balance.* A diet is balanced if it contains appropriate amounts of each nutrient. The Basic Four Food Groups system, devised in 1955 by scientists at Harvard University's Department of Nutrition, grouped foods according to similarity in nutrient content and designated the size and number of servings needed daily from each group to provide nutritional adequacy. This enabled consumers to select foods from groups (fruit and vegetable, grain and cereal, milk and cheese, and meat and alternates) rather than having to calculate the amount of each nutrient in each individual portion of food.[1]

In 1979 the U.S. Department of Agriculture (USDA) modified the Basic Four system and issued a daily food guide that included a fifth group: fats, sweets, and alcoholic beverages. This group, also referred to as "extras," was said to be appropriate for consumption if an individual's basic needs were being met with the nutrient-rich foods from the other four groups.

In 1989 the USDA revised its daily food guide to incorporate the principles of the U.S. Dietary Guidelines and published its recommendations as "A Pattern for Daily Food Choices" (see Table 12-3). This plan designates fruits and vegetables as separate groups and recommends more servings of fruits, vegetables, and grains. (Diets based on this plan get the bulk of their calories from carbohydrates and are limited in fat.) The same principles were then used to construct a "Food Guide Pyramid" that was published in final form in 1992 (see Figure 12-1). The pyramid gives more space to grains, fruits, and vegetables than to meat and dairy groups. This differs from previous charts, which gave equal space to all of the food groups even though fewer portions of meat and dairy products were recommended.

To roughly estimate the adequacy of your diet, use Figure 12-1 to determine the approximate number of calories you consume per day and the recommended number of servings in each food group for your daily calorie level. Then use Figures 12-2 and 12-3 to estimate how many servings you have been consuming and how much fat your daily diet contains.

Junk Food

Many people who use the term "junk food" claim that Americans are filling up on nutritionless foods. The term "junk food" is unpopular with nutrition scientists because all foods contain nutrients. Dr. Helen Guthrie,[9] professor of nutrition at Pennsylvania State University, sums the scientific perspective on this subject as follows:

> As a nutritionist, I contend that the term "junk food" is meaningless and should be discarded. In my opinion, there is no totally worthless food any more than there is a perfect food that meets all our nutritional needs. Obviously, some foods contribute greater amounts of nutrients than others do. But I cannot think of one food that doesn't have some redeeming value under the right circumstances. The problem arises when foods that contribute more calories than nutrients become so important in our diet that foods of higher nutritional value are excluded. It is equally possible to make an unbalanced selection of our most sacred nutritious foods and wind up with a diet overabundant in some nutrients yet deficient in others. In both cases, the result is a junk diet.

Fast Food

The term "fast food" applies to the speed with which a food is prepared and served rather than the nature or content of the food. Sometimes these foods are accused of being junk foods or of having empty calories. The American Council on Science and Health (ACSH)[10] states:

> Contrary to common belief, fast food has substantial nutritional value. Individuals who want to eat healthfully can incorporate fast food meals into a balanced diet by varying their fast food selections, choosing menu items that contribute to nutrient needs, and choosing meals of appropriate calorie content.

ACSH acknowledges that many fast foods are high in sodium, fats, and calories, and recommends eating such foods in moderation. Individuals who eat at fast food outlets can satisfy food group and dietary guidelines by including salad selections and eating a variety of foods in other meals.

U.S. Dietary Guidelines

Although early versions of food group systems provided practical guidelines for avoiding nutrient deficiencies, they did not directly address the preven-

Food Guide Pyramid
A Guide to Daily Food Choices

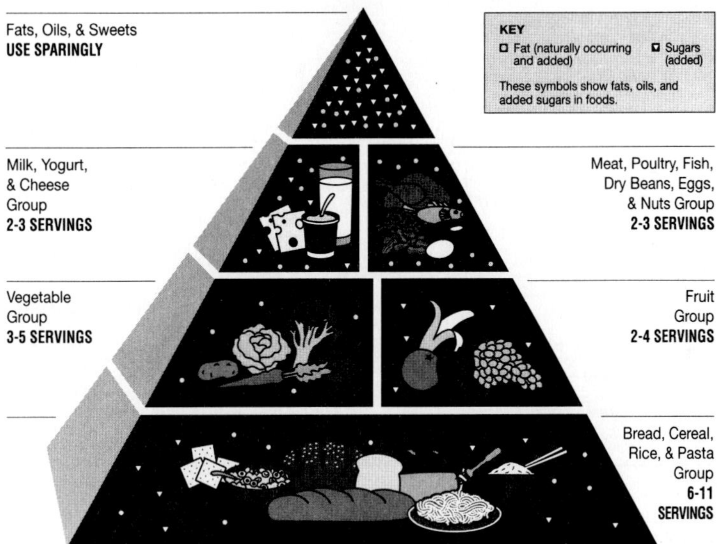

How many servings are right for me?

The Pyramid shows a range of servings for each food group. The number of servings that are right for you depends on how many calories you need, which in turn depends on your age, sex, size, and how active you are. Almost everyone should have at least the lowest number of servings in the ranges.

The following calorie level suggestions are based on recommendations of the National Academy of Sciences and on calorie intakes reported by people in national food consumption surveys.

For adults and teens

1,600 calories is about right for many sedentary women and some older adults.

2,200 calories is about right for most children, teenage girls, active women, and many sedentary men. Women who are pregnant or breastfeeding may need somewhat more.

2,800 calories is about right for teenage boys, many active men, and some very active women.

SAMPLE DIETS FOR A DAY AT 3 CALORIE LEVELS

	Lower about 1,600	Moderate about 2,200	Higher about 2,800
Bread Group Servings	6	9	11
Vegetable Group Servings	3	4	5
Fruit Group Servings	2	3	4
Milk Group Servings	2-3[1]	2-3[1]	2-3[1]
Meat Group[2] (ounces)	5	6	7
Total Fat (grams)	53	73	93

[1]Women who are pregnant or breastfeeding, teenagers, and young adults to age 24 need 3 servings.

FIGURE 12-1. Food guide pyramid.

Bread, Cereal, Rice, and Pasta Group		
Eat 6 to 11 servings daily	**Servings**	**Grams of fat**
▲ Bread, 1 slice	1	1
▲ Hamburger roll, bagel, english muffin, 1	2	2
Tortilla, 1	1	3
▲ Rice, pasta, cooked, ½ cup	1	Trace
Plain crackers, small, 3-4	1	3
Breakfast cereal, 1 oz.	1	*
Pancakes, 4″ diameter, 2	2	3
Croissant, 1 large (2 oz.)	2	12
Doughnut, 1 medium (2 oz.)	2	11
Danish, 1 medium (2 oz.)	2	13
Cake, frosted, 1/16 average	1	13
Cookies, 2 medium	1	4
Pie, fruit, 2-crust, ⅙ 8″ pie	2	19

Fruit Group		
Eat 2 to 4 servings daily		
▲ Whole fruit: medium apple, orange, banana	1	Trace
▲ Fruit, raw or canned, ½ cup	1	Trace
▲ Fruit juice, unsweetened, ¾ cup	1	Trace
Avocado, ¼ whole	1	9

Fats, Oils, and Sweets		
Use sparingly		
Butter, margarine, 1 tsp.	—	4
Mayonnaise, 1 tbsp.	—	11
Salad dressing, 1 tbsp.	—	7
Reduced calorie salad dressing, 1 tbsp.	—	*
Sour cream, 2 tbsp.	—	6
Cream cheese, 1 oz.	—	10
Sugar, jam, jelly, 1 tsp.	—	0
Cola, 12 fl. oz.	—	0
Fruit drink, ade, 12 fl. oz.	—	0
Chocolate bar, 1 oz.	—	9
Sherbet, ½ cup	—	2
Fruit sorbet, ½ cup	—	0
Gelatin dessert, ½ cup	—	0

*CHECK PRODUCT LABEL

▲ Food is one of the lowest fat choices in a food group.

Vegetable Group		
Eat 3 to 5 servings daily	**Servings**	**Grams of fat**
▲ Vegetables, cooked, ½ cup	1	Trace
▲ Vegetables, leafy, raw, 1 cup	1	Trace
▲ Vegetables, nonleafy, raw, chopped, ½ cup	1	Trace
Potatoes, scalloped, ½ cup	1	4
Potato salad, ½ cup	1	8
French fries, 10	1	8

Meat, Poultry, Fish, Dry Beans, Eggs, and Nuts Group		
Eat 5 to 7 oz. daily		
▲ Lean meat, poultry, fish, cooked	3 oz*	6
Ground beef, lean, cooked	3 oz*	16
Chicken, with skin, fried	3 oz*	13
Bologna, 2 slices	1 oz*	16
Egg, 1	1 oz*	5
▲ Dry beans and peas, cooked, ½ cup	1 oz*	Trace
Peanut butter, 2 tbsp.	1 oz*	16
Nuts, ⅓ cup	1 oz*	22

**Ounces of lean meat these items count as*

Milk, Yogurt, and Cheese Group		
Eat 2 to 3 servings daily		
▲ Skim milk, 1 cup	1	Trace
▲ Nonfat yogurt, plain, 8 oz.	1	Trace
Lowfat milk, 2 percent, 1 cup	1	5
Whole milk, 1 cup	1	8
Chocolate milk, 2 percent, 1 cup	1	5
Lowfat yogurt, plain, 8 oz.	1	4
Lowfat yogurt, fruit, 8 oz.	1	3
Natural cheddar cheese, 1½ oz.	1	14
Process cheese, 2 oz.	1	18
Mozzarella, part skim, 1½ oz.	1	7
Ricotta, part skim, ½ cup	1	10
Cottage cheese, 4 percent fat, ½ cup	¼	5
Ice cream, ½ cup	⅓	7
Ice milk, ½ cup	⅓	3
Frozen yogurt, ½ cup	½	2

FIGURE 12-2. Fat content of common foods.

From USDA Human Nutrition Information Service: USDA's food guide pyramid, home and garden bulletin No. 29, Hyattsville, Md, 1992, U.S. Department of Agriculture.

To rate your diet, follow these steps for a few days. Step 3 will indicate whether your diet is generally balanced and adequate in nutrients. Step 4 will evaluate its fat content.

Step 1

Jot down everything you ate yesterday for meals and snacks. | *Grams of fat*

	Grams of fat
______________________________	_____
______________________________	_____
______________________________	_____
______________________________	_____
______________________________	_____
______________________________	_____
______________________________	_____
______________________________	_____
______________________________	_____
______________________________	_____
______________________________	_____
______________________________	_____
______________________________	_____
______________________________	_____
______________________________	_____
______________________________	_____
______________________________	_____
______________________________	_____
______________________________	_____
______________________________	_____
______________________________	_____
______________________________	_____
Total	☐

Step 2

Write down the number of grams of fat in each food you list.

Use the Pyramid Food Choices Chart to get an idea of the number of grams of fat to count for the foods you ate.

Use nutrition labels on packaged foods you ate to find out the grams of fat they contained.

Step 3

Answer these questions:

Did you have the number of servings from the five food groups that are right for you? (See Table 12-1 to determine the number of servings that are right for you.)

	Circle the servings right for you	*Servings you had*
Bread group servings	6 7 8 9 10 11	☐
Vegetable group servings	3 4 5	☐
Fruit group servings	2 3 4	☐
Milk group servings	2 3	☐
Meat group (ounces)	5 6 7	☐

How did you do? Not enough? About right?

Step 4

Add up your grams of fat listed in Step 2. Did you have more fat than the amount right for you? (See Table 12-2.)

	Grams right for you	*Grams you had*
Fat	53 73 93	☐

How did you do? Not enough? About right?

Step 5

Decide what changes you can make for a healthier diet. Start by making small changes, like switching to lowfat salad dressings or adding an extra serving of vegetables. Make additional changes gradually until healthy eating becomes a habit.

FIGURE 12-3. How to rate your diet.

Modified from USDA Human Nutrition Information Service: USDA's food guide pyramid, home and garden bulletin No. 29, Hyattsville, Md, 1992, U.S. Department of Agriculture.

tion of other diet-related health problems. To deal with this matter, the U.S. Department of Agriculture and the Department of Health and Human Services[11] have published *Dietary Guidelines for Americans* for those who want to decrease their chances of developing certain chronic diseases. The guidelines are especially important for people who have risk factors for heart disease (see Chapter 16).

The 1989 report stresses that food alone cannot make people healthy. Smoking, alcohol abuse, other life-style factors and heredity are also important. The American food supply is varied, plentiful, and safe to eat. But many Americans have diets with too many calories, too much fat (especially saturated fat), cholesterol and sodium, and not enough complex carbohydrates and fiber. The guidelines are:

1. *Eat a variety of food.* To ensure variety and a well-balanced diet, choose foods each day from five major food groups: vegetables (3-5 servings); fruits (2-4 servings); breads, cereals, rice, and pasta (6-11 servings); milk, yogurt, and cheese (2-3 servings); and meat, poultry, fish, eggs, and dry beans and peas (2-3 servings). Vitamin or mineral supplements at or below the RDA are safe, but are rarely needed except by women who are menstruating, pregnant, or breast feeding. Many women and adolescent girls need to eat more calcium; children, teenage girls, and women of childbearing age should take care to consume enough iron-rich foods.
2. *Maintain a healthy weight.* Obesity is associated with many serious illnesses. Being too thin is linked to osteoporosis in women and early death in both men and women. For those who are overweight the recommended loss of ½ to 1 pound per week should be accomplished by increasing physical activity and eating less fatty foods, more fruits, vegetables and cereals, less sugar and sweets, and little or no alcohol.
3. *Choose a diet low in fat, saturated fat, and cholesterol.* This advice is tied to the goal of maintaining blood cholesterol level below 200 mg/dl. It recommends a fat intake of 30% or less of calories, with less than 10% of the calories as saturated fat. Have your blood-cholesterol level checked. If it is within a desirable range, help keep it that way with a diet low in saturated fat and cholesterol. If it is high, follow the doctor's advice about diet and medication.
4. *Choose a diet with plenty of vegetables, fruits, and grain products.* Adults should eat at least three servings of vegetables and two servings of fruit daily. It also recommends at least six servings of grain products, with an emphasis on whole grains. Because foods differ in the kinds of fiber they contain, it is best to include a variety of fiber-rich foods. Fiber should be obtained from foods, not supplements.
5. *Use sugars only in moderation.* The major health concern with excess sugar consumption is tooth decay. The risk does not depend simply on the amount of sugar consumed but on the frequency of consumption of sugars and starches and how long they remain in contact with the teeth. Frequent between-meal snacks may be more harmful to teeth than having them at meals. Teeth should be brushed with a fluoride toothpaste and flossed regularly. Fluoridated water or another fluoride source is especially important for children while their teeth are forming.
6. *Use salt and sodium in moderation.* Since high sodium intake can be a factor in high blood pressure, sodium intake should be moderated. This can be accomplished by learning to enjoy the flavors of unsalted foods, adding little or no salt during cooking or at the table, flavoring foods with herbs, spices, or lemon juice, and limiting intake of foods that are obviously salty or contain significant amounts of hidden salt. A blood pressure check is also recommended.
7. *If you drink alcoholic beverages, do so in moderation.* Alcoholic beverages supply calories but few or no nutrients. Drinking them has no proven health benefit, is linked with many health problems, is the cause of many accidents, and can lead to addiction. Since birth defects have been attributed to drinking during pregnancy, women who are pregnant or trying to conceive are advised to abstain completely from alcohol. People planning to drive a car or engage in another activity that requires attention or skill are also advised to abstain.

Single copies of *Nutrition and Your Health: Dietary Guidelines for Americans* (HG 232) are available free from the Consumer Information Center, Department 514-X, Pueblo, CO 81009. Detailed suggestions for implementing the guidelines are included in *Dietary Guidelines and Your Diet,* publication 001-000-04467-2, 1986, available for $4.50 from the Superintendent of Documents, U.S. Government Printing Office, Washington, DC 20402. The National Nutritional Monitoring and Related Research Act of 1990 calls for the report to be updated every 5 years.

Nine Dietary Guidelines

In 1992 the National Academy of Sciences[12] published nine guidelines, some of which are more quantitative than their counterparts in the U.S. Dietary Guidelines:

1. Reduce total fat intake to 30% or less of total calorie consumption. Reduce saturated fatty acid intake to less than 10% of the calories. Reduce cholesterol intake to less than 300 mg daily.
2. Eat five or more servings of a combination of vegetables and fruits daily, especially green and yellow vegetables and citrus fruits. Also, increase the intake of starches and other complex carbohydrates by eating six or more daily servings of a combination of breads, cereals, and legumes.
3. Eat a reasonable amount of protein, maintaining the protein consumption at moderate levels.
4. Balance the amount of food eaten with the amount of exercise to maintain appropriate body weight.
5. It is not recommended to drink alcohol. If one drinks alcoholic beverages, limit the amount consumed per day to no more than two cans of beer, two small glasses of wine, or two average cocktails. Pregnant women should avoid alcoholic beverages.
6. Limit the amount of salt (sodium chloride) intake to 6 g (slightly more than 1 tsp of salt) per day or less. Limit the use of salt in cooking and avoid adding it to food at the table. Salty foods (including highly processed salty foods, salt-preserved foods, and salt-pickled foods) should be eaten sparingly, if at all.
7. Maintain adequate calcium intake.
8. Avoid taking dietary supplements in excess of the RDA in any 1 day.
9. Maintain an optimal level of fluoride in your diet and particularly in the diets of your children when their baby and adult teeth are forming.

Dietary Guidelines for Infants

Consistent with the fact that children below the age of 2 are not "little adults," Gerber Products Company has published *Dietary Guidelines for Infants,* modeled after HHS/USDA's 1985 *Dietary Guidelines for Americans.* Gerber's guidelines are based on published statements by the American Academy of Pediatrics' Committee on Nutrition and were prepared with the help of seven nutrition experts. The guidelines are:

1. *Build to a variety of foods.* Unlike adults, infants do not require a variety of foods to secure nutrition during the first 6 months or so of life. Human milk alone provides the vitamins, minerals, carbohydrates, fats, and proteins needed for normal growth and development during early infancy. Except for fluoride, vitamin D (in the absence of adequate exposure to sunlight), and possibly vitamin K, supplements to human milk are not required during this period. Infant formula is recommended as the best alternative to human milk if breast-feeding is not used or is stopped early. Most babies are ready to start supplemental foods around 4 to 6 months of age. Single-grain cereal is often the first food added after breast milk or formula. Other single-ingredient foods can be added gradually until the baby is eating a variety of foods. New foods should be added one at a time, at intervals of a few days. This allows the baby to get used to the flavor of the food and enables parents to see whether a food might not agree with the baby.
2. *Listen to your baby's appetite to avoid overfeeding or underfeeding.* Although healthy infants can vary considerably from one another in their caloric intake, appetite is likely to be the most efficient way to determine what an infant needs. Most infants instinctively know how much food they need and will not undereat or overeat unless pressured. Babies should be fed when they are hungry but should not be forced to finish the last few ounces of formula or food. The baby's health advisor can chart growth and development to be sure that they are progressing normally.
3. *Don't restrict fat and cholesterol too much.* Although low-fat and low-cholesterol diets are widely recommended for adults, they are not appropriate for infants under the age of 2. Nutritional requirements are higher during infancy than during any other period. At the same time, stomach capacity is limited, so food sources must provide sufficient calories and nutrients in a small vol-

ume. Infants require fat in their diet for normal growth and development.

4. *Don't overdo high-fiber foods.* Infants and small toddlers eating a well-rounded diet probably get enough fiber for their needs. A diet high in fiber may be too low in calories and may interfere with absorption of iron, calcium, magnesium, and zinc. There is no proven benefit from increasing the fiber intake of young children above that provided by a healthy diet.
5. *Sugar is OK, but in moderation.* Sugar, which exists in several forms, is a source of calories and makes some foods taste better. Breast milk, the ideal food for infants, contains lactose, which is similar to table sugar. Other foods in a balanced diet may contain moderate amounts of sugar, but excessive amounts of such foods can crowd out more nutritious foods. Sugar has not been shown to cause hyperactivity, diabetes, obesity, or heart disease. It is, however, linked to tooth decay. Dental care, proper bottle feeding, and the use of fluoride can help control and prevent tooth decay. Bottles of milk or juice should not be used as pacifiers to put a baby to sleep because prolonged contact with the natural sugars in these liquids can cause tooth decay. Artificial sweeteners are not recommended for infants.
6. *Sodium is OK, but in moderation.* Although the amount of sodium in the diet of a small percentage of adults is related to high blood pressure, the amount of sodium in an infant's diet has not been shown to cause high blood pressure in later life. Even though healthy infants can tolerate a range of sodium intakes without ill effects, moderation in sodium intake is urged.
7. *Babies need more iron, pound for pound, than adults.* Infants are born with a stored supply of iron that lasts for the first 4 to 6 months of life. Iron is more likely than any other nutrient to be lacking in the infant's diet. For this reason special efforts should be made to provide infants with iron during the first 2 years. In addition to breast milk the best sources are iron-fortified formula and iron-fortified infant cereal.

According to officials at Gerber, their guidelines were prompted by a telephone survey showing that many parents were inappropriately responding to adult nutritional guidelines by giving their babies skim milk instead of whole milk. In addition, cases have been reported of older children who failed to grow properly because of overzealous, medically unsupervised dietary treatment for high cholesterol levels.

Two versions of the Gerber guidelines have been published, a 20-page booklet for consumers and a 36-page booklet for health professionals. Either can be obtained free of charge by calling Gerber's consumer information center at 1-800-4-GERBER.

Vegetarianism

Vegetarians are individuals who restrict or eliminate foods of animal origin (meat, poultry, fish, eggs, milk) from their diet. The main reasons people choose the vegetarian alternative are: (1) they think it is healthier, (2) they think it is more "natural," (3) they think it is more "ecologic" because it takes less energy to produce vegetarian food than meat, and (4) religious or moral dictates. Dingott and Dwyer[13] classify vegetarians into four categories:

Vegan or strict vegetarians. Eat no animal products at all

Lactovegetarians. Eat milk and cheese products in addition to vegetables. This form of vegetarianism is common among Seventh-day Adventists

Lacto-ovo-vegetarians. Eat no meat, poultry, or fish, but do eat eggs and milk products

Semivegetarians. Eat no red meat, but do include small amounts of poultry or fish in their diet

The USDA estimates that some 10 million Americans, about 5% of our population, now eliminate meat from their diets. Americans have been cutting down on meat consumption during the past several years.

Possible Benefits of Vegetarianism

Dingott and Dwyer[13] state that vegetarianism based on sound nutrition principles can be a healthful choice, but neither vegetarians or omnivores have a monopoly on healthful eating. Similar health benefits can be gained from both well-selected omnivorous and vegetarian diets. The following are possible advantages of a vegetarian diet:

1. Vegetarians, especially those who abstain from all animal foods, generally have lower body weight for their height than nonvegetarians do.
2. Vegetarians have less constipation than meat-eaters.
3. Vegetarianism, as practiced by Seventh-day Adventists, is associated with lower death rates from certain cancers (although abstention from tobacco and alcohol may be responsible for this).

PERSONAL GLIMPSE

Did You Know?

Diet has always had a vital influence on health. Until as recently as the 1940s, diseases such as rickets, pellagra, scurvy, beriberi, xerophthalmia and goiter (caused by lack of adequate dietary vitamin D, niacin, vitamin C, thiamine, vitamin A, and iodine, respectively) were prevalent in this country and throughout the world. Today, thanks to an abundant food supply, fortification of some foods with critical trace nutrients, and better methods for determining and improving the nutrient content of foods, such "deficiency" diseases have been virtually eliminated in developing countries. . . .

As the diseases of nutritional deficiency have diminished, they have been replaced by diseases of dietary excess and imbalance—problems that now rank among the leading causes of death, touch the lives of most Americans, and generate substantial health care costs. . . .

In addition to five of these causes that scientific studies have associated with diet (coronary heart disease, some types of cancer, stroke, diabetes mellitus, and atherosclerosis), another three—cirrhosis of the liver, accidents, and suicides—have been associated with excessive alcohol intake. . . . Dietary excesses or imbalance also contribute to other problems such as high blood pressure, obesity, dental diseases, osteoporosis, and gastrointestinal diseases.

C. Everett Koop, M.D.[14]
Surgeon General
U.S. Public Health Service

4. Vegetarianism may be associated with a lower incidence of atherosclerotic heart disease and high blood pressure. Body weight as well as nondietary factors may contribute to this situation.

Possible Risks of Vegetarianism

It is possible to obtain all the nutrients required for proper growth and health while adhering to a vegetarian diet. However, careful attention must be paid to food selection to ensure that the diet contains an adequate supply of protein, iron, and vitamin B_{12}.

Foods of both animal and vegetable origin provide protein. However, proteins vary in nutritional quality because they differ in the kinds and amounts of amino acids they contain. Proteins from meat, fish, poultry, milk, and eggs rate the highest because they supply all of the essential amino acids in about the same proportions as those needed by the body. The proteins from some legumes (particularly soybeans and chickpeas) are close in nutritional quality to those from animal sources. Combining a small amount of animal protein with plant foods helps to improve the overall protein quality of the diet. High-quality protein can also be obtained by combining plant foods that are complementary in their amino acids; the amino acids insufficient in one food are provided by a complementary food with an adequate amount.

Unless they choose a proper balance of foods, strict vegetarians are at risk for several deficiencies, especially vitamin B_{12}. The other nutrients at risk are riboflavin, calcium, iron, and the essential amino acids lysine and methionine. Vegetarian children not exposed to sunlight are at risk for vitamin D deficiency. Zinc deficiency can occur in vegans because phytic acid in whole grains binds zinc, and there is little zinc in fruits and vegetables. Since B_{12} is present only in animal foods and a limited number of specially fortified foods, vegans should probably take B_{12} supplements prescribed by a physician.

Strict vegetarianism is not desirable for children under the age of 5 because it is difficult for vegans to meet children's high requirements for protein and some other nutrients. Growing adolescents may have difficulty getting adequate caloric and nutrient intake from a vegan diet. Vegetarianism is not a good idea for pregnant or lactating women. Excellent summaries of the special problems of vegetarian eating have been published by the Food and Nutrition Board[15] and the American Academy of Pediatrics,[16] and the American Dietetic Association.[17]

What Vegetarians Should Eat

Stare, Aronson, and Barrett[1] advise vegetarians to select a variety of items daily from each of the following groups:

Protein group: Dried beans and peas, lentils, nuts, and eggs.

Grain and cereal group: Whole grain and enriched breads, cereals, pastas, crackers, and other grain products.

Fruit and vegetable group: All fruits and vegetables, including a citrus fruit daily and a leafy green or bright yellow vegetable every other day.

Milk and milk products group: Milk, yogurt, cheese, and other foods made with milk. This group is especially important for infants, children, and pregnant and nursing women because milk is the single best dietary source of calcium.

Minerals of Special Concern

Certain minerals should be of special concern to consumers. Iron (Chapter 20), fluoride (Chapter 8), and calcium are insufficient in the diets of some segments of the population. Sodium is being consumed in excessive amounts by many persons.

Calcium

Calcium, along with fluoride and vitamin D, is essential for the proper formation and maintenance of bones and teeth. Osteoporosis (thinning of the bones) is a common disease in the aged, especially in women (see Chapter 22). Although hormonal problems may be more important than diet in the development of osteoporosis, the significance of maintaining adequate dietary calcium, fluoride, and vitamin D should not be overlooked.[1]

Milk is the most common source of calcium, but cheese, yogurt, and other foods made with milk also provide significant amounts. If eaten with the bones, sardines and canned salmon are rich in calcium. Dark green leafy vegetables such as spinach and broccoli contain significant amounts of calcium in a less absorbable form. It is difficult to ingest adequate amounts of absorbable calcium if dairy products are eliminated from the diet. Women should discuss with their physician how to ensure adequate intake of calcium through intake of dairy products and/or the use of supplement tablets.

Sodium

The relationship of sodium intake to high blood pressure (hypertension) is of concern because hypertension is an important risk factor in coronary heart disease and stroke. However, a causal relationship has not been proven. Current data indicate that approximately 80% of the population do not appear to be genetically predisposed to hypertension. One third of the remaining 20% appear to be sensitive to sodium; they may be exposed to a higher risk if they consume excess amounts of sodium. Thus, while dietary sodium may not cause hypertension, treatment of people with medically diagnosed hypertension will include sodium restriction for those who are salt-sensitive (this subject is discussed further in Chapter 16).

The average American consumes approximately 10 to 12 g (2 to 2½ teaspoons) of salt per day, of which 3 g occur naturally in foods, 4 to 6 g come from salt-containing ingredients added during food processing, and 3 to 4 g of discretionary intake from the salt shaker. Since salt is about 40% sodium, this amounts to 4 to 5 g of sodium daily. The National Research Council and various government agencies have concluded that reducing salt intake to 3 g per day (which would require eliminating salt during cooking and at the table) would not be harmful. Most people, however, are unwilling to do this.

Significant amounts of sodium are contained in: preservatives, flavor enhancers, cured and processed meats, salted snacks, pickled and canned foods, frozen seasoned convenience foods, baked goods made with baking soda, and certain medicines such as antacids and laxatives. Consumers who wish to limit their salt intake need to read food labels carefully because sodium is contained in the following: disodium phosphate, garlic salt, calcium disodium, monosodium glutamate, trisodium citrate, celery salt, sea salt, salt pork, brine, onion salt, and self-rising flour.[18]

Nutrition Labeling

The U.S. Department of Agriculture regulates the labeling of meat and poultry products. The FDA regulates the labeling of almost all other foods. The FDA's food labeling regulations were established in 1973. Except for fresh seafood, fruits and vegetables, food labels must contain the following information if a nutrient has been added or a nutrition claim is made about the food: (1) serving size, (2) servings per container, (3) calorie content, (4) protein content, (5) carbohydrate content, (6) fat content, (7) sodium content, and (8) percentage of U.S. RDAs of protein, vitamin A, vitamin C, thiamine, riboflavin, niacin, calcium, and iron. An optional listing can also include: the fat content by degree of saturation; the amount of cholesterol; vitamins D, E, and B_6, folic acid, vitamin B_{12}; minerals phosphorus, iodine, magnesium, zinc, copper, biotin, and pantothenic acid.

On most packaged foods, ingredients also have

to be listed, beginning with the ingredient used in the largest amount by weight, followed by others in descending order. However, actual amounts do not have to be stated. Serving size is determined by each manufacturer and often does not correspond to what people typically consume. Fewer details are required on the labels of meat and poultry products.

The FDA and USDA have established "standards of identity" for about 300 foods whose ingredients are fixed by law. These include canned fruit cocktail, peanut butter, margarine, ice cream, catsup, and spaghetti sauce with meat. Ingredient lists are required on some standardized foods but not others.

In the mid-1980s, controversy erupted about whether food labels should be permitted to make health claims, such as "helps prevent cancer" or "helps lower cholesterol." As consumers became more attentive to food choices, there also was considerable public pressure for clearer and more complete nutrition information.[19] During 1990, the FDA began issuing regulations that addressed these problems. Soon afterward, passage of the *Nutrition Labeling and Education Act* strengthened the FDA's authority and requires new rules that take effect by May 8, 1993.

In November 1991 the FDA[21] and USDA[22] proposed additional regulations that include the following:

1. Labeling would be extended to almost all packaged foods.
2. Retailers were urged to voluntarily inform customers about the nutrient content of commonly purchased raw fruits, vegetables, and fish (20 foods in each category). By May 1993, if fewer than 60% of stores are displaying the information, regulations will be written to make the display mandatory.
3. U.S. RDAs would be replaced with U.S. RDIs. These would enable consumers to compare the protein, vitamin, and mineral content of foods, based on the Recommended Dietary Allowances.
4. Daily Reference Values (DRVs) would be set up to provide a similar basis to compare total fat, saturated and unsaturated fat, cholesterol, carbohydrates, dietary fiber, sodium, and potassium. These food components are important to health, but were not addressed by the RDA report.
5. Labels must declare the total number of calories and the number of calories derived from fat; the total amount of fat, saturated fat, and cholesterol; total carbohydrates, complex carbohydrates, and sugars; dietary fiber; protein; sodium; vitamins A and C; calcium; and iron.
6. Labeling of vitamin and mineral dietary supplements, not in the form of ordinary food, would have to identify the quantity and the percentage of RDI for all vitamins, minerals, and other food components present in significant amounts.
7. Serving and portion sizes for 131 food categories, 23 meat categories, and 22 poultry categories would be based on the amount of food customarily consumed per eating occasion by an average person over the age of 4. The units of measurement must appear in common household and metric measurements, such as 1 cup (240 mm).
8. The terms *free, low, light, reduced, less, high, fresh,* and *source of,* as well as various synonyms, have to conform to specific definitions (Table 12-5).[21]
9. Terms related to fat and cholesterol content would be defined (Table 12-5).
10. Health claims would be permitted only if supported by valid and substantial scientific information. Claims would be permitted regarding (1) sodium and high blood pressure, (2) calcium and osteoporosis, (3) dietary fats and cancer, or (4) dietary fats and heart disease. Claims would not be permitted regarding: (1) zinc and immune functions, (2) antioxidant vitamins and cancer, (3) fish oils and heart disease, or (4) folic acid and neural tube defects. The FDA is still studying the possibility of permitting claims relating fiber to cardiovascular disease and cancer. In 1992 the USDA announced a 1-year postponement of the implementation date for the rules pertaining to meat and poultry products.

Figure 12-4 shows examples of nutrition labels under the 1973 rules. Figure 12-5 illustrates the information required under the proposed rules. The FDA is testing various formats and is expected to choose one in the near future.

Macronutrient Percentages

Labels of many food products list the number of grams of protein, carbohydrate, and fat they contain. Proteins and carbohydrates contain 4 calories per gram, while fat contains 9 calories per gram.

TABLE 12–5

PROPOSED TERMS FOR FOODS LABELS

Term	Definition proposed by FDA on November 26, 1991[20]
Free	An amount that is nutritionally trivial and unlikely to have a physiologic consequence
Calorie free	Fewer than 5 calories per serving
Sugar free	Less than 0.5 g per serving
Sodium free or salt free	Less than 5 mg per serving. A claim made for a food normally free of or low in a nutrient must indicate that the situation exists for all similar foods. (for example: "spinach: a low-sodium food")
Low	Low enough to allow frequent consumption without exceeding the dietary guidelines
Low sodium	Less than 140 mg per serving and per 100 g of food (a little less than half a cup)
Very low sodium	Less than 35 mg per serving and per 100 g of food
Low calorie	Less than 40 mg per serving and per 100 g of food
Reduced sodium*	Contains no more than half the sodium of the comparison food
Reduced calories*	Contains ⅓ fewer calories than the referenced food
Light (or lite)	Contains ⅓ fewer calories than the referenced food, with a minimum reduction of more than 40 calories per reference amount and serving size. Products deriving more than half their calories from fat must have their fat content reduced by 50% or more with a minimum reduction of more than 3 g per serving. Other use of "light" must specify if it refers to look, taste or odor (for example, "Light in color")
Less*	Contains at least 25% less of a nutrient than the referenced food
More	Contains at least 10% more of a desirable nutrient than does a comparable food
High	Contains 20% or more of the RDA or DRV
Source of	Contains 10% to 19% of the RDI or DRV
Fat free	Less than 0.5 g of fat per reference amount and serving size, and no added ingredient that is a fat or oil
Low fat	3 g or less of fat per reference amount, per serving size and per 100 g of product
(Percent) fat free	Only for foods that meet the FDA definition of low fat
Reduced fat*	Reduced fat content by 50% or more, with a minimum reduction of more than 3 g per reference amount and per serving size
Low in saturated fat	1 gram or less per serving, with not more than 15% of calories from saturated fat
Reduced saturated fat*	No more than 50% of the saturated fat of the reference food. Foods with at least 25% reduction may use the term "less." When these terms are used, the label must indicate the percentage reduction and the amount of saturated fat in the reference food. The reduction must be at least 1 gram
Cholesterol free	Less than 2 mg of cholesterol and 2 g or less of saturated fat per serving
Low in cholesterol	20 mg or less per serving and per 100 g of food, and 2 g or less of saturated fat per serving

Table 12–5

Proposed Terms for Foods Labels—cont'd

Term	Definition proposed by FDA on November 26, 1991[20]
Reduced cholesterol*	50% or less of cholesterol per serving than its comparison food. The label of a food containing more than 11.5 g of total fat per serving or per 100 g of the food must disclose that fact
Less fat*	At least 25% less fat, with a minimum reduction of more than 3 g per reference amount and per serving size
Fresh	Can only be linked to raw food, food that has not been frozen, processed, or preserved
Freshly	May be used with a verb such as "prepared," "baked" or "roasted" if the food is recently made and has not been frozen, heat-processed, or preserved
Lean	Meat or poultry product with less than 10.5 g of fat, less than 3.5 g of saturated fat, and less than 94.5 mg cholesterol per 100 g
Extra lean	Meat or poultry product with less than 4.9 g of fat, less than 1.8 g of saturated fat and less than 94.5 mg cholesterol per 100 g

From Nutrition Forum Newsletter, Jan/Feb 1992, © 1992 Stephen Barrett, M.D.

*An alternative proposal for the terms "reduced," "less," or "fewer" was drafted in 1992. Under this proposal, the terms would be equivalent and permissible provided they indicate the identity of the comparison food and the percentage by which the nutrient has been reduced. Foods claimed to contain fewer calories must contain at least 40 fewer calories per serving than the referenced food.

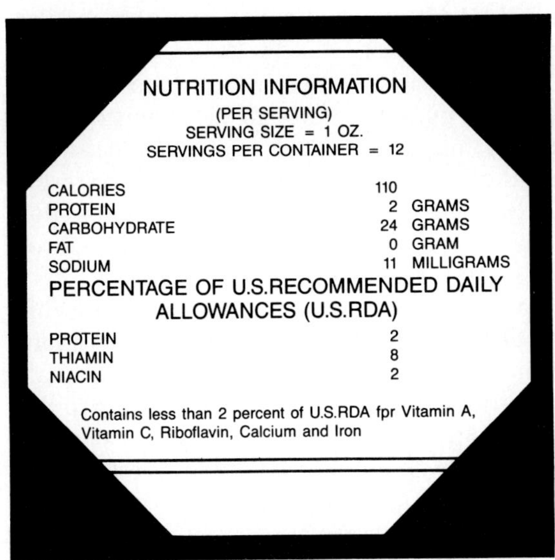

NUTRITION INFORMATION
(PER SERVING)
SERVING SIZE = 1 OZ.
SERVINGS PER CONTAINER = 12
CALORIES 110
PROTEIN 2 GRAMS
CARBOHYDRATE 24 GRAMS
FAT 0 GRAM
SODIUM 11 MILLIGRAMS
PERCENTAGE OF U.S.RECOMMENDED DAILY ALLOWANCES (U.S.RDA)
PROTEIN 2
THIAMIN 8
NIACIN 2
Contains less than 2 percent of U.S.RDA fpr Vitamin A, Vitamin C, Riboflavin, Calcium and Iron

Minimum information now required on nutrition labels

NUTRITION INFORMATION
(PER SERVING)
SERVING SIZE = 8 OZ.
SERVINGS PER CONTAINER = 1

CALORIES 560
PROTEIN 23 GM
CARBOHYDRATE 43 GM
FAT (PERCENT OF CALORIES 53%) 33 GM
POLYUNSATURATED* 2 GM
SATURATED 9 GM
CHOLESTEROL* (20 MG/100 GM) 40 GM
SODIUM (365 MG/100 GM) 830 GM

PERCENTAGE OF U.S.RECOMMENDED DAILY ALLOWANCES (U.S. RDA)

PROTEIN 35
VITAMIN A 35
VITAMIN C (ASCORBIC ACID) 10
THIAMIN (VITAMIN B) 15
RIBOFLAVIN 15
NIACIN 25
CALCIUM 2
IRON 25

*Information on fat and cholesterol content is provided for individuals who, on the advice of a physician, are modifying their total dietary intake of fat and cholesterol.

Optional listings for cholesterol and fat are permissible under current rules

Figure 12-4. Current food label formats.

NUTRITION INFORMATION PER SERVING
Serving Size: 4 ounces condensed
1 cup (244g) as prepared
Servings per Container: 2¾
Calories 170
Calories from fat 30

	AMOUNT	DAILY VALUE (DV)†
Fat	**3 g***	75 g or less
Saturated fat	2 g	25 g or less
Cholesterol	**5 mg***	300 mg or less
Sodium	910 mg	2,400 mg or less
Carbohydrates	27 g	325 g or more
Fiber	**5 g****	25 g
Protein	9 g	

	PERCENT OF DAILY VALUE
Vitamin A	‡
Vitamin C	2
Calcium	4
Iron	15

†As part of a 2,350 calorie diet
‡Contains less than 2 percent of the DV of this nutrient
Meets FDA definitions and is consistent with dietary recommendations as:
*Low or reduced in amount per serving
**High in amount per serving
INGREDIENTS:

FIGURE 12-5. Proposed food label format. Testing by the FDA found that this format, based on the proposed rules, was popular with consumers.

The percentage of calories from each of these macronutrients is calculated with the following formulas:

$$\% \text{ carbohydrate} = \frac{\text{grams of carbohydrate} \times 4}{\text{total calories per serving}} \times 100$$

$$\% \text{ protein} = \frac{\text{grams of protein} \times 4}{\text{total calories per serving}} \times 100$$

$$\% \text{ fat} = \frac{\text{grams of fat} \times 9}{\text{total calories per serving}} \times 100$$

Thus a serving of food that contains 120 calories and 4 g of fat would have a fat content of 30% [(4 × 9) ÷ 120] × 100. The calculation of overall dietary fat content is discussed in Chapter 16.

RELIABLE INFORMATION SOURCES

The dissemination of nutrition advice is poorly regulated by law. For this reason, consumers seeking nutrition advice should be very careful in selecting their advisers. Reliable information can be obtained from nutrition or medical professionals, professional organizations, and publications identified in the remainder of this chapter and in the Appendix. Unreliable sources are identified in Chapter 13.

One's personal physician is probably the most convenient person from whom to obtain advice on nutrition. Medical doctors are often criticized for not knowing enough about nutrition. The American Council on Science and Health disagrees:

> Not all physicians are nutrition experts, just as not all are specialists in cardiology or community medicine. However, the practicing physician has sufficient knowledge of the biochemical and physiological principles of nutrition, and has access to many resources which can aid in answering patients' questions. Most people who read about a "new nutritional discovery" don't have enough knowledge to figure out whether it's a real scientific development or a piece of quack nonsense. Physicians do have the expertise to make this kind of judgment and to evaluate the technical research on which popular reports are based. If you have a question that your doctor can't answer, he or she can refer you to someone who can.[23]

Nutrition Professionals

Nutrition courses offered at accredited universities are based on scientific principles and taught by qualified instructors. A bachelor's degree requires 4 years of full-time study, which qualifies a graduate for entry-level positions in dietetics or food service, often in a hospital. A master's degree in nutrition, which can widen career opportunities, requires 2 more years of full-time study beyond the undergraduate level.

People who wish to become nutrition researchers usually pursue a Ph.D. in biochemistry. This requires a minimum of 2 years of additional study plus a thesis based on original laboratory research. Those wishing to concentrate on teaching or educational research usually seek a degree of Ph.D. or Ed.D. in nutrition education.

In addition to an academic degree, most legitimate nutritionists seek professional certification. Two professional associations are restricted to qualified nutrition scientists. Active membership in the American Institute of Nutrition (AIN) is open to those who have published meritorious research on some aspect of nutrition, who are presently working in the field, and who are sponsored by two AIN members. Nominees are considered by a membership committee, a council of officers, and the membership. The clinical arm of AIN is the American Society for Clinical Nutrition (ASCN), which has similar requirements for membership but specifies clinical research involvement. All ASCN members are also members of AIN, and about 70% of them are physicians. Promoters of nutrition quackery rarely gain admission to these organizations.

Nutritionists at the doctoral level may also seek certification by the American Board of Nutrition as specialists in clinical nutrition (M.D. only) or human nutritional sciences (M.D. and Ph.D.). There are about 400 board-certified nutrition specialists in the United States. Certified nutritionists usually work in medical schools and hospitals, where they conduct clinical research and offer consultation to primary care physicians.

Registered dietitians (R.D.s) are specially trained to translate nutrition research into appropriate diets. Compared to physicians, they usually know less about basic biochemistry, physiology, and metabolism, but more about the nutrient content of specific foods. The R.D. certification is usually sought by bachelor- and master-level nutrition graduates. To qualify, they must have additional professional experience and pass a written test concerning all aspects of nutrition and food service management. They must also participate regularly in continuing education programs approved by the American Dietetic Association.

Most of the 48,000 active R.D.s in the United States work in hospitals. Typically, they counsel patients and conduct classes for pregnant women, patients with heart and kidney disease, diabetics, and other persons with special dietary needs. Dietitians are also employed by community agencies such as geriatric, day care, and drug and alcohol abuse centers. Some dietitians do research. Others engage in private practice where they counsel physician-referred clients.

Consumer Tip

Organizations that evaluate and publish accurate information about nutrition will usually respond to inquiries from individual consumers. The following organizations are considered reliable:

- American Council on Science and Health
- American Dietetic Association
- American Institute of Nutrition
- American Society for Clinical Nutrition
- American Medical Association Department of Personal Health
- Institute of Food Technologists
- National Center for Nutrition and Dietetics
- National Council Against Health Fraud, Inc.
- International Life Sciences Institute/Nutrition Foundation
- U.S. Department of Agriculture Food and Nutrition Information Center
- U.S. Food and Drug Administration

It's Your Decision

1. You plan to obtain a quick dinner at a fast food outlet. How can you assure a nutritious food intake?
2. You have heard that many Americans are not eating properly. How can you check whether your diet contains adequate amounts of all the nutrients you need? Should you take a vitamin/mineral supplement just to be on the safe side? If you are not sure what to do, how can you locate a professional person to help you?

Other Sources

The National Institute for Dental Research, the National Institute of Allergy and Infectious Diseases, the National Cancer Institute, and the National Institute of Arthritis, Metabolism and Digestive and Kidney Diseases all have educational material about nutrition as it applies to their areas of interest. The addresses of these organizations are listed in the Appendix of this book.

State and local dietetic associations are usually eager to be helpful. Dial-A-Dietitian services to answer telephone inquiries are available in a number of cities. Other local sources include: accredited colleges and medical schools, USDA Extension Services of land-grant universities, home economists at USDA county cooperative services (for information on food preparation), state health departments, some local health departments, and state or county medical societies. Available local sources will be listed in the telephone directory.

The National Center for Nutrition and Dietetics, cosponsored by the American Dietetic Association, operates a consumer hotline that permits callers to speak with a registered dietitian, listen to recorded nutrition messages, or leave their name and address for a free brochure. The American Dental Association and several other organizations listed in the Appendix provide information about nutrition as it applies to their areas of special interest.

Table 3-3 lists newsletters and magazines that provide reliable nutrition information. Some cover nutrition only, while others cover health topics with occasional articles on nutrition.

Summary

The basic principles of nutrition are moderation, variety, and balance. These can be achieved by daily selection of appropriate numbers of moderate-sized portions from each of the food groups. Food group systems enable consumers to select foods from groups rather than having to calculate the amount of each nutrient in each individual portion of food. The U.S. Dietary Guidelines provide additional advice about moderating dietary fat (to help prevent heart disease) and consuming adequate amounts of fiber (to help prevent colon cancer). Vitamin deficiencies are rare in the United States, but many women do not consume enough iron or calcium in their diet. Vegetarian diets can be a healthful alternative to those that include meat, but must be constructed carefully to avoid nutrient deficiencies. Many qualified professionals can provide consumers with reliable information and advice about diet and nutrition. New labeling regulations will enable consumers to ascertain the nutrient contents of most foods.

Discussion Questions

1. What are the six major food components?
2. What are the main functions and food sources of proteins, fats, and carbohydrates?
3. Why is glucose called "the universal sugar"?
4. How is food energy stored and released by the body?
5. What is dietary fiber? What are its possible health benefits?
6. What are vitamins? Why are they needed only in tiny amounts?
7. How common are vitamin-deficiency diseases in the United States?
8. Which minerals should be of special concern to consumers?
9. What are Recommended Dietary Allowances (RDAs)?
10. What are the U.S. Dietary Guidelines?
11. What are the similarities and differences between the dietary guidelines for adults and infants?
12. What are food group systems? How do they work?
13. Why do nutrition scientists dislike the term "junk food"?
14. What are fast foods? How may they be integrated prudently into one's diet?
15. What are the possible benefits and risks of vegetarian diets?
16. What is the relationship between sodium intake and high blood pressure? What is meant by sensitivity to salt?
17. What FDA regulations govern food labeling? What changes have been proposed?
18. How can the percentages of fat, protein, and carbohydrate in a food be calculated?
19. Discuss the types of qualified nutrition professionals and their educational requirements.

References

* 1. Stare F, Aronson V, and Barrett S: Your guide to good nutrition, Buffalo, 1991, Prometheus Books.
2. Food and Drug Administration: Food labeling—proposed rules. Federal Register 56:60366-60878, 1991.
3. Pilch SM et al: Physiological effects and health consequences of dietary fiber, Washington, DC, 1987, Federation of American Societies for Experimental Biology.
4. AMA Council on Scientific Affairs: Dietary fiber and health, JAMA 262:542-546, 1989.
5. Food and Nutrition Board: Recommended dietary allowances, ed 10, Washington, DC, 1989, National Academy Press.
6. Barrett S: What happened to the 1985 RDAs? Nutrition Forum 3:1-2, Jan 1986.
7. Herbert V and Barrett S: Vitamins and "health" foods: the great American hustle, Philadelphia, 1981, George F Stickley Co.
8. Food and Drug Administration: Food labeling: reference daily intakes and daily reference values, Federal Register, 55:29476-29533, 1990.
9. Guthrie HA: There's no such thing as "junk food," but there are junk diets, Healthline 5(10):11-12, Nov 1986.
10. American Council on Science and Health: Fast food and the American diet, New York, 1985, The Council.
*11. Nutrition and your health: Dietary guidelines for Americans, Washington, DC, 1985, US Departments of Agriculture and Health and Human Services.
12. Wotecki C and Thomas PR: Eat for life—the Food and Nutrition Board's guide to reducing your risk of chronic disease, Washington, DC, 1992, National Academy Press.
*13. Dingott S and Dwyer J: Benefits and risks of vegetarian diets, Nutrition Forum 8:45-47, 1991.

*Recommended reading

*14. Koop CE: The Surgeon General's report on nutrition and health. DHHS (PHS) Publication No. 88-50210. Washington, DC, 1988, Superintendent of Documents.

15. Food and Nutrition Board, Committee on Nutritional Misinformation: Vegetarian diets, Washington, DC, 1974, National Academy of Sciences.

16. American Academy of Pediatrics: Nutritional aspects of vegetarianism, health fads, and health diets, Pediatrics 59:460-464, 1977.

17. American Dietetic Association: Position of the American Dietetic Association: Vegetarian diets, J Am Diet Assoc 88:351-355, 1988.

18. Lecos C: Tips for the salt-conscious consumer, FDA Consumer 15(9):27-28, 1981.

19. Porter DV and Earl RO: Nutrition labeling—issues and directions for the 1990s, Washington, DC, 1991, National Academy Press.

20. Foulke JE: Wide-sweeping proposals to improve food labeling, FDA Consumer 26(1):9-13, 1992.

21. Food and Drug Administration: FDA Backgrounder: food labeling reform: a progress report (BG 91.4.2), Nov 1991.

22. USDA Food Safety and Inspection Service: Nutrition labeling of meat and poultry products: proposed rule, Federal Register 56:60302-60364, 1991.

23. Meister KA: How much does your doctor know about nutrition? ACSH News & Views 1:4-5, Nov/Dec 1980.

*24. Herbert V, Subak-Sharpe GJ and Hammock DA (eds): The Mount Sinai School of Medicine complete book of nutrition, New York, 1990, St. Martin's Press.

*25. Motulsky AG et al: Diet and health: implications for reducing chronic disease risk, Washington, DC, 1989, National Academy Press.

26. Thomas PR (ed): Improving America's diet and health: from recommendations to action, Washington, DC, 1991, National Academy Press.

27. Brown ML (ed): Present knowledge of nutrition, ed 6, Washington, DC, 1990, International Life Sciences Institute—Nutrition Foundation.

CHAPTER THIRTEEN

NUTRITION FADS, FALLACIES, AND SCAMS

Nutrition seems to be like politics: everyone is an expert.[1]

HAROLD J. MOROWITZ, PH.D.

Did you ever stop to think that your corner grocery, fruit market, meat market and supermarket are also health food stores? They are—and they generally charge less than stores that use the slogan.[2]

VICTOR HERBERT, M.D., J.D.
STEPHEN BARRETT, M.D.

Consumer Decision

How sensible is it to use vitamin and mineral supplements, herbs, and "health" foods?

Will the use of vitamin C prevent colds?

Are "organic" or "natural" foods better than ordinary foods?

How can consumers identify the promotion of questionable nutrition?

Erroneous nutrition concepts lead Americans to waste billions of dollars annually and sometimes to jeopardize their health. Most Americans are probably harmed to some degree by nutrition fads and fallacies. At the core of this problem are individuals and groups whose collective efforts can be referred to as the health food industry. However, pharmaceutical manufacturers and large food companies also foster and exploit public confusion about nutrition. This chapter illustrates how misinformation is used to promote vitamin and mineral supplements, "health foods," "organic" foods, "natural" foods, herbs, related products, and dietary fads. This chapter also discusses the activities and backgrounds of some of the leading promoters of nutrition misinformation. Facts and fads related to weight control are covered in the following chapter.

Food Faddism

Sociologist Robert Schafer and food scientist Elizabeth A. Yetley[3] have defined food faddism as an unusual pattern of food behavior enthusiastically adopted by its adherents. These authors report that faddism is expressed by: (1) acceptance of special virtues of a particular food to cure specific diseases, (2) elimination of certain foods from the diet in the belief that harmful elements are present, or (3) emphasis on "natural" foods. They also state that food faddists use foods not as ends in themselves but as a means of achieving a stable and predictable life pattern. Beal[4] classifies eight types of food faddists noted in Table 13-1.

Dr. William T. Jarvis,[5] professor of public health and preventive medicine at Loma Linda University, notes:

> Faddists utilize the methods of the propagandist by playing on man's deepest fears and prejudices. The purpose of propaganda is to make the respondent hate a perceived enemy and love and give loyalty to a cause. Many aspects of food faddism become social movements which represent symbolic rebellions against authority, society-at-large, or some imagined enermy.

Whorton[6] suggests that the term faddism is misleading because it connotes little more than temporary foolishness. Instead, he suggests, the high levels of devotion, asceticism, and zeal associated with certain health ideologies makes it more appropriate to call them "hygienic religions."

Food Supplements

In ordinary use the term food supplement refers to any food substance, or mixture of such substances, consumed in addition to or in place of food. The most commonly used food supplements are vitamins and minerals. Some products sold as supplements (such as lecithin, PABA, and bioflavonoids) are not essential because they contain nothing the body needs or cannot make.

It is not legal to market any product with therapeutic claims until satisfactory evidence of safety and effectiveness is presented to the FDA. However, many nutritionally related products are marketed as "dietary supplements" even though their actual intended use is for the prevention or treatment of a health problem. This intended use seldom appears on the product label but is communicated to retailers and prospective customers through written or oral claims. Promoters of these products call them supplements, hoping that they will be considered foods rather than drugs and therefore be exempt from the laws regulating the sale of drugs.

Promoters of nutrition quackery are skilled at arousing and exploiting fears and false hopes. Four basic myths are used to encourage the use of health foods and food supplements:

1. It is difficult if not impossible to get the nourishment you need from ordinary foods.
2. Vitamin and mineral deficiencies are common.
3. Virtually all diseases are caused by faulty diet.
4. Virtually all diseases can be prevented or remedied by nutritional means.

TABLE 13–1

EMOTIONAL NEEDS OF FOOD FADDISTS

Type of food faddist	Need served by fad
Miracle-seeker	Patterning need to establish stability regarding health, energy, and so on. Accomplished by diets intended to forestall aging or restore organism to health. Ego defense need to reestablish positive self-concept and feeling of self-worth.
Anti-establishmentarian	Self-realization need to express self in a manner consistent with self-concept and value system.
Super health-seeker	Ego defense need to forestall aging process. Accomplished by diet intended to give super health. Self-realization need to present a front of strength and health.
Distruster of medical profession	Ego defense need to establish control over own destiny and not be dependent on unknown others.
Fashion-follower	Ego defense and patterning need to establish an identity to gain approval and acceptance from others.
Authority-seeker	Self-realization need for recognition of self-competency, provided by apparent knowledge in area of food information.
Truth-seeker	Patterning need to process existing claims concerning nutrition.
One concerned about uncertainities of living	Patterning need for anchors and stability concerning the world.

From Beal VA: Food faddism and organic and natural foods.[4] Reprinted courtesy of American Dietetic Association.

VITAMIN AND MINERAL SUPPLEMENTS

Americans spend about $3 billion a year for vitamin and mineral supplements. Most people who use multivitamins think they are getting "nutrition insurance," but many also believe that extra vitamins can provide extra energy, improve general health, and prevent disease. Most people who use individual supplements believe that these products have medicinal value for the prevention or treatment of disease.[7]

A 1982 Gallup survey found that 37% of American adults were taking vitamin supplements.[8] Most were taking multivitamin or vitamin-mineral preparations. The survey found that the most popular individual supplements were vitamin C, the B vitamins, and vitamin E, in that order. When respondents were asked to state their most important reason for taking vitamins, the answers fell into the following categories:

To supplement diet (31%): "Don't get a balanced diet at all times," "Don't eat right," "Don't get enough vitamins during the day," "I'm an irregular eater"

Healthy/makes me feel better (30%): "To be healthy," "Health supplement," "Good for you," "For general health reasons"

For energy/strength (12%): "Gives me pep," "To keep going," "I am run down," "Pick-me-up"

Doctor recommended/prescribed: (17%)

Pregnant: (5%)

"Nutrition Insurance"

Virtually all nutrition authorities agree that healthy individuals can get all the nutrients they need by eating a balanced variety of foods. Most Americans believe this too, but at the same time many worry that their eating habits place them at risk for deficiency. The fear of "not getting enough" is promoted vigorously, not only by food faddists and health-food industry publicists, but also by major pharmaceutical manufacturers and trade associations. Faddists tend to stress unscientific ideas that one cannot get sufficient nourishment from ordinary foods, while the drug companies use more subtle suggestions that various people may not be getting enough. Both groups fail to suggest how to obtain one's nutrients from foods or how to tell whether one is getting enough. Table 13-2 analyzes common sales pitches for "nutrition insurance."

One of the main arguments used to support recommendations for "insurance" by vitamin supplements is that reputable health and nutrition surveys have found that intakes of some vitamins by some segments of the population are below the Recommended Dietary Allowances (RDA). This statement is true but misleading. As Harper[9] explains:

1. The RDAs are set high enough to encompass the needs of individuals with the highest requirements. Using them directly as standards for evaluating the adequacy of individual nutrient intakes would be like setting the standard for a person's height at 7 feet and concluding that all those under 7 feet have suffered growth retardation.
2. Surveys often identify Vitamin A as a "problem nutrient." However, when the results of dietary surveys are based on measurements of nutrient intakes for a single day, many people who consume adequate amounts of vitamin A over a longer period of time are classified as having a "low" intake. Since vitamin A is stored efficiently in the liver, a surplus consumed on one day will provide a reserve that is available on subsequent days.

The best course of action for individuals who are worried about the adequacy of their diet is to keep a food diary for several days and have it analyzed by a physician or registered dietitian. If a problem is found, it usually is better to correct the diet than to take supplements.

Perspectives on Food Processing

To promote the use of supplements, the health food industry suggests that the processing of food removes the nourishment. It is true that processing can change the nutrient content of food, but the changes are not drastic. Dr. Pavel Jelen[10] at the University of Alberta has noted the following:

1. Only certain nutrients are affected by processing, and most nutrient losses are insignificant to the overall diet. For example, while pasteurization to make milk safe destroys some of its vitamin C content, people do not drink milk to meet their vitamin C needs because milk is a poor source of vitamin C.
2. Some nutrient losses in processing (for example, vitamin losses during the milling of flour) are restored by fortification.
3. The negative effects of some food processing operations that result in losses of certain nutrients are more than compensated by the overall positive effects, especially the continuous availability of most types of food items at reasonable cost.

Food processing and home food preparation can destroy certain vitamins with heat and remove some water-soluble vitamins and minerals through contact with water during cooking. Usually these are only partial losses. Moreover, the nutrients lost from certain foods from the farm to the table are readily obtainable from other foods. Eating moderate amounts of a wide variety of foods, including some uncooked fruits and vegetables, ensures an adequate supply of nutrients.[10]

"Stress Supplements"

Some vitamin manufacturers have advertised that extra vitamins are needed to protect against "stress." While some companies list only physical stresses that supposedly increase vitamin needs, some include mental stress, overwork, and the like. Other companies market products for the "special needs" of athletes, housewives, busy executives, and smokers. Some companies make no health claims at all, relying only on the product's name to sell it.

"Stress vitamins" typically contain 10 or more times the RDA for vitamin C and several of the B vitamins. Although vitamin needs may rise slightly in certain physical conditions, they seldom rise above the RDA, and they are easily met by eating a balanced diet. There is no evidence that

TABLE 13–2

ANALYSIS OF SCARE TACTICS USED TO PROMOTE "NUTRITION INSURANCE"

Claim	Comment
"Remember that the health of your eyes, teeth, bones, and internal systems depends upon a sufficient intake of these vital nutrients."*	Messages of this type, intended to make one nutrient-conscious, are true but misleading. They never say how to tell if one is getting enough.
Of the approximately 40 nutrients that are considered elemental in meeting daily body requirements, many cannot be manufactured or stored by the body. These nutrients must be ingested daily.†	Subtly exaggerates the likelihood of deficiency. The body's storage of water-soluble vitamins is limited, but occasional low dietary intake poses no danger.
How much of your vitamin C gets lost on the way to the table? Picking, packing, processing. All these plus transportation can lead to the destruction of part of the vitamin C in your foods.‡	The real issues are how much remains in one's diet and whether it is enough. Most Americans consume adequate amounts of vitamin C.
No matter how hard you try, in our fast food society, it is often difficult to make sure you are getting enough essential vitamins and minerals in the food you eat.	Exaggerates the difficulty of balancing one's diet.
Getting a balanced diet can be tough, especially when you are busy with other things. So to avoid taking chances, take a supplement.‡	Falsely suggests that it is difficult for busy people to obtain a balanced diet.
Most packaged foods have many, if not all, of the natural nutrients removed during processing and replaced with chemicals.§	Greatly exaggerates the amount of nutrients lost in processing; exploits public fear that our foods contain too many "chemicals."
Our soils are depleted.	Falsely suggests that adequate nutrition can be obtained only by ingesting food supplements or special foods.
"I take my vitamins every day. Just to be on the safe side." (Said by man pictured climbing a steep mountain)‡	Misleading comparison of dangers of mountain climbing and of not taking daily vitamin pills.
Leading medical authorities . . . urge us, as part of a well-balanced diet, to eat more . . . foods that are rich in beta-carotene. That's why beta-carotene is an essential part of the vitamin and mineral formula that makes Centrum more complete than any leading brand. So eat right and take Centrum with beta-carotene. Now there is more reason than ever to take a multivitamin that is more complete."‖	Misleading juxtaposition of truths and half-truths. The cited authorities explicitly recommend getting one's nutrients from foods, not supplements. Centrum is well formulated and is more complete than most of its competitors. However, the addition of beta-carotene is superfluous to anyone eating properly. Nor do people who "eat right" need dietary supplements.
Most of the water soluble vitamins—B-complex and C—should be replaced daily. That is why a good diet is so important. Stresstabs high potency stress formula can help you to back up your diet because they concentrate on vitamins your body cannot store.‖	Water-soluble vitamins do not need to be replaced daily. The body can store them for at least several weeks. Using vitamins to "back up" a good diet is a waste of money. If a supplement is desired, there is no reason to select a "high-potency" (above-RDA) product.
Theragran-M is "fine tuned for the way you live." (TV ad depicting attractive young people doing various athletic activities.)	Life-style characteristics other than food intake have very little to do with vitamin or mineral needs. The imagery may be intended to suggest that the product can make people more vigorous.

*Safeway Stores: Vitamin, mineral and food supplement guide, 1979.
†Sears advertising flyer, Allentown, Penn, 1979.
‡Hoffmann-La Roche: Magazine ads, 1981-1983.
§Neo-Life Corporation: Sharing the new life through better nutrition . . . every day of your life! Counselor, pp 3-5, Feb 1979.
‖Lederle Laboratories, Magazine ads, 1991-1992.

emotional stress increases the body's need for vitamins. Someone who is really in danger of deficiency as a result of illness would feel extremely ill and probably require hospitalization.

Some vitamin manufacturers suggest that strenuous physical activity increases the need for vitamins so that people who engage in vigorous exercise or athletics should take supplements. Strenuous exercise does increase the need for calories, water, and a few nutrients. However, the nutrient needs are unlikely to rise above the RDA. Even if more than the RDA amounts were needed, they would be supplied by the increase in food intake normally associated with exercising. The belief that extra vitamins are useful to athletes is also tied to the idea that extra vitamins provide extra energy—which is untrue.

Smokers tend to have lower levels of vitamin C than do nonsmokers. However, no evidence exists that smokers are deficient in vitamin C.[9] In 1989 the RDA for vitamin C was set at 60 mg for nonsmokers and 100 mg for smokers. Members of the 1980-1985 RDA committee, who did most of the work for the 1989 RDA report, felt strongly that no scientific basis existed for this recommendation.[11] Regardless of which viewpoint is correct, either of these amounts is readily obtainable from food.

No scientific evidence shows that emotional stress increases one's need for vitamins. In 1982 the National Advertising Division (NAD) of the Council of Better Business Bureaus reacted to an ad by Hoffmann-La Roche and noted that the terms "stress" and "acute stress" have one meaning in science and another in popular speech. NAD wondered whether the Roche ads would give a false impression that mental stresses, both minor and acute, might raise the body's requirement for vitamin C. Hoffman-La Roche agreed and pledged to modify its future advertising.[12]

In 1985 E.R. Squibb & Sons, Inc., agreed to pay $15,000 to New York State and to stop making false and misleading claims for its *Theragran Stress Formula.* In 1986 Lederle Laboratories agreed to pay $25,000 and to stop suggesting that *Stresstabs* could reduce the effects of psychologic stress or the ordinary stress of life. Both cases were prosecuted by New York Attorney General Robert Abrams. In a 1985 interview, Lederle's chief of nutrition science acknowledged that "people who eat a balanced diet do not need stress vitamins—or for that matter any vitamin supplement at all."[13] In 1990 Miles Laboratories (makers of *One-A-Day* products) signed a 3-year "assurance of discontinuance" order with the attorneys general of New York, California, and Texas and agreed to pay $10,000 to each of these three states. Without admitting wrongdoing, the company pledged not to claim that: (1) the average consumer needs a supplement to prevent mineral and vitamin loss, (2) vitamins can prevent or reverse lung damage caused by pollution, (3) routine daily stress depletes vitamins, and (4) routine physical exercise (such as the aerobics shown in Miles' television ad) deletes essential minerals.

Types of Over-the-Counter Supplements

Vitamins are sold individually, in combination with other vitamins, and in combination with minerals. Multivitamin-mineral combinations may contain as many as 50 ingredients, but some ingredients, such as rutin, inositol, bioflavonoids, and para-aminobenzoic acid (PABA), are not needed in the human diet.

The variety of products sold as food supplements (including many that contain no essential nutrients) is quite large. Altogether, several hundred companies are marketing more than 7000 such products.

Multivitamins vary greatly in the types and amounts of their individual ingredients. Many products contain ingredients in amounts that exceed the RDA. Vitamin A is present in amounts up to 25,000 IU (international units), or 5 times its RDA; vitamin D is present in amounts up to 1000 IU, 2½ times its RDA; and vitamin E may be found up to 1000 IU, 100 times its RDA; vitamin C up to 1000 mg, 16 times its RDA; single supplement tablets of vitamin C may contain as much as 2000 mg. Dosages this high are unnecessary, costly, and sometimes harmful. Most mineral supplements contain below-RDA amounts, but a few are a bit higher.

These are some of the recommendations made by the FDA expert advisory panel that investigated over-the-counter (OTC) vitamin and mineral products:[14]

1. OTC vitamins and minerals should be labeled for use only for the prevention and treatment of deficiencies when the need for such therapy has been determined by a physician.
2. Only nine vitamins (A,B_6, B_{12}, C, D, folic acid, niacin, riboflavin, and thiamine) and three minerals (calcium, iron, and zinc) should be allowed

to be sold as single-ingredient nonprescription drugs to treat deficiencies.

3. Vitamin E should not be sold by itself as an OTC drug because it has no proven therapeutic value and dietary deficiency is virtually unknown.
4. Vitamin K, biotin, choline, and pantothenic acid should be sold only by prescription. Vitamin K is dangerous for people taking anticoagulant ("blood-thinning" drugs). The other substances should be removed from the OTC market because deficiencies are virtually nonexistent.

The FDA was unable to implement these suggestions because the Proxmire Amendment to the Food, Drug, and Cosmetic Act prevents the agency from regulating the dosages of vitamin products that are not inherently dangerous. The Amendment was passed in 1976 after a massive lobbying campaign spearheaded by the health food industry.[15]

"Natural" Versus Synthetic Vitamins

Many companies sell "natural" vitamins with claims of being better than the synthetic vitamins. Such claims are unfounded. A few synthetic vitamins have slightly different structures than their natural counterparts, but these differences are of no importance inside the body. As noted by Herbert,[16] vitamins are specific molecules; the body makes no distinction between vitamins made in the "factories" of nature and those made in the factories of chemical companies. The prices of "natural" vitamins tend to be higher than those of synthetic vitamins.

"Ergogenic Aids"

More than 100 companies are marketing concoctions of vitamins, minerals, and/or low doses of amino acids with false claims that they can increase stamina and endurance and help build stronger muscles by stimulating release of human growth hormone. Ads for these products typically contain an endorsement from a champion athlete or bodybuilder who attributes success to the products. Some of the products are marketed as weight-loss aids (see chapter 14). Many are touted as "natural steroids" or "growth-hormone releasers," which they are not. Very high doses of certain amino acids have been reported to influence hormone production in laboratory animals. But no such effect from low-dose pills has been demonstrated in humans.

In 1992, the New York City Department of Consumer Affairs[16a] warned consumers to beware of products advertised with terms like "fat burner," "fat fighter," "fat metabolizer," "energy enhancer," "performance booster," "strength booster," "ergogenic aid," "anabolic optimizer," and "genetic optimizer." Manufacturers surveyed by the department were unable to provide a single published report from a scientific journal to back the claims that their products did any of these things. Calling the bodybuilding supplement industry "an economic hoax with unhealthy consequences," the department issued "Notices of Violation" to six companies and challenged the FDA to clean up the marketplace nationwide.

Megavitamin Claims Versus Facts

Claims are widespread that high dosages of vitamins and minerals can prevent or cure a wide variety of ailments. Dr. Linus Pauling, Nobel Prize winner in chemistry and professor emeritus of chemistry at Stanford University, is the chief theoretician for this approach which he calls orthomolecular treatment (*ortho* is Greek for "right"). Orthomolecular treatment supposedly provides the correct amounts of nutritionally "right" molecules normally found in the body. This section examines some of the claims made about megavitamins, the evidence against them, and the dangers involved in their use. Megavitamin treatment for emotional problems is discussed in Chapter 7.

Pauling and Vitamin C

Controversy over the use of massive dosages of vitamin C stems largely from Pauling's publications. His 1970 book, *Vitamin C and the Common Cold,* claimed that taking 1000 mg of vitamin C daily will reduce the incidence of colds by 45% for most people, but that some people need much larger amounts. The 1976 revision of the book, retitled *Vitamin C, the Common Cold and the Flu,* suggests even higher dosages. A third book, published in 1979, claims that high dosages of vitamin C may be effective against cancer.[17] A flyer distributed in 1991 by the Linus Pauling Institute recommends daily doses of 6000 to 18,000 mg of vitamin C, 400 to 1600 IU of vitamin E, and 25,000 IU of vitamin A, plus various other vitamins and minerals. Pauling himself reportedly takes 12,000 mg of vitamin C daily and raises the amount to 40,000 mg if symptoms of a cold appear.[18] However, most medical and nutritional scientists strongly disagree with Pauling's views concerning vitamin C.

Experimental studies of the possible value of vitamin C for preventing infections have been conducted by medical investigators ever since the vitamin became commercially available during the 1930s. At least 15 well-designed, double-blind studies have shown that supplementation with vitamin C does not prevent colds, and at best may slightly reduce the symptoms of a cold.[19] Slight symptom reduction may occur as the result of an antihistamine-like effect, but whether this has practical value is a matter of dispute. Pauling's views are based on analysis of the same studies as other scientists, but his conclusions are different.

The largest clinical trials, involving thousands of volunteers, were directed by Dr. Terence Anderson, professor of epidemiology at the University of Toronto. Taken together, his studies suggest that extra vitamin C intake may slightly reduce the severity of colds, but it is not necessary to take the high dosages suggested by Pauling to achieve this result. Nor is there anything to be gained by taking vitamin C supplements year-round in the hope of preventing colds.[19]

Another important study was reported in 1975 by scientists at the National Institutes of Health who compared the effects of vitamin C pills with a placebo before and during colds. Although the experiment was supposed to be double-blind, half the subjects were able to guess which pill they were getting. When the results were tabulated with all subjects lumped together, the average number of colds reported per person was 1.27 for the vitamin group and 1.36 for the placebo group over a 9-month period. But among the half who did not guess which pill they had been taking, no difference in the incidence or severity was found. This illustrates how people who think they are doing something effective (taking a vitamin) can report a favorable result even when none exists.[20]

In 1976 Pauling and Dr. Ewan Cameron, a Scottish physician, reported that a majority of 100 patients with terminal cancer treated with 10,000 mg of vitamin C daily had survived three to four times longer than similar patients who did not receive vitamin C supplements. However, Dr. William DeWys, chief of clinical investigations at the National Cancer Institute, found that the study was poorly designed because the patient groups were not comparable. The vitamin C patients were Dr. Cameron's, while the other patients were under the care of other physicians. Cameron's patients started taking vitamin C when he labeled them untreatable by other methods, and their subsequent survival was compared to the survival of the "control" patients after they were labeled untreatable by their doctors. Dr. DeWys[21] reasoned that if the two groups were comparable, the lengths of time from entry into the hospital to being labeled untreatable should be equivalent in both groups. However, he found that Cameron's patients were labeled untreatable much earlier in the course of their disease—which means that they entered the hospital before they were as sick as the other doctors' patients and would naturally be expected to live longer.

In 1979 the Mayo Clinic reported a double-blind study of 123 patients with advanced cancer. Half of the patients received 10,000 mg of vitamin C daily, while the others were given a placebo. No differences were found between the two groups in survival time, appetite, weight loss, severity of pain, or amount of nausea and vomiting.[22] An almost identical result was obtained in a study by the North Central Cancer Treatment Group, composed of physicians in seven states and Canada. Survival cures essentially overlapped for 71 patients receiving 10,000 mg of vitamin C and 73 patients receiving a placebo, and median survival time for the placebo group was actually 1 week longer.[23] In 1985 Mayo Clinic researchers reported that 10,000 mg of vitamin C was no better than a placebo in a controlled study of 100 patients with advanced colorectal cancer.[24] The three studies found no consistent benefit among 367 patients with advanced cancer.[25]

Megavitamin E

Claims are being made that large dosages of vitamin E are effective treatment for acne, atherosclerosis, cancer, coronary heart disease, diabetes, sexual frigidity, infertility, habitual abortion, high blood-cholesterol levels, muscular dystrophy, peptic ulcer, rheumatic fever, and blood clots. Proponents claim that vitamin E will increase stamina, prolong life, and protect against the effects of atmospheric pollution. Vitamin E is also being added to after-shave lotion, soaps, underarm deodorants and so-called skin conditioners; however, it has no proven value for any of these purposes.[19]

Vitamin E deficiency symptoms in humans that

are traceable only to an inadequate diet have never been reported, except in premature infants.[19] In adults, deficiency has been observed only in patients with an inability to absorb fat during the digestive process (vitamin E is fat-soluble). About 25 years ago several researchers placed human volunteers on a low vitamin E diet for 4½ years to see whether they could produce signs of deficiency. The volunteers had minor changes in their red blood cells but experienced no symptoms.[19] Thus, it is clearly irrational for healthy persons to take vitamin E supplements as protection against deficiency.

Several years ago, preliminary studies by Dr. Robert London and colleagues at Sinai Hospital of Balitmore suggested that vitamin E supplementation might help women with benign fibrocystic disease of the breast. However, two double-blind studies reported in 1986 found no significant benefit. In one study, the Sinai Hospital group treated 128 patients for two months with either a placebo or 150, 300, or 600 IU of vitamin E. Although slightly more than half of the patients improved during the trial period, those receiving vitamin E did no better than those receiving the placebo. The other study, done by doctors at the University of California in San Francisco, involved 62 women who took either 600 IU of vitamin E or a placebo for 2½ months. No differences in breast findings were observed between the two groups.

Meganutrient Therapy

A small number of physicians (probably a few hundred) believe that large dosages of supplementary nutrients are effective against a wide range of diseases. This approach began during the early 1950s as megavitamin therapy for treatment of schizophrenia (see Chapter 7). It is now called orthomolecular, meganutrient, or nutritional therapy. It is described in such books as *Orthomolecular Psychiatry: A Treatment Approach,* by Drs. Linus Pauling and David Hawkins; *Mega-Nutrition,* by Dr. Richard Kunin; and *Dr. Pfeiffer's Total Nutrition,* by Dr. Carl C. Pfeiffer. Dr. Kunin's book claims that a balanced diet is a practical impossibility and that "the nutrition-prescription movement is . . . a new direction toward which all of medicine is moving." Both he and Dr. Hawkins are psychiatrists; each has served as president of the Orthomolecular Medical Society.

Dr. Pfeiffer was director of the Princeton Brain Bio Center in Skillman, New Jersey, a facility that offers "nutritional" treatment for "the schizophrenias and biochemical deficiencies associated with aging, alcoholism (must be in AA and not drinking), allergies, arthritis, autism, epilepsy, hypertension, hypoglycemia, migraine headaches, depression, learning disabilities, retardation, mental and metabolic disorders, skin problems, and hyperactivity."[26] In 1987 its fee for an initial evaluation was $296, which included $100 for consultation with a doctor and the rest for laboratory tests that most physicians would not consider necessary or useful for diagnosing the above disorders. Nor would most doctors agree that the disorders are associated with biochemical deficiencies. The above costs did not include the 10 or more nutrients typically prescribed for treatment.

Dangers of Excess Vitamins and Minerals

Vitamins in excess of the body's needs usually do not serve a useful function. Excess amounts of fat-soluble vitamins are stored in body fat, where they can build up to toxic levels over a period of time. Excess water-soluble vitamins are excreted through the urine, but these may still have adverse effects. In *Vitamins and Minerals: Help or Harm?* biochemist Charles Marshall reports the following dangers that have been described in medical journals:

1. Daily doses of five times the RDA of vitamin A for several months can result in: lack of appetite, retarded growth in children, drying and cracking of the skin, enlargement of the liver and spleen, increased pressure on the brain, loss of hair, migratory joint pains, menstrual difficulty, bone pain, irritability, and headache.
2. Prolonged excessive intake of vitamin D (usually five times the RDA or more) can cause: loss of appetite, nausea, weakness, weight loss, excess urinary output, constipation, vague aches, stiffness, kidney stones, tissue calcification, high blood pressure, acidosis, and kidney failure (which can lead to death).
3. Doses in the range of 40 to 300 times the RDA of niacin (vitamin B_3) can cause severe flushing, itching, liver damage, skin disorders, gout, ulcers, and blood-sugar disorders. (Despite this, large doses administered under medical supervision can be valuable for controlling abnormal blood-cholesterol levels, as described in Chapter 16.)
4. Excess vitamin E (usually 400 IU or more) can cause headaches, nausea, tiredness, giddiness, inflammation of the mouth, chapped lips, gas-

PERSONAL GLIMPSE

Vitamin A Poisoning

In 1979 a chiropractor in Peoria, Illinois, prescribed massive doses of vitamin A for Lynne Crampton, age 9, and her brother Dale, age 4. Both children suffered from ichthyosis, a congenital disorder in which the skin is scaly and resembles that of a fish. Lynne was prescribed 750,000 international units (IU) daily for several weeks, to be followed by 370,000 IU daily for 2 months. Dale was prescribed 675,000 IU daily for 2 months and then half that amount. The recommended dietary allowance (RDA) of vitamin A is 1665 IU for 4-year-olds and 2331 IU for 9-year-olds.

Within a few months Lynne developed swelling of the brain, manifested by blurred vision and headaches. She also had musculoskeletal pain and tenderness, hair loss for 2 months, and damage to the growth centers of several of her bones. Dale developed bone pain and enlargement of his liver and spleen. Although their acute symptoms subsided after the vitamin A was stopped, both children were permanently harmed. One of Lynne's legs became several inches shorter than the other, which caused her to develop scoliosis. Dale has permanent damage to his liver and spleen. Between 1986 and 1989, suits filed against the chiropractor and the vitamin A manufacturers were settled out of court for a total of $895,000.[30]

Vitamin A toxicity can result from ingesting too much vitamin A on a regular basis for months or years. The signs and symptoms that develop as body stores build up include: dry and itchy skin, headache, hair loss, bone malformation, bleeding tendencies, bone fracture, muscle and joint pain, vision problems, and liver toxicity. Most adverse effects disappear after excessive intake is stopped, but permanent damage can occur to the liver, bones, and eyes. Liver damage in adults has been reported at daily doses of 25,000 IU or more.[31]

trointestinal disturbances, muscle weakness, low blood-sugar levels, and increased bleeding tendency.

5. Various amounts of vitamin C of about 20 times the RDA or more may damage growing bone, produce diarrhea, produce "rebound scurvy" in adults and in newborn infants whose mothers took large doses, cause adverse effects in pregnancy, produce kidney stones, and cause false urine tests for sugar in diabetics. Vitamin C in large doses can also produce false-negative tests for blood in the stool and thereby prevent early detection of serious gastrointestinal diseases, including cancer.[19]
6. Very large doses of B_6 (2000 mg or more; 1000 times the RDA) can cause symptoms resembling those of multiple sclerosis, including numbness and tingling of the hands, difficulty in walking, and the feeling of electric shocks shooting down the spine. Although most of the afflicted individuals recovered after they stopped taking B_6 supplements, some did not.

Recently it was discovered that more than 100 women attending a clinic specializing in treating premenstrual syndrome had developed neurologic symptoms as a result of taking vitamin B_6. Ninety-two had taken less than 200 mg (100 times the RDA) daily for more than 6 months. Twenty of them had taken less than 50 mg per day.[27] The lowest dosage on which anyone developed symptoms was 20 mg per day for 2 years; the shortest time was 2 months of 100 mg per day. All of their symptoms resolved when the B_6 was stopped.

Similar to fat-soluble vitamins, excess amounts of most minerals are stored in the body and can gradually build up to toxic levels. An excess of one mineral can also interfere with the functioning of others. Certain people need to take mineral supplements, but they should never be used without medical supervision.[19,28]

APPROPRIATE USE OF SUPPLEMENTS

In general, supplements are useful for individuals who are unable or unwilling to consume an adequate diet. Physicians commonly recommend vitamins for very young children until they are eating solid foods that contain enough vitamins. After a child reaches the age of 2, however, it is seldom necessary to continue supplements "just to be sure." In 1980 the Committee on Nutrition of the American Academy of Pediatrics[29] stated that supplements might be appropriate as follows:

1. Fluoride supplements should be given to children not drinking fluoridated water. (See Chapter 8 for dosage.)
2. Children with poor eating habits and those using weight-reduction diets can be given a multivi-

tamin-mineral supplement containing nutrients not exceeding RDA levels.

3. Pregnant teenagers are likely to need supplementary iron and folic acid.
4. Children using strict vegetarian diets may need supplementation, particularly of vitamin B_{12}.

Individuals using prolonged weight-reduction diets, particularly diets that are below 1200 calories per day or are nutritionally unbalanced, may benefit from a multivitamin-mineral supplement. Individuals recovering from surgery or serious illnesses that have disrupted normal eating habits may also benefit from supplementation. Elderly individuals who become sedentary or lose interest in eating may not get sufficient nutrients; they also may benefit from multivitamin-mineral supplementation. Unadvertised brands costing about 2¢ per day are available.

Because iron deficiency is not rare, a National Academy of Science committee has recommended that pregnant women take a 30-mg supplement daily during the second and third trimester. Although adequately nourished women do not need supplementation, it is simpler and less costly to supplement the diet than to measure blood iron levels several times during the pregnancy. The committee also suggested that although the best way to obtain nutrients is from food, pregnant women who ordinarily do not consume an adequate diet might benefit from a multivitamin-mineral supplement containing moderate dosages of iron, zinc, copper, calcium, vitamin B_6, folate, vitamin C, and vitamin D.[32]

Postmenopausal women should be sure that their intake of calcium is adequate to prevent thinning of their bones (osteoporosis). This can be done with adequate intake of dairy products, but some women will prefer to take calcium supplements. Women should discuss this matter with their physician or a registered dietitian. Chapter 22 covers this subject further.

Herbert and Barrett[7] state that there are only two situations in which vitamin intake higher than the RDA is legitimate: (1) treatment of medically diagnosed deficiency states—conditions rare except among alcoholics, persons with intestinal absorption defects, and the poor, especially those who are pregnant or elderly; and (2) treatment of certain conditions for which large doses of vitamins are being used experimentally as drugs—with full recognition of the risks involved.

"Health Foods"

"Health foods" are claimed to be special foods that can benefit people's health. The terms health food, natural food, organic food, and organically grown food are often used interchangeably by both sellers and consumers. Vegetarian foods and foods labeled as dietetic may also be referred to as health foods. Nutrition authorities believe that the term health food is inherently misleading, because all foods are healthy when eaten in moderation and can be unhealthy when eaten in excess amounts. Stare, Aronson, and Barrett,[28] state:

> The term is merely a gimmick used to boost sales . . . . Some foods popular as "health foods" are rich in nutrients, but no food has unique health-promoting properties. All foods can contribute to health when eaten as part of a varied and balanced diet. The problem with so-called health foods is that they are promoted with false claims and usually are overpriced.

It is important to remember that the foods eaten are not useful in the body until they are broken down into their component nutrients before being absorbed from the digestive tract; thus claims that certain foods are healthier than others should be evaluated by considering the components of these foods. Confronted with claims about a food, intelligent consumers should ask the following:

1. What is the food's nutritional value?
2. Can special health claims made about it be scientifically justified?
3. How does it compare in price with similar foods?

The following is a list of commonly promoted health foods and related products sold in health food stores. Those marked with an asterisk (*) can cause health difficulties as noted.

Acidophilus: *Lactobacillus acidophilus* is a bacterial organism that ferments the sugars present in milk and milk products such as yogurt. It is claimed that packets of acidophilus supplements aid digestion and promote the health of the digestive tract. This is impractical, however, because oral doses of the bacteria may not survive the acidic environment of the stomach. Acidophilus preparations such as sweet acidophilus milk can be useful to persons who have difficulty digesting lactose (a condition called lactose intolerance). These products are produced by treating milk with acidophilus so that its lactose can be digested. However, individuals with lactose intolerance should have guidance from a physician.

Activated charcoal: Supplements labeled "activated organic charcoal" are usually said to be made from natural organic peat moss. Charcoal supposedly absorbs intestinal gases and "serves as a powerful detoxicant" that combats "gas" and "makes you feel intestinally clean." However, this product is of little value and can add to gastrointestinal distress by interfering with the action of digestive enzymes.

*Alfalfa: Although advocates of alfalfa suggest that it contains certain nutrients that more common plant foods do not, alfalfa actually has less nutritional value than most of the more popular vegetables such as broccoli, carrots, and spinach. Claims have also been made that alfalfa contains all of the essential amino acids, but this is untrue. Alfalfa tea contains saponins, which can adversely affect digestion and respiration.

*Aloe vera: Unsubstantiated claims are being made that aloe vera products can cure or alleviate colitis, bursitis, asthma, glaucoma, hemorrhoids, boils, arthritis, intestinal problems, acne, poison ivy, anemia, tuberculosis, cancer, diabetes, depression, multiple sclerosis, stretch marks, varicose veins, and even blindness. Aloe skin creams or gels are probably harmless; and even though it will not reverse the aging process, topical aloe may exert some skin softening and moisturizing effects. However, aloe juice acts as a laxative and can cause gastrointestinal upset.[33]

*Bee pollen: Bee pollen is claimed to be a "perfect food" but contains no nutrients that are not present in conventional foods. It is also touted as an aid to athletic performance, although actual tests on swimmers and runners have shown no benefit.[34] Bee pollen can cause severe allergic reactions in susceptible individuals.[35]

Bioflavonoids: Bioflavonoids are promoted as essential for good health. It is claimed they aid in resistance to colds and the flu. Scientific tests have shown this claim to be false.[19] Bioflavonoids have never been found to be useful in humans for the treatment of any condition. Bioflavonoids are sometimes referred to as "vitamin P," but they are neither vitamins nor essential for humans.

Blackstrap molasses: Blackstrap molasses is the dark, less-refined form of molasses. It is less sweet than other syrups and has a distinctive flavor. It is touted as a "wonder food" that can restore hair color and cure anemia. Blackstrap molasses is simply another form of sugar. It cannot reverse the graying of hair. It does contain significant amounts of iron; consuming a few tablespoons of molasses at regular intervals can contribute significantly to iron intake.

*Bone meal: Powdered bone is claimed to be a rich source of calcium. Actually, its calcium is poorly absorbed. FDA scientists have found that many bone meal samples contain high levels of lead, a toxic mineral.[36]

*Bran: A fiber of wheat grain, bran is composed mainly of cellulose, an insoluble fiber. It is effective against constipation, but so are whole grains, fruits, and vegetables in the diet. The claim that wheat bran can lower cholesterol is untrue. Excessive intake of bran can cause gastrointestinal disturbances.

Brewer's yeast: Brewer's yeast is used to ferment carbohydrate in making beer. It is a good source of protein and several of the B vitamins, but it is certainly no miracle food.

Carob: Carob beans have been cultivated in Mediterranean countries since ancient times. Carob is now used in dog biscuits, as a flavoring agent in chewing tobacco, and as a chocolate substitute in candy and snack foods. It is lower in fat than chocolate and is caffeine-free, but it is similar in caloric content and does not taste like real chocolate. Claims of wondrous health benefits associated with carob intake are false.

*Chelated minerals: Chelate means "to bind." Minerals in chelated supplements usually are bound to protein, which is claimed to enhance their absorption into the body. However, there is no scientific evidence to support this claim. Individuals with a medically diagnosed need for mineral supplements can get adequate amounts from nonchelated forms, which are less expensive.

Choline: Not essential in the diets of humans, choline is in many foods. Thus, even if one did require a dietary source, supplements would be unnecessary. Although research is being conducted concerning choline compounds in the treatment of certain brain disorders, use of supplements will not improve memory or "counter the aging process" as claimed by faddists.

Cider vinegar: Vinegar made from apples has long been touted as a cure-all, often in conjunction with honey. Cider vinegar is claimed to "keep the body in balance," thin the blood, and aid in digestion—none of which is true. Like the supermarket variety, cider vinegar is an acceptable condiment (flavoring agent), but the myths surrounding its use should be ignored.

Cold-pressed oils: Most vegetable oils are filtered to remove impurities and have antioxidant preservatives added to prevent rapid spoilage. "Cold-pressed" oils undergo a different type of processing. Two types are available: crude, which is dark and still contains sediment and plant solids; and the lighter, filtered version which is more like regular oils. Neither has any health advantage over oils processed by the usual methods. According to *Consumer Reports,* cold pressing takes place between 140°F and 475°F—which is certainly not "cold."[37]

Coenzyme Q_{10}: Preliminary evidence suggests that coenzyme Q_{10}, an enzyme produced in the body, may help keep atherosclerotic plaque from forming by acting as an antioxidant in blood lipid particles. But there is no evidence that coenzyme Q_{10} supplements prevent aging or even increase enzyme levels in body tissues.[38]

Dehydroepiandrosterone (DHEA): "DHEA pills" have been promoted with false claims that they have anti-aging properties and can cause effortless weight loss. In experiments with certain strains of mice, DHEA has blocked tumors and prevented weight gain. Scientists have speculated that declining levels of this adrenal hormone after young adulthood play a role in aging. However, significant dosages can cause unwanted hair growth, liver enlargement, and other adverse effects that make its use impractical. During the mid-1980s, several "DHEA" products marketed through health food stores were found to contain little or no DHEA. In 1985 the FDA ordered manufacturers to stop marketing DHEA products as weight-loss aids.[39]

Desiccated liver: Desiccated liver in pill or powder form contains a number of nutrients. However, it has no advantage over cooked liver and is more expensive.

*Dolomite: Dolomite, mined from rocks, contains calcium and magnesium, but in a poorly absorbable form. Lead, arsenic, mercury, and other contaminants have been found in dolomite samples in amounts ample enough to cause nerve damage and other health problems.

Enzymes: Many products containing enzymes are marketed with claims that they can enhance body processes. Enzymes are proteins that act as catalysts in the body. Enzymes present in food are treated in the body the same way as any other protein: the body—particularly the acid in the stomach—digests them into smaller constituents. Thus enzymes taken orally cannot function the same as enzymes outside of the digestive tract. The tiny amounts of amino acids they provide make no significant nutritional contribution. Pancreatic enzymes have some legitimate medical uses in diseases that cause decreased secretion of pancreatic enzymes into the intestine, but these diseases are not appropriate for self-diagnosis or self-treatment.

Fertile eggs: These eggs supposedly have been fertilized by a rooster, while the supermarket varieties have not. Fertilized eggs tend to spoil faster and cost more. Though claimed to hold a health-promoting quality called "vitalism," they are nutritionally equivalent to their "nonvital" counterparts. Some food faddists claim that brown eggs are nutritionally superior to white eggs. This is untrue—egg color is hereditary and has nothing to do with nutrient composition.

Fish-oil capsules: Epidemiologic research has found that Eskimos and others whose diet is rich in certain fatty acids have less heart disease than other Americans or Europeans. Other research has found that supplements of omega-3 fatty acids (found in fish oils) can help lower blood-cholesterol levels and inhibit clotting, which means they may be useful in preventing atherosclerotic heart disease. However, it is not known what dosage is appropriate or whether long-range use is safe or effective for this purpose. Most authorities believe it is unwise to self-medicate with fish-oil capsules; they should be used only by individuals at high risk for heart disease who are under close medical supervision. However, eating fish once or twice a week may be beneficial.[40] The FDA has ordered manufacturers to stop making claims that fish-oil capsules are effective against various diseases.

*Garlic: Raw garlic and garlic-oil capsules are claimed to "purify the blood," reduce high blood pressure, and prevent cancer, heart disease, and a variety of other ailments. Some studies have found that people given daily garlic or garlic extract had lowered their blood-cholesterol levels. The *Harvard Health Letter* cautions that any evidence of benefit is preliminary and that garlic can produce bad breath, heartburn, flatulence, and can inhibit blood clotting.[41]

*Germanium: "Organic germanium" is touted as a "miracle drug" for a wide range of health problems. Proponents claim that cancer, heart disease, mental deficiency, and many other problems are due to an "oxygen deficiency" that organic germanium can eradicate. There is no scientific evidence to support these claims.[42] A few germanium products have been tested for anti-tumor activity, but no practical application has been found. Although many health food stores sell germanium products, it is illegal to market them with therapeutic claims. The FDA has banned importation of germanium products intended for human consumption and has seized germanium products from several U.S. manufacturers.

*Ginseng: Ginseng herb is being promoted as a healthy tonic, stimulant, aphrodisiac, and a cure-all for many diseases. There is little or no scientific evidence to support these claims. Some studies have found that many "ginseng" products contained little or no ginseng, other products can produce symptoms resembling steroid poisoning.[43] The FDA requires that any product containing whole, ground, or powdered ginseng must be labeled for use only in tea.

Glandular extracts: These products, sold as "food supplements," are claimed to cure diseases by augmenting glandular function in the body. Actually they contain no hormones and therefore can exert no pharmacologic effect upon the body. If they did produce such an effect, they would not be suitable products for self-medication.

Glutamic acid: Health food promoters claim that a variety of substances can increase memory power; one is glutamic acid, the principal amino acid metabolized by the brain. Although scientists are studying the relationship between memory and the intake of certain amino acids, using supplements with the hope of improving brain function is certainly premature. If one's diet is reasonably well balanced, there is no reason to add any amino acid supplement with the hope of improving memory.

*Goat's milk: The milk of goats has been touted as a highly nutritious substitute for cow's milk; it actually is no more nutritious than cow's milk. The late Paavo Airola, naturopath and author of several books advocating questionable nutrition practices, claimed that goat's milk contains special factors effective against arthritis and cancer. This is untrue. Like unpasteurized milk from any animal, goat's milk can carry diseases (see "raw milk," in this section).

Granola: Granola is the common term used to describe various high-priced cereals and candy bars composed largely of oats plus other grains, fruits, seeds, and nuts. Touted as "natural" and rich in nutrients, granola products tend to be high in sugar (usually brown sugar and/or honey), fats (from vegetable oils, nuts, seeds, and coconut), and calories.

Honey: Honey is crude sugar, with only trace amounts of any micronutrients, but not enough to make it significantly more nutritious than sugar. Honey and table sugar are both made of fructose and glucose. Honey, being sticky, is more likely to contribute to tooth decay. It is also more expensive than table sugar.

Inositol: Contrary to popular claims, supplements of inositol will not alleviate baldness, reduce blood cholesterol levels, or aid weight loss. Inositol is not a B vitamin and the body can manufacture all the inositol it needs. Even if it were a vitamin, supplements would be unnecessary because it is readily available in our food supply.

*Kelp: Kelp is a seaweed that is common in the Japanese diet. Tablets of kelp are prepared from dried seaweed and promoted in health food stores as a weight-reduction aid, a rich source of iodide, an energy booster, and a "natural" cure for certain ailments, including goiter. Kelp is high in iodide, a mineral needed to prevent goiter. However, iodized salt furnishes an adequate supply of this mineral to our diet at a fraction of the cost of kelp. Excess iodide can be detrimental to health.

Lecithin: Lecithin is manufactured by the liver and is present in many foods, including soybeans, whole grains, and egg yolks. Claims that lecithin supplements can dissolve blood cholesterol, rid the blood stream of undesirable fats, cure arthritis, improve brain power, and aid in weight reduction are unsupported by scientific evidence.

Octacosanol: Raw wheat germ is claimed to contain an active ingredient called "octacosanol." This substance, present in many plant oils, is not essential in the human diet. Claims that it improves stamina and endurance, reduces blood cholesterol, and helps reproduction are unproven.

PABA (para-aminobenzoic acid): PABA is a vitamin for bacteria, but not for humans. It is claimed that dosages taken orally can prevent or reverse the graying of hair, but no scientific evidence exists to support this claim.

Papain: Papain, an enzyme present in papaya extract, is promoted as a digestive aid, a cure for gum disease, and a weight-reduction aid. As noted earlier, enzymes taken by mouth are rapidly destroyed in the digestive tract. Papain's only significant use is as a meat tenderizer; it can be added to meats before they are consumed and while the enzyme is still chemically active.

*Protein supplements: Protein powders, tablets, and liquids have been advertised as strength-promoting and especially important to athletes. These claims are incorrect. The RDA for protein is easily obtained by eating a well-balanced diet. Meat, poultry, fish, eggs, milk, cheese, and certain plant food combinations are good sources of protein. In excessive amounts, protein supplements can cause nutritional imbalances and kidney problems.[44]

*Raw milk: Raw milk is milk in its natural state. Public health authorities advocate pasteurization to destroy any disease-producing bacteria that may be present. Health faddists claim that it destroys essential nutrients. Although about 10% of the heat-sensitive vitamins (vitamin C and thiamine) are destroyed in the pasteurizing process, milk is not a significant source of these nutrients. On the other hand, contaminated raw milk can be a source of harmful bacteria, such as those that cause undulant fever, dysentery, and tuberculosis. "Certified" milk is unpasteurized milk with a bacteria count below a specified standard, but it still can contain significant numbers of disease-producing organisms. In 1987, in response to a court order, the FDA ordered that milk and milk products in final package form for human consumption in interstate commerce be pasteurized. The agency rejected the idea of merely ordering a warning label because (1) the risks of using raw milk are not related to misuse, and (2) the only step a consumer can take to reduce the risk is not to consume the product. The sale of raw milk has been banned in 27 states, but is still legal within the rest, including California, which contains the largest source.

RNA/DNA: Supplements of these genetic materials are claimed to rejuvenate old cells, improve memory, and prevent skin wrinkling. When taken orally, they are inactivated by the digestive process. Even if they could be absorbed and reach the cells, they would not work because human cells utilize human nucleic acids, not those from lower animals.

Royal jelly: Royal jelly is food for queen bees. Claimed to increase endurance, it has been recommended for athletes. It is also advertised as rich in calcium pantothenate (claimed to be "vitamin B_5"), a supposed antioxidant-antistress nutrient used also in "miracle" skin creams and hair tonics. These claims are unproven.

Rutin: Rutin, chemically related to the bioflavonoids, is not a vitamin for humans. It is illegal for supplements to be labeled with any nutritional claims for rutin, but this substance is often included in multivitamins.

Sea salt: Proponents of sea salt claim that it is unrefined and therefore more nutritious, but actually it is refined to remove impurities. Sea salt contains as much sodium as table salt, but table salt can have the advantage of being iodized. "Seawater concentrates" have been marketed with claims that they can cure cancer, diabetes, and a whole host of other diseases. These claims are both untrue and illegal.

Spirulina: Spirulina is a blue-green algae, some species of which have been used as a dietary staple in several parts of the world. Spirulina is similar to soybeans in nutrient content. It contains protein of fair quality plus some other nutrients, but nothing that cannot be obtained much less expensively from conventional foods. Despite claims by proponents, spirulina has no value as a dietetic aid or as a remedy for any disease. Law enforcement agencies and courts have ordered several multilevel companies to stop making illegal therapeutic claims for spirulina products, but others continue do so. Some products sold as "spirulina" contain no spirulina. Some products have been found to be contaminated with insect parts.

Sprouts: Sprouts add bulk to sandwiches and salads and provide various textures and flavors, depending on the type of bean from which they are sprouted. Their nutrient content depends largely on the bean. The nutritional value of sprouts has been exaggerated. They contain modest amounts of vitamin C, but certainly no "life force," as enthusiasts have claimed.

Superoxide dismutase (SOD): SOD is an enzyme promoted as an "antioxidant" that supposedly protects body tissues against environmental contaminants, heart disease, cancer, and arthritis. The body has its own supply of functioning antioxidants, including various enzymes and vitamins C and E. Enzymes taken orally are simply inactivated in the gastrointestinal tract.

Vitamin B_{15}: "Vitamin B_{15}" is not a vitamin. Also known as pangamate, pangamic acid, or "Russian Formula," it has been claimed to be effective against cancer, heart disease, alcoholism, diabetes, glaucoma, allergies, and schizophrenia. Supposedly it can purify the air, provide the body with instant oxygen, and slow down the aging process.[45] Pangamic acid was patented in 1949 by Ernst T. Krebs and his son, Ernst, Jr., the developers of Laetrile. The American Council on Science and Health states that B_{15} has no health benefit and is hazardous because the chemicals typically present in the supplements may cause cancer and have dangerous side effects.[44] The FDA has banned the sale of "B_{15}" products, but some health food stores still carry them.

Wheat germ: Wheat germ is a good source of some nutrients: protein, several B vitamins, vitamin E, some minerals, and fiber. Wheat germ is neither a cure-all nor a dietary essential. It is amply provided in whole wheat products. As a supplement, it is relatively high in calories and cost.

Yogurt: Yogurt is nutritionally equivalent to whole or low-fat milk (depending on which type of milk it is made from) but costs more. It is a good source of calcium, riboflavin, and other nutrients—as are all milk products—but it is certainly not a "perfect" food with magical antiaging properties, as it is sometimes claimed.

"Organic" Foods

Promoters of "organic" and "organically grown" foods suggest that these are safer and more nutritious than conventionally grown foods. The terms attempt to describe the methods by which foods are produced. Organically grown may be the more appropriate term because in scientific usage, "organic" refers to compounds that contain carbon, which all food substances contain. The most common concept of "organically grown" food was articulated by Robert Rodale in 1972 at a hearing conducted by New York State Attorney General Louis Lefkowitz:

> Food grown without pesticides; grown without artificial fertilizers; grown in soil whose humus content is increased by the additions of organic matter, grown in soil whose mineral content is increased by the application of natural mineral fertilizers; has not been treated with preservatives, hormones, antibiotics, etc.[46]

Many scientists believe this definition is inherently misleading and cite the following facts:

1. "Organic" promoters imply that their products are pesticide-free, but actual surveys have found no significant differences in pesticide levels between organic and conventionally grown foods. Pesticides on the outside of fruits and vegetables may be removed by washing. The tiny amounts of pesticides found in some foods pose no health risk.[47,48] FDA data show that dietary intakes of pesticides are well within recognized safety standards.[49]
2. Plants obtain nutrients from soil in their inorganic state. Organic fertilizers must decompose before their nutrients become available for absorption. What counts is the presence or absence of required nutrients rather than the type of fertilizer.
3. The nutrient content of plants is determined primarily by heredity. Mineral content may be affected by the mineral content of the soil, but this has no significance in the overall diet. If essential nutrients are missing from the soil, the plant will not grow. If plants grow, that means the essential nutrients are present. As noted by Ronald Deutsch,[50] this is logical to believe because a plant does not make its nutrients "as a generous gesture to humans but for its own growth and survival." Studies lasting up to 25 years have found no difference in the nutrient content of organically grown crops and those grown under standard agricultural conditions.[7]
4. The taste of food is determined by heredity, ripeness when harvested, and freshness. A large-scale test of 25 foods at the University of Florida found that many supermarket foods actually looked and tasted better than their "organic" counterparts.[51]

"Organic" agriculture is sometimes referred to as "alternative" or "sustainable" agriculture. Neither of these terms is precisely definable.[52]

Foods labeled organic usually cost more. In 1982 the New York City Department of Consumer Affairs compared the prices of 30 foods in health food stores with conventional outlets. Prices in the health food stores averaged almost double the others.[53] Recent surveys have found similar results.[47] Since organic and conventionally grown foods cannot be told apart by their appearance, some storekeepers have labeled conventionally grown foods as organic in order to increase profits.

Government Involvement

In 1974 the FTC began working on an industrywide rule to cover food advertising, including claims for organic and natural foods. Proponents of these terms attempted to persuade the FTC to legally define them and establish standards. Opponents argued that commercial use of these terms should be prohibited because they are inherently misleading. In 1982 the FTC voted to terminate the rulemaking procedure in favor of a case-by-case approach.

In 1980 a team of scientists appointed by the U.S. Department of Agriculture (USDA) to study "organic farming" concluded that there is no universally accepted definition of the term:

> The organic movement represents a spectrum of practices, attitudes and philosophies. On the one hand are those organic practitioners who would not use chemical fertilizers or pesticides under any circumstances. These producers hold rigidly to their purist philosophy. At the other end of the spectrum, organic farmers espouse a more flexible approach. While striving to avoid the use of chemical fertilizers and pesticides, these practitioners do not rule them out entirely. Instead, when absolutely necessary, some fertilizers and also herbicides are very selectively and sparingly used as a second line of defense. Nevertheless, these farmers, too, consider themselves to be organic farmers.[54]

Despite the apparent lack of a meaningful definition, the USDA Study Team recommended that certification programs be established "to assure that organically produced foods are properly labeled" and that local USDA representatives should help organic producer associations develop criteria for certification standards.

Gradually, in response to pressure from proponents, about half the states passed some type of organic certification law. In 1990 Congress then passed the U.S. Organic Foods Production Act, which directs the U.S. Secretary of Agriculture to establish certification standards and procedures with the help from a 15-member National Organic Standards Board. Once the standards have been established—which may take several years—violators may face civil penalties of up to $10,000 per offense. Commenting on the bill, Larkin[55] stated:

> "Organic certification" *isn't* the answer. It will merely create more confusion and distrust in the marketplace. Foods certified as "organic" will neither be safer nor more nutritious than "regular" foods. They will just cost more. Instead of spending money to legitimize nutrition nonsense, our government should do more to attack its spread.

"Natural" Foods

"Natural" foods are said to be those produced and marketed with a minimum of processing and without the use of additives or artificial ingredients. The word natural, like the word organic, often means that the food product will command a higher price. Advocates of natural foods say that processing reduces nutritional value and that additives are harmful. Critics of the term natural maintain that the American food supply is the safest and best that the world has even seen. They also state that "natural" cannot be meaningfully defined because there is no sharp dividing line between processed and unprocessed foods.

Purposes and Safety of Food Additives

A few basic facts about additive processing should reassure consumers. Today some 2800 substances are intentionally added to foods for one or more of the following reasons:

1. *Maintain or improve nutritional quality:* Vitamins and minerals may be added to enrich (replace those lost in processing) or fortify (add nutrients that may be lacking in the diet). In enriched bread, for example, iron, thiamin, and niacin are restored to the levels found in whole wheat, and riboflavin is added to a higher level.
2. *Maintain product quality:* Preservatives prevent food spoilage from bacteria, molds, fungi, and yeast; extend shelf life; or protect natural color and flavor
3. *Aid in preparation:* Emulsifiers, stabilizers, thickeners, texturizers, and anticaking agents improve homogeneity, consistency, stability, texture, and "mouthfeel" of food; leavening agents affect cooking results; pH control agents affect acidity and alkalinity; humectants cause moisture retention; maturing and bleaching agents and dough conditioners improve baking qualities
4. *Improve taste or appearance:* Flavor enhancers, flavors, and sweeteners may alter the original

taste and/or aroma or restore flavor lost in processing; colors may make foods more appealing

The most widely used additives are sugar, salt, and corn syrup—all found naturally. These three, plus citric acid (found naturally in oranges and lemons), baking soda, vegetable colors, mustard, and pepper, account for 98% by weight of all food additives used in the United States.[56]

To promote natural foods, the health food industry alleges that there are too many chemicals being added to our foods. However, the important issue is not the number of chemicals, but whether they are safe and serve useful purposes. It is illogical to condemn additives with sweeping generalizations; the only proper way to evaluate food additives is to do so individually. This is the responsibility of the FDA, which has paid a great deal of attention to this matter. Food additives, particularly those introduced in the past 20 years, have survived rigid testing procedures not applied to the great majority of natural products. These tests must prove that the additive is not only safe but performs an important function. FDA scientists set tolerance levels in foods and conduct frequent "market basket" studies wherein foods from regions throughout the United States are purchased and analyzed. During the early 1980s, a USDA committee ranked food additives eighth on a list of ten areas of food safety that deserved further research.[57]

Food Industry Involvement

Dr. Elizabeth Whelan,[58] executive director of the American Council on Science and Health, has noted:

> Many of our country's largest and most respected food companies have jumped on the back-to-nature bandwagon. Today the words "natural" and "additive-free" appear on almost every type of edible product. Even beer and candy bars (so-called health bars) bear these magic words. . . . By thus exploiting the growing public fear of additives, many companies are making windfall profits. But they are also ignoring their responsibility to the American public. An educational campaign aimed at exposing food faddism would be a much more commendable course of action.

Some supermarkets are competing directly with health food stores by maintaining "nutrition centers" or sections for natural foods and food supplements. Beech-Nut Corporation and Gerber Products Company are marketing "organic" lines of baby food that cost considerably more than their standard lines.

Herbal Products

Americans spend more than $600 million per year for herb teas, bulk herbs, and other herbal products. Although most of these items are consumed for their flavor, many are also used for supposed medicinal qualities. Herbs are promoted primarily through literature—pamphlets, magazines, and books ranging in quality from cheaply printed flyers to elaborately produced studies in fine bindings with attractive art work. Varro E. Tyler, Ph.D.,[59,60] professor of pharmacognosy at Purdue University, notes that:

1. Practically all of these writings recommend large numbers of herbs for treatment based on hearsay, folklore, and tradition. The only criterion that seems to be avoided in these publications is scientific evidence. Some writings are so comprehensive and indiscriminate that they seem to recommend everything for anything.
2. Many claims are based on treatises written by the 16th century herbalist John Gerard or 17th century apothecary-astrologer Nicholas Culpeper. Many herbs recommended by their books contain cancer-causing compounds.
3. As medical science developed, it became apparent that most herbs did not deserve good reputations, and most that did were replaced by synthetic compounds that are more effective.
4. Potential customers are rarely told that some herbs are dangerous. Even deadly, poisonous herbs are sometimes recommended on the basis of some outdated report or a misunderstanding of the facts. Particularly insidious is the myth that there is something almost magical about herbal drugs that prevents them, in their natural state, from harming people.
5. Many herbs contain hundreds or even thousands of chemicals that have not been completely cataloged. Some of these chemicals may turn out to be useful as therapeutic agents, but others could prove toxic. With safe and effective medicines available, treatment with herbs rarely makes sense. Moreover, many of the conditions for which herbs are recommended are not suitable for self-treatment.
6. For all of these reasons, consumers are less likely to receive a good value for the money spent in the field of herbal medicine than in almost any other.

Herbal teas may have a single ingredient or may be blends of as many as 20 different kinds of leaves, seeds, and flowers. *The Medical Letter* regards the following substances as potentially troublesome: juniper berries, shave grass, horsetail, buckthorn bark, senna leaves, burdock root, catnip, ginseng, hydrangea, lobelia, jimsonweed, wormwood, nutmeg, chamomile, licorice root, devil's claw root, sassafras root bark, Indian tobacco, mistletoe, and pokeweed (especially the root).[61]

In 1984 Canada banned the sale of 57 herbs and required warning labels on 5 others that could pose a risk during pregnancy. The FDA urges caution, but has taken few regulatory actions involving herbs.[62]

Macrobiotic Diets

Macrobiotics is a quasireligious philosophical system founded by the late George Ohsawa. (Macrobiotic means way of long life.) The system advocates a vegetarian diet in which foods of animal origin are used as condiments rather than as full-fledged menu items. The optimal diet is achieved by balancing "yin" and "yang" foods. Ohsawa outlined a 10-stage Zen macrobiotic diet in which each stage became progressively more restricted. The diet was alleged to enable individuals to overcome all forms of illness, which Ohsawa said were due to excesses in diet. In 1971 the AMA Council on Foods and Nutrition said that followers of the diet, particularly the highest level, stood in "great danger" of malnutrition and noted that several deaths had been reported.[63]

Current proponents espouse a diet that is less restrictive but still can be nutritionally inadequate. They recommend whole grains (50% to 60% of each meal), vegetables (25% to 30% of each meal), whole beans or soybean-based products (5% to 10% of daily food), nuts and seeds (small amounts as snacks), miso soup, herbal teas, and small amounts of white meat or seafood once or twice a week.

Today's leading proponent is Michio Kushi, a former student of Ohsawa, who founded and is president of the Kushi Institute in Brookline, Massachusetts. According to Institute publications, the macrobiotic way of life should include chewing food at least 50 times per mouthful (or until it becomes liquid), not wearing synthetic or woolen clothing next to the skin, avoiding long hot baths or showers (unless you have been consuming too much salt or animal food), having large green plants in your house to enrich the oxygen content of the air, and singing a happy song every day.

Kushi[64] claims that macrobiotic eating can help prevent cancer and many other diseases. He also presents case histories of people whose cancers have supposedly disappeared after they adopted the macrobiotic diet. Dwyer[65] states that there is no scientific evidence of benefit and that the diet itself can cause cancer patients to undergo serious weight loss. Raso,[66] who attended a macrobiotic seminar for professionals, reported that astrologic conditions, weather conditions, and a long list of other bizarre factors were said to be relevant to diagnosing patients. Lindner,[67] who had a private consultation at the Institute as part of an assignment for *American Health* magazine, was told that his kidneys were weak, his heart was enlarged because he ate too much fruit, and that deposits of fat and mucus were starting to build up on his intestines. These ideas were preposterous.

Promotion of Questionable Nutrition

Food faddism is promoted through practitioners, health resorts, retail establishments, trade organizations, lectures, books, and magazines. Roth[68] notes that many of the activities of food faddists parallel those of scientific nutrition advocates.

Freedom of speech and freedom of the press make it legal for anyone to make false or unproven health claims about a product as long as the claims are not made while selling the product. Most claims directed to the public about health foods and related products are not found on labels (where they would be illegal) but reach consumers through other channels of communication.

Unproven claims appear in newspapers, magazines, books, newsletters, pamphlets, lectures, and on radio and television talk shows. Many of those who make the claims have no direct connection with supplement manufacturers, while others are paid as "consultants." Retailers absorb misinformation from health food magazines, trade publications, materials distributed by manufacturers, and seminars sponsored by trade organizations. Many health food stores distribute free literature (newsletters, flyers, and article reprints) containing claims that would be illegal on product labels. Illegal oral claims are made quite often in the privacy of health food stores, practitioners' offices, or customers' homes. Products are also promoted through the use of questionable diagnostic tests that supposedly detect vitamin and mineral deficiencies, allergies, or "imbalances."

Books

In 1991 more than $100 million was spent for books purchased in health food stores. Nutri-Books, the largest distributor, stocks more than 2000 titles, most of which promote questionable health ideas and products. Its merchandising manual distributed to bookstores states:

> Books and articles created the nutritional foods industry. . . . They are the number one product-promoters of our industry. Books and magazines are your "silent sales force". . . . Books tell your customers what your products will do. They explain the ways your products may be used. Very often this is information you may not be able to give—or may not be permitted to discuss. . . . Magazines pack a double wallop. Their articles sell products, and so do their ads.[69]

The health food industry is well-organized to promote and capitalize on popular books. *Life Extension,* a bestseller in 1982 and 1983, is based on the medically unacceptable premise that the results of animal experiments can be extrapolated to help humans live to the age of 150. According to advertisements by the book's publisher, the authors Durk Pearson and Sandy Shaw had appeared on the *Merv Griffin Show* 12 times. A Nutri-Books newsletter for health food stores provided the dates and locations of other TV talk show appearances so that the stores would stock the book. *Health Foods Business,* which reports industry trends, noted that sales of "antioxidants, moisturizers and antiaging products" increased following publication of the book. Many companies designed new products to take advantage of the book's popularity. Pearson and Shaw now license several lines of nutritional products based on their formulations.

Similarly, publication in 1985 of *Dr. Berger's Immune Power Diet,* combined with public concern about AIDS, stimulated the health food industry to market dozens of products that supposedly boost the immune system. *Consumer Reports* has expressed skepticism toward "immune-booster" and "life-extension" products.[38,70]

Periodicals

It is illegal for manufacturers to make therapeutic claims for products that are not recognized by experts as safe and effective for their intended use. For example, it would be illegal for a manufacturer to claim that a vitamin C product could prevent colds or that a mineral mixture could cure impotence. It is legal, however, for claims of this type to be made in articles written by "independent" authors. Many specialized magazines, newsletters, and newspapers cater to supplement manufacturers through articles promoting the ingredients of their products. Claims in these articles—no matter how far-fetched—are protected by the doctrine of freedom of the press as long as there is no direct connection between the author and the manufacturer. In some periodicals, ads for supplement products are placed on pages adjacent to the articles about their ingredients.

Multilevel Sales Organizations

Many companies are marketing food supplements, diet plans, homeopathic products, herbs, and other health-related products through person-to-person sales. Almost anyone can become an "independent distributor" by completing an application and paying a small fee (typically $25 to $50) for a kit containing product literature and other sales aids. No knowledge of nutrition or medical care is required. Distributors are urged to use the products themselves and to persuade others to become distributors who, in turn, use the products and recruit more distributors. If the sales volume becomes sufficient, distributors get a percentage of the sales in their "downline." Companies suggest that this process provides a great money-making opportunity. However, it is unlikely that people who do not join during the first few months of operation or do not become one of the early distributors in their community can build enough of a sales pyramid to do well.

Most multilevel companies promote their products with claims that they can prevent or cure a wide range of diseases. A few companies merely suggest that people will feel better, look better, or have more energy if they use supplements. Some companies suggest that the distributors ask how customers feel, and credit any improvement to their products.

The Neo-Life Company of Hayward, CA, has listed the following benefits of working for the company in its *Counselor* magazine: relationships, recognition, self-image, potential income, appreciation, excitement, adventure, freedom, and health.[7]

The Shaklee Corporation was founded in 1956 by Forrest Shaklee, Sr., a retired chiropractor. The biography of Shaklee sold by the company states that at the age of 18 he toured with Bernarr Macfadden to promote Macfadden's methods of "physical culture." Part of Shaklee's performance was the lifting of an iron ball that appeared to weigh over 500 pounds but actually was hollow (see Chapter 2).[71] Shaklee Corporation's official sales policy stresses dietary balance and "nutrition insurance." However, illegal therapeutic claims have been observed at sales meetings. In 1981 two Pennsylvania newspaper reporters who attended Shaklee sales meetings gave this account:

> People stand up at meetings and in the best spirit of an old-fashioned revival tell how Shaklee products have rid them of arthritis, saved their marriage, enabled them to have two bowel movements a day, and kept them from breaking a leg when they fell off a ladder. If there are any doubters, they keep quiet.[72]

Kristan C. Dale, a researcher for the American Council of Science and Health, obtained a Shaklee distributorship, collected training literature, and attended sales meetings in 1982. She encountered claims that vitamin E might make one live longer, B complex was good for coffee jitters, alfalfa has "miraculous" benefits, Herb-Lax cleanses the body of toxins, and many others. She too observed a large variety of testimonial claims. She also found that Shaklee's multivitamin (Vita-Lea) cost $6.32, whereas five comparable products sold in drugstores ranged from $.87 to $1.73 for a 1-month supply. The price was supposedly justified because:

1. Shaklee products have a special composition and method of manufacture.
2. Its vitamins are unique because they are 100% natural and not made from chemicals.
3. Its vitamins are whole foods, not isolates.
4. Customers benefit from Shaklee supplements not only because they are in harmony with nature but because they are "alive"—enzymes kept intact during the special extraction procedure "enliven" various body functions.[73]

United Sciences of America (USA) of Carrollton, Texas, used high-tech videotapes to promote its products. The introductory tape was narrated by William Shatner (Captain Kirk of *Star Trek*) and filled with scenes of laboratories, computers, and prominent medical institutions. Another tape related the ingredients in USA's products—including beta-carotene, fish oils, and fiber—to current research on the prevention of cancer, heart disease, and other conditions. The company claimed that these products comprised a "revolutionary" nutrition program designed and endorsed by a 15-person scientific advisory board that included two Nobel prize winners and several other medical school professors. By August 1986, 8 months after marketing began, the company had over 100,000 distributors and was grossing millions of dollars each month. However, the company drew a great deal of unfavorable publicity when some of the advisors denied endorsing the products and other critics challenged the claims made in the videotapes. The resultant scandal plus action by the FDA and three state attorney-generals quickly drove the company out of business.

Matol Botanical International, a Canadian firm, markets a product called *Km*, a foul-tasting extract of 14 common herbs. Km was originally marketed as Matol, which was claimed to be effective for ailments ranging from arthritis to cancer, as well as for rejuvenation. Canada's Health Protection Branch took action that resulted in an order for the company to advertise only the product name, price, and contents. In 1988 the FDA attempted to block importation of Matol into the United States. However, the company evaded the ban by adding an ingredient and changing the product's name. The product literature acknowledges that Km has never been tested for effectiveness against any disease and states that distributors should not diagnose or prescribe its products for any specific disease. However, many distributors do make therapeutic claims.[74]

Sunrider International, of Torrence, California, markets herbal products with claims that they can help "regenerate" the body. Although some of the ingredients can exert pharmacologic effects on the body, there is little evidence they can cure major diseases or that Sunrider distributors are qualified to advise people how to use them properly. During the mid-1980s, the FDA took several regulatory actions to stop false and misleading health claims for several Sunrider products. In 1989 the company signed a consent agreement to pay $175,000 to the state of California and to stop representing that its products have any effect on disease or medical conditions. The company toned down its literature but continued to make therapeutic claims in testimonial tapes included in its distributor kits.[75]

Nature's Sunshine Products, of Spanish Fork, Utah, is marketing herbs, vitamins, other nutritional supplements, homeopathic remedies, skin and hair-care products, water treatment systems, cooking utensils, and a weight-loss plan. Its more than 400 products include many that are claimed to "nourish" or "support" various body organs. Its salespeople, dubbed "Natural Health Counselors," are taught to use iridology, muscle-testing (a type of applied kinesiology), and other dubious methods to convince people that they need the products.[75a]

Health Food Stores

Health Foods Business estimates that in 1991 there were 7300 "health food" stores in America with total gross sales of $3.9 billion, including $1.5 billion for vitamins and other supplements. No special knowledge or training is required to become a salesperson at a health food store. Personnel in these stores typically obtain information by reading books and magazines that promote supplement products for the treatment of virtually all health problems. Retailers also get information from manufacturers and can attend seminars at trade shows sponsored by industry groups and trade magazines.[76]

Although it is illegal for storekeepers to "diagnose" or "prescribe," it is common for them to do both. Investigators from the American Council on Science and Health demonstrated this in 1983 by making 105 inquiries at stores in a three-state area. When asked about symptoms characteristic of glaucoma, 17 out of 24 suggested a wide variety of products for a person not present; none recognized that urgent medical care was needed. Asked over the telephone about a sudden, unexplained 15-pound weight loss in 1 month's time, 9 out of 17 recommended products sold in their store; only 7 suggested medical evaluation. Seven out of 10 stores carried "starch blockers" despite an FDA ban. Nine out of 10 recommended bone meal and dolomite, products which are considered hazardous because of lead contamination. Nine retailers made false claims of effectiveness for bee pollen, and 10 did so for RNA. The investigators concluded that most health food store clerks give advice that is irrational, unsafe, and illegal.[77]

In 1986 dietitian Clare Aigner posed five similar questions to 10 health food store proprietors in eastern Pennsylvania and concluded that only 46% of the answers were correct.[78] In 1991 Julia M. Haidet,[79] a student at Kent State University, made 30 phone calls to ten stores in Ohio and asked each one for advice about headaches; kidney stones; and abnormal thirst, dizziness, and fatigue. She received no appropriate advice.[79]

General Nutrition, Inc., with more than 1100 outlets, is the largest chain of health food stores in the United States and Canada. In 1984 the company, three of its officers, and two of its store managers were charged with criminal violations of the Federal Food, Drug, and Cosmetic Act. The indictment accused them of conspiring to promote and sell an evening primrose oil product with claims that it is effective against high blood pressure, arthritis, multiple sclerosis, and other diseases. The product had been promoted with newspaper and magazine articles, radio talk show discussions, flyers, and claims made by salespersons to customers. Although the company termed the product a "food supplement," the promotional claims made it a "drug" under federal law. This meant that it could not be legally marketed without FDA approval (which it lacked). In 1986 the company pleaded guilty to four counts of misbranding a drug, and its former president and a vice president pleaded guilty to one count. The company agreed to pay $10,000 to the government as reimbursement for costs of prosecution, and the former president was fined $1000.

Settlement of this case climaxed a series of federal enforcement actions against General Nutrition, Inc. In 1985 the company had signed consent agreements with the U.S. Postal Service to stop making unsubstantiated claims for 14 of its products sold by mail. In 1986 an FTC administrative law judge ruled that ads for another product were deliberately misleading, and he concluded that "General Nutrition's unconscionable, false, and misleading advertising found in this case is not an isolated incident but part of a continuing pattern." In 1988 the FTC charges were settled by a consent agreement in which the company agreed to donate $200,000 each to the American Heart Association, American Cancer Society, and American Diabetes Association for nutrition research. The agreement also prohibited the company from making any future claim for any company-produced product that cannot be substantiated by scientific evidence. Violation of this agreement can trigger penalties of up to $10,000 per day. During 1988 the FTC also obtained a consent agreement prohibiting Great Earth International, the second-largest health food store chain (150 stores), from making unsubstantiated claims for its products.

Between 1986 and 1990, the American Dietetic Association collected more than 500 case reports of people harmed by inappropriate nutrition advice from bogus "nutritionists," health food store operators, and others. In 1987 Florida passed a law forbidding the advertising, labeling, or commercial distribution of any product lacking FDA approval and represented to have an effect on any of a long list of health problems.

Pharmacists

Herbert and Barrett[7] have pointed out that pharmacists play an important role in the selling of vitamin supplements:

> If asked point blank, most pharmacists will admit that few of their customers need supplements and that megadoses of vitamins should be taken only under medical supervision. Why then, do they stock and sell them willingly? . . . In our opinion, pharmacists have as much of an ethical duty to discourage unnecessary use of vitamin and mineral supplements as physicians do to advise against unnecessary surgery. Do you know of any pharmacists who do so?

In 1985 reporters from *Consumer Reports* magazine visited 30 drugstores in Pennsylvania, Missouri, and California. The reporters complained of feeling tired or nervous, and asked whether a vitamin product might help. Seventeen were sold a vitamin product and one was sold an amino acid preparation. Only 9 of the 30 pharmacists suggested that a doctor be consulted.[80] In 1991 Kenneth Smith, a student at Kent State University, was advised to buy a product at 21 out of 25 pharmacies in Ohio where he posed the same questions.[81]

Chiropractors

About 50 companies market supplements through chiropractic offices, where they typically are sold for at least their wholesale cost. Many of these products are intended for the treatment of disease, even though the products are unproven and lack FDA approval for this use. Since it is illegal to place an unproven claim on a product label, claims of this type are conveyed separately through product literature distributed at chiropractic meetings, company-sponsored seminars, and by mail.[82] In 1988 a *Consumer Reports* editor who gained entrance to a company-sponsored seminar was given a 164-page manual describing how to use the company's products to treat 142 diseases and conditions that included epilepsy, heart disease, and whooping cough. The cost of a proposed treatment program for a patient whose case was presented at the meeting was over $5 per day.[83] The company advertises regularly in several chiropractic journals, including *Nutritional Perspectives,* the journal of the American Chiropractic Association Council on Nutrition.

The number of chiropractors engaging in unscientific nutrition practices is unknown, but several studies suggest that it is substantial. In 1988, 74% of about 2400 chiropractors who responded to a survey by the leading chiropractic newspaper reported using nutritional supplements in their practices.[84] Not long afterward, researchers from San Jose State University's Department of Nutrition and Food Science mailed a survey to 438 members of the San Francisco Bay Area Chiropractic Society.[85] Of the 100 who responded, 60% said that they routinely provide nutrition information to their patients, 38% said they provide it on request, 60% said that they treat patients for nutritional deficiencies, 19% said they use hair analysis, and 9% indicated that they use "applied kinesiology" for nutritional assessment. Neither hair analysis (see the following discussion) nor applied kinesiologic methods (see Chapter 9) are valid for the nutritional assessment of patients.

Nonaccredited Schools

Chapter 12 describes the training of dietitians and other nutrition professionals at accredited schools. During the past 15 years, a number of nonaccredited correspondence schools have offered B.S., M.S., and Ph.D. "degrees" in nutrition. The most prominent school was Donsbach University of Huntington Beach, California, whose president, Kurt Donsbach, is discussed later in this chapter. The school was "authorized" to operate by the State of California, which meant only that it had assets of $50,000 and had informed the authorizing agency of its programs. Most of the "textbooks" required for the school's basic curriculum were books written for the general public by promoters of dubious nutrition practices. A typical degree program took less than a year to complete. Graduates refer to themselves as "nutrition consultants," a term also used by some reputable nutritionists. The school ceased operations in 1987, but some of its "graduates" are still in practice.

Bernadean University, of Van Nuys California, offered "nutritionist" and "cancer researcher" certificates, "masters degrees," and "Ph.D. degrees" in acupuncture, reflexology, iridology, naturopathy, homeopathy, and nutrition. Dietitian Virginia Aronson took the "nutritionist" course and reported that she got high grades on all tests whether she put down correct answers or not.[86] In 1982 Bernadean was ordered to cease operations because it was not authorized by the state. Bernadean's most prominent alumnus is "Dr." Richard Passwater, author of *Supernutrition* and several other books.

In response to the rise of nonaccredited schools, dietitians have gained passage of laws to regulate nutritionists in about half of the states. Some make it illegal for unqualified persons to call themselves dietitians or nutritionists, while others define nutrition practice and who is eligible to do it. In states that regulate nutrition practice, health food retailers are still permitted to give limited advice about diet and the use of their products, but are not permitted to do nutritional assessment or counseling.

Questionable Diagnostic Tests

Nutrition consultants, chiropractors, and a small number of other licensed practitioners have been using hair analysis as a method of diagnosis. To obtain the test, customers furnish a sample of hair, usually from the back of the neck, which is sent to a laboratory for analysis. The customer and/or the referring source usually get back a computerized printout that supposedly indicates deficiencies or excesses of minerals. Some also report supposed deficiencies of vitamins. The test usually costs from $25 to $60.

Medical authorities agree that hair analysis is not an appropriate way to assess the body's nutritional state. It has limited usefulness as a screening procedure for the diagnosis of heavy metal poisoning. Hair analysis cannot diagnose vitamin deficiency because there are normally no vitamins in hair except at the root (below the skin surface). Nor can it identify mineral deficiencies because the lower limits of "normal" have not been scientifically established. Moreover, the mineral composition of hair can be affected by a person's age, natural hair color, and rate of hair growth, as well as the use of hair dyes, bleaches, and shampoos.[87]

When 52 hair samples from two healthy teenagers were sent under assumed names to 13 commercial hair analysis laboratories, the reported levels of minerals varied considerably between identical samples sent to the same lab and from lab to lab. The labs also disagreed about what was "normal" or "usual" for many of the minerals. Most reports contained computerized interpretations that were voluminous, bizarre, and potentially frightening to patients. Six labs recommended food supplements, but the types and amounts varied widely from report to report. One report diagnosed 23 "possible or probable conditions," including atherosclerosis and kidney failure, and recommended 56 supplement doses per day. Literature from most of the labs suggested falsely that their reports were useful against a wide variety of diseases and supposed nutrient imbalances.[88]

The owner and medical director of one laboratory—a dentist who had lost his license for insurance fraud—has stated:

> Hair analysis is a super good marketing tool. It's a neat, clean way of telling a customer what he specifically needs. It's the only way, with any specificity, that the health food store owner can tell scientifically what nutrients and minerals a customer needs.[89]

In 1985 the FTC secured a court order forbidding this laboratory from advertising to the public that hair analysis could be used as a basis for recommending supplements.

Live cell analysis is carried out by placing a drop of blood from the patient's fingertip on a microscope slide under a glass coverslip to keep it from drying out. The slide is then viewed with a dark-field microscope to which a television monitor has been attached. Both practitioner and patient can see the blood cells, which appear as dark bodies outlined in white. The practitioner may also take Polaroid photographs of the television picture for himself and the patient. Proponents of live cell analysis claim that it is useful in diagnosing vitamin and mineral deficiencies, tendencies toward allergic reactions, liver weakness, and many other health problems.

Dark-field microscopy is a valid scientific tool in which special lighting is used to examine specimens of cells and tissues. Connecting a television monitor to a microscope for diagnostic purposes is also a legitimate practice. However, experts believe that live cell analysis is useless in diagnosing most of the conditions that its practitioners claim to detect. Lowell,[90] who has observed several practitioners, noted that they failed to clean their microscope slides carefully between patients, which meant that dirt seen under the microscope would be misinterpreted as blood components. He also noted that one practitioner reported blood cell patterns that resulted from his microscope being out of focus and the patterns disappeared when the microscope was properly focused.

"Nutrient Deficiency" Questionnaires

Some nutrition consultants and health food stores use computers to help them decide what their customers need. One type of test involves the completion of a dietary history and another involves completion of a questionnaire about symptoms that supposedly are signs of deficiency. Computer analysis of diet is a valuable tool that reputable nutritionists may find useful when appropriate computer programs are used. However, those used by the health food industry are programmed to tell everyone that they need large numbers of supplements.

In 1988 the Council for Responsible Nutrition began advertising that stress and a fast-paced life made it advisable for women to take supplements. The ads contained a seven-question "National Vitamin Gap Test" with advice that a single "No" answer might indicate a need for supplements. However, the questions were so narrowly written that many people with perfectly adequate diets would give at least one negative answer.[91] (Figure 13-1)

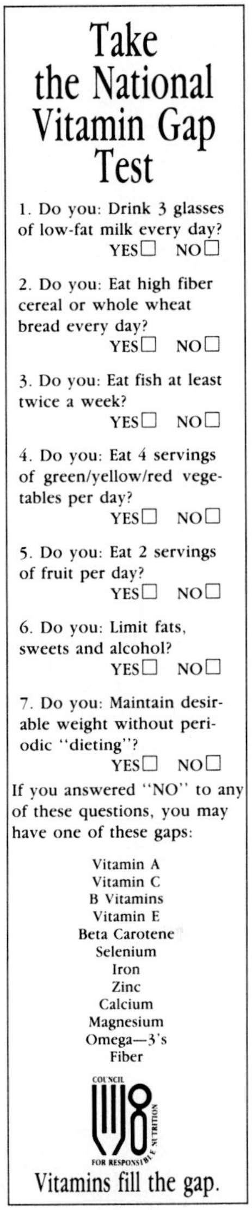

Take the National Vitamin Gap Test

1. Do you: Drink 3 glasses of low-fat milk every day? YES☐ NO☐

2. Do you: Eat high fiber cereal or whole wheat bread every day? YES☐ NO☐

3. Do you: Eat fish at least twice a week? YES☐ NO☐

4. Do you: Eat 4 servings of green/yellow/red vegetables per day? YES☐ NO☐

5. Do you: Eat 2 servings of fruit per day? YES☐ NO☐

6. Do you: Limit fats, sweets and alcohol? YES☐ NO☐

7. Do you: Maintain desirable weight without periodic "dieting"? YES☐ NO☐

If you answered "NO" to any of these questions, you may have one of these gaps:

Vitamin A
Vitamin C
B Vitamins
Vitamin E
Beta Carotene
Selenium
Iron
Zinc
Calcium
Magnesium
Omega—3's
Fiber

COUNCIL FOR RESPONSIBLE NUTRITION

Vitamins fill the gap.

FIGURE 13-1. National "Vitamin Gap" Test.

PROMOTERS OF QUESTIONABLE NUTRITION

Many organizations are involved in promoting unscientific concepts of nutrition that can cause public confusion and lead individuals to make unwise purchases or jeopardize their health. Many of the organizations have respectable or scientific-sounding names, and some even engage in a few activities helpful to the general public. For these reasons, they deserve close scrutiny by consumers.

National Health Federation

The National Health Federation (NHF) is membership organization with headquarters in Monrovia, California, and a legislative office in Washington, D.C. Its members pay from $36 per year for a "regular" membership to $1000 or more for a "perpetual" membership.

NHF's primary theme is "freedom of choice" in health matters. However, it has little interest in scientifically recognized methods. Its magazine, *Health Freedom News,* has carried many ads for questionable treatments and products marketed with illegal claims. Its articles promote unproven treatments and criticize such proven public health measures as pasteurization of milk, immunization, water fluoridation, and food irradiation. Speakers at NHF conventions espouse worthless cancer treatments and a wide range of other dubious practices. Government enforcement actions have been taken against at least 20 of NHF's past or present leaders (or their companies) who engaged in illegal health-related activities.[15]

NHF is very active in the political arena. It presents testimony to regulatory agencies and sponsors legislation aimed at keeping government interference of the health food industry to a minimum. To bolster the influence of its lobbyists, it generates letter-writing campaigns that urge legislators and government officials to support NHF positions. These campaigns typically include charges of persecution, discrimination, and conspiracy.

NHF was founded in 1955 by Fred J. Hart, president of the Electronic Medical Foundation. In 1954 Hart and the Foundation were ordered by a U.S. district court to stop distributing 13 electronic devices with false claims that they could diagnose and treat hundreds of diseases and conditions. In 1962 Hart was fined by the court for violating this order. He died in 1975.

Royal S. Lee, a nonpracticing dentist who died in 1967, helped Hart found NHF and served on its board of governors. In 1962 he and the vitamin company that he owned were convicted of misbranding 115 dietary products by making false claims on the labels for the treatment of more than 500 diseases and conditions. Lee received a 1-year suspended prison term, and his company was fined $7000. In 1973 a prominent FDA official described Lee as "probably the largest publisher of unreliable and false information in the world."[15]

Kurt W. Donsbach, who was chairman of NHF's board of governors from 1975 through 1989, is a nonpracticing chiropractor and naturopath. During the 1960s, he worked for Royal S. Lee as a "research associate" while living in California. In 1970, while Donsbach operated a health food store, agents of the Fraud Division of the California Bureau of Food and Drug observed him represent that vitamins, minerals, and herbal teas were effective against cancer, emphysema, and other conditions. Charged with nine counts of such illegal activity, Donsbach pleaded guilty to practicing medicine without a license and paid a small fine. Today he operates Hospital Santa Monica, a Mexican clinic that offers questionable treatments for cancer and other serious diseases.

NHF's current president is Maureen Salaman, whose husband Frank was convicted in 1977 of conspiracy to smuggle Laetrile into the United States. Other NHF governors have included David Ajay, president of the National Nutritional Foods Association, and Donald F. Pickett, board chairman of the Neo-Life Corporation. Financial difficulties and disputes among its leaders appear to have weakened NHF greatly during the past few years, but the organization is still functioning.

Rodale Press

Rodale Press publishes the magazines *Prevention* and *Organic Gardening* as well as many books and newsletters. Its 1991 gross income was $289 million. The company was founded by J.I. Rodale (1898-1971), who was best known for his interests in "organic farming" and "health foods." For many years, *Prevention* was the leading magazine promoting the health food industry's viewpoints. It attacked ordinary foods and recommended supplements and health foods with claims that often were ludicrous.

During the 1980s, *Prevention* shifted toward the scientific mainstream and acquired a prominent editorial advisory board. Today the magazine emphasizes dietary improvement, appropriate exercise programs, and other health-promoting activities. Although its advice generally is accurate, the coverage of nutrition news is unbalanced and still tends to encourage undue experimentation with dietary supplements. The magazine still publishes some misleading ads.

Rodale's book division and the Prevention Book Club have marketed some authoritative books, but most of their nutrition-related books espouse unproven and unscientific ideas. Ads for the books are even more blatant than the books themselves. For example, a mailer for *The Doctor's Vitamin and Mineral Encyclopedia,* by Sheldon Saul Hendler, M.D., was headlined "The World's Most Powerful Healing Vitamins and Minerals" and promised information on "a substance that reverses the aging process," a "heavy duty smart pill" that "stops the aging process and dramatically improves your memory," and a one-a-day supplement that "could dramatically reduce your chances of breast cancer." The pertinent passages in the book reported speculations based on preliminary or anecdotal evidence.

In 1989 Rodale Press sent readers of *Prevention* an ad for *Nutrition Prescription,* by Brian Morgan, Ph.D. The ad promised that the book would provide "a 'crystal ball' that gives us advance warning of the diseases we are most vulnerable to," plus a nutritional program "specifically designed to defeat the disease, reverse the symptoms and change your medical future for the better." The ad also described Dr. Morgan as "America's leading authority on nutrition." Dr. Stephen Barrett, who labeled the book "an inseparable mixture of good and poor advice," urged the National Advertising Division (NAD) of the Council of Better Business Bureaus to ask Dr. Morgan whether he considered himself "America's leading authority." After reviewing Dr. Morgan's resume, NAD concluded that he was not.[92]

Prominent Individual Promoters

Many individuals have developed and promoted food fads and other dubious nutrition practices. Each of the following has written several books and achieved notoriety during the past 2 decades.

Adelle Davis received a degree in dietetics from the University of California, Berkeley, and a master of science degree in biochemistry from the University of Southern California School of Medicine. Her four books sold 10 million copies: *Let's Eat Right to Keep Fit, Let's Get Well, Let's Cook It Right, and Let's Have Healthy Children.* She criticized the American diet as excessively high in salt, loaded with refined sugar, and contaminated by pesticides, growth hormones, and preservatives. She claimed modern food processing destroys vital nutrients. She proposed that people eat organic fruits and vegetables, whole wheat bread, wheat germ, vitamin supplements, certified raw milk, fresh stone-ground whole-grain bread or cereal, and other "health food" products.

Several critics have noted that many of the claims Adelle Davis made were not even supported by the evidence she cited. Dr. Edward H. Rynearson, emeritus professor of medicine, Mayo Clinic, Rochester, MN, made these comments about *Let's Get Well:*

> She lists 2402 reference. . . . She says . . . "hundreds of studies used as source material for this book have been conducted almost entirely by doctors, perhaps 95% of whom are professors in medical schools" . . . but this simply is not true. Probably less than 10% are professors. I wrote to a number of these eminent scientists (18 responded) . . . in many instances their remarks were either misquoted or taken out of context and not one could recommend this book. . . . I checked her references. I found glaring examples of misquotations and inaccuracies.[93]

Some of the advice in Davis' books is harmful, even potentially fatal. Two cases of children whose mothers followed her advice in *Let's Have Healthy Children* are noteworthy:

> In 1967 an infant girl was given "generous amounts" of vitamin A, which resulted in permanent stunting of her growth. Suit was filed against Adelle Davis and her publisher in 1971. In 1976 the case was settled for $150,000.
>
> In 1978 a 2-month-old infant was given liquid potassium as recommended for colic. Following the second dose he became listless and cyanotic, stopped breathing, and was rushed to a hospital where he died the following day. After a suit was filed against the publisher, the estate of Adelle Davis, and the manufacturer of the potassium product, the book was recalled from bookstores and the defendants settled for a total of $160,000. The book was reissued after changes were made by a physician allied with the health food industry.

Carlton Fredericks was described on some of his book jackets as "America's foremost nutritionist." He considered himself an expert and gave copious advice in books and articles for health food publications. According to the FDA, however, he had virtually no nutrition or health science training. He graduated from the University of Alabama in 1931 with a major in English and a minor in political science. In 1937 he began writing advertising copy for a vitamin company. He also gave sales talks, adopting the title of "nutrition educator."

In 1945, after investigators found that he had been diagnosing patients and prescribing vitamins for their illnesses, Fredericks pleaded guilty to practicing medicine without a license and paid a small fine. He then acquired a master's degree in education and a night-school Ph.D. in communications at New York University. His doctoral thesis was based on the responses of listeners to his radio programs. For 30 years, beginning in 1957, he hosted *Design for Living,* a daily show on the radio station WOR in New York City. Toward the end of his career, he did "nutrition consultations" for $200 each at the offices of Dr. Robert Atkins.

Dr. Atkins, who practices in New York City, claims that "nutrition has been useful in just about every condition I have treated. . . . And there are probably herbal answers for every condition for which there is a pharmacological answer." He describes his method of practice as "complementary medicine," which he defines as a synthesis of orthodox and "alternative" medicine put together to integrate the best of both. He considers Carlton Fredericks to have been his mentor and took over Fredericks' radio program after his death.

Atkins has written four books: *Dr. Atkins' Diet Revolution* (1971), *Dr. Atkins' Superenergy Diet*

(1977), *Dr. Atkins' Nutrition Breakthrough* (1981), and *Dr. Atkins' Health Revolution* (1988). He also markets a "Targeted Nutrition Program" in which "building blocks" are added to a "basic formula" to "help the body to create its own cures." The 17 building blocks include supplements called: Cardiovascular Formula, Heart Rhythm Formula, Hypoglycemia Formula, Anti-Arthritic Formula and Urinary Frequency Formula. A brochure from his office states that the formulas evolved from 25 years of using nutrition to treat more than 40,000 patients. In 1986 he launched the Foundation for the Advancement of Innovative Medicine (FAIM), which holds public meetings and is striving to protect "complementary" physicians from disciplinary action taken by their state medical boards.[94]

During 1991 FAIM campaigned vigorously for a law that would place "alternative" practitioners on the board that regulates professional practice in New York State.

Dr. Stuart Berger is a psychiatrist who practices in New York City as "a specialist in nutritional medicine treating immune disorders, food allergies and obesity." His books include *The Southhampton Diet, How to Be Your Own Nutritionist, What Your Doctor Didn't Tell You in Medical School,* and *Forever Young: 20 Years Younger in 20 Weeks.* All of these books contain many claims for which there is no scientific evidence.

Dr. Berger's Immune Power Diet (1985) states that overweight and numerous other health problems are the result of an "immune hypersensitivity response" to common foods, and that "detoxification" and weight loss followed by food supplements can tune and strengthen the immune system. The *Harvard Medical School Health Letter* said the book "should have been listed in the fiction category" and "is selling a collection of quack ideas about food allergies that have been around for decades."[95]

In 1990 *Inside Edition* aired two television programs describing what happened when a reporter and a prominent New York allergist had visited Berger complaining of fatigue. Both noted that their contact with him lasted about 2 minutes, included no physical examination, and culminated with a diagnosis of chronic fatigue syndrome and allergy to yeast *(Candida).* The reporter's visit was filmed with a hidden camera. The bill was $845 for the first visit and was estimated to be $1500 through the third visit. A former patient described a similar experience that had cost over $1000. A former employee said that Berger had ordered his employees to indicate on blood test reports that every patient was allergic to wheat, dairy products, eggs, and yeast.

Earl Mindell, a co-founder of Great Earth International, has a bachelor's degree in pharmacy from the Univerity of North Dakota and a "Ph.D. in nutrition" from the University of Beverly Hills, a non-accredited school that had no campus or laboratory facilities.[96] His books include *Earl Mindell's Vitamin Bible, Earl Mindell's Vitamin Bible for Kids,* and *Unsafe At Any Meal.* The *Vitamin Bible* recommends self-treatment with supplements for more than 50 health problems. The book also promotes substances that Mindell calls "vitamins" B_{10}, B_{11}, B_{13}, B_{15}, B_{17}, P, T, and U. There is no scientific evidence that any of these substances are vitamins (essential to humans) or that supplements of any of them are beneficial.

Mindell is coeditor, with Richard Passwater, of Keats Publishing Company's "Good Health Guides," a large series of booklets promoting scores of questionable supplements. Mindell has also written information sheets that were distributed free-of-charge in many health food stores. Although all of them warned that the information they contain "is not intended as medical advice but only as a guide in working with your doctor," it is clear that health food stores were using them to boost sales by making claims that would be illegal on product labels. Now retired from active management of his stores, Mindell spends much of his time writing, lecturing, and appearing on talk shows.

Dr. Lendon H. Smith is a pediatrician who claims that allergies, insomnia, alcoholism, hyperactivity in children, and a variety of other ailments are the result of enzyme disturbances that can be helped by dietary changes. He recommends a variety of food supplements and avoidance of white sugar, white flour, pasteurized milk, and other foods that are not "natural." His ideas were promoted widely on his own syndicated TV program and through guest appearances on other shows. His books include *Feed Your Kids Right, Feed Yourself Right,* and *Improving Your Child's Behavior Chemistry.*

In 1973 the Oregon State Board of Medical Examiners placed Smith on probation because he prescribed medication that was "not necessary or medically indicated" for six adult patients, one diagnosed as hyperactive and the other five as heroin addicts. He remained on probation until 1981. In

Consumer Tip

Suggestions for Consumers

The following suggestions should help consumers make healthy and economically sound decisions regarding nutrition:

1. It is virtually impossible for laypersons to sort out nutrition sense from nonsense on a claim-by-claim basis. The more practical approach is to examine the overall philosophy of the individual, organization, or publication making the claim.
2. Be wary of anyone who promotes the fads and fallacies identified in this chapter. Use the reliable sources of information identified in Chapters 3 and 12 and the Appendix of this book.
3. Avoid practitioners who prescribe vitamin supplements for everyone or who sell them in connection with their practice.
4. Be wary of any product promoted for a particular purpose that is not printed on its label. Federal laws require that health products be truthfully labeled and carry adequate directions for use. It is extremely unlikely that a product will do anything that is not claimed on its label.
5. Knowledge of the basic principles of nutrition as outlined in Chapter 12 should enable one to make wise food selections.

It's Your Decision

You have suffered severe tensions both at work and at home. You have read a newspaper advertisement for "stress" vitamins. What action should you take to reach an intelligent decision about using such vitamins?

You visit a health food store to purchase some rice flour. While you are browsing, a clerk engages you in conversation, learns that you suffer from occasional headaches, and suggests that several vitamin products will help you. The clerk also learns that your mother has arthritis and suggests several products for that also. What should you do about these recommendations?

1987 Smith permanently surrendered his medical license rather than face Board action on charges of insurance fraud. According to press reports, the trouble arose because he had signed documents authorizing insurance payments for patients he had not seen. The patients had actually been seen by chiropractors, homeopaths, and other nontraditional practitioners at "nutrition-oriented" clinics in which Smith had worked.[97]

Trade Organizations

Health food retailers have regional and national trade organizations that provide political and educational support. The most active is the National Nutritional Foods Association, which represents several thousand health food retailers, distributors, and producers. Its activities include annual conventions, a newsletter, and lobbying against governmental interference with the industry. Major manufacturers and distributors of vitamins and minerals also are represented by the Council for Responsible Nutrition.

"Nutrition consultants" can join a number of national associations, most notably the American Association of Nutritional Consultants. This group issues certificates suitable for framing and publishes a directory and a monthly newspaper. "Professional membership" is open to virtually anyone who pays the $50 fee. The application asks only for the applicant's name and address. Several investigators have been able to enroll household pets.[98]

During 1991 the health food industry became alarmed that proposed new labeling rules (see Chapter 12) would greatly reduce the number of products it could market and that proposed laws to strengthen federal enforcement agencies would weaken the industry still further. Early in 1992 the Nutritional Health Alliance (NHA) was formed to enable manufacturers, suppliers, distributors, retailers, consumers, and other supplement industry allies to coordinate their efforts to protect the industry. NHA quickly launched a campaign intended to generate 1 million protest letters to Congress. Barrett characterized the situation as a "vitamin war."[99]

Summary

Most Americans are probably harmed to some degree by nutrition fads and fallacies. Promoters of nutrition quackery are well organized and skilled at arousing and exploiting fears and false hopes. Their most persuasive sales pitch is that everyone should take supplements to be sure of getting enough vitamins and minerals. However, it is more sensible for individuals worried about this to keep a food diary for a week and have a physician or registered dietitian determine whether any problem exists.

Supplements and "health foods" have been recommended for virtually every ailment. However, there is little or no scientific evidence to support such recommendations. Megadoses of vitamins and minerals are seldom useful and should never be taken without competent medical advice. Anyone who recommends supplements for everyone should be ignored.

Discussion Questions

1. Define food faddism; list the three ways it can be expressed, the various types of faddists, and the four main myths used to promote "health foods" and food supplements.
2. Define "food supplements" and give some common reasons for their use.
3. Indicate how the concepts of "nutrition insurance" and "stress supplements" are used to promote unnecessary nutrients.
4. To what extent are nutrients lost during food processing?
5. Compare "natural" and synthetic vitamins.
6. What is the prevailing scientific opinion about whether vitamin C supplements are useful against colds or cancer?
7. What evidence exists that large doses of vitamin E or any other nutrients may be effective against diseases?
8. Identify the dangers of megadoses of vitamins and minerals.
9. What are the appropriate uses of vitamin and mineral supplements?
10. Discuss the concepts of "health food," "organic food," and "natural food," including the comparative cost and the extent of government regulation.
11. Identify and evaluate various health foods and related products sold in health food stores.
12. Discuss the purposes and safety of food additives.
13. Discuss the promotion and hazards of herbs.
14. Discuss the nature and risks of macrobiotic diets.
15. Describe some of the ways that dubious nutrition concepts are promoted, both legally and illegally.
16. Explain why hair analysis is not a useful tool for determining the body's nutritional state.
17. Identify the major individuals and organizations promoting questionable nutrition theories and practices.

REFERENCES

1. Morowitz HJ: Drinking hemlock and other nutritional matters, Hosp Pract, pp 155-156, Feb 1978.

*2. Herbert V and Barrett S: Vitamin pushers and food quacks, New York, 1992, American Council on Science and Health.

3. Schafer R and Yetley EA: Social psychology of food faddism, J Am Diet Assoc 66:129-133, 1975.

4. Beal VA: Food faddism and organic and natural foods, presented at National Dairy Council Food Writers' Conference, Newport, RI, May 1972, reported in Schafer R, Yetley EA: Social psychology of food faddism, J Am Diet Assoc 66:129-133, 1975.

5. Jarvis WT: Fads and facts in nutrition (manual for students), Loma Linda, Calif, 1979.

6. Whorton JC: Crusaders for fitness, Mt. Vernon, NY, 1982, Consumer Reports Books.

*7. Herbert V and Barrett S: Vitamins and "health" foods: the great American hustle, Philadelphia, 1981, George F Stickley Co.

8. Gallup study of vitamin use in the United States, survey VI, vol I, Princeton, NJ, Dec 1982, reported in Stanton JL: Vitamin usage: rampant or reasonable? Vitamin Issues 3(2), 1983, Hoffman-La Roche Vitamin Nutrition Information Service.

*9. Harper AE: "Nutrition insurance": a skeptical view, Nutrition Forum 4:33-37, 1987.

10. Jelen P: Food processing for the consumer, Alberta, Canada, 1979, University of Alberta, Department of Food Science.

11. Barrett S: What happened to the 1985 RDAs. Nutrition Forum 3:12, 1986.

12. NAD Case Report 12:15, 1982.

*13. Barrett S et al: The vitamin pushers, In Barrett S et al, eds: Health schemes, scams, and frauds, New York, 1990, Consumer Reports Books.

14. Vitamins and minerals, Consumer Register, April 15, 1979.

*15. Barrett S: The unhealthy alliance—crusaders for "health freedom," New York, 1988, American Council on Science and Health.

16. Herbert V: Separating food facts and myths, In Herbert V, Subak-Sharpe GJ, and Hammock DA eds: The Mount Sinai School of Medicine complete book of nutrition, New York, 1990, St. Martin's Press Inc.

16a. von Nostitz G et al: Magic muscle pills!! Health and fitness quackery in nutrition supplements, New York, 1992, New York City Department of Consumer Affairs.

17. Cameron E and Pauling L: Cancer and vitamin C, New York, 1979, WW Norton & Co Inc.

*Recommended reading.

18. Pauling L: Paper presented at the Natural Foods Exposition, March 29, 1982, reported in Natural Foods Merchandizer, p 65, June 1982.

18a. von Nostitz G et al.: Magic muscle pills! Health and fitness quackery in nutrition supplements, New York, 1992, New York City Department of Consumer Affairs.

*19. Marshall CW: Vitamins and minerals: help or harm? Mt. Vernon, NY, 1985, Consumer Reports Books.

*20. Karlowski TR et al: Ascorbic acid for the common cold: a prophylactic and therapeutic trial, JAMA 231:1038-1042, 1975.

21. DeWys WD: How to evaluate a new treatment for cancer, Your Patient and Cancer, pp 31-36, May 1982.

22. Creagan ET, Moertel CC et al: Failure of high-dose vitamin C (ascorbic acid) therapy to benefit patients with advanced cancer, a controlled trial, N Engl J Med 301:687-690, 1979.

23. Vitamin C goes down for the count in advanced-cancer controlled trial, Medical World News, Aug 22, 1983.

24. Moertel CG et al: High-dose vitamin C versus placebo in the treatment of patients with advanced cancer who had no prior chemotherapy, N Eng J Med 312:137-141, 1985.

25. Moertel CG: Perspective on vitamin C, In Barrett S and Cassileth BR eds: Dubious cancer treatment, Tampa, Fla, 1991, American Cancer Soceity.

26. Princeton Brain Bio Center: Brochure, distributed to patients, Skillman, NJ, 1983, The Center.

27. Dalton K and Dalton MJT: Characteristics of pyridoxine overdose neuropathy syndrome, Acta Neurol Scand 76:8-11, 1987.

*28. Stare FJ, Aronson V and Barrett S: Your guide to good nutrition, Buffalo, 1991, Prometheus Books.

29. American Academy of Pediatrics Committee on Nutrition: Vitamin and mineral supplement needs of normal children in the United States, Pediatrics 66:1015-1020, 1980.

30. Vitamin A cases settled for record sum, Nutrition Forum, 7:31, 1990.

31. Geubel A et al: Liver damage caused by therapeutic vitamin A administration: estimate of dose-related toxicity in 41 cases, Gastroenterology 100:1701-1709, 1991.

32. King JC, Allen L et al: Nutrition during pregnancy, Washington DC, 1990, National Academy Press.

33. Hecht A: The overselling of aloe vera, FDA Consumer 15(6):26-29, 1981.

34. Larkin T: Bee pollen as a health food, FDA Consumer 18:21-22, 1984.

35. Mirkin G: Can bee pollen benefit health? JAMA 262:1854, 1989.

36. Advice on limiting intake of bone meal, FDA Drug Bulletin, 12:5-6, 1982.

37. It's natural! It's organic! Or is it? Consumer Reports 45:410-415, 1980.

38. Can you live longer? What works and what doesn't, Consumer Reports 57:7-15, 1992.

39. Cunningham J: DHEA: facts vs. hype, Nutrition Forum 2:30-31, 1985.

40. Fish: the next health food? Consumer Reports 51:368-370, 1986.

41. Goldfinger SE: Good for what ails you? Harvard Health Letter 16(10)1-2, 1991.

42. Lowell JA: Organic germanium: another health food store junk food, Nutrition Forum 5:53-57, 1988.

43. Tyler VE, Brady LR and Robbers JE: Pharmacognosy, ed 9, Philadelphia, 1988, Lea & Febiger.

44. McPherrin E, Herbert V and Herbert R: "Vitamin B-15": anatomy of a health fraud, New York, 1981, American Council on Science and Health.

45. Hopkins H: Debunking pangamic acid, FDA Consumer 12(7):15-16, Sept 1978.

46. New York State public hearing in the matter of organic foods, New York City, Dec 1, 1972.

47. Newsome R: Organically grown foods: a scientific status summary by the Institute of Food Technologists' expert panel on food safety and nutrition, Food Technology 44(12):123-130, 1990.

48. Jones P: Pesticides and food safety, New York, 1989, American Council on Science and Health.

49. Food and Drug Administration Pesticide Program: Residues in foods—1990, Washington, DC, 1990, The Administration.

50. Deutsch R: Family guide to better food and better health, Des Moines, 1971, Meredith Corp.

51. Appledorf H et al: Sensory evaluation of health foods: a comparison with traditional foods, Florida Agricultural Experimental Stations Series, 5328, 1974.

52. Pesek J et al: Alternative agriculture, Washington DC, 1989, National Academy Press.

53. Traiger WW and Cohen DS: New York City Department of Consumer Affairs' health food stores investigjation, Jan 17, 1983, The Department.

54. Aldrich SA et al: Organic and conventional farming compared, Ames, Iowa, 1980, The Council for Agricultural Science and Technology.

*55. Larkin M: Organic foods get government "blessing" despite claims that aren't kosher, Nutrition Forum 8:25-29, 1991.

56. Lehmann P: More than you ever thought you would know about additives (3-part series), FDA Consumer, April, May, June 13(3):10-16, 12-15, 18-23, 1979.

*57. Kroger M: Food safety: what are the real issues? Nutrition Forum 2:17-18, 1985.

58. Whelan EM: The fear of additives, In Barrett S, ed: The health robbers, ed 2, Philadelphia, 1980, The George F Stickley Co.

*59. Tyler VE: The new honest herbal, Philadelphia, 1987, George F Stickley Co.

*60. Tyler VE: False tenets of paraherbalism, Nutrition Forum 7:41-44, 1989.

61. Toxic plant products sold in health food stores, Medical Letter, April 6, 1979.

62. Snider S: Beware the unknown brew: herbal teas and toxicity, FDA Consumer 25(4):31-33, 1991.

63. AMA Council on Foods and Nutrition: Zen macrobiotic diets, JAMA 218:397, 1971.

64. Kushi M and Jack A: The cancer prevention diet—Michio Kushi's nutritional blueprint for the relief and prevention of disease, New York, 1983, St. Martin's Press Inc.

*65. Dwyer J: The macrobiotic diet: no cancer cure, Nutrition Forum 7:9-11, 1990.

*66. Raso J: A Kushi seminar for professionals, Nutrition Forum 7:17-21, 1990.

67. Lindner L: The new improved macrobiotic diet, American Health 7(4):71-86, 1988.

*68. Roth JA: Health purifiers and their enemies, New York, 1977, Neal Watson Academic Publications (Prodist).

69. Building your nutritional food business with books and magazines—a merchandising manual, Denver, 1982, Nutri-Books.
*70. Power failure for the 'Immune Power' diet, Consumer Reports 51:112-113, 1986.
71. Spunt G: When nature speaks—the life of Forrest C Shaklee, Sr., New York, 1977, Frederick Fell Publishers Inc.
72. Fitzgerald S and Mekeel P: King of the nutrition peddlers, Lancaster, Penn, New Era, pp 26-27, May 1981.
73. Dale KC: "We don't prescribe," but . . . , ACSH News & Views 3:12-13, 1982.
*74. Raso J: Bottled hype: the story of *Km*, Nutrition Forum 8:33-37, 1991.
*75. Barrett S: The multilevel mirage, Priorities, pp 38-40, Summer 1991.
75a. Raso J: The shady business of Nature's Sunshine, Nutrition Forum 9:17-23, 1992.
*76. Fanning O: "Training" for health food retailers, Nutrition Forum 3:33-38, 1986.
*77. Meister KM: Do health food stores give sound nutrition advice? ACSH News and Views, May/June 1983.
78. Aigner C: Advice in health food stores, Nutrition Forum 5:1-4, Jan 1988.
*79. Haidet JM: Poor advice plus doubletalk: a probe of "health food" stores in central Ohio, Nutrition Forum 9:6-7, 1992.
*80. The vitamin pushers, Consumer Reports 51:170-175, 1987.
81. Smith KH: Vitamin pushers in Ohio, Nutrition Forum (in press)
*82. Barrett S: Chiropractors and nutrition: the supplement underground, Nutrition Forum 9:25-28, 1992.
*83. Nutrition against disease: a close look at a chiropractic seminar, Nutrition Forum 5:25-28, 1988.
84. How DCs in the USA practice? Dynamic Chiropractic 6(17):3, 1988.
85. Newman CF et al: Nutrition-related backgrounds and counseling practices of doctors of chiropractic, J Am Diet Assoc 89:939-943, 1989.
86. Aronson V: Bernadean University: a nutrition diploma mill, ACSH News & Views. 4(2):7, 12, 19, 1983.
87. Hambidge KM: Hair analysis: worthless for vitamins, limited for minerals, Am J Clin Nutr 36:943-949, 1982.
*88. Barrett S: Commercial hair analysis: science or scam? JAMA 254:1041-1045, 1985.
89. Geslewitz G: How to analyze your customer's needs, Health Foods Business 29(8):78-79, 1983.
90. Lowell J: Live cell analysis: high-tech hokum, Nutrition Forum 3:81-85, 1986.
*91. Barrett S: Be wary of bogus vitamin questionnaires, Priorities, pp 37-40, Spring 1990.
92. NAD Case Report, Rodale Press, Inc Book Promotion, p 9, April 16, 1990.
93. Rynearson ED: Americans love hogwash, Nutr Rev 32 (suppl):1-14, 1974.
94. Raso J: The FAIM symposium: a "complementary medicine" smorgasbord, Nutrition Forum, 8:17-22, 1991.
95. Bennett W: Review: Dr. Berger's immune power diet, Harvard Medical School Health Letter 10(11):7, 1985.
96. Kenney JJ: An irreverent look at the Vitamin Bible and its author, Nutrition Forum 3:46-47, 1986.
97. Lund D: Lendon Smith loses license! Nutrition Forum 4:56, 1987.
98. Barrett S: The American Association of Nutritional Consultants: who and what does it represent? Nutrition Forum 3:49-54, 1986.
*99. Barrett S: Proposed labeling rules stir controversy, Nutrition Forum 9:9-14, 1992.

CHAPTER FOURTEEN

WEIGHT CONTROL

"It doesn't look that scary to me, either. But my Mom won't even go near it."

Americans brought up in a society full of technological miracles are constantly searching for the easy way out. In desperation, they are willing to try anything offered to them, wasting money, time and sometimes their own lives.

GEORGE L. BLACKBURN, M.D., PH.D.
KONSTANTIN PAVLOU, SC.D.[1]

Q. Can a diet pill really cause people to lose fat while they sleep?
A. If it worked you would be reading about it in the headlines of every newspaper in the country.

ANN LANDERS

Obesity doesn't just happen—it is caused by consuming calories in excess of the amount you are spending. And until you correct the underlying causes of obesity, it will recur.

LYNN J. BENNION, M.D.[2]
EDWIN L. BIERMAN, M.D.
JAMES M. FERGUSON, M.D.

Consumer Decision

What methods can be used to keep one's weight under control?

When is it appropriate to lose weight?

How can commercial weight-loss programs be evaluated?

Americans spend over $30 billion a year for products and services they hope will enable them to control their weight.[3] Much of this money is wasted. The following observation, made in 1972 in the AMA's *Today's Health* magazine, still is appropriate today:

> They will attend reducing clinics and join reducing programs. They will visit doctors who will write weight-reducing prescriptions for them and inject them with hormones. They will enter hospitals for fat-removing operations. They will get themselves hypnotized, and psychoanalyzed individually and in groups. They will purchase books and pamphlets extolling the virtues of high calorie diets, low calorie diets; high fat, carbohydrate and/or protein diets; low fat, carbohydrate and/or protein diets; grapefruit diets, water diets, drinking men's diets, organic food diets and sex-instead-of-supper diets. They will gulp down diet pills, blow on diet soups, chomp on diet cookies and chew on diet gum. Most of the time, for a variety of legitimate reasons, they will emerge in much the same condition as when they began: fat. And much of the time, for a variety of illegitimate reasons, they will also emerge defrauded.[4]

This chapter describes the basic principles of weight control and the various types of products, procedures, and professional services used in the attempt to achieve it. Included in this discussion are diets, pills, special foods, and gadgets, as well as medical, surgical, and psychologic procedures, clinics, and self-help groups. For additional information on exercise, exercise devices, and "spot-reducers," see Chapter 15.

Basic Concepts

The words obese and overweight are often used interchangeably. Strictly speaking, obesity refers to an excess accumulation of fatty tissue in the body, while overweight refers to a weight greater than that listed in an established height-weight table (see Table 14-1). Overweight is commonly defined as 10% to 20% above the weights in a Metropolitan Life Insurance Company table, while obesity is defined as 20% or more above these weights. The causes of obesity are multiple and complex; they include glandular abnormalities (rarely), heredity, improper eating habits, insufficient physical activity, and psychosocial problems. Recent evidence suggests that high-fat diets are more likely than high-carbohydrate diets to produce obesity.[5]

Most people who are overweight are overfat. However, some individuals—particularly muscular young men—can exceed the listed weight without being overfat. Thus, it is more precise to use the term overfat when referring to someone whose weight is too high because of excessive body-fat content. Gabe Mirkin, M.D.,[6] a sports medicine specialist, suggests:

> The sanest definition for all these terms is this: You're fat, overweight or obese if you have an excess of body fat sufficient to impair your health or shorten your life.

The concept of the height-weight table was developed many years ago by Louis Dublin, a Metropolitan Life Insurance Company statistician. After grouping policyholders by age, height, and weight, he found that those who lived longest were the ones who maintained their weight at the average level for 25-year-olds. Since Dublin felt that there is no "ideal" weight for all individuals, he called these ranges "desirable weights." Table 14-1 lists the desirable weights published in 1959 by the Metropolitan Life Insurance Company.

Some statisticians have criticized these weights because they were derived by considering only individuals who had qualified for life insurance. But many authorities believe they are still the best data available that relate weight to life expectancy. The 1959 tables were revised in 1983 to increase the weight ranges by a few pounds. However, most professionals believe that the older tables are more accurate.[7]

Tens of millions of Americans are overfat. Small degrees of overfat are not harmful, but being 20% overfat is clearly a health hazard.[8] The most serious problem associated with being overfat is high blood pressure, but there are also considerably increased risks of sickness and death from diabetes, liver, kidney, heart, and blood vessel diseases, and other problems.

TABLE 14-1

DESIRABLE WEIGHTS FOR MEN AND WOMEN OF AGE 25 AND OVER

	Height in shoes	Weight in pounds (in indoor clothing) Small frame	Medium frame	Large frame
Men	5′-2″	112-120	118-129	126-141
	5′-3″	115-123	121-133	129-144
	5′-4″	118-126	124-136	132-148
	5′-5″	121-129	127-139	135-152
	5′-6″	124-133	130-143	138-156
	5′-7″	128-137	134-147	142-161
	5′-8″	132-141	138-152	147-166
	5′-9″	136-145	142-156	151-170
	5′-10″	140-150	146-160	155-174
	5′-11″	144-154	150-165	159-179
	6′-0″	148-158	154-170	164-184
	6′-1″	152-162	158-175	168-189
	6′-2″	156-167	162-180	173-194
	6′-3″	160-171	167-185	178-199
	6′-4″	164-175	172-190	182-204
Women	4′-10″	92-98	96-107	104-119
	4′-11″	94-101	98-110	106-122
	5′-0″	96-104	101-113	109-125
	5′-1″	99-107	104-116	112-128
	5′-2″	102-110	107-119	115-131
	5′-3″	105-113	110-122	118-134
	5′-4″	108-116	113-126	121-138
	5′-5″	111-119	116-130	125-142
	5′-6″	114-123	120-135	129-146
	5′-7″	118-127	124-139	133-150
	5′-8″	122-131	128-143	137-154
	5′-9″	126-135	132-147	141-158
	5′ 10″	130-140	136-151	145-163
	5′-11″	134-144	140-155	149-168
	6′-0″	138-148	144-159	153-173

From Metropolitan Life Insurance Company. Data are based on weights associated with lowest death rates. To obtain weight for adults younger than 25, subtract 1 pound for each year under 25.

Body fat can be estimated with fair accuracy by measuring the thickness of various skin folds with one's fingers[6,9] or a special skin caliper.[6] More accurate methods exist (such as: underwater weighing, ultrasound, electromagnetic methods, bioelectrical impedance, CT scanning, neutron activation, and nuclear magnetic imaging), but these are expensive and used primarily for research purposes. A rough indication of excessive body fat can be obtained by pinching the flesh on the back of the upper arm, midway between the shoulder and the elbow. Men who can pinch 1 inch or more and women who can pinch more than 1¼ inches are probably overfat. Perhaps the most practical method is to remove one's clothes and look into a full-length mirror.

Obese men tend to accumulate abdominal fat, while women tend to accumulate fat on their hips and thighs. A waist-to-hip ratio (WHR) greater than 1.0 indicates a high risk of adverse health consequences. WHR is determined by dividing the circumference of the waist by the circumference of the buttocks. A man with 35-inch hips and a 42-inch waist, for example, would have a WHR of 1.2. The waist is measured at the level of the umbilicus (belly button), and the hips are measured at the area of maximum protrusion of the buttocks.

With respect to health risks, the location of fat in the body may be more important than the total body fat. In men a high WHR is associated with elevated blood-cholesterol levels and increased risk of coronary artery disease, high blood pressure, and adult-onset diabetes. These problems are related more to fatty tissue located inside the abdominal cavity than to fatty tissue located just under the skin.[2]

The two basic factors involved in weight control are caloric intake and energy expenditure. To lose weight one must eat less or exercise more—but most people need to do both. There are about 3500 calories stored in a pound of fat. Most moderately active people need about 15 calories per pound to maintain their weight (see Table 14-2).[10] To lose 1 pound a week, one must eat an average of 500 fewer calories per day than are metabolized. Nutritionists recommend that diets under 1200 calories per day should not be carried out without medical supervision. Table 14-3 shows how caloric deficit is related to the rate of weight loss.

Most people who are overfat find weight control difficult or impossible to achieve. Long-term studies of overfat individuals have found that more than 95% of those who lose weight by dieting regain it within 1 year.[11] Dietary treatment is most likely to succeed in individuals who are only modestly overweight. Obese individuals tend to burn calories more slowly. They tend to be less active, which compounds the problem, because people tend to eat more when they are sedentary.

Preventing obesity during childhood may lower the chance of obesity in adult life. Obesity is related to both the number of fat cells and the amount of

Table 14–2

Approximate Number of Calories Needed by Moderately Active People to Maintain Weight

Weight	Calories needed
100	1500
110	1650
120	1800
130	1950
140	2100
150	2250
160	2400
170	2550
180	2700
190	2850
200	3000

Table 14–3

Weeks Needed to Lose Weight at Various Calorie Deficits

Pounds to lose	Calorie deficit*											
	100	*200*	*300*	*400*	*500*	*600*	*700*	*800*	*900*	*1000*	*1100*	*1200*
1	5.0	2.5	1.7	1.3	1.0	0.8	0.7	0.6	0.6	0.5	0.5	0.4
2	10.0	5.0	3.3	2.5	2.0	1.7	1.4	1.3	1.1	1.0	0.9	0.8
3	15.0	7.5	5.0	3.8	3.0	2.5	2.1	1.9	1.7	1.5	1.4	1.3
4	20.0	10.0	6.7	5.0	4.0	3.3	2.9	2.5	2.2	2.0	1.8	1.7
5	25.0	12.5	8.3	6.3	5.0	4.2	3.6	3.1	2.8	2.5	2.3	2.1
6	30.0	15.0	10.0	7.5	6.0	5.0	4.3	3.8	3.3	3.0	2.7	2.5
7	35.0	17.5	11.7	8.8	7.0	5.8	5.0	4.4	3.9	3.5	3.2	2.9
8	40.0	20.0	13.3	10.0	8.0	6.7	5.7	5.0	4.4	4.0	3.6	3.3
9	45.0	22.5	15.0	11.3	9.0	7.5	6.4	5.6	5.0	4.5	4.1	3.8
10	50.0	25.0	16.7	12.5	10.0	8.3	7.1	6.3	5.6	5.0	4.5	4.2

© 1992, Stephen Barrett, M.D.

*Calorie deficit equals calories expended minus calories consumed (each 3500-calorie deficit produces a loss of 1 pound.)
Most moderately active people need about 15 calories per pound to maintain their weight.

fat they contain; the more fat cells a person has, the more likely the person will become and remain obese. Excessive calorie intake tends to increase the number of fat cells in the body, particularly during childhood. When people lose weight they decrease the fat content of their cells, but not their number. Thus the more excess weight gained early in life, the more difficult it will be to lose or maintain weight.[2]

A 32-year study of more than 3130 men and women has shown that regardless of initial weight, people whose weight repeatedly goes up and down (referred to as "weight cycling" or "yo-yo dieting") have a higher overall death rate and as much as twice the chance of dying from heart disease.[12] The researchers also found that people who dieted tended to vary their weight more than people who did not. Expressing concern that "the risks due to overweight may not outweigh the risks due to weight fluctuation," the researchers recommended that weight-loss programs give greater emphasis to preventing relapses. Kelley Brownell, Ph.D., the psychologist in charge of the study, said that many women who are not overweight create trouble for themselves by dieting.

Eating Disorders

Our society's preoccupation with body image and dieting has stimulated many people to resort to extreme measures of weight control. Anorexia nervosa is a life-threatening condition manifested by severe limitation of food intake. The victims, most of whom are young women, have an intense fear of gaining weight or becoming fat, even though they are underweight. Bulimia is a disorder manifested by bingeing (episodes of eating large amounts of food) and purging (getting rid of the food by vomiting and/or using laxatives). About half of anorectics are bulimic.

Inadequate food intake or extreme purging can cause metabolic imbalances that result in fatigue, irregular heartbeat, thinning of the bones, and cessation of menstruation. Frequent self-induced vomiting can damage the stomach and esophagus, make the gums recede, and erode tooth enamel. Studies indicate that as many as 1% of females become anorectic between the ages of 12 and 18, and that 4.5% to 18% of female first-year college students have a history of bulimia.[13]

Eating disorders may require psychologic and dietary counseling as well as medical treatment for any physical ailments that have developed. If a patient's weight becomes dangerously low, hospitalization with intensive therapy is recommended. Medical treatment for anorexia may have to include tube feedings or hyperalimentation (complete nutrition through the veins) if the patient will not or cannot eat. Dietary counseling may help an anorectic individual understand the importance of nutrition and instill healthy eating behaviors. Psychologic therapy should aim for greater self-understanding, clarification of family dynamics, and the development of the patient's own individual personality. Additional information about eating disorders can be obtained by sending a self-addressed stamped envelope to the National Association of Anorexia Nervosa and Associated Disorders, or by calling the toll-free number of the Anorexia Bulimia Treatment and Education Center, which are listed in the Appendix of this book.

The Diet and Weight-Loss Marketplace

Surveys have estimated that the percentage of overweight adults in the United States is between 25% and 64%, depending on the criteria and methods used to collect the data. Marketdata Enterprises,[14] an independent market research and consulting firm, estimates the total 1990 sales of $30.2 billion, including: over-the counter (OTC) appetite suppressants ($1.47 billion); low-calorie prepared foods ($1.97 billion); diet soft drinks ($13.3 billion); artificial sweeteners ($1.19 billion); commercial weight-loss centers ($2.0 billion); hospital- and physician-based weight-loss programs ($1.6 billion); nonresidential fitness and exercise clubs/spas ($6.4 billion); residential health spas ($1.55 billion); and diet books and cassette tapes ($0.67 billion). Marketdata also notes:

1. Seventy percent of teenage girls are dieting. The explosion of eating disorder cases is partly exacerbated by misuse of OTC diet products, most notably phenylpropanolamine.
2. Most dieters with money to spend are "cosmetically obese" (20 to 30 pounds to lose) rather than medically at risk.
3. Recent government investigations have pressured many commercial operators to promise to institute methods for collecting and reporting data on their customers' experiences—including their ability to keep weight off once it has been lost.

Questionable Diets

Most fad diets, if followed closely, will result in weight loss—as a result of caloric restriction—but they are monotonous and often dangerous to one's health if followed for long periods. A highly advertised diet will attract large numbers of individuals who try it for a short period of time, lose weight, and encourage others to do the same. Few individuals who participate will retain weight loss; thus the market for "new" diets seems inexhaustible. Many obese individuals are sufficiently desperate or gullible to try one questionable method after another.

The National Council Against Health Fraud warns consumers to be wary of any weight-control program that encourages the use of special products rather than learning how to make wise food choices from the conventional food supply.[16]

Most fad diets lack important nutrients or even whole food groups and are therefore nutritionally unbalanced. The three main types of unbalanced diet plans are: fasting (starvation), supplemented fasting, and low-carbohydrate (high-protein).

Consumer Tip

Dr. Philip L. White, former director of the AMA Department of Foods and Nutrition, warns against trying any method that promises weight loss of more than 2 pounds a week. He gives these additional clues that will help the consumer recognize an unreliable diet promotion:

1. It suggests that a nutrient or food group is either the "key" to weight reduction or the primary "villain" that keeps people overweight.
2. It claims to be a revolutionary new idea.
3. It reports testimonials rather than documented research.
4. It refers to the author's own case histories, but does not describe them in detail.
5. It claims 100% success.
6. It claims persecution by the medical profession.[15]

Complete Fasting

The most drastic way to reduce caloric intake is to stop eating completely. Intake of water, of course, is still necessary. Fasting has been used for weight reduction since ancient times. Losses will be greatest in heaviest subjects and least in individuals who are the lightest. A few days' of fasting are unlikely to be dangerous, but prolonged fasting leads to dangerous metabolic imbalances.

Glucose is essential for the brain and is the preferred fuel for other body tissues. Glucose is easily obtained from carbohydrates, less easily from proteins, but not at all from fats. After a few days of total fasting, body fats and proteins are metabolized to produce energy. The fats are broken down into fatty acids, which can be used as fuel. If sufficient carbohydrate is not available to the body, the fatty acids may by incompletely metabolized and yield ketone bodies, producing a condition known as ketosis. This is hazardous because body proteins must be broken down to ensure an adequate supply of glucose for the brain. During fasting, since no proteins are available from food, they are obtained from muscles and major organs such as the heart and kidneys. A prolonged fast can also lead to anemia, liver impairment, kidney stones, postural hypotension (low blood pressure), mineral imbalances, and other adverse effects. Thus, if used at all, prolonged fasting should never be done without close medical supervision.

Part of the reason for fasting's popularity is that it can produce dramatic weight loss during its early stages. As ketosis begins, large amounts of water will be shed, leading the dieter to think that significant weight reduction is taking place. However, most of the loss is water rather than fat; the lost water is regained quickly when eating is resumed. Appetite, often reduced during ketosis, also returns when a balanced diet is resumed.

Supplemented Fasting

Medical researchers have discovered that if fasting individuals eat small amounts of protein, the protein will break down slowly to provide glucose needed by the brain. Eating carbohydrate for this purpose does not work because it triggers an insulin response that causes intense hunger. In the early 1970s, Dr. George Blackburn and colleagues at the Deaconess Hospital in Boston developed the "protein-sparing modified fast" in which fasting patients were given small amounts of high-quality protein along with noncaloric liquids, vitamins, calcium, potassium, other minerals, and sometimes glucose. Patients were initially hospitalized for a week of evaluation and then followed closely as outpatients. Their diets were carefully calculated by weight. The program emphasized not only diet but also an overall approach that included exercise, instruction in nutrition, and behavior modification.

Today, modified fasting can be done safely on an outpatient basis under skilled medical supervision. But a recent editorial in the *Journal of the American Medical Association* warned that popularization of very-low-calorie (VLC) diets—by such events as Oprah Winfrey's celebrated 67-pound weight-loss (which was followed by regaining a greater amount)—could lead to dangerous misuse. Experts fear that the vigorous marketing of meal-replacement drinks will encourage people to use these products inappropriately. The more meals replaced and the lower the number of calories consumed daily, the greater the risk. The risk is greatest in individuals who are not severely overweight. The FDA now requires a warning label on weight-reduction products if more than half of their calories come from protein.

VLC diets usually contain 400 to 800 calories per day, most of them from high-quality proteins, plus vitamins and minerals, particularly potassium. Some programs use liquid formulas, while others utilize food sources (poultry, fish, and lean meats). Programs this drastic should be restricted to individuals who are at least 30% overweight and be administered only under close medical supervision as part of a comprehensive program. The programs should include a weekly examination by a physician familiar with the metabolic effects of VLC diets, blood tests to detect potentially dangerous metabolic abnormalities, and behavior modification. Patients in controlled investigations have typically consumed the diets for 12 to 16 weeks. Weight gain is common after the eating of food is resumed, but the gain is more likely to occur with do-it-yourself programs than with medically supervised ones.[17] Bennion et al[2] noted that fewer than half of the people who sign up for a VLC program actually reach their goal weight.

Low-Carbohydrate (High-Protein) Diets

Most low-carbohydrate diets do not limit the intake of proteins, fats, or total calories. Promoters claim that unbalancing the diet will lead to increased metabolism of unwanted fat even if the calories are not restricted. This is not true, but calorie reduction is likely to occur because the diet's monotony tends to discourage overeating. A diet that is low in both carbohydrates and calories will produce ketosis and rapid initial weight loss, as noted earlier.

Promoters of low-carbohydrate diets often refer to carbohydrates as "the dieter's number one enemy." This designation is inappropriate, because calories from any source contribute equally to weight gain if consumed in excess. Moreover, because of their high water and fiber content, most carbohydrate foods other than table sugar contain fewer calories per volume of food than most other foods.

Table 14-4 summarizes the shortcomings of various fad diets.

The Atkins Diet

Dr. Atkins' Diet Revolution, published in 1972, sold millions of copies within the first 2 years. The book alleges:

> Carbohydrates—not fat—are the principal elements in food that fatten fat people. They do this by preventing you from burning up your own fat and by stimulating your body to make more fat. . . . Protein and fat combinations alone do not do this.

Atkins stated that these events occur because his diet stimulates production of a "fat-mobilizing hormone." However, the AMA Council on Foods and Nutrition responded to this claim by stating that no such hormone had been identified in humans, that the book makes other biochemical errors, and the unlimited intake of saturated fats and cholesterol-rich foods under Atkins' food plan could increase the dieter's risk of heart disease.[18]

Stung by many critics, Atkins became progressively alienated toward scientific medicine and wrote several more books espousing unscientific nutrition concepts. His latest book, *Dr. Atkins' Health Revolution* (1988), endorses many unorthodox treatments and claims that "nutrients provide a better therapy than do drugs. . . . The body is capable of healing itself, if presented with the proper substances." Chapter 13 contains additional information about Dr. Atkins.

Liquid Protein Diet

The concept of using a very low-calorie protein diet was popularized in 1976 through the book *The Last Chance Diet,* by Robert Linn, D.O. The book's publication spawned production of many do-it-yourself protein supplements in liquid, capsule, tablet, and powder forms. Linn's method bore some resemblance to the protein-sparing modified fast devel-

Table 14–4

Questionable Diet Plans—Past and Present

Diet plan	Brief description	Comments
Bio-Diet	Alternates "crash" diet with binges, plus supplements	Unhealthy practice; supplements do not provide weight-loss benefits as claimed
Bloomingdale's Eat Healthy Diet	Highly restrictive diet based on false premise that certain foods are addictive	Unbalanced; can slow metabolism; semistarvation encourages binge eating
Dr. Stillman's Quick Weight-Loss Diet	Low-carbohydrate diet	Unbalanced, cause ketosis and other serious side effects; weight loss primarily due to temporary fluid loss
F-Plan Diet	Low-calorie, high-fiber diet	May be deficient in calcium; excessive fiber can cause side effects
Fat-Destroyer Foods Diet	Low-carbohydrate high-protein diet	Unbalanced; high in fat/cholesterol; causes ketosis and other serious side effects; weight loss primarily due to temporary fluid loss
Fructose Diet	Low-carbohydrate diet with relatively large intake of fructose	Unbalanced; fructose does not provide weight-loss benefits claimed
Grapefruit Diet	Grapefruit and/or supplements before meals to "burn" fat	Unbalanced and/or ineffective; based on myth that grapefruit facilitates weight loss
I Love New York Diet	Alternates "crash" diet with binges	Unhealthy practice; can slow metabolism; promises unrealistic results
Kelp, Lecithin, Vitamin B_6 and Cider Vinegar Diet	Low-carbohydrate diet plus supplements	Unbalanced; supplements do not provide weight-loss benefits claimed
Mayo Diet	Grapefruit eaten before meals to "burn" fat	Ineffective; based on myth; not connected with the Mayo Clinic
Mono-food diets	Special emphasis given to one food or food type, such as eggs, grapefruit, or fruit only	Unbalanced; can slow metabolism; nutrient deficiencies can develop
Rice Diet	Five phases, beginning with only rice and fruit	Unbalanced; can cause low blood pressure and lead to nutrient deficiencies
Rotation Diet	Low-calorie diet alternating with "normal" eating	Unbalanced; can slow metabolism; binge eating common
Southampton Diet	Low-calorie diet with "mood foods"	Promises unrealistic results; promotes nutrition nonsense
Any more? Unfortunately, yes. As long as the public buys them, the endless parade of questionable diets will continue.	More of the same	Most likely unbalanced, restrictive, and ultimately disappointing; may slow your metabolism and can prove dangerous to your health

Modified from Stare FJ, Aronson V and Barrett S: Your guide to good nutrition, Buffalo, 1991, Prometheus Books.

oped by Dr. Blackburn, but there were significant differences. Most important was the fact that the protein recommended in Linn's book, made from predigested cattle hides, cartilage, and tendons, lacked certain essential amino acids.

Dr. Jean Mayer,[19] former professor of nutrition at Harvard University, warned that limiting food intake to a protein supplement causes serious metabolic changes. He stressed that Dr. Blackburn's program was designed for people who are at least 50 pounds overweight and are dieting under medical supervision. In 1978 the FDA reported that more than 50 deaths had been associated with use of low-calorie protein diets. In addition, hundreds of people had become ill as a result of using protein products. The FDA then proposed that appropriate warnings be placed on the labels of such products.[20] Subsequent studies indicate that the risk of cardiac arrest from a VLC diet is greatly increased in individuals who are mildly to moderately obese.[21]

The Scarsdale Diet

The Scarsdale Medical Diet is a carefully designed regimen that itemizes foods for every day of the week, with no substitutions allowed. The expected intake is 750 to 1000 calories per day. The plan's author, the late Dr. Herman Tarnower, suggested preliminary consultation with a physician, a daily 2-mile walk, and alteration of the 2-week periods of the basic diet with 2-week periods of a more liberal "Keep-Trim Program." Mirkin[7] states that the diet cannot be followed permanently and does not help people change their eating habits.

The Beverly Hills Diet

The Beverly Hills Diet is based on bizarre notions about digestion and metabolism, including the idea that undigested food is what winds up as fat. The author, Judy Mazel, is not a nutrition professional. She claims that for food to be digested properly, only one type (protein, fat, or carbohydrate) should be eaten each day. Her diet calls for just fruit for the first 10 days, then other types of foods are added in various combinations. Three cases of severe diarrhea, muscle weakness, and dizziness on this diet were reported by Mirkin and Shore,[22] who also warned that more serious reactions would not be surprising. Harvard nutritionist D. Mark Hegsted, Ph.D.,[23] noted the diet's low protein content and called it "a sure recipe for malnutrition if you stay on it long enough."

Immune Power Diet

Dr. Berger's Immune Power Diet, by psychiatrist Dr. Stuart Berger, became a best seller in 1985. Its main premise is that obesity and many other health problems are the results of a food allergy that is diagnosable through cytotoxic testing. However, this test, which is performed by examining white blood cells after exposing them to food extracts, is unreliable.[24] Berger's suggested treatment includes dietary advice and large doses of vitamins. Consumers Union's medical consultants stated that "there is no credible evidence that particular foods have either damaging or protective effects on the immune system [or] that food supplements increase the body's resistance to disease."[25] The book helped to create a market for supplement products that "strengthen the immune system."

Fit for Life Diet

Fit for Life is based on theories of "natural hygiene," which allege that eating foods in the wrong combination can cause health problems (see Chapter 9). The book's authors, Harvey and Marilyn Diamond, lack scientific training in nutrition but acquired credentials from the American College of Health Science, an unaccredited correspondence school that in 1986 was ordered by a Texas court to stop granting "degrees" and calling itself a college. According to the Diamonds, when certain foods are eaten together, they "rot" and "decay," creating digestive cesspools that somehow poison your system and make you tired and fat. They recommend a low-fat, high-fiber diet with foods high in water content to "wash out the body from the inside." Katherine Musgrave, a University of Maine nutrition professor, did a computerized analysis of the diet and concluded that it was inadequate in vitamins B_{12} and D, calcium, and zinc.[26] Despite enormous criticism from the scientific community, the book sold close to 2 million copies.

Herbalife

Herbalife International is a multilevel marketing company founded in 1980. Its diet plan was based on four products: (1) a powdered protein meal substitute, (2) an herbal blend whose ingredients include small amounts of laxatives, (3) a multivitamin/multimineral/herb formula, and (4) a linseed oil formula. Initially these products and others were marketed with suggestions that they would produce rapid weight loss, and the herbs they contain were effective against a large number of serious diseases. Testimonials to this effect were spread by personal contact as well as frequent television specials.

In 1985 a U.S. Senate subcommittee held hearings where experts testified that Herbalife had made many false claims, and company officials admitted that many users had experienced headaches, diarrhea, constipation, or other adverse effects from its products.[27] Soon afterward, the California Attorney General charged that Herbalife had made false claims for many of its products and engaged in an illegal pyramid-style marketing scheme. In 1986 the company and its president, Mark Hughes, agreed to pay $850,000 to settle these charges. The court order settling the case forbids representation without reasonable basis that Herbalife products contain herbs that can curb appetite, burn off calories, or cleanse the system.

Prescription Drugs

No drug or drug product currently available appears to be of value in helping individuals to lose weight and keep it off. Some products can suppress appetite temporarily, but the side effects or other negative characteristics limit their usefulness.

Amphetamines ("speed") were once widely prescribed as an appetite suppressant. Their adverse effects outweigh any usefulness as a dieting aid, but a few physicians—contrary to prevailing medical opinion—still prescribe them. Amphetamines are physically and psychologically addicting. Although they can temporarily curb appetite, individuals develop a tolerance to them and higher (dangerous) dosages must be used to maintain this appetite suppression. Amphetamines can produce nervousness, irritability, insomnia, and fatigue. High dosages can cause abnormal heart rhythms, fainting, and psychosis.

In 1971 Dr. John D. Griffith, associate professor at the Vanderbilt University School of Medicine commented:

> Studies show these drugs will suppress appetite and that subjects will lose an average of 6.75 pounds during an 8 to 12 week period. At the end of this time the patient becomes resistant to the effect of the amphetamine and derives little or no further benefit. The cosmetic and health advantages derived from a 6.75-pound weight loss are quite minor. For this reason, responsible physicians are of the opinion that amphetamines should not be prescribed for appetite suppression.[28]

Thyroid hormone helps to control metabolism—the rate at which calories are used up by the body. However, unless there exists a documented deficiency of this hormone, use of thyroid supplements is inadvisable. Small doses given to normal individuals merely suppress normal thyroid hormone production and have no metabolic effect. Large dosages will cause weight reduction, but they will also raise blood pressure and strain the heart. The FDA requires the labels on thyroid products to warn that they should not be used for obesity and that large doses produce serious and life-threatening effects.[29]

Human chorionic gonadotropin (HCG) is a hormone found in the urine of pregnant women. HCG was first used more than 40 years ago by Dr. Albert T. Simeons, a British-born physician who contended that it would enable dieters to subsist comfortably on a 500-calorie-a-day diet. He claimed that HCG would mobilize stored fat, suppress appetite, and redistribute fat from the waist, hips, and thighs. There is no scientific evidence to support these claims. Moreover, a 500-calorie (semistarvation) diet is likely to result in loss of protein from vital organs, and HCG may have additional toxicity.

A controlled study of 200 patients at Lackland Air Force Base, Texas, compared the effectiveness of HCG and a placebo in a weight-reduction program. Those given HCG lost an average of 15 pounds, and those given the placebo lost an average of 15.4 pounds. The FDA and AMA have reviewed all available studies and concluded that HCG has no usefulness in the treatment of obesity. The FDA requires all labeling and advertising of HCG to state that it has not been demonstrated to be effective against obesity. Mirkin[6] states, "At one time, HCG was the most widespread obesity medication administered in the United States. Some doctors liked it because it assured them of a steady clientele. Patients had to come in once a week for an injection."

Fenfluramine (Pondimin) and a few other prescription appetite-suppressant drugs have been able to produce weight loss of ½ to 1½ pounds per week. However, when the drug is discontinued, most users gain weight, and many gain more than they lost while taking the drug. Fenfluramine's adverse effects include diarrhea, drowsiness, high blood pressure, and glaucoma. Bennion et al[2] believe that appetite-suppressant drugs should not be used for weight control because the risk of side effects outweighs the likelihood of a lasting benefit.

Diuretics are substances that cause water loss from the body by increasing the output of urine.

They can be very valuable in the medical treatment of cardiovascular disease, but are inappropriate for use in weight-reduction programs. Any weight loss that results from water loss is temporary and will be reversed when the body is rehydrated. In addition, improper use of diuretics can cause a dangerous depletion of body sodium or potassium.

Nonprescription Products

David Zimmerman,[30] author of *The Essential Guide to Nonprescription Drugs,* notes that over 100 substances have been formulated into weight-loss products. The FDA advisory panel that evaluated these products found that some had no pharmacologic activity at all, and many were unworthy of consideration because no shred of evidence suggested that they could be helpful. Only two ingredients were judged safe and effective: phenylpropanolamine and benzocaine.

Phenylpropanolamine

Phenylpropanolamine (PPA), a nasal decongestant, is the active ingredient in many OTC diet aids, including Acutrim, Appedrine, Control, Dexatrim, Diet Ayds, Diet-Trim, Prolamine, Super Odrinex, Thinz, and Unitrol. Doses high enough to suppress appetite may produce such side effects as headaches, blurred vision, excessive sweating, rapid pulse, nervousness, insomnia, dizziness, heart palpitations, and elevations in blood pressure. The drug should not be used by women who are pregnant or breast feeding, young children, elderly, and those in poor health, especially individuals with high blood pressure, heart disease, diabetes, or thyroid or kidney disorders. The advisory panel judged that 150 mg of PPA daily was safe, but a series of adverse case reports prompted the FDA to set the maximum sanctioned daily dosage at 75 mg. The FDA has also ordered that further studies are needed to resolve questions about the safety of products containing PPA.

The FDA panel released a favorable report on PPA in 1979. Although the report was not endorsed by the FDA itself, sales of PPA products shot up to over $200 million a year. In 1982 *Consumer Reports* noted that mail-order manufacturers were misrepresenting the significance of the panel report and exaggerating the potency of PPA, calling it a "wonder ingredient" able to "neutralize the effect of all incoming calories," "proven safe and effective in government tests," and so on. After reviewing the transcripts of the FDA panel hearings, *Consumer Reports* concluded that: (1) the studies considered by the panel had limitations in size, duration, or design, (2) PPA diet aids may suppress appetites for short periods in some individuals, (3) most of the resultant weight loss occurs during the first 2 weeks of use, and (4) as does fenfluramine, PPA may undermine weight-loss efforts in the long run.[31]

PPA is often an ingredient in fake pep pills that are popular with high school and college students. In 1981 the FDA stated that the proliferation of PPA-containing products has caused PPA overdosage to become an increasingly common problem for poison control centers and hospital emergency rooms. The agency estimated that more than 10,000 poison control cases and 1000 emergency room visits were being made annually for this reason.[31] Cases of moderate and severe anxiety from single doses of 50 to 75 mg have been reported.[32]

Benzocaine

Benzocaine, a local anesthetic, is used in chewing gum, lozenges, and before-meal candies. The theory behind its use is that dulling nerve endings in the mouth can decrease a person's sense of taste and therefore decrease interest in eating. Benzocaine was also judged by the FDA panel as a safe and effective weight-loss aid, but the FDA and the majority of American physicians do not agree with the panel's conclusion. Mirkin[6] states:

> People who lack the will to diet effectively without benzocaine can hardly be expected to put up with the drug indefinitely either. It tastes bad, creates numbness in the mouth, and removes most of the taste in all food, not just fattening food. It can discourage a worthwhile effort to learn good eating habits, and it is never an adequate substitute for those habits.

Bulk Producers

Bulking agents are indigestible, noncaloric substances that absorb water during digestion and supposedly trick the stomach into thinking it is full. The substances include alginic acid, carboxymethylcellulose, carrageen, guar gum, karaya gum, methylcellulose, psyllium, sea kelp, and xanthan gum. The FDA panel judged these substances to be safe but not proven effective. Dr. Ernest Drenick of Los Angeles, who tested methylcellulose tablets in volunteers, found that they experienced no reduction in hunger or appetite. He also demonstrated with x-ray examination that methylcellulose does not actually fill the stomach but quickly passes into the small intestine. Drenick pointed out there is no evidence that increasing the volume of a meal will produce satiety in obese individuals.[33]

Health food stores have promoted two other bulking agents: glucomannan and pectin. Glucomannan is made from the fibers of a Japanese root plant. Some manufacturers of glucomannan products are also promoting them as effective in lowering cholesterol, eliminating ingested chemicals, aiding digestion, and reducing blood-sugar levels. However, there is no scientific evidence to support these claims. In 1980 Dr. Judith Stern of the University of California conducted a double-blind study in which the test group received 1 g of glucomannan before meals, while the control group received a placebo. Both groups participated in a behavior modification program and lost weight, but no statistically significant difference in hunger ratings or weight loss was found between the groups.[27]

Pectin has been marketed in powder and tablet form as a wonder drug for weight reduction. It is naturally present in a number of foods such as apples, apricots, plums, the rinds of cirtus fruits, and root vegetables such as carrots and radishes. However, the quantity of pectin-rich foods that must be consumed to contribute enough bulk for appetite suppression is prohibitive.

In 1989 the FTC charged that Schering Corporation had marketed Fibre Trim with unsubstantiated claims that it is effective for weight loss, weight control, and weight maintenance. In 1991 an FTC administrative law judge[34] ruled that there was no scientific evidence to substantiate such claims. Fibre Trim is composed of natural fiber from citrus and grain compressed into tablets. The recommended daily dosage contains about 4 g of fiber. Ads said the product could provide a feeling of fullness and could "take the edge off hunger." A company document estimated that 70% of Fibre Trim's 1986 sales were to consumers "looking for the magic pill" and who "want a product that will do the work." The judge ordered Schering to refrain from making unsubstantiated claims that Fibre Trim: (a) is a rich source of fiber, (b) could provide any health benefit associated with the intake of fiber, or (c) could provide any appetite-suppressant, weight-loss, or weight-control benefit.

Diet Candies

These products are usually caramels that may contain added vitamins and minerals. Taken before meals, they supposedly cause a rise in blood-sugar levels, which decreases appetite. Candies of this type, such as Ayds, contain 25 calories each and are eaten two at a time before meals. Consumers Union notes that they neither raise blood-sugar levels significantly nor suppress appetite.[35]

Starch Blockers

"Starch blockers" have been promoted as containing an enzyme extracted from beans that, when taken before meals, supposedly blocks digestion of significant amounts of dietary starch. The enzyme works in the test tube, but the body produces more starch-digesting enzymes than starch-blocker pills could possibly block. A 1982 study published in the *New England Journal of Medicine* found no evidence of starch blockade in the feces of pill-takers.[36] Moreover, if undigested starch does reach the large intestine, it is fermented by bacteria normally present, leading to gas production and causing digestive disturbances. Some users of starch blockers have experienced abdominal pain, nausea, vomiting, and diarrhea, probably caused by toxic contaminants in the product. In 1982, the FDA received more than 100 reports of adverse reactions, including 30 cases requiring hospitalization and one death from pancreatitis. As these reports poured in, the agency warned manufacturers to stop marketing these products and obtained injunctions against several companies that refused.

Sugar Blockers

"Sugar blockers" containing an extract of *Gymnema sylvestre,* a plant grown in India, are claimed to cause weight loss by preventing sugar in the diet from being absorbed into the body. According to Purdue University's Varro E. Tyler, Ph.D., a leading authority on plant medicine, chewing the plant's leaves can prevent the taste sensation of sweetness. But there is no reliable evidence that the chemicals they contain can block the absorption of sugar into the body or produce weight loss.

Hormonal Fakery

Following the publication of *Life Extension,* by Durk Pearson and Sandy Shaw, many companies began marketing combinations of the amino acids: arginine, ornithine, and tryptophan. Products of this type (Dream Away, Super-Amino Night, Nite Diet) were claimed to cause weight loss through growth hormone release (GHR). As noted by Lowell,[37] however: (1) amino acid pills do not cause growth hormone release; (2) growth hormone release would be unlikely to cause weight loss; and (3) if significant amounts of this hormone were released in the body, they could cause acromegaly, a disease in which the hands, feet, and face become abnormally large and deformed. In 1988 the FTC charged the makers of Dream Away with false advertising and asked an Arizona federal court to issue an injunction and order them to pay consumer redress.[38] A few months later the defendants agreed to place $1.1 million in an escrow account to repay Dream Away purchasers and pledged not to misrepresent any food, drug, or device in the future.

Cholecystokinin (CCK) is a hormone involved in the digestive process. Products said to contain CCK have been sold by mail and in health food stores with claims that they can decrease hunger and cause sudden and dramatic weight loss. However, although injections of CCK appear to decrease hunger in test animals, doses taken by mouth have no such effect because the hormone is destroyed in the digestive tract.

Dehydroepiandrosterone (DHEA) is a hormone that can reduce weight gain in some strains of mice and rats. Based on this fact, several companies have marketed DHEA products as "miracle weight-reducers." According to Cunningham,[39] people who use DHEA with the hope of losing weight could endanger their health by tampering with their hormones. Moreover, tests of three DHEA products sold in health food stores found that one contained no DHEA at all and the others contained insignificant amounts.

In 1985 the Postal Service forced General Nutrition Corporation to stop making false claims for GHR, CCK, and DHEA products. In 1986 the FDA issued a regulatory letter ordering all manufacturers of DHEA and CCK to stop marketing the products. And in 1988, the FTC forced Great Earth International to agree to stop making unsubstantiated claims for its GHR products. These actions drove most products of this type from the marketplace, but a few still are sold.

Low-Calorie Products

A wide variety of low-calorie foods and beverages are available for use by weight-conscious individuals. These include liquid or powdered preparations (to which water is added) to consume instead of a meal; low-fat foods such as salad dressings made without oil; and foods and beverages made with artificial sweeteners. Well-designed studies to measure the effectiveness of such products are scarce, but many people seem to find these products helpful.

According to FDA guidelines, "low-calorie" foods cannot contain more than 40 calories per serving or 0.4 calories per g. Foods labeled "reduced calorie" are not limited in calories per serving, but they must be at least one third lower in calorie content than similar foods that contain the usual amount of calories. Foods that are labeled "low or reduced calorie" must also bear nutrition labeling that includes serving size and calories per serving in addition to significant nutrients. If a standardized food is modified so that it no longer complies with the standard, the food must be labeled "imitation." Since consumers would reasonably expect food labeled "sugar-free" or "sugarless" to be reduced in calories, the label must alert them if this is not the case. If the word "light" (lite) appears on the label, the food is likely to be reduced in calories. Under FDA regulations proposed in 1991 (see Chapter 12), these words are permissible for foods that contain one third fewer calories than the referenced food; any other use of the term must specify if it refers to look, taste, or odor.

Artificial Sweeteners

Three artificial sweeteners currently have FDA approval: saccharin, aspartame, and acesulfame potassium (acesulfame K). In 1977 the FDA announced its intention to ban saccharin after a single study found that high doses of saccharin caused bladder tumors in rats. However, considerable outcry from both scientists and the general public prompted Congress to enact legislation to prevent the proposed ban. Products that contain saccharin must carry the following warning:

> Use of this product may be hazardous to your health. This product contains saccharin, which has been determined to cause cancer in laboratory animals.

The American Council on Science and Health does not believe that saccharin presents a health hazard at normal levels of use. A 1986 Council report notes that studies of diabetics who used large amounts of saccharin have reported no association between saccharin use and bladder cancer.[40]

Aspartame is formed from the amino acids phenylalanine and aspartic acid. It is used (as

NutraSweet) to sweeten cereals, milk shake mixes, and diet drinks. About 180 times as sweet as sugar, it lacks saccharin's bitter aftertaste. In tabletop form, it is marketed as Equal.

Widespread use of aspartame has provoked reports of headaches and various other reactions. However, a double-blind study of 40 subjects who had reported headaches following ingestion of NutraSweet found that the incidence of symptoms after using aspartame was not significantly different from the incidence after using a placebo.[41]

In 1988 the FDA approved the marketing of acesulfame potassium (acesulfame K; marketed as Sunette) for such products as powdered drinks, puddings, chewing gum, and tabletop sweeteners. The substance is about 200 times sweeter than table sugar and is chemically unrelated to saccharin or aspartame. Unlike saccharin, it leaves no aftertaste. Unlike aspartame, it is not broken down by heat or digestion and passes through the body unchanged.

Fat Substitutes

One product that can substitute for fats has been approved by the FDA. Simplesse is made by the NutraSweet Company. Simplesse is a low-calorie, low-cholesterol product made of natural protein from egg white or milk. It is produced by a cooking process that changes protein into a rich cream that can be used to make products with the taste and texture of butter, cheese spreads, creamy salad dressings, mayonnaise, and ice cream. Trailblazer, a similar product manufactured by Kraft General Foods, is awaiting FDA approval.

Olestra, made by Procter & Gamble, is also awaiting FDA approval. Olestra provides no calories because it passes through the body unchanged. It is made by heating soybean oil with sugar to produce molecules composed of sucrose with 6, 7, or 8 fatty acid groups attached. It is similar to edible fats in most respects, including taste, but cannot be digested into smaller components because the body has no enzymes that can break it down. Once approved by the FDA, Olestra will be blended into cooking oils and similar products. Although it seems likely that fat-substitutes will help individuals lower the fat content of their diet, none have been proven effective as a treatment for obesity. It is not known whether it is safe to replace large amounts of dietary fat with fat-substitutes.[42]

Gadgets and Gimmicks

Over the years, hundreds of bogus gadgets and gimmicks have been marketed with claims that they act in some special way to produce weight control or to slim various parts of the body. For example:

The Vision Dieter was a 2-toned pair of eyeglasses claimed to control appetite if worn 2 hours a day. Its inventor reasoned that if colors could induce shoppers to buy certain products in supermarkets, they also could produce an opposite effect that would reduce food consumption.

Slim-Skins, a plastic suit with an attached hose, was alleged to slim the body if connected to a vacuum cleaner during exercise.

Astro-Trimmer and various other belts or waistbands have been falsely claimed to reduce one's waistline by applying pressure or producing extra heat loss.

Subliminal tapes have been falsely claimed to produce weight loss by reprogramming the brain.

"Walk-on-air" shoes, made of plastic and lined with springs, were claimed to make people move faster, feel better, and burn more calories.

A blue velour blanket was claimed to melt fat during sleep if wrapped around the body after the user took a shower and drank lemon water.

A machine was said to help dieters by counting the number of bites of food and sounding a bell to announce when the user had eaten enough.

Rubber pellets said to resemble maggots were to be wet and sprinkled over a forbidden food. The wriggling motion they develop was claimed to make the user sick enough to avoid the food.

A crossbar contraption that would enable users to hang upside down was claimed to cause calories to rush to the brain where they cannot be absorbed by the intestine.

As far-fetched as items like these may seem, they still may attract large numbers of buyers who are desperate or gullible enough to try almost anything.

Government Regulatory Action

Regimen tablets, claimed to shed pounds without dieting, brought an estimated $16 million in sales between 1956 and 1965. During 1959, they were promoted by 218,000 1-minute television spots and 1,064,000 lines of newspaper advertising.[43] Regimen tablets were of three kinds: benzocaine plus vitamins, ammonium chloride (a mild diuretic), and PPA. In the court case that ended with conviction of the manufacturer and the advertising agency, it was shown that TV models who reduced weight during an advertising campaign had done so by dieting. Participants in the scheme were fined a total of $168,000, and the principle promoter received an 18-month prison sentence.

In 1967 Herman Taller, M.D., author of *Calories Don't Count,* was found guilty by a jury of 12 counts of mail fraud and drug law violations. The government had charged that Dr. Taller had knowingly engaged in a complex scheme to induce the public to buy safflower oil capsules on the basis of principles espoused in his book. The book had sold about 2 million copies, and more than $500,000 worth of safflower oil capsules were sold during the 8 months that they were marketed, before the FDA charged that they were misbranded and ordered their seizure. At the trial Dr. Taller admitted that the advice given in the published book would not work, but he claimed that the book had been ghost-written and that others involved in its promotion had modified the book to give it broader public appeal. Dr. Taller was fined $7000 and placed on 2 years' probation. Five others in the case who had previously pleaded guilty were fined $1000 or $2000 each.

In 1979 the J.B. Williams Co. (makers of Geritol) and its advertising agency agreed to pay a $75,000 fine for violating a 1971 FTC order concerning "P.V.M.," a protein supplement promoted for weight reduction. The FTC had charged that the companies had failed to disclose clearly and conspicuously that any weight reduction would be the result of a diet which restricted calorie intake or an exercise-plus-diet plan.[44]

A federal appeals court has upheld the FTC's contention that it is unlawful and deceptive to represent, directly or by implication, any of the following:

1. That use of an appetite suppressant and/or methylcellulose enables one to lose body weight or fat without dieting or restricting one's accustomed caloric intake.
2. That a weight control product contains a unique ingredient or component, unless the substance is not present in other available weight-control products.
3. That any particular experience with a particular product or plan reflects the typical or ordinary experience of users, unless the representation is true.[45]

"Miracle" weight-loss programs are often sold through the mail. Products are typically claimed to "neutralize food calories," "melt fat off without hunger," and cause weight loss of 10 to 20 pounds in the first week. The programs usually consist of one or more pills or capsules plus a low-calorie diet, which is usually high-protein. Following the diet will result in modest weight loss, but the ads are worded to suggest that the pill or capsule is the key to the program. Since 1979 some of the mail-order programs have used PPA capsules.

In 1983 the Postal Service announced a guilty plea to 40 counts of mail fraud by the Millburn Book Corporation of Montclair, New Jersey. The company grossed $15 million between 1978 and 1981 by advertising six products in more than 600 newspapers and magazines. Included were a book, *The Amazing Diet Secrets of a Desperate Housewife,* and four other dietary schemes (Diet Bullets, Boston Police Diet, Hollywood Emergency Diet, and Dr. Romano's Mega II Rapid Weight Reduction Program). A $150,000 restitution fund was set up to pay back defrauded consumers.[46]

In 1982 Willpower Diet Tablets were advertised for sale by mail with claims that they could "make you skinny in 45 days. . . even if you cheat!!! Or double your money back!" The plan consisted of two types of tablets—Energetic Weight Reduction Appetite Suppressant (methylcellulose plus benzocaine) and S-Energetic (a vitamin mixture)—plus a 1200 calorie diet. Postal officials said that in 1981 the promoter of the plan had been stopped from selling products falsely claimed to promote hair growth and slow the aging process. One of these products was S-Energetic. A few months after the ads for Willpower Diet Tablets appeared, the Postal Service secured a consent agreement that various false claims contained in the ads would be discontinued. The entrepreneur, Leo Daboub, operated under five company names: Health Energetic Company, Vita-Health Research, Nutritional Research, The American Diet Association, and the Diet Stores. In 1985 the Ventura County, California District Attorney obtained a preliminary injunction ordering Daboub to stop making false and misleading claims for his products. He persisted, however, until the court found him in violation of the injunction. He was then permanently enjoined and was ordered to pay over $81,000 in civil penalties.

The most prominent weight-loss scam during the past few years was the marketing of Cal-Ban 3000, a guar gum product claimed to virtually eliminate fat by "short-circuiting the fat-building process." Guar gum is a soluble fiber used in small amounts as a thickener in sauces, desserts, syrups, and various other foods. It has some medically recognized value as a bulk laxative, a cholesterol-lowering agent, and an adjunct to controlling blood-sugar levels in certain diabetics. But it has not been proven effective for weight control; no long-term controlled test of guar gum as a weight-control agent has been reported in the scientific literature. Although weight loss has been reported among individuals who took guar gum during studies related to cholesterol and blood sugar control, this finding has not been consistent.

The marketing of Cal-Ban 3000 began in 1986 and lasted 4 years, despite regulatory action by the Postal Service and the Iowa Attorney General. It was widely promoted through ads showing before-and-after pictures of obese individuals who said they had lost large amounts of weight. Sales were estimated to be $10 to $20 million per year. By 1990, however, the FDA was aware of complaints involving more than 100 people, at least 50 of whom needed medical intervention. The complaints included esophageal obstruction, gastric obstruction, upper and lower intestinal obstruction, nausea, and vomiting. During the summer of 1990, state, local and federal agencies conducted seizures and obtained permanent injunctions that drove the manufacturer out of business.[47]

In 1992, prompted in part by the Cal-Ban situation, the FDA banned guar gum and 110 other ingredients from use in nonprescription weight-loss products. The ingredients include arginine, caffeine, kelp, lecithin, papaya enzymes, phenylalanine, tryptophan, and vitamin B_6.

In 1991 the FTC charged Nu-Day Enterprises, Inc., of Gig Harbor, Washington and its owner, Jeffrey S. Bland, Ph.D., with falsely claiming that their diet program could cause weight loss by turning up the body's "heat-producing machinery" so that fat is lost as body heat instead of the fat being stored. The Nu-Day Diet Program, which cost $59.95 for a 2-week supply, included instructional materials, a meal-replacement formula, and a fiber-containing formula said to be a "natural appetite suppressant." The Nu-Day program was promoted with a 30-minute television program entitled "The Perfect Diet," which offered "amazing true stories of people like yourself losing 20, 30, 50 pounds or more, safely, quickly and naturally." The FTC also charged that format used to make these claims was deceptive. Although the television program appeared to be an independent consumer news show that used interviews to report on its discovery of the Nu-Day Diet, it was actually a paid ad.

The case was settled with a consent agreement in which Dr. Bland agreed to pay $30,000 for redress and to refrain from making the claims that had been challenged. The consent order also requires future programs of 15 minutes or longer to display messages identifying them as paid ads for the products offered.[48]

Dr. Bland, identified during the program as "one of the nation's leading nutritional biochemists," is the health-food industry's most prolific interpreter of nutrition-related scientific developments.[49] His interpretations consistently favor the use of supplements. A former biochemistry professor, he appears frequently at trade shows, writes and edits books, produces audio and video tapes, and conducts seminars for health professionals. He has also been a research associate at the Linus Pauling Institute of Medicine and has directed its nutrient analysis laboratory.

Questionable Devices and Procedures

Many devices and procedures have been marketed with claims that they can help to reduce weight of the entire body or just in selected body parts. "Spot-reducing devices," all of which are fakes, are discussed in Chapter 15.

Acupressure Earrings

Several years ago the Pennsylvania Department of Health and the FDA temporarily blocked the sale of plastic Acu-Ring earrings designed by Dr. Evelyn Lee Sun with the help of her son, an engineer. The devices were claimed to curb appetite when squeezed on an "acupuncture point." The device, now called Acu-Clip, is sold with a low-calorie diet and promoted with claims toned down sufficiently to avoid further government enforcement action. A brochure subsequently mailed to chiropractors stated:

> Patients use the earclip by squeezing it approximately 10 times in succession before meals or whenever they

feel the urge to snack. They then decide whether to forego the food or eat less. This repeated action helps patients to control automatic eating by focusing their attention on what they eat and how much.

Body Wrapping

Many individuals operate salons where it is claimed that clients can trim inches off their waist, hips, thighs, and other areas of the body. These facilities use wraps or garments, with or without special lotions or creams applied to the skin. The garments may be applied to parts of the body or to the entire body. Clients are typically assured that fat will "melt away" and they can lose "up to 2 inches from those problem areas in just 1 hour."[50] However, no product can cause selective reduction of an area of the body. Although wrapping may cause temporary water loss due to perspiration, any fluid will soon be replaced by drinking or eating. Figure 14-1 shows an imaginative ad inviting people to learn how to do body wrapping.

FIGURE 14-1. Local newspaper ad offering "certification" in body wrapping.

Cellulite Removers

Cellulite is a term coined in European salons and spas to describe deposits of dimpled fat found on the thighs and buttocks of many women. Widespread promotion of the concept in the United States followed the 1973 publication of *Cellulite: Those Lumps, Bumps and Bulges You Couldn't Lose Before,* by Nicole Ronsard, owner of a New York City beauty salon that specialized in skin and body care. Cellulite is alleged to be a special type of "fat gone wrong," a combination of fat, water, and "toxic wastes" that the body has failed to eliminate. Anticellulite products sold by mail include "loofah" sponges, cactus fibers, special washcloths, horsehair mitts, creams to "dissolve" cellulite, vitamin-mineral supplements with herbs, bath liquids, massagers, rubberized pants, exercise books, brushes, rollers, and toning lotions. Many salons offer treatment with electrical muscle stimulation, vibrating machines, inflatable hip-high pressurized boots, "hormone" or "enzyme" injections, heating pads, and massage. Some operators claim that 5 to 15 inches can be lost in 1 hour. The FDA states that a series of treatments commonly costs in the range of $200 to $500.[51]

Cellulite is not a medical term. Medical authorities agree that cellulite is simply ordinary fatty tissue. Strands of fibrous tissue connect the skin to deeper tissue layers and also separate compartments that contain fat cells. When fat cells increase in size, these compartments bulge and produce a waffled appearance of the skin. Dr. Neil Solomon, former secretary of Maryland's Department of Health and Mental Hygiene, actually conducted a double-blind study of 100 people to see whether cellulite is different from ordinary fat. Specimens of regular fat and lumpy fat were obtained by a needle biopsy procedure and given to pathologists for analysis and comparison. No difference between the two was found.[51]

Experts agree that no equipment, exercise, or nonsurgical treatment can remove fat exclusively from a single area of the body. The amount of fat in the body is determined by the individual's eating and exercise habits, but the distribution of fat in the body is determined by heredity. In most cases reduction of a particular part can be accomplished only as part of an overall weight reduction program. Liposuction, which may be helpful in some cases, is discussed later in this chapter and in Chapter 21.

Gastric Balloon

In 1985 the FDA approved use of the Garren-Edwards Gastric Bubble, a polyurethane cylinder that could be inserted into the stomach and inflated. Following reports of serious complications, including blockage of the intestine, ulcers, and perforation of the stomach, the manufacturer warned physicians to use it only as a last resort for patients with life-threatening obesity for whom other treatments have not worked. However, a double-blind study showed that the bubble worked no better than a sham procedure in which no bubble was inserted. Although most participants in the study lost weight, their success apparently was due to diet and exercise rather than the device itself.[2]

Surgical Procedures

Surgery for weight-loss purposes is considered a radical approach. Because complication rates are quite high, this approach should be used only for individuals who are morbidly obese (100 or more pounds above desirable weight) and in danger of dying as a result. The following procedures have been used:

Jaw wiring: Wiring the jaw closed allows the patient to feed only on beverages and liquified foods. It leads to rapid loss of weight for the majority of individuals, but most regain their losses once the wiring is undone. Undesirable side effects can occur, such as dental decay from lack of brushing and flossing, atrophy and weakening of jaw muscles, and considerable pain.

Gastric bypass surgery: In some procedures, the small intestine is shortened by looping a section off from the rest to limit caloric absorption. In other procedures, the stomach is constricted and parts of the intestine are bypassed. Side effects can include diarrhea, vitamin deficiencies, anemia, protein deficiency, hair loss, impaired immunity, neurologic disorders, joint pains, kidney stones and gallstones, cardiac irregularities, and liver damage.

Vertical banded gastroplasty: Procedures of this type involve creation of a pouch or other measures to reduce the size of the stomach. This limits the amount that can be eaten at one sitting. Although these procedures are safer than intestinal bypass, postoperative risks include inflammation, hemorrhage, ulceration, and certain nutritional deficiencies. Also, the patient may get around the surgery by ingesting food constantly in small amounts.

The 1991 National Institutes of Health Consensus Development Conference on Gastrointestinal Surgery for Severe Obesity concluded that vertical banded gastroplasty and gastric bypass surgery "dominate practice in the early 1990s and have advanced beyond the experimental stage."[52]

Two types of surgery may be done to remove local fat deposits for cosmetic purposes:

Lipectomy: A lipectomy, usually done for cosmetic purposes, removes fat from beneath the skin. If overeating resumes, the fat simply reaccumulates.

Suction lipectomy (liposuction): Fat is sucked out through a small hollow tube inserted into the fatty area. Proponents state that it can remove 6 pounds of fat with little or no scarring. Complications have included postoperative pain, perforation of internal organs, and fat embolism (also see Chapter 27). *The Medical Letter* states that the procedure has produced satisfactory results in some patients, but the long-term effects are unknown.[53]

Weight-Control Organizations

Many organizations have been established to provide both individual and group counseling for people seeking to lose weight. Some organizations are nonprofit and relatively inexpensive, whereas others are quite costly. Many hospitals and universities conduct obesity clinics. Several self-help organizations have chapters in many cities. Few scientific reports have been published about the effectiveness and complication rates of the methods described in this section.

Inexpensive Organizations

TOPS (Take off Pounds Sensibly) was started in 1948 and claims to have over 11,000 chapters. The members follow diets prescribed by their own physicians and meet weekly to offer moral support to one another. It is based on a group-therapy approach. The cost is $14 to $16 per year, plus a nominal local chapter fee.[54]

Weight Watchers is a franchise started in the 1960s that now includes diet, behavior modification, and exercise. The program focuses on changing one's eating habits rather than counting calories. It attempts to help overweight people to cope with the problems that made them fat and alter their eating habits. The fees are $15 to $21 to register, plus $8 to $12 for weekly meetings until one's weight is within 2 pounds of the client's goal, and free thereafter.[55]

Diet Workshop is a franchise that includes a four-point lifetime program: diet (1200 calories, high in protein), behavior modification, nutrition education, and exercise. Fees are generally $14 for the first meeting and $9 for each weekly meeting thereafter.[56]

The Trims program is an adult education experience that concentrates on individual counseling about nutrition for weight reduction. It also includes behavior modification and exercise. Mail-order courses are also available.

Overeaters Anonymous (OA) is a nonprofit or-

PERSONAL GLIMPSE

Selling It

On April 30, 1991, a sales representative from a diet center in New York City told a 5′-8″ woman who weighed 130 pounds that she was 5 pounds overweight and could afford to lose 7 pounds. This ran counter to advice of the woman's personal physician, who confirmed that she already was at an ideal weight and did not need to lose any more. Moreover, the 7-pound loss would have put her several pounds beneath the ideal target weight listed on the sales representative's own chart. The program would cost $710, which amounted to $100 per pound. When the woman failed to sign up, the sales representative urged her repeatedly and offered reduced payments as an incentive.

On May 8, 1991, a 5′-8″ man who weighed 178 pounds was told at another center that he should lose 18 pounds. No measurements other than weight were taken. The man worked out regularly and was very muscular. He had a low body fat content and did not need to lose weight. On the same day at another center, another man who was 5′-9″ and weighed 142 pounds was urged to sign up for a program to lose 8 pounds in 2 weeks.[14]

ganization for individuals who wish to stop compulsive eating. It operates on the premise that overeating is a progressive illness that cannot be cured but can be arrested. OA expects its members to get general guidance from their own physicians, but it offers three eating plans and suggestions about eating. Members attend weekly meetings when needed. They follow a 12-step life-change plan similar to that of Alcoholics Anonymous. There are no dues or fees. The strength of OA is in its regular meetings where members can openly and safely share their successes and failures, their problems and solutions.

Obesity Clinics

Thousands of commercial obesity clinics and centers are operating in the United States, most of them franchised by large national organizations. Advertisements for these facilities typically promise weight loss of 20 to 30 pounds in the first month and include before-and-after pictures of clients who have supposedly accomplished this. Programs are said to be medically supervised, but the degree of supervision varies. Many clinics are administered by registered nurses. Many clinics employ a physician to do an initial physical examination, but the client might not see the physician again. Prepackaged foods, drinks, or supplement mixtures may be used instead of all or just some meals. Some diets are balanced, whereas others cause ketosis. Fees commonly run from $35 to $75 per week, depending on the program and whether special products are purchased. In several parts of the country, dietitians who have inquired at various clinics have encountered incorrect nutrition concepts and misleading claims for many of these programs.

Diet Center, the largest clinic chain, offers a four-phase program based on a series of highly restrictive diets plus vitamin and mineral supplements. The cost is $35 to $50 per week, plus a registration fee.

Nutri/System, another large chain, offers prepackaged foods for about $9 per day and encourages clients to visit the center several times a week for counseling and support at a small additional fee. A partial refund is offered to those who keep lost weight off for 1 year. A major drawback of this approach is that when participants stop using the prepackaged meals, they must still learn how to make proper food choices. During the past few years, hundreds of former clients have filed lawsuits claiming that the Nutri/System program caused them to develop gallstones.

Medifast, Optifast, Nutrimed, New Direction, and Ultrafast are medically supervised supplemented fasting programs designed for individuals who are 30% or more above their ideal body weight. The initial phase involves the use of prepackaged supplements containing 400 to 800 calories per day. The stabilization phase gradually reintroduces food, and the maintenance phase stresses life-style changes. The cost of these programs ranges from $1000 to $3000, depending on the length of participation and the amount used of the prepackaged products.[56] Optitrim and several other programs are designed for individuals who have smaller weight-loss goals.

Several clinicians have suggested that the following be considered when evaluating a weight-loss facility:

1. Is treatment preceded by a careful medical and behavior assessment?
2. Does the facility offer state-of-the-art therapy? Behavior-modification therapy should be featured for individuals needing to lose less than 50 pounds, whereas those needing to lose more may also require more stringent, medically supervised programs such as modified fasting.
3. Does it offer a close relationship with a therapist who will attempt to help the patient modify behavior?
4. Are the financial arrangements designed to encourage completion of the program?
5. Most importantly, what are the clinic's dropout rates and the average amount of weight lost by clients?[57]

Marsha Hudnall,[58,59] a dietitian who investigated several weight-control programs, found that none of them offered follow-up statistics that could be used to compare one program with another. She concluded, however, that "the relative sensibleness, low cost, and widespread availability may well make Weight Watchers the best option for many people."

Government Investigations

During 1990 a U.S. House of Representatives subcommittee, chaired by Representative Ron Wyden (D-OR), held two hearings focused on deception and fraud in the diet industry. Testimony indicated that a number of commercial programs, where doctors are not involved, refer to their staff as "certified" nutrition counselors, behavior therapists, and the like, even though the only certification they had was by the company offering the program.[60]

During 1991, agents of the New York City Department of Consumer Affairs[14] called or visited 14 weight-loss centers and reported the following:

1. Few of the centers gave advance warning or openly discussed the safety risks of their program (or of rapid weight loss in general), even when directly asked about possible problems. One representative said her center's program was "absolutely safe," even though the health history form that prospective clients had to sign contained a warning about health risks.
2. Some centers attempted to sell their services to people who did not need them, including underweight people.
3. Some centers were engaged more in quackery than medicine. One clinic representative advised that filling the stomach with certain foods would speed up metabolism. Another said her clinic's maintenance program would "close up the body's fat cells."
4. Some centers engaged in high-pressure sales tactics.

Following its study, the Department of Consumer Affairs proposed regulations that would require weight-loss centers to: (1) display a large sign stating that rapid weight loss (more than 1½ to 2 pounds a week) may cause serious health problems, (2) advise consultation with a physician, (3) indicate that only permanent lifestyle changes can promote long-term weight loss, and (4) inform customers that information on dropout rates and staff qualifications were available on request.

Suggestions for Weight Control

Medical and nutrition scientists agree that the key to weight control is to establish prudent and permanent habits of exercise and control of calorie intake. For initial weight loss, they recommend a well-balanced diet with few enough calories to produce a steady loss of 1 to 2 pounds per week. A diet of 1200 to 1300 calories per day is an ideal starting point; it is low enough to achieve weight reduction, yet high enough to be able to supply adequate amounts of the essential nutrients. If food selection is done properly at this caloric level, vitamin supplements are unnecessary. Additional calories can be added to the diet after one's desirable weight is achieved. Since obesity often is associated with a high-fat diet, some researchers suspect that low-fat eating offers promise as a weight-control measure. However, research in this area is in its early stages.[61]

Exercise

Experts agree that exercise plays a critical role in weight control. The idea that exercise is self-defeating is a myth. In most cases exercise does not increase appetite unduly.[62] According to Franklin and Rubenfire,[63] most research on humans indicates either no change in food intake with moderate exercise of extended duration or slight decreases with vigorous exercise of short duration. Mirkin[6] states that the beneficial effects of exercise occur throughout the day, not just during the actual exercise periods. He recommends walking, swimming, or riding a stationary bicycle for individuals who are obese, over 40, or not used to strenuous activities. However, Gwinup[64] has shown that swimming as the *sole* form of exercise is generally not useful for weight control. He believes that rapid heat loss while in contact with water (especially water colder than 80°F) may stimulate the appetite mechanism to increase caloric consumption.[65] Swimming in relatively warm water, or including other aerobic activities in one's exercise program, may prevent this problem.

Consumer Reports on Health[66] suggests that people wishing to lose 10 pounds or less might do best by increasing exercise without dieting. Chapter 15 contains additional information on exercise and weight control.

Behavior Modification

Behavior modification implies a permanent change in habits, rather than a temporary change (such as a diet) that one adheres to until a desired weight level is reached. Various behavior modification procedures are aimed at teaching the overfat individual to change patterns of inappropriate food consumption such as overeating, eating high-calorie foods, or snacking between meals. Individuals who overeat in response to tension may require psychotherapy as well. Gloria Rakita Leon, Ph.D.,[67] associate professor of psychology at the University of Minnesota, identifies these methods as useful when done under professional supervision:

1. Self-monitoring: observing and recording circumstances under which eating takes place
2. Stimulus control and environmental management: using a variety of techniques to curb excessive-eating behavior
3. Positive reinforcement
4. Contingency contracting: use of a signed contract stating what patient will do
5. Self-control strategies: development of mental defenses and more realistic attitude toward eating behavior
6. In many cases, other members of the obese individual's household will have to modify behavior that stimulates overeating

Stare, Aronson, and Barrett[7] offer the following tips for achieving calorie reduction:

1. Use alternatives to food as rewards (for example, long walks, relaxing baths, tickets to a movie or play).
2. Resist the temptation to always "clean the plate."
3. If you eat moderate portions of your favorite foods, you will be less apt to crave them and overindulge.
4. Do not eat while doing anything else, such as talking on the phone or watching television.
5. Find nonfood outlets for release of emotional tension.

Aaron Altschul, Ph.D., of the Georgetown University Clinic, believes that successful dieters achieve the following:

1. They know their weight; they weigh themselves often enough that they are never in doubt about where they stand in relation to their goal.
2. They know what they are eating; if necessary, they keep daily records until they can automatically know what they are eating every day, can anticipate heavy eating events, and can make corrections before and after them.
3. They control their alcohol intake.
4. They engage in a regular program of exercise.
5. They use a personally suitable diet plan—one which they can enjoy or tolerate permanently.

> **IT'S YOUR DECISION**
>
> Many people on television describe how a product has helped them to lose weight. How can you determine whether the product really works?
>
> You have heard about several inexpensive weight-control organizations that offer help with weight control. What information would you need to determine which one might be best?

SUMMARY

To lose weight, people must either eat less, exercise more, or do both. Although hundreds of "miracle" products and "revolutionary" diets have been marketed, no pill, potion, or dietary plan can produce weight loss without exercise or lowering of caloric intake. To lose a pound, it is necessary to burn off 3500 more calories than are taken in. Professional help may be required to clarify and modify the behavior that contributes to overeating. The diet recommended most often by experts is a balanced low-calorie diet that is easily adapted for long-term maintenance. Although unbalanced diets can cause weight loss, they are usually too monotonous for long-term use and are followed by weight gain when the user returns to "normal" eating. Repeated dieting followed by weight gain ("yo-yo dieting") can increase the risk of premature death from heart disease and several other diseases. For most people, the most important factor in successful weight control is exercise.

Discussion Questions

1. Define the terms obese, overweight, and desirable weight.
2. What are the two basic factors involved in weight control?
3. How can an unreliable diet promotion be recognized?
4. What problems are associated with complete fasting, supplemented fasting, and low-carbohydrate diets?
5. What are the shortcomings of the Atkins diet, liquid protein diets, the Scarsdale Diet, the Beverly Hills Diet, and the Fit for Life Diet?
6. Discuss amphetamines, thyroid hormones, HCG, and other drugs prescribed for weight control in terms of their effectiveness and hazards.
7. Discuss the various OTC diet aids, the theories behind their use, and the degree to which they are effective.
8. What is the current status of low-calorie foods, artificial sweeteners, and fat substitutes?
9. Describe some government actions against promoters of questionable weight-control products.
10. What are the various surgical procedures done for weight-loss purposes? For whom are they suitable?
11. What types of services do groups and clinics offer to obese individuals? How can one tell whether a program is reliable?
12. What dietary plan do most medical and nutrition scientists recommend for weight reduction?
13. What role do exercise and behavior modification play in weight control? List some tips for behavior modification.

REFERENCES

1. Blackburn GL and Pavlou K: Fad reducing diets: separating fads from facts, Contemporary Nutrition, July 1983.
*2. Bennion L Bierman EL, and Ferguson JM: Straight talk about weight control, New York, 1991, Consumer Reports Books.
3. The U.S. weight loss and diet control market, Lynbrook, NY, 1991, Marketdata Enterprises.
4. Singer S: When they stop telling you it's easy to lose weight, Today's Health 50:47-49, 62, Nov 1972.
5. Dreon DM et al: Dietary fat: carbohydrate ratio and obesity in middle-aged men, Am J Clin Nutr 47:995-1000, 1988.
*6. Mirkin G: Getting thin, Boston, 1983, Little, Brown & Co Inc.
*7. Stare FJ, Aronson V and Barrett S: Your guide to good nutrition, Buffalo, 1991, Prometheus Books.
8. Garrison RJ et al: Cigarette smoking as a confounder of the relationship between relative weight and long-term mortality, JAMA 249:2199-2203, 1983.
9. Darden E: Your basic guide to fitness, Philadelphia, 1982, The George F Stickley Co.
10. American Medical Association Council on Foods and Nutrition: The healthy approach to slimming, Chicago, 1979, The Association.
11. Wing RR and Jeffrey RW: Outpatient treatments of obesity: a comparison of methodology and clinical results, Int J Obes 3:261-269, 1979.
*12. Lissner L et al: Variability of body weight and health outcomes in the Framingham population, N Engl J Med 324:1839-1844, 1991.
13. Farley D: on the teen scene: eating disorders require medical attention, FDA Consumer 26(2):27-29, 1992.
*14. Winner K: A weighty issue: dangers and deceptions of the weight loss industry, New York, 1991, NY Dept. of Consumer Affairs. Available for $5 from NYC Dept. of Consumer Affairs, 42 Broadway, New York, NY 10004.
*15. Barrett S: Diet facts and fads, In Barrett S, ed: The health robbers, ed 2, Philadelphia, 1980, The George F Stickley Co.
*16. National Council Against Health Fraud: Commercial weight-loss programs, NCAHF position paper, Loma Linda, Calif, 1987, The Council.
*17. Wadden TA, Van Italie TB and Blackburn GL: Responsible and irresponsible use of very-low-calorie diets in the treatment of obesity, JAMA 263:83-85, 1990.
18. White PL: A critique of low-carbohydrate ketogenic weight reduction regimens, a review of Dr. Atkins' diet revolution, JAMA 224:1415-1419, 1973.
19. Mayer J: Liquid protein: the last word on the "last chance" diet, Family Health 10:40-41, Jan 1978.
20. Glick N: Low-calorie protein diets, FDA Consumer 12:(2)7-9, 1978.
21. Van Italie TB and Tang M: Cardiac dysfunction in obese dieters: a potentially lethal complication of rapid, massive weight loss, Am J Clin Nutr 39:695-702, 1984.
*22. Mirkin G and Shore RN: The Beverly Hills Diet—dangers of the newest weight-loss fad, JAMA 246:2235-2237, 1981.
23. Hegsted DM: Rating the diets, Health 15:21-32, Jan 1983.
24. Barrett S and Monaco G: Cytotoxic testing, Nutrition Forum 1:17-19, 1984.
25. Power failure from the immune power diet, Consumer Reports 51:112-113, 1986.
26. Power L: Food combining: fit for laughs, Shape 6(5):38, 1987.

*Recommended reading

27. U.S. Senate Committee on Governmental Affairs: Hearings before the Permanent Subcommittee on Investigations, May 14, 1985, Washington DC, 1985, US Government Printing Office.
28. U.S. Senate Committee on the Judiciary: Hearings before the Subcommittee to Investigate Juvenile Delinquency, Diet Pill Traffic, Abuse, and Regulation, July 15-16, 1971, Washington, D.C., 1972, U.S. Government Printing Office.
29. FDA warns on use of two drugs for obesity, FDA Consumer 11(6):26, 1977.
30. Zimmerman D: The essential guide to nonprescription drugs, New York, 1983, Harper & Row, Publishers Inc.
31. The new diet pills, Consumer Reports 47:14-17, 1982.
32. Dietz AJ: Amphetamine-like reactions to propanolamine, JAMA 245:601-602, 1981.
33. Drenick EJ: Bulk producers, JAMA 234:271, 1975.
34. Parker LF: Initial decision in the matter of Schering Corporation, FTC, Docket No. 9232, Sept 16, 1991.
35. Consumer Reports: The medicine show, ed 4, Mt Vernon NY, 1974, Consumers Union.
36. Bo-Linn GW et al: Starch blockers—their effect on calorie absorption from a high-starch meal, N Engl J Med 23:1413-1416, 1982.
37. Lowell J: "Growth hormone releasers" don't cause weight loss. Nutrition Forum 1:24, 1984.
38. FTC charges "weight-loss while you sleep" ads are false, FTC News Notes, Jan 18, 1988.
39. Cunningham JJ: DHEA: Facts vs. hype, Nutrition Forum 2:30, 1985.
40. Meister KA: Low-calorie sweeteners—aspartame, saccharin, cyclamate, New York, 1986, American Council on Science and Health.
41. Schiffman SS et al: Aspartame and susceptibility to headache, N Engl J Med 317:1181-1184, 1987.
42. Segal M: Fat Substitutes: a taste of the future? FDA Consumer 24(10):25-27, 1990.
43. Schwartz H: Never satisfied—a cultural history of diets, fantasies and fat, New York, 1986, Macmillan Publishing Co.
44. FTC News Summary, March 6, 1979.
45. Porter & Dietsch, Inc., Docket 9047.
46. Postal Inspection Service: Diet entrepreneur fined, Law Enforcement Report, p. 10, Fall 1982.
*47. Barrett S: The rise and fall of Cal-Ban 3000, Nutrition Today 25(6):24-28, 1990.
48. False claims barred for diet program, Nutrition Forum 9:5, 1992.
*49. Fanning O: "Training" for health food retailers, Nutrition Forum 3:33-37, 1985.
50. Wills J: About body wraps, pills, and other magic wands for losing weight, FDA Consumer 16(9):18-20, 1982.
51. Fenner L: Cellulite: hard to budge pudge, FDA Consumer 14(4):5-9, 1980.
52. Grundy S et al: Consensus statement: gastrointestinal surgery for severe obesity, paper presented at the NIH Consensus Development Conference, Vol 9, No. 1, March 25-27, 1991.
53. Suction-assisted lipectomy, The Medical Letter 29:111-112, 1987.
54. Cappellano C: Winning at the weight-loss game: choosing the right program, Environmental Nutrition 13(12):3-5, 1990.
55. Schardt D: A dieter's guide to weight-loss programs, American Health 10(6):56-60, 1991.
56. Dieter beware! The complete consumer guide to weight-loss programs, Lynbrook NY, 1991, Marketdata Enterprises.
57. Gotto AM, Foreyt JP and Goodrick GK: Evaluating commercial weight-loss clinics, Arch Intern Med 142:682-683, 1982.
58. Hudnall M: A look at commercial dieting programs (4 part series), Environmental Nutrition 10(4):2-3, 10(5):2-3, 10(6):4-5, 10(7):5, 1987.
59. Hudnall M: How popular diet programs compare, Environment Nutrition 10(8):4-5, 1987.
60. Deception and fraud in the diet industry, Hearings before the Subcommittee on Regulation, Business Opportunities, and Energy, U.S. House of Representatives Committee on Small Business, March 26, 1990 (Part I) and May 7, 1990 (Part II), Washington DC, Superintendent of Documents, US Government Printing Office.
*61. Datillo AM: Dietary fat and its relationship to body weight, Nutrition Today 27(1):13-19, 1992.
62. Stare FJ and Whelan EM: The Harvard Square diet, Buffalo, 1987, Prometheus Books.
63. Franklin BA and Rubenfire M: Losing weight through exercise, JAMA 244:377-379, 1980.
64. Gwinup G: Weight loss without dietary restriction: efficacy of different forms of aerobic exercise, Am J Sports Med 15(3):275-279, 1987.
65. Steinman S: Study finds swimming ineffective for weight control, Nutrition Forum 5:14-15, 1988.
66. Diet vs. exercise: what's best? Consumer Reports on Health 4:1-3, 1992.
67. Leon GR: The behavior modification approach to weight reduction, Contemporary Nutrition, Aug 1979.

CHAPTER FIFTEEN

Exercise Concepts, Devices, and Services

"He can't come to the phone right now—he's pumping iron!"

(© 1981 Medical Economics Company.)

The great majority know the importance of fitness. But they have not taken the action themselves. Americans are not as fit as they think they are.

MICHAEL MCGINNIS, M.D.
DIRECTOR, OFFICE OF DISEASE PREVENTION AND HEALTH PROMOTION
U.S. DEPARTMENT OF HEALTH AND HUMAN SERVICES

Moderate amounts of exercise can have health benefits and "you don't have to run."

KENNETH H. COOPER, M.D.
INSTITUTE FOR AEROBICS RESEARCH

Consumer Decisions

What type of exercise regimen should a person participate in? Will it be beneficial? Hazardous?

Should a physical exam be conducted first?

Should pregnant women exercise? Continue to jog several miles weekly?

How should a person wisely select an exercise bicycle, a rowing machine, or other exercise equipment?

Should people use hot tubs, whirlpools, or saunas, or have massages?

Should people join health clubs, spas, or exercise centers? Develop an in-home exercise center?

Will exercise help control weight?

Should the elderly participate in an exercise program?

Should a person use anabolic steroids, engage in weight training activities, or participate in a corporation's fitness program?

The preventive health concept that has emerged over the last 25 years was given greater impetus by the U.S. Surgeon General's remark that half of all deaths result from an unhealthy life-style. Most Americans now realize that prudent health habits greatly contribute to the maintenance of wellness and the prevention of illness. This attitude has been instrumental in the rapid growth of the physical fitness movement.

Americans have become involved in a wide variety of fitness activities, especially jogging and walking. They also join health clubs and purchase exercise equipment and supplies for their homes and elsewhere. A Gallup poll several years ago found that 51% of American adults are involved in a daily exercise regimen and 33 million jog regularly (more men than women).

However, Dr. Michael McGinnis,[1] director of the Office of Disease Prevention and Health Promotion of the U.S. Department of Health and Human Services, stated that 80% to 90% of Americans do not get enough exercise, and half of those who start activities stop them shortly afterward. In 1990 retail sales of exercise equipment, clothing, and services were estimated to be:

Athletic and sports clothing	$10 billion
Athletic footware	$3 to $6 billion
Barbells/weights	$250 million
Bicycles	Over $1 billion
Helmets	$2 million
Company fitness programs	$3 billion
Cross-country ski simulators	$200 million
Exercise equipment	$1 billion
Golf equipment	$1 billion
Multipurpose gyms	$1 billion
Roller skates	$400 million
Rowing machines	$200 million
Stationary bikes	$750 million
Tennis equipment	$350 million
Treadmills	$282 million

Nautilus Industries, the largest manufacturer of weight-training machines, makes 26 different types that sell for $500 to $4800 and has annual gross sales of $400 million. There are 2400 Nautilus fitness centers in the United States, with about 1.75 million members. In 1986 indoor fitness equipment had gross annual sales of $230 million. A wide selection of books, pamphlets, audiotapes, and videotapes are also available.

In addition to legitimate manufacturers of quality products, many entrepreneurs have capitalized on people's desire to engage in physical activity. These profiteers often use unfounded claims, fake endorsements, and inaccurate information to confuse consumers about the benefits of exercise equipment and supplies. They sell many items that have little effect on physical fitness.

Consumers have been exposed to many fitness fads, devices, and gadgets; some are useful, many are unessential, and some are dangerous. Isometric equipment, vibrators, massage devices, saunas, electric muscle stimulators, mini trampolines, exercycles, tension bars, weight training items, and rowing machines are some of the items available today.

This chapter is designed to help consumers understand the basic concepts of exercise, including the types, purposes, benefits, and hazards, together with general exercise program suggestions and guidelines. This information, together with a critical review of selected equipment, programs, and ser-

Did You Know

An ideal exercise would improve your aerobic fitness, burn excess body fat, add to muscular strength and endurance, and be easy to start and sustain. However, there is no ideal exercise—at least not for everyone. So aim for a program that helps you accomplish your goals without boredom or guilt.

Consumer Reports Health Letter, Nov 1989.

The word from one fitness specialist to another is that exercise does not have to look like exercise anymore. You can build physical activity into your normal daily routine without ever donning a sweat suit. Climb stairs. Never ride an elevator for less than four flights. Park a half-mile or more from the office and walk in. Carry your own groceries. Use a push mower when cutting grass and then bag the clippings. Weed the garden.

Robert G. Holland[2]

vices, will help consumers make intelligent decisions.

Exercise vs. Fitness

Several definitions of terms are necessary to understand the nature and purposes of exercise:

Health: A condition of the human organism that contributes to the quality of life and is influenced by physical, psychologic, and social factors; exercise and fitness contribute to health.

Physical activity: Any movement produced by skeletal muscles that results in the expenditure of energy.

Exercise: Planned, structured, and repetitive physical activity completed to achieve one or more of the purposes of exercise.

Physical fitness: The ability to carry out daily tasks with vigor, without undue fatigue, and with ample energy to enjoy leisure-time pursuits and to meet unforeseen emergencies. This is achieved through exercise.

These definitions indicate that exercise is a means to an end; an activity that enables one to become physically fit. A fit person therefore has a degree of endurance, strength, flexibility, and cardiorespiratory efficiency to carry out daily tasks. However, although physical fitness is a part of health, it is not synonymous with it. A fit person may not be a healthy person. Individuals who are emotionally disturbed, have cancer or tuberculosis in its early stages, or some other abnormal condition are not in the best of health. They may find it difficult to live productively because of their debilitating condition. Research data reveal that exercise can enhance health status, but it also can contribute to injury and illness.

Types of Exercise

Cooper[3] has classified exercise as isometric, isotonic, isokinetic, aerobic, and anaerobic.

Isometric exercise refers to muscle contractions exerted against resistance in which there is little or no movement of body parts. A person may merely tighten muscles, or may push or pull a stationary object that creates a force or resistance. This form of exercise can be used with minimal or no equipment and be performed while sitting, while in bed recuperating from surgery, and in numerous other confined places. It can help to develop strength and flexibility, but does nothing to aid cardiovascular efficiency or endurance. Isometric exercise has limited value in a program of fitness. It may be useful for sedentary and elderly people, but is dangerous for hypertensive or cardiac patients because it may cause a brief increase in blood pressure. Considerable charlatanism has emerged since the development of this concept. Numerous gadgets and exercises have been marketed with exaggerated claims of benefit from this type of exercise.

Isotonic exercise refers to the contraction of muscles, with or without resistance, in which there is movement of body parts. It will build strength, flexibility, and cardiovascular endurance, depending on its intensity and duration. It may take place through calisthenics, weightlifting, swimming, walking, running, team sports, and many other athletic activities. Many questionable gadgets and procedures for isotonic exercise have been marketed.

Isokinetic exercise is isotonic exercise that involves moving against resistance at a constant speed throughout the entire range of motion. The procedure increases the intensity of the exercise and strengthens muscles faster and with less activity. It increases endurance somewhat.

Aerobic exercise demands large quantities of oxygen for prolonged periods. It forces the heart to pump more blood so that more oxygen can be transported, and increased respiratory activity is needed to provide that oxygen. It promotes heart-lung efficiency and increases the amount of work the body can endure.

Anaerobic means without oxygen and refers to exercise that can be performed without utilizing oxygen a person normally breathes. In some highly competitive sports, such as running the 100-yard dash, performers may not breathe during the entire race.

Purposes of Exercise

Physical fitness is a desirable human condition that is acquired through the development and proper use of the muscles and tissues of the body. Muscles become stronger through use and weaker through inactivity. Regular and periodic movement of muscles through a variety of suitable activities has these fundamental purposes:

Muscle endurance/stamina: The ability to use and contract muscles repeatedly for longer periods. Muscles develop in proportion to the overload effect (intensity) and the amount of resistive exercise provided.

Muscle strength: The amount of force that can be applied by a muscle or group of muscles with a single contraction. Muscles increase in size and develop strength in proportion to the intensity of the exercise.

Flexibility: The extensibility, or stretch, of muscles to allow a full range of movement. Exercise done slowly and deliberately contributes to the efficiency of movement and reduces the chance of injury.

Cardiorespiratory efficiency: The involvement of the heart and circulatory system with the lungs and respiratory system in delivering oxygen and blood to the rest of the body in the most efficient and effective manner.

Benefits of Exercise

There is mounting evidence that just about any physical activity will be beneficial, especially for sedentary people.

Consumer Reports on Health
August 1991

Exercise can have physical, biologic, and psychologic effects on people's health.

Physically, it may result in more strength, stamina, flexibility of muscles and cardiorespiratory efficiency. This leads to more energy, fewer physical complaints, more restful sleep, increased lung and heart capacity (more blood pumped and more oxygen delivered to body tissues with less difficulty), and maintenance of muscle tone.

Biologically, it may reduce the risk of coronary heart disease by increasing the blood levels of high-density lipoproteins (HDL) and lowering the blood levels of low-density lipoproteins (LDL) and triglycerides (fat) (see Chapter 16). Exercise can also lower blood pressure, help control weight, and decrease the rate of bone calcium loss (which helps prevent osteoporosis). Physical activity leads to more efficient digestion, fewer constipation problems, and improves glucose (sugar) tolerance by muscles, thereby reducing need for insulin. Exercise may delay death, primarily due to lowered rates of cardiovascular disease and cancer. It may also help to speed up the recovery of cardiac patients.

Psychologically, exercise may help to combat anxiety, mild to moderate depression, and stress-related problems.

Blair et al[4] reported a study of 10,224 men and 3120 women and concluded that a low level of physical fitness is an important risk factor in men and women. Figure 15-1 identifies some of the significant findings of this research.

Researchers at the Columbia Medical Plan in Maryland and the Francis Scott Key Medical Center in Baltimore tested 52 men with moderate hypertension and exposed them to 10 weeks of aerobics and weightlifting. The men were divided into two groups that received antihypertensive medication and one nondrug group. All three groups lowered pressure to the normal range, and the nondrug group did as well as the two drug groups.[5] Pescatello[6] at the University of Connecticut has conducted two small studies that showed that light exercise can decrease blood pressure.

Dr. William Haskell,[7] deputy director of the Stanford Center for Research in Disease Prevention, studied the benefits of continuous and discontin-

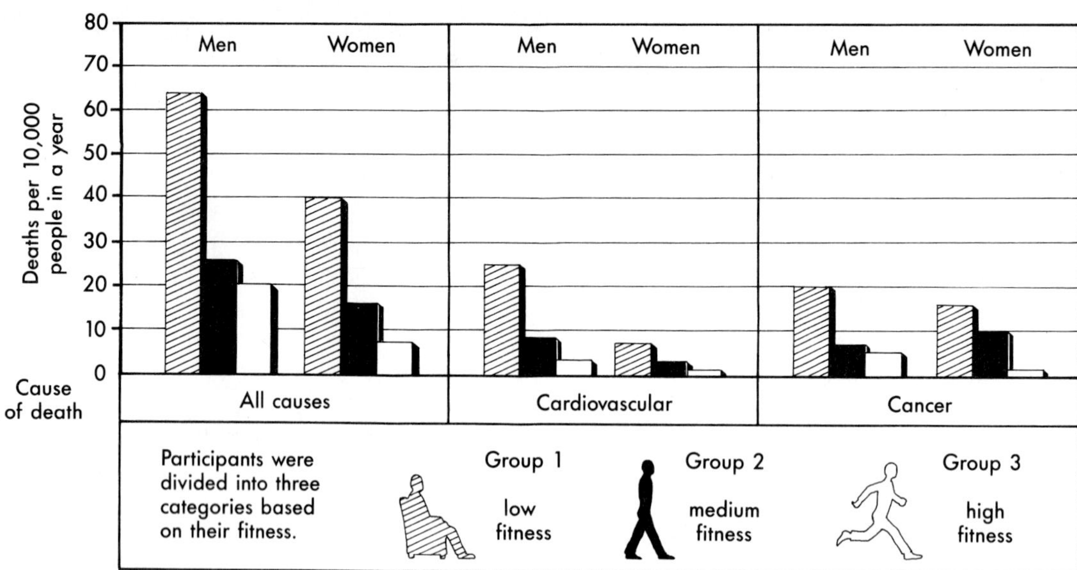

FIGURE 15-1. Fitness decreases the death rate.
Adapted from Take a walk and live, Time 134:90, Nov 13, 1989.

uous exercise (one 30-minute session vs three 10-minute sessions daily) on aerobic capacity, blood pressure, and heart rate. He reported very significant positive changes for the low-intensity and discontinuous groups—almost as great as for the high-intensity and continuous groups. He stated the goal for reducing heart-attack risk with exercise is to expend 250 to 300 calories daily or 1200 to 2000 calories weekly.

Kannel et al[8] stated that epidemiologic evidence linking lack of physical activity to the occurrence of cardiovascular heart disease is substantial but inconclusive. They also stated that overall death rate, cardiovascular activity, and coronary death rate in men are inversely related to the level of physical activity. The Centers for Disease Control, following a 2-year analysis of many studies, concluded that least active people were twice as likely to have heart disease than those who were most active.[9] The researchers added that less-than-vigorous exercise may help protect against heart disease.

Dr. Ralph Paffenbarger, Jr.,[10] Stanford University School of Medicine, reported that regular exercise can prolong life for 1 or more years for sedentary individuals. He also reported on a study of 12,000 men in which the death rate over 8 years decreased about 21% among previously sedentary men who became moderately active in various sports during middle age or later.[6]

At Dr. Kenneth Cooper's Institute for Aerobics Research in Dallas, Duncan[11] demonstrated that modest exercise increases the levels of HDL or "good cholesterol." Harbung, at the University of Hawaii, also showed that HDL levels increased steadily from the least active to the most active people. Springer[11] reported on a Stanford University study in which 127 overweight and sedentary men, ages 30-39, were subjected to a year of exercise and diet. As a result, their triglycerides were lowered and their HDL levels were raised 5 mg/dl. Tucker et al[12] found that adults who walk 2½ to 4 miles or more weekly tend to have less than half the prevalence of total cholesterol/HDL ratios greater than 5.0 compared with those who do not walk or exercise regularly.

Dr. Nancy Love, Stanford University, stated in the *Journal of the American Medical Association* that runners between the ages of 50 and 72 had a 40% higher bone density than those who did not run.[6]

Mellon[13] indicated that exercise is viewed by some authorities as effective therapy for anxious and depressed patients, although a measurable therapeutic response to exercise has been difficult to demonstrate. Blair et al[14] noted that physical activity may indirectly influence such antihealth behaviors as overeating, smoking, substance abuse, stress mismanagement, and risk-taking.

The American College of Sports Medicine believes the maximum benefit from exercise depends on these factors:

Duration: Length of time needed to sustain a suitable level of intensity; how many minutes of exercise

Frequency: Number of times weekly

Intensity: Strenuousness needed to reach a level of exertion to provide maximum oxygen-intake capacity

Mode of activity: What type of activity

Hazards of Exercise

There are 17 million people injured yearly in sports and recreational activities. Injuries range from minor aches and pains to severe overuse syndromes, fractures, and connective tissue tears. The most common problems are orthopedic injuries due to overuse—wear-and-tear to the muscles, ligaments, tendons and joints. The most serious risk is sudden cardiac death.

In 1984 Jim Fixx, an articulate advocate of fitness, died suddenly from coronary heart disease. Such sudden death is rare in people who have no major underlying cardiovascular abnormality. The overall probability of death related to exercise is very low (see Table 15-1). Despite the possible risks, the long-term cardiovascular benefits far outweigh the risks. Experts state that regardless of age, exercise should be started slowly and increased in gradual amounts.[15]

Hastings[16] stated that most fitness-related injuries are minor and do not require the services of a physician. Koplan et al[16a] reported that relatively little is known about the incidence of the risks facing those who exercise regularly. They also noted that injury rates are related to form, frequency, and intensity of activity as well as the characteristics of the environment and the person undertaking the activity. Table 15-2 provides information on some of the injuries that occur. *Consumer Reports*[17] stated that although almost every sport activity has some risk of low-back injury, the condition is self-limiting. It is estimated that 70% recover in 2 to 3 weeks and another 20% recover within 2 months. However, there is a 50% chance of this injury occurring again.

Evidence is mounting that too much strenuous exercise can be hazardous to health. Levine and Wells[18] stated that long-distance runners are especially vulnerable. Teasdale and Hennessey[19] stated that of the 20 million Americans who run for fitness, 70% sustain injuries of sufficient severity to stop them from running at least once a year. Eighty percent of the injuries are to the feet and knees. During 1 mile of running, each foot strikes the ground 800 times and the foot and knee must endure a total of 120 tons of weight.

Exercise hazards are greater for sedentary individuals and for those who suddenly thrust themselves into activities that are too strenuous or prolonged. Table 15-3 illustrates how the incidence of injuries increases sharply as the frequency and duration of exercise increase, as indicated in a 20-week experiment with aerobic exercise programs for sedentary adult men (nonathletes).

Dr. Bergfeld of the American College of Sports Medicine reported that aerobic dance has an injury rate of 50%.[16] Garrick[20] said that instructors are twice as likely to be injured (they work longer and more often), but few require medical care. Shin splints and lower leg pain are common problems. Dr. Michael A. Weintraub, professor of neurology at New York Medical College, stated in the *New England Medical Journal of Medicine* that the jarring forces of high-impact aerobics caused by extended periods of arduous jumping and bobbing can damage the delicate structures of the inner ear. Symptoms include imbalance, vertigo, ringing in the ears, and hearing loss. The extent of this problem is unknown, and the duration of the symptoms is unclear.[21]

Marathon runners can sustain muscle damage that takes longer to heal. Jacobs and Benson[22] compiled responses from 451 entrants in a 10,000 meter race. Of these, 47% had running-related injuries,

Table 15–1

Rates of Sudden Death During Exercise

Sport	Fatalities (per hour of exercise)
Jogging	1/396,000
Rugby	1/50,000
Cross-country skiing	1/600,000
All types of exercise at a community recreation center	1/887,526

TABLE 15–2

EXERCISE INJURIES

Exercise	Findings of clinical studies	Findings of epidemiologic studies
Swimming	Otitis externa; muscle strains and tears; shoulder pain; dental enamel erosion; conjunctivitis	No study
Running	Musculoskeletal ailments such as chondromalacia, achilles tendonitis, shin splints, stress fractures; heat exhaustion	38% of runners injured per year; one third of injuries to knee; data on factors associated with heat exhaustion
Walking	No study	No study
Cycling	Head injuries; fractured limbs; abrasions; lacerations	13% accident rate per year; 62% of cyclists in accidents were injured, one third of whom sought medical care
Calisthenics	Lower leg, foot, and ankle injuries	No study
Racquet sports	Head, eye, and leg injuries; tennis elbow	44.5% injured during playing; 9% incidence of tennis elbow

From Koplan JP et al: The risk of exercise: a public health view of injuries and hazards, Public Health Rep 100:189-195, 1985.

TABLE 15–3

INJURY RATES FOR APPROXIMATELY 100 BEGINNING JOGGERS

Time per session	Percent injured
15 minutes	20%
30 minutes	24%
45 minutes	54%

Sessions per week	Percent injured
1	0.0%
3	14%
5	39%

Data from Scaling the heights of physical fitness, Newsday March 28, 1983.

Did You Know?

Fewer than 10% of Americans over 18 years old exercise vigorously and regularly. Physical activity is inversely associated with morbidity and mortality from several chronic diseases.

70% of the injured sought medical aid, and 76% of these had good to excellent recovery. Figure 15-2 shows the types and numbers of the injuries. Dr. Kenneth Cooper has been free of injury for 15 years and said he has reduced his running to 15 miles weekly (3 miles, five times per week). He believes that marathon running increases the risk of injury.[24]

Women who increase the intensity of their exercise may stop menstruating. Low estrogen levels may occur, causing loss of bone tissue and increased risk of osteoporosis. This condition affects one in four women who exercise, and half of the competitive women runners. The combination of bone loss and vigorous exercise predisposes an athlete to stress fractures. These problems can be reversed by reduction of exercise.

Dr. Kenneth Cooper states that people who run more than 15 miles per week or engage in more than 4 hours a week of aerobic dancing are running for some other reason than cardiovascular fitness.[24] Beside avoiding overuse, runners can lessen their chances of injury by performing gentle stretching exercises, wearing proper shoes, running on soft surfaces (such as a cinder track), and paying heed to proper running style and form.

Dr. James Garrick, director of the Center of

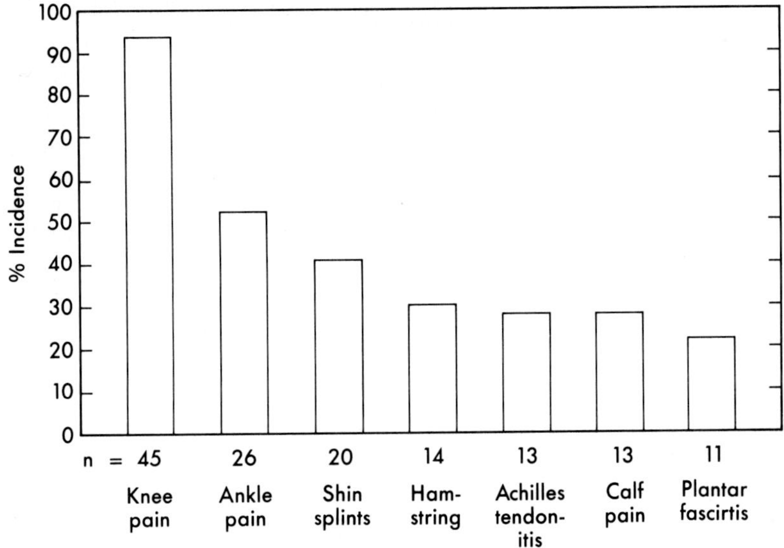

FIGURE 15-2. Injury incidence by site among 210 injured runners.

Sports Medicine at St. Frances Memorial Hospital, San Francisco, has reported that an increasing number of knee and lower back problems related to bench-stepping are appearing.[25] When a bench-stepping program was introduced in 1989, the injury rate was 80%. The majority of the injuries were simple strains and sprains, but 15% of them were serious injuries such as a torn muscle, detached tendon, dislocated joint, stress fracture, or cartilage damage. To reduce the number of such injuries, it has been recommended that the height of the step for beginners be 4 inches and never go above 8 inches.

SPORTS MEDICINE SPECIALISTS

When an injury is sustained and assistance is needed, the first source of help should be from one's primary physician. Other health care professionals who deal with the sports, exercise, and medical needs of active people include:

Exercise physiologist (Ph.D. or M.S.): Someone who helps design exercise programs for a healthy athlete, hospital patient, or fitness club client. Many are research specialists. Those who work in health clubs generally have a master's degree.

Massage therapist: A certified or licensed person who helps speed up recovery after practice or an event by stroking and kneading muscles.

Orthopedist (M.D.): A physician who specializes in the diagnosis and treatment of muscles, bones, joints, and the spine.

Physical therapist (R.P.T.): A trained and licensed individual who helps maintain and restore function to injured limbs and joints using strengthening machines, various exercises, heat, and water; works closely with physicians in rehabilitation.

Podiatrist (D.P.M.): A person medically trained in the prevention, diagnosis, and treatment of injuries, disease, and abnormalities of the foot and ankle.

Sports nutritionist (R.D.): A registered dietician who helps with the nutritional needs of athletes.

Sports psychologist (Ph.D. or M.S.): Someone who works with athletes and teams to provide stress relief and to help meet specific training and competition goals.

EXERCISE PROGRAMS

Individual needs and goals should determine the program of exercise in which to participate. A healthy person should possess sufficient muscular strength to meet the demands of everyday life efficiently and enjoyably. Not all people need the endurance of a marathon runner, the strength of a weightlifter, or the physical fitness of an athlete.

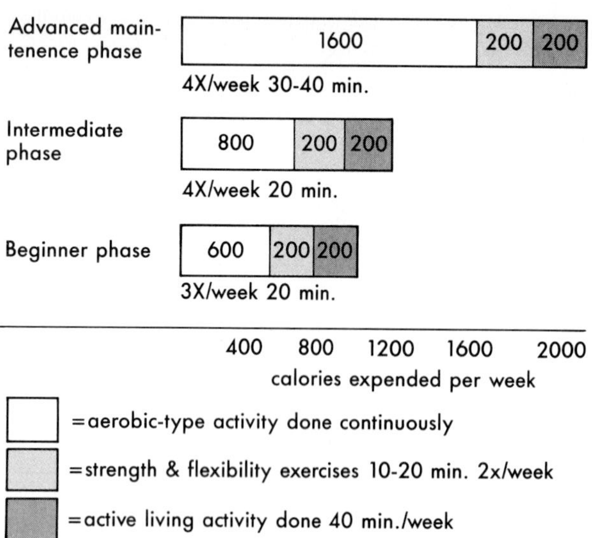

FIGURE 15-3. Recommended amounts of physical activity done per week for healthy adults.
(From Evan T: The Stanford health and exercise handbook, Stanford, Calif, 1987, Stanford Alumni Association/Stanford University Center for Research in Disease Prevention.)

However, almost all people can benefit from regular and systematic exercise with aerobic involvement.

The type and amount of exercise should be adapted to the age and physical fitness of the individual. The American College of Sports Medicine recommends the following guidelines for developing and maintaining cardiorespiratory fitness in the healthy adult:

Frequency: 3 to 5 days per week
Intensity: 60% to 85% of maximum heart rate
Duration: 20 to 30 minutes intensive aerobic activity
Mode of activity: Any activity that uses large muscle groups that can be maintained continuously and is aerobic in nature; for example, jogging, running, walking, hiking, swimming, skating, bicycling, rowing, cross-country skiing, rope jumping, jazzercise, and various other endurance sports activities.

Evan identifies the amounts and types of physical activity to be performed weekly and provides differing maintenance schedules for apparently healthy adults (see Figure 15-3).

Assessing Exercise Intensity

One way to assess the demands on the heart of an activity or exercise is to find its *metabolic equivalents* (METs). A MET is the amount of oxygen consumed while a person sits at rest—approximately 3.5 ml of oxygen per kg of body weight per minute. Performing a 2-MET activity will raise oxygen consumption to 7 ml/kg, while a 3-MET activity will triple the energy demand. Figure 15-4 shows the METs for various activities. MET values can be used to guide doctors who prescribe exercise programs for patients recovering from heart attacks or other cardiovascular problems. For example, if a 5-MET level of exertion on a stress test does not cause symptoms, it is unlikely that the heart will be strained by exercise at home.

The simple way to monitor exercise is to determine the heart rate through the pulse rate. To determine the appropriate intensity of activity, subtract one's age from 220 and take 60% to 75% of the remainder as a starting level of work. The American Heart Association lists the target zone for pulse beats and the average maximum heart rates at different ages, as shown in Table 15-4. As fitness increases, this level should be increased. It should be noted that muscles require movement against resistance to grow in strength and endurance. The best way to strengthen muscles is through exercise that involves gradually increased resistance.

Exercise Guidelines

These suggestions by Dr. Kenneth Cooper are worth considering:

Under 30 years: If there are no medical problems, the individual can participate in any type of exercise activity.
30 to 39 years: Most types of activity are permissible. However, if strenuous exercises are planned, a physician's approval may be advisable.
40 to 59 years: It is advisable to start with a walking program. After conditioning has occurred, running, jogging, and other more demanding activities may be undertaken. However, a physician's approval is advisable before starting. If approval is not given, less strenuous activities such as walking, golf, cycling, and swimming should be permissible.
60 years and over: The average individual should avoid jogging, running, and vigorous competitive sports. Walking, swimming, and stationary cycling will be more beneficial.

Consumers should find these guidelines helpful when they wish to participate in an exercise program:

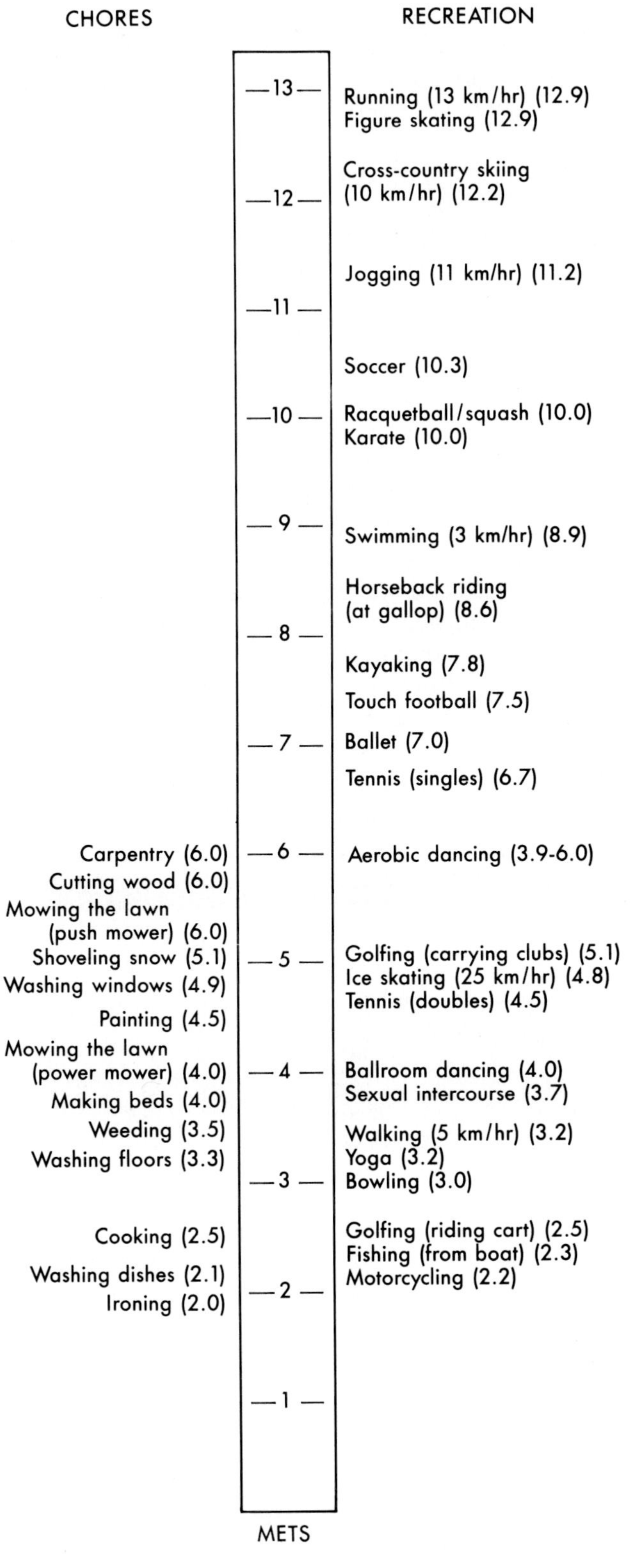

CHORES	METS	RECREATION
	13	Running (13 km/hr) (12.9) Figure skating (12.9)
	12	Cross-country skiing (10 km/hr) (12.2)
		Jogging (11 km/hr) (11.2)
	11	
		Soccer (10.3)
	10	Racquetball/squash (10.0) Karate (10.0)
	9	Swimming (3 km/hr) (8.9)
		Horseback riding (at gallop) (8.6)
	8	Kayaking (7.8) Touch football (7.5)
	7	Ballet (7.0) Tennis (singles) (6.7)
Carpentry (6.0) Cutting wood (6.0) Mowing the lawn (push mower) (6.0)	6	Aerobic dancing (3.9-6.0)
Shoveling snow (5.1) Washing windows (4.9) Painting (4.5)	5	Golfing (carrying clubs) (5.1) Ice skating (25 km/hr) (4.8) Tennis (doubles) (4.5)
Mowing the lawn (power mower) (4.0) Making beds (4.0) Weeding (3.5) Washing floors (3.3)	4	Ballroom dancing (4.0) Sexual intercourse (3.7) Walking (5 km/hr) (3.2) Yoga (3.2)
	3	Bowling (3.0)
Cooking (2.5) Washing dishes (2.1) Ironing (2.0)	2	Golfing (riding cart) (2.5) Fishing (from boat) (2.3) Motorcycling (2.2)
	1	

FIGURE 15-4. METS rating scale of various physical activities. (From METS: a guide to safe exercise, Harvard Heart Letter 1(5):3, 1991.)

TABLE 15-4

CARDIAC TARGET ZONES FOR AEROBIC EXERCISE

Age (years)	Target zone* (beats per minute) 60%-75%	Average maximum heart rate* 100%
20	120-150	200
25	117-146	195
30	114-142	190
35	111-138	185
40	108-135	180
45	105-131	175
50	102-127	170
55	99-123	165
60	96-120	160
65	93-116	155
70	90-113	150

*Maximum heart rate = 220 minus your age.
Target zone is maximum heart rate × 60% to 75%.
©Reproduced with permission. *Exercise and your Heart.* American Heart Association.

1. Determine the physical fitness goal: to increase daily performance; have more energy for pleasure; recover from surgery, pregnancy, or illness; or other.
2. Determine present level of fitness.
3. Consider whether or not to obtain a physician's advice before starting. Authorities do not agree about which individuals should have a health assessment. However, an examination may be appropriate for someone over 35 who is starting an exercise program for the first time. An examination is more appropriate for a person who has been sedentary than for one who has been physically active. The American College of Sports Medicine stated that asymptomatic, physically active persons of any age with no history or risk factors for coronary heart disease usually require little supervision.[26]

Whether to participate in a stress test (assessing heart function while walking on a treadmill or performing some other activity) is a question that should be raised with one's physician. Physicians differ about whether or not to subject individuals to this procedure. A stress test costs several hundred dollars; also, false-positive and false-negative results are common and may create a false sense of security or lead to unnecessary expense. Some authorities believe it should be used only after a thorough clinical examination reveals signs of possible heart disease. The American Heart Association recommends a stress test for individuals over 35 years of age who wish to start an exercise program.[27] Dr. Kenneth Cooper states that the first test should take place at age 35, a second test at 40, and every 3 years thereafter.[28] The American College of Sports Medicine claims an exercise tolerance test (ETT) is not necessary for symptom-free adults under 45 who wish to start an exercise program.[29] (See Chapter 16 for additional information)

4. Select the type of exercise that will be compatible with age and physical condition. In aerobic dance there is a shift in emphasis from high-impact exercise with its hopping, jumping, and jogging movements to low-impact exercise (soft aerobics) with marching, stairway stepping, side-steps, and easygoing dance patterns, especially useful for older persons.
5. Choose exercises that will provide pleasure.
6. Be prudent in the amount of exercise performed; do not attempt an overly intense exercise program, progress gradually at the start. Include warm-up activities: jog in place, ride a stationary bicycle, do calisthenics for a few minutes; stretch muscles to improve flexibility and prevent injury (do not bounce) and cool-off by doing the same activity at a slower pace for 2 to 3 minutes, then stretch again.
7. Whenever possible walk instead of riding by car.
8. Seek information about exercise programs from any of the following:
   a. American Alliance for Health, Physical Education, Recreation and Dance
   b. President's Council on Physical Fitness and Sports (see Appendix for address)
   c. American College of Sports Medicine
   d. Institute for Aerobics Research (Dallas, TX)
   e. Sports and/or exercise clinics at local hospitals
   f. College and university departments of physical education or exercise physiologists

Figure 15-5 should be helpful to those desiring a sport type of exercise. It shows the parts of the body that can be developed.

Kusinitz et al[30] identify in detail the contribution of the various athletic activities to the purposes of exercise as noted in Table 15-5. Table 15-6 lists the

Table 15–5

Selected Sports Activities' Contributions to the Purposes of Exercise*

	Exercise purposes			
Sports activity	**CRE**	**MS**	**ME**	**F**
Aerobics, high-impact	VM	M	VM	M
Aerobics, low-impact	M-VM	S-M	M-VM	M
Aqua exercises	L	S-M	M	M
Basketball	VM	S-M	M	M
Bicycling	VM	M	M	S-M
Bowling	L	L	L	L
Calisthenics	S-M	S	S-M	S
Disco dancing	VM	S-M	M	M
Golf	S-M	S	S	S
Jogging	VM	S-M	M	S-M
Rope jumping	VM	M	M-VM	S
Swimming	VM	S-M	M	M
Tennis	M-VM	S-M	VM	S-M
Walking	S-M	L-S	S-M	L

Adapted from Kusinitz I et al: Physical fitness for practically everybody, Mt Vernon, NY, 1983, Consumer Reports Books.
CRE = Cardiorespiratory efficiency; MS = Muscle strength; ME = Muscle endurance; F = Flexibility; VM = Very much; M = Much; S = Some; L = Little.
*The extent of the benefits from any sport or activity depends on frequency, duration, resistance, and muscles involved.

		Legs				Trunk				Arms				Heart
		Calf/ankle	Thigh/knee	Hips (side)	Buttocks	Stomach	Waistline	Lower back	Upper back	Shoulders	Front, upper	Back, upper	Forearms/wrist	Cardiovascular endurance
Swimming	Crawl		✓		✓		✓		✓	✓	✓	✓	✓	
	Breaststroke		✓	✓	✓			✓	✓	✓	✓	✓	✓	✓
	Backstroke		✓				✓		✓	✓	✓	✓	✓	✓
	Butterfly		✓		✓			✓	✓	✓	✓	✓	✓	✓
	Kicking		✓	✓	✓									✓
	Racing start		✓		✓									
Racket sports	Tennis	✓	✓	✓	✓					✓	✓	✓	✓	
	Racquetball	✓	✓	✓	✓					✓	✓	✓	✓	✓
	Squash	✓	✓	✓	✓					✓	✓	✓	✓	✓
	Paddleball	✓	✓		✓					✓	✓	✓	✓	
Water-skiing			✓		✓				✓	✓	✓	✓	✓	
Jogging	Distance	✓	✓	✓	✓	✓								✓
	Sprints	✓	✓	✓	✓									
Racewalking		✓	✓	✓	✓	✓								✓
Hiking		✓	✓	✓	✓									✓
Bicycling			✓		✓									✓
Golf			✓		✓		✓			✓				
Canoeing, kayaking						✓	✓	✓	✓	✓	✓	✓	✓	✓
Archery									✓	✓	✓		✓	
Fencing			✓		✓				✓	✓	✓	✓	✓	✓
Judo, karate			✓	✓	✓	✓			✓	✓	✓	✓		✓
Team sports	Baseball, softball		✓		✓				✓	✓	✓	✓	✓	
	Basketball	✓	✓	✓	✓					✓	✓	✓	✓	✓
	Field hockey	✓	✓	✓	✓					✓	✓			✓
	Lacrosse	✓	✓	✓	✓					✓	✓	✓	✓	✓
	Soccer	✓	✓	✓	✓									✓
	Volleyball	✓	✓		✓				✓	✓	✓	✓	✓	
	Badminton	✓	✓	✓	✓					✓	✓			
Horseback riding		✓	✓		✓									✓

FIGURE 15-5. Affected body parts and cardiovascular endurance from sports activities.

(Modified from Glamour, p 103, May 1981. Copyright 1981 by The Conde Nast Publication Inc.)

TABLE 15–6

CALORIES EXPENDED PER MINUTE BY ACTIVITY AND WEIGHT

Activity	Calories expended per minute by weight			
	105-115 lbs	127-137 lbs	160-170 lbs	182-192 lbs
Dancing, rock	3.25	3.75	4.41	4.91
Golfing, hand cart	3.25	3.75	4.41	4.01
Lawn mowing, power	3.50	4.00	4.75	5.16
Baseball, fielder	3.66	4.16	4.91	5.41
Walking, 3 mph	3.90	4.50	5.30	5.80
Hiking, 20 lb pack, 2 mph	3.91	4.50	5.25	5.83
Rowing machine, easy	3.91	4.50	5.25	5.83
Sexual intercourse, active partner	3.91	4.50	5.25	5.83
Swimming, crawl, 20 yd/min	3.91	4.50	5.25	5.83
Badminton, singles	4.58	5.16	6.16	6.75
Skating, leisure	4.58	5.16	6.16	6.75
Calisthenics	3.91	4.50	7.33	7.91
Gardening, weeding, digging	5.08	5.75	6.83	7.50
Sawing wood, hand	5.08	5.83	6.83	7.58
Bicycling, 10 mph	5.41	6.16	7.33	7.85
Square dancing	5.50	6.25	7.41	8.00
Tennis, doubles	5.58	6.33	7.50	8.25
Aerobic dancing	5.83	6.58	7.83	8.58
Stair climbing, normal	5.90	6.70	7.90	8.80
Basketball, half-court	7.25	8.25	9.75	10.75
Handball	7.83	8.91	10.50	11.58
Volleyball	7.83	8.91	10.50	11.58
Snow shoveling, light	7.91	9.08	10.75	11.83
Jogging, 5 mph	8.58	9.75	11.50	12.66
Running 6.5 mph	8.90	10.20	12.00	13.20
Skiing cross-country, 5 mph	9.16	10.41	12.25	13.33
Trampolining	10.33	11.75	13.91	15.33
Bicycling, stationary, 20 mph	11.66	13.25	15.58	17.16

Modified from Perry P: Are we having fun yet? American Health 6:59-63, March 1987.

calories expended per minute for selected activities in four weight categories. This information is useful together with Figure 15-5 and Table 15-5. Simon[31] stated that a person who exercises for 20 to 30 minutes three or four times each week at 75% of the maximum heart rate will expend 2000 calories, which is equal to walking or jogging 20 miles.

Women and Exercise

The purposes and benefits of exercise are just as applicable and important to women as they are to men. However, several matters deserve special attention.

Injuries tend to be more prevalent among female than male runners or joggers. The common types are knee problems, shin splints, Achilles tendonitis, stress fractures, sore breasts, and sore nipples. Women who participate in long-distance running also may develop amenorrhea. These precautions may help to minimize the risk of injuries when exercising:

1. Perform slow, stretching warm-up exercises before jogging
2. Wear properly fitting shoes that provide good arch support, heel cushioning, and broad flare at the heel for better stability
3. Wear a brassiere that provides firm support to breast tissue but will not irritate the nipples with improperly placed seams

4. Run on softer surfaces, such as grassy areas or rubberized asphalt, instead of hard pavement
5. Run on flat, straight surfaces as much as possible to prevent undue stress on ankle and knee joints
6. When running daily, mileage should be increased gradually to avoid overuse syndrome by alternating days of hard and easy workouts; this allows time for recovery from trauma to muscles, tendons, and bones

Researchers now believe that weightlifting helps build a large reserve of bone mass needed to prevent osteoporosis. For those women who wish to participate in weightlifting, a program of eight to ten exercises totalling 20 to 30 minutes several times weekly may be advisable.[32]

Dr. William J. Evans, director of the Physiology Laboratory, Human Nutrition Center at Tufts University, stated that women who exercise throughout their life will never have low bone density that leads to osteoporosis. However, they need a balanced program of exercise that includes strengthening of all muscle groups (hips, chest, legs, shoulders, back and abdomen) possibly through weightlifting in addition to aerobic exercise for cardiorespiratory involvement.

There is no indication that exercise during pregnancy is detrimental to fetal development and growth. Moderate exercise can help prevent excessive weight gain and improve recovery after birth. The American College of Obstetricians and Gynecologists advises no more than 15 minutes of exercise at one time for pregnant women.[33] Generally, women who are pregnant should not start new exercise programs and probably should cut back on the intensity of their present activity after consultation with their physicians. For cardiovascular fitness it is advisable to exercise no less than three times weekly for 30 minutes each time. Walking and swimming are especially good for those who have been sedentary. Activities that involve bouncing, jarring, twisting, or that risk trauma to the abdomen should be avoided. The following recommendations should be helpful for women who are pregnant:

1. Do not exercise in hot, humid weather, and drink lots of water to avoid dehydration. Hot tubs and saunas should be limited to 5 to 15 minutes.
2. Activities such as running, cycling, aerobic dancing, and tennis should be decreased in intensity, speed, and frequency as pregnancy advances.
3. Avoid these activities: water skiing, scuba diving, contact sports, racquet sports, and other sports in which lack of balance and coordination might increase the risk of injury. Muscles change and ligaments and joints soften due to hormonal changes. Some weightlifting routines involving the upper body and legs may be continued if modified (lighter weight, fewer repetitions with no straining).
4. Do not exercise while lying on the back after the fourth month, as this may block the blood supply to the uterus.
5. When very tired, or feeling discomfort, stop the activity and rest; do not exercise to exhaustion.
6. Postpartum fitness is improved when pregnant women enter labor and delivery in good physical condition.

Exercise and the Elderly

Of equal importance (to morbidity and mortality) is the potential for regular exercise to preserve function and prolong active life expectancy, not just life expectancy.

E.B. Larsen, M.D.[34]

Exercise conditioning can enable elderly individuals to complete daily activities with less fatigue and it may increase life expectancy. Lack of exercise adversely affects cardiorespiratory function. Lampman[35] states that the benefits include: improved heart-lung efficiency, reduced risk of coronary artery disease, decreased body fat, increased bone density, increased work capacity, greater flexibility and strength, reduced susceptibility to depression, improved self-esteem, and greater independence. He added that to receive the full benefits of regular endurance exercise, an elderly person should start by undergoing a thorough medical evaluation, including a medical history and physical examination and an exercise stress test to evaluate cardiovascular status. With this information the intensity, duration, and frequency of exercise can be determined at the safest level.

The *Mayo Clinic Health Letter* stated that active people have several health advantages over seden-

Consumer Tip

You do not have to use exercise machines or barbells to be fit. Just stay active doing things that you enjoy.

tary people.[36] They are less likely to have coronary heart disease, may have slightly lower blood pressure, be better able to control most cases of adult-onset diabetes, and have a lower incidence of osteoporosis. In addition, those with arthritis will retain more mobility in their joints.

Miller[37] suggests a simple sequence of exercises to loosen joints and stretch and strengthen muscles, combined with an aerobic activity such as walking. This program is recommended for older persons who can walk independently. Miller offers these guidelines: (1) exercise 2 or 3 days a week, (2) do not overdo it, (3) increase workload gradually each session, and (4) report to your doctor any untoward feelings such as breathlessness, faintness, giddiness, pain, or any other unexpected symptom.

Weight Training

Approximately 5 million people train with weights on a regular basis. This is exercise done with resistance. When done correctly, it can increase strength, speed, flexibility, and muscle endurance. It can also improve a person's appearance and self-image. Weight training is not a substitute for aerobic exercise and is not very effective in increasing heart and lung efficiency.[38]

When done improperly and without supervision, weight training may cause injuries that result in sprains, strains, and muscle tears to the shoulders, lower back, and knees. It can increase blood pressure and thus is risky for hypertensive and cardiovascular patients. Menstrual irregularities, like those associated with marathoners, can sometimes occur.[39]

Some experts claim that aerobics has been oversold at the expense of muscle-building. The American College of Sports Medicine suggests in addition to aerobic exercise that individuals engage in weight training is two times per week, performing eight to ten different exercises to strengthen the large muscles of the chest, arms, back and legs.

Anabolic Steroids

Although it may be true that in combination with intensive weight training and a high-calorie, high-protein diet, steroids can augment short-term muscle gain, teens need to ask themselves: Is it worth all the short-term health effects and the possibility of long-term permanent damage? Is it worth the disgrace of being eliminated from competition, or even of being arrested?

Raja Mishra[40]

Anabolic steroids are male hormones, available by prescription, that have legitimate medical uses for certain types of anemias, hereditary angioedema, protein anabolism, and certain gynecologic conditions. They are also useful as an adjunct to growth hormone therapy, and for treating osteoporosis.

Widespread use of steroids has been found among weightlifters, shotputters, discus throwers, football players, and participants in other sports where strength is required. There has been use associated with endurance sports such as Nordic skiing, cycling, and distance running. Steroids have been used by both professional and collegiate athletes. It is estimated that 250,000 high school seniors have used steroids, and their use also has spread to junior high school students. Many steroid abusers take very large doses by combining several different brands of steroids, a practice that is called "stacking."

Steroids are obtained illegally from two main sources: (1) physicians who issue prescriptions and know that they will be used by athletes, and (2) the black market. The FDA estimates that 1 million Americans take anabolic steroids for nonmedical reasons, with annual sales of more than $100 million.[40] These drugs originate mainly from underground laboratories and foreign sources. A recent trend among teenagers has been the use of so-called steroid "alternatives," gamma hydroxybutyrate (GHB) and clenbuterol, both of which can be deadly. The federal Anti-Drug Abuse Act of 1988 increased the penalties for those who distribute steroids, or have steroids in their possession with the intent to distribute them. The Act increases fines and established jail sentences of up to 3 to 6 years for convicted dealers.

The AMA Council on Scientific Affairs has reported that steroid studies show that muscle size and strength can be increased when the drug is used by those who are already training intensively and who combine this activity with a high-protein and high-caloric diet.[41] Body weight is also increased, although much is due to fluid retention. Steroids can increase energy and the ability to train more intensely with shortened recovery period, allowing more frequent training. Many athletes report that large doses result in euphoria, lack of fatigue, greater self-confidence, and enhanced appearance. However, adverse effects can include: acne, genital changes, yellowing of eyes and skin, stunted growth, coronary heart disease, sterility, liver tu-

PERSONAL GLIMPSE

Did You Know?

A 23-year-old bodybuilder, complaining of severe groin pains, was taken to the hospital. Doctors found his liver and kidneys had stopped working. He was immediately rushed to the intensive-care unit. Four days later, he died when his heart stopped. An autopsy revealed that he was a steroid user.

mors, and death. Other possible adverse reactions to steroids may include: abdominal pains, diarrhea, muscle cramps, headache, bone pains, depression, breast development in men, gallstones, high blood pressure, and kidney disease. Women who abuse steroids can develop menstrual irregularities, permanent enlargement of the clitoris, lowered voice pitch, facial hair, increased body hair, decreased breast size, and male-pattern baldness. Taken before puberty, anabolic steroids can stop bone growth and cause permanent stunting of growth.

The AMA Council on Scientific Affairs has made these recommendations:[41]

1. The nonmedical use of steroids by athletes to enhance or sustain athletic performance is inappropriate and should be discontinued.
2. Dealers and distributors of anabolic steroids used for nonmedical purposes should be punished severely.
3. Further research should be done on the short-term and long-term health effects of steroids.

Two studies[42,43] suggest that the use of steroids can cause addiction. The characteristic signs include craving for the substance, use of larger doses, more frequent use, inability to stop, and withdrawal symptoms.

Table 15-7 identifies the most frequent problems reported by steroid users in a survey conducted by the U.S. Department of Health and Human Services.[45]

TABLE 15–7

MOST FREQUENT STEROID-ASSOCIATED HEALTH PROBLEMS CITED BY 72 CURRENT AND FORMER USERS*

Problem	Percent
Liver disease	71
Heart disease	56
Cancer	50
Shrinking of the testicles	49
Adverse personality changes	49
Death	45
Sterility	44
Kidney disease	38
Blood pressure	38
Stunted growth	36

*Respondents were allowed more than one response.
Teenagers blasé about steroid use, FDA Consumer, p 2, Nov 1990.

EXERCISE EQUIPMENT AND SUPPLIES

If things that ring and whistle and buzz and whir and call you a wimp aren't your cup of soup, you might want to consider the advantages of an exercise gizmo that can be had for approximately $2—a Jump Rope.

ROBERT G. HOLLAND[45]

In 1988 an estimated $1.8 billion was spent on over 600,000 home exercise machines at an average cost of $300. Some of these devices have value and contribute greatly to physical fitness, while others have little or no value. Some may cause injuries. Consumers contemplating purchase and use of exercise equipment should consider whether the benefits to be derived will help to achieve any or all of the four essential purposes previously identified: endurance/stamina, flexibility, strength, and cardiorespiratory efficiency. Consumers may also wish to check whether similar benefits can be obtained without equipment or in a less expensive way. (Check the "In-Home Fitness" section at the end of the chapter for suggestions.) Many of the materials on the market are not necessary for fitness. Many items are expensive and poorly constructed. *Most people who purchase exercise equipment waste money, since only 20% of home buyers remain steady users; boredom often sets in.*

The use of exercise equipment involves some risk. Burroughs[46] reported on 18,000 injuries that required emergency room treatment. During 1991 the U.S. Consumer Product Safety Commission identified many exercise devices with faulty springs that had caused bruises, lacerations, and other injuries to users.

It is important for consumers to clearly understand their fitness goals, to obtain expert help in using equipment, and to check the quality of items before purchasing them. Figures 15-6 and 15-7 show several types of equipment useful for aerobic exercise. Table 15-8 compares 29 exercise products, many of which are questionable, that have been advertised in popular magazines and newspapers. The information in Table 15-8 was compiled by Dr. Cornacchia and reviewed by three exercise physiology experts.

Electronic Monitors

Electronic monitors found on many exercise machines provide feedback about such things as heart rate, miles pedaled, and calories burned. Jim Erwin, an exercise physiologist at Centinela Hospital Fitness Center in Inglewood, California, stated that there are no established standards for these machines and some are inaccurate. Actually, they are intended to give approximate readouts, but feedback devices that give distance, speed, repetitions, or elapsed time are usually accurate. Those that give heart rate and calories burned have a larger margin of error; some are as much as 29% inaccurate. He stated that the easiest and perhaps the best way for the average person exercising to gauge a workout, would be as follows: if you work-up a sweat, push harder than the day before (without feeling pain), and end up feeling a "good" tired, then you probably had a good workout.[47]

Exercise Bicycles

More than 100 different brands and models of exercise bicycles are available, ranging in price from $150 to $2000. *Consumer Reports* recommends look-

FIGURE 15-6. Stair-stepping device used with hand weights.
(From Self-Care Catalog, Headsburg, Calif, 1991.)

FIGURE 15-7. Popular equipment used for aerobic exercise.
(From Nordic Track, Chaska, Minnesota.)

ing for these features when shopping for a stationary bicycle:[48]

1. Seat: wide, comfortable, easy to adjust to height
2. Pedals: strap lets you work on upstroke and downstroke; weighted pedals keep the straps on top
3. Handlebars: adjustable ones make long workouts more comfortable
4. Resistance control: a calibrated control is easiest to reset
5. Resistance mechanism: a caliper brake or belt around flywheel to make pedaling harder
6. Gauges: clear and easy to read
7. Frame: rigid

Consumers should try out equipment before making purchases.

Two types of exercise bicycle are marketed: single action and dual action. Single-action bikes are pumped with the legs and turn a flywheel linked to the pedals. Resistance to pumping is provided by a strap around the wheel or a set of caliper brake pads. The tighter the strap or pads, the more difficult it is to turn the wheel, and the greater the workout. Dual-action bikes have the handlebars, linked to the pedals, that move back and forth and are attached to a fan. The faster a person pedals and pumps, the more air resistance takes place and the more energy is expended. The bikes rated highest by *Consumer Reports* are:

Single-action bikes: Tunturi Executive Ergometer, Schwinn Medallion, Schwinn Signature, and Monark Ergo Trainer 810

Dual-action bikes: Ross Futura Air Ergometer, Schwinn Air-Dyne, and Tunturi E702 Air Bike

The list prices of the above single-action bikes ranged from $250 to $400, while the double action bikes cost about $700. Training stands, which support a regular bike and add a resistance device, are listed for $120 to $150.[49]

Mountain Bicycles

Mountain bicycles typically have a sturdy frame, fat, knobby tires, and flat handlebars. (Road bikes have a lighter frame, skinnier, smoother tires, and drop handlebars.) *Consumer Reports* tested 34 mountain bicycles ranging in price from $135 to $535 and concluded that the two best buys are the Giant Iguana at $380 and the Jazz Voltage at $279. Other bikes that received high ratings included: Cannondale SM400, Bianchi Ibex, Trek 380, Specialized Rockhopper, Nishiki Backroads, and Miyata Elevation.[50]

Bicycle Helmets

A study reported in the *New England Journal of Medicine* found that the risk of head injury by cyclists could be reduced 85% by wearing a helmet.[51] Yet fewer than 2% of children and 10% of adults wear helmets while cycling. Helmets cost from $25 to $85. There are no mandatory standards for helmets in the United States, but consumers should buy those that meet the standards of the American National Standards Institute (ANSI) or the Snell Memorial Foundation. These factors should be considered when purchasing a helmet:

Adequate retention system: Straps should be of nonstretch material and helmet should not wiggle, pull, or twist off the head when fastened

Proper fit: Should be snug and sit level on the head

Ventilation: Provide holes for air to keep head cool and comfortable

Color: Select bright colors for visibility; white or yellow

The Washington Area Bicyclist Association[52] has rated these helmets as follows:

Excellent: Bell VI-Pro, Bell Stratos, Giro, Kiwi K-25, Lazer LZ-1, LZ Eddy Merkx, MSR, Nava, Pro-Tec Breeze, and most helmets meeting the Snell 1984 standard

Good: Avenir, Bailen, Bell Tourlite, Brancale SP-4, Cycle Products Co., Targa, Vetta Corsa, and most helmets meeting the ANSI Z90.4 standard

Rowing Machines

High-quality rowing machines cost at least $250. Good equipment has sturdy tubing, parts that fit snugly together, a padded, contoured seat that slides smoothly, and double-piston "oars" with adjustable tension. Before purchasing, ask for a demonstration of the device and try it.

Cross-Country Ski Exercisers

Cross-country ski machines have become quite popular in recent years. This equipment may help produce weight loss, stimulate interest in cross-country skiing, and strengthen and firm many muscle groups, especially in the legs. There is no evidence that this exercise postpones aging, as has sometimes been advertised.

When planning to purchase a cross-country ski exerciser, look for smoothness of operation, overall stability, foot security, a fit that allows adequate adjustment for people of different heights, ease of resistance adjustment, and quiet operation. *Consumer Reports*[53] evaluated a number of exercisers

Text continued on p. 332.

Table 15–8

Comparison of Exercise Equipment

Item	Flexibility	Muscle strength	Muscle stamina/endurance	CRE	Body parts	Muscle groups	Description of equipment
	Benefits*				Affected body areas		
Barbells	N	L-S	L	N	Arms, chest, forearms, shoulders	Biceps, triceps, deltoids, pectorals, forearm muscles	Forms and shapes vary in size and weight; made of iron, rubber plastic; water or sand filled
Bull-worker	N	S-M	L-S	N	Arms, chest, shoulders, forearms	Biceps, triceps, deltoids, pectorals, trapezius, forearm muscles	Two spring-load cylinders about 3 feet long with handles at each end that telescope when compressed
Chinning bar	L	S-M	N-L	N	Arms, back, forearms, shoulders	Biceps, triceps, trapezius, latissimus, forearm muscles	Metal bar hung in doorway or attached to ceiling or wall slightly above reach
Bicycles, stationary (single-action)—some combine rowing features and have fan (dual-action); some have monitors and are computerized	L-S	S-M	M	M-VM	Hips, legs, buttocks, thighs, upper body (rowing)	Biceps, triceps, trapezius, latissimus in rowing; gastrocnemius, gluteals, hamstrings, quadriceps, soleus	A bicycle without the usual wheels, that registers speed and distance; can provide varying degrees of resistance; some also have rowing action
Chest pull/chest expander	L	S-M	L-S	N	Arms, back, chest, forearms, shoulders	Triceps, deltoids, trapezius, pectorals, some forearm muscles	Heavy rubber, elastic bands or springs with handles on each end
Cross-country ski machine also with digital readouts	S-M	S-M	S-M	M-VM	Arms, legs, shoulders, back, buttocks	Biceps, triceps, gastrocnemius, trapezius, deltoids, gluteals, quadriceps, hamstrings	Leg glide with smooth sensation of cross-country motion; resistance of skiing and arm pulls, provide a total execution
Door gym/portable gym	L	M-VM	S-M	S	Arms, calves of legs, chest, shoulders	Biceps, triceps, deltoids, pectorals, gastrocnemius, quadriceps, trapezius, forearm muscles	Varies in complexity of equipment; includes chinning bar, tension items, etc.

TABLE 15–8

COMPARISON OF EXERCISE EQUIPMENT—cont'd

Cost	Advertising claims	Comments
$5 to $18 each set	Tones muscles; very light; easy to store	Provides resistance exercise; especially useful with other equipment; benefits depend on types of exercise, amount of weight, and frequency of use; used as adjunct to jogging—resistive exercises
$40 to $50	Isometric/isotonic exerciser; develops muscles and builds body through push, pull, and press; easy to use; takes 70 seconds a day	Benefits limited as indicated; perhaps some isometric value; limited to upper body excluding abdominals; "70 seconds" advertising claim unreasonable
$10 to $20	Rarely advertised; may be part of a multiple equipment system	Benefits limited to upper body strength development; strenuous for the unfit; easily and cheaply made and installed in home workshop
$150 to $2000	Permits aerobic fitness in home or office; promotes circulation, improves muscle tone and coordination, increases endurance	Extent of resistance and intensity will determine benefits; equipment can vary degrees of resistance; see p. 325 for *Consumer Reports* analysis of quality
$20 to $50	Isometric/isotonic exercise; no long, tiring workouts; tones and shapes all muscle groups in one-fourth time required for barbells and dead weights	Good isotonic trainer for upper body; provides limited resistive exercise benefits; resistive exercise can speed up strength improvement, but time requirement cannot be verified; does not provide isokinetic or isometric exercise
$300 to $1300	Elevates heart rate to fitness level; burns more calories; exercises all muscle groups in upper and lower body	Simulates skiing; fairly good workout; requires good coordination; little strain on body, especially knees
$20 to $100	Provides 30 different body building and shaping exercises—as many as Nautilis and other costly machines; virtually all exercises offered by other expensive weight machines	Depending on type of resistive exercise, might be good weight training device; the several types of equipment do provide a variety of activities; frequency and duration of resistive exercise will determine benefits

Continued

TABLE 15–8

COMPARISON OF EXERCISE EQUIPMENT—cont'd

	Benefits*				Affected body areas		
Item	Flexibility	Muscle strength	Muscle stamina/ endurance	CRE	Body parts	Muscle groups	Description of equipment
Electrical muscle/nerve stimulator	N	L	N	N	Depends on muscles stimulated		Electropulse pads placed in various muscle areas in which three levels of electrical intensity can be applied
Quick-Trim Isotric Exercisor or Rope Tension Gym	L	S-M	L	N	Arms, legs, back	Biceps, hamstrings, quadriceps, latissimus dorsi	Lightweight dynamic tension device; heavy spring pulled and pushed by arms and legs
Gravity Guiding Rack System/ Portable Gravity Guide/Gravity Inversion Boots	N-L	L-S	N-L	N	Abdomen, back, vertabrae or spine	Abdominals, latissimus dorsi, obliques	Simple to complex equipment; individual turned into upside-down position hanging from feet; uses special boots
Grip strengthener	N	S	L	N	Fingers, forearms	Forearm muscles	Rubber ball; fairly hard substance
Hip Cycle, PedaBike, Lazy Slimmer	L	L	N-L	N-L	Legs	Gastrocnemius, hamstrings, quadriceps	Operate pedals like bicycle while lying down or sitting in chair
Multipurpose gyms, Home Fitness System/Portable Gym/Weight Training Complex	S	M-VM	M	L-S	All body parts	Probably most muscles	Contains a variety of weight training equipment with such items as situp/ slant board, leg lifts, etc.; most popular—Nautilus and Universal
Jump rope	L-S	M	M	M-VM	Arms, hips, legs	Biceps, forearm muscles, hamstrings, gluteals, gastrocnemius, quadriceps, soleus	Made of cotton, nylon, polyester material with handles
Minitrampoline	L	S	S-M	S-M	Hips, legs	Hamstrings, quadriceps, gastrocnemius, soleus, gluteals	Steel frame with tough vinyl cover, 34″ × 10″

TABLE 15–8

COMPARISON OF EXERCISE EQUIPMENT—cont'd

Cost	Advertising claims	Comments
Home—$25 to $50 Other—$2500 Services—$25 to $50 per hour	300 sit-ups without moving an inch; 10 miles of jogging lying flat on your back; smooth, flatten tummy, slender thighs, youthful bustline, no-sag backside, wrinkle removal, weight loss	Unrealistic advertising claims; no definitive research indicating value; no aerobic conditioning; FDA approved "electrical nerve/muscle stimulation" to stimulate blood and maintain muscle tone under medical supervision—used in rehabilitation after surgery, injuries and arthritic patients; may help athletes with muscle soreness
$10 to $30	Firms and trims waist, hips, thighs, derriere; flattens stomach; firms and strengthens chest, arms quickly and easily; use only 5 minutes each day	Claims overextended; greatly limited benefits; one cannot spot reduce and trim fat; check quality of equipment
$250 to $1500; boots extra $60 to $85	Relieves backache, stress on spine; relieves back pain without surgery and expensive therapy; restores body flexibility and vigor; gravity flattens stomach, strengthens back and legs; totally safe	No scientific evidence to support claims; hanging upside-down empties leg veins, but so does lying in bed with feet elevated; elevates blood pressure and eye pressure; use with caution, can cause injuries (originally designed as traction apparatus to relieve interdisc pressures)
$7	Builds muscles in wrist/forearm by simply squeezing ball; also exercises toes and instep; great tension reliever	Any round rubber object or other resistant substance will strengthen muscles; frequency and duration important; no evidence of tension relief
$13	Firms hips, trims thighs, shapes calves; makes exercise easier; firms abdomen, buttocks, hips	No resistance exercise, no strength; no involved abdominals, buttocks, hips; stationary bicycle better; note benefit limits
$300 to $4500 and up	Permits a total range of professional gym exercises; 57 simple exercises from heavy body building to general physical fitness; do leg lifts, leg curls, arm curls, and arm rowing	Provides resistive exercise that can speedup strength development and fitness; limited cardiorespiratory involvement; body parts involved depend on choice of exercises; some equipment usable in small space in home; many other less costly equipment and programs
$4 to $25	Involves cardiorespiratory efficiency; leg muscle endurance/stamina	Improves CRE; develops leg strength; excellent activity with inexpensive equipment; can be homemade; weight ropes available
$25 to $100 (small size)	Combines aerobic exercises to work on each muscle in body and heart; easier on knees than jogging; improves posture, balance, digestion; strengthens heart, enjoyable	No effect on digestion; good if intensity is high: study at Arizona State University revealed probable benefit for unfit; must work very hard for aerobic effect; hazard of losing balance and falling; some claims conjecture; less traumatic on body

TABLE 15–8

COMPARISON OF EXERCISE EQUIPMENT—cont'd

Item	Benefits*				Affected body areas		Description of equipment
	Flexibility	Muscle strength	Muscle stamina/ endurance	CRE	Body parts	Muscle groups	
Orthopedic Inversion Machine	N-L	L-S	N-L	L-N	Back, trunk	Latissimus dorsi obliques	Upsidedown stretch and relax back and abdominal muscles
Push-up bars	L	S-M	S	N	Arms, chest, shoulders, upper back	Triceps, deltoids, pectorals, trapezius	Two individual steel bars 6″ from floor
Rowing machine (some have monitors)	S-M	M	M-VM	M-VM	Arms, legs, hips, back, abdomen, shoulders	Biceps, quadriceps, hamstrings, latissimus dorsi, trapezius, abdominals, gastrocnemius, soleus, gluteals	Various styles; some collapsible, some attached to wall, have pulse meter, caloric meter, clock to track elapsed time
Sit-up bar	S	M	M	N-L	Abdomen, lower back	Abdominals, lower back	Bar attached 6″ from wall for hooking feet when exercising
Slant board	L-S	S-M	S	L	Abdomen, back, legs	Abdominals, hamstrings, latissimus dorsi, trapezius	Vinyl covered, padded, board, 12″ to 14″ wide; can be tilted up or down; person lies on it when exercising
Slim/Small Wheel	L	S	L	N	Arms, back, abdomen, shoulders	Biceps, triceps, abdominals, deltoids, pectorals, trapezius, gluteals, latissimus dorsi	6″ to 8″ wheel with bar through center for hands; is rolled to and from body while in kneeling position
Stair climber; digital readouts; some motorized	L-S	S-M	M	M-VM	Legs, buttocks, arms, shoulders (if movable handle)	Quadriceps, hamstrings, gluteals, biceps, deltoids, gastrocnemius	Grasp handle and begin to step and pull working upper body and lower body at same time
Stairway stepping	L-S	S-M	M-VM	M-VM	Legs, buttocks, thighs	Quadriceps, hamstrings, gluteals, gastrocnemius	2 pairs of 2″ blocks and 4″ high platform to step and 4″, 6″ and 8″ plus video
Stomach eliminators	S	S-M	S	L	Lower back, hips, arms	PSOAS, latissimus dorsi, biceps	Crossbar or heavy spring attached; stirrups like foot grips

TABLE 15–8

COMPARISON OF EXERCISE EQUIPMENT—cont'd

Cost	Advertising claims	Comments
$400	Easy and safe; strengthens muscle; supports back; painless inverted abdominal curls; perform trunk twists and hypertensions; improves circulation, releases stress; adds energy and vitality	May strengthen back muscles with some trunk value; no evidence to support release of stress or improve circulation; high cost item—same effect achieved at less or no cost; injury problem (see Gravity Guiding Rack)
$15	Provides better, quicker results than ordinary push-ups; allows greater range of motion	Resistance may quicken benefits; whether better is unproven; same results can be achieved without equipment
$250 to $2000	Strengthens heart, lungs; tones stomach, hip, thighs, and arms; increases endurance; gets rid of tension; rowing is a great all-around fitness program	Good benefits if frequency and intensity and duration maintained; need high degree of motivation to prevent boredom from use; risky for people with back problems
$17	Strengthens middle; shapes legs	Especially helps tone abdominals if knees in bent position; "shaping of legs" claim is puffery; with feet locked, hip flexors are involved
$40 to $80	Firms muscles; orthopedically approved	Greater benefit because of greater resistance from gravity than in flat sit-ups; use of barbells and weights increases resistance and benefits; may be part of home gym equipment
$25	Tightens muscles; takes off inches from waistline without dieting or weight loss; twice a day merely roll back and forth five times; equals same results as a dozen conventional sit-ups	Claims are outrageous, not substantiated; benefits limited; not for people with back or shoulder problems; mostly a latissimus dorsi exercise
$350 to $3000	Work upper and lower body at same time; work every muscle group; for serious training	Good aerobic activity; most muscles involved; limited arm and very limited abdominal and back involvement
Step and video $120 Handouts $29	Latest in low impact video; mix stair climbing and jazz aerobics	Good aerobic and strength activity; limited upper arm and body involvement unless use weights; could be strenuous and should be taken in gradual steps; 6″ to 8″ steps for advanced fitness
$4 to $23	Slimmer, younger look in 2 weeks; flattens stomach, strengthens chest, arms, back, thighs	Benefits limited; some back and arm strength; hazard—breakage of spring

Continued.

Table 15–8

Comparison of Exercise Equipment—cont'd

Item	Benefits* Flexibility	Muscle strength	Muscle stamina/endurance	CRE	Affected body areas: Body parts	Muscle groups	Description of equipment
Tummy Trimming/Stomach Trimmer	N	N	N	N	Abdomen	None	Wide rubber/elastic belt that buttons, tightens, shapes abdominal area
Treadmill	N	S	M	M-VM	Hips, legs	Gluteals, hamstrings, quadriceps, gastrocnemius, soleus	A flat, moving surface on rollers; permits walking at home; some lightweight and portable with adjustable speeds
Thigh machine	N-L	L-S	L	N	Arms, legs, lower back	Hamstrings, quadriceps, gluteals, gastrocnemius, latissimus dorsi	Bar 12″ from floor, movable against some resistance by the arms and legs
Tummy toner	N	L	L	L	Arms, legs, hips	Biceps, triceps, quadriceps, hamstrings, gluteals	Knee pad on rollers attached to steel frame with 12″ high bar in front for hands; glide back and forward on rollers while kneeling
Twister	L	L	L	N-L	Legs, hips	Hamstrings, quadriceps, gluteals, gastrocnemius, soleus	12″ plastic/metal circle/square rotates on ball bearings; person stands on it and twists body

and said that Nordic Track 505 ($470) is best, Fitness Master XC-1 ($529) is good, and Fitness Master LT-35 ($399) and Fit 1 ($495) give a decent workout but have drawbacks.

Portable Pulse Monitors

Pulse monitors check the pulse during exercise to enable individuals to know whether they are performing at an appropriate pulse rate (usually 60% to 85% of maximum). There are two types of monitors: (1) finger or earlobe sensor, and (2) transmitter worn on the chest that broadcasts to a watch that provides the pulse readout. They cost from $40 to $300. The finger or earlobe type is less expensive, but gives inaccurate readings of a high pulse when it is jarred. Some chest devices may be linked to a computer that can generate a printout.

This equipment may be an unnecessary expense because there is another easy way to check the pulse rate. Place the first three fingers of one hand on the inside of the wrist, below where the bone connects to the thumb, and feel the beat. Count the number of pulsations for 15 seconds and multiply by 4 to get the 1-minute pulse rate. For serious

TABLE 15–8

COMPARISON OF EXERCISE EQUIPMENT—cont'd

Cost	Advertising claims	Comments
$8 to $15	Look inches slimmer instantly; flatten stomach; no diet; no exercise	Merely compresses body parts, girdle effect; may result in some local, temporary tissue dehydration
$200 (no motor) to $2500 and up (with motor)	Benefits thighs, legs, stomach, lower back, waist, abdomen, calves, ankles, buttocks, lungs, heart, circulation; improves muscle tone	Benefits good if motivation maintained; costly equipment especially with motor; benefits obtainable in less costly ways
$50	Slims legs; tones and stretches all body parts; over 40 isotonic and isometric exercises	Claims not substantiated; benefits achieved in less costly and probably more effective ways
$23	Helps melt away middle bulge; improves muscle tone; gradually firms muscles from rib cage and pelvis	Claims not substantiated; increase in frequency and duration helps with limited benefits indicated; action primarily aids shoulders and hip flexors
$10	Tones muscles; strengthens legs and hips; slims thighs	Benefits limited; provides some balance and trunk movement, hence some waistline effect; difficult to maintain motivation

exercisers who wish to remain safely within the high end of the target range, the chest transmitter is the only one that is worthwhile. It costs about $100.

Computers and Exercise

Computers are now available in some exercise fitness facilities to help individuals be more precise in achieving their fitness goals and to make training or exercise procedures more efficient. Data fed into computers enable individuals to create exercise programs tailored to specific goals. For example, computers can provide an exercise prescription based on a person's interests, times available, attendance, and fitness scores. This program may require augmentation by a trainer or exercise specialist.

Computerized devices may be used to test muscle strength and to prescribe activities needed to increase strength. Athletes are using the devices to compare their own performances with those of champions to determine weaknesses. To date, little evidence regarding the effectiveness of computers in exercise programs has been published in the scientific literature.

Athletic Shoes

The average person takes 10,000 steps per day. Each step exerts a force greater than the body weight on certain bones and muscles of the feet. Running more than triples that force, and other activities, including aerobics and sports, also greatly increase that force. Thus, cumulative pounding, complicated by poor fitting shoes, can cause aching feet and other foot problems. Foot problems can alter a person's gait and posture, causing pain to progress to the ankles, knees, hips, and lower back. One way to properly take care of the feet is to have proper sport shoes.

The nature of the physical activity determines the type of sport shoe needed; good shoes may cost $40 to $100. They are designed to provide rigidity, durability, flexibility, proper fit, adequate cushioning, and comfort. When purchasing shoes, check these features.[54]

Upper should be nylon mesh or cotton canvas; permits foot to breathe and is lightweight

Heel counter should be rigid plastic or fiberboard to help control side-to-side motion

Outer sole should be of a durable material such as high carbon rubber or polyurethane; for walking or running, should be curved to permit the foot to roll from heel to toe and allow foot to flex; tread to provide traction and some cushioning

Insole may be removable; provides cushioning and arch support

Midsole should be made of a light, springy material that serves as a shock absorber and motion controller

When buying shoes, the most important consideration is a good fit (see Figure 15-8). These guidelines should help when making purchases:[55]

1. Bear full weight on feet when trying on shoes.
2. Wear the kind of socks you plan to wear when exercising.
3. Compare with next larger and smaller sizes to be sure of proper size.
4. Ensure half an inch of space between longest toe and end of shoe.
5. Buy shoes in morning; feet swell in afternoon.
6. Buy shoes that feel comfortable when trying on; do not expect to "break in" shoes.
7. Return them if the shoes feel uncomfortable when you get home.
8. Check stitching, glue, rigidity of heel counter, and flexibility of sole.

Athlete's foot is a fungus infection that causes itching, redness, and skin peeling between the toes. It can cause considerable discomfort. Snug, poorly ventilated shoes, and damp, sweaty socks provide a breeding ground for the fungus. Daily washing of the feet with soap and water is advisable; but the feet, especially between the toes, should be dried thoroughly. Talcum powder can help to keep the feet dry after washing. An antifungal solution or ointment may also help protect against athlete's foot.

Sports Bras

A need for custom sports bras to support female athletes' breasts has not been clearly established. Studies by Hunger and Torgan[56] indicate there is no need for a special type of bra. They reviewed the 5-year injury records of women who partici-

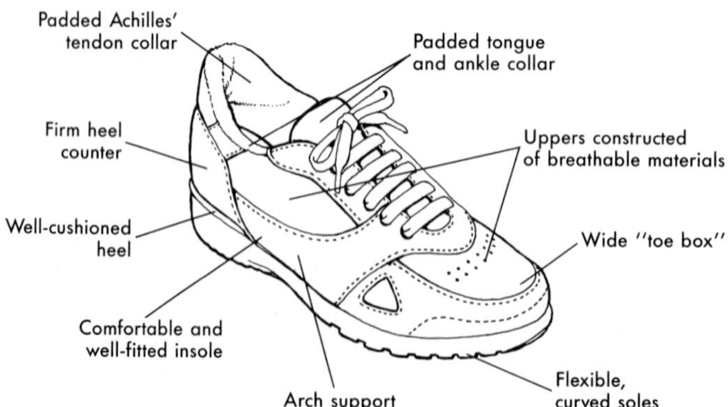

FIGURE 15-8. Basic features of a good walking shoe. Many companies sell shoes specifically designed for walking. However, the same features also can be found in other types of shoes.

(Modified from Mayo Clinic Health Letter 6(6):5, 1988.)

pated in intercollegiate athletics at the University of Washington and found no breast injuries had occurred and no breast pain complaints had been made. Hunger and Torgan also surveyed 85 female athletes who participated in a variety of sports and found no relationship between breast pain and trauma, and the type of bra worn. Only 10 of the women wore sports bras. However, a bra that firmly supports breast tissue with seams that do not irritate nipples is advisable.

Hot Tubs and Whirlpools

Many claims have been made about beneficial effects of hot tubs and whirlpools found in clubs, spas, homes, and hotels. The claims can best be summarized by stating that hot tubs and whirlpools increase blood flow by increasing the circulation of blood to body parts, thereby helping heal some injury problems. They may also help to relax muscles and reduce tension. The 100-degree to 104-degree temperature prevents people with high blood pressure and related heart problems from using them. They present a special safety hazard to small children, since a number of drownings have occurred.

A survey of state epidemiologists from 49 states identified 72 whirlpool-associated outbreaks caused by the *Pseudomonas aeruginosa* bacterium during a 10-year period. These resulted in papular or pustular rashes. Other symptoms included external otitis, mastitis, conjunctivitis, fevers, malaise, and headaches. The rashes lasted from 4 to 14 days. Most of these outbreaks occurred in apartments, motels, and commercial spas. Two additional outbreaks resulted in legionnaires' disease. The risk factors associated with these illnesses are not clear. However, it is believed they are related to the quantity of bacteria in the water, the type of spa construction (concrete, tile, wood, fiberglass, and types of filters), and the type and method of disinfection. It is important that the hot water in these tubs and whirlpools be disinfected adequately, including the periodic addition of an extra disinfectant agent.

Hot tubs, saunas, and whirlpools may be hazardous unless certain educational programs and environmental controls are provided. They are high-risk drowning sites for young children; Shinaberger et al[57] reported the deaths of 74 children under the age of 5 years. The causative factors included lack of supervision, neuromuscular disabilities, and entrapment by suction. To reduce the incidence of drowning, these areas may need fencing, hard covers over them, and supervision. Press[58] noted that 158 adult deaths in hot tubs, saunas, and spas occurred from hypothermia or drowning caused mainly by alcohol ingestion, heart disease, seizure disorders, and cocaine ingestion (alone or with alcohol). These authors recommended that people using these facilities shorten their time of exposure, lower the temperature, and adhere to the warning notices.

Saunas

Saunas are either portable contrivances or built-in rooms that emit steam or dry heat that raises body temperature, thereby causing profuse perspiration. Saunas can be found in homes, health clubs, and other places. Traditionally they have been part of the Finnish culture; however, they have increased in popularity in the United States. Their popularity is undoubtedly related to people's interest in health and to the benefits they expect from applying heat (and also cold) to the body.

Sauna advertisements have claimed that saunas help reduce weight sensibly, clear acne and blemishes, promote fitness, and cure arthritis and bursitis. It is true that some weight is lost in sweating, but it is quickly replaced when water or other fluids are consumed. Soap and water probably do as much for acne and blemished skin as the increased heat. There is no indication of how fitness improvement could take place, and at present there is no known cure for arthritis.

Saunas are not recommended for people with heart or respiratory problems. There are several other dangers, including heat stroke caused by the body's absorption and storage of heat and by dehydration. It is suggested that maximum exposure to a sauna should be 15 minutes.

Portable sauna devices may be purchased for $300 and up. It might cost from $1500 to $3000 or more to build one in a home.

"Sauna shorts" are tight pants that retain body heat and cost from $8 to $20 or more. The advertisements claim that the shorts will keep the heat close to the body, create a saunalike warmth, and, if worn for 15 minutes, provide gentle massage action. There is no evidence that these claims are true.

External Analgesics/Balms

External analgesics are topically applied lotions, creams, and gels, such as Absorbine Jr., Aspercreme, BenGay, Heet, Sloan's Liniment, and Icy

Hot. They are used by people with muscle pain, arthritis pain, and other conditions. In 1990, $64 million was spent in the United States on these products. The principle ingredients can include menthol, camphor, and methyl salicylate.[59] These substances, known as counterirritants, produce irritation of the skin that may counter pain by distracting attention from it. The FDA has approved the substances now marketed as safe and effective when used for the temporary relief of minor aches and pains of the muscles and joints, if used as directed on the label. Aspercreme, Myoflex, and other products have an ingredient similar to aspirin that supposedly relieves pain when applied topically. The FDA considers these safe but not established as effective. Consumers should be aware of these precautions when using these products:

1. Do not apply a bandage or use a heating pad when a counterirritant has been applied; burns are possible.
2. Do not use an external analgesic to mask a serious injury.
3. A hot shower and two aspirin tablets may work as effectively.

Questionable Devices

Many types of exercise devices and equipment are advertised with claims that have no scientific foundation. Bogus claims regarding weight control, body shaping, and effortless muscle-building are the most common.

Continuous passive motion tables. Continuous passive motion (CPM) tables are motorized in segments so that isolated muscle groups can be moved through their range of motion without effort on the part of the user. E.W. Johnson, M.D., chairman of the Department of Physical Medicine at Ohio State University College of Medicine, stated that they have been used in the rehabilitation of injured athletes to restore and maintain joint motions.[60] Dr. J.P. Albright, Department of Orthopedics at University of Iowa, says the CPM units have revolutionized orthopedic surgery.[60] They have been used following joint replacement and ligament reconstruction. The tables are usable by people who are recovering from certain illnesses and operations. They provide passive exercise that could help with joint flexibility for the elderly, sedentary people, and those with neuromuscular disorders. They cost about $30,000 and may be found in health and fitness centers. Claims have been made that individuals can "exercise without exercise" and that the tables can tone muscles, reduce stress, improve posture, cause weight loss, and eliminate excess water retention. These claims have no supporting evidence. Consumers should be aware that CPM units have value in therapy and rehabilitation, but will not benefit healthy, active people.

"Effortless exercisor." The world's first effortless exercisor, a tight-fitting garment perfected by a "leading physician" (unidentified), was advertised to give a new body and new heart in just 2 easy minutes a day. It sold for $11.98 for men and $9.98 for women. The claim was made that a hidden "muscle-girdle" that one never removes would develop the body. Advertisements informed women that the device could squeeze their hips away, firm their bustline, and put a glow in complexions that no cosmetic could ever match. Such possibilities with no exercise are, of course, too good to be true.

Gravity inversion devices. So-called gravity boots are used with support systems that hold people in an upside-down position. The boots alone sell for about $70 a pair and the additional equipment costs from $250 to $1500. The leading manufacturer claimed to have sold 350,000 pairs of shoes in 1982 with gross sales of $12 million. Some of these devices continue to be found in the marketplace and in some health clubs and centers.

The boots were invented in 1965 by Dr. Robert Martin, an orthopedic surgeon, who developed them to relieve stress on spines and joints caused by standing and sitting. He claims that body inversion decompresses spinal disks, stretches back muscles, and improves overall flexibility, posture, and well-being—everything from hemorrhoids to sagging bowels. Members of such sports teams as the Dallas Cowboys, Boston Celtics, and the University of Southern California track team have been identified as users of this equipment. Scientific evidence in support of the claims has not been produced.

Dr. Willibald Nagler, chairman of the Department of Rehabilitation at New York Hospital, has stated, "There is no evidence at all that they help, but there is also no evidence that they do any harm."[61] He warns that people with high blood pressure or circulatory disorders should avoid them. Dr. Ronald Klatz and associates at the Chicago College of Osteopathic Medicine have reported that the use of boots increases the blood pressure at an alarming rate and could be potentially dangerous for anyone with glaucoma, hypertension, weakness in a blood vessel wall, to individuals taking anti-coagulant or aspirin therapy, or to people with spinal instability.[62]

"**Spot-reducers.**" Some products or devices are claimed to reduce or remove fat from specific parts of the body. In controlled studies that compared individuals who performed general exercises with others who performed spot exercises, both groups lost fat where it was most conspicuous, regardless of the type of exercise. Exercise does "burn off" fat and calories, but it does this throughout the body and not just in an exercised area. There is no such thing as spot-reducing.

Belt-vibrating machines. Belt-vibrating machines are still found in some health centers. They do not achieve the purposes claimed. They may feel good, increase circulation, and be somewhat relaxing, but they have no value for weight control or spot-reduction.

Rubber sweatsuits. Sweating is the main cooling mechanism used by the body to cope with heat produced during exercise. As sweat evaporates, it cools the body. Rubber sweatsuits interfere with this procedure: the body sweats more and there is greater water loss, but the suits will cause greater fatigue. When one consumes water, the lost weight will return.

Heat belts. Heat belts are variations of the rubber sweatsuits. Some of them have chemical heat packs to increase the temperature around the waist and the sweat output. Some have elasticized waist cinchers to fit close to the body to keep sweat from evaporating.

Electrical nerve/muscle stimulators ("no-sweat exercise"). Electrical nerve stimulators (ENS)/electrical muscle stimulators (EMS) are sold through the mail or without prescription at $19.95 and up; professional models used in hospitals and other places are priced at $2500. Powered by a 12-volt battery, these machines stimulate nerves that cause muscles to contract. Consumers are purchasing this equipment for home use; others are paying $25 or more for 45-minute sessions at Futureshape, Figuretrim, Ultimate Image, Bodytone parlors, and other such establishments. The advertisements for these products stress an effortless "no-sweat workout," which is a method of moving muscles and obtaining exercise without effort. One advertisement states that an individual can get the equivalent of 10 miles of jogging while lying flat on one's back. Other ads claim that ENS/EMS will strengthen the arm, leg and other muscles, slim and trim the body, shape and contour the body, produce a facelift without surgery (remove wrinkles), control weight, spot-reduce, increase bust size, and remove cellulite. The *Wall Street Journal* reported that these machines are supposed to "battle hanging bellies," "deflate derrieres," and help "pooped-out pecs." The FDA stated that there is no evidence to support these claims and that users are being ripped off.[63]

The low intensity of the electrical stimulation of ENS/EMS equipment makes it suitable for use on athletes to relieve muscle soreness and to speed recovery with almost no risk. The FDA has approved 10 ENS/EMS models for use in physical therapy by trained health practitioners for the following purposes:

1. Relax muscle spasms
2. Prevent clots in leg muscles of bedridden patients after stroke and surgery
3. Increase blood circulation to a part of the body
4. Increase or monitor the range of motion of an arm or leg
5. Retard or prevent muscle atrophy resulting from disease

The hazards of ENS/EMS include electrical shocks and burns. Licensed physical therapists should administer the use of these machines. They should not be used by pregnant women or by persons with heart problems (especially those with pacemakers), cancer, or epilepsy. Electrodes should not be placed where strong current passes through the heart, brain, or spinal cord.

The Relax-A-Cizor was an electrical device that was claimed to provide exercise and reduce the waistline. Like the electrical nerve stimulator (ENS), it provided electrical shocks to the body through contact pads. In the late 1960s the FDA brought suit to stop the sale and distribution of this machine because it was dangerous. More than

CONSUMER TIP

Don't Believe This Ad

"Want a firm body? Re-educate flabby muscles and give you the hard body you've been looking for without the investment in time and sweat."

400,000 units had been sold for $200 to $400 each. At the trial, 40 witnesses testified that they suffered varying degrees of injury while using the machine. The judge concluded that the device could cause miscarriages and aggravate many preexisting medical conditions, including hernias, ulcers, varicose veins, and epilepsy. In 1971 a U.S. district court ruled that Relax-A-Cizors could be used only under a physician's prescription and a permanent injunction was issued prohibiting their sale to the public.

Electrical stimulation is used to strengthen weakened muscles in the rehabilitation of patients after surgery, to prevent muscle atrophy in patients with paralysis from spinal cord injuries or arthritis, to speed recovery of a variety of muscle injuries, and to help with chronic pain. It may be only the first treatment used, and often is followed by traditional exercise. It has been reported that athletic performance can be improved when this procedure is combined with a regular training program. These treatments are usually under medical supervision.

Exercise Facilities

Any program that promises you something for nothing, or a quick cure, is a dead giveaway.

Business Week
September 10, 1984

The thousands of exercise and health facilities in the United States are popular because they provide a variety of benefits, including regimentation, discipline, behavior training, and companionship in a relaxed and pleasant atmosphere. Their effects on fitness and weight control are variable, frequently not predictable, and may be less satisfactory than anticipated or desired. Probably 90% of the activities could be performed at home with very limited expense.

Health Clubs, Spas, Racquet Clubs, and Exercise/Fitness Centers

There are over 40,000 reducing salons, "fat farms," health studios, dance studios, health clubs, figure salons, private gymnasiums, spas, cardiovascular fitness centers, hospital fitness centers, racquet clubs, and fitness and exercise centers. Many are no-frills studios and storefront gyms with such bare essentials as a record player, exercise mats, and an instructor. They attract some 50 million customers from all economic levels, but only 15 million attend regularly.

These facilities gross over $8 billion yearly. Studios, clubs, and figure salons charge annual membership fees from $300 to $3500; most are $500 to $800. "Shoestring" (neighborhood) groups may charge hourly fees from $15 to $25, or weekly fees based on the number of days attended. Racquetball and tennis clubs charge yearly fees of $50 to $850, plus hourly rates of $4 to $25. Health spas or "fat farms" offer many of the services rendered in studios and clubs but provide first-class accommodations and generally pamper their patrons. They give special attention to Spartan diets and extensive exercise programs. Their fees are usually on a weekly residential basis and range from $2000 to $12,000.

The types of facilities can be categorized as follows:

1. Country clubs have a full range of facilities and services. They are plush, expensive establishments that may provide gymnasiums, pools, whirlpools, running tracks, golf, saunas, tennis courts, food, and other services.
2. Full-facility centers, or cardiovascular fitness centers, are on a smaller scale with less space; some are located in shopping centers. They may provide a pool, whirlpool, sauna, steam, dressing rooms, and exercise equipment. Several years ago one such facility placed a full page ad in the *New York Times,* offering a systematic exercise program designed to strengthen the heart. It claimed to be able to safely strengthen the heart and lungs, lower pulse and blood pressure, and reduce serum cholesterol and triglycerides. The advertisement offered supervision by a highly trained staff, whose director had a Ph.D., and all staff members had earned or were working toward a master's degree in exercise physiology.
3. Figure salons and health studios may have pools, saunas, and exercise equipment. They cater to both men and women.
4. Small set-ups, usually in a storefront, have exercise equipment, music, mirrors, and very few employees.
5. "Fat farms," which provide weight reduction and exercise programs.
6. Racquetball and tennis clubs.

Promises are made in these facilities to help patrons improve their physical and mental condition, and reduce tension through weight reduction, active and passive exercise, and special treatments. Numerous health spas are becoming comprehen-

PERSONAL GLIMPSE

Consumer Beware

In San Francisco a nonmember was invited to spend an evening at a health club. He was allowed and encouraged to use every machine available. After 2 hours he was taken to a small room and subjected to a high-pressure sales pitch, while another spa employee locked the door to the building and left. Reluctantly, the young man signed a $349 contract. He later learned that he had signed a bank draft for the full amount of the contract to be withdrawn immediately from his bank account. Fortunately, the consumer action office in the city was able to have the contract rescinded.

sive health centers wherein they provide programs for emotional well-being of their clients. The Association of Quality Clubs stated that 25% of its 1500 members offer seminars in nutrition, stress management, and smoking cessation; 25% have weight-loss programs; and 12% provide programs to boost self-esteem.[64]

Health clubs, spas and fitness centers have been subject to little government regulation. In 1985 Amanda B. Peterson, acting director of the FTC Bureau of Consumer Protection, said she had not seen enough evidence of abuses to warrant establishing a trade regulation rule giving consumers the right to cancel memberships and receive pro rata refunds.[65] However, *Consumer Reports* stated that the FTC had received 3000 complaints, half of them from eight major spas.[66] The Wisconsin attorney general's office received about 5000 complaints. The New York Department of Consumer Affairs accumulated 1000 complaints over a 4-year period. The California attorney general sued the owners of 14 health spas in San Jose for deceiving and overcharging clients. These spas had been taken over by new management, who had tried to elicit a $60 conversion fee from those with long-term contracts by telling them the contracts would be worthless unless the fee was paid. Other charges included:

1. Prospective buyers were discouraged from reading contracts
2. Customers were told that they were signing innocuous documents when they really were signing long-term contracts
3. Bait-and-switch tactics were used, involving advertisement specials that were not available
4. High-quality instruction was advertised despite a lack of trained instructors

People seriously interested in joining a health club should be wary of promotional gimmicks offering free time at the facilities. Deceptive practices are common throughout the health spa industry. Prospective members may be subjected to a sad commentary on the state of their physique and appearance, promised radiant results from the use of equipment, and offered a contract containing doubletalk. Other abuses include: (1) misleading advertising, (2) high-pressure sales, (3) misrepresentation in sales presentations, and (4) collection practices that harass the customer. Consumers should beware of these practices:

A special reduced price: This price is frequently the regular rate.

Bait-and-switch: The customer is frequently made an offer of 10 treatments for $10, only to find that once in the club the 10 sessions are of no value. If the customer demands the special offer, he or she may be told that two treatments must be taken on each visit, or that only limited facilities for limited hours are available under the offer. The salesperson will try to sign the customer up for a more expensive, long-term program.

Free visits: These are sometimes offered to all who sign up at registration tables. "Winners" often find that their "free visit" amounts to a high-pressure sales pitch to accept the prize of a supposed discount on an inflated membership fee.

Before-and-after photographs: These are frequently staged to produce the desired effect. In some cases the person in the picture may never have visited the club, or two different people are shown in the comparison photographs.

Weight loss without exercise: There is no evidence that devices that vibrate or shake the body actually aid in weight reduction or improve muscle tone.

Personal programs: These may prove to be standard calisthenics or other exercises that vary little from one person to another.

Last-day-only rates: The last-day-only offer of a special price may be fraudulent because no price increase was being considered.

Reservation forms: Application forms may be used to deceive a prospective customer into believing that a place is being reserved; the customer may be signing a contract for long-term membership.

Guarantees: Guarantees of weight loss are often meaningless. The spa may be the sole judge of whether the patron followed the program to the letter and can renege on the agreement by judging that the client did not follow the "exact" program.

Reassignment contract: Difficulty may occur when a contract is sold to a third party (such as a loan company) who later demands payment of an unfulfilled contract.

Cancellation: Requests for cancellation of membership contracts often are denied. Apparently a high percentage of people who sign a contract discontinue using the spa in a short time, forfeiting their initial payment. O'Hanlon stated that 75% of those who pay the membership fee never use the facilities after the first 3 weeks.

Spa failures or not opening: After contracts are signed and money is paid, consumers may lose their investment because the spa does not operate.

These suggestions will help to decide whether to sign a contract:

1. Ask members and former members their opinions of the spa and its programs. If necessary, names can be obtained from the organization. If the club refuses to comply, one should beware.
2. Consider checking with a physician about specific exercise and diet needs.
3. Think it over for a few days; a reputable health spa will let one consider joining without applying pressure.
4. Read the contract carefully or get a knowledgeable person to read it, be sure the provisions and agreements are understood.
5. Ask for a short-term program to try out the spa.
6. Understand what happens if a decision is made to cancel the membership. There are many different and confusing refund policies. In an ideal cancellation arrangement, the customer gets a refund based on the proportion of time used during the contract. Under present collection practices used by some spas, however, an individual could be pressured and even sued for the full contract price—even if the spa's facilities were never used.

Individuals who believe that they have been dealt with unjustly or have been improperly pressured into joining by a health club, can seek assistance from a small claims court, local or state consumer affairs office, state attorney general, or county district attorney.

The quality of instructors or supervisory personnel at these various facilities needs careful review by consumers. Employees without adequate credentials may be calling themselves exercise leaders or specialists, or even exercise physiologists. Some college and university-based programs offer training in recreation management that qualifies individuals for employment at a fitness facility. Some instructors are trained in physical education, exercise physiology, or physical therapy, or are former athletes or nurses. Exercise instructors should have had some experience in teaching exercises, plus a minimum of coursework that includes kinesiology (muscle functions), physiology of exercise, psychology, safety, and first aid. Where weight control advice is being provided, personnel should have training in nutrition from a reputable institution. Consumers need to inquire into the training and experience of the instructors (see Table 15-9).

Dietrich and Waggoner[67] investigated 150 clubs in 10 cities in the United States and concluded that 99% of these clubs failed to offer adequate exercise instruction.

Many health clubs provide personal trainers (PTs) for individuals who lack information or are too busy to plan their own fitness regimens. These trainers help consumers complete a total evaluation of their fitness. Planning usually includes a medical history and tests for body fat, flexibility, blood pressure, and heart rate. When an exercise program is prescribed, the consumer is helped on a one-to-one basis, or in a small group, to help with its completion. Some clubs provide this service at no cost, and its extent may be limited. Where extensive personal attention is desired, the cost of the service may be $40 to $100 per hour. Should a person desire a personal trainer, these suggestions should be followed:

1. Ask for credentials
2. Ask for references, talk with references, and watch trainer helping a client
3. Be sure to feel comfortable with the trainer
4. Expect the first consultation to be free; discuss fitness status assessment, type, and implementation of program

TABLE 15–9

EXERCISE INSTRUCTOR CERTIFICATION PROGRAMS

Organization	Requirements (All require CPR certification)
American College of Sports Medicine 401 W. Michigan Indianapolis, IN 46202	*Preventive and rehabilitation fitness* Bachelor's degree or equivalent in allied health field; written and practical exam that includes 10-minute aerobics sequence and correcting errors on exercise video
American Council on Exercise (ACE) P.O. Box 910449 San Diego, CA 92191	*Aerobics certification* Written exam on exercise physiology, anatomy, exercise programming, routine, administrative skills, nutrition and weight control *Personal trainer certification* Health screening, fitness testing, design and implementation of fitness programs
Aerobics and Fitness Association of America 15250 Ventura Boulevard Sherman Oaks, CA 91403	*Personal training* *Aerobics Instructors* *Step Reebok certification* Written exam similar to ACE's: must also do practical exam, including demonstration of a short aerobics session
Institute for Aerobics Research 12330 Preston Road Dallas, TX 75230	*Physical fitness specialist* *Advanced physical fitness specialist* Written and practical exam on exercise physiology, anatomy, fitness assessment, and individual program planning *Group exercise leaders* Written and practical exam on leadership and group programming skills

5. Ask about the cost and number of sessions needed to reach the fitness goal
6. Be wary of any trainer who makes unrealistic promises regarding achievement of the fitness goal

The following questions can help in selecting a club, spa, or exercise center:

1. Does the program serve one's purposes and is it designed to meet individual needs?
2. What is the nature of the facility and equipment? (types, condition, maintenance, sufficient at peak times, time limits on use)
3. Do the locker rooms, showers, bathrooms, and whirlpools show signs of neglect or poor sanitation?
4. What are the costs for services? (initiation fee, rates, additional charges)
5. What is the nature of the staff? (are their qualifications adequate, are they pleasant, attentive, certified by reputable organizations)
6. Is it in a convenient location?
7. Do they have a system to assess fitness, help evaluate progress toward a goal, and is this clearly identified?
8. How does the facility function at peak hours?
9. Will several members' names and telephone numbers be provided?
10. Do you understand the provisions of the contract? Are there hidden clauses? Have you read it carefully? Will you be permitted to take it home to read? Can you get a refund if you cancel? Can you bring friends?
11. Are high-pressure tactics used to get you to join? Are staff members courteous and friendly?
12. Does the local YMCA/YWCA provide facilities and services to meet one's needs?
13. Is the club well-established? (Check with the

CONSUMER TIP

Exercise Myths[68]

- *The best reason to exercise is to burn calories.* In addition to helping with weight control, physical activity can increase bone mass, reduce anxiety and stress, improve blood-cholesterol levels, and provide many other benefits.
- *"No pain, no gain."* Health benefits are achievable by exercising as little as 15 minutes, three times weekly; almost any activity has benefits.
- *Muscle will turn into fat if you stop exercising.* Muscles will grow weaker and become smaller through disuse; activity is necessary to maintain muscle tone.
- *Vitamin supplements provide extra energy.* Vitamins do not provide energy; they are needed for body processes and are readily obtainable from food.
- *Drinking liquids during exercise causes cramps.* Cool drinks of water are recommended during and after exercise to replace lost fluids.
- *The stimulating effects of caffeine improve athletic performance.* Caffeine may provide limited benefit for marathon runners and swimmers; it helps to stimulate the release of fats into the blood for muscles to use as energy and increases the length of time an athlete can endure an activity.
- *Excess weight can be sweated off.* Perspiration loss is fluid loss; it is quickly regained by ingesting fluids.
- *Extra protein helps build stronger muscles.* Excess protein is stored as fat; muscle-building comes through "resistance" exercising such as lifting weights.
- *Exercising can backfire for someone trying to lose weight because it increases appetite and thereby leads to overeating.* Moderate exercise does not markedly increase appetite; weight control involves intake of foods as well as output of energy.
- *Sugary foods eaten before a workout supply quick energy.* Overloading of carbohydrates may have some benefit for endurance runners and swimmers; sugary foods may take several hours to get into the blood stream.
- *Spot-reducing causes more fat to be lost from that area than from the rest of the body.* Fat lost generally comes from deposits throughout the body.
- *"Sport drinks" are the best kind of fluids for exercisers.* The best beverage is plain water. If electrolytes are lost, they can be replaced by ingesting food.
- *Women who participate in strength-training exercises develop oversized muscles.* Muscle strength is increased, but not necessarily size; the male hormone is the reason that men are more prone to muscle enlargement.

local consumer protection agency about complaints.)

14. Can one sample the services before purchasing a membership?

Massage

Massage has had a resurgence of popularity in the United States. Services are available at airports, offices, shopping centers, and in homes. The most familiar form is the Swedish massage that uses oils to reduce friction and involves the use of hands in long, full strokes, along with kneading and pounding motion on muscles. Japanese shiatsu (finger pressure), Chinese acupressure (finger pressure), and reflexology (pressure on hand or foot) are among the numerous other forms of massage. These latter types are promoted with dubious therapeutic claims (see Chapter 9).

Swedish massage frequently does make people feel better. It produces a relaxation of the muscles, temporarily increases the flow of blood, and provides pleasurable activation of the skin touch receptors. It may be helpful in treating some types of skeletal-muscle injuries. Athletes find it useful to help relieve muscle pain and relax. The therapist may also bring about a feeling of confidence, self-assurance, and serenity through verbal and sensory communication. Thus massage may be helpful in temporarily eliminating tension and promoting relaxation.

Massage therapists may provide brief sessions from 10 to 15 minutes with clothes on for $20 to

$25, or a complete massage without clothes on for 1 hour for $40 to $80.

To locate a massage therapist, it may be helpful to talk with people who have had services or to contact the American Massage Therapy Association, P.O. Box 1270, Kingsport, Tennessee 37662 (Telephone: 312-761-AMTA) for the name of an area AMTA representative. Only 15 states license therapists, and their requirements differ widely. A large teaching hospital or your physician may be able to make a recommendation.

Various vibrating devices are available for producing a massage-like effect. There is no evidence that such an effect will occur, although the machines may help in a limited way to relax muscles.

Shower massagers are claimed to melt tension away, put tingle back in one's life, or provide sexual arousal. Prices range from $15 to $35 for the shower-head models and from $25 to $50 for the hose-type units. The pulsating sprays of hot and cold water may be refreshing, but that is the extent of their benefit.

Children's Exercise Centers

Some community centers, health clubs, and local Y's are operating exercise centers for children.[69] It is claimed these programs develop motor skills, balance, and flexibility using a variety of giant balls, hoops, tunnels, mats, and trampolines. The cost ranges from $3 to $15 per hour. There is no evidence that structured exercise benefits infants and preschoolers any more than regular play.

The business community has catered to children and adolescents by providing equipment, sports and fitness clubs, and activity programs. Here are a few illustrations: a 12-station strength-training machine for aspiring high school and college athletes; weights and plastic cones filled with sand for young children to weightlift; a physical education program that focuses on balance, coordination, and agility that uses wooden balance beams, foam balls, climbing apparatus, crawl tunnels, and other items; a club of sports and fitness for kids that offers classes in gymnastics, karate, dance, sport skills, and arts and crafts; cooking and nutrition plus periodic fitness assessment that measures flexibility, muscular endurance, and cardiovascular a condition. Older children can work-out with strength-training machines.

Parents and others considering exercise products and programs should raise certain questions. Are these programs, activities, and products primarily for profit-making purposes? Are they meant to replace free or partially free programs provided by schools, community centers, religious institutions, recreation and parks programs, and others? Are they meant to augment such programs? Are they necessary? What are the benefits and hazards? Who determines the risks involved in the use of the equipment and the participation in the programs? Are they too advanced for some children? Are children being pushed into regimented and possibly harmful programs during their growth and development stages in life?

The American Academy of Pediatrics completed a 2-year study of such programs and concluded that they are not necessary for normal childhood development.[69]

Corporations and Fitness

At least two thirds of American corporations with 50 or more employees offer some kind of health and fitness program.[70] Some corporations have elaborate facilities that include swimming pools, tracks, saunas, and testing laboratories with exercise physiologists in charge, whereas others make a cafeteria available for aerobic exercises. Some programs are run through local Y's or other community organizations, while others have cooperative arrangements with shared facilities and consultants.

Although most programs focus on employee fitness, many have adopted a wellness program that includes weight loss and stress-management instruction. In addition there may be medical screenings, exercise testing, back care, and health education about nutrition, drug abuse, alcoholism, and smoking cessation.

The effectiveness of these programs has been demonstrated by decreased absenteeism and savings by corporations from $1.50 to $2.00 per $1.00 invested. A 10-year-old program conducted by Kimberly-Clark included medical screening, exercise testing, health education, and physical fitness.[71] Many participants increased their fitness level and reduced their weight, body fat content, serum triglyceride level, and systolic and diastolic blood pressure. These results were also reported: 70% fewer accidents, 43% less absenteeism, 76% improvement in job performance, and 76% of those in the program overcame their dependency on drugs and alcohol.

The National Aeronautics and Space Administration (NASA), with the U.S. Public Health Service, conducted a study of 259 employees, ages 35 to 55, who participated in a 1-year, three-times-per-week exercise program. Half of the participants reported better job performance and better attitude toward work, almost all said they felt better, 89% reported improved stamina, 40% said they slept better, 60% lost weight, and absenteeism was reduced by approximately 4 days per year per employee.

Corporations sponsor wellness programs to recruit and retain valued employees, to raise morale and productivity, and to reduce absenteeism. They also hope to reduce medical costs. The programs usually cost the companies from $50 to $500 per employee. Many companies also pay more than $3000 yearly for employee health insurance and medical costs. Although there is some evidence that employees who exercise have lower medical costs than those who do not, there is no proven cause-and-effect relationship. Two other problems face companies with a fitness program: (1) how to reach the people most in need (possibly only 40% or less use them and possibly one-third of these use the facilities and equipment on a regular basis), and (2) measuring the effectiveness of a program is very expensive and may cost more than the program itself.[72]

In-home Fitness

There are several less-costly alternatives to joining a health club or spa. Local YMCAs and YWCAs have programs with membership fees around $300 yearly. In addition, local schools and community recreation organizations may offer sports, exercise, and physical education programs.

Another alternative is a home mini-gym. Expensive equipment is not necessary to achieve fitness. With some ingenuity, simple equipment can be assembled and numerous exercise activities can be performed at little cost or without equipment. The equipment chosen can be selected according to one's goals and budget:

Minimum level. For less than $50 to $75, include a jump rope for $3 to $10; a sit-up bar to fit under any door, $15; a padded mat on which to perform calisthenics, $35; and a 16-pound adjustable-free dumbell set, $15 to $25.

Intermediate level. For $250 more, supplement the minimum level equipment with a stationary bicycle, $100 and up; 100 pounds of weights with long and short bars, $30; a weight bench with a leg lift, $60 to $75; and videotapes of exercise programs, $50.

High level. For $500 to $1000 or more, include a rowing machine, $200 and up; and a total gymnasium or multipurpose machine, $500 to more than $2000.

Listening to music, watching television, or reading during activities can help prevent boredom. Additional motivation may be derived from the daily calisthenics and aerobics programs to be found on radio, television, or videos.

Exercise While Traveling

Numerous exercise opportunities are available to people when traveling, whether housed in a hotel, or confined to a room, plane, bus, train, or car. It may be advisable to plan ahead to take advantage of these exercise opportunities. The following suggestions are not all-inclusive but identify some of the activities that will be helpful to the traveler.

Hotel. Many of the large chains have health clubs with equipment, swimming pools, and saunas. Check the Yellow Pages for a local health club, aerobic dance club, or YMCA/YWCA. Climbing stairs instead of using the elevators, or jogging outside, can be achieved if facilities or equipment in the hotel are not available. Also, there are public and private facilities for tennis, golf, racquetball, and other sports.

Gym in a suitcase. A set of dumbbells, which can be inflated with water, and a jump rope can be carried easily in a suitcase. If an audiotape containing music is included, a self-devised program can easily be arranged. Check the television for early morning exercise programs.

In a plane, train, bus, auto. Isometric exercises while sitting or walking will provide limited muscle activity. Periodic standing, stretching walking exercises can also be managed. When traveling by car, occasional stops to walk or to stretch the various muscles groups can be beneficial. If time permits, jog for 10 to 15 minutes or use a local fitness facility.

Exercise and Weight Control

The American Dietetic Association makes these recommendations to the general public about nutrition and physical fitness:[73]

1. A nutritionally adequate diet and exercise are

major contributing factors to physical fitness and health.
2. Weight maintenance and weight loss can be achieved by a combination of dietary modification, change in eating behavior, and regular aerobic exercise.
3. Skinfold measurements should be used to determine the level of body fitness (amount of fat on body).
4. The generally healthy individual who regularly consumes a diet that supplies the Recommended Dietary Allowances receives all the necessary nutrients for a physical conditioning program.
5. The intensity, duration, and frequency of exercise should be determined according to age, physical condition, and health status of the individual.
6. Habits for a nutritionally balanced diet and physical fitness should be established during childhood and maintained throughout life.
7. An individual who wishes to control weight (see also Chapter 14) through exercise must realize that nothing you can do to your body from the outside—no heating or steaming or pummelling or pounding, and no being jerked or jiggled by some machine—can make you lose weight.[74]

Cooper[3] has said: "Exercise should only be an aid to weight reduction, not the exclusive method . . . it is important to make your diet the crown jewel of your weight reduction program . . . exercise is not an effective way to lose weight rapidly."

Table 15-10 lists a variety of physical activities and the calories burned per minute. To lose 1 pound of weight it is necessary to burn 3500 calories through exercise or physical activity. An individual who walks for 30 minutes daily (7.1 calories per minute) will burn 213 calories. In 16.4 days 1 pound of weight will be lost, provided that the intake of food (calories) remains stable over this period. At the rate of 2 pounds lost per month, a person will lose 24 pounds per year if the intake

TABLE 15–10

CALORIES BURNED IN VARIOUS PHYSICAL ACTIVITIES*†

Activity	Calories per minute	Activity	Calories per minute
Work tasks		**Recreation**	
Carpentry	3.8	Archery	5.2
Chopping wood	7.5	Badminton (recreation-competition)	5.2-10.0
Cleaning windows	3.7		
Clerical work	1.2-1.6	Baseball (except pitcher)	4.7
Dressing	3.4	Basketball half-full court (more for fastbreak)	6.0-9.0
Driving car	2.8		
Driving motorcycle	3.4	Bowling (while active)	7.0
Farming		Calisthenics	5.0
Chores	3.8	Canoeing (2.5-4.0 mph)	3.0-7.0
Haying, plowing with horse	6.7	Cycling (5-15 mph; 10-speed bicycle)	5.0-12.0
Planting, hoeing, raking	4.7		
Gardening		Dancing	
Digging	8.6	Modern: moderate-vigorous	4.2-5.7
Weeding	5.6	Ballroom: waltz-rumba	5.7-7.0
Hiking		Square	7.7
Road-field (3.5 mph)	5.6-7.0	Football (while active)	13.3
Snow: hard-soft (3.5-2.5 mph)	10.0-20.0	Golf (foursome-twosome)	3.7-5.0
Downhill: 5-10% grade (2.5 mph)	3.5-3.6	Handball and squash	10.0
Downhill: 15-20% grade (2.5 mph)	3.7-4.3	Horseshoes	3.8
Uphill: 5-15% grade (3.5 mph)	8.0-15.0	Judo and karate	13.0
40-lb pack: (3.0 mph)	5.0	Mountain climbing	10.0
40-lb pack: 36% grade (1.5 mph)	16.0	Pool or billiards	1.8

Continued.

TABLE 15–10

CALORIES BURNED IN VARIOUS PHYSICAL ACTIVITIES*†—cont'd

Activity	Calories per minute	Activity	Calories per minute
Work tasks		**Recreation**	
House painting	3.5	Rowing (pleasure-vigorous)	5.0-15.0
Ironing clothes	4.2	Running	
Making beds	3.4	12-min mile (5 mph)	10.0
Metal working	3.5	8-min mile (7.5 mph)	15.0
Mixing cement	4.7	6-min mile (10 mph)	20.0
Mopping floors	4.9	5-min mile (12 mph)	25.0
Pick-and-shovel work	6.7	Skating (recreation-vigorous)	5.0-15.0
Plastering walls	4.1	Skiing	
Pulaski ax (depends on rate of work and other factors)	7.8	Moderate to steep	8.0-12.0
		Downhill racing	16.5
Repaving roads	5.0	Cross-country (3-8 mph)	9.0-17.0
Sawing		Snowshoeing (2.5 mph)	9.0
Chain saw	6.2	Soccer	9.0
Crosscut saw	7.5-10.5	Swimming	
Shining shoes	3.2	Pleasure	6.0
Shoveling (depends on weight of load, rate of work, height of lift)	5.4-10.5	Crawl (25-50 yd/min)	6.0-12.5
		Butterfly (50 yd/min)	14.0
Forest Service data (average)	8.0	Backstroke (25-50 yd/min)	6.0-12.5
Showering	3.4	Breaststroke (25-50 yd/min)	6.0-12.5
Stacking lumnber	5.8	Sidestroke (40 yd/min)	11.0
Standing, light activity	2.6	Skipping rope	10.0-15.0
Stone masonry	6.3	Table tennis	4.9-7.0
Sweeping floors	3.9	Tennis (recreation-competition)	7.0-11.0
Tree felling (ax)	8.4-12.7		
Truck and auto repair	4.2	Volleyball (recreation-competition)	3.5-8.0
Walking	7.1		
Downstairs	5.1	Water skiing	8.0
Indoors	3.1	Wrestling	14.4
Upstairs	10.0-18.0		
Washing clothes	3.1		
Washing and dressing	2.6		
Washing and shaving	2.6		

From Sharkey BJ: Fitness and work capacity, U.S. Department of Agriculture, Forest Service, Washington, DC, 1977, Superintendent of Documents.

*Calories burned depends on efficiency and body size. Add 10% for each 15 pounds above 150; subtract 10% for each 15 pounds under 150.

†Also see Table 15-6.

of food is not increased during the year.

Another way to help the consumer control weight is to predict the amount of weight loss that will take place in a specific number of days if there is a reduction in the number of daily calories. For example, deleting 100 calories of food daily from the regular amount ingested will enable a person to lose 1 pound after 35 days (see Table 14-3). Increasing one's activity to include the burning of an additional 100 calories daily will also achieve the same results. The weight-loss process can be speeded up with the reduction of the daily intake of food or the daily calories burned is increased.

IT'S YOUR DECISION

You have never been involved in any type of exercise, but you now believe you can improve your health through such participation. Which of the following actions would you take?

	Reason
1. Enroll in a local exercise center or club	______
2. Purchase an exercycle or rowing machine	______
3. Decide what you want to achieve from your exercise	______
4. Buy a Kenneth Cooper book on aerobics	______
5. Check exercise programs at the local "Y"	______
6. Start jogging/walking 2 to 3 miles daily	______
7. Visit family physician for a physical exam.	______

You have been involved in an exercise program and now want to assess whether it is the best program for you. How would you do this? Is there anyone you would seek out for help? You wish to lose 10 to 20 pounds, and believe this goal can be achieved through exercise. What information must be obtained to determine whether this weight loss is possible? What type of program should you follow? Where can you find help in making this decision?

NUTRITION FOR ATHLETES

The American Dietetic Association[73] stated that a proper well-balanced diet is an essential component of any fitness or sports program. A good mix would contain 50% to 60% carbohydrates, 20% to 30% fat, and 15% to 20% protein.

Individuals engaged in vigorous activity have energy needs from 3000 to 6000 calories per day or more. Complex carbohydrates should comprise 50% to 55% or more of their diet. Carbohydrate-loading is beneficial only to athletes participating in lengthy endurance or multiple-event competitions. However, a diet too low in carbohydrates prior to strenuous exercise can cause fatigue. Endurance athletes may also need to increase their protein intake above the RDA of 0.8 per kg (54 g for a 150-pound man). The *Tufts University Diet and Nutrition Letter* stated that protein intake should be 95 g for a 150-pound man, but notes that "most athletes eat more food than nonathletes, so their higher protein needs are met automatically."[75]

Excessive protein consumption beyond those previously identified has not been demonstrated to enhance athletic performance. Additional vitamins and minerals may be needed, but will be supplied in a balanced diet containing extra calories. Vitamin, mineral, and protein supplementation are unwarranted.

So-called ergogenic aids (for example, wheat germ oil, bee pollen, kelp) provide no benefit and may be harmful (see Chapter 13). More expensive forms of protein, sugars, or vitamins do not provide physiologic benefit.

The pregame meal should be completed 3½ to 4 hours prior to the competition and should be high in complex carbohydrates. Fats and proteins, which require more time for digestion, should be avoided to prevent stomach upsets or indigestion that will affect performance.

Sports Drinks

Americans spend $800 to $900 million yearly on such sports drinks as Gatorade, Exceed, and Quickick, with the belief that the calories and electrolytes they contain will help with fatigue and dehydration. Proper hydration is essential for athletic performance. Extreme exercise levels, prolonged strenuous activity, and certain environmental conditions, may warrant a low-dose electrolyte-replacement beverage during endurance competition. However, cool water can be used to meet the needs of most persons exercising in moderate climates. *Consumer Reports* has noted:[76]

1. For most people, sports drinks are no better than water.
2. Sugars in the drinks are supposed to maintain high levels of blood-sugar to prevent fatigue, however, it takes 1½ hours of strenuous exercise to deplete energy resources.
3. Deliberate replacement of lost electrolytes (primarily sodium) is not necessary for moderate exercise if a person has a normal diet. In very

hot weather, a pinch of salt added to meals for a few days will adequately provide for body needs.

4. These drinks may taste good and cause more to be ingested than needed.
5. People running marathons or involved in intense exercise for hours may possibly benefit from a sports drink to bolster sugar levels and replace electrolytes.

SUMMARY

About half of the adults in the United States participate in daily exercise. However, 80% to 90% do not get enough exercise. Approximately 30 million people (more men than women) jog regularly. Half the individuals who start to exercise soon stop. Consumers should understand the concepts of physical activity, exercise, and fitness, and their relation to health.

Exercises can be classified as isometric, isotonic, isokinetic, aerobic, and anaerobic. The basic goals of exercise are to provide muscle endurance/stamina, muscle strength, flexibility, and cardiorespiratory efficiency. Exercise can produce physical, biologic, psychologic, and social benefits as well as hazards. The hazards are greater for sedentary individuals and those who thrust themselves into activities that are either too strenuous or too prolonged. The type and amount of exercise should be adapted to the age and fitness level of the individual. A minimum program should be 20 to 30 minutes, 3 days a week, at 60% to 85% of one's maximum heart rate. Pregnant women need to know their limitations when it comes to exercise. Exercise programs can enable elderly individuals to complete daily activities with less fatigue, help preserve body functions, reduce high blood pressure, increase bone density, and possibly prolong life expectancy.

Individuals who engage in weight training should clearly understand its benefits, limitations, and hazards. The use of anabolic steroids by athletes is a dangerous practice.

Exercise equipment should be selected by considering potential benefits, effects on body areas, costs, and expert advice. Consumers should be especially critical of advertising claims of benefits, safety, and effectiveness. Many devices have little or no value.

The thousands of health clubs and fitness centers in the United States provide physical benefits, but often are joined for social and psychologic reasons. Prospective members should carefully scrutinize advertisements and contracts from these centers. Children's centers have been established, although their value is questioned. Consumers should know that many of the activities provided in the health clubs can be done at home with less equipment and very limited expense. It also is possible to maintain an exercise regimen while traveling.

Weight loss can be achieved only through a combination of dietary changes, eating behavior changes, and regular aerobic exercise.

ANALYSIS OF EXERCISE EQUIPMENT

There are many advertisements on TV and in magazines and newspapers for exercise equipment. How can consumers judge the value of such devices? The exercise that follows provides one method of analyzing the ads and arriving at intelligent decisions. On a scale of 1 to 5, with 5 being the highest/best number, how would you rate the benefits, body parts claimed to be affected, and the cost value of each of the items illustrated in the photos that follow? Place your number in the appropriate box to the right and total your points for each item.

DISCUSSION QUESTIONS

1. What do each of these terms mean: health, activity, exercise, and physical fitness?
2. What are the types of exercise? Discuss each type.
3. What are the purposes of exercise? Define each purpose.
4. Identify 10 benefits from exercise as outlined by the authorities?
5. What factors are necessary to obtain the maximum benefit from exercise? Outline a program of exercise based on these factors.
6. What are some of the hazards of exercise?
7. What guidelines should be followed by those who desire to participate in an exercise program?
8. Identify five exercise equipment items available in the marketplace. List their benefits or lack of benefits, and their contributions to the purposes of exercise. List the body parts affected.
9. What are the benefits and problems with the

Analysis of Exercise Equipment

	Benefits*				Body parts affected						
Equipment	F	S	E	CRE	Arms	Legs	Shoulder	Abdomen	Back	Cost	Total points
Aqua Jogger											
Curve Shaper											
Lifeline Gym											
No-sweat waist trimmer											
The FLO											
Inversion machine											
Plyo Balls											
PreCor Climber											

*F = flexibility, S = strength, E = endurance, CRE = cardiorespiratory efficiency

use of hot tubs, saunas, massage, and shower massage?

10. Discuss health clubs, spas, and exercise centers in terms of costs, types of facilities available, quality of instructors, and techniques used to persuade consumers to sign contracts.
11. What common practices, identified by the FTC, should consumers be aware of when planning to join a health club or exercise center?
12. Should parents take their children to exercise centers? Why?
13. How are nutrition and exercise related?
14. Should the elderly participate in exercise programs? Why?
15. What is the nature of anabolic steroids? Should they be used by athletes? Are they effective in improving athletic performance?
16. Should consumers establish an in-home exercise center? Why? What might it include?
17. What can a person who travels a great deal do about exercising?

REFERENCES

1. Shape of the nation, Time, p 60, Oct 7, 1985.
2. Holland RG: Moderation in physical fitness, Priorities, pp 32-34, Fall 1990.
3. Cooper K: The aerobics program of total well-being, New York, 1982, M Evans & Co Inc.
4. Blair SN et al: Physical fitness and all-cause mortality, JAMA 262:2395-2401, 1989.
5. Is Exercise a cure for high blood pressure? University of California, Berkeley Wellness Letter 6(11):1-2, 1990.
6. Exercise: Every little bit helps, Consumer Reports on Health 3:57, 60-61, 1991.
7. Haskell W: Training effects of low vs short bouts of exercise in healthy subjects, Am J Cardiol 65:1010-1013, 1990.
8. Kannel WB et al: Epidemiological assessment of the role of physical activity and fitness in development of cardiovascular diseases. Am Heart J 109:876-885, 1985.
9. Exercise and heart disease: the smoking gun, University of California, Berkeley Wellness Letter 4:1, Oct 1987.
10. Elmer-DeWitt P: Extra years for extra effort, Time, 127:66, March 17, 1986.
11. Springer I: A new miracle cure: it's called exercise—you ought to try it, AARP Bulletin, 31:2, 10, Dec 1990.
12. Tucker LA et al: Walking and serum cholesterol in adults, Am J Public Health 80:1111-1113, 1990.
13. Mellon MB: Exercise therapy for anxiety and depression, Postgrad Med 77:59, 1985.
14. Blair SN et al: Relationships between exercise and physical activity and other health behaviors, Public Health Rep 100:172-179, March/April 1985.
15. Sudden death during exercise, Harvard Health Letter, 1(5):1-4, 1991.
16. Hastings AW et al: The fitness boom, Medical World News, pp 45-56, July 23, 1984.

16a. Koplan JP et al: The risk of exercise: a public health view of injuries and hazards, Public Health Rep 100:189-195, Mar/Apr 1985.

17. When exercise hurts, Consumer Reports Health Letter 1:25, 27, 1989.
18. Levine A and Wells S: New rules of exercise, US News and World Report, pp 52-56, Aug 11, 1986.
19. Teasdale R and Hennessey D: Fitness boom or bust, San Francisco, St. Frances Memorial Hospital, Winter 1990.
20. Garrick JG et al: The epidemiology of aerobic dance injuries, Am J Sports Med 14:67-72, 1986.
21. Rosenthal E: Inner-ear damage linked to jarring high-impact aerobics, The New York Times, Dec 6, 1990.

22. Jacobs SJ and Benson BL: Injuries to runners—a study of entrants to a 10,000 meter race, Am J Sports Med 14:151-155, Mar/Apr 1986.
23. Ferrigno R: If 6.2 miles is good, 26 miles is better, San Francisco Examiner, Aug 19, 1984.
24. Holland RG: The aches, pains, joys and jubilation of running, Priorities, pp 8-10, Summer 1991.
25. Fisher L: Step right, American Health 10:66-70, Sept 1991.
26. Walker JG, Walker G: Writing an exercise prescription, J Fam Pract 24:25-34, 1987.
27. American Heart Association: Moderate exercise keeps you fit, Dallas, Tex, Feb 1986, The Association.
28. Reinhold R: An interview with Kenneth Cooper, stress test, The New York Times Good Health Magazine, p 14, Mar 29, 1987.
29. Graham J: A guide to stress tests, the New York Times Good Health Magazine, pp 40, 42-44, Mar 29, 1987.
30. Kusinitz I et al: Physical fitness for practically everybody, Mt. Vernon, NY, 1983, Consumer Reports Books.
31. Simon H: Exercise and well-being, Harvard Medical School Health Letter, pp 3-5, Apr 1985.
32. Mesey T: Health benefits of exercise, Postgrad Med 90:103-110, July 1991.
33. Kaufman E: The new case for woman power, The New York Times, Apr 28, 1991.
34. Larsen EB et al: Ann Intern Med 105:783, 1986.
35. Lampman RM: Evaluating and prescribing exercise for elderly patients, Geriatrics 42:63, 1987.
36. Exercise and aging, Mayo Clinic Health Letter Supplement, June 1991.
37. Miller AP: Realistic exercise goals for the elderly: is feeling good enough? Geriatrics 42:25-29, 1987.
38. Weighting the effects of weight training, Changing Times, 40:22-23, Jan 1986.
39. Talon J: Weighing the merits of weightlifting programs, Newsday, part 2, p 7, Apr 1, 1985.
40. Mishra R: On the teen scene: steroids and sports, FDA Consumer 25(7):25-27, 1991.
41. American Medical Association Council on Scientific Affairs: Medical and nonmedical uses of anabolic-androgenic steroids, JAMA 204:2923-2927, 1990.
42. Leary WE: Uses of steroids risk addiction, two researchers at Yale report, New York Times, Dec 8, 1989.
43. Study shows addiction with anabolic steroids, FDA Consumer 25(10):6-7, 1991.
44. Teenagers blasé about steroid use, FDA Consumer 24(10):2, 1990.
45. Holland RG: Exercise machines, Priorities, pp 6-8, Winter 1990.
46. Burroughs B: Allure of home exercise devices sparks big sales—and many injuries, The Wall Street Journal, p 33, Apr 18, 1985.
47. Roan S: Are exercise machine monitors accurate? San Francisco Chronicle, July 8, 1991.
48. Exercise bikes, Consumer Reports 51:511-512, 1986.
49. Exercise bicycles, Consumer Reports 55:746-750, 1990.
50. Mountain bicycles, Consumer Reports 56:650-655, 1991.
51. Astor-Billian M: A bicycle helmet for every head, Priorities, pp 3-5, Summer, 1991.
52. Washington Area Bicyclist Association: A consumer's guide to bicycle helmets, Washington, DC, 1988, The Association.
53. Cross-country ski exercisers, Consumer Reports 51:747-759, 1986.
54. Shoes to fit the sport, Changing Times 39:62-65, Nov 1985.
55. Running shoes, Consumer Reports 51:650-655, 1986.
56. Hunger LY, Torgan C: The bra controversy: are sports bras a necessity? Physician and Sports Medicine 10(11):75-76, 1982.
57. Shinaberger CS et al: Young children who drown in hot tubs, spas, and whirlpools in California: a 26-year survey, Am J Public Health 80:613-614, 1990.
58. Press E: The health hazards of saunas and spas and how to minimize them, Am J Public Health 81:1034-1037, 1991.
59. Jacknowitz AI: External analgesic products, In Handbook of nonprescription drugs, ed. 9, Washington, DC, 1990, American Pharmaceutical Association.
60. Gauthier MM: Continuous passive motion: the no-exercise exercise, Physician and Sports Medicine (15(8):142-148, 1987.
61. Flipping over gravity boots, Time, p 61, May 2, 1983.
62. A warning about hanging upside down, San Francisco Chronicle, June 19, 1983.
63. Miller RW: EMS: Fraudulent flab remover, FDA Consumer 17(4):29-32, 1983.
64. Horowitz J: From workout to wellness, Time, p 64, July 30, 1990.
65. Health Spa Rule termination, FTC News Notes, p 1, Dec 1985.
66. FTC staff take it easy on spas, Consumer Reports 50:643, 1985.
67. Dietrich J and Waggoner S: The complete health club handbook, New York, 1983, Simon and Schuster Inc.
68. Adapted from The diet/exercise link: separating fact from fiction, Tufts University Diet & Nutrition Letter 6(12):3-5, 1989.
69. Toufexis A: C'mon now, shape it up, baby, Time, 130:61, Oct. 5, 1987.
70. Anderson AD: What's new in the fitness business? The New York Times, p 3, Jan 3, 1988.
71. J & J Data: Fitness up, health costs down, Medical Tribune, p 16, May 27, 1987.
72. Freudenheim M: Assessing the corporate fitness craze, The New York Times, Business Sec, Mar 18, 1991.
73. Position of the American Dietetic Association: Nutrition for physical fitness and athletic performance for adults, J Am Diet Assoc 87:933-939, 1987.
74. Mirkin G: Don't waste time on the wrong exercises, Health 15:37-40, Apr 1983.
75. How much protein do athletes really need? Tufts University Diet and Nutrition Letter 5:1, Oct 1987.
76. Does Gatorade beat water? Consumer Reports on Health, 3:63, 1991.

PART FOUR

MAJOR HEALTH PROBLEMS

CHAPTER SIXTEEN

CARDIOVASCULAR DISEASE

Deaths from heart attack, stroke and other cardiovascular diseases are declining. Advances in medical treatment in recent years have undoubtedly played a part. But there's still a long way to go and no time for complacency. Because someone dies—from cardiovascular disease—every 34 seconds.

AMERICAN HEART ASSOCIATION[1]

CONSUMER DECISION

What are my risk factors for coronary heart disease?

✥

When should one have a cholesterol test?

✥

What percentage of one's diet should be fat? What kinds of fat?

✥

How can people estimate the percentage of fat in their diet?

TABLE 16–1

PREVALENCE OF CARDIOVASCULAR DISEASE (1989 ESTIMATES)

Condition	Prevalence*	Mortality
High blood pressure	62,770,000	31,630
Heart attack and angina	6,160,000	497,850
Stroke	2,980,000	147,470
Rheumatic heart disease	1,310,000	6,000
Congenital heart disease	930,000	5,800

*Some individuals have more than one of the listed conditions.
Source: American Heart Association.[1]

During the past few years, few health-related matters have received as much public attention as the topics of diet, fats, cholesterol, and heart disease. Consumers are being urged to "know their cholesterol number," lower the fat content of their diet, and take other steps to reduce the risk of developing heart disease. The data supporting this advice are voluminous, complex, incomplete, and sometimes confusing. Yet, based on these data, individuals are being urged to make decisions that may affect the length and quality of their life. The information in this chapter should help consumers make intelligent decisions based on the latest available research findings. Most of the research on prevention of heart attacks has been done in men, but there is no reason to believe that the findings do not apply equally to women.

Cardiovascular disease is also an area of explosive technologic development in both diagnostic and treatment procedures. As a result, increasing numbers of consumers will face complex decisions that can affect both their survival and their pocketbook.

This chapter covers the causes, risk factors, and management of the two most prevalent diseases that affect the heart and blood vessels, with emphasis on strategies for prevention and treatment. The main topic is coronary heart disease, but high blood pressure, which can play a role in both heart attacks and strokes, is included because it involves some of the same considerations. Less common types of heart problems, such as rheumatic heart disease, congenital heart disease, and infections of the heart, are not discussed in this book.

PREVALENCE OF CARDIOVASCULAR DISEASE

Cardiovascular diseases (problems affecting the heart and blood vessels) are the leading cause of illness and death for both men and women in the United States. Estimates of the annual cost of treating heart attacks, strokes and other forms of heart disease top $100 billion. About 44% of the deaths in this country are attributable to cardiovascular disease. The majority stem from atherosclerosis.

Before menopause, women tend to have lower blood pressure and fewer heart attacks than do men of equivalent age. (Female hormones exert a protective effect against heart attacks.) After menopause, the rates among women are higher than those of men and increase with advancing age.[1a]

The American Heart Association[1] estimates that 69 million Americans have one or more forms of cardiovascular disease. Table 16-1 indicates the prevalence and mortality of the most common types.

RISK FACTORS FOR CHD

Coronary heart disease (CHD) is a condition in which the arteries to the heart muscle (myocardium) are narrowed. CHD is caused by *atherosclerosis,* a condition in which cholesterol, fat, and fibrous tissue build up in the walls of large and medium-sized arteries. As atherosclerosis progresses, the coronary arteries may narrow and make it difficult for oxygen-rich blood and nutrients to reach the heart muscle.

Reduced blood supply to the heart can result in chest pain (angina pectoris) or other symptoms. If a narrowed blood vessel is completely blocked by a blood clot, the area of the heart just beyond the blockage is denied oxygen and nourishment, resulting in a heart attack (myocardial infarction). The situation often is complicated by the development of an irregular heart rhythm (arrhythmia) and/or heart failure, in which the heart's power to pump blood is inadequate to meet the body's needs.

Like other chronic degenerative disease processes, atherosclerosis can take years to develop. Diet is implicated because the deposits on arterial walls contain high levels of fat and cholesterol. Studies of both humans and animals have shown links between dietary habits and atherosclerosis.

Nine major factors (risk factors) can help predict the likelihood of having a heart attack. The risk factors for coronary heart disease are heredity (family history of heart attack before age 55), being male, advancing age, cigarette smoking, high blood pressure, diabetes, obesity (especially excess abdominal fat), lack of physical activity, and abnormal blood cholesterol levels. The more risk factors a person has, the greater the risk of developing heart disease. Heredity, gender, and age cannot be controlled, but the other risk factors can be influenced by the individual's behavior.

Several of the risk factors are interrelated. Obesity, lack of exercise, and cigarette smoking can raise blood pressure and adversely influence blood cholesterol levels. Some authorities believe that emotional stress is a risk factor, but the evidence for this is not clear-cut.

The Multiple Risk Factor Intervention Trial (MRFIT), funded by the National Institutes of Health, explored whether an intensive educational program could lower the death rate for heart disease. The study involved 12,866 men, aged 35 to 57 years, whose levels of cigarette smoking, blood cholesterol, blood pressure, or a combination of these factors, placed them at high risk for heart disease. After careful evaluation, the men were randomly assigned either to a special intervention program or to their usual sources of health care. The program ended after participants had been followed for more than 6 years. At that time, the researchers were surprised to find no overall difference in death rates between the two groups.[2] However, after 4 additional years, the intervention group had experienced 10.6% fewer heart attacks and had a 7.7% lower overall death rate.[3] Both groups were smoking less and had lower blood cholesterol levels, but the improvement was greater in the intervention group.

Blood Lipid Levels

Lipid is the general term for fatty substances, including triglycerides (fats and oils), phospholipids (such as lecithin), and sterols (including cholesterol). In common usage, fats are lipids that are solid at room temperature, whereas oils are lipids that are liquid at room temperature. (See Chapter 12 for discussion of the types of fat found in foods.) *Blood lipids* is a term used to describe the fatty substances circulating within the blood stream.

Cholesterol is found only in foods of animal origin and is part of every animal cell. It is essential to life, as the body uses cholesterol to make cell membranes, hormones, and bile acids, as well as for other functions. Most of the cholesterol the body uses is manufactured within the body, mainly within the liver. When dietary cholesterol intake is high, the liver tends to compensate by lowering cholesterol production.

Because cholesterol is a fatlike substance and cannot mix with water, the body transports it in protein-containing packages that can flow smoothly throughout the blood stream. These packages, called lipoproteins, are composed of various amounts of cholesterol, triglycerides (fats), phospholipids, and other special proteins.

Serum lipoproteins are classified by their density. The three main cholesterol-protein combinations are high-density lipoproteins (HDL), low-density lipoproteins (LDL), and very-low-density lipoproteins (VLDL). Medical management, however, is based mainly on tests that measure total cholesterol, HDL, and LDL.

People with high blood levels of HDL have a low risk of developing coronary heart disease.[4] Although the reason for this is not certain, many scientists believe that HDL serves as a "scavenger" that transports cholesterol from various cells to the liver, from which it can be excreted in the bile. Because this helps protect blood vessels against atherosclerosis, HDL is commonly referred to as "good cholesterol." HDL may also have some ability to remove cholesterol that has already been deposited in atherosclerotic plaque.

Low-density lipoproteins contain about 60% to

70% of the cholesterol carried in the blood stream. Therefore, when a blood test indicates that total cholesterol is high, this usually means that LDL is undesirably high, but some people (most notably endurance athletes) with high total cholesterol levels have high HDL rather than high LDL. Because the cholesterol from LDL tends to accumulate in the arteries as a component of atherosclerotic plaque, LDL is often called "bad cholesterol," whereas HDL is called "good cholesterol." Actually, because the cholesterol both contain is identical, it would be more accurate to refer to them as good or bad lipoproteins.

A type of LDL called lipoprotein(a), or Lp(a), has been identified as a probable independent risk factor for CHD. Lp(a) has a strong genetic component and is not influenced by diet or most cholesterol-lowering drugs.[5] Although LDL may turn out to be an extremely important factor in the development of heart disease, the study of LDL is in its early stages. Lp(a) measurement is not readily available outside of lipid research centers, and no studies as yet have defined what practical steps can be taken to help people with abnormally high levels.

Long-range studies of large population groups have shown that the higher the total blood cholesterol and LDL levels, the greater the risk of a heart attack (Fig. 16-1). The most important study, begun in 1948 in Framingham, Massachusetts, is still generating valuable information. In 1987, its researchers reported that for people under 50, overall deaths rise 5% and heart-related deaths rise 9% for each 10 mg/dl of total cholesterol.[6] Other studies have shown that lowering the cholesterol level through dietary and/or drug treatment lowers the incidence of heart attacks.[7,8] For middle-aged men, it appears that each 1% reduction in LDL results in a 2% reduction in heart attacks or death from CHD.[9]

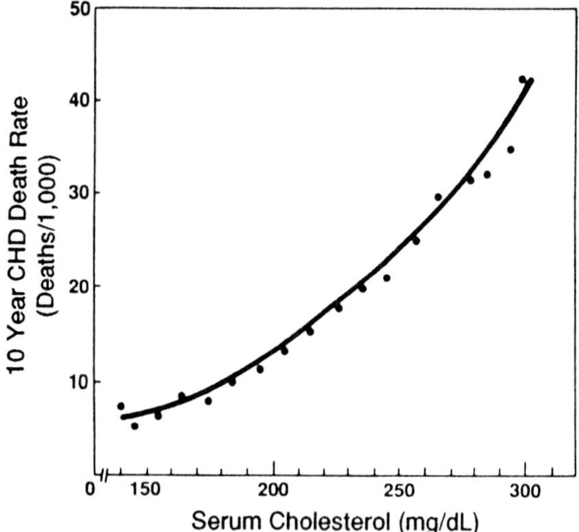

FIGURE 16-1. Relationship between serum cholesterol level and coronary heart disease death rate.

CHOLESTEROL GUIDELINES

Cholesterol and other blood lipids are measured in milligrams per deciliter (mg/dl—a deciliter is about 1/10 of a quart). Total cholesterol, HDL, and triglyceride levels are determined by laboratory tests that measure them directly. LDL is not measured directly but is calculated by subtracting HDL plus one-fifth of the triglyceride level from total cholesterol. Since triglyceride levels are influenced by eating, a blood specimen for LDL determination must be collected after an overnight fast of 12 to 14 hours.

The test to determine total cholesterol, HDL, LDL and triglyceride levels is called a "lipid profile" and should be done when the screening test result is undesirably high.

In 1987, the National Blood, Lung, and Heart Institute's National Cholesterol Education Program (NCEP) recommended that all Americans aged 20 and over have their nonfasting blood cholesterol level measured as part of routine medical evaluation that also considers other risk factors for heart disease. As noted in Figure 16-2, total cholesterol under 200 is considered desirable, 200 to 239 is considered borderline high, and 240 or over is considered high.

According to the Institute's expert panel:

1. If total cholesterol is below 200, the individual should be given general advice about diet and risk reduction and be retested within 5 years.
2. If total cholesterol is over 200, the test should be repeated with a fasting sample.
3. Patients whose total cholesterol values average 200 to 239 should be advised to reduce the fat and cholesterol content of their diet and be retested annually. Fats that should be curtailed include butter fat (in butter, whole milk, cream, ice cream, and cheese), beef fat, pork fat, palm oil, palm kernel oil, and coconut oil. Rich sources of dietary cholesterol include egg yolks, organ meats, and dairy products that contain butterfat. (Although the panel addressed

Chart your heart-health status

Good heart health begins with identifying factors that increase your risk for heart disease. In some families, risk factors for heart disease are inherited. If your parents or grandparents suffered from early coronary heart disease (before age 55) or heart attack, your personal risk of developing coronary heart disease may increase.

Other factors that can increase your risk of heart disease include: being male, smoking, having high blood pressure and high cholesterol. Since high cholesterol and high blood pressure may cause no symptoms, only a checkup can show if you have a problem.

Use this chart to record your heart-health status—and actions you need to take.

Checklist for men: **Cholesterol** ________ **Blood pressure** ________

☑ **Risk factors** (Check any that apply)

Each risk factor increases your chance of developing heart disease.

☐ High cholesterol ☐ High blood pressure ☐ Family history of heart attack before age 55
☐ Male sex ☐ Smoking ☐ Obesity (more than 30% over recommended weight)
☐ Diabetes ☐ Existing blood vessel disease (such as hardening of the arteries)
☐ A level of HDL—"good" cholesterol—under 35, measured by a blood test

☑ **Action** (Check section that applies)

☐ **Total cholesterol under 200—Desirable.** Recheck within five years or sooner if health or diet changes.

☐ **Total cholesterol 200-239—Borderline-high.** (High risk if two other risk factors are present.) Talk to doctor about further evaluation and appropriate management.

☐ **Total cholesterol 240 and over—High risk.** See doctor for further evaluation and appropriate management.

☐ **Blood pressure above 140/90.** See your doctor about treatment steps you may need to take.

Lose weight, if necessary, and **quit smoking** to reduce your risk for heart disease.

Checklist for women: **Cholesterol** ________ **Blood pressure** ________

☑ **Risk factors** (Check any that apply)

Each risk factor increases your chance of developing heart disease. This risk increases even more for postmenopausal women who lose the protective benefits of the hormone estrogen.

☐ High cholesterol ☐ High blood pressure ☐ Family history of heart attack before age 55
☐ Smoking ☐ Obesity (more than 30% over recommended weight)
☐ Diabetes ☐ Existing blood vessel disease (such as hardening of the arteries)
☐ A level of HDL—"good" cholesterol—under 35, measured by a blood test

☑ **Action** (Check section that applies)

☐ **Total cholesterol under 200—Desirable.** Recheck within five years or sooner if health or diet changes.

☐ **Total cholesterol 200-239—Borderline-high.** (High risk if two other risk factors are present.) Talk to doctor about further evaluation and appropriate management.

☐ **Total cholesterol 240 and over—High risk.** See doctor for further evaluation and appropriate management.

☐ **Blood pressure above 140/90.** See your doctor about treatment steps you may need to take.

Lose weight, if necessary, and **quit smoking** to reduce your risk for heart disease.

FIGURE 16-2. Chart your heart health status.

Source: National Cholesterol Education Program. Data from 361,662 men screened for MRFIT study.

Table 16–2

Dietary Therapy of High Blood Cholesterol

Nutrient	Step One diet	Step Two diet
Total fat	Less than 30% calories	Less than 20% calories
Saturated fatty acids	Less than 10% calories	Less than 7% calories
Polyunsaturated fatty acids	Up to 10% of calories	Up to 10%
Monounsaturated fatty acids	10%–15% of calories	10%–15% of calories
Carbohydrates	50%–60% of calories	50%–60% of calories
Protein	10%–20% of calories	10%–20% of calories
Cholesterol	Less than 300 mg/day	Less than 200 mg/day
Total calories	To achieve and maintain desirable weight	

only dietary modification, patients should also engage in aerobic exercise, stop smoking, and take care of other risk factors that can be modified.)

4. About 25% of Americans between the ages of 20 and 74 have a total cholesterol of 240 or higher. These people should have their LDL-cholesterol measured and classified as follows: desirable (below 130), borderline high-risk (130 to 159), high-risk (160 or over), or very high risk (190 or over). Those in the first two groups with no other risk factors can be given general dietary guidelines and followed annually. But those with a high-risk LDL level, or a borderline level with known heart disease or two other risk factors, should receive intensive dietary therapy and more frequent follow-up.
5. Table 16-2 describes the two levels of dietary change recommended for cholesterol reduction. If 3 months on a Step One diet do not yield a desirable result, a Step Two diet should be used. Dietary change must be permanent. Americans currently consume about 37% of their total caloric intake as fat. The Step One diet would reduce this to 30%, the Step Two diet to 20%. Dietary cholesterol intake, which typically is 350 to 450 mg/day, would be reduced to 300 mg/day on the Step One diet and 200 mg/day on the Step Two diet.
6. Therapy with cholesterol-lowering drugs should be considered for those with LDL values of 190 or higher (or 160 with two other risk factors).

In 1991 an NCEP expert panel[10] recommended cholesterol testing for children and adolescents who have a family history of premature cardiovascular disease or at least one parent with high (over 240 mg/dl) blood cholesterol. The panel recommended dietary therapy for children whose LDL was 110 mg/dl or greater and consideration for drug therapy for children over age 10 with persistent LDL levels of 190 mg/dl or more (or 160 mg/dl and other risk factors).

Table 16–3

NCEP Classification of Serum Cholesterol Levels (mg/dl)

Total cholesterol	
Under 200	Desirable
200–239	Borderline high
240 or more	High
LDL cholesterol	
Under 130	Desirable
130–159	Borderline high-risk
160 or more	High risk

In 1992 a National Institutes of Health consensus development panel[11] recognized low HDL (under 35 mg/dl) as a major risk factor for CHD. The panel concluded that all healthy Americans having their total cholesterol checked should be screened for HDL cholesterol as well. The panel also recommended HDL and triglyceride screening for individuals with desirable (under 200) levels of total cholesterol who are known to have coronary heart disease or who have two or more risk factors for it. To increase precision when treatment decisions are involved, at least two (and preferably three)

Personal Glimpse

Snake Oil for the Heart

What could be more timely than a product to reduce blood cholesterol while still allowing you to eat whatever you please? A full-page ad published in 1989 in more than a hundred newspapers claimed that Cho Low Tea would do exactly that.

"Don't cut out your favorite foods," the ad advised. "New Tea from China *Reduces* Cholesterol. Medical studies prove it! Just drinking this refreshing tea every day is as effective as medically prescribed drugs. . . . Cho Low is a rare species of tea grown in China for centuries. Traditionally, the Chinese drink it after every meal as a diet aid. Recently . . . researchers were astonished to discover that besides aiding weight loss, Cho Low Tea contains natural cholesterol-reducing properties. . . . And you get none of the possible side effects of . . . cholesterol-reducing drugs." The ad contained endorsements from seven medical sources and the logo of the Better Business Bureau. The tea cost $29.85 for a 30-day supply.

Fortunately for consumers, a newspaper credit bureau executive became suspicious and alerted law enforcement agencies in California, where the promotion was based. It turned out that the claims were false and the endorsements were complete fabrications. In fact, "Cho Low Tea" did not exist. The perpetrators said that they had planned to repackage another tea but were arrested before they could do so. After pleading "no contest," to false ad misleading advertising, they were sentenced to brief jail terms followed by 3 years' summary probation. Although more than 50,000 people had placed orders totalling over $250,000, the authorities acted so swiftly that none of them lost their money.

samples should be taken at least 1 week apart. Individuals with HDL below 35 mg/dl should attempt to raise their levels by losing weight, stopping smoking, exercising, and eating a low-fat diet. Many experts believe that a ratio of total cholesterol to HDL greater than 4.5 indicates high risk that deserves aggressive treatment. This was considered by the panelists but not included in their recommendations.

The relationship of blood triglyceride levels to cardiovascular disease is unclear. High triglyceride levels do not appear to be a risk factor for coronary heart disease. However, very high levels (over 500 mg/dl) should be treated because they can cause other problems, such as pancreatitis.

Controversy still exists about whether the entire U.S. population should aim to lower their blood cholesterol level or whether efforts should be concentrated on those at highest risk of a heart attack. Some experts, including several affiliated with the American Council on Science and Health (ACSH), believe that the NCEP guidelines are overzealous—particularly for individuals in the 200 to 240 range—and may unduly shift public attention away from other health hazards such as cigarette smoking and high blood pressure.[12] Expert panels in Canada, England and other European countries are not advocating mass screening for cholesterol but suggest treating individuals on a case-by-case basis. Their guidelines are more conservative, with higher action ranges than those of the NCEP. *Consumer Reports*[13] has concluded:

> For those clearly at risk, the decision to adopt a low-fat diet is relatively simple. But for those not clearly at risk, such a decision rests on uncertainties and intangibles. Gaps in the evidence leave room for personal preference to play a big role in a decision that may be more prudent than therapeutic.

Those "clearly at risk" include people with known coronary disease and middle-aged men with high or borderline high cholesterol levels, particularly those with a family history of premature coronary heart disease.

Although the risk factors for women appear similar to those of men, little research has been done to determine the appropriateness of using cholesterol-lowering drugs, particularly in premenopausal women. The female hormone estrogen appears to exert a protective effect against heart disease by lowering LDL levels and raising HDL. After menopause, the level of estrogen drops sharply. The *Harvard Health Letter*[14] states that taking estrogen after menopause may reduce a woman's risk of developing heart disease by almost half. However, there is also some increased risk of cancer of the uterus and possibly of cancer of the breast. This subject is discussed further in Chapter 22.

Problems with Screening Tests

Management of cholesterol levels is complicated by the fact that laboratory tests have considerable margin for error. Test results can vary from sample to sample and some facilities do not perform the test accurately. Levels vary at different times within the individual. The manner in which the test is done also can influence the results. Food intake, changes of position (lying down, sitting, or standing), weight change, alcohol intake, various illnesses, and the technique used to collect the specimen each can cause variations. The Centers for Disease Control recommends using a minimum of two patient specimens to obtain an adequate estimate of the true serum cholesterol concentration.[15] *Consumer Reports on Health*[16] warns that "finger-stick" tests often used in mass screenings are not as accurate as tests using blood drawn from the arm.

An erroneously high reading can cause needless worry and expense. An erroneously low reading can lead an individual to fail to take appropriate action. Considering the test's relatively low cost and the problems that can result from an inaccurate report, it probably is wise to obtain the test from a laboratory recommended by one's personal physician.

Dietary Modification

Most of the cholesterol needed by the body is produced by the body, mainly by the liver. The rest is derived from animal products (meat, fish, milk, eggs) in the diet. Among the dietary factors, the amount and type of fat eaten has the greatest impact on the blood cholesterol level. Decreased consumption of saturated fats usually results in lower blood cholesterol, as does substitution of polyunsaturated fats or monounsaturated for some saturated fats in the diet. Dietary cholesterol affects the level of blood cholesterol, but to a lesser and more variable extent than does the fat content of the diet. A high intake of soluble fiber (found in oat products, beans, and other complex carbohydrate foods) can help to lower blood cholesterol levels.

To assist consumers trying to lower their blood cholesterol, the National Cholesterol Education Program[17] suggests five general guidelines:

1. Eat less high-fat food, especially foods high in saturated fat.
2. Replace part of the saturated fat in the diet with unsaturated fat. There is no biologic need for dietary saturated fat, but it is practically impossible to avoid eating some of it.
3. Eat less high-cholesterol food.
4. Choose food high in complex carbohydrates (starch and fiber), such as fruits, vegetables, whole-grain cereals, beans, and other legumes.
5. Reduce weight if overweight.

At the First National Cholesterol Conference, held in Arlington, Virginia, in 1988, nutrition professionals agreed that the first practical step towards dietary change is to become more aware of one's diet, especially the amount of food eaten and the brands usually purchased. Toward this end, consumers should get into the habit of checking labels to determine the amount of cholesterol and the amount and type of fat. They also need to become cognizant of the "hidden" fats found in processed foods such as cookies, crackers, and snack cakes, and the kinds of fats and oils used in their own cooking.

The next step is to make substitutions. For example, leaner cuts of beef (select or choice rather than prime) should be used, and consumption of fish, poultry, fresh fruits and vegetables, beans, and other legumes should be increased. Foods high in complex carbohydrates—such as whole grains, beans, and vegetables—can be made the "main dish," with small amounts of red meats and cheeses becoming the "side dishes." Mixed dishes such as stews, casseroles, and pasta and rice meals can combine small amounts of meat with other foods, such as grains or vegetables.

Finally, consumers should evaluate their progress by having their blood cholesterol tested within a few months and then periodically as recommended by the professional who is guiding them. The goal should be a gradual but steady reduction in the total cholesterol and LDL-cholesterol levels.

Because the major sources of saturated fat in the American diet traditionally have come from beef and dairy products, dietary advice aimed at lowering blood cholesterol often focuses on cutting back on hamburgers and fatty meats, whole milk, and cheeses—and getting into a habit of preparing foods with less fat. The box at right provides suggestions for reducing fat and cholesterol content of

Dietary Modification for Cholesterol Control

The following can help consumers choose and prepare foods lower in saturated fat and cholesterol:

- Trim all visible fat from beef and poultry, and remove the skin from poultry before eating.
- Bake, broil or roast meat dishes instead of deep-fat frying them. To prevent drying and add flavor, baste with wine, lemon juice, or low fat broths.
- Try experimenting with herbs and spices, such as dill, tarragon, cilantro, and basil.
- Avoid fatty gravies and sauces.
- If pan- or stir-frying, use small amounts of vegetable oils such as canola or safflower oil; also increase your use of olive oil.
- One important change consumers should make is using margarine rather than butter. Many low-calorie margarines, in which water is substituted for some of the oil, are now available. Butter-margarine combinations still contain 80% fat and should be limited.
- To cut down on whole milk products, switch to 2% or 1% milk, and perhaps eventually to skim milk. Many people find it easy to get accustomed to low-fat milk, and that when they do so, whole milk tastes too rich. Use the low-fat or skim-milk versions of ricotta, cottage, and mozzarella cheese. Low-fat farmer or pot cheeses also are available. All these cheeses should contain no more than 2-6 grams of fat per ounce. For desserts, substitute ice milk, frozen yogurt (especially the nonfat variety), sherbert or sorbet for ice cream. If you do eat ice cream, choose regular rather than super premium types.
- Where cholesterol and fat content are not specified on the label, it may still be possible to tell whether a product contains saturated fat or cholesterol by checking the ingredient list. Consumption should be limited of foods that contain palm, palm kernel, and coconut oils, lard, butter, unidentified shortening, egg-yolk solids, and whole-milk solids. Also, cut down on baked goods made from these ingredients or that are fried, such as doughnuts.
- Use yogurt instead of sour cream in dips and toppings.
- Use only the egg whites or discard every other yolk in recipes requiring eggs (2 whites = 1 whole egg in recipes). Or, try commercial cholesterol-free egg substitutes.
- Reduce the amount of fat in recipes by one-third to one-half, and use chiefly polyunsaturated and monounsaturated oils.
- In coffee, use low-fat or skim milk instead of non-dairy creamers containing saturated fats. Skim milk powder also is acceptable.
- Make your own popcorn for a low-calorie snack, but be sure to omit the melted butter. Beware of high-fat microwave popcorn products.
- Avoid nuts that are high in saturated fats, such as coconuts and macadamia nuts.
- Incorporate oat fiber into your diet, for example, in oat bran muffins or in casseroles. To increase total fiber intake, look for the words "whole wheat" or "whole grain" near the top of the ingredient list when buying breads and cereals.
- Use fresh fruit for dessert instead of high-fat desserts.
- Choose low-fat luncheon meats such as turkey breast or pressed turkey instead of salami and bologna. Also eat few frankfurters, other sausages, and bacon. When eating turkey, remember that white meat has less fat than dark meat.
- Shrimp, lobster, and other shellfish may be eaten occasionally because they are lower in cholesterol than previously thought, and do not contain too much saturated fat.
- Buy or make salad dressings with predominantly unsaturated oils. Olive oil is an especially good choice. Or try a nonfat type or just vinegar or lemon juice.
- Limit use of organ meats that are very high in cholesterol, such as liver, kidneys, brain, and sweetbreads.
- Prepare soups and stews containing meat the day before eating them. After refrigerating, skim off the congealed fat on the surface prior to reheating.
- Substitute rice and pasta for egg noodles.
- Be cautious about store-bought baked products such as pies, cakes, croissants, pastries and muffins. Try to find low-fat cookies and crackers. Or eat homemade baked goods prepared with small amounts of unsaturated oils. Angel cake is a good choice because it is low in fat and cholesterol.
- Use some of the many fat-free, cholesterol-free products marketed as substitutes for products that normally are high in fat.
- Make changes gradually to avoid feeling deprived. For most people, enjoying a rich dessert or a prime rib once in a while is not going to significantly affect their cholesterol level as long as the overall cholesterol-lowering diet is followed most of the time. It is better to splurge once in a while than to cheat a little bit each day.

Adapted from Kantor MA: Nutrition, cholesterol and heart disease. Part V: Dietary modification, Nutrition Forum 6:33-37, 1989.

TABLE 16–4

FATTY ACID COMPOSITION OF SELECTED FATS AND OILS

	% Saturated	% Mono-unsaturated	% Poly-unsaturated
Fats and Oils			
Canola (rapeseed) oil	7	58	35
Safflower oil	9	13	78
Walnut oil	10	24	66
Sunflower oil	11	20	69
Corn oil	13	25	62
Olive oil	14	77	9
Soybean oil	15	24	61
Peanut oil	18	48	34
Salmon oil	20	55	25
Wheat germ oil	20	16	64
Cottonseed oil	27	19	54
Tuna fat	30	29	41
Chicken fat	31	47	22
Lard	41	47	12
Mutton (lamb) fat	49	43	8
Palm oil	51	39	10
Beef fat	52	44	4
Palm kernel oil	86	12	2
Coconut oil	92	6	2
Spreads and Shortening			
Mayonnaise (soybean oil)	16	30	54
Mayonnaise (imitation)	18	24	58
Stick margarine (liquid and partially hydrogenated corn oil)	18	51	31
Tub margarine (partially hydrogenated soybean oil)	18	47	35
Shortening (partially hydrogenated soybean and palm oils)	32	53	15
Butter	66	30	4

one's diet. Table 16-4 indicates the fatty acid composition of selected fats and oils.

Overall Fat Percentage

Following the guidelines in the box on page 361 will reduce the fat, saturated fat, and cholesterol content of the diet and should come close to the 30% fat and 10% saturated fat levels recommended in the NCEP Step One Diet. However, the only way to determine how much fat and cholesterol are actually consumed is to add up the amounts contained in the daily diet. While miligrams of cholesterol can be added directly, the percentage of fat must be calculated using information on product labels or from food composition tables. Since there are 9 calories per gram of fat, the percentage of calories from fat equals:

$$\frac{\text{grams of fat consumed during the day} \times 9}{\text{Total calories eaten}} \times 100$$

Thus a person who consumed 2100 calories containing 70 g of fat would have a diet that is $[(70 \times 9)/2100] \times 100 = 30\%$ fat. However, precise self-determination of daily fat and cholesterol intake can be difficult. Many foods do not carry complete nutrition labels, and determining the fat and cholesterol content of many restaurant items is difficult or impossible (although many fast food outlets publish information about their products). Table 16-5 compares several popular books that include food composition tables to help consumers plan their diet. Similar information is also available in government publications.[18]

Computer programs are also available for determining fat and cholesterol intake. The ones containing large databases, including nutritional analyses of brand-name products and fast food items, generally provide the most accurate information. Computer programs are accessible to consumers at certain clinics and through nutrition professionals in private practice. Some are also marketed directly to the public. For home use, Stare, Aronson, and Barrett[19] have identified three programs that are reliable and are updated regularly to include new data on nutrient values and new food products:

"Eat Smart," for Macintosh computers, covers 136 food items and 12 nutrients ($19.95 from Pillsbury Co., Pillsbury Center, Minneapolis, MN 55402).

"You Are What You Eat," for IBM or Macintosh hardware, covers 1000 food items and 13 nutrients ($79.95 from DDA Software, P.O. Box 26, Hamburg, NJ 07419).

"DINE," for IBM or Macintosh hardware, covers 3400 food items and 15 nutrients ($190 from DINE Systems, 2211 Main St., Building B, Buffalo, NY 14214).

Kantor[20] states that despite these self-help aids, most consumers wishing to design a diet that is significantly low in fat would be wise to seek professional advice from a registered dietitian or other professional nutritionist. Chapter 12 describes the training and credentials of professional nutritionists.

Soluble Fiber

It is well established that a diet high in soluble fiber can improve blood cholesterol levels. In 1984, for example, Anderson and colleagues[21] gave 20 men with levels of blood cholesterol above 260 mg/dl diets containing 17 g/day of soluble fiber, derived either from oat bran (100 g/day dry weight) or pinto and navy beans (115 g/day dry weight). Subjects on the oat diet consumed 1 cup of hot oat bran cereal each day plus 5 oat bran muffins. Those eating beans were served cooked beans and bean soup. After 3 weeks, both groups showed favorable changes in their cholesterol levels. Total cholesterol was reduced by about 19%, while LDL levels decreased by approximately 24%. Although the average HDL level also decreased slightly in this study, other researchers have found that HDL usually increased modestly or does not change when subjects increase their soluble fiber intake. The addition of psyllium (the soluble fiber in Metamucil) to a Step One diet has been shown to improve cholesterol levels more than the diet alone.[22]

The foods highest in soluble fiber include oat bran, dry oats, kidney beans, navy beans, pinto beans, lima beans, white beans, Brussels sprouts, kale, broccoli, plums, apples, and oranges and grapefruit (including the fibrous partitions). Large amounts of fiber increase the bulk of the stool and can cause bloating, cramps, and diarrhea. However, discomfort can be minimized or prevented if the amount of dietary fiber is increased gradually, rather than suddenly, so that the body can become accustomed to it.

A controlled experiment suggests that the water-soluble fiber β-glucan is responsible for the cholesterol-lowering effect of oat products. Six groups of about 20 volunteers following a NCEP Step One diet were given either oat bran or oat cereal at daily doses of 1, 2, or 3 oz (dry weight) for 6 weeks, while a seventh group received 1 oz/day of farina, which contains no β-glucan. (A cup of dry oatmeal contains 3 oz.) The groups eating 2 or 3 oz of oat bran or 3 oz of oatmeal had the best results, with total cholesterol falling an average of 7% to 9% and LDL falling an average of 10% to 16%.[23]

Regression of Atherosclerosis

Many studies have shown that improving blood cholesterol levels can reduce the incidence and death rate from heart disease. A few studies have used angiography (an x-ray procedure used to measure blood distribution) to determine whether atherosclerosis within the coronary arteries can be reversed by the treatment program. The studies compare the data obtained before and after the trial period to see whether coronary atherosclerosis has increased (progressed), remained the same, or decreased (regressed). This is done by measuring areas of narrowing and blood flow within the coronary arteries.

The Cholesterol Lowering Atherosclerosis Study involved men aged 40 through 59 with progressive atherosclerosis who had undergone coronary bypass surgery. About 100 men remained in the study

Table 16–5

Cholesterol-Lowering Guidebooks

Title	Author(s)	Method	Food Analyses	Recipe Analysis	Sample Analysis
Beyond Cholesterol: The Johns Hopkins Complete Guide for Avoiding Heart Disease (1989)	Peter Kwiterovich, M.D.	Dietary planning based on selection of foods that are low in saturated fat and/or high in fiber	Calories, total and saturated fat, and cholesterol listed for about 800 foods	Yes	Yes
Controlling Cholesterol (1988)	Kenneth H. Cooper, M.D., Ph.D.	Uses food exchange system to modify sample weekly diet plans	Calories, fat and cholesterol listed for over 500 food items, with fat composition specified for many	Yes	Yes
Count Out Cholesterol (1989)	Art Ulene, M.D.	Provides system for counting levels of saturated fat and dietary fiber to reach goals based on weight or activity level. Cholesterol is tabulated separately.	Ratings assigned for saturated fat, fiber and cholesterol for about 300 foods	No	No
Dr. Dean Ornish's Program for Reversing Heart Disease (1990)	Dean Ornish, M.D.	Dietary planning based on counting grams of fat and saturated fat. Advocates a stringent vegetarian "reversal diet" or a less stringent "prevention" diet, plus multivitamin/mineral supplement	Calories, carbohydrate, protein, total and saturated fat, cholesterol and sodium listed for about 600 foods	Yes	Yes
Eater's Choice (1989)	Ron Goor, Ph.D. Nancy Goor	Dietary planning based mainly on limiting the number of saturated fat calories.	Calories and saturated fat listed for about 1,500 food items	Yes	Yes
Good Fat, Bad Fat (1989)	Glen C. Griffin, M.D. William P. Castelli, M.D.	Dietary planning based on limiting the number of grams of saturated fat	Saturated fat and cholesterol listed for about 270 foods	Yes	No
The American Heart Association Low-Fat, Low-Cholesterol Cookbook (1989)	Scott Grundy, M.D., Ph.D.	Primarily a cookbook	Calories, total and saturated fat, cholesterol and sodium listed for over 500 foods	Yes	Yes
The New American Diet (1986)	William E. Connor, M.D. Sonja L. Conner, M.S., R.D.	Food selection based on "cholesterol-saturated fat index (CSI)," the authors' estimate of the foods' overall effect on blood cholesterol levels	Lists calories and CSI for over 100 foods	Yes	Yes

© 1989, 1992, Mark A. Kantor, Ph.D., and Stephen Barrett, M.D.

for 4 years. Those who received two drugs (colestipol and niacin) had significantly better cholesterol levels and angiographic results than comparable men who received no drugs.[24] Among the no-drug group, those who followed the NCEP Step Two diet were less likely to have progression of their disease than those who did not.[25] The researchers also found that it was better to replace calories from saturated fat with calories from protein and carbohydrate rather than from monounsaturated or polyunsaturated fat.

The Familial Atherosclerosis Study compared high-risk men taking two cholesterol-lowering drugs with a control group given a placebo or one drug. Both groups consumed a low-fat diet. The patients receiving two drugs achieved better blood cholesterol levels and had a greater incidence of regression than those in the control group.[26]

The Lifestyle Heart Trial tested whether regression could be brought about by changes of lifestyle alone—including a 10%-fat vegetarian diet, smoking cessation, stress management techniques, and daily moderate exercise. The only animal products permitted in the treatment group's diet were egg whites and 1 cup per day of nonfat milk or yogurt. Cholesterol intake was 5 mg/day or less. The control group was asked to adhere to a Step One diet. After 1 year, 18 of the 22 members (82%) of the treatment group showed overall regression of coronary atherosclerosis, while the 10 out of 19 members (53%) of the control group showed substantial progression of their disease.[27,28] Dr. Dean Ornish, who directed the trial, reported that the degree of regression was related more to compliance with the low-fat diet than it was to the change in blood cholesterol level. His study is being extended for 3 years to see whether patients will continue to maintain their new life-style and what changes in their atherosclerosis occur over a longer period. Additional studies with larger groups of patients would be desirable but are difficult to conduct because they are very expensive.

Pritikin Diet

The Pritikin diet was designed by the late Nathan Pritikin, a successful inventor who had no professional training in medicine or nutrition. It is very low in fat, high in complex carbohydrates, and low in sodium. Its recommended composition is less than 10% fat, 10% to 15% protein, less than 5% simple carbohydrates, and 75% to 80% complex carbohydrates. It allows 3.5 oz of fish, poultry, or lean meat per day, which resembles a vegetarian diet. The diet is part of an overall program that includes exercise and allows no cigarettes or alcohol.[29] In 1992, the residential program, available at Pritikin Longevity Centers in Santa Monica, California, and Miami, Florida, cost $10,458 for a 26-day stay or $6133 for a 13-day stay. Quaker Oats, which markets Pritikin Foods products, is planning to open community health and fitness centers in several cities.

Pritikin claimed that his program helped many people with heart disease, obesity, diabetes and other health problems. His approach is similar to conventional therapy for cardiac patients but uses a more restrictive diet. The Pritikin diet can achieve considerable reduction in blood cholesterol levels. However, its fiber content is quite high (about 30 g per 1000 calories), which may cause abdominal cramps, bloating, and diarrhea. Dr. Ornish's trial suggests that for some patients, the Pritikin diet may protect the heart better than a less stringent low-fat diet. No direct comparative study has been carried out, however, so it is not clear whether the potential benefits of the Pritikin diet justify the radical dietary changes it requires.

Misleading Advertising

Since the public is much more familiar with "cholesterol" than with "saturated fat," many manufacturers have been making "no-cholesterol" claims even for foods that are high in fat. Unsuspecting consumers interested in trying to adopt healthier eating habits might actually make things worse by eating these foods. A similar situation exists for some products containing oat bran. Although oat bran can play a valuable cholesterol-lowering role as part of a low-fat diet, some "oat bran" products contain insignificant amounts of oat bran or contain undesirable amounts of fat as well.

The New York Department of Consumer Affairs surveyed three supermarket chains in New York City and found 185 products marketed with claims of low or no cholesterol. In some cases the foods were vegetable or grain products that never contained cholesterol to begin with. In other cases, the products were free of cholesterol but contained high levels of fat. In some cases, a heart symbol was displayed on the package or supermarket shelf for foods that were high in fat. The department's report noted:

> Unfortunately, when one product makes a meaningless or deceptive claim, its competitors usually follow suit so they are not competitively disadvantaged. A kind of Gresham's law of grocery shopping ensues as misleading labels push out honest labels. . . .
>
> Vigorous consumer law enforcement at the federal and local levels is needed to ensure that our supermarket shelves serve—rather than sabotage—our consumer interests.[30]

During 1991 the FDA sent regulatory letters to six food companies, warning them to stop making health claims that are not backed by scientific evidence. Ralston Purina was ordered to stop claiming that eating Oat Chex, "may help reduce cholesterol levels." The letter to Ralston said that even if scientific evidence eventually supports a link between eating oat bran and reducing coronary heart disease risk, Oat Chex contains insufficient fiber to support its health claim. The other letters concerned Toasted Oat Bran Shake (J&J Snack Foods Corp.), Rice Bran Oil (Select Origins, Inc.), Oatmeal Goodness Bread Wheat Oatmeal (Continental Baking Co.), Vita Fiber Rice Bran (Pacific Rice Products, Inc.), and Oat Bran Fruit Jumbo Cookies (Health Valley Foods, Inc.). The agency also warned the manufacturers of five corn and canola oils to stop making "no-cholesterol" claims and displaying a heart on their labels.

As noted in Chapter 12, the FDA has proposed regulations to stop misleading claims for the fat and cholesterol content of foods, but they will not take effect before May 1993. Meanwhile, consumers who are concerned about their blood cholesterol level should ignore the slogans and check the ingredients noted on the product label. Current regulations require total fat content to be listed when any type of nutrition claim is made. Under the proposed regulations, almost all packaged foods will have to specify the amounts of fat, saturated fat, and cholesterol.

Cholesterol-Lowering Drugs

The National Cholesterol Education Program considers dietary treatment the cornerstone of therapy to reduce elevated cholesterol levels. The primary goal of dietary therapy is to maintain an LDL level below 130 mg/dl. It is assumed that this will help prevent heart attacks by inhibiting the growth and development of atherosclerotic plaque and may reduce the amount of plaque already present. If a Step One Diet does not succeed, the more rigorous Step Two Diet should be used. If all dietary attempts fail to correct elevated LDL levels within about 6 months, then drug therapy should be considered in addition to diet.

The choice of the drug will depend upon the medical condition of the patient, the nature of the patient's blood lipid abnormalities, concern about adverse effects, and cost. Table 16-6 provides an overview of the commonly used drugs. If one drug is not effective, two may be used together.

Niacin is available in two forms: crystalline (regular) and sustained-release. The usual dosage for cholesterol control is 1 to 3 g daily. Sustained release products have fewer side effects and may be more potent, but they have a much higher incidence of serious adverse effects. Although both varieties are available without a prescription, self-medication is extremely unwise. Near-fatal hepatitis has been reported in a previously healthy 32-year-old man who had taken one 500-mg sustained-release niacin tablet daily for 2 months, purchased at a health food store.[31] Several observers have expressed concern that sustained-released niacin can be purchased without a prescription.[32,33]

Several other products sold through health food stores have been falsely touted as useful for lowering blood cholesterol levels. Garlic may be effective for this purpose but has not been proven safe.[34] Fish oil capsules have variable effects on blood lipids (sometimes raising cholesterol levels) and have little practical use.[35] Lecithin[36] and fiber pills have no proven value. Several companies market products containing various amounts of such substances plus niacin and other ingredients. No product of this type is rationally formulated.[37]

A recent study found that among 333 men who had angina pectoris or previous bypass surgery, those who supplemented with beta-carotene had a lower incidence of heart attacks and strokes. But the study's leaders warn that the data are preliminary and that more research is needed to determine whether supplementation by the general public might be beneficial.[38]

High Blood Pressure

Blood pressure is the force created by the heart as it pushes blood throughout the circulatory system. High blood pressure (hypertension) is defined as blood pressure that is persistently higher than nor-

Table 16–6

Commonly Used Cholesterol-Lowering Drugs

Drugs	Ability to Lower LDL	Ability to Raise HDL	Relative Cost	Advantages	Adverse Effects
Nicotinic acid (niacin)	++	+++	Very low	Most cost-effective; proven effective for reducing heart attacks; may lower Lp(a)	Flushing and itching of the skin; nausea; abnormal liver function; gout. Sustained-release niacin has fewer side effects but greater incidence of serious complications
Cholestipol (Colestid) Cholestyramine (Questran, Cholybar)	++	+	Moderate	Safest; work within the intestine and therefore are not absorbed by the body	Constipation, nausea, bloating, heartburn; can interfere with absorption of fat-soluble vitamins and some drugs
Lovastatin (Mevacor) Pravastatin (Pravachol) Simvastatin (Zocor)	+++	+	High	Most effective for lowering LDL	Side effects are uncommon, but these drugs are too new to have established long-term safety
Gemfibrozil (Lopid)	+	++	Low	Useful for treating elevated triglyceride levels	GI distress, rash, gallstones

mal. Hypertension is sometimes called "the silent disease" because it produces no symptoms until it reaches an advanced state. (Actually, atherosclerosis is equally silent.) High blood pressure often is detected during a routine medical visit or screening program. However, the diagnosis cannot be established with a single reading. Several measurements on different days are required to make a definite diagnosis. Blood pressure measurement and devices are discussed in Chapter 10.

More than 61 million Americans have high blood pressure. It tends to rise as people get older and is more common among blacks than among Caucasians. When it is caused by kidney disease, a tumor, or other identifiable cause, curing the underlying cause usually will cure the problem. However, in the vast majority of cases, there is no identifiable cause and the condition is called essential hypertension.[39] When blood pressure is high, the heart must work harder than normal to pump blood throughout the body. The strain often causes the heart to enlarge, promotes atherosclerosis, and can interfere with the blood supply to the kidneys, heart, or brain, leading to kidney failure, heart attack, or stroke. Early treatment is important to reduce the likelihood of these complications.

Risk Factors for Stroke

A stroke occurs when an artery to the brain bursts or becomes clogged by a blood clot or other particle. Deprived of oxygen, nerve cells in the affected area of the brain cannot function and die within minutes, resulting in loss of function in the parts of the body that are controlled by these cells. The primary risk factors for stroke include heredity, high blood pressure, heart disease, cigarette smoking, being male, advancing age, and diabetes. Secondary risk factors, which contribute to the development of heart disease, include lack of exercise, excessive alcohol intake, and abnormal blood cholesterol levels.

A healthy life-style can lower the incidence of hypertension. Obesity, high alcohol intake, cigarette smoking, physical inactivity, and high sodium intake can contribute to blood pressure elevation. Stamler and colleagues conducted a 5-year study of 201 people with normal blood pressure, 102 of whom who were counseled about these risk factors. When the trial ended, the incidence of hypertension was 8.8% in the intervention group and 19.2% in the control group.[40]

Diagnosis of Hypertension

Blood pressure varies somewhat during the course of a day. It usually is lowest when resting and higher as activity increases. It also can increase when people are nervous about having it tested, a condition referred to as "white-coat hypertension." For this reason it is important to be relaxed when blood pressure readings are taken. Transient elevations usually do not indicate disease or abnormality.

Blood pressure is expressed as a fraction. Systolic pressure, which is the numerator, reflects the pressure when the heart is resting between contractions. Diastolic pressure, the denominator, reflects the pressure between beats. A pressure of 120/80 is considered normal. Abnormal pressure can be classified as follows:

mild hypertension =
 diastolic pressure between 90 and 104
moderate hypertension =
 diastolic pressure between 105 and 115
severe hypertension =
 diastolic pressure above 115
isolated systolic hypertension =
 diastolic below 90
 but systolic above 160[41]

The goal of treatment is diastolic pressure below 90 and systolic below 140.

Nondrug Therapy

For mild hypertension, nondrug treatment should be tried first. The following measures may help:

1. *Weight reduction.* Losing weight usually results in some lowering of blood pressure.
2. *Smoking cessation.* Cigarette smoking raises blood pressure because nicotine causes arteries to constrict.
3. *Increasing exercise.* As noted in Chapter 15, increasing exercise can lower blood pressure, help people lose weight, and increase HDL.
4. *Limiting alcohol intake.* Individuals who consume 6 ounces or more of alcohol per day are twice as likely as nondrinkers to have high blood pressure.
5. *Reducing sodium intake.* As noted in Chapter 12, some people with high blood pressure will benefit from lowering their sodium intake. The treating physician should provide dietary instructions and a protocol to test this possibility.[42] The *Harvard Heart Letter* states that "most people can lower their daily sodium intake to about 1.5 g/day of sodium by following a diet of 'no added salt' . . . by avoiding fast foods and keeping the salt shaker out of reach."[43]
6. *Reducing caffeine intake.* Since caffeine can temporarily raise blood pressure, reducing or eliminating caffeine could be tried.

Consumer Reports states that nearly all hypertensive people can lower their blood pressure to some degree through life-style changes. The benefit depends on how much they change and how high their pressure was to begin with.[44] A recent study involving people with diastolic pressures between 80 and 89 (high normal) found that weight reduction and sodium restriction were effective and that stress management and supplementation with calcium, magnesium, potassium, or fish oil were ineffective in reducing blood pressure.[45]

Drug Therapy

If nondrug measures are unable to normalize blood pressure, drug treatment should be used. The most commonly used antihypertensive drugs fall into four categories:

1. *Diuretics* increase fluid excretion, which reduces blood volume. They are inexpensive.
2. *Beta-blockers* slow the heartbeat and decrease the force of the heart. The cost is moderate.
3. *Calcium channel blockers* keep arteries from constricting. They are expensive.
4. *ACE inhibitors* reduce pressure by keeping arteries from constricting. They have the fewest side effects, but are expensive.[46]

The factors influencing the choice of drug include the doctor's preferences, the extent of the problem, the presence of other health problems, the patient's tolerance of the drugs, side effects, and cost. Side effects can include fatigue, headaches, palpitations, dizziness, loss of sexual desire, and other less common symptoms. Cost varies according to the drug selected, the dosage and frequency used, the availability of a generic version, and the pharmacist's markup. The cost ranges from a few cents a day for generic diuretics to several dollars per day for brandname ACE inhibitors. Some people with mild hypertension are able to discontinue medication safely, but most individuals with moderate or severe hypertension should continue taking it for life.[42] Moderate salt-restriction may enhance the response to some antihypertension medications but can cause difficulty with others.[47]

Heart Attacks

Each year, as many as 1.5 million Americans will have a heart attack, and about 500,000 of them will die.[1] About 60% of heart attack victims die before they reach a hospital. Heart attacks are typically caused by a blood clot that blocks a segment of coronary artery that has been narrowed by atherosclerosis. The resultant lack of blood can cause damage or death to part of the heart muscle, a condition called *myocardial infarction*. The typical symptoms are:

1. Uncomfortable pressure, fullness, squeezing or pain in the center of the chest that lasts more than a few minutes.
2. Pain spreading to the shoulders, neck, jaw, or arms, particularly the left arm.
3. Chest discomfort with lightheadedness, sweating, nausea, and/or shortness of breath.

Not all of these warning signs occur in every heart attack. People who experience them, however, should seek help as soon as possible because early medical intervention can often save a person's life and reduce the amount of damage done to the heart. The American Heart Association advises consumers to know what area hospitals provide 24-hour emergency cardiac care and to call an emergency rescue service if the above symptoms of chest discomfort persist for 10 minutes or more.

Angina pectoris is a condition in which blood supply to the heart is temporarily inadequate to meet the body's needs. It is typically precipitated by exertion. The discomfort of angina can be similar to that of a heart attack but subsides within a few minutes when the individual rests or takes medication (nitroglycerine) that increases the blood supply to the heart. Recurrent attacks of angina indicate that the risk of a heart attack may be high. Medication that dilates coronary arteries often can prevent or reduce the incidence of anginal attacks. In properly selected individuals, coronary bypass surgery or angioplasty (discussed later in this chapter) is curative.

Hospital Care

A myocardial infarction is a medical emergency because it can cause an abnormal rhythm that results in sudden death. What takes place within the first few hours may make the difference between life and death, or between recovery and disability.

Hospital care for a heart attack has five basic goals: (1) to prevent sudden death, (2) to clarify the location and extent of the problem, (3) to minimize damage to the heart muscle, (4) to prevent and treat complications, and (5) to enable the patient to return to as normal a life-style as possible. Upon arrival at the hospital the patient will to be connected to a device that provides a continuous electrocardiogram on an oscillograph screen that hospital staff members monitor. Anticoagulant therapy may be administered to prevent additional blockage from the blood clot. In some cases it is possible to locate and remove the blockage with medication and/or surgery. To take advantage of new developments, it is advisable to obtain care from an up-to-date cardiologist who practices in a well-equipped hospital.

Diagnostic Tests

The tests used to evaluate the structure and function of the heart and its blood supply vary considerably in complexity and cost. A physical examination is likely to include measurement of the pulse, which provides information about the heart's rate and rhythm, percussion (thumping) of the chest, which may indicate whether the heart is enlarged, and listening to the heart with a stethoscope. The stethoscope can reveal murmurs that signify abnormalities of the heart valves. A chest x-ray can detect abnormal enlargement of the heart, which can have a variety of causes.

Electrocardiogram

The test that is best known and most widely used to examine heart function is the electrocardiogram, which is commonly referred to as an "EKG" or "ECG." This test, which usually costs from $35 to $50, detects and measures the flow of tiny electrical currents on the heart's surface. The test is usually performed with the patient lying down, with wires (leads) connected from the patient to the device. The device prints a representation of the electrical activity on graph paper so it can be interpreted by a physician.

Electrocardiograms are especially useful for diagnosing disturbances of heart rhythm. Enlargement of the heart and heart muscle damage may also be indicated. A normal ECG report does not ensure that the heart is normal. Following a heart attack, for example, it may take several hours for abnormal changes to show up on the cardiogram. It is also possible for muscle damage to occur in a part of the heart that a routine ECG procedure does not discern. When a rhythm disturbance is intermittent, a portable device (Holter monitor) that makes a continuous record for 24 hours or more may be needed to demonstrate the abnormality.

Stress Testing

A stress test is basically an electrocardiogram performed during gradually escalated exercise. It is useful to detect unsuspected abnormalities of the heart or help determine the amount of exercise that can be tolerated by an individual with known heart disease. The exercise usually is performed by walking on a treadmill, though another device such as a bicycle may be used for people who have difficulty walking. Before exercise begins, an ordinary ECG is performed to check for abnormalities and provide a basis for comparison. Blood pressure also is measured beforehand and throughout the procedure.

The strenuousness of the exercise will depend upon the individual's health. For those with little or no known impairment, the treadmill speed and elevation will usually be increased until 80% to 90% of the person's maximum heart rate is reached. For individuals with known heart disease the target rate may be set lower. As exercise increases, the attending physician monitors the subject's blood pressure and electrocardiographic pattern on an oscillograph screen. If chest pain, severe shortness of breath, or certain signs of electrical abnormality appear on the screen, the test will be stopped.

A stress test is not appropriate for routine use for people who feel well because it costs about $300 and can yield false-positive results that trigger even greater expense. Testing is likely to be appropriate under the following circumstances:

1. Sedentary individual over age 35 planning to start an exercise program
2. Coronary occlusion or other evidence or coronary heart disease in a blood relative before the age of 55
3. Cigarette smoking, high blood pressure, diabetes, or obesity
4. Chest pain or other symptoms of coronary artery disease during exertion
5. Following a heart attack or heart surgery; used to help determine prognosis and an appropriate heart-strengthening exercise program

Some individuals who develop no symptoms but have an abnormal electrocardiogram during a stress test will need additional testing to clarify whether or not they have coronary artery disease. These individuals may be advised to undergo a thallium stress test, a procedure in which radioactive thallium is injected into an arm vein shortly before the end of the exercise period. A scanning procedure is then used to map the distribution of blood to the heart. This test is far more accurate than ordinary stress testing but costs three to five times as much. A thallium stress test may also be used to measure blood flow to the heart following a cardiac rehabilitation program.

A stress test entails slight risk; it is not risk-free. *The Johns Hopkins Medical Letter*[48] states that the risk of triggering a heart attack is less than 1 in 500, while the risk of dying is less than 1 in 10,000. For this reason, a stress test should be performed in a facility equipped to handle any emergency that may arise, and a physician and at least one technician trained in advanced life support should be present.

Coronary Angiography

Coronary angiography is used to evaluate the blood flow to the heart and visualize the location of narrowed or blocked coronary arteries. It is more accurate than a stress test, but it is more expensive and entails a slightly higher risk of provoking a heart attack. The first step, called catheterization, involves passage of a small hollow plastic tube (catheter) through the large artery in the groin (femoral artery) or the forearm (brachial artery). The cardiologist anesthetizes the skin over the artery and makes a small incision with a scalpel. Then the catheter is inserted into the artery and threaded through arteries until it reaches the openings of the coronary arteries inside the aorta (the main artery emerging from the heart). The patient may feel some pulling or transient pain when the catheter is inserted into the artery, but the rest of the procedure generally produces no discomfort. When the catheter is in place, an opaque dye is injected into the coronary arteries, enabling the pattern of blood flow to the heart muscle to be visualized. The cardiologist observes the flow with a fluoroscope, and x-ray films are taken throughout the procedure. Coronary angiography typically costs from $2000 to $3500, depending partly on whether it is done on an inpatient or outpatient basis. The American Heart Association estimates that 958,000 procedures were performed during 1989.

Other Tests

Echocardiography is a procedure that uses ultrasound to visualize the heart. It is used to gather information about the functioning of heart valves and the structure and functioning of the heart muscle.[49] Images are observed on a screen and photographed for later study. Cardiac catheterization can also be used to measure blood flow within the heart, which is useful for evaluating the structure and function of heart valves. Much research is being done on magnetic resonance imaging (MRI) and other imaging procedures for evaluating cardiac function. (See Chapter 6 for information about ultrasound and MRI tests.)

Surgery to Restore Blood Flow

The heart normally receives its blood supply from the coronary arteries, which connect from the aorta to the heart muscle. If these become clogged near their origin but are open beyond that point, it may be possible to restore the blood supply with a surgical procedure.

Coronary Bypass

In bypass surgery, one or more grafts are connected from the aorta to the unblocked portions of the coronary arteries. The grafts are obtained from the patient's mammary artery (which supplies a portion of the chest wall but is not vital to the area) and/or saphenous veins, which serve the lower part of each leg. During the operation, the patient's heart is stopped so the grafts can be sewn in place while circulation is maintained through a heart-lung machine. If no complications occur, most patients will be discharged from the hospital in 7 to 10 days and recuperate at home for a few months. Bypass surgery can provide dramatic relief for many people with angina and may also be used to restore blood flow following coronary thrombosis. A hospital stay that includes bypass surgery typically costs $30,000 to $35,000. A recent study of 3055 patients at five medical centers found that the inhospital mortality rate for coronary bypass surgery was 3.2% for men and 7.3% for women.[50]

In properly selected patients, bypass surgery can prolong life, particularly for those who are able to reduce their risk factors.[51] There has, however, been considerable controversy over whether the operation is advantageous for people with coronary artery disease who have mild symptoms that can be controlled with drug therapy.[51a] Additional studies are needed to answer this question.

Angioplasty

During the past few years there has been extraordinary progress in the development of instruments and procedures that can unclog arteries from within.

In balloon angioplasty—the medical term for which is percutaneous transluminal angioplasty (PCTA)—a very thin wire is placed into the femoral artery in the thigh and threaded into a coronary artery while the cardiologist watches the wire's progress on an x-ray monitor. Then a guide catheter, a thin, flexible tube about the diameter of a pencil, is passed over the wire and a second catheter tipped with a deflated balloon is threaded through the guide catheter. When the balloon reaches the blockage, it is inflated to compress atherosclerotic plaque against the inner artery walls. The balloon is then deflated and withdrawn. Balloon angioplasty is also used to open arteries in the kidneys, arms, and legs.

The AtheroCath is a motorized device that contains a scraper that shaves plaque from the blocked area and stores it near the tip of the device so it can be removed from the body. It is threaded into the heart vessels through a femoral artery. The device is unsuitable for highly curving vessels or for long segments of plaque.

The AIS Excimer Laser Angioplasty System is a device that can open long segments of coronary artery blockage by vaporizing plaque and may be used together with balloon angioplasty.

Various other devices have FDA approval for unclogging arteries in the legs. These include motorized devices that cut, drill, or pulverize plaque, and laser devices that vaporize it.[52] In some cases a brace (stent) is left within the artery to maintain its patency. The National Heart, Lung, and Blood Institute is collecting long-term data on the safety and effectiveness of these techniques to develop guidelines for their use.

In many cases, angioplasty provides an alternative to coronary bypass surgery.[51a] It costs much less, requires a shorter hospital stay, and has a short recovery period, but has a much higher likelihood of reclogging. (The restenosis rate for angioplasty is in the range of 20% to 45%.) Major studies comparing these two approaches are under way.

The use of bypass surgery and angioplasty has

CONSUMER TIP

Advice to Consumers

Atherosclerosis and high blood pressure develop silently for many years before causing trouble. The difficulty they cause can be prevented or minimized by the following consumer actions:

1. Know the risk factors for atherosclerosis and hypertension and take steps to minimize them. Figure 16-2 provides a convenient summary and checklist for evaluating the status of your risk factors.
2. Do not smoke cigarettes. Smokers develop a much higher incidence of heart disease, stroke, and many cancers.
3. Maintain reasonable weight. Be particularly concerned about developing fatty deposits around the waist (see discussion of waist-hip ratio in Chapter 14).
4. Follow the dietary guidelines in Chapter 12. Eat a balanced diet that is low in fat, particularly saturated fat, adequate in fiber, and moderate sodium. This will not only help prevent cardiovascular disease but may help prevent certain cancers as well.
5. Engage in regular aerobic exercise as outlined in Chapter 15. Exercise can lower total cholesterol and LDL and raise HDL.
6. Have your blood pressure checked at least once a year and take appropriate action if it becomes elevated.
7. Know your "cholesterol number." Have your level checked through a doctor's office and take appropriate action according to the protocols of the National Cholesterol Education Program. If your cholesterol level is high or borderline high, seek expert guidance from a physician who maintains an interest in this subject and pays close attention to recent developments. Usually this can be determined by asking about the physician's level of interest.
8. Do not consume unproven dietary supplements such as fish oil or beta-carotene, but eat fish once or twice a week and have adequate amounts of fruits, vegetables, and whole-grain foods in your diet.
9. If you develop significant cardiovascular disease, seek help from a cardiologist.
10. If you require an invasive diagnostic procedure (such as angiography) or cardiac surgery, select a cardiologist or surgeon who has had adequate experience and works in an up-to-date hospital facility.

risen rapidly during the past 10 years. About 350,000 of each were performed during 1991. Serious questions have been raised about whether these procedures are performed too frequently.[53,54] These questions have no simple answers. Although general guidelines have been developed by several organizations, considerably more research is needed to clarify what is most appropriate in individual cases.

REHABILITATION PROGRAMS

Following cardiac surgery or recovery from a heart attack it is important to take steps to restore function and prevent recurrence. Lack of activity, lack of sleep, medication, the surgery itself, and the stress of being ill can leave patients feeling drained, physically and emotionally. Many hospitals and clinics have established programs to help restore the ability to function. These programs provide gradually escalated exercise, dietary counseling, and attention to the individual's risk factors.[55] A cardiologist performs a stress test to determine the individual's exercise tolerance and prescribes an exercise program. The exercise is then carried out several times a week while the patient is monitored by a specially trained nurse. The patient wears a device that broadcasts an electrocardiogram to an oscillograph observed by the nurse. If the patient's pulse rises too high or the ECG shows signs that the heart is straining, the patient is advised to slow down or stop. Patients are taught how to monitor their pulse and have the opportunity to use many types of exercise equipment. Most programs in-

IT'S YOUR DECISION

At your doctor's suggestion, you have a blood cholesterol test, which shows a total cholesterol level of 220 mg/dl. You obtain a lipid profile 2 weeks later, which shows an LDL level of 135 and an HDL of 40. The doctor says that these levels suggest that your risk of a heart attack is above average. What actions should you consider?

volve three sessions a week for 12 weeks. After that, if all goes well, the patient has learned how to perform heart-strengthening aerobic exercise and will continue a home program indefinitely.

SUMMARY

Cardiovascular diseases are the leading cause of illness and death in the United States. The majority of cases stem from atherosclerosis, a condition in which cholesterol, fat, and fibrous tissue build up in the walls of large and medium-sized arteries. The "risk factors" for coronary heart disease are heredity, being male, advancing age, cigarette smoking, high blood pressure, diabetes, obesity, lack of physical activity, and abnormal blood cholesterol levels. The more risk factors a person has, the greater the risk of developing heart disease. Heredity, gender, and age cannot be controlled, but the other risk factors can be influenced by the individual's behavior.

Medical authorities recommend that all adults have their blood cholesterol and blood pressure checked and take action if abnormal elevations are found. The cornerstone of a cholesterol-reduction program is a balanced, low-fat, high-fiber diet plus regular aerobic exercise. These measures may also be effective in lowering high blood pressure. If nondrug methods are insufficient, drug therapy may be advisable—often on a lifetime basis.

Great progress has been made in both medical and surgical treatment of cardiovascular disease. More research is needed to evaluate newer techniques. If problems arise, expert guidance should be sought from a physician who is well trained and pays close attention to recent developments.

DISCUSSION QUESTIONS

1. Which types of cardiovascular disease are most prevalent?
2. Define atherosclerosis and coronary heart disease.
3. Identify and discuss the risk factors for coronary heart disease. Which ones can consumers modify?
4. How are cholesterol, LDL, and HDL related to heart attack risk?
5. What guidelines for blood cholesterol evaluation have been established by the National Cholesterol Education Program? What should consumers do if their total or LDL-cholesterol levels are in borderline or high-risk ranges?
6. What problems exist regarding the accuracy of cholesterol screening tests? What steps can consumers take to protect themselves against inaccurate test results?
7. What are the relationships between blood cholesterol levels and one's intake of fats and cholesterol?
8. What are the NCEP dietary guidelines for cholesterol control? What practical steps can consumers take to implement these guidelines?
9. What oils and spreads are lowest in the fats that contribute most to raising blood cholesterol levels?
10. What steps can consumers take to determine how much fat and saturated fat their diet contains?
11. What role does soluble fiber play in cholesterol control? What foods are high in soluble fiber?
12. What evidence exists that strict cholesterol control can cause coronary atherosclerosis to regress?
13. What is the Pritikin diet? Discuss the claims made for it and the evidence upon which they are based.
14. What types of misleading claims have been made in food advertising related to the fat and cholesterol content of foods? How can consumers avoid being misled?
15. Discuss the use of cholesterol-lowering drugs and the validity of claims made for nutritional supplement products claims to be helpful.
16. What is high blood pressure? How are abnormal levels classified?
17. Identify and discuss the risk factors for stroke.
18. Discuss drug and nondrug approaches to the treatment of high blood pressure.

19. Briefly discuss the symptoms and hospital treatment of heart attacks.
20. Discuss the use of electrocardiograms, stress tests, coronary angiography, and other imaging procedures used for the diagnosis of heart disease.
21. Discuss coronary bypass and angioplasty.
22. Briefly describe the elements of a cardiac rehabilitation program.
23. Summarize and discuss consumer strategies for preventing coronary heart disease and high blood pressure.
24. Summarize and discuss consumer strategies for obtaining professional help and making appropriate decisions regarding treatment options for cardiovascular disease.

REFERENCES

*1. American Heart Association: 1992 Heart and stroke facts, Dallas, 1991, The Association.

*1a. American Heart Association: Silent epidemic: the truth about women and heart disease, Dallas, 1989, The Association.

2. Multiple Risk Factor Intervention Trial Research Group: Multiple risk factor intervention trial: risk factor changes and mortality results, JAMA 248:1465-1477, 1982.

*3. Multiple Risk Factor Intervention Trial Research Group: Mortality rates after 10.5 years for participants in the Multiple Risk Factor Intervention Trial, JAMA 263:1795-1801, 1990.

4. Castelli WP et al: Incidence of coronary heart disease and lipoprotein cholesterol levels—the Framingham Study, JAMA 256:2835-2838, 1986.

5. Rader DJ and Brewer HB: Lipoprotein(a):clinical approach to a unique atherogenic lipoprotein, JAMA 267:1109-1112, 1992.

6. Anderson KM et al: Cholesterol and mortality: 30 years of follow-up from the Framingham Study, JAMA 257:2176-2180, 1987.

7. Samuelson O et al: Cardiovascular morbidity in relation to change in blood pressure and serum cholesterol levels in treated hypertension, JAMA 258:1768-1776, 1987.

8. Gotto AM Jr et al: The cholesterol facts—a joint statement by the American Heart Association and the National Heart, Lung, and Blood Institute, Dallas, 1990, American Heart Association.

9. Lipid Clinics Research Program: The Lipid Research Clinics Coronary Primary Prevention Trial results. I. Reduction in incidence of coronary artery disease. II. The relationship of reduction in incidence of coronary heart disease to cholesterol lowering, JAMA 251:351-374, 1984.

10. National Institutes of Health: Report of the expert panel on blood cholesterol levels in children and adolescents, Bethesda, 1991, The Institutes.

11. Rapaport E et al: Consensus Development Conference Statement: triglyceride, high density lipoprotein, and coronary heart disease, Bethesda, 1992, National Institutes of Health.

12. Heinz A: Facts and myths about coronary artery disease—a consumer guide. New York, 1989, American Council on Science and Health.

*13. Forget about cholesterol? Consumer Reports 55:152-157, 1990.

14. A woman's heart, Harvard Heart Letter 17(6):5-7, 1992.

15. Cooper GR et al: Blood lipid measurements: variations and practical utility, JAMA 267:1652-1660, 1992.

*16. What's your cholesterol? You need to understand your cholesterol profile to know what to do about it, Consumer Reports on Health 3:81-83, 1991.

*17. Eating to lower your high blood cholesterol, NIH publication no. 89-2920, June 1989. Washington, DC, 1989, Supt of Documents. Single copies available free of charge from National Cholesterol Education Program, National Heart, Lung, and Blood Institute, C-200, Bethesda, MD 20892.

18. USDA: Nutritive value of foods, Home and Garden Bulletin No. 72, is available for $2.75 from the Supt. of Documents, US Govt Printing Office, Washington, DC 20402.

*19. Stare F, Aronson V, and Barrett S: Your guide to good nutrition, Buffalo, NY, 1991, Prometheus Books.

*20. Kantor MA: Nutrition, cholesterol and heart disease. Part V. Dietary modification, Nutrition Forum 6:33-37, 1989.

21. Anderson JW et al: Hypocholesterolemic effects of oat-bran or bean intake for hypercholesterolemic men, Am J Clin Nutr 40:1146-1155, 1984.

22. Bell LP et al: Cholesterol-lowering effects of psyllium hydrophilic mucilloid—adjunct therapy to a prudent diet for patients with mild to moderate hypercholesterolemia, JAMA 261:3419-3423, 1989.

*23. Davidson MH et al: The hypocholesterolemic effects of b-glucan in oatmeal and oat bran, JAMA 265:1833-1839, 1991.

24. Cashin-Hemphill LC et al. Beneficial effects of colestipol-niacin on coronary atherosclerosis. A 4-year follow-up, JAMA 264:3013-3017, 1990.

25. Blankenhorn DH et al: The influence of diet on the appearance of new lesions in human coronary arteries, JAMA 263:1646-1652, 1990.

26. Brown G et al: Regression of coronary artery disease as a result of intensive lipid-lowering therapy in men with high levels of apolipoprotein B, N Engl J Med 323:1289-1298, 1990.

*27. Ornish D et al: Can lifestyle changes reverse coronary heart disease? Lancet 336:129-133, 1990.

28. Gould KL and Ornish D et al. Improved stenosis geometry by quantitative coronary arteriography after vigorous risk factor modification, Am J Cardiol 69:845-853, 1992.

29. Pritikin R: The new Pritikin Program: the easy and delicious way to shed fat, lower your cholesterol, and stay fit, New York, 1990, Simon & Schuster.

*30. New York City Department of Consumer Affairs: Supermarket survey on misleading cholesterol claims. New York, 1991, The Department.

31. Hodes HN: Acute hepatic failure associated with low-dose sustained-release niacin, JAMA 264:181, 1990.

*Recommended reading

32. Henkin Y: Rechallenge with crystalline niacin after drug-induced hepatitis from sustained-release niacin, JAMA 264:241-3, 1990.
*33. Etchason JA et al: Niacin-induced hepatitis: a potential side effect with low-dose time-release niacin, Mayo Clin Proc 66:23-28, 1991.
34. Goldfinger SE: Good for what ails you? Harvard Health Letter 16(10):1-2, 1991.
*35. Kwiterovich P: Beyond cholesterol—the Johns Hopkins complete guide for avoiding heart disease, Baltimore, 1989, The Johns Hopkins University Press.
36. Knuiman A et al: Lecithin intake and serum cholesterol, Am J Clin Nutr 49:266-268, 1989.
37. A vitamin cocktail for cholesterol? Consumer Reports 55:141, 1990.
38. Gaziano MJ and Hennekens CH: A new look at what can unclog your arteries, Executive Health Report 27(8):1, 4-6, 1991.
*39. Farley D: High blood pressure: controlling the silent killer, FDA Consumer 25(10):28-33, 1991.
40. Stamler R et al: Primary prevention of hypertension by nutritional-hygienic means. Final report of a randomized, controlled trial, JAMA 262:1801-1807, 1989.
*41. Systolic hypertension in the elderly, Harvard Heart Letter 2(2):3-7, 1991.
42. Weinberger MH et al: Dietary sodium restriction as adjunctive treatment of hypertension, JAMA 259:2561-2565, 1988.
*43. Lowering blood pressure without drugs, Harvard Heart Letter 2(9):1-5, 1992.
*44. How to lower blood pressure, Consumer Reports 57:300-302, 1992.
45. Hypertension Prevention Collaborative Research Group: The effects of nonpharmacologic interventions on blood pressure of persons with high normal levels, JAMA 267:1213-1220, 1992.
46. ACE inhibitors for hypertension, Harvard Heart Letter 2(6):5-8, 1992.
47. Muntzel M and Drüeke T: A comprehensive review of the salt and blood pressure relationship, Am J Hypertens 5:1S-42S, 1992.
*48. What is an exercise stress test? The Johns Hopkins Medical Letter, Health After 50 3(10):6-7, 1991.
49. Feigenbaum H et al: Tracking the advances in echocardiography, Patient Care, pp 14-45, Mar 15, 1991.
50. O'Connor GT et al: A regional prospective study of in-hospital mortality associated with coronary artery bypass grafting, JAMA 266:803-809, 1991.
*51. Coronary artery bypass surgery today, Harvard Heart Letter 2(7):1-7, 1992.
51a. Bypass surgery. Who really needs it? Consumer Reports on Health 4(7):49-52, 1992.
*52. Farley D: Balloons, lasers and scrapers: help for hearts and blood vessels, FDA consumer 25(3):22-27, 1991.
53. Bypass surgery: making the right choice, Health After 50 3(11):4-5, 1992.
54. Pfeiffer N: The great cardiology debate: angioplasty, Medical World News, pp 28-30, Jan 1992.
55. Zoler ML: Rehabilitation—a boon of the thrombolytic era. Medical World News, pp 35-44, Mar 13, 1989.

CHAPTER SEVENTEEN

ARTHRITIS

"Very well, Mrs. Mooney—then *don't* stop wearing your copper bracelet."

(Reprinted with permission from *Resident & Staff Physician* © [November 1988] by Romaine Pierson Publishers, Inc.)

For some curious reason, the idea lingers that "nothing can be done for arthritis." The very opposite is true. Probably more progress has been made in the fight against arthritis than in the struggle against our other major diseases—cancer, heart disease, and diabetes.

JAMES F. FRIES, M.D.[1]

One of the most striking features of most forms of arthritis is their characteristic flares and periods of lesser disease activity. . . .Patients engaging in alternative treatments frequently do not understand that a "miraculous cure" may simply be a spontaneous remission.

FELIX FERNANDEZ-MADRID, M.D., PH.D.[2]

CONSUMER DECISION

What information is necessary to make intelligent decisions about treatments for arthritis?

When should a physician be consulted?

Where can reliable information about arthritis be obtained?

Arthritis, sometimes referred to as rheumatism, is a general term applied to more than a hundred different conditions characterized by aches and pains of joints, muscles, and/or fibrous tissues. Many forms of arthritis cause considerable suffering and expense. Regardless of the type, early diagnosis and treatment are likely to produce the most favorable results.

People with arthritis often turn to quackery because of fear, loss of hope, inadequate information, and other psychosocial factors. This chapter focuses on the most common forms of arthritis, how they are treated properly and improperly, why patients turn to quackery, and sources of reliable information.

TYPES OF ARTHRITIS

The Arthritis Foundation estimates that the various forms of arthritis affect more than 37 million Americans, several million of whom are significantly disabled. Some forms of arthritis are short-lived and curable, while others are chronic. The most common forms of chronic arthritis are osteoarthritis, rheumatoid arthritis, gout, and ankylosing spondylitis.[3]

Osteoarthritis, the most widespread type of arthritis, is a degenerative disease of the joints. Although sometimes capable of causing acute inflammation, it is most commonly a "wear-and-tear" disease involving degeneration of joint linings and formation of bony spurs within various joints. Most people over 60 years of age have this affliction to some extent, with approximately 16 million sufferers requiring medical care. The main goal of treatment is to relieve pain.

Rheumatoid arthritis is an inflammatory disease that involves episodes of pain and swelling, and in some cases deformity and "freezing" of joints, especially the knuckles and middle joints of the fingers. At least 2 million Americans are afflicted. The disease usually starts between the ages of 20 and 45, affecting about three times as many women as men, but it can occur at any age. *Juvenile rheumatoid arthritis*, a similar condition, affects about 250,000 children and adolescents. The goals of treatment are to reduce pain and inflammation, maintain joint mobility, and prevent deformity.

Gout is a metabolic disorder that affects about 1 million Americans, the majority of whom are men. The inflammation of acute gout commonly strikes the big toe, causing pain and swelling, but it can also begin in the knee, ankle, or other joint. In chronic gout, a buildup of uric acid crystals in various joints can result in disfigurement and disability. The course of gout can vary from a few attacks to a progressive disease that begins at puberty and, if untreated, can disable its host by the age of 40. Fortunately, effective treatment can relieve or prevent attacks and virtually eliminate the danger of permanent disability.

Ankylosing spondylitis is a chronic inflammatory disease of the spine that can also attack the hips and shoulders. It affects men considerably more often than women, usually starting in adolescence or the early twenties. As it progresses, calcium is laid down within the joints of the spine, resulting in stiffness, rigidity, and sometimes deformity of the back. The main goals of treatment are maintenance of spinal mobility and retention of muscle strength.

SCIENTIFIC TREATMENT METHODS

Most patients with chronic forms of arthritis can be helped to lead a productive life if their condition is properly diagnosed and treated. In many cases treatment can help relieve the discomfort and maintain or restore joint function. Medications for gout control the abnormal metabolism of uric acid. The other conditions discussed previously, whose causes are unknown, are treated with drugs, rest, exercise, physical therapy, surgery, and various adaptive devices.

Oral Drugs

A variety of medications can be used to relieve pain and counter inflammation. Finding the best one for an individual patient can be a process of trial and error. Generally, the safest drugs that are likely to help are tried first. Several drugs may be evaluated in varying doses until the best one is found.

The first lines of pharmacologic defense against arthritis are the nonsteroidal anti-inflammatory drugs (NSAIDs), of which aspirin is the most frequently prescribed. Higher dosages of aspirin are needed to reduce inflammation than to relieve pain. For best results, the use of aspirin to treat arthritis should be supervised by a physician. People vary in their tolerance for aspirin, and some cannot take it at all. Large amounts (commonly 10 to 15 5-grain tablets daily) may cause stomach irritation and gastrointestinal bleeding, which can be mild or severe. Other common side effects include ringing in the ears and temporary hearing loss. To control such effects, physicians may reduce the dosage, prescribe aspirin combined with antacid or enteric-coated aspirin (for example, Ecotrin), or try other salicylate drugs similar to aspirin. Further comments on nonprescription pain relievers will be found later in this chapter and in Chapter 20.

Other NSAIDs offer alternative individualized therapy. These drugs include ibuprofen (Motrin), naproxen (Naprosyn), diclofenac (Voltarin), and about a dozen others. In appropriate dosage, they are comparable to aspirin in anti-inflammatory effect, and for some patients the side effects seem milder than those from high doses of aspirin—though they can cause serious gastrointestinal conditions such as bleeding and stomach perforation. All are far more expensive than aspirin, and all but ibuprofen (in low dosage) require a doctor's prescription.

Aspirin and other NSAIDs are considered the safest drugs for long-term treatment. If a patient does not respond adequately, however, other drugs may be used. All involve a greater risk of serious side effects than the NSAIDs, but they can be helpful to patients who might not otherwise obtain relief.

Drug therapy for rheumatoid arthritis has been evolving rapidly. Gold salts and penicillamine have been joined by hydroxychloroquine (an antimalarial drug), methotrexate (a chemotherapeutic agent used against cancer), sulfasalazine (a drug used for treating inflammatory bowel disease), azathioprine and cyclophosphamide (immunosuppressive drugs), and a host of other "second-line" drugs. Unlike aspirin and other NSAIDs, these drugs do not provide immediate pain relief, but they may delay progression of the disease.

Cortisone-related steroids, such as prednisone, are another class of drugs that must be used with caution. Although they can provide dramatic relief of pain and swelling in inflamed joints, their numerous side effects limit their usefulness in prolonged therapy. Unlike gold salts and penicillamine, which can be well tolerated by some patients for years, steroids eventually produce serious side effects in all patients during extended therapy, unless given in very low dosage. Accordingly, in certain cases when oral steroids are the only alternative, they are generally used in the smallest amounts that will improve symptoms, sometimes on an every-other-day basis.

Intra-articular Drugs

When only one or two joints are involved, injection of a steroid drug into the affected joints can provide considerable relief. This technique should be used sparingly, however, because repeated injections can cause cartilage degeneration, rendering the joint useless.

Physical Treatment Measures

Rest is usually important during acute flare-ups. Exercise is helpful to prevent or relieve pain and to maintain joint flexibility and muscle strength. Overweight individuals with arthritis of the legs can benefit from weight reduction. Splinting of affected joints, particularly the fingers, can help in some cases of rheumatoid arthritis.

Physical therapy to relieve pain can include external application of heat by showers, hot or cold packs, whirlpool baths, diathermy, or paraffin baths. Range-of-motion exercises may be included as part of the physical therapy program. Individual joints are sometimes rested in removable, lightweight splints that help lessen inflammation and keep the joint in a normal-use position to protect it against muscle flexion deformities (contractures) that might lead to permanent disfigurement. Splints can also be used to help straighten out a joint that has become fixed in a flexed position. The splints usually are adjusted every few days to move the joint toward the desired position.

Once inflammation and pain subside, more emphasis is placed on exercise. For patients with arthritis, exercise does not mean engaging in athletics or similarly strenuous actitivies. It involves putting joints gently through their full range of motion every day. This helps maintain normal joint movement and helps strengthen muscles that may have been weakened by inactivity. As joint function improves, the exercises may be done against slight resistance, provided there is no pain. Generally, each patient requires an individually prescribed program of exercises.

Adaptive devices include braces to relieve strain on painful body parts and various self-help gadgets to enhance restricted function.

Surgery

Various surgical procedures may relieve the pain of severely arthritic joints, particularly hip and knee joints. The operations include:

Arthroplasty: Reconstruction of a diseased joint using a patient's own tissue

Arthrodesis: Fusion of a diseased joint to relieve pain

Osteotomy: Separation or cutting of a joint that has become fused or has shifted to an abnormal position

Joint replacement: Synthetic materials can be used to replace or rebuild severely afflicted joints

Hundreds of thousands of individuals have undergone satisfactory replacement of hip joints with various ball-and-socket devices. Knee joints are commonly replaced, and operations are sometimes done to replace the joints of the ankles, hands, wrists, and elbows.[4]

Competent Help is Essential

Despite medical advances, treatment of arthritis often can be frustrating to both doctor and patient. Early diagnosis and treatment offer the best results. There are about 2500 arthritis specialists (rheumatologists); far less than are needed to provide optimal care for the huge number of people with arthritis. Thus, most patients must be cared for by their family doctor. According to Arthritis Foundation consultant Diana Benzaia:[5]

> Some family doctors provide good care. Others are sincere in their wish to help but not up-to-date in their knowledge of arthritis treatment . . . . The untrained doctor may sympathize with the patient, shrug his shoulders, indicate that "nothing much can be done," and recommended aspirin to relieve pain. You can't call this approach quackery, but it often drives sufferers to quacks.

Referral to a rheumatologist can be made by one's personal physician or a local chapter of the Arthritis Foundation.

The Patient's Role

Fries[1] states that successful management of arthritis depends upon the afflicted individual as much as it does on the doctor. He states that people with arthritis must decide:

1. How much activity to undertake
2. Whether to see a doctor, and when
3. What kind of doctor to see
4. When to ask for a second opinion
5. Whether to accept the medical advice offered
6. Whether to follow a treatment program offered
7. Whether to seek a quack cure or believe a sensational tabloid story

Fries recommends that a doctor be consulted quickly if joint pain is severe and accompanied by fever or swelling of one or two joints (a possible sign of gout), or if there is inability to use a joint, severe pain from a recent injury, or numbness or tingling related to the joint pain. He also suggests that an appointment should be made for other joint symptoms that have persisted for more than 6 weeks.

Nonprescription Remedies for Arthritis

Widely advertised nonprescription "arthritis pain relievers" should be viewed with skepticism by consumers. Most contain either aspirin, acetaminophen, or ibuprofen, which can relieve pain. But the amounts they contain and the cost per dose are higher than necessary for the purpose. Moreover, acetaminophen has no anti-inflammatory action, so its usefulness for arthritis patients is quite limited. Despite the wide use of salicylates to relieve rheumatic symptoms and related muscular discomfort, an FDA expert panel has advised that nonprescription drugs should not be labeled for this purpose. The panel has recommended that claims such as "for temporary relief of minor arthritic and rheumatic aches and pains" should be forbidden because salicylates act on two levels, depending on dosage. Lower dosages—up to 4000 mg of aspirin daily—can be taken safely for a limited time as self-medication for pain relief and possibly for some limited effect on inflammation. But 5300 mg daily (16 5-grain tablets), a more effective anti-inflammatory dosage, is toxic for some people and should be taken only under close medical supervision.[6]

Cost can be quite significant for patients with arthritis who are taking large amounts of aspirin. For this reason the Arthritis Foundation has suggested that such individuals purchase 5-grain tablets in bottles of 1000. Nonadvertised brands cost the least.

Like aspirin, ibuprofen can be effective against both pain and inflammation. However, the amount contained in the over-the-counter (OTC) products Nuprin and Advil may be too low for optimal results. For this reason ibuprofen should not be used for arthritis without instructions from a physician.

External Analgesics

Liniments, rubs, poultices, plasters, and balms—sometimes referred to as external analgesics—are frequently promoted for the relief of aches and pains due to arthritis. These products depend on one or more skin irritants for their effects. They mildly stimulate nerve endings in the skin, producing warmth, coolness, or pain, which can block or distract attention from more bothersome, deep-seated muscular pains. In addition, the rubbing used to apply these products may loosen tight muscles. Doctors today rarely recommended these remedies, but they have been a part of traditional medical practice and folk healing for thousands of years.

According to Zimmerman,[6] few scientific studies of these external analgesics were conducted; the expert FDA panel assessing their efficacy judged them with less rigorous standards than were applied to other classes of drugs in the FDA OTC drug-review process (described in Chapters 20 and 27). The panel took into account popular appeal, indicated by the amounts sold, as one criterion of product effectiveness, and also noted that complaints have been rare and problems mild. The preferred ingredient is methyl salicylate (oil of wintergreen), found in such products as Gordogesic Cream, Analgesic Balm, Ben-Gay Original Ointment, and Ben-Gay Lotion.

Medical consultants for both the FDA and Consumers Union have warned against the indiscriminate use of external analgesics.[7] Their chemicals can be absorbed through the skin and result in systemic toxicity. Absorption is speeded up if the drug is applied to mucous membranes or cut or inflamed skin. Heating pads should never be used with these products because burns and blistering may result.

Susceptibility to Quackery

As with many chronic diseases, the major forms of arthritis are subject to periods of spontaneous remission. These conditions may flare up unexpectedly for no apparent reason and then suddenly subside, leaving the individual free of pain for days, weeks, or even months. This can make it difficult for individuals to judge the efficacy of treatment measures—particularly in the short run. If a spontaneous remission takes place following use of an unorthodox measure (such as wearing a copper bracelet), while consuming a particular food, or visiting an unorthodox practitioner, the individual may incorrectly conclude that the measure was effective. The Arthritis Foundation believes that far more money is spent on arthritis quackery than for arthritis research.

A 1968 study by the FDA summarizes why patients with arthritic ailments are especially susceptible to quackery:[8]

1. Arthritis is usually a chronic ailment for which there is no cure.
2. Many people do not know how to obtain the best possible help for their condition. Even when they do, treatment may not be effective.
3. Arthritis frequently causes great discomfort; afflicted people often fear that their condition will get worse and affect their ability to function.
4. Faced with frustration and disappointment, they may lose faith in orthodox treatment and grasp at any "miracle" they hear about.

A 1986 FDA survey found that 24% of people with arthritis considered their condition serious or very serious, 18% said that they almost always had a signficant amount of pain, and 22% said that their condition frequently caused significant pain. About one out of three said they would be willing to try anything for their condition, even if it sounds silly or has a small probability of success. About the same percentage said that they had tried at least one method considered questionable by the survey's designers. The most frequently tried methods were vitamins (17%), vibrators (14%), special diets (12%), chiropractic (12%), alfalfa tablets (9%), copper bracelets (9%), honey/vinegar (8%), and cod liver or fish oil (8%).[9]

Unorthodox Treatment Methods

Unorthodox methods include mechanical devices, environmental methods, fad diets, dietary supplements, acupuncture, and medications. They may be promoted through advertisements, books, newspaper and magazine articles, and word-of-mouth. Some are available from questionable practitioners

Consumer Tip

The Arthritis Foundation[10] defines unproven remedies as "treatments that have not shown that they work or are safe." It advises consumers to suspect an unproven remedy if it has any of the following characteristics:

Claimed to work for all types of arthritis
Uses only case histories or testimonials as proof
Only one study is cited as proof that it works
Cited studies that have no control group
Contents are not identified
Has no warnings about side effects
Described as harmless or natural
Claimed to be based on a secret formula
Available from only one source
Promoted only through the media, books, or mail-order

and clinics. Some cause no direct harm but may result in harmful delay in seeking appropriate treatment. Others, however, can result in severe injury or even death. Quackery tends to keep up with the times by developing methods whose supposed actions are based on current scientific discoveries. For example, after astronauts reached the moon, "moondust" was promoted as an arthritis cure. According to Benzaia,[5] gadgets used to be the mainstay of arthritis quackery, but in recent years the emphasis has been on drugs and dietary supplements.

Dr. Cody R. Wasner of the University of Alabama reported that 92 of 98 arthritis patients (94%) interviewed in detail had tried at least one unorthodox remedy.[11] The mean number tried was 3.7, the maximum 13. Dr. Jeffrey Brown of Stanford Medical Center, CA, reported that 123 of 384 patients (32%) who were surveyed by questionnaire had tried such remedies.[11]

Dubious Devices

Devices cannot cure any form of arthritis. Vibrators and whirlpool baths are commonly sold with exaggerated claims. Vibrators may provide some relief of muscle pain caused by overexertion or fatigue and may have a temporary relaxant effect on some muscle tension, but they can sometimes do serious harm by increasing joint inflammation. Many whirlpool baths for self-use are no more effective than simple hot baths. Therefore no such device should be purchased without consulting one's physician.[5]

According to modern folklore, copper bracelets worn on both wrists can set up "curative circuits." To avoid prosecution for fraud, such bracelets are usually advertised as costume jewelry (with no health claims), assuming that readers of the ads are sufficiently familiar with the claims that they will try the product.

The following quack gadgets marketed as arthritis cures have been seized by the FDA and removed from the market:

The Micro-Dynameter, a simple galvanometer made into a complicated-looking box with various dials and wires, was represented as capable of diagnosing and treating virtually all diseases by electronic means.[12] This device was one of many designed by Dr. Albert Abrams, who was considered by the AMA to have been "the dean of gadget quacks."

The Pulse-A-Rhythm, a vibrating mattress, was judged by the FDA to be dangerous and ineffective for people in acute phases of rheumatoid arthritis.[13]

The Vrilium Tube, promoted with supposed radioactive healing powers, was a brass tube about 2 inches long that contained barium chloride. It cost only a few cents to manufacture but was sold for hundreds of dollars.[5]

The Solarama Board (also known as the Earth Board or Vitalator), when placed under the afflicted person's mattress at night, supposedly released curative "free electrons."

The Oxydonor and the *Inducto-Scope* are illustrated in Figure 17-1.

Environmental Approaches

Claims that certain environments offer hope for cure induce many people to spend large sums of money traveling to receive supposedly helpful treatments.

The false claim that radon gas can cure arthritis brought a complaint of misrepresentation against the Elkhorn Mining Company, Boulder, Colorado, by the FTC. People with various diseases, especially arthritis, were taken into an abandoned uranium mine for a fee, supposedly to breathe helpful radioactive rays. The company also claimed falsely that radon gas stimulated the production of ACTH and hydrocortisone, which were helpful in curing arthritis.[14] According to Benazia:[5] "The radiation

facts, fantasies, treatments . . . and future developments in arthritis

INDUCTO-SCOPE

This device (seized by the U.S. Food and Drug Administration), was supposed to "cure" arthritis through "magnetic induction" when the rings were placed over afflicted areas and the plug inserted into a wall socket. Not only was this bizarre device of no value to the sufferer, it exposed him to the hazard of electric shock.

Still being huckstered are pads, pillows, and bags filled with radioactive ore for chronic diseases such as arthritis, rheumatism. An aspirin tablet would do more good!

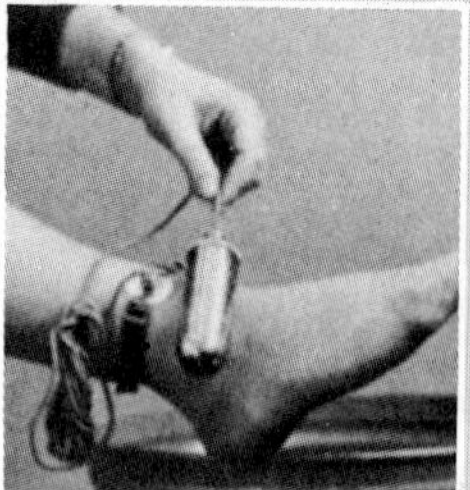

OXYDONOR

The manufacturer claimed this gadget would "reverse the death process into the life process" and "cure" arthritis and rheumatism. The victim was directed to clip the metal disk to his ankle and immerse the cylinder in water—the colder the better. Result: zero. The cost of this phony device: $30.

COPPER JEWELRY

Copper bracelets are just one of the many metal jewelry items foisted on arthritics by deceitful promoters. Greatest benefits are supposedly obtained by wearing one on each wrist to set up a so-called "curative circuit." The theory is hokum in the extreme, but such sales are widespread among desperate arthritis sufferers.

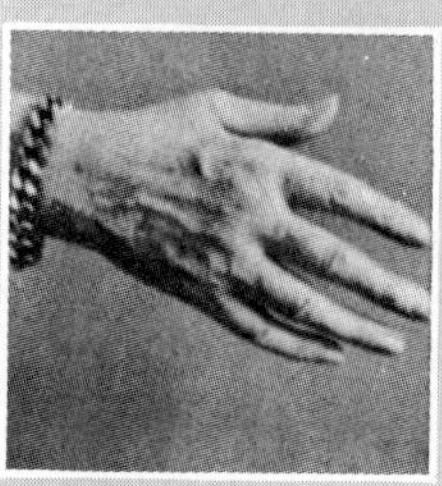

FIGURE 17-1.

level in the mine is so low that it can have no actual effect on the body—which is fortunate—because high levels of radiation can increase people's chances of developing cancer."

Real estate promoters sometimes capitalize on the hope that a warm climate will help people afflicted with arthritis. Noting that rheumatologists in states like Arizona have thriving practices, Benzaia attributes the "weather myth" of arthritis to evidence that some people feel worse when barometric pressure drops. While a stable climate may help some people feel better, weather conditions are never completely stable—nor does weather affect the course of arthritis.

Dietary Methods

The Arthritis Foundation states that no special food, diet, or food supplement can cure arthritis. Gout is partially related to diet, but even the primary treatment is medication rather than diet. The Foundation advises people to beware of claims that any food or food substance can help arthritis. Raw foods, "natural foods," heated milk, honey and vinegar, and alfalfa have been widely promoted as helpful in treating arthritis.

According to an Arthritis Foundation official, any improvement following elimination of the food is probably the result of a placebo effect. The Foundation recommends that rheumatoid arthritis patients who believe their disease is worsened by a food should consult their physicians and avoid that food under medical supervision to see whether any improvement results.

Panush[15] has concluded that a small number (fewer than 5%) of individuals suffering from rheumatoid arthritis may improve after elimination from their diet of a specific food that appears to aggravate their condition. Jarvis reached a similar conclusion after reviewing double-blind studies conducted before 1989.[16]

In 1991 a Norwegian research team reported that a small group of rheumatoid arthritis patients treated with dietary methods for 13 months had fewer symptoms than a control group who ate normally. During the first 7 to 10 days, the treatment group consumed a low-calorie liquid diet with new foods added individually in an attempt to identify foods that might cause arthritis symptoms to worsen. Then these patients followed a vegetarian diet that eliminated dairy products, eggs, refined sugar, citrus fruits, and gluten-containing foods (found in wheat, oats, rye, and barley) for 1 year. The control group ate their usual diet. Patients who had appeared to be helped by the diet had relapsed when they resumed their normal eating habits.[17] *Tufts University Diet & Nutrition Letter* cautions that: (1) the experimental diet can lead to nutritional shortfalls that require professional monitoring; (2) the results were based on the experience of only 17 individuals; and (3) a much larger sample would be required for confirmation.[18]

Dale Alexander claimed that ingested cod liver oil reduces the pain of arthritis by lubricating people's joints.[19] This claim is false because the oil is broken down by digestion into simple substances, before absorption from the intestinal tract, and the oil does not actually reach the joints. Years ago, "immune milk" sold for many times the price of ordinary milk. It was said to produce immunity because the cows producing it had been injected with *streptococcus* and *staphylococcus* vaccines.

Nutritional Supplements

Various vitamin and vitamin-mineral supplements are promoted for the treatment of arthritis through articles in "health food" publications. A number of companies market supplements (for example, Ar Pak) whose names suggest effectiveness against arthritis. To avoid legal trouble, product labels make no actual claims.

Oxycal, a recently promoted product for the treatment of arthritis, is a so-called neutral form of vitamin C that also contains some calcium.

Green-lipped mussel has been promoted by the book *Relief from Arthritis*, by John Croft, and articles in health food magazines and tabloid newspapers. The mussel is harvested in New Zealand, made into supplement capsules, and marketed by various American companies. Although the FDA in 1976 banned importation of green-lipped mussel preparations, they are still being sold in many health food stores. In 1983 the FDA seized a large quantity of products and raw materials from the Aquaculture Corporation of Redwood City, California, manufacturer of Neptone. The company contested the seizure on the grounds that their product was a food rather than a drug. However, FDA documents indicated that the company had distributed literature and suggested in advertisements that green-lipped mussel preparations were effective treatment for arthritis.[20]

Capsules of omega-3 fatty acids, commonly referred to as fish oils, have been marketed with claims that they are effective treatments for several types of arthritis. A few experiments in both animals and humans have had positive results, but it is not known whether there is a dose that is both practical and safe. Fish oil supplements can interfere with blood clotting and increase the risk of stroke, especially when taken with aspirin or other NSAIDs. Fish oils can also cause diarrhea and upset stomach. Responsible medical authorities believe that eating oily fish (mackerel, salmon, sardines, or lake trout) several times a week is preferable to taking fish oil supplements. Eating these fish may help prevent heart attacks as well (see Chapter 16).

Acupuncture

Acupuncture has no known effect on the underlying cause of any form of arthritis. It is alleged that acupuncture provides pain relief in rheumatoid arthritis and osteoarthritis, but controlled experiments suggest that any effect is likely to be temporary. (For details, see the acupuncture discussion in Chapter 9.) The Arthritis Foundation considers acupuncture an unproven remedy because it does not consistently relieve pain and has not been demonstrated to affect the course of any form of arthritis.[21]

Inappropriate Medications

Medications used inappropriately for arthritis treatment can be classifed in two categories: unproven and dangerous.

Clotrimazole. Clotrimazole, an antifungal drug, was acclaimed by a British physician as a cure for rheumatoid arthritis, which he claims is a protozoan infection. Investigation by the Arthritis Foundation revealed that the doctor was unlicensed in Britain at the time of the report, that he was not an arthritis specialist, that the manufacturers of the drug had no knowledge of any antifungal properties, and that no controlled study had been conducted to investigate its effectiveness.[5]

Venoms. Injections of the venoms of bees and snakes have been touted for treatment of arthritis. No evidence of their effectiveness exists, and both products are dangerous. Bee venom can produce severe allergic reactions. Snake venom, which has anticoagulant properties, has been implicated in a case of death caused by brain hemorrhage.[22]

Aloe vera. Products made from aloe vera, a common houseplant, are promoted as effective treatment for hundreds of ailments, including arthritis (see Chapter 13).

Dimethyl sulfoxide (DMSO). DMSO is an industrial solvent that became popular in the 1960s when Dr. Stanley Jacob, University of Oregon Medical School, reported evidence of its use in medical treatment. It has been touted as a "miracle drug," with claims that it relieves pain, decreases swelling, and promotes healing of injured tissue. Its use has been reported for the treatment of sprains, bursitis, scleroderma, rheumatoid arthritis, and other conditions. Veterinarians have been legally using DMSO on animals. It is popular among athletes as a treatment for sore muscles and other injuries. When rubbed into the skin, DMSO is quickly absorbed and produces a garlic-like taste and breath odor. Intravenous use can cause kidney damage and many other serious adverse effects.[2]

The news media—most notably the CBS program *60 Minutes*—have portrayed DMSO as a medical breakthrough. This claim is premature, however, since adequate evidence is not available and long-term effects are not known. The FDA has approved the use of DMSO for the treatment of interstitial cystitis (a rare bladder disorder), but not for the treatment of arthritis or any other ailment. A few states have passed laws permitting the manufacture and sale of DMSO as a nonprescription drug, but it cannot be legally marketed in this way in most states. However, it is available in some health food, surplus, hardware, and other stores, where it is sold as a "solvent" for $5 or more for a 2- to 4-ounce bottle. The Arthritis Foundation considers DMSO "still experimental" and warns that industrial-grade DMSO should never be used because contaminants could produce serious reactions.[23]

"Black pearls." Since the late 1970s, Oriental arthritis remedies said to be "all-natural" herbal products have been illegally marketed in the United States unde the names Chuifong Toukuwan, Black Pearls, and Miracle Herb. Government agencies have found that in addition to herbs, these products contain various potent drugs not listed on their label. The drugs have included antianxiety agents (diazepam [Valium] and chlordiazepoxide [Librium]), anti-inflammatory drugs, (indomethacin, phenylbutazone, prednisone, and dexamethasone), pain-relievers (mefenamic acid, acetaminophen, and aminopyrine), and the male hormone methyltestosterone. Aminopyrine was banned in the United States in 1938 because it can cause agranulocytosis, a life-threatening condition in which the body stops producing white blood cells. Prednisone and dexamethasone are steroids. Some batches of Chuifong Toukuwan have contained amounts of diazepam high enough to cause addiction.[23] In 1975 four users of Chuifong Toukuwan were hospitalized with agranulocytosis and one died. The FDA has banned importation of the product and helped Texas authorities obtain criminal convictions against several marketers.

Homeopathic products (see Chapter 9) are also promoted for arthritis. There is no scientific evidence to support their use.

Clinics

Thousands of arthritis sufferers have received improper treatments in unethical clinics in the United States and several nearby countries. Some of these centers are associated with spas where physical therapy and hydrotherapy are available. Some spas feature mineral waters and baths. The National Institute of Arthritis and Metabolic Disease has stated:

> Some persons with rheumatic complaints . . . believe that trips to the spas where mineral baths are available were helpful to them, but it has not been shown that it was the mineral content of the waters which accompanied such temporary relief as might have been experienced. In many cases . . . it was simply a matter of rest.[24]

Clinics in Mexico, Canada, and the Dominican Republic advocate other costly treatments not based on scientific principles. Some advertise that the cause of arthritis is constipation caused by "toxemia," and that their treatments are "nonmedical and nonsurgical." Treatment at these clinics may include special diets, vitamins, salt rubs, pressurized enemas, massages, and the use of electrical devices. Some clinics dispense steroid drugs such as cortisone or prednisone. Steroid drugs may be included as part of orthodox treatment and can bring about

Deception in Mexico

After reading about a doctor in Mexico, a 44-year-old woman with rheumatoid arthritis paid him a visit.[26] She did this because she had been in severe pain, could hardly walk, and felt desperate. Cortisone had relieved her symptoms but caused severe adverse effects, including liver and kidney trouble and a stroke that required more than a year for full recovery. When she asked the Mexican doctor whether his treatment included any type of steroid drug, he said it did not and it would help her feel better.

Half an hour after receiving an injection, she began to feel dramatically better. She "limbered up," became energetic, and became pain-free for several weeks. However, she then began to experience edema (puffiness) in her face and in other parts of her body and suspected that the injection she had received had contained steroids. The FDA analyzed her medications and confirmed that they contained a combination of steroids. The Mexican doctor had lied to her. She again developed liver and kidney trouble but was able to recover within a few months with appropriate medical treatment.

These events occurred 20 years ago, but the problem of Mexican clinics dispensing unidentified and dangerous drugs still exists.

rapid reduction of pain and inflammation. However, they can have dangerous side effects that make them unsuitable for long-term use in the treatment of arthritis. Steroid drugs should never be used without close medical supervision, yet patients at some foreign clinics are not informed when these drugs are prescribed.[25] As a result many wind up with stomach ulcers, internal bleeding, weakening of bones, infections, and cataracts.

Dr. Robert E. Liefmann, who fled from the United States to Canada, produced Liefcort, which contained three well-known drugs: prednisone, testosterone (a male hormone), and estradiol (a female hormone). In 1969 he was convicted on 16 counts of violating Canada's Food and Drug Act and was fined $2400. He died in 1972 while the case was being appealed. Liefcort still is prescribed in clinics in Canada and Mexico under such names as Balanced Hormone Therapy and Balanced Hormone Treatment for Arthritics.[13] Other potentially dangerous drugs prescribed at these clinics include:

1. Dipyrone, which can cause agranulocytosis, a disease in which the white blood count drops and subsequent infection can lead to death
2. Phenylbutazone, an effective anti-inflammatory drug that requires close medical supervision not offered by the clinics
3. Aminopyrine (described previously)

Some clinics claim to be administering DMSO intravenously and giving patients DMSO pills to take home, but analysis of the pills has shown that they contain phenylbutazone, diazepam, and sometimes aminopyrine.

Sources of Information

Those who desire pamphlets or information about reputable treatment facilites should contact the Arthritis Foundation or one of its local offices (listed in the Yellow Pages). *Arthritis Today*, a bimonthly magazine published by the Foundation, provides consumers with a convenient way to keep informed.

Recommended Books

The following books are reliable and helpful:

Arthritis: A Comprehensive Guide to Understanding Your Arthritis, by James F. Fries, M.D., Reading, Mass, 1990, Addison-Wesley Publishing Co Inc.

The Arthritis Helpbook: A Tested Self-Management Program for Coping with Your Arthritis, by Kate Lorig, R.N., Dr.P.H., and James F. Fries, M.D., Reading, Mass, 1990, Addison-Wesley Publishing Co Inc.

Coping with Arthritis—More Mobility, Less Pain, by Robert P. Sheon, M.D., Roland W. Moskowitz, M.D., Victor M. Goldberg, M.D., with Betty Huber, M.A., New York, 1987, McGraw-Hill Inc.

Taking Control of Arthritis, by Fred G. Kantrowitz, M.D., New York, 1990, Harper-Collins Publishers.

Treating Arthritis—Medicine, Myth, and Magic, by Felix Fernandez-Madrid, M.D., Ph.D., New York, 1989, Plenum Publishing Corp.

Understanding Arthritis: What it is, How it's Treated, How to Cope with it, by the Arthritis Foundation staff, New York, 1987, Charles Scribner's Sons.

Unproven Remedies Resource Manual, by the Arthritis Foundation, Atlanta, 1991.

Nonrecommended Books

The following books promote unproven methods:

Arthritis Can be Cured—a Layman's Guide, by Bernard Aschner, M.D.

Arthritis, Nutrition and Natural Therapy, by Carson Wade.

The Arthritic's Cookbook, by Colin M. Dong, M.D., and Jane Banks.

A Doctor's Proven New Home Cure for Arthritis, by Giraud W. Campbell, D.O., and R. Stone.

Bees Don't Get Arthritis, by Fred Malone.

The Miraculous Holistic Balanced Treatment for Arthritis Diseases, by Henry B. Rothblatt, J.D., L.L.M., Donna Pinorsky, R.N., and Michael Brodsky.

The Nightshades and Health, by Norman Franklin Childers and Gerard M. Russo.

Pain-Free Arthritis, by Dvera Berson with Sander Roy.

There Is a Cure for Arthritis, by Paavo O. Airola, N.D.

You Can Stay Well and *Let's Get Well,* both by Adella Davis, M.S.

Tabloid Newspaper Reports

Tabloid newspapers frequently report so-called arthritis cures—often with front-page headlines. Articles of this type tend to fall into three categories:

1. Sensationalized presentations of useful methods already known to the arthritis community: "New Diet to Ease Pain of Arthritis" (*National Examiner*) was a standard low-fat, high-fiber diet plus vitamin supplments. "How to Wash Away Arthritis Pain Instantly" (*Examiner*) was a hot bath.
2. One-sided reports touting quack nonsense: "Miracle Caves Cure Thousands of Arthritis" (*Sun*) were tunnels in the mines described earlier in this chapter; and "Nature's Miracle Cures for Arthritis and High Blood Pressure" (*Examiner*) were fruits that supposedly rid the body of toxins that cause arthritis.
3. Preliminary reports of research findings: these "breakthroughs" have no practical significance because they are unconfirmed, will not be available for treating people for many years, or might apply to only a tiny percentage of people with arthritis.

It's Your Decision

A friend of yours with rheumatoid arthritis has encountered an herbal product sold person-to-person that is claimed to be helpful for arthritis. The friend has been under medical care, with considerable benefit, but would like to "miss no bets." What would you advise? How can the product be investigated? Is there a way to determine whether the product is safe?

Guidelines for Arthritis Sufferers

These guidelines are provided to help those afflicted with arthritis make intelligent decisions about products and services:

1. Leave the diagnosis of ailments to the physician.
2. Let the physician prescribe the medications.
3. Be wary of testimonials; some are outright lies. Others, sincerely made, may be brought about by the spontaneous remission of the disease.
4. Be on guard against anyone who promises a "sure cure" or claims to have a secret formula for arthritis.
5. Avoid products claimed to offer more than temporary relief from minor pain of arthritis, unless prescribed by your physician. Those that render temporary relief usually contain aspirin or aspirin-like ingredients.
6. Before using nonprescribed products for which claims have been made, check with your physician.
7. Be aware that there is no specific cure for most forms of arthritis.
8. Avoid spas or clinics that urge self-diagnosis by mail or allege therapeutic value of such treatments as mineral salts and baths.
9. Understand that just because a product is marketed does not ensure that the claims for it are justified.
10. Contact a local Arthritis Foundation chapter for assistance.
11. Individuals wishing to use an unproven approach should discuss this with their physician to minimize their chances of deceiving themselves or selecting a dangerous method.

Summary

Arthritis is a general term applied to about 100 different conditions characterized by aches and pains of joints, muscles, or fibrous tissues. Early diagnosis and treatment are likely to produce the most favorable results. Most patients with chronic forms of arthritis can be helped to lead a productive life if their condition is properly diagnosed and treated. In many cases treatment can help relieve the discomfort and maintain or restore joint function. People with arthritis often turn to quackery because of fear, loss of hope, inadequate information, and other psychosocial factors. Since the symptoms of arthritis often vary spontaneously, it may be difficult for people who have arthritis to judge whether an unproven remedy is effective. This chapter describes many types of quackery and tells how to obtain competent professional help.

Discussion Questions

1. Briefly describe the four most common chronic forms of arthritis.
2. What scientific procedures are used to treat arthritis?
3. Discuss the concept of spontaneous remission and its application to people with arthritis.
4. What factors make people susceptible to arthritis quackery?
5. Identify the types of unorthodox procedures used to treat arthritis patients and briefly discuss each one.
6. Where can arthritis sufferers obtain reliable and valid information?
7. What guidelines will aid arthritis-afflicted individuals to make intelligent decisions about products and services?

References

1. Fries JF: Arthritis—a comprehensive guide to understanding your arthritis, Reading, Mass, 1986, Addison-Wesley Publishing Co Inc.

*2. Fernandez-Madrid F: Treating arthritis—medicine, myth, and magic, New York, 1989, Plenum Publishing Corp.

3. Lawrence RC et al: Estimates of the prevalence of selected arthritic and musculoskeletal diseases in the United States, J Rheumatol 16:427-441, 1989.

4. Lewis R: Arthritis: modern treatment for that old pain in the joints, FDA Consumer, 25(6):18-25, 1991.

*5. Benzaia D: The misery merchants, In Barrett S, ed: The health robbers, ed 2, Philadelphia, 1980, George F Stickley Co.

6. Zimmermann DR: The essential guide to nonprescription drugs, New York, 1983, Harper & Row, Publishers Inc.

7. Consumer Reports: The medicine show, ed 4, Mount Vernon, NY, 1974, Consumers Union.

8. Food and Drug Administration: A study of health practices and opinions, Pub 210978, Springfield, Va, 1972, National Technical Information Service, US Dept of Commerce.

9. Louis Harris and Associates: Health, information and the use of questionable treatments: a study of the American public, Rockville, Md, 1987, US Food and Drug Administration.

10. Arthritis Foundation: Unproven arthritis remedies, Atlanta, 1987, The Foundation.

11. International Medical News Service: Most arthritics try at least one unorthodox remedy, Family Practice News, p 7, Sept 1, 1980.

12. Janssen WF: The gadgeteers, In Barrett S, ed: The health robbers, ed 2, Philadelphia, 1980, George F Stickley Co.

*13. Barrett S et al: The mistreatment of arthritis. In Barrett S et al: Health schemes, scams, and frauds, New York 1990, Consumer Reports Books.

14. FTC challenges health claims of mine operator, seeks disclosure of material facts, FTC News Summary, No. 14, Washington, DC, June 28, 1974.

15. Panush RS: Nutritional therapy for rheumatic diseases, Ann Intern Med 106:619-621, 1987.

*16. Jarvis W: Arthritis: folk remedies and quackery, Nutrition Forum 7:1-3, 1990.

17. Kjeldsen-Kragh J et al: Controlled trial of fasting and a 1-year vegetarian diet in rheumatoid arthritis, Lancet 338;899-902, 1991.

*18. A ray of dietary hope for arthritis sufferers, Tufts University Diet & Nutrition Letter 9(12):1-2, 1992.

19. Herbert V and Barrett S: Vitamins and "health" foods: the great American hustle, Philadelphia, 1981, George F Stickley Co.

20. *USA v Articles of Drug . . . Neptone*, Preliminary declarations of Paul J Sage (FDA) and Richard W Dorst (Aquaculture Corporation) in civil case #C-83-0864-EFL, US District Court, Northern District of California, July 22, 1983.

21. Arthritis Foundation: Unproven remedies resource manual, Atlanta, 1991, The Foundation.

22. HHS News, P80-41, Sept 19, 1980.

*23. McCaleb R and Blumenthal M: Black pearls lose luster. Prescription drugs masquerade as Chinese herbal arthritis formula, HerbalGram No. 22, pp 4-5, 38-39, 1990, The American Botanical Association.

24. Smith RL: The health hucksters, New York, 1960, Thomas Y Crowell Co.

25. Diesk A et al: Unconventional arthritis therapies, Arthritis Rheum 25:1145-1147, 1982.

26. Schultz T and Lindeman B: The pain exploiters—a firsthand report on the profiteers who prey on arthritis sufferers, Today's Health, Oct 1973.

*Recommended reading

CHAPTER EIGHTEEN

CANCER

Suppose someone began marketing automobiles with claims that they can run on water. Most people would want this to be proven and guaranteed or they would pass up the offer. Yet many people who feel desperate about a health problem are vulnerable to promises from individuals who . . . use methods that are unproven according to the criteria of the scientific community. This type of analogy might help patients place dubious cancer treatment in proper perspective.

HELENE BROWN[1]

CONSUMER DECISION

How can the risk of cancer be reduced?

How can questionable cancer methods be recognized?

How can someone with cancer obtain the best treatment?

The term cancer encompasses more than 100 diseases characterized by abnormal cell growth. The abnormal cells do not function usefully in the body and can destroy normal tissue. No single form of treatment is best for all types of cancer because each type of tumor has its own characteristics. Since cancer cells are quite similar to normal cells, it is not simple to kill the one while preserving the other. These concepts should be useful in understanding why any method proposed as effective against all cancers should be viewed with great skepticism until all the facts are in. Cancer researchers do not expect to find such a "magic bullet" in the foreseeable future.

Cancer ranks as the second leading cause of death in the United States. The American Cancer Society (ACS) has estimated that in 1992 some 1,130,000 Americans would die of cancer and 520,000 new cases would be discovered.[3] More than 600,000 will be diagnosed with a superficial form of skin cancer not included in these figures because it is easily detected and cured. Another 100,000 will be diagnosed with cancers of the cervix, female breast, or elsewhere, that are so small, localized (in situ), and curable that they are tabulated separately. Except for lung cancer, which has greatly increased, the overall age-adjusted rate of cancer incidence has gradually decreased during the past 30 years.

The American Cancer Society states that one out of four people presently living in the United States will eventually develop cancer, but that half could be saved with early diagnosis and current treatment methods.

This chapter discusses the risk factors for cancer, preventive measures, scientific treatment methods, diet and cancer, susceptibility to quackery, questionable methods, consumer protection laws, and sources of reliable information.

RISK FACTORS FOR CANCER

Cancer is the result of a complex interaction of causative agents, both environmental and genetic. The most common direct cause of human cancer is tobacco smoking, which is responsible for 85% to 90% of lung cancer cases as well as cancers of the bladder, mouth, larynx, esophagus, pancreas, and possibly other organs. About 30% of all cancer deaths in the United States result from tobacco smoking. According to Pitot[4]:

> If all deaths from [cancers] causally related to smoking are removed from the statistics, there is essentially no increase in the overall age-adjusted cancer death rate in men and a continual decreasing cancer death rate in women. Thus, tobacco smoke represents the major cause of human cancer in our society, and it is the only known factor causing a continual increase in the overall . . . cancer death rate in Americans.

Other risk factors related to cancer are diet, alcohol, drugs, sexual patterns, solar radiation, and occupation.

The effect of diet on cancer is not clearly established. However, evidence from human studies suggests that a diet high in fat and calories and low in fiber may increase the chances of cancer of the breast, prostate, colon, and uterus.

Alcohol in large doses increases the cancer risk in the esophagus, mouth, and possibly other sites. In combination with cigarettes it acts synergistically to increase oral cancer risk.

High-dose exposure to ionizing radiation increases the chances of leukemia and skin cancer. Exposure to high indoor levels of radon may be a factor in the incidence of lung cancer.

In rare cases drugs have increased cancer risk. For example, the use of diethylstilbestrol (DES) during pregnancy has been linked to the subsequent development of a rare form of vaginal cancer in a small number of daughters of exposed women.

Risk of cancer of the cervix is increased through poor sexual hygiene, intercourse at an early age, and multiple sexual partners.

The sun's ultraviolet rays cause the majority of skin cancers.

High-dose, long-term exposure to a number of occupational chemicals has been shown to increase the risk of cancer. These include asbestos used for insulating and fireproofing and vinyl chloride used in plastic production.

Some viral infections, most notably AIDs and hepatitis B, are associated with increased incidence of certain cancers.

Despite the presence of carcinogenic substances in the atmosphere, there is no firm evidence that air pollution is a significant cause of cancer.

There is little evidence that food additives used in the United States increase the risk of any form of human cancer.

Preventive Measures

Cancer prevention can take two forms: primary prevention (before it occurs) and secondary prevention (discovery while treatable). The most important primary preventive measure—probably the most important health decision an individual can make—is to avoid cigarettes and other tobacco products. Other important measures are avoidance of overexposure to the sun and of excess alcohol intake. The dietary recommendations of American Cancer Society are discussed later in this chapter.

Secondary methods of prevention include self-examination of the breasts and testes, periodic physical examinations, blood tests (to detect leukemia and prostate cancer), Pap smears, sigmoidoscopy, mammography, and tests to detect blood in the stool. Guidelines for frequency of these examinations are found in Chapter 6. Thermography (a method of measuring heat given off by a part of the body) and transillumination (shining of red and near-infrared light through a body part to illuminate its inner structure)[5] are not valid techniques for breast cancer detection.

Diagnosis

Although cancer is often suspected on the basis of a physical finding, laboratory test, or imaging procedure, standard practice requires confirmation of the diagnosis through microscopic examination by a pathologist. Specimens usually are obtained by biopsy of a small piece of tissue suspected of being cancerous. The diagnosis of cancer is sometimes difficult, and errors do occur. However, although the frequency of diagnostic errors is unknown, it appears to be low.

Once a cancer is identified, the next step is staging, a method of estimating how far the disease has advanced along its usual course. For most cancers this is based on the size of the primary tumor, the involvement of lymph nodes, and the presence of distant metastases. Staging is used to help select appropriate treatment to estimate prognosis, and to evaluate treatment results.

Consumer Tip

Warning Signs

The American Cancer Society lists the following cancer warning signals as reasons to consult a physician:

- Change in bowel or bladder habits
- A sore that does not heal
- Unusual bleeding or discharge
- Thickening or lump in breast or elsewhere
- Indigestion or difficulty in swallowing
- Obvious change in a wart or mole
- Nagging cough or hoarseness

Prognosis

The National Cancer Institute (NCI)[3] estimates that about half the people diagnosed with cancer are likely to live 5 years or more. Its data from 1981 through 1987 include the following 5-year survival rates by sites: uterus 56% to 84%, larynx 54% to 68%, breast 63% to 78%, cervix 57% to 68%, bladder 59% to 79%, prostate 62% to 75%, colon 47% to 58%, and lung 11% to 13%. (The lower number is for blacks, the higher number for Caucasians.) Treatment with anticancer drugs has caused the overall death rate from cancers that usually occur before age 45 to fall sharply and has resulted in long-term survival for many patients. These cancers include Hodgkin's disease and acute childhood leukemia. The overall survival rate from most other cancers has risen slowly.

The outlook for cancer victims depends on the type of tumor, its location, and the extent of its spread. Some tumors grow slowly and remain localized, whereas others grow rapidly and metastasize (spread to distant sites through the blood stream or lymphatic channels). Spontaneous remission of certain cancers occurs, although rarely.

Scientific Treatment Methods

The three main types of conventional treatment are surgery, radiation therapy, and chemotherapy. In some cases a combination of these methods is more effective than one method alone. Treatment may be done with the hope of curing the patient, or it may be done palliatively, with the hope of relieving discomfort or prolonging life.

Surgery is the primary method of treatment for most of the major forms of cancer, especially in their early stages. Cancer surgery chiefly involves removal of the tumor and nearby tissues that may contain cancer cells.

Radiation therapy, also called radiotherapy, involves attacking cancers with x-rays or with rays or particles from such radioactive substances as cobalt or radium. Radiotherapy may be administered externally with a machine or internally by inserting radioactive material into a body cavity or organ. The beams do not kill the cancer cells outright but destroy their ability to reproduce so that once they die, they are not replaced.

Chemotherapy (treatment with anticancer drugs) has become increasingly effective. Because these drugs circulate to all parts of the body, they attack cancer cells that may have spread to distant organs. More than 50 anticancer drugs are in use today, and many others are being tested experimentally. The main drug types are alkylating agents (which block cell reproduction), antimetabolites, steroid hormones, and antibiotics. Because chemotherapy usually has severe side effects, a few facilities have administered less than state-of-the-art dosages to decrease side effects. However, former NCI Director Vincent De Vita has warned that giving such dosages to potentially curable patients is "throwing away the cure rate."[6]

Several other techniques are being studied with the hope that they can enhance the effectiveness of current methods. These include regional hyperthermia (raising the temperature of part of the body to enhance the effect of radiotherapy or chemotherapy), ultrasound (to heat cancer cells, making tumors more susceptible to radiation therapy), hyperbaric oxygen (administration of oxygen in pressurized rooms to enhance the effect of radiation), and "rescue factors" (chemicals used to protect normal cells against otherwise fatal chemotherapy).

Many researchers are investigating "biological response modifiers" that stimulate or use the patient's own immune system to attack cancer cells. These substances, which are quite costly to produce, include interferon, monoclonal antibodies, and interleukin-2. Interferon is the generic name for a group of hormonelike proteins that can combat many types of viruses. In 1986 it received FDA approval for the treatment of hairy cell leukemia, a rare disease. Monoclonal antibodies are antibodies specifically tailored to seek out chosen targets on cancer cells so that they can kill these cells without damaging normal cells. Interleukin-2 (IL-2), produced in the body in tiny amounts, is manufactured by genetic engineering techniques. White blood cells are obtained from the patient, bathed in IL-2 to make them reproduce faster, and reinjected with more IL-2 into the patient's blood stream. They are attracted to and destroy cancer cells. Although these methods have been called "breakthroughs" in the media, they have limited usefulness at this time.

A limited number of patients for whom no established treatment is available may be eligible to enter a clinical trial of a new approach.[7] Information about clinical trials can be obtained from one's treating physician or the National Cancer Institute's Cancer Information Service (described near the end of this chapter).

Scientific treatment facilities maintain a tumor registry in which the details of cases treated at the facility are recorded, with follow-up queries sent annually to patients and/or to their doctors. Data of this type are useful in assessing the results of treatment.

Diet and Cancer

The fact that people with similar hereditary background living in different parts of the world can have different cancer patterns indicates that environmental causes play an important role. In 1982, the National Academy of Sciences' Committee on Diet, Nutrition and Cancer became the first major scientific group to suggest that dietary strategies might help prevent certain cancers. The committee's complete report[8] included four "interim guidelines":

1. Reduce the proportion of calories from fats—all fats, not one particular type—from the

typical 40% fat content of the American diet to about 30%. This is based on a statistical association between fat intake and certain types of cancer. However, a similar association exists between cancer and the intake of proteins and total calories.
2. Include in the daily diet plenty of whole-grain cereals, fruits and vegetables, especially the fruits and vegetables high in vitamin C and beta-carotene (which the body can convert into vitamin A). Citrus fruits are rich in vitamin C, and dark green and deep yellow vegetables are rich in carotenes. The NAS committee also suggested including members of the family Cruciferae: cabbage, broccoli, cauliflower, and Brussels sprouts.
3. Minimize consumption of salt-cured, salt-pickled, and smoked foods. Epidemiologic studies have found that people in some parts of the world who frequently consume such foods have a greater incidence of cancer at certain sites, particularly the stomach and esophagus.
4. Avoid excess consumption of alcohol, especially in combination with cigarettes.'

Many prominent scientists criticized the NAS report's dietary recommendations as inappropriate and premature and expressed concern that they might distract people from avoiding the established causes of cancer, most notably cigarette smoking.[9] However, the recommendations are very close to those of the widely accepted Dietary Guidelines for Americans (see Chapter 12). In 1991, the American Cancer Society[10] endorsed the Dietary Guidelines and issued guidelines based on the points related to cancer prevention:

1. Maintain a desirable body weight.
2. Eat a varied diet.
3. Include a variety of both vegetables and fruits in the daily diet.
4. Eat more high-fiber foods, such as whole-grain cereals, legumes, vegetables, and fruits.
5. Cut down on total fat intake.
6. Limit consumption of alcoholic beverages, if you drink at all.
7. Limit consumption of salt-cured, smoked, and nitrite-preserved foods.

There are no scientific data to indicate what proportion of cancers may be prevented by following this advice. However, following these recommendations is unlikely to produce harm and may produce beneficial results, especially in lowering the incidence of cardiovascular disease (see Chapter 16).

Questionable Anticancer Supplements

The health food industry is usually quick to exploit new scientific information to its advantage. The NAS report on diet, nutrition, and cancer specified that since it is not known which dietary factors, if any, might be helpful, supplementation with individual nutrients is not advisable. Within a few months after the report was issued, however, a number of products containing dehydrated vegetables and various nutrients were marketed as though the report supported their use for cancer prevention. In 1984, the FTC issued complaints against two companies marketing such products: Pharmtech Research, Inc. (Daily Greens), and General Nutrition, Inc. (Healthy Greens). The FTC charged that their advertising was misleading because no proof existed that eating a tiny amount of processed vegetables could help prevent cancer. Pharmtech signed a consent order to stop making unproven claims, while General Nutrition was ordered to do so by an FTC administrative law judge. The FTC's action appears to have driven this type of product from the marketplace.

More recently, fiber-containing pills have been marketed with suggestions that they can help prevent certain cancers. However, this idea has no scientific support and has been criticized by many prominent scientific groups and individual scientists. Kritchevsky,[11] for example, has noted that dietary fibers have value beyond their possible role in preventing colon cancer. He emphasized that "a high-fiber diet is not merely a low-fiber diet with fiber added. . . . All components of diets containing fiber-rich foods are important."

Susceptibility to Cancer Quackery

Cancer is a major field of exploitation of unproven and fraudulent treatments. People use questionable methods mainly because of fears that cancers are incurable and costly to treat, that treatment might be uncomfortable and mutilating, and that they will be socially stigmatized. If treating physicians show signs of discouragement or state that they can do nothing further, patients often lose hope and feel abandoned. Proponents of "sure cures" cater to these feelings by appearing optimistic and caring

FIGURE 18-1. Message designed to undermine public trust in conventional methods of cancer treatment.

while they promote false hopes in cancer victims. Figure 18-1 is an example of literature designed to undermine public trust in orthodox cancer treatment.

The capacity of people to be fooled should not be underestimated. During the 1940s, William Koch, M.D., Ph.D., acquired a large following of believers in a remedy that he claimed was 1.32 parts glyoxylide per trillion parts water. More than 3000 assorted practitioners bought it for $25 per ampule and charged patients up to $300 per injection. Analysis of the product could find only distilled water.

A number of factors can influence people to believe they have been helped by an unconventional method:

1. Some patients who believe they have been cured of cancer never had it in the first place.
2. Patients who use a questionable treatment along with proven treatment may credit the questionable method for any improvement.
3. Even fatal forms of cancer can have some ups and downs in their course so that the patient may feel better on some days than others. A period of well-being following use of an unorthodox method can be misinterpreted as "improvement" or even "cure." (See "Heads I Win, Tails You Lose.")
4. Doctors sometimes give too pessimistic a prognosis. A patient who tries an unorthodox remedy and lives longer than predicted by a doctor may credit the unorthodox remedy instead of realizing that the doctor's prediction was too pessimistic. The placebo effect, which can provide temporary relief of discomfort, can also operate in this manner. Moertel, Taylor, and Roth[12] reported that pain relief occurred in 44 of 112 (39%) cancer patients given a placebo (inert pill). The greatest responses occurred in highly educated people, farmers, professional workers, women working outside the home, and patients who were widowed. The researchers theorized that the pill had acted as a type of self-hypnosis.

Vissing and Petersen[13] state that testimonials offer the most powerful type of persuasion to try an unorthodox method.

Dr. Malcolm Brigden,[14] a Canadian cancer specialist, believes that unorthodox therapy is appealing because its methods are explained in commonsense terms that seem plausible and offer an opportunity to play an active role in fighting the disease: (1) cancer is a symptom, not a disease; (2) symptoms are caused by diet, stress, or environment; (3) proper fitness, nutrition, and mental attitude allow biologic and mental defense against cancer; and (4) conventional therapy weakens the body's reserves, treats the symptoms rather than the disease.

Cassileth and colleagues at the University of Pennsylvania Cancer Center interviewed 304 cancer center inpatients and 356 patients under the care of unorthodox practitioners elsewhere. Among those who used "alternative treatment," many be-

Personal Glimpse

Heads I Win, Tails You Lose

Quacks capitalize on the natural healing powers of the body by *taking credit* whenever possible for improvement in a patient's condition. An opposite tack—*shifting blame*—is used by many cancer quacks. If their treatment does not work, it is because radiation and/or chemotherapy have "knocked out the immune system." Emil J Freireich, M.D., of the M.D. Anderson Hospital and Tumor Institute in Houston, Texas, has combined these two ploys into a tongue-in-cheek plan for becoming a successful quack:

1. Pick a disease that has natural variability.
2. Apply the "treatment" when the patient's disease is getting progressively worse.
3. If the patient's condition improves or stabilizes, take credit. Then stop the treatment or decrease the dosage.
4. If the patient's condition worsens, say that the dosage must be increased or that the treatment was stopped too soon.
5. If the patient dies, say that the treatment was applied too late.

lieved that their cancer could have been prevented through diet (32% of patients), stress reduction (33%), or environmental changes (26%) and therefore was reversible by the same means. Fifty-three patients had rejected conventional treatment of any kind, while 325 had used both conventional and "alternative" treatments.[15]

In 1987 the American Cancer Society found that 452 (9%) of 5047 cancer patients identified through a telephone survey had used questionable treatments. Of these, 49% had used "mind therapies" (mental imagery, hypnosis, or psychic therapy) and 38% had used diets.[15a]

Questionable Methods

Cancer quackery is as old as recorded history and probably has existed since cancer was recognized as a disease. Thousands of worthless folk remedies, diets, drugs, devices, and procedures have been promoted for cancer management. The American Cancer Society has published reports on more than 70 questionable methods that have achieved notoriety during the past 50 years. Until recently these methods were labeled "unproven." However, in 1991, the Society switched to the term "questionable," which is stronger and does not include new methods that are studied responsibly. Responsible experimentation requires a reasonable rationale, full disclosure to the patient, and a system for evaluating the results. It does not involve promoting unproven methods as cures.

In order for science to advance, researchers and clinicians must be free to try new approaches. Before any cancer treatment is accepted for general use by physicians, it must undergo rigorous scientific scrutiny. The American Cancer Society[16] considers these standards for the investigation of unproven methods:

1. Complete examination of the clinical evidence offered by the proponent, including visits and examinations of treated patients, review of microscopic slides of biopsies, and viewings of x-ray films.
2. Reproducible analysis of laboratory tests on animals and/or tissue culture. No drug that has failed laboratory tests has ever been proven effective against human cancer.
3. Evidence of effectiveness in trials on a sufficient number of patients with biopsy-proven cancers. This must include valid statistical comparison of treated and untreated individuals.
4. Evaluation of autopsy data of treated patients who die.
5. Cooperation with other investigating groups such as the National Cancer Institute, the FDA and the Sloane-Kettering Memorial Cancer Center.

The mere fact that something is unproven does not make it "questionable." The American Cancer Society defines *questionable* methods as "diagnostic tests or therapeutic modalities which are promoted for *general* use in cancer prevention, diagnosis, or treatment and which are, on the basis of careful review by scientists and/or clinicians, not deemed proven nor recommended for current use."[17] The Society's reports on questionable methods are prepared with help from its Committee on Questionable Methods (formerly called Commmittee on Unproven Methods), ACS staff members, and many outside consultants.

Questionable methods can be classified in nine broad categories: corrosive agents, plant products, special diets, drugs, correction of "imbalances," biologic methods, devices, psychologic approaches, and worthless diagnostic tests. Many promoters combine methods to make themselves more marketable.

Corrosive agents. Many salves, poultices, and plasters have been applied directly to tumors with the hope of burning them away. Turpentine is an old favorite. It has been claimed that some corrosive agents "draw out" the cancer. The Hoxsey method (see Chapter 2) included a product of this type. In recent years scientists have found chemicals that can destroy some superficial skin cancers. Except for that, however, corrosive agents are worthless against cancer.

Plant products. Most folk remedies fall into the plant category. Brews such as a tea from red clover are used as a beverage or for bathing external cancers. Mucorhicin, said to be produced by cultivating mold on a nutrient, was composed of yeast, salt, whole wheat, and sterile water. Essiac is an herbal remedy whose ingredients have been kept secret. It was developed about 50 years ago by a Canadian nurse named Rene Caisse who was given the recipe by her father. It has never been scientifically tested.

Pau d'arco tea, sold through health food stores and by mail, is said to be an ancient Inca Indian remedy prepared from the inner bark of various species of *Tabebuia,* an evergreen tree native to the West Indies and Central and South America. However, stories about its origins contain a variety of geographic and botanical errors. Proponents claim that pau d'arco tea is effective against cancer and many other ailments. *Tabebuia* woods contain lapachol, a chemical recognized as an antitumor agent. However, human studies have found that as soon as significant blood levels are attained, undesirable effects were severe enough to require that the drug be stopped. Varro E. Tyler, Ph.D., a leading authority on plant medicine, has noted that pau d'arco's "lack of proven effectiveness, potential toxicity, and high cost ($12 to $50 per package) render its use both unwise and extravagant."[18]

ADS, which was claimed to be an herbal tea, was sold for $125 to $150 per quart by Bruce Halstead, M.D., a California physician. Though Halstead maintained that ADS was a "nutritional supplement," analysis revealed it to be 99.4% water and a brown sludge composed mainly of coliform bacteria (the type found in human feces). In 1986, Halstead was fined $10,000 and sentenced to 4 years in prison after being found guilty on 24 counts of cancer fraud and grand theft. Following his trial, the prosecuting attorney call him "a crook selling swamp water." The 4-year sentence is probably the longest ever issued to a physician convicted of health fraud involving patient care. Halstead is appealing his conviction and remains free on $100,000 bail.[19] His medical license was revoked in 1992.

FIGURE 18-2. Pharmacist strikes a blow for public health. Adrian Thomas, owner of the Thomas Pharmacy in Meyersville, Pennsylvania, decided it was hypocritical to give health advice in one part of his store and sell health-destroying products in another. In February 1992, he burned his entire tobacco inventory along with his license to sell tobacco products. He told reporters he was tired of seeing his customers die of cancer and heart disease.

Photo courtesy of Johnstown Tribune-Democrat.

Special diets. Many different dietary approaches have been recommended, including fasting, megadoses of nutrients, consumption of raw foods, and various complicated dietary regimens. The grape cure promoted by Joanna Brandt, N.D., involves eating large quantities of grapes for 1 or 2 weeks, then adding sour milk, raw vegetables, other fruits, nuts, honey, and olive oil. Proponents of the Gerson diet claim to accomplish "detoxificiation" by daily enemas and a diet consisting primarily of fresh fruit and vegetable juices. Salt, spices, sodium bicarbonate, alcohol, and tobacco are forbidden. After several weeks milk proteins, vitamins, and various other food supplements are added. This method was developed by Dr. Max Gerson, a German-born physician who emigrated to the United States in 1936. The treatment, available in Mexico, is still actively promoted by Gerson's daughter, Charlotte Gerson Straus, through lectures, talk show appearances, and publications[20] of the Gerson Institute in Bonita, California. She believes that "by healing the body, you can heal cancer and almost any other chronic disease. . . . All chronic diseases are deficiency diseases."[21] Although Ms. Straus claims high cure rates, there is no evidence that the progress of patients is monitored after they leave the clinic.[22] The macrobiotic diet, discussed in Chapter 13, is a semivegetarian approach claimed to cure cancer and many other health problems.[23]

The American Cancer Society believes that although dietary measures may be helpful in preventing certain cancers, there is no scientific evidence that any nutritionally related regimen is appropriate as a primary treatment for cancer.[24]

Drugs. Iscador, an extract of mistletoe, is claimed to be effective against inoperable tumors. According to a 1962 American Cancer Society report, its proposer, a Swiss physician, claimed that the time of picking the plants was important because they react to the influences of the sun, moon, and planets.[25] It is claimed that Liliverum, said to be an "extract of the ovary part of the Easter lily," surrounds and neutralizes cancer cells within 30 minutes after use.[25]

During the past decade, oxygen-rich compounds (germanium sesquioxide, hydrogen peroxide, and ozone) have been utilized by many promoters of questionable cancer regimens. Their use is based on the erroneous concept that cancer is caused by oxygen deficiency and can be cured by exposing cancer cells to more oxygen than they can tolerate. These compounds have been the subject of legitimate research. However, there is little or no evidence that they are effective for the treatment of any serious disease.[26]

Cancell is a dark brown liquid said to "digest cancer cells." The FDA states that it is composed of ordinary chemicals, including nitric acid, sodium sulfite, potassium hydroxide, sulfuric acid, and catechol.[27] There is not scientific evidence that Cancell is effective against cancer or any other disease. The FDA has taken its promoters to court to try to stop its distribution.

"Antineoplastons" is the name given by Stanislaw R. Burzynski, M.D., to substances that he claims can "normalize" cancer cells that are constantly being produced within the body. He has published many papers in which he claims that antineoplastons extracted from urine or synthesized in his laboratory have proven effective against cancer in laboratory experiments. He also claims to have helped many people with cancer get well. Dr. Saul Green,[27a] a biochemist who worked for many years at Memorial Sloan-Kettering Hospital doing research into the mechanisms and treatment of cancer, has written a detailed analysis of Dr. Burzynski's claims. Dr. Green does not believe that any of the substances Dr. Burzynski calls "antineoplastons" have been proven to "normalize" tumor cells.

Laetrile, a drug that achieved great notoriety during the 1970s and early 1980s, is discussed later in this chapter.

Correction of "imbalances." Revici Cancer Control (also called lipid therapy) is based on the belief that cancer is caused by an imbalance between constructive (anabolic) and destructive (catabolic) body processes. Its proponent has been Dr. Emmanuel Revici, a physician born in Rumania in 1896. To treat the patient, Revici prescribes lipid alcohols, zinc, iron, and caffeine, which he says are "anabolic," and fatty acids, sulfur, selenium and magnesium, which he classifies as "catabolic." His formulations are based on his interpretation of the specific gravity, pH (acidity), and surface tension of single samples of the patient's urine. Revici also claims success against AIDS.

Scientists who have offered to evaluate Revici's methods have never been able to reach an agreement with him on procedures to ensure a valid test. However, his method of urinary interpretation is obviously not valid. The specific gravity of urine reflects the concentration of dissolved substances and depends largely on the amount of fluid a person consumes. The acidity depends mainly on diet, but varies considerably throughout the day. Thus, even when these values are useful for a metabolic determination, information from a single urine sample would be meaningless. The surface tension of urine has no medically recognized diagnostic value.[28]

In December 1983 Revici's medical license was suspended for 60 days while the New York Board of Medical Conduct reviewed charges that he had promised cancer cures to three patients. One was a 49-year-old woman who had consulted Revici after several other doctors had advised her to have a marble-sized lump removed from her left breast. Revici persuaded her to undergo treatment with him. After 14 months, the tumor had filled one breast and spread to the opposite breast and to many lymph nodes—requiring removal of both breasts and treatment with radiation and chemotherapy.

In 1988, state licensing authorities placed Revici on 5 years' probation. The terms of his probation bar him from treating patients for cancer unless they have been: (1) diagnosed by another physician; (2) informed that Revici's treatment is unorthodox; and (3) urged to consult a cancer specialist and a psychiatrist or psychologist before signing a consent form.

In 1989, a jury awarded $1,353,277.50 to the estate of a woman who suffered an agonizing death from colon cancer under Revici's care. When she initially consulted Revici, her tumor was the size of a marble and probably curable by surgery. Testimony at the trial indicated that Revici told her the tumor has almost disappeared despite the fact that it was enlarging. It was also revealed that after the suit was filed, Revici doctored his records to suggest that the woman's cancer was far advanced when she first consulted him.

Biologic methods. "Vaccines" and similar products have been prepared from various substances including pooled cancers, the patient's own blood and/or urine, animal blood and/or urine, and cultures of germs. Anticancergen Z-50 was prepared from either pooled cancer tissues or the patient's blood and urine. In 1966 its promoter, George S. Zuccala, was found guilty in federal court of interstate shipment of an unlicensed vaccine and sentenced to 9 months in prison. Another vaccine was the Radio-Sulpho Cancer Cure, developed by Philip Such, Jr., who claimed he could culture cancer germs direct from the cancer vaccine. Krebiozen and immuno-augmentative cancer therapy are discussed later in this chapter.

Fresh cell therapy, also called live cell therapy or cellular therapy, involves injections of fresh embryonic animal cells taken from the organ or tissue that corresponds to the unhealthy organ or tissue in the patient. Proponents claim that the recipient's body automatically transports the injected cells to the target organ where they repair and rejuvenate the ailing cells. The originator of this approach was Paul Neihans, a Swiss phyisician who died in 1971. The American Cancer Society[29] states that fresh cell therapy has no proven benefit and has caused serious side effects (infections and immunologic reactions to the injected protein) and death.

Hariton Alivizatos, a Greek physician who died during 1991, claimed to have developed a blood test that can determine the type, location, and severity of any cancers. He also claimed to have developed a "serum" designed to help the patient's immune system destroy cancer cells, and to help the body rejuvenate parts destroyed by cancer.[30] Knowledgeable observers believe the principal ingredient was niacin.

Dr. Virginia Livingston, who died in 1990, postulated that cancer is caused by a bacterium that invades the body when resistance is lowered.[31] To combat this, she claimed to strengthen the body's immune system with various vaccines (including one made from the patient's urine); a vegetarian diet that avoids chicken, eggs, and sugar; vitamin and mineral supplements; visualization; and stress reduction. She claimed to have a very high recovery rate but published no clinical data to support this. Attempts by scientists to isolate the organism she postulated were not successful. Researchers at the University of Pennsylvania Cancer Center compared 78 patients with advanced cancer treated at the center with 78 similar patients given various vaccines, a vegetarian diet, and coffee enemas at the Livingston-Wheeler Clinic. The study found no difference between average survival time of the two groups. However, patients in the Livingston-Wheeler program reported more problems with appetite difficulties and pain.[32]

Devices. Numerous gadgets have been falsely claimed to diagnose and/or treat cancer. Some were claimed to use electrical or magnetic energy in curative fashion, while others involved forces not recognized by the scientific community. The Vrilium Tube, or "magic spike," mentioned earlier in this chapter, was alleged to treat cancer as well as arthritis. The Orgone Energy Accumulator was invented by Wilhelm Reich, M.D., to treat diseases by absorbing "blue bions" or "Cosmic Orgone Energy." In 1956 Dr. Reich and an associate were sentenced to prison for violating an earlier injuction against distributing his devices. In 1966 the FDA seized 186 brassieres from a company that falsely advertised that they could prevent breast cancer as well as increasing or decreasing the size of the bosom.[33] Neither quacks nor their victims seem to have any limit to the scope of their imagination.

Psychologic approaches. Dr. O. Carl Simonton, medical director of the Simonton Cancer Center, Pacific Palisades, California, believes that cancers may be affected by meditation. He theorizes that the brain can stimulate endocrine glands to inspire the immune system to attack cancer cells. While in training to become a radiation therapist Dr. Simonton noted that some cancer patients with "positive attitudes" seemed to recover more quickly and live longer than those who seemed less motivated for treatment. Based on this observation, he and his associates developed a system for motivating "positive attitudes," which includes having patients imagine their cancer cells being destroyed by their own immune systems. Basically, the technique involves thinking of benefiting from therapy, enjoying health, standing in a beautiful environment, and other favorable events. A favorite technique is to imagine one's white blood cells fighting cancer cells. However, Friedlander[34] has noted:

> When the Simontons developed this technique, many people thought that the white blood cells of the immune system were the body's major defense against cancer. Cancerous cells supposedly are produced on a steady basis but destroyed by the body's white cells; and malignancies that become evident are the ones that "got away." Unfortunately for the "immune surveillance" theory, we now know that people who are given immunosuppressant drugs . . . or who are immunodeficient because of hereditary disease or AIDS, are not prone to develop any of the common cancers. Rather, they tend to develop unusual cancers—such as Kaposi's sarcoma in AIDS—that arise from cells made abnormal by the underlying diseases. Nevertheless, imagers still meditate about white cells making their cancers go away.

Simonton's book *Getting Well Again* included reports on patients who got better after using his methods. However, Friedlander,[34] who analyzed five of the reports he thought might impress laypersons the most, noted that two of the patients had undergone standard treatment, one had a slow-growing tumor, and one probably did not have cancer. The fifth patient's tumor was treatable by standard means.

Some people suggest Simonton's program may have positive psychologic effects because it may help people relax and give them a feeling that they are "doing something" positive. But scientists who believe that Simonton's methods are ineffective point out that hundreds of scientific studies have found no clear-cut relationship between emotions, personality factors, stresses, and cancer. Simonton has done some studies, but the American Cancer Society and others have questioned the studies' design.[35] Although his method is physically harmless, it may encourage some patients to abandon effective care.

Bernie Siegel, M.D., author of *Love, Medicine & Miracles* and *Peace, Love & Healing,* is a surgeon who espouses meditation, support-group meetings, and other psychological approaches for the treatment of cancer patients. He claims that "happy people generally don't get sick" and that "one's attitude toward oneself is the single most important factor in healing or staying well." He also states that "a vigorous immune system can overcome cancer if it is not interfered with, and emotional growth toward greater self-acceptance and fulfillment helps keep the immune system strong." However, he has done no research to test these notions.

Worthless diagnostic tests. H.H. Beard, a biochemist, claimed that his Beard Anthrone Test could detect cancer within the body within 2 or 3 weeks after it started by measuring a sex hormone in the urine. He was indicted for mail fraud in 1967 and subsequently received a 6-month suspended prison sentence. The Arthur (or Automated) Immunostatus Differential Test (also called the AID test), which Beard claimed could detect cancer before it developed, involved computerized microscopic examination of blood from the earlobe.

Two tests were used by William Kelley, D.D.S., the dentist whose methods were used unsuccessfully to treat actor Steve McQueen. Kelley's Protein Metabolism Evaluation Index was based on the premise that cancer is a foreign protein. His Kelley Malignancy Index was claimed to be " the most

Personal Glimpse

A Victim's Experience

In 1982 my father-in-law was diagnosed as having unresectable, incurable, widely disseminated cancer of the lung, and advised that essentially his condition was terminal. As could be expected, the family was distraught, and we began to grasp at straws and looking into alternative modes of treatment. . . . Some of the local press carried stories about . . . so-called immunoaugmentative therapy. . . . Soon thereafter he went to the Bahamas to get the treatment.

His main symptom had been pain from the tumor. It had metastasized to the bones. When he went down there, he was told to go off pain medication and to begin the serum injections, and that . . . the serum injections, if they work and dissolve the tumor, will cause pain. So he went down there knowing he had a tumor growing in him and causing him pain, and through a pretty good ploy he came back convinced that the pain he was having was a cure. In addition, he was told the tumor was shrinking. The x-ray film they took was overexposed, which has the technical problem of making masses look smaller than they really are.

Upon his return I encouraged him to go to Fox Army Hospital and have another chest x-ray made. Several radiologists corroborated that they could see no evidence of any shrinkage in the tumor. I was then faced with the unpleasant task of telling my father-in-law for the second time he was dying.

It was interesting that both he and his wife came back with total euphoria—that he was cured. They told everyone they saw he was cured. When they realized that they had been fooled, it was really a shock, and, of course one doesn't usually go around telling people you have been fooled.

He died approximately 2 months after he returned. In addition to the emotional turmoil and being away from the rest of the family for essentially half the remaining life he had, this cost them approximately $10,000, including travel and lodging, for this phony cancer cure.

Carl Barnes, M.D.[2]

accurate and extensive cancer detection system ever developed." It was supposed to determine "the presence or absence of cancer, the growth rate of the tumor, the location of the tumor mass, prognosis of the treatment, age of the tumor and the regulation of medication for treatment."[36] A booklet by Kelley claims "at least 86% of all cancer conditions can be treated by diet alone" and that "cancer is nothing more than a pancreatic enzyme deficiency" caused by eating too much of the wrong kind of protein. "If people would not eat protein after 1:00 PM," the booklet states, "83% of cancer in the United States could be eliminated."

According to a report in the newspaper of the American Dental Association,[37] Kelley was convicted in 1970 of practicing without a license after witnesses testified that he had diagnosed lung cancer on the basis of blood from a patient's finger and prescribed supplements and a diet as treatment. In 1973 he was brought before the Texas State Board of Dental Examiners on charges of unprofessional conduct.The complaint contended that he had obtained a fee by fraud or misrepresentation by offering diagnosis and treatment of cancer in his dental office. The board's decision to suspend Kelley's license for 5 years was later upheld in court and went into effect in 1976. However, he continued to promote his methods for several more years through his Dallas-based International Health Institute.[38] Kelley's nutritional approaches are still used today by Dr. Nicholas Gonzales, a physician in New York City who claims to have performed an extensive analysis of Kelley's former patients. Conventional physicians who evaluated 50 case histories from an unpublished manuscript by Gonzales found no evidence of benefit.[39]

Cassileth notes a recent increase in quack claims that cancer is the result of adverse environmental influences, excess protein intake, self-pollution by bad habits, and incorrect spiritual attitudes. Cures promoted by proponents of these ideas include meatless diets; "cleansing" of the body by special diets, enemas, and antioxidants; megadoses of vitamins and trace minerals; and various spiritual approaches. Dr. Cassileth also notes:

> Such programs differ from past cancer quackery. . . . Most are within the control of the patient, who can choose which part of a program to accept, which part to cheat on, and which part to amplify. There is no FDA regulation of most of these programs since the FDA had no jurisdiction over dietary theories, personal vitamin consumption or spiritual improvement. What's more, no action can be taken against the proponents for claiming that orthodox approaches are unnatural and bad.[40]

Krebiozen

The story of krebiozen illustrates how a reputable scientist may become misdirected. In 1949 Dr. Steven Durovic, a physician from Buenos Aires, Argentina, came to the United States to work with scientists at Northwestern University on a "whitish powder" called kositerin, which he thought was useful in treating hypertension. The substance proved to be useless, but Dr. Durovic met Dr. Andrew C. Ivy, a widely known scientist, physiologist, medical researcher, and vice-president of the University of Illinois. He solicited Ivy's help in testing a compound he called krebiozen, which he claimed was produced by injecting 2000 Argentinean horses with *Actinomyces bovis,* the microorganism that causes a disease called "lumpy jaw" in cattle. From the blood of these horses Durovic said he extracted a "whitish powder" that he mixed with mineral oil.

Dr. Ivy, who had served as executive director of the National Cancer Advisory Council, was impressed by the results obtained on a number of cancer patients and publicly supported krebiozen. However, in 1952 six prominent physicians reviewed 500 of Dr. Ivy's 500 cases and concluded there was no acceptable evidence that krebiozen had benefited any of them.[41] Dr. Ivy refused to accept these conclusions, and the controversy continued. In 1961, the National Cancer Institute received a small amount of krebiozen along with clinical data from 4200 patients, of which 504 cases were submitted for review. Twenty-four scientists then conducted a study and concluded that krebiozen was ineffective against cancer.

In 1963 the FDA identified krebiozen powder as creatine, an amino acid constituent of meat and normally found in the body. The FDA reported that krebiozen sold before 1960 consisted of mineral oil only, whereas after 1963 it contained creatine monohydrate, which would not dissolve in mineral oil. Meanwhile, the Cancer Advisory Council of the California State Department of Public Health had concluded that krebiozen "is of no value in the dianosis, treatment, alleviation or cure of cancer."

In 1964, Dr. Steven Durovic, his brother Marko Durovic, Dr. Andrew C. Ivy, and Dr. William P. Phillips were indicted on 49 counts of violating the Food, Drug and Cosmetic Act, mail fraud, mislabeling, making false statements to the government, and conspiracy. All were acquitted in 1966. The American Cancer Society[42] has reiterated that the verdict of acquittal of the Durovic brothers, Ivy, and Phillips did not alter the fact that krebiozen has no anticancer effect in humans.

Paul Sage, an FDA consumer safety officer involved in the enforcement of laws against labeling violations, believed that loss of the krebiozen case discouraged further criminal prosecutions of this type by the FDA. Since 1966 few criminal prosecutions have been brought by the FDA against people who marketed quack products with unproven therapeutic claims.

Immuno-Augmentative Therapy

Immuno-augmentative therapy (IAT) was developed by Lawrence Burton, Ph.D., a zoologist who states that IAT can control all forms of cancer by restoring natural immune defenses. He claims to accomplish this by injecting protein extracts isolated with processes he has patented. However, experts believe that the substances he claims to use cannot be produced by these procedures and have not been demonstrated to exist in the human body. He has not published detailed clinical reports, divulged the details of his methods, published meaningful statistics, conducted a controlled trial, or provided independent investigators with specimens of his treatment materials for analysis. During the mid-1980s, several cases were reported of patients of Dr. Burton who developed serious infections following IAT.

In 1974 Burton declined an offer from the National Cancer Institute to help test his methods. Shortly afterward, after failing to complete a satisfactory application to the FDA to test humans in the United States, he established a clinic on Grand Bahama Island, where patients pay more than $5000 dollars for a few weeks of treatment. A patient information guide provided at Burton's clinic urges patients to seek legal help to force insurance companies to pay for Burton's treatment.[43]

In 1979 Burton's efforts received an enormous

boost when the CBS-TV program *60 Minutes* gave them favorable publicity. A prominent physician stated that one of his patients treated by Burton appeared to have undergone a miraculous recovery. The patient died within 2 weeks after the program was shown, but *60 Minutes* never informed viewers of this fact.

William A. Nolen, M.D., who visited Burton's clinic in 1982, reviewed many records and had follow-up conversations with at least ten patients and some of their doctors. Dr. Nolen concluded that most of the patients had never had cancer or had tumors that typically grow slowly, while some had undergone conventional treatment that was probably responsible for any positive results.[44]

In 1987, the American Medical Association's Diagnostic and Therapeutic Technology Assessment (DATTA) asked an expert panel to evaluate IAT. Of 27 panelists who commented on effectiveness, none rated IAT "established," 6 (22%) called it "investigational," 16 (59%) "unacceptable," and 5 (19%) "indeterminate." Of 26 panelists who commented on safety, none rated IAT "established," 6 (23%) called it "investigational," 19 (73%) "unacceptable," and 1 (4%) "indeterminate."[45]

Dr. Burton's current literature includes a booklet summarizing the experiences of 35 IAT patients and their status as of February 1988. However, Dr. Wallace Sampson, a cancer specialist who examined the data concluded:

> The sampling of cases is not meaningful. To estimate prognosis accurately, the stage and grade of a tumor are needed. Only a few of these vignettes provide both of these. Any facility that treats large numbers of cancer patients will have some patients who survive a long time—with or without treatment. It would not be possible to determine IAT's effectiveness without knowing how these outcomes compare with the rest of Burton's patients who had similar cancers. Moreover, 30 of the 35 received standard or near-standard treatment before undergoing IAT. All of these had a significant probability of living as long as was recorded in the booklet.[46]

In 1982, Florida and Oklahoma passed laws permitting the use of IAT within their borders, but Dr. Burton did not open a clinic in either state. Florida's law was repealed in 1984, and Oklahoma's law was repealed in 1985. During the same year, public health officials found antibodies to the human immunodeficiency virus (HIV) in vials of serum obtained from several patients and were able to culture the virus from one specimen—suggesting that blood infected with HIV had been used to prepare IAT treatment materials.[47]

In 1986, in response to Congressional action, the Congressional Office of Technology Assessment (OTA) appointed a group of technical experts and representatives of Dr. Burton to design a clinical trial to evaluate IAT. According to OTA's report, a protocol was designed in which colon cancer patients would be treated at an accredited medical center in the U.S. However, communication between Dr. Burton and U.S. government authorities broke down after he insisted that a "pre-test" be conducted at his clinic. The OTA report also concluded that "no reliable data are available on which to base a determination of IAT's efficacy."[48]

Laetrile

Laetrile is one of several questionable remedies concocted by the late Ernst T. Krebs, Sr., a San Francisco physician. It is the trade name for the chemical amygdalin, a substance abundant in the pits of apricots and various other plants. Amygdalin is composed of two units of glucose, one unit of benzaldehyde, and one unit of cyanide. Laetrile is also referred to as "vitamin B_{17}," although it is not a vitamin.

There is evidence that Laetrile can be toxic to normal tissues. Dr. Joseph F. Ross, professor of medicine and pathology, UCLA School of Medicine, has documented 37 cases of poisoning and 17 deaths from Laetrile and Laetrile-containing fruit kernels.[49] Dr. Victor Herbert believes that some deaths ascribed to cancer may have been caused or accelerated by cyanide from Laetrile.[50] FDA officials reported in 1977 that Laetrile imported from Mexico and elsewhere varied in its ingredients, potency, and purity. Most tablets and injectable preparations did not contain the amount of Laetrile stated on their labels. Ampules were not tightly sealed, and some even had contamination visible to the naked eye.[51]

Promoters of Laetrile have changed their claims several times.[52-54] and may vary their claims according to the sophistication of the listener. Laetrile is no longer openly proclaimed to cure cancer. Instead, advocates state that it prevents cancer, relieves pain, slows down or controls the disease, and promotes a feeling of well-being. Physicians who treat cancer victims with Laetrile purport to use a "holistic approach," a variable program that may include vitamins A, C, and B complex, pangamic acid (also called "vitamin B_{15}"), fruits and vegetables with little meat, rest, exercise, enzymes, and coffee enemas. They also refer to this treatment as "metabolic therapy."

Many animal studies have demonstrated that Laetrile has no beneficial effect against cancer. Between 1957 and 1975 the National Cancer Institute tested the substance on animal cancers on five different occasions. Four other independent cancer research centers have also performed studies and concluded that Laetrile is not effective. Studies of case reports of humans have also been uniformly negative. In 1953 the Cancer Commission of the California Medical Association published information on 44 cancer patients treated with Laetrile during the previous year. Nineteen had died of their disease, and there was no evidence that Laetrile had helped any of the others. During the 1970s Dr. Ernesto Contreras, a Mexican physician who claimed to have treated more than 16,000 cancer patients with Laetrile, submitted 12 case reports to the FDA to illustrate his successes. Investigation by the FDA revealed that six had died of their disease, one still had cancer, and three could not be located. Two others had been treated with orthodox therapy, which made it impossible to tell whether Laetrile had helped them.[55]

In response to political pressure, a clinical trial was begun in 1982 by the Mayo Clinic and three other cancer centers under the sponsorship of the National Cancer Institute. Laetrile and "metabolic therapy" were administered as recommended by their promoters. The patients had advanced cancer for which no proven treatment was known. Of 178 patients, not one was cured or even stabilized, and none had any lessening of any cancer-related symptoms. The median survival rate was 4.8 months from the start of therapy. In those still alive after 7 months of treatment, tumor size had increased. Several patients experienced symptoms of cyanide toxicity or had blood levels of cyanide approaching the lethal range.[56] Dr. Arnold S. Relman, editor of the *New England Journal of Medicine,* commented on these results as follows:

> Laetrile, I believe, has had its day in court. The evidence, beyond reasonable doubt, is that it doesn't benefit patients with advanced cancer, and there is no reason to believe that it would be any more effective in the earlier stages of the disease. Some undoubtedly will remain unconvinced, but no sensible person will want to advocate its further use and no state legislature should sanction it any longer. The time has come to close the books on Laetrile and get on with our efforts to understand the riddle of cancer and improve its prevention and treatment.[57]

In 1966 Ernst Krebs, Sr., pleaded guilty to contempt charges for shipping Laetrile in violation of injunctions. He received a suspended sentence of 1 year by a California court. Dr. Byron A. Krebs and his brother, Ernst Krebs, Jr., were fined $500 each plus $625 court costs for dispensing the controversial drug in 1973 in San Francisco. Byron was convicted of violating a state health department order not to prescribe the drug and Ernst was convicted of practicing medicine without a license. A sentence of 6 months in jail was also given but was suspended for 3 years on pledges the two would stop advocating Laetrile as a cancer cure. In 1974 Dr. Byron A. Krebs had his doctor of osteopathy license revoked by the State Board of Medical Examiners, who said, "It was found Dr. Krebs was mentally incompetent to practice medicine."[58] In 1977 Ernst Krebs, Jr., was found guilty of violating his 1973 probation by continuing to advocate Laetrile and was sentenced to 6 months in the county jail.

In 1975 a cancer patient named Glenn Rutherford filed a class action suit to stop the FDA from interfering with the sale and distribution of Laetrile. The suit was initially successful to the extent that a federal district court judge in Oklahoma issued a series of orders allowing cancer patients to import a 6-month supply of Laetrile for personal use if they could obtain a physician's affidavit that they were "terminal." A higher court partially upheld this ruling, but in 1979 the U.S. Supreme Court disagreed, stating that drugs offered to "terminal" patients should not be exempted from FDA authority. The court reasoned that it is not possible to determine with certainty who is terminal and that even if it were possible, both terminally ill patients and the general public deserve protection from fraudulent cures. In 1987, after further appeals were denied, the district judge (a strong proponent of Laetrile) finally yielded to the higher courts and terminated the affidavit system.[53] Today few sources of Laetrile are available within the United States, but it still is utilized at at a few Mexican clinics.[58a]

"Metabolic Therapy"

"Metabolic therapy" is based on the idea that cancer and other chronic illnesses result from a disturbance of the body's ability to protect itself. Its most visible proponent was Harold Manner, Ph.D., a former biology professor who left his academic position to market his treatment ideas. Manner defined metabolic therapy as "the use of natural food products and vitamins to prevent and treat disease by building a strong immune system." He theorized that chemicals in food, water and air cause large numbers of primitive cells to become cancerous. He said that when the immune system is functioning normally, the cancer cells are destroyed. But if it is weakened by poor nutrition, environmental pollutants or debilitating stress, cancer cells are uninhibited and multiply rapidly. Therefore, the way to treat cancer is by revitalizing the body's immune system with diet, supplementary nutrients, and "detoxification." In 1982 Manner became affiliated with a clinic in Tijuana, Mexico, which was later renamed the Manner Clinic. During 1988 the clinic charged $7,500 for its 21-day program of vegetable juices, "natural foods," intravenous Laetrile, coffee enemas, and large amounts of vitamins, minerals, enzymes, glandular extracts, other products, and inspirational messages.

Although Manner claimed a 74% success rate in treating cancers, there is no evidence that he kept track of how patients did once they left his clinic. In 1988 a reporter who attended a manner seminar for doctors (mostly chiropractors and naturopaths) uncovered a scheme to defraud insurance companies. The scheme was carried out by a company that files claims on behalf of patients at "alternative" treatment facilities. Instead of indicating what actually took place, the company would enter code numbers for standard treatment on the claim forms.[59] Manner died in 1988, but the clinic is still operating.

The components of metabolic therapy vary from practitioner to practitioner. No controlled study has shown that any of its components has any value against cancer or any other chronic disease. However, many people find its concepts appealing because they do not seem far removed from scientific medicine's concerns with diet, life-style, and the relationship between emotions and bodily responses.

Promotion of Questionable Methods

Promoters of cancer quackery run the gamut from ignorant individuals to highly educated scientists with advanced degrees. A few even hold medical degrees. Such individuals often (1) discount biopsy verification, (2) fail to keep adequate records, (3) spread claims through the media rather than through scientifically acceptable channels subject to peer review, (4) tend to be isolated from established scientific facilities or associates, and (5) claim persecution by the medical establishment.

Cancer patients can obtain information about questionable methods in many ways:

1. *Personal contacts.* Testimonials and other information may be obtained from friends, neighbors, or other individuals who know someone supposedly improved or cured by an unorthodox treatment. In some areas, traffic in questionable methods is so well organized that proponents infiltrate hospitals to tout their methods in "chance meetings" in waiting rooms.
2. *Books.* These are some of the books that have been involved in the promotion of questionable methods of cancer management:

   The Incredible Story of Krebiozen: A Matter of Life or Death, by Herbert Bailey with introduction by Senator Paul H. Douglas, 1962

   Laetrile: Control for Cancer, by Glen D. Kittler, 1963

   Happy People Rarely Get Cancer, by J.I. Rodale, 1972

   Vitamin B-17: Forbidden Weapon Against Cancer, by Michael L. Culbert, 1974

   World Without Cancer, by G. Edward Griffen, 1974

   Laetrile Case Histories, by John A. Richardson, M.D., 1977

   Recalled by Life, by Anthony Satillaro, M.D., 1982.

   The Cancer Industry, by Ralph Moss, 1989.

   A Cancer Therapy, Results of Fifty Cases, revised 1990.

   These books are skillfully written and can cause average readers to conclude that they can make valid judgments based on the information the books contain. Readers are given the impression that the author is impartial and factual, desite the fact that the book strongly advocates a particular method of treatment.
3. *Proponent organizations.* The International Association of Cancer Victors and Friends (IACVF)[60] was founded by Cecile Hoffman, a cancer patient who believed her life had been

saved by the use of Laetrile. Mrs. Hoffman died in 1969 of metastatic cancer. Other groups that promote questionable methods include the Cancer Control Society, which offers tours of the Mexican clinics, the National Health Federation (see Chapter 13),[61] the Committee for Freedom of Choice in Medicine,[62] People Against Cancer, the Foundation for Alternative Cancer Therapy, Ltd, and the Center for Advancement in Cancer Education. Each of these organizations engages in most of the following activities: (a) publishes a magazine or newsletter, (b) sells books, (c) orchestrates letter-writing campaigns, (d) refers patients to "alternative" treatment facilities, and (e) sponsors conventions that attract large numbers of participants. Another organization, Project Cure, promotes questionable treatments through the media and distributes proponent literature. Figure 18-2 illustrates the aggressive language used by some proponents.

4. *Information services.* Several proponents of questionable methods provide individual clients with reports on cancer treatment based on computer searches and other sources. The reports include some information about conventional treatment but are slanted toward unconventional treatment. In 1991, investigative reporter David Zimmerman probed a report from one such service, CANHELP, operated by Pat McGrady, Jr. The report, which had cost $400, said that no effective conventional treatment was available and recommended a restricted diet plus 100 to 150 supplement pills each day. McGrady apparently was unaware of a new treatment that appeared to have extremely good results. The results had not yet been published in a scientific journal but were readily available to physicians and the public from the National Cancer Institute's information services (see below). Zimmerman indicated that McGrady's advice, if followed, would have led to an unnecessary death.[63]
5. *Radio and television programs.* Proponents of controversial remedies are frequently interviewed on talk shows. A few talk show hosts, most notably Gary Null (syndicated from a station in New York City), give a great deal

Fedstapo targeting our medical freedom

U.S. medical orthodoxy and government regulatory agencies have joined forces in an all-out attack on the burgeoning alternative health movement.

To date, the campaign . . . has meant stepped up prosecution of alternative medical practitioners, assembling of "hit lists" of suspect doctors and professional propagandizing in favor of allopathic, drug-industry medicine.

Joined in the alliance against what they choose to call "health fraud" are such governmental agencies as the Food and Drug Administration (FDA) Postal Service, and Federal Trade Commission (FTC), as well as such non-governmental but establishment-lining propaganda groups such as the National Council Against Health Fraud, Inc. (NCAHF), the U.S. Council of Better Business Bureaus, national groups of state and federal health officials and other quasi-official organizations.

FIGURE 18-3. This excerpt, from a newsletter of the Committee for Freedom of Choice in Medicine, implies that organized medicine, drug companies, government agencies, and various consumer-protection groups are conspiring against the public interest. In 1977, the Committee's founder, Robert Bradford, and its vice-president Frank Salaman, were convicted of conspiracy to smuggle Laetrile into the United States. Bradford now operates American Biologics, a Mexican clinic offering a broad spectrum of unorthodox and unproven treatments for cancer, cardiovascular disease, arthritis, multiple sclerosis, and other conditions. Dr. Bruce Halstead, CFCM's vice-president for more than 10 years, was convicted in 1986 of cancer fraud.

of favorable publicity to questionable cancer treatments. A few individuals, such as Harry M. Hoxsey, have had their own radio stations.

6. *Sponsorship by prominent individuals.* Entertainers, socially prominent persons, celebrities, congressional representatives, and others may be persuaded to promote various questionable methods of cancer management. These individuals often are sincere but lack the scientific background to judge the merit of the approach and may not be aware of the strict criteria necessary for scientific investigation before a drug or method is acceptable for medical use.

Cancer Treatment Centers of America, which operates American International Hospital in Zion, Illinois, and another facility in Tulsa, Oklahoma, advertises frequently on television and in health-related magazines and chiropractic journals. Many of its ads feature testimonials from patients who say they received help after other doctors have given up on them. The ads claim that the facilities offer innovative treatment and "specialize in treating cases other hospitals call hopeless." However, no statistics comparing their survival rates with those of other facilities have been published in a scientific journal. Critics charge that in addition to standard approaches, patients at Cancer Treatment Centers of America may be subjected to unproven and disproven treatments, expensive and unnecessary tests, and expensive hospital treatment in situations where less expensive outpatient treatment is standard practice.[64]

Consumer Protection Laws

The U.S. Food and Drug Administration, which has jurisdiction over drugs and devices marketed in interstate commerce, has been able to drive many questionable cancer treatments out of the American marketplace. Regulation of health professionals is handled primarily by state licensing agencies. State attorneys general and local district attorneys can take action against anyone—licensed or not—who violate laws involving fraud and deception. Several states (California was the first) have special laws to control the sale of worthless cancer remedies. The California law has established precise procedures to test and investigate cancer treatment products, with the burden of proof of efficacy and safety being placed on the producer of the substance. Sellers of products must have approval of the State Department of Public Health to sell, prescribe, or adminster a drug or device for the diagnosis or treatment of cancer.

The vigor with which government officials work to protect the public against cancer frauds varies considerably from agency to agency and depends in part on the extent of other matters that compete for their attention. It also depends upon the extent to which fraud victims (or their survivors) make complaints and press for action.

Reliable Information

Reliable information about cancer can be obtained from a local chapter or the national office of the American Cancer Society (1-800-227-2345), as well as from the Cancer Information Service (CIS), Community Special Projects Branch, Division of Cancer Control and Rehabilitation, 8300 Colesville Rd., Silver Spring, MD 20910. Information also can be obtained from CIS Regional Cancer Centers. By dialing 1-800-4-CANCER, callers from most parts of the United States will be connected with the CIS office serving their area. The only areas not tied into the toll-free number are Washington, DC (1-202-636-5700), Alaska (1-800-638-6070), and Hawaii (1-800-524-6070).

The Cancer Information Service can answer questions and may provide literature about the latest cancer treatments, clinical trials, early cancer detection, reducing cancer risk, and community services for patients and their families. Physicians can obtain additional information on treatment protocols, results, and clinical trials through Physician Data Query (PDQ), a computerized database maintained and updated monthly by the National Cancer Institute. This enables most cancer patients to benefit from the latest scientific knowledge without having to travel far.

Cancer Treatment Guidelines

FDA historian Wallace Janssen has suggested the following treatment guidelines for cancer victims:

1. Do not bet your life on any method that has not been approved for marketing or research.
2. Go after the best possible treatment offered by known cancer experts.
3. Avoid any "fad" treatment promoted by some crusading group of laymen.
4. Do not trust testimonials from laypersons who think they have been cured by unrecognized treatments. Such people mean well,

It's Your Decision

You have a serious disease such as cancer or AIDS. A clinic in Tijuana, Mexico, offers to inject various drugs not available in the United States and guarantees that their treatment will help. The treatment program costs several thousand dollars and does not include room, board, or transportation costs. How would you investigate the clinic? What information would you need to make an intelligent decision?

but they are not qualified to diagnose or determine what cured them.

5. Stick with a prescribed treatment even if results are not immediately apparent.
6. Have faith in experts who are devoting their careers to cancer research and treatment.
7. If a specialist "gives up," look for another. A good physician does not abandon a patient to hopelessness.[65]

Reliable Books

The American Cancer Society's Complete Book of Cancer: Prevention, Detection, Treatment, Rehabilitation, Cure, edited by Arthur Holleb, M.D., New York, 1986, Doubleday & Co.

Understanding Cancer (ed 3), by Mark Renneker, M.D. Palo Alto, 1988, Bull Publishing Co.

Cancer Sourcebook, edited by Frank E. Bair. Detroit, 1990, Omnigraphics.

An Almanac of Practical Resources for Cancer Survivors, by Fitzhugh Mullan, M.D., Barbara Hoffman, M.D., and the editors of Consumer Reports Books. New York, 1990, Consumers Union.

Summary

Cancer is a general term applied to more than 100 diseases characterized by cell growth. Early diagnosis and treatment are likely to produce the most favorable results. Victims may turn to quackery because of fear, loss of hope, inadequate information, and other psychosocial factors. This chapter describes many types of quackery and tells how to obtain competent professional help.

Discussion Questions

1. What are the risk factors for cancer? How can it be diagnosed and prevented?
2. Describe the main types of proven cancer treatment.
3. What factors make people susceptible to cancer quackery?
4. Identify and briefly discuss the broad categories of questionable cancer remedies.
5. What was krebiozen? Why is it significant?
6. Describe Laetrile, its effectiveness in the treatment of cancer, and the problems with its use.
7. What is metabolic therapy? What is its appeal?
8. Discuss the Supreme Court ruling on Laetrile.
9. Where and how do people obtain information about questionable cancer treatment methods?
10. What treatment guidelines will help cancer victims?
11. Where can people get reliable information about cancer treatment?

References

1. Brown HG: A final challenge. In Barrett S and Cassileth BR (eds): Dubious cancer treatment, Tampa, 1990, American Cancer Society, Florida Division.
2. Barnes C: Testimony before the subcommittee on health and long-term care of the U.S. House of Representatives Select Committee on Aging. In Pepper C et al: Quackery: a $10 billion scandal, Washington, DC, 1984, U.S. Government Printing Office.
3. Boring CC, Squires TS and Ton T: Cancer statistics 1992, Ca—A Cancer Journal for Clinicians 42:19-38, 1992.
4. Pitot HC: Principles of carcinogenesis: chemical. In DeVita VT, Hellman S, and Rosenberg SA (eds): Cancer, principles and practices of oncology, ed 3, Philadelphia, 1989, JB Lippincott Co.
5. Unreliable breast cancer screening halted, FDA Consumer 25(9):42-43, 1991.
6. Shaving chemotherapy: killing patients with kindness, Medical World News, pp 24-25, Apr 28, 1986.
*7. National Cancer Institute: What are clinical trials all about? NIH Publication No. 90-2706, Washington, DC, 1989, U.S. Government Printing Office.
8. NAS Committee on Diet, Nutrition and Cancer: Diet, nutrition and cancer, Washington, DC, 1982, National Academy of Sciences.
9. Whelan EM: Dietary recommendations for cancer prevention, ACSH News & Views 3:4, 1982.
*10. American Cancer Society guidelines on diet, nutrition, and cancer, Ca—A Cancer Journal for Clinicians 41:334-338, 1991.

*Recommended reading

*11. Kritchevsky D: Diet and Cancer, Ca—A Cancer Journal for Clinicians 41:328-333, 1991.
12. Cancer patients respond to placebos, San Francisco Chronicle, March 20, 1976.
13. Vissing MV and Petersen JC: Taking Laetrile: Conversion to medical deviance, Ca—A Cancer Journal for Clinicians 31:365-369, 1981.
*14. Brigden ML: Unorthodox therapy and your cancer patient, Postgrad Med 81:271-280, 1987.
15. Cassileth BR: Contemporary unorthodox treatments in cancer medicine, Ann Intern Med 101:105-112, 1984.
15a. Lerner IJ, Kennedy BJ: The prevalance of questionable methods of cancer treatment in the United States, Ca—A Cancer Journal for Clinicians 42:181–191, 1992.
*16. American Cancer Society: Unproven methods of cancer management, New York, 1982, The Society.
*17. American Cancer Society: Questionable methods of cancer management. New York, 1992, The Society.
18. Tyler VE: Pau d'arco, Nutrition Forum 2:8, 1985.
19. Doctor sentenced for cancer fraud, Nutrition Forum, 3:39, 1986.
20. Healing, Journal of the Gerson Institute and the Gerson Therapy, vol 1, Fall 1981.
21. Straus CG: The Gerson therapy, Newsreal Series, No 4, Aug 1977.
22. Lowell J: The Gerson clinic, Nutrition Forum 3:9-12, 1986.
23. American Cancer Society: Unproven methods of cancer management: macrobiotic diets for the treatment of cancer, Ca—A Cancer Journal for Clinicians 39:248-251,1989.
24. American Cancer Society: Questionable methods of cancer management: questionable "nutritional" therapies in the treatment of cancer Ca—A Cancer Journal for Clinicians (in press).
25. Wood CG and Pressley BM: The cruellest killers: an update. In Barrett S (ed): The health robbers, ed 2, Philadelphia, 1980, George F Stickley Co.
26. Questionable methods of cancer management: hydrogen peroxide and other "hyperoxygenation" therapies, Ca—A Cancer Journal for Clinicians (in press).
27. Gelb L: Unproven cancer treatments: help or hoax? FDA Consumer 26(2):10-15, 1992.
27a. Green S: "Antineoplastons": an unproved cancer therapy, JAMA 267:2924-2928, 1992.
28. Cancer "cure" challenged, Consumer Reports Health Letter 2:21-22, 1990.
29. American Cancer Society: Unproven methods of cancer management: fresh cell therapy, Ca—A Cancer Journal for Clinicians 41:126-128, 1991.
30. American Cancer Society: Unproven methods of cancer management: Greek cancer cure, Ca—A Cancer Journal for Clinicians 40:368-371, 1990.
31. American Cancer Society: Unproven methods of cancer management: Livingston-Wheeler therapy, Ca—A Cancer Journal for Clinicians 40:103-107, 1990.
32. Cassileth BR et al: Survival and quality of life among patients receiving unproven as compared with conventional cancer therapy, N Engl J Med 324:1180-1985, 1991.
33. American Medical Association Department of Investigation: Facts on quacks, Chicago, 1971, The Association.
34. Friedlander ER: Mental imagery. In Barrett S and Cassileth BR (eds): Dubious cancer treatment, Tampa, 1990, American Cancer Society, Florida Division.
35. American Cancer Society: Unproven methods of cancer management: O Carl Simonton, MD, Ca—A Cancer Journal for Clinicians 32:59, 1982.
36. American Cancer Society: Kelley malignancy index and ecology therapy. In Unproven methods of cancer management, New York, 1971, The Society.
37. Dentist directed McQueen therapy, ADA News, Nov 17, 1980.
38. Herbert V and Barrett S: Vitamins and "health" foods: the great American hustle, Philadelphia, 1981, George F. Stickley Co.
39. Gelband H et al: Unconventional cancer treatment, Washington, DC, 1990, U.S. Government Printing Office.
40. Nourse AE: Quack cancer cures. Good Housekeeping, pp 58-69, Sept 1983.
41. Lasagna L: Doctor's dilemma, New York, 1962, Harper & Row, Publishers.
42. American Cancer Society: Unproven methods of cancer management, New York, 1982, The Society.
43. Patients on unproved cancer therapy told how to make insurance companies pay, Medical World News, June 7, 1982.
44. Nolen, WA: Dr. William Nolen challenges unorthodox healers, 50 Plus, pp 43-45, 70-71, Nov 1983.
45. Diagnostic and Therapeutic Technology Assessment (DATTA): Immunoaugmentative therapy, JAMA 259:3477-3478, 1988.
46. Questionable methods of cancer management: immunoaugmentative therapy (IAT), Ca—A Cancer Journal for Clinicians 41:357-363, 1991.
47. Centers for Disease Control: Isolation of human T-lymphotropic virus type III/lymphadenopathy-associated virus from serum proteins given to cancer patients—Bahamas, MMWR 34:490-491, 1985.
*48. Gelband H et al: Unconventional cancer treatments, Washington, DC, 1990, U.S. Government Printing Office.
49. Stanford Observer, May 13, 1979.
50. Herbert B: Laetrile: the cult of cyanide. In Nutrition cultism: facts and fictions. Philadelphia, 1981, The George F Stickley Co.
51. Top officials cite Laetrile dangers, FDA Consumer 11:3-4, 1977.
52. Young, JH: Laetrile in histoical perspective. In Merkle GE and Petersen JC (eds): Politics, science, and cancer: the Laetrile phenomenon, Boulder, Colo, 1980, Westview Press.
*53. Wilson B: The rise and fall of Laetrile, Nutrition Forum 5:33-40, 1988.
54. American Cancer Society: Laetrile background information, New York, 1977, The Society.
55. Laetrile: the political success of a scientific failure, Consumer Reports 42:444-447, 1977.
56. Moertel C et al: A clinical trial of amygdalin (Laetrile) in the treatment of human cancer, N Engl J Med 306:201-206, 1982.
57. Relman A: Closing the books on Laetrile, N Engl J Med 306:236, 1982.

58. Dr. Krebs' license is revoked, San Francisco Chronicle, July 11, 1974.

58a. American Cancer Society: Questionable methods of cancer management: questionable cancer practices in Tijuana and other Mexican border clinics, Ca—A Cancer Journal for Clinicians 41:310–319, 1991.

59. South J: The Manner clinic, Nutrition Forum 5:61-67, 1988.

60. Unproven methods of cancer management: International Association of Cancer Victors and Friends, Ca—A Cancer Journal for Clinicians 39:58-59, 1991.

61. American Cancer Society: Unproven methods of cancer management: National Health Federation, Ca—A Cancer Journal for Clinicians 41:61-64, 1991.

62. Questionable methods of cancer management: Committee for Freedom of Choice in Medicine, Ca—A Cancer Journal for Clinicians (in press).

*63. Zimmerman D: A case report: how Pat McGrady's 'CAN-HELP' helps patients with cancer, Probe 1(2):4-7, 1991.

64. Weiss J: Critics say cancer ads deceptive, Dallas Morning News, June 21, 1992, pp 1A, 26A.

65. Janssen WF: Cancer quackery: past and present, FDA Consumer 11:27-32, 1977.

CHAPTER NINETEEN

AIDS

AIDS has rightly been called the greatest health threat of the 20th century. AIDS has also been called a quack's dream come true.

FRANK E. YOUNG, M.D., PH.D.
FDA COMMISSIONER
JAMES H. MCILHENNY, PRESIDENT
COUNCIL OF BETTER BUSINESS BUREAUS[1]

In addition to illness, disability, and death, AIDS has brought fear to the hearts of most Americans—fear of disease and fear of the unknown.

C. EVERETT KOOP, M.D., SC.D.[2]
SURGEON GENERAL

Consumer Decision

How can one be reliably tested for AIDS?

How can AIDS be prevented?

What are the most effective treatments for AIDS?

What AIDS-related quackery is found in the health marketplace?

Where can up-to-date information about AIDS be obtained?

Acquired immune deficiency syndrome (AIDS) is a fatal disease caused by the human immunodeficiency virus (HIV). This organism can remain in a person's body for years before symptoms appear and the individual is considered to have AIDS. The virus disrupts the functioning of the body's immune system, rendering the infected individual progressively unable to resist organisms that would normally be harmless.

The incidence of AIDS has been rising rapidly. In March 1992, Secretary of Health and Human Services Louis Sullivan announced that 1 in 250 Americans is now infected with HIV. Since AIDS was recognized in 1981, more than 200,000 cases of AIDS have been reported to the U.S. Centers for Disease Control (CDC), with more than 133,000 deaths.[3] It took 8 years to reach the 100,000 mark, but only 2 years to reach the second. The seriousness of HIV disease, the growing epidemic, and the enormous cost of treating infected individuals will have great impact on our health care system as well as our society as a whole.

This chapter discusses the nature of AIDS, AIDS testing procedures, preventive measures, treatment approaches, economic factors, and AIDS-related quackery.

Course of the Disease

Most people with AIDS are adults in their twenties, thirties, and forties, but the disease can occur at any age. The initial stage of the disease is a brief illness that typically includes fever, sore throat, skin rash, swollen lymph glands, headache, and malaise. This phase, termed *acute HIV syndrome,* usually lasts 1 to 2 weeks and is followed by a prolonged symptom-free period. The median length of the symptom-free period in untreated individuals is about 10 years, but the disease progresses much faster in some individuals and may remain quiescent indefinitely in a small percentage of others. Thus, at any given time, the majority of individuals who carry the AIDS virus exhibit no symptoms. Regardless of the stage of the disease, an infected individual can transmit the virus to others.

Once clinical symptoms appear, the course of the disease can vary considerably, depending in part on the extent of immune damage and the treatment received by the patient. Eventually, most AIDS patients become thin, easily fatigued, and prone to diarrhea, swollen lymph glands, and multiple infections. *Pneumocystis carinii* pneumonia and a skin cancer called Kaposi's sarcoma are life-threatening complications. In addition, some patients suffer from dementia.

Since AIDS was recognized in 1981, the diagnosis of AIDS has been reserved for patients with severe symptoms. The term *AIDS-related complex (ARC)* has been used to designate a relatively mild group of AIDS-related symptoms, but it is now obsolete.

Most authorities believe that it is better to classify the later stages of HIV disease by measuring the number or functioning of certain cells that are part of the body's immune system rather than by just considering the patient's symptoms.[4] These cells, called T-lymphocytes, helper cells, T4 cells, or CD4 cells, are the primary target of the AIDS virus. Recently, CDC proposed to redefine AIDS as an HIV infection in which a person's CD4 cell count drops below 200 per cubic microliter of blood. (A microliter is one millionth of a liter. In healthy people, the number usually ranges from 800 to 1200.) The proposed criteria would provide a larger but more accurate count of the number of infected individuals. Using the old criteria, CDC estimates that about 200,000 of the 1 million Americans infected with HIV have AIDS. If the proposed criteria were adopted, the AIDS total would be boosted considerably. However, their implementation has been postponed indefinitely.[3a]

Testing Procedures

In 1985, the FDA approved a test for use in commercial blood banks and public health clinics to screen blood for antibodies to the AIDS virus. The test, called ELISA (enzyme-linked immunosorbent assay), does not diagnose AIDS but indicates whether an individual has developed antibodies to the AIDS virus. The ELISA test, which is highly sensitive but can yield false-positive results, is also used to screen indivduals. If it is positive twice, more specific tests, such as the Western blot, are used to test for AIDS antigens, which indicate that the disease is present. AIDS testing is not foolproof, however. False-negative results occur when an infected individual has not yet developed antibodies to the AIDS virus.

People who have shared drug needles or who have had sexual contact with a man or woman who could be infected with HIV should consider being tested, even if no symtoms have appeared. Testing can be particularly important for people thinking about entering a new sexual relationship or having children. Testing should be done several months after the potentially risky behavior has taken place. Although most people test positive within 4 months after becoming infected, the virus can take a year to show up in some people. Because a positive test report (even if it is false-positive) can have serious consequences, it is important that HIV testing be preceded by appropriate counseling and that strict confidentiality be maintained.

Public fear of AIDS has encouraged a variety of questionable promotions. In 1991, two dentists in Oakland, California, advertised in local newspapers that they had tested negative for AIDS. According to a report in the *San Francisco Examiner,*[5] the ad attracted no new patients but triggered many phone calls from people who accused the dentists of playing on people's fears. Although transmission of AIDS from a dentist to a patient has been reported (see later in this chapter), the risk is extremely small.

Some dating services require AIDS testing for prospective clients. Although a negative test might reduce the chance of contact with an AIDS-infected individual, it does not guarantee that the person is free of AIDS. Antibodies to HIV are not present during the first few months of infection. In addition, a negative test cannot ensure that an individual will not acquire HIV infection in the future. Some extrepreneurs operating private laboratories have advertised that their AIDS testing can bring "peace of mind by knowing that you are AIDS-free." Other companies have offered "private" AIDS testing my mail. Mail-in test kits do not have FDA approval. The companies marketing them may be unreliable or fraudulent operations. The FDA has stopped two companies that were selling kits for testing saliva for AIDS antibody testing.[6]

Consumers worried about whether they have AIDS should seek testing from a reliable source. In most parts of the country, reliable testing can be obtained anonymously and free of charge through a local health department. It can also be ordered through one's personal physician.

Prevention

AIDS is not acquired through casual contact, such as eating meals, kissing, shaking hands, or being near someone who coughs or sneezes. Intimate contact with body fluids (blood, semen, vaginal secretions, or possibly breast milk) is required. Thus the disease is spread through having sexual intercourse (particularly anal intercourse) with an infected person, sharing contaminated needles and syringes, or being born to an infected mother. Blood transfusions are another potential source of infection, but this problem has decreased greatly since a method of identifying infected blood has been developed. The American Red Cross estimates that the risk of receiving a transfusion unit contaminated with any infectious agent is about 1 in 150,000.[7] CDC states that since 1985, only 20 of the more than 200,000 reported cases of AIDS have been attributed to screened blood.[8] Guidelines are also being developed to prevent transmission of HIV through organ and tissue transplants.[9]

Of the first 200,000 reported American cases, 58% appear to have been spread through homosexual activity, 22% through sharing by intravenous drug abusers, 6% by heterosexual transmission to males, 11% by heterosexual transmission to females, and 2% by blood transfusions performed before current screening procedures were instituted. However, the World Health Organization (WHO)[10] states that heterosexual transmission is growing rapidly and is by far the primary mode of transmission worldwide. In 1992 WHO estimated that 10 to 12 million people are infected by HIV, 2 million people have full-blown AIDS, and up to 40 million will have HIV infection and 18 million will have AIDS by the year 2000.[11] The American Council on Science and Health agrees that heterosexual transmission of AIDS is a serious problem in the United States. Since it takes many years for the disease to become apparent in infected individuals, current figures may under estimate the number of people affected by heterosexual transmission.[12,13]

Many people have wondered whether health care workers who have AIDS or who have contact with AIDS patients are likely to transmit HIV infection to their patients. The evidence so far suggests that this is uncommon. A study of 2500 health workers who cared for very ill AIDS patients found that only 3 of 750 who had stuck themselves with a needle had a positive antibody test for exposure to HIV.[2]

Consumers Union[14] and the American Council on Health[15] recommend the following protective measures:

1. Abstain from sex outside a mutually faithful relationship with a partner whom you know is not infected with the AIDS virus.
2. If you choose to have sexual relations with someone who may be infected with the AIDS virus or whose history is unknown, avoid exchange of body fluids. A latex (rubber) condom should be used during each sexual act, from start to finish. Use of a spermicide provides additional protection.
3. Never use a nonsterile needle or syringe.

Hearst concurs with these recommendations but stresses that avoiding high-risk partners is far more important than anything else.[16] He considers high-risk groups to include "anyone who within the past ten years has engaged in male homesexuality or intravenous drug use, has resided in Haiti or central Africa, has a history of multiple blood transfusions, or is a hemophiliac . . . [and] anyone who has had a regular partner who is a member of any of these groups." (As noted previously, however, the risk from blood transfusions after 1985 is very small.)

Through June 30, 1990, 5425 cases of AIDS were reported among millions of health care workers. A survey by Chamberland et al[17] concluded that most acquired their disease through nonoccupational exposure. The CDC[18] recommends the following:

1. All health care workers should use special care when handling blood specimens or disposing of needles and other sharp instruments.
2. Those who do exposure-prone procedures should know their HIV status.
3. Those who know they are infected with AIDS should not perform exposure-prone procedures unless they have sought counsel from an expert review panel and been advised under what circumstances, if any, they may continue to perform these procedures.
4. Mandatory testing of workers is not advisable.

The American Public Health Association, the National Commission on AIDS, and most health care leaders do not believe that mandatory testing of health care workers would be cost-effective. In January 1991, *Time* magazine reported that no case of transmission from a health care worker to a patient had been confirmed.[19] Subsequent evidence suggests that one dentist who had AIDS probably infected five of his patients. However, the risk of doctor-to-patient transmission still appears to be extremely small.

The American Medical Association House of Delegates has called for voluntary testing of physicians engaged in invasive procedures that risk transmission of HIV and for supervision of doctors who know they are infected with the virus. The invasive procedures are those in which the doctor's hands or instruments enter the patient's body or touch mucous membranes, as in abdominal, heart, or dental surgery. An Illinois law mandates that health care workers and patients inform each other if their contact involves a risk of HIV transmission.

Some entrepreneurs have attempted to exploit public fear of acquiring AIDS. Covers for public toilets and telephone receivers have been marketed with claims that they will prevent transmission of the AIDS virus. Such products are worthless because AIDS is not transmitted in this manner.

Treatment

Finding a cure for AIDS is considered very difficult because HIV infects several types of cells and inserts a copy of itself into their genetic material (DNA). This "tricks" the cells into treating the virus's genes as their own. The virus is then safe from attack by the body's immune system and is reproduced each time the host cells reproduce. The *Harvard Health Letter*[20] notes that it is difficult to envision a drug that could eradicate the virus from multiple sites without doing extensive harm to vital body tissues. In addition, drug resistance occurs readily because the virus constantly evolves into new forms by mutating its own genes. AIDS develops when something happens that triggers rapid reproduction and spillage of the virus into the blood stream, where it destroys CD4 lymphocytes and weakens the immune system of the patient. Researchers hope to find a combination of drugs that, administered early in the disease, will hold the virus in check and make it difficult for drug-resistant strains to develop.

Although no cure for AIDS has been found, significant progress has been made to enable HIV-infected patients to live longer and have fewer complications of their disease. Zidovudine (formerly called azidothymidine, or AZT), the first antiviral drug approved to fight AIDS, can slow the progress of the disease. The *Lahey Clinic Health Letter*[21] notes that treatment with zidovudine is now appropriate when the CD4 count falls below 500, even if the patient has no symptoms of illness. Unfortunately, the length of time it can be administered is limited by the development of side effects (such as bone marrow suppression) and the development of resistant strains. A similar drug, dideoxynosine (DDI), can be prescribed when AZT cannot be tolerated or no longer appears effective. Many other antiviral and immune-related drugs are at various stages of development in the laboratory or in human clinical trials.[22] Progress has also been made in preventing or fighting *Pneumocystis carinii* pneumonia and several other AIDS-related infections. Overall, it has been found that early diagnosis and treatment lead to increased survival.

It is difficult for people with AIDS to maintain adequate nutritional status. This results from a combination of lack of appetite, poor nutrient absorption, and high nutrient losses. Infection of the mouth and throat can make chewing and swallowing painful. Malnourished people are more susceptible to infection than are well-nourished people. Because their resistance is low, AIDS patients should be especially careful to avoid food-borne infections such as dysentery caused by *Salmonella* bacteria. The Task Force on Nutrition Support in AIDS[23] recommends that all HIV patients have a complete nutritional assessment and dietary counseling with a health professional.

The seriousness of AIDS, the growing worldwide epidemic, and political pressure from AIDS activists have led the Food and Drug Administration (FDA) to shorten and streamline its procedures for approving new drugs that can be used for treating HIV infections. Under new regulations, developers of drugs for AIDS and other serious illnesses can make promising drugs available before clinical testing is complete.[24]

Treatment Costs

An economist at the federal Agency for Health Care Policy and Research has estimated the following average costs for treating HIV disease: $5150 per year for treating individuals who test positive but do not have AIDS, $32,000 per year for treating people with AIDS, and $85,333 for lifetime treatment.[25] The U.S. Public Health Service estimates that federal spending budgeted for AIDS during 1992 includes $1262 million for research, $312 million for treatment, and $393 million for prevention, a total of $1967 million.[26] Chapter 26 contains additional information about AIDS treatment costs.

Many insurance companies and self-insured employers have taken steps to minimize or avoid these costs. Some companies, for example, have established lifetime limits on HIV-related claims, ranging from $5000 to $50,000. Some insurers have denied coverage to single men living in certain zip code areas or working as hairdressers. Some insurers require HIV testing of applicants and deny coverage to those who test positive. Critics of these practices claim that they are unfairly discriminatory, and some have filed lawsuits attacking these practices. The American Association of Retired Persons (AARP) has expressed concern about attempts by insurers to limit or exclude by disease category. An AARP official has said, "Once you start with one disease, like AIDS, the next step could be Alzheimer's or other chronic conditions. I think that would be a disaster for the people who need help the most."[27]

When AIDS patients are seriously ill, home care is often an alternative to hospitalization. However, the New York City Department of Consumer Affairs[28] states that private high-tech home care suppliers have been engaging in "bedside robbery." The biggest problem is the provision of total parenteral nutrition (TPN), a liquid protein and fat supplement fed intravenously through a surgically implanted catheter to patients whose digestive systems no longer function normally. The Department's report cited instances in which insurance companies and government agencies have been billed more $15,000 per month for treatment that costs much less to deliver. Only 3 of 12 companies responded to the Department's questionnaire about prices for their services. Several patients reported that buying supplies through a pharmacy and administering TPN themselves could more than halve their home care costs.

Hospice care is another treatment alternative that is more compassionate and less expensive than hospitalization. Buckingham[29] states that many hospice providers have developed innovative programs for people with AIDS.

Burroughs Wellcome Co., which manufactures zidovudine and three other drugs used to treat AIDS patients, is making these products available free of charge to needy patients until they can secure financial assistance from other sources such as state or federal programs.[29a] Physicians can enroll patients in the company's HIV Patient Assistance Program by calling 800-722-9294.

AIDS-Related Quackery

The fact that AIDS causes great suffering and is deadly has encouraged the marketing of hundreds of unproven remedies to AIDS victims. In addition, many companies in the "health food" industry have produced vitamin concoctions claimed to "strengthen the immune system" of healthy individuals.[30] John Renner, M.D., president of the Consumer Health Information Research Institute, who attended meetings of groups promoting unorthodox methods, has commented that "everything has been converted into an AIDS treatment." The remedies he observed have included processed blue-green algae (pond scum), hydrogen peroxide, BHT (a food preservative), pills derived from mice given the AIDS virus, herbal capsules, bottles of "T cells," and thumping on the thymus gland.[31] Young and McIlhenny[1] have noted that some firms have offered to freeze and store bone marrow, claiming that it could be used to restore an AIDS victim's marrow when AIDS began to deplete the body's supply of bone marrow (which manufactures blood cells).

Mexican cancer clinics offer their unproven treatments to AIDS victims, and a black market has developed in drugs that have shown promise but lack FDA approval here because the agency is not convinced they are safe and effective. Several drugs available without a prescription in Mexico are being smuggled into the United States. Drugs are also imported through "buyers' clubs," which obtain the drugs from other countries where they are legally prescribed or used in clinical trials. "Legitimate" buyers' clubs require a prescription written by an American physician who supervises the patient's care. However, some buyers' clubs obtain drugs for people who are not under medical care.

Several studies have shown that a significant percentage of AIDS patients use unproven treatment. A study of 79 patients attending the St. Louis AIDS Clinical Trials Unit found that more than 44 (56%) had tried an "alternative" remedy. The most commonly used were vitamins (46% of patients), herbal therapy (16%), imagery or meditation (14%), and nonapproved drugs (14%).[33] Most patients using these methods thought they had improved their general well-being but readily admitted that the benefit was largely psychological. The average yearly cost was $356, but 14 of the patients spent between $500 and $2700 and 2 patients spent more than $9000 each.

Interviews with 114 patients attending the AIDS Clinic of the University of California San Francisco Medical Center indicated that 25 (22%) had taken one or more herbal products during the 3 months before the survey.[34] The study's authors expressed concern that herbal extracts can produce diarrhea, liver toxicity, and other symptoms common in AIDS itself.

Some AIDS activists have expressed considerable animosity toward government agencies and con-

Personal Glimpse

In 1989, volunteers of the Consumer Health Education Council[32] telephoned 41 Houston-area health food stores and asked to speak with the person who provided nutritional advice. The callers explained that they had a brother with AIDS who was seeking an effective alternative treatment for HIV. The callers also explained that the brother's wife was still having sex with her husband and was seeking products that would reduce her risk of being infected, or make it impossible. All 41 retailers offered products they said could benefit the brother's immune system, improve the woman's immunity, and protect her against harm from HIV. The recommended products included vitamins (41 stores), vitamin C (38 stores), immune boosters (38 stores), coenzyme Q_{10} (26 stores), germanium (26 stores), lecithin (19 stores), ornithine and/or arginine (9 stores), gamma-linolenic acid (7 stores), raw glandulars (7 stores), hydrogen peroxide (5 stores), homeopathic salts (5 stores), Bach flower remedies (4 stores), blue-green algae (4 stores), cysteine (3 stores), and herbal baths (2 stores). Thirty retailers said they carried products that would cure AIDS. None recommended abstinence or use of a condom.

FIGURE 19-1. AIDS activists picketing at the 1990 National Health Fraud Conference. What do you think their activity illustrates about the emotions of desperately ill people?
Photograph courtesy of Lauren Chapman, Kansas City, Mo.

sumer groups that are interested in protecting the public from being exploited by quack methods. About 50 members of the AIDS Coalition to Unleash Power (ACT-UP) staged a protest at the 1990 National Health Fraud Conference in Kansas City, Missouri (Figure 19-1). The demonstrators picketed the hotel and distributed fliers stating, "The goal of this conference is to directly challenge any type of treatment that does not currently meet AMA guidelines or FDA approval! . . . It is not to eliminate any real health fraud that is out there! It represents the efforts of the AMA and the big drug companies to suppress their competition, and the insurance industry to reduce their coverage!" Several protesters were arrested when they stormed into the meeting room blowing loud whistles and shouting their views. Seventeen others were arrested outside the hotel and charged with trespassing.[35]

Since no cure for AIDS is known, victims should be wary of anyone who claims to have one. Up-to-date information can be obtained through the National VD Hotline or the U.S. Public Health Service AIDS Hotline (see the Appendix for toll-free numbers).

IT'S YOUR DECISION

Which of these procedures would you follow if you contemplated having sex with someone?
What is your reasoning?

________ Have partner use a condom

________ Ask whether partner is HIV-infected

________ Ask whether partner uses intravenous drugs

________ All of the above

________ None of the above

SUMMARY

AIDS is a disease of the immune system that is incurable but largely preventable. It is caused by the human immunodeficiency virus (HIV), which escapes the body's immune defenses by incorporating its genes into the genetic material of the body's cells. This organism can remain in a person's body for years before symptoms appear and the individual is considered to have AIDS. By disrupting the functioning of the body's immune system, it renders the infected individual progressively unable to resist organisms that would normally be harmless. Regardless of the stage of the disease, an infected individual can transmit the virus to others. The best way to avoid AIDS is to use a condom and abstain from sex outside a mutually faithful relationship with a partner who is unlikely to be infected with the AIDS virus. In most parts of the country, reliable testing can be obtained anonymously and free of charge through a local health department. It can also be ordered through one's personal physician.

Considerable progress has been made in identifying drugs that can delay the onset of AIDS and control some of its complications. However, the fact that AIDS causes great suffering and is deadly has created a market for many unproven remedies.

DISCUSSION QUESTIONS

1. What is the difference between the terms *HIV disease* and *AIDS?*

2. What is the typical course of HIV disease? Of AIDS?
3. What factors make AIDS difficult to treat?
4. What treatments are available for AIDS and its complications?
5. What observations and predictions have been made about the incidence of AIDS?
6. How is AIDS spread? What measures can prevent its spread?
7. What tests are used to determine whether an individual has AIDS?
8. Identify several dubious products and services related to AIDS or the fear of AIDS.

REFERENCES

1. Young FE and McIlhenny JH: AIDS: False hope from fraudulent treatment. Letter to consumer reporter, May 22, 1989.

* 2. Koop CE: Surgeon General's report on AIDS, Rockville, Md, 1990, US Dept of Health and Human Services.

3. The second 100,000 cases of acquired immunodeficiency syndrome—United States, JAMA 267:788, 1992.

3a. Pfeiffer N: AIDS guidelines: why were they postponed? Medical World News, pp 26-37, 30, May 1992.

4. Volberding P: Management of HIV infection. In Rakel RE, ed: Conn's Current Therapy 1992, Philadelphia, 1992, WB Saunders Co.

5. Garrison J: 2 dentists advertise negative results, San Francisco Examiner, June 30, 1991, p A-12.

6. Sale of unapproved test kits stopped, FDA Consumer 25(8):7, 1991.

7. Red Cross to establish 14 central blood-testing labs, Physicians Financial News, Jan 15, 1992.

8. Say blood supply safe from AIDS infection, Physicians Financial News, May 30, 1992, p 33.

9. Altman LK: Citing AIDS, officials propose tracking transplants, The New York Times, Dec 15, 1991, p 38L.

10. World Health Organization: Current and future dimensions of the HIV-AIDS pandemic, Geneva, 1992, World Health Organization.

11. WHO's new AIDS prevention plan also targets other STDs, American Medical News, May 25, 1992.

12. Carey JM: Heterosexually transmitted AIDS in the United States, New York, 1991, American Council on Science and Health.

*13. Whalen EM: The U.S. AIDS epidemic: an ACSH status report, New York, 1992, American Council on Science and Health.

*14. Hein K, DiGeronimo TF, et al: AIDS: Trading fears for facts, Yonkers, NY, 1991, Consumer Reports Books.

15. Popescu CB: Answers about AIDS, New York, 1988, American Council on Science and Health.

16. Hearst N: Preventing the heterosexual transmission of AIDS, JAMA 259:2428-2432, 1988.

17. Chamberland et al: Health care workers with AIDS—national surveillance update, JAMA 266:3459-3462, 1991.

18. Polder JA, Bell DM et al: Recommendation for preventing transmission of human immunodeficiency virus and hepatitis B virus to patients during exposure-prone invasive procedures, Atlanta, 1991, U.S. Dept. of Health and Human Services.

19. Toufexis A: When the doctor gets infected, Time 137:57, Jan 14, 1991.

*20. Combating HIV in the nineties, Harvard Health Letter 16(11):1-4, 1991.

*21. Living with AIDS, Lahey Clinic Health Letter 3(3):1-4, 1992.

22. AIDS drugs being studied, FDA Consumer 16(2):8-9, 1992.

23. Task Force on Nutrition in AIDS: Guidelines for nutrition support in AIDS, Nutrition Today 24(4):27-33, 1991.

24. Stone B: How AIDS has changed FDA, FDA Consumer 24(1):14-17, 1990.

25. Hellinger FJ: Forecasting the medical care costs of the HIV epidemic: 1991-1994, Inquiry 28(3):213–225, 1991.

26. Haney DQ: Is health lobby robbing Peter to cure Paul? Associated Press story in the Morning Call, Allentown, Pa, May 25, 1992, p A4.

27. Henry S: Health insurance caps—redlining people with AIDS, The Nation, November 11, 1991.

28. DeStefano G: Making a killing on AIDS: home health care and pentamidine, New York, 1991, New York City Department of Consumer Affairs.

29. Buckingham RW: Among friends: hospice care for the person with AIDS, Buffalo, 1992, Prometheus Books.

29a. Drugs free for needy patients, FDA Consumer 26(1):7, 1992.

30. Barrett S: Strengthening the immune system—a growing fad, Nutrition Forum 3:24, 1986.

31. Segal M: Defrauding the desperate, FDA Consumer 21(8):17-19, 1987.

*32. Martin N: AIDS fraud rampant in Houston, Nutrition Forum 7:16, 1990.

33. Rowlands C and Powderly WG: The use of alternative therapies by HIV-positive patients attending the St. Louis AIDS Clinical Trials Unit, Missouri Medicine 88:807-810, 1991.

34. Kassler WJ et al: The use of medicinal herbs by human immunodeficiency virus-infected patients, Arch Intern Med 151:2281-2288, 1991.

35. Barrett S: Sparks fly at health fraud conference, Priorities, Winter 1991, pp 33-35.

*36. Huber JT: How to find information about AIDS, Binghamton, NY, 1992, Haworth Press.

*Recommended reading

Other Products and Services

CHAPTER TWENTY

DRUG PRODUCTS

"When he got up this morning he took an aspirin and some vitamins, then he took pills for his ulcer and pills for iron. Then after some cough medicine he took drugs for a cold, and when he lit a cigarette there was some kind of explosion."

(Reprinted from The Saturday Evening Post. © 1963 The Curtis Publishing Company.)

No drug is perfectly safe. A drug powerful enough to do good is powerful enough to do harm.

MORTON MINTZ
THE THERAPEUTIC NIGHTMARE

Consumer Decisions

Which pain relievers are the most sensible to purchase and use?

Should generic drugs be purchased?

Should laxatives be used?

What over-the-counter cough and cold remedies are effective?

What items should be included in a home medicine cabinet?

Which drug information books are most practical?

Two basic types of medications can be legally purchased in the United States: prescription (℞) drugs and over-the-counter (OTC) drugs. Prescription drugs can be prescribed by a physician or other designated health professional, such as a dentist or podiatrist, and most commonly are dispensed by registered pharmacists. They are also referred to as legend drugs, a term derived from the legend that appears on all packages. They are generally more powerful than OTC products and therefore require professional supervision. By law, a pharmacist cannot fill a prescription without an order that is written or telephoned by the provider. It is also illegal for a pharmacist to fill a prescription without authorization from the provider.

OTC products can be purchased without a prescription from pharmacies, supermarkets, and other outlets. They are generally weaker than prescription drugs and have lesser side effects. They are intended mainly for symptomatic relief of relatively benign self-limiting conditions rather than cure or control of disease. They include such common remedies as pain relievers, antacids, laxatives, and cough and cold remedies.

OTC drugs are occasionally referred to as proprietary (owner), ethical proprietary, patent, or home medicines. The term "patent medicine" emerged during the nineteenth century, when these substances had to be registered with the U.S. Patent Office and the ingredients were kept secret (see Chapter 2). Drug ingredients are no longer kept secret, however, because federal laws require them to be listed on product labels.

Drugs can be marketed under a brand name or their chemical name. New prescription drugs, which are marketed under brand names, are protected by patents that are good for 17 years from the early stages of the drug's development. After this protection period has ended, other manufacturers can copy and market them under their chemical name or another brand name.

Drugs sold under their chemical name are called generic drugs. FDA regulations require that generic drugs undergo limited testing to demonstrate equivalence to their brand-name counterparts. Generic drugs cost less—often considerably less—but some controversy exists over whether they actually are equivalent. Although their active ingredients are identical, their inert ingredients (binders) may affect their absorption and other characteristics of bioavailability. Pharmacists are generally allowed—and in some states are required—to fill prescriptions with generic drugs unless forbidden to do so by the prescribing doctor.

This chapter discusses some commonly used prescription and nonprescription drug products and consumer strategies for using them wisely.

Prescription Drugs

In 1961 there were 656 prescription medicines on the market. Today more than four times that number are available, with total annual sales exceeding $30 billion. About 60% of people in the United States will have at least one prescription this year, with an average of six per person. The National Council on Patient Information and Education[1] states that half of prescriptions are used incorrectly by the patient, and many hospital admissions and deaths can be traced to drug-induced problems.

Many people fail to fill prescriptions they receive, take doses that are too small or too large, take their medication at the wrong intervals, forget to take one or more doses, or discontinue medication too soon. Cramer et al[2] studied the compliance of epileptic patients who used special bottles fitted with a cap that contained a microprocessor to record when the bottles were opened and closed. Even though the patients had a life-threatening disease and were closely monitored, they took an average of only 76% of their medication doses as prescribed.

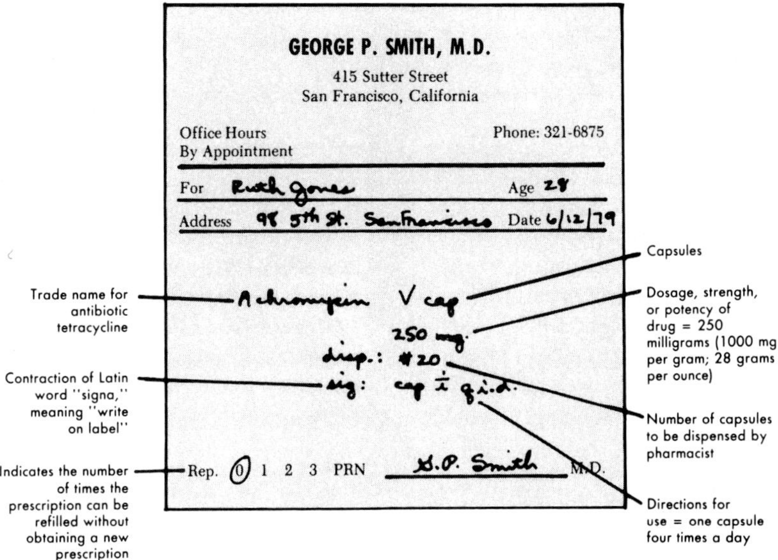

FIGURE 20-1. Contents of a typical prescription.

It is important for consumers to know how to read a physician's prescription. Figure 20-1 illustrates the typical format for prescriptions, and Table 20-1 provides the common Latin abbreviations used by doctors. It is also important be familiar with prescription labels and to understand them. Labels should contain the following information:

1. Patient's name
2. Physician's name
3. Pharmacy name, address, and telephone number
4. Name of the medication, if the physician tells the pharmacist to include it
5. How often and when to take the medication
6. How much to take each time
7. Any special instructions for use
8. Pertinent warnings regarding sedation or sulfite allergy

GENERIC VS. BRAND-NAME DRUGS

Drugs may be identified by generic or brand name. The term generic refers to the name of the active chemical or chemicals in a drug. The brand name of a drug is the name created and used solely by one manufacturer of a product. It is the manufacturer's exclusive property, usually by reason of trademark rights.

Some drugs are marketed under only one brand

TABLE 20–1

COMMON PRESCRIPTION SYMBOLS*

Latin	Abbreviation	Meaning
ad libitum	ad lib	Freely, as needed
ante cibos	a.c.	Before meals
bis in die	b.i.d.	Twice a day
capsula	caps.	Capsule
gutta	gtt.	Drop
hora somni	h.s.	At bedtime
per os	p.o.	Orally
post cibum	p.c.	After meals
pro renata	p.r.n.	As needed
quaque 4 hora	q.4h.	Every 4 hours
quater in die	q.i.d.	Four times a day
quotidie	q.d.	Daily
ter in die	t.i.d.	Three times a day
ut dictum	ut dict.	As directed

*The R in the symbol ℞ is an abbreviation of the Latin verb *recipte,* meaning "take thou." The thou refers to the pharmacist. The "tail" on the R is a contraction of the sign of Jupiter. Thus the symbol is an order to the pharmacist to "take in the name of Jupiter," with the physician invoking the name of Jupiter to ensure that the pharmacist does not make a mistake in carrying out the instructions.

name, while others are marketed under more than one. Major brand-name manufacturers market about half of the generic drugs, while about 350 smaller companies make the rest. The fact that identical drugs are marketed under different names is a potential source of confusion for consumers and possibly even for physicians.

All drug products must meet FDA requirements for form, strength, route of administration (oral or injection), safety, purity, and effectiveness. The official standards of identity, strength, and purity are set forth in the *United States Pharmacopeia (USP)* and the *National Formulary (NF)*. The *USP* covers drug substances and dosage forms, whereas the *NF* covers inactive ingredients in drug products. Both books are revised periodically by experts. In 1980, they were combined into a single volume called the *USP-NF*. The 1990 edition contains about 3000 monographs on drug substances and dosage forms and 250 monographs on inactive ingredients. Product labels sometimes contain the term USP or NF to indicate that the active ingredient meets USP standards. Therapeutic equivalence is established by demonstrating bioequivalence. If the rate of absorption and the blood levels achieved match those of a brand-name drug in the same dosage, a generic substance is considered bioequivalent.

The Federal Drug Price Competition and Patent Term Restoration Act (1984) required the FDA to expedite approval of generic drugs. In approving a generic for marketing, the FDA does not have to approve the safety and effectiveness of its active ingredient(s), since the same chemical substance(s) have been previously approved for use in the drug's brand-name counterpart. However, the FDA must test for and approve the bioequivalency of generic drugs.

In 1987, Dr. Peter Rheinstein,[3] director of the FDA Office of Drug Standards, said that investigations had shown generics to be fully as reliable as their brand-name counterparts. Nightingale and Morrison[4] believe that generic drug products that have been properly evaluated are therapeutically equivalent to their brand-name counterparts. Lunzer[5] has concluded that some brand-name substances are better for treating some serious illnesses. For example, he states that brand-name aspirin may be more effective for rheumatoid arthritis patients,

TABLE 20–2

COMPARATIVE COST OF COMMONLY PRESCRIBED BRAND-NAME AND GENERIC DRUGS*

			Price per 100		
Brand name	**Generic name**	**Dosage**	**Brand**	**Generic**	**Type of drug**
Achromycin V	tetracycline	250 mg	4.10	3.30	Antibiotic
Amoxil	amoxicillin	500 mg	22.25	7.60	Antibiotic
Ativan	lorazepam	1 mg	70.25	4.80	Antianxiety agent
Deltasone	prednisone	10 mg	3.60	4.60	Antiinflammatory drug
Inderal	propanolol	20 mg	36.50	2.95	Beta blocker (for high blood pressure, migraine headaches)
Lasix	furosemide	40 mg	17.25	1.95	Diuretic
Motrin	ibuprofen	400 mg	12.10	4.65	Antiinflammatory drug
Tylenol with codeine	acetaminophen + codeine	300 mg 30 mg	31.70	6.75	Pain reliever
Valium	diazepam	5 mg	58.95	3.95	Antianxiety agent, muscle relaxant

*Source: Modern Medical Supply Co., Rockville Center, NY. These are the spring 1992 catalog prices for physicians who order the products by mail. Retail pharmacy prices for the above items are generally 10% to 50% higher for the brand-name products and 100% to 300% higher for the generic products.

because generic aspirin is formulated poorly and breaks down to salicylic acid and a crystalline substance. At present, more than 400 different generic drugs can be substituted for brand-name drugs.

Generic drugs are estimated to be 30% to 50% cheaper than brand-name drugs. Table 20-2 compares the prices of several commonly prescribed products. Overall, brand names cost 70% more than generics. In order for consumers to realize savings, it is necessary for doctors and pharmacists to make generic drugs available. In all 50 states a pharmacist is allowed to substitute generics if their use has been authorized by a physician.

Generic drugs are not always bargains. Pharmacies buy them at lower prices than brand-name products, but they do not always pass on these savings to the consumer; in some stores consumers have actually paid higher prices for generics. Because prices vary, it is advisable to shop for drugs. Many pharmacies are willing to quote prices over the telephone.

Some manufacturers try to frighten consumers away from generics because brand-name drugs generally are priced higher and yield larger profits. These companies claim that generics are not as safe, that they don't do the job as well and take longer to act, and that patients may suffer side effects. The *FDA Consumer*[6] reported that all of these claims are myths, and *Consumer Reports*[7] also criticized this tactic in an article titled "The Big Lie About Generic Drugs." Authorities generally agree, however, that if a generic drug is used over a long period and appears to be working, it is best to not switch brands when refilling the prescription. Using a single brand will avoid any problem of brand-to-brand variation.

In 1989 it was revealed that several FDA employees had accepted payoffs from generic drug firms and that seven companies had substituted brand-name drugs in tests needed for approval of 57 generic versions. Subsequent investigation revealed that the bribes had not affected the approval process. The FDA banned the 57 products but stated that no evidence was uncovered that they were not actually effective. The agency then analyzed about 3000 samples or 54 different generic drugs obtained from pharmacies and wholesale distributors and found that only a tiny percentage did not comply with FDA standards. *Consumer Reports*[8] again expressed confidence in the safety and effectiveness of generic drugs.

Drug Interactions

When medicine is right
Your ills will take flight
But together with liquor
It may make you sicker

Two or more drugs taken at the same time may interfere with each other's absorption, distribution, or metabolism. For example, taking an anticoagulant (which helps prevent blood clots) with an antacid may slow the rate of absorption to a point below that required for either to be effective. Aspirin increases the clot-preventing ability of oral anticoagulants and can cause someone on anticoagulant therapy to have a hemorrhage. Thousands of people who combine alcohol with other drugs are treated in hospital emergency rooms yearly, and some die. Alcohol is a central nervous system (CNS) depressant, as are narcotics, barbiturates, tranquilizers, sedatives, and prescription painkillers. Alcohol causes drowsiness and, depending on the amount consumed, can affect walking, talking, and driving. When mixed with another depressant drug, the combined effect is compounded. This cumulative or synergistic effect causes a result that is greater than the sum of the two drug actions.[9]

Many cough, cold, and allergy remedies sold over the counter contain antihistamines, and some also contain alcohol. When these products are taken with alcoholic beverages, they can increase drowsiness and be dangerous when driving an automobile or operating machinery.

Foods can interact with drugs, making them work faster or slower or preventing them from working at all. For example, the calcium in dairy products impairs the absorption of tetracycline (an antibiotic), and carbonated beverages and fruit juices with a high acid content can cause some drugs to dissolve in the stomach rather than in the intestine.

Consumers can minimize the likelihood of taking an adverse combination of drugs by telling their physician when they are taking drugs from another source and by carefully following the directions when using any nonprescription product.

New Drug Delivery Methods

Increasing numbers of drugs are becoming available in delivery systems that deliver the drug at a slow rate for a long time rather than immediately releasing them into the body.[10]

Medicine-impregnated skin patches permit absorption through the skin at a steady rate. This maintains blood levels high enough to be effective but low enough to prevent toxicity. This controlled release reduces the frequency with which the drug must be taken and makes it easier for the patient to follow the physician's orders. Transderm-Nitro, for example, is a disk that contains a 24-hour supply of nitroglycerin and is placed on the chest to prevent angina pectoris (heart-related chest pain). Transderm-S is a thumbnail-sized disk that contains a 3-day supply of scopolamine; the disk is placed behind the ear to control motion sickness. Severals brands of patches that release nicotine are available to help people stop smoking cigarettes (see section on smoking deterrents).

Pumps have also been developed to deliver drugs at a controlled rate. Infusion pumps can be programmed to deliver drugs at precise dosages and delivery rates. To date, pumps have been approved for the delivery of insulin, a cancer drug, and morphine (for severe chronic pain). The Norplant system (see Chapter 22), implanted under the skin, protects against pregnancy for about 5 years. It consists of flexible silicon tubes filled with a hormone that is released gradually.

Over-the-Counter Drugs

OTC drugs are those available without prescriptions. They frequently provide temporary relief from simple discomforts. The FDA estimates that the number of OTC products marketed in the United States is between 125,000 and 300,000, with several hundred basic ingredients. They include acne products, antacid products, antimicrobials, antiperspirants, analgesics, corn and callus removers, cough and cold remedies, hormones, menstrual products, laxatives, ophthalmics, skin protectants, and sunscreen products. The Nonprescription Drug Manufacturers Association estimates that $11.2 billion was spent in 1990 in the United States for OTC products.

Consumers self-medicate extensively, and 75% use OTC drugs. These substances can help relieve minor complaints if used properly; however, they can create numerous problems if used improperly.

For many people the chief source of information about OTC drugs is television advertising. Ads generally are poor sources of drug information. Their message is often deliberately unclear and misleading. Their primary purpose is to increase usage of the product, even if this involves inappropriate or unnecessary use.

Federal law requires the following information to appear on all OTC labels:

1. Name or statement of identity of the product
2. Net quantity of the contents; also the number of tablets or ounces of fluid or ointment
3. Active ingredients
4. Name and address of the manufacturer, distributor, or packer
5. Directions for the safe use by the consumer, including the following:
   a. Individual dose or unit dose
   b. Frequency of use
   c. Maximum dose for one day
   d. Maximum number of days product should be used
   e. Cautions or warnings such as, "If symptoms persist more than 24 hours, see your doctor," or "Should not be taken by persons with high blood pressure or heart disease unless directed by a doctor"
   f. Side effects such as drowsiness
   g. Date of expiration of use when drug is no longer effective
   h. Drug interaction precautions
   i. Warning about serious allergic reactions if the product contains sulfites.

The labels of most OTC medicines sold in the United States list the inactive ingredients such as flavors, colors, binders, emulsifiers, and preservatives on their labels. This is a voluntary action on the part of manufacturers.

FDA's OTC Review

In 1972 the FDA began an extensive evaluation of over-the-counter drugs to ensure their effectiveness and safety. Rather than attempting to examine the huge number of products individually, it divided the ingredients into categories and appointed expert advisory panels to evaluate the categories. The following sequence of events was planned: As each panel report was completed, the FDA would publish a proposed monograph in the *Federal Register* for public comment. After comments were received and revisions made, a tentative final monograph would be published to provide manufacturers with an additional opportunity for comments. Following this comment period, a final monograph would be issued and ingredients that had not been judged both safe and effective would be banned.

Initially, each ingredient would be placed into one of three categories:

1. Generally recognized as safe and effective and not mislabeled.
2. Not generally recognized as safe and effective, or mislabeled.
3. Available data insufficient to permit final classification at this time.

The Health Research Group[11] thought this process would take too long to remove unsafe and ineffective products from the marketplace. It also opposed Category III because it permitted hazardous drugs to remain on the market for 2 or more years. A successful suit by the group caused the FDA in 1981 to remove this classification from the final monographs and reduced the length of time that insufficiently tested ingredients could remain on the market.[12]

The expert advisory review process concluded that only one third of the about 730 active ingredients in OTC drugs were safe and effective. As a result, manufacturers reformulated many products by removing unsafe and ineffective ingredients or by adding others. To date, only about half of the 71 proposed monographs had been promulgated into final rules,[13] but most of the remaining OTC products are safe and effective for their intended purposes. Daytime sedatives, aphrodisiacs, hair restorers, and drugs for benign prostatic hypertrophy were banned because no safe and effective ingredient was found for use in OTC products of this type.

The advisory panel recommended shifting a number of active ingredients from prescription to over-the-counter marketing status. The Nonprescription Manufacturers Association estimates that more than 200 drug products (involving a total of about 40 active ingredients) that were available only by prescription 10 years ago are now available over the counter. These include certain antihistamines and nasal decongestants for colds and allergies, sleep aids, pain relievers, cough medicines, antimicrobial products, and anti-itch medicines.[14] Some examples are sodium and stannous fluoride rinse (anticaries), chlorpheniramine maleate (antihistamine), hydrocortisone (topical-external analgesic), ibuprofen (pain reliever), and oxymetazoline hydrochloride (oral-nasal decongestant).

The panels' efforts have also led to more understandable product label statements. New warnings were printed against the misuse of such products as analgesics and antipyretic products containing salicylates and acetaminophen. New labeling was prepared for sunscreen products to better explain the amount of protection they provided.

Suggestions for Using OTC Medicines

Before purchasing an OTC drug, one should be certain that the substance is actually needed. One might ask whether a physician should be seen instead. If there is a need for temporary relief, one may wish to ask a pharmacist for advice. The best way to choose OTC drugs is to identify the chemical names of the ingredients useful for the condition in question and check product labels to obtain what you need. A reputable pharmacist can help select a suitable compound. Before using any OTC drug, learn its purposes, side effects, recommended dosage, precautions for use, and limitations. Directions for use will be found on the product label or an accompanying instruction sheet. Generally these directions are accurate and conservative. Medicines should not be taken in greater dosage or more frequently than indicated unless specified by a physician.

Many OTC products contain more than one ingredient. Some contain one ingredient that is effective when taken alone and others that are unproven or ineffective. The combination is then potentially more dangerous and at best no more effective than the single ingredient. Former FDA Commissioner Donald Kennedy, the AMA Council on Drugs, and the National Academy of Sciences Drug Efficacy Study[11] have criticized OTC combination drugs and said that a mixture can be "irrational" even though one or more ingredients in the mixture are effective. In addition, it may be advisable to adjust the dosage of one ingredient more than another. This can only be done if the ingredients are available separately. Thus it is generally best to select single-ingredient products.

Allergy Products

Allergy is the hypersensitivity of blood cells to a specific substance (called an antigen or allergen) that results in a condition such as hay fever, asthma, urticaria (hives) or other skin eruption, itching of the eyes, and certain types of headaches. About 50 million people in the United States suffer from allergic reactions, the most common of which is seasonal allergic rhinitis (hay fever). The common substances that may trigger allergic reactions include the following:

Inhaled substances: Pollens from weeds, grasses, trees, and plants; dusts in the home and in industry; mold spores; animal skin and hair; feathers; cosmetics; hair lotions; tobacco smoke; insecticide sprays; and many other chemicals.

Foods: Lobster, crab, other shellfish, and fish; chocolate; nuts; spices; eggs; milk; wheat; soy products; some fruits and vegetables

Substances that contact the skin: Plastics; metal; rubber; fabrics; dyes; cosmetics; resins; drugs; insecticides; the foliage of certain plants such as poison ivy

Medications: Aspirin, various antibiotics, and other drugs

Common Allergic Conditions

Eczema is a skin eruption characterized by itching, swelling, blisters, oozing, and scaling. It may begin in one area of the body and spread to others. It has many causes, and often there is a family history of allergy.

Bronchial asthma is marked by difficulty in breathing accompanied by wheezing, a sense of constriction in the chest, cough, and expectoration. It afflicts several million people in the United States.

Contact dermatitis is a skin eruption that occurs following contact with various industrial chemicals, metals (hairpins, curlers, bobby pins, thimbles, needles, scissors, coins, items with nickel in them), plastics, cosmetics, deodorants, mouthwashes, dyes (bleaching peroxides, shampoos, rinses), certain textiles, adhesive tape, rubber (garments, swim suits, surgical bandages, support hose, dress shields), medicines, resins, insecticides, and plants (poison ivy, poison oak, poison sumac).

Drug allergies may occur in the form of skin rashes, fever, and other reactions.

Food allergies usually result in digestive disturbances, but hay fever, asthma, eczema, hives, and anaphylaxis can also occur.

Seasonal allergic rhinitis (hay fever) is characterized by nasal congestion and discharge, sneezing, and redness and itching of the eyes in response to allergens that are inhaled. The most common allergens are dust mites, mold, ragweed pollen, and grasses.

Insect stings can cause allergic reactions. Both immediate and delayed reactions can result from the stings of bees, wasps, hornets, and yellow jackets. Desensitization injections may be recommended for persons who experience a severe reaction.

Urticaria is characterized by itching welts (hives) on the face, lips, tongue, eyelids, ears, or other parts of the body. Infections, emotional stresses, foods, drugs, and inhalants may be causative factors.

Management of Allergies

Medical treatment of an allergy may entail more than the mere prescription of a drug. It may require a thorough review of the patient's life situation for clues to the causes. Consultation with an allergy specialist may be advisable, particularly when the cause is not readily apparent. Skin tests or blood tests may be performed. However, although these can identify suspected allergens, they must be interpreted in light of the patient's history. Substances that test positive do not always cause the patient to develop symptoms. Once an offending substance is identified, it may be possible to avoid it or desensitize the individual with a series of injections.

Although self-treatment with OTC medications is suitable for mild allergies, it is probably advisable to have at least one consultation with a physician to confirm the diagnosis and discuss the various treatment options. Unsupervised self-treatment is not suitable for severe or chronic allergies. However, well-informed patients can play a major role in managing their treatment.

Drug Products for Allergies

Many products are available to relieve the symptoms of allergies. *Antihistamines* may provide temporary relief, especially for hay fever and itching skin. Table 20-3 compares the effectiveness and side effects of several such products. Most OTC antihistamines can cause drowsiness; the extent depends on the particular ingredient, the dosage, and the susceptibility of the individual. Drowsiness is rarely a problem with Seldane and Hismanal, but these are available only by prescription and cost considerably more than the others. Several products also contain the decongestant pseudoephedrine, which can counteract the sedative effect of the antihistamine. However, it may be best to purchase the ingredients separately so that their dosages can be adjusted separately.

TABLE 20–3

COMPARISON OF SELECTED ANTIHISTAMINES

Chemical name	Brand names	Generic available	Antihistamine effect	Sedative effect	Drying effect
Brompheniramine	Dimetane	✓	+ + + + +	+	+ + +
Chlorpheniramine	Aller-Chlor Chlorate Chlor-Trimeton	✓	+ + +	+	+ + +
Dexbrompheni-rame	*Drixoral		+ + + +	+	+ + +
Dexchlorpheni-ramine	Polaramine	✓	+ + + + +	+	+ + +
Triprolidine	Actidil *Actifed *Alleract	✓	+ + + +	+	+ + +
Pyrilamine	Dormarex	✓	+	+	–
Diphenhydramine	Benadryl 25 Nervine Nighttime Nytol Sleep-Eze-3 Sominex 2	✓	+ +	+ + + + +	+ + + + +
Doxylamine	Unisom Night-Time Sleep Aid		+ +	+ + + + +	+ + + + +
Phenindamine	Nolahist		+ + +	–	+ + +
Terfenadine	Seldane (prescription only)		+ + +	–	–
Astemizole	Hismanal (prescription only)		+ + +	–	–

*Combined with pseudoephedrine to counteract sedation
+ + + + + = High + + + + = Moderate to high + + + = Moderate + + = Low to moderate + = Low – = Low to zero
Sources: AMA Drug Evaluations, Handbook of Nonprescription Drugs

The response to antihistamines varies from one person to another. Therefore, it is best to experiment with different ones to find one that works without causing oversedation. It may be prudent to take a nonsedating product during the day and a sedating one at bedtime.[15] *Consumer Reports Health Letter*[16] states that antihistamines are most effective when allergy symptoms are mild or if used before symptoms become severe. It also suggests that sustained-release products be avoided because their rate of absorption into the bloodstream and onset of action are unpredictable.

When one is using antihistamines, alcohol and psychiatric drugs that cause sedation should be avoided because they may multiply each other's sedative effect. Pregnant and breast-feeding women, men with prostate problems, and people with glaucoma should not use antihistamines without consulting a physician. It is inadvisable for someone using a potentially sedating antihistamine to drive a car or operate industrial equipment unless it is known from experience that a drug will not interfere. *Consumer Reports Health Letter*[17] states that the long-held idea that asthmatics should avoid antihistamines is no longer regarded as correct.

Chromalyn (Nasalcrom) is a prescription nasal spray that can prevent allergy symptoms but must be used 2 to 4 weeks before it takes effect. It has no side effects but costs about $13 a week.

Corticosteroid hormones (cortisone, hydrocortisone, and prednisone) are presciption drugs that may be taken orally for short periods to treat severe allergic reactions. However, for most conditions, the risk of side effects is too great for long-term use.

Steroid drugs can also be very helpful when used in nasal sprays or inhalants.

Epinephrine (adrenaline) is a prescription drug that may be injected for the treatment of acute allergic attacks. It is a powerful drug that takes effect quickly. Other useful measures for asthma include aerosols to be inhaled to dilate the air passageways, antibiotics for acute infection, cough-controlling agents, expectorants for loosening bronchial secretions, and steroid inhalants.

Nasal decongestants, available as OTC products, are sprayed into the nose to shrink nasal blood vessels and membranes. Since frequent use can cause rebound congestion, they are not appropriate for the treatment of hay fever or other chronic conditions.

Emergency Medical Identification

Individuals with severe or life-threatening allergies should carry some form of emergency medical identification. This can take the form of (1) a health card to be carried in the person's pocket, purse, or wallet or (2) a plastic card or metal tag worn about the neck or wrist. Information on these identification cards or tags should specify any major allergies or sensitivities and the drugs (penicillin, tetanus antitoxin) likely to produce reactions. If an individual is found unconscious or is a victim in an accident and is unable to communicate, the information will be valuable to those giving first aid.

Poison Ivy, Poison Oak, Poison Sumac

Each year millions of persons suffer from contact dermatitis due to poison ivy, poison oak, or poison sumac. It may be acute or chronic, depending on the intensity of the exposure and the degree of sensitivity to the allergens. It can develop as a result of direct contact with plants or indirectly from contaminated clothing, pets, or other sources. About 70% of adults are sensitive to the oily resin produced by these plants. A thorough washing with soap and water within 10 to 20 minutes after exposure may remove the resin from the skin before it causes trouble. Clothing is decontaminated by machine washing with laundry detergent.

Severe dermatitis due to poison ivy, oak, or sumac can be dangerous and painful. The eyelids may be swollen shut; there may be swollen lymph nodes, flulike symptoms, or kidney damage; even blood changes are possible. Extreme cases may require hospitalization. However, most cases clear up within 1 to 3 weeks.

The itching of the rash may be relieved by applying cold compresses, a paste made of baking soda and water, calamine lotion (without phenol), or a nonprescription hydrocortisone cream. Nonprescription products containing a local anesthetic or antihistamine should be avoided. Although these measures may be helpful for mild cases, a prescription product containing higher dosage of a topical steroid is likely to be far more effective. The medical treatment of severe cases may include an antihistamine and a few days of oral steroid medication.

Some physicians inject or orally administer extracts of the offending plant to try to desensitize (build up an immunity) to dermatitis. Desensitization is at best temporary, expensive, and relatively inconvenient.

External Analgesics

External analgesics are topically applied substances that have analgesic, anesthetic, antipruritic, or counterirritant effects. The analgesic, anesthetic, and antipruritic substances depress skin receptors for pain, itching, and burning and act directly to diminish or remove symptoms resulting from burns, cuts, abrasions, insect bites, and other lesions. Topical counterirritants are applied to the intact skin for the relief of pain. They differ from the other agents because their effect results from irritation of the skin that draws attention away from deeper-seated sources of discomfort. Similar relief often can be obtained from the application of heat with a warm compress, hot water bottle, or other means.

Counterirritants produce a mild inflammatory reaction. Some products bring extra blood to the surface of the skin by dilating the small blood vessels, thus warming the area; the heat supposedly provides pain relief. The most widely used counterirritant is methyl salicylate, the active substance in oil of wintergreen. The use of counterirritants has a strong psychological component and may exert a placebo effect.

The FDA advisory panel said the following substances were safe and effective for topical analgesia:

Analgesics: Benzocaine, dibucaine, dibucaine hydrochloride, dimethisoquin hydrochloride, dyclonine hydrochloride, lidocaine, pramoxine hydrochloride, tetracaine, and tetracaine hydrochloride

Anesthetics: Benzocaine, dibucaine, menthol, and phenol

Antipruritics: Diphenhydramine hydrochloride, tripelennamine hydrochloride, hydrocortisone, and hydrocortisone acetate

Counterirritants: Allyl isothiocyanate, stronger ammonia water, methyl salicylate (most widely used, especially as athletic rubs in locker rooms), and turpentine oil, histamine dihydrochloride, methyl nicotinate, camphor and menthol, capsicum, capsicum oleoresin, choral hydrate, and eucalyptus oil

Many external analgesic products contain active ingredients from more than one group. However, it is irrational to combine counterirritants with local anesthetics, topical antipruritics, or topical analgesics, all of which depress skin sensation and exert an effect opposite to the counterirritant. External analgesics can cause contact dermatitis in individuals with sensitive skin.

Several precautions should be considered in using these substances: (1) do not use when there is severely restricted blood circulation in the legs, (2) do not bandage the area, since the skin may blister, (3) to prevent irritations, do not bring the preparations in contact with the eyes, (4) do not apply to wounds, (5) do not apply to large parts of the body, and (6) discontinue use if an adverse reaction occurs.

Internal Analgesics

Internal analgesics are used for pain relief but have other uses as well. Americans spend about $2 billion a year for them. The three most prominent and widely used ingredients are aspirin, acetaminophen, and ibuprofen. These substances are remarkably safe when used as directed but produce adverse reactions in some people. Table 20-4 summarizes potential benefits, dosage, adverse effects, and cost.

Aspirin

Aspirin (acetylsalicylic acid) is effective against pain, fever, and inflammation. The adult dose of two 5-grain tablets (650 mg) provides substantial relief from mild to moderate pain. *Consumer Reports*[18] says that although buffered aspirin (magnesium carbonate) is advertised to be faster and gentler, studies show that these effects are no different from those of other marketed substances. Enteric-coated tablets are slow to dissolve and cause less stomach irritation. They benefit those who are arthritic and need to be helped all day, but they do not give prompt pain relief.

Aspirin can deteriorate. If it has a furry look or a vinegar-like odor, it should be discarded.

Aspirin hazards. All drugs have potential dangers, and aspirin is no exception. Prolonged use of aspirin without a physician's counsel is poor self-treatment. The hazards of using aspirin include the following:

Hypersensitivity: Allergic reactions include asthma, angioneurotic edema (vasomotor nerve disorder), skin eruptions, and rarely, anaphylactic shock.

Gastrointestinal disturbances with internal bleeding: Approximately 5% of the individuals who take one dose complain of heartburn and dyspepsia. The incidence of gastroduodenal bleeding is high. Of those who take two tablets three times daily, 70% lose 2 to 6 ml (½ to 1 tsp) of blood daily, and 10% lose as much as 10 ml (2 tsp) per day. This level of blood loss is usually not clinically significant.

Ototoxicity: Large doses of aspirin (9 to 25 tablets, 5 grains each) may cause tinnitus (ringing in ears), vertigo (dizziness), and bilateral hearing loss. The conditions generally disappear within a few days after use of the drug is stopped.

Prothrombin depression: In large doses, salicylates reduce plasma prothrombin (involved in blood coagulation) levels, and in some cases increase the time it takes blood to clot. This condition may be significant in patients with fever, rheumatic patients taking large doses, people with liver damage, people with vitamin K deficiency, and surgical candidates. No one taking anticoagulants should take aspirin without a doctor's supervision.

Overdose: A dose of 25 to 35 tablets (1¼ grains each) can kill a child 1 to 5 years of age. Signs of overdose include bloody urine, diarrhea, dizziness, severe drowsiness, and ringing and buzzing in the ears.

Reye's syndrome: Aspirin taken by children who have chickenpox or flu can cause Reye's syndrome, a rare disease that can be fatal. Therefore, children with chickenpox, flu, or an undiagnosed viral illness should be given only acetaminophen for fever.

Pregnancy: Large amounts during the latter months of pregnancy may cause adverse effects for both mother and fetus. Over 3250 mg/day (10 tablets) can delay or prolong labor, cause greater blood loss at delivery, increased perinatal mortality, and decreased neonatal birth weight.

During the past few years it has been found that taking low doses of aspirin can be effective in preventing heart attacks and may cut the risk of strokes

TABLE 20–4

COMPARISON OF SINGLE-INGREDIENT PAIN RELIEVERS

	Aspirin	Acetominophen	Ibuprofen
Common brand names	Bayer Bufferin Emprin Norwich	Anacin-3 Datril Tylenol	Advil Medipren Motrin IB Nuprin
Therapeutic uses	Pain relief Fever reduction Antiinflammatory effect in higher doses (requires medical supervision) Heart attack prevention with small doses (requires medical supervision)	Pain relief Fever reduction	Pain relief Fever reduction Menstrual pain Dental pain Soft tissue injuries Antiinflammatory effect in higher doses (requires medical supervision)
Appropriate amount per tablet	325 mg	325 mg	200 mg
Standard dosage	Adults: 2 every 4 hours	Adults 2 every 4-6 hours	Adults: 2 every 4-6 hours
Cost (per 100)	1-4¢ per tablet	3-5¢ per tablet	5-7¢ per tablet
Advantages	Lowest cost	Fewer side effects than aspirin	Fewer side effects than aspirin; antiinflammatory doses better tolerated
Adverse effects	Stomach irritation Interferes with blood clotting Allergic reactions ranging from itching to asthma Ringing in ears (very high doses) Should never be given to children under 16 with viral illness, because of risk of Reye's syndrome	Stomach upset, but milder than aspirin Some risk of kidney disease with prolonged daily use	Stomach upset (in between aspirin and acetaminophen)

due to blood clots.[19] This use, however, should not be attempted without discussion with one's medical doctor.

The FDA expert panel that reviewed internal analgesics concluded that the addition of alkaline buffers makes aspirin dissolve more quickly, speeding its absorption into the system. This reduces but does not eliminate the effect of aspirin on the stomach. However, the panel indicated there had been no well-controlled clinical studies to prove that buffered aspirin works faster or is more effective than plain aspirin. Also, not all brands of buffered aspirin dissolve at the same rate, and not all dissolve faster than plain aspirin.

Acetaminophen

Acetaminophen is as effective as aspirin in analgesic (although a little slower) and antipyretic (fever-reducing) effect. However, it has little antiinflammatory effect. Therefore, it should not be relied upon for treating arthritis or other types of inflammation. Tylenol is the leading pain reliever; its market share is far greater than that of any other brand. Its manufacturer has promoted the nonaspirin feature and the possible hazards from the use of aspirin.

Acetaminophen has these advantages over aspirin: (1) it can be used by people allergic to aspirin, (2) it does not cause gastric mucosal damage and bleeding, and (3) it may be used by people receiving anticoagulant therapy. Its disadvantages resulting from excessive ingestion are kidney damage and liver toxicity.

Ibuprofen

Ibuprofen was approved for over-the-counter sale by the FDA in 1984. Like aspirin, it offers antiinflammatory action as well as pain relief and fever reduction. The best known brands are Advil, Nuprin, and Motrin B. Ibuprofen is the active ingredient in Motrin, a prescription drug used for the treatment of arthritis (see Chapter 17) and menstrual pain. However, OTC products contain 200 mg per tablet, whereas Motrin contains 300 to 800 mg per tablet.

Combination Products

No carefully controlled studies indicate that mixtures of analgesic compounds have any greater effectiveness than individual ingredients. The Public Citizen Health Research Group[11] states that increasing the number of ingredients in a product rarely makes the product better or more effective. *Consumer Reports Health Letter*[20] states that caffeine has not been proven to make a pain reliever more effective and that antacids have not been shown to buffer the stomach—a full glass of water or other liquid with each dose is the best buffer.

Costs

An effective dose of pain relief can cost anywhere from 1 cent to more than 13 cents. Generic products are generally less expensive than brand-name products. Aspirin generally is the cheapest of the pain relievers. The usual adult dose of acetaminophen or aspirin is two 325 mg tablets. The usual adult dose of ibuprofen is 200 to 400 mg. Higher doses are usually unnecessary unless pain is intense, but intense pain is probably reason to consult a physician. Extra-strength products, which contain higher doses per tablet, are more expensive than regular-strength products and are unnecessary. An individual wishing to take more than the regular dose can easily use regular-strength tablets to do so. For example, someone wishing to take 1000 mg of acetaminophen can save money by using 3 325 mg tablets instead of 2 500-mg tablets.

Suggestions for Using Pain Relievers

These guidelines provide suggestions for the use of internal analgesics by the consumer:

1. Prolonged use for such chronic conditions as rheumatoid arthritis should be supervised by a physician.
2. When one is taking aspirin, a full glass of water or other liquid should be drunk to minimize possible stomach irritation.
3. Individuals allergic to aspirin or who get stomach upsets should consider using acetaminophen.
4. Persons who experience mild stomach distress when taking aspirin should consider using acetaminophen or a soluble form of aspirin that can be dissolved in a glass of water.
5. Patients with bleeding disorders and anticoagulant users should not take aspirin.
6. Sufferers of stomach ulcers or gout should consult a physician before taking aspirin.
7. Individuals should not take more than 10 or 15 grains (two or three tablets) at a time more often than every 4 hours or more than 10 tablets in 24 hours unless instructed to do so by physician.
8. Parents should not buy flavored aspirin, which can be mistaken for candy by small children.
9. People taking high doses of aspirin or taking them for long periods should not drink alcoholic beverages because they may increase stomach irritation.
10. The cheapest pain reliever will usually do the job. Brands with similar amounts of the same ingredients should do the job equally well.
11. Avoid "shotgun formulas" that contain combinations of aspirin, acetaminophen, caffeine, and antacids.
12. Refrain from buying more than one year's supply of aspirin. Drugs break down and lose their potency if stored for long periods. The bathroom is the worst place for storage, since heat and humidity accelerate decomposition.

ANTACIDS

Overeating or eating certain foods may cause distention, or stretching, of the stomach owing to delayed gastric emptying and swallowed air. Nausea, vomiting, and heartburn may also occur. This condition, for which people in the United States spend close to $1 billion yearly, may be identified as sour stomach, upset stomach, heartburn, and indigestion. Individuals seeking relief may reach for an antacid. It should be noted that similar symptoms can be caused by other conditions such as heart attacks, gallstones, and peptic ulcers.

Antacids function by neutralizing excess hydrochloric acid present in gastric juice. Labels must list the possible interaction problems involved with a particular OTC drug. By reading the label, individuals can learn if the product should not be used while taking other drugs. It is not necessary to see a doctor for occasional heartburn or indigestion. If symptoms persist for more than two weeks or are severe, however, a doctor should be consulted.

Simethicone, which is approved by the FDA as an antigas ingredient, is said to relieve gas symptoms by breaking up gas bubbles, making them easier to eliminate from the body. Simethicone is found in several antacid products. However, Consumers Union's medical consultants believe that it does not help relieve heartburn and is "effective only in increasing the price of those antacids that contain it."[21]

Some products combine calcium and magnesium compounds in an attempt to balance the tendency of some ingredients to cause diarrhea while others cause constipation. Consumers Union's medical consultants say that aluminum/calcium/magnesium combinations are more sensible than calcium/magnesium combinations but are far more expensive. Combination products that contain antacids and other drugs are not advisable unless there is evidence that each ingredient is needed to provide the relief that is claimed. For example, some products contain both an antacid and aspirin (salicylate). Aspirin is undesirable in a product intended solely for relief of acid indigestion because aspirin has no antacid action and can irritate the stomach. Combining aspirin and an antacid ingredient is permissible if the combined product is intended for treatment of acid indigestion and headache occurring at the same time, because both ingredients are needed to treat both symptoms together. Use of an anticholinergic ingredient, which decreases stomach activity, in combination with an antacid is not advised. Also not advised are products that combine an antacid with a laxative, a sleep aid, bile salts, or an ingredient that decreases nausea. Such combinations are either ineffective or unsafe.

All antacids are safe when used occasionally by healthy individuals. However, if taken on a regular basis they may cause bowel irregularities, aggravate kidney disorders, or mask a serious problem such as a peptic ulcer. Regular use requires medical diagnosis and supervision. Table 20-5 compares the major antacid ingredients.

These suggestions will help the consumer in the safe and effective use of antacids:

1. Try to eliminate the cause of frequent heartburn or upset stomach (excess fatty food, alcohol, stress) instead of making antacid use a part of your daily life.
2. Use antacids only occasionally for indigestion or heartburn. Don't exceed maximum dosage or frequency without consulting a physician. If symptoms persist, see your doctor.
3. Liquid or powered antacids neutralize acid more effectively than tablets. Chew tablets thoroughly to help them dissolve or disperse quickly in the stomach.
4. To increase effectiveness, take antacids half an hour to two hours after a meal.
5. Antacids may interfere with the absorption of other drugs (tetracyclines, digitalis, anticoagulants), so consult your pharmacist or doctor before combining medications.
6. If on a salt-restricted diet, avoid antacids containing sodium.
7. Seek medical help immediately if your heartburn is severe and accompanied by chest pain, weakness, breathlessness, or sweating.
8. Pregnant women and people with ulcers or kidney problems should consult a physician before using any antacid.
9. If using antacids only to increase calcium consumption, take doses yielding no more than 1000 to 1500 mg of calcium a day, and avoid aluminum-based antacids, which can actually deplete calcium.[22]

ANTIBIOTICS

Antibiotics (also called antimicrobial drugs) are substances used to fight infections caused by disease-producing microorganisms. They are prescrip-

TABLE 20–5

COMPARISON OF ANTACID INGREDIENTS

Ingredient/brands	Relative potency	Disadvantages	Drug interactions
Sodium bicarbonate Alka Selzer Bromo-Selzer	Fast-acting, high potency	Can cause belching and flatulence; high sodium content makes it unsuitable for individuals on high-sodium diet	
Calcium carbonate Tums Alka-2 Titrilac	Fast-acting, highly potent and lasts long	Frequent or heavy use can cause constipation, kidney damage, kidney stones; can cause "acid rebound" (increased acid production) when stopped	Increases absorption of several drugs; delays effectiveness of several others
Magnesium compounds Maalox Mylanta Wingel Riopan Gelusil	Fast-acting, medium potency	Can cause diarrhea, kidney stones, drop in blood pressure	Interferes with bioavailability of several drugs
Aluminum compounds Rolaids AlternaGEL Amphogel	Relatively weak and slow-acting, but lasts long	Heavy use can weaken bones of people with kidney disease	Slows absorption or interferes with action of several drugs

tion items and should not be used without the advice of a physician. They can be harmful if misused. More than 100 antibiotics have been developed. The physician may conduct culture and sensitivity tests to help determine the appropriate drug to prescribe for a patient's illness.

Penicillin is effective against common types of blood poisoning, boils, scarlet fever, ear and bone infections, and many types of nonviral pneumonia. It usually cures gonorrhea and syphilis. It is widely used and is among the safest of antibiotics. It can, however, cause allergic reactions in some people, and bacteria may develop a resistance to it. The allergic reactions include hives, skin rash, and edema—a small percentage involve anaphylactic shock, an extreme form of sensitivity that can be fatal.

Amoxicillin is similar to penicillin but is effective against a broader spectrum of bacteria.

Cephalosporins resemble penicillin chemically and are used in staphylococcal infections that are resistant to penicillin. They are often considered to be safe substitutes for patients with minor allergy to penicillin. Diarrhea is a possible side effect.

Erythromycin is one of the safer, more effective agents against certain strains of streptococci and staphylococci in pneumonia, infections of the heart lining, and carbuncles. However, many strains of staphylococci are resistant to the drug.

Fluoroquinolones are useful for treating bronchitis and urinary tract infections.

Chloramphenicol, because it can cause aplastic anemia, is used only for the treatment of typhoid fever, certain types of meningitis, and a few other severe infections.

Tetracyclines, including chlortetracycline and oxytetracycline, are used to treat urinary tract infection, gonorrhea, chlamydia, cholera, brucellosis, trachoma, and infections caused by Rickettsia (organisms transmitted by ticks, lice, and mites). Side

Consumer Tip

A Difficult Germ

Clostridium difficile can produce toxins that damage the large intestine (colon). The bacterium is carried harmlessly by about 1 person in 50 but is more common among patients in hospitals and nursing homes. It is usually held in check by friendly bacteria that inhabit the colon, but when the normal balance is disturbed, it may overgrow. This can happen when any antibiotic is administered but most often occurs with clindamycin, ampicillin, or the cephalosporins.

Clostridium difficile overgrowth can result in a mild, self-limiting diarrhea, a more severe diarrheal illness (colitis), or a life-threatening disease called pseudomembraneous colitis. The symptoms can range from simple loosening of the stools to relentless bloody diarrhea with fever and severe abdominal pain. They can begin during the period of antibiotic therapy, a few days afterward, or even as long as six weeks later.

These infections are expensive and sometimes difficult to diagnose and treat. Hospitalization may be required. Vancomycin, the principal antibiotic used to cure the infection, can cost up to $400 for a 1-week supply. (Gram for gram, it is four times as expensive as gold.) Relapses occur in 20% to 40% percent of cases.

The point of this story is that antibiotics are a two-edged sword and should not be taken promiscuously. Intelligent consumers should adhere to four strategies:

- Don't take antibiotics unless they are prescribed for you.
- Don't press a doctor to prescribe antibiotics for colds or for other viral infections for which there is no proven benefit.
- If you develop diarrhea while taking an antibiotic, stop taking it and notify your doctor quickly. Failing to do so could result in serious worsening of the diarrhea.
- If you have taken an antibiotic within six weeks before contracting a diarrheal illness, mention this fact when you consult your doctor.

effects may include vomiting, diarrhea, sore tongue, and rectal itching.

Antibiotics are also used in nonprescription products for the treatment of cuts, abrasions, and burns. An FDA advisory panel recommended that (1) wound protectants should be labeled as "first-aid products" or "protectants," with a warning that they should not be used longer than 1 week, and (2) that skin wounds should be washed gently.

Antibiotics have been called miracle drugs. They have dramatically reduced death rates and prevented much suffering among people. However, as a result of the vast increase in the use of these substances, the incidence of adverse reactions has increased. Certain organisms have grown more resistant to certain antibiotics, rendering these drugs less useful. There are also indications that the drugs are being misused and overused.

Antibiotics are useless against most viruses. For this reason, physicians do not generally prescribe antibiotics for most common viral infections, such as colds and influenza. They may be appropriate, however, if a secondary bacterial infection occurs.

Acyclovir for Genital Herpes

Infection with the herpes simplex virus can cause clusters of small red lumps that turn into painful blisters. Type 1 (HSV-1) is responsible for cold sores (fever blisters) on or near the lips. Type 2 (HSV-2), a venereal disease that affects millions of Americans, causes blisters on the genitalia and sometimes on the buttocks and thighs. Following the first outbreak, the HSV virus remains latent in the cranial nerves or spinal cord until some stimulus triggers migration down a nerve to where it produces the characteristic skin eruptions. Type 2 infections occur far more commonly and more frequently than those of Type 1 and are potentially more serious.

Acyclovir (Zovirax) is used to treat genital herpes. It speeds the healing of herpes sores and reduces the multiplication of the causative virus. It helps prevent recurrences and can reduce the duration of outbreaks. Acyclovir works by preventing the herpesvirus from spreading to uninfected cells,[23] but it does not cure the infection or eredicate the virus from the body. The drug is usually administered by mouth but may be used intravenously in immunosuppressed individuals (such as people with AIDS). An ointment is also available. No other drug or diet, vaccine, or other product has been shown to be effective in preventing, curing, or alleviating genital herpes.

Individuals with genital herpes may need to decide with their doctor whether to use acyclovir to minimize recurrences or to take it only when outbreaks occur. Kaplowitz et al[24] completed a 3-year study of acyclovir in 525 patients who had had more than six recurrences per year. Daily dosage of acyclovir reduced the overall recurrence rate about 90% and enabled 61% of patients who completed the study to be recurrence-free during the third year. About 10% of the patients experienced side effects, which included weakness, headache, abdominal pain, nausea, and diarrhea. Whether daily dosage of Zovirax is practical depends on the frequency and severity of recurrences, the individual's tolerance for the drug, and the ability to afford the drug's cost, which is about $5 a day.

Antimicrobials

Antimicrobials are substances that kill germs or inhibit their growth. They are included in such products as soaps, hand washes for health care personnel, preoperative skin cleansers, skin antiseptics, skin wound cleansers, skin wound protectants, and surgical hand scrubs.

The FDA has identified five ingredients that are safe and effective for consumers to use to clean small superficial skin wounds: hexylresorcinol, benzalkonium chloride, benzethonium chloride, methylbenzethonium chloride, and poloxamer 188. A sixth ingredient, tincture of iodine, is considered safe and effective only when used as a preoperative skin cleanser. Hexachlorophene, once a popular soap ingredient, is now available only on prescription. It is allowed as a preservative in nonprescription drugs and cosmetics in concentrations of 0.1% if there is no other suitable preservative.

Aphrodisiacs (Sex Enhancers)

In 1990, the FDA banned the sale of nonprescription aphrodisiac drug products. An FDA advisory panel had examined various ingredients, including gotu kola, ginseng, licorice, sarsaparilla, nux vomica, cantharides (Spanish fly), Pega Palo, strychnine, and yohimbine, as well as the hormones testosterone and methyltestosterone. They concluded that there was no scientific evidence to support claims that these products can increase sexual arousal or desire or improve sexual performance.[25] Herbal products, if taken in quantity, can cause high blood pressure and sleeplessness. Spanish fly can irritate the urinary tract. The FDA states that individuals with sexual problems should seek professional medical help.

Poppers sold under the trade names of Rush, Thrush, Hardware, Locker Room, and Bolt are used as inhalant drugs to enhance sexual pleasure but are sold as room odorizers or liquid incense; thus they have avoided FDA jurisdiction. The products are readily available in bars, discos, and some bookstores. They contain either amyl nitrite or butyl nitrite, which causes dilation of blood vessels in the hands, feet, and face. This increased blood flow causes a "pleasurable experience." Little is known about their long-term effects, but they can cause burns around the nose, and bronchitis.[26] Amyl nitrite has been a prescription drug to relieve heart pain.

Harvey and Beckman[27] report that a study of sexually active women between the ages of 18 and 34 failed to show any significant effects of alcohol on sexual arousal, pleasure, or orgasm. Large amounts of alcohol can cause temporary impotence in men.

Remedies for Athlete's Foot and Other Foot Conditions

The most prevalent superficial infection in humans is athlete's foot (tinea pedis). It is classified symptomatically as acute (weeping and inflammatory lesions) or subacute/chronic (dry, scaly skin). In both cases itching, burning, and stinging are the primary complaints. The fungus is probably acquired most often by people walking barefoot on infected floors. Treatment preparations are available in cream, ointment, liquid, and powder forms.

The FDA expert advisory panel judged the following ingredients in OTC antifungal medications as safe and effective: clioquinol, tolnaftate, and undecylenic acid and its salts, haloprogin, miconazole nitrate, and nystatin. Tolnaftate can be used to prevent as well as to treat athlete's foot.

Effective therapy for athlete's foot involves proper hygiene that includes (1) cleaning and thoroughly drying the feet daily, (2) reducing heat and perspiration by wearing light shoes and cotton socks for ventilation, (3) changing clothing and towels frequently, (4) using a drying powder between toes, and (5) wearing protective footwear in public and home shower and bathing areas. If the eruptions are oozing, if the space between the toes has a foul odor, if the foot looks inflamed or swollen, or if the patient has diabetes or eczema, a medical doctor or podiatrist should be consulted.

Corn and Callus Remedies

Corns and calluses are protective responses to friction or pressure, usually caused by ill-fitting shoes, improperly fitted hosiery, or orthopedic problems. Calluses are skin thickenings with no central core, usually found on the palms of the hands and soles of the feet. Corns are skin thickenings with central cores that press on nerve ends, causing pain. The types include (1) hard corns, most commonly found on joint surfaces, (2) soft corns, resulting in a whitish thickening of the skin between the fourth and fifth toes, (3) intermediate corns, which are hard rimmed, soft in the center, and painful, and (4) neurovascular corns, which contain a large amount of blood and occasionally rupture.

Most OTC products contain an acid that softens and destroys the outer layer of skin. When carelessly applied it may cause serious burns. An FDA advisory panel found that salicylic acid was safe and effective for removing calluses and hard corns. This substance is in Freezone Corn and Callus Remover, Dr. Scholl's Waterproof Corn Remover, and several other products. Applications should be limited to five treatments. If no improvement occurs within two weeks, professional help should be sought from a medical doctor or podiatrist.

Cough and Cold Remedies

Almost any congestion in the nose is often labeled a cold, even though the congestion may be caused by pollutants or allergens rather than by one of the 120 or so viruses that cause cold symptoms. Colds can be classified as abortive (symptoms subside in 24 hours), mild, moderate, and severe. Medical science cannot cure a cold, but several types of medicines can help to control the symptoms.

Most coughs are caused by acute respiratory tract infections, such as the common cold. Coughs are usually mild and self-limiting. The cough reflex, controlled by a cough center in the brain, helps the lower respiratory tract rid itself of secretions and foreign matter. Dry, hacking coughs, which are usually caused by irritation rather than secretions that need to be cleared, often can be controlled by OTC medication that suppresses the cough reflex. Productive coughs reflect the body's need to clear the respiratory passageways of secretions. Coughs that are productive or last for more than a week indicate a need for medical attention.

Ingredients in OTC Products

Americans spend over $2 billion annually for cold, cough, allergy, bronchodilator, and antiasthmatic drug products. OTC cough and cold remedies may contain the following ingredients:

Antihistamines: Table 20-3 lists the characteristics of commonly used antihistamines. They are most useful for controlling seasonal allergic rhinitis. They have no ability to prevent or abort the common cold. They are found in almost all cold remedies. Many of them have a drying effect on mucus secretion in the nose. Some can cause drowsiness. *Consumer Reports*[28] believes that antihistamines have not been proven more effective than a placebo in stopping a runny nose and should be removed from OTC cold remedies.

Topical decongestants: Various sympathomimetic amines are available in nosedrops or inhalants to provide temporary relief from nasal stuffiness. They work by constricting dilated blood vessels and opening the nasal passages. The substances include phenylephrine, oxymetazoline, and xylometazoline. Although topical decongestants are more effective than oral decongestants, frequent use can cause rebound nasal stuffiness that is worse than the original stuffiness.

Oral decongestants: Sympathomimetic amines ingested orally last longer but cause less intense vasoconstriction than topical sprays or drops. They do not produce rebound congestion but can produce insomnia and irritability. The most commonly used ingredients identified as safe and effective by the FDA[29] are phenylephrine and pseudoephedrine. Phenylpropanolamine (PPA), which is still under review, is marketed as a single-ingredient decongestant in cold remedies and in diet pills (see Chapter 14). Consumer's Union's medical consultants recommend that PPA be avoided because it can cause dangerous blood pressure elevation.[30]

Expectorants: Expectorants are administered orally to stimulate the flow of respiratory tract secretions to help with dry coughs. The only currently approved substance is guaifenesin, which has been shown to loosen phlegm but not to help relieve a cough.[31]

Oral cough suppressants: Cough suppressants are used for dry, hacking coughs. The two most widely used safe and effective ingredients approved for OTC use are codeine (in combination products) and dextromethorphan.[32] These ingredients work by inhibiting the brain's cough reflex. OTC products containing codeine can be marketed in about half the states. Single-ingredient codeine is available by prescription only.

Topical cough suppressants: Camphor and menthol may be used in hot steam vaporizers and in ointments rubbed on the chest. Their label must read: "For steam inhalation only. Do not take by mouth." They can quiet coughs by acting locally on the throat.

Antipyretic analgesics: In adults 325 to 650 mg (5 to 10 grains: 1 to 2 tablets) of aspirin or acetaminophen or 200 mg ibuprofen every 4 to 6 hours should help relieve discomfort and fever.

There is no evidence that vitamin C supplements are effective in preventing the common cold. At best they may slightly reduce symptoms. (See Chapter 13.) Vitamin C is not an approved ingredient in OTC products for colds but is promoted as a cold remedy by the health food industry.

Suggestions for Treating Colds

The best a person can do about a cold is to get symptomatic relief. However, remember the cliché, "You can cure a cold with treatment in 1 week and without treatment in 7 days." These suggestions are worth considering when cold symptoms appear.

1. Rest in bed for a day or so, especially if the symptoms are severe.
2. Take aspirin for aches and pains, or take acetaminophen or ibuprofen if allergic to aspirin.
3. Decongestant nose drops can provide temporary relief from a stuffy nose, but symptoms may worsen if they are used too frequently.
4. The use of antihistamines to stop a running nose is controversial. Some authorities believe that antihistamines are effective, while other authorities are skeptical.
5. A vaporizer can help relieve a cough by putting moisture into the air and loosening secretions.
6. Sucking cough drops or lozenges, increasing fluid intake, and drinking hot beverages may be beneficial. Lozenges and cough drops offer no advantages over less expensive hard candies.
7. A cough suppressant is appropriate for a dry, hacking cough but not for a productive one. The best choice is single-ingredient dextromethorphan. A physician should be consulted if a cough lasts longer than 1 week.

Diarrhea Remedies

Most attacks of diarrhea are self-limiting; the symptoms are relieved within a day or two, with or without treatment. However, if the symptoms do not subside after a brief time or if they are accompanied by fever, severe abdominal pain, severe malaise, or bloody stools, a physician should be consulted.

OTC preparations provide symptomatic relief mainly through the ability to modify the physical characteristics of the intestinal contents without regard to the cause of the diarrheal symptoms. There are a variety of substances used in trying to accomplish this change, but the drugs used most frequently are called adsorbents. Adsorption is the property of a substance to attract and hold to its surface a gas, liquid, or a substance in solution or in fine suspension, and thus to concentrate it. The principal adsorbent drugs used are kaolin, pectin, activated attapulgite, and bismuth salts. Two commercial products on the market are Kaopectate and Pepto-Bismol.

An FDA advisory review panel has classified only two antidiarrheal ingredients as acceptable. These are opiates, including opium powder, tincture of opium, and paregoric; and polycarbophil. Polycarbophil is an adsorbent substance that binds fecal matter. Opiates such as paregoric in 15 to 20 mg doses help slow passage of the intestinal contents. The panel stated that the following substances need further study: activated attapulgite, activated charcoal, kaolin, pectin, atropine sulfate, homatropine, methyl bromide, hyoscyamine sulfate, alumina powder, bismuth salts, calcium hydroxide, phenyl salicylate, zinc phenolsulfonate, calcium carbonate, *Lactobacillus acidophilus, L. bulgaricus,* and sodium carboxymethylcellulose.

In mild and moderate diarrhea, if the patient is not vomiting, the replacement of lost fluid is important and can be safely prescribed. To help maintain fluid and electrolyte balance, ingest fruit juices, caffeine-free soft drinks, and salted crackers. Avoid alcohol and caffeine-containing beverages. Table 20-6 suggests a home treatment procedure for this type of diarrhea. Traveler's diarrhea can often be prevented if these simple rules are followed: do not eat anything that is not cooked, except for fruit that you peel yourself; do not eat salads; do not drink beverages with ice in them; do not brush your teeth with water that you would not consider safe to drink; drink only bottled water, soft drinks, beer,

Table 20–6

Home Treatment of Diarrhea

Glass number 1	Glass number 2
8 oz orange, apple, or other fruit juice (rich in potassium)	8 oz tap water (boiled or carbonated if purity of source is unknown)
½ tsp honey or corn syrup (rich in glucose necessary for absorption of essential salts)	¼ tsp baking soda (sodium bicarbonate)
1 pinch table salt (sodium chloride)	

Drink alternately from each glass. Supplement with carbonated beverages, water (boiled if necessary), decaffeinated tea or coffee, as desired.

Adapted from Plorde JJ: Drug therapy (hosp ed), Aug 1979, p 62. In Lange RL: Antidiarrheal and other gastrointestinal products. In: Handbook of nonprescription drugs, ed 8, Washington DC, 1986 American Pharmaceutical Association. Copyright 1986 by the American Pharmaceutical Association. Reprinted by permission.

or wine. The basic rule is "boil it, cook it, peel it, or forget it."

Bismuth subsalicylate (Pepto-Bismol) is somewhat effective for preventing and treating traveler's diarrhea. The prophylactic dose is 30 to 60 ml or two tablets four times each day during the first 2 weeks of travel. For acute illness, 30 to 60 ml should be taken every 30 minutes for a total of eight doses. The salicylate content can be a problem for people who are taking other salicylate-containing drugs (if the combined total is too high) or who are allergic to aspirin.

Ophthalmic Products

Nonprescription ophthalmic products are basically safe and effective only to relieve minor symptoms such as itching, tearing, tired eyes, or eyestrain caused by minor irritation and redness of the eyes. These problems are usually self-limiting. OTC products may cause allergic reactions due to the active ingredients or to preservatives.

Smarting, burning, itching, conjunctivitis, and blepharitis (inflammation of the eyelid) are often caused by infection by bacteria or viruses, or by allergic sensitivity to dust, pollens, and molds. These can generally be cured fairly quickly by appropriate antibiotic drops or ointments prescribed by a physician.

Eye fatigue may be the result of errors of refraction (nearsightedness, farsightedness, and astigmatism), or it may be associated with general fatigue caused by a sleepless night, for example. There are also some systemic conditions that affect eye muscles and lids and cause fatigue. However, these conditions are not suitable for OTC treatment but require medical aid.

Should a simple eye irritation occur from smog, strong light, sea bathing, or swimming in chlorinated water, placing one or two drops of cold tap water on the lower lid with a clean eye dropper is generally helpful. The application of iced, wet compresses for about 15 minutes safely relieves tired, though otherwise healthy, eyes.

Here are some suggestions for consumers:

1. Use OTC ophthalmic products only when the vision is not threatened and for no longer than 48 hours without medical attention.
2. Check the expiration dates on product labels and discard them within 3 months after day of opening.
3. Do not use solutions that are cloudy or discolored or that contain foreign particles.
4. Prevent bacterial contamination by not touching the tip of the dispenser and by keeping the container tightly closed when not in use.

Consumers Union's medical consultants believe that boric acid solution should not be used as an eyewash because of possible toxicity. Such solutions have not been demonstrated to be more effective than plain water for the relief of eye discomfort. Consumers Union also states:

> Beyond any claimed therapeutic effect, some of the OTC eye solutions seem to offer a cosmetic effect: "Get the red out," says one ad. A topical vasoconstrictor (such as tetrahydrozoline in Visine) should not be used regularly for cosmetic purposes. Such use risks a rebound effect in which the condition returns with increasing severity, which would require increasing frequency of dosage.[33]

Eyelid infections in the form of styes are caused by the staphylococcus bacterium. The symptoms are a red, swollen, tender area and some pain. The condition is usually self-limiting, but if it worsens, a physician should be consulted. Warm compresses for temporary relief and an antibacterial ointment (a pharmacist may help with the selection) may be applied.

Hangover Products

Although several popular drinks (Singapore Sling, Suffering Bastard, Bloody Mary, and Rasputin) are alleged to relieve hangovers, the FDA's advisory panel[34] could not identify any product or single ingredient that would relieve the symptoms of a hangover or any ingredient that could entirely prevent inebriation. To relieve hangovers, the panel recommended the use of pain relievers for headaches, antacid for gastric distress, and caffeine for fatigue and dullness. The panel concluded that activated charcoal is safe to use in the doses found in products for reducing and minimizing hangover symptoms, but its effectiveness had not been demonstrated. Some evidence indicates that the use of fructose prevents and reduces inebriation, but the panel stated that the evidence was not clinically significant and recommended further research.

Hemorrhoidals

Hemorrhoids are clusters of dilated (varicose) veins in the lower rectum and anus; they generally occur in individuals between 30 and 50 years of age. They may be internal or may protrude outward. Internal hemorrhoids are rarely painful, but external hemorrhoids can be painful.

Hemorrhoids are frequently self-treatable. They may be related to erect posture, eating refined foods, drinking fewer liquids, the overuse of laxatives, chronic constipation, pregnancy, and lifting heavy objects. Some symptoms that lead people to believe they have hemorrhoids may be caused by a different problem. Itching can be the result of poor anal hygiene, perianal warts, intestinal worms, medication allergies, psoriasis, or nervous scratching.

These suggestions can help individuals to minimize the symptoms of hemorrhoids:

1. Increase the amount of fiber in the diet. This helps to soften the stool and reduce constipation. Eat fruits, vegetables, whole-grain breads, and whole-grain cereals.
2. Practice good anal hygiene to control irritation and itching by keeping the skin around the anus clean and dry.
   a. Avoid vigorous wiping with dry toilet paper; use cotton or a rag moistened with warm water and pat dry.
   b. Completely remove soap residue after showering or bathing.
   c. Use sitz baths in warm water two to three times daily for 10 to 15 minutes at a time.
   d. Wear loose cotton underwear and lightly sprinkle anus with talcum powder.
3. If hemorrhoid symptoms persist despite self-treatment, professional help may be needed.

Consumer Reports[35] has expressed reservations about the use of OTC products containing anesthetics, astringents, counterirritants, and skin protectants. Some of the ingredients can cause allergic reactions and make irritations worse. Hemorrhoidal products are marketed in three basic forms: cleansers, suppositories, and creams or ointments.

Cleansers: The best products keep the anal area clean; for example, Tucks and Preparation H pads.

Suppositories: They can lubricate the rectum and make hard bowel movements less painful, but they have minimal effect.

Creams and ointments: These may soothe irritation. Creams are preferable because ointments are greasier, retain moisture, and encourage itching and irritation. Hydrocortisone in some products is an effective antiitch ingredient, but its overuse may lead to dependency and cause thinning of the skin.

Consumer Reports[35] states: "There is no acceptable evidence that the heavily promoted Preparation H . . . can shrink hemorrhoids, reduce inflammation, or heal injured tissue." Preparation H contains live yeast cell derivative and shark liver oil in addition to petroleum jelly. The *Public Citizen Health Research Group Health Letter*[36] states that yeast cell derivative has not been proven beneficial and that the product contains too little shark liver oil to protect the skin around the anus.

Iron-Containing Products

Victor H. Lindlahr (osteopath, naturopath, nutrition theorist, sanitorium lecturer, publisher, and radio commentator) was the guiding spirit behind Geritol and some other products that began marketing in 1934. In 1945 the FTC reported that Lindlahr had admitted that the St. Louis College of Physicians and Surgeons, from which he claimed to have been graduated, was a diploma mill. He said he never was licensed to practice medicine but testified that he considered himself entitled to use the

M.D. degree for writing purposes.

In the 1950s Lindlahr employed Dr. Norman Jollife, chief of the Nutrition Division of the New York City Health Department, as a medical consultant. Lindlahr wrote booklets about the benefits to be obtained from Geritol, Serutan, Sominex, and other products that were reviewed by Jollife for scientfic accuracy.

Geritol, "for those with tired blood," contained 100 mg of iron per fluid ounce in combination with vitamins. This amount apparently was appropriate for treating iron deficiency. There was disagreement, however, about whether an iron tonic such as Geritol should be taken and whether iron taken in that form was significantly absorbed and used by the body. Jollife estimated that 15% of people in the United States had iron deficiency caused by deficient diets. To the contrary, Dr. William J. Darby stated in the *Journal of the American Medical Association* that by adulthood, even the poorest dietary regimens were sufficient to prevent this condition, except in the presence of chronic blood loss. In 1968 the FTC charged that TV commercials had misrepresented the likelihood that Geritol would relieve tiredness, loss of strength, run-down feeling, nervousness, and irritability. In 1975 the J.B. Williams Company of New York City settled the matter by agreeing to pay $125,000 in penalties to the government. The company had previously paid a $175,000 settlement in connection with advertisements for Fem-Iron, a product similar to Geritol.

A well-balanced diet usually supplies enough iron, even for women with heavy menstrual periods. The body normally absorbs the correct amount of iron that it needs. However, some people are susceptible to iron overload (hemochromatosis), which can cause serious damage to body organs. It is inadvisable to take iron-containing supplements without first determining they are needed.

Although advertisers have suggested that many people have "tired blood," it is important to remember that (1) many illnesses cause fatigue and lack of energy and (2) if a person has anemia, iron tablets by themselves may not help. Anemia is a condition in which there are not enough red blood cells. The causes include iron deficiency, abnormal absorption of vitamin B_{12}, liver and thyroid diseases, hidden infections, and internal bleeding from an ulcer or cancer. Blood tests are necessary to make an accurate diagnosis.

Iron-containing products should be stored carefully if there are children in the home. An analysis of 3.8 million cases of poisoning among children has concluded that iron was the single most common cause of accidental death by ingestion. During 1991, 11 children died following iron supplement ingestion.[37]

LAXATIVES

Constipation (overly hard stools) is a functional impairment of the colon, which normally produces properly formed stools at regular intervals. Constipation is related to an individual's habits and can occur when the customary pattern of bowel action is disrupted. The most common cause is too little fiber in the diet. Various medications have constipation among their side effects.

A misconception exists among some individuals that the colon is an unsanitary sewer that must be periodically and vigorously cleaned out. Many quacks have thrived by promoting this concept. There is no scientific support for this idea. Nor is it necessary for all people to have a daily bowel movement. Some people normally have a bowel movement only once every 2 or 3 days. Others do so only once per week, although this is not common and need not be encouraged. After limited irregularity, bowel rhythm usually returns to regular action with no treatment; there should be no ill effects except a slight feeling of discomfort. If it fails to return after 1 week, one might check with a physician.

When bowel change occurs, it may be temporary, resulting from travel, change of diet, or emotional tension, or it may be a side effect of medication. In such cases, if the consumption of additional fruits, vegetables, fluids, and high-fiber foods is not successful, a prepackaged saline enema or glycerin suppository is generally the quickest and safest approach. Properly administered, an enema cleans only the distal colon and most nearly approximates a normal bowel movement. Increasing exercise can also help.

Consumer Reports Health Letter[38] recommends that if these measures don't work, use of a bulk-forming laxative or stool softener should be the next step. If that does not work, a mild laxative for a day or two may be advisable. However, overdependence on laxatives may be harmful; they should not be used on a regular basis. Americans spend about $400 million per year on laxatives. Table 20-7 compares various types.

TABLE 20–7

COMPARISON OF OTC LAXATIVE INGREDIENTS

Type	Examples	Products	Mechanism of action	Comments
Bulk-forming agents	Psyllium, polycarbophil, cellulose, bran, methylcellulose	FiberCon, Metamucil, Serutan	Absorb water in the intestine and swell the stool into an easily passed soft mass	Safe to take indefinitely
Lubricant	Mineral oil	Agoral Plain, Fleet Mineral Oil Enema	"Grease" stools to fascilitate excretion	Should be used only sparingly and for short periods; can interfere with absorption of fat-soluble vitamins, and can leak from rectum
Stool softeners	Docusate	Colase, Dialose, Regutol, Surfak	Merge with feces to soften their consistency. Useful for people who are temporarily bedridden, have hard, dry stools, or must avoid straining. Not effective for chronic constipation	Should be used only sparingly and for short periods
Saline laxatives	Sorbitol, magnesium salts, sulfate salts	Milk of Magnesia, Citrate of Magnesia, Epsom Salts	Promote secretion of water into the intestine	Safe with prolonged use but promote dependency
Chemical stimulants	Bisacodyl, casanthral, cascara, castor oil, phenolphthalein, senna	Carter's Little Pills, castor oil, Modane, Feen-A-Mint, Fletcher's Castoria, Ex-Lax	Promote secretion of water into the intestine; some stimulate more vigorous contractions of the colon. Should be considered a last resort	Can lead to dependency and can damage the bowel with daily use for months or years

Pain in the abdomen can be caused by a variety of conditions. Some of them, such as cancer, an inflamed appendix, or a bowel obstruction, are serious and require skilled medical assistance. The use of laxatives in such cases is dangerous. A laxative should not be used when nausea or vomiting is present or for longer than 1 week. Overuse suppresses the normal urge to defecate and leads to dependency. Rectal bleeding or failure to have a bowel movement after the use of a laxative may indicate a serious condition and is reason to consult a physician.

Consumers may find these tips helpful in preventing constipation:

1. Eat a well-balanced diet that includes whole-grain breads or cereals, prunes and prune juice, fresh fruit, and vegetables.
2. Drink plenty of liquids.
3. Exercise regularly.
4. Set aside time after breakfast or dinner to allow for an undisturbed visit to the toilet.
5. Whenever possible, defecate soon after feeling the urge to do so.

Motion Sickness Remedies

The FDA has reported these ingredients in nonprescription motion sickness drugs to be safe and effective: cyclizine hydrochloride, meclizine hydrochloride, dimenhydrinate, and diphenhydramine hydrochloride. The most common ingredient is dimenhydrinate, which is found in Dramamine and most other products. These drugs are antiemetics (products that prevent vomiting). They may cause drowsiness and should not be combined with alcoholic beverages. Transderm Scop, a prescription product for adults, can prevent motion sickness without causing sedation. The product is a patch that is placed behind the ear of the user at least 4 hours before its effect is desired. The patch releases small amounts of scopolamine over a 3-day period.

Sleep Aids

Nonprescription preparations rely primarily on antihistamine agents for their sedative effects. Sedation effects vary from individual to individual. An FDA advisory panel stated that occasional use of a sleep aid is not harmful, but a person with a chronic sleep problem should consult a physician. Their investigation revealed that many sleep-aid products contained ingredients that were ineffective (for example, aspirin, vitamins, passionflower extract) or unsafe (for example, bromides, scopolamine). The experts believed that an antihistamine could be safe and effective if given in proper dosage. As a result of their findings, OTC sleep aids were reformulated to include an antihistamine, either diphenhydramine (used in Compoz, Nytol, Sleep-eze 3, Sleepinal, Sominex, and Sominex 2) or doxylamine succinate (used in Unisom, Doxysom, and Ultra Sleep), as their sole active ingredient.

Prescription sleep aids are far more potent than nonprescription products and can have more significant side effects. These, too, should not be used for long periods.

Alcohol has sedative qualities, but if used on a regular basis the quantity may have to be continually increased to induce sleep. In addition, the user

Consumer Tip

Self-Help for Sleepless Nights

Self-Help and traditional remedies may be sufficient to cope with occasional bouts of insomnia. Before reaching for drugs, insomniacs may want to try one or more of these measures:

- Cut back on caffeine consumption, particularly in late afternoon or evening. Avoid daytimenaps.
- Before bedtime, take a warm shower or, better yet, a warm bath.
- Retire to an environment conducive to sleep; use bedding that's clean and comfortable, and be sure the bedroom is cool, quiet, andark.
- Stick to a regular sleep schedule throughout the week and avoid oversleeping on weekends.
- Regular exercise can help, but avoid exercising within a couple of hours of bedtime.
- Avoid excitement before retiring. Relax with light reading, restful music, or television.
- Don't eat large meals before bedtime. Instead, eat a light snack high in carbohydrates.
- When anxiety is a problem, set aside a time during the day as a regular worry period; meanwhile, be mentally armed with a list of pleasant, relaxing subjects to crowd out anxieties at bedtime—and try not to worry about going to sleep.

Egon Weck[40]

may awaken in the middle of the night when the sedative effect wears off. A warm glass of milk is safer and might work.

A common but frequently unsuspected cause of insomnia is the consumption of caffeine-containing beverages such as coffee, tea, and cola drinks. Caffeine can interfere with sleep even when it is ingested during the early part of the day. A National Institutes of Health Consensus Conference concluded that insomnia for more than 3 weeks may warrant an extensive diagnostic evaluation.[39]

L-Tryptophan, an amino acid that was available for many years as a food supplement, was promoted as a sleep aid although it had never been proven safe and effective for this purpose. The FDA banned it from the marketplace in 1989, after it was implicated in an outbreak of eosinophilia-myalgia syndrome, a rare but serious disorder characterized by severe muscle and joint pain. More than 1,500 cases and 38 deaths were reported. The difficulty was due to a contaminant introduced during the manufacturing of L-tryptophan by a Japanese supplier.

Smoking Deterrents

An FDA expert advisory panel[41] said there was no OTC ingredient available that is considered safe and effective as a smoking deterrent. The ingredients they reviewed included ground cloves, ground coriander, eucalyptus oil, ground Jamaica ginger, lemon oil, licorice root extract, menthol, menthol salicylate, quinine ascorbate, silver nitrate, thymol, and povidone-silver nitrate. Since that time several effective products have been developed, but all of them are available only by prescription.

Nicotine Chewing Gum

In 1984 nicotine gum was approved for use in smoking cessation under a physician's prescription. It is being marketed under the brand name Nicorette by Merrell Dow Pharmaceuticals, Inc., a subsidiary of the Dow Chemical Company. A 96-piece package of Nicorette costs about $20. Each piece of gum contains 2 mg of nicotine, which is slowly absorbed through the lining of the mouth over a 20- to 30-minute period. Chewing one piece of gum per hour produces blood nicotine levels comparable to those obtained with hourly cigarette smoking. Any nicotine that is swallowed has little effect on the body. The gum provides a substitute for oral activity and can prevent nicotine withdrawal symptoms, allowing the smoker to break the behavioral habits of smoking without suffering the discomforts of nicotine withdrawal at the same time. After a few months, use is tapered off. Forty-eight percent of the subjects of one study were not smoking 6 months after discontinuing use of the gum.

An FDA Drug Abuse Advisory Committee, which reviewed the evidence on nicotine gum, concluded that it increases the likelihood of smoking cessation when used together with an acceptable counseling program.[42] The Merrell Dow company supplies doctors with detailed information on how to select and prepare patients for using the gum. Patients receive a 24-page booklet and, on request, two newsletters about smoking cessation and nicotine gum treatment. Doctors are urged to provide at least one follow-up visit per month over the treatment period (usually 3 to 4 months). However, some experts are worried that physicians may not prescribe it properly or provide the necessary counseling.

Transdermal Nicotine Patches

Three companies are now marketing prescription products (Nicoderm, Habitrol, PROSTEP) that deliver nicotine into the body through the skin. Approval of a fourth product (Nicotrol) is expected soon. The products are small patches that release nicotine slowly and steadily when placed on the upper body or upper outer part of the arm. The recommended period of use is 6 to 8 weeks, with dosage decreased as the user becomes more accustomed to not smoking. The effects of use for more than 3 months are unknown. The side effects, which usually are dose-related, include diarrhea, nausea, dry mouth, joint pains, abnormal dreams, insomnia, nervousness, and headache. *The Medical Letter*[43] states that none of these products has been proven more effective or better tolerated than the others.

Sore Throat Products

Most sore throats are caused by an infection; more throat infections are viral than bacterial in origin. Use of an antiseptic gargle or medicated lozenges can do nothing to cure a cold or throat infection. The offending organisms are deep in the throat tissues and cannot be eliminated by gargling. Lozenges promoted for relief of pain from sore throats usually contain a topical anesthetic such as benzocaine. At best, the pain relief obtained may be short-lived.

An FDA advisory panel[44] has recommended these sore throat ingredients as safe and effective: aspirin, benzocaine, benzyl alcohol, dyclonine hydrochloride (prescription only), hexylresorcinol, menthol, phenol, phenolate sodium, and salicyl alcohol.

OTC mouthwashes are dilute solutions of aromatic substances that may be sweetened with saccharin and colored in some fashion. They may contain ethanol, astringents (zinc salts), surface-active agents (for foam), and quaternary ammonium halides (antiseptic agents). The halides have no significant ability to kill germs during a gargle. In 1978 the Supreme Court upheld a 1975 FTC order that $10 million worth of Listerine ads must carry the statement, "Listerine will not help prevent colds or sore throats or lessen their severity." This was the first time the high court had ruled in a case of corrective advertising. The FTC said that false claims had been made about Listerine's power to prevent colds. The commission said that comparable relief could be obtained from salt water. The FDA no longer will permit manufacturers of mouthwashes to claim their products have medicinal value or can stop bad breath.

In 1981 the FTC released the findings of an 18-month study of the corrective advertising conducted by the Warner-Lambert Company. The study revealed that consumers were more aware that Listerine mouthwash does not prevent colds and sore throats or lessen their severity. It also indicated that there was a 40% drop in the amount of the product used for colds and sore throats, but the total quantity used was not reduced.

Some medical consultants recommend warm salt water (1/2 tsp of salt to an 8-oz glass of warm water) both as a gargle and a mouthwash. In addition, a pain reliever might help to relieve general discomfort.

It should be noted that untreated throat infections caused by streptococci may lead to rheumatic fever or kidney disease. An attempt to treat a sore throat with a patent medicine may delay proper diagnosis and treatment by a physician.

If a sore throat lasts more than a day or two or is accompanied by fever or severe malaise, a physician should be consulted to assess the likelihood of a streptococcal infection.

Stimulants for Fatigue

Fatigue is a normal physiologic result of physical exertion. It disappears after adequate rest has been obtained. However, students who want to avoid fatigue and stay awake while cramming for exams, truck drivers wishing to be alert on long trips, or those seeking pick-me-ups for whatever reason may resort to OTC drugs or illegally obtained prescription drugs that contain a stimulating substance.

The ingredient most commonly found in the OTC products is the stimulant caffeine. It can help to reduce drowsiness and fatigue and stimulate muscular function. An FDA advisory panel said, "In cases where mental alertness or motor performance is necessary, such drugs (caffeine) can modify fatigue states to allow successful completion of a required task."[45] The FDA panel stated that caffeine in doses of 100 to 200 mg every 3 to 4 hours is safe and effective in OTC products. Table 20-8 illustrates the caffeine contents of selected sources.

Too much caffeine can create a number of prob-

Table 20–8

Caffeine Content from Selected Sources*

Source	Caffeine (approximate amount)
Beverages	
Brewed coffee	100 to 150 mg/cup
Instant coffee	86 to 99 mg/cup
Tea	60 to 75 mg/cup
Decaffeinated coffee	2 to 4 mg/cup
Cola drinks/many soft drinks	36 to 60 mg/12 oz
Cocoa	50 mg/cup
Milk chocolate	3-6 mg/oz
OTC products	
Caffedrine Capsules	200 mg
Vivarin Tablets	200 mg
Wakoz	200 mg
Quick-Pep Tablets	150 mg
Nodoz Tablets	100 mg
Summit	100 mg

*From Caro JP and Walker CA: Stimulant products. In: Handbook of nonprescription drugs, ed 8, Washington DC, 1986, American Pharmaceutical Association. Adapted with permission.

lems. It can mask fatigue to the point where a person may suddenly collapse from exhaustion. It may make a person excessively nervous and irritable, cause palpitations and heart irregularity, and stimulate excess stomach acidity. Tolerance and physical dependence can occur with habitual ingestion of caffeine.

Caffeine is not advisable for people with high blood pressure. It may cause palpitations and tachycardia. It should also be avoided by ulcer patients because it can increase gastric secretion.

Some OTC analgesic (pain-relief) products contain as much as 64 mg (1/2 cup of coffee) of caffeine per dose. The inclusion of caffeine in product mixtures for relief of headache is questionable.

Some individuals will experience withdrawal symptoms (headache, irritability, restlessness, fatigue) if they suddenly abstain from a daily regimen of coffee consumption.

Consumers also should be wary of products that are claimed to improve one's personality, marriage, sex life, or other farfetched benefits. The main ingredient may be caffeine.

Home Medicine Cabinet

It is prudent to have medical supplies and drug products available for self-treatment of certain illnesses, injuries, and emergency situations. Select from Table 20-9 according to the anticipated needs of your household.

Keep drug items out of reach of children. Discard medications that have reached their expiration date or have changed in color, odor, or consistency. The telephone numbers of your doctor, hospital, poison control center, ambulance or rescue squad, and police and fire emergency switchboards should be kept handy.

Prudent Use of Medication

Safe, effective drug use depends upon the patient's understanding of the drug regimen, its risks and benefits, and the necessary precautions associated with each medication. In many cases, the key to safe and effective use of medication is open communication with the prescriber.[46] Prudent use of medication requires knowledge of the following:

1. *The name of the drug.* Knowing the name will not only enable you to look up information about the drug, it will also enable you to discuss it with your doctor (or another doctor) should this be necessary.
2. *The drug's purpose.* This information will help you understand your treatment and whether or not it is working.
3. *How and when should it be taken?* This basic information will be on the product's label. Some medications are best taken on an empty stomach (before meals) for maximum absorption. Some are best taken on a full stomach to prevent the medications from irritating the stomach. Some are inactivated by food and must be taken on an empty stomach. Some have to be taken on an exact schedule, while others do not. It may be helpful to keep a written record of what you are doing—particularly when several medications are being taken on different schedules.
4. *Are there any special instructions?* Sometimes specific foods, alcoholic beverages, or other medicines will react unfavorably with the medicine just prescribed.
5. *What side effects might occur?* All drugs have possible side effects. If they occur, in some cases nothing need be done and the medication can be continued. In others, a change of dosage or a different medication will be advised. The occurrence of certain side effects would be a reason to stop using the drug. It can help to be aware of the common side effects and what to do if they occur. One of the most important side effects is drowsiness—a common characteristic of antihistamines, sedatives, and drugs for mental and emotional problems. People taking any of these drugs should not drive a car until they have determined that the drugs will not interfere with their ability to do so safely. Information about side effects can be obtained by asking your physician or pharmacist or consulting a reliable reference.
6. *How long should the drug be taken?* Some drugs need be taken only until symptoms stop, while others should be taken for a period specified in advance. For example, pain relievers can be stopped when your pain goes away, but antibiotics are typically prescribed for 7 to 14 days to eradicate germs that remain even though symptoms of the infection have disappeared.
7. *What should I do if I miss a dose?* In some cases it will be advisable to make up the dose to maintain an adequate blood level of a medication. In other cases it won't matter, and doubling the

TABLE 20–9

HOME MEDICINE CABINET

First aid and medical supplies	
Band-aids of various sizes	Hydrogen peroxide (for cleansing wounds)*
Absorbent cotton	Sterile gauze pads
Ace bandage	Adhesive tape
Tongue depressors	Cotton-tipped applicators
Ice bag	Hot water bottle or heating pad
Sunscreen product	Safety pins
Flashlight	Small blunt-edged scissors
Eye cup	Oral and rectal thermometers
Dosage spoon	Petroleum jelly
Fine-point tweezers and sewing needle (for removing splinters)	First-aid manual
Drug items	**For treatment of**
Aspirin, acetaminophen, and/or ibuprofen	Fever, headache, other aches and pains
Antacid	Heartburn and upset stomach
Hydrocortisone ointment or cream	Minor skin irritations and allergies
Antibiotic ointment or cream	Minor skin infections
Antidiarrhetic	Diarrhea
Antihistamine (chlorpheniramine)	Allergic reactions and colds
Cough syrup (suppressant)	To reduce the intensity of a cough
Decongestant (pseudoephedrine)	Stuffy nose
Antinausea (dimenhydrinate)	Nausea (including motion sickness)
Mild laxative (Milk of Magnesia)	Occasional constipation
Glycerine suppositories or prepackaged enemas	Occasional constipation
Calamine lotion	Contact dermatitis (such as poison ivy)
Additional products for children	
Pediatric acetaminophen	Fever
Syrup of ipecac	Poisoning (to induce vomiting only if use is advised by a physician or poison control center)

*Years ago it was thought that wounds should be disinfected by swabbing an antiseptic such as tincture of iodine into the wound. This practice is no longer recommended because anything that kills germs on contact can also kill healthy tissue. The best way to cleanse most wounds is to wash them with soap and water. However, hydrogen peroxide can also be useful for this purpose.

dose will increase the likelihood of side effects.

8. *Is written information about the drug available?* Some doctors provide instruction sheets on common prescription drugs. A package insert may be available from the pharmacist who fills the prescription, but these tend to be overly technical. Practical information can be obtained from a guidebook such as *About Your Medicines* or *The Essential Guide to Prescription Drugs,* listed at the end of this chapter. The *Physicians' Desk Reference (PDR),* which contains extensive lists of precautions and side effects, is impractical for laypersons because it provides little perspective on the frequency of side effects and what to do if they occur.
9. *Is a generic form available?* Generic drugs usually cost less and are just as potent as name brands. Some doctors routinely prescribe them, but others simply don't bother. With a few medicines for serious diseases, there may be a medical reason to avoid a generic drug. But in most cases, there is no reason they cannot be used.

It should not be necessary to ask all the above questions each time you visit a doctor and receive a prescription. A good doctor will communicate most of this information when the medicine is prescribed. But don't expect or demand a lengthy discussion on the uncommon side effects and complications of common drugs. If you think your doctor is not communicating enough, a tactful question may clarify the situation.

When traveling, try to take along enough medicine to meet your needs. Carrying an extra prescription may be wise in case your luggage is lost or your supply runs out. If a childproof container is hard to handle, ask the pharmacist for one that is easy to open.

Drug Safety Precautions

1. If you go to more than one doctor, tell each about any prescription and OTC medications you are taking. It is a good idea to keep a record with you. Also tell the doctor about any adverse drug reaction you have had.
2. Stick to the dosage the doctor prescribes. Taking extra may increase the chances of adverse reactions without increasing the chances of benefit. And don't stop a medicine because you don't think it is working. Some drugs have to be taken for several days or even weeks before their effect is apparent. Instead, contact your doctor for instructions. Keep a daily record of all drugs being taken, especially if treatment schedules are complicated.
3. Remember that alcohol and sedatives can multiply each other's effect on the brain. Don't mix alcohol and sleeping pills, antianxiety agents, or any other drugs that have sedative effects. If you drink regularly, make sure your doctor knows about it.
4. Keep your drugs in their original containers so no mix-up occurs about which drug is which.
5. Remember that it may be risky to share medicines with others. When prescribing medications, doctors take into account the patient's age, weight, sex, other medications being taken, and other factors. What is good for one person may not be good for someone else.
6. Clean out your medicine cabinet periodically. Throw away any drugs that reach their expiration date or change in color, odor, or texture. Flush them down the toilet so that no one else can use them. Drugs prescribed for a previous illness or for another person should not be taken without first checking with the physician. The drug may have lost its strength or changed its composition, or a more appropriate drug may be available for the illness.
7. Call the doctor promptly if an unusual drug reaction occurs.

IT'S YOUR DECISION

Your doctor has prescribed an antibiotic for the treatment of a respiratory tract infection. On the second day you took the drug, you developed nausea and diarrhea. Would you:

(Check all that apply)

Inspect the *Physician's Desk Reference* to see whether this is a common side effect?	_______
Telephone your doctor to report the new symptom?	_______
Wait 24 hours to see what happens?	_______
Stop taking the drug?	_______
Telephone the pharmacist?	_______
Other	_______

RECOMMENDED REFERENCE BOOKS

The following books contain practical information for consumers. Most of them are updated every 1 to 4 years. Table 10-6 contains additional information on drug reference books.

AARP pharmacy service prescription drug handbook, Glenview, IL, 1988, Scott, Foresman & Co.

Drug information for the consumer, Yonkers, NY, 1992, Consumer Report Books.

About your medicines, Rockville, MD, 1992, United States Pharmacopeial Convention.

Long JW: *The essential guide to prescription drugs,* New York, 1991, Harper Collins.

Prescription drugs, by the editors of Consumers Guide with Nicola Giacona, PharmD, New York, 1991, Crown Publishers.

Handbook of nonprescription drugs, ed 9, Washington, DC, 1990, American Pharmaceutical Association.

Zimmerman D: *Zimmerman's complete guide to nonprescription drugs,* Detroit, 1992, Gale Research Co.

Summary

The two basic types of medicines that can be purchased in the United States are prescription and over-the-counter (OTC) drugs. Generic drugs are generally bioequivalent to brand-name drugs and are less expensive and therefore can save money for the consumer.

Prescription drugs in general are more powerful and have more side effects. Prudent consumers learn the name, purpose, dosage, side effects, and other significant characteristics of drugs that are prescribed for them. This information can be obtained from one's physician, a pharmacist, product labels, package inserts, drug reference books, or a combination of sources.

OTC drugs are intended mainly for self-treatment of minor illnesses and injuries. Since 1972, expert advisory panels have reviewed the ingredients in these products to determine their safety and efficacy. As a result, many ingredients that were hazardous or ineffective have been removed from the marketplace. The commonly used OTC products include pain relievers, antacids, antihistamines, cough and cold remedies, laxatives, and remedies for diarrhea and motion sickness. The best way to choose an OTC remedy is to determine what ingredients are desirable and select products that contain them. In most cases, single-ingredient products are best. It is also prudent to have medical supplies and drug products available at home for the self-treatment of minor illnesses and injuries and for first aid in emergencies.

Discussion Questions

1. What are the basic types of drugs and their synonyms?
2. What suggestions should be considered when using or planning to use, or is using, prescription drugs?
3. Illustrate the nature of a physician's prescription and list some of the common abbreviations found thereon.
4. Identify some of the antibiotics and their purposes. Should they be prescribed on a patient's mere request?
5. What are the similarities and differences between generic and brand-name drugs? Should they be prescribed by physicians? Why?
6. What are over-the-counter drugs? What suggestions should be followed by a consumer when purchasing OTC products?
7. Describe the FDA's OTC drug review process and its outcome.
8. How should contact dermatitis from poison ivy, poison oak, or poison sumac be treated?
9. How do external analgesics affect the body?
10. Compare the uses, side effects, and costs of the three main types of internal analgesics.
11. What is iron deficiency anemia? What are its causes and methods of diagnosis?
12. Identify and compare the major ingredients in antacids.
13. What are antimicrobials? What safe and effective ingredients have been identified by the FDA?
14. What are some of the substances claimed to be aphrodisiacs? How effective are they?
15. What are the common ingredients in athlete's foot products? Describe the effective therapy for the condition.
16. What are the common ingredients found in cough and cold remedies? What substances are safe and effective?
17. What are the safe and effective OTC nasal decongestants and antitussive substances?
18. What antidiarrheal ingredients are considered acceptable by the FDA? What ingredients may be found in a home treatment remedy?
19. What can be done by the consumer for simple eye irritations?
20. What are the ingredients found in OTC hemorrhoidal products? What can be done to minimize the symptoms of hemorrhoids?
21. Compare the general types of substances used in laxative products.
22. What therapeutic agents are found in OTC eyewashes? Which specific substances are safe and effective according to the FDA?
23. Discuss sleep aids in terms of their effectiveness, ingredients, and hazards.
24. What substance is safe and effective to use as a stimulant against fatigue? In what dosage and in what frequency?
25. What information should a patient have about a prescribed medicine before leaving a physician's office?
26. Why do people fail to use prescription drugs properly?
27. What are the hazards of drug interactions and food and drug interactions?

28. What drug and nondrug items should be found in a home medicine cabinet? How should this cabinet be maintained?
29. Identify several drug reference books that provide reliable information for consumers.

REFERENCES

1. National Council on Patient Information and Education: Talk about prescriptions, Washington, DC, 1990, The Council.
2. Cramer JA et al: How often is medication taken as prescribed? A novel assessment technique JAMA 261:3273-3277, 1989.
3. Generic drug wars, AARP News Bulletin 28:11, Oct 1987.
4. Nightingale SL and Morrison JC: Generic drugs and the prescribing physician, JAMA 258:1200-1204, 1987.
5. Lunzer FZ: Are bargain drugs right for you? American Health 6:68-69, July 1987.
6. Myths and facts of generic drugs, FDA Consumer 21(7):13-14, 1987.
7. The big lie about generic drugs, Consumer Reports 52:480-485, 1987.
8. Generic drugs: still safe? Consumer Reports 55:310-311, 1990.
9. Alcohol, caffeine, and tobacco are drugs, too. Consumer Reports Health Letter 3:12, 1991.
10. Segal M: Patches, pumps, and timed release: new ways to deliver drugs, FDA Consumer 25(8):15-17, 1991.
11. Public Citizen Health Research Group: Over the counter pills that don't work, Washington, DC, 1983, The Group.
12. Nonprescription drug review, FDA Consumer 15(10):23, 1981.
13. Chelimsky E: Nonprescription drugs: over the counter and underemphasized, Washington, DC, 1992, U.S. General Accounting Office.
14. Segal M: Rx to OTC: the switch is on, FDA Consumer 25(2):9-11, 1991.
15. How to relieve allergy symptoms—and stay awake, Consumer Reports Health Letter 4:37, 1992.
16. Antihistamines. Consumer Reports Health Letter 1:12-13, 1989.
17. Antihistamines and asthma, Consumer Reports Health Letter 3:47, 1991.
18. The search for the right pain reliever, Consumer Reports 52:82-85, 1987.
19. Aspirin: the all-time wonder drug. The Johns Hopkins Medical Letter, Health After 50 3(12):4-6, 1992.
20. Pain relievers, Consumer Reports Health Letter 1:1,4,8, 1989.
21. Antacids, Consumer Reports Health Letter 2:12-13, 1990.
22. How to use antacids safely and effectively, University of California, Berkeley Wellness Letter 2(6):3, 1986.
23. The pill for herpes—for whom? Harvard Medical School Health Letter 10(2):6, 1985.
24. Kaplowitz LG et al: Prolonged continuous acyclovir treatment with normal adults with frequently recurring genital herpes simplex virus infection, JAMA 265:747-551, 1991.
25. Hecht A: Of hangovers and love potions, FDA Consumer 16(10):10-11, 1982.
26. Hse E: Warning on gay enhancers, San Francisco Chronicle, March 24, 1983.
27. Harvey SM and Beckman ZD: Alcohol consumption, female sexual behavior, and contraceptive use, J Stud Alcohol 47:327-332, 1986.

*28. Cold remedies: which ones work best? Consumer Reports 54:8-11, 1989.

29. Hecht A: More yesses, no's and maybes for OTC drugs, FDA Consumer 19(3):16-19, 1985.
30. Decongestants, Consumer Reports Health Letter 1:21, 1989.
31. Cough remedies, Consumer Reports Health Letter 1:30-31, 1989.
32. Final rule issued on OTC cough medicines, FDA Consumer 21(9):3, 1987.
33. Consumer reports: The medicine show, Mt Vernon, NY, 1974, Consumers Union.
34. Herndon ML: Guaranteed hangover remedy revealed! FDA Consumer 17(10):16-17, 1983.
35. Help for hemorrhoids, Consumer Reports 51:578-580, 1986.
36. Hemorrhoids, Public Citizen Health Research Group Health Letter 7(3):1-6, 1992.
37. Litovitz T and Manoguerra A: Comparison of pediatric poisoning hazards: an analysis of 3.8 million exposure incidents, Pediatrics 89:999–1006, 1992.
38. Laxatives, Consumer Reports Health Letter 2:85, 1990.
39. Freedman DX: Drugs and insomnia, Consensus Development Conference Summary, 4:1, Bethesda, 1984, National Institutes of Health.
40. Weck E: From awake to zzzzzzz, FDA Consumer 23(8):14-15, 1989.
41. No smoking deterrents, FDA Consumer 19(8):2-3, 1985.
42. Whelan EM: A smoking gun: how the tobacco companies get away with murder, Philadelphia, 1984, George F Stickley Co.
43. Nicotine patches, The Medical Letter 34:37-38, 1992.
44. Hecht A: Aspirin vs acetaminophen, FDA Consumer 17(1):7-9, 1983.
45. Hecht A: Panel reports on sleep aids, FDA Consumer 10(1):10-13, 1976.
46. Council on Better Business Bureaus: Tips on prescription drugs and pharmacies. Arlington, VA, 1990, The Council.

*Recommended reading.

CHAPTER TWENTY-ONE

SKIN AND BEAUTY AIDS

Man can be cured of every folly but vanity.

ROUSSEAU

Beauty is a conspiracy of pain forced upon women. . . . In the boardroom and in the bedroom, women are entrapped by a cult that is the equivalent of the iron maiden.

NAOMI WOLF[1]

CONSUMER DECISIONS

What kinds of cosmetics and beauty aids should be purchased?

Will skin bleaching creams be helpful?

How can aging and wrinkling of skin be prevented?

Should one have breast augmentation, reduction, or liposuction performed?

Which antiperspirants/deodorants should one use?

What can be done about baldness? Excess hair?

How can you protect yourself against the sun's hazards?

The human need for social acceptance is undoubtedly the motivating force that drives people to seek the fountain of youth. Author Naomi Wolf[2] stated that women learn as young girls that sexual attraction is the "desire to be desired." Betty Friedan, pioneer feminist, stated that women often go to extremes in their pursuit of good looks. They endure face-lifts and possibly risk their health with silicone injections into their breasts.

Manufacturers exploit this need by promoting products they claim will help individuals achieve a measure of self-esteem. Incomplete or unscientific data are often utilized to make inaccurate, misleading, and unsubstantiated advertising claims. Cosmetics may be helpful, but they cannot perform miracles. Thus, consumers are likely to be disappointed with "instant face-lifts," cream masks, cream peels, and other procedures claimed to help them look younger. No cream, salve, or gel can provide eternal youth. Such ingredients as vitamin E, jojoba oil, aloe vera, almond collagen, and avocado may give cream a lush look or a smooth consistency, but they do little more than add to the cost of the product.

It is estimated that over $24 billion yearly is spent on skin and beauty aids in the United States. The leading categories, in their order of sales, are cosmetics, hair products, women's fragrances, and skin preparations. Several billion dollars are spent each year on substances claimed to prevent or remedy lines, wrinkles, loss of skin elasticity, and other effects of aging. Additional billions are spent on cosmetic surgery. At least half a billion dollars is spent yearly on facial cleaners.

This chapter focuses on cosmetics, cosmetic surgery, breast implants, deodorants and antiperspirants, acne, hair and scalp care, skin protection, and the treatment of warts.

COSMETICS

Except in rare situations, most cosmetics have been safe and have caused little difficulty in the past 30 years.

ANDREW P. LAZAR, M.D.,
PAUL LAZAR, M.D.
DERMATOLOGISTS, NORTHWESTERN UNIVERSITY
MEDICAL SCHOOL, JANUARY, 1987

The Federal Food, Drug, and Cosmetic Act defines cosmetics as substances intended to be rubbed, poured, sprinkled, or sprayed on the body to cleanse, beautify, promote attractiveness, or alter appearance. FDA regulations are limited to the mislabeling of products. However, all ingredients that make up 1% or more of a cosmetic must be listed on the label, in the order of predominance, with the ingredient present in the largest amount listed first. This should enable allergic individuals to identify and avoid irritating materials and help consumers compare the ingredients of inexpensive products with those of expensive ones. In addition, manufacturers must substantiate the safety (not efficacy) of ingredients prior to marketing. If the safety has not been determined, a warning must appear on the label. Color additives to be used must be approved by the FDA.

Cosmetics can keep the skin clean, moist, and soft. They can also temporarily close pores, plump up skin to make wrinkles less noticeable, and provide an artificial glow. Such effects are transient and sometimes so slight that they may go unnoticed.

Soaps

Don't be taken in by the perfumes, the fancy packaging, and the pretty colors. Differences in cleansing effectiveness among soaps are slight. . . .

CONSUMER REPORTS
JANUARY 1985

PERSONAL GLIMPSE

Consumers: How many of these advertised and promoted cosmetic aids have you tried or plan to try?

Face-lifts	Body tucks
Liposuction	Electrolysis
Collagen implants	Breast lifts
Wrinkle creams	Face masks
Mud baths	Chemical peels
Wrinkle fills	Liquid diets
Cellulite reduction	Tweezing
Plucking	Waxing
Straightening	Waving
Herbal heat wraps	

CONSUMER TIP

Ounce for ounce, the longest-lasting bar soap, Pears, should give three times as many hand washes as the quickest to vanish, Neutrogena.

Soaping Up
Consumer Reports, Oct. 1990

Soap cleans the skin more effectively than any other product. It is the best cleanser for most people. It is traditionally made of natural ingredients: fatty acids from animal fat or vegetable oils, alkalis, scent, and coloring materials. Some soaps, including the new liquid type, may be detergent or part detergent, made of synthetic, often petroleum-based ingredients. Liquid soaps generally are more expensive than bar soaps. There are clear soaps, medicated soaps, and soaps marketed by perfume and cosmetic companies. Bar soaps range from 30¢ to $15 or more. Liquid soaps range from 99¢ to $8.50 or more. Personal preference usually determines which soap will be purchased.

Adverse reactions to alkaline soap occur in a small percentage of people. The pH of the soap indicates the extent of acidity or alkalinity. A pH of 7 is neutral, a higher number means the product is alkaline, and a lower number means it is acidic. *Consumer Reports*[3] found that Caress Body Bar and Bath Oil, Estee Lauder bar, Johnson's Baby Bar, and Liqua 4 Liquid were very close to neutral. Alkaline soaps can cause rough, red, dry skin. Individuals with dry skin may find that a superfatted soap (contaning additional fats or oils such as moisturizing cream, lanolin, or cocoa butter) will leave the skin feeling more comfortable. But soaps are not really soothing; they can dry and irritate skin. Using a moisturizing lotion that contians an emollient after bathing is a good preventive measure.

Deodorant soaps include an antibacterial agent. Perspiration has no odor; body odor is caused by bacteria that act on perspiration. However, all soaps provide some protection from unwanted odors by floating off bacteria along with dirt and grease. *Consumer Reports*[4] studied 42 of the best-selling brands of soap and made these recommendations:

Best buys @ 6¢ per wash: Palmolive Green and Pure & Natural
High Rated Deodorant Bars: Safeguard, Shield
Best Liquid Soap:Liquid Dial Anti-bacterial
Lasted Longest: Pears, Tone Creme with Cocoa Butter

Soap and water act on the skin surface to loosen and remove soil and grime, body secretions, skin cell debris, microorganisms, and the many substances applied to it by design such as cosmetics, toiletries, and medications. General rules for washing the skin follow:

1. Avoid using very hot water and scrubbing with strong soap because these cause excessive oil removal from the skin and subsequent dryness, chapping, and itching. Use soft water when possible.
2. Do not massage soap into the skin unless advised to do so by your physician for a specific reason. Use your fingertips, not a facecloth or brush.
3. Do not use a medicated soap unless advised to do so by your physician. The potential harm outweighs the benefits because of possible allergic reactions and photosensitivity. Hexachlorophene was removed from deodorant soaps several years ago.
4. Use enough water to rinse away all traces of soap.
5. If you have oily skin, wash your face with soap and water frequently instead of with cleansing cream. You may wish to follow with a cold water wash.
6. If you have dry skin because of water loss from cells, use soap and water but alternate with

cleansing cream. Use a bland soap and pat your face dry with a towel.
7. Avoid too frequent bathing, especially during the winter, since this can dry and irritate the skin.

Facial Cleansers and Creams

The main purpose of a facial cleanser is to remove makeup and grime. Soap and water can do this, but soap can remove the skin's natural oils and leave it rough, chapped and tender. A typical cleanser contains water, glycerin or other moisturizer oils, fats or greases (for consistence and to dissolve grime), detergents (wash grime), preservatives (forestall spoilage), and dyes and scent (make it look and feel good). *Consumer Reports*[5] recruited a panel of 90 women who wore makeup to test cleansers. Most of the women concluded that Olay Beauty Cleanser at 85¢ per ounce was best. Other preferences were Elizabeth Arden Moisture-Rich Skin Wash, and Revlon European Collagen Complex. The products were easy to apply and remove, took off makeup efficiently, smelled pleasant, felt good on the skin during use, and left the skin feeling nice after use.

Facial creams are sealants that assist in the retention of moisture so the skin can remain soft and pliable. Skin-care products that cost 10 times more than other products do not work better. *The New Medicine Show*[6] reported that in 1986, 600 women tested 48 products and found that all of them worked. The products cost from 10¢ to $6.10 per ounce. The only way to alleviate dry skin is to restore the proper balanace of moisture to the skin. Moisturizers can help do this by:

1. Containing some kind of oil to retard water evaporation; e.g., glycerin.
2. Containing humectants (ingredients that attract and hold water). The best time to apply them is after bathing. The moisturizing ingredients generally found in facial creams are listed in Table 21-1.

There are no miracles in nonprescription preparations for the skin at any price. There is no evidence that products containing such ingredients as vitamin E, estrogen, or avocado will improve skin texture.

Table 21-1

Moisturizer Ingredients

Ingredients	Comments
Collagen and elastin	Found in connective tissue, cartilage and bone; bind moisture to skin; give creams and lotions satiny feel
Lanolin and petrolatum	Retard evaporation of water; smoothen and soften skin
Cocoa butter	Slows evaporation of moisture
Aloe	Soothing and mild humectant; cannot heal, nourish, or rejuvenate skin
Vitamin E	Like other oils is barrier to evaporation; is potential allergen- may cause itchy skin reaction

From The new medicine show.[6]

Skin Bleaching Creams

Skin bleaches are used for skin disoloration (hyperpigmentation) caused by freckles, flat moles, liver spots, and melasma, which may occur during pregnancy and among women taking oral contraceptives. Skin bleaches are used to lighten abnormal skin, which in severe cases can be disfiguring and emotionally stressful as well. They make the skin especially sensitive to the sun, and the label warning should indicate this fact. An FDA expert panel reported that the only safe and effective skin bleaching ingredient is hydroquinone in concentrations from 1.56% to 2%. Nonprescription products containing 2% hydroquinone include Esoterica, Porcelana, and Artra. Engasser and Maibach[7] said bleaching creams (2% to 5%, by prescription only) for severe conditions are modestly effective in treating pigmentary disorders.

Hydroquinone does not actually bleach the skin, but inhibits its pigment-producing cells (melanocytes). Since these cells are deep in the skin, lightening products work slowly, if at all. Results may not be apparent for 3 months. Users (including those who do not sunbathe) should apply a sunscreen because fade creams increase sensitivity to the sun. *Consumer Reports*[8] offers these remarks for fade cream users:

1. When they work, they work only against freckles and age spots.

2. They will not cause blemishes to completely disappear.
3. Apply them only to the pigmented areas and not the surrounding skin.
4. If no results are obtained after 3 months, consider professional treatment.
5. Protect hands and face from excessive exposure to the sun to prevent pigmentation production.
6. Foundation creams can cover skin blemishes and serve as an alternative to fade creams.

Lipsticks

Lipstick dermatitis used to be a common allergic reaction. Since manufacturers stopped using eosin, this condition has become rare. However, on occasion, the skin reacts to other ingredients such as base, colors, or perfume.

Eye Cosmetics

Eye cosmetics are used to highlight and emphasize the eyes. Available eye cosmetics include eye shadows, eye shadow setting creams, under-eye concealers, eye liners, mascaras, artificial eyelashes, and eyebrow pencils. Special care in their selection must be taken by individuals with sensitive skin or contact lens wearers. Eye cosmetics may cause irritant or allergic contact dermatitis.[9]

Shampoos

Shampoos generally contain: (1) a synthetic detergent (alone or with soap) as the main cleansing agent, (2) a sudsing agent that makes rinsing easier, (3) fragrance, and (4) various other substances such as jojoba, henna, aloe, chamomile, lanolin, and coconut oil. The main function of shampoo is to clean the hair by removing dirt, dead skin scales, and excess sebum. Just about every shampoo product will do well.

Unless soap is used in soft water, it leaves a film on the hair. Soap will clean the hair, but it may look dull because oil has been removed from hair shafts. The detergents in shampoos form no film. Manufacturers add conditioners to their products to reduce the depletion of natural hair oils. Thus the hair is not only clean but remains shiny and manageable. Some so-called natural ingredients in shampoos, such as jojoba, henna, and aloe, may have conditioning effects, but these are not well documented. People with dandruff have a scalp problem, not a hair difficulty. Severe flaking of the scalp may be a symptom of seborrheic dermatitis or psoriasis that warrants the attention of a physician. Most people who wash their hair frequently have no need for a medicated shampoo. The FDA[6] has identified 5 ingredients in OTC dandruff shampoos that are safe and effective:

Coal-tar preparations—Denorex, Tegrin
Salicylic acid—P & S, X-Seb
Selenium sulfide—Selsun
Zinc pyrithione—Head & Shoulders, Sebulin, Zincon
Sulphur preparations—Sebulex, Vanseb

Consumer Reports stated: (1) there is no "best"shampoo; a brand that makes the hair feel good should be continued, and (2) inexpensive shampoos contain adequate cleaning and conditioning agents.

Aging Skin and Wrinkles

When your friends begin to flatter you on how young you look, it's a sure sign you're getting old.

Mark Twain

Aging and wrinkling are changes of the skin and the subcutaneous tissue that result from the degeneration of elastic tissue, loss of subcutaneous fat, and loss of fluid content. Overexposure to sun dries the skin and hastens aging and wrinkling. Repeated exposure to ultraviolet rays also increases the like-

Can Aging Be Reversed?

In 1990, researchers reported the test results of a drug that might reverse the aging process. A synthetic human growth hormone (HGH), produced naturally in the pituitary gland, was injected for 6 months into 12 men ages 61 to 81 with startling results. Skin thickness and lean body mass increased, and fat decreased. Researchers noted, the effect reversed "changes incurred during 10 to 20 years of aging." This is an expensive and experimental drug, tried on only 12 men at a cost of $14,000 for a year's supply.

Changing Times, Feb 1991

Questions: Can these results be repeated? Will it work on a larger population? Will it work on women?

lihood of developing premalignant tumors. Sun-damaged skin, referred to as "sailor's skin," is wrinkled, thickened, and uneven in color. Cigarette smoking can accelerate wrinkles and rough skin. Cosmetic products at best provide temporary improvements in appearance. Cosmetic counters display hundreds of moisturizers, many of which are touted to help the aging process and wrinkles. These materials contain various oils that trap water in the skin and prevent its evaporation. By masking tiny lines that detract from one's appearance, they may help the skin look and feel better for a few hours. An inexpensive brand will probably provide as much benefitt as a more expensive one. There is no evidence that Vitamin E in moisturizers penetrates the skin. Vitamin A does not affect the skin the way Retin-A does. Appropriate cosmetic surgery (discussed later) performed by a qualified surgeon may be the most rewarding approach to improving the appearance of the skin.

Medical professionals use a variety of procedures to help people with damaged and disfigured skin. Dermatologists[10] can provide any of the following treatments:

- *Topical tretinoin (Retin-A):* Originally prescribed for severe acne, tretinoin is a derivative of Vitamin A. It is a prescription skin cream that has been widely touted as an antiwrinkle treatment for fine wrinkles. There is some evidence that it may reverse photodamage to the skin. Its side effects include skin irritation, increased susceptibility to sunburn, and severe inflammation of the skin. The treatment must be continued for life to sustain benefits. The long-term safety and effectiveness of Retin-A has not been well established. The product costs $20 to $60 monthly.
- *Alpha hydroxy acids.* Available by prescription; loosen dead cells from the skin's surface, leaving a smoother, softer layer; also help return moisture in severely dry skin.
- *Soft-tissue implants (cow collagen).* These are placed in large and deep wrinkles to "puff-up" the skin; used from nose to lips, between eyes and around eyes (see later report on collagen).
- *Lipotransplantation.* Small amount of fat is removed from the thigh and injected into skin depressions around the eyes, nose, and mouth. The procedure's effectiveness has not been established.
- *Chemical peels.* Chemicals are applied to the skin to peel off the top layer. There may be temporary pain and burning afterwards. Takes several weeks to heal and effect may last for years.
- *Dermabrasion.* High-speed rotating brushes remove damaged skin. Is used mostly for scars. May cause swelling and redness and leave splotchy coloring and minor scars. Recovery time is 3 to 6 weeks.
- *Silicone Injections.* Have been used for many years
- *Fibril Injections.* Patient's blood is mixed with chemicals in a sponge implanted in a wrinkle. It stimulates collagen growth.

Collagen

In 1981, the FDA approved the use of cow collagen for wrinkles, lines, and scars. Since then physicians have injected many patients with protein collagen, which is a support material found in muscles, skin, and tendons. The substance can temporarily smooth out imperfections, such as shallow scars or lines around the eyes and mouth. It also has been marketed to puff up the lips. Injections must be repeated every 6 months, or sooner, because the body breaks down the collagen.[11] The cost ranges from $300 to $600 for a 30-minute visit.

Some people have an allergic reaction at the injection site that results in redness, itching, swelling, and hardening of the skin. Some researchers suspect that collagen can trigger autoimmune diseases, in which the body's immune system turns against its own tissues. Two such potentially fatal diseases that inflame the skin and weaken muscles are polymyositis and dermatomyositis (PM/DM). The FDA[12] concluded there was no evidence to support a connection between collagen injections and PM/DM. The FDA continues to monitor scientific studies to determine if collagen has long-term effects. However, pressure has been increasing to have the FDA reevaluate its conclusions and to reopen its investigation of collagen practices.

The FDA now requires that collagen products be labeled with a warning to consumers and physicians about a possible association between injectable collagen and connective tissue diseases such as rheumatoid arthritis and scleroderma. The FDA has also expressed concern that the Collagen Corporation, a large producer of collagen, has not been adequately reporting patient complaints and has been downgrading the severity of problems. For example, it had not recorded scars and reactions such as abscesses serious enough to require treatment with steroids or antibiotics. It failed to report

54 complaints about side effects such as swelling, stinging, and burning after injections into the red part of the lips. However, the corporation has promised to pay legal fees for doctors who are sued by patients.[13]

There have been many illegal, misrepresented, and unproven treatment for wrinkles, some of which may have been harmful. Several illustrations are discussed next.

Glycel, a product promoted by Dr. Christiaan Barnard, the South African surgeon who performed the first successful heart transplant, is a cosmetic containing glycosphingolipid (GSL) that was claimed to be a "rejuvenating" ingredient. Advertisements claimed that an absence of GSL causes wrinkles. This product sold for $75 a jar. Dr. Vincent DeLeo,[14] a dermatologist at Columbia Presbyterian Medical Center in New York, said that it was merely a moisturizer that smoothes out lines and wrinkles temporarily.

In 1988 the FDA[15] sent regulatory letters to Alfin Fragrances, Inc. (manufacturer of Glycel), Estee Lauder, Inc., Christian Dior Perfumes, Inc., Avon Products, Inc., and several other manufacturers, ordering them to stop making antiaging claims for their skin care products. Statements that a product can counteract or retard the aging process or rejuvenate or repair the skin are drug claims because they indicate that the product is intended to affect a bodily function or the body's structure. The FDA said that since "antiaging" creams had not been proven safe and effective for their intended purposes, drug claims for such products were illegal.

In their book *Life Extension,* Durk Pearson and Sandy Shaw recommended many substances they claimed might extend life. They suggested using 31 substances, including prescription drugs (e.g., L-Dopa, Hydergine), essential nutrients (zinc, selenium, large doses of most vitamins), other substances naturally found in foods (e.g., choline, RNA, bioflavonoids), and antioxidant food additives (e.g., BHT). Some of these items may be dangerous in large quantities, although they are safe in small amounts. The U.S. House of Representatives Select Committee on Aging noted that "Most experts believe this book represents a misinterpretation of sound aging research . . . . Isolated, unsubstantiated reports are used to validate hypotheses." The regimen it describes involves visits to physicians willing to prescribe the drugs, frequent medical examinations, and laboratory tests to detect possible adverse effects—at an annual cost of $1000 to $2000.[16]

The *Johns Hopkins Medical Letter, Health After 50*[17] stated that new animal studies indicate that past skin photodamage may be somewhat reversible. If the sun is avoided or a sunscreen is used, the skin will partially repair itself.

CONSUMER TIP

Preventing Wrinkles

Although wrinkles cannot be totally prevented, there are ways to reduce their incidence and severity:

- Avoid exposure to the sun (see pp 471-473)
- Reduce or avoid such facial expressions as pursing the lips, arching eyebrows, or grimacing
- Avoid smoking
- Sleep on both sides of the face
- Avoid cycles of gaining and losing weight

Camouflage Cosmetics

Regular cosmetics have limited usefulness in masking skin imperfections such as scars, burns, or pigment changes. Corrective cosmetics have an opaque foundation that is more effective for concealing skin blemishes. Corrective cosmetics are waterproof and smudgeless. They are recommended by dermatologists and plastic surgeons when medical treatment cannot further improve appearance. They can camouflage birthmarks, broken capillaries, postoperative discolorations, dark circles under the eyes, pigmentation problems, cleft lip, varicose veins, and strech marks. Such cosmetics provide "natural" colors and textures to the skin, and can remain on the skin for a long time.

Cosmetic Safety

The average female consumer uses more than 12 cosmetics daily, yet few catastrophes occur. The *Harvard Medical School Health Letter*[18] stated cosmetics generally are safe and do not cause serious harm. The FDA receives 500 complaints yearly, but there is no formal mechanism for collecting these complaints. Also, the Food, Drug, and Cosmetic Act does not require cosmetics manufacturers to test their products for safety. Representative Ron Wyden (D-OR)[19] wants to modify the Act to force companies to safety test their products and make the data available to the FDA. Manufacturers are expected to report consumer injuries.

According to Tolchin,[20] only 3% of some 4000 to 5000 cosmetic manufacturers file injury reports. Despite the claim by the Cosmetic, Toiletry and Fragrance Association that cosmetics are safe, Representative Wyden believes no one knows the extent of the problems. He claimed there are products on the market that have led to life-threatening disease and disfigurement through illegal and improper promotion. He wants companies to be registered with the FDA, keep adequate safety data, and disclose and file injury reports. FDA Commissioner Dr. David Kessler[19] identified three potentially hazardous substances and said he would clamp down on unapproved use of approved drugs and promotional literature disguised as medical literature:

- *Retin-A* was approved to treat severe acne but not for preventing wrinkles. It potentially increases the risk of cancer.
- *Collagen* was approved for certain cosmetic purposes, such as acne scars, but not for lip augmentation. The Collagen Corporation has agreed to stop this promotion.
- *Liquid silicone injections* have never been approved for any use, including the removal of wrinkles and other facial deformities.

A 5-year study by 12 dermatologists funded by the FDA[21] revealed that skin products (lotions, creams) and hair preparations (including colors) caused 52% of the cosmetic problems and makeup caused 11%. Lazar[22] said the most common difficulties are irritants and nonallergic reactions followed by allergic reactions, photosensitivity reactions, and physiochemical interactions. The most common offenders are the fragrances, preservatives, and lanolin in hair products and facial makeup.

No ingredient that causes cancer may be used in cosmetics. Some coal-tar products are used, but their long-term effects are unknown. Arndt[18] indicated that nitrosamines, which are potent carcinogens, have been found in some cosmetics due to impurities in the production process. Although nitrosamines have been detected in the urine of people who use cosmetics, their concentration is low and the risk of cancer is negligible. Estrogen hormones that affect feminine characteristics and can penetrate the skin are found in cosmetics. It is not known how many products contain hormones. The FDA says the amount is inadequate to make skin look younger.

Contamination of eye shadow, mascara, eye lotion, and eye drops, and prolonged use of contact lenses present possible hazards. Eye infections, some of a serious nature, can result. Eyeliner, shadow, and mascara normally pose no danger to the user. Well-packaged eye makeup is almost always clean and uncontaminated (due to preservative). Yet each year some women acquire eye infections. No makeup can be kept sterile, and care should be taken when using them. These suggestions should be helpful:

Do's

1. Wash hands before application.
2. Keep applicators and containers clean.
3. Buy mascara in small amounts.

Don'ts

1. Don't scratch the eye during application.
2. Don't use saliva to wet makeup; water is safer.
3. Don't share makeup.
4. Don't try eye products from testers in department stores.
5. Don't buy an open package that may have been sampled.

Consider these safety rules when using cosmetics:

1. Read the labels carefully and follow directions exactly. This is especially important when using antiperspirants, depilatory (hair-removing) preparations, hair dyes, home permanents, and skin packs.
2. Apply a small amount on the inside of your forearm and leave it for 24 hours to determine if you are allergic to the cosmetic.
3. Stop using the cosmetic immediately if it causes an adverse effect such as burning, breaking out, stinging, or itching. See your physician if the condition appears serious.
4. To prevent contamination wash your hands before applying a cosmetic.
5. Close containers after each use to prevent contamination.
6. Do not borrow cosmetics from others.
7. Do not buy cosmetics without preservatives; help prevent contamination.

8. Avoid scented soaps; fragrance may be responsible for allergy and irritation.
9. Be extremely cautious when using cosmetics around the eyes.
10. Report adverse effects of cosmetics to the manufacturer and the FDA as a public service.
11. Use aerosol products in well-ventilated rooms.
12. Bear in mind: (a) No product is foolproof against allergies. No product is truly nonallergenic. (b) Medicated cosmetics will not cure skin diseases. A physician should be consulted.

Did You Know?

Surgeons can cure many of the side effects of aging without any wonder drug! Wrinkly neck? Bags under eyes? Love handles? Large tummy? It can be done with a needle, a knife, a laser, or an injection. Oh! yes, and with a check.

Changing Times, Feb 1991

COSMETIC SURGERY

Plastic surgery refers to the repair, remodeling, or restoration of injured or defective tissue or body parts. It is performed by plastic surgeons as well as ophthalmologists (eyelid tucks and repairs around eyes), otolaryngologists (repair and reconstruction of fractures of head and neck region), dermatologists, and general surgeons. For congenital abnormalities (e.g., cleft lip), trauma rehabilitiation (accidents), and cancer-related surgery (breast implants), most plastic surgical procedures are reconstructive. The remaining procedures are for aesthetic reasons or to improve body contours.

This section deals primarily with cosmetic or aesthetic surgery—the improvement of physical appearance by repairing and restoring damaged areas of the skin and by remodeling the face and other parts of the body.

The demand for cosmetic surgery or body contouring (a term widely used) in the United States has increased tremendously in the past few years. The desires to increase self-esteem and social acceptance and to preserve youth and beauty have been the reasons for this interest. Two other factors have contributed to the growth of cosmetic surgery: new surgical procedures using safer anesthetics, and physician advertising. Two years ago a Los Angeles magazine contained more than 25 advertisements about the miracles of cosmetic surgery. The advertised procedures cost from $50 to $5000.

More than $500 million is spent each year to eliminate double chins, modify the nose or derriere, and acquire tummy tucks and facelifts. People who want to look young will undergo considerable cost and inconvenience. Such surgery can be costly and painful, may take weeks or months to recovery, is generally not covered by insurance, and involves risk. Infection is the greatest risk, but surgical procedures may also lead to bleeding, adverse reactions to anesthetic, and on rare occasions, even death. Breasts have been severely disfigured and noses have been made unsightly. One woman reportedly awakened from tummy-tuck surgery to find her belly button 2 inches off center.

Types of Cosmetic Surgery

Walzer[23] identifies the following types of cosmetic surgery:

Laser surgery. Lasers are instruments that produce high-energy light that can cut tissue like a scalpel. Laser surgery is bloodless because it seals off blood vessels as it cuts. It is used to treat skin disorders—moles, brown spots, tattoos, warts, and skin growths. Complications are on the par with other surgical techniques. The cost and maintenance of equipment ranges from $25,000 to $100,000.

Electrosurgery. This procedure can cut and destroy tissue. It seals severed blood vessels to control bleeding. It is used for dilated veins, dilated blood vessels, liver spots, small cysts, keratoses, warts, and some forms of skin cancer. It is a more versatile technique than laser surgery and less expensive.

Sclerosurgery. This technique injects small veins with a solution containing an irritating chemical. Subsequently a clot or scar forms that causes the veins to shrink and fade away.

Liposuction. This procedure removes fat deposits and is used to remodel body contours. It is the most common cosmetic surgical procedure. A hollow, blunt-ended tube is inserted under the skin and a suction machine vacuums out the fat. Patients may experience soreness and black and blue discolorations due to bleeding. The procedure is used on the flanks, buttocks, abdomen, and fatty areas around the knees, ankles and under the chin. Complications include: excess bleeding, shock, in-

Buyer Beware

A young mother in Texas went to a physician for liposuction. The doctor had advertised he was an expert when actually he was a general practitioner who had taken a weekend course in liposuction. Three days after surgery the women died from a massive infection. The Texas State Board of Medical Examiners investigated and revoked the license of the physician.

Question: How can consumers locate a competent plastic surgeon?

fection if unsterile instruments are used, "rapping" (ridging of skin surface), and skin death. In 1987 the American Society of Plastic and Reconstructive Surgeons[24] reported that 11 deaths had occurred from the use of this procedure.

The *Mayo Clinic Health Letter*[25] says that body contouring through liposuction may be safe if you have the right doctor, but there is no panacea for a less-than-perfect body.

Skin peel. Acid is applied to the skin using cotton-tipped applicator sticks to modify superficial lines, furrows, and discolorations due to chronic sun damage. May produce pain and burning that disappears after several hours. Healing is usually complete in 2 weeks. May cause an increase or decrease in pigmentation.

Dermabrasion. Skin that has been frozen is removed in layers using a wire brush that is motor driven. The procedure is used for acne scars, injury scars, and tattoos.

Collagen injections. Refer to page 457.

Eyeline surgery. This involves the implanting of permanent eyelash lines in the dermis of the lashline using metallic oxide pigment (analogous to tattooing). The procedure has not been approved by the FDA, and some physicians are questioning its value. It costs $450 to $1500 and involves some risks including hypersensitivity to the pigment and infection. Swelling and bruising may last several weeks. The long-term effects of this surgery are not known.

Fees for cosmetic surgery

These are some of the cosmetic procedures and their fees, according to the American Society of Plastic and Reconstructive Surgeons[26] and several other sources.[27,28]

Abdominoplasty (stomach)	$2000–$6000
Blepharoplasty (eyelids)	$1000–$4000
Breast augmentation	$1800–$4000
Breast reduction	$2000–$7000
Breast lift	$1500–$5000
Surgical body contouring	$1000–$8000
Chemical peel (chemosurgery)	$1200–$3000
Dermabrasion (skin planing)	$600–$2500
Face-lift	$2000–$10,000
Forehead lift	$1200–$5800
Hair transplant	$250–$4000
Chin augmentation	$250–$3000
Rhinoplasty (reshaping of nose)	$1500–$6000
Otoplasty (reshaping of ear)	$1000–$3500

Liposuction (suction lipectomy):

Thigh	$750–$4000
Abdomen	$2000–$6000
Buttocks	$500–$3000
Face	$500–$4000

Since 1991 the cost of breast enlargements, face-lifts, and other cosmetic surgical procedures is not tax-deductible. The IRS will also tax reimbursements for surgery paid for through company-sponsored health plans. According to *U.S. News & World Report*[29] the most commonly performed procedures during 1989 included:

Liposuction	250,000
Breast augmentation	100,000
Eyelid tuck	100,000
Rhinoplasty (nose)	95,000
Face-lift	75,000
Chin implant	17,000

Face-lifts can improve appearance by obliterating wrinkles, bags, pouches, or sagging skin that has lost its elasticity. The procedures involve removal of excess skin and tightening of the skin to make wrinkles less noticeable. The surgery takes 2 to 5 hours. It is usually done under local anesthesia

PERSONAL GLIMPSE

Did You Know?

In 1988, 39% of the 48,480 people who had face-lifts were under the age of 51. The average cost of the operation was $3420.

in a hospital or the surgeon's outpatient operating room. It is not possible to predict how long a face-lift will last, but 3 to 12 years is generally the length of time. A face-lift can usually be repeated.

Breast Implants

It is estimated that 2 million women have received breast implants during the past 20 years. Approximately 100,000 yearly undergo surgery for breast augmentation. The usual reasons for the operation are: (1) replacement after cancer surgery, (2) to make nonmatching breasts the same size, or (3) a desire for larger breasts. A study of 600 women with breast implants found that 93% were satisfied with the results and 80% said they would have surgery again if needed.[30] Table 21-2 describes the types, nature, and risks of breast implants used for augmentation and reconstructive surgery.

Breast implants last for many years in some women, while in others frequent replacement seems to be necessary. In recent years there have been numerous reports of women who have experienced disfigurement, hard breasts, severe pain, and other unpleasant complications. Consumer groups believe the number of women affected may be in the thousands despite the lack of published evidence to substantiate these numbers. Many surgeons claim the surgery is safe and effective, and complications that arise are usually correctable and not life-threatening. In 1989, Dr. William Shaw,[31] Chairperson, Department of Plastic Surgery, UCLA, stated that an unlucky 5% of women who have augmentation and reconstruction operations have complications, but most are reversible. He also said that one in five women will need repeat surgery due to painful capsular contraction, asymmetry, infection, blood clots, or rupture of the implant.

The medical literature reports that up to 75% of women with implants have some capsular contraction, with 20% experiencing severe contractures. In 1990, health experts reported that 40% of women have serious problems and Kassousky,[32] a pathologist at UCLA, said complications occur in 40% of implant cases. In 1991, FDA scientists[24,33] said that 25% of implants produce a substance that causes cancer in laboratory animals. They stated that polyurethane in implants breaks down into a substance called TDA (2-toluene diamine) that could trigger cancer. They added that the risk of cancer in humans is not known, however the estimated cancer risk from polyurethane could be 1 in 12,000.[34]

A panel of medical experts that met in San Francisco in June 1991 played down the risks of breast implants.[35] These are some of their remarks:

Ralph K. Davies, University of California, Medical Center, San Francisco: alarm sounded too loudly

T. Roderick Hesbi, Emory University School of Medicine: Polyurethane breaks down very slowly; is no scientific evidence it releases carcinogens

Noel R. Rose, Johns Hopkins School of Hygiene: report unfounded of implants causing connective tissue and skin disorders

Susan Roux, Memorial Breast Center, California: stainless steel must be used to have totally unbreakable breast implants.

In April, 1991, the FDA gave breast plant manufacturers 90 days to provide data on the safety and effectiveness of their products or have them removed from the marketplace. In January 1992 FDA Commissioner Dr. David Kessler declared a moratorium on silicone-implant surgery until an Expert Advisory Panel could review new evidence received. He urged manufacturers to halt marketing the devices and surgeons to stop inserting them in women.

In May, 1992, the FDA[35a] announced that silicone-gel breast implants will be available only to women enrolled in clinical studies. However, they will be widely available for women for reconstructive surgery following breast cancer surgery and certain other medical conditions. Use of these devices for breast augmentation will be greatly limited. Saline-gel implants will continue to be obtainable without restriction. Manufacturers will be required to periodically submit safety and effectiveness information of their products to the FDA.

Meanwhile, women who have had breast implants may wish to consult their doctor for information, advice, or reassurance about their own

TABLE 21–2

TYPES OF BREAST IMPLANTS

Type	Nature	Comments
Silicone-Gel	Rubber balloon filled with gel; feels similar to normal breast	Leak or rupture ("gel break") may require surgery; silicone not absorbing may move; forms scar tissue (lumps) that are hard (capsular contraction); may cause pain, nipple changes, autoimmune (connective tissue) diseases—lupus, scleroderma, and others
Saline	Inflatable implants filled with salt-water solution; many surgeons reluctant to use	Leak or rupture likely; will deflate and require surgical removal; may lead to scar tissue and calcium deposits; body can absorb solution and less likely risk of autoimmune diseases and cancer
Double-lumen	Two balloons, one inserted in other; contains silicone-gel and saline solution	Similar to silicone-gel and saline filled
Textured	Silicone-gel balloon with coating of polyurethane; designed to reduce scarring and capsular contraction	May leak or rupture and release small amounts of TDA (2,4-toluene diamine), which causes cancer in animals; not known whether causes cancer in humans; estimated cancer risk is 1 in 12,000; short- and long-term risks unknown except as indicated in silicone gel; manufacturers have removed from marketplace
TRAM	Transverse rectus abdominus myocutaneous Extra fat taken from stomach to form new breast	Feels more natural to touch; cannot be rejected by body; will not rupture or break; leave additional scar tissue where fat removed; need more time on operating table and blood transfusion; not for smokers and diabetics

Note: Silicone and salt implants may "hide" suspicious lesions because mammography is difficult to perform and calcium deposits found in scar tissue interferes with the interpretation. Compression of breast in mammography may cause implant rupture.
From Greenberg J: Putting on a good front, Priorities, Summer 1991 and Important information on breast implants, FDA Backgrounder, Aug 1991.

condition. Additional information can be obtained from:

FDA/CDRH HF2-210
5600 Fishers Lane
Rockville, MD 20857

Maryland Dept. of Health & Mental Hygiene
Division of Cancer Control
201 W. Preston St.
Baltimore, MD 21201

Command Trust Network, Inc. (nonprofit clearinghouse for breast implant information),
P.O. Box 17082
Covington, KY 41017 (send business size self-addressed envelope with two first-class stamps)

Liquid Silicone

Liquid silicone injections apparently may continue to be available in Mexico for those women in desperate need of breast change and who desire to pay less and save money. These injections originally used to be the procedure used by physicians to implant the breasts. Women frequently went to Mexico for these injections because of convenience and probably cost. Over a period of 7 years, San Diego physicians treated 400 women who suffered mutilated breasts and infections traced to injections given by physicians in Mexican border cities. About 20% of the women required amputation of both breasts because of the extreme damage. Injections were prohibited in the United States by the FDA some years ago. This action occurred because 4 women died in 1971. There were also reported cases of blindness, severe pain, infection, and discoloration. In addition, the FDA concluded that liquid silicone could mask malignancies, and small amounts could move from the site of the injection. Silicone injections may still be obtainable in Tijuana and other Mexican cities for as little as $800 for eight injections plus the use of plastic molds to shape the breasts. Physicians in Mexico may continue to engage in such "get-rich" medical practices. Consumers need to understand that silicone injections may be hazardous. Women should be wary of physicians who encourage their use and engage in such a practice.

Frauds and Quackery

An estimated 3 million Americans undergo plastic surgery each year to improve their appearance and the damage caused by accidents or disease. Of this number, 1 million individuals undergo this surgery for cosmetic reasons. Apparently, most of the people are satisfied with the results. However, the $3.5-billion-a-year industry includes unscrupulous and unskilled practitioners who have bilked patients out of thousands of dollars and left many with mutilated bodies. For example, a young Los Angeles man who wanted his nose straightened had consulted a doctor who claimed to be a "board-certified specialist in cosmetic surgery." Four operations later he had lost most of his nose and he had to undergo ten additional operations and spend over $50,000 for reconstruction. His doctor had been a general practitioner who had no formal training in plastic surgery.[36]

Only about 4000 physicians are board-certified in plastic surgery, but other physicians can acquire skills pertinent to their area of specialty. (For example, ear, nose, and throat specialists can study reconstructive surgery of the head and neck, while ophthalmologists may study plastic surgery of the eyelids.) Much of the problem rests with those physicians who have taken up cosmetic surgery with little or no formal training or those who use the media to mislead or misrepresent their competence and results. One get-rich-quick operator, who offered clinical face-peel franchises to doctors, promised a $400,000 income. The franchise cost $40,000 to $50,000, which included a week's training and help with advertising procedures.

Cosmetic Surgery Tips for Consumers

Consumers should protect themselves against charlatans and quacks if they seek cosmetic surgery. They should seek the most qualified surgeons and not be rushed into a decision until they have surveyed the field. These consumer tips will provide assistance:

1. Ask your family physician, the local medical society, or the American Society of Plastic and Reconstructive Surgeons (see Appendix for address) for the names of qualified board-certified surgeons. This might include plastic surgeons, ophthalmologists, otolaryngologists, or dermatologists, depending upon the nature of the surgery.
2. Consult several physicians before making a selection even though your family physician may have suggested a qualified doctor. Do not hesitate to ask questions about qualifications, and number and types of operations performed, success rates, and risks. Note the patience and thoroughness of the answers.
3. Ask physicians to show you photographs of their patients before and after successful surgeries to be able to estimate the potential benefit of the operation to you. If the doctor uses an image on a computer screen to show personal changes that may take place, do not be swayed by a flattering image; it can be manipulated.
4. Try to discover if any lawsuits are pending against the doctor.

Cellulite

Cosmetic manufacturers have produced lotions, creams, and gels that they claim will thwart the wrinkly ravages of aging and will smooth cellulite. U.S. sales of these skin products has reached $3.7 billion yearly. Individual items cost from $12 to $150 and more.[37]

There is no scientific evidence to support the sweeping claims made by the manufacturers of these cosmetics products. The aggressive marketing that implies certain substances can alter body physiology cannot be verified through scientific studies. Since 1987, the FDA has sent complaints to 50 cosmetic companies about specific claims. Most firms as a result have changed their pitches.[38] As noted in Chapters 14 and 15, cellulite is a nonmedical term commonly used to describe deposits of dimpled fat found on the thighs and buttocks of many women.

CONSUMER TIP

Picking A Plastic Surgeon

- Check the doctor's credentials or call the American Board of Plastic and Reconstructive Surgeons at 1-800-776-2378 or the American Board of Medical Specialities at 1-800-776-2378 for information. If a doctor is offended or objects to your queries, go elsewhere.
- Ask how often the doctor has performed the procedure and request names and telephones of several patients.
- Ask doctor to carefully and completely identify all risks involved in the surgery. Be sure you understand these risks.
- Be wary of doctors who advertise and claim great results, safe and easy surgery, and do not provide details of possible risks and complications.
- Ask if the doctor is a staff member of a major hospital. Check hospital and find out if doctor has privileges to perform desired surgical procedure. If the reply is negative, seek another doctor.
- Check the clinic (surgicenter) to ascertain whether it is accredited if you are to be a patient. Does the clinic have adequate emergency equipment and an experienced anesthetist.
- Unless you have had one recently, be sure the doctor completes a thorough medical history and physical examination.

A surgical procedure also is available. It is done using a sharpened tube (cannula) in some cases to cut fibers, but the procedure is not guaranteed to be effective. This surgery costs $3000 to $4000.

DEODORANTS AND ANTIPERSPIRANTS

Perspiring is a natural body function that helps regulate body temperature, eliminate certain waste products, and protect the skin against dryness. Normal skin secretions do not have objectionable odors. However, when skin bacteria interact with sweat, the result may be unpleasant odors.

The eccrine and apocrine glands are the main producers of perspiration. Eccrine glands, the major source of perspiration, are found on all surfaces of the body except the margin of the lips and certain portions of the sex organs. They secrete watery or water-soluble substances. The body has relatively few apocrine glands; they are found in the axillae (underarms), around the nipples, on the abdomen, and in the genital area. They produce a milky sweat, rich in organic material, that has a characteristic but not objectionable odor.

Two approaches can be used to control body odor:

1. Controlling or masking the odor by impeding bacterial action through the use of deodorants or deodorant soaps.
2. Stopping or reducing perspiration through the use of antiperspirants.

Deodorants

Deodorants control body odor resulting from bacterial decomposition of sweat from the apocrine glands. They are considered by the FDA to be cosmetics and therefore do not need premarket approval for safety and efficacy. Deodorants either reduce the number of odor-causing bacteria in the underarm area or cover up the odor. No deodorant is guaranteed to control odor.

Perhaps the most effective way to control odor is by washing daily with a mild antibacterial soap to remove gland secretions and bacteria. However, some people are sensitive to antiseptic agents. Some dermatologists believe that their labels should carry a warning that people who use them may experience severe reactions such as swelling and blistering when exposed to sunlight. The substances implicated have included trichlorocarbanilide (triclocarban, or TCC), and tribromosalicylanilide (TBS), found in a number of popular soaps. Hexachlorophene can be absorbed through the skin and under certain circumstances have adverse effects on nerve tissue. It has been removed from the general market and can be purchased by prescription only.

Table 21-3 provides information that can help consumers evaluate OTC deodorant products.

Antiperspirants

Antiperspirants reduce secretions from eccrine glands by astringent action, which contracts the skin to prevent the flow of perspiration. The FDA considers these products drugs. Therefore, their active ingredients require approval. The FDA has approved these substances as safe and effective: aluminum chlorohydrates, aluminum chloride, buffered aluminum sulfate, and aluminum zirconium chlorohydrate for topical application.[39] For aerosol application only aluminum chlorohydrate has been approved.

Table 21–3

Antiperspirants vs. Deodorants

	Active ingredient	Actions	Comment
Antiperspirant*	Aluminum compound (e.g., aluminum chlorohydrate or aluminum-zirconium chlorohydrate)	Diffuses into sweat glands and retards flow of perspiration. Many are also effective against odor-causing bacteria.	Effectiveness varies according to ingredients and type of applicator. Aerosols are generally less effective and shorter lasting.
Deodorant**	Benzalkonium chloride, methylbenzenthonium chloride, neomycin sulfate, fragrance	Controls odor either by reducing bacteria or masking smell.	Doesn't reduce perspiration. Good for people who are allergic or sensitive to aluminum compounds.

Safety note: Though approved by the FDA, aerosols may cause lung problems after many years of use. They can cause pain and irritation if accidentally sprayed in the eyes. Deodorants and antiperspirants should be used only on underarms.

*Drugs must be approved by FDA
**Cosmetic ingredients do not need FDA approval
Source: Buying guide: Antiperspirants and deodorants, Unviersity of California, Berkeley Wellness Letter 2:3, April 1986. Reprinted permission of University of California, Berkeley Wellness Letter, P.O. Box 10922, Des Moines, IA 50340. © Health Letter Associates, 1986, 1987.

The effectiveness of specific antiperspirants varies with each individual. It also depends on the type (roll-on or spray), the brand, the active ingredient, and the formula. Deodorant sticks, roll-ons, and creams generally are more effective than aerosols. The reduction is sweating by antiperspirants ranges from 15% to 70%. OTC products rarely control wetness totally. For greater reduction of wetness, a prescription product is necessary. Some people who use antiperspirants have an allergic reaction or skin irritation. Table 21-3 will help consumers when they are deciding to purchase antiperspirants.

Consumers will find these suggestions helpful when using antiperspirants:[40]

1. Repeat application regularly; they work for limited periods of time.
2. Dry underarms thoroughly before application; this enhances penetration of active ingredients.
3. Avoid irritation; do not apply to freshly shaved skin.
4. If one product does not work, try another.

Antiperspirants should not be used for hyperhidrosis (excessive perspiration), bromidrosis (offensive odor), or chromidrosis (colored sweat). These are abnormal conditions that need medical attention.

Some people who cannot tolerate antiperspirants or deodorants may be helped by an antibacterial product like chlorhexidine soap (Hibiclens), povidone-iodine solution (Betadine or Efudine), or a topical antibiotic such as Neosporin cream (with prescription) or ointment (without prescription).

No deodorant or antiperspirant is a substitute for cleanliness through washing with soap and water. However, controlling body odor may require a combination of things previously described.

Consumers Union's medical consultants recommend that a roll-on, cream, lotion, or sticktype deodorant or antiperspirant be used rather than an aerosol. They warn that repeated use of aerosol sprays may be potentially harmful. The cans have been known to explode, some gases and solvents are flammable, and accidental ignition has been reported. Inhalation of some gaseous propellants has produced abnormal heart rhythms in laboratory animals.

Acne

Acne vulgaris is a disorder of the sebaceous (oil) glands. Approximately 75% of teenagers are afflicted, and it remains a problem for millions of people into their twenties and sometimes beyond. At puberty these glands increase in size and activity

TABLE 21–4

NONPRESCRIPTION ACNE PRODUCTS

Type	Comments
Benzoyl peroxide*	Most effective of FDA approved ingredients. For sensitive skin start with 5%; for nonsensitive skin start with 10%. If skin becomes overly dry and scaly, stop application and also cut down on soap use.
Sulphur	Helps heal existing lesions by peeling and drying out; safe and effective for mild acne.
Sulphur plus resorcinol	Safe and effective only in mild cases.
Salicylic acid	May help to unseat blackheads in mild acne; helps remove some surface oil.
Alcohol cleansers	Have no effect on acne; help remove surface oil, but ordinary soap does just as well.
Soaps	Medicated soaps are no more effective than ordinary soaps. Many of the touted soaps contain benzoyl peroxide or sulfur, which are effective ingredients when left on the skin but have little value in soaps that are immediately washed away.

*FDA has reclassified Benzyol peroxide from Category I: safe and effective, to Category III: more data needed; there is evidence it produces cancer in mice. From FDA, Federal Register, August 1, 1991

and secrete more sebum (oil), which can collect in the shafts of the hair follicles, become infected by surface bacteria, and result in pimples and blackheads. With some young people the condition may be extensive and chronic, resulting in pain and disfiguring scars that may create emotional problems. However, most cases of acne are mild.

In adult women, cosmetics (especially greasy, heavy creams) may be the cause. In older women, acne can be caused by abnormal hormone production. Certain jobs, such as chronic exposure to mineral oils used in industry, may aggravate the condition or make people more susceptible.

Acne cannot be prevented or cured, but it can be controlled and minimized. Dermatologists recommend washing the face several times daily with ordinary soap and warm water. There is no proof that this practice helps, but scrubbing with a soapy washcloth does remove some oils, dead skin, and surface bacteria and help to keep the pores open. It also produces minor irritation, causing increased capillary blood flow to the skin, which may help in some cases. Ultraviolet light from sunlight or a sunlamp can be effective but is no longer used to treat acne because it increases the risk of skin cancer.

Acne is not primarily a dietary disease. Authorities differ about the importance attached to diet control. A strict diet by itself will not clear the skin, yet some people who eat sweets, nuts, chocolate, and fried foods find these foods aggravate the condition.

Most moderate or mild cases respond to self-treatment with nonprescription drugs, although a physician might produce quicker and better results. Only 1 in 10 cases need medical supervision. The FDA[5] has approved four over-the-counter ingredients. Products that fail to contain at least one of these active ingredients should not be used: Benzoyl peroxide (2.5% to 10%), sulfur (3% to 10%), sulfur and resorcinol (8% sulfur, 2% resorcinol), and salicylic acid. Table 21-4 gives Consumer Union's analysis of nonprescription products with comments.

The New Medicine Show[6] suggests these procedures for the self-treatment of acne:

1. Wash the face daily 2 to 3 times. Use soap and warm water and rinse thoroughly; scrub gently with soapy washcloth to remove some oils, dead skin, and some bacteria.
2. Use of cleansing products such as Noxzema Medicated Skin Cream, Cuticura Medicated Soap, and "Acne" soaps are no more useful than plain bar soap. Abrasive soaps have limited

Table 21–5

Prescription Acne Medications*

Type	Form	Trade name	Comments
Antibiotic	Oral, lotion, or gel	Various	Benefit for moderate cases; daily doses for months/years; most side effects when taken orally at times.
Benzoyl peroxide with antibiotics	Oral, gel, topical	Benoxyl 10, Fostex, Oxy-5, Loroxide, Vanoxide	For severe acne
Tretinoin (vitamin A acid)	Liquid, gel, cream	Retin-A	Cleans follicle openings, reduces number of acne lesions.
Estrogen	Large doses		Reduces sebaceous gland secretions; uncommon since oral Accutane
Isotretinoin (synthetic of vitamin A acid)	Oral	Accutane	For severe cystic acne; completely clears lesions in 80% patients after 4–5 months; needs physician supervision due to side effects, which include dry chapped lips, itchy skin, eye irritations, muscle and joint pain.

*From The new medicine show.[6]

value and can be harsh on sensitive skin.

3. It is not wise to use face creams in place of soap and water; greases and creams plug pores.
4. Avoid so-called skin foods, skin tonics, lubricating creams, and vanishing creams.
5. Avoid squeezing and picking blackheads and plump pimples; it may cause infection. If acne cannot be controlled through cleansing or the use of any of the OTC products identified, medical care is needed. Physicians use a variety of prescription medications as shown in Table 21-5.

Walzer[23] suggests these treatments for acne:

Mild acne. Use external medications only. OTC products containing sulphur, salicylic acid and benzoyl peroxide, medicated soaps and prescription topicals (tretinoin, antibiotic lotions, and gels).

Moderate Acne. Above plus oral antibiotics

Severe Acne. Above plus injection of steroids into acne cysts; also estrogen, isotretinoin (Accutane).

Acne scar. Dermabrasion or facial planing is a restorative, operative procedure. Healing takes several weeks and skin remains red and sensitive. Is not an impressive method and has possible complications—alterations of skin pigmentation, keloids (thick scar tissue). It is better to wait. Time and patience go a long way and nature may eliminate some of the scarring. Cystic acne is the most severe form; it causes inflammatory areas that result in deep pitting and scarring of the skin.

Dermatologists and plastic surgeons treat acne scars through cryosurgery, dermabrasion, tissue elevation (injections of minute amounts of silicone liquid under the scar), and induced collagen or collagen augmentation (also see liquid silicone and collagen p. 457).

Accutane, a powerful prescription drug that has been available since 1981, can be very effective for severe acne that does not respond to other forms of therapy. The results have been dramatic and often provide a permanent solution. Treatment takes 4 to 5 months at a cost of over $500 for the medication. However, Accutane use is unsafe for pregnant women. The manufacturer has estimated that between 1982 and 1986, the manufacturer reported that 62 babies whose mothers took the drug were born with defects. However, the FDA estimated that total number of cases was about 1300.

In 1988, an FDA expert advisory committee recommended severe restrictive use in young women. The American Academy of Dermatology has established guidelines whereby women who plan to use

Accutane complete a negative pregnancy test 2 weeks before starting the drug. Also, women who intend to become pregnant should stop using the drug at least 3 weeks before conception.

Hair, Nail, and Scalp Care

Oiliness and flaking of the scalp are normal. All skin, including that of the scalp, sloughs off its dead outer layer. When this occurs, some oil from the sebaceous glands is added, and the combination forms dandruff.

Washing the hair once or twice weekly, depending on the extent of oiliness, can maintain a reasonably clean and healthy scalp. Bar soaps are generally poor for cleaning hair; they tend to leave a deposit of film on hair shafts. It is better to use a shampoo that will retain the natural oils or that contains lanolin as a replacement.

Seborrheic dermatitis is a condition characterized by redness, inflammation, itching, and flaking of the skin. It most commonly affects the scalp and face but can also occur on the ears, chest, and other parts of the body. Its internal causes may be hormonal, dietary, or emotional. It may also be caused by external use of medications, cosmetics, or other substances. A prescribed medicated shampoo together with other action may be necessary; therefore a physician's guidance is advisable.

Baldness

The healthy scalp of a young adult normally has 100,000 hairs and loses 50 to 100 each day, most of which begin to regrow in a few months. As a person gets older, the rate of loss increases, and a permanent thinning may be inevitable.

Temporary hair loss may be associated with hormonal imbalance and can occasionally occur following surgery, childbirth, radiation, cancer treatment, or certain diseases accompanied by a high fever. Other causes of temporary hair loss include reactions to hair products and procedures (permanent waving, drying, and weaving), iron deficiency, toxic amounts of vitamin A or mercury, and medications such as heparin and warfarin (anticoagulants), amphetamines, L-dopa, and propranolol (Inderal). In such instances, regrowth usually occurs within a few months.

There is no specific therapy for temporary hair loss. To minimize it, one should avoid excessive manipulation, brush hair moderately with a soft brush, shampoo regularly and gently with a mild shampoo, dry hair by letting the towel soak up moisture rather than by vigorous toweling, and avoid hair styles that require pulling the hair excessively.

The so-called normal or common baldness is the male pattern baldness (androgenic alopecia). Although the specific cause cannot be identified it is probably related to hereditary factors (especially among Caucasians), an excess of male hormones (androgens) such as testosterone, and possibly attacks on scalp hair follicles by the body's immune system.

Alopecia areata, a condition in which hair falls out in patches, occurs with equal frequency in men and women. The cause is unknown, but it may be related to heredity or to the body's immune system.

Nutritional deficiencies are not the cause of ordinary baldness. Some deficiencies of vitamins resulting from dieting, severe protein deficiency, or severe digestive disturbances may contribute to dryness and lack of luster. In chronic starvation some hair loss may occur.

There is no single treatment that helps everyone, and some medical treatments for baldness have only limited success. Individuals concerned about baldness should discuss it with their doctor and possibly see a dermatologist. Despite claims to the contrary, however, there is no nonprescription hair treatment or remedy that can prevent, postpone, or correct baldness.

An FDA expert advisory panel that reviewed numerous hair treatment products, including lanolin, olive oil, wheat germ oil, and vitamins, found no scientific evidence that any such substances are effective for preventing or curing baldness. The FDA then banned the sale of all nonprescription creams, lotions or other externally applied products that are claimed to grow hair or prevent baldness. Any manufacturer claiming to have such a product will have to present proof to the FDA prior to its sale.[42] In announcing the ban, the agency noted that nothing done to a hair shaft once it emerges from the surface of the scalp will influence hair growth. One observer has remarked that if anything did work, there would be no bald dermatologists.

Treatments with new drugs to alter the body's response to male hormones are available through physicians. However, these drugs are absorbed into the body, have feminizing effects, are more useful for women, and have minimal benefits.

Minoxidil (Rogaine). Minoxidil was originally approved by the FDA and marketed as Loniten for lowering blood pressure. However, in certain concentrations it was found to spur the growth of body hair. In 1988, the FDA approved the use of minoxidil as a prescription drug for the treatment of hair loss. Now marketed as Rogaine, it has been widely advertised. A 2% solution of this product when extensively applied, is the only approved substance useful for stimulating hair growth on the crown of the head for individuals with male pattern baldness. Studies have indicated that the medication can restore hair growth in some men with thinning hair. It cannot restore hair to the density that existed when the user was young. It cannot help bald men. When topical applications of Rogaine are stopped, the benefits disappear. Twice daily, applications must be continued indefinitely to retain the restored hair. Its long-term effects are not known. The annual cost for treatment is $600 to $700 plus physician fees.

Rogaine's manufacturer, the Upjohn Company, completed a study of 2300 men between the ages of 18 and 49 with male-pattern baldness who used a 2% solution of minoxidil for 1 year. These were their findings: 8% had dense new hair growth, 31% had moderate new hair growth, and 61% had little or no new hair growth. *The New Medicine Show,*[6] however, reported that: (1) no men over 49 years were included in the study (2) no bald men with hair only on the sides or with a smooth shiny crown were included, (3) only a 1-inch circle of baldness at the crown of the head was part of the study (4) the control group used minoxidil for 4 months, and 20% of the placebo group grew new hair, and (5) the product has not been tested on older men and those with cardiovascular disease.

Stein[43] reported that in a random sampling of 900 dermatologists of the American Academy of Dermatology, with more than 500 reporting, 70% said they had prescribed topical minoxidil for hair loss. But fewer than 10% of the respondents were responsible for more than half of the prescriptions. Degroot et al[44] reached these conclusions about minoxidil: (1) it probably has less than a 10% chance of providing cosmetically satisfactory hair growth, and (2) the results of costs/benefits analysis raise questions regarding use.

Toupees or wigs have been helpful for some people. Ready-made hairpieces cost $100 to $200, but custom-made pieces with natural or synthetic hair average $500. For others, hair implants, and hair transplants, have been attempted. These procedures can be slow, tedious, painful, hazardous, and costly, and may be of limited benefit in selected cases. Individuals with hair problems should consult their family physician or a dermatologist.

Is Minoxidil Practical?

It is impossible to predict the outcome of the use of Rogaine (minoxidil), but your chances of some new hair growth are better if:

- You are in your 20s and have been losing your hair for the past 5 years.
- You have a small bald area on the crown of your head.
- You have a scattering of hairs that lightly covers your bald spot.
- You have an ample supply of cash (Author's addition)

Mayo Clinic Health Letter 7(6):1-2, 1989

Hairpieces

Hairpieces are perhaps the most acceptable form of hair covering. However, some people find them uncomfortably hot. They must be attached to the scalp by tape, elastic bindings, or some surgical procedure (may cause chronic irritation and infection). They generally contain 40% human hair and 60% synthetic hair. They must be replaced every 1 to 4 years. Their cost ranges from $500 to $2500.

Hair Transplants/Implants

Hair transplant procedures include punch grafts, strip grafts, scalp reduction, scalp expansion, and hair-bearing flaps with variations and combinations. Walzer[23] stated these methods are the most widely used and the most acceptable ways to restore hair. Most people are satisfied with the results. This is not a total solution to baldness. Only a thin hair covering can be established, and repeated operations are necessary as hair loss continues. Dermatologists debate whether enough improvement takes place to warrant the time, cost, and discomfort.

Grafting involves the transfer of permanently growing hair from the sides and back of the head to the areas of baldness. Small sections of skin containing a few hairs and their follicles are sliced out and the plugs inserted into bare parts of the scalp after similarly shaped sections are removed. This procedure involves the use of 50 or more plugs and after several weeks the hair grows normally. At $20 to $30 or more per plug, the cost of a major transplant could be thousands of dollars.

Scalp reduction is a surgical procedure that shrinks a bald spot the size of one's palm to the width of a finger. An incision is made in the crown and sides of the head and pulling areas with hair together toward the bare spot. The remaining bald spot can be filled with transplanted hair plugs. The surgery can be performed without hospitalization at an approximate cost of $1200. In one of four patients the skin of the scalp is too tight and cannot be stretched.

Scalp or tissue expansion is a surgical procedure using balloon-like devices to move hair across bare patches of skin.

Transplants can result in infection, scarring, and excessive bleeding. Surgeons continually improve their techniques, however, and often are able to provide a more natural-looking hairline and reduce the size of bald areas.

If a person has the time, money and a stoic attitude toward pain, hair transplant surgery may provide a satisfactory alternative to baldness. Some 250,000 Americans have selected this method, which costs up to $15,000 and takes a considerable length of time to complete. The problem of finding a surgeon who can produce good results can be formidable. Here are a few suggestions:

1. Consult with a dermatologist whose practice does not include transplants and ask for a referral.
2. Call the dermatology department of the local medical school and ask for a referral.
3. Ask the surgeon to show before-and-after photos of some patients.
4. Ask for complete information on risks and adverse effects.

In 1983 the FDA[45] banned the use of synthetic hair fibers for scalp implantation. The fibers were not effective in simulating natural hair or concealing baldness. The FDA said no hair fiber or synthetic hair implant technique was safe and effective. Over 300 complaints had been received that fibers had fallen out, broken off, or been rejected by the body.

Hair Straighteners

Three methods used to straighten naturally curly hair are (1) applications of pomades or resinous fixatives (heavy oils or petroleum products), (2) passing a heated comb through the hair (hot pressing), and (3) chemical straighteners.

Some chemical substances for permanently uncurling hair that may create health hazards include (1) alkaline or sodium hydroxide creams, (2) thioglycolate lotions or creams, and (3) ammonium or sodium bisulfite lotions.

Excess Hair Removal

Excess hair (hirsutism) results from an overabundance of androgens produced in the adrenal glands and ovaries. It is estimated that one third of all women of reproductive age have at least a few long, coarse facial hairs. Cosmetic treatment for minor problems of excess hair may include:

Makeup. A heavy cosmetic base serves to disguise mild excess facial hair.

Bleaching. Works best on mild upper lip fuzz.

Plucking. An effective but painful process (hair does grow back). Applying wax to skin as a warm liquid is advisable so that upon cooling hair comes out with the wax. The skin remains smooth with no stubble and may last for 6 weeks. Plucking may lead to infection and cause pits, scars, or ingrown hairs.

Pumice stone. May irritate skin.

Shaving. The easiest, cleanest, cheapest way to remove hair. Shaving does not increase rate of hair growth or make hair coarser. If hair is dark, the typical "five o'clock shadow" will appear.

Chemical depilatories. These contain salts of thioglycolic acid and are available in pastes, lotions, and creams. A thick layer is applied to the skin and left for 5 to 15 minutes. It can be wiped away with a washcloth. Some people may be allergic or suffer skin irritations. A test sample should be placed on the anterior wrist for 20 minutes prior to use. If there is no irritation, it is safe to use.

Electrolysis. This is the only safe way to remove unwanted hair permanently. This method uses an electric current to destroy the hair papilla. Its safety and effectiveness depend on the expertise of the operator. Competence of nonmedical electrolysis operators varies widely. Some states have no standard training and licensing requirements. Electrolysis may be tedious, time-consuming, expensive, and uncomfortable, depending on the areas involved and the amount of unwanted hair to be removed. In addition, the excessive exposure to electric current may damage the skin and cause scarring or infection.

A dermatologist should be consulted to determine whether electrolysis is advisable and to obtain the name of a suitable practitioner. Growths that contain hair, such as moles, should be diagnosed and evaluated by a physician.

Some women may need medical treatment for hirsutism. A physician may advise the use of drugs to inhibit androgen production or block its effect on hair follicles. These substances all have undesirable side effects, and none is uniformly effective. The limitations of the therapy and the extent of the side effects should be discussed thoroughly before submitting to treatment.

Hair Dyes and Bleaches

Although the incidence of allergy is low considering the widespread use of hair dyes and bleaches, there is a danger of dermatitis for some people. Individuals who have sensitive skin or are not sure of their degree of sensitivity should conduct a patch test before using these substances. The test is performed by placing a small amount of the dye on the skin and noticing if the skin turns red.

Excessive bleaching of hair can cause it to become dry, lusterless, and brittle. Peroxide is a slow bleaching agent to which boosters such as ammonium and potassium persulfates may be added to speed up the process. Peroxide attacks the hair protein (keratin), as well as the hair color pigment, causing hair to lose elasticity, resilience, and tensile strength. Future hair growth is generally not affected.

Hair-Growth Frauds

Hundreds of bogus baldness products have been marketed by mail and through health-food and department stores. Most include vitamin combinations said to provide the nutrients needed to nourish the hair. Although severe malnutrition can result in hair loss, there is no evidence that dietary supplements will increase hair growth for anyone who is eating normally. The following cases illustrates government action against bogus hair products.

In 1983, to settle charges by the FTC, Braswell, Inc., and its director, A. Glenn Braswell, agreed to pay $610,000 in civil penalties and to stop claiming that any product or service could cure or prevent hereditary baldness. Mr. Braswell also was convicted of mail fraud and perjury and served a brief prison sentence. The mail fraud charges involved the faking of before-and-after advertising photographs that supposedly showed positive results of bust developer, hair growth, and cosmetic products. Evidence indicated that Braswell received over $2 million for a worthless baldness cure in one 6-month period.[46]

In 1989, in response to action by the Pennsylvania Department of Health, General Nutrition Corporation agreed to stop marketing a "Helsinki formula" hair treatment. The product, which included a shampoo, a conditioner, and a vitamin tablet, had been marketed with false claims that it was a proven treatment for thinning hair and that the vitamin supplement contained "those special nutrients that have been proven helpful in an overall hair-care regimen."[47]

In 1991, the FTC ordered a California manufacturer to pay $2 million plus court costs for falsely and deceptively claiming "New Generation" products prevent baldness and stimulate hair growth in those with male-pattern baldness.[48] The products included shampoos and cleanser/conditioners, one of which contained polysorbate 60 in a formula allegedly developed and tested at the University of Helsinki.

Acrylic Fingernails

Acrylic nails can be nails that are repaired with acrylic glue, plastic nails that are secured to the nail plate with acrylic glue, or sculptured nails formed with various acrylic polymers that are shaped or sculptured onto the nail plate. They have the following possible risks:[49]

Trauma. Longer nails are subject to frequent and greater trauma; may cause separation of the nail plate from the nail bed.

Overhydration. Acrylic nails impede the evaporation of water from the nail plate. It remains waterlogged for longer periods and can become infected by bacteria and yeast.

Contact Allergy. Acrylic glues may cause allergic reactions, dermatitis (skin inflammation), and dermatitis at sites distant from the fingers (nail tissue disorders), and even permanent nail loss.[50]

Krazy glue used to repair breaks in the nail plate, and acrylics used in "sculptured" nails, may cause problems in sensitive individuals. It is important that careful sanitary procedures be followed in the application of these nails by: (1) thoroughly drying the nail surface to prevent bacteria and fungi from growing, (2) keeping air out to prevent the nail bed from swelling, (3) selecting salons that use disinfectants and equipment such as dry-heat sterilizers and autoclave machines, and (4) being aware of one's own sensitivities.

Sun Protection

The sun emits several types of light rays. The two that consumers should be aware of are ultraviolet A (UVA) and ultraviolet B (UVB) rays. When the skin is exposed to sunlight the body tries to protect itself by producing melanin, a dark pigment in certain skin cells, that blocks out the sun's rays. The darker a person's skin, the more melanin and natural protection it contains. However, even the darkest-skinned people can burn when sufficiently exposed to the sun. Skin cancers are most common among individuals with lightly pigmented skin (fair skinned). UVB rays can burn the skin, causing redness and blistering. Repeated exposure to these rays may be a cancer risk. Sunscreens can block UVB rays, and the SPF (Sun Protection Factor) numbers on product labels relate just to them. UVA rays are the major cause of skin cancers.

There are three types of skin cancer:

1. *Basal cell carcinomas.* These usually appear on the face, ears, or scalp as pale, waxlike, pearly nodules. They do not metastasize (spread through the body) but if untreated can harm surrounding tissues.
2. *Squamous cell carcinomas.* These appear as red, scaly, sharply outlined patches. If untreated, they can metastasize.
3. *Melanomas.* These typically start as a molelike growth that increases in size and darkness. They metastasize early and are highly malignant.

More than 95% of basal and squamous carcinomas are easily cured when detected early. About 600,000 cases are diagnosed annually. The American Cancer Society[51] estimates that in 1992 about 32,000 melanomas of the skin will be diagnosed and about 6700 people will die from the disease.

UVA rays are also the probable cause of photochemical changes in the eyes that cause cataracts. These rays lead to premature aging of the skin that results in wrinkling, irregular thickening, drying, loss of elasticity, and sagging. Photosensitivity reactions to sunlight may occur when taking such drugs as tetracycline, chlorpromazine, or sulfonamides.

Consumer Tip

Consumer Warnings

UVA and UVB radiation should be avoided like the plague—a plague of skin cancer. What is needed is a change in habits and attitudes about sun exposure, including public perception that tanned skin is healthy and aesthetically ideal.

C. and F. Garland
University of California School of Medicine
San Diego

There's no such thing as a safe tan.

Darrell Rigel, M.D.[53]
NYU Medical School

Protection from the sun requires consumers to take preventive action that includes the use of sunscreens that will absorb, reflect and scatter ultraviolet light, the avoidance of sun at particular hours, the careful control of sun exposure when tanning (also see tanning salons, tanning accelerators, and tanning pills) and the use of sunglasses (see chapter 23).

Sunscreens are available as lotions, creams, gels, oils, alcohol solutions and wax substances for lips. The common ingredients are:[54]

Anthranilates (methyl anthranilate): moderate protection UVA/UVB

Benzophenones (oxybenzone, sulisobenzone, dioxybenzone): UVA/UVB combinations offer "broad-spectrum" protection; usually found in SPFs 15 or higher

Cinnamates (e.g., octyl methoxycinnamate): common in UVB filter)

PABA (para-aminobenzoic acid): extremely effective against UVB rays; rarely used due to skin infections

PABA derivatives (e.g., octyl dimethyl PABA): Good UVB protection with less irritation

Zinc oxide: used in lip pomade to block UVA and UVB rays

Parsol 1789: the only FDA-approved UVA protectant.

Correct use of sun blocks will reduce the likelihood and intensity of sunburn and block UVB rays that create burns and some may provide protection against UVA radiation. Consumers should be aware that products vary in terms of their formulations by manufacturers. Sunscreen products therefore may have differing effects on individuals. It is advisable to purchase a small amount of a product to determine whether it feels good and does not irritate the skin.

Sun blocks are rated according to the sun protection they provide. This rating can be identified by the letters SPF (sun protection factor) and a number that follows. The higher the number, the greater the protection. To determine the extent of protection needed, it is necessary to know the type and sensitivity of your skin, check the average number of minutes it will take to turn the skin red, and multiply this number by the SPF number (see Tables 21-6 and 21-7). For example, if it takes 20 minutes for the skin to turn red and the SPF is 15, the product will provide up to 300 minutes or 5 hours of protection. Individuals with sensitive skin and who burn easily need greater protection than those with darker skin and a greater amount of melanin. The American Academy of Dermatology and the National Institutes of Health[53] have stated that individuals should use products that are SPF 15 or higher. They also have indicated that products that exceed SPF 30 do not make sense because ample protection can be achieved at other values. An FDA official has said that SPFs over 30 are unnecessary and new rules would ban these products.[55]

The SPF values system for sunscreens applies only to UVB radiation. The *Journal of the American*

Table 21–6

Skin Types and Sensitivity to Sun*

If you	Your skin type is
Always burn easily, never tan	1 (very sensitive)
Burn easily, tan minimally	2 (very sensitive)
Burn moderately, tan gradually	3 (sensitive)
Burn minimally, always tan well (moderate brown)	4 (moderately sensitive)
Rarely burn, tan profusely (dark brown)	5 (minimally sensitive)
Never burn, are deeply pigmented (black skin)	6 (insensitive)

*Based on 45 to 60 minutes of unprotected skin exposure to sun.
Modified from The darker side of indoor tanning.[52]

Table 21–7

Skin Protection by SPF 15 Products

Skin type	Skin and tanning characteristics	Average minutes to MED*	Estimated hours of protection with SPF 15
1	Fair skin, usually blue eyes, freckles, white skin, burns easily, severely, tans little	20a	5
		12b	3
2	Fair skin, red, blond, or brown hair, blue, brown or hazel eyes, white skin, usually burns easily, severely	25-30a	6.25-7.5
		15-18b	3.75-4.5
3	Average Caucasian, white skin, burns moderately, tans average	35-40a	8.75-10.0
		20-24b	5-6
4	White, light brown skin, dark brown hair, skin burns minimally, tans easily	40-50a	10.0-12.5
		30-35b	7.5-8.75
5	Brown skin, rarely burns, tans easily	50-60a	12.5-15.0
		35-40b	8.75-10.0
6	Black/dark brown skin, burns only with severe exposure	70-75a	17.5-18.75
		40-50b	10.0-12.5

*MED (minimum erythema [redness] dose)—smallest amount of sunlight exposure necessary to induce barely perceptible redness of unprotected skin with 24 hours of exposure. Varies by skin type, location, time of year, and time of day. Time needed to reach 1 MED will increase earlier or later in the day or in cooler seasons in Spring and Fall; will decrease at higher altitudes.
a—at 40 to 44 degrees latitude in Northern California, Kansas City, New York, Indianapolis.
b—at 20 to 25 degrees latitude in Miami and Brownsville, Texas.
Modified from the Skin Cancer Foundation and M.A. Pathak, Dept. of Dermatology, Harvard Medical Center Massachusetts General Hospital, Boston, and as reported in Sunscreens, Consumer Reports 56:400-403, 1991.

Medical Association[56] reported that UVA sun rays have been considered harmless, however there is strong evidence that this type of radiation can cause skin damage including premature aging and skin cancers. *Consumer Reports* stated that protection from UVA rays is necessary. DeLeo,[57] said there is no rating system to measure UVA protection. Although new sunscreens claim to be providing UVA blocking agents, many are not adequate since the quality of protection has not been determined.

Many manufacturers claim that sunscreens provide some protection from UVA radiation but none of the substances has received FDA approval. The FDA has warned producers that label displays and other UVA protective claims may be subjected to regulatory action. Only one substance, Parsol 1789, has received FDA approval. *Consumer Reports* says two effective products containing the FDA-approved substance are Filteray and Photoplex. After conducting tests, *Consumer Reports* made these recommendations for purchasing sunscreens:

1. Choose one with SPF 15 that is water-resistant.
2. Buy according to price, and select a product that is PABA free. They conclude the top three products to be: K Mart Solice at 66¢ per oz, Rite Aid at 75¢ per oz, and Avon Sun Seeker at $1.09 per oz.
3. Consider using Filteray or Photoplex if you have fair skin, a history of skin cancer, or a job that exposes you to long hours in the sun.
4. Buy a "broad-spectrum" labeled product that provides protection against UVA and UVB radiation. These suggestions should help to obtain the most effective sun protection:
   a. Identify your skin type and sensitivity to ultraviolet light and the recommended SPF needed by reviewing Tables 21-6 and 21-7.
   b. Determine the amount of time for the initial exposure according to your skin type. Table 21-7 will provide help.
   c. Use a special sunscreen product for the eye area that will not run into the eyes and cause irritation. Lips are especially sensitive and need a special screen. Avoid PABA product ingredients.
4. Decide on the time of day for exposure. The burning rays of the sun are most intense between 10 AM and 3 PM (standard time).
5. When applying the sunscreen: (a) Put on at least 30 minutes before exposure to allow the ingredients to penetrate the skin; (b) use generous amounts of the sunscreen in order to form a protective film on the skin's surface, but do not rub it in; and (c) Reapply frequently during the day, because sweat and water can wash away the product. Reapplication does not increase the length of time to stay out in the sun without skin damage.
6. Use a wide-brimmed hat and clothing to help protect against the sun's rays.

Tanning Salons

There are about 25,000 tanning salons in the United States. The original units provided UVB rays, but operators had to be extremely cautious in regulating exposure to avoid severe sunburn and other problems. These units have now been replaced mainly with UVA claimed to be safe. The FDA has stated that UVA sunlamps are not safer than UVB sunlamps. Dr. Irene Markin stated that tanning devices may cause premature aging of skin, skin cancer, and cataracts. They may also affect blood vessels. In 1986 and 1987, the Wisconsin Department of Health surveyed opthalmologists, dermatologists, and emergency room physicians to ascertain the number of burns caused by tanning devices ranging from home-use sunlamps to commercial tanning booths. The 132 ophthalmologists who responded reported treating 152 patients for corneal, retinal, and other injuries to the eye. The 344 dermatologists and emergency room physicians responding to the survey reported treating 220 patients for burns, 105 of which were first-degree burns.[58]

Manufacturers and operators of UVA tanning facilities claim a golden brown tan can be obtained in five 20-minute sessions, with one or two sessions weekly thereafter for maintenance. Single tanning sessions cost $5 to $25. Tanning salons are unregulated and unlicensed in most states. They do not always warn patrons of health risks or follow the safety procedures recommended by the FDA. These safety measures include provision of timing devices, warning labels, safe exposure schedules and goggles. The FDA recommends 30 minutes as the maximum duration of a tanning session. Tanning devices should not be used by individuals who: (1) burn easily, (2) get frequent cold sores, or (3) use medicines that make a person sunburn more easily.[59]

Individuals who desire to use tanning units should follow these precautions:

1. Start exposure time in short intervals; know your skin type and exposure limits.
2. Do not increase the exposure time in an attempt to obtain a darker tan; it can result in serious injury.
3. Avoid direct contact with the lamps to avoid burns.
4. Be cautious about exposing body parts that usually do not get sun: armpits, breasts, genitals.
5. Wear protective goggles; do not rely on closed eyes, sunglasses, or cotton wads. Be sure the goggles fit snugly around the eyes are are not cracked.
6. Consult your physician if you are using prescription medications; some antibiotics, tranquilizers, and high blood pressure medicines increase the body's sensitivity to ultraviolet light.
7. Be sure someone is standing nearby in case of an emergency.

Tanning Accelerators

The cosmetic industry has marketed "tan accelerators" in the form of creams that they claim will provide a deeper tan with less time spent in the sun. Tyrosine, the active ingredient in these creams, is naturally present in the skin's cells and is needed for melanin production. The companies conclude that tyrosine leads to more melanin and therefore tanning occurs. The *Journal of the American Academy of Dermatology*[60] reported that such a claim cannot be documented. Jaworsky et al[61] studied tan accelerators and concluded their efficacy could not be substantiated. DeLeo said they do not work.[53]

Tanning Pills

So-called tanning pills do not provide a tan but rather a "dye-job." The palms and soles of the feet will have a distinct orange tinge. Some pills contain synthetic food colors (carotenes) like those found naturally in apricots, carrots, and peaches that create the "tan." The color fades when the pills are no longer taken. The amount of color additive found in these tablets is 20 to 30 times more than the amount consumed in the normal diet. The pills range from $20 to $30 for a month's supply. Some tanning pills contain canthaxanthin, a fat-soluble carotenoid that the human body cannot convert to vitamin A.

Canthaxanthin is legally used in tiny amounts as a food coloring agent. Despite a warning by the FDA, it has been illegally sold in tanning parlors and by mail as a tablet for skin tanning, under such names as Orobronze, Darker Tan, and BronzGlo. Ads for Darker Tan promised "a rich dark bronze glowing tan without risking skin cancer. A case has been reported of a 20-year-old woman who took high doses and developed aplastic anemia, a serious condition in which the production of blood cells is impaired. Previous reports have linked canthaxanthin use to hepatitis, generalized itching, hives, and eye problems.[62] The FDA[63] has continued to warn consumers that canthaxanthin, the major ingredient in tanning pills has not been approved to be safe by the agency; such products therefore are illegal.

Wart Treatments

Warts are a thickening and piling up of skin resulting from abnormal local cell growth. They are caused by a viral infection of the epidermis (outer layer of the skin). They are contagious, and scratching can spread them. They can occur on any part of the body but most often appear on the hands, fingers, and soles of the feet. Those occurring on the feet (plantar warts) tend to be painful because of the pressure and irritation of weight-bearing. Warts rarely become cancerous. It may be necessary to have a physician remove them. Many warts disappear eventually without treatment.

Many treatments are available for treating warts, including freezing with liquid nitrogen or dry ice, burning with an electric needle, surgical excision, various acids, and other chemicals. Most of the methods must be applied by a physician. OTC products contain an acid or other caustic agents and can be hazardous if directions are not carefully followed. An FDA expert panel concluded that salicylic acid was the only substance both safe and effective. The panel summarily dismissed benzocaine, camphor, castor oil, iodine, and menthol because it found no data about their safety or effectiveness. When using salicylic acid, protect the surrounding skin with a ring of petrolatum.

Summary

Consumers spend over $24 billion yearly on skin and beauty aids that may be helpful but will not perform miracles. Cosmetics are substances that are

IT'S YOUR DECISION

Suppose you have unusually large or small breasts and want to change their size. Which one or more of the following actions would you take?

	Reason
1. Purchase a product guaranteed to increase (or reduce) breast size by rubbing it on	______
2. Purchase an exercise device claimed to increase size after use	______
3. Wear different styles of clothing	______
4. Undergo cosmetic surgery by your local physician	______
5. Undergo cosmetic surgery by a dermatologist	______
6. Undergo cosmetic surgery by a board-certified plastic surgeon	______
7. Enroll in a weight-training program	______
8. Other	______

rubbed, poured, or sprinkled on the body to alter appearance. They help to keep the skin clean, moist, and soft, and generally are safe to use. Although the FDA expects manufacturers to substantiate product safety, there are no regulations regarding efficacy since the ingredients are not considered to be drugs. Soaps, creams, lipsticks, and shampoos are generally safe, but consumers should be aware of their comparative costs, possible allergic reactions, and misleading advertisements.

There are many unproven remedies and treatments for wrinkles on the market, some of which may be dangerous. Aging and wrinkling of the skin are generally irreversible processes that may be temporarily helped with the use of collagens and other products and procedures. Plastic surgery may improve physical appearance. Consumers should realize that any surgery involves risks and may be costly, and they should seek qualified practitioners. Neither Retin-A nor liquid silicone have been approved for treating wrinkles. Collagen has not been approved for lip augmentation. Laser surgery has been effective in the treatment of some eye problems and skin disorders. It is an expensive treatment. Breast implants are under severe criticism by consumer advocates due to possible connection with cancer in animals. The FDA is reviewing the evidence regarding safety.

Acne is a disorder of the sebaceous glands. Minor conditions can be improved through hygienic practices and generally can be treated with OTC products. Severe conditions need the help of a dermatologist or plastic surgeon. Accutane may be helpful.

Deodorants control body odor, and antiperspirants control perspiration. Consumers need to be aware of the functions of available products and realize that some may cause allergic reactions. There is no substitute for soap and water for cleanliness.

The hair and scalp generally can be kept clean and healthy by washing once or twice weekly. There is no nonprescription product that can prevent, postpone, or correct baldness. Minoxidil may effect some hair restoration for some people. Electrolysis is the safest way to remove surplus hair permanently.

There is no scientific evidence supporting the claims that cosmetic products can eliminate dimpled fat (cellulite) from the body. There is no safe way to obtain a tan. Sunlight can be hazardous. Overexposure may cause burning, aging and wrinkling, cancers and cataracts. However, a product with an SPF 15 rating is probably the best way to block UVB sun rays. Most sunscreens available do little, if anything, to protect against UVA rays that are also dangerous. Consumers should use a "broad-spectrum" sun blocker when outdoors.

Discussion Questions

1. What is the legal definition of cosmetics? What control does the FDA have over cosmetic products?
2. What are the general rules to be followed when washing the skin?
3. What are the purposes of facial cleansers? How can dry skin be avoided?
4. What happens to the skin when it ages? What are some of the products and procedures advertised to remove wrinkles and restore youthful appearance of the skin?
5. What action should be taken to prevent wrinkles and skin aging?
6. What are the ingredients found in shampoos? Which ones are safe to use? What action occurs when the hair is shampooed?
7. What safety precautions should be followed when using cosmetics?
8. What types of breast implants are available? What are several risks involved when undergoing this surgery?
9. What is the difference between cosmetic, reconstructive, and plastic surgery? What are some of the cosmetic body contouring procedures being performed? What are the costs, benefits, and risks?
10. How can a consumer locate a qualified plastic surgeon?
11. What is the nature of acne? What are the different types of acne and identify treatment and risk procedures?
12. What methods can be used to control body odor? What are some of the products that will help to control body odor?
13. What is dandruff and how can it be controlled?
14. What is baldness? What procedures can be used to control this condition? Are they effective?
15. What are the effects and the hazards of the use of hair dyes?
16. What are the hazards of sun exposure? What sun rays are involved? What are sunscreens and how can they protect the body? What are thet best ways to be protected from the sun's rays?
17. Are skin bleaching creams effective? Hazardous?
18. What procedures can be used to remove excess hair? Are they effective? Hazardous? What is the best and safest way to remove hair on a permanent basis?
20. How can consumers best protect themselves when visiting a tanning salon?

REFERENCES

1. Wolf N: The beauty myth, New York, 1991, William Morrow.
2. The bad side of looking good, Time p. 68, Mar 4, 1991.
3. Hand and bath soaps, Consumer Reports 50:52-55, 1985.
4. Soaping up, Consumer Reports 55:644-646, 1990.

*5. Facial cleansers, Consumer Reports 54:408-410, 1989.

6. Editors of Consumer Books: The new medicine show, Mount Vernon, NY, 1989, Consumers Union.
7. Engasser PG and Maibach H: Cosmetics and dermatology: bleaching creams, J Am Acad Dermatol 5:143-147, Aug 1981.
8. Fade creams, Consumer Reports 50:12, 1985.
9. Draelos ZK: Eye cosmetics, cosmetics and cosmetic surgery, Dermatology 9:1-7, 1991.
10. Facial wrinkles, Mayo Clinic Health Letter 9(7):3-4, 1991.
11. Can collagen injections erase wrinkles safely? Consumer Reports Health Letter 3:36, 1991.
12. FDA Reviews collagen studies, FDA Consumer 25(5):5, 1991.
13. Collagen to protect doctors, San Francisco Chronicle, pp. B1, B4, Sept 18, 1991.
14. Fisher AA: Cosmetic warning: this product may be detrimental to your purse, Cutis 39:23-24, 1987.
15. Antiaging creams challenged, FDA Talk Paper, May 14, 1987.
16. Barrett S: Book review of Life extension: a practical scientific approach, ACSH News & Views 4(5):13-14, 1983.
17. The way to eliminate wrinkles, Johns Hopkins Medical Letter, Health After 50 3(5):6-7, 1991.
18. Arndt K: Beauty and health, Harvard Medical School Health Letter 12(2):3-5, 1986.
19. Beauty drugs made them ugly, women tell house probers, San Francisco Chronicle, pp 2, 4, June 12, 1991.
20. Tolchin M: Who's monitoring cosmetic safety? The New York Times, p A40, April 14, 1990.
21. Stehlin D: Cosmetic allergies, FDA Consumer 20(9):28-31, 1986.
22. Lazar R: Cosmetics, Barnum and science, Cutis 39:335-336, 1987.
23. Walzer RA et al: Healthy skin: a guide to lifelong skin care, Mount Vernon, NY, 1989, Consumers Union.
24. Hilt J: Scientists tie breast implants to cancer, The New York Times, p A18, Apr 14, 1991.
25. Liposuction, Mayo Clinic Health Letter 7(7):4-5, 1989.
26. Behbehani D: Cosmetic surgery, San Francisco Magazine p 38, Oct 1987.
27. The dark side of cosmetic surgery, The New York Times, Apr 17, 1988.
28. There are no antiaging wonder drugs, Changing Times, Feb 1991.

*Recommended reading

29. Findlay S: Buying the perfect body, U.S. News & World Report, pp 68-75, May 1, 1989.
30. Greenberg J: Putting on a good front, Priorities, p 6-7, Summer 1991.
31. Breast implant surgery, The New York Times, Dec 28, 1989.
32. U.S. to begin regulation of breast implants '91, The New York Times, Dec 19, 1990.
33. Purvis A: Time bomb in breasts, Time p 70, April 29, 1991.
34. Important information on breast implants, FDA Backgrounder, Aug 1991.
35. Dowling T: Doctors claim breast implants safe, San Francisco Chronicle, June 30, 1991.
35a. Segal M: Silicone breast implants, FDA Consumer 26:6-9, 1992.
36. Robinson D: The truth about cosmetic surgery, Readers Digest, Feb 1991.
37. The truth about cellulite, San Francisco Chronicle, July 3, 1991.
38. Donnelly SB: Fountain of youth in a jar, Time p 83, Oct 14, 1991.
39. American Pharmaceutical Association: Handbook of nonprescription drugs, ed 9. Washington, DC, 1991, The Association.
40. Farley D: Sweating it out, FDA Consumer 19(10):21-25, 1985.
41. FDA, Federal Register, August 1, 1991.
42. FDA Press release, July 7, 1989.
43. Stein RS: Topical minoxidil: a survey of use and complications, Arch Dermatology 123:62-65, Jan 1987.
44. DeGroot A et al: Minoxidil: hope for the bald? Lancet 8:1019-1021, 1987.
45. Hair fiber implants banned, FDA Press Office, June 3, 1983.
46. Nelson CP: Testimony before the subcommittee on health and long-term care of the U.S. House of Representatives Select Committee on Aging. In Pepper C et al: Quackery: a $10 billion scandal, Washington, DC, 1984, U.S. Government Printing Office.
47. Helsinki Hair Formula, Nutrition Forum 6:30, 1989.
48. FTC News Notes, Sept 9, 1991.
49. Nail care: our recommendation, Mayo Clinic Health Letter 8(8):4, 1990.
50. Why you should think twice about acrylic fingernails, Scripps Clinic Personal Health Letter 1(4):5, 1990.
51. Boring CB, Squires TS, and Tong T: Cancer statistics 1992, Ca—A Cancer Journal for Clinicians 42(1):19-38, 1992.
52. The darker side of indoor tanning. Dept of Health and Human Services, Rockville, MD, 1987.
53. Greeley A: No safe tan, FDA Consumer 25(4):18-21, 1991.
54. Willensky D: Sunscreen talk, American Health 10(6):29-31, 1991.
55. Gellene D: FDA rewrites rules for tanning products, San Francisco Chronicle, p A4, July 3, 1991.
56. Revised regulation for sunscreen labeling expected soon from FDA, JAMA 265:3217, 1991.
57. Sunscreens, Consumer Reports 56:400-408, 1991.
58. Burns and eye injuries from tanning devices, FDA Consumer 23(8):3-4, 1989.
59. The darker side of indoor tanning, HHS Publication No. (FDA) 87-8270, 1987.
60. How about an accelerated tan? University of California, Berkeley Wellness Letter 3(11):7, 1987.
61. Jaworsky C et al: Efficacy of tan accelerators, J Am Acad Dermatol 16:769-778, 1987.
62. Bluhm R et al: Aplastic anemia associated with canthaxanthin ingested for 'tanning purposes,' JAMA 264:1141-1142, 1990.
63. Update on tanning pills, In-home report of FDA, T90-45, Oct. 1, 1990.

CHAPTER TWENTY TWO

ESPECIALLY FOR WOMEN

"Let's play doctor. I'll give you a list of my ailments and you blame it all on my hormones."

(© Glasbergen.)

One need spend only a day in a women's clinic or hospital emergency room to appreciate the difficulties that can visit the female reproductive system when women are not educated to be vigilant in self-protection.[1]

SADJA GOLDSMITH GREENWOOD, M.D.
UNIVERSITY OF CALIFORNIA MEDICAL CENTER
SAN FRANCISCO

Consumer Decisions

What should be done about premenstrual syndrome?

What type of birth control method should be used?

Should feminine hygiene products be used?

Women are faced with a variety of health problems related to the anatomy and physiology of their reproductive organs. This chapter discusses menstrual discomfort, feminine hygiene, vaginitis, and birth control methods (including the methods used by men). Comments are also made about osteoporosis, pregnancy testing, mastectomy prostheses, "breast developers," and excessive use of certain procedures by gynecologists.

Menstrual Problems

A majority of women who menstruate experience unpleasant symptoms before or during their monthly periods. Symptoms fall into three general categories: dysmenorrhea (painful menstruation), premenstrual syndrome (PMS), and menstrual irregularities.

Dysmenorrhea

Dysmenorrhea typically is experienced as cramp-like lower-abdominal discomfort, which may come and go in waves. There may also be dull lower backache and, in some women, nausea and vomiting. These complaints begin shortly before the onset of menstrual flow and usually last 2 or 3 days. About 10% of women have symptoms severe enough to interfere with their usual activities.

Dysmenorrhea may be primary or secondary. Primary dysmenorrhea, by far the more common type, begins during the first year or two after the onset of menstruation, usually lasts only a few years, and is dramatically relieved after childbirth. Primary dysmenorrhea does not usually require consultation with a physician unless symptoms are severe and do not respond to self-treatment of aspirin, ibuprofen, or acetaminophen.

Secondary dysmenorrhea refers to menstrual pain that develops in women who previously had little or no cramping with their periods. It is usually associated with some type of abnormality of the reproductive organs such as benign uterine tumor (polyp or fibroid), a pelvic infection, or endometriosis. It can also be caused by an intrauterine device (IUD) used for birth control. A physician should be consulted in all cases of secondary dysmenorrhea to determine the presence of any underlying disease that requires treatment. In most cases of secondary dysmenorrhea, treatment by a physician is more effective than self-treatment.

Premenstrual Syndrome

Premenstrual syndrome (PMS; also called premenstrual tension) can be defined as a combination of physical and/or emotional symptoms that occur before menstruation and disappear or become minimal during periods. PMS is said to be very common, but estimates of its incidence are clouded by the fact that it has not been clearly defined. The symptoms vary from person to person, but are usually consistent for each individual; they include: tension, depression, irritability, fatigue, difficulty in concentration, crying spells, aggression, headaches, abdominal bloating, swelling of the hands and feet, breast tenderness, constipation, acne, abnormal thirst, and cravings for sweets and/or salty foods. Usually relief occurs when the menstrual period begins, but if the period is delayed, the severity of the symptoms increases. In contrast to dysmenorrhea, PMS usually starts during the late 20s or 30s and worsens with age and after childbearing.

The cause of PMS is unknown, but it seems unlikely that a single cause is responsible for the wide variety of symptoms involved. Hormonal, nutritional, and psychologic factors have been suggested but not proven.

Most women with PMS do not need treatment by a physician. Only symptoms that disrupt their lives need medical intervention. Understanding what occurs in the body when symptoms are present often provides significant relief. The following suggestions may also help:

1. For premenstrual water retention (abdominal bloating and swelling of the hands and feet), refrain from adding salt to meals and restrict sodium-containing foods for a few days before the time of the menstrual cycle when the symptoms typically occur.

2. For breast discomfort or symptoms of anxiety, avoid or limit coffee, tea, cocoa, cola, other foods, and medications that contain caffeine or related compounds. Although this may not help, it is harmless and relatively easy to do.
3. Try to identify and deal with psychosocial stresses.
4. If eating sweets appears to produce symptoms, try to satisfy cravings with complex carbohydrates, such as fruits, rather than simple sugars.[2]

Over-the-Counter Drugs for Menstrual Distress

The ingredients found in over-the-counter (OTC) menstrual products have included pain-relievers (analgesics), antihistamines, diuretics, smooth-muscle relaxants, plant products, and vitamins. However, the FDA Advisory Review Panel on OTC Miscellaneous Internal Drug Products has graded as safe and effective only the following ingredients:

Analgesics: Aspirin or acetaminophen have about the same effect on pain. The recommended dosage of either drug is 5 to 10 grains (300 to 600 mg) every 4 hours, not to exceed 4000 mg in 24 hours. The usual dosage of ibuprofen (which was granted OTC status after the advisory panel report), is 200 mg every 4 to 6 hours. Unadvertised brands cost the least.

Antihistamines: Pyrilamine maleate may help relieve premenstrual irritability, depression, and tension. The recommended dosage is 25 mg every 3 to 4 hours, or 60 mg every 12 hours, not to exceed 200 mg in 24 hours.

Diuretics: OTC diuretic products are weak compared to those available by prescription, but they may alleviate the symptoms of premenstrual tension by helping the body shed water. The recommended dosages are as follows: ammonium chloride, 1 g 3 times daily for up to 5 days; pamabrom, 50 mg per dose, not to exceed 200 mg daily; and caffeine, 100 to 200 mg every 3 to 4 hours (the amount in 1 to 2 cups of coffee). Caffeine, in addition to being a mild diuretic, is a stimulant that can relieve mild fatigue, but it may also interfere with sleep and increase breast symptoms.

A number of other substances found in OTC menstrual products were judged by the FDA advisory panel to be unproven or ineffective:

Smooth-muscle relaxants: The theory behind their use is that they can relieve menstrual cramps by relaxing uterine spasm. However, cinnamedrine was judged safe, but of unproven efficacy; hydrochloridehomatropine methylbromide was judged safe but ineffective.

Plant products (herbs): All ingredients in this category were disapproved. Pleurisy root, black cohosh, and life root were judged unsafe as well as ineffective.

Vitamins: Some doctors prescribe pyridoxine (vitamin B_6) for the treatment of PMS. The FDA panel concluded that usual dosages are safe, but that pyridoxine is not proven effective because the few studies supporting its effectiveness are small and not well designed.[3] However, subsequent reports of nervous system toxicity indicate that pyridoxine supplementation is unsafe (see Chapter 13). Other supplementary vitamins were summarily disapproved by the expert panel.

Prescription Drugs

Primary dysmenorrhea probably results from the action of prostaglandins, which are hormone-like organic acids produced in the uterine lining while the egg is being readied to leave the ovary. Therefore drugs that inhibit ovulation or prostaglandin action are often effective. Patients who require contraceptive protection and relief from primary dysmenorrhea often benefit from oral contraceptive drugs. Aspirin or ibuprofen, which have antiprostaglandin activity, may be effective when taken the day before a menstrual period. More potent prostaglandin inhibitors include the prescription drugs idomethacin (Indocin), mefenamic acid (Ponstel), and naproxen (Naprosyn), all of which have analgesic activity as well. Diuretic drugs may also be prescribed for PMS.

Menstrual Irregularities

Hormonal imbalances may result in frequent or irregular periods with continuous or intermittent spotting. During the first and last few years of menstruation, irregularity is common and may not be abnormal. However, persistent irregularity is a reason to consult a physician. Bleeding for longer than 7 days is considered excessive and may be caused by a uterine polyp or fibroma that interferes with the uterine mechanism for limiting menstrual blood loss. Bleeding that occurs a year or more after menstrual periods cease (postmenopausal bleeding) should be evaluated promptly because it may be a sign of cancer.

Women normally lose 1 to 4 tablespoons of blood during a menstrual period, with a daily iron loss of up to 1.4 mg. This amount of iron can be provided by a balanced diet. When blood flow is a little heavier than usual, clots may form. Individuals with a heavy blood flow should be sure that their iron intake is adequate. This can be accomplished by eating iron-rich foods (liver, veal, other meats, fish, soybeans), cooking in an iron pot, or using iron supplements. However, self-medication with supplementary iron is not wise unless a deficiency is medically diagnosed by means of a blood test. Even if iron deficiency is present in an individual, the cause should be established before treatment is begun.

Menstrual Products

Two basic types of menstrual protection are available: external (pads) and internal (tampons). A 1977 survey by Consumers Union found that more women seemed satisfied with tampons than with conventional pads. Women who favored tampons mentioned these reasons: comfort, lack of mess and unpleasant odor, invisibility under clothes, ease of use, and ease of disposal. Women who favored pads liked their comfort and absorbency, but one third of them had never tried tampons.[4]

Menstrual Pads

Rinzler[5] defined the perfect menstrual pad as one that does not chafe, rub, leak, or show under one's clothes. She stated that powders used to deodorize pads may be irritating, and pads with built-in deodorant or masking perfume may provoke allergic reactions as well. Therefore the most practical way to prevent odor is to use plain pads, changing them as frequently as needed.

Tampons and Toxic Shock

An effective tampon is one absorbent enough to protect against leaks, but not so absorbent that it dries out delicate vaginal tissues. It should also be easy to insert, comfortable to wear, and easy to remove. It may be helpful to use a more absorbent one on days when menstrual flow is heavy and a less absorbent one when flow is light. Use of a highly absorbent tampon when flow is light may result in excess absorption of natural vaginal lubrication.

Excessive drying of the vaginal tissue can render a woman susceptible to toxic shock syndrome (TSS), a rare but potentially fatal infection caused by staphylococcus bacteria. TSS is characterized by high fever, vomiting, diarrhea, sunburnlike rash, liver or kidney failure, and a rapid drop in blood pressure that can cause shock. In 1989 the FDA ordered manufacturers to standardize tampon labeling so that "junior," "regular," "super," and "super plus" means the same thing regardless of a manufacturer's brand. Packages now must explain the basis for the rating and advise on choosing the lowest appropriate absorbency.

> **Consumer Tip**
>
> The following measures can help prevent toxic shock syndrome:
>
> - Wash hands with soap and water before and after inserting or removing a tampon. Use care to avoid carrying bacteria from the skin or rectum into the vagina.
> - Choose the lowest absorbency product that is effective. Use no applicator, or use a cardboard applicator, because plastic applicators may be more likely to scratch the vagina. On days when secretions in the vagina are scanty, use a water-soluble lubricating jelly on the tampon applicator to avoid nicking the vaginal surface.
> - Change tampons often—at least as frequently as every 6 to 8 hours.
> - Alternate tampon use with pads during a given menstrual period. Do not use a tampon on days when bleeding is light.
> - If symptoms of high fever (102.7° F or higher), vomiting, diarrhea, or sunburnlike rash occur, discontinue tampon use and immediately consult a physician.

Vaginal Hygiene

Under normal circumstances the healthy vagina cleans itself. Like the eyes, nose, and mouth, it is lined with epithelial cells that produce secretions that wash away surface debris as they move toward the outside. At the same time, bacteria normally present maintain the normal acidity of the vagina and fight off potential disease-causing bacteria.

Douching

Most physicians agree that for healthy individuals douching is unnecessary and may be harmful.[6]

Many of the preparations on the market are too strong for delicate tissues of the vagina and disturb the normal acid balance of the vagina. Douches may also contain local anesthetics (phenol, menthol) that can mask symptoms of infection. A povidone-iodine douche (such as Betadine Douche) can be very helpful in certain types of vaginal infections, but it should never be used before a physician establishes the diagnosis.[1] Douching within 3 days before a pelvic examination or Pap smear can interfere with the accuracy of these procedures.

The FDA, which previously considered douches as cosmetics, now requires that all products for douching be labeled: "For cleansing purposes only. Do not use more than twice weekly unless directed by a physician," or "For cleansing purposes only, after menstruation and after marital relations." (However, it should be noted that postcoital douching is not an effective means of birth control.) The FDA Advisory Panel on OTC Contraceptives and Other Vaginal Drug Products has recommended that any douche that contains a medicinal amount of an active drug ingredient should be regulated as a drug—meaning that no claim of effectiveness against disease could be made without proof that it is true.[3]

External Hygiene

Vaginal secretions and perspiration can collect on the external surfaces of the vaginal folds, where they can break down and become odorous if allowed to accumulate. This is more likely to happen with the use of pantyhose and nylon panties, which increase the accumulation of perspiration. These garments should be washed after each wearing in mild, nonperfumed, nondetergent soaps. If pantyhose are used, cotton panties should be worn underneath for better absorption of perspiration.

For adequate hygiene, washing with soap and water is all that is needed. So-called feminine deodorant sprays are not necessary and can cause trouble not only for women but also for their male sexual partners. Some women who have used these products have experienced infections, irritations, burns, and rashes.[7] Women who choose to use a spray despite these facts should follow the manufacturer's directions carefully. The FDA requires the following label warning:

> CAUTION: For external use only. Spray at least 8 inches from skin. Use sparingly and not more than once daily to avoid irritation. Do not use this product with a sanitary napkin. Do not apply to broken, irritated, or itching skin. Persistent or unusual odor may indicate the presence of a condition for which a physician should be consulted. If a rash, irritation, unusual vaginal discharge, or discomfort develops, discontinue use immediately and consult a physician.

Boston gynecologist Daniel W. Cramer, M.D., has warned that women should not use talcum powder around the genital area because talc that enters the pelvic area can cause cancer. In a 3-year study, he found that women who regularly dusted their genitals and/or sanitary napkins with talcum powder were several times more likely to develop ovarian cancer than women who did not.[8]

Vaginitis

Vaginitis is an irritation of the vagina or the vulva (soft folds of skin outside the vagina). Most women have vaginitis at some time during their life; it usually has little to do with personal cleanliness. Its symptoms are itching or burning of the vagina or vulva, often accompanied by an abnormal vaginal discharge that may be malodorous. There also may be burning when urine flows over the inflamed tissues. The most common cause is an infection inside the vagina, but some cases involved no infection. The most common organism is a fungus, *Candida albicans,* which also is referred to as "yeast" or "monilia." Vaginitis can also be caused by trichomoniasis, chlamydia, and several other types of sexually transmitted diseases.

When no infection can be identified, the irritation is called nonspecific vaginitis. The causes of this condition include: hormonal factors, douches that are too strong or used too often, forgeting to remove tampons or a contraceptive sponge from the vagina, wearing clothing that does not permit sufficient ventilation of the genital area, or adverse reactions to the chemicals in perfumed soaps or toilet paper, "feminine hygiene" sprays, home remedies, or swimming pool water. The treatment of the infection depends on the cause.

Nonprescription products are now available to treat vaginal candidiasis. However, since some causes of vaginitis are potentially serious, a doctor should be consulted unless the woman is certain that she has a recurrence of a previously medically diagnosed problem that is suitable for self-treatment. When a sexually transmitted disease is present, the woman's sexual partner will require treatment to prevent reinfection.

Birth Control

Throughout history, both men and women have sought effective ways to control their fertility. Many of these treatments were not effective, and many caused infections and burns. As far back as 1850 B.C., in ancient Egypt, recipes for barrier methods of birth control were buried with the dead to prevent pregnancy in the afterlife. They advised using honey, carbonate of soda, and crocodile dung as spermicides.

Five major types of birth control methods are used today in the United States: surgical sterilization, hormonal methods (oral contraceptives, implants), barrier methods, fertility awareness (rhythm) methods, and intrauterine devices (IUDs). Despite recent medical advances, a completely safe, effective, and reversible method has yet to be developed. Planned Parenthood Federation of America suggests five standards to consider when selecting a method:[9]

1. *Personal preference:* Choose a method with which you are physically and emotionally comfortable and can use consistently.
2. *Safety:* Be aware of any health risks involved.
3. *Effectiveness:* Choose a method that provides the amount of protection you need to feel secure. For maximum effectiveness, the method must be understood and used carefully and consistently.
4. *Convenience:* Choose a method that is available and affordable.
5. *Partner perference:* This also may be a factor in deciding which method is most appropriate.

Table 22-1 compares the failure rates, risks, side effects, and other noteworthy features of the various methods. Additional information and services can be obtained from physicians, women's centers, or Planned Parenthood clinics.

Fertility Awareness Methods

Fertility awareness (rhythm) methods depend on abstaining from intercourse or using other forms of contraception during the fertile days of the menstrual cycle. The fertile days are those just before and after ovulation, which occurs about 14 days before the onset of the next menstrual period. Ovulation can be determined by counting days (calendar method), by noting changes in body temperature taken each morning, by noting changes in the character of cervical mucus, or by a combination of these methods. Rhythm methods are economical, free of side effects, and practiced successfully by many women, but these methods are among the least successful. They work best in women whose menstrual cycles are regular.

Test kits that attempt to predict ovulation are available for home use. They may be useful for planning pregnancies, but are not reliable for purposes of birth control. Since sperm can live in the vagina for a few days, pregnancy can result from having unprotected intercourse a few days before the test indicates that ovulation has occurred.

Barrier Methods

Barrier methods work in one of two ways: the sperm is either immobilized by a chemical (cream, jelly, foam, or suppository) or mechanically blocked (diaphragm, cervical cap, condom, or sponge) from entering the uterus. Effectiveness depends upon how conscientiously the method is used. Combinations of a mechanical and a chemical method are far more effective than either type used alone. Barrier products include the following:

Diaphragm: The diaphragm is a flexible rubber barrier that covers the cervix. It must be fitted by a doctor. Learning to use it may take time and patience. It is most effective when used together with contraceptive jelly. It may be left in place for up to 24 hours.

Condom, male: The male condom is a sheath of thin latex or animal tissue that fits over the penis; it offers good protection against sexually transmitted diseases, though this protection is not absolute. Simultaneous use of a spermicide provides additional protection and also can kill sperm if the condom breaks. Some condoms contain spermicide, but the extra protection is likely to be greater with the other large amounts of spermicide used in the vagina. Marketing surveys show that 40% to 50% of condoms are purchased by women. *Consumer Reports* states that skin condoms (made from part of the intestine of a lamb) are less likely to break than latex condoms, but may not be as effective in preventing transmission of the AIDS virus.[10]

Condom, female ("vaginal pouch"): The female condom is a soft, loose-fitting polyurethane sheath and two diaphragm-like, flexible polyurethane rings. One ring, which lies inside the sheath, fits internally like a diaphragm and anchors the sheath inside the vagina. The other ring forms the outer edge of the sheath and remains outside the vagina. The female condom is easy to use and does not require fitting by a health professional. It is thicker and covers more of the genitals than the male con-

TABLE 22–1

COMPARISON OF CONTRACEPTIVE METHODS

Method	Typical yearly pregnancy rate per 100 women*	Typical cost†	Risks and side effects	Comments
Subdermal implant (Norplant)	0.04	$350 plus doctor fee of $200-$300	Menstrual cycle irregularity	Effective for up to 5 years
Male sterilization	0.15	$250-$750	Pain, swelling, bleeding	Success must be confirmed by a negative sperm count after several ejaculations have taken place
Female sterilization	0.4	$350-$2500	Risks associated with surgery	Cost varies with type of operation
Birth control pills	3	Cost of doctor's exam plus $5 to $15 per month for the pills	Minor problems include tender breasts, nausea, gain or loss of weight Mild high blood pressure Slight increase in incidence of gallbladder disease Thromboembolic phenomena: blood clots in legs (1 in 2000 yearly), less commonly in lungs, heart, or brain; incidence of heart attack is dangerously increased in heavy smokers	Must be taken daily to be effective. Reduces menstrual bleeding and cramping Reduces risk of several cancers and heart disease No protection against socially transmitted diseases (STDs)
Intrauterine device	3	$300 for device, exam, insertion, and follow-up	Menstrual cramps, bleeding, and spotting Pelvic infection Perforation of uterine wall (rare) Ectopic pregnancy (pregnancy outside uterus) Infection or miscarriage can result if pregnancy occurs during use of IUD	Protasert is effective for 1 year Copper T 380A is effective for up to 8 years No protection against STDs

Condom (female)	n.a.	$2.25 each		FDA approval expected during 1992
Condom (male)	12	50¢-$2.50 each	Allergic reaction (rare) Rough handling may tear product	Significant protection against STDs, especially when combined with spermicide Skin condoms may not protect as well as latex condoms
Cervical cap	18	Doctor's visit plus $13-$25 for diaphragm	Abnormal pap smears	Some protection against certain STDs
Diaphragm	18	Doctor's visit plus $13-$25 for diaphragm	Bladder infections Allergic reaction (rare)	Should be checked for weak spots or holes before insertion
Coitus interruptus (withdrawal)	18	No cost	No physical risk	May make female satisfaction less likely Pregnancy can result from sperm in pre-ejaculatory fluid
Vaginal sponge		$1.50 each	Allergic reaction Toxic shock syndrome (rare)	Some protection against certain STDs
No previous childbirth	18			
After previous childbirth	28			
Fertility awareness methods (rhythm)	20	Charts and kits are inexpensive	No physical risk	The frequency of unwanted pregnancy varies with the type of method used
Foam, cream, jelly	21	$1 per use	Allergic reaction (rare)	Some protection against certain STDs
Vaginal suppository	40	70¢ per use	None reported	Some protection against certain STDs
No method used	85	—	Very high risk of unwanted pregnancy	No protection against STDs

*More conscientious use will greatly decrease the failure rates for users of birth control pills, barrier methods, and rhythm methods, but relative effectiveness remains approximately the same.

†Clinics offer some of these services at lower cost.

Based partially on data from Hatcher RA et al: Contraceptive technology 1990-1992, New York, 1990, Irvington Publishers; and Facts about birth control, 1990, Planned Parenthood.

PERSONAL GLIMPSE

Sample Script for Safer Sex[12]

If your partner says: What's that?
You can say: A condom, sweetheart.

If your partner says: What for?
You can say: To use when we're making love.

If your partner says: Rubbers are gross.
You can say: Being pregnant when I don't want to be is more gross. Getting AIDS is totally gross.

If your partner says: Rubbers aren't romantic.
You can say: What's more romantic than making love and protecting each other's health at the same time?

If your partner says: Let's face it. Making love with a rubber on is like taking a shower with a raincoat on.
You can say: You face it. Doing it without a rubber isn't making love; it's playing Russian roulette.

If your partner says: But I love you.
You can say: That won't protect me against disease or pregnancy.

If your partner says: I guess you don't love me.
You can say: I do, but I'm not risking my future to prove it.

If your partner says: We're not using a rubber and that's it.
You can say: O.K. You know how to play checkers?

dom, which means it may offer complete protection against sexually transmitted diseases.

Cervical cap: The cervical cap is a flexible cup-like device about 1½ inches in diameter that fits snugly over the cervix and may be left in place for up to 48 hours. A pelvic examination by a physician is needed to determine the correct size. The cap is recommended only for women with a normal Pap smear, and another Pap smear should be obtained after 3 months of use to be sure that abnormal changes have not occurred in the cervical tissue. (They occur in about 4% of users.) It is also recommended that users apply spermicide with each use and remove the device within 48 hours after insertion.

Foam, cream, jelly, suppositories: A number of products contain a chemical that kills sperm on contact. To be effective, the product must cover the cervix. The combination of foam plus a condom greatly enhances effectiveness. Used alone, aerosol foams are the most effective in this group. Suppositories tend to lose their effectiveness rapidly, within 30 minutes after they are inserted. Planned Parenthood suggests that creams and gels should not be used alone and should be combined with a condom, diaphragm, or cervical cap.

Vaginal contraceptive sponge: The vaginal sponge is a soft, round sponge, approximately 2 inches in diameter, made of polyurethane and impregnated with a spermicide that is activated by moistening the sponge with water. When properly inserted, it covers the cervix. The sponge is considered effective for 24 hours after insertion. During this period it continuously releases a spermicide and acts as a barrier to block sperm from entering the cervix. A polyester loop attached across the bottom of the sponge permits easy removal. Clinical trials indicate that the sponge is similar to the diaphragm in effectiveness. Itching, genital irritation, persistent unpleasant odor, unusual vaginal discharge, or symptoms of toxic shock syndrome are uncommon and should be promptly reported to a physician.

Intrauterine Devices

The IUD is the world's most often used method of temporary birth control for women. It involves the insertion by a doctor of a small piece of shaped plastic into the uterus, where it prevents the fertilized egg from implanting in the uterine wall. When the IUD is in place, an attached string hangs through the opening of the cervix so the position of the IUD can be checked. Protection is increased if the sexual partners use a condom and/or foam during the woman's most fertile period (usually the week beginning 19 days before the next period is due).

IUDs offer convenience and a high rate of effectiveness as long as they stay in place. The disadvantage is that they sometimes have major side effects: bleeding, menstrual cramping, and infections. One IUD, the Dalkon Shield, was withdrawn from the market in 1974 because of a high incidence of complications, including rare instances of fatal pelvic infections. Negative publicity and lawsuits led other manufacturers to withdraw IUDs from the American market, even though there was little or no evidence that the products were unsafe.[11]

Two types of IUDs are available in the United States today: Protasert, a progesterone-releasing IUD that must be replaced annually, and the Copper T 380A, which now is FDA-approved for up to 8 years of use. IUDs are not recommended for women with multiple partners or those who have had a recent or recurrent pelvic infection, tubal pregnancy, very heavy periods, or previous trouble with an IUD.

Hormonal Methods

Two types of contraceptives prevent pregnancy through the effects of female hormones: oral contraceptives and contraceptive implants.

Oral contraceptives, available only by prescription, contain one or two hormones similar to those that naturally regulate menstruation. Pills that contain estrogen and progestin prevent ovulation from taking place. Those that contain only progestin (called minipills) decrease the incidence of ovulation and do various other things to prevent pregnancy. Pills provide the best protection available with a temporary method if they are taken properly, with no missed doses. Some users have an additional benefit of decreased menstrual pain and bleeding. Extensive studies by the U.S. Centers for Disease Control indicate no evidence that long-term use of oral contraceptives increases the incidence of breast cancer. The researchers also noted that oral contraceptives appear to offer some protection against ovarian and uterine (endometrial) cancer.

The list of possible side effects is long, but serious problems are rare. Mild side effects, such as nausea, weight gain, fluid retention, spotting between periods, and breast tenderness, usualy subside within a few months. Moderately troublesome side effects include headaches and depression. The incidence of side effects is less with the minipill, but its effectiveness is a bit lower. Most women who take either type of pill have no side effects or complications. Birth control pills should not be taken by individuals with a history of blood clots in the legs or elsewhere, or by heavy smokers. Pills should not be taken by women who are pregnant, have active liver disease, cancer of the breast or internal sexual organs, or abnormal vaginal bleeding.

In addition to its contraceptive effects, the pill has proven to have significant health benefits. Studies show that the use of the pill decreases the incidence of ovarian and endometrial cancers, benign cysts of the ovaries and breasts, and pelvic inflammatory disease. The pill also prevents heavy and irregular menstrual periods.[13]

In 1990 the FDA approved use of the contraceptive implant, Norplant, which consists of six silicone tubes that are about the size of matchsticks.[14] The tubes are implanted in the woman's arm in a fanlike arrangement that can be felt but not easily seen. Once in place, the tubes steadily release a low dose of progestin into the blood stream. The implant procedure takes 10 to 15 minutes. Norplant is highly effective for up to 5 years but often causes menstrual irregularities. During 1991 the median fee for the implant and its insertion was $580.

Surgical Sterilization

Close to half of the married couples using contraception have one partner who has been sterilized. Sterilization has the advantage of being permanent. Because of this, however, a decision to undergo sterilization should be made only after careful consideration and discussion with one's physician. Although sterilization procedures can sometimes be reversed, it is important to be certain that no more pregnancies are desired.

Female sterilization can be accomplished by preventing the passage of eggs down the fallopian tubes from the ovary to the uterus. The tubes can be separated by cutting, blocked with clips or bands, or sealed with electric current. The most popular method is with laparoscopy. The surgeon makes a tiny incision just inside the navel and inserts a laparoscope (a rodlike instrument with a viewing scope) to locate the tubes, which usually are cut with a second instrument inserted through another small opening. Other methods of sterilization include the following types of surgery: minilaparotomy (using a nonvisualizing instrument through a small skin incision in the abdomen), laparotomy (through a larger skin incision), culdoscopy (inserting a visualizing instrument through an incision in the vagina), and colpotomy (a vaginal approach without a visualizing instrument). The procedures usually are performed in the hospital, and most take between 15 and 30 minutes.[15]

Male sterilization (vasectomy) is accomplished by cutting and sealing off the tube (vas deferens) to each testicle, through which sperm travel before they are stored for ejaculation. In the traditional method, a local anesthetic is injected into the area, an incision is made on each side of the scrotum, and the tubes are located and blocked. Minor complications (swelling, tenderness, blood clots, infections, and sperm leakage under the skin) occur in a small percentage of cases.[16] In a newer procedure (microvasectomy), the scrotal skin is not cut but is punctured to reach the vas deferens. Microvasectomy decreases the possibility of complications. The procedures take about 20 minutes and are done on an outpatient basis. A number of ejaculations must take place (typically 15) before sperm stored in the testis are expelled and success of the operation can be confirmed by laboratory examination of a specimen of semen.

Therapeutic Abortions

A 1973 Supreme Court decision permits abortions to be performed during the first and second trimesters of pregnancy. About 1.5 million abortions are performed annually.

The surgical technique used depends on the stage of pregnancy and the preference of the physician.[17] During the first 12 weeks of pregnancy, uterine contents are evacuated by a suction procedure (vacuum curettage) usually performed on an outpatient basis using local anesthesia to numb the cervix. From 13 to 16 weeks the cervix requires additional stretching before the uterine contents can be evacuated; a dilation and evacuation procedure (D&E) is commonly performed under general anesthesia. From 17 to 24 weeks a D&E may still be performed, or a solution of saline (salt), prostaglandin, and/or urea is injected into the uterus. Prostaglandin can also be administered by vaginal suppository. These substances cause the uterus to become irritable and contract, expelling its contents in a procedure that resembles labor. The complication rate of therapeutic abortion is under 1% during the first trimester, but rises gradually (to 2% to 3%) the later the procedure is performed.

Abortion is a subject of considerable controversy. "Pro-choice" advocates believe that women should have the freedom to choose whether to terminate unwanted pregnancies. "Pro-life" advocates believe that abortion is morally wrong because it involves the destruction of human life. Counseling is available to women who need help in deciding whether or not to terminate their pregnancy. Information about abortion may be obtained from some physicians, local family planning clinics, women's centers, and Planned Parenthood offices. Information about the "pro-life" viewpoint can be obtained from some physicians and religious leaders, as well as from Birthright USA and Alternatives to Abortion, which have facilities in hundreds of cities nationwide. In 1991 the U.S. Supreme Court upheld a law that forbids federally funded facilities from discussing abortion in their clients.

Mifepristone, commonly called RU 486, is a drug that can induce abortion if taken within the first 6 weeks of pregnancy. When prescribed with prostaglandin, it is about 95% effective and has a low incidence of side effects. It was developed and is prescribed in France, but is not marketed in the United States.[18]

Osteoporosis

Osteoporosis is a condition, occurring mostly in women, in which bones become less dense (more porous) and more brittle. It occurs most commonly in postmenopausal women, whose ovaries no longer produce the estrogen needed to help maintain bone mass. Caucasian women who are fair and thin-skinned have increased risk of developing osteoporosis. Other risk factors are cigarette smoking, lack of weight-bearing exercise (see Chapter 15), insufficient calcium intake, alcohol abuse, and early menopause.

The early stages of osteoporosis produce no symptoms. Often the first sign is a fracture of the hip or wrist after a minor fall. Lost bone tissue cannot easily be replaced, but further bone loss can be minimized by preventive measures. About half of the women who reach age 75 suffer at least one fracture due to osteoporosis.

In 1991 the FDA Advisory Committee on Maternal Health recommended that estrogen-replacement therapy be made available to virtually all postmenopausal women. This therapy also can decrease unpleasant menopausal symptoms and protect women against heart disease. Although it may increase the risks of breast and uterine cancer, these risks appear small compared to the probable benefits. Consumers Union's medical consultants belive that women at high risk for osteoporosis or heart disease should consider taking estrogen if they have no medical reason not to do so.[19]

In recent years, x-ray examination (densitometry) of the wrists or spine has been promoted as a screening test by "storefront" osteoporosis centers and various physicians who claim that by detecting decreased bone mass they can identify women at risk for fractures due to osteoporosis. The spinal examination is more accurate but costs more and involves considerably more radiation. However, most authorities believe that densitometry should be done only when the information it yields might help in deciding a course of action (for example, in evaluating whether certain postmenopausal women should take estrogen). Regardless of what a bone scan might show, women should minimize their chance of developing osteoporosis by heeding its risk factors throughout their adult life. They should consume adequate amounts of calcium, engage in weight-bearing exercise, and not smoke cigarettes or abuse alcohol. Before menopause, there is little reason to screen women for bone loss.

Pregnancy Testing

When a woman is pregnant, human chorionic gonadotropin (HCG) becomes present in her urine. This hormone, which is produced by the chorion (the membrane surrounding the embryo in the uterus), is the substance tested for by pregnancy tests performed on urine. The most accurate tests (radioreceptor assay or radioimmunoassay) are performed by laboratories on blood samples.

Do-it-yourself test kits are available (see Chapter 10). If done carefully, the tests are usually accurate when positive, but there is a significant incidence of false-negative results. Moreover, do-it-yourself testing may be a needless purchase. If the result is positive, indicating a probable pregnancy, a visit to a physician is advisable. If the physician insists on confirming the diagnosis, the woman will wind up paying for two pregnancy tests.

Infertility

About 1 out of every 12 American couples that try to have a baby fail to do so. The term infertility is reserved for couples that have not achieved a pregnancy despite at least a year of regular sexual intercourse without birth control. The problem is attributable to the man in about one third of couples, and to the woman in about another third. In some couples, both are impaired; and in others, no problem can be identified. Evaluation of the male begins with a sperm count and may later involve testicular biopsy. Evaluation of the woman begins with temperature-taking to identify ovulation and urine tests to identify certain hormones. If necessary, various tests can be used to evaluate the structure of the uterus and other internal reproductive organs. With specialized help, about half of the infertile couples achieve pregnancy.

The FDA[20] suggests that couples seeking infertility services should check the doctor's qualifications carefully, rather than relying on advertisements. One's family physician may be a good source of referral to a specialist. For women, the best doctor may be a board-certified obstetrician-gynecologist who has had 2 years of further training in reproductive endocrinology. For men, the best doctor may be a board-certified urologist with a special interest in infertility. Resolve, a nonprofit group, maintains a list of specialists and can provide additional information about infertility. Many communities have a Resolve chapter listed in their local telephone book. The FTC advises consumers to question providers carefully about their previous experience and success rates.[21]

Mastectomy Prostheses

Women who undergo breast removal surgery for cancer or other conditions may wish to retain a normal breast contour as much as possible. Sometimes plastic surgery can be performed to reconstruct the breast. If the surgery is not too radical, reconstructive surgery may be relatively simple. At other times, the plastic surgery may involve using skin grafts from other parts of the body.

An alternative approach is the use of a mastectomy prosthesis. Ready-made devices, which cost $100 or more, may be filled with silicone gel, air, liquid, weighted or unweighted foam rubber, or polyester. The liquid or silicone gel forms are generally heavier and more expensive, but are usually preferable because they assume a natural breastlike contour and do not slip out of position.[22] Custom-made devices, made from molds, cost $300 or more. Comparison shopping is advisable. One should not buy a product until completely satisfied with both appearance and comfort. Particular attention should be paid to fit; one should be sure that both breasts appear matched from the side, top, and bottom. Breast prostheses are often covered by medical insurance, but many insurers only pay for the first one after the surgery.

Advice and emotional support after mastectomy can be obtained from the American Cancer Society program called Reach to Recovery, a network of local support groups composed of women who have undergone mastectomy.

Breast Developers

Various creams, protein powders, and gadgets have been sold by mail with claims that they can enlarge the female breast. All of these products are fakes. In 1977 the Good Housekeeping Institute ran a controlled test on four bust developers advertised in leading magazines: a water-massage type and three "tension" devices (one clam-shaped, one rod-shaped, and one that used an oversized rubber band). The cost of these items ranged from $9.95 to $19.95. The test results showed that none of these devices had any effect on breast size.[23]

The breast itself is a gland and has no muscles. Since bust size is measured around the torso, resistance exercises that increase the size of chest and back muscles will slightly increase the bust measurement; but the actual breast and cup size are not affected. The growth of the breasts is influenced only by hormones—released during puberty and pregnancy—and by general weight gain. Estrogen prescribed for menstrual difficulty or birth control may produce some temporary breast enlargement, but the breasts return to their original size when the drug is stopped. As noted in Chapter 21, plastic surgery is the only procedure that can be used to permanently augment breast size.

Unnecessary Procedures

The general subject of unnecessary surgery is discussed in Chapter 6. Herbert H. Keyser, M.D., clinical associate professor of obstetrics and gynecology at the University of Texas, believes that insufficient attention has been given to certain procedures commonly performed on women. He states the following:

1. Ultrasound, which can be used to visualize a baby in the uterus, should not be done routinely or to determine the baby's gender. Although no harm in humans has been reported, experiments have shown that high doses of ultrasound can cause chromosomal damage and low birth weights in mice. Chapters 6 and 23 contain additional information about ultrasound devices.
2. A small number of surgeons are doing excessive numbers of dilation and curettages (D&Cs), particularly on women under the age of 30. D&C is a procedure in which the lining of the uterus is scraped off (curetted) after the opening to the uterus has been stretched (dilated). Although commonly regarded as minor surgery, this operation is not risk-free. Serious complications are rare and include: death from anesthesia, perforation of the uterus, excessive bleeding, infec-

It's Your Decision

You have encountered unusual difficulty with premenstrual syndrome. Which of the following actions would you take?

	Reason
1. Take a pain reliever	______
2. Attempt to reduce tension and stress	______
3. Increase vitamin intake	______
4. Increase intake of herbal tea	______
5. Get more rest by going to bed earlier	______
6. See a doctor	______
7. Other	______

tion, and scarring of the uterine lining.

3. The cesarian rate has risen steadily and is now performed in more than 20% of deliveries. The main reason for this is that obstetricians are afraid of being sued if they do not rescue the baby at the first sign of possible complications. The best defense against unnecessary cesarian sections is to choose an ethical doctor who works in a hospital with stringent peer review.[24]

Consumer Reports recommends that women who are selecting an obstetrician should ask about the doctor's percentage of cesarian deliveries (12% to 14% is usually reasonable).[25] Inquiries also should be made about the doctor's practice style and hospital policies regarding labor and delivery.

SUMMARY

Women are faced with a variety of health problems related to the anatomy and physiology of their reproductive organs. Menstrual cramps that begin during the first year after the onset of menstruation are usually mild and self-treatable. Premenstrual syndrome is a combination of physical and/or emotional symptoms that occur before menstruation and disappear during periods. PMS usually will respond to self-help measures. Persistent menstrual irregularity is a reason to consult a physician. All women should attempt to prevent osteoporosis by avoiding or correcting the life-style factors that tend to increase its risk of developing. After menopause, estrogen-replacement therapy should be considered.

Many choices are available to sexually active individuals who wish to prevent pregnancy. Contraceptive methods should be judged by considering effectiveness, safety, convenience, and personal acceptability.

Women should be aware that D&Cs, cesarian sections, uterine ultrasound tests, and bone scans for osteoporosis are performed more often than necessary.

DISCUSSION QUESTIONS

1. What are the three main types of menstrual disorders? How are they treated?
2. How do the various types of menstrual aids compare?
3. What is toxic shock syndrome? How can it be prevented?
4. How should "vaginal hygiene" products be regarded?
5. What are the advantages, disadvantages, and possible complications of the various types of birth control measures?
6. Who is most at risk for osteoporosis? What can be done to prevent it? When is it appropriate to have a bone scan to detect osteoporosis?
7. What procedures may be performed too commonly on women?

REFERENCES

1. Shephard BD and Shephard CA: The complete guide to women's health, Tampa, Fla, 1983, Mariner Publishing Co.

*2. Beaudette T: Premenstrual syndrome: is it nutrition-related? Nutrition Forum, Aug 1987.

3. Zimmerman DR: The essential guide to nonprescription drugs, New York, 1983, Harper & Row, Publishers Inc.

4. Consumer Reports, eds: The medicine show, Mount Vernon, NY, 1980, Consumers Union.

5. Rinzler CA: Strictly female: an evaluation of brand-name health and hygiene products for women, New York, 1981, New American Library.

6. California Medical Association: Feminine hygiene in the age of advertising, Health Tips, index 70, July/Aug 1978.

7. Holt LH and Weber M: The American Medical Association book of womancare, New York, 1984, Random House Inc.

8. Hewitt JH: Warn your patients against talc use in feminine hygiene, Primary Care & Cancer, pp 27-29, May 1985.

9. Planned Parenthood Federation of America: Over the counter birth control for women, New York, 1988, The Federation.

*10. Can you rely on condoms? Consumer Reports 54:135-141, 1989.

11. Mastroianni LM, Donaldson PJ and Kane TT (eds): Developing new contraceptives—obstacles and opportunities, Washington, DC, 1990, National Academy Press.

12. Knowles J: The condom: what it is, what is it for, how to use it, New York, 1990, Planned Parenthood Federation of America.

13. Snider S: The pill: 30 years of safety concerns, FDA Consumer 24(10):8-11, 1990.

14. Segal M: Norplant—birth control at arm's reach, FDA Consumer 25(4):8-11, 1991.

15. Planned Parenthood Federation of America: Voluntary sterilization for women, New York, 1987, The Federation.

16. Planned Parenthood Federation of America: All about vasectomy, New York, 1991, The Federation.

17. Cook AT: Fact sheet: What is abortion? Washington, DC, 1992, National Abortion Federation.

18. Gooding J and Williams R: RU 486—the fuss, the fears and the facts, American Health 10(10):65-69, 1991.

*19. The estrogen question: is it a natural supplement or a dangerous drug? Consumer Reports 56:587-591, 1991.

*Recommended reading

20. Randal J: Trying to outsmart infertility, FDA Consumer 25(4):22-29, 1991.
21. Facts for consumers: infertility services, Washington, DC, March 1990, FTC Office of Consumer/Business Education.
*22. Kushner R: Why me? Philadelphia, 1982, WB Saunders.
23. Do the bust developers really work? Good Housekeeping 185:153-154, Aug 1977.
*24. Keyser HH: Women under the knife: a gynecologist's report on hazardous medicine, New York, 1984, Warner Books Inc.
*25. Too many cesarians, Consumer Reports 56:120-126, 1991.
*26. Knowles J: Facts about birth control, New York, 1990, Planned Parenthood Federation of America.
27. Hatcher RA et al: Contraceptive Technology 1990-1992, New York, 1990, Irvington Publishers.

CHAPTER TWENTY-THREE

HEALTH DEVICES

"It's not like the old days."

Consumer Decision

What should a person do who has a hearing problem?

What type of hearing aid should be purchased?

What type of eyeglasses should be purchased?

Are contact lenses safe to use? Do they need special care?

Should a person undergo radial keratotomy surgery?

When a pacemaker, heart valve, or hip socket replacement has been recommended, what information is needed to arrive at an intelligent decision whether or not to approve of this replacement?

What information is needed to select a heating pad or an air purifier?

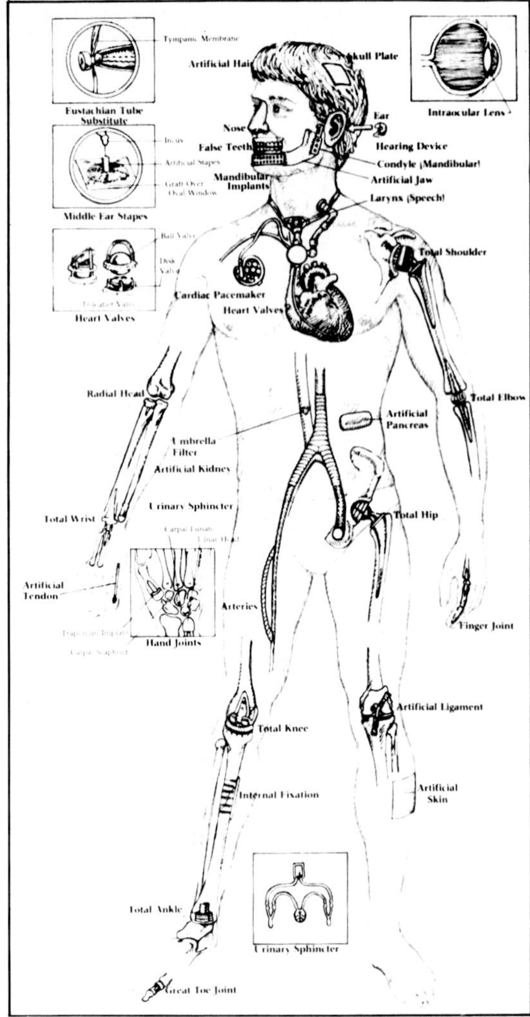

FIGURE 23-1. Human medical device implants.

Individuals who are unable to hear properly may be advised by a physician to purchase a hearing aid. People who have difficulty seeing may need to purchase eyeglasses or possibly contact lenses. Sunglasses may be advisable to protect one's eyes from the sun's glare and prevent cataracts. Some consumers may need to purify the air in their homes to help with allergies. The purchase of an electric heating pad to help relieve menstrual cramps or a muscle injury may be necessary. Many homeowners are considering whether to install water treatment systems to assure safe water supplies. Physicians must select artificial hearts and heart valves, pacemakers, hip replacement sockets, ultrsound equipment, and numerous other medical devices for their patients. Figure 23-1 illustrates many of the implant devices used by surgeons.

These devices are only a few of the more than 1700 types and over 100,000 products being marketed. It is estimated that $14 billion is spent yearly on these devices. The FDA, under various provisions of the Food, Drug, and Cosmetic Act, is responsible for overseeing the safety and efficacy of devices in the United States (see Chapter 27). The Act defines the term device as follows:

> An instrument, apparatus, implement, machine, contrivance, implant, in vitro reagent, or other similar or related article . . . which is . . . intended for use in the diagnosis . . . cure, mitigation, treatment or prevention of disease . . . or intended to affect the structure of any function of the body . . . and which does not achieve any of its principal intended purposes through chemical action within or on the body . . . and which is not dependent upon being metabolized for the achievement . . . of any of its principal intended purposes.[1]

This definition encompasses a wide spectrum of devices that may be categorized as appliances, equipment, and mechanical items. They incude such items as eyeglasses, sunglasses, contact lenses, hearing aids, shower massagers, pregnancy test kits

CONSUMER TIP

Some Devices May be a Needless Expense

The self-help movement in the United States brought many entrepreneurs into the health marketplace. The 32-page catalog of one New York company advertised 188 devices that included: hearing aid, electric pain reliever, end-snoring gadget, therapeutic footrest, weak joints security, callous remover, back pain support, wheelchair, incontinence pants, invisible girdle, silicone comfort bra, hygienic pants, flossing tooth pick, bunion pain-relief gadget, electric massager, and tension-relief pillow. Some of these items may provide limited relief, whereas others may be a waste of money. Chapters 3, 4, and 5 of this textbook will help consumers to make intelligent decisions about the items found in this catalog.

(Chapter 10), bicycles, rowing machines (Chapter 15), heating pads, sphygmomanometers (Chapter 10), thermometers, pacemakers, and heart valves.

MEDICAL DEVICE LAWS

The need for legislation to control medical devices to ensure safety and effectiveness has been known for many years. Dangerous, harmful, and ineffective products had been on the market for a long time. In 1969 a search of the medical literature by the U.S. Department of Health, Education, and Welfare uncovered 10,000 verified injuries related to medical devices in a 10-year period, 751 of which had proved fatal. In addition, the FDA reviewed death certificates in 10 states and found 858 deaths directly related to devices over a 10-year period. The Commission on Professional and Hospital Activities, an independent health group, estimated that 36,000 complications from medical devices occurred in 1 year. Over the years the FDA has had to deal with the following problems: intrauterine devices that could perforate the uterus, poorly designed and manufactured heart valves, faulty cardiac pacemakers, improperly designed respirators, electric beds that killed people, unsafe x-ray machines, inaccurate thermometers, defective hearing aids, improperly functioning kidney dialysis machines, defective defibrillators (applies electrical impulses to normalize irregular heart beats), as well as various other devices promoted by quacks and other entrepreneurs in the health marketplace.

The 1976 Medical Device Amendments to the Federal Food, Drug, and Cosmetic Act required premarket approval of implanted and life-support devices. Before the law was passed, the FDA had to prove that items were hazardous or ineffective to stop their sale. This often involved much time, effort, and expense for research and court procedures. The burden of proof of safety and efficacy is now on manufacturer. However, no reporting system for adverse reactions to the use of health devices was established until the Mandatory Device Reports Act was passed in 1984. During 1985 to 1987 the FDA received reports of 1554 deaths that resulted from malfunctions of medical devices; one third of these were from heart valve or defibrillator failures.[2] There were 29,176 injuries, with 56% from malfunctioning pacemakers or pacemaker electrodes. In 1990 Rep. John Dingell (D-MI) criticized the FDA for failure to monitor devices.[3]

After it became apparent that the 1976 Medical Device Amendments needed reform, Congress passed the Safe Medical Devices Act of 1990. This Act reclassified devices that were intended for humans as follows:

Class I: *General controls.* Devices that do not appear to present an unreasonable risk of illness or injury are subject only to the general controls that apply to all devices. These controls include registration of the manufacturer, recordkeeping requirements, labeling requirements, and good manufacturing practice regulations.

Class II: *Special controls.* Devices for which general controls are not sufficient to assure safety and effectivness and for which there is sufficient information to establish special controls to provide this assurance. Special controls include performance standards, postmarket surveillance, patient registries, and guidelines for submitting clinical data to the FDA before the device is marketed. The Safe Medical Devices Act of 1990 requires the Secretary of Health and Human Services to determine what controls are necessary to regulate life-supporting and life-sustaining devices.

Class III: *Premarket approval.* Devices for which insufficient information is available to establish special controls or which may pose unreasonable risk of illness or injury. Before the marketing of such a device is permitted:

1. Controlled studies must be conducted, including clinical investigation by qualified experts.
2. The manufacturer must obtain an Independent Device Exemption (IDE) from the FDA to develop clinical data. An IDE permits limited distribution of a product to specific locations for animal and laboratory tests to predict whether or not the device will be helpful to people.
3. Safety and effectiveness must be determined for the intended users of the device. The probable benefits must be weighed against the probable risks of injury or illness.

The 1976 law requires manufacturers to notify the FDA if a device is implicated in the death or serious injury of a user. The 1990 law extends this requirement to hospitals, nursing homes, and outpatient facilities (except physicians' offices) and also requires notification of the manufacturer. The 1990 law also enables the FDA to order an immediate recall of a device it deems unsafe. Manufacturers can be assessed civil penalties of $15,000 for each violation of the law and a maximum of $1,000,000 for each proceeding in an FDA civil case before an administrative judge.

Problem Reporting Program

The Medical Device and Laboratory Product Problem Reporting Program is coordinated by the U.S. Pharmacopeial Convention with financial support from the FDA and the National Center for Devices and Radiological Health. The program is designed to identify problems such as improper labeling, defective components, performance failures, poor packaging, incomplete and confusing instructions, and/or erroneous information. It provides a way to promptly bring health hazards to the attention of government and industry officials.

Consumers who encounter a problem with any medical device should report it (or have their doctor report it) to the Practitioners Reporting Network (800-638-6725, or 301-881-0256 call "collect" in MD). Callers will be asked to give the product's name, lot number, expiration date, the model and serial number, and the manufacturer's name and address. Consumers may also wish to write to the U.S. Pharmacopeial Convention, Medical Device and Laboratory Product Problem Report Program (see Appendix for address).

Individuals with an implanted device also should register with a national registry, such as Medic Alert (800-344-3226), which will provide notification if the device is recalled or develops an identifiable problem.

Hearing Aids

The National Hearing Aid Society states that nearly 21 million Americans are deaf or hearing-impaired. The society estimates that 80% to 85% of them might be helped by a hearing aid, but only 4 million use one.[4] Retirees surveyed by Franks and Beckman[5] gave these reasons for not using a hearing aid: (1) cost, (2) do not wish to call attention to disability, (3) dealer practices, (4) amplified sounds are not clear, (5) difficulty in manipulating controls, and (6) not knowing where to obtain a hearing aid.

Eighty percent of those who wear hearing aids are 60 years old or older. Hearing loss is most common among the elderly. One person in four over 65 years, and one in three over 75 years experience this problem. However, the rate of noise-induced hearing loss is rising among young and middle-aged people resulting from the use of motorcycles, snowmobiles, powerboats, radios with headphones, poorly designed telephones, and rock music. The average age for first-time users of hearing aids is decreasing from 60 years to 50 years. Many individuals who purchase a hearing aid get no benefit from it or would be better served by medical or surgical treatment. Some of these people may have only moderate hearing loss. Many of these individuals rely solely upon the advice of a salesperson.

Signs and Symptoms of Hearing Loss

People with friends or family members who experience any of the following symptoms should advise them to have their ears checked for possible hearing loss:

1. Words are difficult to distinguish
2. Sounds seem subdued
3. Another's speech appears mumbled and slurred
4. Sounds such as the ticking of a watch, dripping of a faucet, or high tones of a musical instrument are difficult or impossible to hear
5. Continual hissing or ringing background noise (tinnitus) is heard
6. Turns up the television or radio volume excessively
7. Asks people to repeat themselves
8. Favors one ear
9. Strains to hear

The questions below are designed to evaluate your ability to hear in different circumstances. Your answers will aid in determining if hearing help is needed.

Please answer *each* statement below by placing an "X" in the "Yes" column or "No" column.

	YES	NO
1. Can you usually hear and understand what a person says, without seeing his face, if that person *whispers* to you from across a quiet room?	___	___
2. Can you usually hear and understand what a person says, without seeing his face, if that person *talks in a normal voice* to you from across a quiet room?	___	___
3. Can you usually hear and understand what a person says, without seeing his face, if that person *shouts to you* from across a quiet room?	___	___
4. Can you usually hear and understand a person if that person *speaks loudly into your better ear?* (note: either ear if you believe them to be the same)	___	___
5. Can you usually distinguish the sound of speech from other sounds and noises?	___	___
6. Can you usually tell one kind of noise from another?	___	___
7. Can you *only* hear loud noises?	___	___

Please answer the question below by circling the letter above the answer that most accurately describes your experiences.

8. How difficult do you find it to follow conversations if there is surrounding noise (for instance, while several people are talking at the same time as in a restaurant)?

A	B	C	D	E
Not at all Difficult	Slightly Difficult	Somewhat Difficult	Quite Difficult	Extremely Difficult

Screening Chart for Hearing Acuity Test

	1	2	3	4	5	6	7
A				X	X	X	X
B				X	X	X	X
C			X	X	X	X	X
D		X	X	X	X	X	X
E	X	X	X	X	X	X	X

DIRECTIONS FOR SCORING TEST

Indicate the *first* question number ________________ (1-7) in which you answered "YES".

Indicate the *letter* circled in question #8. ____________ (A-E)

Take the *number* you just wrote above and find the matching number column at the top of the chart. Move *down* that column until you come to the *letter* that you indicated. This is your Scoring Square.

If there *is* an "X" in your Scoring Square, a need for hearing help is indicated.

If there is *no* "X" in the Scoring Square, hearing help is probably *not* necessary.

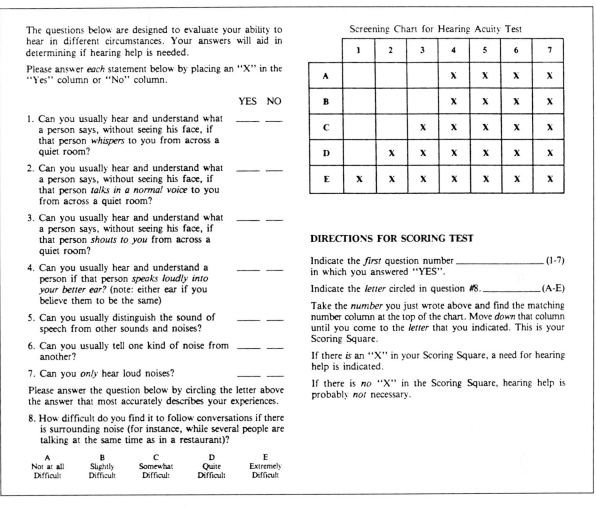

FIGURE 23-2. Self-hearing test.
Source: Better Hearing Institute, Washington, D.C.

Individuals who wish to evaluate their ability to hear in different circumstances can use the Self Hearing Test (Figure 23-2); answers will help determine whether hearing assistance is needed.

Types of Hearing Loss

There are two major types of hearing loss: *conductive* and *sensorineural.* In conductive deafness, which is the less common of the two, sound waves cannot be transmitted to the audtiory (hearing) nerve. Conductive deafness is related to the outer and middle portions of the ear and can be caused by: (1) impacted wax in the external ear, (2) injury to the eardrum (tympanic membrane) by an explosion, blow to the ear, infection, or sharp implement, or (3) arthritic disease, middle ear infection (otitis media), and other conditions that prevent the three inner ear bones (malleus, incus, stapes) from vibrating.

Sensorineural deafness, also called perceptive or nerve deafness, is more common. It is caused by damage to the auditory nerve, which connects the inner part of the ear to the brain. Nerve deafness can result from birth defects, illness producing a high fever, overexposure to high noise levels, use of certain medications, head injuries, vascular problems, and tumors. Nerve deafness often is related to aging, and is the most common reason for using a hearing aid. Some impairments can be medically or surgically treated. If there is partial hearing, a hearing aid may be effective. Some individuals have "mixed" hearing loss—both conductive and sen-

Table 23–1

Significance of Hearing Loss Levels

Level of loss (dB)	Description	Effect	Need for hearing aid
25 to 40	Mild	Difficulty understanding normal speech	Some situations
41 to 55	Moderate	Difficulty understanding loud speech	Frequent need
56 to 80	Severe	Can understand only amplified speech	All communication
81 or more	Profound	Difficulty understanding amplified speech	May need to supplement hearing aid with speech-reading, aural rehabilitation, or sign language

From American Association of Retired Persons: AARP product report: hearing aids, Washington, DC, Dec 1989, The Association.

sorineural. Elderly individuals with a hearing loss often have damage to the auditory nerve as well as a defect in the ear mechanism that relays sound to that nerve.

Diagnosis of a Hearing Problem

The evaluation for suspected hearing loss will include a discussion by a physician specialist (otolaryngologist) of the symptoms and past medical history, examination of the ears and throat, an audiometric test, and other special tests that are appropriate. The audiometric test is performed in a special soundproof room, usually by an audiologist. Some otolaryngologists employ an audiologist in their office, while others refer the patient to one located elsewhere. During the test, various levels of sound (low to high volume) are transmitted to the patient through an earphone. The patient responds by signaling to the tester which sounds can be heard. The levels of sound heard are recorded on a graph (audiogram). The collected information is analyzed and the hearing level, measured in decibels (dB), is established. When all tests are completed, the otolaryngologist informs the patient of the nature and extent of the problem, if any, and whether a hearing aid might be helpful. Table 23-1 indicates when a hearing aid might be useful.

Selecting a Hearing Aid

The best way to select a hearing aid dealer is probably through the recommendation of a physician. One's family doctor or otolaryngologist may be able to make a suitable recommendation. A few otolaryngologists employ a qualified person in their office who fits hearing aids. Before visiting a dealer, it may be helpful to visit a local noncommercial hearing aid center.[6] Such centers are usually connected with a hospital and are staffed by qualified personnel who help to determine the proper type of hearing aid. They do not sell hearing aids, but they recommend specific brands and models and will also check the one a consumer purchases to be sure it is appropriate for that person's needs.

Types of Hearing Aids

Most hearing aids work in a similar manner, although designs may differ somewhat. A hearing aid is a miniature, battery-powered, amplifier system with a microphone that picks sound waves and sends them to the ear canal. A "monaural" system consists of a hearing aid for one ear and a "binaural" system uses hearing aids for both ears.

There are four genral types of hearing aids:

1. *On-the-body models* have strong power for severe and profound hearing losses. They are carried in pockets or on clasps that are attached to clothing; some models have a variable tone control.
2. *Behind-the-ear models* have moderate power for mild to severe hearing losses; these are 2-inch long crescent-shaped devices that hook over the ear.
3. *Eyeglass models* are similar to behind-the-ear models except that they are built into an eyeglass

TABLE 23–2

COMPARISON OF HEARING AIDS[7,8]

Site/range of hearing loss	Extent of hearing loss	Average cost	Advantages	Disadvantages
On-the-body 40-110dB	Moderate to profound	$1500-$2000	Most powerful; prevents feedback; high amplification	Bulky; requires long wire; cosmetically displeasing; high frequency response loss
Behind-the-ear 25-80dB	Mild to severe	$500-$700	Most versatile; 2″ hook over ear; cosmetic appeal; no wires	Feedback amplification limited
In-the-ear 25-55dB	Mild to moderate	$500-$700	One piece; custom fitted; easily concealed; sound directly to inner ear	Size limits power; more repairs; volume controls malfunction; ear wax damage
In-ear-canal 25-55dB	Mild to moderate	$700-$1000	Barely visible; cosmetic appeal	Power limits; volume controls smaller; more repairs; ear wax damage
Eyeglass models 25-70dB	Mild to severe	$500-$800	Glass frame conceals hidden wires; greater range with special modifications	Must wear glasses; bulky; not very popular

Note: Selection depends on size, power, ease of use, and cosmetic appeal; 98% of types used are behind-the-ear, in-the-ear, or in-the canal.

Modified from Sataloff RT and Vassalo LA: Choosing the right hearing aid, Hosp Pract 16:32A, May 1981; and American Association of Retired Persons: AARP product report: hearing aids, Washington, DC, 1989, The Association.

frame; they are no longer very popular.

4. *In-the-ear models* are molded to fit the ear or may be placed directly into the ear canal; these are for mild to moderate losses. They are less visible but the smaller size limits sound output. Manipulation of volume control and replacement of batteries is more difficult.

One should not be influenced solely by the price or appearance of hearing aids, but should obtain answers to these questions:

1. What is the quality of the sound?
2. Does the aid help you to understand speech in quiet places? In noisy places?
3. Is the aid comfortable to wear?
4. Are the controls (tone, volume) easy to operate?
5. Can the aid be easily handled (especially for young children, the infirm, and elderly people)?
6. Does the price include all parts?
7. Is there a charge for fitting the aid?
8. What are the costs of maintenance?

Table 23-2 provides information about the types of hearing aids, their average costs, and some of the advantages and disadvantages of each type. Table 23-3 describes the characteristics of nine models of hearing aids selected from an extensive list prepared by the American Association of Retired Persons (AARP). They are for illustrative purposes and not endorsed nor recommended by AARP.

Obtaining the proper fit of a hearing aid may require several visits to the dealer. In addition, adjusting to the device may take weeks or months.

Before making a purchase, one should rent the hearing aid for a trial period. Many manufacturers will offer a trial rental or purchase-option plan,

Table 23–3

Characteristics of Selected Hearing Aid Models[8]

Brand/model	Hearing loss	Frequency response*	Selected features	Cost
Behind-the-ear models				
3M Memory Mate	Mild to severe	Varies with memory selected	Automatic gain control; 8 separate program memories	$1300-$2000
Oticon E40	Mild to severe	165-5600 Hz	Automatic gain control; feedback control; noise suppressor	$500-$700
SearsXL	Mild to moderate	650-6262 Hz	Automatic gain control; high frequency aid	$625
In-the-ear-canal models				
ArgosyCCA	Mild to moderate	Varies with circuit	Automatic signal control; feedback control	$650-$800
Beltone Ode	Mild to moderate	Varies with circuit	Feedback control; tone control	$950-$1200
GN Danavox Discretion	Mild to moderately severe	200-6300 Hz	Automatic signal control; automatic gain; feedback control	$500-$800
In-the-ear models				
MaicoFPR	Mild to severe	230-6000 Hz	Automatic signal processing; gain control; noise suppressor	$500-$800
Miracle Ear JS	Mild to severe	200-7500 Hz	T-switch; tone control	$595-$850
Telex 28A	Mild to severe	Varies with circuit	Automatic gain control; noise suppressor; feedback control	$525-$700

*Hertz (Hz) is a measurement of sound frequency (pitch); for example, traffic noise = 250 Hz, flute high note = 9000 Hz.
Note: These are examples of aids and are not endorsed or recommended by AARP.
Modified from American Association of Retired Persons: AARP product report: hearing aids, Washington, DC, Dec 1989, The Association.

usually up to 30 days. There may be a fee for this service, but the fee may be applied to the total cost of the device at the time of purchase. Sometimes community agencies provide a rental service at little or no cost.

One should be wary of salespeople who come to homes unannounced. They may attempt to make a sale by offering to provide a ride to the store or bank to get money. One's name and address should not be given to a telephone caller who claims to be giving away a free hearing aid or gift.

Mail-Order Aids

Fitting a hearing aid so that it is comfortable and functions properly is an art rather than a science.

Consumers may be sadly disappointed if they purchase a hearing aid through the mail with the hope of saving money. Selection of a hearing aid requires the talent of an expert to obtain the proper fit, and to help in the selection process. There is no standard "one-size-fits-all" hearing aid. Hearing loss in the mild to moderate range can have many individual variations. For pieces to fit properly, a professional should take the proper impressions of the ear.[7]

Consumer Tip

Checklist for Hearing Aid Selection

Do not hesitate to ask:

- ✔ Which brand and model should be considered?
- ✔ Which brand works best with one's hearing loss?
- ✔ What special features are available? How will they help?
- ✔ Which batteries are used? How long will they last? How much do they cost?
- ✔ What is the frequency response of the aid?
- ✔ What kind of warranty is offered?
- ✔ How much does it cost?
- ✔ Is there a 30-day trial period?

From American Association of Retired Persons: AARP Product report: hearing aids, Washington, DC, Dec 1989, The Association.

Hearing Aid Dealers

Hearing aid dealers sell, lease, or rent equipment. They conduct hearing tests for selection and fitting, encourage prospective users to try amplification, make impressions for ear models, counsel the hearing impaired on ways to adapt to the aid, and repair malfunctioning hearing aids.

The National Hearing Aid Society has a voluntary certification program for qualified dispensers. In most states hearing aid dispensers are licensed under standards of competence and a strict code of ethics. In New Jersey a dealer must provide a written receipt that contains the date of sale, model specifications of product, serial number or model number of the hearing aid, and the address of the principal place of business of the licensee. If the hearing aid has been used or reconditioned, the receipt must state this and list the dispenser's license number and the terms of guarantee or warranty. In Washington the customer must receive a receipt and a description of the aid purchased, including whether it has been used or reconditioned; in addition, the customer must be told the amount charged, the terms of sale, and the consumer's rights that include the right to rescind the transaction if a licensed physician advises against the purchase by the customer by sending a notice of cancellation by certified mail within 30 days of the date of purchase.

There are three methods of evaluating a hearing aid dealer or hearing aid specialist:

1. *Licensure.* Licensure, based on an examination, is required in all states except Colorado, Massachusetts, Minnesota, and New York. It is also required in the District of Columbia.
2. *Certification.* The National Board of Hearing Instrument Specialists grants this certification status. Dealers who qualify may be designated by the letters BC-HIS. Some dealers inaccurately call themselves "certified hearing specialists." The National Hearing Aid society is another source to check for certification.
3. *Reputation.* Information frequently can be obtained from the Better Business Bureau, the local consumer protection agency, the attorney general's office, or the board that licenses dealers and audiologists. Additional clues may be obtained by consulting with several clients of the dealer.

When visiting a dealer, be aware of high pressure sales approaches and "free consultation" offers. Be prepared to ask questions such as:

1. How long has the dealer been in business?
2. Does the dealer have an established office?
3. Is the dealer a member of the National Hearing Aid Society?
4. Is the dealer a member of the state or city hearing aid dealers guild or society?
5. Does the dealer hold a license, if one's state licenses such dealers?
6. Does the dealer stand behind the product and clearly spell out the terms of the warranty or guarantee?
7. Can the dealer provide rapid and efficient repairs if the hearing aid needs to be serviced?

Consumers should understand that no hearing aid is perfect. Even the most expensive aids have limited ability to improve hearing. At best they provide an inexact amplification of sounds. These points are also important:

1. No hearing aid can restore normal or natural hearing.
2. Using a hearing aid cannot reverse, halt, or even retard the progression of hearing loss.
3. Many persons with hearing loss will not benefit from the use of a hearing aid and will not be able to consistently distinguish and understand speech sounds in noisy or group situations.

Federal Regulation

In 1977 the following federal regulations promulgated by the FDA became effective:

1. Hearing aids may be sold only to people who have a statement from a physician that a hearing aid may help, unless medical evaluation of the hearing loss is specifically waived by the purchaser. The evaluation must have occurred within 6 months before purchase. Waiver is not permissible for persons under 18 years of age. Hearing aid dispensers are not allowed to encourage prospective buyers to waive the medical examinations.
2. Patients must be advised to consult a physician or ear specialist if any of the following conditions are discovered: visible congenital deformity of the ear; history of active drainage from the ear within the previous 90 days; acute and chronic dizziness; one-sided hearing loss within the previous 90 days; evidence of wax accumulation or the presence of a foreign body in the ear canal; pain or discomfort in the ear; audiometric airborne gap equal to or greater than 15 dB at 500 Hz, 1000 Hz, and 2000 Hz.
3. Manufacturers must provide consumers with a detailed brochure that describes what hearing aids can do, how they work, and how to use them. This is intended to help prospective buyers avoid inaccurate information and misunderstandings. Dealers must let the buyers read the brochure before completing the sale.
4. Sellers of hearing aids are required to keep records for 3 years after the sale, including the required medical statement or waiver.

Several regulations outlined by the FTC further protect the consumer:

1. The buyer has the right to cancel the sale by returning the hearing aid within 30 days of delivery and receiving most of the money back.
2. People selling aids are required to identify themselves as salespersons and not "experts" when visiting homes or places of employment.
3. Misleading advertising, misrepresentations by sellers, and high-pressure sales tactics are prohibited.

Problems in Selection

Many people with hearing difficulties face problems in the selection of the appropriate aid:

1. The degree and quality of hearing loss are difficult to determine even by the experts.
2. There is no single aid that can completely compensate for any particular type of hearing loss.
3. There are hundreds of aids from which to make a selection, but there is only limited unbiased technical information to help make the decision.
4. The quality and reliability of hearing aids vary widely.
5. The quality of hearing aid services varies. Some hearing aid dealers have inadequate training and are unable to help select an aid that has performance characteristics best suited to a patient's needs.
6. The FTC has reported numerous instances of misrepresentation, insufficient information, and price fixing. Many hearing aids are sold to uninformed consumers who later find out that they cannot hear any better with them. Many sales are made in people's homes. Many salespeople exaggerate claims, are incompetent to fit devices, identify people with problems through false telephone surveys, offer free booklets or prizes, arrive unannounced, and use high-pressure sales tactics.
7. Costs may be excessive, especially for the elderly. Medicare does not pay for hearing aids, Medicaid does pay for them in some states, and private insurance companies rarely pay.

Hearing aid selection requires expert assistance. Itinerant salespeople and mail-order purchases should be avoided.[9] Here are some common deceptions in advertisements that the FTC has identified:

1. Representations, directly or by implication, that hearing aids will help all persons in all situations.
2. A promise of a "free gift" or "free valuable information"—not disclosing that respondents will be visited in their home by a salesperson.
3. A promise of a "free replica of a hearing aid," which turns out to be a nonoperative, plastic display that is brought to a person's home by a salesperson.

The attorney general of Vermont has reported these problems that have surfaced in that state: (1) unnecessarily prescribed hearing aids, (2) questionable competence of hearing aid dealer, and (3) deceptive advertising.

Cost of Hearing Aids

Hundreds of hearing aid models are available from about 40 manufacturers. The devices vary in size and shape and cost from $300 to $2000 or more. The average cost is $500 to $700. Before selecting a hearing aid, consumers should compare prices because they vary from dealer to dealer. The full cost, including a year's service, should be checked.

CONSUMER TIP

Buying A Hearing Aid

- Do not buy through the mail
- See a hearing specialist, an audiologist trained to test hearing; or an ear, nose, and throat specialist
- Insist on a 30-day trial period
- Be sure the dealer observes all the conditions for sale

One should carefully review and understand the contract and guarantee before making a purchase or signing an agreement to purchase. Answers to the following questions may be helpful.

1. Is the cost of the ear mold included in the price?
2. How long will the dealer provide free service?
3. Will the dealer lend another aid if one needs to be repaired?
4. Will a written warranty be given? Is it backed by the dealer as well as the manufacturer? Are the provisions understood?
5. Does the installment credit contract state the finance charges, annual percentage rate, and total cost?
6. Is there a fee for the 30-day trial period?
7. Can the aid be returned and exchanged? On what terms?

Since the average life of a hearing aid in daily use is about 3 years, repairs and service will probably be needed. It is important to know whether the dealer can provide service and do minor repairs. If one needs financial assistance, a physician, dealer, or local speech and hearing center can help. If not, one should write or call one of the following:

1. The local United Fund or any other social service organization
2. The state vocational rehabilitation office of the public health department
3. The Medicaid office (if eligible)
4. Veterans Administration office (if a veteran).

Sources of Information

Information about local certified hearing aid dealers can be obtained from the National Hearing Aid Society or the Better Hearing Institute. To receive information about local qualified audiologists, or to learn about the location of speech and hearing centers in one's neighborhood, one may write to the American Speech-Language-Hearing Association. Also, check the local telephone directory, hospitals, or universities for speech and hearing agencies. Information about hearing aids is available from:

National Information Center on Deafness
Gallaudet University
800 Florida Ave., N.E.
Washington, DC 20002
202-651-5051 (voice)
202-651-5052 (telecommunications device for deaf; TDD)

Self Help for Hard of Hearing People
7800 Wisconsin Ave.
Bethesda, MD 20814
301-657-2249 TDD

National Hearing Aid Society
20361 Middlebelt
Livonia, MI 48152

Better Hearing Institute
5021B Backlick Road
Annandale, VA 22003
1-800-EAR WELL

Cochlear Implants

A cochlear implant is an auditory prosthesis designed to stimulate the cochlea, the organ of the internal ear responsible for hearing. The implant system includes a small speech processor, which the patient wears in a pocket or on a belt; an external transmitter, which is positioned behind the ear; and a surgically implanted internal receiver/stimulator with one or more electrodes. The speech processor receives sound through a microphone and converts the sound into an electrical signal, which is then sent to the external transmitter and from there to the implanted receiver/stimulator. The receiver/stimulator transmits the signal to the cochlea, or inner ear, via the electrode(s). This enables the deaf person to detect medium and loud environmental sounds and speech at comfortable listening levels. The device may improve lip-reading skills. Implants are appropriate for profoundly deaf persons who cannot benefit from a hearing aid or tactile device. There are 200,000 to 250,000 individuals with profound hearing impairment in the United States. This surgical procedure should be performed by a qualified otologic surgeon. The risks of this procedure include infection, bleeding, facial nerve injury, damage to the cochlea, and anesthetic complications. The total cost for the device, hospital and surgical fees, and rehabilitation ranges from $15,000 to $25,000.

VISION AIDS

Vision aids include eyeglasses, contact lenses, and sunglasses. Annual sales of these devices in the United States total $11 billion. Ninety-five percent of people over 45 years of age wear glasses. 13% of those 65 years of age and older have some visual impairment and up to 25% may be using incorrect lens prescriptions.[10]

Individuals with poor vision face these problems:

1. Eye examinations, improperly performed, that lead to inaccurate prescriptions; as a result, many consumers purchase inappropriate lenses and possibly unneeded glasses.
2. Incompetent lens makers do not properly complete prescriptions. Willens[11] conducted a study of lenses prepared by several opticians in one city and found only one set—the cheapest—free of flaws. Most problems were minor; the lens was not lined up with the center of the eye or the bifocal dividing line was not even with the lower eyelashes. These deficiencies could lead to headaches and other discomforts.
3. Unfair, deceptive, and inaccurate advertising by eyeglass dealers. In a survey of six optical stores in New York City, Willens found that prices ranged between $65 and $129.95, and that the most expensive lenses had the most flaws.

The FTC permitted eyeglass advertising in the 1970s, with the result that numerous outlet stores emerged in many cities in the United States. Pearle Inc. has about 1000 stores, Lenscrafters has about 330 stores, Cole Vision has 800 stores, and Royal International has 644 stores. These stores offer a variety of attractive inducements such as cut-rate prices, "two-for-one" promotions, in-house optometrists, and rapid delivery of lenses. Thus priviate optometerists' business has been reduced from 80% to 50%. The American Optometric Association and many individuals claim that these chains do not provide quality care.[12] However, evidence of this has not been published.

Professional Evaluation for Eyeglasses

To identify vision problems properly, it is necessary to conduct an examination that takes 40 minutes or longer, costs $50 to $100 or more, and includes the following: general health history, external eye examination, internal eye examination (using an ophthalmoscope to illuminate the interior of the eye), test of ocular motility (coordination of eye movements), examination of the cornea, glaucoma test (tonometry), and refraction (nearsightedness/farsightedness). These tests can be completed by an ophthalmologst (M.D.) or optometrist (O.D.) (see Chapter 6 information about optometrists).

The U.S. Preventive Services Task Force stated there is no basis for visual screening of asymptomatic adults below the age of 40. The Task Force also said that there are no data to determine the optimal interval for vision screening: however, the recommended frequency comes from arbitrary opinions of experts. John O'Neil,[13] a pediatric ophthalmologist at Georgetown University Hospital in Washington, DC, stated that people aged 20 to 40 years who have healthy eyes and no eye problems present in the family, could limit examinations to one every 5 years.[13] Beyond age 40, these examinations should take place more frequently (perhaps every 2 years).

Selection of Eyeglasses

When eyes have been examined and glasses are indicated, the doctor prepares a prescription for the appropriate type of lenses. Glasses may be purchased from an opthalmologist, optometrist, or dispensing optician. Prices vary widely, so it is wise to do some shopping to compare prices. The cost of ordinary glasses depends on the nature of the lenses (plastic, glass, bifocals, tinted), the type of frame, and whether a person is covered by insurance or participates in a cooperative service. The total cost, including an eye examination, can be from $100 to $300 or more; for bifocals or trifocals, the total cost might be as much as $100 higher.

The FTC Eyeglass Rule, which requires that the consumer receives a copy of the prescription, enables consumers to shop for the best price. A study conducted by the FTC Bureau of Economics covering 12 metropolitan areas found that the average cost of eyeglasses with an examination was 24% less in cities where advertising was permitted. Large chain stores have reduced prices in many communities.

It is important that glasses be checked by the doctor or office staff after they have been received from the dispenser to be certain that the prescription has been accurately filled.

Lenses are made of plastic, glass, or a laminated combination of plastic and glass. The majority of lenses today are plastic. The FDA requires that all lenses pass a test to show they are resistant to shattering on impact. Plastic lenses are more easily scratched but weigh less and are more resistant to breakage.

Consumers with vision problems may find these guidelines useful:

1. Obtain a thorough examination by a competent ophthalmologist or optometrist
2. Shop for eyeglasses and compare prices
3. Be skeptical of the hard sell, especially of attempts to sell special ultraviolet filters for an additional $100; they probably are not needed
4. Wear the glasses for a few days, and have them checked if they do not feel right
5. If the glasses prove to be defective, do not hesitate to return them to the source of purchase to rectify the problem

Some prescription glass lenses are photochromatic (sensitive to ultraviolet light). They darken in sunlight and lighten in shade. Such lenses take a minute or two to make their changes. They do not work as well in an automobile because sufficient ultraviolet light may not filter through the windows and the darkening process may not occur. About half the lenses sold yearly are bifocals (two sets of lenses in one) or trifocals (three sets of lenses in one).

Refractive Keratotomy

It is possible to alter the refractive state of the eye by making appropriate incisions in the cornea. These incisions change the shape of the cornea and enable light rays to converge properly on the retina, thereby reducing and possibly correcting the nearsightedness. Radial keratotomy, in which radial incisons are made in the cornea, is used to correct myopia (nearsightedness).

During the early 1980s, when radial keratotomy was new, medical authorities cautioned that there were no long-term data showing that the procedure was safe and likely to permanently improve vision permanently. Many authorities also objected to the idea of surgery being performed on eyes that were not diseased when the use of eyeglasses could enable them to see adequately. Early studies found that significant percentages of people who underwent the procedure did not get the results for which they had hoped. In 1988 a panel of 35 experts consulted through the AMA Diagnostic and Therapeutic Technology Assessment (DATTA) procedure indicated a lack of consensus about the safety and effectiveness of radial keratotomy for people with a small refractive error. For people with a large refractive error (greater than −6.00 diopters), the panel concluded that RK had not been established as safe and effective.[14]

When radial keratotomy was introduced, the surgery used razor blade fragments to make many incisions in the eye. In 1982 the Prospective Evaluation Radial Keratotomy (PERK) Study was begun at nine medical centers, with 10 surgeons using a standardized technique that included diamond-bladed knives, fewer incisions, and ultrasonic measurements of the corneal thickness. The PERK study involved 435 patients who had moderate myopia in the range of −2.00 to −8.00 diopters.

The study's outcome was reported in 1990 in the *Journal of the American Medical Association.*[15] The results involved measurements on about 400 patients, most of whom were followed for 4 years. Before the operation, 69% of the eyes that were evaluated scored 20/200 or worse on the Snellen eye chart, with 48% unable to read the top line. Another 30% saw 20/50 to 20/160, and one eye saw 20/40. As of the latest follow-up, 52% of the people operated on saw 20/20 or better and 76% of the subjects saw 20/40 or better. Only 2% saw 20/200 or worse. Of the 323 patients with both eyes operated on, 64% stated that they wore no optical correction after the surgery.

The PERK researchers concluded that further changes in the shape of the cornea may occur for several years after the operation, which makes it difficult to accurately predict the outcome for an individual eye. The researchers reported these additional findings:

1. Losses of vision after surgery were not usually severe. Only two of the subjects had eye conditions that were not correctable with glasses or contact lenses to 20/25 or better. One year after surgery, 48% of the patients were very satisfied, 42% were moderately satisfied, and 10% were dissatisfied.
2. Many patients reported the presence of radiating light around light sources such as headlights or street lights at night. The extent or severity of night glare was unknown. Most patients reported that it did not interfere with their normal activities, but some stated that it interfered severely with night driving.
3. Severe complications were exceedingly rare and

did not occur in the PERK study.

Bender[16] made the following supportive comments about radial keratotomy:

1. The use of diamond-bladed knives and ultrasonic measurements of the corneal thickness have reduced the tendency toward overcorrection and improved the predictability of the procedure.
2. This is not a perfect method. The major complications are refractive ones. Overcorrection will reduce distance acuity and near acuity, especially in patients with presbyopia. These people will need reading glasses or bifocals.
3. Two thirds of the patients achieved their goal of eliminating glasses or contact lenses. Myopia can be reduced and uncorrected visual acuity can be improved in all cases.
4. Radial keratotomy is the most widely applied and most predictable refractive procedure, but it is not suitable for all myopic patients.

Newer techniques involving computerized assessment, precisely calculated cutting patterns, and lasers have made refractive keratotomy much more predictable than it was only a few years ago. Astigmatic keratotomy is used to correct uneven curvatures of the eye. This procedure is gaining wide use, especially after lens-implant surgery for cataracts, because it may correct all refractive error and free the patient from dependence upon eyeglasses. Hexagonal keratotomy is being performed to correct farsightedness, but long-term follow-up data are not yet available.

People contemplating refractive surgery should discuss the potential benefits and risks with an ophthalmologist who is well regarded by the medical and optometric communities. Although the procedures (especially radial keratotomy) have few complications, the risk involved may not justify their use if adequate vision can be achieved with eyeglasses or contact lenses.

Contact Lenses

It is estimated that 20 million people wear contact lenses. Not everyone can wear them, and they do not correct all vision problems. At least half of these people use soft contacts, and about 4 million wear extended-wear lenses. The new types of lenses are the rigid gas-permeable lenses and the disposable extended-wear lenses. However, except for extreme nearsightedness, one's vision is no better with contacts than with regular glasses. Many individuals nevertheless purchase them for cosmetic reasons and they also serve a useful purpose in athletics. They are especially helpful for correcting nearsighted problems and after cataract surgery. Contacts should not be used by individuals with these problems: allergies, eyelid infections, blocked tear ducts, use of antihistamines or blood pressure medications that have a drying effect on the eyes, and inability to manage the insertion or proper care of contacts.

Contact lenses are plastic discs worn in front of the pupil and in contact with the cornea. They adhere to the cornea by capillary action on the normal layer of tear fluids. There are many types of lenses, but the major ones are described in Table 23-4.

A person who wants contact lenses should follow these procedures:

Eye examination: This should be thorough and completed by an ophthalmologist or optometrist. It will reveal whether an individual is a good candidate for contacts through the use of tests for corneal sensitivity and lacrimal (tear) secretion. The examination will also involve a refraction test to prepare a prescription for correcting the vision problem.

Fitting examination: This procedure involves measuring the curvature of the eye to determine the type of lens needed. The examination is performed by an ophthalmologist, optometrist, or optician.

The FTC's "Eyeglass Rule" mandates that an eye specialist must give a copy of the prescription to the patient when requested after the examination. These specialists are not required to provide the results of the fitting examination. However, some will do it voluntarily.

The following people should not wear contact lenses:

1. Elderly people with chronic dryness of eyes, who are often predisposed to inflammation and infection if contacts are worn.
2. Certain people with such medical problems as hand tremors, Parkinson's disease, severe arthritis (causing insertion and removal difficulties), hay fever (pollen may lodge behind the lens), diabetes, epilepsy, or other conditions that might involve loss of consciousness should wear contacts with caution.
3. Workers exposed to dust, fumes, chemicals, high temperatures, foreign bodies, and other materials that could become trapped under the contact lens and damage the cornea.

Cost of Contact Lenses

The prices charged for contact lenses include the actual cost of the lenses, the amount of time spent to fit the lenses and to provide follow-up care, the nature of the warranty, and the value of the services as determined by the practitioner. Table 23-4 compares the advantages, disadvantages, and prices of different types of contact lenses together with their problems and risks. Prices should be interpreted carefully because they may or may not include the initial examination, follow-up care, a good lens care kit, or a good warranty.

Soft Contact Lenses

Soft contact lenses are very popular. However, they are more expensive, correct a limited number of visual problems, must be stored wet, and are more likely to act as a breeding ground for bacteria that may cause eye infections. Soft contact lenses and rigid gas-permeable lenses are useful after injuries and postcataract surgery. The FDA recommended that manufacturers advertise that soft lenses should not be worn continuously for more than 7 days. Physicians advise daily removal of the lenses for cleaning and to rest the eyes.

Interference With Lens Function

These factors can interfere with lens function:[19]

Very low humidity. Dry heat, air conditioning, extremely dry weather, airplane cabins, wind, and hair blow-dryers can make the lenses uncomfortable

Slow blinking rate. When watching television the eyes may become dry

Cold pills and diuretics. Use of these substances can decrease the amount of tears; colds and watery eyes can make lenses uncomfortable

Pregnancy, menstruation, or birth control pills. These conditions and drugs may cause dry eyes in some women

Table 23–4

Comparison of Contact Lenses[17,18]

Type	Material	Advantages	Disadvantages	Problems/risks
Daily Wear				
Hard lens $75-$200	PMMA (polymethyl methylacrylate)	Good acuity; stable; resists deposit formation; relatively inexpensive; little care needed; can be worn 10-16 hours without too much discomfort	Covers small area; easier to dislodge; dust can get under; uncomfortable 2-4 weeks; often irritability; not for extended wear	Fatigue; corneal infection
Soft lens $150-$200	Hydrogel (30%-80% water)	Comfortable from first day; covers large eye area; less likely to dislodge; good for sports; fits snugly; wears longer	Vision may not be as sharp as hard lens; more prone to deposits and bacterial contamination; needs more cleaning and disinfecting; replacement may be needed every 6-8 months; will not withstand heat disinfection; not useful for severe astigmatism	Greater possibility for infection, corneal ulcers

Continued.

Table 23–4

Comparison of Contact Lenses[17,18]—cont'd

Type	Material	Advantages	Disadvantages	Problems/risks
Extended Wear				
Gas-permeable lens approximately $400 pair	Silicone acrylate polymer Cellulose acetate butyrate	More comfortable for those who must wear rigid lens; midway between rigid and soft; hard yet flexible; sharper vision; more durable than soft lens; wear 1 to 7 days; contamination more easily handled	Easier to scratch, chip; requires more care; more costly; longer to get used to; requires more expert fitting than soft lens	Possible corneal ulcers; risks not completely known
Soft lens $250-$450	Hydrogel	Wear up to 7 days; wear while asleep; most comfortable; good for some cataract removal patients	Need careful cleaning and disinfecting; protein deposits form; specialist must check 3-4 times in first 6 months; costly; may require more frequent replacement; more complications; will not withstand heat disinfection	Corneal ulcer; conjunctivitis
Disposable soft lens $500 yearly	Hydrogel	Lesser risk of infection; no maintenance; minimized protein deposit formation; wear up to 7 days and discard	Need professional eye checks 4 times yearly (vs. 1-2 times yearly for other soft contact lenses); less infection safe	Corneal ulcer; conjunctivitis risks not known

Note: These lenses are best for myopia. Bifocal contacts have not been generally successful in providing good vision for reading and distance.
Annual maintenance costs for cleaning and disinfection: hard lens = $30-$40; soft lens = $40-$80; extended lens = $70-$100.
From Turturo MA et al: Contact lens complications, Am J Emerg Med 8:228-233, 1990; and Pros and cons of soft lenses, Public Citizen Health Research Group Health Letter, 6(11):7, 1990.

Aerosol sprays. They can be irritating if sprayed into the eyes

Care of Contact Lenses

Contact lenses require special care to protect wearers from irritations, infection, and other eye problems. Improper lens care can also damage lenses and shorten lens life. Surveys have shown that most lens wearers do not follow lens care instructions. Table 23-5 provides useful information for contact wearers.

These are the procedures that wearers should

Table 23-5

Caring For Contact Lenses*

	Clean Remove surface dirt	Rinse Rinse dirt away	Enzyme* Removes deep deposits	Disinfect/store To eliminate bacteria	Rinse* Rinse dirt away	Wet Prepare lens surface	Insert	Lubricate/rewet For comfort	Clean lens case
Hard	✓	✓				✓	✓	✓	✓
Rigid Gas-Permeable	✓	✓	✓	✓		✓	✓	✓	✓
Soft (Daily and Extended-Wear)	✓	✓	✓	✓	✓			✓	✓

*NOTE: *Always wash your hands before you handle your lenses. This is the most effective infection control procedure you can practice. The optional procedures, marked by an asterisk, should be followed as needed or as recommended by your eye-care practitioner. For extended-wear lenses, the routine should be followed every time they are removed (as often as directed by your practitioner). This is a guideline; some procedures require more specific directions for use. Always follow your practitioner's directions.*

Source: Contact Lenses: The Better The Care The Safer The Wear. DHHS Public. No (FDA)91-4220, 1991.

follow after washing hands:

Hard lens care: Hard lenses are the simplest to care for and should be:

1. Cleaned daily with a chemical solution to remove tears, mucus, and other materials.
2. Rinsed and soaked in a commercially available sterile-saline solution to keep lenses sterile. Do not use homemade saline solutions using tap water or distilled water (not sterile). Leave the lenses in the solution overnight to clean and prevent dehydration.
3. Lubricated by using a commercial contact lens wetting solution before the lenses are placed in the eye.
4. Have lens polished yearly by a professional to remove built-up materials.
5. Clean and disinfect the storage box regularly.

Soft lens care: Plastic may serve as a breeding place for bacteria. Plastic also tends to collect surface debris from tears, dust, smoke, hair sprays, mascara, and other substances that may cause irritation and infection of the cornea.

1. The lenses should be cleaned after each wearing by placing several drops of the cleaner on each side of the lens and rubbing each side vigorously with the forefinger. The lenses should then be thoroughly rinsed to remove residue that can irritate the eye or cloud the lenses. They should be air-dryed between uses. Cleaning solutions should be used every time lenses are removed from the eyes.
2. After cleaning, the lenses should be disinfected by one of two methods: (1) chemical disinfection and hydrogen peroxide sterilization are procedures whereby lenses are immersed in a chemical solution for at least 4 hours, preferably at night, to kill bacteria. (2) Heat disinfection (hot sterilization) involves the use of a saline solution, a plastic carrying case, and an electric heating unit ($40 to $60). The lenses are immersed in the saline solution in the carrying case and placed in the heating unit, where they are left until the temperature is high enough to kill any contaminating microorganisms. The yearly cost of the materials needed is about $150. (The procedure works best on hard lenses.)
3. Rinse and wet the lenses using a wetting solution before insertion in the eye. Do not use saliva; it may cause infection.
4. Clean and disinfect storage case frequently.

Extended wear lens care: These lenses are too fragile to be heat sterilized. Therefore, a chemical disinfectant should be used. Follow the same procedures listed for soft lens care.

Gas-permeable lens care: These lenses should be washed daily in a chemical solution and stored overnight in a conditioner. Clean them weekly with an enzyme solution. Rinse them with distilled water; tap water leaves a residue.

Lens Wearer Problems

Contact lens wearers are more prone to ophthalmologic conditions than the general population.

The *Mayo Clinic Health Letter* identified the nature of these problems as follows:[20]

Overuse. The cornea can be without oxygen; this may result in blurred vision, pain, tearing, redness, and sensitivity to light.

Corneal vascularization. Tiny blood vessels may appear if an adequate amount of oxygen is not provided; blurred vision may occur.

Corneal warpage. Shape may change; usually associated with hard lenses.

Giant papillary conjunctivitis. "Pink-eye" is relatively common among soft lenses wearers.

Sensitivity to solutions. Sensitivity to light or allergic reactions may take place; may require use of a different cleaning solution.

Corneal abrasion. Scratching of lens may interfere with vision.

Corneal ulcer. Vision may decrease from a corneal ulcer, with eye becoming red, painful, and sensitive to light; corneal perforation and vision loss may occur.

Smith and McRae[21] reported that contact lenses continually collect eye-irritating protein and muscinous deposits, bacteria, and that hard lenses may decrease blood supply to the cornea. These factors may cause many of the conditions previously identified. Individuals who remove lenses daily generally have only a small risk of infection, redness and pain.

Smith and McRae[21] noted, however, that two studies completed at Massachusetts Eye and Ear Infirmary and the Harvard Medical School revealed that people who used extended-wear soft lenses have a 10% to 15% greater risk of eye problems than those people who used soft lenses. The risk increases with the number of days the lenses are worn without removal. One of the studies found that the overall incidence of ulcerative keratitis was 1 in 300 to 450 people per year.

Extended-wear lens users, who wear them overnight, have a 5 times greater risk of problems than those who remove the lenses nightly. Extended-wear-rigid-gas-permeable lens and disposable lens risks are not completely known. It is assumed the risks may be less than other extended-wear lenses since less care is required. Olsen,[22] however, indicated that he is not sure that their use will reduce the incidence of ulcers. It has been reported that users of disposable lenses for 1 to 2 weeks are vulnerable to many eye problems.

Problems with extended-wear contact lenses can be greatly reduced with hygienic care that includes periodic replacement and removal of lenses from the eyes and systematic cleaning with solutions, tablets, cleaners, enzymes, and sterilizing equipment.

Tips for Lens Wearers

1. Do not wear lenses longer than is normal or prescribed, even if they feel comfortable; this may cause unnecessary problems.
2. Remove lenses and consult a physician immediately when these signs of problems appear: red or painful eyes, sudden change in vision, repeated eye irritation, excess secretions, or "spectacular blur."
3. Wait about 20 minutes after arising in the morning before inserting lenses; corneas may be slightly swollen and need to return to normal shape.
4. Use cosmetics with care when wearing contact lenses. Mascara, eye shadow, eye liners, and face powder may lead to ocular discomfort if the cosmetic gets into the eyes. Hair sprays, perfume, cologne, and nail polish contain solvents that can cause corneal edema and affect refraction. Contaminated substances can lead to infection. It is important to wash the hands and rinse them thoroughly before handling lenses.
5. Insert lenses before applying makeup; foundation or powder base, whether liquid, cream, or powder, is difficult to completely wash off hands.
6. Replace mascara supplies three to four times per year; contamination with bacteria is common and can lead to a corneal infection.
7. Athletes (such as baseball or tennis players) who must stare intently at a ball should consider using soft contact lenses, which cover the cornea completely and reduce blurred vision.[23]

Consumer Guidelines When Shopping for Contact Lenses

1. Be leery of stores that advertise cut rates; lenses may be inferior, older designs that were bought by the store at bargain prices.
2. Find out whether follow-up care is provided; some stores merely provide a booklet or kit.
3. Judge practitioners by the amount of time devoted to prescribing and fitting lenses and the provision of follow-up care; do not judge by price alone. The first fitting should take at least 1 hour, and the practitioner should give precise instructions for insertion, removal, and proper care.
4. Inquire about initial and ongoing costs.
5. Shop around for lenses and beware of fitters offering only one kind.
6. Seek answers to these questions:
   a. What is the charge for an eye examination, fitting, adjustments, a lens care kit, and follow-up visits? An unlimited, reasonably priced package may be the best deal.

CONSUMER TIP

Care of Contact Lenses

- Contact lenses must be kept clean to prevent infections
- Do not wear contact lenses longer than recommended
- Disinfect contact lenses before storing
- Periodically clean and disinfect the storage case
- Redisinfect any lens stored longer than 1 day
- In disk systems, keep the disk dry and drain residual fluid from the case

Louis Wilson, M.D.
Emory University Clinic

b. What is the refund policy? Does it apply if one is unable adapt to the lenses.
c. How many types and brands of lenses are sold? It takes several tries to find the right lens; a large selection increases one's chances of a good fit.
d. How much is the charge for replacement lenses? How long must one wait for a replacement lens?
e. Will a copy be provided of the complete prescription for eyeglasses and contact lenses? A prescription will be useful for comparative shopping.

Ready-to-Wear Glasses

Ready-to-wear reading glasses are available in many stores and are priced from $10 to $20. They are available in 10 different powers. The power is indicated by a "focus number" on each pair, which can be translated into the standard prescription unit, the diopter, as shown here:

Focus number	Equivalent diopters
32	+1.25
26	+1.50
22	+1.75
20	+2.00
18	+2.25
16	+2.50
14	+2.75
12	+3.25
10	+4.00
8	+5.00

As a temporary measure, if all one needs are magnifying lenses to make print look larger, one might check with an eye doctor to see if these glasses are usable and which focus number is best. An eye specialist should be consulted for eyeglass needs. These commercial reading glasses may cause headaches, tired eyes, and other symptoms of eyestrain.

Glasses By Mail

Glasses are available by mail from various sources but may present these problems: (1) the lenses may not be ground according to prescription specifications, (2) the glasses cannot be fitted properly, which may result in discomfort and difficulty in use, (3) the consumer has little or no recourse to complain about deficiencies, and (4) mail-back attempts together with communication complexities may make it impossible to obtain satisfactory results.

The cost savings may be important to the consumer, but they must be weighed against the identified problems. However, an alternative to buying glasses by mail may be to take advantage of the discount prices advertised in the local newspapers and magazines. These suppliers may also warrant careful investigation, but problems are more easily handled in one's community than by mail. In addition, eye specialists may be more readily available to check the accuracy of prescription specifications.

Sunglasses

The eyes need protection from sun rays and from special sunlamps that emit ultraviolet light blue light. Ultraviolet B (UVB) light can damage the cornea and produce a painful condition known as photokeratitis. Scientists also believe that prolonged exposure to UVB light may cause cataracts. Ultraviolet A (UVA) light may also cause cataracts, and it may cause retinal damage and be related to the loss of vision in old age. Blue light has been linked to retinal damage. Sunglasses offer the best protection from the sun. They are better than visor hats and parasols, although the later can provide additional protection. The FDA and the Sunglass Association of America have developed a labeling agreement whereby sunglass labels will indicate the "use category" of the product.[24] The different levels of protection for different environments are:[25]

Cosmetic. Lightly tinted lenses for use in nonharsh light; screens at least 70% of UVB, 20% of UVA, and less than 60% of visible light.

General Purpose. Medium to dark tinted lenses for use in outdoor activities, such as boating, flying, and hiking; screens at least 96% of UVB, 60% of UVA, and 60% to 92% of visible light.

Special Purpose. Recommended for use in very bright environments, such as when skiing, mountain climbing, or at tropical beaches; screens at least 99% of UVB, at least 60% of UVA, and 20% to 97% of visible light.

When selecting sunglasses, consumers may find these recommendations helpful:[26]

1. *Buy glasses that meet the standards of the American National Standard Institute (ANSI).* This is the organization that established the standards accepted by the FDA and the Sunglass Association of America. Look for these ANSI labels: General

Purpose, Special Purpose, and Cosmetic. People who spend much time outdoors should be sure that their glasses provide 100% protection against UVA and UVB rays.

2. *Lens darkness and color.* Glasses should block 75% to 90% of visible light and should have a transmission value of 10% to 25%. If no value is listed, look in a mirror, if you see your eyes in the mirror then the lenses are not dark enough. Dark green or dark gray lenses cause least distortion of natural colors. Amber lenses ("blue-blocking") are favored by boaters, pilots, hunters, and skiers only for clarity.
3. *Large shape and size.* Wraparound frames keep lenses close to eyes and offer the most protection. When driving be sure peripheral vision is not blocked.
4. *Style and fit.* Glasses should fit snugly and comfortably and not press on nose, temples, bone, or cartilage around ears. Put glasses on and bend head forward to see if they stay in place.
5. *Type of lens.* Select from these types:

   Polarized: Cuts glare; use when driving or boating.

   Gradient: Single-gradient lenses are dark on top and light on bottom; cuts glare; useful in driving. Double-gradient lenses are dark on top and bottom and lighter in middle; for sports that include skiing, tennis, and sailing; useful in sand and snow where glare is above and below; not good for driving.

   Photochromatic: Lenses change color with varying light intensity; different times needed to change color (30 seconds needed to darken lenses and 5 minutes needed to lighten lenses).

   Mirrored: Easily scratched and often thin; glare protection provided, but little ultraviolet light protection.
6. *Material in lens.* Polycarbonate plastic for safety is tough but easily scratched; better quality lenses have scratched-resistant coating.
7. *Quality of lens.* Check for distortion; hold glasses at arms length and look through lenses at a straight line in distance, then slowly move lens across the line and if it sways or bends, lenses are imperfect.
8. *Blue light.* Glasses that block 75% of visible light will block a significant amount of blue light.
9. *Price.* Cost can vary from $2 to $145 and an additional $10 to $15 for scratch-resistant coating. Bausch and Lomb's Ray-Bans sell for at least $50 and meet ANSI standards. A less expensive alternative, less than $20, is Akorn Inc.'s Solar Shield glasses. For about $50 an optician will sell nonprescription glasses with a coating that blocks UVA and UBV rays.[27]

Sunglasses are available with or without prescription lenses. Prescription lenses may be necessary for people with vision problems, especially for those who plan to work, read, or play in sunlight. They can be made of plastic, glass, or both with light-inhibiting substances mixed into the color to coat the lens. Plastic lenses are lighter than glass and are less likely to shatter from blows, but are more easily scratched.

The American Optometric Association says "quality" nonprescription glasses have lenses that are free of distortion, imperfection, and mismatching of color and absorptive power. A simple test, stated in #7 of the previous recommendations, is recommended to check refractive quality. Also check to see that the coloring in the lens is even and that one lens is not darker than the other.

Consumers should consider these tips before buying a pair of sunglasses:

1. Do not use cost as the only guide to quality. Check the manufacturer's tag to be sure that the glasses meet or exceed the minimum standards of the FDA or the ANSI.
2. Advertising claims such as "guaranteed safe," "certified," "sharpens color," "eliminates headlight glare," "penetrates haze," and "helps you see better" are essentially meaningless.
3. Look carefully for scratches, bubbles, and other flaws on lenses. Such irregularities often cause distored images and may lead to headaches, eye strain, nausea, and dizziness.
4. Lenses should filter out 70% to 85% of the sunlight or glare in a car and 85% to 95% at the beach or on a ski slope. Manufacturers are not required to list these percentages on their labels, although some are doing so voluntarily. Visual comfort should be the main criterion for selection. Lenses should be made of high-quality glass or impact-resistant plastic.
5. The lenses should be equally dark throughout the entire surface.
6. For nonprescription glasses, the wraparound lenses are better because they avoid distortion and fit closer to the eyes, giving more complete coverage. For skiing, wrap-arounds may protect

peripheral vision against sun glare.

7. Polarization helps reduce glare and makes objects look clearer.
8. Plastic lenses are lighter and safer for children but scratch easily. Since January 1972, most lenses must be labeled "impact resistant," as required by the FDA.
9. Glasses should fit comfortably at the nose, temples, and ears. They should be as close to the eyes as possible without touching the lashes, and side pieces of the frame should not block vision.

These following considerations about sunglasses are also important. Never wear them while driving at night; people, poles, and other vehicles become more difficult to see. Do not wear glasses indoors or in dim illumination, except on the advice of an eye specialist; this will make your eyes more sensitive to light outdoors. Never look at the sun directly, either with or without glasses; the rays may burn the retina and result in permanent damage and loss of vision. When boating, wear glasses that will not cloud or mist. Those who are partially colorblind should obtain prescription glasses from an eye specialist. Those who depend on sunglasses for eye comfort most of the time should also consult an eye specialist.

Equipment Used by Physicians

Numerous devices are used in medical practice. Among these devices are: x-ray machines, electrocardiographs, fluoroscopes, artificial heart valves and pacemakers, surgical implant materials, clinical thermometers, heart-lung machines, ultrasound equipment, CAT scanners, and prostheses. It is estimated that 3000 to 4000 manufacturers make about 20,000 devices that support a $3 to $5 billion industry. The growth of scientific knowledge and technology, together with the advances in medicine, have resulted in the continual creation of new instruments, equipment, and materials.

It would be impossible in this section to provide information about all the medical devices used by physicians. This section discusses several types that have received media attention.

The application of electronics to an increasing number of new materials in medical care has resulted in thousands of lives being saved through such techniques and devices as intensive-care monitoring, internal pacemakers, and artificial heart valves. These major advances have been accompanied by the potential for significant hazards. The nature and extent of these problems were reported by the National Center for Health Statistics from its 1988 survey of 122,000 people. In February 1991 the Center released information from 5592 individuals who said they had used one or more implanted medical devices. Depending on the type of device, 20% to 50% of the recipients claimed to have had problems, and 10% required a replacement. Table 23-6 summarizes the data.

This section emphasizes several types of "high-technology" equipment, while the following section covers equipment used primarily in home care. Consumers who have questions about the risks and effectiveness of any medical device should not hesitate to seek answers from their physicians. Decisions involving some of the newly developed devices and procedures can be complex and should receive appropriate deliberation.

Table 23–6

Problems with Implanted Devices*

Type of device	Number of devices	Approximate percentage of people reporting problems
Intraocular lens	3765	(50%)
Artificial Joint	1625	(33%)
Ear Vent Tubes	1494	(33%)
Pacemaker	460	(25%)
Artificial heart valve	253	(20%)

From More than one million implants needed to be replaced annually: better pre-market testing needed, Public Citizen Health Research Group Health Letter, 7(5):11-12, 1991.

*122,000 people were surveyed.

Pacemakers

Pacemakers are implanted to correct abnormal heart rhythms. They provide electrical nerve impulses that are needed when the normal impulses fail. It is estimated that over 175,000 pacemakers are implanted annually, and some 700,000 people now wear these devices. The cost of this procedure, including hospitalization, is about $15,000. Dr. Brendon Phibbs stated that the best physicians cannot be absolutely certain when pacemakers are necessary or desirable.[28] He advised physicians to be sure that a patient's irregularity is not caused by a drug reaction, a temporary abnormality, or a passing, correctable disease. Dr. Phibbs also reported that 25% of pacemakers implanted each year should be removed because they could trigger medical complications, including thrombosis and embolism, infection, and irregular heart beat. If infection appears and the pacemaker is not removed, the death rate could reach as high as 66%. The FDA has estimated that as many as 20% of pacemakers fail after 3 years.

In 1985 the U.S. Senate Special Committee on Aging[29] concluded that one third of the implanted pacemakers were unnecessary, and of the 30,000 replacements, two thirds were unnecessary. It was reported to the Committee that some companies paid physicians as much as $150 or more for each device they implanted, with some physicians completing as many as 15 implants a week. Senator John Heinz, chairman of the Committee, estimated that at least half of the $2 billion that Medicare paid for these devices was wasted.

The FDA has established a pacemaker registry to which physicians who implant, remove, or replace cardiac pacemakers and leads are to provide certain information about their patients and the devices. Failure to comply can result in the loss of Medicare payments. This information will be used to track the performance of pacemakers and pacemaker leads.

The Public Citizen Health Research Group study in 1982 concluded that 22.7% of implanted cardiac pacemakers in Maryland in 1979–1980 were unnecessary and another 13.4% were questionable.[30] In 1988 the *New England Journal of Medicine* reported a study in Philadelphia in which 20% of the pacemakers were implanted without adequate indication of need and an additional 35% were only possibly indicated. The National Center for Health Statistics study in 1988 showed that 25% of the implanted pacemakers developed problems.

Consumers faced with a decision about a pacemaker should obtain advice from a board-certified cardiologist. They should know the risks of not obtaining a pacemaker and whether alternative forms of treatment might be available. Do not hesitate to obtain a second opinion. The consumer should be ready to raise such questions as: Is the coronary irregularity due to a drug reaction or to a temporary abnormality? Is the pacemaker likely to need replacement? The consumer should also ask about the surgeon's experience and success rate.

Artificial Hearts

Dr. William DeVries was the first surgeon to implant a total artificial heart (TAH) in humans. All four of his patients died, but one survived 620 days and another 488 days. Cole[31] reported that research with artificial hearts has also been conducted at Pennsylvania State University with somewhat better results. However, the researchers used the artificial heart as a "bridge" to transplantation; it was used to keep patients alive until a transplant was available. Seventeen patients were maintained on the artificial heart while awaiting transplantation with these results: three were fully rehabilitated, three were discharged from the hospital and recuperated at home, several remained in the hospital, and seven died awaiting or following the transplant.

Dr. Barney Clark, a dentist in Seattle, was the first recipient of the Jarvik-7 permanent artificial heart in 1982. He died of an infection. Strokes and infections doomed experiments with the Jarvik-7. About 150 more patients received temporary Jarvik-7 artificial hearts as a bridge to heart transplants. Approval for the use of the Jarvik heart was withdrawn by the government in 1990 because of manufacturer deficiencies. Boffey[32] said that expert heart surgeons believe that the artificial heart is not as good as the human heart transplant.

The majority of physicians who have implanted artificial hearts and who specialize in human heart transplants believe that the current artificial heart is a temporary bridge until human heart transplants can be arranged.

The estimated survival rate for those patients with artificial hearts is 3.5 years at an approximate cost of $200,000 for implantation. There are between 17,000 and 35,000 patients each year who may be considered candidates for artificial hearts.

There are some 1000 individuals who qualify each year for transplants, but only 600 human hearts become available.

The FDA has allowed artificial heart implant research to continue under more controlled conditions.[33] They will more closely supervise clinical trials and only give approval to experimentation on a case-by-case basis.

The FDA has given a Houston hospital approval to begin experimental use of a portable, battery-powered mechanical device to help a failing heart to pump blood until a donor can be found.[34] It is called a "left ventricle assist device" because it takes over or boosts the work of a failing left ventricle. It will be the first heart device to keep a person alive while letting the patient move freely. The new artificial ventricle was implanted in five patients while they awaited a heart transplant.

A panel from the Institute of Medicine stated that self-contained mechanical pumps (total artificial hearts) will be implanted in patients to replace human hearts in 20 years at an estimated cost of $100,000 per heart.[35] The Institute also stated that 58,000 to 70,000 patients annually could be candidates for some type of mechanical heart device (implanted ventricle assist device that costs $50,000) and 10,000 to 20,000 patients will need a complete artificial heart.

Artificial Heart Valves

About 15,000 people each year in the United States undergo cardiac valve surgery. Approximately 85,000 men, women, and children have been helped by the implantation of an artificial valve in their heart.

There are two categories of artificial heart valves used: mechanical and tissue. The mechanical types include: (1) the cage-ball design, which has been on the market the longest; valve-related deaths using this device have dropped 50% and the 5-year survival rate has climbed to 76% with the failure rate being less than 1%, (2) the pivoting disk, and (3) the bileaflet type (very new). Tissue valves work more like human valves and are made of either pig heart valves or cow pericardium (tissue covering the heart). The patients with tissue valves do not require follow-up medication. However, such valves do not wear as well as mechanical valves and may weaken in time.[36]

Starting in 1984 the Public Citizen Health Research Group (HRG) tried to persuade the FDA to recall the Bjork-Shiley Converse-Concave heart valve from the marketplace. HRG claimed that 389 had failed because of strut failure (fracture) with 178 deaths. Early in 1990 a subcommittee of the Energy and Commerce Committee of Congress criticized the company for not reporting critical failures to the FDA and stated that it had ignored warnings from a FDA district office. After HRG filed a class action suit against the manufacturer in 1990, the company finally yielded and agreed to notify 20,000 patients with implants about the hazards of their valves.[38,39] The FDA accepted the company's plan, which also included notifying 19,000 heart specialists and over 450 hospitals in the United States.[40]

Individuals who may need heart valve surgery should become aware of the types of devices available and be ready to select a highly qualified surgeon to perform the operation. They should also ask questions concerning the failure rate, risks and benefits, and alternative procedures.

Hip Replacement Operations

Almost 100,000 hip replacement operations, at a cost of $15,000 each, are completed each year in the United States. Replacements are advisable for individuals with severe pain and major disability from arthritis (osteoarthritis, rheumatoid arthritis) or after an injury.

Nine out of ten operations are successful, with a death rate of 1%. Two major problems remain: infection and long-term loosening of the hardware, which necessitates repeated surgery in about 10% of the patients. Almost half of the artificial hip replacements fail within 15 years because stress loosens the cement that binds the artificial hip bone. The main factors that determine successful outcome are the ability of the surgeon and hospital support team. Consumers are wise to ask questions before having this surgery performed, and to select a surgeon who has a good success rate.

Microwave Diathermy

Microwave diathermy is the medical use of heat produced by microwave radiation. This form of treatment produces a deep-heating effect on muscles 2 inches beneath the skin. It helps to increase the flow of blood and increases cellular membrane permeability and metabolic rate. It can reduce pain and promote quicker healing of tissues.

Diathermy is used by physical therapists, family

Personal Glimpse

Did You Know?

Surgeons in operating rooms may be calling out for "Krazy Glue, plaster of paris, or a zipper." Physicians are using household products daily as medical devices:

- *Krazy Glue* (cyanoacrylate) is used to suture skin wounds; it can patch an aneurysm (weakened part of blood vessel). If injected into the blood stream, it can shut off circulation to a tumor, thereby shrinking it and enabling surgical removal.
- *Plaster of paris* (calcium sulfate hemihydrate) is used to fill holes and cracks in bones. Plaster of paris may be mixed with a mineral derived from sea coral that results in a compound that is identical to freeze-dried human bone.
- *Zippers* are used to close the abdomen of some patients who are undergoing pancreatic surgery; zippers reduce bleeding and enzyme leakage into the abdominal cavity.

Although these items have not been approved by the FDA under the Medical Device Law, they did not have to be demonstrated as safe and effective because they were marketed before 1976. However, the Safe Medical Device Act of 1990 may change this if problems develop.

San Francisco Chronicle, Sept. 12, 1991

physicians, chiropractors, and various medical technicians. Proponents of this treatment may recommend its use for bursitis, tendonitis, arthritis, fractures, sinus conditions, eye conditions, and other problems. College and university athletic trainers routinely use this procedure in the treatment of muscle pulls and sprains.

Microwave radiation has resulted in cataracts in patients treated for sinus conditions, damage to the eyes when neck and shoulder injuries are treated, and severe skin and underlying tissue burns. The FDA cautions consumers to check with qualified medical experts before undergoing microwave diathermy treatment.

Ultrasound Equipment

In diagnostic ultrasound, a small hand-held transducer (an electronic device that transforms electrical energy into sound energy) is moved across the surface of the patient's body or inserted into a body cavity (such as the vagina or rectum). High-frequency, inaudible sound waves travel into the body and bounce back as they encounter bones and soft tissues. The pattern that these waves produce appears on a screen and can be studied and photographed for later reference. The use of diagnostic ultrasound is increasing rapidly.

There are four general areas for ultrasound use: surgery, dentistry, physical therapy, and diagnosis. In surgery, a focused ultrasound beam or a vibrating probe (scalpel) produces an intended cutting effect on tissue. These procedures are fairly common in other parts of the world, but are largely experimental in the United States. In dentistry, an ultrasonic scaler vibrates at high speed to remove calculus from tooth surfaces and for gum (gingival) curettage. In physical therapy, ultrasound has long been used to produce deep-heat effects to treat muscle and joint pain and stiffness. It is a standard treatment by physical therapists and chiropractors and now it shows promise of being an adjunctive treatment to cancer chemotherapy. In diagnosis, ultrasound is increasingly being used for head-to-toe identification of illness and disease conditions and as a routine part of maternal and prenatal care. It is the latter use that especially concerns FDA and others who urge more action in its use.

A significant number of pregnant women receive at least one ultrasound examination. Ultrasound is invaluable in high-risk pregnancies where the known benefits outweigh the theoretical risks. However, the National Center for Devices and Radiological Health of the FDA has found no scientific evidence to support routine use during pregnancy.

Ultrasound can be used to check the well-being of the fetus during pregnancy and labor.[41] It can reveal the number of fetuses, age, size, fetal position, some birth defects, and other vital information. Three kinds of utlrasound can be used during pregnancy, for different purposes:

1. *Real-time.* Still pictures are taken in rapid succes-

sion that will detect heart beat, placenta, movement of arms and legs, and the number and position of fetuses.
2. *Doppler.* This is used before and during labor to provide audible heart beat signals.
3. *Vaginal.* Helps to diagnose the cause of bleeding and pain, or an ectopic pregnancy (egg growing outside uterus); vaginal ultrasound also can detect some birth defects early in the pregnancy.

In more than 20 years of use, there have been no reports of harmful effects associated with the use of ultrasound. However, reasonable caution in using ultrasound during pregnancy is advised by scientists and medical groups. The American College of Radiology Commission on Ultrasound has urged that ultrasound examinations of the pregnant uterus be limited to medically indicated cases and not be performed routinely.[42]

A transrectal ultrasound device uses high-frequency sound waves that may improve the efficiency of detecting prostate cancer (rather than by a doctor's examining finger) has had encouraging success for only small tumors. However, studies completed at St. Joseph Mercy Hospital in Ann Arbor and the Memorial Sloan-Kettering Cancer Institute have questioned the accuracy and selectivity of the device to screen ambulatory patients.[43]

TENS Devices

Transcutaneous electrical nerve stimulation (TENS) device has become popular for the treatment of pain through the skin. There are about 40 brands that cost from $600 to $700 or more and are available only by prescription.

The TENS device is a small battery-powered generator about the size of a deck of playing cards that can be carried by hand or worn on a belt clip. Wire leads run from the generator to a pair of electrodes about the size of half dollars. The electrodes are coated with a conductive gel and are placed either directly on or near the area of pain. When the generator is turned on, electric current passes through the area and deadens or alleviates certain kinds of pain. The patient may feel nothing or just a slight tingling at the point of contact. Relief can last for hours or days, but for chronic pain the device must be used continuously. Treatment of some acute pain is possible.

TENS may provide relief for patients with chronic low back pain, phantom limb pain (a sensation that an amputated limb is still there and hurts), and osteoarthritis, but it is less effective for cancer pain or pain caused by abnormalities of the nervous system, according to Dr. Donlin Long, professor and chairman of the Department of Neurosurgery, Johns Hopkins University School of Medicine.[44] He studied 200 patients with chronic pain and reported that 78 experienced excellent relief 3 to 6 days after treatment, 54 had good relief, and 65 had little or no relief. In follow-up interviews with the 78 people who had reported excellent relief and had used TENS at home, 10 stated that they had excellent relief, 33 had good relief, and 32 had fair relief. In a survey done for the FDA several years ago by physical therapists, 82.8% stated TENS had given satisfactory relief to patients with chronic pain, while 8.2% stated that the results were partially satisfactory, and the remainder stated the treatment was unsatisfactory.

Assessing the effectiveness of TENS devices is not easy because: the intensity of pain is difficult to measure; pain is a subjective experience influenced by the psychologic state of the patient; environmental influences, domestic and work pressures, cultural customs, and economic values can influence a patient's perception of pain; and the proximity of pain to the site of the electrodes can have some influence.

TENS should not be used by a patient wearing a demand-type cardiac pacemaker or during pregnancy or delivery, and the device should not be placed on the neck over the carotid arteries because the electrical current could interrupt heart rhythm and cause cardiac arrest.

Intraocular Lenses

About 60% of older people, with an estimated 1 million yearly, are affected with cataracts that may require treatment.[45] A cataract is an opacity of the lens of the eye that impairs vision. The cause is unknown, but it is believed that the ultraviolet light from the sun is an important factor. Cataracts can cause double or blurred vision, sensitivity to light and glare, less vivid perception of color, and frequent changes in eyeglass prescription. Some cataracts remain small and never need treatment, while others grow more quickly and progressively larger. Only when a cataract interferes with normal activities is it time to consider surgery. When cataracts are ready for removal, surgery is performed and a plastic intraocular lens (IOL) replaces the clouded lens. The procedure can be completed in an hour-long operation and usually does not require hospitalization. Dr. Carl Kupfer, director of the National Eye Institute in Bethesda, stated, "Implantation of the lens is one of the most successful operations in medicine." Some experts estimate that 88% of persons receiving IOLs will achieve 20/40 visual acuity or better; if there are no other eye diseases or complicating factors, 94% of the patients will achieve 20/40 visual acuity or better.

IOLs remain permanently in place, are not felt by the patient or noticed by others, and require no maintenance. Eyeglasses with lenses for near and distant vision may still be required. The standard surgical procedure for IOLs ranges in cost from $3000 to $5000 and is performed in a hospital or doctor's office.

The operation is not risk-free. After IOL implantation, a clouding of the lens capsule, known as secondary cataract, occurs in roughly 40% of the cases. This can be corrected quickly and easily using laser treatment. Postoperative infection is uncommon. Other problems that occur in a small percentage of patients include swelling of the cornea, glaucoma, and swelling of the retina. Consumers seeking to have lenses implanted should seek the best qualified surgeon possible.

Home Care Devices

Increasing numbers of home care devices are appearing in the marketplace. Some of these are described in Chapter 10. Some additional types of equipment used primarily for personal care are described in this section.

Personal Emergency Response System

Emergency medical help for elderly people, or people convalescing from surgery, illness, or injury, is now available by the push of a button.[46] A relatively inexpensive device, the personal emergency response system (PERS) contains a transmitter mounted on a lightweight medallion-sized unit that can be worn on the wrist, a belt, or around the neck. When its button is pressed, a radio signal prompts a machine connected to the telephone to call the monitoring center for help. The monitoring center usually tries to call back to find out what is wrong. If they are unable to reach the person or help is needed, the center will try to reach a designated person (friend, family member) to follow up the call. If a medical emergency appears evident, an ambulance will be dispatched. Here is how to obtain the best PERS service:

1. Contact a local or state department of aging, hospital, social service agency, or nonprofit health care organization.
2. Rent or lease a unit. Lifeline, the largest supplier, generally rents these units for $25 to $50 a month, plus installation charges.
3. Ask to try out a system. Be sure the transmitter functions up to 200 feet throughout different parts of the house; buttons should be easy to operate and batteries should be easy to replace.
4. Inquire about power failures; is auxiliary power such as batteries available?
5. Discuss company policy about nonemergency calls; some companies desire use only in dire emergencies.

Bottled Water

According to a Roper poll, Americans are greatly concerned about contamination of their drinking water. In 1990, they spent $2 billion on bottled water and purifying systems. Public health control measures of public water have improved general sanitation throughout the years and epidemics of

PERSONAL GLIMPSE

A Patented Device for Nausea?

The following information was reported in The New York Times.[47] A device has been patented that is intended to meet the needs of pregnant women and other people who must avoid antinausea medications. The instrument looks like a wristwatch and emits a continuous stream of electric impulses that are said to mimic the effects of acupuncture needles; theoretically, the stimulations will block nerves and thereby relieve pain and discomfort. According to a manufacturer who plans to market the device, tests conducted on 24 pregnant women at the University of California at Davis Medical Center showed a statistically significant reduction in nausea.

What additional information might help you evaluate this report?

water-borne bacterial diseases have been exceedingly rare in the United States. However, new technologies, the expansion of agricultural use of new and larger amounts of pesticides, industrial pollution of streams and lakes, and the expansion of garage dumps have dumped contaminants into underground surface water supplies. The most important pollutants apparently are radon, lead, and nitrite. The EPA has placed levels on the number and amounts of pollutants permitted in drinking water. Some states have also placed limits on chemicals that may be found in water. However, these restrictions apply only to municipal water supplies. People who have private sources of water or private wells therefore have become alarmed over the health risks to which they are being exposed. Also, if the water looks, tastes, or smells different then these people may worry about its purity. As a result, many individuals have resorted to purchasing bottled water and water-purifiers or welcome tests of their water supplies.[50]

If your tap water meets current federal standards, there is no need to drink bottled water. Bottled water is not necessarily safer than tap water; it may come out of someone else's tap. The *University of California, Berkeley Wellness Letter*[51] stated that many people drink bottled water because they think it is "healthier" and "purer." About 25% of the bottled water in the United States comes from tap water and municipal systems. Some are high in sodium and most include fluoride (added to many water supplies to help control dental decay). Bottled water may contain levels of potentially harmful contaminants not allowed in public drinking water.

Water Treatment Devices

The water treatment or purification business has been rife with scams and hokum. The less a person knows about water, the easier it is for a salesperson to sell equipment that is unreliable or unnecessary. The FTC warns that not all companies selling water tests are legitimate.[48] Fraudulent sellers that advertise "free home water testing" may be interested in selling a water treatment device whether it is needed or not. Some salespeople add chemicals to tap water to change its color or to form particles that supposedly prove it is contaminated. Other entrepreneurs try to sell a device without testing the water or may offer a water purifier as part of a prize promotion. They may notify people by telephone or mail that they have been selected to win a prize.

CONSUMER TIP

Information on Water Safety

Individuals concerned about the safety of their water supply can call the EPA's Safe Drinking Water Hotline (800-426-4791) or obtain the free booklet, "Is Your Drinking Water Safe" from the EPA Office of Drinking Water, WH-550, 401 M St., Washington, DC 20460.

To qualify they are required to buy a water treatment device costing hundreds of dollars. Consumers should never give their credit card number to someone they do not know over the phone.

The FTC suggests taking the following steps before having water tested or before purchasing any type of water treatment system:

1. Avoid "free" home water tests: checking for acidity/alkalinity, iron, manganese, or color is meaningless since none are harmful.
2. Be wary of claims of government approval: the government does not endorse water tests, water treatment, or purification systems. If the Environmental Protection Agency (EPA) registration number appears on a treatment product label, it merely means that the product has been registered with the EPA.
3. Determine the quality of water independently: check local water superintendents for latest test results of the water supply. If you have your own water supply, ask local or state health department if free testing is available; most will test for bacterial contents. A consumer can also engage a private laboratory that is certified by the state health department or the state environmental agency. Tests for bacteria cost from $15 to $45, while tests for chemicals can cost hundreds or even thousands of dollars. *Consumer Reports*[49] has identified three mail-order laboratories it considers reliable:[49]

   Water Test, 33 So. Commercial St., Manchester, NH 03101; 800-426-8378

   National Testing Laboratories, 6151 Wilson Mills Rd., Cleveland, OH 44143; 800-458-3330

   Suburban Water Testing Laboratories, 4600 Kutztown Rd., Temple, PA 19560; 800-433-6595
4. Decide what you need: if water tests indicate

problems, there is a wide variety of water purifiers. They range from inexpensive, simple filter devices for a kitchen faucet to expensive sophisticated systems. No one water treatment device can solve every problem. Ask the testing firm or local government official what system is best for your needs.

5. Comparison shop: after you identify the problem, shop for the right device or filter. Write to the FTC for a copy of "Buying a Home Water Treatment Unit."

Tap Water Filters

Devices to filter tap water are heavily promoted. Some can remove certain contaminants, but none removes all. Eventually filters become saturated with contaminants and become ineffective. You cannot tell this by looking at a filter. It is impossible to tell when a filter is saturated; it may become a bacterial breeding ground.[52]

Electric Heating Pads

It is estimated that 4 million heating pads are sold yearly in the United States at prices ranging from $25 to $50. If used prudently, a heating pad in good condition may safely relieve superficial muscular aches and pains, treat certain skin ailments, and even comfort cold feet.

Heating pads transform electrical energy into heat energy, which is applied locally to the body. The heating element is covered by a layer of asbestos or other insulating material. The element is then enclosed between two sheets of fibrous filler material and heat-sealed in a vinyl sheath. As long as the vinyl sheath is intact, the user is relatively safe from dangerous electrical shock.

The possible hazards from the use of an electric pad are: (1) lethal shock if moisture gets into the wire heating element as a result of a pinhole leak, (2) burns of the skin, and (3) danger of fire caused by heating pad failure. One safety practice is to purchase a pad that is approved by Underwriter's Laboratories (UL), since they require limits on the use of the electrical current.

Heating pads should not be used on an unconscious person, on a person with poor blood circulation, on skin treated with liniment, salve, or ointment, over a recent wound, by individuals with diabetes, or by a person taking cortisone or similar medications. One should never sleep on a heating pad.

Vaporizers

A vaporizer may help relieve a dry, hacking cough or discomfort from an acute respiratory infection or dry air, especially in the winter heating season. However, studies have shown that harmful bacteria and molds can multiply in the water tank of a humidifier and be spewed into the air. Some humidifiers may emit toxic substances like lead and asbestos if they are present in the water in the tank. Ultrasonic humidifiers have been a public concern because of these emissions and are no longer popular. Ultrasonic humidifiers use high frequency sound to break up water into mist. Steam units make steam by boiling water. A 1989 study at the Oak Ridge National Laboratories in Tennessee reported that ultrasound and cool-mist units released the most bacteria and warm-mist units released insignificant amounts. Cool-mist units also released significant amounts of mold.[53]

Bacteria can cause a respiratory disease similar to pneumonia, and molds can produce allergic reactions. Therefore it is important to keep humidifiers scrupulously clean by keeping them dust-free, aerated, and sterilized. A double-blind study of 66 patients found that inhalation of heated, humidified air had no more effect than a placebo in relieving common cold symptoms.[54]

Air Cleaners

Public concern about air pollution has led to the production of a variety of indoor devices designed to clear the air of tobacco smoke, odors, dust, pollen, and other pollutants. *Consumer Reports* stated that these devices have limited usefulness. They cannot do much to filter formaldehyde and other pollutant gases. The best way to clean air of smoke and odors is to open a window and use a fan. Air filters can do a creditable job in removing smoke and dust, but the best devices are rather expensive.

The kind and amount of impurities that can be removed from air depend on the following: (1) the type of air cleaner, its efficiency, and its capacity, (2) the nature and quantity of the particulates to be removed, (3) the amount of loose particles on floors, walls, ceilings, and furnishings that can easily become airborne, and (4) the rate of new air coming into the room from inlets, floor leaks, and open doors.

Consumer Reports has identified these types of air cleaners:[55]

Fan/filter systems are those in which a fan is used to draw air through a filter. The filters may consist of: (1) activated carbon, silica gel, or a proprietary resin bead, which are inexpensive but not very effective cleaners, or (2) synthetic or glass fiber, which is quite effective, especially if electrically charged.

Electrostatic precipitators draw air with a fan past an electrode that gives airborne particles an electric charge. The air then passes a collector plate with an appropriate opposite charge, and the pollutants stick to it. This system could be a component of a forced-air heating system if an entire house is to be cleaned. New and smaller models are on the market that work fairly well.

Negative-ion generators spew electrons into the air and turn molecules into negative ions. These ions give a negative charge to airborne particles that drift and stick to ground surfaces, walls, and ceilings. They can be effective in smoke removal, but confer no special health benefit.

Consumer Reports made the following recommendations in regard to air cleaning:

1. Open a window and use a fan when possible; when opening a window is not possible, an air cleaner might be helpful.
2. Install an air cleaner as a component in a house with a forced-air heating system at a cost of $300 to $400 plus installation. This will be effective in helping to relieve allergies.
3. Select an air cleaner from some of the best ones tested:

   Bionaire 1000 ($299)—ion generator; fan/filter

   Pollenex ionizer 1801 ($100)—ion generator; fan/filter

   Norelco HB9000 ($100)—fan/filter for smoke and dust

   Space-Gard 2275 ($140)—fan/filter for smoke and dust

   Oster ($158)—electrostatic precipitator

These guidelines will assist the consumer in making a decision to purchase an air cleaner:

1. Little benefit will be derived from an air cleaner if a person does not remain in the purified area most of the time.
2. A physician's advice should be obtained to determine the need for a device and the kind to purchase; individuals cannot determine the value to health or identify the contaminants that should be removed. A person allergic to ragweed may have to minimize outdoor activity and/or reduce the moisture content or air temperature when indoors to obtain a measure of relief.

When a medical or health claim made for an air cleaner device—that the product cures or alleviates illness, protects against infections, prevents lung cancer, halts asthma attacks, ends allergic reactions, reduces emphysema symptoms, or wards off colds—the product will be regarded by the FDA as a medical device subject to regulation under the Federal Food, Drug, and Cosmetic Act. The manufacturer would therefore have to produce evidence to support such claims to be able to sell these products legally.

Quack Devices

The FDA has grouped quack devices into nine general categories. The following devices can be considered complete fakes:[56]

1. Figure enhancers such as bust developers and spot-reducers
2. Arthritis and pain relievers claimed to relieve all types of pain
3. Sleep aids claimed to produce electrical impulses that cause natural sleep
4. Hair and scalp devices claimed to eliminate baldness or remove unwanted hair painlessly and permanently
5. Youth prolongers claimed to eliminate wrinkles and restore youthful facial contours

It's Your Decision

You are nearsighted and dislike wearing glasses. You have tried hard and soft contact lenses, but they are expensive and need a great deal of care. A friend has told you about radial keratotomy as an answer to your problem. What should you know and do to decide whether to undergo this surgery?

Your friend apparently has difficulty hearing sounds and voices. You have detected this problem because the person frequently asks you to repeat comments or explain music sounds when you attend concerts or watch television programs together. What action should you take or propose to help this person? Should you first encourage this person to visit a local hearing aid dealer? Why?

6. Sex aids claimed to cure impotence or frigidity
7. Air purifiers claimed to destroy bacteria and TB germs and reduce the aging process
8. Disease diagnosers claimed to be capable of diagnosing all diseases or a wide variety of diseases
9. Cure-all devices claimed to be effective against a wide variety of illness.

SUMMARY

There are many thousands of health devices. Amendments to the Food, Drug, and Cosmetic Act have now classified devices into three classes. Implanted and life-saving devices need premarket approval before they can be sold to the public. The FDA has been severely criticized for its failure to implement several major provisions of these amendments.

Although 25 million Americans could benefit from the use of hearing aid, only 5 million use them on a regular basis. However, many individuals who purchase hearing aids do not need them. There are hundreds of models to choose from, and those people who are in need should first obtain an examination by a qualified person, select a reliable hearing aid dealer, and follow the established guidelines in the selection process.

Vision aids should be carefully selected. Consumers should be aware of the various types of practitioners and choose the one best qualified. A thorough and complete examination should be conducted by an ophthalmologist or an optometrist, and the prescribed lenses should be prepared correctly. Contact lenses, especially soft lenses, require special care to prevent infection and corneal ulcers. Lens wearers must follow specified procedures when using contacts. Glasses ordered through the mail may present problems for consumers.

The devices used in standard medical practice include artificial hearts, heart valves, pacemakers, ultrasound equipment, and clinical thermometers. These items are regulated by the FDA and should function safely and efficiently. Unfortunately, pacemakers, heart valves, and hip prostheses are occasionally found to be defective. Although consumers do not have much choice in their selection, they can discuss their options with their physicians.

Consumers should make intelligent choices when purchasing from the vast array of heating pads, air vaporizers, air purifiers, and self-diagnosis kits. Many of these items can help to relieve pain, speed up the healing process, and assist in the diagnosis of conditions.

In recent years, TENS devices for pain relief and healing and laser equipment for surgery have been available. Patients should follow the guidelines provided in this chapter to make intelligent decisions whether or not to use these items.

DISCUSSION QUESTIONS

1. What is the legal definition of a medical device?
2. How are devices classified in the Safe Medical Device Act of 1990? What are the provisions for each classification?
3. What are the symptoms of hearing loss?
4. What are the types and causes of hearing loss?
5. How can it be determined that a hearing aid is needed?
6. What are the decibel levels of hearing loss and describe the nature of each?
7. What are the types of hearing aids? What are some of the advantages and disadvantages of each type?
8. How should a person select a hearing aid dealer? Who can help with this process?
9. What problems may be encountered in the selection of a hearing aid? What guidelines should be followed?
10. What federal regulations have been promulgated to help the consumer purchase a hearing aid?
11. What are cochlear implants? Why may they be necessary? Who can benefit from their implantation?
12. What guidelines will help the consumer in selecting eyeglasses?
13. What procedures should be included in an eye examination? Who should perform the examination? What should be the frequency of this examination?
14. What is radial keratotomy? How effective is it? Are there any risks with this procedure?
15. What are the major types of contact lenses? What are the advantages, disadvantages, and problems of each type? What procedures should be followed when using these lenses?
16. What tips are important for lens wearers to follow?
17. What is the proper way to care for hard and soft contact lenses?

18. What are several problems that contact lens wearers may have to face?
19. What are the guidelines to follow when shopping for contact lenses?
20. When may ready-to-wear glasses be appropriate to use? With whom should a consumer consult about purchase?
21. What types of sunlight may cause damage to one's eyes?
22. What useful information is found on sunglass labels about the levels of protection from ultraviolet light?
23. When selecting sunglasses, what factors should receive consideration?
24. What are some of the devices used in medical treatment? What are some of the problems that have occurred with several of these devices?
25. What guidelines will help a consumer who plans to undergo pacemaker implantation surgery?
26. What steps are recommended for consumers to follow to have their home water supply tested or to purchase a water treatment system?

REFERENCES

*1. Food and Drug Administration: Federal food, drug, and cosmetic act, as amended, and related laws. HHS Publication No. (FDA) 89-1051, Washington, DC, 1989, US Government Printing Office.
2. GAO finds FDA drags feet in medical device safety, Public Citizen Health Research Group Health Letter, 5(6):10-11, 1989.
3. Commerce challenges FDA medical device oversight, The Nation's Health, Apr 1990.
4. Weinstock CP: Hearing aids: a link to the world, FDA Consumer, 24(1):18-23, 1990.
5. Franks JR and Beckman NJ: Rejection of hearing aids: attitudes of geriatric sample, Ear Hear 6:161-166, 1985.
*6. National Bureau of Standards: Hearing aids, Pub #117, Washington, DC, 1981, US Government Printing Office.
7. Sataloff RT and Vassalo LA: Choosing the right hearing aid, Hosp Pract 16:32A, May 1981.
*8. AARP Product report: hearing aids, Washington, DC, Dec 1989, American Association of Retired Persons.
9. Mail order hearing aids, American Speech and Hearing Association, Apr 1990.
10. Lawrence RS et al: Guide to clinical preventive services, report of the US Preventive Services Task Force, Baltimore, 1989, Williams & Wilkins.
11. Willens M: Buying eyeglasses: a money survey finds disturbing defects at any price, Money, 16:157-159, July 1987.
12. Deutsch CH: The big battle over eye wear, The New York Times, Nov 26, 1989.
13. Farley D: Eyeing glasses: the focus of function, FDA Consumer 19(3):10-14, 1985.
14. Diagnostic and Therapeutic Technology Assessment (DATTA): Radial keratotomy for simple myopia. JAMA 260:264-267, 1988.
*15. Waring GO et al: Results of the Prospective Evaluation of Radial Keratotomy (PERK) Study 4 years after surgery for myopia, JAMA 263:1083-1091, 1990.
16. Bender P: Radial keratotomy in the 1990s and the PERK Study, JAMA 63:1127, 1990.
17. Turturo MA et al: Contact lens complications, Am J Emerg Med 8:228-233, 1990.
18. Pros and cons of soft lenses, Public Citizen Health Research Group Health Letter 6(11):7, 1990.
19. Wrap-up: contact lenses, University of California, Berkeley Wellness Letter 2(10):4-5, 1986.
20. Contact lenses, Mayo Clinic Health Letter 6(6):2-4, 1988.
*21. Smith RE and McRae SM: Contact lenses—convenience and complications, N Engl J Med 321:823-826, 1989.
22. Olsen M: Increasing use of contact lenses prompts issuing of infection-prevention guidelines, JAMA 261:343-344, 1989.
*23. Contact lenses (part 2), Consumer Reports 45:382-386, 1980.
24. Auerbach J: Protecting your eyes from everyday hazards, FDA Consumer, 24(5):29-31, 1990.
25. Sunglasses: the safety/quality question, University of California, Berkeley Wellness Letter 6(10):3, 1990.
26. Sun and shades, Harvard Medical School Health Letter 15(9):1-3, 1990.
27. What's wrong with inexpensive sunglasses, Kiplinger's Personal Finance Magazine 45:77, Aug 1991.
28. Some pacemakers should be removed, physician reports, AARP News Bulletin, p 5, Nov 1985.
29. US Senate Special Committee on Aging: Committee investigation pacemaker probe uncovers continued industry abuses, Summer 1985, US Government Printing Office.
30. Unnecessary pacemakers, Public Citizen Health Research Group Health Letter 4(4):9, 1988.
*31. Cole HM: Four years of replacing ailing hearts: surgeons assess the data, questions remain, JAMA 256:2921-2925, 1986.
32. Boffey PM: Artificial heart: should it be scaled back? The New York Times, Dec 3, 1985.
33. Artificial heart implants can continue, FDA Consumer 20(2):5-6, 1986.
34. Altman LK: FDA approves use in tests of pump to aid failing heart, The New York Times, Jan 4, 1991.
35. A study conducted at the request of the National, Lung and Blood Institute, as reported in the San Francisco Chronicle, July 24, 1991.
36. Asner M: Artificial valves: a heart rending story, FDA Consumer, 15(8):4-7, 1981.
37. Stewart RW: FDA assailed over faulty heart valves, San Francisco Chronicle, Feb 26, 1990.
38. Unger M: Class-action suit on Pfizer's heart valve, Newsday, Mar 22, 1990.
39. Search scheduled for heart valve patients, The New York Times, Dec 12, 1990.
40. Yields on notifying patients with heart valves, Public Citizen Health Research Group Health Letter 6(9):8, 1990.
41. The perplexities of pregnancy, FDA Consumer 24(9):19, 1990.

42. Thompson RC: The unknowns of ultrasound, FDA Consumer 17(2):9-11, 1983.
43. Detecting prostate cancer: ultrasound, Harvard Medical School Health Letter 15(9):6-8, 1990.
44. Asner M: TENS: current that switches off pain, FDA Consumer, 16(9):5-7, 1982.
45. Hale E: Lifting the clouds of cataracts, FDA Consumer, 23(10):27-30, 1989/1990.
46. Emergency help at your fingertips, Johns Hopkins Medical Letter, Health After 50 2(1):7, 1991.
47. Andrews EA: Device said to provide nausea relief, The New York Times, p 30, Jan 5, 1991.
48. Water testing scams, FTC Bureau of Consumer Education, Aug 1990.
49. The selling of water safety, Consumer Reports 55:27-43, 1990.
50. Is your drinking water safe? University of California, Berkeley Wellness Letter 7(9):4-5, 1991.
51. Bottled water, University of California, Berkeley Wellness Letter 7(9):5, 1991.
52. Bottled and tapwater, Harvard Medical School Health Letter 14(1):4, 1988.
53. The search for the safe humidifier, The New York Times, Jan 12, 1991.
54. Macknin ML et al: Effect of inhaling heated vapor on symptoms of common cold, JAMA 264:989-991, 1990.
55. Air cleaners, Consumer Reports 50:7-11, 1985.
*56. FDA: The big quack attack: medical devices, HHS publication No (FDA) 80-442, Washington, DC, 1980, US Government Printing Office.

---

*Recommended reading

Protection of the Consumer

CHAPTER TWENTY-FOUR

COPING WITH DYING

It is a myth to think that death is only for the old. Death is there from the very beginning.

HERMAN FEIFEL[1]

"I have terminal cancer," says a delicate white-haired woman in a hospital bed, "and to endure pain is absolute hell. I want to choose treatment on my own terms in a dignified manner."

NEWSDAY[2]

The notion that terminal patients have nothing to lose by turning to quackery is dead wrong. Most people faced with a life-threatening disease can make a reasonable psychological adjustment. Those who face reality experience five classical stages: denial, anger, bargaining, depression and acceptance. Those who accept their fate are in the best position to use their remaining time wisely. . . . Quacks discourage people from making the difficult adjustment by reinforcing their denial. Such people usually die unprepared because preparation for death is an admission of failure.

WILLIAM T. JARVIS, PH.D.[3]

CONSUMER DECISION

How can people cope with a terminal illness or the death of a loved one?

Should I have a living will or advanced medical directive?

How can appropriate hospice care be located and selected?

Can anything be done to extend one's life span?

PERSONAL GLIMPSE 

Who Should Determine When Someone Has the Right to Die?

In 1990, the U.S. Supreme Court affirmed that competent people have a right to refuse life-sustaining treatment, including artificially given food and fluids. But when patients are incompetent, the court said, they are unable to make informed and voluntary choices. States are therefore justified in requiring "clear and convincing evidence" of the patient's wishes before allowing withdrawal of such support measures. The ruling was applied to the case of 32-year-old Nancy Cruzan, who had been in a coma as a result of irreversible brain damage since a 1983 car accident. By a 5–4 vote, the Supreme Court upheld a Missouri Supreme Court ruling that Ms. Cruzan's guardian could not terminate her treatment because there was not sufficient evidence of her wishes. The verdict has stimulated many hospitals to become more aggressive about having patients sign living wills or other "advance directives" to be used if they become irreversibly ill and are unable to speak for themselves.

What is your reaction to the court's decision?

Death, an unpleasant expectation, is inevitable in everyone's life. It is an occasion that can have traumatic effects on the family and friends of the deceased. The burden can be eased by understanding the emotions involved and planning ahead to deal with various issues that pertain to dying. This chapter can help consumers make intelligent decisions about dealing with grief, preparing an advanced medical directive, donating body parts, euthanasia, hospice care, and quackery related to aging.

GRIEF

Grief is the sadness, pain, and suffering that take place when a family member or friend is terminally ill or dies. The intensity and duration of these emotions depend on the nature of the relationship to the dying person and the emotional makeup of the grieved persons.

The *Mayo Clinic Health Letter*[4] states that adult grief predominantly involves four reactions:

1. *Shock, numbness, and disbelief.* Bereaved individuals may appear to be holding up well even though inside they feel terrible.
2. *Pining, yearning, and sadness.* Usually numbness turns to intense feelings of separation and mental pain in the months after the death.
3. *Acceptance of loss.* When death occurs, complete failure to mourn is a sign that something may be wrong.
4. *Resolution of grief.* As the individual "lets go," it becomes possible to reinvest in continuing life—for example, resuming former behavior patterns, seeking new relationships.

Bereavement (grief over the loss of a loved one) can cause reactions of guilt, shame, sadness, and/or fear of dying. Bereaved individuals must learn to cope with reality. This process involves gradual acceptance of the fact that a loved one has passed on, followed by gradual reinvolvement in day-to-day activities. People who mourn typically must cope with a feeling of emptiness related to the fact that a part of their emotional investment has been lost. When mourning is successful, the emotions are "reinvested" as the individual becomes reinvolved in activities.

Many people believe that crying and other expressions of sadness are abnormal and a sign of emotional weakness. The presence of emotions may be painful to other people. However, expressions of grief are normal and healthy. Cassem[5] has noted:

> Allowing the bereaved to express feelings is essential. The most important part of this process is to avoid the maneuvers that nullify grieving. Clichés ("It's God's will"), self-evident but irrelevant reassurances ("After all,

you've got three other children"), and outright exhortations to stop grieving ("Life must go on") should carefully be avoided.

Bereaved individuals can best deal with grief by recognizing that the sadness they feel is normal and resuming activity when they are able to do so. Friends often can help simply by expressing their sympathy and acknowledging the upset of the bereaved. In many cases, religious involvement is helpful.

Physicians often see people who feel that it is wrong to feel upset. Usually all such people need to proceed with mourning is reassurance that it is all right to grieve. An opportunity to ventilate both positive and negative feelings toward the ill or deceased individual may be helpful. Antidepressant drugs usually are not appropriate in the treatment of uncompleted grief. The act of giving them may convey a message that grieving is abnormal. Some communities have support groups for those who need help.

Normal Versus Abnormal Grief

The length of the grieving or mourning process varies among individuals. When a loved one has passed on, most people take 6 to 12 months, but some take less and some take considerably more. Horowitz[6] has noted:

> In normal grief . . . the person passes through such states of mind with a sense of progressing along a mourning process. However, in pathological [abnormal] grief, the person may become frozen in one or more of these states, without progress over weeks or even months. There may be additional signs of inertia, hypochondriasis, numbness, unaccountable irritability, feelings of gross worthlessness, and apathy.

The Johns Hopkins Medical Letter states that "success" of the grieving process should not be measured by a predetermined timetable but by the griever's acceptance of the loss. The signs of unresolved grief include suicidal thoughts, chronic sleep difficulty, overuse of alcohol or drugs, persistent depression, failure to carry out normal daily routines, and persistent symptoms resembling those of the deceased. A shift to positive and realistic plans for the future is a sign that mourning is becoming complete.[7] Professional help is unlikely to be needed unless severe depression or social isolation persists for 6 to 12 months.

Advance Medical Directives

Consumer Reports Health Letter states that the need to prepare for death appears more pressing today than ever because machines often can keep a dying or permanently unconscious patient alive, sometimes indefinitely, with no hope of recovery. However, people do have certain rights to refuse treatment.[8] Someone who wishes to invoke the right to refuse medical treatment should prepare what is known as an *advance medical directive* (see Figure 24-2). This directive may be in the form of a *living will* or a *durable power of attorney for health care (DPAHC)*.

A *living will* is a document (Figure 24-1) in which a patient states whether artificial life-support procedures such as a respirator or intravenous feeding should be used. This document is activated if a patient becomes terminally ill (when death is imminent in days, weeks, or months and usually certified by two doctors) or is too ill (e.g., in coma) to communicate treatment preferences. However, family members may counteract the wishes of a patient. A study of 175 nursing home residents with living wills revealed that in 25% of the cases, doctors and nurses made decisions that were contrary to the instructions of a living will.[9]

Living will documents have two limitations: (1) the wishes of the patient may be counteracted by family members and others, and (2) the term *heroic measures* may be difficult to define. Each state interprets this phrase differently. Michael R. Schuster, a lawyer for the American Association of Retired Persons, states that the durable power of attorney is a better procedure.[9]

Emanuel and Emanuel[10] indicate that although living wills have been strongly endorsed in principle, they rarely are used in clinical practice because they are vague and difficult to apply. These authors have proposed an *advance medical directive* (Figure 24-2), that specifies what to do about 12 types of medical intervention. Emanuel and Emanuel believe their proposal makes it clear what patients would like done if they become unable to communicate.

Durable power of attorney is a document (Figure 24-3) in which the patient designates another individual (proxy), usually a family member or intimate friend, to make treatment decisions in the place of the patient if the patient is unable to make the necessary decisions.

TO MY FAMILY, MY PHYSICIAN, MY LAWYER, MY CLERGYMAN
TO ANY MEDICAL FACILITY IN WHOSE CARE I HAPPEN TO BE
TO ANY INDIVIDUAL WHO MAY BECOME RESPONSIBLE FOR MY HEALTH, WELFARE OR AFFAIRS

Death is a much a reality as birth, growth, maturity and old age—it is the one certainty of life. If the time comes when I, ______________________________ can no longer take part in decisions for my own future, let this statement stand as an expression of my wishes, while I am still of sound mind.

If the situation should arise in which there is no reasonable expectation of my recovery from physical or mental disability, I request that I be allowed to die and not be kept alive by artificial means or "heroic measures." I do not fear death itself as much as the indignities of deterioration, dependence and hopeless pain. I, therefore, ask that medication be mercifully administered to me to alleviate suffering even though this may hasten the moment of death.

This request is made after careful consideration. I hope you who care for me will feel morally bound to follow its mandate. I recognize that this appears to place a heavy responsibility upon you, but it is with the intention of relieving you of such responsibility and of placing it upon myself in accordance with my strong convictions, that this statement is made.

Signed ______________________________

Date ______________________________

Witness ______________________________

Witness ______________________________

Copies of this request have been given to ______________________________

____

____

____

FIGURE 24-1. A sample living will.

New Law

The Patient Self Determination Act, which took effect on December 1, 1991, applies to hospitals, nursing homes, hospices, health maintenance organizations, and home health care agencies that receive Medicare or Medicaid funding. The law provides that when a person enters a health facility, the medical staff is required to:

1. Identify the person's right to make decisions to accept or refuse treatment about medical care under state law
2. Inform the individual of the right and procedures to follow in preparing a living will or other advance directive
3. Make the person's living will or advanced directive part of the person's medical record
4. Take no discriminatory action because of any decision regarding life-sustaining medical treatment

MY MEDICAL DIRECTIVE

This Medical Directive expresses, and shall stand for, my wishes regarding medical treatments in the event that illness should make me unable to communicate them directly. I make this Directive, being 18 years or more of age, of sound mind and appreciating the consequences of my decisisons.

SITUATION (A)

If I am in a coma or in a persistent vegetative state, and in the opinion of my physician and several consultants have no known hope of regaining awareness and higher mental functions no matter what is done, then my wishes regarding use of the following, if considered medically reasonable would be:

SITUATION (B)

If I am in a coma, and I have a small likelihood of recovering fully, a slightly larger likelihood of surviving with permanent brain damage, and a much larger likelihood of dying, then my wishes regarding the use of the following, if considered medically reasonable, would be:

SITUATION (C)

If I have brain damage or some brain disease which cannot be reversed and which makes me unable to recognize people, or to speak understandably, *and I also have a terminal illness,* such as incurable cancer which will likely be the cause of my death, then my wishes regarding use of the following, if considered medically reasonable, would be:

SITUATION (D)

If I have brain damage or some brain disease which cannot be reversed and which makes me unable to recognize people, or to speak understandably, *but I have no terminal illness,* and I can live in this condition for a long time, then my wishes regarding use of the following, if considered medically reasonable, would be:

	(A) I WANT	(A) I DO NOT WANT	(A) I AM UNDECIDED	(A) I WANT A TRIAL: IF NO CLEAR IMPROVEMENT STOP TREATMENT	(B) I WANT	(B) I DO NOT WANT	(B) I AM UNDECIDED	(B) I WANT A TRIAL: IF NO CLEAR IMPROVEMENT STOP TREATMENT	(C) I WANT	(C) I DO NOT WANT	(C) I AM UNDECIDED	(C) I WANT A TRIAL: IF NO CLEAR IMPROVEMENT STOP TREATMENT	(D) I WANT	(D) I DO NOT WANT	(D) I AM UNDECIDED	(D) I WANT A TRIAL: IF NO CLEAR IMPROVEMENT STOP TREATMENT
1) **CARDIOPULMONARY RESUSCITATION—** if on the point of dying the use of drugs and electric shock to start the heart beating, and artificial breathing.																
2) **MECHANICAL BREATHING—** breathing by a machine.																
3) **ARTIFICIAL NUTRITIONA AND HYDRATION—** nutritions and fluid given through a tube in the veins, nose, or stomach.																
4) **MAJOR SURGERY—** such as removing the gall bladder or part of the intestines.																
5) **KIDNEY DIALYSIS—** cleaning the blood by machine or by fluid passed through the belly.																
6) **CHEMOTHERAPY—** drugs to fight cancer																
7) **MINOR SURGERY—** such as removing some tissue from an infected toe.																
8) **INVASIVE DIAGNOSTIC TESTS—** such as using a flexible tube to look into the stomach.																
9) **BLOOD OR BLOOD PRODUCTS—**																
10) **ANTIBIOTICS—** drugs to fight infection																
11) **SIMPLE DIAGNOSTIC TESTS—** such as blood tests or x-rays.																
12) **PAIN MEDICATIONS, EVEN IF THEY DULL CONSCIOUSNESS AND INDIRECTLY SHORTEN MY LIFE—**																

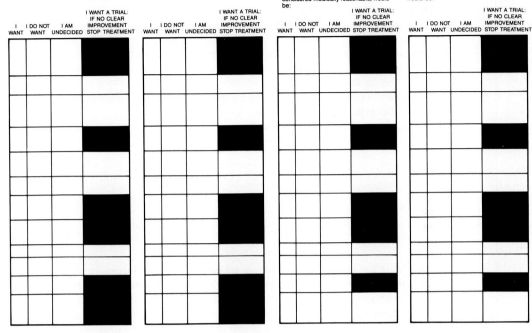

FIGURE 24-2. My medical directive.

Copyright 1990 by Linda L. Emanuel, M.D., and Ezekiel J. Emanuel, M.D.[10] The authors advise that the form be completed pursuant to discussions with the patient and the physician and made part of the patient's medical record. See page 535 for information on availability of copies.

Twelve Types of Medical Intervention[11]

Before making an advanced medical directive, you may want to discuss the following medical interventions with your doctor:

1. Cardiopulmonary resuscitation (CPR): a manual or mechanical technique to start a stopped heart.
2. Mechanical breathing: use of a machine (a ventilator) to pump air in and out of the lungs; usually requires that a breathing tube be inserted into the windpipe.
3. Artificial nutrition and hydration: feeding liquid nourishment and fluids through a tube placed in a vein (IV), passed through the nose down into the stomach (nasogastric intubation), or placed directly into the stomach through a surgically created opening (gastrostomy).
4. Major surgery: an important, difficult, and potentially hazardous operation, such as removal of part of the intestines because of obstruction.
5. Minor surgery: a less extensive operative procedure, such as removal of damaged tissue so that a bedsore can heal.
6. Kidney dialysis: mechanical clearing of accumulated waste from the blood.
7. Chemotherapy: drug treatment used to fight cancer.
8. Invasive diagnostic test: a test requiring that the skin be punctured or cut or that an instrument such as a cardiac catheter be inserted into the body.
9. Simple diagnostic test: a basic noninvasive procedure (blood test or simply x-ray).
10. Transfusion: introducing whole blood or blood components into a vein.
11. Antibiotic treatment: using drugs to fight bacterial infection.
12. Pain medication: the use of painkilling drugs, including narcotics, which may dull consciousness and indirectly hasten death.

POWER OF ATTORNEY FOR HEALTH CARE

I, *(your name)*, hereby appoint: *(name, address and phone numbers)* as my attorney-in-fact to make health care decisions for me if I become unable to make my own health care decisions. This gives my attorney-in-fact the power to grant, refuse or withdraw consent on my behalf for any health care service, treatment or procedure. My attorney-in-fact also has the authority to talk to health care personnel, get information and sign forms necessary to carry out these decisions.

With this document, I intend to create a power of attorney for health care, which shall take effect if I become incapable of making my own health care decisions and shall continue during that incapacity.

My attorney-in-fact shall make health care decisions as I direct below or as I make known to my attorney-in-fact in some other way.

(a) Statement of directives concerning life-prolonging care, treatment, services and procedures:

(b) Special provisions and limitations:

By my signiature I indicate that I understand the purpose and effect of this document. I sign my name to this form on *(date)*, at *(address)*.

____

____

Your signature

WITNESS

I declare that the person who signed or acknowledged this document is personally known to me, that the person signed or acknowledged this durable power of attorney for health care in my presence, and that the person appears to be of sound mind and under no duress, fraud or undue influence. I am not the person appointed as the attorney-in-fact by this document, nor am I the health care provider of the principal or an employee of the health care provider of the principal.

(Date, and print names, signatures and addresses of two witnesses)

At least one of the witnesses listed above shall also sign the following declaration: I further declare that I am not related to the principal by blood, marriage or adoption, and, to the best of my knowledge, I am not entitled to any part of the estate of the principal under a currently existing will or by operation of law.

____

____

(Signatures)

FIGURE 24-3. A sample power of attorney for health care form.

Drafting an Advance Directive

The Johns Hopkins Medical Letter[11] suggests following these procedures when preparing an advance directive:

1. Contact your lawyer or state attorney general's office to get information on living will and DPAHC legislation in your state as well as appropriate forms.
2. Sign your advance directive and designation of DPAHC before two witnesses (neither being the assigned DPAHC, a potential heir, or a doctor or other health care professional who is caring for you) and, if required by your state, a notary. A lawyer is not required, although you might want to consult one.
3. Give copies to your family, your doctor, your lawyer, and your cleric. Do not store your living will in a safe deposit box, where it may be inaccessible to anyone but you.
4. To keep the living will current (and more likely to be upheld should it ever go to court), reexamine the document every 2 years or so, and

sign and date it again. Every 5 years, sign again in front of witnesses and a notary.

Guidelines for Decisions to Forego Medical Treatment

Guidelines were prepared for physicians at an international conference in 1989 to assist them in making decisions about (1) patients who were competent and had executed an advance directive before becoming incompetent, (2) those who were competent and now are not competent with no written statement, (3) those who are not now competent or ever have been competent, and (4) the scarcity of medical resources. The proposed guidelines were based on fundamental values needed to make ethical decisions. The guidelines included:

For all persons. (1) Have a moral obligation not to inflict or risk harm to others, (2) must respect patients' choices selected according to their own conscience, values, and religious convictions, and (3) must act fairly and justly in the distribution of scarce resources.

For competent patients who become incompetent with advanced directive. Should patients refuse treatment: (1) physician should not impose treatment even if potentially life-prolonging, and (2) physician should not be obliged to provide physiologically futile treatments.

For competent patients who become incompetent without advanced directive. Physician: (1) should ensure patients' preferences as far as possible, (2) has duty to share all alternatives with family or related others regarding plan of action and gain acceptance, (3) should consult widely with consultants and others if patient has no family or friends, (4) if requested, should not provide futile treatment, and (5) should not provide treatment if sole purpose is death.

For patients who are not now competent and never have been competent. Physician: (1) does not have absolute duty to life-prolonging treatment, (2) must weigh benefits and burdens of treatment in terms of quality of life, (3) must involve family, surrogates, physicians, and other care givers in decisions, (4) must act in trustworthy manner, and (5) may withhold life-prolonging treatment if burdens outweigh benefits.

Scarcity of resources. (1) Society must establish limits and priorities, (2) processes used to establish limits should be open and fair, (3) established policies that are restrictive must be publicized in advance of patient admission, and (4) patient has no right to treatment that has no reasonable expectation of benefit.[12]

Additional information about advance medical directives can be obtained from the Society for the Right to Die (see Appendix for address). A copy of "My Medical Directive" is available from the Harvard Medical School Health Publications Group, P.O. Box 380, Boston, MA 02117 at 2 copies for $5 or 5 copies for $10; bulk orders also available.

Donations of Organs and Other Body Parts

Organ transplantation usually is thought of in terms of major organs such as the heart, kidney, or lung. However, about 70 nonorgan tissues can be used to help the living. Corneal transplants can restore sight. Skin grafts can help burn victims. Heart valves can aid those with congenital heart disease. Ligaments can help people who acquire sport injuries. It is estimated the average bone donor can help 51 people.[13] The focus of this discussion is on body organs because their use is generally related to whether a person lives or dies.

Monaco[14] stated the success rate for organ transplants has been remarkable:

Living-related kidneys = over 90% were 1-year graft survivals.
Cadaver kidneys = over 80% success with 5% mortality
Liver = 75% of 1-year graft survivals
Heart = 85% survival; 50% of retransplants are successful
Heart-lung = 50% survival
Pancreas and single lung = experimental

The United Network for Organ Sharing (UNOS) stated that through 1988, 4083 donors yielded 1647 hearts, 1680 livers, and 74 both hearts and lungs. Of the 9123 kidney transplants performed, 7200 were from cadavers and about 2000 were from living-related donors.[14] However, the supply of cadaver organs and tissues does not come close to meeting the needs of patients awaiting transplantation. It is estimated that of the 25,000 potential donors that become available each year, fewer than 20% become donors.[15] In 1989, UNOS reported that 15,721 people were waiting for a cadaver kidney, 1227 for a heart, 743 for a liver, and 231 for both heart and lungs. About 10% to 15%

The Search for a Donor

Jean-Pierre Bosze is not likely to be alive a year from now if he does not receive a bone marrow transplant. Diagnosed with leukemia in 1988, the 12-year-old boy from Illinois has searched in vain for a suitable donor. His father, his mother, and other relatives have had their blood tested, but none had the right type. His doctors have consulted the National Marrow Donor Program of 180,000 potential donors, but the odds of unrelated people matching are 1 in 20,000.[17]

What Do You Think?[19]

Patients who need kidney and heart transplants are dying because not enough people donate organs. Is it time to treat organs as private property that people can buy and sell?

of those eligible for a heart transplant die before a suitable organ can be found.

The shortage of donors has created several problems. Kjellstrand[16] stated there is an unequal distribution of body parts. The availability of kidney transplants in the United States depends on sex, race, age, and income. Women and nonwhite patients in 1983 had only two-thirds the chance that men and white patients had of receiving a transplant. Patients aged 11 years to 35 years had an 85% chance of receiving an organ. In terms of renal transplants, men get more than women, whites more than blacks, rich more than poor, and young more than old.

In some parts of the world the selling of body organs is a commercial enterprise. Commercialism in the western world has been outlawed and is considered to be not only illegal but also immoral. However, because of the shortage of donors and the large number of patients awaiting body parts, there are some proposals to provide financial aid or material incentives to the heirs. This might come in several ways: (1) burial expenses, (2) rebates or deferral of state and federal income taxes, (3) a fixed grant for the widow and/or dependent children, (4) a government-sponsored or paid-for insurance policy payable to a designated beneficiary.

It is feared that if organ transplants become a commercial business, the poor may sacrifice their bodies and the rich will gain unfair access to scarce resources. In the Middle East the practice of trading in human organs is prevalent, whereby the poor and the needy are the victim donors.

Sells[18] has indicated that operations should be performed for therapeutic reasons, and a financial reward does not represent a therapeutic indication for surgery. He added that all commerce in human organs is morally unacceptable. Kjellstrand[16] believes that physicians owe justice and advocacy to patients. There must be no difference in how patients are treated.

How to Donate

The Uniform Anatomical Gift Act, or its equivalent, has been adopted in all states that permit individuals to bequeath their bodies for immediate use after death. However, people must register before death occurs. Those planning to take this action should thoroughly familiarize themselves with the requirements and possible costs. In some states, permission to use tissues after death is communicated by a card that is signed and attached to one's driver's license. The most widely used plan for donating parts is through the use of a Uniform Donor Card available from the National Kidney Foundation (Figure 24-4). Identification bracelets indicating a wish to donate are available from Medic Alert Foundation. Information is also available from Living Bank, which maintains a national registry (see Appendix for addresses).

Euthanasia

This section does not discuss the philosophical or moral issues involved in euthanasia. Rather, it presents information intended to provide understanding about its nature, related laws, ethics of physician responsibilities, and guidelines for responsible decisions.

Euthanasia has been described as legalized killing, mercy killing, aid-in-dying, death with dignity, physician-assisted suicide, and physician-administered death by lethal injection. Nowell-Smith[20] has classified two types: (1) *active voluntary euthanasia* (intervention by a doctor to end life; to assist in suicide) and (2) *passive euthanasia* (a decision not to prolong life by withdrawing or withholding

UNIFORM DONOR CARD

OF ______________________________
Print or type name of donor

In the hope that I may help others, I hereby make this anatomical gift, if medically acceptable, to take effect upon my death. The words and marks below indicate my desires.

I give: (a) _____ any needed organs or parts
(b) _____ only the following organs or parts

____
Specify the organ(s) or part(s)

for the purposes of transplantation, therapy, medical research or education;

(c) _____ my body for anatomical study if needed.

Limitations or special wishes, if any: ______________________________

Signed by the donor and the following two witnesses in the presence of each other:

______________________ Signature of Donor | ______________________ Date of Birth of Donor

______________________ Date Signed | ______________________ City & State

______________________ Witness | ______________________ Witness

This is a legal document under the Uniform Anatomical Gift Act or similar laws.

For further information consult your physician or

National Kidney Foundation
116 East 27th Street, New York, N.Y. 10016

FIGURE 24-4. A sample organ donor card.

treatment). Passive euthanasia can include nonresuscitation after cardiac arrest, withdrawal of a respirator, abstention from intrusive feeding regimens, and administration of analgesics in doses to relieve pain even though this hastens the death of the patient.

Carton[21] stated that American medicine is moving along the road to euthanasia (physician-assisted termination of human life). Life-sustaining technology now enables severely ill persons to survive coma, chronic vegetative states, and other conditions of great impairment. Formerly, these people would have died rather promptly. Now their lives can be maintained by ventilators and mechanized feeding devices. Parker[22] argues that in certain cases ordinary medical practitioners are duty bound to assist death.

Euthanasia in some form has a measure of support in the medical community. A study of general practitioners in France, Canada, and the United States found 30% strongly or mostly agreed with euthanasia and 59% strongly or most strongly disagreed. Another poll of general practitioners indicated that 35% would definitely consider its use, and an additional 10% said they would consider it if it became legal.[20]

Although euthanasia is illegal in all jurisdictions in the United States, there are indications that it occurs. The American Hospital Association estimates that many of the 6000 deaths occurring daily in this country in some way are planned by patients, families, and physicians. There are no data regarding the number of assisted suicides.[23]

Attempts are being made to legalize euthanasia in some form. Voters in the state of Washington have rejected an attempt to become the first jurisdiction in the Western world to legally permit physician-administered death on request of the patient. Passage of the referendum would have permitted removal of all artificial life-support systems from patients who had made a request in a living will, a directive to physicians, or a durable power of attorney. It would also have permitted discontinuance of tube feeding and would define irreversible coma and vegetative states as terminal illness. California and Oregon advocates have contemplated placing this issue on the ballot.

DO YOU AGREE?

Dr. Jack Kevorkian, a Detroit physician, advocates doctor-assisted suicide for people suffering from terminal or severely painful diseases. He assisted in the suicide deaths of Sherry Miller and Marjorie Wantz on October 23, 1991. Ms. Miller was 43 and had multiple sclerosis. Ms. Wantz was 58 years old and suffered a painful but not terminal disease that required 10 pelvic operations. The two women killed themselves in a remote cabin north of Detroit using machines provided by the doctor.

The New York Times, November 3, 1991

Forty-one states have enacted natural death acts, which allow anyone to sign a living will—a document stating that if a person is suffering from a terminal illness that is certified by one (or two) doctors, the person's life should not be sustained by medication, artificial means, or heroic measures.[24]

Sherwood[25] identifies possible abuses that may arise from the loosening of restraints on euthanasia. These include (1) improper application to the poor, homeless, elderly, and uninsured, (2) pushing the medical community down the "slippery slope," leading to decisions that permit others to die such as chronically ill, disabled, and retarded persons, and victims of Alzheimer's disease, (3) coercing the terminally ill to make fatal decisions in a hurry; many worry about the burden on family and take the "quick and easy" way out.

The manual on ethics of the American College of Physicians[26] states that (1) "active euthanasia" is a euphemism for the intentional killing of a person, (2) a physician engaged in euthanasia would be guilty of homicide, (3) euthanasia is contrary to public policy, medical tradition, and the most fundamental measures of human value and worth, (4) physicians are obligated to prevent disease and untimely death and to care for the sick, treat and cure when possible, help patients cope with illness, disability, and death, and relieve suffering, and (5) in all instances, the physician must help maintain the dignity of the person.[27]

Stolinsky[26] has observed that newspapers discuss euthanasia without mentioning the Ten Commandments, the Hippocratic Oath, or any other source of ethical principles: "Everything is just a matter of would you want to be cared for by someone whose only guide to life-and-death decisions was a public opinion poll."

Hospice Care

Hospice care is a way of helping people who have only a few weeks or months to live. It is provided mostly in the home by family and friends with the support of health professionals and volunteers.

The first hospice program appeared in London in 1970. The first U.S. program was founded in 1975 in Connecticut. In 1989 there were approximately 1700 hospices in the United States, including 322 (19%) that were Medicare-certified.

These are the types of hospice organizations and programs[28]:

1. *Freestanding (independent).* Privately owned groups that provide comprehensive services with their own administrations and staffs. Inpatient care may be provided through arrangements with a hospital or nursing home.
2. *Home health agency–based.* Type of organization with its own staff; includes visiting nurse associations, for-profit home care agencies, and public agencies. Provides county home care services.
3. *Hospital-based.* Services available through their own home care units or with community health agencies.
4. *All-volunteer organizations.* Programs coordinated with home health agencies and hospitals in community. Coordinator is the only paid staff person.

Hospice care was originally designed to help terminally ill individuals (particularly cancer patients) who wished to die in a peaceful, homelike setting and be free from as much pain as possible. This has been broadened so that programs now cover general care for anyone who may be dying. However, the emphasis is on, but not limited to, the control of pain and terminal stages of cancer. Ninety percent of those serviced by hospices are dying of cancer.

Hospice care today provides palliative (not curative) support services to patients and families in both home and hospital settings. These services include physical (medications), psychological (fear, anxiety, grief), social (individual and family support), and spiritual (religious) aid by a medically supervised, interdisciplinary team of professionals and volunteers. Specialists in death awareness are available. Medical help and emotional support are offered during bereavement. Medications are given not to prolong life but to relieve distressing symptoms and pain.

A basic hospice program should also include:

1. Placing control of care in the patient's hands and encouraging family and staff to establish good working relationships.
2. Being on call 24 hours a day every day of the week.
3. Making the patient comfortable in the management of pain and other troubling symptoms.
4. Creating a pleasant environment, whether the patient is at home or in a different setting, that allows for the frequent presence of family and friends.

The costs for services depend on the nature and

extent of care (inpatient or outpatient) and typically range from $60 to $500 per day. Payment can come from a variety of sources: private (individuals and foundations) and third-party payers, including private insurance companies, Medicare (with limitations), Medicaid (some states), and other state and local government programs. Rhymes[29] reported that several studies showed hospice care to be less expensive than conventional care in the last year of life. The savings are greater in the final month or two of life. However, if there is heavy use of home services before the last 2 months, hospice care may cost more than conventional care.

Greer and Mor[30] stated the average length of stay in a hospice program was 63 to 72 days. Half the patients die within 35 days, 20% die in 10 days or less, 8% stay more than 210 days, and 10% are discharged alive. Those discharged were long-term patients, many without cancer.

Rhymes[29] stated that patients generally feel that hospice care is equal to or better than conventional care. However, inpatient units may be more successful at reducing patient pain and stress than home care programs.

In 1982, the U.S. Congress approved payment for certain hospice services under Medicare. These services include physician fees, nursing care, counseling, medical social services, short-term inpatient care, medical supplies, home health aides and homemakers. To qualify for Medicare benefits, the patient must (1) be terminally ill with a life expectancy of 6 months or less and (2) relinquish all other Medicare benefits except those services of the attending physician. The patient would be limited to 210 days of services, but Medicare would not pay more than $6884 for the care of one patient and 80% of the care would have to take place at home. To qualify for participation in the Medicare program, a hospice must be certified by the Joint Commission on Accreditation of Healthcare Organizations.

Lukashok[31] reported that in 1985 the average number of days for which hospice services were provided for a Medicare patient was 32.1. This average was less than time spent in most hospices, yet only 22 patients exceeded the 210-day maximum allowed. Lukashok stated the average expenditure per beneficiary in 1985 was $2088. This was somewhat lower than the expense of other hospices. The government neither saved nor spent any meaningful amounts of money.

Rhymes[29] indicated that hospices served a small percentage of terminally ill patients and Medicare hospice benefits were used by fewer people than originally projected. In 1985, less than 13,000 were serviced of a projected number of 40,000 people. This was due to two factors: (1) Medicare requirements for hospice certification were viewed as burdensome, and (2) primary care providers were unaware that hospice services were available.

CONSUMER TIP

When to Decide on a Hospice

The answer depends on the individual situation and may not be easy to determine.

These two indicators should be considered:

- ✔ The doctor advises that further treatment is not likely to be effective.
- ✔ The patient decides not to continue treatment that may have painful side effects and will merely delay death a little longer.

Locating and Selecting a Hospice

The names and addresses of hospice care organizations and agencies may be obtained from the National Cancer Institute (telephone 800-4-CANCER); a discharge planner, community relations person, or social worker at a local hospital; a local church or synagogue; Visiting Nurse Association; health department; social services office; or American Cancer Society office. The answers to these questions will provide the information needed for hospice selection[28]:

About the Hospice

What nurses, doctors, volunteers, or others will provide services? What services will they provide?

What will the doctor's role be and will the hospice be in communication?

Will service be provided on a 24-hour basis daily?

Will someone help with the insurance forms?

How often will the nurse, doctor, or other visit the home or provide services?

Will bereavement counseling be available after death of the patient?

How are middle-of-the-night crises handled?

What follow-up services are provided if the patient must return to the hospital?

About Costs

What are the fees? Are they charged by the hour, day, or visit?

Will the hospice accept fee payments by private insurance, Medicare, or other payee? Will there be additional charges not covered by these providers?

Will the hospice handle billing with Medicare or private insurance carrier? Will the hospice negotiate with insurance carrier should charges be denied?

About the Program

Does the hospice mainly involve home or hospital care? How does the hospice arrange for hospital care if necessary?

Does the hospice have a home care program if hospice program is in a hospital or other facility? Will this staff provide service if patient must go home?

About Standards

What kind of accreditation does the hospice have? Does the hospital have state approval?

Additional Sources of Information

Other organizations that can provide information are the National Hospice Organization, American Cancer Society, National Consumers League, National Homecaring Council, and Joint Commission on Accreditation of Healthcare Organizations. Their addresses are listed in the Appendix.

Quackery Related to Aging

The wish to delay aging and prolong life is almost universal. Many entrepreneurs have capitalized on these wishes and proposed modern equivalents of the "fountain of youth." Chapter 21 describes how cosmetics manufacturers have made unproven claims that their products can rejuvenate the skin and/or remove wrinkles. Some product lines include vitamin supplements in addition to skin creams. Other manufacturers have marketed products claimed to prevent or delay aging, boost immunity, cure chronic disease, and/or improve memory.

Some spas offer therapeutic baths (in mineral water or seawater), mud packs, seaweed wraps, and a variety of other services claimed to promote rejuvenation or healing. Van Italie and Hadley[32] note that whereas most American spas offer fitness activities, European facilities are more likely to feature "cures," stress reduction, or various forms of pampering. Rejuvenation claims are also made by physicians engaged in unproven practices here and abroad. Fresh cell therapy, which is claimed to rejuvenate body organs, is described in Chapter 18.

Life Extension Claims

During the early 1980s a series of books suggested to the public that life can be extended by manipulating certain body systems with dietary methods, nutritional supplements, and/or drugs. The theories were based mainly on misinterpretations or inappropriate extrapolations of animal experiments.

In 1980, Saul Kent, author of *The Life Extension Revolution*,[33] founded the Life Extension Foundation in Hollywood, Florida. Its stated purpose was to "mobilize support for life extension, provide the public with products and services, and raise money for life extension research." Regular membership in the foundation costs $50 a year and entitles members to product discounts, a directory of "life extension" doctors, a directory of "innovative medical clinics," a copy of *The Physician's Guide to Life Extension Drugs*, and two monthly newsletters.

Kent's book was followed in 1982 by *Life Extension—A Practical Scientific Approach*, a 900-page book that outlined an extensive program of supplements and drugs, combined with laboratory testing to look for signs of improvement or toxicity. The book's authors, Durk Pearson and Sandy Shaw, claimed that their program might extend an average individual's life span by several decades and improve quality of life as well. Yetiv,[34] however, who published a detailed review of the book, found it to be "extremely inaccurate." He said that some of its recommendations were potentially life-threatening, many of the references cited did not support the book's claims, and some of the references directly contradicted the book's claims.

Another book, *Maximum Life Span*, by Roy L. Walford, M.D.,[35] suggested that human life span could be extended by eating fewer than 1500 calories a day and taking certain supplements. Walford's theories are based on experiments in which laboratory animals fed a high-nutrient, low-calorie diet lived longer than normal.

Each of the three books was followed by a sequel providing detailed advice on following the programs that they recommended. The resultant publicity inspired many manufacturers to market products claimed to influence some aspect of aging. The Food and Drug Administration (FDA) has driven some products of this type from the marketplace, but others still are sold.

In 1987, FDA officials and U.S. marshals seized large quantities of products marketed by the Life Extension Foundation, including BHT (promoted for herpes and AIDS), DMSO (for arthritis and bursitis), Coenzyme Q_{10} (for cardiovascular disorders and increased longevity), and Cognitex (to enhance mental function). In 1991 Saul Kent and the foundation's vice president were charged with 28 criminal counts related to importing and selling unapproved new drugs and misbranded prescription drugs.

Gerovital H3 (GH3) was developed by Dr. Anna Aslan, a Rumanian physician. It has been promoted by the Rumanian National Tourist Office and a few American physicians as an antiaging substance—"the secret of eternal vigor and youth." Claims have been made that GH3 can prevent or relieve a wide variety of disorders, including arthritis, arteriosclerosis, angina pectoris and other heart conditions, neuritis, deafness, Parkinson's disease, depression, senile psychosis, and impotence. It is also claimed to stimulate hair growth, restore pigments to gray hair, and tighten and smooth skin. The main ingredient in GH3 is procaine, a substance used for local anesthesia. Although many uncontrolled studies describe great benefits from the use of GH3, controlled trials using procaine have failed to demonstrate any. Noting that para-aminobenzoic acid (PABA) appears in the urine of people receiving procaine injections, a few American manufacturers have been selling procaine tablets containing PABA with false claims similar to those made for GH3. The FDA has taken regulatory action against several companies marketing "GH3" products, but other brands still are marketed.

Scientific Responses

Schneider and Reed[36] and Yetiv[37] have summarized and evaluated life extension strategies proposed in both popular books and the scientific literature. Their findings include:

1. Several studies in animals have shown that cutting calories 50% to 60% can significantly increase maximum life span. However, the restriction also retards their growth and development and thus is not suitable for humans.
2. Exercise has beneficial effects on several aging processes as well as cardiovascular disease. However, it has not been demonstrated that exercise is related to longevity.
3. Many types of immunologic manipulation have been proposed, including the transplantation of immune cells from young animals. However, no such approach has been demonstrated safe or effective in humans.
4. Antioxidant nutrients such as selenium, vitamins C and E, and BHT are claimed to delay aging by soaking up "free radicals" that have escaped the body's own "free radical patrols." Although antioxidants can deactivate free radicals in the test tube, they have not been proved to do so in humans.
5. Superoxide dismutase (SOD) is an enzyme whose tissue levels in various animal species appears related to their life span. However, consumption of SOD supplements has no effect in humans because SOD (a protein) is digested into its component amino acids and does not reach the tissues as intact SOD.

Much research is being done to see whether antioxidant supplements can protect against heart disease, cancer, and other diseases. After reviewing current research data, *Consumer Reports* concluded:

> No one has yet proven the theory that antioxidants slow aging and fight disease by protecting the body from free radicals, although evidence is accumulating. Very few studies so far have examined the effect of supplements directly, and prospective clinical trials are still essential.[38]

No controlled clinical trial has tested whether taking high dosages of vitamins or minerals can prolong life. However, a study of the death rates of elderly readers of *Prevention* magazine, most of whom took high doses of supplements, found no evidence of this.[39] Another epidemiologic study[40] found that people who consumed 300 to 400 mg of vitamin C daily (with roughly half from food) tended to live longer and have less heart disease than those who averaged 50 mg per day. (The RDA is 60 mg per day.) However, the study does not prove that supplementation is beneficial because the people with higher vitamin C intake had generally healthier life-styles.

Cryonics

Cryonics is defined by its proponents as "the freezing of humans as shortly as possible after death with the hope of eventual return to life."[41] Proponents claim that it is possible to preserve "with reasonable fidelity" the basic biologic components of the brain and that future technology will be able to repair

IT'S YOUR DECISION

One of your parents is in the hospital with a terminal illness from which there is no hope of recovery. How can you resolve the following questions?

1. Should a discussion be made with the physician to clarify what medical interventions might be used or withheld?
2. Should your parent be encouraged to prepare—or should you prepare—a living will, durable power of attorney, or other type of advance medical directive?
3. Which friends or family members, if any, should participate in helping to resolve these questions?

brain damage caused by "imperfect preservation, premortal disease, and postmortem changes." In 1989 the cost was a minimum of $100,000 for whole-body freezing and perpetual maintenance in liquid nitrogen, or $35,000 for preservation of just the brain within the head.

National Council Against Health Fraud president William T. Jarvis, Ph.D., calls cryonics "quackery's last shot at you." In a recent interview he said:

> Cryonic technology has not been demonstrated to work in laboratory animals. Even if the rest of a person's body could be revived after hundreds of years, the brain could not. Brain cells deteriorate within minutes after death, and any still viable when the body is frozen would be burst by the freezing process. Cryonics might be a suitable subject for scientific research, but marketing an unproven method to the public is quackery.[42]

SUMMARY

Death, an unpleasant expectation, is inevitable in everyone's life. It is an occasion that can have traumatic effects on the family and friends of the deceased. The burden may be eased by understanding the emotions involved and planning ahead to deal with various issues that pertain to dying. The intensity and duration of grief and mourning depend on the nature of the relationship to the dying person and emotional makeup of the survivors.

The need to prepare for death has become more pressing because machines often can keep a dying, permanently unconscious patient alive, sometimes indefinitely. A living will, advance directive, or durable power of attorney can help people control the nature of the care they receive when terminally ill. Hospice care provides another way to reduce suffering for patients with a terminal illness.

The technology and success rates of organ transplantation have improved greatly during recent years, but there is a serious shortage of available organs. Many entrepreneurs have capitalized on people's wish to prolong life and delay aging.

DISCUSSION QUESTIONS

1. What is the meaning of grief? What adult reactions are involved?
2. How should grief be handled?
3. What is the meaning of the terms *living will, durable power of attorney,* and *advance medical directive?*
4. Name five types of medical intervention that might be discussed with your doctor before making an advance medical directive.
5. What four things are medical facilities required to do by the Patient Self Determination Act of 1991?
6. What procedures should be followed when preparing an advance medical directive?
7. What guidelines for decisions to forego medical treatment should physicians follow?
8. How successful are organ and body part transplantations?
9. What measures have been proposed to increase the supply of transplantable body parts?
10. How can individuals donate organs and body parts? Where can they obtain information about making donations?
11. What is euthanasia? Identify the various types.
12. What are some pros and cons of euthanasia?
13. What general types of hospice organizations and programs exist in the United States?
14. What is the fundamental purpose of a hospice?
15. What are some reasons for hospice care? What advantages may it have over conventional care?
16. How can individuals locate and select a hospice?
17. Identify and discuss several unproven methods claimed to delay aging or prolong life.
18. Discuss cryonics, including its cost and effectiveness.

REFERENCES

1. The New York Times, July 21, 1974.
2. Life & death choice in Washington, Newsday, Nov 3, 1991.
*3. Jarvis WT: How quackery harms. In Barrett S and Cassileth BR, eds: Dubious cancer treament, Tampa, 1991, American Cancer Society Florida Division.
*4. Grief—time can be the greatest healer of all, Mayo Clinic Health Letter 8(3):3–4, 1990.
5. Cassem NH: The person confronting death. In Nicholi AM, Jr. (ed): New Harvard guide to psychiatry, Cambridge, Mass, 1988, Harvard University Press.
6. Horowitz MJ: Posttraumatic stress disorders. In American Psychiatric Association Task Force on Treatments of Psychiatric Disorders: treatments of psychiatric disorders, vol 3, Washington, DC, 1989, American Psychiatric Association, pp. 2069-2070.
7. Charting a course through grief, The Johns Hopkins Medical Letter, Health After 50 3(12):6–7, 1992.
8. Avoiding prolonged death, Consumer Reports Health Letter 2(8):1–2, 1990.
9. Gates M: Patients due facts on treatment rights, AARP Bulletin 32:1, 14, Nov 1991.
10. Emanuel LL, Emanuel EJ: The medical directive: a new comprehensive advance care document, JAMA 261:3288–3293, 1989.
11. Living wills: limitations and alternatives, The Johns Hopkins Medical Letter, Health After 50 2(8):4–5, 1990.
12. Stanley JM: The Appleton Consensus: suggested international guidelines for decisions to forego medical treatment, J Med Ethics 15:129–136, 1989.
13. Richmond S: The gift of a better life, Changing Times 44:92–93, 1990.
14. Monaco AP: Transplantation: the state of the art, Transplantation Proceedings 22:896–901, 1990.
15. Jonasson O: Obligation of the health care community in organ procurement, Transplantation Proceedings 22:1010–1011, 1990.
16. Kjellstrand C: The distribution of renal transplants—are physicians just? Transplantation Proceedings 22:964–965, 1990.
17. Gibbs N: The gift of life—or else, Time 136:70, 1990.
18. Sells RA: Organ commerce: ethics and expediency, Transplantation Proceedings 22:931–932, 1990.
19. Slutsker G: Should I be allowed to buy your kidney? Forbes 145:365–384, May 28, 1990.
20. Nowell-Smith P: Euthanasia and the doctors—a rejection of the BMA's report, J Med Ethics 15:124–128, 1989.
21. Carton RW: The road to euthanasia, JAMA 263:2221, 1990.
22. Parker M: Moral intuition, good deaths and ordinary medical practitioners, J Med Ethics, 16:28–34, 1990.
23. Cassell CK and Meier DG: Morals and moralism in the debate over euthanasia and assisted suicide, N Engl J Med 323:750–752, 1990.
24. Insel MS: Dying and death. In Insel PM and Roth WT: Core concepts in health, ed 6, Palo Alto, Calif, 1991, Mayfield Publishing Co.
25. Sherwood J: Washington sets euthanasia vote, AARP Bulletin 32:1,15, Nov. 1991.
26. Stolinsky DC: Euthanasia and the American College of Physicians ethics manual, Ann Intern Med 112:312, 1990.
27. Benson DC: Euthanasia and the American College of Physicians ethics manual, Ann Intern Med 111:952–953, 1989.
28. Coleman B: A consumer guide to hospice care, Washington, DC, 1990, National Consumers League.
29. Rhymes J: Hospice care in America, JAMA 264:369–372, 1990.
30. Greer DS, Mor V: How Medicare is altering the hospice movement, Hasting Center Report 15:5–9, 1985.
31. Lukashok H: Hospice care under Medicare: an early look, Prev Med 19:730–743, 1990.
32. Van Italie TB, Hadley L: The best spas, New York, 1989, Harper & Row.
33. Kent S: The life extension revolution—the source book for optimum health and maximum life-span, New York, 1980, William Morrow and Company.
*34. Yetiv JZ: Popular nutritional practices: a scientific appraisal, New York, 1988, Dell Publishing.
35. Walford RL: Maximum life span, New York, 1983, W.W. Norton & Co.
36. Schneider EL, Reed JD: Life extension, N Engl J Med 312:1159-1168, 1985.
37. Yetiv J: Life extension, part I: theories of aging, Nutrition Forum, Oct 1986.
38. Can you live longer? What works and what doesn't, Consumer Reports 57:7–15, 1992.
39. Enstrom JE and Pauling L: Mortality among health-conscious elderly Californians, Proc Natl Acad Sci U S A 79:6023–6027, 1982.
40. Enstrom JE, Kanin LE, Klein, MA: Vitamin C intake and mortality among a sample of the United States population, Epidemiology 3:194–200, 1992.
41. The cryobiological case for cryonics, undated paper distributed in 1989 by Alcor Life Extension Corporation, Riverside, Calif.
42. Jarvis WT, quotation in Butler K: A consumer's guide to "alternative" medicine, Buffalo, 1992, Prometheus Books.

*Recommended reading

CHAPTER TWENTY-FIVE

HEALTH INSURANCE

"It's a get-well card from your hospitalization insurance company."

(Reprinted with permission from Changing Times Magazine, © Kiplinger Washington Editors, Inc., August, 1971.)

Getting the right kind of health insurance is generally far more difficult than getting the right kind of life insurance.

CHANGING TIMES

Shopping for health insurance ranks somewhere between grouting the tub and giving blood. A good thing, a necessary thing, but, at best, a chore.

PAUL COHEN[1]

Health insurance policies contain hidden benefits that you can't tap into because you aren't told about them. It's like you're being mugged without even knowing it.

THE COMPLETE GUIDE TO HEALTH INSURANCE[2]

CONSUMER DECISIONS

What types of health insurance will provide the best coverage?

Should consumers purchase health insurance advertised through the mail?

What type of supplementary health insurance coverage is needed by elderly consumers?

What guidelines will help consumers select health insurance?

Where can one obtain information about health insurance policies and coverage?

 **PERSONAL GLIMPSE** 

Did You Know?

- The days are gone when a person went to a doctor of choice, filed a claim with the employing union or group and waited for a check covering 80% or more of the bill. More patients are now finding they must obtain permission for treatment beforehand, choose a doctor less on competency than cost and what insurance plan the doctor is in. There is a new breed of insurance watchdogs who have enormous power over patients' and doctors' decisions.

  Newsday, Dec. 1, 1991
- Insurance companies are systematically driving away thousands of people with costly health problems each year, creating a new population of uninsured with no way to pay for medical care. The increasingly high costs of medical services are causing private health insurers to limit risks by drastically increasing premiums, refusing to pay claims, blacklisting entire occupations or canceling groups with high medical bills.

  San Francisco Chronicle, Feb 20, 1990

Modern health insurance in the United States began as hospital insurance in 1929. In the 1930s and through World War II, it expanded to cover hospital, surgical, and medical services. Employers began to include insurance in collective bargaining contracts. The 1950s saw the emergence of catastrophic insurance or extended illness and long hospital stays. Protection grew rapidly, and by the mid-1950s, 77 million people had coverage for hospital expenses. During the next few years, insurance companies began to offer high-benefit major medical plans and comprehensive coverage with limits placed on out-of-pocket expenses (100% of costs beyond set limits were covered by most insurance plans). The 1970s and 1980s brought the growth of managed care plans, including health maintenance organizations (HMOs) and preferred provider organizations (PPOs). By 1990, 50 million to 60 million people (28% to 30% of all those insured) were enrolled in managed care plans. There have also been more self-funded employer plans. By 1989, approximately 213.6 million (87% of the total population in the United States) were covered to some extent by private and/or public insurance. Of these, 184.5 million were under 65 years of age, and 29.1 million were over 65 years of age. Table 25-1 provides additional information about the number of Americans covered by health insurance.[3]

Many people have far less insurance than is necessary to ensure that they will not be bankrupted or forced to mortgage their future because of health-care bills. Most individuals do not understand what is covered by their health insurance until they receive hospital and doctor bills. Frequently they are surprised and chagrined to discover they must pay sizable out-of-pocket sums of money. In 1990 it was estimated that 31 million to 37 million (12% to 15% of the population)[4] Americans, the majority of whom were poor or economically disadvantaged, had no health insurance protection. Most of these individuals fall outside the protection of Medicaid. Many more millions are underinsured.

Health insurance has more varieties than almost any other type of insurance. Hundreds of commercial companies are writing thousands of different policies yearly. In addition there are numerous Blue Cross–Blue Shield plans, self-funded plans, and prepayments plans (HMOs and PPOs). Their benefits, options, limitations, and exclusions have been described by one state insurance commissioner as "uniformly nonuniform." Their complexity often bewilders people. The terms and language of their policies often are difficult to understand. Comparison of various policies may be difficult or impossible. Most people accept without question the group policies provided and/or recommended by their employer, union, or other organization.

TABLE 25–1

HEALTH INSURANCE COVERAGE (1989)

Type of coverage	Number covered in millions	% of total number insured	% of population*
Private insurance	189.0	88.4	77
Employer-related	153.8	72	62.8
Blue Cross/Blue Shield	72.5	33.9	30.4
Other plans	77.1	36.1	29.3
Individual/family plans	9.7	4.5	4.4
Public insurance (includes Medicaid)	24.7	11.6	10.1
No health insurance	31.3	—	12.8

*U.S. population = 244.9 million
Source: Health Insurance Association of America.[3]

This chapter discusses the various types of health insurance plans, provides guidelines for selecting insurance, and reviews several proposals for national health insurance.

HEALTH INSURANCE PLAN BENEFITS

Health insurance plans differ widely in the variety of services they cover. The plans can be categorized as (1) basic health insurance and (2) major medical/extended/catastrophic benefits. Consumers should be knowledgeable about these benefits when selecting health insurance policies.

Basic Health Insurance

Basic health insurance includes benefits for hospital, surgical, and medical expenses. The extent of these benefits differs from contract to contract. Individuals should read their policies carefully to understand the nature of the expenses covered.

Hospital benefits may provide payment of specified amounts of money for a specified number of days, which may or may not pay all the costs. Many policies, however, cover the full charges for daily room (usually a semiprivate room), board, routine nursing services, and intensive care up to a maximum number of days. The insured individual may be required to pay a specific dollar amount (a deductible of $100 to $500 a year) before the insurance takes effect or may be required to pay a certain percentage of costs (known as coinsurance). Additional benefits may be provided up to a fixed dollar amount or for the full cost of other inpatient or outpatient hospital services (other than physicians' fees). Inpatient services are services one receives while confined as a bed patient in a hospital and may include laboratory tests, drugs, x-ray procedures, operating room, anesthesia, surgical dressings, and physical therapy. Outpatient services are those rendered in the outpatient department or emergency room of a hospital. Some individual policies provide cash benefits for each day in the hospital.

Surgical benefits after any deductible generally pay a surgeon's fee up to a specific limit set forth in the contract (commonly 80% of charges), or the insurer may agree to pay the full amount, up to but not exceeding the surgeon's usual and customary fee. Should a surgical fee exceed the amount allowed under a usual and customary fee policy, one of two outcomes may result. Under many policies, the physician (medical as well as surgical) may elect to accept the allowance under the plan in return for a guarantee that payment by the insurance company will be made directly to the physician rather than to the patient. This procedure is known as accepting assignment. When a physician accepts assignment, the patient may not be billed for the difference between the usual fee and the amount paid by the insurance company (except for amounts that involve deductibles or coinsurance). Physicians are likely to accept assignment when patients have financial difficulties or when the physicians think that a patient might pocket a direct insurance payment without paying the medical bill. If the physician does not belong to a fixed fee plan and has not accepted assignment, the patient will be liable for the difference between the physician's fee and the policy allowance.

Medical benefits provide for payment of nonsurgical physician's fees. They may include usual and customary charges or a stated amount for each hospital visit by the attending physician. They generally pay 80% of the bills including prescription drugs, laboratory tests, private nurses, and other out-of-hospital care. They may also include the maximum number of visits or dollar amounts to be paid for office and home calls plus other professional services. These medical benefits are usually available only with other basic coverages such as hospital and surgical insurance.

Maternity care may be considered a medical benefit, but some policies treat it as a separate category. Hospital care for childbirth may be paid in full, or a maximum amount may be specified. Physicians' fees are usually covered according to a schedule of benefits, with higher amounts permitted for complicated procedures. When available, major medical contracts often cover complications of pregnancy (for example, cesarean section) if expenses exceed maximum benefits of the basic health insurance plan.

Extended care or skilled nursing institution benefits may be covered as a basic benefit, but more often they are included only in major medical contracts. When included, benefits may specify a fixed allowance per day or full charges for a certain type room for a maximum number of days. Such contracts usually cover only care within a limited number of days after discharge from a hospital. Payment is provided only for medically necessary services, not for mere residence or for custodial care.

Benefits for mental or emotional disorders are often treated as a separate category. Some policies have a deductible or coinsurance provision that applies to psychiatric treatment. Other contracts exclude or limit coverage. Some policies provide coverage for vision care, dental care, and prescribed drugs.

Major Medical Insurance

Major medical or extended benefits contracts (also referred to as catastrophic coverage) are designed to help offset heavy medical expenses that result from prolonged illness or serious injury. They take over where the basic health insurance plan leaves off and provide broad coverage of all medical expenses. They may be supplementary to the basic plan or comprehensive, in which both basic and catastrophic plans are included. Generally major medical policies contain deductible and coinsurance provisions. The deductible amount may vary from $50 to $1000 or more. Coinsurance (what the insured pays) is usually 20%, but some contracts have an upper limit on coinsurance expense, after which the insurer pays all charges.

Many policies have a stop-loss feature that limits out-of-pocket expenses (for example, $1500 for one person and $3000 for a family) in any one year; 100% of medical bills over these amounts is paid for by the insurer. Maximum lifetime benefits can range from $50,000 to $1 million or can be unlimited.

The coverage under major medical insurance is generally quite extensive and can include nursing care (including special duty nurses), physical therapy, durable medical equipment (such as a respirator or feeding device), emergency ambulance service, prescription drugs, prosthetic appliances, and psychiatric care or rehabilitation. It generally covers every type of care prescribed by a physician both in and out of the hospital.

Major medical insurance serves as a supplement to basic health insurance. Because most health insurance claims fall within basic coverage provisions, it is possible to purchase high maximum benefits under major medical policies for a relatively small increase in premium. Some companies combine the basic and major medical plans into what is called comprehensive major medical insurance.

These are the desirable components of a major medical policy:

Convertibility: Ensures conversion to an individual policy if one changes jobs or is divorced.

Renewability: Guarantees renewability to age 65 and conversion to Medicare.

Maximum benefits: Covers expenses of $1 million or more for each family member.

Amount of deductible: Should not exceed $750 to $1000.

When deductible qualifies: Policy should start to pay for services when deductible has been met within a 12-month period.

Coinsurance: Should pay 20% to 25% up to a cutoff point of $1500 to $3000, after which the insurer should pay 100%.

Changes in coverage: Insurer may not reduce benefits or coverage.

Hospital expense limit: Should be at least as high as

the daily semiprivate room charges in one's area.

Intensive and cardiac care: Should be fully covered.

Private nursing: Provision should include care both in and out of the hospital when specified by physician, usually with a limit.

Psychiatric: At least 50% of the psychiatric bills in and out of the hospital; should have a $10,000 or higher limit to be paid.

Convalescent home care: Coverage should include 60 to 120 days; benefits usually run up to about half of the daily hospital limits.

Blood, plasma, and prosthetics: Should be fully covered.

Contract Provisions

A health insurance policy is a business arrangement formalized by a written contract that details both benefits and obligations. When selecting insurance, consumers should make certain that they understand the terms of the contract.

Dependent coverage: Dependents can be protected under a family plan. Individuals must be alert to the age at which benefits begin and end. Infants should be covered from birth. Other children are usually covered until age 19 years (sometimes longer if full-time students). Coverage is usually dropped automatically when children reach the maximum age listed in the contract, marry, or enter the armed forces, but some policies continue coverage for totally disabled or handicapped children as long as they are dependent.

Dependents often have the option of converting their terminating coverage to their own individual policy, regardless of medical history. Because the premiums for such individual coverage are higher, it is a good idea to keep dependents under family coverage for as long as the policy allows.

Some policies provide fewer benefits to family members than they do to the principal insured person.

Waiting periods: When medical examinations are not required, coverage generally does not become effective until a probationary period, usually 2 weeks to a month, has elapsed. Maternity benefits may not be granted until 10 months or a year after a policy has been issued. There may also be waiting periods for surgery involving the tonsils, adenoids, and appendix, as well as for hemorrhoid surgery and hernia repair. Specific waiting periods may be imposed if an illness or disorder is identified in a subscriber's health history.

Preexisting illness: An illness or a condition due to injury that is present prior to the contract's date is often excluded from coverage for a specific time, often a year. In some instances the exclusions may be permanent. Clauses in contracts may cause refusal to pay for the treatment of an illness that was present when the policy was taken out even though an individual was unaware of its existence at the time of issuance of the policy.

Conversion privileges: Many group contracts contain a clause that allows an employee, when leaving a job or in the case of marriage, death, divorce, having a child, or reaching maximum age, to convert all or part of the contract to an individual or family plan. There is usually a time limit of 15 to 30 days during which the conversion privileges can be exercised.

Cancellation and renewal provisions: Policies may include these provisions and therefore should be carefully reviewed:

1. Cancellation may occur at the wish of the company.
2. A noncancelable guaranteed renewable clause means the policy cannot be canceled as long as one pays the premiums. The company may not alter any of the provisions or the premium rates despite high medical and hospital bills that an individual incurs. Some of these policies may be renewable for life.
3. A guaranteed renewable clause prevents the termination of policies as long as the premiums are paid, but the company can raise rates at its discretion for everyone having the same kind of coverage. Thus the rates may be changed but not the provisions of the policy.
4. An optional renewal clause means that changes and cancellation are at the discretion of the insuring company when the policy comes up for renewal, although any current claims must be paid.

Limitations: Some plans limit the choice of physician or location of the hospital or other place of care. They should not impose limitations when the insured person is traveling within the United States.

Coverage in other countries: Many contracts provide for payment of medical care wherever received. This is an important provision that should be stated in the agreement, and individuals should check for its inclusion.

Exclusions: Most contracts exclude coverage for care in hospitals owned and operated by the federal government and for industrial injuries or diseases ordinarily covered by workmen's compensation laws. In addition, conditions resulting from acts of war, riot, and injuries and illnesses sustained while serving in the armed forces are excluded. Most policies do not pay for dental services, hearing aids, or eyeglasses. One should read contracts carefully to understand these exclusions.

Coordination of benefits: When an individual is eligible for benefits under more than one contract or policy, a coordination of benefits provision may apply. This limits payment so the total amount paid under all contracts does not exceed the medical expenses incurred.

TYPES OF HEALTH INSURANCE PLANS

Health insurance plans may be classified as private or public. The private sector includes individual plans, managed care, and plans offered by corporations, unions, and other employer groups. The public plans include Medicare and Medicaid.

Fee-for-Service Plans

Fee-for-Service (FFS or traditional) is a method of purchasing health care whereby a physician or hospital bills the patient (or insurance carrier) for each visit or service rendered. Fee-for-service plans are often referred to as traditional or prepaid insurance. They are usually obtained through labor unions, professional organizations, or employers. They include both *group* and *individual* plans and are usually paid with monthly or quarterly premiums. The coverage may include hospital, surgical, medical, and major medical benefits plus other services on predetermined schedules. Fee-for-service plans are provided by Blue Cross–Blue Shield, private insurance companies, and employers who self-insure their programs.

Individual policies have coverage similar to that of group policies but offer fewer benefits at higher cost. For example, only 70% or less of daily hospital costs may be paid in the basic individual health plan. Many people buy these plans to supplement group coverage. About 5% of the people in the United States carry additional individual supplementary policies, including 80% of the elderly who supplement Medicare. Exclusions and restrictions are more common. Some companies are more selective about whom they will accept into these plans. They may refuse to insure a person whose health history indicates a poor risk. Also, provisions for cancellation and renewal of policies may be at the option of the company. The biggest problem is to find a carrier one can afford. An individual plan may cost $2000 yearly or more. Consumers not covered by group insurance may find these suggestions helpful:

1. Survey professional and fraternal organizations or universities, if a student or alumnus member, for possible group plans. Also, group plans may cost less than individual insurance, but the waiting time for coverage of preexisting conditions may be shorter, and they may not require a physical examination or AIDS testing.
2. Make sure that any private insurer you consider has at least a B+ rating from *Best's Insurance Reports* (Life/Health Edition). This reference can be found in most large libraries.
3. Check employed spouse's coverage to learn whether one qualifies as a dependent.
4. Ask several companies whether they offer group insurance for self-employed persons.
5. If a group plan must be terminated, find out whether it can be converted to an individual plan. Group continuation is permissible under the Consolidated Omnibus Budget Reconciliation Act of 1985 (COBRA). The spouse, widow, or widower of an employee or an employee who quits or has been laid off has the right to remain in the company's plan for 18 months (or 36 months for the family if the person dies or gets divorced). This law applies only to companies with 20 or more employees. Those individuals involved pay a 2% higher rate than that charged to the group. A 1989 amendment provides additional help for disabled employees who leave their job.
6. After COBRA runs out, the next option beyond an individual policy is a conversion policy. By law in all but 15 states, a conversion option is mandatory. However, a person must sign up for this conversion within 31 days after the COBRA benefits end. The benefits from such a policy may be low and the price may be high. It may cost $2000 to $3000 to sign up for a conversion policy.
7. If the above items do not apply, purchase an

individual policy at a higher premium with less coverage; the higher the deductible, the lower the premium. Contact a variety of companies regarding coverage and costs. A local chapter of the National Association of Life Underwriters, 1922 F Street, NW, Washington, DC 20006, will provide the names of representatives who offer policies.
8. Obtain a temporary individual policy while waiting for a permanent or group policy to take effect.

Benefits of Fee-for-Service Plans

The benefits provided by private prepaid fee-for-service policies vary widely. The extent and cost are based on the breadth of coverage provided and whether the insurance is obtained as an individual or as a member of a group. Group plans generally offer the most extensive coverage. It is also true that the more benefits included in a policy, the higher the premium.

When purchasing private prepaid health insurance or reviewing policies in force, look for these four factors to ensure the best protection:

1. Basic health insurance includes coverage of hospital, surgical, and regular medical expenses.
2. Major medical insurance includes high maximum benefits ($300,000 to $1 million or more), and a deductible amount as high as you can afford (often $100 to $1000) before the insurer starts paying for services.
3. The out-of-pocket expenses to be paid by the individual should be reasonable (perhaps 25%). A health insurance policy that covered every possible contingency would be prohibitively expensive.
4. Contract provisions, such as exclusions, omission, cancellation, renewal, and conversion clauses, should fit your needs.

Many insurance companies pay for certain preventative services. Those now available include mammography (test for breast cancer), diabetes education, cardiac rehabilitation, and Pap tests (primarily for detecting cervical cancer). In major studies, Blue Cross–Blue Shield companies discovered that they saved between $1.92 and $2.50 for every $1 invested. A Stanford University study found a 7% to 17% reduction in number of doctor visits by elderly patients.[5]

Comprehensive health insurance, which includes a basic plan and a major medical plan, is perhaps the best protection one can have. Table 25-2 illustrates the essential benefits of a plan offered by PERS Care.

Table 25-3 shows the premiums charged for Blue Cross policies in 1989 in the states of Washington and Alaska. It illustrates how policies with higher deductibles have lower premiums.

Managed Care

Managed care refers to several procedures used by insurance carriers to try to hold the line on benefit costs and yet be able to provide quality medicine. These controls, called utilization management, are used to determine whether medical services are appropriate for a person's condition in or out of the hospital. Many employers use this system to make traditional insurance affordable, but it is a standard feature of HMOs, PPOs, and other such organizations. Managed care may involve any or all of these features[6]:

1. *Preadmission review.* Nonemergency hospitalization must be approved before admission.
2. *Mandatory second opinion for elective surgery.*
3. *Preadmission testing.* Certain tests must be done on an outpatient basis before admission.
4. *Concurrent review.* Care is reviewed to determine whether treatment can be rendered at home.
5. *Discharge planning.* This determines the nature of equipment and support services needed for home service.
6. *Case management.* This assesses complicated or high-cost cases to determine appropriate setting for continued treatment.

Health Maintenance Organizations (HMOs)

Once promoted as an alternative to fee-for-service (FFS) health insurance plans, HMOs are becoming increasingly difficult to distinguish from other plans.

Feldman R et al.
Health Services Research, June 1990

Health maintenance organizations are closed systems of health care in a defined geographical area that provide basic, comprehensive, and preventive services to voluntarily enrolled persons for a fixed monthly fee. HMOs may also be loosely organized associations of physicians who practice medicine in their own offices. These closed or open groups can be independently owned or can be sponsored by an insurance company, hospital, phy-

TABLE 25–2

PERS CARE*

Covered services	Basic benefits
Hospital	
Inpatient	
Room & board and all medically necessary services, including general nursing care service, operating and special care room fees, diagnostic and x-ray and laboratory services.	No charge
Outpatient	
Surgical room fee, radiation & chemotherapy treatment, renal dialysis.	No charge
Physician care	
Office/home/hospital visits	No charge
Allergy testing	No charge
Vision exam	Excess charges
Hearing testing	20%
Immunization/inoculation	No charge
Gynecological exam	20%
Periodic health exam	Not covered
Diagnostic x-ray/lab	
Outpatient diagnostic x-ray & laboratory services	No charge
Prescription drugs	
All prescription drugs to include diabetic supplies, insulin, needles, syringes, & blood glucose testing strips	\$4—generic \$8—nongeneric
Durable medical equipment	No charge; rental or purchase by physician approval if for therapeutic value
Ambulance	No charge
Emergency care/services	No charge
Mental health	
Inpatient	No charge
Outpatient	Excess charges; maximum per year \$1000; physician charges limit = \$32 daily
Alcohol/drug abuse	
Inpatient/outpatient	Not covered
Home health services	
Medically necessary; custodial care not covered	No charge
Speech/physical/occupational therapy	No charge
Acupuncture	20%; 20-visit limit per year
Biofeedback/chiropractic	No charge
Other	
Unreplaced blood & blood products	20% 1st three units
Hospice	No charge

From: California Public Employees' Retirement System, Health Plans, August 1, 1991. Sacramento, CA, 1991.
*Monthly premiums: 1 party, \$123.49; 2 party, \$246.99; 3 party, \$355.47

Table 25–3

Traditional Deductibles, Monthly/Annual Premiums for Health Insurance Policies in Washington and Alaska (Blue Cross, 1989)

Traditional deductible	Single monthly/annual	Couple monthly/annual	Family monthly/annual
$200	$91/1092	$183/2196	$247/2964
$500	$73/876	$146/1752	$197/2364
$1000	$59/708	$117/1404	$158/1896

Source: Berman H, Rose L: Choosing the right health care plan. New York, 1990, Consumer Reports Books.

sicians' association, employer, union, or other entity. This type of group practice approach to health insurance began several years before World War II and has steadily grown since that time. Three of the largest long-established plans are the Kaiser Foundation Health Plan (California, Portland), the Health Insurance Plan (HIP) of Greater New York, and the Group Health Cooperative of Puget Sound (Seattle). These groups are now referred to as health maintenance organizations.

HMOs received impetus from the Health Maintenance Organization Act of 1973 passed by the U.S. Congress. This was an effort by the federal government to find a way to help control the escalating medical costs and to improve the quality of health care in the United States. The law requires all employers with 25 or more employees to offer workers an opportunity to join a qualified HMO if one exists in the area. This legislation allocated $375 million in seed money to start these prepaid organizations. Applications for $100,000 to $200,000 were given consideration for anyone who wished to start an HMO. Today, HMOs must meet government standards to become federally qualified. These standards require providers to assure financial solvency and to meet certain requirements to staff, facility, and services offered. This financial stimulus has led to over 60 million enrollees (29% of the health-insured). About 30 large corporations operate HMOs in two or more states.

There are five general models of HMOs:

IPA (independent practice association): An HMO contracts with an association (group) of physicians in various settings and specialties. These doctors include solo and group practitioners. Physicians are paid on a fee-for-service basis. These fees may be 15% or 20% less than the usual and customary fees. Patients see physicians in their individual offices. This model has the largest enrollment and number of plans and is continuing to grow.

Network: An HMO contracts with two or more independent physician group practices to provide services to its members.

Group: An HMO contracts with a single multispecialty group of physicians to provide health services to its members. A capitation payment is made to the group for each HMO member services regardless of the number of office visits made by members.

Staff: This is the original model (Kaiser), in which physicians are employed directly by the HMO and practice in a central office facility with the necessary administrative support. Doctors receive a salary and bonuses based on the HMO's profits, costs of operation, physician performance, and other factors. Patients can select a primary care physician who can direct them to staff specialists as needed.

Point-of-service (open-ended): A relatively new plan in which enrollees can choose providers (physicians, and so on) outside the plan, but they receive strong incentive to use affiliated providers.

Although HMO enrollment has been growing, the number of plans has been decreasing. However, the IPAs have expanded to the extent that about half are functioning like fee-for-service plans. Table 25-4 gives the number of plans and their enrollments in 1989.

The following kinds of services may be available through HMOs:

1. Physician services (including consultant and referral services)
2. Inpatient and outpatient hospital services
3. Emergency health services, as medically necessary

TABLE 25–4

HMO ENROLLMENT, 1989

Model	Number of plans	Enrollment	Percent
Group	85	9,844,770	28
IPA	386	15,428,000	44
Network	86	5,431,530	16
Staff	66	4,326,860	12
Totals	623	35,031,160	100

Source: Marion Managed Care Digest, HMO Edition[7]

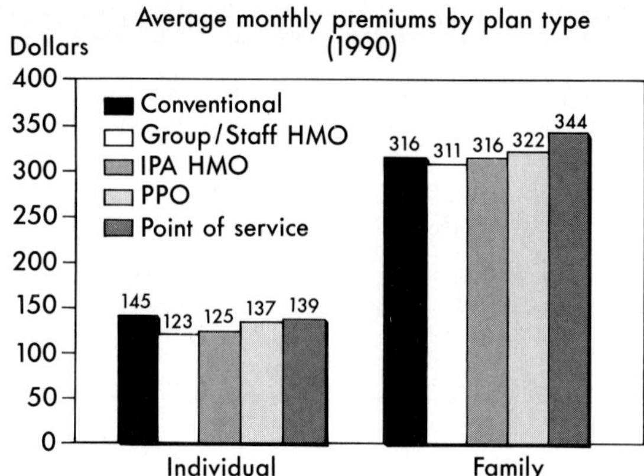

FIGURE 25-1. Premiums for HMO.

4. Short-term (20 or fewer visits) outpatient evaluative and crisis intervention mental health services
5. Medical treatment and referral services for abuse of and/or addiction to alcohol and drugs
6. Diagnostic laboratory, and diagnostic and therapeutic x-ray services
7. Home health services
8. Preventive health services (including immunizations, well-child care from birth, periodic health evaluations for adults, voluntary family planning services, infertility services, and children's eye and ear examination).

An HMO may also include any or all of the following services:

1. Intermediate or long-term care
2. Vision care, not part of basic services
3. Dental service
4. Mental health services, not part of basic services
5. Long-term physical medicine and rehabilitative services, including physical therapy
6. Prescription drugs

In addition to the basic premium, some HMOs make small additional charges for certain services (for example, office visits, prescriptions). By operating within a fixed budget, however, the HMO has a financial incentive to provide early care and to minimize use of expensive hospital facilities. Table 25-5 illustrates one basic HMO insurance plan available in California.

HMO Premiums

The premiums for HMO plans have been rising with medical costs and today are probably equal and may be higher than those of fee-for-service plans. *Consumer Reports*[4] evaluated health insurance policies and found the following premium ranges:

Men— $658 to $3100 yearly
Women—$716 to $3167 yearly
Family—$1928 to $6100 yearly

The Health Insurance Association of America surveyed 2621 employer groups and found the monthly premium costs for traditional plans, HMOs, and PPOs as shown in Figure 25-1.

In the New York City metropolitan area[8] in 1989 the monthly premiums for HMO insurance were as follows:

Single—$111 to $205
Family—$256 to $576.

HMO Quality

The quality of services provided by HMOs has received varying reports as indicated in the list of advantages and disadvantages in this section. However, a few studies listed next provide some evidence of the quality of their services.

Chase[9] reported that a study published in the *New England Journal of Medicine* described the quality of care as "at least as good at HMOs as at private hospitals and doctors' offices."

Schaefer[10] and Wolfe[11] have commented on a Puget Sound study that found that hospital admissions were 40% less for HMOs than for fee-for-service groups, and the costs for all services were 25% less. However, not everyone agrees that HMOs are better than other forms of health insurance.

TABLE 25–5

FOUNDATION HEALTH PLAN (BASIC HEALTH INSURANCE)

		Member pays
Hospital		
Inpatient Outpatient	Room and board and all medically necessary services	No charge
	Surgery; radiation, chemotherapy; renal dialysis	No charge
Physician care	Surgery; hospital visits; well-baby care	No charge
	Office visits; home visits	No charge
	Allergy treatment including antigen; immunizations and inoculations	No charge
	Annual physical exams, including pap smears, breast exams, lab and x-ray	No charge
	Hearing exams to determine condition	No charge
	Vision testing not a covered benefit	Not covered
Diagnostic/x-ray/lab	Diagnostic, x-ray, and laboratory services for medical diagnosis; allergy testing	No charge
Prescription drugs	When ordered by a Plan physician, oral drugs, diabetic supplies and birth control pills, excluding psychotropic drugs, except for approved medical diagnosis	$4/prescription
Durable medical equipment	Prosthetic devices; rental or purchase of durable medical equipment, including crutches, wheelchairs, braces, etc., as approved by Medicare	No charge
Maternity	Treated as any other illness, prenatal, postnatal, nursery care, nonelective and elective abortions	No charge
	Natural childbirthing classes not covered	Not covered
Family planning	Sterilization procedures	No charge
	Infertility diagnosis and treatment as covered by Medicare	No charge
	Contraceptives—IUD/diaphragm	No charge
Ambulance	Ambulance services provided when medically necessary. Includes air ambulance. Does not include other forms of public conveyance.	No charge
	Worldwide coverage if you are temporarily outside service area and require emergency treatment	No charge
Emergency care/services	An emergency is an unforeseen medical condition that would result in further disability or death if not immediately diagnosed and treated.	
	Worldwide coverage. Regular Plan benefits for medically necessary emergency care out of the service area or when a participating provider is not available.	No charge
	Hospital emergency room	No charge
Mental health	Inpatient: Up to 190 days, including physician services, in your lifetime	No charge
	Outpatient: Up to 20 visits per calendar year upon referral of primary care physician	No charge
Alcohol/drug abuse	Inpatient diagnosis, detoxification, and treatment provided, as approved by Medicare	No charge
	Rehabilitation as covered by Medicare	No charge

Continued.

TABLE 25-5

FOUNDATION HEALTH PLAN (BASIC HEALTH INSURANCE)—cont'd

		Member pays
Home health services	Intermittent skilled nursing care when medically necessary and approved by Medicare Custodial care is not a benefit	No charge
Speech/physical/occupational therapy	Short-term speech, physical, and occupational therapy for acute conditions until significant improvement can be expected and as approved by Medicare	No charge
Chiropractic/	As approved by Medicare	No charge
Acupuncture/biofeedback	Not a covered benefit	Not covered
Other:	Blood and blood administration	No charge
	Organ transplants—nonexperimental	No charge
	Hospice care—as approved by Medicare	No charge
Health education	Health Education Department provides a variety of counseling and educational services designed to enhance the health knowledge of our membership and has various programs designed specifically for seniors	Varies

Source: Public Employees Retirement System, Health Benefits Division, Health Plans, Aug 1, 1987, Sacramento, California State Printing Office.
Est. Fees 1991: employee = $118; plus one dependent = $233; plus two dependents = $307.

Patient dissatisfaction has increased as a result of efforts to hold down costs. Complaints regarding quality of care are greater, according to a RAND Corporation study and reports from state agencies in Florida and Minnesota.

Dr. Ronald Bronow,[12] a Los Angeles dermatologist, stated that three out of every four HMO plans were in deep trouble because they could not hold down costs. They could not raise premiums in order to make money because they had to remain competitive with other HMOs and employers applied pressures to keep prices down. Bronow added that 16 HMOs disappeared in 1987, and 29 plans did not renew Medicare contracts in 1988. This condition apparently stabilized in 1990, when there were fewer HMOs and almost 90% reported profits for the year.[13]

Some HMOs have experienced severe financial difficulty. *Consumer Reports*[4] indicated that a number of HMOs in the past have gone broke, leaving many people without health insurance coverage. The question of what action to take should this problem arise cannot be easily resolved. Many states have provided conversion policies or continuation coverage for such unfortunate people. However, there is no assurance that the same coverage will be provided. Nevertheless, consumers who find themselves without insurance due to the collapse of an HMO should explore the availability of this option.

HMO Advantages/Disadvantages

Some of the advantages and disadvantages of HMOs are listed in Table 25-6. A family with two

TABLE 25-7

NUMBER OF HMOS OFFERING SPECIALTY PROGRAMS

Specialty program	Percentage of HMOs
Dental	27
Vision	43
Psychiatric/Mental health	57
Prescription drug	52
Occupational health/Workers compensation	7
Other specialties*	3

*Other specialties include social HMOs and senior health plans.
From Marion Managed Care Digest, HMO edition, Kansas City, Mo, 1990, Marion Merril Dow, Inc.

Table 25–6

Advantages and Disadvantages of HMOs

Advantages	Disadvantages
Lower health costs; no deductible; rarely coinsurance & less out-of-pocket expenses	Some do not have board-certified physicians
No charge or low charge or low charge at time of service; e.g., $2 for office visit	Possible long waits for service in staff model
One-stop care for staff model; services in one building	Possible problems of access to physicians and personnel
Preventive care in some plans; in some plans well-baby care, Pap tests, mammography, flu shots and other immunizations	Limited choice of primary physician
Greater protection against unnecessary surgery	May be seen by nurse practitioner or physician's assistant in some plans
Fewer laboratory tests	Cost-effectiveness may take priority over patient needs
More likely to cover office visits	Restricted choice of hospitals and physicians in most plans
No paperwork to file claims	Location may not be convenient
Specialty programs provided by some; see Table 25-7	No coverage of costs of doctor's fee outside of HMO plan
Can request change of doctors	Limited coverage when traveling
	Change of jobs may make it difficult to remain in HMO

Consumer Tip

"Survival" in an HMO

- Learn the system: what people will and won't do; talk to other patients.
- Ask members who the best doctors are.
- Arrange to see your primary physician; don't wait until sick.
- Be a good listener when visiting a doctor.
- Bring a short list of questions, but be brief. Remember, the doctor may have a productivity quota and be able to give you only 10 to 15 minutes of attention.
- Be prepared to have a nurse practitioner see you; may take more time with you.
- Ask to change doctors if not satisfied with the assigned person.

Victor Cohn[14]

or more children who will need vaccinations and treatment for childhood diseases, and other people who make frequent visits to doctors' offices, may find an HMO to be the best value.

HMO Selection Guidelines

These guidelines will help to select an HMO:

1. Ask consumer agencies and state regulators about complaints and check the HMO's financial health.
2. Consult friends and coworkers who belong to HMOs.
3. Visit the HMO clinic or doctor. Ask whether doctors are board-certified in their specialties. Check the turnover rate for physicians. Talk to members. Check waiting-room times and how long it takes to get an appointment. Ask whether doctors will see you on all visits or whether minor matters will be handled by a nurse practitioner or physician's assistant.
4. Ask whether the HMO is federally qualified and whether it belongs to the Group Health Association of America, a trade group that inspects members' facilities.
5. Ask about costs for premiums and out-of-pocket expenses.

6. Ask about major medical coverage.
7. Ask about the services offered, the hospitals or clinics used, the length of time in business, the extent to which the plan is "managed," or restricted in services.

PPOs and PPAs

Preferred provider organizations (PPOs) and preferred provider associations (PPAs) were started in the 1980s as fee-for-serivce alternatives to traditional health insurance (basic and comprehensive). In 1989, there were 708 such programs operating in the United States, servicing over 30 million employees (including dependents over 69 million people).[15] Some are operated by insurance companies (the largest group includes Blue Cross–Blue Shield), while others are operated by physicians and hospitals, physicians and medical groups, or hospitals. Contracts are made with panels or networks of providers to provide services to a defined group of consumers. These providers are paid on a negotiated fee schedule that in 1989 averaged 22% lower than customary rates. The providers may include pharmacists, chiropractors, chiropodists, and optometrists. Those enrolled in a PPO must select services from a designated panel of providers. Beneficiaries who use providers from a closed panel pay lower fees for services. For example, they may pay a $150 deductible, 5% to 10% of most charges, and no fee for hospitalization. Patients have the option of going to providers not affiliated with the panel but receive less reimbursement. They may have to pay a $200 to $300 deductible plus 20% to 25% of the costs of services. Like HMOs, PPOs regulate costs of services (managed care) by directing patients to providers who are committed to cost-control measures. These panels, however, also provide a variety of services in addition to basic and comprehensive care as identified in Table 25-8.

Many PPOs offered exclusive provider options (EPOs) in 1989. Enrollees in EPO programs must pay all costs if they go to a provider who is not designated by the program. Approximately 33% of the PPOs provide this option. The Health Insurance Association of America[3] stated that the distinctions between HMOs, EPOs, are becoming blurred.

Table 25-9 compares the coverage, costs, advantages, and disadvantages of traditional plans, HMOs, and PPOs.

Table 25–8

Special Services Provided by PPOs, 1989

Type of service	% PPOs offering service
Well-baby care	62
Adult physical exams	42
Diagnostic procedures	71
Medical/surgical	95
Mental health/psychiatric care	66
Vision care	32
Chiropractic	25
Dental care	22
Substance abuse treatment	87

Source: Managed Care Digest, PPO Edition[15]

Corporations and Health Insurance

Business establishments in the United States have provided insurance benefits to their employees and retirees for many years. They have made available a variety of fee-for-service, HMO, PPO, and other types of policies. Forty-three percent of all companies offer health insurance for employees, with large companies providing insurance for all of their workers. Employers have been able to deduct their health-care costs from their total income, and employees have not had to declare these benefits as taxable income. The costs for these health benefits have escalated to a point that for many companies, it is no longer possible to raise product costs to compensate—and unless they solve the problem, their profits could disappear. As a result, many business establishments are making efforts to manage the health care of their employees to reduce expenditures. These efforts include the following:

1. More of the financial burden for health care is being shifted to employees by forcing them to relinquish their freedom to choose health providers. Companies are buying into, establishing their own, or contracting with HMOs, PPOs, and similar organizations. Employees may not benefit from these plans due to the provision of deductibles, copayments, and other cost-sharing devices. Also, employees may have to pay part of the premium costs.
2. Large establishments are self-insuring their

health plans, thereby assuming the financial risks involved. A small percentage also self-administer, but most hire a commercial insurance company to administer the plan.

3. Some companies have been paying employees not to go to the doctor; they have introduced cash incentives. The procedure varies somewhat, but typically $300 to $500 has been deposited in the account of each employee. At the end of the year each individual receives what is left after medical expenditures have been deducted. Employees seem to be happy with the plan. However, members of unions and insurance companies, as well as some of the executives of the corporations involved, indicated this procedure may merely be payment to the young, who normally don't run up large medical bills. The plan has not been a solution to escalating medical costs. In addition, some observers believe the procedure can be dangerous for individuals who postpone care with the result that acute or minor conditions become chronic or serious. In recent years, the popularity of this plan has diminished.

Table 25–9

Comparison of Typical HMO, PPO, and Traditional Insurance Plans

Traditional plan	Health maintenance organization (HMO)	Preferred provider organization (PPO)
What's covered		
Hospital stays, doctor visits, prescription drugs, lab tests, alcohol and drug abuse treatment, mental health care in and out of hospital, nursing care for recovery at home (if recommended by your doctor, limited to 90 days). Though dental coverage is not the rule, traditional policies are more likely to offer it than other plans.	Hospital stays, doctor visits, prescription drugs, lab tests, mental health care in and out of hospital, alcohol and drug abuse treatment, nursing care for recovery at home, annual physical exams, regular baby checkups, immunizations, Pap smears, birth control, allergy tests.	Hospital stays, doctor visits, prescription drugs, lab tests, mental health care in and out of hospital, alcohol and drug abuse treatment, nursing care for recovery at home, regular baby checkups, immunizations, Pap smears, birth control, allergy tests.
Costs		
Monthly premium: $130 to $200 for an individual, $350 to $500 for a family.*	Monthly premium: $120 to $190 for an individual, $330 to $470 for a family.	Monthly premium: $120 to $180 for an individual, $310 to $450 for a family.
Deductible: $150 for an individual, $300 for a family each year.	Deductible: none	Deductible: $100 for an individual, $250 for a family each year.
Out-of-pocket expenses: Besides deductible and your share of premium, you pay 20% of bills up to a ceiling of $500 to $5000 each year.	Out-of-pocket expenses: Besides your share of premium, you pay $5 to $20 per office visit.	Out-of-pocket expenses: Besides deductible and your share of premium, you pay 20% of bills up to a ceiling of $500 to $2000 each year. "Preferred" physicians and hospitals charge cheaper fees than what you'd be charged by nonparticipants.
Maximum the company will pay: $1 million over the policy's lifetime.	Maximum the company will pay: No stated limit.	Maximum the company will pay: $1 million over the policy's lifetime.

Continued.

Table 25–9

Comparison of Typical HMO, PPO, and Traditional Insurance Plans—cont'd

	Traditional plan	Health maintenance organization (HMO)	Preferred provider organization (PPO)
Advantages	The most flexible. Consumers can go to virtually any doctor or hospital they choose.	Potentially the cheapest of all three plans, it provides the broadest coverage. No claim forms to fill out.	Combines features of traditional and HMO plans. By choosing doctors and hospitals affiliated with the plan, you pay lower fees (for some plans, your copayment also drops from 20 to 10 percent). For costlier outside services, plan provides traditional coverage.
Drawbacks	Potentially the most expensive of the three plans. Requires record keeping because you often pay up front and file forms for reimbursement. Doesn't cover such preventive services as annual physical exams, regular baby checkups, immunizations, Pap smears, and birth control. Mental health care restricted to a cost of $1000 per year for outpatient treatment, 90 days for inpatient. Alcohol and drug detox treatment limited to 30 days of inpatient care. Companies may rule a cost exceeds usual, reasonable, or customary charge for a given service, then pay less than your full claim. Increasingly, freedom of traditional plans is being replaced by requirements such as second opinions for operations and prior approval for hospital visits.	Limits your choice of doctors and facilities to those in the plan; if you go outside, it won't pay any of the cost. Visits to specialists, hospitals, and other services must be okayed by primary doctor. Psychiatric visits limited to 10 to 20 per year, approved only if primary doctor believes you'll be helped by short-term treatment. Some limits on out-of-town nonemergency care, a concern for frequent travelers. Some subscribers complain about requirement to see a nurse practitioner before seeing a doctor and about lengthy waits for appointments. Most HMO's don't cover dental care.	Since participating doctors also see nonplan patients and receive higher fees from them, you may get second-class treatment. Most PPOs don't cover annual physical exams or dental care. Most require a second opinion for surgery and lab tests before admission to a hospital. PPOs use financial incentives to limit your use of hospitals—both for operations and recovery.

Research by Valerie Fahey
*When considering the premium, remember that if you're employed it's probably your company, not you, who's paying most of it.
From Cohen P: Health plan roulette, In Health 4(4):78-82, 1990. Reproduced with permission.

Problems with Corporate Health Insurance

Corporate health insurance has developed these problems:

Employees in small companies without coverage. Eighty-seven percent of Americans without health insurance are workers living in a family headed by a worker. Almost half of those uninsured are either self-employed (21%) or work with firms with fewer than 25 employees (28%).[16] Federal and state laws have been changed to help companies with few employees to self-insure and thus become exempt from compliance with mandated benefits (for example, cover chiropractic and mental health services). Others have introduced high deductibles and workers assuming payment of part of the premiums. Blue Cross–Blue Shield plans have proposed insurance reforms to make private coverage available to employees in small firms. The American Medical Association has proposed a minimum benefits package (Table 25-10) that would cost em-

Table 25–10

AMA Proposed Minimum Benefits Package

Covered

- Physician services—office visits limited to 20 per person per year; inpatient visits limited to 45 days per person per year.
  - Services include
  - Diagnosis and treatment of illness or injury
  - Prenatal and postnatal care of mother and infant
  - Immunizations and well-child care in accordance with American Academy of Pediatrics guidelines
- Outpatient facility services, including
  - Diagnostic services such as x-rays and lab tests
  - Use of operating room and supplies
  - Use of emergency room and supplies
  - Dialysis care
- Inpatient hospital care, including:
  - Semiprivate room, board, and nursing services
  - ICU at three times semiprivate room rate
  - Drugs, oxygen, blood, biologicals, supplies, and equipment
  - Operating, delivery, and recovery room charges
  - All medically necessary special types of care, including but not limited to intensive, coronary, dialysis, and rehabilitation unit charges
  - Diagnostic services
  - Care for pregnancy and complications
  - Medically necessary ancillary services
- Skilled nursing facility services—limited to 180 days per person per year
- Dental services (office and hospital)—limited to repair necessitated by injury to sound teeth or jaw
- Home health care (medically necessary services prescribed by a physician)—limited to 240 visits per person per year. Includes
  - Services of physicians, home health aids, medical social workers, and nurses under physician supervision
  - Ancillary services, medical supplies, and appliances
  - Oxygen, blood, and biologicals
  - Rental of durable medical equipment
- Ambulance services
- $1 million lifetime limit on overall benefits per person

Not covered

- Routine physicals, including routine screening tests
- Detoxification
- Family planning
- Sterilization, reversal of sterilization, artificial insemination
- Cosmetic surgery
- Obesity treatment and weight loss programs
- Custodial or domiciliary care
- Eyeglasses
- Hearing aids
- Orthopedic shoes
- Orthodontic appliances
- Personal comfort items
- Hospice
- Outpatient prescription and nonprescription drugs
- Outpatient physical, speech, and occupational therapy

Source: Benefits package gets leaner, Medical World News, July 1990.

ployees about $1700 annually per employee (70% family policies and 30% individual policies), with employers paying 80% of the premiums.[17]

Bankruptcy of some insurers. Since 1989 at least 51 mostly small commercial health insurers have been unable to meet financial obligations.[18] Here are a few suggestions for consumers:

1. Be alert to signs of trouble, such as dramatic increases in premium costs.
2. Check company ratings in *Best's Insurance Reports* (Life/Health Edition) in your local library. The rating should be at least B+. Another rating service is Weiss Research (800-239-9222), which will give you a company's rating for $15.
3. Be aware that Blue Cross–Blue Shield plans are not regulated as an insurance company and generally are not rated.
4. Check the financial condition of the HMO enrolled in; some have been having financial problems. If any of these cause uneasiness or concerns, consumers may wish to (1) report suspicions of insurer problems to their employers, (2) consider changing from a fee-for-service plans to an HMO if offered by employers, (3) consider changing to another insurer with a higher premium but top rating if present insurer is having financial problems. Should your plan go into bankruptcy, unpaid claims may be covered by a state guaranty fund (48 states have such a fund). However, if an employer is self-insured, there is no coverage for unpaid claims.

Corporations changing retirees' heath insurance benefits. Corporations are beginning to challenge the security of health insurance benefits because of escalating costs, increased number of retirees, retirees living longer, failure to set aside money in advance to pay for promised benefits, failure of cost controls to function, and other factors. Most companies believe they have the right to modify or terminate existing retiree medical plans.[19] As a result, some coverage has been cancelled; premiums, deductibles, and copayments have been increased; and some retirees have been paid off in some manner. Some of the changes that companies are instituting include eliminating dependency coverage; requiring employees to work longer for medical coverage as a retiree; allowing retirees to pay for their own health coverage after retirement; and limiting payment of cost increases, with retirees paying the additional fees.

The Retiree Benefits Bankruptcy Protection Act of 1988 prohibits firms seeking reorganization from changing health benefits without court approval. Any retiree who believes health benefits are to be terminated or modified may well consider these suggestions:

1. Ask to see a copy of the statement of benefits; check that it includes a statement about the right to terminate or change benefits.
2. Keep all statements or documents of entitled health benefits.
3. Check all options offered by the company.
4. Compare costs of retiree coverage with costs of private insurer.
5. Form or participate in a retiree club to seek group insurance.
6. Question all proposed changes for accuracy.
7. Consider consulting an experienced lawyer for action.

CONSUMER TIP

When Selecting Health Insurance

On leaving a job

- Consider COBRA (Consolidated Omnibus Budget Reconstruction Act 1985). You can retain your insurance up to 18 months even if fired or firm goes broke. You pay premiums. Does not apply if firm has fewer than 20 employees or is self-insured.

On your own

- Get into a group. May provide more coverage at less cost.
- Check Blue Cross–Blue Shield for open enrollment periods.
- Consider increase of deductible. Can save on premium.
- Purchase only benefits needed. Family members covered?
- Remember tax benefits. Self-employed deduct 25% from taxable income.
- Review monthly premiums, deductible, out-of-pocket costs.
- Check whether spouse has plan.

Joseph Anthony[20]

HEALTH INSURANCE PROBLEMS

Health insurance companies and consumers are faced with a variety of problems that need attention. The following are some of the most important problems today:

Uninsured and Underinsured Consumers

The majority of the uninsured are people who are employed. Congress has made unsuccessful efforts to have these individuals covered. However, their plans have been tied to the development of a national health insurance program for all Americans. It is estimated that an additional 56 million people in 1984 were underinsured. They were inadequately protected against large medical bills.[22]

Insurers in many states have attempted to help the uninsured (particularly workers) through the offering of bare-bones policies at fairly low costs; 23 states have altered their laws to permit such policies, and 12 more are considering allowing such plans. However, employers show little interest in these policies. Consumer advocates oppose the proposals because of their limited coverage. These advocates claim they are attempts to avoid more fundamental reforms that threaten the insurance industry.[23]

High-Risk Consumers

Twenty-three states have high-risk pools for people who are unable to purchase insurance because insurers believe the risk of insuring them is too great. The coverage is similar to major-medical plans but has more exclusions. The application rules differ from state to state, but generally a person must have been a resident for at least 6 months and have been rejected by at least one carrier. The policies usually require a high deductible, greater coinsurance, and provide relatively low lifetime benefits ($250,000 to $500,000). For a 45-year-old man, an individual policy with a $500 deductible would cost $3844 yearly in Chicago; that is double the cost of most such policies for lower-risk individuals.[4]

Financial Problems of Insurers

The increasingly high costs of medical care have caused many commercial companies to lose money on group insurance policies. During 1988, many paid out more in claims than they received in premiums. Loss ratio should not be lower than 75% to 80%, but many had loss ratios over 100%[25] See Tables 25-11, 25-12, 25-13, and 25-14 for information. As a result, some companies closed shop, refused to renew policies, or sharply increased premiums, with the result that many individuals and groups lost their coverage.

The Wall Street Journal reported that eight Blue Cross–Blue Shield companies in five eastern states had 1990 deficits. Apparently their rate increases and cost-cutting efforts were not sufficient. Experts believe most plans are stable and consumers should not seek other coverage at this time.[26]

Fraud

The most common frauds that occur are claims for medical services not performed such as diagnostic tests and physical examinations, claims for non-

Table 25–11

Calculation of Loss Ratios

Average benefits paid to policyholders	÷	Estimated annual premium	=	Loss ratio (%)
$1140		$1200		95
960		1200		80
780		1200		65
600		1200		50
420		1200		35

Table 25–12

Premiums, Claims and Loss/Expense Ratio of 768 Companies and 18 Blue Cross-Blue Shield Plans in 1990

Plans	Premiums	Claims	Loss ratio	Expenses	Expense ratio %	Combined ratio %
Group	$45,359,491	$35,589,891	78.4	$9,431,884	20.8	100.2
Individual	14,895,290	8,500,875	66.6	6,211,932	41.7	108.5
Totals	60,254,781	44,090,766	72.5	15,643,816	31.25	103.8
Blue Cross	12,332,793	10,755,769	87.3	1,307,276	10.6	97.9

Source: Collected from National Underwriter: Profiles 1991 Health Insurers, Cincinnati, National Underwriter Co., 1991.

Table 25-13

Loss Ratios of 10 Leading Health Insurance Companies Offering Group Policies in 1990

Company	Percent
Life Insurance Co. of North America	96.8
Continental Assurance Co.	87.6
Blue Cross-Blue Shield, Conn.	87.6
Conn. General Life Insurance Co.	86.7
Mutual of Omaha	86.0
Travelers Insurance Co.	84.6
Health Care Service Corp.	84.4
Prudential Insurance Co. of America	83.8
Guardian Life Insurance Co. of America	80.2
New York Life Insurance Co.	79.1

Source: National Underwriter: Profiles 1991 Health Insurers, Cincinnati, National Underwriter Co., 1991.[21]

Table 25-14

Loss Ratios of 10 Leading Health Insurance Companies Offering Individual Policies in 1990

Company	Percent
Provident Life & Accident Insurance Co.	86.8
Equitable Life Assurance Society of the U.S.	80.7
State Farm Mutual Auto Insurance Co.	79.3
Paul Revere Life Insurance Co.	73.4
Time Insurance Co.	66.8
United American Insurance Co.	65.6
Physicians Mutual Insurance Co.	65.1
Bankers Life & Casualty Co.	62.1
Golden Rule Insurance Co.	61.8
Mutual of Omaha Co.	59.1

Source: National Underwriter: Profiles 1991 Health Insurers, Cincinnati, National Underwriter Co., 1991.

covered services such as cosmetic surgery, weight-loss programs, prescriptions for narcotics, and other forms of overbilling. In Michigan in 1989 there were 8324 investigations, 709 warrants, 643 arrests, and 472 convictions of providers, subscribers, and employers.[27]

Consumers should be alert for people who sell bogus health insurance policies to the public from companies that don't exist. These individuals may disappear after collecting premiums. The California Department of Insurance has issued warnings about such individuals and advised that the department be called to verify the authenticity of the company or agent.

Collecting Claims

Although a 1990 survey by the Health Insurance Association of America found that insurers process most claims within 14 days, The president of Claimcare, a firm that files claims for frustrated policy holders, said that 30% of the claims his company had reviewed had been submitted improperly. Some claims were too old, others omitted the claimant's birthday, listed an incorrect service code, or made another type of error. The following suggestions can help consumers facilitate the claims process:

1. Keep careful and complete records.
2. Be sure that claim forms are completed accurately.
3. If a problem arises, contact the company for an explanation or to register a complaint. Start with the claims supervisor; then write to the president and/or the board of directors if necessary.
4. If you feel you are not receiving proper attention, threaten to turn the matter over to the state insurance commission if no action is taken in 15 days.[28]

Loss Ratios

Numerous insurance companies do not use an adequate percentage of their premiums to pay claims for services rendered to their clients. The amount of money a company pays out in claims is a factor often overlooked in selecting a health insurance policy. This factor is often expressed as the benefit-cost ratio or simply the *loss ratio.* This compares the amount paid in claims with the amount received in premiums. It is one way that consumers can assess the value of health insurance policies. A high loss ratio is a sign of a good company to deal with. The Better Business Bureau[1] stated that for group policies a minimum of $75 should be returned for every $100 collected and for individual policies a minimum of $60 should be returned. Thus the loss ratios should be 75% or 60%.

Table 25-11 illustrates how loss ratios are calculated, and Table 25-12 provides information about the extent of the health insurance business in 1990 together with data about total premiums received, claims paid, and loss and expense ratios of insurers in the United States. Note that while commercial companies average a 66.6% loss ratio on individual policies and a 78.4% loss ratio on group policies, the Blue Cross–Blue Shield loss ratio for group policies was 87.3%. Also note that the administrative expenses for individual policies were considerably higher than group policies. Many insurers lose money on individual policies because the expenses are very high. Consumers may want to see whether the Blue Cross–Blue Shield policies available to them have favorable loss ratios. Tables 25-13 and 25-14 show the loss ratios for 10 of the leading companies marketing individual and group policies.

Misleading Advertising

The field of commercial health insurance often contains deceptive advertising. Ads stating that no medical examination is needed may fail to indicate that there is a clause in the policy that can deny a person benefits if a defect is uncovered after the insurance becomes operative. There may be a provision in fine print that excludes coverage for preexisting ailments for up to 2 years following the date the policy becomes effective. Other ads claim that hospital benefits paid by companies are tax-free, which may not be true. Indemnity policies that pay the policyholder a fixed sum of money for a specified period, such as $50 a day for up to 50 days' hospitalization, are not deductible.

A number of state insurance departments have put teeth into their regulations governing health insurance advertising and have established this Advertising Code of Conduct:

Deceptive language: Certain misleading words and phrases may not be used. Among these are full, complete, replace, income, fill gaps in medicine, liberal, generous, tax-free, extra income while confined, only, just, merely, and benefit builder. In California these words are prohibited: chartered by, regulated by, supervised by, audited by, examined by, state approved, all, complete, 100% coverage, and unlimited, except when health plans actually provide such health coverage. Also in California, ads must list all limitations, exclusions, exceptions, and waiting periods.

Stampede tactics: There shall be no suggestions of special rates for prompt response or the existence of enrollment periods when this is contrary to fact.

Celebrity solicitations: Anyone endorsing a policy in print or on the air must disclose any financial interest other than receipt of the normal talent fee for performance of services.

Disappearing coverage: No claim may be made that "no medical exam is required" if a clause in the policy excludes preexisting conditions. Exclusion clauses must be defined and described.

Government endorsements: Any implication that a special relationship with a government exists is expressly forbidden.

Slippery Tactics: Unusual amounts for unique claims cannot be spotlighted in an attempt to spruce up common coverage. When marketing hospital indemnity policies, an advertiser may not imply that a small daily benefit such as $25 could amount to a potential payment of $10,000. To illustrate, the average length of stay in a hospital is 7.1 days, and the total possible return for that period would be $178 at the $25 rate. To acquire a return of $10,000 an individual would have to spend 56 periods of 7.1 days in a hospital, which is virtually impossible.

When reviewing an advertisement for health insurance, these questions will help to assess the benefits intelligently:

1. What does the policy cover specifically? If the ad does not disclose all the limitations and exceptions, obtain a copy of the policy and study it to be sure it meets your needs.
2. Does it apply to both accidents and sickness?
3. How much will the policy pay? Reread the statement made previously about slippery tactics.
4. How much of the actual costs will be covered? If the policy pays $350 weekly at $50 daily, this will be less than 20% of a $284-per-day room in a hospital.
5. When do the benefits begin? There may be no sickness benefit until the policy is in force 30 days, or there may be a 4-day waiting period if hospitalized for illness, a 6-month wait for attention to specific conditions such as diabetes, hernia, or cancer, or a 2-year wait on preexisting conditions.
6. On what basis can you renew the policy? Check this carefully and obtain clarification when needed.

7. How does the policy supplement Medicare? Services such as dental services, eyeglasses, medical examinations, and drugs are not covered by Medicare. Medicare may pay for only 40% or less of some services provided by hosptials and physicians.
8. Is the company licensed in your state? Check with your state insurance office for this information.

Mail-Order Health Insurance

Mail-order insurance refers to policies sold by mail through advertising in circulars, letters, newpapers, or magazines and radio or television broadcasts. Generally no agents participate in the process. Many insurance companies in the United States are involved in the mail-order business. They handle about 2% of the total $70 billion health insurance sales. Unfortunately, mail-order policies often have limited benefits, so considerable caution should be used by individuals who contemplate their purchase.

Most mail-order policies offer indemnity benefits paying cash directly to the insured person. Usually the benefits are based on the number of days a person is hospitalized, with a maximum amount specified. For example, one policy pays the following for a $108 yearly premium for an individual:

$50 per day after the 8th day ($350 weekly)
$75 per day for the 61st to 90th day ($525 weekly)
$100 per day for the 91st to 371st day ($700 weekly).

Since the average hospital stay is 7.1 days (approximately 11 days for the elderly), with an average daily cost for room and board of over $400, it should be obvious that such insurance may not be very helpful. Adequate comprehensive health insurance, including supplementary insurance for the elderly, should provide greater protection and make cash-benefit coverage unnecessary.

Loss ratios of mail-order insurance companies often are low. These are usually individual policies. Mail-order insurance companies often exclude claims for preexisting conditions and totally deny a greater percentage of claims than other insurance companies.

Referring to mail-order insurance, Herbert Denenberg, a former Pennsylvania insurance commissioner, commented at a Congressional hearing:

> They offer "junk" insurance, gimmick insurance . . . . The companies engage in widespread practices of fraud and misrepresentation . . . the industry admits abuses but . . . does little or nothing about it . . . much mail-order coverage emphasizes in-hospital coverage . . . . The mail-order insurance companies imply that going to the hospital could be a source of profit.

Potential purchasers of mail-order policies should carefully examine the details regarding exclusions, waiting period, and other clauses. Don't be misled by complicated language. Most policies are written in a style that is difficult for the average person to understand. Consult a reputable insurance agent or other knowledgeable person for help.

Many companies that sell insurance by mail use deceptive practices. The word "hospital" may be defined so narrowly that more than 80% of the hospitals in the country would not be included. Offers of what appears to be maximum coverage for hospital expenses may provide benefits that are far less.

One company advertised "guaranteed continuable" and "only you can cancel." However, despite the advertising, policies can be canceled and rates raised under certain circumstances. One should be sure to read the fine print.

Insurance sold by mail may require no medical examination, but the application form requires the person to state whether medical attention has been received in the past 5 years and to list any diseases or physical disabilities. Unless the form is checked carefully, one may find when making a claim that the company will refuse to make payment, contending there were "preexisting conditions" that the person failed to mention on the application form.

Some advertisers claim to have the "lowest regular premium of any company." One should be aware that an initial low premium may greatly increase in a few years. Low rates do not guarantee the honesty of the company and may indicate the company rejects most claims.

Claims that the insurance is a better buy because of the elimination of commissions and underwriting costs associated with policies sold by salespeople may be untrue. The percentage of premiums returned to policyholders as benefits may not be high. It may range from 20% to 50%.

Mail-order insurance companies do not become licensed in many states in which they are soliciting. Therefore it might be advisable to check out the company in any, or all, of the following ways. The local office of the FTC may be contacted if there is a question about misleading or deceptive advertising. Information about the reputation of a company as well as answers to questions or problems may be obtained from the state insurance commissioner's office or the Better Business Bureau. Above all, one should remember that these companies are in business to make a profit, often a big one.

Limited Coverage for Preventive Measures

Except for HMOs, most basic insurance policies continue to provide little reimbursement for preventive health services. There is a growing belief that medical care must go beyond its orientation to illness to focus on the total health needs of the individual, with greater concern for the individual as a person, and therefore to more comprehensive health care. Many group prepaid health plans have accepted this approach and use it to identify one of the benefits of their system of health care over other approaches.

Exclusions and Limitations of Policies

Many individuals are unfamiliar with the exlusions, limitations, waiting periods, and other contract provisions found in policies. Frequently these conditions are found in small print, or the language is not clear enough for people to understand.

High Cost of AIDS

The AIDS epidemic is having a tremendous impact of public and private health care programs and on the insurance industry in the United States. Hospital costs and health insurance premiums undoubtedly will be affected as the incidence and deaths continue to rise.

The Centers for Disease Control in the United States has estimated that there are 1.5 million Americans infected with the HIV virus. As of 1990 there were 136,204 cases of AIDS reported, with 83,145 deaths. Public hospitals have provided 50% of inpatient care and 75% of outpatient care. The annual cost of care for an AIDS patient is estimated to be $32,000, with public hospitals losing $5818 per patient and private hospitals losing $2381 per patient.[29] The cumulative cost for AIDS care has not been determined, but estimates indicate that during the 1986-1991 period it ranged from $19 billion to $112 billion.

A survey conducted by the Office of Technology Assessment (OTA) found that 86% of commerical insurers and over 50% of Blue Cross–Blue Shield and HMO plans who responded said that they screen or plan to screen health insurance applicants for HIV infection. Some are requesting a physician's statement from selected applicants, while others are routinely testing those seeking insurance. Companies are addressing the AIDS problem in order to reduce the financial impact by expanding testing, denying insurance to applicants with sexually transmitted diseases, and placing dollar limits on coverage in new policies.[30]

Dread-Disease and Hospital Indemnity Plans

Many insurance companies provide coverage for dread-disease and hospital indemnity plans that reimburse consumers with fixed amounts of dollars. These payments are made directly to individuals rather than to providers of services. Some policies specify coverage for such items as hospitalization, surgery, prescription drugs, vision care, and/or cancer treatment. For example, a hospital indemnity policy may pay $50, $75, $100 or more for each day a patient is hospitalized. Where the average stay may be approximately 7 days at $500 or more per day, it is obvious that unless this is supplementary coverage, the cash reimbursement will only cover a limited amount of the cost.

Consumers should be wary of insurance policies for cancer, diabetes, or other specified diseases. These policies often are referred to as dread-disease policies. Insurance companies have sold millions of such policies, amounting to billions of premium dollars, to many elderly people by using scare techniques. This may be a waste of money because it may duplicate existing coverage or because it does not cover expenses. *Consumer Reports*[21] compared the reimbursements of two insurers for a $19,774 claim for colon-cancer surgery with follow-up chemotherapy. They discovered that one company paid $4100 and the other paid $6210.

Companies frequently advertise that such a plan is supplementary to present insurance when it actually is an unnecessary expenditure if one's insurance includes major medical coverage.

These plans often have provisions that warrant careful review and understanding. They may include a waiting period before the policy becomes operative, fail to cover preexisting conditions, charge additional premiums for added benefits, among others.

The late Claude Pepper, former chairman of the House of Representatives Select Committee on Aging, recommended that state laws regulate the sale of dread-disease insurance. His committee's report stated that cancer insurance is a big rip-off. These policies often have uncommon restrictions and limitations that are frequently hidden. They also heighten the fear and costs of the disease. A few states have banned or restricted the sale of policies limited to specific diseases.

Consumer Reports[21] considers dread-disease and hospital indemnity policies to be the worst buys in health insurance.

Dental Insurance

The National Center for Health Statistics estimates that in 1986, 88.6 million Americans (37.8% of the population over the age of 2) had private dental insurance.[31] Dental insurance programs were originally started by nonprofit dental service corporations sponsored by local dental societies. Currently most policies are provided by commerical insurance companies and HMOs and PPOs. Medicaid also provides coverage in some states.

Practically all private dental insurance plans are group plans that provide open-ended (no restrictions on the selection of dentist), or closed-ended plans with services from a specified group of dentists. These plans are available through unions, organizations, and industrial companies. The cost of monthly premiums range from $20 to $30 for individuals and $40 to $60 per family. Individual plans, purchasable directly from an insurance company, have higher premiums, with more limited coverage and larger out-of-pocket expenses.

Dental insurance usually covers examinations, fillings, x-ray films, extractions, cleaning, and dentures. Orthodontic and endodontic care, bridgework, oral surgery, and periodontics are often limited or excluded unless a higher premium is paid. Other common exclusions or limitations apply to care for preexisting conditions, replacement of lost dentures, dentures and bridgework to replace teeth lost prior to coverage, and expenses covered by other insurance.

There are three general types of prepaid dental plans: comprehensive deductible, scheduled fee, and fixed fee.

In a *comprehensive deductible plan,* the deductible clause may require the individual to pay the first $25 to $50 for each family member each year. At this point coinsurance would function and possibly 57% to 80% of the cost would be covered by insurance. The policy may further limit payments to 50% to 60% for such service as orthodontic and periodontic care. Yearly limits might be $750 per individual, with a $1000 or larger lifetime limit for orthodontics.

In a *scheduled fee plan* the insurer agrees to pay a fixed amount for each type of dental procedure. The fee is usually less than the fee normally charged. The balance is an out-of-pocket cost to the individual. The premium for this type of insurance is usually less than the comprehensive plan.

Fixed fee plans are similar to scheduled fee plans, except the dentist agrees not to charge more than specified fees. Hence, there is no out-of-pocket expense.

Table 25-15 illustrates two prepaid dental care plans.

Dental insurance policies are available from three sources: (1) private insurance companies, (2) dental service nonprofit corporations, generally operated by dental societies, and (3) group dentists' practices and clincs.

Many dental authorities believe that insurance companies should provide lower rates for communities that fluoridate their water supplies. Fluoridation of water is a very effective procedure to reduce the incidence of dental decay and can reduce the need for some professional services.

Consumers wishing to evaluate a dental insurance plan should seek answers to these questions:

1. How comprehensive is the plan? Does it cover preventive as well as restorative treatment? Are there limits to the number of visits within a specified period?
2. Is there a dollar limit on the amount of treatment for each covered individual?
3. How can a person know that quality care will be rendered?
4. Is there a lifetime limit in dollars per person for some types of infrequent, expensive treatment such as orthodontics and prosthetics?
5. Are the fee schedules in line with the customary and reasonable charges required of dentists practicing in the area?
6. Does the patient have freedom of choice in the selection of a dentist?
7. What percentage of the charges for services will be covered by the insurance?

Long-Term Care Insurance

Long-term care refers to a broad range of nursing, medical, and social services provided to an individ-

TABLE 25–15

TWO ILLUSTRATIVE DENTAL PLANS

Benefits	Charges	Monthly premium*
Plan 1—Open-end		
Diagnostic and preventive care: examinations, cleaning, fluoride treatment	75%; no deductible	Subscriber = $30 per month; with one dependent = $45; with two dependents = $60
Basic benefits:	75%; $50 deductible per person; $1500 per year	
Restorative: amalgam; synthetic porcelain and plastic restoration (fillings)		
Endodontic: tooth pulp		
Periodontic: gums and bones; supporting teeth		
Prosthetic appliance repair: crowns, inlays, bridgework, dentures, relining dentures		
Injection of antibiotic drugs		
Crowns, jackets, and gold cast restoration	50%; $50 deductible	
Prosthodontic	50%; $50 deductible	
Orthodontic	50%; $1000 lifetime	
Plan 2—closed-end		
Preventive care: examinations, x-ray films, cleaning, office visits, education	None	Subscriber $25; subscriber and one dependent, $40; subscriber and two dependents, $60
Treatment: additional fees on scheduled basis such as:		
Amalgam restoration—one tooth surface	$ 35	
Amalgam restoration—two tooth surfaces	55	
Acrylic crown	250	
Full crown	400	
Periodontics—emergency	125 per quadrant	
Oral surgery—single extractions	50	
Prosthetics—complete maxillary denture	550	
Dentists: selection permitted from provided list		

*Estimates

ual over a prolonged period of time (see Chapter 11). The most common settings are nursing homes and individual homes.

The levels of service provided in nursing homes are classified as skilled nursing care (intensive medical and rehabilitative care by trained personnel), intermediate nursing care (less intensive care by trained personnel), and custodial care (daily activities such as meals, bathing, and dressing). In home care, patients may receive skilled nursing care (also occupational and physical therapy), home-health aides (personal and custodial care), and homemaker services (cleaning, cooking, and running errands).

Consumer Reports[32] stated that 43% of all Americans who reach the age of 65 will eventually enter a nursing home. The California Advocates for Nursing Home Reform[33] indicated that 50% of those who enter a nursing home remain for 3 months or less, 37% remain for 3 months to 3 years, and 11% remain for more than 3 years.

Nursing home costs can range from $40 to $120 daily ($15,000 to $45,000 yearly), and home care costs may be $15 to $75 or more daily. These costs have encouraged the elderly to seek protection and has stimulated insurance companies to offer policies to offset some of the expenditures for long-term care. An estimated 1 million to 1.5 million people are covered by some form of long-term care insurance.

The cost of long-term care insurance depends on the city, type of coverage, age of person, benefits, and other variables. *Consumer Reports*[32] said that a 65-year-old can obtain an $80 daily benefit payable for 4 years with a 30-day waiting period for $706 to $3020. Pear[34] reported that the average insurance premium that pays $50 to $100 daily would be $505 yearly for 50-year-olds, $1055 yearly for 65-year olds, and $3815 yearly for 79-year olds.

Consumers should be aware that a number of abuses that have occurred in the solicitation and administration of long-term care insurance:

1. Use of misleading and deceitful sales tactics; providing misrepresentations and confusing information about policy terms and benefits.
2. Failure to clearly explain benefits, restrictions, and policy limitations.
3. Failure to adequately inform about the increase of premiums due to age and inflation.
4. Use of scare tactics to intimidate clients.
5. Failure to leave sample copies of policy and other written information.
6. Arbitrary denial of benefits and failure to process claims. *Consumer Reports* indicated that companies rarely pay all claims. Several said that their percentage of denied claims ranged from 22% to 80%.[32]
7. Selling policies to low-income individuals who probably were eligible for Medicaid.

Consumers seeking long-term care insurance policies should obtain answers to these questions:

1. Is the entire spectrum of nursing covered? Skilled? Custodial? Home?
2. What is the daily benefit (per day, per hour, per visit)? It should pay half to two-thirds of the cost.
3. How long to the benefits last?
4. What is the cost of the coverage? Will the premiums increase with age or in response to inflation? Is protection against inflation provided? A $30,000-a-year nursing home cost with a 5% yearly inflation will escalate to $50,000 per year in 10 years.
5. Are policies guaranteed renewable?
6. When do benefits begin?
7. Do benefits hinge on prior hospitalization? Doctor approval? Anything else?
8. Are illness or injuries excluded from coverage? If yes, don't buy the policy.
9. What are the restrictions on preexisting conditions? Waiting periods? Deductible?
10. Are home health care services included? What are they?
11. Will you leave a sample copy of the policy?
12. Is the company's loss ratio 80% or more?
13. Has the company reinsured its long-term care policies (paid another company to assume some risk)?
14. Will I receive a copy of the outline of coverage?
15. Can I receive a 30-day free look at the policy with refund of the premium if requested?
16. What are the limitations and exclusions?
17. Is Alzheimer's disease covered? To what extent?
18. What is Best's rating of the company? Check *Best's Insurance Reports* (Life/Health Edition) in the library. Should be A+ or A.

Consumers who need help in choosing a long-term care insurance policy may obtain free literature from the following sources:

The Consumer's Guide to Long Term Health Insurance
Health Insurance Association of America
P.O. Box 41455
Washington, D.C. 20018

Shopper's Guide to Long-Term Care Insurance
National Association of Insurance Commisions
(from State insurance departments)

Public Plans

The two major types of public health insurance plans in the United States are Medicare and Medicaid. Their essential features are compared in Table 25-16. Further information is available from local welfare and Social Security offices.

Medicare

Medicare is a federal government insurance program created by amendments to the Social Security Act. It provides health insurance benefits for persons 65 years or older and for certain disabled persons under 65 years of age. It is composed of two parts. Part A provides compulsory hospital insurance financed through Social Security taxes paid by employers, employees, and the self-employed. Part B is a voluntary program of medical insurance to help pay for physicians' services and various other medical costs. Part B is financed through the monthly premiums paid by subscribers of the plan.

Table 25–16

Comparison of Medicare and Medicaid Services

	Medicare	Medicaid
Administration	Social Security office Federal insurance program	Local welfare office Federal-state partnership assistance program
Financing	Trust funds from Social Security Contributions from insured	Taxes from federal, state, local sources
Eligibility	People 65 years and older	Needy and low-income people, people 65 years and older, blind and disabled people, members of families with dependent children, some other children, possibly others†
Benefits	Same in all states Hospital insurance (Part A) Inpatient: up to 60 days in a semiprivate room for each benefit period, patient pays first $628 and $157 daily in coinsurance 61st through 90th day for covered services and supplies; also, 60 reserve days (nonrenewable—once in a lifetime) if needed, patient pays $314 in coinsurance per day Blood: all but first three pints yearly Skilled nursing facility (after 3-day hospital care: all covered services paid for first 20 days; patient pays $78.50 a day in coinsurance for the 21st through 100th day Hospice care; up to 210 days if terminally ill certified by doctor	Varies from state to state Hospital services At least these services: inpatient hospital care, outpatient hospital services, other laboratory and x-ray services, physician's services, screening, diagnosis, and treatment of children; home health care services Pays what Medicare does not pay for eligible people
	Medical insurance (Part B) Deductible $100 annually Coinsurance pays for 80% of reasonable charges* after deductible	Medical services Many states pay for dental care, prescribed drugs, eyeglasses, clinic services, and other diagnostic, screening, preventive, and rehabilitative services

Continued.

Table 25–16

Comparison of Medicare and Medicaid Services

	Medicare	Medicaid
Benefits (cont'd)	Services and benefits: Physician and medical and surgical care in office, hospital, skilled nursing facility or in home; radiology and pathology services in hospital; 50% of costs up to $250 after first $75 for outpatient treatment of mental illness. Mammography x-ray: women over 65 years; every other year; pay $44 or 80% up to $55 Outpatient hospital: emergency room, laboratory tests, x-ray services, and supplies; pays 80% of reasonable charges Outpatient physical therapy and speech pathology: pays 80% of reasonable charges up to $500 yearly Ambulance transporatation, prosthetic devices, medical equipment, and blood except first three pints Home health care: part-time skilled nursing care, physical and speech therapy provided at full costs up to 21 home visits in one calendar year Exclusions: regular dental care, glasses, hearing aids, eye or ear examinations to prescribe hearing aids or fit glasses, immunizations, cosmetic surgery, routine physical examinations	Medicaid pays the $100 Medicare does not pay for eligible people; pays deductibles, coinsurance for medicare enrollees
Premium costs	Hospital insurance (Part A): none Medical insurance (Part B): $29.90 monthly by eligible person; 1992 = $31.80; 1993 = $36.60; 1994 = $41.10; 1995 = $46.20	None; federal government contributes to states 50% to 80% of costs for needy and low-income people

Modified from U.S. Department of Health and Human Services, Social Security Administration: Your Medicare handbook, Baltimore, 1990, Social Security Administration

*The "reasonable charge" for a physician's service is the lowest of three kinds of charges: the actual charge, the physician's customary charge, and the prevailing charge. The actual charge is the charge the physician billed for the service. The customary charge is the charge the physician usually bills most patients for the same service. The prevailing charge is the lowest charge made by at least three fourths of the physicians in the same area. Whichever one of these charges is lowest is called the "reasonable charge." If the prevailing charge for a service is $40 and a physician charges $36 (customary charge) but bills $42 for the service (actual charge), the "reasonable charge" is $36.

†*Spousal Impoverishment.* If one spouse enters a nursing home and seeks Medicaid while other remains home, the at-home spouse can keep at least $992 of the couple's income. Also, spouse will be allowed to keep $12,000 in assets or half of couples' resources, whichever is greater, up to $60,000, in addition to the couple's house.

Note: A supplementary commercial Medigap health insurance policy will help to cover deductibles, coinsurance and other costs.

Diagnosis-Related Groups (DRGs)

Since 1983, Medicare has paid for hospital services according to a predetermined schedule for about 500 diagnosis-related groups (DRGs). The DRG system replaced the system whereby hospitals in various parts of the United States received widely divergent fees for the same services. It was instituted as an effort to control medical costs. Hospitals able to provide services for less than the government rate could retain the difference. Thus, a hospital that kept a patient for 2 days would receive as much as one that kept a similar patient for 6 days. To assure that the quality of care would not be affected, hospitals treating Medicare patients must conduct strict peer review.

Hospitals claim that DRG procedures have helped them to reduce costs by 5% by reducing the average length of hospital stay from 9.5 days to 7.5 days. Tests previously performed in the hospital are now often done on an outpatient basis. The *Mayo Clinic Health Letter* said it is not known whether the care delivered to senior citizens has become more efficient.[35] The American Association of Retired Persons (AARP) has suggested that the system provides an economic incentive to skimp on the quality of care and to cost-shift the matter to private insurance companies.[36] AARP reported that hospitals were discharging elderly patients who still needed treatment. To prevent this early release from happening, patients are advised that if they believe they are too sick to be released and an early discharge is planned, they should: (1) ask for a written notice, which will be needed for appeal, (2) request assistance from their doctor, and (3) immediately appeal to the hospital Peer Review Organization (PRO). Strasser[37] stated that the DRGs have not been able to stem the continuous rise in medical costs, and other dramatic action may be necessary by the U.S. Congress.

Insurance Problems of the Elderly

The U.S. Congress in 1989 passed the Physicians Payment Reform Act, which included two features of importance to Medicare beneficiaries. Starting in 1991, doctors not accepting assignment are able to charge elderly patients more than 25% of the fees approved by Medicare. This percentage dropped to 20% in 1992 and drops to 15% in 1993. In addition, physicians are responsible for the filing of all Medicare claims for the services they perform. Physicians have up to a year in which to file claims. This has created a problem for some consumers. Doctors who do not accept assignment can request full payment for services at the time provided. Therefore, if physicians who have received payment delay filing of claims, patients can have a long wait before obtaining reimbursement.[38] Consumers may find it useful to ask when the doctor plans to file the Medicare claim and also to request such action be taken within a reasonable length of time.

Spiraling costs have created a heavy financial burden for many elderly persons. Medicare pays less than half the total health bill for persons age 65 and older. In addition, certain special needs of the aged are not covered or are only partially covered.

As people become older, they are more likely to become disabled and to need medical care. It is estimated that only 34% of people 45 to 64 years old have no chronic condition, 20% of those 65 to 74 have none, and fewer than 13% of those over 75 have none.

Many elderly people need long-term care exceeding 30 days in the hospital. Coverage for long-term care is not provided by Medicare. The elderly occupy a high percentage of hospital beds. The median age for individuals in nursing homes is 80 years.

Outlays for out-of-hospital drugs are greater for old people than for all other age groups. Those with severe disabilities spend three times more money for drugs than do those without such conditions.

Dental care for the elderly is a sizable problem. More than half the people over 65 years have not seen a dentist in 5 years, 50% to 60% have lost all their teeth, and a very small percentage have dental insurance.

Resolution of the health problems identified here may be difficult or impossible for many older persons. However, it may be possible to minimize out-of-pocket expenses by (1) asking physicians to accept assignment for fees under Medicare (In 1988, 72% of physicians accepted assignment), (2) purchasing supplementary (Medigap) insurance, (3) joining an HMO that accepts Medicare patients, or (4) applying for Medicaid, if eligible.

Supplementary Health Insurance (Medigap)

Approximately 25% to 30% (7 million) of the elderly have no Medigap coverage. More than 3 million of these are eligible for Medicaid. It is estimated that 23 million retirees have acquired Medigap insurance policies to supplement their Medicare coverage. Their purpose was to reduce out-of-pocket expenses (Medicare pays about 40% of medical costs) and to provide increased benefits. Medicare does not cover the cost of drugs, dentures, nursing home care, eyeglasses, hearing aids, and other materials and services. In 1990, senior citizens spent $10 billion to $15 billion for such insurance. Freudenheim[39] claims many elderly have been ripped off.

The problems that have arisen in the marketing of supplementary health insurance plans include the following:

1. Medigap rates have been rising each year at a rate higher than inflation. In 1990, the average monthly premium was $69.96. Critics have said the increases have been excessive.
2. The loss ratio standards established by the National Association of Insurance Commissioners (NAIC) of 60% for individual policies and 76% for group policies have not been reached by 34% of insurers providing individual plans and by 66% of insurers providing group plans. Critics have stated that loss ratios of 60% to 75% are too low and should be 70% to 80%.[40]
3. Insurance solicitors have taken advantage of the elderly with these abuses: unfair sales tactics, sale of unnecessary policies, scare tactics, unwarranted rate increase, and encouraging policyholders to cancel one policy for another one at a considerably higher rate despite adequacy of present one.[41]

To help resolve Medigap problems, the National Association of Insurance Commissioners created 10 standardized packages of supplementary insurance policie for distributuion to consumers, beginning in 1992. These will replace the variety of confusing policies previously marketed and will be the only supplementary health insurance policies available. Table 25-17 identifies the plans and their coverage. The cost will vary according to the extent of coverage and probably will range from $400 to $2000 yearly. Consumers who already have adequate supplementary policies need not switch to one of the newer ones. However, individuals who seek new Medigap policies should heed these suggestions offered by *Consumer Reports:*[42]

1. Don't buy more than one policy.
2. Part B deductible: buying coverage of the first $100 of any physician or hospital charges is dollar trading. You pay an extra premium for this coverage.
3. Part B excess charges: if your physician accepts assignment, this is unnecessary. However, a specialist or team of specialists may not accept assignment.
4. At home care after hospitalization: if you already have a long-term care policy, this coverage will not be needed.
5. Prescription drugs. If your expenditures do not exceed the deductible, this coverage is unnecessary. However, it may be advisable at some time in the future.
6. Buy Medigap insurance when first eligible for Medicare; it is cheaper then, and no medical exam is required if application is made within the first 6 months.

A federal law that took effect in the middle of 1992 to help with Medigap problems provided that counseling be made available at Social Security offices. The law also states that (1) policies must be written in uniform language, (2) loss ratios must be 65% to 75%, (3) renewability must be guaranteed, (4) sale of duplicate policies to Medicare beneficiaries or persons eligible for Medicaid is prohibited, and (5) violators can be punished by penalties of up to 5 years in prison and a $25,000 fine.[43]

Table 25-18 compares the estimated annual out-of-pocket costs for elderly persons with and without supplementary insurance. It should be noted that these expenses are subject to inflationary factors and individual differences in coverage and services. It must be kept in mind that no affordable insurance could ever be written to cover all out-of-pocket expenses. In budgeting for health insurance, one should seek the most comprehensive coverage possible at the lowest possible cost.

Supplementary health insurance is no guarantee that all the inadequacies of Medicare will be covered. The Medicare Supplement Policy Checklist on page 586 should help to review the terms of a plan under consideration.

In addition, consider these suggestions:

1. Buy only one Medigap policy to augment Medicare coverage.
2. Be certain that the policy includes major medical or catastrophic coverage.
3. Obtain a sample copy of the policy under consideration for thorough review.
4. Check out the following:
   a. Inquire of the state insurance commissioner, the Better Business Bureau, or a local consumer organization about complaints received, whether or not the company is li-

Table 25–17

10 Standard Medigap Health Insurance Plans Approved by the National Association of Insurance Commissioners

Yearly est. costs	Plan	Part A hospital coinsurance, days 61-90 ($157 per day)	Part A hospital coinsurance, days 91-150 ($314 per day)	All charges for extra 365 days in hospital	Part A blood deductible, 3 pints	Part B blood deductible, 3 pints	Part B coinsurance (20% of allowable charges)	Skilled-nursing facility coinsurance, days 21-100	Part A deductible ($628 per year)	Emergency care in foreign countries	Part B deductible ($100 per year)	Part B excess charges	At-home care after a hospital stay	Prescription drugs	Preventive medical care
$400-$600	A	✓	✓	✓	✓	✓	✓	—	—	—	—	—	—	—	—
$500-$700	B	✓	✓	✓	✓	✓	✓	✓	✓	—	—	—	—	—	—
$500-$700	C	✓	✓	✓	✓	✓	✓	✓	✓	✓	✓	—	—	—	—
$550-$800	D	✓	✓	✓	✓	✓	✓	✓	✓	✓	—	—	✓	—	—
$700-$1000	E	✓	✓	✓	✓	✓	✓	✓	✓	✓	—	—	—	—	✓
$700-$900	F	✓	✓	✓	✓	✓	✓	✓	✓	✓	✓	[1]	—	—	—
$500-$700	G	✓	✓	✓	✓	✓	✓	✓	✓	✓	—	[2]	✓	—	—
$700-$900	H	✓	✓	✓	✓	✓	✓	✓	✓	✓	—	—	—	[3]	—
$1000-$140	I	✓	✓	✓	✓	✓	✓	✓	✓	✓	—	[1]	✓	[3]	—
$1200-$180	J	✓	✓	✓	✓	✓	✓	✓	✓	✓	✓	[1]	✓	[4]	✓

[1] Pays 100% of difference between doctor's bill and amount Medicare pays.
[2] Pays 80% of difference between doctor's bill and amount Medicare pays.
[3] $1250 maximum yearly benefit; $250 deductible; 50% coinsurance.
[4] $3000 maximum yearly benefit; $250 deductible; 50% coinsurance.
Source: The New Medigap Plans, Consumer Reports 56:616-617, 1991.

TABLE 25–18

EST. AVERAGE OUT-OF-POCKET COST OF HEALTH CARE FOR ELDERLY INDIVIDUALS WITH AND WITHOUT SUPPLEMENTARY INSURANCE COVERAGE*

Coverage	Without supplementary insurance	With supplementary insurance
Medicare		
Part A deductible	$ 540	$ 0
Part B premium at $13.20 monthly	482	482
Part B deductible	100	0
Additional out-of-pocket expenses (est.)	1800	350
Supplementary premium	0	400-1800
Total (est.)	$2922	1232-2632

*Estimated overall per capita health care expenditure for those 65 and over was over $5000.

censed to operate, and length of time in business.

b. Ascertain the loss ratio. The payout should be at least $75 per $100 of premiums for a group policy and at least $60 per $100 of premiums for an individual policy. Further information about this can be obtained by writing to Argus Health Chart, National Underwriter Company, 420 E. 4th St., Cincinnati, OH 45202.
c. Check the rating (A+ to C) in *Best's Insurance Reports* (Life/Health Edition).

5. Don't purchase specialized coverage such as hospital indemnity, accident, intensive care, and cancer policies. These policies usually provide limited coverage for items that usually have adequate coverage by supplementary and catastrophic coverages.
6. You should be allowed 10 days to cancel the policy if you change your mind.
7. Pay by check, money order, or bank draft payable to the insurance company, and obtain a written receipt on company stationary.
8. Consider participation in an HMO as an alternative to purchasing a supplementary insurance policy.

HMOs, PPOs,and Medicare

Medicare now permits senior citizens to enroll in an HMO by paying an extra premium ($20 to $50 per month) on Part B of Medicare insurance. This arrangement has been offered to help reduce the escalating costs of medical care, enable the elderly to obtain more comprehensive treatment without having to expend large out-of-pocket funds, and provide quality care on a cost-effective basis. Additional benefits include more hospital days, preventive care, prescription drugs, routine eye examinations, and eyeglasses.

Individuals who wish to select an HMO may arrange for one through a local Social Security office, which will direct premiums originally paid to Medicare to the organizations chosen.

The program has been in operation since 1986, with approximately 150 HMOs serving over 1 million people. A few problems, however, are causing some organizations to pull out of the arrangement and others to be dropped. Many elderly are high users of services, and their last years of life are medically costly. HMOs claim the fees received are too low, and they are losing money. The American Association of Retired Persons (AARP) and others have stated that cost-cutting procedures have led some HMOs to provide poor care and bad management. Certain organizations have been operating dishonestly, misrepresenting benefits through unscrupulous marketing practices, using deceptive sales pitches, and denial of services. The Health Care Financing Administration, which runs Medicare, has investigated complaints and decided not to renew the contract of 10 organizations. AARP has also identified these problems: (1) "biased selection," whereby illegal strategies were used to screen out the least healthy beneficiares, (2) confusion about the lock-in provision, which requires that clients visit only HMO doctors and facilities, and (3) high-pressure sales tactics.

Despite these uncertainties, this prepaid care provides an appealing alternative for Medicare beneficiaries who desire comprehensive coverage if they can find an efficient HMO. These are some of the advantages and disadvantages:[44]

Advantages	Disadvantages
No claim forms to file	May be locked in to panel physicians
Provides extra benefits and reduced premiums	Location may be inconvenient
Guaranteed renewal	Limited coverage when traveling
Provides preventive care	May employ few specialists
No deductibles or copayments	Nonemergency appointments may be time consuming
Services may be in one location	

AARP publishes a booklet of helpful tips for selecting an HMO. For a free copy of "Choosing an HMO: An Evalution Checklist," write to

Fulfillment Section
AARP
1909 "K" Street, N.W.,
Washington, DC 20049.

Another possible source of supplementary health insurance to Medicare is to join a PPO. They function in the same manner as HMOs, providing similiar services with comparable advantages and disadvantages. However, they are not available in all areas because the federal government only recently has started to promote them.

Medicare Fraud

Some medical practitioners and suppliers of medical devices are bilking the federal government by charging for services not rendered, overcharging, or engaging in other abuses. Since 1987, more than 70 individuals and companies have been convicted of fraud and other crimes in the sales of medical equipment such as wheelchairs, portable ventilators, artifical limbs, and muscle stimulators.[45] Some mobile health centers (laboratories on wheels) have enticed people to obtain "free" tests for cholesterol, hearing, vision, or blood pressure, and then submitted multiple bills for the same service. Medical practitioners are involved in fraud practices such as the following:[46]

1. A cardiac specialist does a 20-minute EKG and bills for a much costlier 24-hour procedure.
2. An anesthesiologist bills for periods totalling more than 24 hours in a single day.
3. A dermatologist removes a simple growth but bills for removing multiple growths.

U.S. Attorney General William P. Barr has stated that health care scams were costing Americans $50 billion a year.[47] However, no detailed information to support this allegation has been published.

Consumers need to be alert for fraudulent practices and should report them to the Inspector General's Office by calling 1-800-368-5779.

Medicaid

Medicaid is a federal grant-in-aid program under which the states may contract with the Secretary of Health and Human Services to finance health care services for public assistance recipients. It provides for certain categories of indigent and medically indigent persons. There are 25 million eligible persons, including the aged, blind, disabled, and members of single-parent families with dependent children. The proportion of state to federal funding of the program is determined by a formula based on each state's per capita income.

Eligibility requirements differ from state to state. Table 25-16 provides some of the details of eligibility and services rendered. Of those eligible for Medicaid, 41% are 65 years and older and therefore eligible to receive Medicare.

Guidelines for Selecting Health Insurance

When choosing health insurance, become familiar with all the literature provided. It is best to obtain a copy of the policy and read it carefully. If the language appears conflicting or difficult to understand, don't hesitate to ask the company representative for clarification. Be sure the coverage is suitable, and don't hesitate to shop around. Policies vary greatly in terms of services rendered and costs.

To assist in the search for an appropriate health insurance policy, the following questions should be helpful:

Type of policy

1. Is the policy a group or individual one?
2. Is the insurance comprehensive, providing basic health insurance that also includes hospital, surgical, medical, and maternity benefits? Does it

also include major medical insurance or is such insurance available?

Hospital insurance

1. How many days are covered for each illness? What is the per diem rate? Is the allowance sufficient to cover the entire daily rate? Is there coverage for intensive care?
2. What are the services provided? Are added services included?
3. Is there a deductible clause?
4. Are there limits on the choice of hospitals?
5. Are in-hospital physicians' services covered?
6. Is consultation permissible? Under what conditions?
7. Are the covered days limited to one period of hospitalization, or is there more than one period covered up to a maximum number of days?
8. Are there limitations on readmission to a hospital for the same illness?

Surgical insurance

1. What surgical procedures are covered, and to what extent? What is the surgical fee schedule? Will the insurance cover all or partial costs?
2. Are there provisions for consultant services?
3. Are there limits in choice of surgeons or where they may conduct their surgery?
4. How do the fees allowed compare with the local surgeons' charges in general?

Medical insurance

1. Which services are covered? Excluded? Limited?
2. Are there provisions for home and office visits? Limitations?
3. Is there a deductible clause?
4. Does it include service for accidents?
5. Is the choice of physicians limited?
6. Is mental illness covered?
7. Are there provisions for concurrent services of more than one physician if medically necessary?

Maternity care

1. What services are rendered? What are the limitations? What complications are covered?
2. When available? For whom?

Major medical insurance

1. What services are covered?
2. What is the maximum coverage? The minimum recommended is $1 million. What is the stop-loss limit?
3. Is there a deductible? How much?
4. Is coinsurance required? Limits?
5. Can maximum limits be restored after illness?
6. What percentage above the deductible is paid by the company?

Extended care

1. What services are covered? For how many days? Per diem allowance? Must it follow hospitalization?
2. Are services of RNs, LVNs, LPNs, or other allied health professionals covered?

Contract provisions

1. Are all family members covered? To what ages?
2. Are there waiting periods? What is the effective policy date?
3. What are the conditions and limitations in regard to preexisting conditions? Do they apply for more than 1 year?
4. Can the policy be converted to an individual plan? To a family plan if an individual marries? Is it convertible after retirement?
5. What are the conditions regarding cancellation and renewal of policy? By whom? Is it a guaranteed renewable policy?
6. What are the exclusions? Are they more restrictive than the usual ones, such as dental, vision, hearing?
7. Does coverage include other countries?
8. Are provisions made for coordination of benefits with other policies that an insured person may have?
9. Can rates be changed? What are the conditions for rate changes? How do they compare with those of other companies?

Selecting an insuring organization

1. Is the company licensed in your state?
2. Is the company or agent a reliable and reputable one? Are claims paid promptly and without hassels?
3. Are the loss ratios high? Are they at least 60% and preferably 70% or more?

Selection Procedures

1. Choose a policy with high maximum benefits and comprehensive coverage. Mesh basic insurance protection and major medical so there are few gaps in coverage. Preferably, buy both policies from one company. Medicare should be coordinated with a supplementary policy.
2. Buy only as much insurance as needed. Avoid overlapping and duplicating coverages. Check the benefits you have before purchasing a new policy.

3. Purchase a group policy if possible. It will be less costly and provide greater benefits.
4. Avoid buying a dread-disease policy that pays for only one kind of ailment, such as cancer. A policy with comprehensive coverage will provide adequate protection.
5. Obtain sample policies from several different companies to compare benefits. Ask advice of an insurance agent. Raise questions about unclear information.

Sources of Health Insurance Information

Additional health insurance information may be obtained from an insurance agent, insurance company, Blue Cross—Blue Shield representative physician, local medical society, Better Business Bureau, state insurance commissioner, or state or local consumer affairs office. One can also write to the American Hospital Association, Blue Cross-Blue Shield Association, Council of Better Business Bureaus, Delta Dental Plans Association, Group Health Association of America, Inc., and Health Insurance Association of America. (See Appendix for addresses.)

National Health Insurance (NHI)

More than 25 years ago, former U.S. Senator Everett M. Dirkson said:

> It is our aim that medical care be available to all Americans under a system providing (1) the greatest freedom of choice, (2) with minimal financial burdens, (3) with optimum personal dignity, and (4) with maximum flexibility for continued growth of the world's finest medical care.
>
> In achieving this purpose, there is a role for government . . . it should be held to the minimum practical, if the primary role of individual responsibility with freedom is not cramped.

Despite the noble goal of universal health insurance for all Americans, numerous proposals have been made but none have become operational. The need for a coordinated plan has never been greater than it is today.

The U.S. spends more money and a larger share of its resources than any other country in the world for medical and health care. In 1990, this expense amounted to $666.2 billion ($2566 per person), which was 12.2% of the gross national product. However, Americans are receiving far less than full value for their health expenditures. More than 31 million are uninsured, and many more millions are underinsured. Escalating costs for health services, increased out-of-pocket expenses for the elderly and the chronically ill, and widespread lack of protection from catastrophic illness are compounding the problem.

In recent years there has been considerable dissatisfaction among consumers with the present health-care system. A study conducted by the Harvard Community Health Plan and Louis Harris Associates as reported in the *Journal of the American Medical Association* found 55% were satisfied with their own and their family's health care, but only 10% were satisfied with the current health-care system. In addition 58% of the labor union leaders favored an all-government insurance plan.[48] A survey of 2733 readers of the *AARP Bulletin*[49] indicated that 87% favor a government-sponsored national health insurance plan. Polls by NBC and the *Los Angeles Times* revealed that 67% of Americans preferred a Canadian-style comprehensive health insurance plan.[50]

Since 1930, many comprehensive health insurance laws have been proposed in the U.S. Congress. During the past 10 years, many more programs have been suggested, but none has become a reality.[24,48] Table 25-19 compares a variety of plans that have been proposed. These programs can be grouped into four general approaches:

1. A compulsory employed-based private insurance program with government-insured nonworkers and the poor.
2. A requirement by employers to provide employees with health insurance or pay a tax, with the government insuring nonworkers and the poor.
3. An income-related tax-credited arrangement for individuals independent of their employers to purchase private insurance.
4. An all-government insurance system.

Although there is a consensus that our society must provide medical and health care for all people in the United States, there is no consensus on how to do this. There appear to be three general suggestions for change:

1. Modify the present private insurance involvement with some increased government support.
2. Combine greater employer-employee participation with government help for the poor and uninsured.

Table 25–19

13 Proposals for the Reform of the U.S. Health Care Insurance System

Author of proposal	Coverage	Administration	Financing	Cost containment/ provider reimbursement	Other distinctive features
Type I: Compulsory private insurance through employers, with government insuring nonworkers and the poor					
Kirkman-Liff	Universal	Private: insurers offer community-rated plans Government: Medicare/ Medicaid enrollees get vouchers to buy private insurance	Employer/employee premium sharing; federal government pays employer share of premium for nonworkers	Copayments/cost sharing; managed care optional; reimbursement negotiated between provider and payer representatives	Copies some features of German and Dutch systems; long-term care benefits unmentioned
Todd et al (American Medical Association)	Nearly universal; excludes non-poor nonworkers	Private; insurers offer private plans or state risk pool for uninsurable and others Government: unchanged	No change	Changes tax treatment of employee benefits; health promotion; repeals state-mandated benefits; seeks reduction in administrative costs; improves Medicaid reimbursement levels; private insurance unchanged	Adds private long-term care benefits and expands Medicaid; catastrophic coverage; reforms Medicare trust fund
Rockefeller (Pepper Commission)	Universal	Private: insurers offer private plans Government: replaces Medicaid with new program for poor nonworkers, and self-employed, with buy-in option for employed	Employer/employee premium sharing; existing government sources plus new taxes	Encourages use of managed care; cost sharing; improves consumers' knowledge; malpractice reform; public program pays Medicare rates; private insurance unchanged	Insurance reform; universal coverage of long-term care

Bronow et al (Physicians Who Care)	Nearly universal; excludes non-poor nonworkers	Private: community-rated insurance plans with high deductibles Government: expanded Medicaid coverage	Employer/employee premium sharing plus individual medical savings accounts; government unchanged	High cost sharing; reimbursement unchanged	Adds public-private long-term care coverage and catastrophic coverage
Nutter et al (Medical Schools Section, American Medical Association)	Nearly universal; excludes non-poor nonworkers	Private: insurance plus insurance risk pools Government: expanded Medicaid coverage	Employer/employee premium sharing; employment-based tax to cover new Medicaid costs; elderly pay for Medicare expansion	All-payer, prospective payment for hospital and professional services	Eliminates deductibility of employer contributions; adds long-term care and catastrophic coverage to Medicare
Type II: Law requiring employers to provide private insurance to employees or pay equivalent tax, with government insuring nonworkers and the poor					
Davis	Universal	Private: insurers offer private plans Government: Medicare coverage for all others	Employer/employee premium sharing or employer payroll tax; income tax; general revenues	All payers adopt Medicare rates and volume performance standards for hospitals and physicians	Allows states to buy Medicaid enrollees into Medicare long-term care expansion optional for states
Schwartz (Kansas Employer Coalition on Health)	Universal	Private: insurers offer private plans Government: regional public sponsors and Medicare	Employer/employee premium sharing; tax on individuals in pool; general revenue	Malpractice reform; increased cost sharing; health promotion; insurance price increases tied to consumer price index, with government adjustments; mandatory community rating of insurance	Insurers join reinsurance pools
Enthoven and Kronick	Universal	Private insurance, Medicare, and public sponsors for all others	Employer/employee premium sharing; other sources unchanged	Increased cost sharing; market forces growing from competing managed care plans; changes the tax deductibility of employer health benefits	Emphasizes managed care delivery systems; no change in long-term care benefits

Continued.

TABLE 25–19

13 PROPOSALS FOR THE REFORM OF THE U.S. HEALTH CARE INSURANCE SYSTEM — cont'd

Author of proposal	Coverage	Administration	Financing	Cost containment/ provider reimbursement	Other distinctive features
Holahan et al	Universal	New federal-state program for anyone not covered by an employer or Medicare	Employer/employee premium sharing or tax; existing and new state and federal tax revenue	Federal share of health expenditures tied growth in GNP; states have strong cost-containment incentives; tax deductibility of benefits limited to standard benefit package; reimbursement unchanged	Federalizes long-term care benefits; cost containment left to the states; eliminates Medicaid
Type III: Tax credit for purchase of private insurance					
Butler (Heritage Foundation)	Universal	Individuals purchase private coverage from competing insurers independent of employers; Medicare/Medicaid beneficiaries get vouchers	Individual payment for all premiums or care; government pays for poor	Changes in tax treatment of health benefits to discourage overinsuring and overuse; reimbursement unchanged	Purchase of long-term care coverage at discretion of individuals
Type IV: All-government insurance system					
Roybal (US Health Act)	Universal	Single insurance system run by new agency; role for private insurers	Same sources of revenue to be paid into single account	Prospective payment, with total budget cap of 12% to 13% of GNP; all reimbursement based on Medicare rules	Adds broad range of health and long-term care benefits

Grumbach et al (Physicians for a National Health Program)	Universal	Public administrator replaces Medicare, Medicaid, and private insurance	Payroll tax; existing government revenue sources; new taxes	Annual hospital budget negotiated with state plan based on past expenditures, performance, and cost and use projections; physicians paid on negotiated fee schedule	Each state determines who runs the plan; no copayments and deductibles; long-term care fully covered
Fein (Committee for National Health Insurance)	Universal	States have much flexibility with federally specified benefits and budget oversight	Federal and state taxes and premiums paid into single state agency; agency pays insurers or providers on capitated basis; federal contribution increases based on growth in GNP	State and national health care budgets; negotiated payments to institutional providers; negotiated physician fee schedule; expansion of capitated systems; consolidated administration; government review of technology and treatment effectiveness; administrative savings	Encourages state experimentation; long-term care benefits unchanged

*LTC indicates long-term care; GNP, gross national product.
Source: Blendon RJ and Edwards JN: Caring for the Uninsured: Choices for Reform, JAMA, 265:2563–2565, 1991.

3. Establish a completely public plan that is controlled, supported, and administered by the federal government. Canada's plan is often mentioned as an exemplary one.

The Canadian plan for health care is a publicly funded system consisting of 10 provincial plans that cover medically necessary hospital and physician services for all Canadians. It is funded by general tax revenues from income taxes, lottery profits, and corporate taxes and is supplemented by sales taxes, employer taxes, and others. Each provincial government in Canada determines its own budget, including overall increases in hospital costs and physician fees as well as the acquisition of expensive equipment and services. The only out-of-pocket expenses are for services not covered by the provincial plans such as routine adult dental care, prescription drugs, cosmetic surgery, eyeglasses, medical expenses in foreign countries, and hospital room amenities. Doctors are reimbursed on a fee-for-service basis according to government schedules.

In 1987, the administrative cost for health care in the U.S. was $96.8 billion to $120.4 billion, which was 19.3% to 24.1% of the total amount spent.[51] The Congressional Research Service found the U.S. administration costs be 6.9% versus 1.5% to 2% in Canada. A report in the *New England Journal of Medicine* said the U.S. could save $29 billion in administrative costs.[52]

The U.S. Government Accounting Office (GAO)[53] stated that a single payer of health-care costs, with responsibility to oversee the system, could save enough money in administrative costs to finance the uninsured millions of Americans and have enough left over to cover copayments and deductibles. However, the GAO identified a problem in the Canadian system that is the result of the control of hospital costs and the limited use of high-tech diagnostic and surgical procedures. Waiting lists have developed for some speciality care services such as cardiac bypass surgery, lens implants, and magnetic-resonance imagery (MRI). However, all emergencies receive immediate treatment. Although it has been claimed that the quality of medicine is high, there are some concerns over the longer waits to see doctors, the use of outdated technology, and the rationing of some services.

Some of the advantages and disadvantages of the Canadian system of health insurance are summarized in Table 25-20.

State Programs

Many states have passed or are contemplating laws to assist the millions of Americans who are uninsured. A few states have decided to subsidize basic insurance projects for some of the uninsured, and several states have changed laws to encourage pri-

Table 25–20

Advantages and Disadvantages of the Canadian Health Care System

Advantages	Disadvantages
Comprehensive care for all	May be significant delays in obtaining services, including doctor appointments and elective surgery
Single payer of costs by provincial governments; no claim forms, deductibles, coinsurance, out-of-pocket expenses	Limited use of high-tech equipment
Patient can choose doctor; specialist visits only on referral from primary care doctor; 95% of people satisfied with system	Everything accessible but not accessible enough
Hospitals are 95% full; in U.S., 66%	Less aggressive in treating chronic conditions; few open heart surgery centers
No acutely ill person denied prompt care	Limited number of specialists; ratio is 4 to 1; U.S. is 1 to 1
Provincial governments set budgets for each hospital and doctor fees through negotiations with medical associations; gross incomes of physicians have some limitations	Excess use of system by patients; diagnostic test ordered by doctor but patient may have to wait or travel to obtain
	Health care research not as extensive; some waiting periods: hip replacement, 6 to 10 mos.; most cataracts, 2 mos. or more; elective and urgent general surgery, 4 weeks

vate insurers to sell basic low-cost policies to the working uninsured. The cost might be $60 monthly, which is 25% to 40% below policies with broad coverage. Critics claim these measures are poor substitutes for comprehensive health care for all Americans. These state health insurance projects all emphasize primary care and prevention but are targeted at different groups of people. Also, the the benefits are limited to order to keep costs low. For example, Hawaii limits hospitalization benefits to 5 days with a $2500 limit. In Washington there are no coverages for mental health care, mammography screening, and treatment of alchoholism and drug abuse.[54]

Several states are considering broader legislation to cover all people with a Canadian-type health care plan with a single state government payer. California has introduced a plan that initially would require employees of five or more people to offer a basic low-cost health insurance plan to workers and their dependents. By 1999 this plan would be extended to cover all uninsured Californians.

Seventeen states have established high-risk pools of funds or trust funds to assist people with chronic health problems who have difficulty in obtaining insurance.

The Oregon Health Service Commission created a list of health care services, ranking them from the most important to the least important ones to receive treatment, in its Medicaid program. It is an attempt to maximize benefits within severe budget limitations. Criticism has arisen because it seems to favor minor treatments over lifesaving ones. The arrangement creates a conflict between cost-effectiveness and the rescue of endangered life, referred to as the Rule of Rescue. It has been concluded that the use of cost-effectiveness analysis is unlikely to produce a socially or politically acceptable definition of what is necessary care.

Summary

Health insurance benefits may be categorized as basic health insurance and major medical/extended/catastrophic.

When selecting health insurance, consumers should understand the meaning of waiting periods, conversion privileges, cancellations, limitations, exclusions, and other contract provisions.

Health insurance can be categorized as private (group or individual) or public (Medicare, Medicaid). The main types of private plans are fee-for-service and managed care (HMOs, PPOs, PPAs).

Health maintenance organizations and preferred provider organizations have become popular. There are five general types: IPA, network, group, staff, and point-of-service. Consumers should be aware of the advantages and disadvantages of these plans.

Many corporations provide one or more of the types of health insurance for their employees. Some

It's Your Decision

You will soon have the opportunity to select a health insurance plan for yourself or your family from several offered by your employer. Which of the following actions would you take?

	Action	Reason
1. ______	Ask a friend, neighbor, or relative for advice	______
2. ______	Select an HMO policy	______
3. ______	Select a fee-for-service policy	______
4. ______	Try to determine your health insurance needs	______
5. ______	Obtain sample policies for review	______
6. ______	Compare sample policies using a list of guidelines to determine benefits and needs	______
7. ______	Ask your family doctor for assistance	______

MEDICARE SUPPLEMENT POLICY CHECKLIST

Check the column to the right that identifies the coverage and benefits provided in the policy under review*

	Yes	No	Comments
Hospitalization (part A) Pays initial $620 deductible (1st 60 days)			
Pays $157 per day coinsurance for 61st to 90th day			
Pays $314 per day coinsurance for 60 lifetime reserve days			
Pays $78.50 per day coinsurance for skilled nursing facility for 21st to 100th day			
Pays costs in skilled nursing facility after 21st day			
Pays for first three pints of blood			
Pays costs of emergency outpatient services			
Pays 90% of all hospital expenses for 365 days after Medicare inpatient coverage including lifetime services			
Medical insurance (part B) Pays $100 yearly deductible; 1992 = $125; 1993 = $150			
Pays 20% of reasonable charges after 80% paid by Medicare (At least $5000 maximum per year)			
Pays for home health care services beyond Medicare			
Pays 20% for blood (after first 3 pints) after 80% paid by Medicare			
Pays for: 1. Prescription drugs			
2. Private duty nurses			
3. Psychiatric care			
4. Eyeglasses, hearing aids, dentures			
5. Regular medical checkups			
6. Dental care			
7. Others			
Catastrophic coverage Provides $1 million or more			
Monthly premium cost = ____________			

*State insurance commissioner can be called to see whether company is licensed to sell policies in the state.

plans are entirely subsidized by the companies, and others expect the employees to pay part of the premiums. Employees should know about COBRA and its significance in case their firms go bankrupt or they lose their jobs.

One way to measure the quality of a health insurer is to check its loss ratio in the National Underwriter's Profiles 1991 Health Insurance.

Several other types of health insurance include dread-disease and hospital indemnity plans, fixed dollar amounts, dental, and long-term care.

Medicare and Medicaid are the public health insurance plans available for selected groups of people who are elderly, poor, or handicapped. The elderly should have a Medigap supplementary policy to reduce out-of-pocket expenses and for greater protection. The federal government has standardized 10 Medigap plans to prevent deceptive promotion of Medigap policies.

The guidelines for selecting heath insurance will help consumers when they contemplate the purchase of health insurance.

Many people are dissatisfied with the health care system. There are many proposals for change, and some type of national health insurance may be available in the future. The Canadian plan has some advantages worth reviewing.

Discussion Questions

1. What are the general types of health insurance plans? Briefly discuss each one.
2. What are the basic benefits to be derived from health insurance plans? What are the inclusions of each benefit?
3. What suggestions will help consumers locate individual fee-for-service health insurance plans?
4. What are the components of major medical insurance? Briefly comment on each.
5. What is managed care? What are four features of this service?
6. What are HMOs and PPOs? What are the advantages and disadvantages of these organizations? What are the types of HMOs? Briefly discuss each one.
7. What is the quality of medical care provided by HMOs?
8. What are dread-disease and hospital indemnity health insurance plans? Are they recommended for purchase? Why?
9. What are the types and benefits of prepaid dental insurance plans? What guidelines will help consumers to purchase dental health insurance?
10. What is the meaning of the term *loss ratio?* Why is it important?
11. What are four health insurance problems that may be faced by consumers? Discuss each one briefly.
12. How are corporations trying to manage their health insurance programs? Identify several problems related to this action.
13. What guidelines will help consumers in the selection of HMO insurance?
14. What is long-term health insurance? What are several abuses that sales personnel have used? List five questions consumers should ask when seeking the purchase of this type of insurance.
15. What are five contract provisions found in health insurance policies that consumers must understand?
16. What are the types and what is the nature of the major public health insurance plans?
17. What is the meaning of the term Medigap health insurance? What standards have been established by the federal government to control the sale of this type of insurance? What guidelines will help consumers to purchase medigap insurance? Are there advantages or disadvantages for Medicare enrollees to subscribe to HMO or PPO insurance?
18. What are diagnosis-related groups (DRGs)? Why are they important?
19. What guidelines can help consumers select health insurance policies?
20. What sources are available to consumers who desire health insurance information?
21. Should there be national health insurance for all people in the United States? Describe three general proposals for universal health insurance in this country. What are the nature, advantages, and disadvantages of the Canadian plan?

REFERENCES

1. Cohen P: Health plan roulette, In Health 4(4):78–82, 1990.
2. Complete guide to health insurance, New York, 1988, Avon Books.

*3. Health Insurance Association of America: Souce book of health insurance data, 1991, Washington, DC, 1992, The Association.

*4. Crisis in health insurance, Consumer Reports 55:533–549, 1990.
5. Barnhill W: Preventive action begins to catch on, AARP Bulletin 32:12-13, April 1991.
6. Isaacs F: Health insurance today, Chicago, 1990, Blue Cross–Blue Shield.
*7. Marion managed care digest, HMO edition, Kansas City MO, 1990, Marion Merrill Dow, Inc.
*8. A guide to health maintenance organizations, Washington, DC, 1989, National Consumers League.
9. Chase M: HMOs, hospitals rated equal in care of chronically ill, *The Wall Street Journal,* April 12, 1985.
10. Schaefer C: Second thoughts on HMOs, Changing Times, 41:33–34, May 1987.
11. Wolfe S: Rating our health care systems, Public Citizen, Spring 1984.
12. Bronow R: Why the prognosis is poor for the HMO system, The San Francisco Chronicle, Aug. 8, 1988.
13. Which way will managed care take you? Medical Economics, Apr 22, 1990.
14. Cohn V: Making your health plan work for you, Washington Post Health Section, Nov 28, 1989, reprinted in Public Citizen Health research group Health Letter 6(1):4–7, 1990.
15. Managed care digest, PPO edition, Kansas City, MO, 1990, Marion Merrill Dow, Inc.
16. "Bare bones" insurance plans: filling the small business gap, The Nation's Health, Aug. 1991.
17. Benefits package gets leaner, Medical World News, July 1990.
18. How healthy is your health insurance? Kiplinger's Personal Finance Magazine 45:78–80, July 1991.
19. A promise not kept, Modern Maturity 33:30–38, June-July 1990.
20. Anthony J: Aaarrghh? Making your health insurance work for you, American Health 10(6):76–79, 1991.
21. National Underwriter: Profiles 1991 Health Insurors, Cincinnati, 1991, National Underwriter Co.
22. Friedman E: The uninsured: from dilemma to crisis, JAMA 265:2491–2495, 1991.
23. deCourcyHinds M: Insurers drive to sell "bare bones" health policy falter for lack of interst, The New York Times, Nov 10, 1991.
24. Health system proposals compared to APHA policies, The Nation's Health, March 1990.
25. Wright G: Health care insurance cost increases to continue, Indiana Medicine 82:202–203, March 1989.
26. Simon R: What cracks in the Blue Cross system can mean to you, Money 20:27–28, May, 1991.
27. Plan investigation reveals diet center fraud, Consumer Exchange, Chicago: Blue Cross–Blue Shield, Oct. 1990.
28. Bodner T and Wilcox MD: When your health insurance makes you sick, Kiplinger's Personal Finance Magazine 45:64–66+, Oct. 1991.
*29. AIDS update: An executive report, Hosptials, May 5, 1990.
30. U.S. Congress, Office of Technology Assessment, AIDS and health insurance, Washington, D.C., Feb. 1988.
31. National Center for Health Statistics: Current estimates from the National Heath Survey, Series 10, No. 165, Oct 1988.
32. An empty promise to the elderly, Consumer Reports 56:425–442, 1991.
33. California advocates for nursing home reform, Long Term Care Insurance, San Francisco, 1989.
34. Pear R: U.S. investigations tell of abuses in sale of nursing home insurance, The New York Times, April 12, 1991.
35. Diagnosis-related groups (DRGs), Mayo Clinic Health Letter 8(6):7, 1990.
36. Carlson E and Oriol W: DRGs: surviving Medicare's new obstacle course, Modern Maturity 28:25, Dec. 1985.
37. Strasser AL: Rising costs of Medicare may cause medical care rationing for the elderly, Occupational Health and Safety 58:62, Sept. 1989.
38. Kelso JE: A Medicare problem, CRTA contact, California Retired Teachers Association 6:4, Nov. 1990.
39. Freudenheim M: Health insurance rates for elderly, The New York Times, April 16, 1990.
40. Dolan L: Medigap abuses are targeted, AARP Bulletin, 31:1+, July-August 1991.
41. Carlsen E: Float like a butterfly, sting like a bee, AARP Bulletin, 31:1, March 1990.
*42. The new medigap plans, Consumer Reports 56:616–617, 1991.
43. Medigap insurance: shopping made (a little) easier, Consumer Reports 56:6, 1991.
*44. Berman H and Rose L: Choosing the right health care plan, Consumer Report Books, Mt. Vernon, NY, 1990, Consumers Union.
45. Pear R: U.S. to crack down on medical abuse, The New York Times, Nov 3, 1991.
46. Cole A: The $10 billion dollar blank check, Modern Maturity, April/May, 1990.
47. Gianelli DM: Final rules list penalties for fraud, patient abuse. American Medical News, pp 3, 47, Feb 24, 1992.
48. Blendon RJ and Edwards JN: Caring for the uninsured: choices for reform, JAMA 265:2563–64, 1991.
49. Carlsen F: A call for change: readers assail U.S. system, AARP Bulletin 31:1, May 1990.
50. Which countries are satisfied with their health care? Public Citizen Health Research Group Health Letter 6(8):9–10, 1990.
*51. Woodhandler B and Himmelstein DV: The deteriorating administrative efficiency of the U.S. health care system, N Eng J Med 324:1253–58, 1991.
52. Insurance Canadian style: states start to explore the option, The Nation's Health, June 1991.
*53. U.S. General Accounting Office: Canadian health insurance: lessons for the U.S., Report of Chairman, Committee on Government Operations, U.S. House of Representatives, July 1991.
54. "Basic" state health insurance plans: no substitute for a national program, Public Citizen Health Research Group Health Letter 7(3):7, 1991.

*Recommended reading

CHAPTER TWENTY-SIX

HEALTH CARE ECONOMICS

The American health care system, and especially its cost, is out of control, inhibiting access to care for many, lessening quality of care for some, and creating an almost palpable angst among physicians and others concerned with this enormous national problem.

NICHOLAS E. DAVIES, M.D.
LOUIS H. FELDER, M.D.[1]

From some Wall Street junk bond traders to certain Midwest sports millionaires to many California real estate developers, greed is in fashion. Physicians are not immune to the pandemic caused by the greed virus.

GEORGE D. LUNDBERG, M.D.[2]

What else could anyone expect in America but rapidly rising health care costs, with 3 million desperate drug abusers at large on our streets, 18 million alcohol abusers loose on our highways, 55 million tobacco abusers causing 1000 costly, painful deaths every day, and nearly 1 million new cases of venereal disease adding to our society's existing burden every year. . . . Waiting in the wings are growing crises involving long-term care, homelessness, Alzheimer's disease, and the uninsured and underinsured working poor, not to mention the burgeoning tragedy of a million or more men, women, and children infected with the AIDS virus.

TIMOTHY B. NORBECK[3]
EXECUTIVE DIRECTOR
CONNECTICUT MEDICAL SOCIETY

CONSUMER DECISIONS

How can consumers reduce expenditures for health products and services?

How can consumers plan ahead for health care expenses?

 **PERSONAL GLIMPSE** 

After a middle-aged woman was left comatose following a routine gallbladder operation, her son filed a malpractice suit. He settled out of court for more than $1 million from the hospital's insurance company and another million from the surgeon's insurance company. The surgeon then sued the son for unpaid medical fees of $115,000—including $4000 for the original surgery and the rest for 931 visits to the comatose patient's bedside. The doctor denied wrongdoing and expressed compassion and sorrow for the family. He said, "I am merely seeking fair and reasonable payment for my services."

Do you think the physician was justified in sending the bill?

What impact do you think million-dollar verdicts have on the cost of medical care in this country?

In 1990, expenditures for health care in the United States represented 12.2% of the gross national product (GNP) and totaled $666.2 billion.[4] The per capita cost for all health services was $2566. As shown in Table 26-1, $585.3 billion was spent on personal health care.

The cost of America's health care has been rising steadily at an alarming rate. The Health Care Financing Administration (HCFA)[4] has reported that the average yearly rise was 10.5% between 1960 and 1970, 13% between 1970 and 1980, and 10.3% between 1980 and 1990. HCFA[5] predicts that if circumstances don't change, the total cost will reach $1.45 trillion in 2000, which would be $5,155 per person with $1452 out-of-pocket per family.

The reasons for the fast rising costs include (1) increasing use of costly high-tech equipment,[6] (2) innovative treatment of such illnesses as AIDS and cancer, (3) aging population, (4) fraudulent practices by some physicians, (5) the large number and cost of malpractice suits, (6) administrative costs of complying with government regulations,[7] and (7) the practice of defensive medicine—testing that is medically unnecessary but done to protect the physician against the danger of a malpractice suit—which adds tens of billions of dollars yearly to the cost of medical care.[3]

A Health Insurance Association of America (HIAA)[8] survey of American householders' views of health care revealed that 80% were highly satisfied or somewhat satisfied with health care, and 84% to 88% were satisfied with their own physician(s). However, 70% were somewhat or very dissatisfied with the costs of health care.

In the world's richest nation, where billions of dollars are spent yearly on health care, many people are unable to obtain adequate medical attention. Those primarily involved are the so-called working poor, the homeless, and the elderly. Great burdens

TABLE 26–1

PERSONAL HEALTH CARE EXPENDITURES, 1990

	Amount ($ billions)	Percentage
Hospital care	256.0	43.7
Physician services	125.7	21.5
Dental services	34.0	5.6
Other professional services	31.6	5.4
Home health care	6.9	1.2
Drugs and other nondurable products	54.6	54.6
Vision products and other medical durables	12.1	2.1
Nursing home care	53.1	9.1
Other personal care	11.3	1.9
Total	585.3*	

*88% of total expenditures ($662.2 billion)

Source: Levit KR et al: National health care expenditures, 1990. Health Care Financing Review 13(1)29-54, 1991.

TABLE 26–2

PER CAPITA AND OUT-OF-POCKET EXPENDITURES BY TYPES OF SERVICE, 1990

	Per capita		Out-of-Pocket	
Types of services	Amount	Percent	Amount	Percent
Personal health care				
Hospital care	$ 986	43.7	$ 49	9.3
Physician services	484	21.5	90	17.2
Dental services	130	5.8	69	13.1
Other professional services	122	5.4	34	6.5
Home health care	27	1.2	3	0.6
Drugs and other nondurable medical products	210	9.3	155	29.6
Vision products and other medical durables	47	2.1	32	6.1
Nursing home care	204	9.1	92	17.6
Other personal care	44	1.9	—	
Total personal health care cost	$2255	100.0	524	100.0
Administration, government public health activities, research, and construction	311			
Total per capital cost	$2566			

Note: The average person age 65 or over pays four to five times as much out of pocket as the total shown in the table.
Data from Levit KR et al: National health care expenditures, 1990. Health Care Financing Review 13(1)29-54, 1991.

are also placed on a substantial segment of the population, including some middle-income families who are financially devastated when serious, chronic, or catastrophic illness occurs.

This chapter provides only limited attention to the solution of the tremendously important health-related financial problems facing Americans. Instead, in keeping with the theme of the text, it will try to help consumers understand some of the types of expenses they encounter when purchasing health services and products. It offers suggestions to help control these expenses.

PERSONAL HEALTH CARE EXPENDITURES

In 1989, 76% ($406 billion) of personal health expenses were paid by third parties (private health insurers and public agencies) and 24% ($116 billion) were paid directly by individuals. U.S. Department of Commerce data indicated that in 1988 health care was the third largest expense (after food and clothing) for the average American. The total expenses for personal health needs in 1986 amounted to approximately 13.7% of the average budget.[9]

Table 26-2 shows the per capita and out-of-pocket expenditures for health-care services utilized in 1990. The largest dollar amount was for hospital services, whereas the greatest percentage paid out of pocket was for drugs and other nondurable medical products. People over 65 had out-of-pocket expenses averaging more than $1800, and their per capita costs were as follows: Ages 65 to 69, $3728; 70 to 74, $4424; 80 to 84, $6717; 85 and over, $9178. It should be apparent that the elderly have greater health-care costs than people below the age of 65 years.

Table 26-3 shows the personal health care expenditures by type of services and by out-of-pocket and third party payments. The government pays the largest amount, private health insurance pays almost 36%, and out-of-pocket expenses make up 23.5%.

Table 26-4 shows the average annual expenditures per person by age groups for 1990. There is an upward progression of costs as a person grows

TABLE 26–3

SOURCES OF PAYMENT FOR HEALTH PRODUCTS AND SERVICES IN 1990 (BILLIONS OF DOLLARS)

Categories of service	Out-of-pocket payments	Private health insurance	Government programs
Hospital care	12.8	89.4	140.0
Physician services	23.5	58.2	43.9
Dental services	18.0	15.1	0.9
Other professional services	8.6	12.8	6.4
Home health care	0.8	0.5	5.1
Drugs & other nondurable products	40.2	8.3	6.1
Vision products and other medical durables	8.2	1.3	2.7
Nursing home care	23.9	0.6	27.7
Other personal care	—	—	9.1
Totals	136.1	186.2	241.9
Percent	24.1%	33.0%	42.7%

Source: Levit KR et al: National health care expenditures, 1990. Health Care Financing Review 13(1)29-54, 1991.

TABLE 26–4

ESTIMATED AMOUNTS SPENT FOR HEALTH CARE IN 1990 BY PEOPLE IN VARIOUS AGE GROUPS

Age group	Individual average	Percent of U.S. total	Health insurance	Medical services	Prescription drugs, etc.
Under 25	$ 486	6.6	$125	$288	$ 73
25-44	1065	14.4	244	668	153
25-64	1607	21.6	450	867	290
65-74	2010	27.2	906	726	378
75 & older	2231	30.2	985	833	413

Source: Original data from 1984 as reported in U.S. Department of Commerce, Statistical abstract of the United States, 107th edition, Washington, D.C., 1987, Government Printing Office. The 1984 data were extended to include an estimated 50% rise for the 6 years to 1990.

older. Such average expenditures are almost five times as great for those over 75 than for those under 25.

Consumers should understand that despite third party payments, no insurance is going to pay all health care costs. Individuals must realize that they will have to share some of the financial responsibility for their health care. This usually occurs through deductibles and coinsurance. This responsibility may increase in the future for some people if coverage is to be provided for everyone. Chapter 25 describes the various types of insurance plans.

When planning for health care, consumers should consider the following: (1) out-of-pocket expenses will occur each year and average at least $500; (2) costs for health care will increase as one grows older, (3) a sizable portion of one's yearly income should be budgeted for health care, including dental and vision care not covered by insurance, and (4) the amount to be budgeted will depend on the size of one's family and nature of one's insurance coverage.

Physicians' Fees

Physicians generally base fees on (1) the nature, extent, and complication of the service, (2) the time involved, (3) the operating costs—rent, heat, lighting, salaries of personnel, (4) the experience and expertise of the practitioner, (5) the area of the country in which the physician practices, (6) the customary fees charged by physicians in the community, and (7) in some circumstances, the economic status of the patient. Federal regulations prohibit medical organizations from establishing fee guidelines or fee schedules. This is considered a restraint of trade.

Insurance plans pay for medical services in three ways. Physicians may be compensated for each service they render, the so-called *fee-for-service* method. The second method is a *salary* from a hospital, group health insurance plan, or governmental or private organization or agency. Some members of group health plans may also receive a share of the profits at the end of each year, based upon the amount of service rendered. The third method is *capitation,* a fixed monthly amount paid for each patient (per capita) regardless of the amount of services used.

For many years, insurance companies have based fee-for-service payments to practitioners on a UCR (usual, customary, and reasonable) reimbursement approach. *Usual* refers to a physician's own charges for the previous year or years. *Customary* refers to the range of fees charged by all physicians in a given region. *Reasonable* refers to a fee within a given region or area that falls below the 90th percentile of the customary charges. Medicare has used the 75th percentile and pays 80% of this amount.

Many attempts have been made to control escalating medical and hospital costs without affecting the quality of care. They have included (1) reduction of time patients stay in hospitals, (2) elimination of unnecessary surgery by obtaining second opinions, (3) establishment by Medicare of the DRG program, whereby hospitals are reimbursed at set fees for over 400 medical procedures (see Table 26-5), (4) emphasis on preventive care, (5) operation of storefront medical centers and clinics, (6) development of HMOs, PPOs, and other group associations, and (7) encouragement of outpatient surgery for the repair of hernias, removal of tonsils, breast biopsies and other procedures. This last strategy has cut the average cost of these operations in half.

Table 26–5

Reduced Payment to Hospitals Under DRG Program

Service	Normal charge	DRG payment
Hip replacement	$ 8,100	$ 7,900
Total mastectomy	3,300	3,100
Heart valve	27,600	21,000
Orthopedic	14,091	11,521
Rehabilitation for substance abuse	45,000	32,000

Source: Gilbert S: America abandoning sick patients? The Good Health Section, The New York Times, April 29, 1990.[10]

Another practice to control medical costs has been the publishing of physician fees for consumer review and appraisal. Colorado, Florida, Iowa, Minnesota, Nebraska, New Hampshire, North Carolina, Oregon, and Wyoming have taken steps to inform people about doctor charges.[11] In Baltimore, Maryland, a published directory lists 12,000 physicians and the fees they charge for commonly performed procedures. Such a document, if available in other communities, could be useful in selecting a physician. However, consumers should not select a physician solely on fees charged. Qualifications and the ability to render the highest quality of medical care should be the primary factors.

In 1992, Medicare implemented the resource-based relative value system, a method of payment (described below) quite different from the UCR method. The new system is an effort to control the escalating costs of medical care and to provide a more equitable reimbursement for services rendered. It will be phased in over a 5-year period and includes these provisions.[12]

1. Payment will be made according to the resource-based relative value scale (RBRVS), a nationwide fee scale that takes into account (a) the extent of history taking and physician examination, (b) the complexity of medical decision making, (c) the time spent counseling the patient, (d) the severity of the patient's health

Table 26–6

Selected Medical Procedures and Physicians' Fees 1990

	Approximate range of fees ($)
Medicine	
Office visits	
New patient	
Brief evaluation, examination	38 to 50
Initial comprehensive history and physical examination	100 to 155
Established patient	
Brief evaluation, examination, and/or treatment	25 to 35
Periodic examination (adult)	50 to 75
Well-baby care without immunizations	40 to 57
Home visits	
New patient	40 to 160
Established patient	30 to 100
Consultations	
Including limited examination	65 to 90
Requiring comprehensive history, examination, and evaluation	140 to 210
Immunizations	11 to 45
Psychiatric services	
Psychotherapy—50 minutes	75 to 115
Psychotherapy—25 minutes	55 to 75
Group therapy (maximum eight persons) for 1.5 hours	25 to 50
Diagnostic services	
Eye examination (E visual)	55 to 75
Eye examination (basic comprehensive audiometric tests)	65 to 90
Electrocardiogram with interpretation and report	50 to 65
Electrocardiogram with exercise test	190 to 290
Allergy testing, 1 to 10 tests (per test) (intradermal)	8 to 11
Surgery	
Skin	
Sebaceous cyst excision	66 to 100
Biopsy	58 to 80
Breast	
Biopsy (needle)	65 to 95
Unilateral mastectomy	683 to 1,225
Musculoskeletal system	
Fractures—Ankle	720 to 2,650
Cardiovascular system	
Aortic valve repair	1,300 to 7,150
Aneurysm repair	2,000 to 2,412
Digestive system	
Hemorrhoidectomy	112 to 1,700
Inguinal hernia	832 to 1,785
Tonsillectomy with or without adenoidectomy (under 12 years)	432 to 750
Urinary system	
Kidney transplant	3,800 to 5,000
Prostatectomy, TUR (transurethral section)	1,782 to 2,650
Maternity care	
Total obstetrical care	1,380 to 2,000

TABLE 26–6

SELECTED MEDICAL PROCEDURES AND PHYSICIANS' FEES 1990—cont'd

	Approximate range of fees ($)
Radiology	
Chest x-ray (2 views)	55 to 75
Pathology	
Basal metabolic rate; blood count, complete	16 to 25
Insulin, blood	34 to 40
Pap smear test	15 to 25
Red blood cell count	6 to 10
Skin test, tuberculosis	10 to 20
Sugar (glucose) blood	8 to 15
White blood cell count	8 to 10
Urinalysis routine, complete	10 to 15
Panel test (20 or more)	42 to 65
AIDS screens	40 to 60

Source: This information was compiled by a reliable California provider in 1991.

problem, and (e) the time spent with the patient.

2. Fees that Medicare patients can be charged by doctors who do not accept assignment are limited. In 1991, physicians could exceed Medicare-approved fees by only 25% in 1991, 20% in 1992, and 15% in 1993 and thereafter. Several states have passed laws with similar provisions.
3. Doctors have been instructed not to attempt to offset fee reductions by ordering more tests, doing more procedures, or submitting a higher proportion of claims for higher-priced services.
4. Restrictions were placed on referral of patients to clinical laboratories or other health-care facilities in which the referring physician has a financial interest.

Physicians' fees vary from community to community. Table 26-6 shows the range of fees for the services of private practitioners in one western state. They were prepared by a large private insurance company in 1991 based on UCR charges.

Table 26-7 lists the median physician fees for selected surgical and OBG procedures in the United States. Table 26-8 shows the mean physician fees in dollars charged for new and established patients and follow-up hospital visits by specialty in 1990.

TABLE 26–7

MEDIAN PHYSICIAN FEES FOR SELECTED SURGICAL AND OBG PROCEDURES IN THE UNITED STATES, 1989

Procedure	Median fee
Hysterectomy	$1770
Complete OB care	1569
Dilation and curettage	450
Cesarian section	2053
Appendectomy	801
Inguinal hernia repair	800
Modified radical mastectomy	1489
Total hip arthroplasty	3500
Coronary bypass operation	4834
Pacemaker insertion	1500
Breast augmentation (bilateral)	2397
Breast reduction (bilateral)	3501
Lumbar laminectomy	2501
Excision of knee cartilage	1501

Sources: Medical economics, Oct. 2, 1989, Oradell, NJ Medical Economics Co., Inc. and Health Insurance Association of America: Sourcebook of health insurance data 1990, Washington, DC, 1990, The Association.

TABLE 26–8

MEAN PHYSICIAN FEES FOR OFFICE VISITS FOR NEW AND ESTABLISHED PATIENTS AND FOLLOW-UP HOSPITAL VISITS BY SPECIALTY (1990)

	Office visits		
Physicians	New patient	Established patient	Hospital visits follow-up
All	$ 74.84	$39.87	$43.23
General family	44.46	31.24	35.81
Internal medicine	101.37	42.75	45.85
Surgery	68.86	39.00	41.85
Pediatrics	54.27	35.73	45.50
Obstetrics and gynecology	76.06	49.80	49.43

Source: Gonzalez ML (ed): Socioeconomic characteristics of medical practice, 1990/1991. Chicago, 1991, American Medical Association.

TABLE 26–9

COST OF SELECTED HIGH-TECHNOLOGY MEDICAL PROCEDURES (1989)

Procedure	Cost*
Cardiovascular	
Thrombolytic agents (blood clot dissolver)	$ 8,000
PTCA (coronary angioplasty)	4,000
Pacemaker (advanced)	7,000
Implantable defibrillator	12,000
Peripheral vascular angioplasty	4,000
Valvuloplasty (opening blocked artery)	
Ear nose and throat	
Cochlear implants	4,000
Diagnostic imaging	
MRI (magnetic resonance image)	850
High-speed Cine-CT	700

*Medical fees not included
Source: Sourcebook of health insurance data 1990, Washington, D.C., 1990, Health Insurance Association of America.

TABLE 26–10

PHYSICIAN NET INCOME BEFORE TAXES (1989)

Specialty	Median	Mean
General family practice	$ 90,000	$ 95,900
Internal medicine	120,000	146,500
Surgery	180,000	220,500
Pediatrics	93,000	104,700
Obstetrics and gynecology	164,000	194,300
Radiology	180,000	210,500
Psychiatry	100,000	111,700
Anesthesiology	180,000	185,800
Pathology	148,000	154,500
All physicians	125,000	155,000

Source: Gonzalez ML (ed): Socioeconomic characteristics of medical practice, 1990/1991. Chicago, 1991, American Medical Association.

Table 26-9 identifies the cost of several high-technology procedures. Table 26-10 reveals the median and mean physician net income after expenses by specialty.

Money[13] magazine stated the fastest-rising component in health care costs from 1982 to 1988 was doctor wages. They increased 48% during this period, twice the inflation rate. An AMA survey in 1989 found two thirds of Americans think doctors are too interested in making money.[14] Dr. Laurens White, former president, California Medical Association, believes physician fraud is increasing health costs by $65 billion yearly. In *The Wall Street Journal*, December 5, 1989, he charged, "at least 5%

[of physicians] are out-and-out crooks and my bet is another 30% are overcharging in forms that vary from the trivial to obscure." He identified these causes:

1. Cancer specialists who charge $1000 for a series of chemotherapy treatments that cost the doctor $100.
2. Gynecologists "unbundling" their charges for a hysterectomy (billing separately for incision, scar removal, and the procedure), thereby increasing the cost tenfold.

Luciano[13] identifies these physician practices that increase health costs:

1. One in eight doctors (12%) own a health-care business to which patients are referred; 25% own independent clinical laboratories causing more patients to have more tests than generally needed. The excess costs of these actions are estimated to be $140 million.
2. A significant number of surgical claims are submitted improperly by doctors, thereby increasing their fees. He stated unbundling to be a technique of multilisting insurance codes to overstate the actual amount of work done; excess costs equal $6 billion annually.
3. Up to one third of medical treatments are unnecessary; excess costs equal $50 billion.

Consumers may not be able to change the system, but to obtain protection these actions are suggested:

1. *Talk money with your doctor.* Ask for costs and make it clear you are not just interested in out-of-pocket expenses but total costs.
2. *Talk value.* Ask how much a test or procedure will add to knowledge about your condition or improve your health.
3. *Don't use price as a substitute for quality.* How many times has the doctor performed the procedure? What is his or her success rate? Ask if there are less expensive alternatives of equal quality.
4. *Report suspected fraud and abuse* to your insurer, to Medicare, and others.
5. *Don't be greedy.* Don't ask your doctor to mislabel a visit so you can obtain reimbursement for something not covered by your insurance policy.

Professional Advertising

Now that physicians are free to advertise (see Chapter 5), numerous ads are appearing in telephone directories, newspapers, and magazines and on radio and TV. A few physicians who have hired public relations companies to help publicize their practices spend $10,000 to $100,000 or more a year for media coverage. Public relations firms may groom physicians for talk shows and prepare slick press kits touting their specialties. Other firms turn clients into authors by developing a book idea, finding a ghost writer, and even obtaining a contract for the book's publication. The number of physicians who hire press agents is not known, but these agents claim their "doctor business" is on the increase.

Although the AMA has withdrawn its objection to advertising by its members as long as they do not mislead consumers or imply exclusive remedies, the critics of media advertising list these reasons for their objections: (1) publicized claims can mislead the public; (2) some self-promoters are practitioners on the fringe of their profession who may advocate unusual and controversial remedies and cures; (3) when medical reports are printed in medical journals, they can be evaluated through peer review, whereas claims made during television or radio interviews are virtually impossible to evaluate; and (4) when physicians challenge questionable claims of treatment in the media, the controversy gives additional free publicity to the claimant.

Fee Conclusions

These conclusions may be drawn from the information about physician fees:

1. Medical costs vary according to the section of the United States in which one lives.
2. Fees for services depend on a variety of factors, including inflation.
3. Physicians have considerable freedom to establish their own fees. Should professional directories become more prevalent, consumers should be able to compare fees and credentials.
4. Some physicians who appear frequently on television and radio or who write books are promoting questionable procedures.
5. Physician ownership of a commercial laboratory, medical imaging facility, or expensive diagnostic equipment may lead to excessive testing or inappropriate self-referrals.
6. Consumers should not hesitate to ask questions about fees, medical procedures, and laboratory tests to determine need, value, and quality of care.
7. Reporting suspected fraud or overcharging of patients is a consumer responsibility.

TABLE 26–11

ESTIMATED DENTAL FEES, 1990

Services	Average fees	Range of fees
Diagnostic		
Periodic oral examination	$ 15	$ 10-20
Initial oral examination	20	18-38
Full mouth x-ray (4 bitewings)	30	25-45
Preventive		
Prophylaxis—adult	34	28-46
—child	25	30-40
Topical application of fluoride (excluding prophylaxis)—child	15	18-30
Restorative		
Amalgam—one surface, primary	33	27-40
—three surfaces, permanent	46	43-76
Inlay, metallic, one surface	310	246-374
Crown, procelain on gold	451	440-593
Crown, full high noble metal	435	394-506
Periodontics		
Gingivectomy or gingivoplasty, per quandrant	212	187-364
Endodontics		
Therapeutic pulpotomy (excluding final restoration)	75	52-98
Root canal, one canal	250	215-312
Oral surgery		
Extraction, single tooth	46	38-60
Orthodontics		
Comprehensive treatment (transitional dentition), Class I malocclusion	2500	2000-3000
Comprehensive treatment (permanent dentition), Class I malocclusion	2779	2307-3250
Prosthodontics (removable)		
Complete upper or lower denture (fixed)	682	548-816
Bridge retainers, crown, porcelain fused to high noble metal	538	460-618
Cosmetic Bonding	133	125-141

Sources: Bentley, J et al: Dental Fees and Inflation: Good News or Bad News, J Am Dent Assoc, 123:91-92, January, 1992. Dollars and Sense, American Health, X:30, June, 1991. (From Dental Management Mag, Feb, 1991)

DENTISTS' FEES

Table 26-11 estimates average fees charged by general dentists and selected specialists in the United States in 1990. Consumers should be aware that fees vary widely in metropolitan as well as nonmetropolitan areas. The list of fees may be helpful when preparing a budget for dental care and when considering the purchase of dental insurance (see Chapter 25). Table 26-12 provides information about the income of dentists in the United States in 1991.

Considerable evidence indicates that preventive dentistry can save consumers money. More important, however, are the benefits of freedom from pain and discomfort, retention of teeth, and less time lost obtaining dental care. The incidence of dental caries and periodontal disease can be reduced through the fluoridation of water supplies, topical application of fluorides, and plaque control measures (see Chapter 8).

Table 26–12

Income of Dentists

Type of dentist	Mean net income	Mean gross income
General practitioners	84,320	319,170
Specialists	135,390	417,100

Source: Bureau of Economic and Behavioral Research: The 1991 survey of dental practice, Chicago, 1992, American Dental Association.

Consumer Action Regarding Fees

Every consumer should be prepared to take these important actions in regard to professional fees: (1) discuss them with practitioners before services are rendered, (2) don't hesitate to ask questions, and (3) seek explanations when overcharges or inequities occur.

Unfortunately, patients are often too intimidated to ask about fees. This may be caused in part by the individual's dependence on the services of the practitioner and to some physicians taking offense if individuals decide to shop around. People need to set aside such fears and understand that the doctor may be just as anxious as the patient to clarify charges. Some practitioners post signs in their offices indicating their willingness to discuss fees, whereas others accommodate individuals on request. After discussing costs, the consumer may decide to try another physician or dentist, and that is a decision that must be permitted. Should a professional be unwilling to take the time to communicate, it may be advisable to seek someone else to provide one's care.

It should not be necessary to discuss fees with a physician on every office visit. It should be done during one of the initial visits and when some major service is to be rendered. A number of questions may be asked:

1. What are the usual and customary charges, and for what services?
2. How do these charges compare with the fees of other physicians in the community?
3. Will the payments from the insurance company be acceptable? If not, what will be the approximate out-of-pocket expense?
4. Can the out-of-pocket expenses be budgeted over a period of months, or will a single payment be required? How is the budgeted arrangement to be handled?
5. Will the physician bill the patient directly or bill the insurance company?
6. If well-baby care is necessary up to a specific age, is there a package fee arrangement for such services? How are the payments to be made?

If an individual believes that unfairness, injustice, or overcharging has occurred, these actions are suggested:

1. First attempt to obtain clarification through the office assistant, and if that is not satisfactory, from the physician directly.
2. If you cannot reach the physician or if you are dissatisfied with the initial communication with the physician, send a certified letter to the practitioner, giving all the facts and requesting a written explanation.
3. If you are still dissatisfied, file a formal complaint with the local medical or dental society. Its grievance committee should investigate the matter, discuss your case with the physician, and try to arrive at an equitable and mutually satisfactory solution.
4. The final step, if all else fails, is to decide whether the problem deserves the attention of an attorney or the state licensing board.

One final thought about fees. If one is uncertain about a charge or wishes information about the customary rates in the community and it is not possible to obtain a satisfactory answer from one's own physician, these actions may be advisable: (1) contact the local medical or dental association or (2) call several local doctors' offices.

Consumers should be cautious about equating cost with quality of services. Individuals may find it necessary to reduce their health expenditures and should seek ways to do so. However, if a person wants the best qualified professional, or one with an outstanding performance record and who may be more expensive, it may be necessary to reconsider and find alternative ways of financing the service.

The use of less costly practitioners or services may not always be in the best interests of the consumer. The selection of a health practitioner or service should not be based solely on price but rather on the faith the individual has in the person and the quality of the help received. An attentive, competent, communicative practitioner, one with integrity, is certainly most desirable.

Hospital and Nursing Home Costs

Hospital room charges have increased nearly 130% since 1980, when the average cost was $127. In 1990, the cost of a semiprivate room averaged $297 (plus tests, drugs, doctor bills, and so on), with Connecticut ($456) and California ($453) being the most expensive states and Mississippi ($167) and Arkansas ($170) the least expensive. The average cost for treating a patient in 1988 in a community hospital was $586 a day, with a range of $360 (South Dakota) to $961 (Alaska). The average cost of a hospital stay (7.2 days) in 1988 was $4219. These figures do not include surgical or other medical bills.

The reasons for the spiraling costs include the following:

1. Inflation caused by wage increases and other factors
2. Growing public interest in health care
3. Expensive new technology (such as magnetic resonance imaging and computed tomography)
4. Rising malpractice premiums
5. Unused hospital beds
6. Need for more services by the aging population
7. Physicians ordering more laboratory tests than necessary
8. Patients allowed to remain in hospitals longer than necessary. This practice is changing with the advent of DRGs by Medicare and the increase in the use of clinics and outpatient services. Schwartz and Mendelson[15] stated that the reduction of inpatient hospital days in the 1980s briefly slowed hospital costs. However, once the potential savings from inappropriate days has been exhausted, real hospital costs will rise unless other effective measures to contain costs are implemented.
9. Cost of complying with accreditation standards and government regulations.

The cost of having a baby continues to skyrocket. Table 26-13 provides information regarding the average cost of maternity care for a normal delivery and a cesarean section. The average cost for a vaginal delivery in a hospital in 1989 was $4334; for a cesarean it was $7186. Since an additional cost of $500 to $800 for well-baby care during the first 18 months is to be anticipated, consumers should (1) be sure that their health insurance plan covers these costs or (2) consider changing to an HMO or a PPO that provides these additional services.

The Marine Engineers Beneficial Association, a private health care plan, publicized two hospital bills that have sent shock waves through the health insurance industry.[16] A patient in a Houston hospital for five months was charged $447,574. Of this amount, $73,000 was for professional medical services, with an average daily cost of about $2500. A patient in a Boston hospital incurred a hospital bill of $238,000 for 37 days plus $3450 for surgeon fees, an average of $6525 per day.

Here are several additional illustrative costs for procedures performed in hospitals:

Kidney transplants	$75,000 up
Coronary bypass	$30,000 up
Total hip replacement	$8,000 to $12,000

Table 26–13

Average Cost of Maternity Care (1988-1989)

	Normal delivery			Cesarean section		
Census region	Hospital charges	Physician fees*	Total	Hospital charges	Physician fees*	Total
Northeast	$2964	$1492	$4456	$5826	$2053	$7879
Midwest	2657	1492	4149	4688	2053	6741
South	2712	1492	4204	5034	2053	7087
West	2745	1492	4237	5533	2053	7586

*Physician fees include prenatal and delivery fees.
Source: Health Insurance Association of America[9]

Substance abuse rehabilitation	$30,000 to $45,000
Heart valve replacement	$30,000 to $40,000
Bone marrow transplants	$100,000
Pacemaker implant	$6000 to $9000
Liver transplant	$216,000

In freestanding birthing centers, children can be born in a cliniclike atmosphere outside of a hospital. These centers claim that their fees, including obstetrical professional charges, are half the cost of those in a hospital. Consumers wishing to save money may discuss the possible use of a center with their own physician. However, although most deliveries do not require hospital care, emergencies can arise that do. Thus, delivery in a freestanding facility entails an extra risk.

The National Council of Senior Citizens[17] said the costs and charges in for-profit hospitals are higher than those in nonprofit hospitals. They claim that when nonprofits are acquired by for-profit corporations, the costs often increase. About 24% of the hospitals in the United States are for-profit.[18] A study by the Institute of Medicine[15] reported that these hospitals had somewhat higher prices and provided less care for the uninsured than the not-for-profit facilities.

Consumers may be able to reduce hospital and surgery costs by (1) obtaining a second opinion where elective surgery is advised, (2) refraining from hospital stays that are extended merely for the convenience of the patient, (3) with the help of a physician, shopping for a hospital, since rates differ (some areas in the United States have developed consumer guides to hospitals that provide information about charges, services, and other matters), and (4) monitoring hospital bills carefully to be certain all charges are valid. Billing errors, which are common, can include overcharges as well as charges for unreceived services.

The cost per day at a nursing home depends on the nature of the care rendered, the type of facility, the region of the United States, and a number of other factors. It is estimated the average daily cost is $65 to $100, the weekly cost is $455 to $700, the monthly cost is $2000 to $3000, and the yearly cost is $24,000 to $36,000. Some 70% to 80% of the elderly cannot afford one year in a nursing home, and two thirds who can pay initially would run out of funds within the first year. Most nursing home care is financed by private sources and paid directly by patients and families. For many people, nursing home expenses are by far the largest out-of-pocket burden of all the health care services.

Reducing nursing home costs may be difficult but these are several procedures that may help: (1) check Medicare coverage and whether Medicaid is obtainable, (2) determine whether additional insurance is needed and available, (3) consider purchasing long-term insurance (Chapter 25), and (4) explore alternatives to nursing home care (Chapter 25).

Health Insurance

The cost of health insurance varies according to a number of factors, such as size of family, nature and extent of the coverage, and whether the insurance includes major medical protection. When deciding to select a policy, the reader might wish to review Chapter 25 for details.

In 1990, premiums for 20 health insurance policies available to California state employees were as follows:[19]

Employee only: $115 to $204 monthly, or $1380 to $2448 yearly, for the basic plan with major medical (catastrophic) coverage.

Employee with one dependent: $233 to $385 monthly, or $2796 to $4620 yearly, for the basic plan with major medical (catastrophic) coverage.

Employee with two or more dependents: $338 to $514 monthly or $4056 to $6168 for the basic plan with major medical (catastrophic) coverage.

Supplementary insurance for the elderly:

Employee only: $80 to $134 monthly, or $960 to $1608 yearly.

Employee and one dependent: $156 to $272 monthly, or $1872 to $3264 yearly.

Employee with two or more dependents: $209 to $408 monthly, or $2508 to $4896 yearly.

Table 26-14 identifies the average percentages of personal health expenditures covered by private insurance, governmental insurance plans, and out-of-pocket payments in 1989. It should be apparent that direct out-of-pocket expenses (23.5%) will be necessary for noncovered health care services. Private health insurance provides about 36% of the overall costs.

The information presented should help individuals anticipate needs and budget for health care. Individuals should review their current health insurance coverage to determine the extent to which

TABLE 26–14

PERCENTAGES OF PERSONAL HEALTH EXPENDITURES COVERED BY PRIVATE AND GOVERNMENTAL INSURANCE PLANS (1990)

Services	Private health insurance	Government	Out-of pocket payments	Other private
Hospital care	34.9	54.7	5	5.4
Physician services	46.3	34.9	18.7	—
Dental care	44.4	2.6	52.9	—
Nursing home care	1.1	52.2	45.0	1.9
Other professional services	40.5	20.2	27.8	11.4
Home health care	11.6	73.9	7.2	7.2
Drugs and other non durable products	15.2	11.2	73.6	—
Vision products and other medical durables	10.7	22.3	67.8	—
Total personal health care expenditures	31.8	41.3	23.2	3.6

Source: Levit KR et al: National health care expenditures, 1990. Health Care Financing Review 13(1)29-54, 1991.

IT'S YOUR DECISION

An insurance company received a hospital bill totaling $1.25 million for a 26-year-old woman who was the first person to receive a new heart, liver, and kidney in the same operation.[20] The operation took 21 hours and involved at least 36 people: 11 surgeons, 6 anesthesiologists, 15 nurses, 1 physician assistant, 2 blood technicians, and 1 liver technician. During her hospital stay, the woman had seven more operations and spent 113 days in the intensive care unit while doctors struggled unsuccessfully to save her.

When queried by a reporter from *The New York Times*, the hospital refused to release a copy of the bill. But it did provide information on the average payment it receives from Blue Cross-Blue Shield for a $120,000 liver transplantation when there are no complications. The main items include the following:

$28,000 for hospital and intensive care rooms

$20,000 to acquire donor organ

$20,000 for surgeons, anesthesiologists, a radiologist, an internist, and a neurologist

$15,000 for tests including radiology, ultrasound, and CT scans

$8000 to administer blood

$7000 each for use of the operating room and pharmacy charges

$4000 each for anesthesia and pulmonary services

The insurance company balked at paying the bill without conducting an audit. The hospital refused to permit an audit until the bill was paid. The reporter noted that a bill this size could have considerable impact on even a large employer's annual health insurance premiums.

The surgeons who operated on the patient acknowledged that even with a single-organ transplant there is a 15% to 25% chance of death within months. Do you think insurance companies should pay for very expensive procedures where the likelihood of prolonging life is small? Do you think the insurance company should pay this bill?

it will provide for hospitalization and other medical care that may be necessary. If this review indicates that large out-of-pocket expense may occur, it would be advisable to increase the protection under the present policy, change to another type of insurance such as an HMO or PPO, or purchase supplementary health insurance. One should bear in mind that it may be exorbitantly expensive, unwise, or simply not possible to have insurance to cover every possible expense. Out-of-pocket expenses that do not exceed 20% of the total costs are not unreasonable. However, an individual needs the greatest protection possible, especially for catastrophic illness. Periodic review of one's health insurance status is strongly advisable.

Dental health insurance policies (see Chapter 25) are becoming more readily available. The cost depends on the same variety of factors outlined under medical insurance. A typical policy costs $250 to $300 yearly for an employee only, $500 to $600 yearly for an employee with one dependent, and $700 to $800 yearly for an employee with two or more dependents. Group plans are obtainable through unions, professional and governmental organizations, or corporations. Some employers pay the entire cost of premiums, whereas others pay only part of the cost. Group policies are usually less expensive and provide wider coverage than individual policies. Therefore it is advisable to try to obtain a group policy.

It should be noted that additional out-of-pocket expenses will be necessary for such things as eyeglasses, drugs, medical and dental services, toothbrushes, and other items. The amount will depend on the extent of the insurance coverage and need.

Individuals over 65 years of age have higher health-care costs than those who are younger. Chapter 25 pointed out the need for supplementary health insurance when out-of-pocket expenses for the elderly may total as much as 62% of their costs. Even with supplementary insurance there will be additional costs. Unfortunately, many elderly are unable to afford such supplementary expenditures.

People planning to retire should plan to budget at least $2000 a year for health insurance. The following figures provide some guidance as to the amounts. They include insurance premiums and out-of-pocket expenses and assume 10% yearly increase in costs due to inflation.[21]

Year	Age 65[a]	Age 62[b]
1990	$2100	$2900
1995	$3382	$4670
2000	$5447	$7521

[a]Assuming coverage by Medicare and additional coverage through a private "medigap" policy.
[b]Assuming retiree is too young for Medicare and is in an employer-sponsored insurance program. Premiums may be higher if this isn't true.

Suggestions for Consumers

These guidelines can help consumers plan or budget for health insurance:

1. Identify the size of your family and the type and quantity of coverage needed.
2. Ascertain the nature of family health problems.
3. Check your records of expenditures over the past year or years to obtain indications of insurance and out-of-pocket expenses. Budget accordingly for out-of-pocket expenses, unless you decide on supplemental insurance.
4. Find out the general costs of medical services in the area in which you live to help assess your overall expenditures.
5. Determine the type of coverage (Chapter 25) that you want, such as a basic plan with hospitalization, surgery, and medical protection, or major medical.
6. Consider a variety of plans unless this is impractical because of membership in a union or an industrial or professional group. In any event, check the nature of the coverage. Also investigate HMOs, PPOs, Medicare, and Medicaid (Chapter 25).
7. Consider whether you need and can afford additional insurance.

Long-Term Care Insurance

There are two reasons to buy long-term care insurance: (1) to prevent depletion of assets if a person must go into a nursing home and (2) to pay the costs of nursing home care that a person could not afford without insurance.

Long-term care insurance is expensive and may only partially offset the high costs of the care. The premiums may range from $2000 to $10,000 a year, depending on one's age, the benefits, the deductible, and other factors. When seeking such insurance, people should be sure the policy contains these provisions: not require prior hospitalization or skilled nursing home care, have a minimum benefit period of 2 years, have a minimum deductible period not to exceed 100 days, pay a minimum of $80 a day, and provide for guaranteed renewability.[22,23]

People with an annual income of less than $20,000 and assets (including a home) of less than $50,000 probably don't need commercial long-term care insurance. They probably can qualify for Medicaid on admission to a nursing home or could spend their available funds in 6 to 12 months in order to qualify.[21]

About 9 million American veterans of various wars are elderly. Some who need a nursing home can obtain help through the U.S. Department of Veterans Affairs. This office maintains over 13,000 beds in 127 of its 172 medical centers. Interested veterans should contact local offices for information.[24]

AIDS Costs

AIDS patient care is concentrated in a few large hospitals in major metropolitan areas. About 5% of the nation's hospitals are treating 50% of the AIDS patients. Public hospitals provide more than half of inpatient and 78% of outpatient care. In 1987, treatment losses for inpatient AIDS cases was $5,818 per patient in public hospitals and $2,381 in private hospitals, with yearly costs totaling $38,000 per patient. These were the daily per person costs:

	Costs	Revenues	Loss
Inpatients			
Private hospitals	$666	$574	$ 92
Public hospitals	709	491	218
Outpatients			
Private hospitals	125	104	94
Public hospitals	308	44	264

The source of payer costs by percentages for inpatient care were as follows:[25]

Payer	Private hospitals	Public hospitals
Private insurance	48	13
Medicaid	34	52
Self-pay	13	31
Medicare	3	2
Prisoner	2	2

The Department of Health and Human Services has estimated that if current trends continue, about $10.4 billion will be needed to treat AIDS in the United States in 1994.

People without insurance who become HIV-infected and wish to have coverage generally are rejected by private insurers. Individuals with insurance who test positive usually can renew coverage but cannot obtain new policies or increased limits. However, they may lose their insurance later in the illness.

AIDS patients who desire insurance protection should consider the following:

1. Try to retain insurance with the firm where employed if it provides adequate coverage.
2. Use Medicare, if covered, as the major source of payment for services.
3. Investigate Medicaid eligibility. However, Medicaid may not provide full reimbursement coverage for treatments. HIV-infected persons may have difficulty establishing eligibility and may have to try to qualify for disability coverage under the Supplementary Security Income (SSI) of the Social Security System.
4. Seek out insurance companies that cover home care benefits; policies may be expensive.[26]

Drugs

Prescription and OTC drugs are the two broad categories of substances about which consumers must make intelligent decisions. The $5 billion yearly advertising campaigns of the $50 billion drug industry continually pressure individuals to buy products. Over $20 billion is spent yearly on OTC drugs and over $30 billion on prescription drugs. Generally, the profit margins of drug companies have been considerably higher than those of other manufacturers.

Prescription Drugs

In Chapter 20 evidence was presented showing little or no difference chemically or therapeutically between generic and brand-name drugs. Many patients can save significant sums of money by requesting physicians to prescribe substances by common name rather than brand name. However, consumers should realize that generic versions are not available for recently released drugs and that physicians feel that for certain medical conditions, a brand name may be more effective. Consumers should also be aware that there are disparities in prices of identical prescriptions at different pharmacies. Therefore it may be advisable to shop for the best prices.

An FTC study concluded that the use of generic drugs could save Americans $130 million to $236 million a year.[27] Such savings may diminish in the future because manufacturers have raised many generic prices as well as brand-name prices.

In Florida several years ago a survey involving 60 pharmacies and 132,000 prescriptions showed the average saving by purchasing generic drugs to be $1.92 per prescription. A Consumer Federation of America survey of 147 outlets in 17 states discovered a wide range in generic and brand-name prescription drug prices. A consumer action group in San Francisco's East Bay surveyed 113 pharmacies and reported similar price variations. Discount stores appeared to provide drugs at cheaper prices but did not provide such services as personal medication records, emergency services, and delivery of drugs. The American Association of Retired Persons[28] surveyed more than 1000 pharmacies in 165 communities and reported these findings:

1. The average price of prescription drugs at pharmacies within the same community varied greatly. Some pharmacies charged almost 50% more than others. Prices varied even more from community to community.
2. Brand-name drugs tended to cost twice as much as generic equivalents.
3. Pharmacies that provide free delivery service, emergency service, and medicine management aids tended to have slightly higher drug prices.

Older Americans use about 30% of the prescription drugs dispensed in the United States, yet the elderly make up only 12% of the population. It has been reported that 15% of the elderly are unable to pay for their medications. Many states have begun to address this problem.[29]

New York State passed prescription drug assistance legislation for the elderly.[30] It is a two-level program for low- and moderate-income older people. Individuals who are 65 or older pay a registration fee and can purchase generic and brand-name drugs at 40% of generally charged cost. Similar legislation has been enacted in Delaware, Illinois, Maryland, New Jersey, Maine, Connecticut, Pennsylvania, and Rhode Island.

Prices of prescription drugs are climbing rapidly, due in part to a new federal law that forces manufacturers to cut prices to state Medicaid programs. This action has caused manufacturers to increase the prices of drugs sold to the general public, the Veteran's Administration, HMOs and others.

Consumers who use prescription drugs routinely and who can wait a week or longer to obtain them may find the use of discount mail-order service a way to help reduce costs. Many such pharmacies are open only to members, but some are available to anyone (see Table 26-15). Members of the American Association of Retired Persons (AARP) must be 50 years of age and pay a $5-a-year fee. National Pharmacies makes prescriptions available to members of the National Council of Senior Citizens, membership in which is available to people of all ages and costs $12 per year. Table 26-15 compares the prices of 12 drugs at six mail-order pharmacies and a typical drugstore. Some drugs may be cheaper at local pharmacies. No single mail-order pharmacy is consistently less expensive than the others. These companies may also save money for the consumer through volume orders (ask your physician to permit larger amounts to be ordered) and for some over-the-counter products such as cold remedies and vitamins.

Reducing Prescription Drug Costs

These suggestions may be helpful in reducing prescription costs:

1. Discuss prices with your physician.
2. Ask your physician to prescribe your drug by generic or chemical name rather than by brand name.
3. Check the prices at several outlets; they should be willing to give this information by telephone.
4. If you must take prescribed medication for a long-term illness, inquire whether it is advisable to purchase pills and capsules in the more economical quantities of 100 and 200. However, do not insist on quantities larger than your physician thinks you need to treat the illness.
5. Do not press your physician to prescribe drugs unnecessarily. It has been estimated that a great

TABLE 26–15

COMPARING MAIL-ORDER PHARMACIES*

	Action-mail order 800-452-1976	AARP* 202-872-4700	Family pharmaceuticals 800-922-3444	Medi-mail 800-331-1458	National pharmacies* 202-347-8800	Pharmail 800-237-8927	Typical drugstore
Cardizem, 60mg (for angina)	$ 43.39	$ 47.95	$ 52.31	$ 49.95	$ 44.80	$ 48.99	$ 50.99
Diazepam, 5mg (generic of Valium)	11.99	9.45	12.75	6.95	7.95	4.99	10.99
Dyazide, 25/50mg (diuretic, antihypertensive)	26.99	28.95	27.54	29.95	29.95	26.99	27.99
Feldene, 20mg (for arthritis)	173.39	169.65	167.67	187.95	134.39	176.00	177.59
Furosemide, 40mg (diuretic)	6.69	5.95	5.37	4.95	6.48	4.99	6.99
Ibuprofen, 600mg (for arthritis)	14.99	10.95	14.29	8.69	9.99	5.99	11.99
Mevacor, 20mg (for cholesterol)	163.39	154.95	174.35	158.95	185.35	155.00	158.29
Prozac, 20mg (antidepressant)	140.39	147.85	157.82	156.95	168.82	152.00	159.19
Tenormin, 50mg (for angina and hypertension)	63.99	64.70	70.27	68.95	58.95	67.99	62.99
Valium, 5mg (for anxiety)	38.39	47.25	47.29	47.50	36.98	46.99	46.99
Zantac, 150mg (for ulcer)	119.99	120.45	120.15	130.95	106.98	125.00	120.29
Acetaminophen, 325mg (nonprescription)	1.99	3.49	2.73	2.81	3.88	1.99	5.39
POSTAGE & HANDLING (per order)	0.50	1.00	1.50	1.48	0.50 Max.	none†	

*Available to members only.
†$10 minimum purchase per order.
*All prices are for quantities of 100.
Source: Henderson N: Cut the cost of prescription drugs, Changing Times 45:83, June 1991.

deal of money is wasted because of unnecessarily prescribed drugs.

6. Ask the pharmacist whether the store or company provides a discount for the elderly. Many pharmacies provide a 10% discount.
7. Consider purchasing drugs at discount mail-order pharmacies. *Consumer Reports Health Letter*[31] states that these tend to charge less than discount chain drugstores.
8. If the physician fails to prescribe a generic drug, the pharmacist may have the option to substitute one (see Chapter 20).
9. Give careful consideration to the selection of a pharmacy. Price should not be the sole reason for selection. Convenience, courtesy, and service may be worth the extra price paid for a product. Besides the cost of traveling to a distant store, the time involved may make the trip not worthwhile. The pharmacist may be able to help you assess the quality of a drug and should be willing to answer questions readily. A higher-priced drug is not necessarily a better one.

OTC Drugs

Remember that the purpose of OTC drug advertising is not to educate consumers but to sell products. Most ads for nonprescription drugs are misleading. It is not unusual for ads for competing drugs with identical ingredients to attempt to persuade consumers that the drugs differ in quality—with each one claiming to be the most effective.

The intelligent consumer will learn the names, dosages, and purposes of common active ingredients and will develop a list of those that seem to be useful for the self-treatment of minor ailments. This information will make it possible to select the least expensive brands that contain the desired ingredients. As with prescription drugs, prices vary from product to product and from store to store. One can compare prices over the telephone. Also, do not hesitate to have the pharmacist clarify the safety and efficacy of drugs and their ingredients. If you desire information about the ingredients in drugs, check your local library for the latest edition of the American Pharmaceutical Association's *Handbook of Nonprescription Drugs*.

Guidelines for Reducing Health Care Costs

Health care costs and benefits can be defined both in terms of dollars and in terms of the presence or absence of disease. The following suggestions are presented to help consumers protect their health and avoid unnecessary expense. Some are simple to carry out, whereas others require diligent and continuous effort.

1. Acquire a primary physician, preferably before you are ill. Chapter 6 will help you find one. Check fees and costs in advance.
2. Take action to prevent illness. Do not smoke; maintain optimum weight; avoid excessive intake of alcohol; get sufficient exercise; keep immunizations up-to-date; wear safety belts in automobiles.
3. Have periodic health examinations as recommended in Chapter 6.
4. Ask your physician to consider lowering the price for services if you are unable to meet costs; some fees are negotiable. If you have insurance, inquire whether the doctor will accept assignment for services allowed by Medicare or your insurance company.
5. Use the telephone discriminately to obtain needed information from your personal physician. However, do not expect this procedure always to be a substitute for an office visit. Remember that the physician's time is valuable; have your thoughts well organized before telephoning.
6. Local clinics run by health departments may provide certain tests without cost and will inform your physician of the results. Keep in mind, however, that isolated tests are not a substitute for an overall diagnostic evaluation.
7. Take advantage of outpatient services, including surgery, whenever possible, since this is less costly than inpatient services.
8. Do not pressure physicians to allow you to remain in a hospital longer than necessary. Avoid entering the hospital on a weekend if possible; costs are higher because your tests and procedures may not begin until Monday.
9. The local health department may provide immunizations and other health services without charge.
10. Become familiar with local health facilities and organizations. Know ahead of time what to do and whom to call in case of emergency. (For example, The American Cancer Society and the American Lung Association can help people who want to stop smoking.)
11. Clinics at dental schools may be able to provide services at lower cost.

12. When elective surgery is recommended, seek a reasonable explanation of what it entails, why it is recommended, and what are the risks. Ask if a medical alternative is available and consider getting a second opinion (see Chapter 6). Your primary physician's opinion may be as valuable as that of a second surgeon, or even more valuable.
13. Mental health care may be less expensive through group therapy, self-help groups (Chapter 7), or clinics.
14. Appropriate home care services, where available, are generally less expensive than hospital and nursing home care. Medicare, Medicaid, and insurance companies are often willing to pay for these services.
15. Attempt to purchase prescription drugs by generic name rather than brand name. Compare prices in several pharmacies and follow the other suggestions presented earlier in this chapter.
16. Do not waste money on vitamins and other food supplements. Unless you have a specific medical condition that necessitates supplements prescribed by your physician, a balanced variety of foods will provide all the nutrients you need. If you wish to take supplements regardless, multivitamin and mineral tablets are available for 5 cents per day or less. Do not ingest doses exceeding the recommended dietary allowances (RDAs).
17. Read labels carefully on all products purchased and adhere to instructions and warnings thereon.
18. Learn the names of all medications you use; take them as prescribed.
19. Brush and floss your teeth daily. Invest in periodic dental checkups at intervals recommended by your dentist. Support fluoridation of local drinking water and use other means of fluoride supplementation if recommended by your dentist. Give consideration to the purchase of dental insurance.
20. Be skeptical about the health information you receive unless you are certain that its source is reliable. Be especially skeptical of information in the news media and in advertisements.
21. Purchase health insurance and make sure that its coverage is adequate (Chapter 25) to prevent financial catastrophe in case of serious or prolonged illness. An HMO or PPO (Chapter 25) may be less expensive and provide appropriate medical services.
22. Visit your doctor during regular office hours except in emergencies.
23. Acquire several basic health reference books for reliable information about illnesses and conditions you might experience and medications you may need to take (see Chapter 11).

SUMMARY

Health care expenditures in the United States in 1990 represented 12.2% of the GNP and totaled $666.2 billion, with a per capita outlay of $2566. Personal out-of-pocket expenditures were approximately 23.2% of health care costs. Individual out-of-pocket costs averaged $524, with the elderly paying almost 5 times that amount.

The increasing cost of medical care has been influenced by such factors as high-tech equipment, AIDS and cancer treatment, care for the aged, malpractice insurance premiums, and fraudulent professional practices.

Consumers should understand that health insurance can never completely pay for medical services. There will always be out-of-pocket expenses for deductibles, coinsurance, and for other reasons.

Physicians' fees are determined by a variety of factors, and insurance companies reimburse doctors based on the UCR principle. Physicians are paid for their services on a fee-for-service method, by a specified salary, or by capitation fees. Fees vary from area to area. Numerous ways to control dental and medical costs have been attempted, including preventive dentistry and health care.

Consumers should always ask questions and discuss professional fees before obtaining medical services. Always seek explanations for overcharges and inequities.

In 1990 the average cost of a semiprivate hospital room was $297 per day. The cost of having a baby was $4000 to $5000 plus $500 to $800 for well-baby services. The estimated average daily cost in 1990 for a nursing home was $65 to $100 or $24,000 to $36,000 yearly. The advent of for-profit hospitals has increased the cost of services in these facilities.

Health insurance premiums are escalating and consumers need to carefully assess policies in the selection process. Dental insurance policies appear to be increasing in availability.

Consumers must make intelligent decisions regarding the purchase of drugs, for which the authors' suggestions can be helpful.

To reduce health care costs: (1) take preventive action, (2) use local diagnostic clinics and local health facilities and organizations, (3) consider purchasing drugs by mail, (4) obtain second opinions when elective surgery is suggested, (5) purchase generic drugs whenever possible, (6) don't waste funds on vitamins and other food supplements, and (7) purchase adequate health insurance.

Discussion Questions

1. How much was spent on health care in the United States in 1989? What percentage of the GNP does this represent? What are the trend for these costs by the year 2000?
2. What is the meaning of the phrase "shared financial responsibility" for health care costs as it applies to the individual?
3. What are five reasons for the continued rising costs of medical care in the United States?
4. What factors are involved in determining physicians' fees? What is the meaning of UCR? How are physicians paid for their services?
5. What attempts have been used to control the escalating costs of medical care?
6. Should physicians advertise their services? What problems may arise?
7. What conclusions may be drawn from the information provided in the text in regard to physicians' fees?
8. What actions should consumers take, and what questions should be asked about medical and dental fees?
9. Why is long-term health insurance advisable? What are the costs? What should the coverage include?
10. What can AIDS patients do to help pay for the costs of treatment services?
11. What are the present costs for hospital and nursing home services? How can they be reduced?
12. What guidelines will help consumers to budget for health insurance?
13. How can consumers reduce prescription and OTC costs?
14. What guidelines should consumers follow to help reduce the cost of health care?

REFERENCES

*1. Davies NE and Felder LH: Applying brakes to the runaway American health care system—a proposed agenda, JAMA 263:73-76, 1990.
2. Lundberg GD: Countdown to millenium—balancing the professionalism and business side of medicine, JAMA 263:86, 1990.
3. Norbeck TB: Private practice, Feb 1990, pp 11-17.
*4. Levit KR et al: National health care expenditures, 1990, Health Care Financing Review 13(1)29-54, 1991.
*5. Sonnefels ST et al: Projections of national health expenditures through the year 2000. Health Care Financing Review 13(1):127, 1991.
6. Ginzberg E: High-tech medicine and rising health care costs, JAMA 263:1820-1822, 1990.
7. Cooper W and Shulkin DJ: Can we monitor the monitors of medical costs? Pennsylvania Medicine 93(5):28-29, 1990.
8. Gabel J et al: America's views on health care: foolish inconsistencies. Health Affairs 8:103-118, spring 1989.
*9. Health Insurance Association of America: Sourcebook of health insurance data, 1990, Washington, D.C., 1990, the Association.
10. Gilbert S: America abandoning sick patients? The Good Health Section, The New York Times, April 29, 1990.
11. Doctors' directory to list fees, Medical World News, May 24, 1986.
12. Stephens R: Doctors' fee overhaul wins congress approval, AARP Bulletin, Jan 1990.
*13. Luciano L: A cure your MD won't like. Money Extra, Special Year End Edition, 19:54-59, 1990.
14. Mendleson D: Fraud, abuse inflate health costs, The California State Retiree, Dec 1990.
15. Schwartz WB and Mendelson DN: Hospital cost containment in the 1980s, N Eng J Med 324:1037-1042, 1991.
16. Pair of patient bills leaves insurance with financial pain. AARP Bulletin 28:2, April, 1987.
17. For-profit hospital care: who profits? who cares? A Study by the National Council of Senior Citizens, Washington, DC, March 1986.
18. Friedman E: Sorting myths from reality: the for-profits. Medical World News, Feb 27, 1989.
19. California Public Employees' Retirement System: Supplement to Medicare Health Plans, Sacramento, August 1, 1991.
20. Freudenheim M: Employers balk at high cost of high-tech medical care, The New York Times, April 29, 1990, pp. 1, 24.
21. Rowland D: Playing retirement roulette, The New York Times, April 22, 1991.
22. Long-term care insurance, Public Citizen Health Research Group Health Letter 7(10):10-11, 1991.
23. Long-term care insurance, part 2, Public Citizen Health Research Group Health Letter 7(12):1-4, 1991.
24. Long-term care: a little known option for veterans, Public Citizen Health Research Group Health Letter 7(11):5, 1991.
25. Lackin H: AIDS update: an executive report, Hospitals, April-June, 1990.

26. Bailey MA et al: Economic consequences for Medicaid of human immunodeficiency virus infection. Health Care Financing Review, 1990 Annual Supplement.
27. Wood J: 10 Ways to save money on drugs, Modern Maturity, 30:103, Oct/Nov 1987.
*28. American Association of Retired Persons: A report on pharmacy services in 165 communities: 100 pills of Procardia—$58.50 on Main Avenue, $26.99 on First Street, Washington, DC, 1989, the Association.
29. U.S. Senate, Special Committee on Aging: Rising drug prices prompt committee investigations, Aging Reports, winter 1990.
30. New York eases costs for prescriptions, AARP News Bulletin 28:2, Apr 1987.
31. Should you buy drugs by mail? Consumer Reports Health Letter 2(5):1-2, 1990.

*Recommended reading

CHAPTER TWENTY-SEVEN

CONSUMER LAWS, AGENCIES, AND STRATEGIES

When a situation can be solved with education, we will serve as the instructor. When a sterner approach is called for, we will be the "cop."[1]

FRANK E. YOUNG, M.D., PH.D.
FDA COMMISSIONER, 1984–1989

CONSUMER DECISIONS

What laws and agencies help protect consumers in the health marketplace?

What action should consumers take if they encounter a false or misleading advertisement, a fraudulent or inappropriate service, or a bogus health product?

How can consumers make intelligent decisions about health products and services?

Protection for the consumer of health products and services is encompassed by the basic principles of the Consumer Bill of Rights, which President John F. Kennedy outlined in a message to Congress in 1962. People must be provided with safe and effective foods, drugs, cosmetics, medical devices, and services by health practitioners. They must receive accurate information, through advertising and other media, that will enable them to make intelligent and free choices. Individuals have the right to speak out and be heard, to complain, and to know where to render complaints when they have been misled by charlatans or fraudulently exploited by manufacturers.

Responsibility for implementing the basic rights is reciprocal, involving community agencies and individuals. Consumer protection thus requires all of the following:

1. Laws ensuring that health products are safe and effective and that health professionals are competent
2. Government agencies that enforce the laws and keep the public informed
3. Professional, voluntary, and business organizations that serve as consumer advocates, monitor goverment agencies that issue safety regulations, and provide reliable information about health products and services
4. Education of the consumer to permit freedom of choice based on an understanding of scientific data rather than misleading information
5. Action by individuals to register complaints when they have been deceived, misled, overcharged, or victimized by frauds

Many agencies help to protect the American people in health matters. This chapter highlights the laws that control the three main federal consumer protection agencies: the Food and Drug Administration (FDA), the Federal Trade Commission (FTC), and the United States Postal Service (USPS). Information is also provided about state and local agencies, voluntary, business, and professional groups, consumer education, and actions that intelligent consumers can take to help protect themselves in the health marketplace. Additional sources of information are listed in the Appendix.

U.S. FOOD AND DRUG ADMINISTRATION

The FDA is part of the U.S. Public Health Service, a basic component of the Department of Health and Human Services (formerly HEW). Its main function is to protect the public from health hazards involving foods, drugs, cosmetics, and medical devices. Approximately 25 cents of every consumer dollar in the United States is spent on FDA-regulated products that are produced or distributed by close to 90,000 companies.

The FDA sets performance standards; conducts inspections, surveys, and analyses to measure compliance with these standards; evaluates drugs and devices that require premarket clearance; initiates enforcement actions when necessary; and helps inform and educate industry, health professionals, and the public. In fiscal year 1991 (October 1, 1990, through September 30, 1991), the agency had approximately 8400 full-time employees and a budget of $682 million.[2]

The FDA is organized into six regions with 22 district offices and many field offices located throughout the country. Its headquarters offices are located in the Washington, D.C., area and include the Office of the Commissioner, Center for Food Safety and Applied Nutrition, Center for Biologics Evaluation and Research, Center for Drug Evaluation and Research, Center for Veterinary Medicine, and Center for Devices and Radiological Health. Another component, the National Center for Toxicological Research, is in Jefferson, Arkansas. The FDA Commissioner is appointed by the president and confirmed by the U.S. Senate.

Legislative History

The original *Pure Food and Drug Act* (1906) was passed in response to public concern about the safety of foods and drugs. After the Spanish-American War, it was discovered that the army had been supplied with spoiled canned meat and sawdust-adulterated flour. There were also reports that toxic chemicals such as formaldehyde had been used to preserve milk sold in neighborhood grocery stores. The final impetus to passage of a law was publication in 1905 of Upton Sinclair's exposé, *The Jungle,* which described the filthy conditions in Chicago meat-packing plants and revealed that rats, other vermin, and even human fingers were being processed along with sausage meat. The 1906 act required that foods be pure and wholesome.

The act also contained drug provisions aimed at controlling the patent medicines that for years had contained alcohol, opiates, and other undesirable substances without public knowledge of the materials' contents. Truthful labeling of medicines became mandatory. It was not the whole truth, however; only identification of constituents was required. There was limited supervision of the interstate sale of foods and drugs and no provision requiring safety or efficacy of these products. Cosmetics were not a part of this early legislation.

The *Sherley Amendment to the Food and Drug Act* (1912) prohibited the labeling of medicines with false therapeutic claims intended to defraud the purchaser.

The *Food, Drug, and Cosmetic (FDC) Act* (1938) replaced the 1906 law with new and stronger provisions. The mounting death toll from elixir of sulfanilamide gave great impetus to the ultimate passage of this act. The product was sold over the counter for the treatment of infections, especially gonorrhea. It was the first antibiotic drug and at first was considered a miracle drug. Unfortunately, it contained the toxic substance diethyleneglycol and had not been tested for safety. In 1937, 107 people, many of them children, died. The FDC Act sought to protect consumers with the following provisions:

1. Foods must be pure and wholesome, safe to eat, and produced under sanitary conditions.
2. Drugs and therapeutic devices must be safe.
3. New drugs must be approved for safety by the FDA before they can go on the market. (Products marketed before 1938 did not have to meet this requirement.)
4. Cosmetics must be safe.
5. Labeling must be truthful and not misleading; common names of all ingredients are required; quantities and proportions of potent and habit-forming narcotic and hypnotic substances must be given.
6. Drug labeling must include warnings needed for safe use.
7. Drugs not safe for self-treatment are restricted to sale by prescription.
8. Drug-manufacturing plants must be registered and be inspected by the FDA at least once every 2 years.
9. Antibiotics, insulin, and colors used in foods, drugs, and cosmetics must be tested in FDA laboratories before they can go on sale.
10. Chemicals added to foods must be proven safe before their use is allowed.
11. Pesticide residues on raw crops must not exceed safe tolerances. (The Environmental Protection Agency now establishes the limits, and the FDA enforces them.)
12. Penalties are heavier for second offenses and fraud. First offenses might bring up to 1 year in jail.

The *Public Health Service Act* (1944) contained two sections now enforced by the FDA. Their provisions cover the safety, purity, and potency of biologic products, such as vaccines, sera, and blood for interstate sale and the safety of pasteurized milk and shellfish, as well as the sanitation of food, water, food services, and facilities for travelers on trains, airplanes, and buses.

The *Durham-Humphrey Amendment* (1951) specified that drugs that cannot be safely used without medical supervision must be so labeled and dispensed only by prescription of a licensed health practitioner. Thus a distinction was made between over-the-counter (OTC) and prescription drugs. Before this law took effect, manufacturers decided whether to classify drugs as prescription or OTC drugs. If the FDA disagreed, it could bring the case to court and charge that the product was misbranded.

The *Food Additives Amendment* (1958) prohibited the use of new food additives until the manufacturer had established their safety.

The *Delaney Amendment* (1958) gave the FDA additional authority to ban the use of food additives that can cause cancer in humans or animals.

The *Color Additive Amendments* (1960) permitted the FDA to regulate the conditions for the safe use of color additives in foods, drugs, and cosmetics and to require manufacturers to make the necessary scientific investigations to establish safety.

The *Federal Hazardous Substances Labeling Act* (1960) required that labels display prominent warnings regarding household products with hazardous chemicals. This is now enforced by the Consumer Product Safety Commission.

The *Kefauver-Harris Drug Amendments* (1962) overhauled and strengthened the drug provisions of the FDC Act of 1938. They came about as a result of the foresight of Dr. Frances Kelsey, an FDA medical officer who prevented the release of thalidomide on the U.S. market because of suspected side effects (see Chapter 2). These 1962 amendments included the following provisions:

1. Manufacturers must provide substantial evidence that a new drug is effective and safe before it can be approved for marketing.
2. Previously cleared new drugs may be ordered off the market immediately if new information indicates an imminent hazard to health, and any prior approval may be withdrawn.
3. Manufacturers are required to get the patient's consent if experimental drugs are to be used, unless this is not feasible or the investigator believes that obtaining such consent would be contrary to the patient's best interest.
4. All drug products must be registered annually with the FDA, and each establishment will be inspected at least once every 2 years.
5. Drug labels must bear the established generic name of the drug, and prescription drug labels must list the quantity of each active ingredient.
6. Prescription drug advertisements must include a summary of side effects, contraindications, and effectiveness.
7. Control over the advertising of prescription drugs was passed from the FTC to the FDA.
8. Pharmaceutical manufacturers must comply with the Code of Good Manufacturing Practices in testing, processing, packaging, and holding drugs.
9. The FDA was given broad inspection authority over prescription drugs.

The *Drug Abuse Control Amendments* (1965) were enacted to control the manufacture and distribution of depressants, stimulants, and hallucinogens. The amendments required wholesalers and jobbers of these drugs to register annually with the FDA. The agency was also authorized to seize illegal supplies, serve warrants, arrest violators, and require all legal handlers of controlled drugs to keep records of their supplies and sales. A new Bureau of Drug Abuse Control (BDAC) was established for these purposes. In 1968, to consolidate the policing of illegal drug traffic, BDAC was transferred from the FDA to the new Bureau of Narcotics and Dangerous Drugs (BNDD) in the Department of Justice.

The *Fair Packaging and Labeling Act* (1966) provided additional support for the FDA to ensure that food, drugs, medical devices, and cosmetics were honestly and informatively labeled. It required more complete information on labels and packages. The information was to be clearly and prominently stated in terms that would enable consumers to make value comparisons between competing products. Food package labels were required to contain the identity of the food; the name and address of the manufacturer, packer, or distributor; the net quantity of the contents; and a list of the ingredients. The FTC retained jurisdiction over advertising for OTC drugs.

The *Poison Prevention Act* (1970) required special packaging to protect children from accidentally ingesting toxic substances. Poisons identified by the Secretary of Health, Education, and Welfare must be packaged so that most children under the age of 5 would find them difficult to open.

The *Radiation Control for Health and Safety Act* (1971) was designed to protect the public from unnecessary exposure to radiation from electronic products such as color television sets, microwave ovens, and x-ray machines. The FDA sets performance standards for these and similar products.

The *Medical Device Amendments* (1976) supplemented the 1938 FDC Act, which permitted action only if a defect in a product was discovered after the product had been in use. The amendments gave the FDA new authority to ensure the safety and effectiveness of devices. They enabled the FDA to require premarket approval for some items and performance standards for others.

The *Infant Formula Act* (1980) requires strict controls to ensure the nutritional content and safety of commercial baby foods.

The *Orphan Drug Act* (1983) was passed to facilitate the development of new drugs for more than 5000 rare diseases affecting an estimated 10 to 20 million Americans. A disease is considered "rare" if it affects fewer than 200,000 people. Drug companies can now take tax deductions for about three fourths the cost of conducting clinical trials on orphan drug products. Companies might otherwise be reluctant to develop such drugs and gain FDA approval because the cost is prohibitive. The legislation also authorized grants to fund research to discover useful substances. About 60 orphan drugs have received FDA approval and more than 400 others have been granted orphan status and are working their way through the approval process. Following approval the manufacturer is entitled to 7 years of marketing exclusivity.

The *Drug Price Competition and Patent Term Restoration Act* (1984) permits the FDA to approve generic versions of previously approved new drugs without requiring their sponsors to duplicate the costly human tests required for the original drugs. It allows the term of patents on medicines (17 years) to be extended up to 5 years to compensate for the time required to get FDA approval.

The *Prescription Drug Marketing Act* (1988) prohibits selling, buying, trading, or offering to sell, buy, or trade prescription drug samples.

The *Safe Medical Devices Act* (1990) gave the FDA the power to (1) obtain earlier knowledge of serious device problems, (2) order recalls to quickly remove defective products from the marketplace, (3) track devices from the manufacturer to the consumer, and (4) apply large civil penalties for violations of the act. The act requires hospitals and other health care providers to report device-related deaths directly to the FDA instead of to the device manufacturer. Additional provisions are discussed in Chapter 23.

The *Nutrition Labeling and Education Act* (1990) provided for (1) mandatory labeling on most food products, (2) standardization of portion sizes, (3) more apppropriate disclosure of fat and cholesterol contents, (4) determination of whether disease-prevention claims can be made for various nutrients, and (5) voluntary guidelines to retailers for nutrition information on raw fruits, vegetables, and fish. Chapter 12 discusses these provisions in detail.

Food, Drug, and Cosmetic Act

The Food, Drug, and Cosmetic Act, including amendments, is the primary federal consumer protection law in the United States.[3] It deals with imported products as well as domestic ones. Its purpose is to ensure that (1) foods are safe to eat, (2) drugs and health devices are safe and effective for their intended uses, and (3) cosmetics are safe and are not advertised deceptively. Its main provisions are as follows.

Food provisions. Food is considered adulterated if it contains (1) poisonous or deleterious substances that are injurious to health, (2) filthy, putrid, or decomposed substances or substances prepared and packed under unsanitary conditions, or (3) unsafe color additives.

Food is said to be misbranded when (1) the labeling is false and misleading, (2) the food is offered for sale under the name of another food, (3) the food is an imitation of a food and the label does not bear the word *imitation,* (4) the container is so made, formed, or filled to be misleading about its contents, (5) the food is represented for special dietary use without the label bearing information about the product's vitamin, mineral, and dietary properties, (6) the food contains artificial flavoring, artificial coloring, or chemical preservatives that are not listed on the labels, or (7) the labeling is not conspicuously displayed in terms that consumers are likely to read and understand.

Regulations adopted in 1973 require manufacturers to provide nutrition information on their product labels when one or more nutrients are added to the food or if a nutritional claim is made about the product. The required information includes the amount per serving of calories, protein, fat, carbohydrate, and several vitamins and minerals. Additives must be supported by evidence substantiating their safety before they may be included in a product. New regulations are pending (see Chapter 12).

Food additives. The Food Additives Amendment of 1958 authorized the FDA to establish the quantities of certain substances that could be added safely. In addition, the FDA could prevent the use of substances that showed evidence of carcinogenic effect when consumed in any amount, not only by humans but also by experimental animals. This is the controversial Delaney Amendment (also called the Delaney Clause).

The Delaney Amendment resulted in the removal of cyclamates from low-calorie soft drinks and was involved in the debate over the removal of saccharin from the marketplace. The food industry, various government regulatory agencies, and the American Council on Science and Health believe this amendment should be repealed or modified because it is rigid and does not attempt to quantify the risk to humans and compare it to a product's possible benefits. Jukes[4] states that (1) the amounts of carcinogens in food and food additives are small, (2) the quantities found naturally in the diet vastly exceed those from human-made sources, and (3) antioxidants protect against low levels of carcinogens. The Council for Agricultural Science and Technology (CAST)[5] has noted that substances can now be detected in amounts too small to have a significant effect on health. CAST regards the Delaney Clause as "hopelessly obsolete" and believes a "de minimus" concept should be substituted. (The term comes from a judicial doctrine, *de minimus non curat lex,* which means "the law does not concern itself with trifles.") Various others argue that the Delaney Amendment should be retained because it makes it easy for the FDA to protect the public from the inclusion of carcinogenic substances in foods.

Food additives may be categorized as regulated food additives or GRAS (generally recognized as safe) substances. Several thousand compounds can be classified as additives. Regulated food additives are substances that can be added directly to food (such as vitamins to milk or bread) or that get into food from its surroundings, including packaging, manufacturing equipment, and other sources. The GRAS list includes about 700 additives that scientists recognize as safe as a result of long-established use without evidence of harm to individuals.

Many additives come from food itself. Lecithin, for example, is found in all plants and animals. It is obtained primarily from soybeans and is used mostly as an emulsifier to keep ingredients in processed foods from separating. Calcium and sodium propionate are used in the fermentation of Swiss cheese. Propionate is used primarily as a mold inhibitor in baked goods. Vitamin and mineral additives are identical to the vitamins and minerals found naturally in food.

Food additives are used as (1) nutrient supplements (such as vitamins and minerals), (2) nonnutritive sweeteners (sugar substitutes), (3) preservatives (to prevent spoilage and chemical change), (4) stabilizers and thickeners (as in ice cream, candy, frozen desserts, pectins, vegetable gums, and gelatin), (5) flavors or flavoring agents (such as spices, liquid derivatives of onion and garlic, and monosodium glutamate from corn), (6) bleaching and maturing agents (which speed the aging process of flour), and (7) colors.

Any new substance proposed for addition to food must undergo rigid testing. The FDA also requires information about the chemical composition of the substance, how it is manufactured, and the methods used to detect and measure its presence at the expected levels of use. Data must show that the proposed testing methods are sensitive enough to determine compliance with established regulations. Finally, proof must be provided that the substance is safe for its intended use. This requires tests that administer the additives in various concentrations in the diets of two or more species of animals. The FDA will allow the use of a food additive only if it concludes there is practical certainty that no harm will result from its normal use over a lifetime.

FIGURE 27-1. International food irradiation symbol.

Food irradiation. During the 1960s, food irradiation received FDA approval for use on potatoes to control sprout growth and for insect disinfection of wheat and wheat flour. More recently, it was approved for spices and dried herbs (1983), pork (1985), fresh fruits and dry vegetable substances (1986), and poultry (1990). The process uses ionizing irradiation (electrically charged particles) to retard spoilage or make foods safer to eat. The American Council on Science and Health[6] believes this procedure has great potential for use on meats, poultry, fish, fruits, and vegetables. For example, irradiation can kill *Salmonella* bacteria in poultry and trichinosis organisms in pork and can retard spoilage of fruits and vegetables. Extensive studies indicate that foods exposed to low doses of irradiation are safe to eat.[7] The foods do not become radioactive or undergo significant changes in nutrient composition. Irradiation is also used to sterilize medical instruments and to prepare special foods for astronauts, military personnel, and cancer patients with impaired immunity. The labels of irradiated foods must carry the internationally used logo of the stylized rose with two petals (Figure 27-1).

Like fluoridation, irradiation has been unfairly attacked by the health food industry, food faddists, and affiliated "consumer" groups. These attacks

TELL THE FDA
DON'T NUKE MY FRUIT

FIGURE 27-2. Bumper sticker used by opponents of food irradiation.

have persuaded three states to ban the sale of irradiated foods and made many manufacturers reluctant to market these foods to the general public. However, a large facility for irradiating fruits, vegetables, and poultry opened in Florida in 1992.

Drug provisions for humans. The FDC Act prohibits misbranding or adulteration of any drug. Drugs are categorized as new, investigational, prescription, or nonprescription.

New drugs are considered to be any drug that (1) contains a newly developed chemical, (2) contains a chemical or substance not previously used in medicine, (3) has previously been used in medicine but not in the dosages or conditions for which the sponsor now recommends use, or (4) has not been recognized by experts as safe and effective for its intended use. New drugs cannot be introduced into interstate commerce unless they have been approved by the FDA. Approval is obtained by filing a new drug application (NDA), which includes acceptable scientific data that demonstrate the drug's safety and efficacy.

Investigational drugs are new drugs intended solely for research use by experts who are qualified by training and experience to investigate the drugs' safety and effectiveness. Their use is permitted under regulations established by the FDA.

Prescription drugs may be dispensed only when prescribed by a licensed health professional.

Nonprescription drugs are those considered safe for consumer use when label directions and warnings are followed. These are OTC drugs, and no prescription is required. Many are now undergoing review for safety and efficacy.

Imported drugs must comply with FDA provisions. Those that have been considered safe and effective outside the United States must still undergo the NDA procedure in this country.

The labeling of a drug must include the following:

1. The name and address of the manufacturer, packer, and shipper
2. The strength and quantity
3. The active ingredients
4. An expiration date
5. A warning if a habit-forming substance such as codeine is used
6. The quantity of ingredients such as alcohol, bromides, and ether
7. If a prescription drug, a caution that the drug may be dispensed only by prescription
8. The established name and trade name clearly identified
9. Adequate directions for use, such as conditions of use, dosage, frequency, and time of administration
10. Adequate warnings, when necessary, to protect the user
11. No false or misleading statement.

Other drug provisions of the FDC Act include:

1. Drugs must not consist of filthy, putrid, or decomposed substances.
2. Drugs must not be dangerous to health when used as directed by the label.
3. Nonofficial drugs (those not in any of the official compendia) are considered adulterated if their strength differs from or their purity or quality falls below that which they claim to possess.
4. Manufacturers may not ship prescription drugs directly to the public. They may be sent only to firms that are regularly and lawfully engaged in the wholesale or retail distribution of prescription drugs or to hospitals, clinics, physicians, or others who are licensed to prescribe such drugs.
5. The official drug compendia are *The United States Pharmacopeia (USP)* (which includes the *National Formulary [NF])* and the *Homeopathic Pharmacopeia of the United States.* By law, all substances in these references must meet the standards of strength, quality, and purity they set forth.

Clinical testing of drugs. Before new drugs can be approved and marketed, the manufacturer must submit substantial evidence of safety and efficacy. These steps are generally followed:[8]

1. The drug must be subjected to laboratory screening and animal tests that indicate it can be safely tested in humans.
2. Before the drug is given to people, the sponsor must submit a notice of clinical investigation exemption for a new drug (IND) and submit the results of the animal studies. This IND contains a detailed outline (protocol) describing the planned testing, composition of the substance,

standards to follow to ensure safety, training and experience of the investigators, progress reports, and other information.

3. On FDA approval to proceed, the clinical investigation of human testing follows three phases: Phase I—About 50 people are exposed to the drug to determine the toxicity, metabolic absorption and elimination, and other pharmacologic reactions; the preferred route of administration; and the safe dosage. Phase II—Initial trials are conducted on a small number of people for treatment or prevention of the specific disease. Additional animal studies to indicate safety may be conducted concurrently. Phase III—Extensive clinical trials take place if Phases I and II demonstrate reasonable assurance of safety and effectiveness, suggesting that the drug's potential value outweighs its possible hazards.
4. The manufacturer submits an NDA together with all the data collected. In addition, a sample of the package insert and the label to be used are forwarded.
5. The FDA approves the NDA, asks for further evidence, or rejects the application.
6. The FDA can withdraw appproval of a drug found to produce unexpected side effects or to be less effective than anticipated.

The process used by the FDA to approve drugs usually takes several years and has been criticized for delaying the speed with which beneficial new drugs can be marketed. On the other hand, some authorities have expressed concern that speeding up the process may weaken protection against unsafe and ineffective drugs. In 1987, in response to the AIDS crisis, the FDA established regulations permitting promising investigational new drugs to be used outside of clinical trials to treat serious or life-threatening conditions when no satisfactory alternative is available.[9]

In 1972 the FDA began the enormous task of reviewing approximately 300,000 OTC products and 800 ingredients for safety and efficacy (see Chapter 20). Because the number of drugs was so large, the agency decided to investigate the ingredients according to categories rather than each product individually. Each group of drugs was investigated by an expert panel.

As the panel reports were issued, many manufacturers reformulated their products by removing ingredients judged unsafe or ineffective and/or adding effective ones. By 1989, new rules were proposed for about 60 categories of drugs, but final rules had been issued for fewer than half of these categories.[10]

Device provisions. Before the 1976 Medical Device Amendments, any device could be sold to the public provided it was properly labeled. If the device needed the supervision of a licensed practitioner, the label had to caution that use was restricted. A prescription device could be shipped to a licensed practitioner but not to the patient unless ordered by the practitioner. A device became illegal if it was dangerous to the health of consumers when used as prescribed or suggested on the label. Labels had to contain adequate directions and include warnings to ensure safe use. Despite these rules, numerous worthless, ineffective, dangerous, and often expensive products were marketed.

The 1976 amendments gave the FDA the authority to ensure the safety and efficacy of all devices both on the market and before they are marketed. Although this law gave the FDA great power to supervise the device market, the agency did very little to implement the law.[11] The 1990 Safe Medical Devices Act strengthened the FDA's ability to monitor the marketplace, order recalls, and initiate large civil penalties for violations of the act (see Chapter 23 for details).

Cosmetic provisions. Cosmetic preparations may be distributed in the United States or imported only if they comply with the cosmetic provisions of the FDC Act and the Fair Packaging and Labeling Act. Cosmetics are subject to the drug provisions of the FDC Act if they are offered to prevent or cure ailments or to affect the structure and function of the body. Cosmetics that may be considered drugs include antibiotic deodorants, hormone creams, baldness remedies, and products that are claimed to remove wrinkles, cure skin diseases, or treat or prevent dandruff.

Products must not be injurious to the skin when used as directed on the label. Hair dye preparations that contain skin irritants are an exception. These may be marketed for use as hair dyes if the label bears this statement:

> CAUTION: This product contains ingredients which may cause skin irritation on certain individuals, and a preliminary test according to accompanying directions should first be made. The product must not be used for the dyeing of eyelashes or eyebrows, which may cause blindness.

The labeling must contain adequate directions for making the preliminary test.

Color additives used in cosmetics must be approved as safe and certified by the FDA. No coal tar dye is certified for use around the eyes. Containers must not be composed of harmful substances. False and misleading statements are not permitted on labels.

Enforcement Actions

During an average year, the FDA investigators inspect about 20,000 companies in the United States and 400 abroad.[12] When a food, drug, device, or cosmetic product is defective or hazardous to human health or violates FDA regulations, the FDA can ask the manufacturer to correct the situation. Usually the request will lead to a voluntary recall or correction of faulty labeling. If a manufacturer does not comply, the FDA can seek a court order authorizing the agency to seize the product. A U.S. marshal will then be directed to take possession of the goods until the matter is resolved. During fiscal year 1988, 1526 recalls and 3614 voluntary corrections were undertaken by industry and verified by the FDA.[13]

When products are marketed with improper claims, the FDA may issue a letter specifying the law violations and demanding to know how the problem will be corrected. If the letter is ignored or if the FDA decides to begin with more forceful action, the agency can initiate court proceedings for a seizure, injunction, or criminal prosecution.

If a product is seized, it may be returned to its owner if its labeling can be corrected. If a product is basically unfit to market or if its owner does not contest the seizure, the court will order it destroyed. Injunctions are court orders that tell individuals or companies to discontinue illegal practices (such as marketing drugs that lack FDA approval as safe and effective). If an injunction is violated, the court has considerable discretion in determining the punishment and can order imprisonment or a large fine. In criminal cases, first-time violators of the Food, Drug, and Cosmetic Act can be imprisoned up to 1 year and repeat offenders can be imprisoned for up to 3 years. The 1984 Criminal Fine Enhancement Act amended all federal criminal laws to allow fines of up to $100,000 (or $250,000 if death results) per offense for up to two offenses. Recalls and seizures are listed in the *FDA Enforcement Report*, which is issued weekly.

In health fraud cases, warning letters are used most often, and prosecutions are rarely used. The FDA does not routinely maintain statistics indicating how many of its enforcement actions involve health frauds. However, the agency has reported that during fiscal year 1987 it initiated 38 regulatory letters, 7 seizures, 3 injunctions, and 1 criminal prosecution involving health fraud. Table 27-1 describes three cases in which seizures and court action by the FDA have stopped companies from marketing products with illegal therapeutic claims.

The FDA concentrates its efforts against health frauds on products that are inherently unsafe or are illegally marketed for the treatment of disease. Worthless yet harmless articles promoted to improve health, athletic ability, or appearance—which the agency considers mere "economic frauds"—are considered low priority and are virtually unregulated. Critics of this policy believe that routine use of criminal prosecution against health frauds would enable the FDA to deter the marketing of bogus products. As noted by Barrett[14]:

> The Internal Revenue Service has made it clear that cheating on income tax can cost people dearly and land them in jail. The FDA should make it clear that cheating on product labels (as well as accompanying literature) can cost just as dearly.

Educational Activities

The FDA distributes many publications about foods, drugs, devices, cosmetics, and hazardous substances. Also, consumer affairs officers are available to answer questions and to participate in educational programs at schools and elsewhere throughout their districts. The addresses and telephone numbers of FDA consumer affairs offices are listed in the Appendix of this book. *FDA Consumer*, issued monthly, provides excellent educational articles and summaries of regulatory actions. "Talk Papers," written primarily to help FDA spokespeople answer questions about agency positions on health frauds, may be given to people who make inquiries. Details of specific enforcement actions may be obtained by writing to the FDA Freedom of Information Staff, HFI-35, 5600 Fishers Lane, Rockville, MD 20857. Requests should indicate why the information is needed and express willingness to pay a small fee if the fee cannot be waived.

Since 1984, the FDA administration has given high priority to public education about health fraud, which the agency defines as "the promotion,

Table 27–1

FDA Seizure Actions

Company	Product	Disposition
Padma Marketing Corporation, Berkeley, California	Padma 28 Tibetan herbal food supplement held for sale accompanied by leaflets stating that it was "more effective for treating circulatory disorders than any pharmaceutical drug!"	Considered an unapproved new drug whose label lacked adequate directions for use. Ordered destroyed by default decree.
Swanson Health Products, Fargo, North Dakota	Oil of evening primrose capsules, promoted as effective against high blood pressure.	Ordered destroyed by default decree because it contained the nonconforming food additive gamma linolenic acid.
Potentials Unlimited, Inc., Grand Rapids, Michigan	"Hypnotic sleep tapes" on 31 subjects marketed with false and misleading claims for enuresis, facial tic, allergies, acne, teeth and gum problems, high blood pressure, and many other health problems.	Court ruled that the tapes were "devices" under the law because they were marketed with (illegal) therapeutic claims. The court ordered the tapes constructively destroyed by erasure of their content.

for profit, of a medical remedy known to be false or unproven." During that year the FDA and the Council of Better Business Bureaus sent information packets to the advertising managers of 19,500 newspapers, magazines, and radio and television stations, asking them to check advertising copy more carefully before accepting it for publication. Citing common characteristics of misleading health ads, both agencies offered to evaluate questionable claims. Between 1985 and 1988, the FDA cosponsored two national health fraud conferences and many regional ones.

Federal Trade Commission

The FTC is an independent federal agency directed by five commissioners nominated by the president and confirmed by the Senate, each serving a 7-year term. The president chooses one commissioner to act as chairman. The FTC's law enforcement work is divided among its Bureaus of Consumer protection, Competition, and Economics.

The Bureau of Consumer Protection aims to keep the marketplace free from unfair, deceptive, or fraudulent practices. Its five divisions are credit practices, marketing practices, advertising practices, service industry practices, and enforcement. The Bureau of Competition is the FTC's antitrust arm and seeks to prevent business practices that restrain competition. The Bureau of Economics provides economic analysis and support to the FTC's consumer protection activities. The FTC has 10 regional offices, whose addresses are listed in the Appendix.

Legislative History

The *Federal Trade Commission Act* (1914) was intended to preserve competition in the growing industrial society by providing safeguards against business monopoly. It was designed to prevent unfair methods of competition in commerce by making unfair practices unlawful, thereby protecting consumers as well as other entrepreneurs. The FTC was given authority to investigate, publicize, and prohibit such procedures. The first five commissioners were sworn into office in 1915.

The *Wheeler-Lea Amendment* (1938) to the FTC Act provided for the control of advertising:

> It shall be unlawful for any person, partnership, or corporation to disseminate, or cause to be disseminated, any false advertisements—by the United States mails, or in commerce by any means, for the purpose of inducing . . . the purchase of food, drugs, devices, or cosmetics . . . the dissemination . . . of any false advertisement . . . shall be an unfair or deceptive act or practice in commerce.

Labeling was not included in this act.

The *Fair Packaging and Labeling Act* (1966) was designed to prevent unfair and deceptive packaging and labeling of consumer commodities. The FTC was given responsibility in all areas except food, drugs, devices, and cosmetics, which were still delegated to the FDA.

The *Magnuson-Moss Act* (1975) gave the FTC the authority to adopt trade regulation rules that define unfair or deceptive acts in a particular industry.

Enforcement Actions

When the Commission feels that a company is making a false or deceptive advertising claim, it may seek to stop the advertisement or require some other appropriate remedy.[15] FTC actions can be triggered by letters from consumers, businesses, members of Congress, or other interested parties. However, the agency will not usually act unless the matter involves interstate commerce and is believed to involve a significant problem such as a safety hazard or substantial economic harm to the public.

The first step is an investigation. If the agency concludes that the law has been violated, it may attempt to obtain voluntary compliance by entering into a consent order with the company. A company that signs a consent order need not admit that it violated the law but must agree to stop the practices described in an accompanying complaint. If a consent agreement cannot be reached, the FTC may issue an administrative complaint or seek a court order (injunction) to stop the practice.

When the administrative complaint is disputed, an administrative law judge holds a formal hearing similar to a court trial. Evidence is submitted, testimony is heard, and witnesses are examined and cross-examined. If the judge finds the law has been violated, a cease-and-desist order or other appropriate relief can be issued. Initial decisions by administrative law judges can be appealed to the full Commission, which acts like a court of appeal. Respondents who are dissatisfied with the Commission's decision can appeal their case to the U.S. Court of Appeals and ultimately to the U.S. Supreme Court. The FTC staff may not appeal the Commission's decision.

If a consent agreement is reached or the FTC is upheld on appeal, a financial penalty may be assessed that can include making restitution available to consumers or donating money for research. Occasionally, a company must do "corrective advertising," in which future ads must indicate that previous ads had been false, inaccurate, or misleading. Future violations of consent agreements or cease-and-desist orders can result in fines of up to $10,000 per day for each violation.

Companies going through the administrative or court procedures described previously can continue the disputed practice(s) if they choose to do so. When the FTC believes that an unfair practice will cause great public harm if allowed to continue, it may ask a federal court to issue an injunction. If a permanent injunction is issued, it may include financial penalties and consumer redress.

When the FTC believes that a problem affects an entire industry, it may promulgate an industry guide or trade regulation rule. Guides are interpretive statements without the force of law. Rules represent the conclusions of the Commission about what it considers unlawful. Before guides and rules are established, interested parties are given the opportunity to comment. Once a rule is established, the Commission can take enforcement action without lengthy explanations about why a particular ad is unfair or deceptive. A reference to the rule is enough. In health matters, problems are almost always handled on a case-by-case basis rather than through rule making.

Although FTC actions are powerful, the agency's ability to protect consumers is quite limited. The agency does not have sufficient resources to investigate most of the complaints it receives. When action is taken, it may take years to complete, particularly when contested. Months or even years may go by before an investigation begins or is completed. Unless a consent agreement or injunction is obtained, further delays can occur with each step in the process. This enables some operators to make considerable profits before their improprieties are stopped. Perhaps the most famous case of this type was the FTC's action to remove the word *liver* from *Carter's Little Liver Pills.* Although the pills did nothing for the liver, it took the agency 16 years to win the case. In another prominent case, the FTC began investigating the J.B. Williams Company's *Geritol* ads in 1959 and the final settlement (a $302,000 fine) did not occur until 1976.

During recent years, the FTC has prosecuted 5 to 10 cases per year involving health claims, including the following.

In 1981, American Home Products Corporation was ordered to stop claiming that its products contained "the pain reliever most recommended by doctors" without disclosing the ingredient to be aspirin.

In 1983, two Florida chiropractors were stopped from claiming that their $7,501,500 "laser facelifts" were effective.

In 1985, Joseph Weider and Weider Fitness, Inc., agreed to pay a minimum of $400,000 to settle FTC charges that they had misrepresented two mineral supplements, *Anabolic Mega-Pak* and *Dynamic Life Essence*. Weider and the company agreed not to falsely claim that these products could help build muscles or were effective substitutes for anabolic steroids. They also agreed to make refunds to anyone who had purchased these products and, if the amount refunded was less than $400,000, to donate the difference to fund research on the relationship of nutrition to muscle development.

In 1986, Meadow Fresh Farms and its president, Roy Brog, agreed to stop claiming that the company's milk-based dairy substitute could reduce the incidence of cardiovascular disease because it contained less xanthine oxidase (a milk enzyme) than does homogenized milk.

In 1986, after being charged with false advertising, A.H. Robins Company agreed to stop claiming that *Viobin Wheat Germ Oil* could help consumers improve endurance, stamina, vigor, or other aspects of athletic fitness.

In 1987, Kraft, Inc., was prohibited from falsely representing that a slice of *Kraft Singles* had the same calcium content as five ounces of milk.

In 1987, Phillipe LaFrance USA, Ltd., agreed to pay $600,000 in civil penalties and to make no false claims in the future. The FTC had charged the company with falsely claiming that its "sex nutrient pills" could improve the sexual performance of otherwise healthy men low in "the sex nutrient."

In 1990, Nature's Way and its president, Kenneth Murdock, agreed to stop making unsubstantiated claims that *Cantrol* is helpful against yeast infections caused by *Candida albicans*. The product, which contains acidophilus, evening primrose oil, vitamin E, linseed oil, caprylic acid, pau d'arco, and several other substances, had been promoted with a self-test based on common symptoms the manufacturer claimed were associated with yeast problems. The FTC charged that the test was not valid for this purpose. The company also agreed to pay $30,000 to the National Institutes of Health to support research on yeast infections.

In 1991, Slender You, Inc., signed a consent agreement to stop making unsubstantiated weight loss claims for continuous passive motion exercise tables it manufactures and sells to health and fitness centers.

U.S. Postal Service

The Postal Service has jurisdiction over situations in which money is sent through the mail for products or services. Postal inspectors look for misleading advertisements in magazines and newspapers and on radio and television. They also receive complaints from the public and from other government agencies. Postal inspection offices exist in 39 cities, with about 1900 inspectors available to investigate all types of violations. Eight attorneys in the Postal Service's law department plus ten postal inspectors with law degrees are available to prosecute cases. The case selection process is decentralized, so that different types of cases are emphasized in different regions of the country.

Postal Laws

Title 39, Section 3005, of the United States Code can be used to block promoters of misleading schemes from receiving money through the mail. If sufficient health hazard or economic detriment exists, an immediate court order to impound mail may be sought under Section 3007 of the code. However, the Postal Service cannot proceed unless the Justice Department approves such action or takes the case itself.

Title 18, Section 1341, provides for criminal prosecution but requires proof of intent to deceive. The maximum penalties are 5 years in prison and a fine for each instance proved. The 1984 Criminal Fine Enhancement Act allows fines of up to $100,000 (or $250,000 if death results) per offense for up to two offenses. However, criminal prosecution is rarely used in cases involving claims made for mail-order health products because (1) administrative procedures are simpler and quicker and (2) intent to deceive is difficult to prove when a perpetrator pretends to believe that the product works. The Postal Service does not have jurisdiction when companies take credit card orders by telephone and deliver through private carriers such as United Parcel Service. However, the Justice Department may seek such an injunction under Section 1345, which allows federal district courts to enjoin acts of mail and wire fraud.

When a mail fraud is detected, postal attorneys can file a complaint or seek an agreement with the perpetrator. When a complaint is contested, a hearing is held by an administrative law judge assigned to the Postal Service. If the evidence is sufficient, this judge will recommend that the Postal Service issue a False Representation Order (FRO) blocking money sent through the mail in response to the misleading ads. Although the order can be appealed to the courts, very few companies do this. Each voluntary agreement and FRO is accompanied by a cease-and-desist order that forbids both the challenged acts and similar acts. Under the *Mail Order Consumer Protection Amendments of 1983,* if this order is violated, the agency can seek a civil penalty in federal court of up to $10,000 per day for each violation.

Criminal cases, consent agreements, and false representation orders are noted in the *Law Enforcement Report,* which is issued four times a year, free of charge, to interested media and consumer protection agencies. The agency probably handles between 25 and 40 health-related cases per year, but exact figures are not available.

In most cases in which health-related products are falsely advertised, the FDA and FTC also have jurisdiction. The FDA can regulate any product intended for use in the cure, mitigation, treatment, or prevention of any ailment, and the FTC has jurisdiction over advertising of all health-related products except prescription drugs. However, the FDA rarely becomes involved with mail-order sales, and the FTC handles relatively few.

Enforcement Actions

Most mail-order health schemes attempt to exploit people's fear of being unattractive. Their promoters are usually "hit-and-run" artists who hope to make a profit before the Postal Service stops their false ads.[16] Common products include "miracle" weight loss plans, fitness and bodybuilding products, spot-reducing devices (claimed to reduce specific parts of the body), antiaging products, and supposed sex aids.[17]

Before the 1983 law was implemented, many unscrupulous mail-order promoters considered legal defense costs and occasional fines as a normal part of their operating overhead. If prosecuted, they would remain in business by changing the wording of an ad, the name of the product, or their company name. However, the huge penalties made possible by the new law appear to have decreased the number of mail-order health schemes. Some examples of recent actions by the U.S. Postal Service follow.

In the case of Braswell, Inc., the Postal Service obtained 32 false representation orders and 15 consent agreements prohibiting the marketing of many bogus health and beauty products. But the company remained in business until its president, Glen Braswell, was successfully prosecuted for mail fraud involving the faking of "before-and-after" photographs for ads for bust developer, hair growth, and cosmetic products. Although he had grossed $75 million over a 12-year period, his sentence was only 5 years' probation. However, he also was given a 3-year prison term for federal income tax evasion and perjury charges developed during the mail fraud investigation.

In 1981 the Robertson-Taylor Company began marketing a series of products claimed to be effective against various health problems. Among them were *Metabolite 2050* ("the ultimate cure for fat"), *Arthrex* (for arthritis), *Derma-Tec* (wrinkle remover), *Cellulase-EFX* ("cellulite dissolver"), *Libutol 1500* (sexual stimulant), *Medi-Tec 90* (for baldness), and *Tranquinol* (nerve relaxer). During 1983 and 1984, the Postal Service secured mail-stop orders enabling it to return to the sender orders for several of the company products. (Despite this, the company had estimated sales of $4 million in 1984.) In 1985, at the request of the FDA, U.S. marshals seized 24 products with an estimated retail value of $2.2 million. Florida authorities then shut down company operations by seizing its mailing lists and additional products and charging its president with 42 counts of criminal fraud.[18]

In 1983, Jacob W. Kulp, D.C., a chiropractor from Cheetowaga, New York, entered a plea bargain in which he pleaded guilty to violating a federal food and drug law, and the Postal Service agreed not to prosecute him for mailing out a worthless "nutrient deficiency test." To gather evidence, postal inspectors used an undercover "patient" who took the test and was advised to use wheat fiber tablets to cure "black intestinal plaque."[19]

During 1985, the president of Encore House, Inc., and its advertising director pleaded guilty to criminal mail fraud and received prison sentences for falsely promoting a device called Figure-Tron II. Ads for the device had claimed that "tiny micro-electro impulses tone your muscles 500 times a minute," providing the exercise benefit of "3000 sit-ups without moving an inch" or "10 miles of jogging while lying flat on your back." The company also signed a consent agreement with the Postal Service and FTC in which it was assessed $100,000 and a $250,000 restitution fund was set up.[18]

In 1990 postal officials filed a false representation complaint against Nature's Bounty, Inc., of Bohemia, New York (doing business as Puritan's Pride). The complaint charged that at least 19 of the company's nutritional products were falsely advertised in Puritan Pride mail-order catalogs. The products include Cholesto-Flush, Fatbuster Diet Tea, Kidney Flush, Memory Booster, Prostex, and Stress B with 500 mg of vitamin C. The case was settled with a consent agreement under which Nature's Bounty admitted no wrongdoing but agreed to stop making the challenged claims. The agreement also authorized a Postal Service judicial officer to determine at a later date whether Nature's Bounty should be required to substantiate all future health-related claims for its mail-order products.

Other Federal Agencies

The Office of Consumer Affairs was created in 1971 as part of the Executive Office of the President of the United States. It replaced the President's Committee on Consumer Interest, which was established in 1964. In 1976 the office became part of the Department of Health, Education and Welfare (now the Department of Health and Human Services). The director of this office is the special adviser to the president for consumer affairs. The Office of Consumer Affairs helps develop information of interest to consumers and other government agencies.

The Consumer Information Center stocks and distributes many consumer publications, some free and some for a modest fee. Its catalog lists more than 50 publications on health and nutrition topics.

The Consumer Product Safety Commission distributes information and receives complaints about the safety of products.

The Environmental Protection Agency, among its many duties, sets standards for water quality and pesticide tolerances for foods (which the FDA enforces).

The Health Care Financing Administration (HCFA) administers Medicare and Medicaid programs, maintains statistics on health care costs, and oversees federal quality control programs related to health care. Its quarterly journal, *Health Care Financing Review,* reports on the economics of health care.

The National Health Service Corps recruits and places health care professionals in medically underserved communities.

The National Institutes of Health (NIH) is the federal government's primary agency for supporting and conducting biomedical research and training. Its 306-acre campus in Bethesda, Maryland, houses 13 institutes and a 500-bed hospital. NIH also holds conferences and distributes publications on health matters.

The National Health Information Center (NHIC) was established in 1979 as a service of the Office of Disease Prevention and Health promotion of the U.S. Public Health Service. NHIC operates a toll-free hot line through which it refers callers to more than 1000 organizations that can provide health-related information. It also issues a newsletter *(Prevention Report)* and many other reports about information resources. Although NHIC's leads usually are reliable, it may refer people who inquire about nonscientific methods to organizations that espouse them.

The U.S. Centers for Disease Control studies environmental health problems and administers national programs for disease prevention. Its numerous activities include tracing the source of epidemics and publishing the *Morbidity and Mortality Weekly Report (MMWR).*

The U.S. Department of Agriculture conducts nutrition research and enforces standards for meat and poultry products. It also publishes periodicals and other reports on nutrition research, food safety, and the food marketplace.

The addresses of these and other federal agencies are listed in the Appendix of this book.

State and Local Agencies

State and local agencies that offer information or other help to consumers include health departments, professional licensing boards, consumer protection bureaus, attorneys general, and agriculture departments. Hundreds of counties and cities have offices that deal with consumer affairs, including health matters. Consumers should investigate the resources in their area if they have problems regarding health products or services. The *Consumer Protection Report,* published 10 times a year by the National Association of Attorneys General, summarizes enforcement actions by state and federal agencies.

Nongovernmental Organizations

Hundreds of organizations play a significant role in helping to educate and protect consumers in health matters. These organizations can be broadly classified as voluntary, business, or professional. Their activities can include research, publications, advice to consumers, media contacts, testimony to government agencies, lawsuits, and promotion of legislation.

Voluntary Organizations

Voluntary organizations generally are nonprofit corporations formed to assist the public in various ways. Some are supported primarily by dues from their members, some are supported primarily by contributions, and some receive both. Consumer groups may address a broad range of consumer issues or focus on limited areas, such as health or health fraud. Many voluntary organizations support research and provide consumer education about a specific disease or diseases. The American Cancer Society and Arthritis Foundation are two of the most prominent groups of this type. Other organizations, designated as self-help groups, provide information and emotional support for individuals and families affected by particular diseases.

Some voluntary organizations that have had significant impact on the consumer movement in the United States are described as follows. Their addresses and those of many others are listed in the Appendix.

Consumers Union (CU), founded in 1936, conducts research and produces *Consumer Reports, Consumer Reports on Health, Consumers Union News Digest,* and many books, pamphlets, films, newspaper columns, radio and television programs, and teaching aids. *Consumer Reports* usually covers one or two health topics per month. CU's Washington office monitors government activities and represents consumers through lawsuits and testimony before regulatory agencies.

Consumer Federation of America, founded in 1967, is suppported by dues and contributions from its more than 200 member organizations. It addresses a wide range of issues, most of them economic, and presents its views to Congress and various government agencies. It publishes a bimonthly newsletter, compiles voting records of congressional representatives on consumer issues, and sponsors an annual assembly on important issues. Its member organizations pay dues and are accorded votes according to the size of their membership; the largest member is Consumers Union.

The National Consumers League, founded in 1899, has a scope of political activity similar to that of Consumer Federation of America. In addition, it develops research and shoppers' guides and helps to resolve grievances. Its members receive a monthly bulletin and a copy of *Consumers' Almanac,* which contains a great deal of useful consumer information.

The Public Citizen Health Research Group (HRG), founded in 1971 by Ralph Nader and Sidney Wolfe, M.D., is now directed by Dr. Wolfe and staffed by health professionals, attorneys, and researchers. They publish a monthly newsletter, monitor government health agencies, analyze proposed legislation and take vigorous action—including lawsuits—when they believe that the government is lax in protecting consumers from dangerous foods, drugs, or medical practices. In 1987, for example, HRG forced the FDA to ban interstate sale of unpasteurized milk. HRG also investigates and issues reports on economic and quality-of-care issues. The reports have covered medical fees, hospital evaluation, unnecessary surgery, mental health care, vision care, medical discipline, and many other topics.

The Center for Science in the Public Interest (CSPI) was founded in 1971 by former associates of Ralph Nader and reportedly has 250,000 members. It publishes the monthly *Nutrition Action Healthletter,* as well as booklets, posters, computer software, and other materials, most of which concern foods and food choices. It also engages in lawsuits and political activities intended to foster what it believes are better policies toward health and environmental issues by government and industry. CSPI has stimulated many significant government actions to protect consumers. But it also promotes organic foods, suggests that everyone should take vitamin supplements, and maintains an alarmist attitude toward the American diet and food supply.

The American Association of Retired Persons (AARP), founded in 1958, provides its 32 million members with guidance on a wide variety of economic and health issues. It publishes the magazine *Modern Maturity* as well as many pamphlets and books. AARP's mail-order pharmacy fills prescriptions and sells many nonprescription products at discount prices. AARP members can participate in myriad social, recreational, educational, and political activities through 4000 local chapters, most of which hold monthly meetings. AARP's health-related publications are usually excellent. However, its pharmacy service has been sharply criticized for "hyping" stress vitamins and selling bee pollen and other questionable products.[20] Much of this problem was corrected after the appointment of a nutrition advisory board.[21]

The National Council Against Health Fraud (NCAHF) began in 1977 as the Southern California Council Against Health Fraud and became national in 1984. It has more than 1200 members and chapters in 13 states. Its activities include a bimonthly newsletter, a media clearinghouse, consumer complaint referral services, legislative action, research on unproven methods of health care, and seminars for professionals and the general public. The Council also appoints task forces to conduct extensive investigations and issue position papers. Its Task Force on Victim Redress helps victims of quackery who want to file suit. Other task forces are concerned with acupuncture, chiropractic, diet and behavior, nutrition diploma mills, broadcast media abuse, dubious dental practices, vitamin abuse, ergogenic aids, herbs, medical neglect of children, cancer quackery, and the quality of information in health periodicals.

The Committee for the Scientific Investigation of Claims of the Paranormal (CSICOP) was founded in 1976 to encourage critical investigation of paranormal and fringe-science claims. It is composed of prominent scientists, educators, and journalists and is assisted by more than 50 scientific and technical consultants. It publishes a quarterly scientific journal, *The Skeptical Inquirer,* and maintains subcommittees on astrology, education, paranormal health claims, parapsychology, and UFOs. Groups similar to CSICOP exist in many areas of the United States and in several foreign countries.

The American Council on Science and Health (ACSH) was founded in 1978 to evaluate issues involving food, drugs, chemicals, the environment, life-style, and health. ACSH has more than 200 prominent scientific and policy advisers. It produces peer-reviewed reports, and a quarterly magazine, *Priorities.* It also hosts seminars and press conferences and serves as a clearinghouse for the news media and answers individual inquiries from the public.

The Consumer Health Information Research Institute (CHIRI) was established in 1989 to promote consumer and patient education activities, including studies of misinformation, fraud, and quackery. It maintains a publications list and can answer individual questions.

Business Organizations

Many business organizations provide information and educational materials to consumers. The Health Insurance Institute, for example, provides excellent information about the insurance marketplace, and the National Dairy Council provides reliable information about food and nutrition. The Council of Better Business Bureaus is unique among business groups because it also takes an advocacy role in encouraging truth in advertising and other good business practices through industrial self-regulation. It has published a code for advertising and selling as well as pamphlets to help consumers make wise purchasing decisions.

In recent years, the Council has helped the FDA to discourage media outlets from accepting misleading ads for health products. The Council's National Advertising Division (NAD) receives and adjudicates complaints about nationally circulated advertising and has persuaded a few manufacturers to withdraw health-related ads that have been challenged. However, NAD has exhibited little interest in adjudicating complaints related to vitamin supplements and has even endorsed a fraudulent ad for "nutrition insurance" (see Chapter 5). Local Better Business Bureau offices can sometimes help consumers with complaints about health products and services provided by local businesses; however, problems with licensed practitioners usually are referred to medical societies or state licensing boards.

Professional Organizations

Health professionals can join a multitude of local, state, and national groups interested in promoting their profession or specialty. The largest such group is the American Medical Association, which evaluates information, publishes books and journals, conducts seminars, engages in lawsuits and legislative activity, offers information to the public and the media, and engages in many other activities. The publications of recognized professional groups are generally reliable and well written; the names and addresses of many such groups are listed in the Appendix.

Consumer Action

It is fitting to conclude this book with probably the most important segment of the Consumer Bill of Rights: the right to be heard.

Table 27-2 summarizes where consumer complaints can be sent. Complaints to federal agencies may receive extra attention when a member of Congress is involved, so it is often a good idea to send a copy of your complaint to your congressional representatives. Where more than one enforcement agency appears to have jurisdiction, it is best to contact all of them.

To make a complaint, record what you have observed and what you think is wrong, and send or deliver this information to the appropriate agency along with any evidence you have collected. If your complaint involves a food or drug, enclose the label or a complete description of the label (including code marks) and indicate where you obtained the product. If your complaint involves a product you have used, check first to be sure you followed the directions. If you have what appears to be an adverse effect to a medication, the problem is most likely an allergy or a side effect known to the FDA rather than poor quality of the medication. Your doctor can be consulted to find this out. If you complain about an advertisement, indicate when

Table 27–2

Where to Complain or Seek Help*

Problem	Agencies to contact
False advertising	FTC Bureau of Consumer Protection Regional FTC office National Advertising Division, Council of Better Business Bureaus Editor or station manager of media outlet where ad appeared
Product marketed with false or misleading claims	Regional FDA office State attorney general State health department Local Better Business Bureau Congressional representatives
Bogus mail-order promotion	Chief Postal Inspector, U.S. Postal Service Editor or station manager of media outlet where ad appeared
Improper treatment by licensed practitioner	Local or state professional society (if practitioner is a member) Local hospital (if practitioner is a staff member) State licensing board National Council Against Health Fraud Task Force on Victim Redress
Improper treatment by unlicensed individual	Local district attorney State attorney general National Council Against Health Fraud Task Force on Victim Redress
Advice needed about questionable product or service	National Council Against Health Fraud Consumer Health Information Research Institute Local, state, or national professional or voluntary health groups

© 1985, 1989, 1991, Stephen Barrett, M.D.

*See Appendix for addresses. When more than one regulatory agency appears to have jurisdiction, contact each of them.

PERSONAL GLIMPSE

For society to improve, people must speak out loudly and clearly when they have been misled. Individual consumers as well as agencies and organizations must assume responsibility in this regard. Individuals often feel helpless when cheated, but they must fight back by registering complaints. The system will not change unless peopple want it to be modified and are willing to take action on their own behalf.

If you encounter a food, drug, device, cosmetic, or other health-related product that appears to be mislabeled or otherwise defective, you can perform a public service by reporting it to the FDA. If you encounter false advertising, you can perform a similar service by reporting it to the FTC or to your state attorney general. When sale through the mail is involved, contact the Postal Service. When services rather than products are involved, a state or local agency is likely to be most helpful.

CONSUMER TIP

The intelligent health consumer does the following:

- ✔ Identifies and uses reliable sources of information. Chapter 3 and the Appendix list sources that the authors of this textbook consider reliable.
- ✔ Is skeptical and investigates the accuracy of health advertising before making purchasing decisions.
- ✔ Understands which types of health problems can be self-treated and which should receive professional care.
- ✔ Takes an active role in dealing with health professionals; is assertive but tactful; endeavors to learn the nature of any ailment and the mechanism and potential hazards of treatment; is aware of fees involved.
- ✔ Locates and uses a primary physician (or medical group) who provides scientific, considerate, and compassionate care.
- ✔ Uses medication properly; carefully reads labels and follows directions for safe use; is aware of common side effects; requests generic drugs when appropriate.
- ✔ Is aware of the signs of quackery and health fraud; avoids products and procedures that are unscientific or unproven and practitioners who recommend them.
- ✔ Is familiar with the laws, regulations, and rights that protect consumers.
- ✔ Supports, participates in, and seeks help when needed from appropriate consumer organizations.
- ✔ Writes letters, makes phone calls, and takes other appropriate action to protest deceptive or fraudulent health practices.

and where you observed it.

Information supplied by consumers often leads to detection and correction of a problem. Many people are afraid that making a complaint will subject them to legal action or involve them in a time-consuming process. This is unlikely, however. Complaints made in good faith are privileged—which means the complainant is shielded from liability. Nor is a complainant likely to be needed as a witness in a court proceeding. Regulatory agencies almost always conduct their own investigations and proceed on the evidence gathered by their trained investigators.

The Intelligent Health Consumer

Intelligent consumers accept personal and public responsibility for the protection of health. They actively pursue the information and understanding necessary to make wise decisions about health products and services. They are willing to speak out and encourage social action when misrepresentations or fraudulent practices are encountered.

SUMMARY

Consumer protection in health matters has two components: education and law enforcement. Intelligent consumers actively pursue the information needed to make wise decisions about health products and services. They are also willing to support government action against health frauds and misrepresentations. Government agencies, in turn, must establish and enforce standards for professional competence and honest marketing of products and services.

DISCUSSION QUESTIONS

1. Which three main federal agencies protect consumers in health matters? What laws define their scope and purposes?

2. What is a "new drug"?
3. List the steps involved in the drug approval process.
4. What are the principal responsibilities of the FDA, FTC, and Postal Service? Describe the enforcement actions they can take.
5. What is the Delaney Amendment? Why is it controversial?
6. What is the GRAS list?
7. Which types of products are typically involved in mail-order health scams?
8. What should consumers do when they encounter a questionable food or drug product or advertisement?
9. Describe the purposes and activities of five voluntary groups involved in protecting consumers in health matters.
10. Describe the activities of the Council of Better Business Bureaus and its local affiliates.
11. Describe the intelligent health consumer.

REFERENCES

1. Young FE: FDA: the cop on the consumer beat, FDA Consumer 22(3):6–7, 1988.
2. Edwards CE et al: Final report of the advisory committee of the Food and Drug Administration, Washington, DC, 1991, U.S. Department of Health and Human Services.
3. Federal Food, Drug, and Cosmetic Act, as amended, and related laws, Washington, DC, 1989, U.S. Government Printing Office publication no. 017-012-00347-8. (Obtainable for $7.50 from the Superintendent of Documents, U.S. Government Printing Office, Washington, DC 20402.)
4. Jukes TH: The Delaney clause—a 1990 apppraisal, Priorities, Winter 1991, pp 23–24.
5. Francis FJ: Food safety: interpretation of risk, Ames, Iowa, 1992, Council for Agricultural Science and Technology.
6. Meister KM: Irradiated foods, New York, 1985, American Council on Science and Health.
7. Blumenthal B: Food irradiation toxic to bacteria, safe for humans, FDA Consumer 24(9):11–15, 1990.
8. From test tube to patient: new drug development in the United States, an FDA consumer special report, HHS publication no. (FDA) 88-3168, Rockville, Md, 1988, US Food and Drug Administration.
9. Young FE: Investigational new drug, antibiotic, and biological drug product regulations; treatment use and sale; final rule, Federal Register 52:19476–19477, 1987.
10. Doyle C: Milestone status of OTC review documents, October 3, 1989.
11. Kessler DA et al: The federal regulation of medical devices, N Engl J Med 317:357–366, 1987.
12. Benson JS: FDA enforcement activities protect public, FDA Consumer 25(1)7–9, 1991.
13. Young FE: FDA enforcement actions 1987–1988, FDA Consumer 22(3):5, 1989.
14. Barrett S: Quackery and the FDA: a complicated story, Nutrition Forum 8:41–44, 1991.
15. Federal Trade Commission: A guide to the Federal Trade Commission, Washington, DC, 1991, U.S. Government Printing Office.
*16. Barrett S: Quackery by mail, New York, 1991, American Council on Health.
17. Delusions of vigor: better health by mail, Consumer Reports 44:50–54, 1979.
18. Shearing the suckers, Consumer Reports 51:87–94, 1986.
19. Postal Inspection Service: Chiropractor causes fiber tablets to become a misbranded drug, Law Enforcement Report, Winter 1983/1984, p 10.
20. Vitamin hype for senior citizens, Consumer Reports 51(10):627, 1986.
*21. Barrett S et al: Health schemes, scams, and frauds, New York, 1990, Consumer Reports Books.

---

*Recommended reading

Appendix

Reliable Sources of Information

§These sources have toll-free numbers.

Federal Government Agencies

U.S. Department of Agriculture, Washington, DC 20250

Food and Nutrition Information Center: 301-504-5414 [for consumer questions]

Food and Nutrition Service: 3101 Park Center Dr., Alexandria, VA 22302

Human Nutrition Information Service: [primarily a research agency] 6505 Belcrest Rd., Hyattsville, MD 20782

Cooperative Extension Services are located in many cities

Centers for Disease Control, Office of Public Inquiries, 1600 Clifton Road, N.E., Atlanta, GA 30333

Clearinghouse on Child Abuse and Neglect Information, P.O. Box 1182, Washington, DC 20013

Consumer Information Center, P.O. Box 100, Pueblo CO 81002 [Free and low-cost publications]

§Consumer Product Safety Commission, 5401 Westbard Ave., Bethesda, MD 20207

§Environmental Protection Agency (EPA), 401 M St., S.W., Washington, DC 20460

Food and Drug Administration, 5600 Fishers Lane, Rockville, MD 20857

Consumer Affairs Offices:

201 E. Indianola, Phoenix AZ 85012

1521 W. Pico Blvd., Los Angeles, CA 90015, 213-252-7597

50 United Nations Plaza, San Francisco, CA 94102, 415-556-1458

P.O. Box 25087, Denver, CO 80225, 303-236-3018

6601 N.W. 25th St., Miami, FL 33159, 305-526-2919

7200 Lake Ellenor Drive, Orlando, FL 32809, 407-648-6922

60-8th St., N.E., Atlanta, GA 30309, 404-347-7355

300 S. Riverside Plaza, Chicago, IL 60606, 312-353-7126

101 W. Ohio St., Indianapolis, IN 46204, 317-226-6500

4298 Elysian Fields Ave., New Orleans, LA 70122, 504-589-2420

One Montvale Ave., Stoneham, MA 02180, 617-279-1479

900 Madison Ave., Baltimore, MD 21201, 301-962-3731

1560 E. Jefferson Ave., Detroit, MI 48207, 313-226-6260

240 Hennepin Ave., Minneapolis, MN 55401, 612-334-4103

1009 Cherry St., Kansas City, MO 63106, 816-374-6086

808 N. Collins Alley, St. Louis, MO 63102, 314-425-5021

200 S. 16th St., Omaha, NE 68102, 402-221-4675

61 Main St., West Orange, NJ 07052, 201-645-6365

850 Third Ave., Brooklyn, NY 11232, 718-965-5043

599 Delaware Ave., Buffalo, NY 14202, 716-846-4483

320 Central Ave., Brunswich, OH 44212, 216-273-1038

1141 Central Parkway, Cincinnati, OH 45202, 513-684-3501

Room 900 U.S. Customhouse, 2nd & Chestnut Sts., Philadelphia, PA 19106, 215-597-0837

P.O. Box 5719, Puerto de Tierra Sta., San Juan, PR 00906, 809-729-6852

297 Plus Park Blvd., Nashville, TN 37217, 615-781-5372

3032 Bryan St., Dallas, TX 75204, 214-655-5315

1445 North Loop West, Houston, TX 77008, 713-220-2322

10127 Morocco, San Antonio, TX 78216, 512-229-4531

1110 N. Glebe Rd., Arlington, VA 22201, 703-285-2578

22201 23rd Drive, S.E., Bothell, WA 98021, 206-483-4953

U.S. Court House Rm. 5-B-06, 517 E. Wisconsin Ave., Milwaukee, WI 53202, 414-297-3097

Federal Trade Commission, 6th & Pennsylvania Ave., N.W., Washington, DC 20580

Regional Offices:

1718 Peachtree St., N.W., Atlanta, GA 30367, 404-347-4836

10 Causeway St., Boston, MA 02222, 617-565-7240

55 E. Monroe St., Chicago, IL 60603, 312-353-4423

668 Euclid Ave., Cleveland, OH 44114, 216-522-4207

100 N. Central Expressway, Dallas, TX 75201, 214-767-5501

1405 Curtis St., Denver, CO 80202, 303-844-2271

11000 Wilshire Blvd., Los Angeles, CA 90024, 213-575-7575

150 William St., New York, NY 10038, 212-264-1207

901 Market St., San Francisco, CA 94103, 415-744-7920

915 Second Ave., Seattle, WA 98174, 206-553-4656

Health Care Financing Administration (HCFA), 200 Independence Ave., S.W., Washington, DC 20201

National AIDS Information Center, P.O. Box 6003, Bethesda, MD 20850

National Cholesterol Information Education Program Information Center, 4733 Bethesda Ave., Room 530, Bethesda, MD 20814

§National Health Information Clearinghouse, P.O. Box 1133, Washington, DC 20013

*National Information Center for Rare Diseases and Orphan Drugs, 450 5th St., Washington, DC 20001

National Institutes of Health, 9000 Rockville Pike, Bethesda, MD 20892

National Cancer Institute

National Eye Institute

National Heart, Lung, and Blood Institute

National Institute of Allergy and Infectious Diseases

National Institute of Arthritis and Musculoskeletal and Skin Diseases

National Institute of Diabetes and Digestive and Kidney Diseases

National Institute of Child Health and Human Development

National Institute of Dental Research

National Institute of Mental Health

National Institute of Neurological Disorders and Stroke

National Institute on Aging

National Institute on Alcohol Abuse and Alcoholism

National Institute on Drug Abuse

National Maternal and Child Health Clearinghouse, 38th & R St., N.W., Washington, DC 20057

Office of Technology Assessment, U.S. Congress, Washington, DC 20510

Office on Smoking and Health, 5600 Fishers Lane, Rockville, MD 20857

U.S. Postal Service, 475 L'Enfant Plaza, Washington, DC 20260

President's Council on Physical Fitness and Sports, 450 E. 5th St., Washington, DC 20201

Voluntary and Professional Organizations

Most of the organizations listed below are voluntary groups that draw support and members from the general public as well as professionals. Some have a single national office, while others have chapters in various cities. Most of these organizations provide educational materials on request. Some raise and distribute funds for research. Some conduct educational programs for the public and encourage and develop local support groups. Some offer individual counseling.

Business and professional groups, indicated by an asterisk (*), are composed exclusively or primarily of health professionals or other professionally trained individuals. Most of these groups publish a scientific journal and hold educational meetings for their members. Most of them also help the public by setting professional standards, disseminating information through the news media, and responding to inquiries from individual consumers.

Additional information on most of these organizations can be obtained from (1) the *Encyclopedia of Medical Organizations and Agencies* [Gale Research Company, published periodically and available in the reference department of most public libraries]; (2) the *Encyclopedia of Associations* [Gale Research Company]; (3) *Voluntary Health Organizations: A Guide to Patient Services,* by L. Scheinberg and D.M. Schneider [New York, 1987, Demos Publications]; and (4) *National Healthlines Directory,* by L. Marinos et al [New York, 1992, Information Resources Press].

Action on Smoking and Health, 2013 H St., N.W., Washington, DC 20006 [nonsmokers' rights]

§Al-Anon Family Group Headquarters, P.O. Box 862, Midtown Station, New York, NY 10018

Alcoholics Anonymous, P.O. Box 459, Grand Central Station, New York, NY 10163

Alexander Graham Bell Institute for the Deaf, 3417 Volta Pl., N.W., Washington, DC 20007

Amytrophic Lateral Sclerosis Association, 21021 Ventura Blvd., Woodland Hills, CA 91364

§Alzheimer's Disease and Related Disorders Association, 70 E. Lake St., Chicago, IL 60601

*§American Academy of Allergy and Immunology, 611 E. Wells St., Milwaukee, WI 53202

*§American Academy of Family Physicians, 8880 Ward Parkway, Kansas City, MO 64114

*American Academy of Ophthalmology, 655 Beach St., P.O. Box 7424, San Francisco, CA 94109

*American Academy of Otolaryngology-Head and Neck Surgery, 1 Prince St., Alexandria, VA 22314

*§American Academy of Pediatrics, 141 Northwest Point Blvd., Elk Grove Village, IL 60009

American Alliance for Health, Physical Education, Recreation and Dance, 1900 Association Drive, Reston, VA 22091

*American Association for Counseling and Development, 5999 Stevenson Ave., Alexandria, VA 22304

*American Association for the History of Medicine, Boston Univ. School of Medicine, 80 E. Concord St., Boston, MA 02118

*American Association for Marriage and Family Therapy, 1100 17th St., N.W., Washington, DC 20036

*American Association for Partial Hospitalization, 1411 K St., N.W., Washington, DC 20005

*American Association for the Study of Headache, 875 Kings Highway, West Deptford, NJ 08096

*American Association of Blood Banks, 1117 N. 19th St., Arlington, VA 22209

American Association of Homes for the Aging, 1129 20th St., N.W., Suite 400, Washington, DC 20036

American Association of Kidney Patients, 1 Davis Blvd., Tampa, FL 33306

*American Association of Pastoral Counselors, 9508A Lee Highway, Fairfax, VA 22031

*American Association of Plastic Surgeons, 10666 N. Torrey Pines Rd., La Jolla, CA 92037

American Association of Retired Persons, 601 E St., N.W., Washington, DC 20049

*American Association of Sex Educators, Counselors, and Therapists, 435 N. Michigan Ave., Chicago, IL 60611

*American Association of Suicidology, 2459 S. Ash, Denver, CO 80222

§American Association on Mental Retardation, 1719 Kalorama Rd., N.W., Washington, DC 20009

*§American Board of Medical Specialties, 1 Rotary Center, Evanston, IL 60201

*American Burn Association, Francis Scott Key Hospital, 4940 Eastern Ave., Baltimore, MD 21224

§American Cancer Society, 1599 Clifton Road, N.E., Atlanta, GA 30329

American Celiac Society, 58 Musano Ct., West Orange, NJ 07052 [dietary guidance for celiac disease]

*American Cleft Palate Association, 1218 Grandview Ave., Pittsburgh, PA 15211

*American College Health Association, 1300 Piccard Dr., Suite 200, Rockville, MD 20850

*§American College of Cardiology, 9111 Old Georgetown Road, Bethesda, MD 20814

*American College of Health Care Administrators, 325 S. Patrick St., Alexandria, VA 22314 [nursing homes]

*American College of Obstetricians and Gynecologists, 409 12th St., S.W., Washington, DC 20024

*American College of Physicians, Independence Mall W., 6th St. at Race, Philadelphia, PA 19106

*American College of Radiology, 1891 Preston White Dr., Reston, VA 22091

*American College of Sports Medicine, P.O. Box 1440, Indianapolis, IN 46206

*American College of Surgeons, 55 E. Erie St., Chicago, IL 60611

American Council on Science and Health, 1995 Broadway, 16th Floor, New York, NY 10023

*American Dental Association, 211 E. Chicago Ave., Chicago, IL 60611

§American Diabetes Association, 1660 Duke St., Alexandria, VA 22314

*American Dietetic Association, 216 W. Jackson Blvd., Chicago, IL 60606

*American Epilepsy Society, 638 Prospect Ave., Hartford, CT 06105

American Family Foundation, P.O. Box 2265, Bonita Springs, FL 33959 [cults]

*American Federation of Home Health Agencies, 1320 Fenwick Lane, Silver Spring, MD 20910

*American Fertility Society, 2140 11th Ave., Suite 200, Birmingham, AL 35205

American Foundation for AIDS Research, 5900 Wilshire Blvd., Los Angeles, CA 90036

§American Foundation for the Blind, 15 W. 16th St., New York, NY 10011

*American Geriatrics Society, 770 Lexington Ave., New York, NY 10021

American Group Psychotherapy Association, 25 E. 21st St., New York, NY 10010

*American Health Care Association, 1201 L St., N.W., Washington, DC 20005 [nursing home standards]

§American Heart Association, 7320 Greenville Ave., Dallas, TX 75231

*American Hospital Association, 840 N. Lake Shore Drive, Chicago, IL 60611

*American Industrial Hygiene Association, P.O. Box 8390, 345 White Pond Dr., Akron, OH 44320

*American Institute of Nutrition, 9650 Rockville Pike, Bethesda, MD 20814

§American Kidney Fund, 6110 Executive Blvd., Rockville, MD 20852

§American Liver Foundation, 1425 Pompton Ave., Cedar Grove, NJ 07009

American Lung Association, 1740 Broadway, New York, NY 10019

*American Medical Association, 515 N. State St., Chicago, IL 60610

*American Medical Women's Association, 801 N. Fairfax St., Alexandria, VA 22314

*American Medical Writers Association, 9650 Rockville Pike, Bethesda, MD 20814

*§American Mental Health Counselors Association, 5999 Stevenson Ave., Alexandria, VA 22304

American Narcolepsy Association, P.O. Box 1187, San Carlos, CA 94070

*American Nurses' Association, 2420 Pershing Rd., Kansas City, MO 64108

*American Occupational Therapy Association, 1383 Piccard Dr., Rockville, MD 20850

*American Ophthalmological Society, Duke University Eye Center, Durham, NC 27710

*American Optometric Association, 243 N. Lindbergh Blvd., St. Louis, MO 63141

*§American Osteopathic Association, 142 East Ontario St., Chicago, IL 60611

American Parkinson Disease Association, 60 Bay St., Suite 401, Staten Island, NY 10301

*American Pharmaceutical Association, 2215 Constitution Ave., N.W., Washington, DC 20037

*§American Physical Therapy Association, 1111 N. Fairfax St., Alexandria, VA 22314

*American Podiatric Medical Association, 9312 Old Georgetown Road, Bethesda, MD 20814

*American Psychiatric Association, 1400 K St., N.W., Washington, DC 20005

*American Psychoanalytic Association, 309 E. 49th St., New York, NY 10022

*American Psychological Association, 1200 17th St., N.W., Washington, DC 20036

*American Public Health Association, 1015 15th St., Washington, DC 20005

American Red Cross, 17th & D Sts., N.W., Washington, DC 20006

*American School Health Association, P.O. Box 708, Kent, OH 44240

*American Sleep Disorders Association, 604 Second St., S.W., Rochester, MN 55902

American Social Health Association, P.O. Box 13827, Research Triangle Park, NC 27709 [venereal disease]

*American Society for Artificial Internal Organs, P.O. Box C, Boca Raton, FL 33429

*American Society for Clinical Nutrition, 9650 Rockville Pike, Bethesda, MD 20814

*American Society of Clinical Hypnosis, 2200 E. Devon Ave., Des Plaines, IL 60018

*American Society of Clinical Oncology, 435 N. Michigan Ave., Chicago, IL 60611

*American Society of Hematology, 6900 Grove Rd., Thorofare, NJ 08086

*American Society of Internal Medicine, 1101 Vermont Ave., Washington, DC 20005

*American Society of Law and Medicine, 765 Commonwealth Ave., Boston, MA 02215

*§American Society of Plastic and Reconstructive Surgeons, 444 E. Algonquin Rd., Arlington Heights, IL 60005

*§American Speech-Language-Hearing Association, 10801 Rockville Pike, Rockville, MD 20852

American Tinnitus Association, P.O. Box 5, Portland, OR 97207

*American Urological Association, 1120 N. Charles St., Baltimore, MD 21201

American Transplant Association, P.O. Box 822123, Dallas, TX 75382

American Venereal Disease Association, P.O. Box 1753, Baltimore, MD 21203

*American Veterinary Medical Association, 930 N. Mecham Rd., Schaumburg, IL 60196

Americans for Nonsmokers' Rights, 2530 San Pablo Ave., Berkeley, CA 94702

§Arthritis Foundation, 1314 Spring St., N.W., Atlanta, GA 30309

Association for Retarded Citizens, P.O. Box 6109, Arlington, TX 76005

*Association for the Advancement of Health Education, 1900 Association Dr., Reston, VA 22091

Association for the Care of Children's Health, 7910 Woodmont Ave., Bethesda, MD 20814

Association for Macular Diseases, 210 E. 64 St., New York, NY 10021

Association for Voluntary Sterilization, 122 42nd St., New York, NY 10168

§Asthma and Allergy Foundation of America, 1125 15th St., N.W., Washington, DC 20005

Autism Society of America, 8601 Georgia Ave., Silver Spring, MD 20910

Bald-Headed Men of America, 3819 Bridges St., Morehead City, NC 28557

*Better Hearing Institute, Box 1840, Washington, DC 20013

Better Vision Institute, 1800 N. Kent St., Rosslyn, VA 22209

*Blue Cross and Blue Shield Association of America, 676 N. St. Clair St., Chicago, IL 60611

Braille Institute of America, 741 N. Vermont Ave., Los Angeles, CA 90029

Cancer Care, Inc., 1180 Avenue of the Americas, New York, NY 10036

§Candlelighters Childhood Cancer Foundation, 1312 18th St., N.W., Washington, DC 20006

Children of Aging Parents, 2761 Trenton Road, Levittown, PA 19056

Children's Healthcare Is a Legal Duty (CHILD), P.O. Box 2604, Sioux City, IA 51106

Children's Hearing Education and Research, 928 McLean Ave., Yonkers, NY 10704

Child Welfare League of America, 440 1st St., N.W., Washington, DC 20001

Committee for the Scientific Investigation of Claims of the Paranormal (CSICOP), P.O. Box 703, Amherst, NY 14226

Concern for Dying, 250 W. 57th St., New York, NY 10107 [death with dignity]

Consumer Federation of America, 1424 16th St., N.W., Washington, DC 20036

§Consumer Health Information Research Institute (CHIRI), 3521 Broadway, Kansas City, MO 64111.

Consumers Union, 101 Truman Ave. Yonkers, NY 10703

§Cooley's Anemia Foundation, 105 E. 22nd St., New York, NY 10010

*Council for Agricultural Science and Technology (CAST), 137 Lynn Ave., Ames, IA 50010 [nutrition]

*Council of Better Business Bureaus

Headquarters Office: 1515 Wilson Blvd., Arlington, VA 22209

National Advertising Division: 845 Third Ave., New York, NY 10017

Crohn's & Colitis Foundation, 444 Park Ave. South, New York, NY 10016

§Cystic Fibrosis Foundation, 6931 Arlington Rd., 200, Bethesda, MD 20814

Deafness Research Foundation, 9 E. 38th St., New York, NY 10016

*Delta Dental Plans Association, 211 E. Chicago Ave., Chicago, IL 60611 [dental insurance]

Doctors Ought to Care (DOC), 5510 Greenbriar, Suite 235, Houston, TX 77005 [tobacco and other preventive health issues]

Dysautonomia Foundation, 20 E. 46th St., New York, NY 10017

Dystonia Medical Research Foundation, 8383 Wilshire Blvd., Beverly Hills, CA 90211

*ECRI, 5200 Butler Pike, Plymouth Meeting, PA 19462 [medical devices]

Emphysema Anonymous, P.O. Box 3224, Seminole, FL 34642

§Endometriosis Association, 8585 N. 76th Pl., Milwaukee, WI 53223

§Epilepsy Foundation of America, 4351 Garden City Dr., Landover, MD 20785

Eye Bank Association of America, 1725 I St., N.W., Washington, DC 20006

Family Service America, 11700 W. Lake Park Dr., Milwaukee, WI 53224

Gamblers Anonymous, 3255 Wilshire Blvd., Los Angeles, CA 90015

*Federated Ambulatory Surgery Association, 700 N. Fairfax St., Alexandria, VA 22314

*Federation of Societies for Experimental Biology, 9650 Rockville Pike, Bethesda, MD 20814

*Food and Nutrition Board, National Academy of Sciences, 2101 Constitution Blvd., N.W., Washington, DC 20418

Foundation for Hospice and Home Care (see National Homecaring Council for address)

*Gerontological Society, 1275 K St., N.W., Washington, DC 20005

Group Against Smoking Pollution (GASP), P.O. Box 632, College Park, MD 20740

*Group Health Association of America, 1129 20th St., N.W., Washington, DC 20036

Guide Dog Users, c/o Kim Charlson, 57 Grandview Ave., Watertown, MA 02172

*Health Insurance Association of America, 1025 Connecticut Ave., N.W., Washington, DC 20036

Help for Incontinent People, P.O. Box 544, Union, SC 29379

§Huntington's Disease Society of America, 140 W. 22nd St., New York, NY 10011

Information Exchange on Young Adult Chronic Patients, 151 S. Main St., New York, NY 10956 [mental illness]

§*Institute for Aerobics Research, 12330 Preston Road, Dallas, TX 75230

*Institute of Food Technologists, 221 N. LaSalle St., Chicago, IL 60601

International Association for Medical Assistance to Travelers (IAMAT), 417 Center St., Lewiston, NY 14092

International Association of Laryngectomees, c/o American Cancer Society

*International Health Society, 1001 E. Oxford Lane, Englewood, CO 80110 [public health]

*International Life Sciences Institute, 1126 16th St., N.W., Washington, DC 20036 [nutrition, toxicology, technology risk assessment]

Interstitial Cystitis Association, 38 Cedar Lane, Ossining, NY 10562

Jewish Guild for the Blind, 15 W. 65th St., New York, NY 10023

*Joint Commission on Accreditation of Healthcare Organizations, One Renaissance Blvd., Oakbrook Terrace, IL 60181

§Juvenile Diabetes Foundation, 432 Park Ave. S., New York, NY 10016

La Leche League International, 9616 Minneapolis Ave., Franklin Park, IL 60131 [breastfeeding]

Learning Disabilities Association of America, 4156 Library Rd., Pittsburgh, PA 15234

Lehigh Valley Committee Against Health Fraud, P.O. Box 1747, Allentown, PA 18150 [quackery]

Leukemia Society of America, 733 Third Ave., New York, NY 10017

Little People of America, 7238 Piedmont Drive, Dallas, TX 75227 [dwarfism]

§Living Bank, P.O. Box 6725, Houston TX 77265 [organ donor registry]

§Lupus Foundation of America, 1717 Massachusetts Ave., N.W., Washington, DC 20036

Make Today Count, 101½ S. Union St., Alexandria, VA 22314 [support groups for cancer patients]

March of Dimes Birth Defects Foundation, 1275 Mamaroneck Ave., White Plains, NY 10605

Maternity Center Association, 48 E. 92nd St., New York, NY 10128

§Medic Alert Foundation International, 2353 Colorado Ave., Turlock, CA 95380 [warning bracelets, organ donor registry]

*Medical Library Association, 6 N. Michigan Ave., Chicago, IL 60602

Mended Hearts, c/o American Heart Association [support group for cardiac surgery patients]

Mental Health Association, 1021 Prince St., Alexandria, VA 22314

Muscular Dystrophy Association, 810 7th Ave., New York, NY 10019

§Myasthenia Gravis Foundation, 53 W. Jackson Blvd., Chicago, IL 60604

Narcotics Anonymous, P.O. Box 9999, Van Nuys, CA 91409

§National Alliance for the Mentally Ill, 2101 Wilson Blvd., Arlington, VA 22201

National Amputation Foundation, 12-45 150th St., Whitestone, NY 11357

*National Association for Ambulatory Care, 21 Michigan St., Grand Rapids, MI 49503

*National Association for Chiropractic Medicine, P.O. Box 794, Middleton, WI 53562

§National Association for Hearing and Speech Action, 10801 Rockville Pike, Rockville, MD 20852

*National Association for Home Care, 519 C St., N.E., Washington, DC 20002

§National Association for Sickle Cell Disease, 3345 Wilshire Blvd., Los Angeles, CA 90010

National Association of Anorexia Nervosa and Associated Disorders, P.O. Box 7, Highland Park, IL 60035

National Association of Area Agencies on Aging, 600 Maryland Ave., Washington, DC 20024

National Association of Attorneys General, 444 N. Capitol St., Washington, DC 20001

National Association of the Deaf, 814 Thayer Ave., Silver Spring, MD 20910

National Association of the Physically Handicapped, Bethesda Scarlet Oaks, 440 Lafayette Ave., Cincinnati, OH 45220

*§National Association of Social Workers, 750 First St., Washington, DC 20002

National Ataxia Foundation, 600 Twelve Oaks Center, 15500 Wayzata Blvd., Wayzata, MN 55391 [loss of muscle coordination and balance]

National Burn Federation

*§National Center for Nutrition and Dietetics, 216 W. Jackson Blvd., Chicago, IL 60606

National CFS Association, 3251 Broadway, Kansas City, MO 64111 [chronic fatigue syndrome]

National Committee for the Prevention of Child Abuse, 332 S. Michigan Ave., Chicago, IL 60604

National Consumers League, 815 15th St., N.W., Washington, DC 20005

National Council Against Health Fraud

Headquarters: P.O. Box 1276, Loma Linda, CA 92354

Resource Center: 2800 Main St., Kansas City, MO 64108

Task Force on Victim Redress, P.O. Box 1747, Allentown, PA 18105

National Council on Alcoholism and Drug Dependence, 12 W. 21st St., New York, NY 10010

National Council on Family Relations, 3939 Central Ave., St. Paul, MN 55421

§National Council on the Aging, 600 Maryland Ave., S.W., Washington, DC 20024

National Council on Patient Information and Education, 666 11th St., N.W., Washington, DC 20001

*National Dairy Council, 6300 North River Road, Rosemont, IL 60018

§National Easter Seal Society, 70 E. Lake St., Chicago, IL 60601 [handicapped children and adults]

National Family Planning and Reproductive Health Association, 122 C St., N.W., Washington, DC 20001

National Federation of the Blind, 1800 Johnson St., Baltimore, MD 21230

National Foundation for Asthma, P.O. Box 30069, Tucson, AZ 85751

National Genetics Foundation, 180 W. 58th St., New York, NY 10019

National Headache Foundation, 5252 N. Western Ave., Chicago, IL 60625

§National Head Injury Foundation, 333 Turnpike Rd., Southborough, MA 01772

*National Health Council, 1730 M St., N.W., Washington, DC 20036

*National Hearing Aid Society, 20361 Middlebelt Rd., Livonia, MI 48152

§National Hemophilia Foundation, 110 Green St., New York, NY 10012

*National Homecaring Council, 519 C St., N.E., Washington, DC 20002

*§National Hospice Organization, 1901 N. Moore St., Arlington, VA 22209

§National Kidney Foundation, 30 E. 33rd St., New York, NY 10016

*National League for Nursing, 350 Hudson St., New York, NY 10014

National Leukemia Foundation, 585 Stewart Ave., Garden City, NY 11530

National Lupus Erythematosus Foundation, 2635 N. 1st St., San Jose, CA 95134

§National Mental Health Association, 1021 Prince St., Alexandria, VA 22314

§National Multiple Sclerosis Society, 205 E. 42nd St., New York, NY 10017

§National Neurofibromatosis Foundation, 141 Fifth Ave., New York, NY 10010

§National Organization for Rare Disorders (NORD), 4960 Sentinel Drive, Bethesda, MD 20816

National Organization on Disability, 910 16th St., N.W., Washington, DC 20006

National Osteoporosis Foundation, 2100 M St., Washington, DC 20037

*National Parkinson Foundation, 1501 N.W. Ninth Ave., Miami, FL 33136 [Parkinson's disease and related neurological disorders]

National Psoriasis Foundation, 6443 S.W. Beaverton Highway, Portland, OR 97221

*National Rehabilitation Association, 633 S. Washington St., Alexandria, VA 22314

National Resource Center for Worksite Health Promotion, 777 N. Capitol St., N.E., Washington, DC 20002.

National Safety Council, 444 W. Michigan Ave., Chicago, IL 60611

National Self-Help Clearinghouse, 25 W. 43rd St., Room 620, New York, NY 10036

*National Society of Patient Representatives, c/o American Hospital Association, 840 N. Lake Shore Dr., Chicago, IL 60611

§National Society to Prevent Blindness, 500 E. Remington Rd., Schaumburg, IL 60173

§National Spinal Cord Injury Association, 600 W. Cummings Park, Woburn, MA 01801

National Sudden Infant Death Syndrome Foundation, 10500 Little Patuxent Parkway, Columbia, MD 21044

National Tay-Sachs and Allied Diseases Association, 385 Eliot St., Newton, MA 02164

§National Tuberous Sclerosis Association, 8000 Corporate Drive, Landover, MD 20785

National Wheelchair Athletic Association, 3595 E. Fountain Blvd., Colorado Springs, CO 80910

Neurotics Anonymous International Liaison, 11140 Bainbridge Dr., Little Rock, AR 72212

§Orton Dyslexia Society, 724 York Rd., Baltimore, MD 21204

Osteogenesis Imperfecta Foundation, P.O. Box 14807, Clearwater, FL 34629

Overeaters Anonymous, 4025 Spencer St., Torrance, CA 90503

Paget's Disease Foundation, P.O. Box 2772, Brooklyn, NY 11202

§Parents Anonymous, 6733 S. Sepulveda, Los Angeles, CA 90045 [child abuse]

People-to-People Committee for the Handicapped, P.O. Box 18131, Washington, DC 20036

§Phoenix Society, 11 Rust Hill Rd., Levittown, PA 19056 [burn injuries]

§Planned Parenthood—World Population, 902 Broadway, 10th Floor, New York, NY 10010

Psoriasis Research Institute, P.O. Box V, Stanford, CA 94305

Public Citizen Health Research Group, 2000 P St., N.W., Washington, DC 20036

RAND Corporation, P.O. Box 2138, Santa Monica, CA 90407

Reach to Recovery, c/o American Cancer Society [mastectomy support group]

Recovery, 802 N. Dearborn St., Chicago, IL 60610 [mental illness]

§Resolve, 5 Water St., Arlington, MA 02174 [infertility]

§RP Foundation Fighting Blindness, 1401 Mt. Royal Ave., Baltimore, MD 21217 [retinitis pigmentosa and similar degenerative diseases]

Secular Organizations for Sobriety (SOS), Box 5, Buffalo, NY 14215

Self-Help Center, 1600 Dodge Ave., Evanston, IL 60201

Scoliosis Association, P.O. Box 51353, Raleigh, NC 27609

*Sister Kenny Institute, 800 E. 28th St., at Chicago Ave., Minneapolis, MN 55407

*Society for Clinical and Experimental Hypnosis, 128-A Kings Park Drive, Liverpool, NY 13090

*Society for Computer Medicine, 1901 Fort Meyer Drive, Arlington, VA 22208

Society for the Right to Die, 250 W. 57th St., New York, NY 10017.

§Spina Bifida Association of America, 1700 Rockville Pike, Rockville, MD 20852

Stroke Club International, 805 12th St., Galveston, TX 77550

Suicide Prevention Center of Los Angeles, 626 S. Kingsley Dr., Los Angeles, CA 90005

Take Off Pounds Sensibly (TOPS), P.O. Box 07360, Milwaukee, WI 53207

§Tourette Syndrome Association, 42-40 Bell Blvd., Bayside, NY 11361

§United Cerebral Palsy Associations, 7 Penn Plaza, New York, NY 10001

United Network for Organ Sharing (UNOS), P.O. Box 13770, Richmond, VA 23225.

§United Ostomy Association, 36 Executive Park, Irvine, CA 92714

United Parkinson Foundation, 360 W. Superior St., Chicago, IL 60610

§United Scleroderma Foundation, P.O. Box 350, Watsonville, CA 95077

*United States Pharmacopeial Convention, Inc., 12601 Twinbrook Parkway, Rockville, MD 20852 [Drug publications]

Weight Watchers International, Jericho Atrium, 500 N. Broadway, Jericho, NY 11753

Wellness and Health Activation Networks, P.O. Box 923, Vienna, VA 22182 [self-help and healthy lifestyles]

Toll-Free Numbers

Government Agencies and Services

AIDS Clinical Trials Information Service	(800) 874-2572	
AIDS Information Hotline (Public Health Service)	(800) 342-2437	
AIDS National Information Clearinghouse	(800) 458-5231	
Cancer Information Service	(800) 422-6237	HI (800) 524-1234 MD (301) 427-8656
Consumer Product Safety Commission	(800) 638-2772	AK, HI (800) 638-8270 MD (800) 492-8104
Drug-Free Workplace Helpline	(800) 843-4971	
Fraud Hotline (office of Inspector General)	(800) 424-5210	
Hill-Burton Hospital Free Care [referrals for free care]	(800) 638-0742	MD (800) 492-0359
Medicare Fraud	(800) 237-2832	
National Clearinghouse for Alcohol and Drug Information	(800) 729-6686	
National Drug Abuse Treatment Hotline	(800) 662-4357	
National Health Information Center	(800) 336-4797	MD (301) 565-4167
National Information Center on Orphan Drugs and Rare Diseases (FDA)	(800) 456-3505	MD (301) 565-4167
National Institute for Occupational Safety and Health	(800) 356-4674	
National Rehabilitation Information Center	(800) 346-2742	
National Resource Center on Child Abuse and Neglect	(800) 227-5242	

National Second Surgical Opinion Program	(800) 638-6833	MD (800) 492-6833
Safety Drinking Water Hotline (EPA)	(800) 426-4791	DC (202) 382-5533
U.S. Pharmacopeial Reporting Program [problems with devices]	(800) 638-6725	MD (301) 881-0256
USDA Meat and Poultry Hotline	(800) 535-4555	

Nongovernmental Hotlines

Aerobics and Fitness Association of America	(800) 446-2322	
AIDS Hotline (American Social Health Association)	(800) 342-7514	
Al-Anon Family Group Headquarters	(800) 356-9996	
Alcoholism and Drug Addiction Treatment Center	(800) 382-4357	
Alliance of Genetic Support Groups	(800) 336-4363	
Alzheimer's Association	(800) 272-3900	IL (312) 335-3900
American Academy of Allergy and Immunology	(800) 822-2762	
American Academy of Family Physicians	(800) 274-2237	
American Academy of Pediatrics	(800) 433-9016	
American Association of Oral and Maxillofacial Surgeons	(800) 467-5268	
American Association on Mental Retardation	(800) 387-1968	
American Board of Medical Specialties	(800) 776-2378	
American Cancer Society Cancer Response Line	(800) 227-2345	
American College of Cardiology	(800) 253-4636	MD (301) 897-5400
American Council of the Blind	(800) 424-8666	
American Council on Alcoholism	(800) 527-5344	
American Diabetes Association	(800) 232-3472	DC, VA (703) 549-1500
American Foundation for the Blind	(800) 232-5463	NY (212) 620-2147
American Heart Association	(800) 242-1793	
American Kidney Fund	(800) 638-8299	MD (800) 492-8361
American Leprosy Missions	(800) 543-3131	NJ (201) 794-8650
American Liver Foundation	(800) 223-0179	NJ (201) 857-2626
American Mental Health Counselors Association	(800) 326-2642	
American Mental Health Fund	(800) 433-5959	IL (800) 826-2336
American Narcolepsy Association	(800) 222-6085	
American Osteopathic Association	(800) 621-1773	
American Paralysis Association	(800) 225-0292	NJ (201) 379-2690
American Physical Therapy Association [sports injuries]	(800) 955-7848	
American SIDS Institute (sudden infant death syndrome)	(800) 232-7437	GA (800) 847-7437
American Society of Plastic and Reconstructive Surgeons	(800) 635-0635	
American Speech-Language-Hearing Association	(800) 638-8255	MD (301) 897-8682
American Trauma Society	(800) 556-7890	MD (301) 420-4189
Amyotrophic Lateral Sclerosis (ALS) Association	(800) 782-4747	
Anorexia Bulimia Treatment and Education Center	(800) 332-2832	MD (301) 332-9800
Arthritis Foundation Information Line	(800) 283-7800	
Asthma and Allergy Foundation	(800) 727-8462	
Birth Control Information Line	(800) 468-3637	
Bulimia Anorexia Self-Help Crisis Hotline	(800) 227-4785	
Candlelighters Childhood Cancer Foundation	(800) 366-2223	
Chemical Referral Center [health and safety information]	(800) 262-8200	DC, AK (202) 887-1315
Children's Craniofacial Association	(800) 535-3643	
Children's Hospice International	(800) 242-4453	VA (703) 684-0330
Cleft Palate Foundation	(800) 242-5338	
Cochlear Implant Center	(800) 458-4999	
Consumer Health Information Research Institute	(800) 821-6671	
Cooley's Anemia Foundation	(800) 221-3571	NY (212) 522-7222
Cornelia De Lange Syndrome Foundation	(800) 223-8355	CT (203) 693-0159
Crisis Line [depression, suicide, sexual abuse, pregnancy]	(800) 866-9600	
Crohn's and Colitis Foundation of America	(800) 343-3637	NY (212) 683-3440
Cystic Fibrosis Foundation	(800) 344-4823	VA, DC (703) 549-1500

Endometriosis Association	(800) 992-3636	WI (414) 962-8972
Epilepsy Foundation of America	(800) 332-1000	MD (301) 459-1000
Guide Dog Foundation for the Blind	(800) 548-4337	
Heart Information Service (Texas Heart Institute)	(800) 292-2221	
Histiocytosis Association of America	(800) 548-2758	
HIV Patient Assistance Program [free medication for needy]	(800) 722-9294	
Hospice Education Institute	(800) 331-1620	
Human Growth Foundation	(800) 451-6434	
Huntington's Disease Society of America	(800) 345-4372	NY (212) 242-1968
Impotence Information Center	(800) 843-4315	
Institute for Aerobics Research	(800) 635-7050	
Juvenile Diabetes Foundation International	(800) 223-1138	NY (212) 889-7575
Lighthouse National Center for Vision and Aging	(800) 334-5497	
Living Bank Organ Donor Registry	(800) 528-2971	TX (713) 528-2971
Look Good . . . Feel Better [beauty advice for cancer patients]	(800) 395-5665	
Lung Line Information Service	(800) 222-5864	
Lupus Foundation of America	(800) 558-0121	MD (301) 670-9292
Medic-Alert Foundation International [emergency medical identification]	(800) 432-5378	
Mothers Against Drunk Driving (MADD)	(800) 438-6233	
Myasthenia Gravis Foundation	(800) 541-5454	
National Abortion Federation	(800) 772-9100	DC (202) 546-9060
National Alliance for the Mentally Ill	(800) 950-6264	
National Association for Hearing and Speech	(800) 638-8225	HI, AK, MD (301) 897-0039 call collect
National Association for Parents of the Visually Impaired	(800) 562-6265	
National Association for Sickle Cell Disease	(800) 421-8453	CA (213) 736-5455
National Association of Social Workers	(800) 638-8799	
National Center for Nutrition and Dietetics	(800) 366-1655	
National Center for Stuttering	(800) 221-2483	
National Child Abuse Hotline	(800) 422-4253	
National Child Safety Council Childwatch	(800) 222-1464	
National Cocaine Hotline	(800) 262-1463	
National Council on Alcoholism and Drug Dependence	(800) 622-2255	
National Council on Child Abuse and Family Violence	(800) 222-2000	
National Council on the Aging	(800) 424-9046	
National Domestic Violence Hotline	(800) 333-7233	
National Down Syndrome Society Hotline	(800) 221-4602	NY (212) 460-9330
National Easter Seal Society [rehabilitation]	(800) 221-6827	
National Emergency Medicine Association	(800) 332-6362	
National Enuresis Society	(800) 637-5379	
National Eye Care Project Helpline	(800) 222-3937	
National Food Addiction Hotline	(800) 872-0088	
National Foundation for Depressive Illness	(800) 248-4344	
National Gaucher Foundation	(800) 925-8885	
National Head Injury Foundation	(800) 444-6443	
National Headache Foundation	(800) 843-2256	IL (800) 523-8858
National Hemophilia Foundation	(800) 424-2634	
National Hepatitis Hotline	(800) 233-1079	
National Hospice Organization	(800) 658-8898	
National Information System and Clearinghouse [disabilities in children]	(800) 922-9234	SC (800) 922-1107
National Kidney Foundation	(800) 622-9010	
National Lymphedema Network	(800) 541-3259	
National Marrow Donor Program	(800) 654-1257	

National Mental Health Association	(800) 969-6642	
National Multiple Sclerosis Society	(800) 624-8236	
National Neurofibromatosis Foundation	(800) 323-7938	NY (212) 460-8980
National Organization for Rare Disorders	(800) 447-6673	CT (203) 746-6518
National Parkinson Foundation	(800) 327-4545	FL (800) 433-7022
National Pesticide Telecommunications Network	(800) 858-7378	
National Pregnancy Hotline	(800) 852-5683	CA (800) 831-5881
National Retinitis Pigmentosa Foundation	(800) 683-5555	
National Reye's Syndrome Foundation	(800) 233-7393	
National Runaway Switchboard [crisis intervention]	(800) 621-4000	
National Sexual Addiction Hotline	(800) 321-2066	
National SIDS Foundation [sudden infant death syndrome]	(800) 221-7437	MD (301) 459-3388
National Society to Prevent Blindness	(800) 331-2020	
National Spinal Cord Injury Association	(800) 962-9629	
National STD Hotline [sexually transmitted diseases]	(800) 227-8922	
National Stroke Association	(800) 367-1990	
National Tuberous Sclerosis Association	(800) 225-6872	
Organ Donor Hotline (UNOS)	(800) 243-6667	
Orton Dyslexia Society	(800) 222-3123	MD (301) 296-0232
Parents Anonymous [child abuse]	(800) 421-0353	CA (800) 352-0386
Parkinson's Disease Foundation	(800) 457-6676	
Peyronia's Society of America	(800) 346-4875	KS (316) 283-2456
Phoenix Society [burns]	(800) 888-2876	
Planned Parenthood Federation of America	(800) 829-7732	
Prostate Information Line	(800) 543-9632	
Recovery of Male Potency	(800) 835-7667	MI (313) 966-3219
Resolve [infertility]	(800) 662-1016	
RP Fighting Blindness [retinitis pigmentosa]	(800) 638-2300	
Simon Foundation [urinary incontinence]	(800) 237-4666	
Spinal Bifida Information and Referral	(800) 621-3141	MD (301) 770-7222
Sturge-Weber Foundation	(800) 627-5482	
Suicide and Rape 24-Hour Emergency Services	(800) 333-4444	
Target Resource Center [alcohol and drug abuse education]	(800) 366-6667	
Tourette Syndrome Association	(800) 237-0717	
United Cerebral Palsy	(800) 872-1827	
United Leukodystrophy Foundation	(800) 728-5483	
United Ostomy Association	(800) 826-0826	
United Scleroderma Foundation	(800) 722-4673	
University of Alabama Nutrition Hotline	(800) 231-3438	
Visiting Nurse Associations of America	(800) 426-2547	
Women's Sports Foundation	(800) 227-3988	AK, HI, CA (212) 972-9170
Y-Me Breast Cancer Support Program	(800) 221-2141	(708) 799-8228

Magazines

Consumer Reports, P.O. Box 53029, Boulder, CO 80322

FDA Consumer, Superintendent of Documents, P.O. Box 371954, Pittsburgh, PA 15250

Health, P.O. Box 54218, Boulder, CO 80322

Living Well, P.O. Box 7550, Red Oak, IA 51591

Priorities, American Council on Science and Health, 1995 Broadway, New York, NY 10023

Skeptical Inquirer, Box 703, Buffalo, NY 14226

Food News for Consumers, Superintendent of Documents, Washington, DC 20402 [food safety]

Food Review, ERS-NASS, P.O. Box 1608, Rockville, MD 20849 [food safety and economics]

Your Health & Fitness, General Learning Corp., 60 Revere Drive, Northbrook, IL 60062

Newsletters

Consumer Reports on Health, Box 36356, Boulder, CO 80322.

Contemporary Nutrition, P.O. Box 3588, Wyoming, MN 55092 [free to qualified professionals]

Dairy Council Digest, 6300 N. River Rd., Rosemont, IL 60018

Edell Health Letter, P.O. Box 57812, Boulder, COL 80322

Environmental Nutrition, 2112 Broadway, New York, NY 10023

FTC News Notes, Federal Trade Commission, Washington, DC 20580 [free to eligible persons]

Harvard Health Letter, P.O. Box 420300, Palm Coast, FL 32142

Harvard Heart Letter, P.O. Box 420379, Palm Coast, FL 32142

Healthline, Mosby–Year Book, Inc., 11830 Westline Industrial Drive, St. Louis, MO 63146

Johns Hopkins Medical Letter, Health after 50, P.O. Box 420179, Palm Coast, FL 32142

Lahey Clinic Health Letter, P.O. Box 541, Burlington, MA 01805

Law Enforcement Report, U.S. Postal Service, Washington, DC 20260 [free to eligible persons]

Lawrence Review of Natural Products, Facts and Comparisons, 111 West Port Plaza, Suite 423, St. Louis, MO 63146 [herbs and other naturally occurring products]

Living Well, P.O. Box 7550, Red Oak, IA 51591

Mayo Clinic Health Letter, P.O. Box 53889, Boulder, CO 80322

Mirkin Report, P.O. Box 6608, Silver Spring, MD 20916

NCAHF Newsletter, National Council Against Health Fraud, P.O. Box 1276, Loma Linda, CA 92354

Nutrition Forum, P.O. Box 1747, Allentown, PA 18105

Obesity and Health, Rt. 2, Box 905, Hettinger, ND 58639

Prevention Report, USPHS Office of Disease Promotion, 330 C St., S.W., Room 2137, Washington, DC 20201

The Health Letter, 1703 Kaiser Ave., Irvine, CA 92714

Tufts University Diet and Nutrition Letter, P.O. Box 57857, Boulder, CO 80322

University of California, Berkeley Wellness Letter, P.O. Box 10922, Des Moines, IA 50340

University of Texas Lifetime Health Letter, P.O. Box 420342, Palm Coast, FL 32142

Glossary

accreditation: Certification by an accrediting organization that a facility meets its standards. Hospitals and other health care facilities are accredited by the Joint Commission on Accreditation of Healthcare Organizations. Colleges and professional schools are accredited by agencies approved by the U.S. Secretary of Education or the Council on Postsecondary Accreditation.

acetaminophen: Nonprescription drug used to relieve pain and reduce fever; the active ingredient in Tylenol and Datril.

acidosis: State in which the blood is more acidic than normal.

acupuncture: System of treatment that purports to balance the body's "life force" by inserting needles (or using other procedures) at points where imaginary horizontal and vertical lines meet on the surface of the body.

acupressure (shiatsu): A technique that uses finger pressure instead of needles at "acupuncture points."

addiction: Dependence on a substance that can cause withdrawal symptoms when stopped.

administrative complaint: Civil complaint alleging that a law has been broken, which can lead to a formal hearing before an administrative law judge.

adrenaline: Hormone, produced and stored by the adrenal glands, which can cause increased heartbeat and other reactions that prepare the body to meet emergency situations.

advance directive: Document in which a person states choices for medical treatment or designates who should make treatment choices if the person should lose decision-making capacity.

aerobic exercise: Exercise that uses large quantities of oxygen and promotes cardiorespiratory fitness.

AIDS (acquired immunodeficiency syndrome): Fatal disease in which the body's immune system breaks down, leaving the body susceptible to certain cancers and serious infections.

alkalosis: State in which the blood is more alkaline (less acidic) than normal.

allergen: Substance that, in contact with the body, produces an allergic reaction.

allergic reaction: Excessive reaction of the body's immune system to a food, drug, or other substance that is ordinarily harmless. In susceptible individuals, exposure to an allergen can cause certain cells to release histamine, which can cause sneezing, wheezing, hives, and other allergic reactions.

allopathy: Term coined by Samuel Hahnemann (founder of homeopathy) to designate the conventional medical practice of his time. Used in this manner, allopathy today would encompass all of medical science. However, the term falsely implies that scientific medicine is just one of many alternative approaches, as are homeopathy, chiropractic, Chinese medicine, and holistic medicine.

alopecia: Medical term for baldness.

"alternative" health care: Misleading term used to characterize many types of unscientific methods. Since ineffective methods are not true alternatives to effective ones, the terms "unscientific" or "dubious" are more appropriate.

AMA: abbreviation for American Medical Association.

ambulatory care: Outpatient care.

amino acid: Building block of proteins.

anaerobic exercise: Exercise, such as sprinting, done without using the oxygen one breathes.

analgesia: Pain relief.

analgesic, external: Topically applied substance that can relieve pain.

analgesic, internal: Drug taken by mouth to relieve pain.

anecdotal evidence: Reports of personal observations that have not been made under strict experimental conditions.

anesthesia: Loss of sensation, with or without loss of consciousness.

angioplasty: Reconstruction of a blood vessel.

anorexia: Loss of appetite.

anorexia nervosa: Dangerous condition whose victims lose interest in eating and become dangerously thin, usually as a result of false beliefs about being too fat.

antacid: OTC product used to neutralize hydrochloric acid produced by the stomach.

anthroposophical medicine: Practice based on an occult philosophy said to relate humankind to the natural environment, with emphasis on color and rhythm.

antigen: Substance that, as a result of coming in contact with appropriate tissues of an animal body, induces antibody formation.

antihistamine: Drug that counteracts histamine, a substance released during allergic reactions, which can cause localized redness, edema, and mucus production.

antimicrobial: Substance that kills germs or inhibits their growth.

antipruritic: Substance that prevents or relieves itching.

antipyretic: Drug that reduces fever.

aphrodisiac: Substance (falsely) claimed to increase a sexual stimulation.

aplastic anemia: Life-threatening disorder in which the bone marrow fails to produce adequate numbers of circulating blood cells.

applied kinesiology: Pseudoscience based on the belief that every organ dysfunction is accompanied by a specific muscle weakness.

arrythmia: Irregular heart rhythm.

arteriosclerosis: Chronic disease characterized by hardening and thickening of artery walls.

aseptic: Free of microorganisms.

astigmatism: Uneven curvature of the cornea or surface of the lens of the eye, which distorts vision by preventing light rays from focusing properly on the light-sensitive membrane at the back of the eye (retina).

atherosclerosis: Accumulation of deposits of cholesterol and fibrous tissue within the inner walls of large and medium-sized arteries; extensive build-up can result in blockage of blood flow.

autointoxication: Unfounded concept that intestinal contents stagnate and putrefy to form toxins that are absorbed and cause chronic poisoning of the body.

ayurvedic medicine: Pseudoscience said to be based on a traditional Indian approach that combines herbs, purifying therapies, and so-called rejuvenation techniques.

balanced diet: Selection of a wide variety of foods from each of the various food groups.

bile: Yellow or greenish fluid secreted by the liver and passed into the small intestine, where it helps in the digestion and absorption of fats.

bioequivalent: Term used to describe drugs whose absorption, blood levels, and therapeutic actions are equivalent.

biofeedback: Relaxation technique using an electronic device that continuously signals pulse rate, muscle tension, or other body function by tone or visual signal.

bioflavonoid: Pigmented substance, not essential in humans, once thought to have vitamin activity. No evidence exists that bioflavonoids are useful for the treatment of any human ailment.

biopsy: Removal and examination of a sample of tissue from a living patient for the purpose of diagnosis or prognosis of disease.

biorhythms: Pseudoscience based on the theory that human behavior is characterized by regular body rhythms that begin at the moment of birth.

board-certified specialist: Health professional who has completed accredited training and passed the examination given by a specialty board.

board-eligible: One who has the required training and experience to take a certifying examination but has not taken or passed the examination. Although the American Board of Medical Specialties has officially abandoned the term, it is still in common use.

bran: Outer coat of a cereal grain.

calculus: Hard substance, such as a kidney stone, gallstone, or the hard substance (calcified plaque) that can accumulate on the surface of teeth.

calorie: Unit that expresses the energy value of foods. Carbohydrates and proteins contain 4 calories per gram; fat contains 9 calories per gram.

candidiasis hypersensitivity: Fad diagnosis based on the notion that multiple common symptoms are the result of sensitivity to the common yeast *Candida albicans.*

capitation: Method of paying health care providers according to the number of patients they agree to serve rather than the amount of service rendered per visit.

caplet: A drug tablet shaped like a capsule.

carcinogenic: Cancer-causing.

carcinoma: A malignant tumor of the epithelium. Epithelial cells form the outer layer of the skin and line the gastrointestinal tract, the genitourinary tract, the glands, and other free surfaces within the body.

carcinoma in situ: A cancer that lies within the epithelium and has not invaded adjacent tissues; *see carcinoma.*

cardiovascular: Pertaining to the heart and blood vessels.

cardiorespiratory efficiency: Ability of the heart, blood vessels, and lungs to deliver oxygen to body parts.

caries: Tooth decay.

carotene: Yellow pigment found in various plant and animal tissues that is the precursor of vitamin A. An excessive amount of carotene can cause carotenemia, a condition in which the skin turns yellow.

cataract: Clouding of the lens of the eye.

CAT scan: Imaging method in which the density of an area of the body is determined with the use of x-rays fed into a computer to create a picture on a screen similar to a cross-sectional photograph; used in study of body structures.

caveat emptor: Let the buyer beware.

caveat vendor: Let the seller beware.

cease and desist order: Order given by an administrative law judge to stop unlawful activity; if not appealed, the order becomes final.

cellulite: Medically unrecognized term sometimes used to describe dimpled fat commonly found on the thighs of women.

cellulose: Main component of plant cell walls. A component of dietary fiber, cellulose absorbs water readily and makes stools bulkier and softer.

cervix: Lower part of the uterus. An opening in the cervix connects the uterus to the vagina.

CHAMPUS: Federal insurance program for military dependents and retirees.

chemosurgery: Use of caustic chemicals to remove diseased or unwanted tissue.

Chinese medicine: A collection of practices that includes acupuncture, the use of herbs and dietary procedures, pulse diagnosis, and other procedures.

chiropractic: Pseudoscience based on the false belief that most ailments are caused by misaligned spinal bones.

cholesterol level: The amount of cholesterol in the blood, a factor that can help indicate the risk of heart disease.

chronic fatigue syndrome: Illness in which profound fatigue persists or recurs for at least six months and is accompanied by several flulike symptoms such as throat inflammation, enlarged lymph nodes, low-grade fever, muscle and joint pains, headache, difficulty in concentrating, and exercise intolerance.

civil procedure: Noncriminal legal action such as an administrative hearing or a civil court action.

clinical: Related to the treatment or examination of patients, for example, clinical study, clinical practice, clinical psychology.

clinical ecology: Pseudoscience based on the belief that multiple symptoms are triggered by hypersensitivity to common foods and chemicals.

closed panel HMO: Insurance plan that covers services only from specific providers.

coinsurance: Partial payment required from policyholder for services rendered.

colonic irrigation: High-colonic enema performed through a rubber tube inserted through the rectum for a distance of 20 to 30 inches. Warm water is pumped in and out through the tube, typically using 20 or more gallons. The procedure has no medical justification but is used by proponents of "autointoxication."

colonoscope: Instrument passed through the rectum to examine almost the entire length of the large intestine.

complete protein: Protein that contains all of the essential amino acids.

complex carbohydrates (starches): Compounds composed of long chains of glucose molecules.

comprehensive health insurance: Broad coverage that includes basic health insurance plus major medical and/or catastrophic coverage.

confidentiality: Ethical principal that information disclosed during the course of treatment may not be revealed without the patient's consent.

congenital: Present at birth.

consent decree (or order): Court-approved agreement (usually to stop behavior that has been challenged by a regulatory agency) that has the force of law.

Consumer Bill of Rights: Principles devised by President Kennedy, who stated that consumers have the right to safety, to be informed, to choose, and to be heard.

consumer health: Information pertaining to the intelligent purchase and use of products and services that will directly affect one's health.

continuing medical education (CME): Postgraduate educational activities aimed at maintaining, updating, and extending professional skills. Many professional organizations, state licensing boards, and hospitals require CME participation.

contraceptive: Substance or device used to prevent pregnancy.

coordination of benefits: Provision of an insurance policy that prohibits collecting benefits from two or more policies for medical care, thereby profiting when you are ill. After the primary company pays, other companies will calculate their coverage of the remainder. All group policies contain a coordination clause, but most individual policies do not.

coronary: Pertaining to the heart.

cosmetics: Substances intended to be rubbed, poured, sprinkled, or sprayed on the body to cleanse, beautify, increase attractiveness, or alter appearance.

crown: The portion of the tooth normally visible above the gum line.

cryosurgery: Destruction of diseased or unwanted tissues by freezing.

cystoscope: Instrument used to look inside the bladder and urinary passageway (urethra).

daily reference values (DRVs): A system of food component standards which the FDA has proposed to make food produce labels more useful (see Chapter 12).

decongestant: Drug that constricts blood vessels and membranes of the nose to relieve stuffiness.

deductible: Amount paid out of pocket before insurance coverage takes effect.

defensive medicine: Use of medically questionable procedures (such as x-ray examinations following minor head injuries) done to protect the doctor in the event of a malpractice suit.

defibrillator: Device used to administer an electric shock to attempt to restart a heart that has stopped beating.

delusion: False belief, not ordinarily accepted by other members of the person's culture, which is firmly held despite obvious proof or evidence to the contrary.

dentifrice: Toothpaste, gel, or powder used in brushing the teeth.

denturist: Technician who provides dentures directly to the public without supervision or referral from a dentist. Denturism is illegal in most states.

dermabrasion: Process that removes the upper layers of the skin to improve the appearance of scars.

dermatitis: Inflammation of the skin.

diathermy: Generation of heat in tissue by electric currents for medical or surgical purposes.

dietary guidelines: see U.S. Dietary Guidelines.

dilate: Expand or widen.

diploma mill: Unaccredited organization that awards degrees without requiring its students to meet educational standards for degrees established and traditionally followed by reputable educational institutions.

diplomate: One who has passed an examination given by the National Board of Medical Examiners (one route to state licensure) or a specialty board.

diuretic: Drug that increases the output of urine.

DNR: Abbreviation for "do not resuscitate," a medical order to refrain from cardiopulmonary resuscitation if a patient's heart stops beating.

double-blind test: An experiment in which neither the experimental subjects nor those responsible for the treatment or data collection know which subjects receive the treatment being tested and which receive something else (such as a placebo).

DRGs (diagnosis-related groups): Categories created under Medicare for payment of hospital bills according to the patient's diagnosis rather than the length of stay or specific treatment rendered.

drug (under federal law): Any substance intended to be used in the prevention, care, mitigation, or treatment of disease.

dysmenorrhea: Menstrual pain.

edema: Swelling of tissues as a result of the presence of abnormally large amounts of fluid between the cells.

elective procedure: Procedure (usually surgical) that is not an emergency.

electrosurgery: Use of electricity to destroy benign lesions on skin.

emphysema: Chronic disease in which the ability to move air in and out of the lungs is impaired.

energy medicine: Term used by practitioners who claim to be able to detect and manipulate "subtle energies," some of which cannot be measured. This category includes the alleged energies involved in psychic healing, prayer, meditation, hope, faith, and the will to live. Energy medicine also is said to encompass acupuncture, electrodiagnosis, homeopathy, and magnet therapy.

endometrium: The lining of the uterus.

endorphins: Narcotic-like substances produced by the body that may relieve pain and produce euphoria.

enrichment: Addition of specific nutrients to a food to maintain established standards of identity for that food.

environmental illness: Term clinical ecologists use to describe what they consider dysregulation of the immune system. Its proponents claim that multiple symptoms can be triggered by hypersensitivity to common foods and chemicals.

enzymes: Protein substances that trigger and speed up (catalyze) chemical reactions within the body.

ESADDI: abbreviation for estimated safe and adequate daily dietary intake for certain essential vitamins and minerals for which data are sufficient to estimate a range of requirements but insufficient for developing an RDA.

essential nutrients: Specific nutrients that cannot be synthesized by the body and therefore must be obtained from food.

estrogens: Female sex hormones involved in the development of secondary sexual characteristics and in the maintenance of menstruation; estrogens are contained in birth control pills and may be administered to control menopausal or postmenopausal symptoms.

expectorant: Drug that stimulates the flow of respiratory tract secretions.

extended care: Long-term care with less nursing and rehabilitative service than that provided at a skilled nursing facility.

false-negative test: Test result that wrongly indicates normalcy.

false-positive test: Test result that wrongly indicates an abnormality.

fee-for-service-care: Professional care for which a fee is earned for each service rendered, as opposed to payment through salary or capitation.

fermentable carbohydrates: Carbohydrates, such as sugars and starches, that can be split into relatively simple substances. In the mouth, saliva and the bacteria in plaque act on these carbohydrates to produce acids that can attack tooth enamel.

fetus: Baby developing in the uterus.

fiber (dietary): Plant constituents of food that are resistant to digestion by human gastrointestinal secretions; also called roughage.

flatulence: Excessive gassiness.

flexibility exercise: Stretching of muscles to increase range of movement.

fluoridation: Addition of fluoride to a community's water supply to prevent tooth decay.

food combining: Dietary practice based on the incorrect notion that various food combinations eaten during the same meal can cause or correct ill health.

food group system: System of classifying foods according to their "leader" nutrients to simplify selection of a balanced diet.

food irradiation: Application of ionizing radiation (x-rays or beta rays) to foods to kill organisms, inhibit sprouting, or delay ripening.

food supplement: Product used to provide nutrients in addition to those found in one's diet.

fortification: The addition of nutrients originally not present (or not present in significant amounts).

gangrene: Local death of tissue resulting from loss of blood supply.

gastrointestinal tract: Digestive pathway, including the esophagus, stomach, small intestine, and large intestine.

generic drug: Drug marketed under its chemical name rather than a trade name. Most generic drugs are less expensive but equal in potency to their brand-name equivalents.

genetic engineering: Techniques of altering plants and animals by modifying their genes. Genetic manipulation has enabled commercial production of insulin, produced several types of hardy crop plants, and shown promise in the treatment of several diseases.

genital: Pertaining to sexual organs.

gingivitis: Inflammation of the gums; the earliest stage of periodontal disease.

glaucoma: Disease in which pressure inside the eye increases; can cause blindness if untreated.

glucose: Simple sugar that is the basic form of food energy for life.

glycogen: Form of glucose that is stored in the liver and muscles.

granola: Common term to describe various mixtures of oats, other grains, fruits, seeds, and nuts. Although granola products are often promoted as "health foods," many of them are high in calories and fat.

hair implantation: Surgical procedure of questionable safety and efficacy in which hair or a hairpiece is anchored to the scalp by use of sutures or other means.

hair transplantation: Surgical grafting of hair-producing tissue from one part of the body to another.

HDL (high-density lipoproteins): Substances in the blood that transport cholesterol from various cells to the liver, from which it can be excreted in the bile. Since this helps to protect blood vessels against heart disease, HDL is often referred to as "good cholesterol."

health freedom (freedom of choice): The right to free choice of health practitioners, practices, and products. Although it is desirable for consumers to be free to make informed choices, promoters of quackery promote this slogan to oppose government interference with their activities.

health maintenance organization (HMO): Prepaid health plan in which patients receive care from designated providers.

heart failure: Inability of the heart to pump enough blood to meet the needs of the body.

hemorrhage: Excessive bleeding.

herb: Plant or plant part valued for its medicinal, savory, or aromatic qualities.

herpes: Family of viruses that can cause acute or periodic skin eruptions, including cold sores (herpes simplex type 1), genital herpes (herpes simplex type 2), shingles (herpes zoster), and chickenpox (herpes zoster).

heterosexual transmission (of disease): Transmission from male to female or from female to male.

holistic medicine: Treatment of the "whole person" (physical and psychologic); the term is often used to promote the use of a wide variety of unscientific methods.

homeopathy: Pseudoscience based on the belief that greatly diluted substances can exert powerful therapeutic effects on the body.

hormone: Substance made in one part of the body that circulates through body fluids to exert its effect on another part of the body.

hospice: Program that enables terminally ill individuals to die comfortably in a homelike setting.

hypercholesterolemia: Medical term for high blood cholesterol level.

hypertension: Medical term for high blood pressure.

hyperthermia: Treatment method in which the temperature of the body or a body part is raised.

hypoglycemia: Low blood sugar. Physiologic hypoglycemia is normal and helps make a person feel hungry. Pathologic hypoglycemia is a rare condition in which severe symptoms occur when the blood sugar drops very low.

hysterectomy: Operation to remove the uterus.

iatrogenic: Pertaining to a health problem that results from a diagnostic or treatment procedure.

ibuprofen: Chemical (generic) name for the analgesic/antiinflammatory drug found in such products as Motrin and Advil.

imaging procedures: Examinations that use x-rays, ultrasound, radioactive chemicals, magnetic waves, or other modalities to visualize the structure or function of specified body parts.

impaired physician: Loosely defined term encompassing any form of physical, mental, or behavioral problem that interferes with a doctor's ability to provide appropriate patient care. The problems can include unethical conduct, mental illness, senility, drug abuse, and/or failure to keep up-to-date.

incidence: The number of new cases of a disease that develop in a population during a specified period, usually a year.

infertility: Inability to conceive a child.

inflammation: Local tissue reaction consisting of swelling, redness, and warmth.

injunction: Court order forbidding a particular act or acts. When an injunction is violated, the court has great leeway in ordering punishment.

inpatient: Person who is treated at a facility while in residence.

insomnia: Inability to sleep.

interferon: Protein molecule, made in tiny amounts by the body's immune system, that helps the body to combat viral diseases and possibly cancer.

intramuscular injection: Injection into a muscle.

intraocular lens: Plastic lens used to replace an abnormal lens (cataract) of the eye.

intravenous: Administered into a vein.

iridology: Pseudoscience based on the theory that most body abnormalities cause abnormal markings in the eye.

isokinetic exercise: Isotonic activity involving maximum contraction of muscles throughout the full range of motion.

Isometric exercise: Contraction of muscles with little or no movement of body parts.

isotonic exercise: Contraction of muscles with movement of body parts.

jaundice: Yellowish pigmentation of the skin, eyes, and other tissues caused by accumulation of bile pigments.

JCAHO: A commonly used abbreviation for the Joint Commission on Accreditation of Healthcare Organizations, formerly called Joint Commission on Accreditation of Hospitals (JCAH); see *accreditation*. The organization itself never uses "JCAHO" but refers to itself as the Joint Commission.

ketosis: Abnormal metabolic state brought about by incomplete breakdown of fatty acids into ketone bodies; may result from low-carbohydrate or starvation diet.

kinesiology: Study of the mechanics and anatomy of motion and the functions of muscles; a respectable science, as distinguished from "applied kinesiology," a pseudoscience based on the theory that muscular imbalance is a major factor in most diseases.

laparoscope: Instrument that can be inserted into the abdominal cavity to visualize its contents or perform surgery (such as female sterilization or gallbladder removal).

LDL (low-density lipoproteins): Substances that contribute to fatty deposits (atherosclerosis) in the major arteries and are associated with increased risk of atherosclerosis. For this reason they are often called "bad cholesterol."

legumes: A group of vegetables that includes peas and beans, including black beans, black-eyed peas, broad beans, chickpeas, kidney beans, lima beans, pinto beans, soybeans, lentils, split peas, and peanuts.

lesion: Abnormal change in the structure of an organ or body part resulting from injury or disease, especially a change that is circumscribed and well defined. Examples are cuts, burns, skin eruptions, and tumors.

leukoplakia: Precancerous condition in which thickened white patches occur on mucous membranes, most commonly those of the tongue, mouth, or female genitalia.

life expectancy: Average number of years that people a certain age are likely to live.

lipid: Chemical name for fat.

living will: Document in which the signer requests to be allowed to die rather than be kept alive by artificial means in the event of becoming terminally ill.

long-term care: The continuum of broad-ranged maintenance and health services to chronically ill, disabled, or mentally retarded persons. Services may be provided on an inpatient (rehabilitation facility, nursing home, mental hospital), outpatient, or at-home basis.

loss ratio: Percentage of premium dollars an insurance company pays in benefits to policyholders; also called benefit-cost ratio.

macrobiotic diet: Restricted diet, high in whole grains, claimed by its advocates to improve health and prolong life.

macronutrient: Nutrient needed in large amounts.

major medical insurance: Coverage to offset heavy medical expenses from prolonged illness or serious injury.

malaise: Medical term for general discomfort or uneasiness, which often is an early sign of illness.

malocclusion: Improper alignment of the jaws or teeth.

managed care: Health-care system (such as HMO or PPO) that integrates the financing and delivery of services by using selected providers, utilization review, and financial incentives for members who use the providers and procedures authorized by the plan.

mania: Excitement of psychotic proportions manifested by mental and physical hyperactivity, disorganized behavior, and/or elevation of mood.

manic-depressive psychosis: Also called manic-depressive illness. A mental impairment characterized by recurrent periods of mania, depression, or both.

marker: A substance whose blood level is followed to measure the progress of treatment, mainly of certain types of cancer.

media: Information sources, including radio, television, newspapers, magazines, books, newsletters, and pamphlets.

Medicaid: Federally subsidized, state-run program of health care for indigent persons.

medically indigent: Term referring to people who have enough money for most expenses but are unable to pay for sudden high costs of health care. Most medically indigent individuals are employed but cannot afford (or cannot obtain) adequate health insurance.

Medicare: Federal health insurance program for persons 65 years of age or older and for certain disabled younger persons.

megavitamin therapy: Unorthodox treatment using high dosages of vitamins, usually 10 times the RDA or more.

menopause: The period of life during which menstruation normally stops—often referred to as the change of life.

metaanalysis: A scientific review process in which conclusions are reached by quantifying a large number of research studies rather than interpreting them subjectively.

metabolic therapy: Loosely defined unorthodox program that may include megadoses of vitamins, oral enzymes, pangamic acid, coffee enemas, and a low-protein diet.

metabolism: Sum of the physical and chemical processes by which the body is maintained; also, the reactions involved in energy production.

METs (metabolic equivalents): A measure of the intensity of physical activity. METS are multiples of the resting metabolic rate, which can be expressed in terms of total oxygen consumption or oxygen consumption per unit of body weight. One MET is the amount of oxygen consumed while a person sits at rest: approximately 3.5 ml of oxygen per kilogram of body weight per minute.

micronutrient: Nutrient needed in only tiny amounts.

misbranding: Misrepresentation, as defined by the Federal Food, Drug, and Cosmetic Act, in the labeling or advertising of a food or drug.

morbidity: Measure of the effects of disease on a population. Incidence and prevalence are both measures of morbidity.

mortality (of a disease): The total number of deaths from a given disease in a population during a specific interval of time, usually a year.

mucous membrane: Mucus-producing tissue that lines the body's air passageways and digestive tract.

naprapathy: A variant of chiropractic based on the philosophy that contractions of the body's soft tissue cause illness by interfering with neurovascular function.

natural hygiene: A philosophy of health and "natural living" that emphasizes fasting and food combining; *see* food combining.

naturopathy: Pseudoscience based on the belief that the basic cause of disease is violation of nature's laws.

neurotic reaction: Nervous response resulting from inner emotional conflict in which the person is generally able to separate what is real from what is not.

new drug: Drug that is not generally recognized by experts as safe and effective; see *safe and effective.* Drugs cannot be legally marketed in interstate commerce unless they have FDA approval or are generally recognized as safe and effective for their intended use. Intended use can be determined from claims in labeling, advertising, or other statements to prospective buyers.

nutripathy: Pseudoscience in which urine and saliva tests are used to detect "energy imbalances" that can be corrected with a variety of supplements and special formulas. The data are interpreted using "a mathematical formula for perfect health, based on the biological frequencies of living matter." The formula was developed by Carey Reams, a self-proclaimed biophysicist who was prosecuted during the 1970s for practicing medicine without a license.

obese: Having excess body weight as a result of the presence of surplus fat.

obsessive-compulsive disorder: Mental problem in which people have recurrent ideas, thoughts, images, or impulses that they know are irrational but cannot control. They also may engage in repetitive actions such as excessive handwashing, which they recognize as irrational.

occlusion: The act of closure or state of being closed or obstructed. In dentistry the term refers to the contact between upper and lower teeth (for example, malocclusion). In medical practice it is used to describe blockage of a body passageway such as a blood vessel or duct.

oncologist: Physician who specializes in the treatment of cancers.

open panel: Prepaid insurance plan in which any physician (or other covered type of health professional) can become a provider under the plan.

opportunistic infection: Infection by an organism that normally is harmless but is able to thrive when an individual's immunity is impaired by a serious disease (such as cancer or AIDS) or by treatment with drugs that suppress the immune system.

orthomolecular treatment: Dubious treatment method claimed to treat diseases by administering the "right" nutrient molecules (for example, vitamins, minerals) at the right time; also called meganutrient therapy.

osteopath: Physician who is a graduate of an osteopathic medical school. Osteopathy was originally based on false beliefs but gradually abandoned them and incorporated the theories and practices of scientific medicine.

osteoporosis: Thinning of the bones, common in postmenopausal women.

otitis: Inflammation of the ear. Otitis media, the most common cause of earaches, is an inflammation of the middle ear.

outpatient: Person who is treated at a facility without residing there.

over-the-counter (OTC) drugs: Nonprescription drugs.

overweight: Weighing more than the amount listed in a standard height-weight table.

ovulation: Release of a mature egg from an ovary.

palliation: Treatment that lessens symptoms but does not cure.

palpate: To examine by touching with the hands.

palpitation: Noticeably forceful heartbeat.

paradigm: A model or overall understanding of how things work. If a new concept doesn't fit, scientists must determine whether the new concept is flawed or the current paradigm must be altered. An example of a faulty paradigm is the claim by "alternative" practitioners that disease is caused by body "weaknesses" that their various methods can correct.

paranormal: Not measurable or explainable by currently accepted scientific methods or theories.

patent medicine: Formerly, medicine whose formula was protected from being copied by a patent from the U.S. Patent Office.

Patient's Bill of Rights: Lists of ethical principles that define considerate and ethical treatment in a hospital or nursing home.

patient package insert (PPI): Leaflet that tells how to use a drug; includes information on the drug's purposes, hazards, and side effects.

pedal: Pertaining to the foot.

percussion: Technique of physical examination in which a body part, usually the chest or abdomen, is tapped with the hand in order to produce a sound that reflects the density of the underlying organ(s).

periodontal disease: General term for inflammatory and degenerative diseases of the gums and other structures that surround the teeth and attach them to their sockets. The word *periodontal* comes from two Greek words meaning "around the tooth."

pharmacognosy: The science of medicines from natural sources.

photochromatic: Term applied to some eyeglass lenses that lighten or darken in response to the amount of ultraviolet light present.

phrenology: Pseudoscience based on the belief that the contours of the skull reflect the person's mental faculties and character.

placebo: Inert substance given with the hope that it will relieve symptoms.

placebo effect: Response to a treatment that does not result from pharmacological effect or other direct physical action.

plantar: Pertaining to the sole of the foot.

plaque (atherosclerotic): Deposit that builds up on the inner wall of an artery; see *atherosclerosis.*

plaque (dental): Soft, sticky, colorless, almost invisible film that continuously forms on the teeth and contains bacteria that cause dental decay and periodontal disease.

positive test: Test result that is abnormal.

precertification: Component of managed care in which a plan representative must authorize use of a procedure in order for it to be covered by the plan; also called preauthorization. Precertification is required most often for nonemergency hospital admissions, elective surgery, or psychiatric care.

precursor: Substance from which another substance is derived, commonly used to describe an inactive substance that is converted into an active enzyme, vitamin, or hormone. Beta-carotene, for example, is a precursor of vitamin A.

preferred provider organization (PPO): Prepaid insurance plan in which member hospitals and/or physicians contract with a third party payer to deliver services for negotiated fees, usually at a reduced rate. Beneficiaries may seek care from nonmember providers, but if they do, the out-of-pocket cost is likely to be higher.

premenstrual syndrome (PMS): A combination of physical and/or emotional symptoms that occur before menstruation and disappear or become minimal during menstrual periods; also called premenstrual tension (PMT).

prescription drugs: Drugs that cannot be obtained unless ordered by a physician or other designated health professional.

prevalence: The total number of cases of a given disease that exist in a population at a specific time.

primary care: health care provided by the first professional to see the patient—typically a family practitioner, internist, or pediatrician.

prosthesis: Artificial device to replace a missing body part, such as an eye or a leg.

protocol (experimental): A written description of the background, objective, design, and intended interpretation of an experiment.

pseudoscientists: Individuals who invent, misuse, and/or distort scientific evidence to support their beliefs or practices.

psychic surgery: Sleight-of-hand fakery by individuals who pretend to remove diseased organs during "surgical procedures" that leave the skin intact.

psychosomatic (or psychophysiologic): Pertaining to the effect of emotions on the body.

psychosurgery: Effective but rarely needed method of relieving severe nervous symptoms by severing selected nervous pathways within the brain.

psychosis: Severe form of mental disturbance in which contact with reality is impaired.

psychotherapy: Conversational method used to treat emotional problems.

puffery: Advertising that uses vague superlatives, exaggerations, or subjective opinions without specific facts.

pyorrhea: Lay term for gum disease.

RDAs (Recommended Dietary Allowances): Levels of certain nutrients adequate to meet the needs of practically all healthy persons. Some scientists use the abbreviation RDA for both the singular and plural of the term.

RDIs (Reference Daily Intakes): A system of nutrient standards, based on the 1989 RDAs, which the FDA has proposed to replace the U.S. RDAs on product labels (see Chapter 12).

rebound (from a medication): Situation in which stopping a medication produces a withdrawal reaction opposite to that of the medication. Overuse of nosedrops, for example, can cause rebound congestion, and the use of large doses of vitamin C can cause rebound scurvy.

reflexology: Pseudoscience based on beliefs that each body part is represented on the hands and feet and that pressing on the hands and feet can have therapeutic effects in other parts of the body.

regulatory letter: Letter from the FDA warning a seller to stop breaking the law. If corrective action is not taken promptly, the FDA may initiate a seizure or seek an injunction.

renal: Pertaining to the kidney.

respirator: Device for maintaining artificial respiration.

risk factor: Factor that increases the probability of getting a particular disease, such as atherosclerotic heart disease, cancer, or osteoporosis.

roots (of a tooth): The lower portions of the teeth below the gum.

rubella: German measles.

safe and effective: Legal term used by the FDA to describe drugs that are generally recognized by experts as both safe and effective. Drugs recognized as safe or effective but not both are still considered "not safe and effective."

salt-sensitivity: A tendency toward abnormal elevation of blood pressure in response to salt (sodium) intake.

scientific method: Principles and procedures for the systematic pursuit of knowledge, involving data collected through observations and experiments and the formulation and testing of hypotheses.

screening test: Efficient method to identify an unrecognized health problem. Screening tests sort out people who probably have a specific problem from those who probably do not. Findings that are abnormal or equivocal indicate that further evaluation is needed.

self-help groups: Groups of laypersons who help each other cope with specific problems.

semen: Whitish fluid that carries the male sperm.

sensitivity (of a test): The likelihood that a test will correctly identify people having the condition that the test is intended to detect. A highly sensitive test will detect most or all of those who have the condition and will have few false-negative results.

serum: The fluid portion of the blood obtained after removal of blood cells and fibrin clot.

sexually transmitted disease (STD): Disease caused by a virus, bacterium, parasite, or fungus that is transmitted from one person to another through intimate (usually sexual) contact.

side effect: An effect of a drug that is undesirable or unrelated to the main reason for which it is prescribed.

sigmoidoscope: Hollow tubular instrument that can be passed through the anus into the rectum and part of the large intestine for diagnostic or therapeutic purposes.

simple carbohydrate: Sugar composed of one or two sugar molecules.

skilled nursing facility: Patient care center that provides rehabilitative services and 24-hour nursing for convalescent patients.

specificity (of a test): The likelihood that a positive result indicates that an individual has the specific condition that the test is intended to detect. A highly specific test will have few false-positive results and often will establish the diagnosis.

speculum: Tubular instrument used to look into an opening of the body, such as the nose or ear.

sphygmomanometer: Instrument for measuring blood pressure.

spontaneous remission: Recovery from illness without treatment.

STD: Abbreviation for sexually transmitted disease.

stenosis: Narrowing of a body passageway such as an artery or duct.

stress test: Evaluation in which an electrocardiogram is taken during gradually escalated exercise.

sun protection factor (SPF): Number indicating the degree of protection provided by a sunscreen product against ultraviolet rays.

suppository: Drug product administered by insertion into a body opening, usually the rectum or vagina, where it melts to release its active ingredient(s).

systemic: Term referring to the body as a whole rather than to a part of the body.

TENS device: Battery-powered device that delivers an electric current to an area of the body to relieve certain types of pain.

testimonial: Claim by the user that a treatment method has been effective; not a reliable form of evidence.

thermography: Imaging procedure based on the measurement of heat radiating from the body's surface. Scientific practitioners consider thermography unreliable, but it is popular among chiropractors. In 1991 the AMA House of Delegates adopted the position that thermography has not been demonstrated to have any value as a medical diagnostic test.

third party payer: Payment source other than patient or provider (for example, insurance company or government program).

TMJ (temporomandibular joint): The jaw joint, which is located in front of the ear near the external ear canal.

tolerance (to a drug): Adaptation to a drug so that higher doses become required to achieve the same effect.

topical use (of a drug): Application to a body surface.

treatment planning: A formal process whereby various staff members of a health-care facility meet regularly to discuss patients, set goals, record the steps necessary to reach the goals, and evaluate the progress of the patients. It is required for the accreditation of psychiatric facilities.

tremor: Abnormal trembling or shaking of a body part.

ultrasound device: Mechanism that transforms electrical energy into sound energy for use in diagnosis, surgery, dental care, or other therapeutic procedures.

unbundling of fees: Making separate charges for the components of a medical encounter that normally has a single charge. An example would be separate charges for an operation and postoperative hospital care when it is customary to include the postoperative care in the original fee.

United States Pharmacopoeia (USP): Authoritative volume on drugs that contains the official standards for identity, strength, and purity.

USDA: Abbreviation for United States Department of Agriculture.

U.S. Dietary Guidelines: Seven general dietary guidelines, developed by the U.S. Department of Agriculture and the Department of Health and Human Services, for people who want to decrease their chances of developing certain chronic diseases.

U.S. RDAs (U.S. Recommended Daily Allowances): Simplified FDA version of the RDAs used for many years in food labeling; may be replaced by RDI; see *RDIs*.

utilization review: Review, based mainly on medical records, intended to determine the quality and necessity of services provided to the patient.

varicose: Abnormally swollen or dilated.

vascular: Pertaining to blood vessel(s).

vegan: Strict vegetarian; one who eats no products of animal origin (red meat, poultry, fish, eggs, milk, cheese, and milk products).

vertebra: Spinal bone.

vision therapy: Unscientific system of eye exercises claimed to strengthen eyesight and improve learning disabilities.

vitalism: The concept that the functions of an organism are due to a vital principle or "life force" distinct from the physical forces that can be explained by the laws of physics and chemistry. Nonscientific health systems based on this philosophy (for example, chiropractic, naturopathy, homeopathy) maintain that diseases should be treated by "stimulating the body's ability to heal itself" rather than by "treating symptoms."

withdrawal reaction: Symptoms that occur following stoppage of an addicting drug.

yo-yo dieting: Repeated weight loss (through dieting) followed by weight gain; also called weight cycling.

INDEX

t indicates table.

E

G

H

I

J

K

N

830
PBMT
12895 E-70 70
CLB
ICI INFORMATION CONSERVATION INC.